Chambers
Office Oracle

Chambers
Office Oracle

Consultant Editor: Doreen Sharp

Published in association with the
Royal Mail

Chambers

Published by W & R Chambers Ltd, Edinburgh, 1987

British Library Cataloguing in Publication Data

Chambers office oracle.
    1. Office practice—Dictionaries
    I. Sharp, Doreen
    651'.03'21   HF5547.5

ISBN 0 550 18075 3

Typeset by Blackwood Pillans & Wilson Ltd, Edinburgh

Printed by
Charles Letts & Co Ltd
London Edinburgh & New York

Acknowledgments
The Royal Mail
Tom Pinder, Consultant in Speech-in-Management
Inspector Waddington, Metropolitan Police Crime Prevention
  Service
Todd Research Ltd
Acco Company Ltd
SASCO
Business Education Service
Talisman Chauffeurs (defensive driving techniques)
British Telecom
Institute of Freight Forwarders Ltd
Trans Global Air Limited
British Standards Institution
British Rail
Susan Shatto

Contents

PART I:
Business Communication

Chapter 5
BUSINESS COMMUNICATION—*Written*

Chapter 6
ADVERTISING AND PUBLICITY

Chapter 7
GRAPHS, CHARTS AND VISUAL PLANNING

PART II:
Business Procedures

Chapter 8
BUSINESS ENTERTAINING

Chapter 9
MEETINGS

Chapter 10
PLANNING A CONFERENCE/EXHIBITION

Chapter 11
INTERVIEWING SKILLS

PART III:
Organisation and Finance

Chapter 12
BUSINESS STRUCTURES

Chapter 13
FINANCE AND BANKING

Chapter 14
SECURITY

Chapter 15
DISTRIBUTION OF GOODS

PART IV:
Government and Law

Chapter 16
GOVERNMENT IN THE UNITED KINGDOM

PART V:
Office Safety, Equipment and Services

Chapter 21
TELECOMMUNICATIONS

PART VI:
Useful Information

Chapter 22
GEOGRAPHICAL AND TRAVEL INFORMATION

Chapter 23
CALENDARS

Chapter 24
MAPS

Chapter 25
WEIGHTS AND MEASURES

Chapter 26
MEDIA

Chapter 27
GLOSSARIES

Chapter 28
ABBREVIATIONS IN COMMON USE

PART VII:
Dictionary

Consultant Editor Doreen Sharp

Widely known and respected author, lecturer, examiner and moderator in Business Education. Formerly Head of Secretarial Studies, Department of Business and Social Sciences, Bromley College of Technology.

Author (and co-author) of 20 books on various aspects of business training for Pitman, McGraw-Hill and Macmillan including Pitman shorthand textbooks, *Electronic Keyboarding* and *The PA's Handbook* (Papermac 3rd edition 1986).

Founder member (Joint Chairman 1979–82) of the European Association of Professional Secretaries and member of the European Association of Teachers.

Presently a member of the Syllabus Committee of the Examinations Board of the London Chamber of Commerce and Industry (LCCI). Previously served on the Royal Society of Arts (RSA) Advisory Committee in Secretarial Subjects and the Secretarial Studies Committee of the Business and Technician Education Council (BTEC).

Editor Virginia Tebbit

Contributors

Ian Derbyshire	Research Fellow at Cambridge University. Author of Chambers *Political Spotlights* series on modern world politics.
Pamela Forrester	Education Liaison Officer for the LCCI Examinations Board and Chief Examiner for the Meetings component of the LCCI Private and Executive Secretary's Diploma. Formerly in charge of secretarial training for British Petroleum. Has lectured in many parts of the world including Singapore, Lagos and Perth (Australia).
Doreen Lowe	Head of School of Information Processing, Wigan College of Technology. Author of four word processing textbooks (Wigantec).

Elizabeth McCall-Smith	General Medical Practitioner in Edinburgh.
Joan Moncrieff	Formerly Lecturer in Secretarial Studies, Mid-Warwickshire College of Further Education and Senior Lecturer in Business Studies, Bromley College of Technology. Co-author of *The PA's Handbook* (Papermac 3rd edition 1986). A member of the SIMpleton's Club (Speech in Management), for practice and promotion of Public Speaking.
Arthur Trimnell	Company Secretary/Accountant in the electrical industry before entering Further Education as Lecturer and Senior Lecturer in Business Studies at Bromley, Woolwich and Southwark Colleges. Examiner in Law and Accounts for professional bodies.
Doreen Trimnell	Formerly Principal Lecturer and Deputy Head of Department of Business Studies, Hackney College, 1976–86. Previously RSA Chief Examiner for Audio-Typewriting and presently Assessor for RSA Integrated Schemes. Co-author of textbooks on Keyboarding and Typewriting (McGraw-Hill) and Shorthand (Pitman).
Malcolm Wood	Solicitor working in private practice in Edinburgh.

Preface

Chambers Office Oracle provides a wide range of information and advice for staff in every type and size of office and has been designed to help office workers deal quickly and efficiently with many everyday queries—both common and uncommon—that can take time and effort to answer. *Chambers Office Oracle* is in fact one book and many books, blending up-to-date factual material with more general information *and* a handy Chambers dictionary.

Chambers Office Oracle represents the work of many individuals and organisations. In order to ensure the accuracy and usefulness of *all* the information in the book educational and business advisers have been consulted at each stage. The specialist sections have been written by experts in their fields.

The variety of information is mirrored in the variety of presentation. Articles, glossaries, lists, tables, charts, diagrams and maps have been used to guarantee ease of use and great flexibility.

Chambers Office Oracle will be an indispensable reference text no modern office can afford to be without.

The publishers welcome suggestions from readers for additional material which they would find useful in subsequent editions.

Part I
BUSINESS COMMUNICATION

1 English Standard Usage

2 Forms of Address

3 Business Communication
Oral

4 Effective Speaking in Public

5 Business Communication
Written

6 Advertising and Publicity

7 Graphs, Charts and Visual Planning

1 ENGLISH STANDARD USAGE

1.1 Clarity of expression

In business communication clarity of expression is all-important. The ability to communicate one's purpose, requirements and conclusions clearly and concisely saves time, money and unnecessary labour.

When composing a business letter, report or article, it is essential to keep its intended function in mind constantly and to be aware of how the structure and style of language works to fulfil that function. (See also Chapter 5.2.) Here are some helpful guidelines:

Structure

Before starting to write, establish and note down the objectives, the main points to be made and any firm conclusions to be conveyed; refer to those notes frequently.

Use a separate paragraph to deal with every major subject or idea; within each paragraph, make sure that every sentence connects logically with the preceding one.

Remember that every finite verb in a sentence marks a separate clause; each clause should be linked to the next by a conjunction, a colon or a semi-colon, rather than a comma.

In general, avoid forming sentences by joining a number of clauses with 'and' or 'but'.

Stay in one tense as far as possible.

Place descriptive phrases, adjectives and adverbs as close as possible to their subject.

Check that it is always clear what subject a pronoun refers to.

Style

Form sentences of different lengths and of varied structure.

Look for the most direct way of expressing your meaning; use clear and specific vocabulary, avoiding jargon, ambiguous phrases and unnecessarily technical language, e.g. 'I enclose' *not* 'Herewith please find enclosed', 'Soon' *not* 'In the near future'.

Make positive statements rather than negative ones.

Delete words that are not strictly necessary for meaning; they serve only to obscure the subject and lengthen the text, e.g. 'Though seriously ill, he came to the office daily' *not* 'In spite of the fact that he was seriously ill, he came to the office daily'.

1

Check that you have not repeated either vocabulary or subject matter needlessly; if a word recurs frequently, consult a thesaurus for an alternative.

Ensure that major points are not swamped by minor details.

Accuracy

Check all facts and details carefully.

Consult a dictionary whenever there is any doubt about the spelling or meaning of a word.

Consult an English usage dictionary if there is any doubt about how a term should be used.

Finally, always re-read your work several times, revising it according to these guidelines. Ensure that it fulfils its purpose concisely and clearly, that the main points have been sufficiently emphasised, and that no important facts have been omitted. If necessary, seek a second opinion from a colleague who can offer constructive advice.

1.2 Correct grammatical usage

There are a number of areas in which grammatical errors are commonly made in everyday English. Some simple rules can be applied to avoid these errors.

Who and whom

(1) Use *who* when the pronoun is the subject of a verb:

The man who *(subject)* phoned yesterday came to the office today.

(2) Use *whom* when the pronoun is the object of a verb:

The man whom *(object)* you *(subject)* phoned yesterday came to the office today.

(3) Use *whom* when the relative pronoun is governed by a preposition and try to keep the preposition and the relative pronoun together:

The man *to whom* you spoke on the phone yesterday came to the office today.

Like and as

(1)   Use *like* to compare things or people, i.e. to qualify nouns or pronouns:

> Your *desk* is like *mine*.
> My electric *typewriter* is like *Anne's*.
> *He* looks like a *man* who has a lot of problems. (Here two people are compared.)

(2)   Use *as* to compare actions, i.e. to join clauses and thus govern verbs (sometimes the verb is only implied):

> *You work* very much as *I do*.
> *Operate* the shift-key as I *told* you.
> We *shall give* the staff a bonus, as last year. (Here 'we *did*' is implied.)

Due to, owing to, because of

(1)   Use *due to* only when preceded by some tense of the verb 'to be':

> My absence *was* due to illness.
> If mistakes occur they *will be* due to carelessness.

(2)   Do not begin a sentence with *due to*.

(3)   If a choice can be made between the phrases *because of, owing to* and *due to*, use the first. (*Owing to* and *due to* often cause ugly as well as dubious constructions.)

Shall and will, should and would

(1)   When making a statement of fact without special emphasis *I* and *we* are usually followed by *shall* or *should* (not will or would):

> I should be glad if you would write to me without delay.
> We should be grateful if you would let us have a reply at once.

(2)   *Shall* is used with *will* (future tense):

> I shall be glad if you will let me have a reply at once.
> If you will let us have your cheque we shall despatch the goods immediately.

Do not join a future tense to a conditional tense in one sentence.

I and me

(1)   Use *I* as the subject of a sentence. Mistakes often occur when *I* or *me* is linked with another noun or pronoun. Avoid these mistakes by

mentally taking away the intervening noun or pronoun and checking the sense of what remains:

> The managing director and I will interview you.
>
> *not*
>
> Please meet the managing director and I for an interview. (*I* is wrongly used here instead of the object *me*. 'Please meet I for an interview' is obviously incorrect.)

(2) Use *I* if the pronoun is linked to a following clause:

> It was I who wrote the report.

(3) Use *me* after a preposition e.g. Come with me. Errors sometimes occur when the object of a preposition is two pronouns linked by 'and' e.g. Between you and me (*not* I), Like you and me (*not* I).

Either and or, neither and nor

(1) Use *either* or *neither* with two persons or things:

> I have examined both machines and find that either (neither) will suit our purpose.

(2) Use *either* or *neither* with the singular as they refer to one person or thing to the exclusion of the other:

> You will find that either (neither) of these typewriters *is* suitable.

(3) Always follow *either* by *or*, and *neither* by *nor*, in a comparison:

> Either (Neither) Miss Brown or (nor) Miss Green is to take dictation in the Manager's office.

(4) Always place *either* or *neither* next to the words they qualify:

> I shall buy either (neither) a magazine or (nor) a newspaper.
>
> *not*
>
> I shall either (neither) buy a magazine or (nor) a newspaper.

Each and none

Use *each* and *none* with the singular as they refer to one person or thing:

> Each of you *is* to receive a rise in salary next month.
> As none of the clerks *is* willing to work overtime we are behind schedule this week.

Using the infinitive

The infinitive has two forms; present and past:

> e.g. to do (present infinitive)
> to have done (past infinitive).

(1)   Use the *present infinitive* after a past tense or any compound tense:

> I meant *to telephone* you yesterday.
>> *not*
> I meant to have telephoned you yesterday.
> The staff would have preferred *to work* a five-day week.
>> *not*
> The staff would have preferred to have worked a five-day week.

(2)   Use the *past infinitive* when a present tense is followed by an infinitive which describes a past event:

> Henry Ford *is* said *to have been* a millionaire by the age of forty.

The split infinitive

The infinitive of a verb consists of two words, e.g. to forecast, to announce, to move. The two words are a unity and should not be separated (split) by the insertion of additional words or phrases. Opinions differ on the gravity of this error but all agree that gross infringements of the rule should be avoided.

> I should like, on behalf of all our members, *to move* a vote of thanks to the chairman.
>> *not*
> I should like *to*, on behalf of all our members, *move* a vote of thanks to the chairman.

Comparative and superlative

(1)   Use the comparative degree when two things are compared, and the superlative for more than two:

> Mary has taken the *better* of the two typewriters and the *best* of the three dictating machines.
> Which of these two cloths is the *more* hard-wearing?

(2)   Use *less* for quantity or amount; use *fewer* for number:

> The industry has bought *less* steel than it did last year and thus produces *fewer* cars. (Quantity and number)
> I paid £3 *less* than the market price for a ton of cotton waste. (Amount)

(3) *Unique* means the only one of its kind and has *no comparative*. It should not be used casually to mean novel, scarce or rare. 'Almost unique' is allowable, but 'comparatively unique' or 'very unique' reduce the word to absurdity and should not be used.

Verbal nouns

In the following sentences the words in italic are nouns made from verbs (verbal nouns) and not participles:

> The chairman likes *travelling*.
> He hates *leaving* work unfinished.
> *Taking* a holiday is very refreshing.

(1) Qualify verbal nouns by possessive adjectives, not by pronouns (i.e. use *my, his, our, your, their* NOT *me, him, us, you, them*):

> The error was caused by *his typing* so carelessly.
> The supervisor criticised *our leaving* early.
> Do you agree to *my taking* a day's holiday.

(2) Similarly, use the possessive form for a noun qualifying a verbal noun:

> I don't object to *Mary's* talking provided she lowers her voice.
> He is unemployed because of the *firm's* going into liquidation.
> The department has been disorganised by the *Manager's* leaving.

1.3 Punctuation

A **full stop** (.) is used at the end of a statement and often after a command; a **question mark** (?) comes after a question and an **exclamation mark** (!) after an exclamation or interjection, and sometimes after a command:

> This is a useful report. Show it to the Chairman tomorrow.
> Would you make a copy for me? Cheerio! Don't forget what I said!

A **comma** (,) shows a slight break in a sentence. It is used:

(1) between two clauses joined by *but* or *or* if the second one has a subject:

> I'll come to see you tomorrow, but I don't know when I will arrive.

(2) after a subordinate clause:

> When he returned, I made a cup of tea.

(3) around the kind of relative clause that gives *additional information*:

> The salesman, who had driven from Southampton, was tired.

but *not* around the kind of relative clause that *identifies* a person or thing:

> Those people who would like tickets should write to the secretary.

(4) around a descriptive or explanatory phrase referring to a person or thing:

> Mrs Cook, our local councillor, has joined the committee.

(5) after introductory words, or around words which form a comment:

> However, I wasn't late after all.
>
> I must leave now, unfortunately.
>
> Philip, I'm sorry to say, has left the company.

(6) before *please*, after *yes* and *no*, and before or after the name of the person who is being spoken to:

> May I see the file, please?
>
> No, I'm sorry.
>
> Hurry up, Christopher.

(7) in a list of more than two things and often between adjectives preceding a noun, where there are two or more:

> a pen, a pencil and a rubber
>
> a busy, overcrowded room (but no commas in e.g. a *cheerful old man*, because *old man* is regarded as a single unit).

A **colon (:)** is used to introduce the answer that the first part of the sentence expects:

> There's one thing I'd really like: a new car.
>
> You'll need the following: passport, ticket, boarding pass.

A **semicolon** (;) separates parts of a sentence that are equally important and are not linked by *and, but, or*, etc. Sometimes a semicolon is used to separate items in a list:

> One tray of sandwiches will be sufficient; to prepare more would be wasteful.
> I have three ambitions: to set up my own business; to buy a boat and sail around the world; to live in Sydney.

Quotation marks (' ') or (" ") are used before and after direct speech; a **comma** is usually put before or after the direct speech:

> Mary said, 'You're late'.
> 'You're late', said Mary.

Both single and double quotes are correct, but modern usage prefers single quotes. However, if there is a quotation or highlighted passage within another quotation, both single and double quotes must be used:

> 'Did she say "You're late"?', John asked.

An **apostrophe** (') is used:

(1) to form possessive nouns; it is placed before the *s* with singular nouns and with plural nouns not ending in —*s*, and after the *s* with plural nouns ending in —*s*:

> Anne's desk; the women's coats; the residents' car park.

(2) in shortened forms, showing where part of a word has been left out:

> I've only two appointments today.
> Aren't you coming with us?

A **hyphen** (-) is used:

(1) in many nouns (others are written as one word or as two words without a hyphen):

> air-conditioning (but *aircraft* and *air force*).

(2) in compound adjectives placed before the noun:

> a six-page contract; a twenty-year-old building: a well-deserved award.

(3) sometimes with a prefix:

> The votes must be re-counted.

1.4 **Spelling rules**

To a large extent the ability to spell English words correctly depends on becoming familiar with the *look* of them when they are spelt in the accepted way. Much help with spelling is given in the Dictionary (Part VII) and, in cases of doubt, words should always be looked up there.

There are, however, a few general rules *though one must always be on the watch for exceptions.*

Derivatives of words ending in *-y*

(1) The plural of a noun in **-y, -ey** (also **-ay, -oy, -uy**):

A noun in **-y** following a consonant has its plural in **-ies.**

baby	*babies*	*country*	*countries*

Nouns in **-ey,** etc., have their plural in **-eys,** etc.

donkey	*donkeys*	*valley*	*valleys*
day	*days*	*Monday*	*Mondays*
alloy	*alloys*	*guy*	*guys*

(2) The parts of a verb when the verb ends in **-y, -ey** (etc.):

The formation is similar to that of noun plurals in (1) above.

	cry	*cries*	*cried*
	certify	*certifies*	*certified*
but	*convey*	*conveys*	*conveyed*
	delay	*delays*	*delayed*
	destroy	*destroys*	*destroyed*
	buy	*buys*	

(3) Comparison of adjectives, or the formation of nouns or adverbs from them:

A rule similar to the above holds for words in **-y,** and in some cases for those in **-ey** (etc.).

	shady	*shadier*	*shadiest*	*shadiness*	*shadily*
	pretty	*prettier*	*prettiest*	*prettiness*	*prettily*
but	*grey*	*greyer*	*greyest*	*greyness*	*greyly*
	coy	*coyer*	*coyest*	*coyness*	*coyly*

There are, however, exceptions and irregularities for which a dictionary should be consulted.

Derivatives of words ending in -*c*

When a suffix beginning with a vowel is added, and the consonant still has a hard *k* sound, -**c** becomes -**ck**:

picnic	*picnicking*	*picnicked*	*picnicker*
mimic	*mimicking*	*mimicked*	*mimicker*

-**k**- is not added in words such as *musician, electricity*, etc., where the consonant has the soft sound of *sh* or *s*.

-ie- or -ei-?

i before *e*

except after *c*.

(This rule applies only to words in which the sound is long *ē*.)

e.g.	*belief*	*believe*	*grief*	*pier*	*siege*
	ceiling	*conceit*	*deceit*	*deceive*	

Exceptions are *seize, weird* and personal names (e.g. *Neil, Sheila*) and certain surnames.

The doubling of a final consonant before a following vowel

(1)   In a word of one syllable with a short vowel, the final consonant is doubled:

e.g.	*man*	*manning*	*manned*	*mannish*
	red	*redder*	*reddest*	*redden*
	sin	*sinning*	*sinned*	*sinner*
	stop	*stopping*	*stopped*	*stopper*
	drum	*drumming*	*drummed*	*drummer*

(2)   In a word of more than one syllable with a short final vowel, the final consonant is doubled only if the accent is on the final syllable:

e.g.	*entrap'*	*entrapping*	*entrapped*	
	regret'	*regretting*	*regretted*	
	begin'	*beginning*	*beginner*	
	occur'	*occurring*	*occurred*	*occurrence*
but	*en'ter*	*entering*	*entered*	
	prof'it	*profiting*	*profited*	
	gall'op	*galloping*	*galloped*	
	hicc'up	*hiccuping*	*hiccuped*	

(3) In British English (but not in American) **-l** is doubled no matter where the accent falls:

| e.g. | *compel'* | *compelling* | *compelled* | |
| and also | *trav'el* | *travelling* | *travelled* | *traveller* |

(4) Some derivatives of words ending in **-s** can be spelt in two ways: e.g. *bias*.

Certain words ending in **-p** are not treated strictly in accordance with the rule stated in (2) above, e.g. *kidnap*, *handicap*.

Derivatives of words with final *-e*

(1) Before a vowel (including **y**), **-e** is usually dropped:

e.g.	*come*	*coming*	*hate*	*hating*	*rage*	*raging*
	fame	*famous*	*pale*	*palish*	*use*	*usable*
	ice	*icy*	*noise*	*noisy*	*stone*	*stony*

Some exceptions are intended to distinguish one word from another:

e.g. *holey* (=full of holes), *holy*; *dyeing*, *dying*.

(2) Before a consonant, **-e** is usually kept:

| e.g. | *hateful* | *useless* | *movement* | *paleness* |

but see *true*, *whole*, *judge* for exceptions.

(3) **-e-** is kept after soft **-c-** or **-g-** before **-a, -o-**:

| e.g. | *noticeable* | *traceable* | *manageable* | *advantageous* |

Plural of words ending in *-f*

It is usual to add *s* to make the plural form, e.g. *roof, roofs*, but there are several exceptions, e.g. *calves, elves, knives, leaves*.

Some words have optional spellings, e.g. *hoof* (*hoofs*, or *hooves*), *scarf, wharf, handkerchief*.

The suffix *-ful*

Take care in spelling adjectives formed by the addition of *-ful*, e.g.
care + full = careful
help + full = helpful

Irregular plurals

Where a noun has an irregular plural form it is usually shown in its entry in the Dictionary (Part VII).

1.5 Words confused and misused

accept	check	currant	fiancé
except	cheque	current	fiancée
access	choir	deduce	forceful
excess	quire	deduct	forcible
advice	chord	defective	foreward
advise	cord	deficient	forward
adverse	collaborate	deprecate	formally
averse	corroborate	depreciate	formerly
affect	complement	desert	gaol
effect	compliment	dessert	goal
allude	comprise	device	gild
elude	consist	devise	guild
allusion	concert	draft	gilt
delusion	consort	draught	guilt
illusion			
	concise	dual	gorilla
amend	precise	duel	guerrilla
emend	confidant	elicit	hangar
amoral	confident	illicit	hanger
immoral	confidante		
		eligible	hoard
aural	contemptuous	legible	horde
oral	contemptible	emigrant	illegible
bail	continual	immigrant	ineligible
bale	continuous		
		eminent	imaginary
berth	correspondent	imminent	imaginative
birth	co-respondent	ensure	imply
born	corps	insure	infer
borne	corpse	exceedingly	impractical
breath	council	excessively	unpractical
breathe	counsel	exercise	inapt
cannon	councillor	exorcise	inept
canon	counsellor	faint	ingenious
canvas	credible	feint	ingenuous
canvass	creditable		

interment	motif	pray	shear
internment	motive	prey	sheer
lair	naught	premier	stationary
layer	nought	première	stationery
lath	negligent	principle	storey
lathe	negligible	principal	story
lay	noxious	prophecy	straight
lie	obnoxious	prophesy	strait
licence	oculist	quiet	superficial
license	optician	quite	superfluous
lightening	official	raise	surplice
lightning	officious	raze	surplus
liqueur	peal	rare	swingeing
liquor	peel	unique	swinging
loath	persecute	recourse	team
loathe	prosecute	resource	teem
loose	personal	reverend	venal
lose	personnel	reverent	venial
metal	pore	review	veracity
mettle	pour	revue	voracity
meter	practice	sceptic	waive
metre	practise	septic	wave

2 FORMS OF ADDRESS

2.1 Correct forms of address

At some time you may wish to write to a peer of the realm or to a person holding some official title or position. You may be aware that etiquette requires the use of certain phrases such as 'His Grace' 'His Worship' or 'My Lord', but may be uncertain about which is the correct form to use.

To help with this problem, information is given below on how to address and begin a formal letter to such people, and also on how to address them when speaking to them. Where no form of spoken address is given, you may assume that no special style exists. *Note*: in the forms of address given below, 'S——' stands for surname and 'F——' for forename.

Air Force—see **Officers.**

Ambassador, British ——*Address on envelope*: 'His/Her Excellency' (HE) (in other respects according to the ambassador's rank), followed if desired by 'HM Ambassador'. *Note*: His/Her Excellency (HE) is not used in the United Kingdom. The wife of an ambassador is not entitled to the style 'Her Excellency'. *Begin*: 'Sir' or 'Madam' (or according to rank). *Close*: 'I have the honour to be, Sir/Madam (or according to rank) Your Excellency's obedient servant'. *Spoken address*: 'Your Excellency' at least once, thereafter 'Sir' or 'Madam', or by name.

Ambassador, foreign ——*Address on envelope*: 'His/Her Excellency the Ambassador of ——' or 'His/Her Excellency the —— Ambassador'. The wife of an ambassador is not entitled to the style 'Her Excellency'. *Begin*: 'Your Excellency', refer to as 'Your Excellency' once, thereafter as 'you'. *Close*: 'I have the honour to be, Sir/Madam (or according to rank), Your Excellency's obedient servant'. *Spoken address*: 'Your Excellency' at least once, thereafter 'Sir' or 'Madam', or by name.

Archbishop (Church of England and Churches in the Anglican Communion) ——*Address on envelope*: 'The Most Reverend the Lord Archbishop of ——'; the Archbishops of Canterbury and York are Privy Counsellors and should be addressed as 'The Most Reverend and Right Hon. the Lord Archbishop of ——'. *Begin*: 'Dear Archbishop' or 'My Lord Archbishop'. *Spoken address*: 'Your Grace'; begin an official speech 'My Lord Archbishop'.

Archbishop (Church of England, etc.) retired —— reverts to Bishop; see **Bishop (Church of England, etc.) retired.**

Archbishop (Roman Catholic) ——*Address on envelope*: 'His Grace the Archbishop of ——'. *Begin*: 'My Lord Archbishop'. *Close*: 'I remain, Your Grace, Yours faithfully' or 'Yours faithfully'. *Spoken address*: 'Your Grace'.

Archbishop (Roman Catholic) retired ——*Address on envelope*: 'The Most Reverend Archbishop [S——]'. Otherwise as for a Roman Catholic archbishop.

Archdeacon ——*Address on envelope*: 'The Venerable the Archdeacon of ——'. *Begin*: 'Dear Archdeacon' or 'Venerable Sir'. *Spoken address*: 'Archdeacon'; begin an official speech 'Venerable Sir'.

Army—see **Officers.**

Attorney-General—as for a Secretary of State.

Baron ——*Address on envelope*: 'The Right Hon. the Lord ——'. *Begin*: 'My Lord'. *Spoken address*: 'My Lord'.

Baroness (Baron's wife) ——*Address on envelope*: 'The Right Hon. the Lady [S——]. *Begin*: 'Dear Madam'. *Spoken address*: 'Madam'.

Baroness (in her own right) ——*Address on envelope*: either in the same way as a Baron's wife, or, if she prefers, as 'The Right Hon. the Baroness [S——]'. Otherwise as for a Baron's wife.

Baron's daughter ——*Address on envelope*: if unmarried, 'The Hon. [F—— S——]'; if married to a commoner, 'The Hon. Mrs [husband's surname]'; if married to a Baron or Knight, 'The Hon. Lady [husband's surname]'; if the wife of a peer or courtesy peer, address as such. *Begin*: 'Dear Madam', or according to rank. *Spoken address*: 'Miss/Mrs [S——]', or according to rank.

Baron's son ——*Address on envelope*: 'The Hon. [F—— S——]'; the eldest sons of Barons in the peerage of Scotland are usually addressed 'The Master of [peerage title]'. *Begin*: 'Dear Sir'. *Spoken address*: 'Mr [S——]' or 'Sir'; a Master may also be addressed as 'Master'.

Baron's son's wife ——*Address on envelope*: 'The Hon. Mrs [husband's forename and surname]'; if the daughter of a Viscount or Baron, 'The Hon. Mrs [husband's surname]'; if the daughter of a Duke, Marquess or Earl, address as such. *Begin*: 'Dear Madam', or according to rank. *Spoken address*: according to rank.

Baronet ——*Address on envelope*: 'Sir [F—— S——], Bt'. *Begin*: 'Dear Sir'. *Spoken address*: 'Sir [F——]'.

Baronet's wife ——*Address on envelope*: 'Lady [S——]'; if she has the title 'Lady' by courtesy, 'Lady [F—— S——]'; if she has the courtesy style 'The Hon.', this precedes 'Lady'. *Begin*: 'Dear Madam'. *Spoken address*: 'Madam'.

Bishop, Diocesan (Church of England and Churches in the

Anglican Communion) —*Address on envelope*: 'The Right Reverend the Lord Bishop of —'; the Bishop of London is a Privy Counsellor, so is addressed as 'The Right Rev. and Right Hon. the Lord Bishop of London'; the Bishop of Meath is styled 'The Most Reverend', not 'The Right Reverend'. *Begin*: 'Dear Bishop' or 'My Lord'. *Spoken address*: 'Bishop'; begin an official speech 'My Lord'.

Bishop (Church of England, etc.) retired —*Address on envelope*: 'The Right Reverend [F— S—]'; if a Privy Counsellor, 'The Right Rev. and Right Hon. [F— S—]'. *Begin*: 'Dear Bishop', 'My Lord' or 'Right Reverend Sir'. *Spoken address*: 'Bishop'; begin an official speech 'My Lord' or 'Right Reverend Sir'.

Bishop (Episcopal Church in Scotland) —*Address on envelope*: 'The Right Reverend [F— S—], Bishop of —'. Otherwise as for a bishop of the Church of England. The bishop who holds the position of Primus is addressed as 'The Most Reverend the Primus'. *Begin*: 'Dear Primus'. *Spoken address*: 'Primus'.

Bishop (Roman Catholic) —*Address on envelope*: 'His Lordship the Bishop of —' or 'The Right Reverend [F— S—], Bishop of —'; in Ireland, 'The Most Reverend' is used instead of 'The Right Reverend'; if an auxiliary bishop, address as 'The Right Reverend [F— S—], Auxiliary Bishop of —'. *Begin*: 'My Lord' or, more rarely, 'My Lord Bishop'. *Close*: 'I remain, My Lord (or, more rarely, 'My Lord Bishop'), Yours faithfully', or Yours faithfully'. *Spoken address*: 'My Lord' or, more rarely, 'My Lord Bishop'.

Bishop, Suffragan (Church of England and Churches in the Anglican Communion) —*Address on envelope*: 'The Right Reverend the Bishop of —'. *Begin*: 'Dear Bishop', 'My Lord' or 'Right Reverend Sir'; begin an official speech 'My Lord' or 'Right Reverend Sir'. Otherwise as for a Diocesan Bishop.

Bishop, US (1) Protestant Episcopal Church —*Address on envelope*: 'The Right Reverend [F— S—]'. *Begin*: 'Right Reverend Sir' or 'Dear Bishop'. *Spoken address*: 'Bishop [S—]'.

(2) **Methodist Church** —*Address on envelope*: 'The Reverend [F— S—]'. *Begin*: 'Reverend Sir' or 'Dear Bishop'. *Spoken address*: 'Bishop [S—]'.

Cabinet Minister—see **Secretary of State.**

Canon (Church of England and Churches in the Anglican Communion) —*Address on envelope*: 'The Reverend Canon [F— S—]'. *Begin*: 'Dear Canon' or 'Dear Canon [S—]'. *Spoken address*: 'Canon' or 'Canon [S—]'.

Canon (Roman Catholic) —*Address on envelope*: 'The Very

Reverend Canon [F—— S——]'. *Begin*: 'Very Reverend Sir'. *Spoken address*: 'Canon [S——]'.

Cardinal ——*Address on envelope*: 'His Eminence Cardinal [S——]'; if an archbishop, 'His Eminence the Cardinal Archbishop of ——'. *Begin*: 'Your Eminence' or, more rarely, 'My Lord Cardinal'. *Close*: 'I remain, Your Eminence (or 'My Lord Cardinal'), Yours faithfully'. *Spoken address*: 'Your Eminence'.

Chairman of County Council, Regional Council, etc. ——*Address on envelope*: 'The Chairman of the —— Council'. *Begin*: 'Dear Mr Chairman', even if the holder of the office is a woman. *Spoken address*: 'Mr Chairman', even to a woman, or by name.

Clergy (1) **Church of England and Churches in the Anglican Communion.** *Address on envelope*: 'The Reverend [F—— S——]'. *Begin*: 'Dear Sir' or 'Dear Mr [S——]'.

(2) **Roman Catholic** ——*Address on envelope*: 'The Reverend [F—— S——]'; if a member of a religious order, the initials of the order should be added after the name. *Begin*: 'Dear Reverend Father'.

(3) **Church of Scotland and other churches** ——*Address on envelope*: 'The Reverend F——' S——. *Begin*: 'Dear Sir/Madam' or 'Dear Mr/Mrs etc. [S——]'.

Companion of an order of knighthood ——the initials 'CB', 'CMG' or 'CH' (as it may be) follow the ordinary form of address.

Consul, British ——*Address on envelope*: [F—— S——], Esq., British Consul-General/Consul/Vice-Consul'; a Consul-General, Consul or Vice-Consul holding Her Majesty's Commission is addressed as 'HM Consul', etc., rather than as 'British Consul', etc.

Countess ——*Address on envelope*: 'The Right Hon. the Countess of ——'. *Begin*: 'Dear Madam'. *Spoken address*: 'Madam'.

Dame ——*Address on envelope*: 'Dame [F—— S——]', followed by the letters of the order; if a peeress or the daughter of a Duke, Marquess or Earl, 'Lady [F—— S——]' followed by the letters of the order; if styled 'The Hon.' then this precedes 'Dame'. *Begin*: 'Dear Madam'. *Spoken address*: 'Madam'.

Dean (Anglican) ——*Address on envelope*: 'The Very Reverend the Dean of ——'. *Begin*: 'Dear Dean' or 'Very Reverend Sir'. *Spoken address*: 'Dean'; begin an official speech 'Very Reverend Sir'.

Doctor ——physicians, anaesthetists, pathologists and radiologists are addressed as 'Doctor'. Surgeons, whether they hold the degree of Doctor of Medicine or not, are known as Mr/Mrs. In England and Wales, obstetricians and gynaecologists are addressed as Mr/Mrs, but in Scotland, Ireland and elsewhere as 'Doctor'. In addressing a letter to the holder of a doctorate, the initials DD, LLD, MD, MusD, etc., are placed after the ordinary form of address, as 'The Rev. John Smith, DD', 'John Brown, Esq., LLD', but 'The Rev. Dr Smith' and 'Dr John Brown' are also frequently used.

Dowager —*Address on envelope*: on the marriage of a peer or baronet, the widow of the previous holder of the title becomes 'Dowager' and is addressed 'The Right Hon. the Dowager Countess of —', 'The Right Hon. the Dowager Lady —', etc. If there already is a Dowager still living, she retains this title, the later widow being addressed 'The Most Hon. [F—], Marchioness of —', 'The Right Hon. [F—], Lady —', etc. It should be noted, however, that many Dowagers prefer the style which includes their Christian names to that including the title Dowager. (*Begin*, etc. as for a peer's wife).

Duchess —*Address on envelope*: 'Her Grace the Duchess of —'. *Begin*: 'Dear Madam'. *Spoken address*: 'Your Grace'. (For Royal Duchess, see **Princess**).

Duke —*Address on envelope*: 'His Grace the Duke of —'. *Begin*: 'My Lord Duke'. *Spoken address*: 'Your Grace'. (For Royal Duke, see **Prince**).

Duke's daughter —*Address on envelope*: 'Lady [F— S—]', the surname being that of her husband if she is married. If married to a peer, she is addressed according to her husband's rank only; this, however, does not necessarily hold in the case of peers by courtesy. If married to a person with the style 'The Hon.', she does not adopt this but retains the title 'Lady'. *Begin*: 'Dear Madam'. *Spoken address*: 'Madam'.

Duke's eldest son and son's heir —*Address on envelope*: A Duke's eldest son takes his father's second title. This courtesy title is treated as if it were an actual peerage (but see notes p 24). The son's eldest son takes his grandfather's third title, also being addressed as if a peer. (*Begin*, etc. according to rank).

Duke's eldest son's wife —*Address on envelope*: as if her husband's courtesy title were an actual peerage (but see notes p 24).

Duke's younger son —*Address on envelope*: 'Lord [F— S—]'. *Begin*: 'My Lord'. *Spoken address*: 'My Lord'.

Duke's younger son's wife —*Address on envelope*: 'Lady [husband's forename and surname]'. *Begin*: 'Dear Madam'. *Spoken address*: 'Madam'.

Earl —*Address on envelope*: 'The Right Hon. the Earl of —'. *Begin*: 'My Lord'. *Spoken address*: 'My Lord'. (For Earl's wife, see **Countess**).

Earl's daughter—as Duke's daughter.
Earl's eldest son and son's wife—as Duke's eldest son and son's wife.
Earl's younger son and son's wife—as Baron's son and son's wife.

Firms ——*Address on envelope*: the term 'Messrs' is becoming archaic. It cannot be used with the name of a limited company, nor in addressing a firm (a) which does not trade under a surname, (b) whose name includes a rank or title, or (c) which bears the name of a woman. *Begin*: 'Dear Sirs'.

Governor of a colony or **Governor-General** ——*Address on envelope*: 'His Excellency [ordinary designation], Governor (-General) of ——'. The Governor-General of Canada has the rank of 'Right Honourable' which he retains for life. The wife of a Governor-General is styled 'Her Excellency' within the country her husband administers. *Begin*: according to rank. *Close*: 'I have the honour to be, Sir (or 'My Lord' if a peer), Your Excellency's obedient servant'. *Spoken address*: 'Your Excellency'.

Judge, High Court ——*Address on envelope*: if a man, 'The Hon. Mr Justice [S——]'; if a woman, 'The Hon. Mrs Justice [S——]'. *Begin*: 'Dear Sir/Madam'; if on judicial matters, 'My Lord/Lady'. *Spoken address*: 'Sir/Madam'; only on the bench or when dealing with judicial matters should a High Court Judge be addressed as 'My Lord/Lady' or referred to as 'Your Lordship/Ladyship'.

Judge, Circuit ——*Address on envelope*: 'His/Her Honour Judge [S——]'; if a Knight, 'His Honour Judge Sir [F—— S——]'. *Begin*: 'Dear Sir/Madam'. *Spoken address*: 'Sir/Madam'; address as 'Your Honour' only when on the bench or dealing with judicial matters.

Judge, Irish—as English Circuit Judge.
Judge, Scottish—see **Lord of Session.**
Justice of the Peace (England and Wales) ——when on the bench, refer to and address as 'Your Worship'. Otherwise according to rank. The letters 'JP' may be added after the person's name in addressing a letter, if desired.

Knight Bachelor—as Baronet, except that 'Bt' is omitted.
Knight of the Bath, of St Michael and St George, etc. ——*Address on envelope*: 'Sir [F—— S——]', with the initials 'GCB', 'KCB', KCMG' (as it may be) added. *Begin*: 'Dear Sir'.
Knight of the Garter, or of the Thistle ——*Address on envelope*: The initials 'KG' or 'KT' are to be added to the address. (*Begin*, etc. according to rank).

Knight's wife, (whether wife of a Knight Bachelor or of a Knight of an order of chivalry)—as Baronet's wife or according to rank.

Lady Mayoress ——*Address on envelope*: 'The Lady Mayoress of ——'. *Begin*: 'My Lady Mayoress'. *Spoken address*: '(My) Lady Mayoress'.

Lady Provost ——*Address on envelope*: 'The Lady Provost of ——'. *Begin*: 'My Lady Provost'. *Spoken address*: '(My) Lady Provost'.

Lord Advocate of Scotland ——*Address on envelope*: 'The Right Hon. the Lord Advocate, QC' or 'The Right Hon. [F—— S——], QC'. *Begin*: 'Dear Sir', or 'My Lord' if a peer. Otherwise according to rank.

Lord Chancellor ——*Address on envelope*: 'The Right Hon. the Lord Chancellor'. *Begin*: 'My Lord'. Otherwise according to rank.

Lord Chief Justice ——*Address on envelope*: 'The Right Hon. the Lord Chief Justice of England'. *Begin*: 'My Lord'. Otherwise according to his rank as a peer. The Lord Chief Justice of Northern Ireland is addressed in the same manner unless he is a knight, in which case he is addressed as 'The Right Hon. Sir [F—— S——], Lord Chief Justice of Northern Ireland'.

Lord High Commissioner to the General Assembly ——*Address on envelope*: 'His/Her Grace the Lord High Commissioner'. *Begin*: 'Your Grace'. *Close*: 'I have the honour to remain, Your Grace's most devoted and obedient servant'. *Spoken address*: 'Your Grace'.

Lord Justice-Clerk ——*Address on envelope*: 'The Hon. the Lord Justice-Clerk'; if a Privy Counsellor, 'The Right Hon.'. *Begin*: 'My Lord'. *Spoken address*: 'My Lord'; refer to as 'Your Lordship'. The wife of the Lord Justice-Clerk is styled and addressed in the same manner as the wife of a Lord of Session.

Lord Justice-General of Scotland ——*Address on envelope*: 'The Right Hon. the Lord Justice-General'. *Begin*: 'My Lord'. *Spoken address*: 'My Lord'; refer to as 'Your Lordship'. The wife of the Lord Justice-General is styled and addressed as for the wife of a Lord of Session.

Lord Justice of the Court of Appeal ——*Address on envelope*: 'The Right Hon. Lord Justice [S——]'. *Begin*: 'My Lord'. *Spoken address*: 'My Lord'; refer to as 'Your Lordship'.

Lord Mayor ——*Address on envelope*: The Lord Mayors of London, York, Belfast, Cardiff, Dublin and also Melbourne, Sydney, Adelaide, Perth, Brisbane and Hobart are styled 'The Right Hon. the Lord Mayor of ——'; other Lord Mayors are styled 'The Right Worshipful the Lord Mayor of ——'. *Begin*: 'My Lord Mayor', even if the holder of the office is a woman. *Spoken address*: '(My) Lord Mayor'.

Lord Mayor's wife—see **Lady Mayoress.**

Lord of Appeal in Ordinary and his wife—as Baron and Baroness. Their children are styled as those of a Baron.

Lord of Session in Scotland —*Address on envelope*: 'The Hon. Lord [S——]'; if a Privy Counsellor, 'The Right Hon.'. *Begin*: 'My Lord'. *Spoken address*: 'My Lord'; refer to as 'Your Lordship'. The wife of a Lord of Session is styled 'Lady' and is addressed as for the wife of a Baron, but without the prefix 'The Right Hon.'.

Lord Provost —*Address on envelope*: 'The Right Hon. the Lord Provost of Edinburgh/Glasgow', but 'The Lord Provost of Aberdeen/Dundee'. *Begin*: 'My Lord Provost'. *Spoken address*: 'My Lord Provost'.

Lord Provost's wife—see **Lady Provost.**

Marchioness —*Address on envelope*: 'The Most Hon. the Marchioness of ——'. *Begin*: 'Dear Madam'. *Spoken address*: 'Madam'.

Marquess —*Address on envelope*: 'The Most Hon. the Marquess of ——'. *Begin*: 'My Lord'. *Spoken address*: 'My Lord'.

Marquess's daughter—as Duke's daughter.

Marquess's sons and sons' wives—as Duke's sons and sons' wives.

Master—a title borne by the eldest son of a Baron or Viscount in the peerage of Scotland. See **Baron's son.**

Mayor —*Address on envelope*: 'The Worshipful the Mayor of ——'; in the case of cities and certain towns, 'The Right Worshipful'. *Begin*: 'Mr Mayor', even if the mayor is a woman, although some women prefer 'Madam Mayor'. *Spoken address*: 'Mr Mayor'.

Mayoress —*Address on envelope*: 'The Mayoress of ——'. *Begin*: 'Madam Mayoress'. *Spoken address*: 'Mayoress'.

Member of Parliament —*Address on envelope*: add 'MP' to the usual form of address. (*Begin*, etc. according to rank).

Moderator of the General Assembly of the Church of Scotland —*Address on envelope*: 'The Right Reverend the Moderator of the General Assembly of the Church of Scotland' or 'The Right Reverend [F—— S——]'. *Begin*: 'Dear Sir' or 'Dear Moderator'. *Spoken address*: 'Moderator'. Ex-moderators are styled 'The Very Reverend'.

Moderator of the General Assembly of the United Reformed Church —*Address on envelope*: 'The Right Reverend [F—— S——]'. *Begin*: 'Dear Moderator'. *Spoken address*: 'Moderator' or 'Mr Moderator'. Ex-moderators are styled 'The Reverend'.

Monsignor ——*Address on envelope*: 'The Reverend Monsignor [F—— S——]'; if a canon, 'The Very Reverend Monsignor (Canon) [F—— S——]'. *Begin*: 'Reverend Sir'. *Spoken address*: 'Monsignor [S——]'.

Officers in the Army, Navy and Air Force ——*Address on envelope*: the professional rank is prefixed to any other rank, e.g. 'Admiral the Right Hon. the Earl of ——', 'Lieut.-Col. Sir [F—— S——], KCB'; officers below the rank of Rear-Admiral, and Marshal of the Royal Air Force are entitled to 'RN' (or 'Royal Navy'), and 'RAF' respectively after their name. Army officers of the rank of Colonel or below may follow their name with the name of their regiment or corps (or an abbreviation thereof). Officers in the women's services add 'WRNS', 'WRAF', 'WRAC'. *Begin*: according to social rank.

Officers, retired and former ——*Address on envelope*: officers above the rank of Lieutenant (in the Royal Navy), Captain (in the Army) and Flight Lieutenant may continue to use and be addressed by their armed forces rank after being placed on the retired list. The word 'retired', or any abbreviation thereof, should not normally be placed after the person's name. Former officers in the women's services do not normally continue to use their ranks.

Pope ——*Address on envelope*: 'His Holiness, the Pope'. *Begin*: 'Your Holiness' or 'Most Holy Father'. *Close*: if a Roman Catholic, 'I have the honour to be, your Holiness's most devoted and obedient child' (or 'most humble child'); if not Roman Catholic, 'I have the honour to be (or 'remain') Your Holiness's obedient servant'. *Spoken address*: 'Your Holiness'.

Prebendary—as Church of England Canon.

Prime Minister ——*Address on envelope*: according to rank; the Prime Minister is a Privy Counsellor (see separate entry) and the letter should be addressed accordingly. (*Begin*, etc. according to rank).

Prince ——*Address on envelope*: if a Duke, 'His Royal Highness the Duke of ——'; if not a Duke, 'His Royal Highness the Prince [F——]', if a child of the sovereign, otherwise, 'His Royal Highness Prince [F——] of [Kent or Gloucester]' but see notes p 24. *Begin*: 'Sir'. Refer to as 'Your Royal Highness'. *Close*: 'I have the honour to remain (or be), Sir, Your Royal Highness's most humble and obedient servant'. *Spoken address*: 'Your Royal Highness' once, thereafter 'Sir'.

Princess ——*Address on envelope*: if a Duchess, 'Her Royal Highness the Duchess of ——'; if not a Duchess, the daughter of a sovereign is addressed as 'Her Royal Highness the Princess [F——]' followed by any title she holds by marriage; 'the' is omitted in addressing a princess who is not the daughter of a sovereign; a Princess by marriage is addressed 'HRH Princess [husband's forename] of —'; but see notes p 24. *Begin*: 'Madam'. Refer to as 'Your Royal Highness'. *Close*: as for Prince, substituting 'Madam' for 'Sir'. *Spoken address*: 'Your Royal Highness' once, thereafter 'Ma'am'.

Privy Counsellor —*Address on envelope*: if a peer, 'The Right Hon. the Earl of —, PC'; if not a peer, 'The Right Hon. [F— S—]', without the 'PC'. (*Begin*, etc. according to rank).

Professor —*Address on envelope*: 'Professor [F— S—]'; the styles 'Professor Lord [S—]', 'Professor Sir [F— S—]', etc. are frequently used but are deprecated by some people; if the professor is in holy orders, 'The Reverend Professor'. *Begin*: 'Dear Sir/Madam', or according to rank. *Spoken address*: according to rank.

Provost, Roman Catholic—as Roman Catholic Canon.

Provost, Town —*Address on envelope*: 'The Provost of —'. *Begin*: 'Dear Provost'. *Spoken address*: 'Provost'.

Queen —*Address on envelope*: 'Her Majesty the Queen'. *Begin*: 'Madam, with my humble duty' but see notes p 24. Refer to as 'Your Majesty'. *Close*: 'I have the honour to remain (or be), Madam, Your Majesty's most humble and obedient servant'. *Spoken address*: 'Your Majesty' once, thereafter 'Ma'am'; begin an official speech 'May it please Your Majesty'.

Queen Mother—as for the Queen, substituting 'Queen Elizabeth The Queen Mother' for 'The Queen'.

Queen's Counsel—append 'QC' to ordinary address, but not if addressing a letter to a person holding one of the higher legal appointments such as a High Court Judge or Lord of Appeal in Ordinary.

Rabbi —*Address on envelope*: 'Rabbi [initial and surname]' or, if a doctor, 'Rabbi Doctor [initial and surname]'. *Begin*: 'Dear Sir'. *Spoken address*: 'Rabbi [S—]' or Doctor [S—]'.

Secretary of State —*Address on envelope*: 'The Right Hon. [F— S—], MP, Secretary of State for —', or 'The Secretary of State for —'. Otherwise according to rank.

Viscount —*Address on envelope*: 'The Right Hon. the Viscount —'. *Begin*: 'My Lord'. *Spoken address*: 'My Lord'.

Viscountess —*Address on envelope*: 'The Right Hon. the Viscountess —'. *Begin*: 'Dear Madam'. *Spoken address*: 'Madam'.

Viscount's daughter, son and son's wife—as Baron's daughter, son and son's wife.

Some general notes

Closing a letter The simplest correct way of closing a formal letter is 'Yours faithfully'. The longer very formal ceremonial styles are now seldom used, but they have been noted in the preceding list where they are still appropriate.

Courtesy titles Holders of courtesy titles are addressed according to their rank, but without 'The', 'The Right Hon.' or 'The Most Hon.'.

Ranks Ranks in the armed forces and ecclesiastical and ambassadorial ranks *precede* titles in the peerage, e.g. 'Colonel the Earl of ——' or 'The Rev. the Marquess of ——'.

Royal family Although the correct forms of address are given in this section for use in communications addressed to members of the Royal family, it should be noted that it is more normal practice for letters to be addressed to their private secretary, equerry or lady-in-waiting.

For more detailed information, see especially Debrett's *Correct Form*, Black's *Titles and Forms of Address*, or contact the Foreign and Commonwealth Office's Protocol Department.

2.2 Orders, decorations and medals

General rules

The correct order for post-nominal letters is as follows:

1. Decorations and honours according to precedence.
2. Royal appointments (PC, ADC, QHP, QHS, QHDS, QHNS, QHC, QC, JP, DL). Of these only QC must be used in addressing. PC is rarely used, and JP and DL are only required if the letter concerns matters directly connected with that office.
3. University degrees.
4. Medical qualifications.
5. Fellowships and memberships (of professional bodies, societies etc.). Election to certain distinguished bodies should always be recognised, e.g. FRS, RA, ARA, RSA, FBA.
6. Appointments/offices, e.g. MP, WS.

Bt (for Baronet) must precede all other post-nominal letters; VC, GC and CV then take precedence over all other honours.

Kt (for Knight Bachelor) should never be used after the name.
PC (if used) follows KG.

British and Commonwealth honours

The following list shows British and Commonwealth honours in order of precedence. Any honours indicated by * carry the title 'Sir' or 'Lady', unless the holder has a higher rank e.g. Baron, which carries the title 'Lord'.

VC	Victoria Cross
GC	George Cross
CV	Cross of Valour (Aus.)
*KG	Knight of the Garter
*KT	Knight of the Thistle
*KP	Knight of the Order of St Patrick
*GCB	Knight/Dame Grand Cross of the Order of the Bath
*OM	Order of Merit
*AK	Knight of the Order of Australia
*AD	Dame of the Order of Australia
*GCSI	Knight Grand Commander of the Order of the Star of India
*GCMG	Knight/Dame Grand Cross of the Order of St Michael and St George
*GCIE	Knight Grand Commander of the Order of the Indian Empire
*CI	Imperial Order of the Crown of India
*GCVO	Knight/Dame Grand Cross of the Royal Victorian Order
*GBE	Knight/Dame Grand Cross of the Order of the British Empire
AC	Companion of the Order of Australia
CH	Companion of Honour
*KCB	Knight Commander of the Order of the Bath
*DCB	Dame Commander of the Order of the Bath
*KCSI	Knight Commander of the Order of The Star of India
*KCMG	Knight Commander of the Order of St Michael and St George
*DCMG	Dame Commander of the Order of St Michael and St George
*KCIE	Knight Commander of the Order of the Indian Empire
*KCVO	Knight Commander of the Royal Victorian Order
*DCVO	Dame Commander of the Royal Victorian Order

*KBE	Knight Commander of the Order of the British Empire
*DBE	Dame Commander of the Order of the British Empire
*Knight Bachelor	
AO	Officer of the Order of Australia
CB	Companion of the Order of the Bath
CSI	Companion of the Order of the Star of India
CMG	Companion of the Order of St Michael and St George
CIE	Companion of the Order of the Indian Empire
CVO	Commander of the Royal Victorian Order
CBE	Commander of the Order of the British Empire
SC	Star of Courage
DSO	Companion of the Distinguished Service Order
AM	Member of the Order of Australia
LVO	Member (now Lieutenant) of the Royal Victorian Order (4th Class)
OBE	Officer of the Order of the British Empire
ISO	Companion of the Imperial Service Order
MVO	Member of the Royal Victorian Order (5th Class)
MBE	Member of the Order of the British Empire
RRC	Member of the Royal Red Cross (1st Class)
DSC	Distinguished Service Cross
MC	Military Cross
DFC	Distinguished Flying Cross
AFC	Air Force Cross
ARRC	Member of the Royal Red Cross (2nd Class)
GCStJ	Bailiff Grand Cross of the Order of St John of Jerusalem
AM	Albert Medal
DCM	Distinguished Conduct Medal
CGM	Conspicuous Gallantry Medal
GM	George Medal
BM	Bravery Medal (Aus.)
QPM	Queen's Police Medal for Gallantry
QFSM	Queen's Fire Service Medal for Gallantry
DSM	Distinguished Service Medal
MM	Military Medal
DFM	Distinguished Flying Medal
AFM	Air Force Medal
QGM	Queen's Gallantry Medal
BEM	British Empire Medal
QPM	Queen's Police Medal for Distinguished Service
QFSM	Queen's Fire Service Medal for Distinguished Service
Commendation for Brave Conduct	(Aus.)

Queen's Commendation for Brave Conduct
War Medals and Stars—in order of the date of campaign for which they were awarded
Polar Medals—in order of date
RVM   Royal Victorian Medal
Imperial Service Medal
Defence Force Service Medal
Reserve Force Decoration
Reserve Force Medal
National Medal
Coronation, Jubilee and other commemorative medals
Long Service Medals
VD   Victorian Decoration
ERD   Emergency Reserve Decoration
TD   Territorial Decoration
ED   Efficiency Decoration
RD   Royal Navy and Royal Marine Forces Reserve
                Decoration
AE   Air Efficiency Award
Foreign orders, decorations and medals (respectively)—in order of date

Commonwealth orders

The Order of Australia grades are shown in their appropriate positions in the above list, but for citizens of other Commonwealth countries the letters designating their own national orders should *precede* any other honours (other than VC or GC).

Thus, for Canadian citizens:

    CC   Companion of the Order of Canada
    OC   Officer of the Order of Canada
    CM   Member of the Order of Canada

follow VC or GC and *precede* any other honours.

For New Zealand citizens:

    QSO   Queens Service Order of New Zealand   *precedes* OBE.
    QSM   Queens Service Medal of New Zealand   *follows* QGM.

3 BUSINESS COMMUNICATION

Oral

Good communication is the key factor in business. Despite the increasing application of microchip technology good relationships between people are built up through effective oral communication. It is important to develop a clear, natural speaking voice, a courteous manner and a tactful approach.

The spoken word is the least costly method of communication but to be effective demands the full attention of both the speaker and the hearer. Ideas can be exchanged, difficulties and problems solved, often more amicably by face-to-face conversation than by any other means. When sitting opposite one another personal reactions can be judged more precisely and a shift of emphasis or change of approach can often achieve the desired outcome. The main disadvantage of business deals transacted in this way is that there may be no record of the conversation. This can, of course, be overcome by a subsequent letter of confirmation.

Courteousness should always be maintained even in the most frustrating circumstances. In busy offices it is often necessary to interrupt other people at work but this is usually accepted with good grace if an apology introduces the request and a suitable tone of voice is adopted. Politeness between office personnel helps to make a more pleasant working atmosphere, although it is not always possible, of course, to like every member of staff.

A tactful manner should be cultivated. The ability to judge when and how to approach colleagues is an important asset in business life. When making a request, or discussing a new idea, choosing the right time can have a crucial effect upon the outcome.

How to address colleagues is a matter of protocol within each firm. Today first names seem to be the norm but it is wise to retain a degree of formality when addressing top executives, or people being introduced and met for the first time. An over-friendly manner may be misinterpreted and may not assist in promoting a good business relationship.

3.1 Reception of visitors to an office

Arrangements for receiving callers vary according to the size and type of organisation. Whether a full-time receptionist is employed or a secretary has to combine this role with other work, the receptionist is the first contact callers have with the firm.

Receptionist
Personal attributes of a receptionist:
> a pleasant personality and speaking voice
> a willingness to be helpful to visitors
> a smart appearance
> some work experience within the firm, in order to have gained a good understanding of its work.

To perform the role efficiently a receptionist needs:
> details of all employees i.e. name, status within the firm, department and telephone extension
> point of contact for executives i.e. personal assistant or secretary
> a copy of the daily appointments register (see p 30)
> up-to-date information on changes within the firm, i.e. movement of staff, absences, those on flexitime (if appropriate) and any other unusual occurrence which may affect callers
> a good internal communication system for contacting persons required by callers i.e. internal telephone, paging device, loudspeaker intercom (depending upon the requirements of the organisation).

Reception
The reception area or room should:
> be adequately furnished with comfortable chairs
> be well lighted, heated and ventilated
> contain magazines, as well as trade and company literature, if appropriate
> have facilities for refreshments if a caller is kept waiting.

Visitors
Visitors may be:
> people with appointments—business customers, clients or representatives, personal friends of executives/staff

members of the firm who need access to executives or managers (*Note:* This is sometimes arranged through a secretary.)

people without appointments—may be genuine contacts or 'time wasters'.

Procedure

(1) *Callers with appointments*

Welcome callers courteously; frequent visitors should be greeted by name.

Check the appointments register, which should list the names of expected visitors, time of arrival, and the persons they wish to see.

Contact any persons required to see if they are free. When using intercom devices speak slowly and clearly. Make sure names are pronounced correctly. Remember that what is said can be heard by the visitor. Never carry on a private conversation when attending to a visitor.

If the person required is available, ask the messenger (if one is employed), secretary or designated person to accompany the caller to the meeting place. Do not leave callers to find their own way.

If the person required is not immediately available, apologise and ask the caller to wait in reception.

If there is prolonged delay explain the reason and apologise again. At this stage it may be prudent to find another person to see the caller, or to arrange another appointment.

If a receptionist has a combined role (e.g. switchboard operator or typist) care should be taken to ensure that the visitor is given priority over other duties.

(2) *Callers without appointments*

These visitors require careful handling to discover if they are genuine or 'time wasting'.

Find out the purpose of the visit and if an immediate interview is necessary see if the person required is available.

It is the policy of some firms not to see casual callers and in this case an appointment should be made.

If the caller is an obvious 'time waster' the receptionist should say firmly but tactfully that there is no one available. Suggest that a message is left or an appointment made for another time.

Do not get involved in arguments with visitors. If they become hostile try to remain cool and courteous; seek the help of a senior member of staff if necessary.

3.2 Scheduling appointments

It is usually the secretary's role to prepare a daily appointments sheet for an executive and keep the desk diary up to date. A check should always be made to record any appointments booked directly by the executive. In the first instance appointments should be entered in the desk diary in pencil and inked in when confirmed.

Checklist for booking appointments:

avoid times allocated to routine tasks and meetings

space out appointments in case meetings and discussions run beyond the allotted time

confirm telephone appointments by letter, stating time and place

follow up when appointments are not kept and try to find out the reason

if appointments need to be cancelled through illness or unavoidable urgent business, do this by telephoning and making a new appointment.

3.3 Dictating correspondence

Shorthand

There are a number of advantages in having a shorthand secretary (or shorthand-typist) despite the economy of time in using an audio dictating machine. The personal contact provides greater interest and job satisfaction to the secretary; queries can be raised and settled quickly as they occur. A shorthand secretary should be well informed about the firm and able to advise and assist in many ways. A well-trained and experienced shorthand secretary should be capable of dealing with routine correspondence by composing letters from brief notes.

Guidelines for dictation to a shorthand-typist

Prepare notes for dictation before calling in the shorthand-typist.

Speak clearly. Do not try to dictate whilst smoking or eating.

An experienced shorthand-typist is able to punctuate and paragraph according to the sense of the passage and inflection in the dictator's voice. However, if there are individual preferences regarding punctuation it is as well to indicate them.

31

Give instructions regarding any special requirements, e.g. extra copies for distribution.

If there are interruptions during dictation (e.g. a difficult or confidential telephone call) signal the shorthand-typist to leave so that time is not wasted.

Avoid mistakes over names, specialist or technical data by giving the shorthand-typist relevant correspondence.

Audio

The use of a dictating machine saves time because recording can be done at any time most convenient to the dictator. A regular flow of small amounts of dictation throughout the day will help the audio-typist to achieve an even output of work. Where dictation tapes can be shared between several audio-typists this further improves the work flow. Dictation can also be recorded after office hours, at home or on the move, i.e. in a car, train or aircraft.

Other advantages of audio are:

the audio-typist is not interrupted by telephone or other calls whilst transcribing

the recording media can be mailed easily so that transcription need not wait until the dictator returns to the office

dictating machines can be used for other purposes: recording interviews and telephone conversations for later transcription; leaving instructions for work to be done during absence; dictating notes for the secretary to compose letters.

Guidelines for dictation to an audio-typist

Make sure the machine is working properly and the controls are understood.

Organise materials and thoughts before starting to dictate. Make any necessary notes to avoid mental blocks occurring during dictation.

Do not switch on until ready to start dictating as gaps in the recording will be confusing to the audio-typist. However, it is wise to leave a space between dictated passages in case it is necessary to insert instructions. Switch off when 'thinking' time is required.

Hold the microphone about 6″ from the mouth. Enunciate words carefully, emphasising word endings and plurals. Do not let the voice fade at the end of a sentence. Use the telephone phonetic alphabet for single letters which might be confused (see p 37).

The audio-typist must be able to understand quickly what is to be typed. Meaning and expression should be indicated by intonation of the voice. Vary the tone and speak more quickly when dictating instructions.

At the beginning of each passage indicate the length of the letter or document (i.e. short, medium or long), the number of copies required and any other particular requirements, e.g. distribution. Index strips are often used to indicate document lengths but it is helpful to the audio-typist in selecting stationery to be told on the recording medium also.

Dictate all punctuation marks and paragraphing, also any special requirements regarding headings, the use of capitals, brackets, etc. The audio-typist will not be able to produce good copy at the first typing unless clear instructions are given.

Erase errors by playing back and recording over.

Remote control system

This involves a pool of dictating machines. Dictators can dial over the internal telephone system, or a special circuit, to a bank of recording machines and dictate when convenient. It is preferable to record in small batches to spread the load in the audio centre. A supervisor controls and distributes the work between the audio-typists, and then arranges for the completed transcripts to be checked and returned to the originator. Although this is an impersonal system because the dictator and audio-typist may never meet, it is efficient and well suited to part-time employees and job-sharing.

3.4 Using the telephone

The telephone system provides a quick and easy form of instant communication between subscribers in homes, shops, offices, hospitals or factories situated almost anywhere in the world. All telephone subscribers are permanently connected to exchanges and exchanges can all be connected together. Via the exchange system, telephone calls are temporarily set up for the duration of the call.

General information

Dialling codes are needed to make calls to telephones on other exchanges and to call countries where there is direct dialling. Each telephone subscriber is given a booklet listing local, national and international dialling codes.

Telephone directories are issued free for a customer's own area. All customers are listed in strict alphabetical order, i.e. surname, initials, address. Directories explain how to get emergency services (on 999) and give details of operator and information services, e.g. directory enquiries.

Yellow page directories list all business subscribers under their respective trade or profession.

Telephone numbers in major cities are in all-figure form, e.g. 01-246 8071 (London). Elsewhere in the UK all telephone numbers have an exchange name associated with the number. The dialling codes for all exchanges in the UK are given in the dialling code booklet provided by British Telecom. Information on international dialling codes and tones is also given in the booklet.

Tones

Dial tone is a continuous purring or high pitched hum meaning that the equipment is ready for a call to be dialled.

Ringing tone is a repeated 'burr-burr' which indicates that the equipment is trying to call the dialled number.

Busy tone is a repeated simple tone meaning that the dialled number or British Telecom lines are in use.

Number unobtainable tone is a steady high pitched note indicating that the called number is unobtainable for one of the following reasons:

    the number was incorrectly dialled
    the number is a spare or ceased line
    the number is out of order
    the number is temporarily out of service.

No tone means a fault on the line or on the equipment. The code and number should be checked before re-dialling.

Pay-on-answer tone is a series of rapid pips telling the caller to insert money, and the called person that the call is from a payphone. Many coin boxes now require payment by credit card purchased from a post office.

Special information tone is a repeated series of three tones in ascending pitch indicating that a recorded message is about to be given.

Costs

All dialled telephone calls are charged in units. The time allowed per unit depends upon the time of day, day of the week, distance of the call and the destination. A map is available showing the extent of local call areas and calls within that area are all charged at local rate.

Monday to Friday

Cheap rate operates from midnight to 0800 and 1800 to midnight

Standard rate operates from 0800 to 0900 and 1300 to 1800

Peak rate operates from 0900 to 1300

Saturday and Sunday

Cheap rate operates over each 24 hours

Operator services

Operators help over difficulties and offer a range of services. See Chapter 21.3.

Guidelines

These give recorded information on specific topics and are obtained simply by dialling a special number (see p 218).

Making a telephone call

Check that the number and dialling code are correct. (Refer to telephone directory, dialling code booklet or directory enquiry service if necessary.)

Lift the receiver, listen for the dial tone (continuous purr or high pitched hum).

Dial code, if required, followed by the number. Dial carefully taking the dial right round to the finger stop and letting it return freely. For a press button telephone, press each button carefully to its full extent. Press at a steady rate. If a mistake is made replace the receiver for a moment or two and then re-dial.

When the call is answered ask for the person required and/or extension number if known, and give the caller's name.

Costs in time and money can be reduced if a note is prepared, in advance of making a telephone call, of the salient points for discussion or areas of enquiry. This is especially so when a message has to be left with a third party, or on an answering/recording machine (see p 37).

If a call is cut off replace the receiver for a few seconds before dialling again.

Answering a telephone call

Answer promptly and announce the number. If answering on an extension telephone announce your name or the department, whichever would be most helpful. Pick up the receiver with the hand not normally used to write with.

Keep a message pad and pencil by the telephone. A message should be repeated to ensure it is correct. Take the caller's name and telephone number. Make sure the message is given immediately to (or left for) the person for whom it is intended. If an enquiry involves collecting information, offer to call back and say what the delay is expected to be. An example of a useful message form is given below.

Telephone Message		
FOR_____		
DATE_____TIME_____		
WHILE YOU WERE OUT		
M_____		
FROM_____		
PHONE NO._____		
TELEPHONED		PLEASE PHONE
RETURNED YOUR CALL		WANTS TO SEE YOU
CAME TO SEE YOU		WILL CALL AGAIN
MESSAGE_____		
_____		
_____		
_____		
_____		
_____		
_____		
TAKEN BY		

If an incoming call is cut off, replace the handset and wait for the other person to call again.

Using an answering/recording machine

The use of one of these machines when no-one is available to answer the telephone personally means that no calls or messages are missed. An announcement is recorded which invites the caller to leave a message. A bleep signifies when to start dictating the message. Business firms and private households have been quick to recognise the value and convenience of installing answering/recording machines and the majority of callers now find them acceptable.

The benefits of installing a machine, especially to the business user, are:

customers are not restricted to calling during normal office hours but can call when convenient to them

prospective customers can call immediately they read an advertisement, whether in the evening or during the week-end

incoming calls are spread so that congested lines are avoided during normally busy periods

if messages can be received before opening time it is possible to plan certain work schedules more economically, e.g. maintenance engineer, sales follow-up, ex stock goods delivery, staff absence

work flow is improved when outside staff can telephone in and indicate reports or messages for immediate action at any time of the day

meetings and work routines need not be interrupted by telephone calls at inconvenient times.

Pronunciation

Do not shout on the telephone; talk quietly but distinctly into the mouthpiece. Change the pitch of your voice and speak more slowly if there is difficulty in being heard. Clear and careful pronunciation prevents errors and aids efficiency. Use the telephone alphabet given below when spelling out words:

A	Alfred	J	Jack	S	Samuel
B	Benjamin	K	King	T	Tommy
C	Charlie	L	London	U	Uncle
D	David	M	Mary	V	Victor
E	Edward	N	Nellie	W	William
F	Frederick	O	Oliver	X	X-Ray
G	George	P	Peter	Y	Yellow
H	Harry	Q	Queen	Z	Zebra
I	Isaac	R	Robert		

Some numbers can be confused over the telephone. Here is a guide to pronunciation:

0	Long 'O'
1	Emphasise 'N'
2	Emphasise 'T' and long 'OO'
3	Slightly rolled 'R' and long 'E'
4	One syllable, long 'O'
5	Emphasise first 'F' pronounce as 'Fife'
6	Long 'X'
7	Two syllables
8	Long 'A' emphasise 'T' as in 'Ate'
9	One syllable, emphasise 'N' and long 'I'

When saying telephone numbers, groups of two or three numbers come most naturally; more than four can be confusing for the listener.

4 EFFECTIVE SPEAKING IN PUBLIC

The ability to speak fluently and effectively is a tremendous asset in business life and it carries no particular mystique. Contrary to popular belief everyone is capable of being a good speaker, providing sufficient attention has been paid beforehand to certain basic principles. Lack of confidence deters many people from volunteering to speak in public, but after the first time, and with practice, this becomes less and less of a problem.

Talks fall naturally into the following categories or combinations of these categories:

to inform
to persuade
to solve a problem
social speaking.

The first thing a prospective speaker must do, therefore, is to identify the main purpose of his or her talk.

4.1 Identification and purpose

To inform

This is the most straightforward type of talk, and the most effective way to deal with it is to find a sequence to build upon. For instance, an account of a journey provides its own sequence, so does a progression of events or ideas, or a description of someone's life and achievements.

If possible, build from basic facts which the audience already know to the new information to be imparted, working from the known to the unknown. Some kind of structural sequence can usually be found with a little thought.

Be absolutely certain that all your facts are accurate; it is not wise to risk a public correction from someone in the audience.

To persuade

A sales talk is one variety of this kind of talk ('Our products are the best'), or a call to action ('We want production figures doubled by next month') or simply a talk to the board to prove that your point of view is better than theirs. There can be many variations on the theme of persuasion. Barristers and politicians are experts in this technique. However, it is not effective just to state a point of view, a preference or even a strong belief and to expect your audience to agree. They need good reasons, if not absolute proof.

Bring in all the ammunition you can to support your argument. Use all your cunning to make your theme look attractive. If you are selling an idea, quote instances where similar ideas were successful. Set out the advantages to follow from the adoption of your proposals. Say what will happen if your advice is *not* adopted.

Quote references and sources of support. Your recommendations must be clear and understandable, and you must, of course, be totally convinced of the value of your cause. Anticipate any counter-objections that may come up and demolish them with sound argument before anyone has a chance to voice them (e.g. 'You may say that this is not going to work but I can prove that it will') and give your reasons with good examples.

Sound argument backed up by clear reasoning, combined with enthusiasm and conviction, should bring success; the more vitality and conviction you can show in your manner the more convincing you will be.

To solve a problem

You may already have the answer to the problem or, as in a committee meeting, you may hope to find it with the help of your audience.

To start with, muster all the information possible. Understand the different points of view that are held, so that the problem is clear in your own mind and you can explain it as simply as possible to your hearers. You should also know why the problem has arisen and the developments arising from it, and what may happen if it is *not* solved. You may suggest your own ideas for solving it, quote the various alternative ways put forward by others, and recommend a particular one if you have a preference.

This type of talk should be especially clear and constructive, with sensible suggestions put forward, and it may well have a set 'question time' afterwards, with general discussion and vote-taking in order to come to a final decision.

Social speaking

It is not unusual to be asked, sometimes at short notice, to propose a vote of thanks, open a new department, welcome a newcomer, say farewell to a colleague on retirement, propose a toast to a special guest or perform any other necessary social ceremony with grace and competence.

Between five and ten minutes is probably a suitable length for such speeches; more time could make them tedious. Keep the treatment light and amusing. Little anecdotes can be incorporated, provided that they have a bearing on the subject. Try to avoid saying 'And that reminds me of . . .' before bringing in a funny story, as it is usually obvious that this is not strictly the case.

Bring in personal but kindly references to those present (topical touches are appropriate) and mention familiar matters with which the audience can identify. All of these can combine to make a warm, humorous little speech. Risqué stories and controversial subjects must be avoided. You are there to contribute to the festive occasion and to combine the necessary formalities with a cheerful and light touch. Both speaker and audience should be enjoying themselves.

Two special variations on social speaking are set out below; the formula to introduce a guest speaker and the little vote of thanks that should follow.

To **introduce** a guest speaker:
state the qualifications of the speaker
remind the audience of the subject
give the speaker's name
give a signal that it is time to be quiet and attentive.

For instance (these are brief pointers and can of course be adapted):
'Ladies and Gentlemen, it is my great pleasure this evening to welcome someone whose talents and achievements in the world of business are well known. He is the Principal of the Royal College of Commercial Communicators and he is going to tell us about the latest work they are doing there. He is the author of those two well-known books "Electronics for Everyone" and "Technical Analysis in Business" and I am sure we are going to hear a highly interesting talk. Ladies and Gentlemen, I am delighted to introduce . . .'

Pause slightly, give his name, look at him and smile, then sit down and start the clapping. The audience will clap, quieten down, and then settle down to listen.

To give a **vote of thanks**, stand up and say something on the following lines (again using your own adaptation):

'Ladies and Gentlemen, I am sure you would wish me, on your behalf, to thank Professor Peabody for her most interesting (amusing/instructive) talk. I was most interested to learn that (quote something appropriate that you have heard) and I am sure we are all now much the wiser about (whatever the subject was). I for one have enjoyed it tremendously, as I am sure we all have. Thank you, Professor Peabody, for a most interesting (exciting/informative) talk.'

Look at her, smile, start the clapping, and the audience will join in.

4.2 The audience

There may be only a few people present, as at a board meeting, or a vast number, as for a large formal lecture, and a speaker needs to know the size of group and the type of people who will make up their audience. Find out beforehand and plan your talk accordingly. Speak naturally, in your own style, but with proper consideration for those listening. Guard against appearing insufferably clever, and never talk down to an audience. A group of qualified engineers, for instance, will understand technical language but young trainee managers will need more general terms. The setting itself may be formal or informal and your manner and vocabulary should be adjusted sensibly to the occasion.

4.3 Content and construction

Theme

When you have decided on the type of talk you are going to give, take pen and paper and set down your main themes, with wide spacing between the lines for additions and notes. Then add notes to fill out your first draft, developing the headlines into paragraphs. Give your talk a beginning, a middle and an end. You might treat this as introduction, main theme(s) and conclusion. Adding a brief summary at the end is often useful, to remind the audience finally of your main points.

Develop your subject so that ideas move naturally from one to another in a way that makes it easy for your listeners to follow. Link ideas together; do not jump like a grasshopper from one subject to another unconnected one.

Timing

When your script is finally written out, read through it, revise and polish, and then talk it through, timing it carefully with a stopwatch. A tape-recorder is very helpful as you can play a recording back to yourself. Perhaps you have been asked to speak for twenty minutes; if you are speaking for twenty-five minutes prune carefully, tighten up the wording and re-record. If you are only speaking for fifteen minutes, add more material or suitably expand your existing paragraphs. Re-time, alter and adjust until your talk is exactly right for length at the rate at which you will be speaking. In this way you can make any talk fit exactly the time you wish it to take.

When rehearsing the talk, infuse an element of vitality and enthusiasm into what you are saying. This will bring the whole thing to life and make all the difference to the way your audience will receive it.

Check cards

The next step is to transfer the main paragraph headings onto a small card, to hold in your hand as a reminder while you are actually speaking. The main points should be written briefly in clear bold lettering, easy to pick up with a quick glance during your talk, to keep you on course, to ensure that you make your points in the right order, and to prevent you from omitting anything or actually drying up. It will not matter that you are seen to refer to your little card from time to time. If you need several, they can be held unobtrusively in a small pack, and you will be able to remove the top one from time to time and replace it at the back of the pack as you go confidently on your way.

Visual aids

If you are planning to use visual aids, make sure beforehand that they are in good order, and check that there will be no missing charts, non-existent projectors, chalkless blackboards or other embarrassments. Equipment must be up-to-date and in good working order, and of course this includes microphones. If you have an article to demonstrate, see that it will actually be there when you want it, that it works, and that you can anticipate and answer questions about it. It may be necessary to get to the hall or room early to see that everything is ready for you, or to check with your chairperson.

4.4 Presentation and delivery

Stance and gesture

Stand still and do not fidget. Keep gestures moderate and controlled. Do your best to appear relaxed. Do not pace restlessly up and down, jingle keys or coins in your pockets, toss a piece of chalk up and down, rub your nose, polish your spectacles or adjust your tie. Many people find it useful to hold something (check cards, for instance, or a pointer if you have slides or wallcharts to talk about). On the other hand, do not appear rooted to the spot or taut with nervous anxiety. Natural movement and an occasional gesture for emphasis are acceptable and quite sufficient.

Clarity

Speak clearly, perhaps a little more slowly than your natural conversational pace. If you are using a microphone, hold it a few inches away from your mouth, not too close or the sound will be loud and distorted. Try it out beforehand if you can. Should there be no microphone, pitch your voice as naturally and distinctly as you can, so that you can be heard at the back of the room or hall. There is no need to be self-conscious about a regional accent if you have one, but it *is* vitally important to be clear. Never mutter or mumble, and do not indulge in any ums and ers and y'knows, or any of the other irritating little clichés of sloppy and careless present-day speech.

Eye-contact

Remember that you have something to share with your audience and that your main purpose is to hold their interest and attention. Look at them, let your eyes make contact with different individuals, talk *to* them and not *at* them or beyond and past them. Be interested in your own talk and make that enthusiasm personal and infectious.

4.5 Interruptions

This is a difficult problem but it can be dealt with sensibly. Usually it is best for a speaker to ignore it altogether, relying on the chairperson to deal with it by having the offenders removed if necessary. A well-judged retort to a heckler may silence him or her temporarily and can make the heckler look foolish, but never do anything to start a slanging match. If you can score a point with good humour then do so, but to deal successfully with such nuisances is really a matter for the experts and the amateur is best advised to take as little notice as possible of rude interruptions, relying on the chairperson, or whoever has introduced them, to deal with the situation.

4.6 Conclusion and questions

Finish your talk definitely and finally. Do not tail off in a vague way so that the audience is uncertain whether you have finished or not. If the talk has been well constructed they will sense when you are coming to your conclusion, because you will be summarising or winding up your material. When you have done this and have reached the end, stop decisively and sit down.

To bring questions to an end when time is running out, say 'I think there is just time for one more question'. When this final question has been put and answered, the speaker can say 'I'm afraid that has to be the last one, as time has now run out', or the chairperson may do this for the speaker. There is no reason why talks and lectures should run overtime to the inconvenience of both speaker and audience.

4.7 Self-confidence

Self-confidence comes with good preparation and practice, and a self-confident speaker is usually a good one. Nervousness is every beginner's problem, but this need only be a temporary disadvantage if a speaker takes a little trouble to learn and persevere.

There are a number of excellent books on effective speaking, some of them listed below. You will find a selection on the shelves of your local public library.

Bibliography:
Stand and Deliver: Handbook for Speakers, Chairmen and Committee Members, by Kenneth P Brown. Pub. Thorsons Publishers Ltd, 1983.
The Art of Speaking Made Simple, Gondin & Mammen. Pub. Heinemann, 1983.
Tips on Talking. Pub. BACIE, 1960, 14th impr. 1983.

5 BUSINESS COMMUNICATION

Written

5.1 Business stationery

International paper sizes

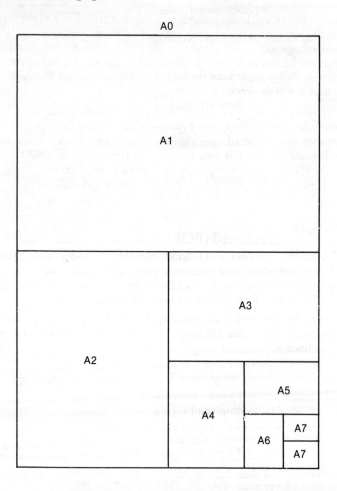

Sizes

A0 = 841 × 1189 mm	A4 = 210 × 297 mm
A1 = 594 × 841 mm	A5 = 148 × 210 mm
A2 = 420 × 594 mm	A6 = 105 × 148 mm
A3 = 297 × 420 mm	A7 = 74 × 105 mm

Types of paper

Bond A good quality paper which should not crease or tear easily. Usually white although pastel colours are obtainable. Used for top copy and business correspondence, when the firm's letter heading is printed at the top of the page. Normal weight 70–90 gsm (grammes per square metre).

Bank A flimsy paper used for carbon copies and sets of forms. White or coloured and weighing 40–45 gsm. When regular multi-person/ department distributions are made, coloured copies can be used to identify specific areas.

Air mail A thin lightweight paper which reduces the cost of overseas air mail postage.

NCR (no carbon required) The reverse side of the top copy and top sides of subsequent sheets are treated with a special substance to produce copies.

Post Office Preferred (POP) envelopes and cards

There is a preferred range of sizes known as POP which is based on its suitability for Royal Mail equipment, and this range is recommended for all users, big and small. To fall within the POP range envelopes must be:

no smaller than 90 × 140 mm
no bigger than 120 × 235 mm
oblong in shape, the longer side should be at least 1.4 times the shorter side
made from paper weighing at least 63 gsm including contents.

The most widely-used International Standards Organisation envelope sizes fall within the POP range, i.e. DL (110 × 220 mm) and C6 (114 × 162 mm).

The above rules apply equally to window envelopes and cards. Rigidity is especially important for cards; to be sufficiently rigid they must not be less than 0.01 in. thick with a tolerance to an absolute minimum of 0.009 in.

Other types of envelope

A stock of the following shapes in varying sizes should be kept in the stationery store:

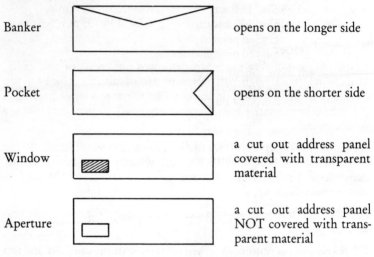

Banker	opens on the longer side
Pocket	opens on the shorter side
Window	a cut out address panel covered with transparent material
Aperture	a cut out address panel NOT covered with transparent material

Window and aperture envelopes save time as the name and address does not have to be typed twice, but care should be taken to position the window correctly so that no detail is lost. Enclosures must be secured so that they do not move and obscure the address.

Letterheads, business cards, compliment slips

Letterheads   Most firms use a letter heading detailing:

 registered name
 registered office
 logo (if any)
 directors, company officials' or principals' names
 branch offices and/or subsidiary companies
 telephone number(s) and STD code
 telex number
 VAT number (if any).

The modern tendency is for the printed letterhead to be blocked to the left hand margin which then matches fully blocked letter layout. (See 5.2).

An advertising slogan may be incorporated on the headed notepaper. The quality and style of letterheading should reflect the firm's image and create in the public a feeling of confidence.

Business cards   Standard size cards (88×55mm) are most popular as they fit easily into wallets and cardholders. Business cards may contain most of the information printed on the firm's letterhead, with the card owner's name displayed prominently.

Compliment slips   Small pieces of paper which have details of the firm and *With Compliments* printed on them. These details are usually the same as those printed on the firm's letterhead. Compliment slips are used to accompany leaflets and small items where a letter is not considered necessary. They may be square or oblong. If printed as part of the firm's stationery order, i.e. on an A4 sheet, two thirds for the letter heading and one third for the compliment slip is the most economical layout.

Memoranda

Commonly called 'memos', these are used internally for sending messages to employees of a particular organisation, i.e. in the same building, or to representatives/agents based elsewhere in the country or abroad.

Printed forms are usual, specifying: To; From; Date; Reference; Subject heading.

No formal salutation or complimentary close is used. If there are enclosures ENC(S) should be marked at the end of the memo, against the left hand margin. A copy should be retained for filing.

5.2 Correspondence

Business letters—setting out

The most widely used and economical layout for a business letter is the fully blocked style with 'open' punctuation. All the parts of the letter are set against the left hand margin which should be aligned with the firm's printed letter heading. No punctuation is used except to ensure clarity in the address and text of the letter. Abbreviations do not need full stops.

Example showing letter parts and style:

Our reference	AD/DT (author's/typist's initials)
Date	12 April 198–
Addressee	Mr J Brown
	Brown, Green & Co Ltd
	3 Prince John Street
	LONDON N16 0RH
Salutation	Dear Sir
Subject heading	CHAMBERS OFFICE ORACLE
Text of letter:	
—introduction	I was very pleased to receive your letter of 8 April asking for an advance copy of our above publication to be released shortly.
—development	I am sending you two copies as requested so that you can circulate them amongst your staff and gauge their reaction to its suitability as an office reference book. I feel confident that they will find it the most comprehensive combined office manual and dictionary on the market today. The detailed index makes it very quick and easy to use.
—conclusion	I look forward to receiving your favourable comments in due course.
Complimentary close	Yours faithfully
Name of firm	W & R CHAMBERS LTD
Allow	
5/6 line spaces	
for signature	
Signatory's name	(A N Other)
Signatory's designation	Sales Manager
Enclosure(s)	ENCS

Note: The usual salutation and complimentary close for a business letter is:

'Dear Sir(s)/Madam' followed by 'Yours faithfully'.

or

'Dear Miss, Mrs, Ms or Mr' followed by 'Yours sincerely'.

If a *For attention* line is used it should be inserted before or after the addressee's name and address. The letter, however, should be addressed to the company (i.e. Dear Sirs).

Letters should be typed on the company letterhead in single-line spacing, unless they are very short, when double-line spacing can be used. Continuation sheets are usually typed on plain matching paper with details of page number, date and addressee's name at the top of the page against the left hand margin.

Business letters—composing

A good business letter should be concise, courteous and correct in tone. It is usually set out in three paragraphs as indicated in the example above but that arrangement should not become artificial. Use the following logical arrangement for paragraphing:

(1) Introduction (one paragraph)	states subject of letter acknowledges a correspondent's letter (quotes date and reference, if any)
(2) Development (one or more paragraphs)	deals in a methodical way with the subject previously referred to in the introduction, i.e. lists facts or arguments, gives detailed explanation, outlines a course of action
(3) Conclusion (one paragraph)	usually kept for expressions of courtesy and goodwill which leave a favourable impression in the reader's mind.

The use of a subject heading, especially in a complicated matter, helps the letter to be correctly routed, gains the reader's interest and saves time.

Be specific and give full details, e.g. relevant dates, prices and description of articles, specification numbers and components.

Check that all the correspondent's queries have been answered.

Consider the letter from the reader's standpoint; what the writer takes for granted may not be obvious to the person receiving the letter.

Avoid opening the final sentence of the conclusion with a present participle such as hoping, trusting, wishing. For example, 'Thanking you for your prompt attention to our order, I am, Yours faithfully' . . . This sentence would be incomplete without the words 'I am'. The plain statement 'We thank you for your prompt attention to our order' is preferable.

Style Keep sentences short and to the point. Paragraphs will vary; they should not consist of one short sentence, nor must they be too long. Long paragraphs are more difficult to read and to understand than short paragraphs. (See also Chapter 1.1).

Tone   Courtesy is more than the occasional use of a polite word or phrase. The reader's response should be borne in mind constantly and tactful phrasing sought. For example:

'May I clarify several points'
not
'You appear to have misunderstood several points'.

The tone of a letter reveals the writer's personality; a co-operative person writes a friendly, constructive letter.

'As we do not appear to have received . . .'
not
'As you forgot to enclose . . .'

Business letters help to create good public relations; they indicate an efficient organisation.

Direct mail—planning the letter

The four most common components of a direct mail package are: a letter; a reply service; an envelope; other inserts.

Direct mail tends to be a 'words' medium, an individual communication between advertiser and prospective customer, in which illustration and graphics are supportive of a message already expressed in words. The letter is the primary consideration in any mailing as it is the 'salesman'.

Construction and presentation

Write from the recipient's point of view, presenting the advantages and benefits to be gained from buying the product or service. Stress how it will help the prospective customer, what problems it will solve, why it is the most suitable product of its kind and the most cost-effective. A successful letter will:

gain attention by identifying a problem and offering to solve it
convince the recipient the product is the solution by describing how well it does what it is meant to do, how pretty it looks, how reasonably priced it is, etc.
stimulate desire to buy or find out more about the product (—case histories or glowing testimonies from people whose business efficiency or lifestyle the product has enhanced)
encourage immediate action (—include a reply card or envelope).

There are two key areas for attention in the presentation of a direct mail letter:

(1) *Salutation*   Use a name if possible, or 'Dear Gardener' or 'Dear

Wine Lover'. Avoid 'Dear Sir' and never use 'Dear Sir/Madam'. Consider a heading promoting the product's benefits.

(2) *After the complimentary close*   A PS can enhance the response rates by, for example, announcing a discount or a special gift for people who reply before a certain date.

The body of the letter should be broken up into easy-to-read paragraphs, with sub-headings, indentations and underlinings to emphasise key points. Anything that makes the letter easier or more exciting to read will be advantageous.

Refer to Royal Mail leaflet *A Guide to Effective Direct Mail* for more detailed help. (See also Chapters 6.4 and 26.6).

Telemessages—composing

The telemessage is an electronic letter service which combines easy telecommunications access with reliable postal delivery. Telemessages can be sent from telephones, telex machines or the customer's own computer terminal equipment. Telemessages may be dictated from any telephone (with the sole exception of cardphones) by simply dialling 100 (190 in London) and asking for the Telemessage Service. Telex users should refer to the telex director for their access code.

Telemessages are printed on single sheets on A4 Telecom headed notepaper and delivered with the first class post on the next working day. They follow the format of a business letter with the sender's name and address, and the date printed in the top right hand corner. The text can be a short note, technical letter, lists with tabulating, or just a simple greetings message. The advice given on planning a business letter applies equally to telemessages. There is a limitation on the length of text (up to 35 lines). Telemessages are charged in blocks of 50 words at varying rates. Operators will help customers to lay out their message to achieve the desired impact.

A senders-copy service and business reply service are available.

5.3 Reports

In the business world a written report is often required for meetings and conferences or to summarise the result of an investigation. It provides information, reports on findings, puts forward ideas and may make recommendations. Reports must be carefully structured and the facts arranged logically so that the reader can grasp the meaning quickly and easily.

Reports deal with a wide range of topics and vary greatly in length, e.g. a single sheet of paper, a brochure, a book with chapter headings, footnotes, index and appendices.

It is important to note the difference between minutes and a report. Whereas minutes concentrate on recording decisions reached, a report analyses the reasons which lead to the decisions recorded.

Main types of report

Company   This is a report required by statute to be made annually to shareholders. The Directors' Report, the audited statement of accounts and the Chairman's Annual Review are often contained in one booklet.

Annual (of a voluntary organisation)   The Honorary Secretary usually presents this at the Annual General Meeting. It may also incorporate the Treasurer's accounts.

Committee   A committee may be set up to study and report on a given problem. It will investigate, hear evidence and issue joint findings (e.g. Government Reports published by HMSO).

Conference   A conference is usually held to exchange ideas, disseminate and/or formulate policy. A report is made setting out the factors involved and the reasoning which led to an acceptable solution.

Expert   This is a report commissioned from one who possesses specialised knowledge (e.g. engineer, surveyor).

Unusual occurrences   Fire, accident, theft: usually forms are used in the first instance to ensure that all the relevant information is given in a logical order. If an enquiry is later set up a report may be required setting out the findings.

Routine   In industry and commerce all firms need a constant flow of up-to-date information on such matters as raw materials, stocks, liquid assets and sales. In the normal course of work, responsible persons may be asked to provide reports on problems within their organisation. These may be written out formally or, if short, may be in the form of a letter or memorandum. Reports required urgently may be given orally—face to face or as part of a telephone conversation.

Preparation

Subject   Make sure of the concise terms of reference and be clear on the scope and purpose of the report.

Reader   Bear in mind: (a) what the reader knows already and wants to know; (b) the terminology that will be understood; (c) how the report may be used.

Material   Collect facts and ideas and file them under selected topics. Check for accuracy.

Structure

The following arrangement is frequently used:

terms of reference—statement of instructions/purpose
presentation of facts—analysed, then set out in the most effective order
conclusions—after study of the facts
recommendations—after study of the conclusions.

Method

Use this sequence in composing a report:

define the purpose briefly, then choose a suitable title
consider the facts and decide upon the conclusions and recommendations
select sufficient facts to support the conclusions and recommendations
arrange the material in logical order under appropriate headings
review and revise the material.

Style

Keep the following points in mind:

the tone should be impersonal and economical in wording
all views should be balanced and fair, free from bias
the facts should speak for themselves
keep the language: (a) brief, e.g. use 'if' not 'according as to whether'; (b) clear and definite, e.g. avoid expressions like 'in the region of'; (c) simple, e.g. use 'find out' not 'endeavour to ascertain'
use active constructions as they are more forceful and save words
avoid jargon and clichés—they will not impress the reader
keep sentences short, as involved sentences can impede understanding.

(See also Chapter 1.1).

Content

Checklist

Does the report state clearly: (a) subject and purpose?; (b) date?; (c) scope?; (d) by whom it was drawn up?

Does the main part of the report contain all the relevant facts?

Is the order of the main part of the report in logical sequence?

Is the problem clearly stated?

Is the main issue obscured by small details?

Are the sources of facts clearly set out?

Do the conclusions follow logically from the facts?

Have abbreviations and symbols been used consistently?

Are there any statements where the meaning is not quite clear?

Are all facts, figures and calculations accurate?

Format

Layouts vary widely. A routine report will not be set out in the same way as the findings of a conference, but this checklist covers the main requirements:

Is the layout clear and easy to follow?

Are the main parts of the structure in the most suitable order?

Do the headings stand out clearly?

Is the numbering of pages and paragraphs uniform?

Are the appendices clear and helpful?

Presentation

Reports should be accurately typed and attractively presented in a neat cover. If the report is to be duplicated or printed check the typescript carefully before it is submitted.

5.4 Summarising

The ability to summarise accurately is a valuable skill for noting messages, instructions, interviews with clients, dealing with correspondence and reports, and in minuting meetings.

A summary is a condensed form of verbal or written work. Brevity is secured by selecting the essentials and stating these tersely. However, a summary must remain faithful to the original work and must cover all essential points.

Skill in summarising requires:

> common sense
> an ability to listen
> careful reading
> frequent practice.

Using reported speech

For business purposes a summary is a record of a past event and is thus written in reported speech. When converting a passage to reported speech these guidelines should be followed:

> present tenses become past tenses
> verbs already in the past may need changing to the remoter past to keep the correct relationship
> future tenses must be changed to the conditional
> pronouns must be changed to the third person
> question marks and exclamation marks must not appear in reported speech.

> 'Are we all agreed that our next meeting will be held on the first Wednesday in March?' asked the chairman
> *becomes*
> The chairman asked if members agreed that their next meeting should be held on the first Wednesday in March.

Note: The past tenses of 'may' and 'can' are 'might' and 'could'.

Basic technique for summarising

Read the document carefully several times so that the theme or central argument becomes clear.

Study each section in turn. Pick out the main points, underscore and number them.

All paragraphs may not be of equal importance, e.g. the introductory paragraph may have little to underscore whereas the central paragraphs may contain many important points.

Eliminate any repetition, lists, examples and detailed description. Retain technical terms or names.

Use your own words to note in short sentences the points underscored.

Check each point against the original passage making slight modifications if necessary.

Combine the notes into a continuous narrative, paragraphing appropriately. Be as brief as possible without changing the facts or sense.

Avoid disconnected statements and aim for a logical flow of sentences to provide continuity of thought.

Make sure that the summary is a clear and fair impression of the original and will make sense to the reader.

Summarising correspondence

Follow the basic summarising technique, using reported speech.

The layout should emphasise the following:

a title heading incorporating the names and addresses of correspondents
the subject of the correspondence
the date of each letter.

Keep to an active construction and avoid lengthy introductory statements, e.g.

'Bowes & Co complained . . .'

not

'Bowes & Co wrote saying that they wished to complain that . . .'.

5.5 Copy preparation and proof correction

There are certain basic rules for the preparation of manuscript for publication. A well prepared manuscript saves time and money.

Copy preparation

Style of presentation should be decided and adhered to consistently throughout the work.

Copy should be typed in double-line spacing on one side only of good quality A4 paper using a good quality black ribbon. A copy should be kept against loss of the original. Electronic typewriters and word processors allow for corrections and amendments to be made easily, and a variety of founts can be used quickly. Copy can also be prepared on disk for direct processing by the printer.

Headings—the importance of main, shoulder, side and sub-headings must be made clear to the editor and printer.

Margins should be kept uniform at top, base and sides. A quick estimation of the number of words per page or per chapter can then be made. A wide left-hand margin is usual so that the printer can add instructions for printing where necessary.

Punctuation marks and symbols, including use of single and double quotes, must follow a consistent pattern. Use open punctuation for abbreviations and acronyms.

Spelling should be kept consistent where dictionaries give alternatives for certain words.

Time—it is preferable to use the 24-hour clock (e.g. 1400 hrs not 2 o'clock or 2 pm).

Dates can be given as '1 November 1987' and 'in the 1980s' (no apostrophe). In tables and schedules months can be abbreviated to three letters.

Mathematical and scientific symbols should be inserted by hand if they cannot be typed exactly.

Metric system is now used almost worldwide (see Chapter 25.1). Use a written letter 'l' for litre as the typed 'l' could be confused with the figure '1'.

Footnotes add detail to the text and should be inserted at the end of the page carrying the text reference, at the end of the chapter, at the end of the completed work, or at the base of a tabulation. The standard symbols are * † ‡ § or superior numerals, with or without brackets, running serially throughout an article or chapter.

Illustrations should be kept separate from the main typescript but their exact position in the printed work should be clearly marked. As illustrations greatly increase the cost of printing their inclusion should be carefully considered. Photographs should not be folded, written on or clipped to a manuscript. Keep flat and pack carefully between stiff card if posted.

Pages should be numbered consecutively throughout the work. Attach a front page giving the name and address of the author(s) and title of the article or book. It is better not to staple or pin the completed manuscript.

Proof correction

The printer's readers check the proofs and mark any literal errors and queries before passing them on to the author. Alterations or corrections made by the author should be in a different colour from

Group B   Deletion, insertion and substitution

Note: The letters M and P in the notes column indicate marks for marking-up copy and for correcting proofs respectively.

Number	Instruction	Textual mark	Marginal mark	Notes
B1	Insert in text the matter indicated in the margin	λ	New matter followed by λ	M P Identical to B2
B2	Insert additional matter identified by a letter in a diamond	λ	λ Followed by for example Ⓐ	M P The relevant section of the copy should be supplied with the corresponding letter marked on it in a diamond e.g. Ⓐ
B3	Delete	/ through character(s) or ⊢———⊣ through words to be deleted	⌀	M P
B4	Delete and close up	⌒ through character or ⌒⌒⌒ ⊢———⊣ through character e.g. chara̓cter charaͦcter	⌀̑	M P
B5	Substitute character or substitute part of one or more word(s)	/ through character or ⊢———⊣ through word(s)	New character or new word(s)	M P
B6	Wrong fount. Replace by character(s) of correct fount	Encircle character(s) to be changed	⊗	P
B6.1	Change damaged character(s)	Encircle character(s) to be changed	✕	P
B7	Set in or change to italic	——— under character(s) to be set or changed	⊔	M P Where space does not permit textual marks encircle the affected area instead
B8	Set in or change to capital letters	≡≡≡ under character(s) to be set or changed	≡	

Extract from BS 5261 : Part 2 : 1976 reproduced by permission of the British Standards Institution. Complete copies can be obtained from BSI at Linford Wood, Milton Keynes, MK14 6LE.

that used by the printer. Ideally corrections should be confined to misprints; alterations, other than minor adjustments, are very costly.

Standard correction marks   The British Standards Institution issue a classified list of standard marks for use in copy preparation and proof correction (BS 5261C:1976). An extract is shown opposite. Each correction is shown by a mark in the text with a corresponding mark in the left- or right-hand margin.

Return of proofs to printer   Clear written instructions should be made on the proofs in answer to any queries raised by the printer. If further page proofs are necessary, subject to the final corrections being made, the printer should be told. (For a glossary of printing terms see Chapter 27.5.)

6 ADVERTISING AND PUBLICITY

6.1 Choosing an advertising medium

The range of outlets available for successful advertising continues to increase and so reach a wider audience. The methods available to the businessman or private individual are specified below.

Broadcasting Commercial television and independent local radio.

The Press National and local newspapers; monthly and weekly magazines catering for every kind of interest; trade and technical journals.

Direct mail e.g. Reader's Digest.

Outdoor advertising All kinds of transport: rail, bus, underground, and stations; posters and signs on hoardings and shop fronts; aerial banners, etc.

Other Cinema screen; exhibitions; point of sale.

Faced with this diverse range of options, the advertiser needs to formulate a clear set of principles upon which a choice can be based. In evaluating cost-effectiveness, the price of the product, the size of company and the type of operation required are all factors which should affect choice.

Target group
Define: the sex, age group and social economic group (e.g. high, middle or low income group, or retired) of readership or audience.

Media
Consider: which medium will reach the greatest number in the chosen target group, in the required depth, at the right time and in the right place

the advantages and disadvantages of each type

which media are used by competitors

the importance of speed and timing

the volume and frequency required

whether the various methods are easily available

whether surveys are available showing the effectiveness of the preferred medium.

Cost

Compare: the production costs

the comparative costs with other media

any rate concessions offered.

At the top end of the market, advertising at national level requires expert budgeting, planning, creation, placing, publishing and checking of advertising campaigns. This is a three-way operation involving the advertiser, advertising agency and media owners, as well as other ancillary services.

Advertising agencies

Advertising agencies are experts who prepare campaigns, known as 'accounts', for customers. They are media independents who plan and buy space and air time; they may arrange for other creative agencies to prepare materials. It is worth noting that whereas agents do not usually incur any liability on a contract, an advertising agent becomes responsible for paying the media and, should the need arise, may have to pursue the client for the debt.

Publicity

Publicity may not necessarily be bought but may be built up through good public relations. It is an important part of any business's marketing process. (See Chapter 12.6).

The press, radio and television are always keen to get a good story and the keen businessman should build up good relations with the media, using opportunities for news about his firm. This can be done by the firm issuing a **press release,** or employing a **public relations consultant** who can advise and prepare an appropriate campaign.

When issuing a press release make sure: that it is noticed (print *Press Release* across the letterhead); that it has eye appeal; that it has an attractive heading; that it is suitably brief; that it is simple in style; that it includes prices where applicable. If there is a human interest story involved this will add to the appeal.

A **press agency** will take a story or press release and distribute it. The timing of the release is vital; it is wise to get it to the editor early in the day, preferably on a Monday when news may be sparse. Allow ample time for consideration by the editor and for possible changes.

6.2 Independent broadcasting

Time can be bought on ITV, Channel 4, Independent Local Radio (ILR) and *Oracle* teletext just as space can be bought in newspapers. Independent broadcasting is financed in this way. Television advertising time is restricted to a total of six minutes in any hour averaged over the day's programmes, whilst radio advertising is normally limited to a maximum of nine minutes in each hour. Advertising breaks are carefully controlled: there must be a clear distinction between programmes and advertisements; they should occur in natural breaks, and there should be an even spread of advertising.

The Independent Broadcasting Authority enforces a strict code of advertising standards and practice by examining over 10000 new television scripts and 8800 new radio scripts per annum. A copy of *The IBA Code of Advertising Standards and Practice* is available from IBA on request.

Television is an intimate form of advertising, reaching as it does millions of homes daily. This method of advertising is for the multi-national companies; production and air time costs are high. Expert advice and assistance is essential in the production of professional programmes in order to ensure customer appeal and impact.

Independent local radio is a powerful advertising medium which offers cost-effective advertising over 46 local radio stations. Charges are about one third of television costs for the same length of commercial. The programme style consists of news bulletins, short features and entertainment items, with music catering for all tastes across the musical spectrum. Each local radio station broadcasts programmes to suit local needs and interests. Listeners are encouraged to phone in to express opinions, seek advice on solving problems or participate in locally sponsored events, all of which suggests that commercials are likely to be well received. Radio is available all day—in the home, garden, car, street or at work.

ILR stresses listener loyalty. Its research shows that 73% of all radio listeners tune into one station and there are high levels of repeat listening. This produces an unusually stable audience around which it is easy to plan and buy advertising space. It is an immediate medium, peak listening time being early in the morning before people go shopping. With stations covering almost the whole country, radio offers flexibility in the selection of geographical markets suited to the needs of the individual advertiser.

Radio commercials offer low creative costs; they are quick to make and can be tested and varied easily, thus making them an attractive marketing opportunity. They do however require the assistance of experienced radio copy writers to achieve the greatest impact.

Advertising packages are available from stations to meet advertisers differing needs. For example, the advertiser can opt for evenly spaced spots throughout a broadcasting week, or a 'Target Group Plan' where a specified reach and frequency is guaranteed for target groups over seven days. There are only three buying points:

Broadcast Marketing Services
7 Duke of York Street, London SW1Y 6LA   Tel: 01-839 4151

Independent Radio Sales
86/88 Edgware Road, London W2 2EA   Tel: 01-258 0408

Capital Radio Sales
356 Euston Road, London NW1 3BW   Tel: 01-388 6801

Local advertisers can buy direct from their ILR station.

The *Radio Marketing Bureau* (259–269 Old Marylebone Road, London NW1 5RA. Tel: 01-258 3705) promotes independent radio to the advertising industry and is ready to give advice on all aspects of radio advertising. It has also developed various services to aid the planning of radio campaigns and these are available free of charge to enquirers.

Chapter 26 lists addresses of television and radio stations.

6.3 Press

National

Advertising in the national newspapers is a high cost operation but it has the advantage that people throughout the country will get the same advertising message in the same newspaper on the same day. Care must be taken to select the paper which will reach the right target group for the product or service offered. Some nationals have days and sections devoted to specific businesses (e.g. holiday, entertainment, cars, property). *British Rate and Data,* known as BRAD, is useful for studying the market. It is available in most libraries and lists different types of magazines, newspapers, etc., together with advertising rates and technical data, including circulation figures.

(For addresses see Chapter 26).

Regional

It is claimed that around 75% of adults in Britain see a local 'paid for' paper each week, as well as seeing one or more of the proliferation of free papers. This indicates that more people read a local paper than all the nationals put together. These statistics place the local press in an advantageous position for the advertiser. Local papers mirror the characteristics of their areas and so it is possible to plan advertising campaigns tailored to a particular section of the public. By using regional advertising it is easier to pin-point specific target groups geographically and less wastage occurs.

The *Regional Newspaper Advertising Bureau Ltd* (Grosvenor House, 141 Drury Lane, London WC2B 5TB. Tel. 01-836 8251) promotes national advertising in the regional press, covering some 1500 local papers. It keeps the advertising industry aware of its existence by selling the benefits of local and regional newspapers and providing services in the planning and use of the medium. Its computerised database and mapping facility has produced *Where,* a definitive guide to the regional press which has become an essential reference work in promoting and improving access to regional newspapers. The Bureau also operates a central booking facility for agencies who do not employ staff experienced in handling a booking service. The Co-operative Advertising Division is another expanding area of service to advertisers.

6.4 Direct mail

Direct mail has become increasingly popular in recent years for business and consumer advertising. It is now the third largest advertising medium in the United Kingdom, absorbing more of the total national advertising budgets than posters, cinema and radio put together. (See also Chapters 5.2, 26.6).

Developments within the industry have improved the quality of mailshots and made it a more effective advertising medium, either standing alone or as part of a multi-media campaign. However, unless direct mail is professionally organised it can result in wasted energy. Successful direct marketing is based on three factors: an accurate mailing list, correctly targeted to a potential target group of users; the product or service on offer; well-produced sales copy which carries impact and reflects the value of the product or service to the target group.

There are professional consultants who can provide a range of sophisticated services, e.g. a specially-generated marketing file validated against the National Household File, demographic data, response analysis and facilities for promotions to be enclosed and mailed. Royal Mail offer an extensive range of discount programmes which includes a free trial run for first time users of their Business Reply Service and Freepost. (See *The Guide to Effective Direct Mail* issued by Royal Mail).

The advantages of direct mail are that it can:

select potential customers with great precision

provide a choice of formats and creative approaches

be directed personally to the target user.

Consumer direct mail
The most common uses for consumer direct mail are:

selling direct to the customer without the need for middlemen

generating sales where a product requires a meeting between customer and sales force (e.g. fitted kitchens, central heating)

sales promotion of special offers with 'money off' vouchers

seeking enrolment of club members (e.g. book and record clubs)

mail order to recruit new customers and local agents

fund raising by charitable organisations.

Business direct mail
Business markets usually consist of quite tightly defined groups of people for whom mass advertising is not suited. Direct mail can accurately pin-point different market sectors to suit different requirements such as launching a new industrial product or business service, sales lead generation to help minimise wasted calls, dealer support, conferences, etc.

The strategy of a well organised direct mail campaign comprises:

(1) *Initial planning* Decide the role direct mail will play within the overall marketing strategy.

(2) *List selection* Define the target market. If this is unknown employ market research consultants.

(3) *Designing and writing material* Decide what is going to be said to the identified audience. (See p 52).

(4) *Printing* Translate the words and pictures (if any) into print and production.

(5) *Mailing* Physically collating all the items and despatching them. Except for small mailings this work is best done by a mailing house.

(6) *Response and fulfilling* It is vital that this is carried out promptly, e.g. supplying goods, arranging for salesmen to call, etc.

(7) *Analysis of results* The advantage of direct mail is that it is easily measurable, i.e. new business set against expenditure involved.

(See also Chapters 20.1, 26.6).

6.5 Outdoor advertising

Posters, cards and signs are the main media used in outdoor advertising. They are pasted on hoardings, inside and outside all kinds of transport, on sites at railway and bus stations, in bus shelters and at airports. Electric signs appear mostly in crowded urban streets, and on panels on the fascias of shops. In fact, any site can be used if planning permission has been granted for advertising purposes.

More specialised outdoor advertising can be by aerial means, e.g. trailing banners from aircraft, hot air and tethered balloons, airships, etc. There is also a developing advertising area known as *Newscaster* which uses an electronic device to show a moving strip of words; one application alternates news with advertisements. It has a versatile application ranging from signs on high buildings to a video strip in a shop window.

At Heathrow Airport Terminal Four underground station there is a video wall. Television monitors in banks of three are set into the cross-track wall of the single loopline station. Advertising time is sold in 60 or 30 second slots for up to twelve months, the advertiser's message being repeated every six minutes throughout the day.

Posters and signs are a mass advertising material which cannot be thrown away or turned off. They can be most effective when used to augment advertising in other media—television, radio or the press—by keeping a particular message or brand name constantly in the public eye. Success is dependent upon booking a selection of sites where there is a guaranteed audience.

Basic guidelines for posters are that they must be seen frequently and demand attention; the message must be brief, easily read and quickly understood by people on the move. Conversely, posters placed inside transport or in station waiting-rooms can be more informative; there the travelling public are a captive audience who have time to read more detailed copy. It is the place to give more information, to use illustrations or a series of posters, and to add some humour so that interest is maintained.

Posters and signs

Questions for consideration

What role will the poster play in the overall advertising strategy—remind or inform?

Does the size conform to the specification on the rate card?

Has colour been used for impact and realism?

Will the budget buy sufficient sites to ensure repetition value?

Are the best materials being used to give long life, and what is the possible replacement cost if one is mutilated?

What are comparative costs and can the scheme be tested?

Has geographical flexibility been utilised to ensure that the right kind of people see the poster?

Can a visit be made to assess the value of the site(s)?

Does the copy comply with the rules of advertising?

Poster Marketing (21 Tothill Street, London SW1H 9II. Tel: 01-222 7988) and *Outside Site Classification and Audience Research* (OSCAR) act together as a marketing bureau for the poster trade and will help and advise potential advertisers.

London Transport Authority (LTA)

London Transport Advertising offers extensive poster space distributed across the richest market-place in Britain—Greater London. It provides a comprehensive, versatile and sophisticated method of communicating with a potential daily advertising audience of over seven and half million consumers—residents, commuters and tourists. The LTA have analysed by demographics and life style their captive audience and the result is fully illustrated in their brochure *Advertising on the Move*. Details of costs and campaign planning are given in their brochure *Rate Card 18* together with information on eight campaigns which have produced impressive results.

Underground Research has shown that each year over 750 million passenger journeys are made on the London Underground. A recent survey of the attitudes to advertising by regular users of the Underground showed that the majority noticed posters and appreciated the impact, colour and information they provided. The average commuter stands face-to-face with a cross-track poster for at least three minutes before catching a train so can read and digest even the longest copy.

Buses LTA's fleet of double-decker buses is an advertising medium unique to the capital and moves for 18 hours every day through areas where it is often impossible to buy any other form of advertising. The campaign thus reaches passengers, pedestrians and motorists simultaneously. The high coverage and frequency offered make it equally effective as a single medium or as part of a mixed media schedule.

Recent research and development has produced a new technique in poster display on London buses. This has improved the quality of display and provided advertisers with a wider choice of format and more space. Posters are printed on vinyl or paper and mounted on tough, rigid, lightweight plastic boards. These boards are then slid into existing frames and locked tight to give all-round protection.

All over painted buses are available in Central London. The Cityrama fleet of 22 buses are advertising vehicles with an audience potential of commuters, London residents, overseas visitors and other UK tourists. Twelve open-top double-decker buses normally operate in the high tourist season, from May to September, and ten closed-top buses operate for twelve months of the year. They run exclusively on the London sightseeing tour which takes between one and a half and two hours to complete.

There are no design restrictions, all exterior bodywork of the bus, apart from the windows and destination blinds, being available. The interior of the bus can also be used for advertising, and leaflets or products distributed. Advertisers may also hire their painted bus for promotional purposes.

For further advice and information contact: The Sales Manager, London Transport Advertising, 10 Jamestown Road, Camden, London NW1 7BY. (Tel: 01-482 3000).

7 GRAPHS, CHARTS AND VISUAL PLANNING

There are many ways of presenting figures—from a small tabulated statement to a large display board. Graphic presentation of information is much more revealing than columns of figures. Whatever type of work is being conducted there are generally figures to be analysed—wages, exports, sales, prices, expenses, crime figures, births and deaths—the list is endless.

Obviously the method of presentation of facts must fit the purpose for which it is intended. Where figures are constantly fluctuating, perhaps weekly or even daily, an easily adjustable method needs to be used. Before selecting the type of graph or chart to be used it is important to identify the kind of comparison which is called for. Concentrate on key points and choose the chart form which brings out these points most graphically. Unnecessary detail weakens the impact.

Charts do not supersede other forms of records but they present existing records in pictorial form. There are many business areas where charting can considerably improve efficiency.

7.1 Line graphs

Much statistical information can be effectively displayed in line graph form—purchases of raw materials, sales figures for exports, monthly salary figures, daily temperature readings in the factory, orders for newly marketed products, etc.

The graph has a two-dimensional display of data. The two dimensions (axes) are the *index* (vertical axis) and the *scale* (horizontal axis). The graph is formed by plotting one against the other.

There are several points to remember when compiling a line graph:

give a suitable heading or title
annotate each axis adequately
time is usually shown on the horizontal scale, reading from left to right
the vertical scale must read from the base upwards and must be marked at regular intervals according to the data given; choose as large a scale as possible
plot each point carefully and join to the following point by a straight line

if possible draw on squared paper so that a set number of squares
   can be given for each unit along each of the axes
multi-line graphs must have a key displayed showing the colour or
   line formation adopted.

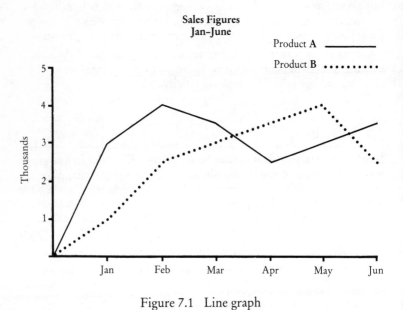

Figure 7.1   Line graph

7.2 Bar charts

A bar chart is the best way to display comparative figures, month by month or year by year. It can be displayed either vertically or horizontally.

Vertical

The information conveyed by the line graph (Fig. 7.1) could be given just as effectively in a bar chart (Fig. 7.2).

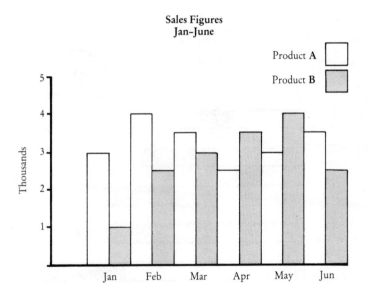

Figure 7.2   Vertical bar chart

Horizontal

Here the vertical dimension is not a scale but is merely used for labelling the items measured. The bars can therefore be used in any sequence.

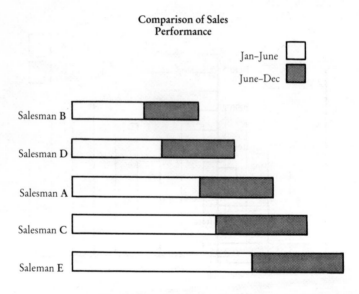

Figure 7.3   Horizontal bar chart

Deviation

Items are ranked in a rising scale from the least profitable to the most profitable. A vertical line separates the winners from the losers with the bars extending to the right of the centre line for winners and to the left for the losers.

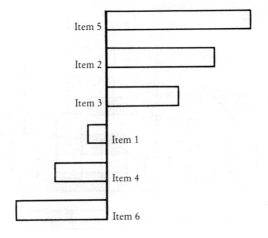

Ranking of Items

Figure 7.4   Deviation bar chart

Combined bar and curve

This type of chart shows both the fluctuation in each month's figures and the cumulative trend since the beginning of the year.

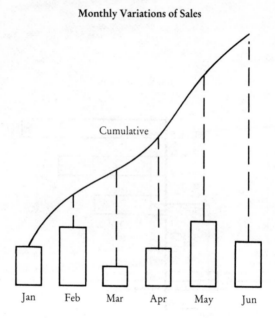

Figure 7.5   Combined bar and curve

7.3 **Histogram**

This is a specialised form of bar chart showing frequency distribution, where the peak is at the centre of the distribution.

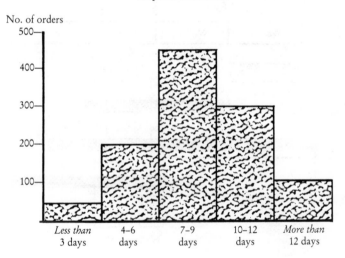

Figure 7.6   Histogram

7.4 Gantt chart

This is used to show the comparison between work which has been scheduled and work which has actually been accomplished in relation to time. In Figure 7.7 the work scheduled is shown by heavy lines and the work completed by the end of the second week by light lines.

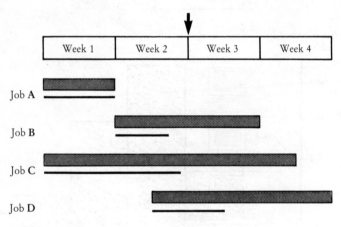

Figure 7.7 Gantt chart

7.5 Pictogram

This is a form of graph which is represented pictorially and is very useful for presentation to the general public. There are three important points to note:

    the drawing must be clear and simple

    each drawing must represent a stated amount

    further amounts have to be shown by *further* pictures and not by larger pictures.

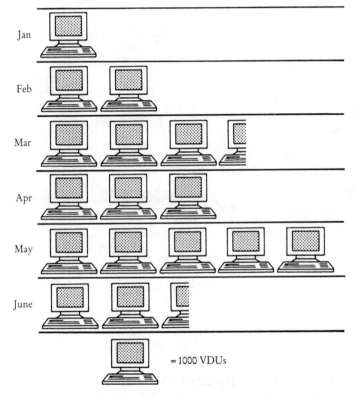

Figure 7.8   Pictogram

7.6 Pie chart

Pie charts are often used when it is necessary to show the relationship of parts to a whole. It is best to use as few component parts as possible and preferably not more than four or five.

There are two ways of focusing special attention on a single component:

using a darker shading or colour
separating the segment from the remainder of the pie.

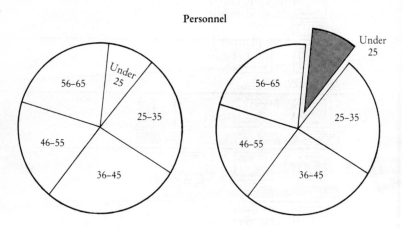

Figure 7.9   Pie charts

7.7 Visual planning control boards

Visual planning is quite simply a means of presenting the essential facts of a complex situation immediately and clearly. Properly used, visual planning ensures that the overall situation is grasped quickly, decisions can be taken faster and with greater confidence, problems can be more accurately defined and future trends and needs can be more effectively assessed.

The five stages for effective visual planning on control boards are:

defining the system and establishing the two axes

choosing an appropriate grid

displaying information to the best advantage, using chart pens, self-adhesive or magnetic shapes and tapes

selecting accessories for assembling and maintenance of the chart—uncomplicated in design, flexible in use and easy to assemble and re-assemble

providing suitable mountings for single charts, groups of charts and for transporting charts from one location to another—with provision for confidentiality where this is required.

The **perpetual year planner** (Fig. 7.10) is a popular form of visual planning control board. Printed on a metal board, this has magnetic moveable date strips and can be used year after year.

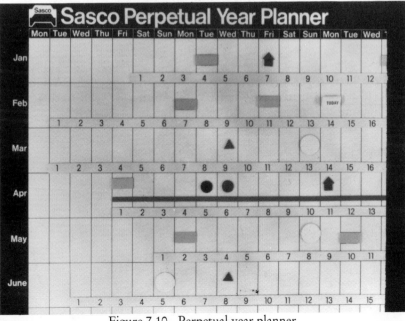

Figure 7.10 Perpetual year planner

A variant of this is the **fiscal planner** (Fig. 7.11) for use by accountants, local government officers and anybody who plans an April to March year.

Figure 7.11   Fiscal planner

A wide range of matching visual planning components is available and more sophisticated equipment, such as executive chart cabinets which house up to nine grid charts in sliding tracks. These are ideal for housing information which requires a measure of security.

Part II
BUSINESS PROCEDURES

8 BUSINESS ENTERTAINING

Much goodwill can be derived from successful business entertaining; insufficient care and preparation may create a bad first impression and never lead to a good business relationship. Often the organisation of visits and the entertainment of visitors is the responsibility of a separate department which needs to be informed of the names of visitors, the purpose and length of the visit, dates and times of arrival and departure and any special requirements.

Those lacking expert assistance may find it helpful to create a 'Visitor Profile' with the following headings: Who?; Length of visit?; Purpose?; Where?; How much can we spend? Possible sub-headings are: Accommodation; Food and Drink; Transport; Excursions; Staff assistance; Outside agencies. The 'Who' section will cover not only name, designation and other background details but also whether the person to be entertained comes from the home country or abroad.

8.1 Home and overseas visitors

Whoever the visitors are, a warm welcome is essential, therefore:

confirm appointments in writing so that there is no confusion on either side

ensure that the visitors know how to reach the venue

supply the home visitor with a map accompanied by details of public transport and clear road and parking directions.

An overseas visitor may need to be met at an airport or station and must be told how to make contact and where to wait if necessary. Those meeting visitors should overestimate (rather than under-estimate) the time allowed to reach the meeting point and both visitor and host need a mutual telephone number to contact in case of difficulty. The onus is on the host who has the advantage of local road/ rail/air timetables and information services. If the guest has come straight from an intercontinental flight, allowances must be made for time differences and jet-lag, leaving an interval for rest and refreshment before the commencement of an important meeting or an exhausting tour.

The length of visit will dictate the type of hospitality to be offered.

8.2 **Short term visits**

Short term visits, such as half-day or full-day factory or office visits, invitations to drinks, lunch or dinner (possibly requiring overnight accommodation), need careful planning to ensure that the guest is suitably entertained and supplied with the maximum information without being rushed or made to feel part of a public relations exercise. To keep the personal touch:

  inform the receptionist of the expected time of arrival of the visitors

  make sure they are met at reception and personally escorted to the host's office or the meeting room

  appoint a member of staff to take care of the guests, arranging cloakroom facilities, providing refreshments and taking care of personal needs e.g. confirming travel times, checking appointments, making telephone calls

  if there is an interval between the arrival of visitors and the beginning of the meeting or tour, ensure that the callers are not allowed to wander about the premises unattended and that the waiting period is made as comfortable as possible.

If the visitor is to be shown round the factory or work site:

  obtain clearance from heads of departments

  arrange special safety equipment as needed, e.g. in 'hard hat' areas

  check with security services whether passes or identity tags are required

  organise transport to facilitate movement throughout the site

  give clear instructions on safety precautions and warnings of 'No smoking' zones.

An office visit may mean liaison between several departments with a carefully arranged timetable so that departmental heads, supervisors and other essential staff are available when required. In these circumstances:

  ensure that each department has a copy of the itinerary and that it is clear which member of staff is responsible for welcoming visitors and handing them on to the next department

  allocate departmental responsibility for provision of refreshments e.g. coffee/tea/lunch arrange for the tour to end in plenty of time so that visitors can catch trains/planes or keep their next appointment

at the end of the tour make sure visitors are returned to the starting point so that questions can be answered, future action settled, belongings collected and the host can bid them farewell

occasionally it may be necessary for visitors to stay overnight and for accommodation to be provided; an invitation to dinner may be appropriate followed by some entertainment e.g. theatre, concert, cabaret—the host should make the necessary arrangements having regard to budget limits and the visitors' preferences.

8.3 Long term visits

Long term visits e.g. for a weekend or for several days, require more detailed planning, a careful choice of venue and a wider selection of leisure activities involving the considerations laid out below. The 'Visitor Profile' will show who is to be entertained and the length and purpose of the visit. Background details will give some clues as to the visitors' possible requirements and tastes. Authorities such as a national's embassy may be able to help with suggestions regarding entertainment, food and drink, particularly when there are restrictions on the grounds of religion or custom.

Budget

Before any arrangements can be made it is essential for the host to know how much can be spent. Most organisations have an annual allocation of funds for business entertaining and many have clear guidelines on the standard and extent of entertainment which can be provided. Towards the end of the financial year funds may be running low. Therefore whatever is available must be used to the best advantage.

Venue

Check what can be offered within the company e.g. meeting rooms, catering facilities (ranging from the supply of tea or coffee to providing informal drinks, lunches, formal and informal dinners), conference accommodation, printing (for invitations, publicity material, handouts).

If the required facilities are not available some research is necessary.

Never accept an estimate at face value; always visit, see the accommodation, take a check list of requirements and make sure the objectives can be met. Having selected a venue, establish a contact who will be responsible for seeing that the arrangements are carried out efficiently.

Menus

Ensure that the contact knows the limits of the budget and is able to provide a choice of menu to allow for special diets for vegetarians, diabetics, etc. Remember religious restrictions e.g. Jewish, Islamic. To such visitors some food and drink may be unacceptable e.g. meat (especially pork) and alcohol.

Staff

Involve as many staff as possible; inevitably there will be some who can relate to the visitors for various reasons; utilise their services; look to them for guidance e.g. on dietary and religious requirements; ask for assistance in interpreting, hosting and escorting; remember to thank them for any help they give.

Transport

If visitors have to be met or conveyed from one site to another, check available transport, company cars, public or private transport, referring to budget, time schedule and 'Visitor Profile'.

Social activities

If the visit is long term the 'Visitor Profile' needs to be expanded to highlight leisure activities and preferences, therefore:

> find out what leisure activities are available at the venue and within a convenient distance

> research local resources—theatres, concerts, sight-seeing excursions

> enlist the assistance of hotels, theatre/travel agents, visitors' centres and tourist boards.

Reservations

Confirm all reservations and requirements in writing. Keep to deadlines, particularly for catering when extra numbers and last minute orders for special meals can upset schedules. Check all arrangements by personal contact to avoid any misunderstandings thus ensuring the maximum comfort of guests.

Bibliography and useful sources of information:

Hotels and Restaurants in Great Britain. Pub. Automobile Association, annually.

Good Food Guide. Pub. Consumers' Association and Hodder & Stoughton, annually.

AA and *RAC Handbooks.*

Yellow Pages and *Thomson Local Directory* (for local catering services).

National and local newspapers; telephone information services (for entertainment and leisure activities).

The P.A.'s Handbook (Ch.17 Social and Business Entertaining), by Joan Moncrieff and Doreen Sharp. Pub. Macmillan Press, 3rd edn 1987.

9 MEETINGS

A meeting is a means by which a group of people with a common interest can share ideas, pool experiences and participate in decision-making. A properly conducted meeting is a method of two-way communication enabling information to be given and received, problems discussed, grievances aired, tactics explained and decisions taken.

9.1 Types of meeting

Formal meetings

A formal meeting is one which is closely controlled by regulations. The rules governing the conduct of meetings are set out in the Articles of Association of a company, a club's constitution or the standing orders of a local authority. A breach of these regulations may invalidate proceedings at a meeting. Examples of formal meetings:

Statutory Meetings required by law, e.g. the first meeting of the shareholders of a public limited company.

Ordinary general Often called **annual general** meetings, these are the regular yearly meetings of the members of an organisation. The Companies Acts require a public limited company to hold ordinary general meetings at intervals of not more than 15 months, and 21 clear days' notice must be given to all members who have the right to attend. Formal business only can be conducted at these meetings e.g. the presentation and adoption of the annual report and accounts and the appointment of officers and auditors. It is usual for the chairperson to review the past year, outline plans for the future and answer members' questions.

Extraordinary/special These are meetings called at the request of members or officers to discuss and vote upon urgent issues which are outside the scope of a general meeting. Such meetings are not held regularly but only when required to transact extraordinary or special business. Special regulations in the constitution or standing orders govern the convening and conduct of such meetings.

Shareholders Shareholders are members of a company and have the right to attend these meetings. A company may also call meetings of different classes of shareholders, e.g. preference shareholders and ordinary shareholders, when matters have to be discussed which affect one category of shareholders only.

Creditors The Companies Acts also provide for meetings of a company's creditors in the event of the company going into liquidation.

Board Those appointed by members to run the organisation on their behalf, e.g. directors, meet regularly to discuss strategy and make policy decisions. As the members of the board are accountable to the members of the company, provisions for the formal conduct of such meetings are made in the relevant legislation, e.g. the Companies Acts and the internal regulations of the organisations concerned.

Informal meetings

An informal meeting may be said to be one which is not closely constrained by legislation or internal regulations. Those attending the meeting are often well known to each other; the atmosphere is therefore more relaxed and the discussions less restrained. Such meetings may be called at short notice but any decisions taken may have to be confirmed by a higher authority. Examples of informal meetings:

Committee Meetings may be held at regular or irregular intervals depending upon the type of committee. The degree of formality depends upon the regulations governing the committee's formation.

Staff Staff meetings are generally informal, e.g. departmental meetings or meetings of certain categories of staff such as sales representatives. When a Staff Association is formed formal regulations are drawn up governing the appointment of representatives and the convening of meetings.

Working parties These may be formed by a parent committee for the purpose of discussing and reporting back on certain matters. Recommendations can be made but action cannot be taken without the approval of the parent committee.

Managers Intercommunication between departments and divisions is essential to good management. Managerial meetings, although informal, may have considerable influence upon the running of an organisation.

9.2 **Preparation**

Venue

The place in which a meeting is held can influence the effectiveness of the meeting. If the meeting place is too large communication between those attending may be limited; if it is too small discussion may be stifled. When making preparations for a meeting consideration must be given to:

the size of the meeting room
its availability and accessibility
seating accommodation
lighting and heating (or air conditioning)
resources available, e.g. microphones, audio-visual aids, toilet facilities and cloakroom accommodation, availability of refreshments.

Notice

The notice of a meeting states the date, time and place of the meeting and the type of meeting to be held. The notice must be sent to all those entitled to attend; the length of notice required depends upon the type of meeting and the regulations governing it. Frequently the notice is sent out with the agenda and may appear on the same document as the agenda, e.g. as part of an internal memorandum calling an informal meeting.

Agenda

A list of items to be discussed at a meeting. It is the first step towards an effective meeting because it should:

define the purpose of the meeting
plan the content of the meeting
give members the opportunity to prepare for the meeting.

A customary order for agenda items is:

appointment of chairperson (if not already appointed)
apologies for absence
approval of the minutes of the previous meeting
matters arising from the minutes
correspondence
reports of committees, working parties or officers

general business of the meeting
date of the next meeting
any other business.

The agenda for a meeting at which formal motions are to be discussed should contain the full wording of such motions.

9.3 Procedures

For a meeting to be effective and valid it is important that procedures and regulations are strictly followed. The chairperson, secretary and other officers are the persons most concerned with ensuring this.

Chairperson

The person appointed by members to take the chair is responsible for:

the correct conduct of the meeting, e.g. ensuring that the agenda is followed, that minutes are accurate, properly approved and signed, that regulations and procedures are observed
maintenance of order
deciding who shall speak; anyone addressing a meeting does so 'through the chair' and fair opportunity should be given for all aspects of an argument to be considered
ensuring that discussion keeps to the point of the business in hand
guiding the discussion and summing up when appropriate
formulating proposals and amendments
taking decisions on points of order
ascertaining the 'sense' of the meeting i.e. taking votes and declaring the results
closing or adjourning the meeting
ensuring that any necessary follow-up action is taken.

Secretary

The secretary must be thoroughly conversant with regulations and be prepared to assist the person in the chair with procedures before, during and after the meeting. The specific responsibilities of the secretary are:

to send out the notice convening the meeting in the required form and within the prescribed time
to draw up the agenda in consultation with the chairperson
to prepare the meeting room

    to keep the attendance register

    to make arrangements for recording votes

    to draft the minutes and maintain the minute book

    to remind members of any follow-up action required of them and ensure that reports and/or supporting documents are submitted in time for the next meeting.

The secretary may be a paid official or an honorary secretary. Sometimes a separate minutes secretary is appointed to be solely responsible for minuting the meeting.

Officers

Other officers may have specific duties to perform at a meeting. For example, the treasurer of a club or society may be required to report regularly upon the financial position of the organisation; chairpersons of sub-committees or working parties may be required to attend certain meetings to report back on the work of their groups.

9.4 Terminology

Some terms commonly used in connection with meetings are explained below:

ad hoc committee One appointed to deal with a particular job, on completion of which the committee is disbanded. (Sometimes called a *special purpose* committee.)

adjournment The postponement of completion of the business of a meeting. A meeting may be adjourned by the chairperson, with the consent of the meeting and subject to the regulations. Notice of an adjourned meeting must be given.

amendment A proposed alteration to a motion which adds, inserts, deletes or substitutes words.

ballot A secret vote by means of voting slips placed in a sealed ballot box.

casting vote A second vote which may be allowed to a chairperson to resolve a deadlock when an equal number of votes are cast for and against a motion.

closure A motion proposed with the object of ending discussion on a matter before the meeting.

co-option The power to invite other members to serve on a committee by majority vote of the elected members.

ex officio This term means 'by virtue of office'. A person who is not an elected member may be invited to attend a meeting by reason of his or her office, e.g. the official secretary to a committee.

in attendance Persons invited to attend a meeting to give expert advice, help or information.

in camera In private i.e. not open to the public.

intra vires Within the power of the person or organisation concerned.

lie on the table A motion or document (e.g. an application for membership of a club) on which no decision will be taken at present is said to 'lie on the table'.

majority The number of votes required to carry a motion. A *simple* majority is one vote more in favour of the motion than the number cast against. The regulations of an organisation define the number of votes required to pass a resolution.

motion A motion is a proposal, moved by a member, that certain action be taken. The motion must be seconded by another member before the chairperson puts the question to the vote. A motion passed by a majority vote becomes a resolution.

nem con No votes cast against a motion (although some members may have abstained from voting).

point of order A question raised by a member regarding procedure at a meeting or about a possible infringement of the regulations.

poll A method of voting which enables account to be taken of the number of votes each person holds. The way in which a poll is to be conducted is laid down in the regulations.

proxy One acting for another. A person may be appointed to vote on behalf of another who is unable to attend the meeting.

quorum The minimum number of persons required by the regulations to be in attendance to constitute a valid meeting.

show of hands A method of voting. The chairperson calls upon all those members in favour of a motion to raise one hand. When these have been counted by the tellers the chairperson asks for those against the motion and then those who wish to abstain, to raise their hands. The total number of votes cast for and against a motion, with the abstentions, should add up to the number of voters present at the meeting.

standing committee A permanent committee e.g. a local government housing committee.

sub-committee A small committee appointed by a main committee to deal with some specific part of the main committee's work.

teller One who is appointed to count votes at a meeting.

ultra vires Outside the power of the person or authority concerned.

unanimous A vote is unanimous when all members have voted in favour.

9.5 Minutes

The purpose of minutes is to keep a brief and accurate record of the business transacted at a meeting. Minutes need not be detailed but should be sufficiently clear to enable those absent from the meeting to follow the course of the meeting and to understand the reasons for the decisions taken.

Minutes should be in the third person and past tense. They must be approved by members, signed by the chairperson and should be kept in chronological order in a minute book for future reference.

All minutes should contain:

a description of the type of meeting
date, time and place of the meeting
names of those present with the chairperson's name first
a summary of the business discussed in the agenda order.

Minutes of a formal meeting such as an annual general meeting should include the full wording of motions put to the meeting with names of the proposer and seconder and a declaration by the chairperson of the result of the vote. If the result is not unanimous the minutes should record the number of votes cast for and against the motion and the number of abstentions. When a motion has been agreed by the correct majority according to the regulations governing the meeting, it becomes a resolution and the minutes should record 'It was resolved that . . .' followed by the full wording of the resolution.

When an amendment to a motion is proposed the amendment must be discussed and voted upon before the main motion. If the amendment is passed it is incorporated into the original motion, called the *substantive* motion, on which a vote is taken and recorded as above. If the amendment is not carried the chairperson will put the original motion to the vote. If the substantive motion is defeated the original motion cannot be voted upon.

An informal meeting, such as a staff meeting, may require more detailed minutes giving a summary of points made during discussion and including suggestions which were not accepted, as well as recording the decisions taken. These *minutes of narration* may also include the names of speakers for and against a proposal and the names of those from whom further action is required.

Copies of minutes of formal meetings are usually sent to members before the next meeting so that members can check their accuracy. The minutes of a company's annual general meeting may be approved at the next board meeting. Minutes of informal meetings are often read to members by the secretary at the next meeting.

If members agree to an alteration to the minutes the chairperson should make the alteration and initial it before signing the minutes as a correct record.

10 PLANNING A CONFERENCE/EXHIBITION

No two conferences or exhibitions can ever be alike; every business will have different aims and ideas and therefore guidelines can only be given in a very general way. The object of such occasions is to gather people together for a purpose and the first consideration is to define clearly what that purpose is. To set up a conference or exhibition is an expensive procedure, not to be undertaken lightly. Planning, strategy and timing are of vital importance if the occasion is to be sufficiently worthwhile and cost-effective. The following checklist will help prospective organisers to work out a campaign according to their own particular requirements and resources.

10.1 Aims and objectives

Conferences are held for one or a combination of the following reasons:

to increase or renew business and professional contacts

to exhibit and demonstrate goods and artefacts of all kinds

to build up public relations

to give or exchange information, including training sessions

to explain future planning and policies

to achieve and expand publicity

to investigate and solve problems

to build up morale.

10.2 Strategy and planning

Delegation

The principal Conference Organiser should make out a preliminary schedule of events, after which the operation becomes a group activity. Duties may be delegated to separate departments, although if the project is not over-ambitious a small group of two or three people may be able to organise the whole programme competently on their own. Delegation can of course be infinitely flexible, according to the firm's staff structure.

Naturally there should be a considerable amount of contact and co-operation between all the departments involved to ensure smooth progressive planning with the minimum amount of hold-ups and hiccups.

Chairperson

The ideal chairperson is someone willing to take on the job, who has a good platform presence, a quiet authority and a sense of humour. (There may be a different chairperson for different days if the conference is a lengthy one.)

The chairperson must be fully briefed on all matters concerning the conference, be firmly in control at all times, and amongst his or her general duties the following take priority:

  to open the proceedings, welcome delegates and re-state the programme (announcing any changes that may have been necessary)

  to be available to introduce speakers and be in control of 'question and answer' sessions

  to keep the programme within its planned limits, keeping talks or demonstrations from running beyond their scheduled time

  to close the conference formally and thank everyone concerned in its success.

Speakers and Guest of Honour

Speakers must be selected and approached early (months or even a year ahead) and asked if they will accept an invitation to lecture or give a talk and demonstration. The guest of honour will also need plenty of notice, allowing as much time as possible for the preparation of a speech. See that all acceptances are confirmed in writing and, in case of an unavoidable cancellation at a later stage, have one or two other names on a reserve list.

Write to or telephone the speakers to ascertain whether they need visual aids of any kind and take steps to see that these are provided; it may be necessary to hire microphones or other equipment. Make sure all electrical fittings are adequate and in good order, that acoustics and ventilation are good. The lecture room should be made quite ready beforehand, probably necessitating an early inspection with the caretaker and electrician.

Costs

Make a sensible forecast of possible costs and then add half as much again, since costs have a way of escalating. Many firms keep contingency funds for regular projects of this kind, but when arranging a first-time conference careful financial forecasting is vital. Costs are likely to go up during the period between the initial estimates and the presentation of final bills. As the project goes forward constant running checks should be made to ensure that expenses are kept as closely as possible within budget limits. A special extra fund should be kept available for unexpected emergencies.

Suitable dates

A conference may be contained in a single day, extend over a weekend or run for several days consecutively. Avoid clashing with bank and other public holidays or church festivals. If the conference is of interest to foreigners their holiday dates should also be considered (see Chapter 23.2). Peak working periods of the year should be avoided; these vary for different trades and professions. It is also as well to find out whether there are likely to be any rival conferences which could provide unwelcome competition.

Accommodation and venue

These depend entirely on the type of conference proposed, whether it is to be long or short term, residential or non-residential, held on the firm's own premises or away in another area. Probable requirements will be:

lecture hall (or halls) with platform, comfortable seating and good
  acoustics

exhibition halls with adequate display areas

rooms suitable for discussion groups and seminars

studios or workshops for training

lounge for coffee and bar facilities

dining room for lunches or formal dinners

adequate and suitable cloakrooms and toilet facilities

good kitchen accommodation if catering staff are involved

easy access and sufficient car-parking space for visitors.

When selecting accommodation attention must be given to cleanliness, heating and ventilation, possible draughty areas, pillars that could obstruct the view during lectures or demonstrations. If any handicapped people are likely to attend, staff should be asked to stand by to give assistance if and where required. Remember that handicapped delegates may have difficulty with swing-doors and lifts.

If delegates are to stay overnight, hotel accommodation will be required with clean and comfortable bedrooms and other amenities. Any good hotel manager will be happy to show you the accommodation beforehand and discuss terms for single or block bookings.

The actual location of a conference or exhibition centre deserves attention. Quiet surroundings are best; avoid premises with adjacent building sites or goods yards at any time and school playgrounds during term-time.

The host's own business premises will probably be the most appropriate venue, but if they are not entirely suitable they may be made so with the help of an outside catering firm and local hotels to assist with overnight accommodation. Alternatively, another location may be more suitable, such as:

Purpose-built conference centre There are plenty of big modern conference centres that can be hired in many localities, providing every possible facility for large or small events of all kinds.

Hotels and guesthouses These can often provide excellent rooms specially adapted and equipped for conferences and exhibitions. Enquiries in the district via the local paper or *Yellow Pages* will provide a selection of possibilities.

Local authorities and other large organisations Many big concerns have their own colleges and training centres, often in converted country houses and mansions, with good accommodation and catering facilities. These are often available for booking during their holiday periods.

Universities Accommodation is available during the long vacation in many colleges in university towns and cities. Delegates and visitors usually appreciate the opportunity of using lecture rooms and halls of residence within interesting and historic settings of this kind.

Guest list and invitations

Invitations will be sent out according to the names on your guest list and it is as well to keep a record of acceptances and refusals so that, in the event of there not being as many acceptances as was hoped, a secondary reserve list can be made up to augment the numbers.

Invitation cards and a printed programme can be sent out separately, or an attractively printed brochure or leaflet may be produced with a separate or detachable tear-off reservation slip to be filled in and returned as an acceptance. The information printed on this reservation form should include the following:

announcement of the event, its aims and subject

the date or dates

the precise location and address

an introductory paragraph with any necessary explanatory notes

the programme for each day, setting out the various events and including the names of the speakers

administrative details, e.g. the fee to be paid, an address and telephone number for enquiries, a list of available hotels if the conference lasts more than a day

an acceptance slip to be returned with the fee, giving space for the delegate's name and address, the company represented, his or her status within that company and a telephone number for contact

a small sketch map of the district may be included, with directions as to how to find the conference buildings. The nearest railway station, airport, bus station and car-parking areas should be clearly indicated.

Programme construction

Naturally programmes will depend on the nature of the event and its duration. The following guidelines are very general and can be adapted as appropriate. Items to consider are:

a general assembly on the first day, when the Chairperson will welcome the delegates and formally open the conference

a series of related demonstrations and lectures

special seminars, discussions and practical workshops

films and illustrated talks

an exhibition (pictures, models, artefacts of all kinds)

excursions during 'leisure' time, perhaps on the last day, to a theatre or local place of interest

coffee and tea-breaks, formal or informal lunches, formal dinner on the last evening with a special guest-speaker.

Working events should not be timetabled to run too closely together; delegates will need a short break between talks and seminars. The printed programme might cover one specimen day as under:

Day I	(Chairperson's name)
9.00	Arrival and coffee
9.30	Welcoming address by the Chairperson
9.35	Talk or lecture (subject, speaker's name and degrees or qualifications)
10.45	Coffee
11.00	Workshops of some kind, demonstrations, training sessions etc. (subject, instructor's name and qualifications)
12.00 –12.30	Reports and assessment on previous session
13.00	Lunch
14.30	Talk or lecture (subject, speaker's name, etc.)
15.30	Tea
15.50	Lecture or seminar (subject, speaker's name, etc.)
16.30 –17.00	Open discussion
17.00 –17.05	Chairperson's winding up address
19.30	Dinner

Catering

This may be carried out by your own company if the facilities are there, or left to outside caterers. If the former, consult the Catering Manager early so that he or she may order extra goods and equipment in plenty of time.

If outside caterers are to be engaged, write to several for specimen menus and estimates, stating your approximate requirements. It is not possible to give exact numbers before the acceptances come in or all tickets have been sold. The firm with the lowest charges may not necessarily be the best or most suitable. A personally recommended firm may be your best choice. Your reputation will be at stake, so do not make a snap decision but choose with care.

For a formal dinner ensure that flowers, printed menus, place-cards, etc., are not forgotten and put up a seating plan where the guests can see it before entering the dining-room.

Seating plans should be tactfully drawn up; the Chairperson and

Guest of Honour should be seated at the top table with any other principal after-dinner speakers and other important visitors.

Exhibits and reception area

Ways of exhibiting products are many and various since different articles require different display methods. Objects may be tastefully displayed in purpose-designed showcases, films specifically commissioned for information purposes and shown in a small cinema, video films shown on VDU screens, technical equipment demonstrated in working order by a trained operator, charts, graphs and diagrams put up for inspection on large display frames (see Chapter 7). Large exhibits, such as a building scheme, can be shown by means of scale models and photographs. Showcases and lighting, by today's sophisticated methods, can be skilfully and attractively combined.

By contrast some exhibits, pictures and prints for example, need only good wallspace and soft indirect lighting to be seen to the best advantage.

A reception area can provide a useful focal point for delegates on arrival, in addition to being a general meeting place and information centre. It is the ideal place to position the following:

Notice boards for plans of the area with directions to conference rooms, cloakrooms, etc., individual telephone messages, lists of names of the delegates attending.

Counter with attendant issuing leaflets and brochures such as those giving information about the firm (history, products, progress and development), details of training and career opportunities, extra printed programmes, information about local places of interest, travel facilities (train timetables, bus schedules and taxi services with telephone numbers), conference assessment forms for delegates to fill in and return when the conference is over, folders to hold papers conveniently and personal identification lapel badges (if these have not previously been sent out through the post).

General enquiry desk with a qualified and informed member of staff in attendance.

Display stands with posters and other exhibits concerning the theme of the conference.

Publicity and the press

Publicity for a conference is not always required, but, in cases where it is needed, the first thing to do is to contact the local or national press and send them the printed programme, with a covering letter saying that it would be appreciated if they would send a representative and a photographer to report on the event. When they arrive they should have all the assistance they require. Select a reliable member of staff to look after them and answer questions, but choose someone discreet and tactful enough to know that not *all* information is necessarily to be divulged.

The Public Relations Officer may also contact local or national radio and television stations if the occasion is of sufficient importance. (See Chapter 26 for useful addresses).

Safety and security

Insurance is of vital importance. Extra electrical equipment, temporary fittings and extensions, large groups of people, litter and cigarette ends all provide risks and nothing should be left to chance. Check carefully to see where there may be problems of safety and take steps to minimise the hazards and insure against them.

Fire exits must be clearly signposted, fire-doors *never* locked when people are on the premises, and fire-extinguishers should be placed at strategic points (all members of staff should be instructed in their use). Night watchmen or guard dogs may be employed for the hours when the buildings are virtually empty. The installation of a burglar-alarm system may be thought necessary. (See also Chapter 14).

Outside assistance and agencies

There are plenty of individuals and companies who would be happy to arrange everything for you, but the specialised conference agencies, though highly efficient, are expensive. However, smaller, single organisations may be employed separately, such as:

    printers for brochures, programmes, posters, etc.
    temporary clerical staff to assist with extra paperwork
    security firms for overall safety planning
    interpreter services if foreign delegates are to be present
    bar staff and catering firms to help with meals and snacks
    publicity agents to spread the news far and wide

display unit designers to set out your products in the most enticing way

video and photographic suppliers for display purposes.

The *Yellow pages* are an invaluable source of outside help, also the advertisements in the trade and technical papers concerned. You are not alone, help is at hand.

Winding up

A few last minute duties are important as soon as the conference is over. These include:

Tipping A tangible mark of appreciation for services rendered (caretaker, telephone operator, kitchen staff and so on) will be deserved and much appreciated.

Safety All electrical equipment should be checked and all rooms inspected and locked up before the building is finally vacated.

Acknowledgments Letters of thanks and appreciation to those concerned are a priority when the programme is safely completed. They should be sent off as promptly as possible.

An informal post-conference meeting of the various organisers and helpers should be held at a short time after the event, when delegates' assessments have come in and retrospective opinions can be formed as to how successful the conference proved to be. Good strategy will be worth repeating on future occasions; alternatively, much can be learnt from any miscalculations or mistakes.

All relevant records and copies of correspondence should be kept in a special 'Conferences' file for helpful reference on other similar occasions. Good contacts will be required again, others will need to be avoided.

Cuttings from press reports and photographs, when they appear, should also go into the 'Conferences' file, which will then form a valuable set of records on which to base future events.

10.3 Press conferences

A press conference has a different character and, because of its particular nature, requires special timing. The press are middlemen, passing on news to their own publications, and usually their information has to be up-to-the-minute and relayed swiftly. Early in the day, therefore, is the best time for a press conference. This allows reporters to contact their offices promptly and there should be a number of telephone booths and telex terminals within easy distance for their specific use.

A discussion period should be scheduled, after the information-giving session, so that the press can ask questions and fill out their facts as they wish before finally putting in their reports.

When a press conference is to be set up a suggested list of contacts for the organiser might be:

local newspapers
national daily and evening papers
chief news agencies
appropriate trade and technical or professional journals
radio and television networks
(see Chapter 26 for addresses).

Printed information may be given out at a press conference, confirming and augmenting any information given orally (—this should not be issued beforehand).

10.4 Confravision

If it is not practicable to bring delegates from various far-flung locations together conveniently, the British Telecom *Confravision* service may be the answer. Links between widely separated groups, using sound and vision lines of communication, make it possible to hold a 'meeting' even though the participants are not in the same room. Television screens at each terminal provide a visual and aural link each with the others. (See also Chapter 21.5)

Information about this service can be obtained from British Telecom Headquarters on 01-357 3982. *Confravision* studios are currently located in eight major cities, and international links have been developed between the UK and a number of foreign countries.

11 INTERVIEWING SKILLS

Training and experience are necessary if an interviewer is to become skilful enough to conduct an interview which is satisfactory to both sides. An interview should not be a one-sided affair; it should be a conversation of which the interviewer always has control. Its purpose is the exchange of information, both factual and behavioural, between interviewer and interviewee for a specific purpose. The responsibility for success rests with the interviewer who should always be fully prepared.

Before the interview the interviewer should consider:

the type of interview: its aim; the right approach to adopt

length of interview: allow sufficient time to achieve the objective and refer to a checklist of essential points to be covered

background information: documents to be read *before* the interview and to be available *during* the interview

location: size of room (too large becomes impersonal; too small, uncomfortable); adequate furniture and facilities (ashtrays, tea/coffee) to create a relaxed atmosphere; privacy, without noise and distractions.

During the interview the interviewer should:

establish confidence by putting the interviewee at ease

vary the types of questions asked in order to obtain the maximum information, avoiding questions which require only yes/no answers

listen and show interest in the interviewee noting the interviewee's voice tone and physical reactions, which will help the interviewer to understand better the answers to the questions

sum up from time to time to ensure that the interviewee understands the points made at each stage of the interview

take notes as the interview proceeds to avoid forgetting important points or repeating questions, but note-taking should be unobtrusive so that the interviewee is not distracted

be prepared to give information and clear up misunderstandings but encourage the interviewee to talk freely; the interviewer should not monopolise the conversation

clearly indicate when the interview has come to an end and make sure that the interviewee leaves in no doubt as to further action to be taken by both parties.

11.1 Recruitment interview

The aim of a recruitment interview is to select the best person to fill a staff vacancy either by internal or external recruitment. In terms of cost, public relations and future teamwork and achievement within the organisation, the outcome of such an interview is so important that the interviewer must prepare with care. A wrong decision can have lasting effects.

The approach should be to create a good impression of the organisation while being honest about the requirements of the job.

The interview cannot be hurried; it is necessary not only to assess the candidate's ability to do the job but also how he or she will fit into the working team.

Background material required includes:

> job description and specification of the person required
> candidate's application form or personal file (if internally recruited)
> company information which, in the case of an external recruit, needs to cover areas such as wage/salary structure, pensions, conditions of service, social amenities.

The location will probably be the interviewer's office. Whether across a desk or at a table the interview should be conducted so that both parties can see each other and neither is at a disadvantage, from misplaced light or inappropriate seating. There should be no interruptions, such as telephone calls, to stem the flow of the interview.

To put a candidate at ease the interviewer may start with open questions, i.e. those starting with *why, what, when* or *how,* or leading questions, i.e. those which indicate the required answer. As the interview progresses information can be extracted by specific questions and the interviewee's ability to deal with problem situations can be deduced from answers to hypothetical questions which have been already prepared by the interviewer.

Listening also involves watching to assess the candidate's reactions. Questions which are dodged or only partially answered may be re-stated in a different way. Eye-contact is important. Interviewers who keep their eyes on their notes miss a great deal of unspoken information.

A final summary of the interview should confirm the points covered; check that the interviewee has no further questions, ascertain whether or not the applicant is still interested if the job is offered and give a time within which the offer will be confirmed or withdrawn.

11.2 Counselling interview

Most people, at some time, seek expert advice to help them deal with problems which affect their personal or working lives. Sometimes the counsellor whose advice is sought is a member of an organisation which deals with specific problems, such as income tax queries or matrimonial difficulties; usually an appointment is made in such a case, and the interviewer has adequate time to prepare. Sometimes an interview is sought at short notice, however, and the interviewer has no advance warning of the problems to be discussed—a frequent occurrence when the person from whom advice is sought is a worker's manager or personnel officer.

The object of a counselling interview is to proffer advice, but the counsellor should remember that, at first, the interviewee may simply be seeking someone to whom the problem can be explained—perhaps an opportunity to voice a complaint which has never been put into words before.

The interviewer's attitude should be understanding and reassuring. A counselling interview must be unhurried, uninterrupted and private. Confidentiality must be assured.

Background material, such as a staff member's private file, may not be readily available at an unplanned interview but can be read and acted upon before the follow-up interview, which is essential when counselling.

An office environment is not suitable for a counselling interview unless telephone calls are re-routed and only those whose presence is requested are allowed to enter the office during the interview. The possibility of interruption can undermine confidence and so, when counselling interviews are frequent, a small room with comfortable furniture should be made available, where both parties can relax; this can create a more informal atmosphere and result in a more satisfactory outcome.

Counselling skills

All the interviewing skills are required when counselling, but tactics may differ from those used for other types of interview. These include:

using 'open' questions to start the person talking (specific questions may be used to clarify)

allowing the individual to talk freely, without interruption, until the problem has been determined, giving more than usual attention to listening and observing; remembering that it is important to be seen to be listening and that a pause in the narration may lead to further revelations if not interrupted; respecting silence but being prepared to re-start the flow of information by discreet questioning

showing an understanding of the other person's position unemotionally, bearing in mind possible alternative interpretations of the problem

advising: in other types of interview the interviewer is expected to give the interviewee information but in a counselling interview the individual is seeking advice; this must be given with discretion, since few people take advice easily and fewer act upon advice given.

The role of the counsellor is to:

obtain the maximum information with the utmost care and the minimum interruption

listen, understand and instil confidence

help the interviewee to think through the problem and see possible solutions

assist in the realisation of these solutions by providing names, addresses and telephone numbers of specialists in dealing with problems, e.g. Citizens' Advice Bureaux, Local Authorities' Social Services

advise but not dictate; the decision must be made by the person concerned if he or she is to make future decisions without guidance and if the result of the present decision is not to be blamed upon the interviewer.

A follow-up interview is essential in order to:

show the result of any action the interviewer has promised to take

check developments and offer additional assistance if necessary

encourage the interviewee to continue in a course of action or to take further action as required discover whether or not the action advised has been followed and has proved successful; this will help the interviewer in subsequent cases.

11.3 Disciplinary interview

Mistakes, wrong attitudes or breaches of a company's code of discipline by an employee require a carefully handled interview, the object of which is to inform the person concerned of the errors made, suggest remedial action and take measures to prevent a recurrence of the fault.

The interviewer's approach should depend upon:

the seriousness of the offence

whether the employee has been called upon to attend a previous disciplinary interview

knowledge of the individual's temperament; some are easily upset by the mildest criticism, others become belligerent or defensive.

Before the interview the interviewer should:

get up to date with current employment legislation, particularly that concerning unfair dismissal

know all the facts about the current misdemeanour and what action can be taken e.g. a warning and/or further disciplinary proceedings

read previous reports on the employee's work

acquire background information about the person to be interviewed in order to understand behaviour and attitude

follow the company's guidelines and correct procedures e.g. liaise with union officials, inform the interviewee of entitlement to the presence of a representative and arrange for an interviewer's representative to attend if deemed necessary.

Written reports or complaints which have led to the employee being called for interview should be available for reference; also the company's handbook and appropriate guidelines e.g. safety rules.

During the interview the interviewer should:

adopt an informal approach initially, although the interview may become more formal as it progresses

be fair but firm

ensure that the person concerned understands the reason for the interview

listen to the interviewee's point of view

be prepared to explain company policy and the seriousness of the offence, particularly the effect on fellow workers

suggest remedies and improvements which can be made in attitudes and work; note reactions as these help the interviewer to determine whether to proceed further or whether a warning and another follow-up interview is sufficient action at this stage

leave the interviewee in no doubt as to what is expected of him/her and what further action is being taken by the interviewer.

After the interview the interviewer should:

write a full report immediately, recording action taken and warnings given

send a copy of the report to all concerned, including the individual and the union representative, and place a copy on file.

11.4 Appraisal interview

A successful appraisal interview requires careful preparation by both the interviewer and the interviewee, who must be given adequate notice of when and where the interview is to take place and with whom. The aim of an appraisal interview is frequently misunderstood. It is not a confrontation to highlight the worker's faults or to voice mutual complaints. It should be a discussion between a manager and a member of staff the purpose of which is to:

ensure that the scope of the job and its areas of responsibility are fully understood

define objectives and standards

assess performance, identify strengths and weaknesses and find means of improvement

determine training needs

consider potential for development.

Before the interview the interviewer should study:

the employee's job description

previous assessments, performance reviews and targets attained

the worker's self appraisal form if one has been completed (many companies use this method to help the interviewee prepare for the appraisal and, if copies are made available to interviewers, the information can be of considerable help to them).

During the interview the approach should be relaxed, considerate and friendly. As with all interviews uninterrupted privacy is essential and it is very important that the discussion should not be hurried. Unheeded grievances may impede progress in the coming year and lead to lack of co-operation and problems with other members of the staff. Difficulties may not be resolved immediately but, if the job-holder feels that they have been discussed and action will be taken, relations with management will be improved.

For the discussion to be of value both parties must listen carefully. The appraiser, particularly, should avoid talking too much, but should encourage the interviewee to present a point of view at the same time knowing when, tactfully, to halt the over-talkative.

Producing a summary of points made and actions decided upon at each stage of the interview can prevent repetitions and misunderstandings.

Finally, the manager's report or comments on the appraisal form should be seen by the employee who is then invited to make comments, the completed form being signed by both parties.

The interview should end on a positive note, with the interviewee clear about past performance, future prospects and action agreed. The interviewer must ensure that any action promised is undertaken without delay. A satisfactory appraisal interview can assist a manager's forward planning, boost staff morale and considerably improve staff/management relations.

Bibliography:
Interviewing in 26 Steps, John S. Gough. Pub. BACIE, 11th impr. March 1981.
A Guide to Interviewing Skills, Janis Grummit. Pub. The Industrial Society, repr. July 1985.
Selection Interviewing, Peter Whitaker. Pub. The Industrial Society, 1973, repr. May 1985.
Appraisal and Appraisal Interviewing, Brian Scott and Barry Edwards. Pub. The Industrial Society, 1972, repr. May 1986.

Part III
ORGANISATION AND FINANCE

12 BUSINESS STRUCTURES

12.1 Sole trader

Law

There is no legal formality required for setting up in business as a sole trader but every business has to comply with both local and state laws. For example, enquiry should be made with the local authority regarding the details of any bye-laws regarding fire regulations or whether planning permission is required for advertising on premises. Such local rules affect not only shops, offices and factory premises but also the use of private homes for business purposes.

Government statutes (Acts of Parliament) affect the conduct of business life in a wide variety of ways. Some of the areas and statutes are:

Goods   Consumer Safety and Protection, Weights and Measures, Trade Descriptions

Employees   Equal Pay, Race Relations

Premises   Factories, Health and Safety, Control of Pollution

Finance   Consumer Credit, Income Tax, PAYE, VAT.

Registration of business names

The Business Names Act 1985 stipulates that if the business is conducted under a name which is not the actual name of the proprietor then the following requirement must be met. At the place of business there must be prominently displayed: the business name, the activity of the business and the actual name of the owner. All business stationery must also carry the two names. The registration address varies according to the country in which the business is carried on, namely:

England and Wales   Registrar of Companies, Companies Registration Office (CRO), Crown House, Crown Way, Maindy, Cardiff CF4 3UZ

Scotland   102 George Street, Edinburgh EH2 3DJ

Northern Ireland   IDB House, 64 Chichester Street, Belfast BT1 4JX

Notification

Customs and Excise (VAT), the Inspector of Taxes and the DHSS must be told that trading has commenced, even if the sole trader's full-time employment is continuing.

Costs

Apart from the cost of any professional advice from a solicitor or accountant (prudence suggests this should be taken) there is no other legally required expense when starting a business. Profits will be taxed as personal income and liabilities will eventually be the responsibility of the person running the business.

12.2 Partnership

Partnerships are governed by the Partnership Act 1890 which specifies that persons carrying on business for profit constitute a partnership. Twenty is the maximum number of partners for all except special categories of business; at the present time these are: accountants, solicitors, members of the Stock Exchange, estate agents, auctioneers, surveyors and patent agents. Other businesses may be added at the discretion of the Secretary of State.

The legal requirements for setting up in business are basically the same for a partnership as for a sole trader (see p 113) with the addition of the points laid out below.

Deed of partnership

The Partnership Act 1890 sets out the consequences of partnership including financial arrangements, for example:

profits and losses shared equally

no entitlement to a salary or wage, nor to interest on capital invested in the business

interest at 5% will be paid to a partner who makes a loan, additional to capital; no interest will be charged on partnership withdrawals.

However, the partners can vary conduct within the partnership as decided between themselves when drawing up the deed of partnership. Professional advice should be sought for this.

Registration of business names

When the name of the business is not the names of the partners, then the same law applies as for the sole trader (see p 113).

If the partnership has more than twenty members the law stipulates that provided a list of all members is kept and is available at the main place of business the stationery does not have to contain these names.

Termination

Technically the partnership ends if a partner dies, becomes bankrupt, retires, becomes insane or if a new partner joins. The accounts should be finalised and creditors told of the change.

Management

All partners (unless they are limited partners) can participate in the management of the business and all have authority to bind the others and have access to the books of account.

Liability

Provided there is at least one general partner with unlimited liability, there can be partners who are specifically limited in their liability i.e. *sleeping partners*. Every limited partnership must be registered with the Registrar of Companies (see p 113). All general partners are jointly and severally liable for debts of the partnership. If for example they are equal partners and one cannot pay his or her portion of a partnership debt, the other(s) must shoulder it.

12.3 Limited companies

The limited company must be registered either as a *public* or a *private* company.

Public limited companies (plc)

Public limited companies are governed by the Companies Acts 1948-85. The 1985 Act is a consolidating Act which is expected to be fully implemented by the end of 1986. The Companies Acts are affected by the Insolvency Act 1985. All companies are required to register the following two documents with the Registrar of Companies (for address see p 113):

Memorandum of Association   This must state that it is a public company, and gives:
the name of the company
domicile (it is usual to give the full address) of the company
a statement that the liability of its members is limited by shares or by guarantee, or a statement that members have unlimited liability
its share capital with details of number, value and category of share

the areas of activity in which the business will deal (known as the *objects clause*)

details of each subscriber and a witnessed signature to their undertaking to take up the shares stated to be their portion of the capital (there must be at least seven subscribers).

Articles of Association This governs the relationship between the members and the company e.g.

how alterations to the share capital have to be made

rules regarding notice of and proceedings at meetings

rules governing directors, etc.

There are model forms of the Memorandum and Articles which may be adopted or amended in 'Statutory Instrument 1985 No 805' for public and private companies with or without share capital, those with guaranteed liability, or unlimited liability.

When a company is formed, initial legal and accountancy fees and registration charges are incurred. There are then continuing costs in maintaining a register of shareholders and sending statutory returns to the Registrar of Companies (CRO) namely:

the annual return

the annual accounts

notices of change of directors of a limited company.

A company's shares can be bought and sold if they have been quoted on the Stock Exchange.

Private companies

The private company is governed by the rules and regulations of the public company with the following changes:

it does not have the statement in its Memorandum that it is a public company, but states that shares will not be offered to the public

there is a minimum of two subscribers to the Memorandum

its shares are not quoted on the Stock Exchange, but any changes of ownership need to be recorded.

12.4 Co-operatives

A co-operative is a business enterprise which is jointly owned by its members; as a rule these are the people who work in it although sometimes friends, relations or suppliers may also be members. Each member has one vote, but day-to-day business decisions come within the sphere of an appointed management often shared by rotation. Ownership may be:

proportional—when the members own a share in the assets in proportion to their investment

common—meaning that all members have an equal share in the assets regardless of the investment they have made.

Co-operatives registered under the Industrial and Provident Societies Acts must have at least seven members, all members of a co-operative may have limited liability if it has not registered as a limited company. The Act also lays down strict rules about interest paid on loans and the distribution of profit, and the business must be run for the mutual benefit of the members or of the community.

A co-operative may: (a) form as an original enterprise, e.g. Society for Worldwide Interbank Financial Telecommunications (SWIFT); (b) be a development of a partnership or (c) take over an ailing firm.

A co-operative must be registered with the Registrar of Friendly Societies (see address p 118), or if an incorporated limited company with the Registrar of Companies (see p 113).

Agencies

Co-operative Development Agency (CDA)

Broadmead House, 21 Panton Street, London SW1Y 4DR (Tel: 01-839 2987)

Holyoake House, Hanover Street, Manchester M60 0AS (Tel: 061-833 9379)

This is an organisation set up in 1978 by the Government to advise. Since 1984 it has made grants and loans to help establish, develop or provide training courses for co-operators and partnerships.

Highlands and Islands Development Board (HIDB)

Bridge House, Bank Street, Inverness IV1 1QR (Tel: 0463-234171)

Established in 1965 to provide finance and assistance for setting up and running community projects in the Highlands and Islands not only to co-operatives but also to manufacturing, service, agriculture, tourism and fisheries businesses.

Industrial Common Ownership Finance Co. (ICOF)
1st Floor, 4 Giles Street, Northampton NN1 1AA (Tel: 0604 37563)
Works closely with local authorities and offers advice, consultancy, and loan funds. Funds are available only to co-operatives which have registered with ICOM (see below).

Industrial Common Ownership Movement (ICOM)
7 The Corn Exchange, Leeds LS1 7BP (Tel: 0532-461737)
Advises on financial, management, legal and all aspects of common ownership. Provides model rules.

Job Ownership Ltd (JOL)
9 Poland Street, London W1V 3DG (Tel: 01-437 5511)
Sometimes known as the *Mondragon* system named after a town in the Basque region of Spain where a 1956 successful worker ownership has spread. A non-profit organisation which promotes conversion of existing firms to worker ownership. Advice free on first consultation. Provides model rules.

The Registry of Friendly Societies
England and Wales: 15 Great Marlborough Street, London W1V 2AX
(Tel: 01-437 9992)
Scotland: The Assistant Registrar for Scotland, 58 Frederick Street, Edinburgh EH2 1NB (Tel: 031-226 3224)
Northern Ireland: Department of Economic Development, IDB House, 64 Chichester Street, Belfast BT1 4JX (Tel: 0232 234488).
Information and advice about rules and registration is given for each separate part of the UK.

The Scottish Co-operative Development Committee
Templeton Business Centre, Templeton Street, Bridgeton, Glasgow G40 1DA (Tel: 041-554 3797)
Offers guidance similar to JOL but does not provide model rules.

12.5 Franchise

Franchise is a rapidly growing method of expanding or starting up in business with a proven product or service. It is not a business format but rather the taking on of an existing product or service which has a brand or product name. A franchisee may be a sole trader, partnership or limited company.

The franchisor is the organisation which is the innovator of the idea, has the rights in it and lays down the way in which the business is to be run. The franchisor ensures uniformity in such things as presentation, layout, format, recipes, premises, prices, stationery.

The person taking up and operating the business (the franchisee) pays a fee for the help and advice given during the starting up and initial launch period plus a continuing royalty and/or commission on goods supplied. The franchisee is assured of exclusive rights within an agreed area for a product range that has been successfully market tested and, often, advertised nationally. The franchisee and staff usually receive not only initial training but also subsequent updating when the franchisor introduces new lines or methods. To ensure a national standard of service and quality, the franchisor exercises control and supervision throughout the contract period.

From the end of the Second World War until about the early 1970s this type of business organisation was principally connected with major car manufacturers, oil companies and soft drink bottlers. There are now over 200 different franchise schemes in the UK. They include Holland and Barratt, the Body Shop, Prontaprint and Wimpy, as well as professional, rental, cleaning and educational services.

All of the high street banks offer special facilities to prospective franchisees and most franchisors will be able to suggest a bank which has been particularly helpful in the past. Personal investment is required and amounts start at around £3000.

The *British Franchise Association* publishes a guide and a list of its membership (see Bibliography p 122).

12.6 Starting a new small business

Definition
This concerns the person or persons considering starting a new

business (whether full or part-time) and having control of it (whether employing others or not). The business can be manufacturing, providing a service, or selling either retail or wholesale.

Skills

Apart from technical ability in the particular business the person (or persons) starting up in business will need a range of skills covering marketing, legal matters, accountancy principles and management techniques. They will need to possess:

durability, in handling great demands on time and energy especially until established

flexibility, in coping with changes in legislation, customer demand, materials supply, economic and political climate

ability to update by keeping abreast of technical changes, improved methods, etc.

ability to delegate when possible (and profitable to do so)

decisiveness, in assessing the consequences of alternatives both in daily problem-solving and in forming a long-term objective

enthusiasm to be conveyed to any employees and to customers.

Initial considerations

Market research

A new business must have established the market to whom its product/service is to be offered, from the following categories: male; female; employed; unemployed; home-based; teenagers; children; age-band e.g. 12-18, 18-30, 30-50, 50 upwards; social/economic group.

Premises

If the business is to be operated from home permission will be required. The local authority may stipulate that planning regulations must be observed. If the house is not personally owned the landlord, or mortgagor, must agree to the change of use. A household insurance policy for public liability, theft, fire and burglary may be invalidated unless the company has been told and agrees to continue indemnity.

Finance

Professional advice may be obtained from a solicitor, accountant or a bank manager. The Banking Information Service publishes a book, *The Banks and Small Firms*, which contains information on: eligibility

for aid and loans; capital investment appraisement; business systems; a list of some of the support that has been given to small firms by seven banks over the past five years (see Bibliography p 122).
Other useful addresses and contacts are:

Small Business Capital Fund   88 Baker Street, London W1M 1DC

Council for Small Industries in Rural Areas   35 Camp Road, Wimbledon Common, London SW19 4UP

Local council offices

Manpower Services Commission

Government help and funding: small firms centres of the Department of Industry

Ring Freefone and ask for *Enterprise.*

Type of business organisation

A small business may be: a sole trader; a partnership; a limited company or a co-operative (see 12.1, 12.2, 12.3, 12.4). *Note:* There is a legal requirement to notify Customs and Excise (VAT), Inspector of Taxes and the DHSS on commencement of business, even if full-time employment is continued.

Accounts

If financial help is needed from a bank or another source it will be necessary to submit at least the following forecasts when considering starting up in business:

- a forecasted **profit and loss account** stating the expected sales, cost of sales and all expenses likely to be incurred in making the target profit for the first year
- a forecasted **balance sheet** containing a list of all the assets, liabilities and capital at the end of the first year
- a **cash flow forecast** setting out how much money has to be spent and how much is actually received, month by month for the first year.

When the business is operating, the proprietor should compare the estimates with the actual results to ensure that any imbalance is corrected quickly. This is called *management accounting*.

Bibliography:

Starting Your Own Business. Pub. 'Which?' Magazine, 14 Buckingham Street, London WC2N 6DS, rev. edn 1986.

How to Start, Run and Succeed in Your Own Business, D Jones and W H Perry. Pub. Wheatsheaf Books Ltd, 1983, repr. 1984.

Working for Yourself, Godfrey Golzen. Pub. Kogan Page, 1986.

The Guardian Guide to Running a Small Business, Clive Woodcock. Pub. Kogan Page, 1986.

Accountants Digest No 162 (covering co-operatives). Produced and published by the Technical Services Dept of the Institute of Chartered Accountants in England and Wales, Autumn 1984.

Co-operating For Work (Booklet MS14). Pub. Manpower Services Commission Dept CW, 1983.

A Comprehensive Guide To Franchising. Pub. The British Franchise Association, Franchise Chambers, 75a Bell Street, Henley-upon-Thames, Oxon RG9 2BD.

The Banks and Small Firms. Pub. The Banking Information Service, 10 Lombard Street, London EC3V 9AR, 1985.

Advice and leaflets on all topics in this chapter are available from high street banks.

13 FINANCE AND BANKING

13.1 Banking services

Special services offered to business customers by high street banks

Home factoring
The bank acts as the sales ledger accounts department for the client regarding the credit sales. To arrive at the discount rate to charge for this service, the bank considers the type of business, the average monthly sales and average value of each invoice and the average settlement date. The bank pays the monthly credit sales, less the discount, to the client. The client ceases to have the slow payer problem and can utilise the prompt cash payment to best advantage. The bank receives settlement from the debtors or suffers any eventual bad debt.

Foreign factoring
Similar to the home scheme but the bank sends the invoices in the currency of the buyer and chances the fluctuations in rates of exchange.

Hire purchase facilities
Through a subsidiary of the bank an arrangement is made by which the subsidiary company buys capital equipment and leases it to the client—this facility has possible tax benefits.

Bills—for export/import operations
These may be for collection, negotiation or documentary credit. For example, where it is a British business making an export, the British bank makes contact with a foreign bank in the locality of the exporter. Documents of title are prepared by the British firm whose bank sends them to the foreign bank of the exporter in exchange for payment. If all is in order payment is made and the goods are despatched. The banks charge a commission for this service.

Forward exchange
In circumstances where an importer needs to pay in the currency of the foreign supplier by a specified date, the amount can be predetermined by relating to the spot (today's) price. The currency is bought at a premium or discount which is quoted daily in the financial press.

Performance bond

In the building and construction industry it is usual for the tender to be accompanied by a performance bond. This is an assurance by a bank that their customer (the tenderer) is able to do the job to the standards and by the time limit specified.

Status enquiries

The bank can take up on behalf of a client a report from a prospective new customer's banker. The client then has an indication of the creditworthiness of the new customer.

Merchant banks

The bank can provide a specialist service for such situations as business mergers, registration services, management of pension or loan syndication.

Information and advisory services

The major banks offer a wide range of specialist knowledge to manufacturing and commercial businesses, thus ensuring that businesses consider the aid offered by the Government and other agencies. Some areas covered are:

starting your own business
financial control and planning for the small business
financial incentives and assistance for industry.

Services offered to personal customers by high street banks

Borrowing

Bank loans are available to pay for furniture, holidays, car, caravan, boat, season ticket, improvements to the home or to buy a home on mortgage—provided that the borrower's bank manager is satisfied regarding repayment. The borrower should make comparisons to ascertain which bank offers the best rate of interest and terms. The law requires that annual percentage rate (APR) is clearly stated on all advertisements for loans.

Credit cards

Three credit cards—Access, Visa and Trustcard—have been issued by banks and it is estimated that 20 million have been issued in the UK. There is no charge to the cardholder who has one monthly account for all purchases with an option to pay in full, or over a period; the latter involves additional payment in the form of interest. These cards have almost worldwide acceptance.

Cash cards

In the UK over 17 million people have cash cards enabling them to obtain cash from over 14000 branches in the UK and over 8000 dispensing machines, many of which operate 24 hours a day.

Travel

Apart from the use of a credit card abroad, the banks provide other facilities for travellers. These include foreign currency, travellers' cheques in both sterling and foreign currencies which can be replaced if lost or stolen, and uniform Eurocheques which can be used in over five million shops, restaurants, garages, banks, etc. in the UK, Europe and Mediterranean countries. Most banks provide an emergency service to get cash to you quickly wherever you are, in case of need.

Insurance

The major banks have insurance subsidiaries which are staffed by specialists whose job is to get the best possible cover for customers at the most competitive price. The need may be simple, such as insuring holiday luggage, or complex, requiring a range of life policies or pension plans.

Investment

Not only will banks look after all aspects of any stock market investment(s), but they also offer unit trusts and a range of personal equity plans (PEPs) which were officially started on 1 January 1987.

Executor

Banks have long been operating the service of executorship at modest cost and they also give advice on minimising any possible Inheritance Tax, and help in the drawing up of a will.

Saving

This is the area covered by the bulk of the 200 different services provided by banks and where competition is greatest. A variety of schemes are aimed at children and regular savers, whilst investors are offered good terms for seven-day deposits, extra interest accounts and high interest cheque accounts.

13.2 Girobank

Girobank is the trading name of Girobank plc—an established clearing bank and wholly owned subsidiary of the Post Office Corporation.

The bank provides a comprehensive range of services using the national network of almost 20000 post offices for counter facilities.

Girobank is at the forefront of advanced computer technology which enables the bank to provide a fast and efficient service. The system is ideal for money movement between accounts, whether for rapid marshalling of funds, improved financial control or access to money markets. Money market dealings are handled from the bank's head office in the heart of London's financial sector.

A network of offices around the country, together with Girobank Scotland and Girobank Northern Ireland, provides close contact with business and personal customers and enables enquiries to be dealt with quickly and efficiently.

Services available to business customers

Services include:

full current account banking

nationwide service for the deposit of branch and agent takings at post offices, during long weekday business hours and Saturday mornings

withdrawal facilities and a change-giving service at local post offices

rapid marshalling of funds into central accounts to facilitate efficient cash management

full payment and collection services, including cheque, credit transfer, standing order and direct debit; Girobank is a sponsoring bank in the Bankers' Automated Clearing Services (BACS)

money market deposits for short, medium or long term investments

specialist investment services including wholesale deposits and certificates of deposit

cash transfer through Clearing House Automated Payments System (CHAPS) and Town Clearing

full international money transmission service for payments and receipts, foreign currency and travel finance facilities; rapid payments abroad can be arranged by a variety of methods from telex to SWIFT (Society for Worldwide Interbank Financial Telecommunications) credit facilities, including overdrafts, short and medium term loans, acceptance credits and leasing finance, advanced payment and deferred purchase schemes and financing for the purchase of local authority mortgages

direct credit of pay, allowances, expenses and occupational pensions; payment instructions can be in list form, on computer tape, or through another bank via BACS; cashcheques, encashable at post offices, can be used to make payment where the payee does not have a bank account

dividend payments

Transcash—whereby cash (and cheque by arrangement) may be paid in at post offices for credit to a Girobank account; ideal for paying accounts, mail order purchases and the collection of insurance premiums; the Transcash slips are forwarded to the payee after crediting by the bank

collection services enabling local authorities and housing associations to have rent, rates and mortgages paid by tenants and householders at convenient post offices

a facility for building societies allowing investors to make deposits to and withdrawals from their building society accounts at post offices.

Services available to personal customers

Services include:

full current account banking, without charges when in credit, withdrawal up to £50 every other day at either of two designated post offices, and a debit-only charging system on overdrawn accounts which operates only on the days an account is actually overdrawn

a free transfer service for payments to other Girobank account holders (this covers most household bills and many mail order payments)

a cheque card giving cheque cashing facilities at 20000 post offices and at branches of other banks, and guaranteeing cheques and transfer payments for up to £50; this card also allows you to draw up to £100 cash daily at a nominated post office

frequent statements of account (after every credit or ten debits)

high interest-bearing deposit account

personal loans and revolving credit, mortgage and bridging finance

travellers' cheques, foreign currency and postcheques which can be cashed at more than 90000 post offices in most European and several other countries automated banking, through the (LINK) network of automated teller machines (ATMs) for cash withdrawals, balance enquiries and statement ordering 24 hours a day, every day

a Visa credit card allowing instant credit and acceptable at nearly four million outlets worldwide, can also be used for cash withdrawals from Girobank ATMs in the UK and from Visa ATMs worldwide

a range of insurance services through leading UK insurance companies and specially designed for Girobank customers.

13.3 Building societies

Traditionally the purpose of a building society was to receive subscriptions from members to create a fund to make loans to them for the purchase of their residential homes. The loans were secured on the member's land. The first Act of Parliament governing building societies was passed in 1836 and the latest in 1986. The societies do not make a profit nor distribute a dividend. The scope and extent of the industry is shown in the following table:

Year	Number of societies	Value of assets	Owner-occupiers as % of all houses
1900	2286	£60 million	10 per cent
1984	190	£102 billion	61 per cent

In 1984 26 million building society subscribers created funds which enabled 6 million loans to be made to home owner-occupiers. In the same year between 15-20% of these loans were from insurance companies, local authorities and banks. The remaining 80-85% of home buyers were building society members. A person becomes a member whether lending or borrowing money from a building society.

Loans

Building society loans are of two kinds:

Annuity mortgages The borrower makes equal monthly repayments over 20 or 25 years to pay off the loan and interest. Charges in interest rates may vary the 'equal' monthly payments. In the early years of the loan the repayment covers mainly the interest charges, but in later years the capital sum borrowed takes the larger proportion of the repayments.

Endowment mortgages Monthly repayments cover the interest only but simultaneously premiums have to be paid for a life assurance policy which on maturity provides the means of repaying the capital sum. Such policies offer a 'with profits' option which may repay a larger amount at the end of the term.

Investment

Some of the schemes offered for investment are:

Ordinary shares About a third of all savers use this type of investment which allows a minimum deposit of £1, immediate withdrawal and competitive interest rates.

High interest share accounts These require a minimum deposit (e.g. £500 or £1000), allow withdrawal on demand and pay a higher rate of interest than ordinary shares.

Short notice accounts Similar to high interest share accounts but a specified number of days notice of withdrawal is required, or there is a loss of interest. The rate of interest paid is higher than for high interest share accounts.

Term shares A specified period of years is agreed (three to five years) for the deposit to remain untouched except for the death of the investor, otherwise a penalty is paid on the interest. A higher rate of interest is paid than on short notice accounts.

Regular savings A commitment is made that a regular amount will be saved each month which will attract a preferential rate of interest over the ordinary share savings rate. It is mainly used by prospective home-owners who are saving for the amount needed as a deposit.

Save as you earn (SAYE) This is another form of regular savings over a set period of time with a tax-free bonus at the end of the term.

New powers and services

The Building Society Act which came into force on 1 January 1987 gave societies wider powers in housing and banking services. Eighty per cent of a society's funds has to be raised from the investing public and mainly lent to home buyers. However, additional services may be offered to members, whilst for the first time in the history of the industry, non-members can be clients. The new services are as follows:

> loans other than for home buying, possibly unsecured, may be granted to first time owner-occupiers to buy carpets and furniture for their house, and to other clients to buy e.g. cars, boats, caravans, or pay for holidays

the insurance facilities previously enjoyed by members are now available to non-members whilst the range is increased by the addition of life, sickness, accident, home and contents cover

the range of savings described above is extended to include: stocks and shares dealings; unit trust management; management of personal equity plans (PEPs); financial and investment advice to the public and provide savings schemes through employers

foreign exchange services

surveys and valuations of land, estate agency and conveyancing services

loans on a second mortgage

land and property purchase

paying and collecting services for other organisations.

13.4 The Stock Exchange

The Stock Exchange was formed in 1773 to establish a market and code of conduct for the purchase and sale of securities. Historically companies were formed to finance exploration and trade and ended with the conclusion of the venture. The backers could withdraw their stake if successful in persuading someone else to buy their 'share'. The principle of shares originated in the late 17th century and has continued and developed through the industrial revolution to today's varied demands. The Stock Exchange has also progressed to meet the varying capital investment requirements of governments, industry and commerce through the same time scale.

Shares are bought and sold through stockbrokers who are also independent advisers on a wide range of financial subjects. The expertise thus required involves research by analysts to evaluate the prospects of industries, companies and their management to assess current and future share values. To buy or sell shares an approach can be made directly to a member of the Stock Exchange, to a local bank manager, solicitor or accountant, except for shares offered directly to the public. When a company offers shares to the public it must issue details (known as a *Prospectus*) of its assets and liabilities, and a summary of its history and trading results, etc. This enables the prospective purchaser to decide whether or not to buy shares.

On 27th October 1986 changes were made to consolidate the Stock

Exchange's position of pre-eminence in Europe and the international money market. Changes were also necessary to meet the government's budgeted increase in individual share ownership visualised by the Finance Act 1986. This Act outlined the personal equity plans (PEPs) which grant income tax relief on capital gains and investment income on shares within specified limits. The increasing interest of the individual investor was reflected in the response throughout the country to the British Telecom, Trustee Savings Bank and British Gas share issues.

Equities is the term given to 'ordinary' shares held by an investor. These shares are called *stock* when certain procedures have been taken to convert them from shares. If the business fails shareholders lose their investment, but usually a dividend is paid to them out of profits and there is the prospect of an increase in the value of the investment. A few companies offer shareholders a discount on their purchase of the company product or service e.g. travel, hotel bills, DIY or wine.

Securities is the term which includes not only equities but gilts, debentures, bonds, loans and stocks. See the glossary of Stock Exchange terms (Chapter 27.6) for a full list of terms.

When a deal is made on the Stock Exchange the parties receive a contract note which is an important legal document setting out the price and settlement date. This is the date when the seller transfers shares to the buyer who then pays for them.

The year is divided into two working week periods, labelled *accounts*. Settlement of all transactions during the account is usually made on the second Monday following the account and is called Account Day.

The stockbroker makes a charge for the service given in either selling or buying shares. After 27th October 1986 the fee ceased to be based on a fixed commission scale. There is also a stamp duty payable which can be varied by the Chancellor of the Exchequer's budget. Income from any of these investments is subject to income tax, and the sale of investments (other than gilts) is liable for Capital Gains Tax, again depending on the current budget ruling.

Some newspapers print details of the shares which are listed on the Stock Exchange in a form similar to that laid out on p 132.

1	2	3	4	5	6	7
High 224	**Low** 160	**Name of company** CBA 5p	**Price** 182-2	**Cover** 3.5	**Yield** 3.3	**P/E** 11.3

Columns 1 and 2 show the highest and lowest price paid (in pence) during the previous twelve months.

Column 3 gives the name of the company and in this example indicates that each share is a 5p share.

Column 4 quotes the current price in pence (182) and '−2' indicates that the price is 2p down on the previous trading day.

Column 5 means 'dividend cover' and indicates that had all profit been distributed instead of some being retained the dividend could have been 3.5 times higher than it was.

Column 6 makes an assumption that if a dividend is paid out at the previously declared rate, and that the price paid for the shares is at today's price (182p) then a £100 investment would give a return of £3.30.

Column 7 means 'price:earnings ratio' and relates the current price being paid for shares with the earnings the company is making. It is a reflection of the confidence which investors have in the company (which should be compared with other companies in the same line of business).

Note: Columns 6 and 7 are the opinions of the financial staff of the newspaper publisher.

14 SECURITY

Almost all large firms now have their own Safety Officer, someone who will deal with small routine matters as well as major security problems. If there is no Safety Officer, the General Manager or Head Caretaker should have the authority to maintain general conditions of safety on the firm's behalf.

Sensible basic vigilance is a vital part of any security system; the expense involved may well be much less than any possible consequent insurance claims against the company. Regular checking and renewal of worn fittings and furniture, careful inspection and care of electrical equipment, plumbing, locks, bolts and window catches, are all a matter of common sense in order to reduce the likelihood of painful and expensive accidents. All staff have a personal responsibility to notice, and to report to the proper quarter, any items of worn or otherwise faulty equipment (see Chapter 18.1).

14.1 Confidential information

Telephone conversations
If there are people within hearing when a confidential telephone call comes through, several courses of action are possible. One is to ask whether you may call back at a more convenient time, making sure that you know the caller's telephone number. Another is to ask the caller to hold while you move to a more privately situated extension, and a third is to ask the caller to ring back at a time when you know that you will be alone and able to take the call.

It should go without saying that anyone in possession of confidential information must guard at all times against being inadvertently drawn or tricked into divulging any part of it, whether on the telephone or in general conversation. 'I'm afraid I can't discuss that' or a flat 'I'm sorry, no comment' may be the only answer if a caller persists in being too inquisitive.

Documents
Confidential documents must be kept in their own private filing system, under lock and key, with only authorised staff having access to them. Letters, reports, minutes of meetings and company accounts which are only for restricted circulation must never be left about on desk tops or carried freely in folders that can be put down and

forgotten or easily stolen. Outdated confidential documents to be destroyed should be burnt or put through a shredding machine.

Computerised data

Computerised information carries its own special risks, as the data can be tapped and read by anyone who knows how to retrieve it. Confidential computers should therefore be housed in their own separate, protected security room, or at least fitted with security locks and covers, a range of which is now on the market.

14.2 Financial responsibility

No single individual should be in charge of accounts. A second or even a third person should be available to check figures regularly, even in the case of something as minor as a petty cash box, to provide a safeguard against inaccuracies or any possible charge of pilfering. It is an accepted practice to double-check in this way and therefore no one should raise any objection. Larger accounts are of course dealt with by several members of staff and are eventually audited by a qualified firm of accountants. Continuous checking and cross-checking of all financial matters by a number of reliable people reduces the possibility of accounts being falsified.

Protection of cash

Banking and collection of money is frequently carried out too casually for safety. Various precautions should be taken when such journeys are made on a regular basis, e.g. the route taken to and from the bank should be varied; the day of the week, and the time of day when collection or delivery is made, should differ. It is always advisable for the person acting as courier to be accompanied, and at least one of the party should be male.

Firms such as *Securicor* undertake the protection of cash or other valuables in transit and the *Yellow Pages* directory provides a number of names of other security firms who can make suggestions and offer assistance for this and allied problems.

14.3 Outside organisations

Professional advice is always worth having. The Crime Prevention Officer at your local police station gives free help and advice on any aspect of security.

A wide choice of firms and agencies is to be found in *Yellow Pages* under 'Security Services'. There are companies providing equipment such as burglar alarm systems, grilles and gates, special safes and locks, as well as shredders and computer-locking devices. There are confidential enquiry agents, private detectives, personal guard services and dog patrols. Banks will guard special valuables in their safe-deposit vaults; safety-printers will produce documents or accounts and keep them confidential until their authorised disclosure date.

The *British Safety Council* issues publications advising on every aspect of business and industrial security. Helpful brochures and leaflets can also be obtained from the *Royal Society for the Prevention of Accidents* and from the *Fire Protection Association* (see Bibliography p 146 for addresses). The safety industry is extensive and constantly expanding to keep pace with present-day risks.

14.4 Office visitors

From a security aspect, and also as a matter of common courtesy, visitors should always be supervised. Expected callers with definite appointments pose no problem, but always consider the possibility that the man in overalls, wandering down a corridor, is not really an authorised workman. No stranger should ever be able to walk into a building and wander around it unsupervised.

A reliable and comfortable reception area is of vital importance, where callers can be received, checked in by internal telephone from reception to the person they are visiting, wait for an appointment if necessary, and then be personally escorted to the right destination.

When the visitor leaves the process should be reversed; a telephone call to the reception desk will ensure that the visitor is taken right to the door and is seen to leave the building.

Visitors can be issued with temporary badges or passes at the reception desk, when entry has been authorised, showing their name and the date. These temporary passes must be handed back by the visitors when they leave. In a big firm with a large number of personnel a system of entry passes for regular staff is a good one, although to work effectively this system must apply to the top management level as well as the general workforce.

Theft is an ever-present risk, especially in shops, stores and supermarkets, and any good security firm will advise on the precautionary measures to take. Closed-circuit television cameras may be of assistance, or a system of alarm tags to fix to portable goods which activate if the goods are taken away without being paid for.

14.5 **Industrial safety**

Safety in workshops, warehouses and factories is a specialised subject which depends on the nature of the premises and it is best to take the advice of specialists. Professional advice on all aspects of safe storage of goods can be obtained from the *British Safety Council*. Methods of storage vary enormously, according to the products concerned. For instance chemicals, paints, dry goods, special liquids, etc., all need special conditions consistent with complete safety. (See also 14.7.)

Machinery poses its own particular hazards. Moving parts are dangerous unless adequately screened; electricity, chemicals and molten metals can be highly dangerous unless properly protected and should be approached only by those who understand them.

The *British Safety Council* can offer invaluable advice on all risks of this kind and issues an extensive range of pamphlets which includes helpful information concerning the main causes of industrial accidents. (See Bibliography p 146.) It gives guidance on the conveying of heavy loads, safety measures affecting transport, different types of protective clothing and many other matters regarding prevention of accidents in business and industry.

14.6 **Industrial espionage**

Industrial spying is a flourishing and profitable industry as the acquisition of secret information can be worth a fortune. For instance, a new cost-cutting manufacturing process, the result of a long line of research, the likelihood of a takeover bid or an imaginative publicity project would be matters of very great interest to an industrial spy who could pass on information to a rival organisation.

Staff

It is vital for all employees always to be on guard against letting information escape inadvertently, whether written, verbal or on computer. Matters apparently trivial to one person can be of great importance to another. It is not possible to be too careful in conversation or with the transmission and storage of confidential data and documents.

Members of staff have been known to have been planted, sometimes for years, within a firm with the express purpose of becoming trusted and, at the same time, achieving a position where they can steal confidential information and pass it on. Many government departments have security staff to investigate prospective personnel thoroughly before taking them on, and again in considerable depth before promotion. All personnel managers, when engaging new employees for any kind of confidential or high security work, have a responsibility to make detailed enquiries into an applicant's previous contacts and work experience, in order to reduce the risk of infiltration into the firm by someone undesirable and dangerous.

Equipment

Competent industrial spies are patient and unobtrusive. They have access to various up-to-date specialised devices to help them and may be backed by an unscrupulous and efficient organisation willing to pay well for their services. They may use any of the following gadgets, singly or together:

> tiny transmitters to fit into a telephone, capable of relaying a conversation to a van or house several streets away
>
> suction microphones that can be attached almost invisibly to walls, windows or articles of furniture
>
> cameras that can photograph prints, plans or typescript from any distance up to 100 metres away
>
> short-wave recorders and receivers that can fit into a hat, a book or a briefcase
>
> tiny microphones, transmitters and recorders small enough to fit neatly into a matchbox, cigarette packet, wrist-watch, desk diary, etc., which can be placed casually on a desk or table or brought out during conversation.

There are confidential security agencies who will check office premises for hidden bugging devices, before important meetings.

14.7 Fire prevention

Foresight and planning are of vital importance in fire prevention and selected staff should be trained to undertake fire duties, as part of a set procedure under a designated Chief Fire Officer.

Setting up typical fire prevention scheme

The Chairman or Managing Director heads the campaign.

A Fire Prevention Committee is set up including, for example, a fire brigade representative, insurers, architects and a representative of HM Factory Inspectorate, to decide on a strategy to minimise fire risks. It is also useful to invite a risk assessor from an insurance company.

A Chief Fire Officer is appointed and a deputy to substitute for him/her when the Chief is away or otherwise unavailable. Both will have undergone training in fire prevention and precautions. He/she will work out a set procedure with full authority for setting off fire-alarms, calling out the fire brigade, calling up a private fire-fighting team and evacuating the building if necessary.

Selected personnel are trained to make regular checks at possible risk areas. Checks at night, when staff have left the premises, are quite as important as daytime inspections. Departmental managers or foremen with regular supervisory duties are suitable candidates for this task.

All employees are trained in the location of escape routes and fire exits and the positions and use of fire-fighting appliances, so that they know what to do when they hear a fire alarm, and where the nearest fire exit is to be found.

All exits should be clearly signposted and escape routes clearly marked. It must be possible to hear and recognise the sound of the alarm bell in all parts of the premises. Escape doors must *not* be locked when staff are on the premises and lifts should *not* be used in emergencies.

Fire-fighting equipment should be regularly and frequently checked to ensure that it is all in good working order; if it is not, replacements should be made immediately. The installation of smoke alarms or sprinkler systems may be worth consideration.

Occasional unscheduled fire-drills provide useful lessons in establishing how long it takes to evacuate a department or building. These exercises may be inconvenient and expensive in terms of business time lost, but if the result is that staff learn exactly how to take the quickest route out of the building with no panic, they prove well worthwhile.

Hazards

The following fire hazards merit special attention:

Smoking Cigarettes and matches are sometimes thrown aside carelessly.

Electricity Wiring and equipment can become worn, out-of-date or overloaded; trailing wires and flexes can be dangerous.

Portable heaters These should never be placed where there are draughts, nor put close to any flammable materials.

Rubbish Metal bins are the best containers for waste. Bonfires should be kept at a safe distance from buildings and sensibly supervised.

Dangerous goods Gas cylinders, chemicals, aerosols, paint, etc. require specialised storage.

Arson Regrettably these days precautions have to be taken against deliberate vandalism. All doors, windows and other means of access should be securely closed and locked when staff are away from the premises.

The local fire brigade can assist with suggestions for a fire prevention scheme for your particular business, and the *Fire Protection Association* exists to advise on planning, the provision of suitable equipment and training schemes for fire-safety personnel. Details of all these items are obtainable on request and useful leaflets, brochures and posters are also available. (See Bibliography p 146.)

14.8 Bomb scares

Dealing with a telephone warning

Any advance warning of an unexploded bomb usually comes over the telephone. When this happens the person receiving the warning call must keep calm and try to obtain as much information as possible. The following suggestions are recommended by the *Crime Prevention Section of New Scotland Yard*:

> ask (1) *where* the bomb is located, (2) *when* it is timed to explode, (3) *what* it looks like, (4) *who* and *where* the caller is and (5) *why* the bomb has been planted

> keep the caller talking, at the same time listening for an accent and trying to detect background noises; write down everything—the police will want as much information as possible when they arrive

> inform the firm's Safety Officer at once, if there is one, or the most responsible person available; the police must be called immediately and the decision taken as to whether the building has to be evacuated.

Some firms like to have two different alarm systems, one for fire and one for bomb threats, as the procedure in each case may differ. A public address system may be used to give the alarm, providing that the person using it is absolutely calm and constructive in giving directions.

Staff should be asked to leave the building by routes leading *away* from the danger area if possible, and should *not* be sent past glass partitions or plate glass windows if this can be avoided. If personnel are already accustomed to fire-drills it ought to be possible to empty the building quickly and efficiently, with the minimum of confusion (see 14.7). There may, however, be good reasons for keeping staff inside the building, for instance if a car bomb has been planted in an outside car park.

The Safety Officer should arrange for the police to be met on arrival. There will then be a search. It is particularly important to remember that any place of shelter is checked before people are allowed to enter.

Letter bombs

Some innocent-looking objects can in fact be lethal. The *Crime Prevention Section of New Scotland Yard* recommends that any letter or packet which appears suspicious should be carefully inspected for any of the following:

a tiny hole, as if made by a pin, in envelope or wrapping

a foreign or otherwise strange style of writing

no apparent airspace between the contents and the crease or fold of the envelope, the spare spaces being sealed down closely

oil or grease marks

visible wires

a heavier weight than the size seems to merit

a smell of almonds

an unsolicited book

something hard or stiff in a package or letter (about 2 oz or more in weight)

an inner envelope with any of the above features, inside a normal outer envelope or wrapping.

Look for the postmark, the original source or the name of the sender; if in doubt, check with the sender. If you still feel you have something suspicious:

put the letter or packet carefully on a flat surface, desk top or table, but *not* on the floor as it will later have to be inspected from all angles by the Crime Prevention Officer

do not attempt to open it and do not allow anyone else to touch it do not put it in water or any kind of container

    leave it in an empty room with the door locked, keep the corridor outside clear and keep the key available for the police when they arrive.

It is worth noting that efficient mail bomb detector equipment is obtainable in a variety of types and sizes. A small desk model, for instance, can X-ray letters and small parcels, a conveyor-belt unit can feed a continuous stream of mail past the inspection area, and larger installations can screen suspect parcels and luggage. A typical all-purpose model is shown in Figure 14.1. An increasing number of major organisations are installing detector equipment in mail-rooms as part of their overall security systems, to provide reassurance and protection for staff.

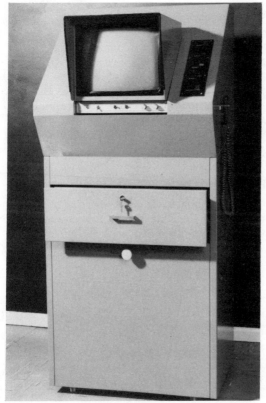

Figure 14.1 Typical mail-bomb detector unit

Car bombs

It is common sense always to leave a car with the windows closed, the bonnet internally fastened and the boot and doors securely locked whenever it has to be left unattended.

Places to check for explosive devices are under the car, along the exhaust pipe and under the engine, as well as under the wings and wheel arches. If you see unexplained wires or wooden switches, strange packages or anything else that arouses suspicion, *do not touch anything* but inform the police immediately.

14.9 Kidnapping and terrorist activities

Precautions

Everyone must now be aware that kidnapping is a common and recognised method of terrorism, undertaken for the purpose of obtaining money or bargaining power. Any person of wealth or influence, political or industrial, could be a prospective target in the violent world of today. It should not be necessary to state categorically that this is primarily and above all a matter for the police. *Department A7(3) of New Scotland Yard* are the people to contact. They offer comprehensive guidance on sensible precautions to be taken by anyone considered to be a possible target. The rest of this section lays out the main points contained in their advice.

Place of business

A security report should be made out on the building and grounds, location and surrounding areas of the business, and any overlooking vantage points.

Access to top-level offices and business suites should be controlled (special 'access control' schemes are obtainable from New Scotland Yard).

All reliable and responsible staff connected with VIPs should be trained in the action to take in the event of attack or violent intrusion.

A procedures plan should be worked out in advance, for use if the alarm system is activated.

Advance information on a VIP's movements should be restricted on a 'need to know' basis. This includes appointments in diaries, information in the press or special publicity notices, travel documents, etc., all of which should be kept concealed at all times.

Place of residence

A survey of the location, its position and surroundings should be made, including a check on neighbouring property and access routes. New Scotland Yard can advise on alarm systems and the prevention of unauthorised entry. Social visits and non-business appointments should be undertaken only with suitable precautions.

Travel

For **train journeys** made on a regular and therefore predictable basis, it is advisable to make a habit of choosing different places to sit, using a compartment already occupied, and not wearing or carrying anything distinctive such as an eye-catching buttonhole or conspicuous suitcase.

For **air travel** the booking should be made in a different name, and then changed at the last minute to the correct one. Again, plain inconspicuous luggage is advisable, which should always be kept locked and if possible within sight all the time, or checked immediately on return. Security arrangements needed abroad should be quietly planned and organised beforehand and should be confirmed before the journey is started.

It may be worth noting that a Hollywood firm, Trans World Entertainment, has produced a video guide to survival techniques in a hijack or kidnapping. In the video, a former Israeli army officer who lectures on terrorism in the United States gives much useful advice to travellers on personal conduct and behaviour in planes, airports and hotels to minimise the dangers of a terrorist attack. First distributed in America, the tape is scheduled to be released to British video outlets in 1987 and is entitled 'Travel without Terror'.

For **car travel** it is recommended that starting times be varied, that an inconspicuous car is used, with a plain-clothes chauffeur, and that the specially reserved VIP bay in the car park is not taken but an ordinary staff allocation used instead. The car should have a radio or telephone link with a base or headquarters, so that regular checks may be made during the journey.

The chauffeur should be qualified in defensive anti-terrorist driving techniques. Recognised courses of training along these lines are now available, intended to equip drivers and chauffeurs with the necessary expertise to get their passengers out of trouble. An advanced practical driving course of this kind, for training your chauffeur in anti-terrorist skills, may be worth very serious consideration.

The car should have sufficient petrol, be fully lockable, reliably roadworthy and with no distinguishing badges or stickers. The chauffeur should be wary of following cars and suspicious of unexpected diversions or roadblocks. In the event of trouble he or she will have to make a quick decision as to whether or not to make a detour.

Prior planning of journeys should always include taking note of alternative routes and places of safety, such as police stations, fire stations, ambulance depots, etc.

Prior precautions should include a telephone call, just before leaving, to a responsible contact at the destination point, to inform him or her of the time of departure and expected time of arrival. A special code-word should be chosen, to be used if confirmation is required later that any messages sent by the VIP are genuine. This code-word should only be known to the VIP, his or her family and the chauffeur.

Scotland Yard is very specific on one point. Its pamphlet, *Advice to persons considered vulnerable to kidnap*, states:

> 'It is understood that many small companies, in countries where this type of crime is prevalent, pay small ransoms and do not inform the police. IT IS VITAL THAT POLICE BE CALLED AND ASSUME RESPONSIBILITY IMMEDIATELY ON EVERY OCCASION, FOR ONCE A RANSOM HAS BEEN PAID ANOTHER DEMAND MAY BE MADE SOON AFTER.'

(The capital letters are theirs.)

Dealing with a kidnap call

If a kidnap has taken place there will be a telephone call some time later from the kidnappers. There are then several important things to remember and the person taking the call should *keep calm* and *keep the kidnapper talking*. They must try to remember everything that is said and to *write down* as much as possible so that an accurate report can be given later to the police. A foreign or regional accent, background noises and any other distinctive sounds are all significant. If you are ever in receipt of such a call:

ask for as much information about the hostage as possible, whether they are well and if they may come to the telephone (if so, get the pre-arranged code-word from them)

> if you cannot speak directly to the hostage, ask for any of their special physical characteristics, which their family or friends could confirm
>
> ask who and where the kidnapper is, what money is wanted and how and where delivery is to be made
>
> ask how the person collecting it can be identified and how soon the hostage will be released after payment is made
>
> try to judge whether the call is a hoax or a genuine threat
>
> do anything you can to keep the caller talking (e.g. say that you cannot hear them, that the telephone line is faulty, ask them to repeat the information).

The results of such an attempted conversation may not be encouraging, but the main thing is to *keep talking, keep calm* and *inform the police* immediately afterwards.

The Crime Prevention Section of New Scotland Yard is located at Peel House, 105 Regency Street, London SW1P 4AN (Tel. 01-230 2367).

14.10 Insurance

In all matters of risk and security, insurance has a business priority that can hardly be overestimated. Policies must of course be updated regularly to keep pace with today's requirements, and premiums paid before their expiry date. Insurance premiums may seem expensive but, on the other hand, ignoring insurance cover can turn out to be an extremely costly mistake.

A risk assessor from an insurance company can give advice on ways of reducing the hazards in your firm as much as possible, perhaps by recommending minor alterations or rearrangements. When these risks have been minimised an adequate insurance scheme can be planned on the most sensible cost-effective basis.

Managements have a clear duty and responsibility to safeguard the interests of everyone concerned with their business activities. No firm operates in a vacuum; every company is part of a network and a major accident of any kind in one firm can have wide-ranging consequences of all kinds—physical, mental and financial—throughout the industry. An inadequate or lapsed policy or a carelessly unpaid premium can make all the difference between a minor nuisance and a major tragedy.

Bibliography:

Yellow Pages, for lists of security firms, safety equipment, etc.

British Safety Council Publications, lists obtainable from the BSC, National Safety Centre, Chancellor's Road, London W6 9RS.

Fire Protection Association Publications, lists obtainable from 140 Aldersgate Street, London EC1A 4HX.

Royal Society for the Prevention of Accidents (RoSPA) Publications, on all aspects of safety, available from the Industrial Safety Training Centre, 22 Summer Road, Acocks Green, Birmingham B27 7UT.

15 DISTRIBUTION OF GOODS

15.1 Regulations

There is a legal duty to report to HM Customs when goods are moved out of the country, to ensure that customs dues and tariffs are met. Unlike the law in many other countries, there is no statute in English law requiring the exporter (or importer) to employ a freight forwarder. However, the volume of regulations and rules and the consequent potential loss through error are a strong recommendation for utilising the services of a freight forwarder. All products have a tariff number which enables HM Customs and Excise officers to identify the declared contents of any export.

Varying regulations apply depending on the goods being exported and the country of destination. The British Overseas Trade Board (BOTB) publishes a free booklet *Help for Exporters* which includes a list of the telephone contact points where specialist market advice for an area can be obtained. The 48-page booklet provides a mine of information regarding the support available not only from the BOTB but from other organisations. Some examples are: Technical Help for Exporters (THE); Simplification of International Trade Procedures Board (SITPRO); local Chambers of Commerce; banks.

The import regulations of the destination country are of equal importance to the exporter. Items such as labelling, certification of origin, weights and measures, tariffs, vehicle regulations, etc., need to be observed scrupulously to ensure effective delivery to the customer. Delay at the port of entry will not impress the foreign customer and may involve storage charges until the documentation is clarified. Documentation varies according to category of goods, country of destination and method of transport. The following is an indication of the documentation likely to be involved with the export of goods:

HM Customs require the exporter (or agent) to 'make an entry' which provides a reference number which must be entered on the shipping documents

a commercial invoice setting out a description and the quantity of the consignment, with the requisite number of copies and, if required, a translation into the language of the consignee

a consular invoice is also required in some cases

certificate of origin

an air waybill *(if sent by air)*

CMR conditions of carriage *(if sent by road)*

      CIM conditions of carriage *(if sent by rail)*

      a bill of lading *(if sent by sea)*

      insurance certificate.

The present nomenclature listing the codes for tariffs, Customs Co-operation Council Nomenclature (CCCN), is to be replaced on 1 January 1988 with a new worldwide system of coding and classifying goods. The new system is referred to as the **Harmonised System** (HS). At the same time the European Community's integrated tariff (TARIC) will be incorporated in the HS coding.

The two co-ordinating changes in the UK are named **Customs 88 Project.** More detailed information is available from: Customs 88 Project, HM Customs & Excise, Room 301, Dorset House, Stamford Street, London SE1 9PS.

Another move which will come into effect at that time to bring about more simplification is the **Single Administrative Document** (SAD).

15.2 Transportation

Air transport

There has been a dramatic increase in recent years in the volume of air freight. Some international airports have loading arrangements which enable a 747 jumbo jet freighter to dock straight into the warehouse building so that cargoes can be loaded quickly without being left out in the open. Some airports also have automated conveyor and storage systems. Loading is facilitated by the use of containers, pallets and the *igloo* (an air-consignment rigid box, sized for above-floor loading).

Because of the complex nature of the air freight industry it is advisable to seek the services of a member of the Institute of Freight Forwarders to obtain the most cost-effective service available. The range of this service can cover packages from one kilo in weight to a consignment requiring the chartering of a 747-200C aircraft which has a payload of 104 780 kgs. Freight forwarders can quickly arrange and assemble 'consolidated' consignments which achieve reduced charges for the consignor. 'Consolidated' means that several consignments are amalgamated into one so that, for air freight purposes, the combined packages are treated as a single consignment. Tariffs vary depending on:

whether the goods are from an industrial or a commercial user

the destination area (because different volume to weight ratios apply).

Leading international air freight forwarders, such as Trans Global Air Ltd, book regular cargo space and thus obtain concession rates which enable customers to save up to 60% off normal rates to many destinations. They also accumulate specialist knowledge of local rules and regulations regarding imports and exports which increases their ability to ensure efficient onward transhipment to outlying destinations. Trans Global have established an excellent reputation through their work with over 60 governments and government agencies around the world and have been employed as air freight specialists on building projects such as hotels, road construction and hydroelectrics. They have established a book division to cater for the special needs of British publishing houses regarding distribution and special cargo rates. Other services to customers are:

a fleet of vehicles providing a feeder link to seaports and airports

packing on the customer's premises

provision of all categories of insurance

granting permission to use a central warehouse as a receiving depot

a courier service for documents and time-sensitive items

a 'home move' service covering packing, collection, air transportation, customs clearance, delivery and unpacking at the new address.

Road transport

There are two major associations for the road transport industry:

Freight Transport Association Ltd (FTA)
St. John's Road, Tunbridge Wells, Kent TN4 9UZ

Road Haulage Association Ltd (RHA)
Roadway House, 104 New King's Road, London SW6 4LN.

Both associations keep members informed of legislation and other matters affecting the industry. They have a current list of members who offer specialist services ranging from 65 bhp vans for parcel services to 430 bhp tractors to haul trailers, or a combination of truck and draw-bar trailer for large lightweight goods. Bulk-load handling, tanker and refrigerated trucks cater for every business requirement. Manufacturers are offered a complete warehousing facility including a selection and packing operation.

The European Commission is committed to the removal of trade barriers by 1992, which means that continental hauliers will be seeking business throughout the UK. Eurotunnel have set a target date of 1993 for completion of the Channel Fixed Link. These two '90s projections will bring new factors into the haulage business in England and the RHA has begun preparations to meet the challenge.

When lorries operate in Europe and the Middle East additional requirements are:

the appropriate 'T' form

usually a TIR *(Transports Internationaux Routiers)* carnet to ensure free passage of containerised goods at intermediary customs point(s) en route

vehicle registration document and driver's passport

authority to drive the vehicle, rules of the road, speed, hours of driving and rest

international driving licence (needed for some European countries)

pre-arranged checkpoints for two-way relay of messages

all documentary customs and tariff details, i.e. packing notes, value of each kind of goods carried, and the relevant customs codes for tariff purposes.

Rail transport

In his 1986 address, the President of the Chartered Institute of Transport said that rail's share of freight traffic had dropped in the previous twenty years from 21% to 9%. He explained that 70% of all goods were moved less than 30 miles and at least 90% of goods have an origin or destination away from a railway line, thus he acknowledged the economies and logistics which foster co-existence of the complementary transporters.

Railfreight International has specialist representatives located at Bristol, Glasgow, London and Manchester to cover the surrounding areas. It provides a service in refrigerated and insulated transport, as well as a list of freight forwarders and wagon operators. Charges are usually on a simple per-wagon basis but special contracts can be arranged. Uniform conditions of carriage with the various railways is assured through the CIM Convention. The EEC's Community Transit Procedure has eliminated the need for 'T' forms. Customs clearance, whether at ports or inland, is handled through British Rail or its accredited freight forwarders.

A useful publication is the *Documentation Handbook* available on request from: Railfreight International, Publicity Store, British Rail, Room 5, Melbury House, Melbury Terrace, London NW1 6JU.

Sea transport

The International Standards Organisation (ISO) has achieved a rationalisation of the sizes and range of containers to enable significant reductions in the time needed to load and unload vessels. Containerisation has resulted in a speedy turnaround of ships. Breakages and pilfering losses have also been reduced. Standardisation of facilities at ports of call, plus limiting the number of stops en route, has further reduced the voyage time for consignments. Containers can be loaded directly on to the large road haulage vehicles and trailers. The network of motorways linking European ports ensures fast road movement.

Businesses involved with shipping often use the services of freight forwarders to handle the documentation, viz: insurance, certificates of origin, customs licences, transportation to and/or from ports, and groupage (e.g. collecting sufficient freight to fill a container which is charged at a lower tariff than a part-loaded one). Cases have to be marked by a four-line code which has international acceptance, for example:

Code	Indicating
987	order number
HULL	destination
ICI	abbreviated name of consignee (Imperial Chemical Industries)
2/10	case identity (the second case in a consignment of ten to the same place, for the same consignee).

There are other standardised markings to indicate that a case has to be kept upright, that the goods are fragile or inflammable, and so on. Integrated shipment of goods by air/road/rail/sea has resulted in increased competition within the industry, resulting in transport becoming more cost-effective.

Courier service

See Chapter 20.2, 20.5.

Bibliography

Send It Anywhere Directory. Pub. Kogan Page, 1983.

Croner's Reference Book for Exporters. Pub. Croner Publications Ltd, November 1986.

Help for Exporters. Pub. British Overseas Trade Board, January 1986.

Selling to Western Europe. Pub. British Overseas Trade Board, 1986.

Railfreight International. Pub. British Rail, 1984.

A Brief Introduction to Freight Forwarding. Pub. Institute of Freight Forwarders Ltd, February 1985.

Part IV
GOVERNMENT AND LAW

● John
O'Groats

All this extra distance and no extra cost.

● Land's End

We can go near. Or we can go far. Either way you'll have no extra to pay.

Just a simple single charge that will guarantee delivery to any address the length and breadth of Britain.

It's a service no other national carrier could even begin to match. And it's just one of an outstanding range we can offer your business.

Call 01-200 0200 and ask for Royal Mail Parcels.

You'll find no other carrier goes quite so far to help you.

Royal Mail Parcels

16 GOVERNMENT IN THE UNITED KINGDOM

16.1 The UK system of government

The United Kingdom is a unitary state with a constitutional Monarch, Queen Elizabeth II (*b* 1926), at its head. Legislative power resides in Parliament, which is a trinity of the Crown and two chambers, an upper house—the Lords, and a lower house—the Commons. The House of Commons, whose members alone are elected, is the dominant of these three branches of government. The majority party within this chamber forms the government of the day and from its ranks are drawn the Prime Minister and Cabinet, who assume day-to-day control of the nation's affairs. They work with the permanent government machine and frame new policies for passage through the Commons and the Lords. Outside Parliament, the judiciary ensures that these laws are adhered to, while local government and quangos (quasi-autonomous non-governmental organisations) carry out functions 'devolved' by Parliament.

16.2 Principal political institutions

Executive institutions

At the apex of the UK system of government stands an hereditary **Monarch**, whose powers are, in theory, extensive, including the right to appoint ministers, dissolve Parliament and give final approval (the Royal Assent) to all legislation. In practice, however, the Monarch's role is largely formal and ceremonial. She is constrained by the laws and conventions of the constitution and must act on the advice of the Prime Minister. The Queen is thus an apolitical figure who provides a stable and unifying focal point for the nation. Real executive power is wielded by her elected ministers within Parliament.

The political executive numbers around a hundred and is composed of members from the party or coalition which commands a majority in the House of Commons. It is chosen by the Prime Minister, who is the party's leader, with about 80% drawn from the Commons and the rest from the Lords. A quarter of this government team comprises 'whips', whose task is to ensure party discipline and loyalty in Parliament, and specialist law officers. The remainder of the team is primarily concerned with policy-making and overseeing the permanent executive machine, the Civil Service. They are assigned to different government departments, each usually having at its head a Secretary of State, with lower-ranking Ministers of State and junior Under-Secretaries of State below.

The top 20–25 members of the government meet together to co-ordinate policy making and executive actions in a **Cabinet**, which is selected by the Prime Minister. It convenes weekly in full session on Thursday mornings at the Prime Minister's offices at 10 Downing Street, while smaller specialised Cabinet committees and sub-committees meet more regularly, most of these enjoying independent decision-making powers. The Cabinet is the centrepiece of political authority in Britain, with its members being collectively responsible for decisions taken. Within the Cabinet, the **Prime Minister** is, in theory, 'first among equals', but is, in reality, the most important single member. Lacking detailed departmental responsibilities, the Prime Minister is able to concentrate on co-ordinating activities and determining priorities, as well as acting as the chief public spokesman for the government. The Prime Minister also enjoys extensive patronage powers, being able to award honours and appoint ministers, peers, ambassadors, senior civil servants, judges, Church of England bishops and the heads of Royal Commissions, quangos and nationalised industries.

Legislative institutions

The two chambers of Parliament—the Commons and the Lords—act as a vital check on the executive and form the links between the public and the government of the day.

The **House of Commons** is unquestionably the more important chamber, its support being essential to maintain the government in power. It also enjoys exclusive rights over financial bills and can override the Lords' vetos. The Commons comprises 650 members (MPs), who are elected on a 'first-past-the-post' basis in single member constituencies which, on average, comprise 65 000 electors. Elections are held at least every five years, with the Prime Minister exercising the right to ask the Monarch to dissolve Parliament and call fresh elections at an earlier date.

The Commons is concerned chiefly with three activities:

the passage of legislation
the debate of public issues
the scrutiny of executive actions.

It meets in annual sessions beginning in November and ending in late October and sits for between 150 and 250 days per year. The timetable of the House is concerned overwhelmingly with government business, but time is also set aside for the opposition and for private members.

Legislation introduced in the House is almost exclusively framed by the government, although a few uncontroversial Private Members' Bills do find their way on to the statute book each year. This legislation needs to pass through a series of stages before it can become law. Firstly it is carefully scrutinised by government departments and lawyers and the views of interested bodies are sought, special Royal Commissions sometimes being set up for this purpose. It is then put before a Cabinet committee or full Cabinet, after which a **'Green Paper'** for discussion or **'White Paper'** for public and parliamentary notification is issued. The legislation is then presented to Parliament as a Bill and is given a general **First Reading** before the full House.

The principles behind the Bill are debated during its **Second Reading** and, if approved, it is sent to a legislative Standing Committee, composed of 20-50 members reflecting party strengths, or, if the Bill concerns important financial or constitutional matters, to a committee of the full House. During this **Committee Stage** each clause of the Bill is scrutinised and voted on in detail, with minor amendments improving the clarity of the measure frequently being made. The government can expedite discussion during the Committee Stage by applying the 'guillotine', setting a timetable for each clause.

The Bill with its amendments is subsequently put before the House again for the **Report Stage**. Last-minute changes can be made on this occasion and, if approved, it is sent to the full House for final approval after its **Third Reading**. For a Bill to become law, it needs to pass through a similar process in the House of Lords, after which it is given the **Royal Assent**. Between 50 and 70 such Bills gain approval each year. During this legislative procedure, backbench and opposition MPs are able to debate, scrutinise and propose amendments to government legislation. In addition, they keep a check on the work of the executive:

during the hour set aside for the questioning of government ministers at the start of each parliamentary day (between 2.30 and 3.30 pm, Tuesdays and Thursdays being set aside for questions to the Prime Minister)

during the 19 days allocated for debate on issues raised by the opposition through the new institutions of the 14 specialist Select Committees.

The **Select Committees**, twelve of which were set up in 1979, cover all departments except the Lord Chancellor's Law Office and comprise between nine and eleven MPs each, drawn from all parties, with chairmanships divided between the two major parties. They have the power to call witnesses and send for official papers.

The **House of Lords** forms a second chamber for scrutiny and debate. It is composed of 770 hereditary peers and 350 life peers, but its average daily attendance is only 300. Its membership is both elderly (many of the life peerages being awarded to those who have distinguished themselves in public service), and varied (including 24 Bishops of the Church of England, 2 Archbishops and 11 Law Lords). In party terms, almost 49% of its regular attenders support the Conservatives, 16% Labour, 10% the Liberal-SDP Alliance and 25% are independent crossbenchers. The Lords is of value in 'polishing up' Commons' legislation and as a forum for debate. It is also used for the introduction of non-controversial legislation, thus saving Commons' time. It lacks the power to veto Commons' legislation however, being able only to delay the implementation of non-financial Bills passed by the Commons in two successive sessions for a one-year period.

Judicial institutions

Outside Parliament, a vast judicial machine operates to ensure that parliamentary statutes and the common law are upheld. This judicial system is divided into functional branches and hierarchies. The major division is between **Civil** and **Criminal Law**, the former being concerned with damages against individuals and claims for compensation, the latter with offences against society in general which require exemplary punishment. Minor civil cases are dealt with by Circuit judges at the County Court level, more important cases being sent before the High Court. Minor (summary) criminal offences, for example driving misdeeds, are tried in Magistrates' Courts by Lay Magistrates (JPs).

More serious (indictable) criminal offences are sent to Crown Courts to be tried before a judge, and if the defendant pleads not guilty, a jury of twelve randomly selected lay people. Within each branch of the law, appeal to a higher court—the Crown Court, High Court, Court of Appeal and the House of Lords or, in certain instances, the European Court of Justice—is permissible. More than 2000 administrative tribunals also operate to hear disputes between the citizen and government agencies, dealing with issues such as rents, rates, pensions and social security benefits.

The judicial system deals with more than two million cases a year, at a cost to the State of more than £0.5 billion. Employed in its functioning are more than 44 000 solicitors, 4800 barristers, 27 000 JPs and 450 full-time judges.

JPs work part-time and are prominent members of the local community who have been recommended to the Lord Chancellor (a Cabinet member). They undergo a period of basic legal training, are advised by qualified clerks and are paid attendance allowances. **Solicitors and barristers** undergo specialised training and must pass examinations set by their professional bodies.

Judges are appointed from the ranks of barristers on the recommendation of the Lord Chancellor and, in the cases of the highest judges, the Prime Minister. Once appointed, they cannot be removed before their retirement at the age of 72 or 75. They thus enjoy considerable independence in decision-making, but are required to interpret the law on the basis of previous decisions ('judicial precedent') and in accordance with the strict wording of parliamentary statutes.

The Scottish judicial system differs somewhat, with the Sheriff Court taking the place of County Courts in civil cases, and with the Police, JP and Sheriff Courts replacing the Magistrates' Courts and Crown Courts in criminal offences. The Court of Sessions is the supreme civil court in Scotland and the High Court of Justiciary is the foremost criminal court.

16.3 Local government in the UK

Parliament enjoys sovereignty (supremacy) in the legislative sphere. No other body has law-making powers or can overrule an Act of Parliament. However, for convenience and to bring decision-making closer to the people, powers in specified areas have been delegated to lower tiers of government.

At the national level, there is a devolution of administrative and executive powers in the cases of Scotland, Wales and Northern Ireland, in recognition of their strong and specific identities. Both the Principality of Wales (population 3 million) and the Kingdom of Scotland (population 5.2 million), which were respectively united with England by Acts of Union in 1535 and 1707, have their own Secretaries of State in the Cabinet (usually a fellow national), junior ministers and 'offices', which take over many of the administrative and executive functions carried out by central government departments in England (population 46.5 million).

The **Welsh Office**, which is based primarily in Cardiff (although an additional small ministerial office exists in London), has full responsibility in Wales for health, housing, local government, primary and secondary education, town and country planning, water and sewerage, roads, forestry, tourism, national parks and historic buildings. The **Scottish Office**, based in Edinburgh, has even greater powers, being concerned additionally with economic planning (running the Scottish Development Agency), agriculture, fisheries, the police and fire services. It employs 9000 civil servants in five functionally divided departments. These offices are dependent upon central government for funding, but are often able to frame independent and innovative policies of their own.

Arrangements for Northern Ireland (population 1.7 million) have traditionally differed. The Province, while also sending MPs to the House of Commons, was unique in possessing its own two-chambered Parliament at Stormont between 1921 and 1972, to which Westminster devolved extensive powers, as well as its own prime minister and civil service. Direct rule from Westminster had, however, to be imposed following sectarian violence between 1968 and 1972. The Stormont Parliament was suspended in March 1972 and a **Northern Ireland Office** was set up instead, based in Belfast and London. It has responsibilities for health and social services, finance, manpower services, education, the environment, commerce and agriculture. It is functionally divided into departments, with its public servants drawn largely from the old Northern Ireland Civil Service, but its Secretary of State and junior ministers are, of necessity, of English descent. Attempts to resurrect a locally elected national assembly in Northern Ireland in the years since 1972 have so far failed.

Throughout the UK there are also subnational tiers of local government to which Westminster has devolved policy-making and administrative powers in specific fields. Its political members are elected and raise a portion of their income locally through the imposition of rates. In broad terms, local government is responsible for the provision of primary and secondary education, public housing, local buses, refuse collection, the personal social and health services, the police and fire services, roads (excluding motorways), environmental health, as well as regulating standards and local activities. They also provide leisure and cultural amenities and often promote local tourism and industries. Taken together, the local government machine is vast, its spending amounting to almost 10% of gross domestic product (GDP), or a quarter of total public spending, and it employs almost three million people. It is under the political direction of more than 100 000 locally elected 'amateur' councillors, elected for four-year terms, who are paid attendance allowances and are served by professional local government officers.

The local government system in the UK today follows a three-tier structure. The top and most important tier is that of the **County Council** (or **Regional Council** in Scotland) which is responsible for overall planning, transport, the police and fire services, education, personal social services and waste disposal facilities. Below these councils, but not subservient to them, are the **District and Metropolitan District Councils** which are concerned with housing, local planning, environmental health, leisure activities and waste collection. At the bottommost rung are the **Parish, Town or Community Councils** with responsibility for local parish amenities.

In England's seven major cities, London, Birmingham (West Midlands), Liverpool (Merseyside), Greater Manchester, Leeds (West Yorkshire), Sheffield (South Yorkshire) and Newcastle (Tyne and Wear), Metropolitan Councils used to exist, but were abolished in 1986, their functions being transferred to Metropolitan District and Borough Councils and, in a number of cases, to new **Joint Boards** composed of members nominated by the District and Borough Councils. In Northern Ireland, the democratic element is far weaker because of Direct Rule and sectarian problems. The distribution of local councils in England, Scotland, Wales and Northern Ireland is as follows:

England: 39 'Shire' County Councils; 36 Metropolitan District Councils; 296 Non-Metropolitan District Councils; 32 London Borough Councils; over 8000 Parish/Town Councils.

Scotland: 9 Regional Councils; 53 District Councils; over 1200 Community Councils; 3 Island Councils for the Western Isles, Orkneys and Shetlands (with the powers of Regional and District Councils).

Wales: 8 County Councils; 37 District Councils; over 500 Community Councils.

N Ireland: Area Boards (appointed directly by the Secretary of State); 26 District Councils (concerned with local environmental and recreational services).

The funds for local government are partly obtained from rates imposed on local householders and businesses, from council house rents and from leisure amenity charges. More than 60% of local government's income is, however, provided by central government in the form of the Rate Support Grant and specific grants for services such as the police and transport. In recent years, central government's control over local government spending and revenue raising has been tightened, with penalties being set for councils which raise rates above specified limits.

16.4 The permanent government machine

Government today is involved in a wide range of regulative, promotional and service activities. State spending accounts for more than 45% of GDP and almost 30% of the national workforce is employed in the public sector. In charge of this labyrinth of activities are more than 100000 elected officials, who are served in turn by 1.6 million full-time, professional public servants.

The central government's **Civil Service** numbers 620000 and is divided on departmental and functional rank lines. There are currently 15 major Departments of State and 16 more minor or sub-departments.

Major departments

Ministry of Agriculture, Fisheries and Food (MAFF); Ministry of Defence (MOD); Dept of Education and Science (DES); Dept of Employment (DE); Dept of Energy; Dept of the Environment (DOE); Foreign and Commonwealth Office (FCO); Dept of Health and Social Security (DHSS); Home Office; Northern Ireland Office; Scottish Office; Dept of Trade and Industry (DTI); Dept of Transport; HM Treasury; Welsh Office.

Minor Departments

Lord Chancellor's Dept; Office of Arts and Libraries; HM Customs and Excise; Export Credits Guarantee Dept; Central Office of Information (COI); Board of Inland Revenue; Law Officers' Dept; Management and Personnel Office (MPO); Ordnance Survey Dept;

Overseas Development Administration (ODA); Parliamentary Counsel's Office; Paymaster General's Office; Office of Population Censuses and Surveys; Procurator General and Treasury Solicitor's Dept; HM Stationery Office (HMSO); Office of Telecommunications (Oftel).

The largest departments are Defence (which, including the Royal Ordnance Factories, employs 98 000), Health and Social Security (90 000), Employment (55 000), the Home Office (33 000), Environment (21 000), Transport (13 000) and Trade and Industry (12 000). Within these departments, civil servants are divided functionally into grades, namely Administrative Officers, concerned with policy, and Executive and Clerical Officers, with its implementation. There are also specialist technical personnel. A number of departments, such as the DOE, DTI, DHSS and the Department of Employment, have a regional structure; the latter two also boast a large network of local offices.

The remainder of white-collar public servants work at the local government level, in public corporations (nationalised industries) and **quangos**. The latter are government agencies which have been set up by statute to carry out executive actions or to operate in an advisory, regulatory or promotional capacity. There are more than 1000, prominent examples being the Regional Health and Water Authorities, the Manpower Services Commission, the University Grants Committee, the Housing Corporation, the Milk Marketing Board, the National Consumer Council, the Equal Opportunities Commission and the Atomic Energy Authority. Quango heads are appointed by government, but are given considerable freedom of action, within financial limits, and are expected to manage their enterprises in an efficient, non-political manner.

16.5 Political parties and organised interest groups

Political power is exercised in the UK by **parties** organised at the national and local levels. These parties are based on broad ideologies and philosophies of government and appeal to different social groups and areas. They present detailed policy programmes and manifestos to the public at election-time and, once elected, serve as their representatives and form a vital bridge in the political system.

In England, Scotland and Wales four parties dominate: on the right of the political spectrum the Conservatives (membership 1.2 million, leader Mrs Margaret Thatcher), on the left, the Labour Party (membership 270000, leader Mr Neil Kinnock). In between stand two parties, the Liberals (membership 105000, leader Mr David Steel) and the Social Democratic Party (SDP) (membership 55000, leader Dr David Owen), which temporarily combine as the Liberal-Social Democratic Alliance for election contests. In Scotland and Wales nationalist parties, Plaid Cymru (PC) and the Scottish National Party (SNP), are also significant entities and have seats inside the Commons. The most important minor party in Britain is the ecologist Green Party, although it enjoys no parliamentary representation.

Party politics in Northern Ireland differ substantially from that on the British mainland. The Conservative, Labour and Liberal-SDP Alliance parties do not contest elections in the Province. Instead sectarian-based Protestant and Catholic parties vie for power in local and parliamentary elections. On the Protestant side, two major Unionist parties dominate, the Official Unionist Party (OUP) (leader Mr James Molyneaux) and the hardline Democratic Unionist Party (DUP) (leader Rev. Ian Paisley), with the smaller Ulster Popular Unionist Party (UPUP) also being of importance. On the Catholic Nationalist side stand the moderate Social Democratic and Labour Party (SDLP) (leader Mr John Hume) and the extreme nationalist Provisional Sinn Fein (PSF) (leader Mr Gerry Adams), the political offshoot of the Irish Republican Army (IRA). In addition to these parties, there are a large number of minor parties, the most important of which is the non-sectarian Alliance Party of Northern Ireland.

SEATS WON BY PARTIES IN THE JUNE 1983 GENERAL ELECTION

	England	*Scotland*	*Wales*	*N Ireland*	*Total*
Conservative	362	21	14	—	397
Labour	148	41	20	—	209
Liberal	10	5	2	—	17
Social Democratic	3	3	0	—	6
Scottish Nationalist	—	2	—	—	2
Plaid Cymru	—	—	2	—	2
Official Unionist	—	—	—	11	11
Democratic Unionist	—	—	—	3	3
Social Democratic and Labour	—	—	—	1	1
Provisional Sinn Fein	—	—	—	1	1
Ulster Popular Unionist	—	—	—	1	1
Total	523	72	38	17	650

The **franchise** in elections is granted to all UK subjects over the age of 18 with the exception of peers, those certified as mentally ill and persons serving more than twelve months' imprisonment. Voting is by the simple majority system in single member constituencies, except in the case of local elections in Northern Ireland, where a proportional representation system applies. Candidates in parliamentary elections must be over the age of 21, be nominated by ten electors and provide a deposit of £500, which is reimbursed if 5% or more of the vote is achieved. Civil servants, judges, members of the armed forces, peers, Church of England and Roman Catholic clergymen, undischarged bankrupts, the certified insane and prisoners serving more than twelve months are debarred from standing for the Commons. Candidates in local elections must be over the age of 21 and must, in addition, have employment or residency connections with the area for which they stand, but cannot be an employee of the local authority in question.

While political parties seek to exercise power directly over the full range of government affairs, numerous smaller **interest groups** and **pressure groups** work outside Parliament and local government chambers, attempting to influence policy decisions in more narrowly specific spheres. These groups seek variously to promote or to defend their interest in the face of government legislation and are concerned with a wide variety of matters, economic, professional and political. Prominent economic interest groups include the Trades Union Congress (membership 9 million) and its constituent trade unions, the Confederation of British Industry, the British Road Federation and the National Farmers' Union.

Prominent professional interest groups include the British Medical Association, the Law Society and the Police Federation. Examples of political interest groups are Greenpeace and the Campaign for Nuclear Disarmament. These groups use a variety of tactics in an effort to influence public opinion and political decision makers.

Political interest groups concentrate, in particular, upon demonstrations and other forms of public action. Economic and professional interest groups involve themselves most prominently in consultation with and in the lobbying of politicians and civil service and quango leaders at Westminster, Whitehall and in the provinces. A number of the groups sponsor MPs, either directly or indirectly, the Labour and Conservative parties being significantly dependent upon trade union and business funding. Many pressure groups are quasi-permanent, others are temporarily formed to oppose specific decisions of local or national government.

163

17 LEGISLATION IN THE EIGHTIES

Since 1 January 1980 over 400 new public general Acts of Parliament have appeared on the statute books. Some of them have yet to come fully into force and some have very limited relevance to the general public. There remain, however, a large number of statutes which have come into force in the present decade which have considerable importance to a large number of people. It is clearly beyond the scope of this work to deal with all of these and this section focuses, therefore, on certain features of recent legislation which have an impact on commercial life. The matters discussed below arise from complex legislation and contain many pitfalls for the unwary. Specialist advice from a solicitor or other professional adviser is highly recommended for anyone affected by this legislation.

17.1 The Business Expansion Scheme

As part of a general government policy to encourage the formation of new businesses financed by private capital, the Business Start-Up Scheme was introduced by the Finance Act 1981. The basic idea of this scheme was to allow individuals relief from income tax on the amount of money paid for shares in new unquoted companies, provided that various conditions were met—including a requirement that the company in question should carry on a 'new' trade. The problem which the scheme was designed to help alleviate was the difficulty experienced by entrepreneurs in finding risk capital for new ventures. Inevitably, a significant proportion of new ventures do not succeed, and a private individual risks losing his or her investment. However, if tax relief is given on the investment, the net effect is that the government pays a proportion of the investment, reducing the risk of the individual by a proportion equivalent to that person's highest rate of tax.

The Business Start-Up Scheme attracted a great deal of interest but it was soon found to be too restrictive in its operation, and the **Finance Act 1983** replaced it with the Business Expansion Scheme, often referred to by its initials BES. The BES is not confined to new companies or new trades and although, as explained below, it is subject to a number of conditions, it can provide a considerable incentive for investment in unquoted companies.

The relief

Briefly, the BES allows an individual who is UK resident and who subscribes up to £40 000 in any tax year for 'eligible shares' in one or more 'qualifying' companies, to set the cost of that investment against his or her total taxable income for the year in question. An additional benefit introduced by the Finance Act 1986 is that shares issued under the BES after 18 March 1986 will be exempt from capital gains tax on their first disposal, provided that the BES relief applying to those shares has not been withdrawn.

Conditions

BES relief can only be claimed by a qualifying individual who subscribes for new eligible shares in a qualifying unquoted company. Those shares must have been issued for the purpose of raising money for a qualifying trade which is being carried on or will be carried on within two years by the company or by a qualifying subsidiary. Eligible shares are ordinary shares which carry no preferential rights. The concepts of 'qualifying individual', 'qualifying company' and 'qualifying trade' are explained below.

Indirect investment

The subscription may be made either directly or through an approved investment fund. In the case of direct investment, relief is not available for investments of less than £500 in any one company in any tax year. This lower limit does not apply to indirect investments through a fund, however, and this enables investors to spread risk in comparatively small investments over a number of companies in which a fund invests on their behalf.

Qualifying individuals

In order to qualify for relief, an individual must be resident and ordinarily resident in the UK within the meaning of the tax legislation at the time of the investment. Also, the individual must not be connected with the company which issues the shares or become so connected within the five years after making the investment.
The main rules relating to connection with a company are:

the individual or his/her associate must not be an employee, partner or paid director of the company
the individual and his/her associates must not control the

company or possess more than 30% of the ordinary share capital, or loan capital and issued share capital or voting power in the company.

For this purpose, an associate includes a husband or wife, lineal ancestor or descendant, a partner and certain persons with whom the individual has connections through a trust. A director is not regarded as a paid director when they are only repaid travelling and other expenses, but he or she must not be paid any remuneration.

Qualifying companies

For a company to be 'qualifying':

> it must have been incorporated in the UK and must be resident only in the UK
>
> it must not be quoted on the Stock Exchange and its shares must not be dealt in on the Unlisted Securities Market
>
> it must not be a subsidiary of or be controlled by any other company and any subsidiaries it has must be at least 90% owned by it
>
> all of its share capital must be fully paid up
>
> it must either carry on a qualifying trade or exist for the purpose of holding shares in its subsidiaries, which must all carry on qualifying trades.

Qualifying trades

The purpose of the BES is to encourage investment in risky ventures which might otherwise have difficulty raising capital. Because of this, the **Finance Act 1983** excluded from the definition of 'qualifying trade' certain activities, principally in the financial sector, which the scheme was not designed to encourage. These included commodity and securities dealing, banking, insurance and the provision of legal and accountancy services. After the introduction of the BES, there was some concern that too much BES money was being channelled into low-risk, asset-backed ventures such as property development, investment in fine wines, etc. To combat this, recent Finance Acts have placed considerable restrictions on the applicability of the BES to activities such as these and the Government has powers to bring in further restrictions by statutory instrument if further action is necessary.

Claiming relief

Claims for relief can be made when the qualifying trade has been carried on for at least four months and must be made within two years of that date, or (if later) two years from the end of the tax year in which the investment is made. The procedure for claiming relief firstly involves the company applying to the Inland Revenue for approval of the company and its trade for the purposes of the BES. Once approval has been obtained, the company may issue forms to its BES shareholders containing a certificate which the shareholders must pass on to the Inland Revenue when claiming relief in their personal taxation.

Limitation and withdrawal of relief

Relief cannot be claimed on more than £40 000 invested by an individual investor (and his/her spouse) in any one tax year.

If the conditions of relief relating to the company cease to be satisfied within three years after the date of the investment or (if later) three years after the company began to carry on a qualifying trade, the relief is withdrawn. Relief is also wholly or partly withdrawn if the individual receives value from the company or disposes of his or her shares within five years. Value is received from the company if, for example, it redeems the shares or provides a loan or some other benefit to the individual.

Relief is not available unless the shares are subscribed for and issued for a bona fide commercial purpose and not as a scheme or arrangement one of the main purposes of which is the avoidance of tax.

Seeking BES finance

The BES has proved to be a considerable success and, because of this, it has been extended indefinitely by the **Finance Act 1986**. It still remains difficult, however, for companies seeking BES investment to make contact with individuals wishing to take advantage of the scheme, owing to the very considerable restrictions which the law places on the ability of companies to offer shares to individuals. These restrictions are contained in the Companies Act 1985 and the Prevention of Fraud (Investments) Act 1958, replaced by the **Financial Services Act 1986**. Contravention of these provisions is a very serious matter and companies seeking BES investment from members of the public should always seek professional advice. However, contacting an approved investment fund would not amount to an offer to the public and might provide a company with more straightforward access to BES funds.

17.2 Share incentive schemes

There has been a trend in several industrial countries, over the last two or three decades, to encourage employees to acquire shares in the companies for which they work. In this way, the employees receive an additional incentive to work hard and this benefits both the company and, more indirectly, the economy of the country in question.

The incentive can be provided to the employee in a number of different ways, but the two main methods involve either the acquisition of shares by the employer (or a trust on his or her behalf) wholly or partly paid for by the company itself or the acquisition by the employee of options to buy shares at a later date. An option is simply a right to call upon the company to issue shares to the option holder at a particular price. The advantage to employees arises if, say, they have an option to buy shares at £1 each and the share price has moved up to £5 each. They can realise a profit by buying at the lower price and selling at the higher.

In the UK, the basic taxing provisions are structured so as to tax as income any benefits obtained from employment, including shares and share options. In ordinary cases, the disposal of shares or options by an individual gives rise to a charge to capital gains tax rather than income tax. In the case of shares or options acquired by employees in their employment, however, income tax is in many instances payable on any gain on disposal or deemed gain where shares are acquired on special terms and held for a specified period. The treatment of capital gains as income is particularly unattractive for higher rate tax payers, who find themselves paying tax at rates higher than the uniform rate for capital gains tax. It may also be disadvantageous for many basic rate tax payers, however, if their gain would otherwise fall within the annual allowance for capital gains tax, bearing no tax at all.

To encourage employee share ownership, specific exemptions from the basic taxing provisions have been enacted in various Finance Acts. Each of these involves the establishment of a scheme which must be approved by the Inland Revenue before relief is given. Details of the schemes are given below. It is important to appreciate that these schemes provide exceptions to the basic taxing provisions and that relief from income tax will not be available unless the schemes are properly set up and operated.

Approved Profit-Sharing Schemes

Approved Profit-Sharing Schemes were introduced by the **Finance Act 1978** and involve an employing company paying a part of its profits to trustees, who use these funds to buy shares in the company (or its parent company) for the benefit of eligible employees. The shares are appropriated to the individual employees but must normally be retained by the trustees for a two-year retention period. After this period, the employees may instruct the trustees to dispose of the shares, but the disposal is only exempt from income tax in normal circumstances if it takes place after a further three years. The company is allowed relief from corporation tax on the amount of profits which it applies towards the acquisition of shares for employees by the trustees of the scheme.

Participants

The scheme must be open to all individuals who are full-time directors and employees of the company concerned and have been such for the qualifying period (not exceeding five years) laid down by the rules of the particular scheme. A participant must be someone who pays tax under Schedule E and must not have had shares appropriated to him or her under another approved scheme run by the same or a connected company. No relief is available to an individual if the employing company is a close company and the individual or his/her associates hold more than 25% of the ordinary shares.

Shares

The scheme shares must be shares of the employing company or its parent company. They must be fully paid up and must be part of the ordinary share capital of the company. Except in the case of workers' co-operatives, the shares cannot be redeemable and must not be subject to any special restrictions which do not apply to all shares of the class. It is permissible for companies to include a provision in their Articles of Association which obliges employees or directors to sell their shares when they cease to hold their office or employment with the company, but this will only be allowed if it applies to all shares of the class—not only to scheme shares—and if the compulsory sale is for a cash consideration. Except in the case of employee-controlled companies, the company concerned must only have one class of ordinary share or, if it has more than one, the majority of the class of shares used in the scheme must not be held by employees.

Approval

Relief from income tax will not be given unless the scheme is set up in accordance with the provisions of the Finance Act 1978 and is approved by the Inland Revenue. Relief will not be available if the conditions of the scheme are not observed. The scheme must provide for shares, acquired by the trustees, to be appropriated to eligible employees or directors within 18 months of purchase by the trustees. In general, the shares must be retained by the Trustees for two years after appropriation (the *retention period*) although there are special provisions to deal with takeover bids, mergers, etc. which may occur during this period. The retention period comes to an end before two years in the event of the death of the participant, if he or she reaches pensionable age or if he or she ceases to be employed by reason of disability or redundancy. In the case of a workers' co-operative where the scheme shares are redeemable, the retention period comes to an end when the employee ceases to be employed by the co-operative, for any reason.

At the end of the retention period, the participant can instruct the trustees to sell his or her shares, but if the disposal takes place before the fifth anniversary of the date when the shares were appropriated to that person (the *release date*), they will be subject to income tax on the value of the shares at the date of appropriation. This provision does not apply in the case of the death of a participant before the release date and if the participant reaches pensionable age or loses his or her job through disability or redundancy, the income tax charge is levied only on 50% of the relevant value. If the participant instructed disposal of his or her shares in the year prior to the release date, the appropriate percentage will be 75%.

The value of shares which may be apportioned to any participant in any one tax year must not exceed 10% of his or her salary for the year in question or £1250, whichever is greater, subject to an overall limit of £5000.

Savings-Related Share Option Schemes

Savings-Related Share Option Schemes were introduced by the **Finance Act 1980** and provided an opportunity for employees to benefit from the increase in the share price in their employer company or its parent by exercising an option to acquire shares at the end of a prescribed period. Such a scheme operates by the relevant company granting to a participant an option to acquire shares at a price not less than 90% of the market value of those shares at the time of the grant of the option. The participant must enter into an approved Save As You Earn (SAYE) contract at the same time as he or she receives his or her option and the acquisition of shares by the exercise of the option must be paid for out of the proceeds of the SAYE contract—i.e. the savings which he or she makes and the tax free bonus paid at the end of the contract period (the *bonus date*). The SAYE contract must provide for a monthly payment into a building society or other approved savings body not exceeding £100 and must last for between five and seven years.

Participants are not obliged to use the savings from the SAYE contract to buy shares, but if they decide to do so, they must exercise their option within the six months after the bonus date. If the participant dies within this six month period, his or her executors have twelve months from the bonus date to exercise the option.

Participant and shares

The qualifications for participants in Savings-Related Share Option Schemes are similar to those which apply to participants in Approved Profit Sharing Schemes, and the shares must satisfy similar criteria.

There are no special provisions relating to workers' co-operatives.

Approval

A scheme requires to be approved by the Inland Revenue before relief is given. The scheme must allow participants to exercise options prior to the bonus date on the attainment of pensionable age, on termination of employment through injury, disability or redundancy or (after three years from the grant of the option) on termination of employment for any other reason. In each of these circumstances, the option must be exercised within six months after the relevant event and will be eligible for the taxation relief provided by the scheme. The scheme must also provide the executors of a deceased participant with the opportunity to exercise the option within the twelve months following the participant's death even if this occurs before the bonus date. Again, this exercise will be eligible for relief. The scheme may provide for the exercise of options prior to the bonus date in the event of a takeover bid and in other similar circumstances, but in this case, if the option is exercised pursuant to such a provision within three years of the grant of the option, no relief will be available.

Approved Share Option Schemes

The Share Incentive Schemes introduced by the 1978 and 1980 Finance Acts were generally welcomed but met with criticism in some quarters on two main grounds—(1) they were both relatively limited in their extent, the 1978 Scheme being limited to £5000 per annum and the 1980 Scheme being limited to £1200 per annum plus bonuses; (2) in order to obtain approval, they had to be open to all employees and directors who met the relevant criteria. In response to these points, the **Finance Act 1984** introduced a new Approved Share Option Scheme, which could relate to considerably larger sums and could be offered to employees or directors selected, largely, at the discretion of the board of directors of the relevant company.

Under the scheme, a company may award options to selected employees or directors. The aggregate value of unexercised options held by a participant must not exceed, at any time, the greater of £100 000 or four times that person's current or preceding year's salary, provided that the salary is subject to PAYE. The value of shares covered by an option must normally be the market value of the shares assessed in the period of 30 days prior to the grant of the option.

Participants

Participants must be either full-time directors (normally 25 hours per week) or qualifying employees, who are required to work at least 20 hours per week. As in other schemes, a person will not be eligible to be a participant if the employing company or its parent is a close company and he or she has a material interest in it.

Shares

The shares which may be the subject of an Approved Share Option Scheme are subject to criteria similar to those which apply to Approved Profit Sharing Schemes and Savings-Related Share Option Schemes.

Approval

A scheme requires to be approved by the Inland Revenue before any options may be granted under it. The scheme may allow a participant to exercise an option at various times, but relief from income tax will only be obtained if the time of exercise of an option is not less than three years nor more than ten years after the date of the grant of the option. In addition, an option may not be exercised less than three years after the participant last exercised an option under an Approved Share Option Scheme. If the participant dies, his or her executors may exercise any options which he or she had and obtain tax relief without being subject to the 'three year' rules provided that they exercise the options not later than one year after the participant's death and not later than ten years after the grant of the options in question.

17.3 Purchase by a company of its own shares

It has been an established rule of UK company law for nearly 100 years that a limited company may not purchase its own shares and this basic prohibition is now contained in the **Companies Act 1985**. The rule was created to avoid a company reducing its capital without the authority of the court and to prevent a company from artificially manipulating its share price by 'trafficking' in its own shares.

There are some instances, however, particularly in the case of private companies, when the capacity of a company to buy its own shares may be of considerable benefit. In family-owned companies, for example, one shareholder may die or may wish to have no further active involvement in the business. In these circumstances, there may be a need to release capital represented by that shareholder's holding in the company while at the same time a desire on the part of the other shareholders not to allow the sale of the shares to any outsiders. If the other shareholders do not have or cannot raise sufficient funds to purchase the shares for themselves, the options open to them were often liquidation or a complicated petition to the court for authority to reduce the company's capital. The Companies Act 1981 introduced provisions allowing for the purchase by limited companies of their own shares in certain circumstances. These provisions are now contained in the Companies Act 1985 and operate by way of an exception to the general prohibition referred to above. They apply both to public and private limited companies but only the provisions which relate to the latter will be considered below.

Procedure

In order to purchase its own shares, a company must have power to do so contained in its Articles of Association. Shares may not be purchased unless, after the purchase, there are at least two shareholders in the company and there remains in issue at least one share which is not redeemable. All purchases by a company of its own shares must be approved by a special resolution of the company in general meeting. A copy of the contract for the purchase (or, if there is no written contract, a memorandum of its terms) must be available at the meeting at which the resolution is passed and must also be available for inspection at the registered office of the company for at least 15 days prior to the meeting. The special resolution would be ineffective if it had not been passed, had it not been for the fact that the votes attached to the shares which were to be purchased by the company were cast in favour of the resolution.

Shares may be purchased out of distributable profits, the proceeds of a fresh issue of shares and, subject to certain conditions, out of capital. Payment for shares out of capital is only permitted if, and to the extent that, the available profits of the company together with the proceeds from any fresh issue of shares, are insufficient to make the required purchase. 'Available profits' are determined by reference to accounts prepared as at a date within three months prior to the date of the statutory declaration of the company's directors referred to below.

It is illegal for a company to purchase shares out of capital unless the directors make a statutory declaration to the effect that the company will, during the twelve months after the payment for shares out of capital, be able to pay its debts as they fall due. This statutory declaration must be supported by a report from the company's auditors. No later than one week after the statutory declaration the company must pass a special resolution approving the purchase, and the special resolution will be ineffective unless the statutory declaration and auditors' report are available for inspection at the meeting at which the resolution is passed. The purchase must take place no earlier than five weeks and no later than seven weeks after the date of the special resolution.

In the week following the special resolution, the company must publish, in the *London Gazette* and in an appropriate national newspaper, a notice with details of the resolution and the proposed purchase, informing any creditor of the company of their right, within five weeks of the resolution, to apply to the court for an order prohibiting the purchase. The court may, on the application of such a creditor or a shareholder of the company who did not vote in favour of the special resolution, either confirm or cancel the purchase or make such other order as it thinks fit. The Act also makes provision for notification to be given in the prescribed manner to the Registrar of Companies at appropriate stages in the procedure.

Taxation

In ordinary circumstances, the purchase by a company of its own shares for more than the subscription price originally paid for those shares would be treated as a distribution by the company equal to the amount of the excess. This would give rise to an advance corporation tax liability on the part of the company and the distribution would be investment income in the hands of the shareholder, with the appropriate tax credit. However, the Finance Act 1982 introduced provisions which prevented such treatment in two cases, both of which involve unquoted companies.

The first case concerns the purchase of shares by a company to raise money for the payment of capital transfer tax, provided that substantially all of the purchase price is used for such a payment, that the payment is made within two years of death and that the capital transfer tax liability could not otherwise have been paid without undue hardship.

The second case arises where the whole or main purpose of the purchase is to benefit a trade carried on by the company or by any of its 75% subsidiaries, provided that certain conditions are satisfied and provided also that the purchase is not mainly aimed at avoiding tax or enabling the seller of the shares to participate in the company's profits without receiving a dividend. In order to satisfy the conditions contained in the Finance Act, the selling shareholder must be resident and ordinarily resident in the UK in the tax year when the purchase is made and must have held the shares for at least five years. Special provisions apply where the seller has acquired the shares from his or her spouse or under a will or intestacy or where the seller holds the shares as an executor.

After the transaction, the selling shareholder and his or her associates must have reduced the nominal value of their shareholding in the company and their entitlement to a share in the company's profits by at least one quarter. The selling shareholder (and his or her associates) must also have no control over the company after the transaction and there must be no arrangements in place which would result in such control being regained after a period of time. A procedure exists for obtaining prior clearance from the Inland Revenue. Stamp duty is payable on the transfer of shares from the seller to the company at the normal rates.

17.4 Personal liability and disqualification of directors

Personal liability of directors

It has always been a fundamental feature of a limited liability company that its directors are not personally liable for the debts and obligations of the company. There have always been some exceptions to this general rule, but it has only been in rare cases, normally involving conduct which is clearly fraudulent, that ordinary creditors of a company have had any recourse against directors themselves. This position has been altered by the introduction of the concept of 'wrongful trading' in the Insolvency Act 1985, now replaced by the **Insolvency Act 1986**.

If a company has gone into insolvent liquidation, it is now possible for a liquidator to apply to the court for an order declaring that a director should contribute, from his or her own funds, to the company's assets. The court will not make such an order, however, if it is satisfied that the person concerned took every step which he or she should have taken to minimise potential loss to the company's creditors when they knew, or ought to have known, that the company had no reasonable prospect of avoiding insolvent liquidation.

Disqualification of directors

The Insolvency Act 1985 also introduced provisions, now contained in the **Company Directors Disqualification Act 1986**, giving the court wider powers to disqualify directors. In every liquidation, receivership or administration, the relevant officer now has a duty to report to the Department of Trade on the conduct of directors. On the basis of this report, the Secretary of State may apply to the court for a disqualification order if it appears expedient in the public interest. If such an application is made in the case of directors of an insolvent company, the court has a duty to make an order if it is satisfied that their conduct makes them unfit to be concerned in the management of a company.

17.5 The Data Protection Act 1984

The Data Protection Act 1984 introduced important new controls on the use of computers for holding information on living individuals. The Act uses a number of new expressions, the meanings of which are explained below.

A new Register has been established, under the control of the Data Protection Registrar, and with effect from 11 May 1986 data users who hold personal data on computers have been obliged to register details of the data they hold, the purposes for which the data is held, the sources of the data, the categories of person to whom the data may be disclosed and the foreign countries to which the data may be transferred. Failure to register will constitute an offence. There is also an obligation on computer bureaux to register particulars of their names and addresses.

The Act also imposes a duty on data users to adhere to certain principles regarding the collection, holding and disclosure of personal data. A further feature of the Act is that data subjects are now given the right to obtain access to personal data concerning them, the right to have that information rectified if it is inaccurate and the right to seek compensation for damage and distress caused by the loss, destruction or unauthorised disclosure of personal data.

There are a number of exceptions from the effects of the Act, including an exception for personal data held by an individual and 'concerned only with the management of his personal, family and household affairs or held by him only for recreational purposes'. The Act is, therefore, unlikely to affect the ordinary domestic use of home computers for Christmas card lists, etc. Anyone contemplating more extensive use of a computer in connection with personal data, however, should obtain further information (see p 178).

Terminology

The following are key expressions used in the Data Protection Act 1984:

computer bureau A person (including a company or firm) who processes personal data for data users or allows data users to process personal data on his or her equipment.

data Information recorded in a form in which it can be processed by equipment operating automatically in response to instructions given for that purpose.

data subject An individual who is the subject of personal data.

data user A person (including a company or firm) who controls the contents and use of a collection of personal data which is, or is to be, processed automatically.

personal data Information about a living individual (not a company or corporation), including expressions of opinion but excluding indications of the intentions of the data user relating to that individual.

Further information

Booklets containing guidance on the Act are available from the Office of the Data Protection Registrar, Springfield House, Water Lane, Wilmslow, Cheshire SK9 5AX (Tel. 0625 535777). Application packs for registration containing the Registrar's notes on procedure may be obtained from post offices.

Part V
OFFICE SAFETY, EQUIPMENT AND SERVICES

18 HEALTH AND SAFETY

18.1 Health and safety at work: checklist

First aid   YES/NO

  Is first aid kit regularly inspected and replenished? ☐ ☐
  Are there trained first aiders always available? ☐ ☐
  Are the names and the location of first aiders
  prominently displayed? ☐ ☐
  Has any provision been made for a permanent/
  temporary first aid room? ☐ ☐

Accidents

  Is there a standard procedure for reporting
  accidents? ☐ ☐

Fire

  Are fire notices prominently displayed? ☐ ☐
  Are fire doors closed but never locked? ☐ ☐
  Are flammable liquids handled with caution and
  stored safely? ☐ ☐
  Is the fire alarm in good working order? ☐ ☐
  Is a regular fire drill carried out? ☐ ☐
  Is adequate fire-fighting equipment installed and is
  it checked at regular intervals? ☐ ☐

Radiators

  Are these kept completely free? ☐ ☐

Electrical equipment

  Are there any unguarded electric fires? ☐ ☐
  Are there any trailing flexes? ☐ ☐
  Are machines switched off/unplugged when not in
  use? ☐ ☐
  Are any electric points overloaded? ☐ ☐
  Are all electrical appliances regularly serviced? ☐ ☐

Machinery

  Are guards fitted to any dangerous machinery? ☐ ☐

Protective clothing

  If special clothing has been issued against a
  particular hazard is it being used correctly? ☐ ☐

Passages

  Are these free from obstructions of any kind? ☐ ☐

Stairs

    Is there a handrail? □ □

    Are the stair treads at all worn? □ □

Flooring

    Are any floor coverings badly worn? □ □

    Are floors clean but not highly polished? □ □

Ventilation

    Is there a flow of fresh air without draughts? □ □

Lighting

    Is the lighting completely adequate in all parts of
the rooms and corridors? □ □

Temperature

    Is the minimum standard 16°C? □ □

Space

    Is there 400 cubic feet of working space per person? □ □

Toilets

    Are the sanitary provisions and supply of
wash-basins adequate? □ □

Drinking water

    Is there a constant supply of fresh drinking water? □ □

Filing

    Are files kept at the right height? □ □

    Are cabinets placed so that there is ample room
when any drawer is fully extended? □ □

    Are drawers ever left open to trip up the unwary? □ □

Waste paper

    Are there sufficient waste paper baskets? □ □

Noise

    Is the level of noise acceptable? □ □

Safety Officer

    Is there a Safety Officer or Representative on the
staff? □ □

Safety policy

    Is there a written policy statement on safety and
are staff aware of it? □ □

18.2 Emergency first aid in the office

Serious emergencies

Cardiac arrest

This is the most serious medical emergency likely to be encountered in the office. Although it is likely to be an extremely rare occurrence, it is important to know what action to take. The patient will certainly die if nothing is done, but if resuscitation is attempted there may be as much as a 50% chance of saving his life. Resuscitation must be begun urgently—within three to four minutes—or permanent brain damage may occur.

The main signs of cardiac arrest are:

  unconsciousness

  absent pulses

  absent respiration

  dilated pupils (after a few minutes).

The most likely sufferers are males aged 45-64. The loss of consciousness is sudden and the patient will look pale. You will not be able to feel a pulse at the wrist (below the thumb) or below the chin (at the angle of the jaw). Most cardiac arrests are due to heart attacks and the patient may have complained of chest pain before collapsing.

Action to be taken:

  summon others to help you; one person should immediately dial 999 and call an ambulance

  strike the lower half of the sternum (breast bone) with a hard blow of the fist. If this fails to work within ten seconds and there is still no pulse, external cardiac massage should be attempted

  working together, one person should perform external cardiac massage (Fig. 18.1) while another should apply artificial respiration (Fig. 18.2). Lay the patient on the floor on his back. The neck should be arched and the chin braced to establish a clear air passage (Fig. 18.3). Loosen clothing around the neck, waist and chest and remove dentures.

The first person places the heel of one hand over the lower third of the patient's sternum (breast bone) with the heel of the other hand on top of the first hand. With arms straight, the rescuer rocks forward, pressing on the lower half of the sternum, depressing it 3-5 cms. This is done at the rate of approximately one depression per second.

Fig. 18.1 Cardiac massage

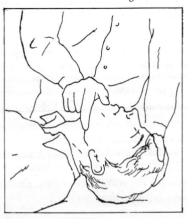

The second person performs mouth to nose or mouth to mouth respiration. He takes a deep breath through the mouth, sealing his lips round the patient's mouth (in which case the nostrils should be pinched shut) or round the nose, blowing into the patient's lungs until the chest rises. The rescuer then takes away his mouth and watches the chest fall. This is repeated 12-15 times per minute—about once for every five times the sternum is depressed as above. The first person should stop depressing the sternum while air is being blown into the patient's lungs by the second person. Both should continue until medical help arrives.

Fig. 18.2 Artificial respiration

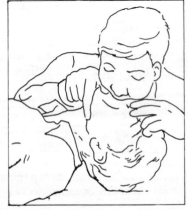

Fig. 18.3 Making a clear air passage

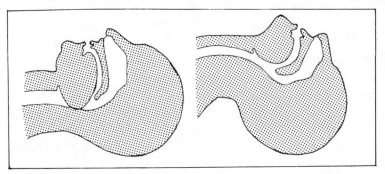

Unconsciousness

(The patient is still breathing, the heart is beating, and the pulse is present). Possible causes:

stroke
drug or alcohol overdose
diabetes
epileptic fit
simple faint.

Lay the patient on the floor on his side. This is the easiest position for the patient to breathe in without choking. Loosen tight clothing around the neck and waist and remove dentures.

In the case of a simple faint the patient will rapidly recover when lying down. If consciousness is not regained within a few minutes, call an ambulance. If the patient is frothing at the mouth and making odd noises, if his limbs are jerking or if he is very stiff rather than limp, he is likely to be having an epileptic fit. He will be unconscious and will not hear what is being said to him. Clear a space so that he cannot injure himself by knocking against furniture. If possible, remove dentures, which may obstruct breathing. It is not necessary to put anything in the mouth; even if the patient does bite his tongue it will heal rapidly.

Wait two to three minutes. Recovery will probably occur quite quickly and consciousness will be regained. The patient will probably be sleepy and may complain of aches and pains. At this stage it may be helpful to seek advice from the patient's general practitioner if he or she can be contacted by telephone. If the fit does not stop in the space of two or three minutes help should be summoned urgently.

Electric shock

Action to be taken:

switch off the current

if necessary, pull the patient away from the electricity source by his clothes

if cardiac arrest has occurred, proceed as in the previous section.

Major fall

(A fall from a height where serious injury to spine or legs could have occurred)

Action to be taken:

do not move the patient if serious injury is suspected

call an ambulance

give nothing to eat or drink.

Minor emergencies

It is useful to have a **first aid kit** to deal with minor emergencies. The suggested contents of such a kit are:

soluble aspirin and paracetamol tablets for headaches and minor aches and pains

adhesive dressings such as Elastoplast in various shapes and sizes for cuts and bruises

non-sticky dressings such as Melolin to cover temporarily more serious wounds which will require stitches or other treatment in a doctor's surgery or a casualty department (also crêpe bandages to hold these dressings in place)

cotton wool and antiseptic solution to clean grazes and small cuts (a small bowl is useful for this purpose)

gauze swabs (several layers of these may be applied to a cut which is bleeding heavily; pressure is then applied with hands or by bandaging the swabs in place to stop the bleeding)

triangular bandage to make a sling to support an injured arm, wrist or hand (this may be done before treatment is sought from a doctor)

scissors, safety pins and tweezers.

Nose bleeds

The patient should sit or lie down quietly. An assistant, or the patient himself, should then press over the bleeding nostril for ten minutes without moving. This is almost certain to stop the bleeding. Afterwards the patient should avoid blowing or cleaning his nose and thus disturbing the newly-formed blood clot.

Eye accidents

It is possible to remove an eyelash or small dust particle from the corner of the eye using a rolled-up tissue. It is best to seek medical help with other foreign bodies. If anything is sprayed or splashed in the eye, wash the eye immediately with plenty of water.

Burns

Run the burned part under a cold tap. If skin is broken or blistered, cover with a clean, dry, non-stick dressing. If it is extensive, cover in the same way and seek medical help.

18.3 Disablement

In order to register as disabled, a person must have injuries, disease or congenital deformities which have lasted for more than twelve months and which cause substantial difficulty in finding suitable employment. A registered disabled person then becomes the holder of a **green card**. This system is entirely voluntary and many people with disabilities are not registered, either because they do not wish to be or because they are not eligible. They and their employers, however, may need advice and practical help to enable them to find work.

The Manpower Services Commissions Disablement Advisory Service, which can be contacted through local job centres (listed in the telephone directory under *Manpower Services Commission*) provides a comprehensive service of advice and practical and financial help to allow people with all sorts of disabilities to work. They provide many information booklets, including those covering specific medical conditions. They may finance necessary adaptation of work premises or equipment, or may loan (permanently) expensive equipment to help a disabled individual to work. They can also arrange for assessment of capability at an employment rehabilitation centre.

Types of disability

Arthritis

This is the most common cause of long-standing disability and affects both sexes and all ages. The extent of disability depends on which joint or joints are involved. The usual problems are pain and restriction of movement. Pain can often be controlled with drugs but, if inadequately controlled, can affect concentration and work performance. Restriction of movement leads to many problems, but it is often possible to get round these. An occupational therapist can visit the office and assess the problems of the disabled individual, and then any adaptation required may be financed by the Manpower Services Commission.

A 'Fares to Work' scheme organised by the same body will help meet the cost of a taxi or pay a fee to a colleague for transporting a disabled person who is unable to use public transport. Even when a person is severely disabled and, for example, confined to a wheelchair (also through conditions other than arthritis) work may be feasible with alterations to the office and to the facilities.

Epilepsy

There is no reason why an epileptic should not work normally in an office. Most epileptics are normal in every way, except during fits. The majority of epileptics are on drugs which are very effective in preventing fits; this is certainly the aim of treatment. If a fit does occur, it may be very alarming to an observer who has not previously seen one, and it is desirable that colleagues should have some idea of what to expect should a fit occur and of how to deal with it. Anticonvulsant drugs used in epilepsy may cause drowsiness and impaired concentration and co-ordination, and therefore affect work performance. Epileptics who have had a daytime fit during the last three years may not drive a motor vehicle.

Diabetes

This condition should normally present no problems at work. Diabetics should eat regularly and should not miss meals. They should carry a supply of glucose in case of hypoglycaemia or low blood sugar, which may be caused by insufficient food or too much exercise. Colleagues should know about the person's diabetic condition. Drowsiness, faintness and uncharacteristically irritable, difficult or confused behaviour may be an indication that the blood sugar is too high or too low.

Many diabetics must test their urine for sugar before meals in order to keep their blood sugar well-controlled. They may also need to give themselves insulin injections: toilet facilities should therefore be adequate.

Heart problems

These may arise when a person convalescing from a heart attack or heart surgery returns to work. The return should be gradual. Initially it would be preferable for the person to work part-time and at a slower pace, but there is no reason why both the hours and the pace should not be increased gradually to the previous level over the course of a few weeks. It is very important for the affected individual not to smoke.

Psychiatric problems

Psychiatric illness is one of the most difficult disabilities to deal with for both the sufferer and for colleagues. A person who is mentally ill is likely to be unable to cope with work and either may not realise that he is ill, or may realise it but be unable to do anything about it. As a result, extra pressure is put on colleagues and goodwill may be exhausted. It may then be very difficult for an individual who has already suffered considerable loss of confidence to get back to work. What is required in dealing with such a person is great patience and understanding, together with an ability to disregard events leading up to the breakdown, which may have caused a fair degree of disruption. Communication with the individual's general practitioner, with his permission, may be helpful in dealing with him.

Eye problems

In an office it may be difficult for a person who develops a visual handicap to work normally. It is important to make things as easy as possible by ensuring that light is good. In the case of blindness or partial blindness, the Royal National Institute for the Blind can give advice on aids and financial assistance may be provided for the blind person to engage a part-time reader.

Severe kidney disease

A person suffering from severe kidney disease, chronic renal failure, will feel permanently tired and below par, and as a result will function below his or her optimum. Shorter working hours and perhaps longer breaks may help, and part-time work may be needed if dialysis is required. The Manpower Services Commission may provide a grant to allow for job-splitting or job-sharing in this situation. Following a kidney transplant, a person should be able to get back to working at full capacity.

Respiratory diseases

People disabled by respiratory diseases such as asthma, bronchitis and emphysema, will be mainly limited by how much moving round, climbing stairs, etc. is required. As in other conditions, the Manpower Services Commission may be able to fund modifications to premises, such as lift installation. Affected individuals will benefit from a clean, smoke-free atmosphere.

Ileostomy and colostomy

Even teenagers may require ileostomy and colostomy for serious bowel disease and once convalescence is complete there is no reason why colleagues should even know about the disability. The colostomy or ileostomy, which is an opening of the bowel on the abdomen over which a bag is worn for the collection of excrement, should not smell or cause any risk to others as far as hygiene is concerned, and the person should lead a normal life with it. Adequate toilet facilities should be provided.

Multiple sclerosis

This is the most common neurological disease affecting young adults. It is difficult to deal with because its symptoms and time course are so variable. Modification of duties and responsibilities should take this variability into account. This disease may cause problems with mobility and eyesight, or possibly psychiatric symptoms. Dealing with these difficulties should be as discussed in previous sections.

AIDS

This disease has only been described recently; people are inexperienced in dealing with it and therefore it causes a great deal of fear, panic and hysteria. A person who is known to have been infected with the AIDS virus should work normally. A proportion of these people, perhaps 10%, will later become ill with AIDS and when ill will probably be unable to work. Spread of the disease is by sexual intercourse or by contact with the blood of an infected person through broken skin. If someone with the AIDS virus has a bleeding cut or abrasion, it should be dealt with by someone with medical knowledge. Spilled blood should be cleaned with diluted household bleach by someone wearing rubber gloves. Sharing a room, chair, coffee cup or toilet will *not* cause another to catch AIDS from an individual who is infected with the virus.

18.4 The use of drugs

The drugs considered here are those prescribed to individuals under medical supervision, those purchased over the counter for minor illnesses, and drugs of abuse which may be legally prescribed but misused or which are illegally obtained. Alcohol and nicotine also fall into the category of drugs which, though legal and freely available, may nonetheless be abused.

Prescribed drugs

The majority of these are unlikely to affect an individual's work performance or have any effect noticeable to colleagues or workmates. The category of drugs which may cause difficulties are those which act on the nervous system such as sedatives, tranquillisers and anti-depressants. Tranquillisers and antidepressants are prescribed for moderately severe psychological disturbances such as anxiety or depression. These drugs may very well cause drowsiness or slowing up of mental faculties, but as the underlying illness may also cause slowing up and difficulty with concentration it may be difficult to distinguish between the effect of drugs and the effect of the illness. If the problem is severe, it would be better for the affected individual to remain off work until recovery.

Over-the-counter drugs

Antihistamines are an example of a commonly used group of drugs which although bought for allergies and hay fever may also affect the central nervous system. These drugs can cause drowsiness and impaired work performance.

Illegal drug use

This is not likely to be a very common problem in the office as the individuals who are users of illegal drugs, such as heroin, usually have great difficulty holding down a job and are rarely in regular employment for any length of time. This problem would therefore be more likely to be found in the case of a new or temporary employee who is relatively unknown to other staff.

Signs to look for in someone who is using illegal drugs:

    drowsy, slowed up, or dreamy behaviour

    appearing 'high' in a manner not appropriate to situation or surroundings

    loss of judgement

    irritability

    shakiness

    unexplained sudden absence from work

    spending long periods in toilet

    intravenous injection needle marks on hands, forearms at the elbow, or on the neck

    very small pupils

    thin, pale, unhealthy appearance.

If there is a suspicion that illegal drugs are being used, the police should be notified.

Alcohol

This is the 'drug' problem which is most likely to arise in the office. Alcohol abuse is all too frequent nowadays and in times of stress moderate drinking may very well get out of control.

Signs to look for:

    unreliable time-keeping, particularly in the mornings, and absentee-ism, particularly on Mondays

    shakiness, particularly in the mornings

    smell of alcohol on the breath in the mornings

    reddish/purplish complexion with bloodshot eyes

    obvious drunkenness at work with slurred speech, drowsiness and poor co-ordination

    frequent lunch-time or afternoon drinking with consumption habitually greater than others

    domestic, marital, social or relationship problems.

Alcohol misuse is a very difficult problem to deal with and sometimes it seems easier to overlook it and to cover up for the individual concerned. Affected individuals often deny the problem to family, friends, colleagues and even to themselves. To cover up for and overlook the problem is in fact more likely to harm than help the unfortunate victim; it usually delays the person from seeking medical help or making any attempt to deal personally with the problem. Therefore, although it may seem brutal, it is preferable to confront the individual, suggest appropriate help, and issue warnings if work is suffering.

Smoking

Nowadays there is evidence that cigarette smoke can harm the health not only of the smoker but also of people in the vicinity who inhale the smoke passively. It would be preferable for smoking to be banned from any office where there are non-smokers present and allowed only in a specially designated area.

19 OFFICE MACHINERY AND EQUIPMENT

19.1 Binding machines

Binding units enable loose sheets of paper to be bound together into booklets.

Comb binding A two-stage operation in which the papers are first punched and then spiral bound, either with metal or plastic.

Thermal binding The papers are placed inside pre-glued covers which are then put into the machine. When the sheets are firmly bonded into the covers a timer activates a buzzer and a warning light.

19.2 Communications equipment

Telephone answering machine

A telephone answering machine is switched on when a telephone is unmanned. It plays a pre-recorded message inviting the caller to leave a message which is then recorded and can be played back later. If the machine is linked to a computer the number of messages recorded can be visually displayed. Some machines allow a remote playback to be activated which means that the user can phone in and have the messages played back over the telephone.

Radiopaging system

Members of staff who are not based in an office can be contacted by means of a radiopaging system. A high frequency signal or bleep alerts the user of a call. Several messages can be stored on the pocket-sized receiver and messages can be received from more than one source by using different bleeps for different callers.

Qwertyphone

A qwertyphone is a compact 'memory-phone-cum-computer-terminal' with a typewriter keyboard and liquid crystal display. It can be used as a 'memotyper' as well as providing access to on-line databases and electronic mailbox systems. Numbers can be stored, then amended and searched by name, address, occupation or number.

Interactive video

Communication takes place by means of a video display. The system can be used for sales promotions and training purposes. Information is stored on a laser disk controlled by a microcomputer with suitable software. Video disks can also be used to store archive material.

Electronic mail

Messages are sent and received using a microcomputer linked to a telephone system by means of a modem. A modem is a tele-communications device which enables microcomputer users to transmit and receive data over a communications system. Messages can be filed electronically and retrieved later.

Telex, fax and videotex

See Chapter 21.8.

19.3 Calculators and computers

Calculators

Electronic calculators vary in size from wafer-thin pocket calculators to desk-top models with print-out facilities. The size of a calculator does not reflect its power. Some models are programmable and may have extra features such as time and date display, electronic diary and notepad facilities.

Computers

Networks

Integrated computer systems capable of handling text, data, image, graph and voice are now available providing the business user with a complete information processing facility. Work stations situated at different locations can be linked to the computer network to provide distributed data processing facilities. An open system network allows different makes and standards of system to be interconnected.

Microcomputers

It is very difficult to define a typical microcomputer. There are many makes and models available, ranging from powerful desk-top business microcomputers, with as much processing power as small

193

minicomputers, to portable home computers. Off-the-shelf applications software is readily available for the business user including database management systems, accounts, word processing and spreadsheet packages. Many systems now feature the use of a *mouse*, a small hand-held device connected to a microcomputer. When the mouse is rolled across the desk surface a pointer is moved across the screen and when the pointer is positioned on a word or pictorial image (*icon*) a button can be pressed on the mouse initiating an activity, e.g. loading a file from disk or editing text.

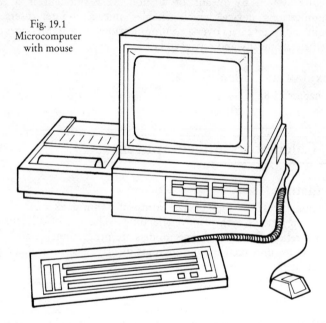

Fig. 19.1
Microcomputer
with mouse

Minicomputer

Minicomputers are usually smaller than mainframes but may in fact be more powerful than small, old mainframe equipment. A minicomputer can support several programming languages and multiprogramming as well as offering more processing power and storage capacity than a micro.

Mainframe computer

A large, fast, powerful general-purpose mainframe computer provides centralised computing facilities for an organisation and is capable of supporting a large number of terminals.

Mainframe and minicomputers are used to carry out traditional data processing functions such as payroll, customer accounts and stock control. The type of equipment used depends upon the needs of the user.

19.4 Copiers

Office copiers are used to produce exact copies from an original document. Copying falls into three main categories; low, medium and high volume.

Low and medium volume

Low and medium volume copiers use a dry toner process and feature the latest technology. Different types of paper can be used and the print enlarged or reduced in size. The number of copies required is selected from a touch-sensitive console and a self-diagnostic panel displays symbols visually to indicate when the paper is getting low or if more toner should be added.

High volume

High volume copiers are usually faster and more robust, with the option to print on both sides of the paper. Other facilities include automatic collating and stapling of documents and automatic reset so that a long-run job may be interrupted to make a single copy. Offset machines can be used for high speed, high volume printing in black and white or colour. Sophisticated technology allows all functions to be done at the touch of a button.

Copier control

It is possible to monitor the use of copiers using a management information system which can give a precise account of photocopier use. Identity codes and account numbers are allocated to departments.

19.5 Dictating machines

Pocket dictating machines

A dictating machine is used either in or out of the office to record speech. The recording is stored on magnetic tape and transcribed later.

New machines are slimline in shape, with electronic touch control and a digital display in minutes and seconds. They are often advertised as electronic notebooks.

Centralised dictating

A centralised dictating system provides audio-typing facilities for all departments. Documents are dictated using a remote control microphone. Transcriptions are carried out in a typing pool under the direction of a supervisor.

19.6 Mailing equipment

The type of mailing equipment used depends upon the volume and nature of mail that needs to be handled.

Mobile sorting trolley

A mobile sorting trolley can be used to sort and distribute incoming mail after it has been time and date stamped.

Electronic postal scales

Electronic postal scales feature a digital display of weight and postage rates with touch selection for different classes of mail, e.g. first class, second class or recorded delivery.

Franking machine

Envelopes or adhesive labels are fed into the franking machine and endorsed with the pre-selected date and postage rate. A logo or advertising slogan can be printed on the envelopes at the same time. On some models envelopes are automatically fed in, sealed and franked.

Users of franking machines must conform to the following conditions:

(1) Authority must be obtained from the local head post office before starting to use a machine.

(2) Payments in advance for postage or value cards must be made at a specified post office.

(3) Franked correspondence must be faced, bundled (as detailed in the poster 'How to post franked mail', or as required by the local Head

Postmaster) and either handed in at a specified post office or posted within special envelopes in posting boxes agreed by the Head Postmaster. Enquiries about these conditions should be addressed to the local Head Postmaster.

(4) The Royal Mail needs to have a completed control card at the close of business each working week, whether or not the machine has been used, to check that the machine is working properly.

(5) Only the supplying company may repair or modify machines. Users must have the machine inspected and maintained by the supplying company not less than twice in each six-month period, or as specified by the Royal Mail, in order to ensure clear impressions and complete accuracy in recording.

(6) Machines are available from supplying companies authorised by the Royal Mail. Enquiries about the supply of franking machines and the types available should be addressed to these firms:

Envopak Ltd
Powerscroft Road, Sidcup, Kent   DA14 5EF   01-302 2500
Hasler (Great Britain) Ltd
Hasler Works, Commerce Way, Croydon   CR0 4XA   01-680 6050
Pitney Bowes Ltd
The Pinnacles, Harlow, Essex   CM19 5BD   (0279) 26731
Roneo Alcatel Ltd
Mailroom Division
PO Box 66, South Street, Romford   RM1 2AR   (0708) 46000
Scriptomatic Ltd
Scriptomatic House, Torrington Park, London   N12 9SU 01-445 0163

Addressing machines

Addressing machines can be used to select, sort and print addresses from a mailing list, although computerised systems linked to word processors are being used increasingly to deal with high volume direct mail.

Computerised mailing machines

A computerised system enables forms to be separated, folded, inserted, sealed and franked. Computerised mailing machines are efficient when dealing with large amounts of outgoing mail.

Miscellaneous mailing equipment

Other items of equipment used in the mailing room include joggers and collators to sort papers into order, perforators to punch holes and automatic folding, inserting, tying and sealing machines.

Shredding machines are generally housed in the mailing room; they are used for disposing of used envelopes, unwanted papers and confidential waste.

19.7 Storage of information

Indexing

Strip indexing Information is entered on a strip which is then inserted into a holder. All the strips are visible and the system can be updated by simply adding or removing the strips.

Visible indexing Visible index cards overlap displaying the bottom section of the card so that it is visible when the card is filed.

Blind indexing Index cards are stored one behind the other in a box, tray or cabinet.

Rotary indexing Rotary index cards are secured to a central spindle which rotates when cards are being searched. There are both horizontal and vertical systems.

Filing

Vertical filing In a vertical filing cabinet documents are filed one behind another in drawers. The files may be suspended from rails and subdivided according to the indexing system in use.

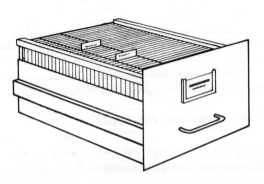

Lateral filing In a lateral filing cabinet documents are stored side by side, like books on a shelf. The files may be suspended from rails. Lateral filing systems hold more files and take up less space than vertical systems.

Horizontal filing Paper records are stored flat one on top of another in drawers. This method is suitable for filing large plans and drawings.

Microfiling Papers are photographed and reduced in size then stored as microfilm in rolls, on sheets, in transparent jackets or aperture cards. Microfilm can be processed directly from a computer.

The documents are read by inserting the film into a microfilm reader. This method of filing is useful for storing archival materials, parts manuals, bank records and for library work.

Computerised filing

Computer aided microfilm retrieval Microfilmed documents, and relevant information about them, are fed into a computer along with film and frame references. Frames have an image which can be detected by a photocell which enables the frames to be counted. Documents can be searched, sorted, indexed and retrieved.

Database management systems Customer records, personnel files and other records can be stored on a computer then searched, sorted and retrieved electronically using a database management system. Records can be printed or merged with other documents to produce a report.

Documents prepared on a word processor can be stored on disks and retrieved electronically.

19.8 Text handling equipment

Electronic lettering systems

An electronic lettering system is used to produce type on an adhesive-backed tape to be inserted into text and used for headlines or subheadings.

Electronic typewriters

Electronic typewriters are replacing manual and electric models. Electronic machines have fewer moving parts and usually have at least a single line visual display and an internal memory. The display allows editing to take place before a document is printed. Text can be stored and if amendments are needed the whole document does not have to be re-typed.

Video typewriters

A screen and external disk storage drive can be added to some electronic typewriters. These machines do not have full word processing facilities but are popular with typists who feel comfortable using a familiar keyboard.

Word processors

A word processor consists of a *keyboard* to enter text, a *screen* to view what has been typed, a *disk drive* to store the documents, and a *printer*. Once a document has been typed it can be stored and retrieved. Text can be inserted and deleted, sections can be moved within the document or transferred to another document. The layout can be altered and pages numbered automatically without any re-typing. Standard letters can be produced and automatically merged with a mailing list. Spelling can be checked against a dictionary.

Phototypesetters

Publication-quality print can be prepared for printing using a small computer-assisted typesetting system. Reports, accounts, price lists, etc., prepared on a word processor, can be input into phototypesetters. The type, in digital form, can then be slanted to form italics, compressed, enlarged, reduced or expanded before being printed. Type takes up less space than typewritten text.

Printers

The quality of the printed document depends upon the type of printer used.

Dot matrix printers Dot matrix printers operate at high speeds and offer a choice of type sizes and styles. They are comparatively cheap to purchase but the quality of the print may be poorer than that produced by a daisy wheel or laser printer. Models are available which can be switched to near letter quality print mode.

Daisy wheel printers A daisy wheel printer with a carbon ribbon will produce high quality print. The print wheel must be changed if different type sizes or type fonts are required.

Ink jet printers Ink jet printers are fast and quiet. The ink is sprayed onto the paper.

Laser printers A laser printer is an intelligent copier. Printing takes place at high speed producing superb quality documents. Many types and styles of text can be printed as well as graphics and the machine is virtually silent.

20 THE ROYAL MAIL

20.1 Business economy services

Mailsort 1

If a company can pre-sort a first class mailing of 4000 or more items, it could qualify for a discount of up to 14% on the postage and still get the normal first class delivery. This high level of discount has a number of conditions:

at least 90% of the addresses to be correctly postcoded

pre-sortation down to delivery offices in bundles of at least 25 letters.

(*Note:* Assistance may be available on sortation software changes for pre-sort services users.)

An extra 2% discount is available to those companies who are able to post Mailsort items early in the day (i.e. before 1.00 pm). As the postcode is the key to efficient pre-sortation, the Royal Mail can provide assistance in the postcoding of address lists.

Volume	Delivery Office Sortation Discount	County/Post Town Residue
4000—25000	11%	For early
25000—50000	12%	posting or
50000—300000	13%	OCR readable
over 300000	14%	only

This service replaces the first class letter contract service.

Mailsort 2

If a company can pre-sort a second class mailing of 4000 or more letters it could qualify for a discount of up to 14% on the postage and still get the normal second class delivery. Similarly the high level of discount involves conditions which have to be met:

at least 90% of the addresses to be correctly postcoded

pre-sortation down to delivery offices in bundles of at least 25 letters

(County or Post Town residues qualify for a reduced discount—
see below).

Volume	Delivery Office Sortation Discount	County/Post Town Sortation Discount
4000—25000	11%	7%
25000—50000	12%	7%
50000—300000	13%	7%
over 300000	14%	7%

Plus an extra 2% discount on all OCR readable residues.
This service replaces the second class discount service.

Mailsort 3

For scheduled advertising or less time-sensitive mailsorts, i.e. with a
delivery span of seven working days, mailings of over 4000 letters
which can be pre-sorted to delivery offices, a company could qualify
for a discount of up to 32% off the standard price. The conditions of
postcoding and pre-sortation common through Mailsort 1 and
Mailsort 2 apply. This facility can save money for companies who send
large quantities of non-urgent mail-circulars, price lists, reports and
direct mail, etc. Because postage costs are significantly reduced,
Mailsort 3 allows more frequent mailings and/or the mailings of more
items.

Volume	Delivery Office Sortation Discount	County/Post Town Sortation Discount
4000—10000	18%	15%
10000—25000	22%	15%
25000—50000	25%	15%
50000—300000	26%	15%
300000—1 million	29%	15%
over 1 million	32%	15%

Plus an extra 2% discount on all OCR readable residues.
This service replaces the bulk rebate service.

Response services

Business Reply, *Freepost* and *Admail* are designed to stimulate customer
response by simplifying the response process—whether answering
advertising messages or paying bills.

Business Reply

A company can make it easier and quicker for customers to pay bills by enclosing a pre-printed *Business Reply* card, envelope or label (first or second class). It is ideal for:

obtaining immediate orders from direct mail shots

offering follow-up literature

facilitating communications between agents and head offices

enhancing a company's image in terms of efficiency, enthusiasm and customer service

improving cash flow.

Freepost

Freepost offers three services:

First class pre-printed

Second class pre-printed

Second class non-pre-printed.

Freepost is ideal for:

press advertising

television and radio advertising

direct mail or door-to-door

special on-pack offers.

Admail

This is a redirection service which enables direct response advertisers to quote a local or prestigious address but to have replies re-routed direct to their fulfilment house anywhere in the UK. Postage can be paid by the respondents or the service can be used in conjunction with *Freepost*.

Incentive discount for growth (IDG)

This facility is designed for companies who spend over £20000 a year on postage—and whose volume of postage increases year by year. Such companies can qualify for up to 20% discount on the real value of the year's increase. If the amount of business mail sent out by a company is increasing, with an IDG contract it may be possible to save money on the extra real postage costs.

A company involved in direct mail, direct marketing, or with large customer lists, can benefit in particular—with savings on spin-off mailings, statements, or reminders—because IDG allows more mail to be despatched without a proportionately increased postage cost.

The Postcode Project

To help postcode firms' mailing lists, the Royal Mail has introduced *The Postcode Project*. This project offers advice, assistance and under certain conditions a financial contribution that may help substantially with the cost of postcoding a company's computer-based address list.

Any company which frequently uses computerised mailing lists of at least 20 000 addresses held in a format that the bureaux, with whom the Royal Mail has contacts, can handle may be eligible for financial aid to assist with the computerised postcoding of the list. This process may leave some manual postcoding left to be done for which no assistance is given.

A number of computer agencies have devised programs for adding postcodes to addresses, using the Royal Mail's *Postcode Address File* as the database. The Royal Mail has contracts with such agencies and has used independent research to confirm the agencies' high standards.

Printed postage impression

Printed postage impressions (PPI) are a pre-printed alternative to traditional stamps and franking machines. If large quantities of identical letters, packets or parcels are despatched a PPI simplifies the handling and accountancy procedures. It is only necessary to stock the pre-printed envelopes in readiness for use. This time-saving facility is particularly valuable when used in conjunction with Royal Mail discounts.

There are separate designs which cover Mailsort 1, 2 and 3 service indicators.

Making the most of postal weight allowances

When a company sends out a business letter—or an invoice statement or receipt—it is usually lightweight (probably less than 15g), but the initial weight allowance is 60g before any extra postage is incurred. So it would surely make sense to enclose a sales leaflet, a price list, a special message, for no extra postage. Regular POP or similar sized envelopes normally have sufficient strength and flexibility to carry additional leaflets.

Intelpost

Intelpost is one of the largest electronic messaging services in the world. It transmits clear facsimiles of any document up to A4 size—letters, reports, contracts, quotations, drawings, plans, graphs. It is fast, reliable and confidential. It is also widespread—there are over 100 *Intelpost* centres in Britain and 2000 overseas; no other electronic mail service can offer anything approaching this vast level of coverage.

Intelpost can speed communication for every type and size of business. Companies with fax machines, telex or computers can use it from their own premises; companies without these facilities can use it from Intelpost centres throughout Britain. Fast collection and delivery services mean Intelpost works well even if the recipient has no equivalent technology.

Intelpost is not expensive. There are no fees, subscriptions or electronic mailbox costs; prices are very competitive and are based entirely on the number of pages, the destination and the method of delivery.

Household Delivery Service

The Household Delivery Service enables a company to advertise its services or products through the mail without needing to address an envelope. The advertising material is delivered by professionals—the regular postman with the normal mail and it is therefore more likely to be read.

Household Delivery can be particularly useful when linked to a press, TV or radio campaign and it can include a reply-paid card to encourage potential customers to respond—also a useful way to build up a customer list.

Household Delivery is therefore an exceptionally valuable way to advertise a product or service to a specific area or areas—which can range from one postcode sector to the whole country (by *Acorn* if you wish), including Northern Ireland. Any enquiries should be addressed to:

Royal Mail Services for Business Economy
Freepost (no stamp required)
33 Grosvenor Place
London
SW1X 1EE

20.2 Datapost services

Sameday

Facilities: a same-day door-to-door service by radio controlled motorcycles and vans. Ideal for goods and documents needing rapid pickup and high speed delivery. The service gives a money-back same-day guarantee within 80 UK cities and towns and between centres directly linked by rail.

Advantages: high security, extremely competitive prices, and locally based service.

Overnight

Facilities: guaranteed next-day delivery of goods up to 27·5 kg to any point in Britain. Separate, fast-stream handling and supervision, signatures against transfer en route. An exclusive air network supplements Inter-City rail and the biggest delivery fleet in the country. Special staff are employed as necessary to reach remote destinations.

Advantages: a service for parcels that have to be there tomorrow— both regular consignments and one-off packages. Delivery by 10.00 am or noon and backed by the *Datapost Double Guarantee*—money-back promise and free insurance against loss, damage or delay. Security guaranteed by Royal Mail's unmatched experience and resources.

International

Facilities: fast delivery to key commercial centres worldwide. Backed by the *Datapost Double Guarantee* (see above).

Sample times	
London to Bahrain	24 hours
Aberdeen to Zürich	48 hours
Birmingham to Tokyo	72 hours
Manchester to The Hague	24 hours

Advantages: competitive pricing with no hidden extras. Datapost packs available for still further economy. Minimal paperwork and a variety of contract options. Datapost is available through 2500 post offices, or contract pickup, or same-day collection via Freefone Datapost.

Any enquiries should be addressed to:

Datapost Marketing Department
Freepost (no stamp required)
33 Grosvenor Place
London
SW1X 1EE

20.3 Special services

Special Delivery

Extra assurance for first class letter mail.

This service provides delivery by a Royal Mail messenger for letters and packets arriving at a delivery office centre on the next working day after posting but too late for normal delivery on that day.

In addition to first class postage a Royal Mail Special Delivery fee of £1.50 must be paid. A *Certificate of Posting* will be issued. Items must be posted at post office counters by the *Latest Recommended Posting Times* for next working day delivery. The special delivery fee will be refunded automatically to the sender if an item posted by the latest recommended posting time does not receive delivery on the next working day after posting.

This service is *not* available to the Isle of Man, the Channel Islands or the Irish Republic.

Express Delivery

The Express Delivery Service is available for letter packets addressed to places in the Channel Islands or the Isle of Man and for both letters and parcels to the Irish Republic. It is not available for second class letters.

This service allows for delivery of a postal packet by special messenger after arrival which will ensure earlier delivery than by normal handling. Express Delivery items are sent from the office of posting to the office of delivery in ordinary mails. The fee is £1·50 in addition to full ordinary postage. In the Irish Republic additional charges are collected from the addressee when delivery is made by messenger more than one mile from the delivery office.

Express Delivery items arriving at the office of delivery after the first ordinary delivery of letters may sometimes be included in a normal delivery. In such cases a refund of the Express Delivery fee will be made on application.

Any enquiries should be addressed to:

Royal Mail Special Services
Freepost (no stamp required)
33 Grosvenor Place
London
SW1X 1EE

20.4 Parcels services

National goods distribution

Packages up to 25 kg can be delivered anywhere in the country, normally within three days. A contract service is available which saves having to weigh and stamp each individual parcel. Any company sending over 20 parcels weekly is eligible and can obtain a printed postage impression (PPI). Royal Mail Parcels can bill the customer at regular intervals and collect from their premises. Large consignments (usually 200 or more a week) qualify for flat rates when collection is free.

Lightweight parcels can be posted at letter post rates. Recorded delivery is possible and there is additional compensation for loss or damage if items are sent by registered post. Worthwhile rebates are available for bulk (over 4250) mailings of identical packets.

Zonal distribution

County parcels

This service offers a reduced rate for parcels posted and delivered within a specified area, usually a group of counties (see map opposite). It is especially attractive for firms with a sizeable proportion of their customers fairly close at hand.

(See *Rider* services p 212 for details of overnight parcel delivery within the London Postal Area and within the North East, Northern Ireland and Thames Valley.)

Reduced-rate county parcels

County areas

1. Avon/Gloucestershire/Somerset/
   Wiltshire
2. Staffordshire/Warwickshire/West
   Midlands/Worcestershire
3. Bedfordshire/Leicestershire/
   Northamptonshire
4. Derbyshire/Nottinghamshire
5. Cambridgeshire/Lincolnshire/
   Norfolk/South Humberside/
   Suffolk
6. Dyfed/Gwent/Herefordshire/
   Mid-Glamorgan/South
   Glamorgan/West Glamorgan
7. Cheshire/Lancashire
8. Cumbria/Dumfriesshire/
   Kirkcudbrightshire/Wigtownshire

9. Northern Ireland
10. Berwickshire/East Lothian/Fife/
    Kinross-shire/Midlothian/
    Peeblesshire/Roxburghshire/
    Selkirkshire/West Lothian
11. Aberdeenshire/Banffshire/
    Kincardineshire
12. Argyll/Arran/Ayrshire/Bute/
    Clackmannanshire/Coll/Colonsay/
    Dunbartonshire/Gigha/Iona/
    Islay/Jura/Lanarkshire/Mull/
    Renfrewshire/Stirlingshire/Tiree
13. Angus/Caithness/Canna/Eigg/
    Inverness-shire/Moray/
    Nairnshire/Perthshire/Rhum/
    Ross-shire/Skye/Sutherland
14. North Humberside/North
    Yorkshire/South Yorkshire/West
    Yorkshire
15. Berkshire/Buckinghamshire/
    Oxfordshire

16. Dorset/Hampshire/Isle of Wight
17. East Sussex/Kent/West Sussex
18. Clwyd/Gwynedd
19. Powys/Shropshire
20. Cornwall/Devon
21. Barra/Benbecula/Harris/Lewis/
    North Uist/South Uist
22. Orkney
23. Shetland Islands

**In these areas, delivery is within a
single county:**

24. Surrey
25. Middlesex
26. Hertfordshire
27. Essex
28. Merseyside (including South Wirral)

'Rider' services

A new range of services is being developed specifically for local business. *Rider* services operate in areas where a particular need for local overnight collection and delivery service exists. There are four *Rider* services in operation:

Nightrider (serving the London Postal Area)

Parcel Rider (serving Northern Ireland)

Tyne Rider (serving the North East)

Thames Rider (serving Berks, Bucks, Oxon and adjacent areas of the Thames Valley).

Watch out for further introductions of *Rider* Services.

Trakback

This new signed delivery service, available to parcel contract holders only, gives verbal confirmation of delivery normally five days after posting and a copy of the recipient's signature as an optional extra. Royal Mail Parcels will supply a *Trakback* bar-coded label which must be attached to each parcel—which is then sent in the normal way. The recipient signs for the parcel on delivery, the bar-code being read and entered into a computer. To confirm delivery a free call is made to the *Trakback Response Centre*.

For further information telephone 01-200 0200 and ask for Royal Mail Parcels.

Royal Mail Parcels
Signed Delivery Service

20.5 International services

Airstream

A new Royal Mail International letter service for customers sending more than 2 kg of international letters per collection. It is available worldwide and offers substantial financial savings for large users. It is an ideal service for correspondence, financial mail, travel schedules, reports and personalised mailshots.

Contract facilities (printed papers)
Bulk airmail (BAM)
This is a fast service—3 to 4 days delivery—specifically geared to large quantity despatches of printed papers to **Europe**. It is ideal for books, magazines, direct mailshots or any type of printed paper traffic with a European destination.

Accelerated surface post (ASP)
This covers destinations **outside Europe** and uses air transport for speed compared with surface transport for economy.

ASP takes a fraction of the time of ordinary surface mail, yet often costs very little more. This means that you can get all sorts of printed paper/material direct to people overseas in a matter of days—instead of several weeks or months. In fact ASP is the perfect 'happy medium'; it provides for a service intermediate in price and speed between existing air and surface mail services.

Contract facilities (parcels)
Air and surface parcel services; anyone sending in excess of 30 parcels per week may qualify for special tariffs. Payment is on account using postage paid impressions.

Direct agents bag service
A special service for customers wishing to send books, periodicals or other printed matter by a surface route to a single addressee (e.g. a retail outlet or agent abroad). The service is available **worldwide**; delivery 4–8 weeks.

Worldwide high speed courier
Datapost International (see p 208).

Swiftair
This is a high-speed letter post service available to all countries. Items must be handed over a post office counter, or included in firms' collections (but kept separate from other correspondence to ensure proper handling). Each item must bear a *Swiftair* label and this should

be affixed at the top left hand corner of the address side—in the case of items going outside Europe, immediately below the blue airmail label.

A Royal Mail Service

The Royal Mail aims for *Swiftair* items to be flown to the country of destination on the day after posting (subject to availability of flights) and delivered at least one day earlier than the ordinary airmail services. Any enquiries should be addressed to:

Royal Mail International Marketing Department
Freepost (no stamp required)
33 Grosvenor Place
London
SW1X 1EE

International Business Reply Service

This service enables businesses who wish to obtain replies from their clients overseas, without putting those clients to the expense of paying the return postage, to enclose in their communication unstamped reply cards or envelopes bearing the special International Business Reply Service design. Their clients can then post the reply cards or envelopes back to the UK in the normal way but without having to buy and affix postage stamps. Instead, the addressee in the UK will pay the charges on all the replies that he or she receives.

Completed *International Business Reply* cards and envelopes will be returned as European All-Up mail.

The service is currently available to twelve major European countries and there are plans to extend it to other countries in the near future. Any enquiries should be addressed to:

Sally Bennett
Freepost (no stamp required)
Royal Mail International Letters
Room 320
52 Grosvenor Gardens
London
SW1W 0YA

21 TELECOMMUNICATIONS

21.1 Business telephone systems

This is a highly technical and rapidly changing area because of the development of new technologies and the convergence of micro-processor based computing and telecommunication facilities.

Public telephone network (PTN)

Telecommunications apparatus must be approved and must undergo stringent tests for safety and operational performance. It is possible to choose from a variety of sources whether to buy, rent or lease the telephone apparatus to be connected to the line. Equipment is covered by a *Branch Systems General Licence* and users must abide by its terms.

The Government has laid down marking orders which require all apparatus to be clearly marked to show whether or not it has been approved for connection to the British Telecom network.

 Green circle
APPROVED for
connection

 Red Triangle
NOT approved for
connection

Private branch exchange (PBX)

A private branch exchange is a customers' switching apparatus which routes calls between extensions and the public telephone network, and internally between extensions.

Private automatic branch exchange (PABX)

PABX is an automatic version of PBX which permits calls to be dialled direct from extensions. If it is desirable to control the number of outgoing calls then some extensions can have restricted external dialling. Incoming calls are usually routed through the switchboard but the system may incorporate a direct dialling-in facility which enables callers to dial extensions directly without going via the operator.

Key telephone systems

A key telephone system allows groups of incoming lines to be associated with a number of telephone stations; any extension user can then take an incoming call and transfer it, if necessary, to the wanted section. An operator is not required. For economy this system can be used with simple approved plug-in telephones.

Call connect systems

Advances in microelectronics have resulted in sophisticated PBX systems which now offer the following additional facilities to business users:

long numbers can be coded

the telephone system can re-direct calls to other extensions when the first one is engaged, or automatically re-dial when the number called is engaged

internal and external calls can be initiated from each extension

the user can put a bar on incoming calls or alternatively put a bar on outgoing calls

all incoming calls can be directed to another telephone

calls can be diverted to another extension if the call remains unanswered or if the called telephone is engaged

loudspeaker telephones leave the user's hands free and can be used when several people need to be involved in a call

a call waiting facility provides a means of answering an incoming call when the user is already engaged upon another call

the three party service enables the customer to set up a three-way conversation on his or her telephone.

Call cost indicators

The cost of calls can be monitored either as they are being made or over a period of time. A print-out records the time, date, number called, duration and cost of each call.

Cordless telephones

Cordless telephones allow staff who work in small businesses, such as garages, hairdressers or on building sites, easy access to a telephone so that business is not lost.

Payphones

Traditional pay-on-answer coinphones are being replaced by micro-processor-controlled public and rented payphones with credit display and follow-on call facilities.

21.2 Cashless calling

Account call
For account calls a special code is entered instead of money and the cost is charged to the phone bill.

Credit call
This is a credit call payment system for national and international calls. Calls are charged to the customer's credit card.

Freefone
Freefone calls are available through the operator and are good for business since they encourage people to communicate. A business may use a Freefone number which enables customers to make a call without charge and the Freefone subscriber pays the bill.

Linkline
The Linkline service is designed for advertisers of a wide variety of goods and services. Customers can call Linkline 0800 free or Linkline 0345 at a local charge, wherever they may be on British Telecom's network in the UK. The rest of the charge will be met by the renter.

Phonecard
Phonecard allows payment for calls in advance. Phonecards which entitle the user to a specific number of units can be purchased at post offices, tobacconists and newsagents displaying the Phonecard logo.

21.3 Operator services

Advice of duration and charge (ADC)
ADC calls are available through the operator who will ring back at the end of a call to advise the caller of the charge and duration.

Alarm call
The alarm call service is available through the operator who will ring a given number at the time requested.

Transferred charge call

The operator speaks to the called number and, if the incoming call is accepted, the charge is transferred to that number.

21.4 Information services

CityDirect

A service for frequent callers to North America.

CityCall

A SuperCall financial information service providing nine bulletins of continually updated financial information.

Guidelines

This is the general term given to British Telecom recorded information services which are obtained by dialling the appropriate number (see your local phone book). Guidelines include:

FT Cityline Information provided through the Financial Times industrial ordinary share index to keep customers in touch with the Stock Market. The information is updated seven times a day.

Traveline Information on rail, road, sea and air provided by the BBC and available to the public.

Timeline Timeline gives the caller the correct time.

Weatherline Local weather forecasts provided by the Meteorological Office.

Other Guideline information services include: Albumline, Cricketline, Discline, Leisureline, Carebear Bedtime Storyline, Raceline, Radioline, Skiline and Sportsline.

Touch screen

Touch screen systems can be used to eliminate the use of a keyboard. Examples of users include:

> city currency dealers (City Business System)
> airport control (Touchdown)
> police communications (Touchline).

21.5 Conferencing

Audio conferencing

National and International Conference Call Services permit several users at various locations to conduct a business meeting using the telephone as a link. It is possible to connect calls between several countries.

Video conferencing

Videostream is a service which links participants in sound and vision. The system is available in the UK and internationally. It enables groups of people to see and speak to each other, making it possible to hold board meetings, sales meetings and seminars without the expense of long distance travel. Special studios are not required.

Confravision is a public videoconferencing service. Studios which can accommodate up to six people are located in eight major cities (see p 105).

21.6 Mobile communications

Cellular radio network

Radiophone   Office staff who have to spend a lot of time away from the office but who need to keep in touch with the office or with customers will find the radiophone useful. Models are available that work from the car battery, other models work in or out of the car and some are small enough to fit in a handbag or briefcase.

Radiopaging

Radiopaging is available nationwide; the latest radiopagers have the facility to receive and display written messages. Messages can be sent to the pager via telex, datel or through an answering bureau. Some pagers have the option to vibrate rather than bleep; this facility is particularly useful when the wearer is in a meeting or working in a noisy environment such as in an airport or on a building site.

Pinpoint

Using radio technology this service enables fleet operators and security firms to keep track of vehicles. It provides a considerable defence against crime.

Voicebank

A computerised voice storage and forward system. Voicebank mailboxes store a total of 48 messages each up to one minute long. The Voicebank service provides the businessman with an efficient and cost-effective method of keeping in touch 24 hours a day.

Voicemail

Telephone system users are provided with a voice message facility. Voicemail is a modular minicomputer system with disk message store.

Mobile radiopayphones

Trainphone Mobile radiopayphones are available on several main-line rail routes.

Ferryphone Trials involving the use of radiopayphones are being carried out on selected ferry routes.

Mobile radiopayphones are also being used on certain long distance coach routes.

21.7 Data transmission systems

Integrated digital exchanges

An integrated digital network such as *System X* can connect voice and data to a customer concurrently or change from one to the other midway through a call. With integrated digital access customers can be connected to advance network services including telex, fast facsimile, electronic mail, picture videotex, graphics, electronic fund transfer and slow scan TV.

Public switched telephone network (PSTN)

Wide area networks offer immediate access to a computer regardless of distance. A visual display unit at one location is linked to a computer at another location, e.g. airline reservations terminals. Remote offices can be linked to a central computer saving overheads on payroll, personnel and other business functions. Scientists, engineers and designers can benefit from on-line access to stored information and the problem-solving capability of computers.

Packet Switchstream (PSS)

Packet Switchstream is a switched data network providing a public computer data transmission service.

Multistream

Multistream is an enhanced version of Packet Switchstream currently offering videotex access and an error protection facility. The range of facilities will soon be extended in readiness for the 'cashless society'.

An electronic funds transfer at point-of-sale service will link shops with banks and credit card companies allowing anyone with a bank account to pay electronically for goods and service with an encoded plastic card.

It will also be a message-handling service for Packet Switchstream allowing electronic mail, telex and teletex all to interconnect.

Private circuits

A line can be leased to connect two sites. Private circuits may be connected through switching apparatus, data terminals or other apparatus.

Kilostream

Kilostream supplies fast links between customers' premises and can carry voice, data or vision.

Megastream

Megastream circuits of even greater speed and capacity are being used by large businesses in the design of their corporate networks.

Satstream

Satstream offers private satellite links for business communication. Voice and data communications are aimed at the satellite by dish aerials. The signal is carried to the satellite where it is bounced back and re-transmitted around the world to a receiving aerial. Satstream is a service primarily for large organisations. It is used for international telecommunication transmission, telephone, computer traffic, videoconferencing, fax and electronic distribution of mail.

21.8 Data transmission services

Imtran

A system which links telephone conversation with still television pictures and enables graphic designers, architects and engineers to see and advise on drawings and plans at remote locations. X-ray and body-scan pictures can be sent over the telephone network which enables surgeons away from hospitals to examine records or pictures seconds after they are available.

Photo videotex

Photo videotex enables full colour photographic images to be displayed with text and graphics. This can be used in many service areas including travel, mail order shopping and by estate agencies.

Teleshopping

This is a grocery delivery service linked to *Prestel* for Central London customers.

Telemessages

Specifications, quotations or other messages may be sent by telephone, telex, *Prestel, Dialcom* or through a customer's computer terminal. The telemessages are delivered by post on the next working day. For a small extra charge an exact copy of the telemessage can be delivered to the sender.

Telex

For legal and security reasons many messages have to be in writing. Telex provides a fast, clear textual communication facility between national and international subscribers. Proof of sending and receiving is made possible by the use of answerback codes which are printed at the top and bottom of all telex messages. Subscribers are issued with a Telex Directory which lists telex numbers and answerback codes.

The *TextDirect* service enables registered users to send and receive telexes through electronic typewriters, word processors or personal computers.

Telex plus

Network facilities now include short-code number selection, call re-direction and broadcast calls. Telex equipment may be connected to computer-controlled exchanges. Telex with electronic terminals can interconnect with Packet Switchstream into other services such as teletex.

Teletex

Teletex is a fully automatic international telecommunications service for sending messages between terminals. Business correspondence, statistics and simple messages can be sent to users around the world at thirty times the speed of telex. Messages are sent memory to memory which means that messages can be prepared, stored and sent when appropriate. Repeated attempts are automatically made to get a message through and all attempts are recorded on a log. Each terminal has a unique identity to provide secure communications. Each message is headed by a call identification line which includes the date and time sent, the identification of the sender and the called teletex number.

The service conforms to international standards but is also flexible. Teletex terminals may be electronic typewriters with a teletex adapter, modern electronic telephone exchanges, multi-purpose computers or small business microcomputers.

Electronic mail

BT Gold has over 200 000 electronic mailboxes compatible with the Dialcom worldwide electronic mail system. The mailboxes operate through a computer linked to the telephone network. A user must have an identity number and a password. Documents can be prepared 'off-line' and then sent at high speed to one mailbox or to a number of different mailboxes simultaneously. Using a small microcomputer text can be sent and received from any location as long as there is a telephone line.

Facsimile transmission (Fax)

Facsimile systems allow companies to keep pace with modern business communication needs. Fax machines linked to the telephone system are similar in appearance to desk-top copiers. Many paper communications are drawings, diagrams or pictures and these can be sent electronically by using facsimile machines. Equipment compatible with defined international standards can connect with a national and international fax network making it possible to exchange information with businesses all over the world.

Delayed transmission features allow documents to be sent automatically at any time of day or night. The original is exactly reproduced at its destination, normally in black and white, although some equipment can reproduce in full colour. Both parties must have compatible equipment. Delegates travelling to conferences or business meetings do not need to carry all the necessary documentation with them but can use delayed-timer polling facilities to collect their documents from other machines.

Bureaufax

Bureaufax is used to transmit documents overseas and does away with compatibility problems. A business does not even need to have its own fax machine to use the service, neither does the addressee. The customer in the country of origin can send a document by hand, post or fax to a Bureaufax Counter Office; it is then transmitted to a similar office in the destination country. From there the copy can be transmitted by fax to the final destination if that business has a fax machine. Alternatively the copy could be delivered by post or collected by the addressee.

Videotex

Videotex is a generic term for teletext and viewdata.

Teletext uses television channels to transmit information over the air via broadcast signals e.g. *Ceefax* and *Oracle*.

Viewdata falls into two categories: public and private. *Prestel* is the registered trademark for public viewdata in the United Kingdom. It is a generally available mass service and can be used by businesses, by private individuals at home or in public places such as libraries. Each user is given a number and a password and can use either a *Prestel* set or a microcomputer linked to the telephone line with a modem, to access pages of information. *Prestel* offers a variety of services including news and information. Export information, investment statistics, company information and tax guides are a few examples. *Prestel* is a two-way system; users can receive information and send messages to other users or to the information providers. Response pages allow users to order goods, book a hotel or theatre seat or purchase services such as insurance.

Private viewdata systems can be set up to disseminate information within an organisation.

21.9 International communications

International Direct Dialling (IDD)
It is possible to dial direct to hundreds of countries in the world.

International Linkline
Customers abroad can call companies in the UK free of charge. The cost of the call is met by the renter.

International Packet Switchstream (IPSS)
International Packet Switchstream offers data transmission connections to networks in 40 countries.

International Kilostream
International Kilostream is a private digital circuit service currently available to the USA, Hong Kong, Japan, South Africa, Singapore and Bahrain.

International business services
International telex, telemessage and telegram services transmit data abroad via the telephone or packet switching networks. Electronic mail and conferencing facilities are available internationally.

International telemessages This service is available only to the USA.

International telegrams International telegrams are available world-wide and are charged according to length of message and distance sent.

Data Direct This is an international high speed public data service linking the UK and the USA.

International travel

INMARSAT (Maritime satellite) On the seas worldwide, vessels and rigs which are equipped for satellite services can use the direct-dial satellite services. A ship's number can be obtained by dialling International Directory Enquiries. Services provided include telephone, telex, telegrams, data transmission, fax, access to Prestel, International Packet Switchstream and electronic mail.

MAR (Maritime and aeronautical radio) Public air-to-ground telephone and telex services are provided through MAR. An earth station is being commissioned that will allow airlines to provide an automatic telephone service via satellite to aircraft passengers.

Part VI
USEFUL INFORMATION

Your company could be better off if your customers didn't pay...

Your customers would be more likely to contact you by post if they didn't have to pay for the stamp.

So if you had a FREEPOST address, they'd be encouraged to reply to your ads – and your sales could increase.

Or if you had a BUSINESS REPLY licence, you could send them reply-paid envelopes with your invoices – and many bills would be paid sooner.

What's more, the first time you use either of these response services you could qualify for special introductory offers.

FREEPOST and BUSINESS REPLY are part of the Royal Mail Services For Business Economy – services that help businesses save money, improve cash flow, create extra sales.

For further information contact Tony Groom, FREEPOST (no stamp required), Financial Mail Group, 33 Grosvenor Place, London SW1X 1EE

Royal Mail
Saving business money

22 GEOGRAPHICAL AND TRAVEL INFORMATION

22.1 Countries of the world

Country	Capital	Official language(s)	Currency
Afghanistan	Kabul	Pushtu, Dari	Afghani (Af) = 100 puls
Albania	Tirana/Tiranë	Albanian	Lek (L) = 100 quintars
Algeria	El Djazair/ Algiers	Arabic	Dinar (AD) = 100 centimes
Andorra	Andorra la Vella	Catalan	French Franc and Spanish Peseta
Angola	Luanda	Portuguese	Kwanza (Kz) = 100 lweis
Antigua and Barbuda	St John's	English	East Caribbean Dollar (EC$) = 100 cents
Argentina	Buenos Aires	Spanish	Austral (Arg$) = 100 centavos
Australia	Canberra	English	Dollar (A$) = 100 cents
Austria	Vienna	German	Schilling (Sch) = 100 groschen
Bahamas	Nassau	English	Dollar (BA$) = 100 cents
Bahrain	Manama	Arabic	Dinar (BD) = 1000 fils
Bangladesh	Dhaka	Bangla (Bengali)	Taka (Tk) = 100 poisha
Barbados	Bridgetown	English	Dollar (Bds$) = 100 cents
Belgium	Brussels	Flemish, French	Franc (BFr) = 100 centimes
Belize	Belmopan	English	Dollar (Bz$) = 100 cents
Benin	Porto Novo	French, English	CFA Franc (CFAFr) = 100 centimes
Bhutan	Thimphu	Dzongkha (Tibetan/ Burmese)	Ngultrum (N) = 100 chetrums
Bolivia	La Paz	Spanish	Peso (B$) = 100 centavos

227

Country	Capital	Official language(s)	Currency
Botswana	Gaborone	English	Pula (Pu) = 100 thebe
Brazil	Brasilia	Portuguese	Cruzado/Cruziero (Cr) = 100 centavos
Brunei	Bandar Seri Begawan	Malay	Dollar (Br$) = 100 cents
Bulgaria	Sofia	Bulgarian	Lev (Lv) = 100 stotinki
Burkina Faso	Ouagadougou	French	CFA Franc (CFAFr) = 100 centimes
Burma	Rangoon	Burmese	Kyat (K) = 100 pyas
Burundi	Bujumbura	Kirundi, French	Franc (BuFr) = 100 centimes
Cameroon	Yaoundé	French, English	CFA Franc (CFAFr) = 100 centimes
Canada	Ottawa	English, French	Dollar (C$) = 100 cents
Cape Verde Islands	Praia	Creole Portuguese	Escudo (CVEsc) = 100 centavos
Central African Republic	Bangui	French	CFA Franc (CFAFr) = 100 centimes
Chad	N' Djamena	French	CFA Franc (CFAFr) = 100 centimes
Chile	Santiago	Spanish	Peso (Ch$) = 100 centesimos
China	Beijing (Peking)	Puronghua (Mandarin Chinese)	Renminbi Yuan (RMBY or $) = 100 fen
Colombia	Bogotá	Spanish	Peso (Col$) = 100 centavos
The Comoros	Moroni	French, Arabic	CFA Franc (CFAFr) = 100 centimes
Congo	Brazzaville	French	CFA Franc (CFAFr) = 100 centimes
Cook Islands	Avarua	English, Polynesian dialects	New Zealand Dollar (NZ$) = 100 cents
Costa Rica	San José	Spanish	Colon (CR₡) = 100 centimos
Cuba	Havana	Spanish	Peso (Cub$) = 100 centavos

Country	Capital	Official language(s)	Currency
Cyprus	Nicosia	Greek, Turkish	Pound (C£) = 1000 mills
Czechoslovakia	Prague	Czech, Slovak	Koruna (Kčs) = 100 heller
Denmark	Copenhagen	Danish	Krone (DKr) = 100 øre
Djibouti	Djibouti-Ville	French, Arabic	Franc (DjFr) = 100 centimes
Dominica	Roseau	English	East Caribbean Dollar (EC$) = 100 cents
Dominican Republic	Santo Domingo	Spanish	Peso (DR$) = 100 centavos
Ecuador	Quito	Spanish	Sucre (Su) = 100 centavos
Egypt	Cairo	Arabic	Pound (E£) = 100 piastres
El Salvador	San Salvador	Spanish	Colón (ES₡) = 100 centavos
Equatorial Guinea	Malabo	Spanish	Ekuele (E) = 100 centimes
Ethiopia	Addis Ababa	Amharic	Birr (Br) = 100 cents
Fiji	Suva	English, Fijian, Hindi	Dollar (F$) = 100 cents
Finland	Helsinki	Finnish	Markka (FMk) = 100 penniä
France	Paris	French	Franc (Fr) = 100 centimes
Gabon	Libreville	French	CFP Franc (CFPFr) = 100 centimes
The Gambia	Banjul	English	Dalasi (Di) = 100 butut
German Democratic Republic (E Germany)	East Berlin	German	GDR Mark/ Ostmark (M) = 100 pfennig
Germany, Federal Republic of (W Germany)	Bonn	German	Deutsche Mark (DM) = 100 pfennig
Ghana	Accra	English	Cedi (₡) = 100 pesawas

229

Country	Capital	Official language(s)	Currency
Greece	Athens	Greek	Drachma (Dr) = 100 lepta
Grenada	St George's	English	East Caribbean dollar (EC$) = 100 cents
Guatemala	Guatemala City	Spanish	Quetzal (Q) = 100 centavos
Guinea	Conakry	French	Syli (Sy) = 100 cauris
Guinea-Bissau	Bissau	Portuguese	Peso (GBP) = 100 centavos
Guyana	Georgetown	English	Dollar (G$) = 100 cents
Haiti	Port-au-Prince	French	Gourde (Gde) = 100 centimes
Honduras	Tegucigalpa	Spanish	Lempira (La) = 100 centavos
Hong Kong	Victoria	Engiish, Chinese	Dollar (HK$) = 100 cents
Hungary	Budapest	Hungarian	Forint (Ft) = 100 fillér
Iceland	Reykjavik	Icelandic	Króna (IKr) = 100 aurar
India	New Delhi	Hindi	Rupee (Re) = 100 paisa
Indonesia	Jakarta	Bahasa Indonesian	Rupiah (Rp) = 100 sen
Iran	Tehran	Farsi	Rial (RI) = 100 dinar
Iraq	Baghdad	Arabic	Dinar (ID) = 1000 fils
Ireland, Republic of	Dublin	Irish, English	Pound/punt (IR£) = 100 pence/pighne
Israel	Jerusalem	Hebrew	Shekel (IS) = 100 agorot
Italy	Rome	Italian	Lira (L) = 100 centesimi
Ivory Coast	Abidjan (commercial) Yamoussoukro (political and administrative)	French	CFA Franc (CFAFr) = 100 centimes
Jamaica	Kingston	English	Dollar (J$) = 100 cents

Country	Capital	Official language(s)	Currency
Japan	Tokyo	Japanese	Yen (Y) =100 sen
Jordan	Amman	Arabic	Dinar (JD) =1000 fils
Kampuchea (Cambodia)	Phnom Penh	Khmer	Riel (CRI) =100 sen
Kenya	Nairobi	Kiswahili	Shilling (KSh) =100 cents
Kiribati	Tarawa	I-Kiribati, English	Australian Dollar (A$) =100 cents
Korea, Democratic People's Republic of (N Korea)	Pyongyang	Korean	Won (NKW) =100 chon
Korea, Republic of (S Korea)	Seoul	Korean	Won (W) =100 chun
Kuwait	Kuwait City	Arabic	Dinar (KD) =1000 fils
Laos	Vientiane	Lao	Kip (Kp) =100 at
Lebanon	Beirut	Arabic	Livre/Pound (L£) =100 piastres
Lesotho	Maseru	Sesotho, English	Malote (LSM) =100 licente
Liberia	Monrovia	English	Dollar (L$) =100 cents
Libya	Tripoli	Arabic	Dinar (LD) =1000 dirhams
Liechtenstein	Vaduz	German	Swiss Franc (SFr) =100 centimes
Luxembourg	Luxembourg- Ville	German	Franc (LFr) =100 centimes
Macao	Macao City	Portuguese	Pataca (Pat) =100 avos
Madagascar	Antananarivo	French, Malagasy	Franc (MgFr) =100 centimes
Malawi	Lilongwe	Chichewa, English	Kwacha (MK) =100 tambala
Malaysia	Kuala Lumpur	Bahasa Malaysia (Malay)	Dollar (M$) =100 cents

Country	Capital	Official language(s)	Currency
Maldives	Malé	Dhivehi	Rufiyaa (MRf) = 100 laris
Mali	Bamako	French	CFA Franc (CFAFr) = 100 centimes
Malta	Valletta	English, Maltese	Pound (M£) = 100 cents
Mauritania	Nouakchott	French, Arabic	Ouguiya (U) = 5 khoums
Mauritius	Port Louis	English, French	Rupee (MR) = 100 cents
Mexico	Mexico City	Spanish	Peso (Mex$) = 100 centavos
Monaco	Monaco	French	Franc (MnFr) = 100 centimes
Mongolia	Ulan Bator	Mongolian	Tugrik (Tug) = 100 möngö
Morocco	Rabat	Arabic	Dirham (DH) = 100 centimes
Mozambique	Maputo	Portuguese	Metical (MZM) = 100 centavos
Namibia	Windhoek	Afrikaans, English	Rand (R) = 100 cents
Nauru	Yaren District	English, Nauruan	Australian Dollar (A$) = 100 cents
Nepal	Kathmandu	Nepali	Rupee (NRp) = 100 pice
Netherlands	Amsterdam (The Hague— seat of government)	Dutch	Guilder (Gld) or Florin = 100 cents
New Zealand	Wellington	English	Dollar (NZ$) = 100 cents
Nicaragua	Managua	Spanish	Córdoba (C) = 100 centavos
Niger	Niamey	French	CFA Franc (CFAFr) = 100 centimes
Nigeria	Lagos	English	Naira (N) = 100 kobo
Norway	Oslo	Norwegian	Krone (NKr) = 100 ore
Oman	Muscat	Arabic	Rial Omani (RO) = 1000 baizas

Country	Capital	Official language(s)	Currency
Pakistan	Islamabad	Urdu	Rupee (Rp) = 100 paisa
Panama	Panama City	Spanish	Balboa (Ba) = 100 centesimos
Papua New Guinea	Port Moresby	English, Hiri Motu, Melanesian Pidgin	Kina (K) = 100 toca
Paraguay	Asunción	Spanish	Guarani (G) = 100 centimos
Peru	Lima	Spanish	Sol (S) or Inti = 100 centavos
Philippines	Manila	Tagalog, Cebuano	Peso (PP) = 100 centavos
Poland	Warsaw	Polish	Zloty (Zl) = 100 groszy
Portugal	Lisbon	Portuguese	Escudo (ESc) = 100 centavos
Puerto Rico	San Juan	Spanish	Dollar ($) = 100 cents
Qatar	Doha	Arabic	Riyal (QR) = 100 dirhams
Romania	Bucharest	Romanian	Leu (pl. Lei) = 100 bani
Rwanda	Kigali	French, Kinyarwanda	Franc (RWFr) = 100 centimes
St Kitts-Nevis	Basseterre	English	East Caribbean Dollar (EC$) = 100 cents
St Lucia	Castries	English	East Caribbean Dollar (EC$) = 100 cents
St Vincent	Kingstown	English	East Caribbean Dollar (EC$) = 100 cents
San Marino	San Marino	Italian	Lira (SML) = 100 centesimi
São Tomé and Principe	São Tomé	Portuguese	Dobra or Escudo (ESP) = 100 centavos
Saudi Arabia	Riyadh	Arabic	Riyal (SAR) = 100 halalas
Senegal	Dakar	French	CFA Franc (CFAFr) = 100 centimes

Country	Capital	Official language(s)	Currency
Seychelles	Victoria	English, Creole	Rupee (SR) = 100 cents
Sierra Leone	Freetown	English	Leone (Le) = 100 cents
Singapore	Singapore City	Chinese, English, Malay, Tamil	Ringgit or Dollar (S$) = 100 cents
Solomon Islands	Honiara	English	Dollar (SI$) = 100 cents
Somalia	Mogadishu	Somali, Arabic	Shilling (SoSh) = 100 centesimi
South Africa	Pretoria (administrative)	Afrikaans	Rand (R) = 100 cents
	Cape Town (legislative)	English	
Spain	Madrid	Spanish	Peseta (Pa) = 100 centimos
Sri Lanka	Colombo	Sinhala, Tamil	Rupee (SLR) = 100 cents
Sudan	Khartoum	Arabic	Pound (S£) = 100 piastres
Surinam	Paramaribo	Dutch	Guilder (SGld) or Florin = 100 cents
Swaziland	Mbabane	English, SiSwati	Lilangeni (Li) = 100 cents
Sweden	Stockholm	Swedish	Krona (SKr) = 100 øre
Switzerland	Berne	German, French, Italian, Romansch	Swiss Franc (SFr) = 100 centimes
Syria	Damascus	Arabic	Pound (Syr£) = 100 piastres
Taiwan	Taipei	Mandarin Chinese	New Dollar (NT$) = 100 cents
Tanzania	Dar es Salaam	Swahili, English	Shilling (TSh) = 100 cents
Thailand	Bangkok	Thai	Baht (Bt) = 100 satang
Togo	Lomé	French, Kabiye, Ewe	CFA Franc (CFAFr) = 100 centimes
Tonga	Nuku'alofa	Tongan	Pa'anga or Tongan Dollar (T$) = 100 seniti

Country	Capital	Official language(s)	Currency
Trinidad and Tobago	Port of Spain	English	Dollar (TT$) = 100 cents
Tunisia	Tunis	Arabic	Dinar (TD) = 1000 millemes
Turkey	Ankara	Turkish	Lira (TL) = 100 kuros
Tuvalu	Funafuti	Tuvaluan (Samoan)	Australian Dollar (A$) = 100 cents
Uganda	Kampala	English	Shilling (USh) = 100 cents
Union of Soviet Socialist Republics	Moscow	Russian	Rouble (Rub) = 100 kopeks
United Arab Emirates	Abu Dhabi	Arabic	Dirham (DH) = 100 fils
United Kingdom	London	English	Pound sterling (£) = 100 pence
United States of America	Washington DC	English	Dollar ($) = 100 cents
Uruguay	Montevideo	Spanish	New Peso (UrugN$) = 100 centesimos
Vanuatu	Port Vila	Bislama, English, French	Vatu (V) = 100 centimes
Venezuela	Caracas	Spanish	Bolivar (B) = 100 centimos
Vietnam	Hanoi	Vietnamese	Dồng (D) = 100 hào
Western Samoa	Apia	English, Samoan	Tala or Western Samoan Dollar (WS$) = 100 sene
Yemen Arab Republic (N Yemen)	Sana'a	Arabic	Riyal (YR) = 100 fils
Yemen People's Democratic Republic (S Yemen)	Aden	Arabic	Dinar (YD) = 1000 fils
Yugoslavia	Belgrade	Serbo-Croat, Slovene, Macedonian	Dinar (D) = 100 paras
Zaire	Kinshasa	French	Zaire (Z) = 100 makuta

235

Country	Capital	Official language(s)	Currency
Zambia	Lusaka	English	Kwacha (K) = 100 ngwee
Zimbabwe	Harare	English	Dollar (Z$) = 100 cents

22.2 World time zones

World standard times

Since the end of the 19th century a system of World Standard Time by zones has been used. By this system the world is divided into 24 time zones, each comprising of approximately 15° of longitude and representing one hour of time. Individual countries adopt a convenient standard time, although some large countries, e.g. USA, Canada, USSR, are divided into several time zones.

The measurement of the time follows the East-West progress of the sun across the world's surface, using the **Greenwich Meridian** as the starting point and **Greenwich Mean Time** (GMT) as the base time. All countries East of the Greenwich Meridian are ahead of GMT and those to the West are behind GMT. The date changes on the **International Date Line** (an imaginary division, approximately 180° from the Greenwich Meridian, passing through the Pacific Ocean). *(For map see Chapter 24.4).*

Hours ahead of or behind GMT

Abu Dhabi +4	Brisbane +10	Djakarta +7	Kuwait +3
Accra 0	Brussels +1	Doha +3	Lagos +1
Adelaide +9½	Bucharest +2	Dubai +4	Lima −5
Algiers 0	Budapest +1	Dublin 0	Lisbon 0
Amman +2	Buenos Aires −3	Frankfurt +1	London 0
Amsterdam +1	Cairo +2	Geneva +1	Luxembourg +1
Ankara +2	Calcutta +5½	Gibraltar +1	Madeira −1
Athens +2	Canberra +10	Hanoi +7	Madras +5½
Auckland +12	Cape Town +2	Helsinki +2	Madrid +1
Baghdad +3	Caracas −4	Hobart +10	Malta +1
Beijing +8	Chicago −6	Hong Kong +8	Manila +8
Beirut +2	Copenhagen +1	Islamabad +5	Mauritius +4
Belgrade +1	Dallas −6½	Istanbul +3	Melbourne +10
Berlin +1	Damascus +3	Jakarta +8	Mexico City −6
Berne +1	Darwin +9½	Jerusalem +2	Milan +1
Bombay +5½	Delhi +5½	Johannesburg +2	Montevideo −3
Bonn +1	Detroit −5	Karachi +5½	Montreal −5
Brindisi +1	Dhaka +6½	Kuala Lumpur +7½	Moscow +3

Munich +1	Perth +8	Rotterdam +1	Tokyo +9
Muscat +4	Prague +1	Sana'a +3	Toronto −5
Nairobi +3	Pretoria +2	San Francisco −8	Tripoli +2
Naples +1	Quebec −5	Santiago −4	Tunis +1
New York −5	Rabat 0	Seoul +9	Vancouver −8
Nice +1	Rangoon +6½	Singapore +7½	Vienna +1
Nicosia +2	Rawalpindi +5	Sofia +2	Warsaw +1
Oslo +1	Reykjavik 0	Stockholm +1	Washington −5
Ottawa −5	Rio de Janiero −3	Suez +2	Wellington +12
Panama −5	Riyadh +3	Sydney +10	Winnipeg −6
Paris +1	Rome +1	Tehran +3½	Zurich +1

Note: In some countries Summer Time or **Daylight Saving Time** operates during part of the year. These variations from Standard Time are decided annually.

22.3 International airports and airlines

Airports

Abu Dhabi (Abu Dhabi International)	77277/77335	Durban (Louis Botha International)	(031) 42-6184
Accra (Kotoka International)	76171	East Berlin (Schonefeld)	672 4068
Amsterdam (Schipol)	(020) 5179111	Frankfurt (Frankfurt/Main)	(0611) 69-01
Athens (Athinai)	(01) 97991	Freetown (Lungi International)	025 215
Auckland (Auckland International)	275 3899	Gaborone (Gaborone International)	53731/53732
Baghdad (Baghdad International)	5518888/5519999	Geneva (Geneva Intercontinental)	(022) 98-11-22
Bahrain (Bahrain International)	32133/321640	Harare (Harare International)	50422
Bangkok (Don Muang)	511 0121	Helsinki (Vantaa International)	82921
Basel (Basel-Mulhousen)	(061) 57-31-11	Hong Kong (Kai Tak International)	(3) 829751
Benghazi (Benina)	97147/86329	Houston (Houston Intercontinental)	(713) 443 4364
Berlin (Tempelhof)	(030) 690 9601		
Bombay (Santa Cruz International)	535491		
Boston (Logan)	(617) 482 2930	Jeddah (Jeddah International)	27211
Brunei (Bandar Seri Bagawan)	6531	Johannesburg (Jan Smuts)	(011) 975 1185
Buenos Aires (Ezeiza)	6200043		
		Kingston (Norman Manley International)	928 6057
Cairo (Cairo International)	968866	Kuala Lumpur (Subang International)	03-760717/760723/760833
Chicago (O'Hare International)	(312) 686 2200		
Copenhagen (Kastrup)	(01) 41-1-31	Kuwait (Kuwait International)	740296
Damascus (Damascus International)	555601	Lagos (Murtala Muhammed)	31631
		Lima (Jorge Chavet International)	529570
Dar es Salaam (Dar es Salaam International)	42211	Lisbon (Lisbonne)	82591/881101/885011
Delhi (Palam)	392719	London (see UK Airports: 22.4)	

Los Angeles (Los Angeles International)	(213) 646 5252
Lusaka (Lusaka International)	(011) 74331/74213
Madrid (Barajas)	(1) 222-11-65
Manila (Luzon International)	828 1784
Mexico City (Benito Juárez International)	571-36-00/571-30-07/571-34-32
Montreal (Dorval)	(514) 636 3223
Moscow (Sheremetyevo)	294-18-31/158-79-35
Nairobi (Jomo Kenyatta International)	822111
Nassau (Nassau International)	(809) 77281
New York (J F Kennedy International)	(212) 471 7594
Oman (Seeb International)	619210
Osaka (Itami International)	(06) 863 1121
Oslo (Furnebu)	(02) 12-13-40
Ottawa (Ottawa International)	(613) 998 3151
Paris (Charles de Gaulle International)	(1) 862-12-12/862-19-14
Peking (Beijing Capital)	555531
Prague (Ruzyné)	334
Puerto Rico (Puerto Rico International)	(809) 791-0030/791-0054
Rangoon (Mingaladon)	40111/40221/40231
Reykjavik (Reykjavik)	(91) 17430
Rio de Janeiro (Galeao)	398 6060
Rome (Leonardo da Vinci International)	(4867) 601541
Rotterdam (Zestienhoven)	(010) 371144
Santiago (Arturo Merino Benitez)	719152/733968
Shanghai (Hung-Chaio)	536530
Singapore (Changi International)	5421122
Sofia (Sofia International)	451121/26
Stockholm (Arlanda)	(08) 24-40-00
Sydney (Kingsford Smith)	(02) 667-0544
Taipei (Chiang Kai Chek International)	(033) 832001/832004
Tehran (Mehrabad)	641171
Tel Aviv (Ben Gurion International)	(03) 972610/972615
Tokyo (Haneda International)	(03) 747 0511
Tokyo (Narita International)	(0476) 32-2102/32-6417
Toronto (Toronto International)	(416) 676 3000
Vancouver (Vancouver International)	(604) 273-2311
Vienna (Schwechat)	(0222) 77700
Warsaw (Okecie)	46-11-82/46-99-56
Washington DC (Dulles International)	(301) 787 7079
Wellington (Wellington International)	888 500
Zurich (Zurich Intercontinental)	(01) 816-22-11

Airlines

Airline	Reservations	Flight enquiries
Aer Lingus	01-734 1212	01-734 1212
Aeroflot	01-493 7436	01-759 2529
Air Canada	01-759 2636	01-897 1331
Air France	01-499 9511	01-759 2311
Air India	01-491 7979	01-897 6311
Air Jamaica	01-734 1782	01-759 2595
Air Lanka	01-439 0291/3	01-439 0291
Air New Zealand	01-930 3434	(0293) 518033
Alia (Royal Jordanian Airlines)	01-734 2557	01-745 7031
Alitalia (Italian Airlines)	01-602 7111	01-759 1198
Austrian Airlines	01-439 0741	01-745 7191
British Airways	01-897 4000	01-759 2525
British Caledonian	01-668 4222	(0293) 25555
BWIA International	01-734 3796	01-839 7155
Caribbean Airways	01-636 2151/4	(0293) 28822
Cathay Pacific	01-930 7878	(0293) 502087
Cyprus Airways	01-388 5411	01-388 5425
Egyptair	01-734 2395/6	01-759 1520
El Al (Israel Airlines)	01-437 9255	01-759 9771
Finnair	01-408 1222	01-759 1258
Gulf Air	01-408 1717	01-897 0402
Iberia (International Airlines of Spain)	01-437 5622	01-759 4321
Icelandair	01-499 9971	01-745 7051
JAL (Japan Air Lines)	01-408 1000	01-759 9880

Airline	Reservations	Flight enquiries
KLM (Royal Dutch Airlines)	01-568 9144	01-750 9820
Kuwait Airways	01-935 8795	01-745 7772
Lufthansa (German Airlines)	01-408 0442	01-759 5642
MAS (Malaysian Airline System)	01-491 4542	01-759 2595
Middle East Airlines	01-493 5681	01-759 9211
Olympic Airways	01-846 9080	01-846 9080
Pakistan International Airlines	01-734 5544	01-759 2544
Pan Am (Pan American World Airways)	01-409 0688	01-409 0688
Qantas	(0345) 747767	(0345) 747767
SAA (South African Airways)	01-734 9841	01-897 3645
Sabena (Belgian World Airlines)	01-437 6950	01-437 6950
SAS (Scandinavian Airlines)	01-734 4020	01-734 4020
Singapore Airlines	01-747 0007	01-745 4151
Swissair	01-439 4144	01-745 7191
TAP (Air Portugal)	01-828 0262	01-828 0262
Thai Airways International	01-499 9113	01-897 1331
TWA (Trans World Airlines)	01-636 4090	01-636 4090
Virgin Atlantic	(0293) 38222	(0293) 38222
World Airways	01-434 3252	(0293) 502073

For UK airlines see p 241.

22.4 UK travel information

Air commuter services

British Airways Super Shuttle	01-897 4000
London Heathrow *to* Belfast/Edinburgh/Glasgow/Manchester	
British Caledonian	01-668 4222
London Gatwick *to* Aberdeen/Glasgow/Edinburgh/Manchester	
British Midland Diamond Service	01-581 0864
London Heathrow *to* Edinburgh/Glasgow	
Edinburgh *to* Amsterdam	
Glasgow *to* Amsterdam/East Midlands/Jersey/Guernsey	

UK airlines

Air Atlantique	(0203) 307566	Channel Express Air Services	(0202) 570701
Air Europe	01-651 3611		
Air UK	01-551 4988	Dan-Air	01-680 1011
Airways International Cymru	(0446) 711811	Guernsey Airlines	(0481) 35727
		Highland Express Airways	(0292) 79822
Anglo Airlines	(0293) 510131	Jersey European Airways	(0392) 64440
Aurigny Air Services	(0481) 822886		
		Loganair	041-889 3181
Britannia Airways	01-568 9144	Manx Airlines	01-493 0803
British Airways	01-897 4000	Monarch Airlines	(0582) 424211
British Caledonian	01-668 4222	Orion Airways	(0332) 812469
British Midland	01-581 0864	Virgin Atlantic Airways	(0293) 38222
Brymon Airways	01-549 6535		
Cal Air International	01-409 0814		

UK airports

(For map see p 279)

Aberdeen (Dyce)	(0224) 722331	Birmingham International	021-767 5511
Alderney (The Blaye)	(0481) 822711	Blackpool (Squire's Gate)	(0253) 43061
Barra (North Bay)	041-889 1311	Bournemouth (Hurn)	(0202) 579751
Belfast International (Aldergrove)	(0232) 229271		
		Bristol (Lulsgate)	(0275) 874441
Belfast Harbour (Sydenham)	(0232) 57745	Cardiff—Wales (Rhoose)	(0446) 711211
Benbecula (Balivanich)	(0870) 2051	Carlisle (Crosby)	(0228) 73641
		Cork	965388

241

Coventry (Baginton)	(0203) 301717
Dublin	(0001) 379900
Dundee (Riverside Park)	(0382) 643242
East Midlands (Derby)	(0332) 810621
Edinburgh (Turnhouse)	031-333 1000
Exeter (Clyst Honiton)	(0392) 67433
Fetlar	095783 267
Fort William Heliport	(0397) 4182
Galway (Carnmore)	(0009) 84300/ 84392
Glasgow/(Paisley)	041-887 1111
Gloucester/ Cheltenham (Staverton)	(0452) 856681
Guernsey	(0481) 37766
Humberside (Ulceby)	(0652) 688456
Inverness (Dalcross)	(0463) 232471
Islay (Glenegadale/ Port Ellen)	(0496) 2361
Isle of Man (Ronaldsway)	(0624) 823311
Isle of Skye (Ashaig/Broadford)	(04712) 202
Isles of Scilly (St Mary's)	(0720) 22677
Jersey (States)	(0534) 46111
Kirkwall (Orkney)	(0856) 2421
Leeds/Bradford	(0532) 509696
Lerwick (Sumburgh)	(0950) 60645
(Tingwall)	(059) 584 306
Liverpool (Speke)	051-486 8877
London-Battersea Heliport	01-228 0181
London City (Stolport)	01-568 9111 (opening late 1987)
London (Gatwick)	(0293) 28822
London (Heathrow)	01-759 4321
Londonderry (Eglinton)	(0504) 810784
Luton	(0582) 36061
Manchester International	061-489 3000
Newcastle (Woolsington)	091-286 0966
Newquay (RAF St Mawgan)	(0637) 860551
Norwich	(0603) 411923
Papa Westray	(0856) 3535
Penzance Heliport	(07366) 4296
Plymouth (Roborough)	(0752) 705151
Prestwick	(0292) 79822
Rothesay Heliport	(0292) 79822
Shannon	61444
Shoreham (Brighton/Hove/Worthing)	(0273) 452304
Southampton (Eastleigh)	(0703) 612341
Southend	(0702) 340201
Stansted	(0279) 502380
Stornoway (Lewis)	(0851) 2256
Teesside	(0325) 332811
Tiree (Reef)	(08792) 456
Tresco Heliport (Scilly)	(0720) 22083
Unst (Baltasound)	(095781) 404/5/6/7
Waterford (Portlaw)	(0005) 75580
Weston-super-Mare Heliport	(0934) 28726
Wick	(0955) 2215

British Rail

Services from London:

(*to* East Anglia and Essex)	01-283 7171
(*to* Midlands, N Wales, North West, W Coast to Scotland)	01-387 7070
(*to* Southern England)	01-928 5100
(*to* W of England, W Midlands, S Wales)	01-262 6767
(*to* W Yorkshire, North East, E Coast to Scotland)	01-287 2477

Services from Birmingham (New Street):	021-643 2711
from Bristol (Temple Meads):	(0272) 294255
from Cardiff (Central):	(0222) 28000
from Edinburgh (Waverley):	031-556 2451
from Glasgow (Central):	041-204 2844
from Leeds (City):	(0532) 448133
from Liverpool (Lime Street):	051-709 9696
from Manchester (Piccadilly):	061-832 8353
from Newcastle (Central):	(0632) 326262
from Sheffield:	(0742) 26411

Eastern Region:

(York)	(0904) 53022

London:

(Charing Cross)	01-928 5100
(Euston and St Pancras)	01-387 7070
(Fenchurch Street)	01-283 7171
(King's Cross)	01-278 2477
(Liverpool Street)	01-283 7171

London Midland Region:

(Birmingham)	021-643 2711

Scottish Region:

(Glasgow)	041-204 2844
(Edinburgh)	031-556 2451

Southern Region:

(Waterloo and Victoria)	01-928 5100

Western Region:

(Paddington)	01-262 6767

Motorail Services:	01-387 8541

Sleeper Services:

(Euston)	01-388 6061
(King's Cross)	01-278 2411
(Paddington)	01-723 781

Hoverspeed City Link:

(London *to* Paris)	(0304) 216205
	01-554 7061

Car ferry services

B & I Line

    (Liverpool *to* Dublin)   051-227 3131

    (Holyhead *to* Dublin and Dun Laoghaire)   (0407) 50222

    (Fishguard *to* Rosslare)   (0348) 872881

Brittany Ferries

    (Portsmouth *to* St Malo)   (0705) 827701

    (Plymouth *to* Roscoff and Santander)   (07527) 21321

    (Cork *to* Roscoff)   021-507 666

DFDS Seaways

    (Harwich *to* Esbjerg, Hamburg and Gothenburg)   (0255) 554681

    (Newcastle *to* Esbjerg, Bergen and Gothenburg)   (0632) 575655

Hoverspeed Ltd

    (Dover *to* Boulogne and Calais)   (0843) 595555/594881

                                                            01-554 7061

North Sea Ferries Ltd

    (Hull *to* Zeebrugge; Ipswich *to* Rotterdam)   (0482) 795141

P & O Ferries

    (Dover *to* Boulogne)   (0304) 203399

    (Southampton *to* Le Havre)   (0703) 32131

Sealink British Ferries   01-834 8122

    (Dover *to* Boulogne, Calais, Dunkirk and Ostend; Fishguard *to* Rosslare; Folkestone *to* Boulogne; Harwich *to* Hook of Holland; Heysham *to* Douglas (Isle of Man); Holyhead *to* Dun Laoghaire; Newhaven *to* Dieppe; Portsmouth *to* Channel Islands and Cherbourg; Stranraer *to* Larne; Weymouth *to* Channel Islands and Portsmouth)

Sealink Isle of Wight Services   (0705) 827744

    (Portsmouth and Lymington *to* Isle of Wight)

Townsend Thoresen   (0304) 203388

    (Dover *to* Boulogne, Calais and Zeebrugge; Felixstowe *to* Zeebrugge; Portsmouth *to* Cherbourg and Le Havre; Larne *to* Cairnryan)

Car hire services

Alamo Rent A Car	01-897 0536	Telex 261863
Avis	01-848 8733	Telex 933936
Avis Chauffeur Drive	01-897 2621	Telex 905016
Budget	(0800) 181181	Telex 877994
Godfrey Davis Chauffeur Drive	01-834 6701	Telex 22819
Godfrey Davis Europcar	01-950 5050	Telex 25468

Guy Salmon	01-408 1255	Telex 21213
Hertz	01-679 1777	Telex 8812947
Key Rent-a-Car	01-897 7777	Telex 917061
Swan	01-995 4665	Telex 935102
Travelwise	01-582 1769	Telex 21120

Consult *Yellow Pages* for your local branches.

Passport offices

Belfast
Hampton House, 47–53 High Street, Belfast BT1 2AB   (0232) 232371
Glasgow
Empire House, 131 West Nile Street, Glasgow G1 2RY   041-332 0271
Liverpool
5th Floor, India Building, Water Street, Liverpool L2 0QZ   051-237 3010
London
Clive House, 70–78 Petty France, London SW1H 9HD   01-213 3000
(A–D)   01-213 3261   (E–K)   01-213 7272
(L–Q)   01-213 6098   (R–Z)   01-213 6915
Newport
Olympia House, Upper Dock Street, Newport NPT 1XA   (0633) 56292
Peterborough
55 Westfield Road, Westwood PE3 6TG   (0733) 895555

Travel associations and bodies

Air Transport Operators Association   (0428) 4804
Clembro House, Weydown Road, Haslemere, Surrey GU27 2QE
Air Transport Users Committee   01-242 3882
129 Kingsway, London WC2B 6NN
Association of British Travel Agents   01-637 2444
55/57 Newman Street, London W1P 4AH
British Airports Authority   (0293) 517755
Gatwick Airport, Gatwick, W Sussex RH6 0HZ
British Vehicle Rental Leasing Association   (0243) 786782
13 St John's Street, Chichester, W Sussex PO19 1UU
Civil Aviation Authority   01-379 7311
CAA House, 45/59 Kingsway, London WC2B 6TE
Guild of British Travel Agents   01-930 2278
60/61 Trafalgar Square, London WC2N 5DS

22.5 UK counties and regions

Common written abbreviations of the English counties preferred by the Royal Mail are given in brackets after each county. The form *Salop* (for Shropshire) is also used in speech. There are no commonly used abbreviations for Welsh and Northern Irish counties or Scottish regions. *(For map see p 276.)*

England

Avon
Bedfordshire
 (Beds)
Berkshire
 (Berks)
Buckinghamshire
 (Bucks)
Cambridgeshire
 (Cambs)
Cheshire
Cleveland
Cornwall
Cumbria
Derbyshire
Devon
Dorset
Durham
East Sussex
Essex
Gloucestershire
 (Glos)
Greater London
Greater Manchester

Hampshire
 (Hants)
Hereford and
 Worcester
Hertfordshire
 (Herts)
Humberside
Isle of Wight (IOW)
Kent
Lancashire
 (Lancs)
Leicestershire
 (Leics)
Lincolnshire
 (Lincs)
Merseyside
Middlesex
 (Middx)
Norfolk
Northamptonshire
 (Northants)
Northumberland
 (Northd)
North Yorkshire
 (N Yorks)

Nottinghamshire
 (Notts)
Oxfordshire
 (Oxon)
Shropshire
 (Salop)
Somerset
South Yorkshire
 (S Yorkshire)
Staffordshire
 (Staffs)
Suffolk
Surrey
Tyne and Wear
Warwickshire
 (Warwicks)
West Midlands
West Sussex
West Yorkshire
 (W Yorkshire)
Wiltshire
 (Wilts)

Wales

Clwyd
Dyfed
Gwent

Gwynedd
Mid Glamorgan
Powys

South Glamorgan
West Glamorgan

Northern Ireland

Antrim
Armagh
Down

Fermanagh
Londonderry
 (Co. Derry)

Tyrone

Scotland

Borders
Central
Dumfries and
  Galloway
Fife

Grampian
Highland
Lothian
Orkney

Shetland
Strathclyde
Tayside
Western Isles

23 CALENDARS

23.1 Calendars 1987-2000

1987

	January	February	March	April	May	June
M	5 12 19 26	2 9 16 23	2 9 16 23 30	6 13 20 27	4 11 18 25	1 8 15 22 29
T	6 13 20 27	3 10 17 24	3 10 17 24 31	7 14 21 28	5 12 19 26	2 9 16 23 30
W	7 14 21 28	4 11 18 25	4 11 18 25	1 8 15 22 29	6 13 20 27	3 10 17 24
T	1 8 15 22 29	5 12 19 26	5 12 19 26	2 9 16 23 30	7 14 21 28	4 11 18 25
F	2 9 16 23 30	6 13 20 27	6 13 20 27	3 10 17 24	1 8 15 22 29	5 12 19 26
S	3 10 17 24 31	7 14 21 28	7 14 21 28	4 11 18 25	2 9 16 23 30	6 13 20 27
S	4 11 18 25	1 8 15 22	1 8 15 22 29	5 12 19 26	3 10 17 24 31	7 14 21 28

	July	August	September	October	November	December
M	6 13 20 27	3 10 17 24 31	7 14 21 28	5 12 19 26	2 9 16 23 30	7 14 21 28
T	7 14 21 28	4 11 18 25	1 8 15 22 29	6 13 20 27	3 10 17 24	1 8 15 22 29
W	1 8 15 22 29	5 12 19 26	2 9 16 23 30	7 14 21 28	4 11 18 25	2 9 16 23 30
T	2 9 16 23 30	6 13 20 27	3 10 17 24	1 8 15 22 29	5 12 19 26	3 10 17 24 31
F	3 10 17 24 31	7 14 21 28	4 11 18 25	2 9 16 23 30	6 13 20 27	4 11 18 25
S	4 11 18 25	1 8 15 22 29	5 12 19 26	3 10 17 24 31	7 14 21 28	5 12 19 26
S	5 12 19 26	2 9 16 23 30	6 13 20 27	4 11 18 25	1 8 15 22 29	6 13 20 27

1988

	January	February	March	April	May	June
M	4 11 18 25	1 8 15 22 29	7 14 21 28	4 11 18 25	2 9 16 23 30	6 13 20 27
T	5 12 19 26	2 9 16 23	1 8 15 22 29	5 12 19 26	3 10 17 24 31	7 14 21 28
W	6 13 20 27	3 10 17 24	2 9 16 23 30	6 13 20 27	4 11 18 25	1 8 15 22 29
T	7 14 21 28	4 11 18 25	3 10 17 24 31	7 14 21 28	5 12 19 26	2 9 16 23 30
F	1 8 15 22 29	5 12 19 26	4 11 18 25	1 8 15 22 29	6 13 20 27	3 10 17 24
S	2 9 16 23 30	6 13 20 27	5 12 19 26	2 9 16 23 30	7 14 21 28	4 11 18 25
S	3 10 17 24 31	7 14 21 28	6 13 20 27	3 10 17 24	1 8 15 22 29	5 12 19 26

	July	August	September	October	November	December
M	4 11 18 25	1 8 15 22 29	5 12 19 26	3 10 17 24 31	7 14 21 28	5 12 19 26
T	5 12 19 26	2 9 16 23 30	6 13 20 27	4 11 18 25	1 8 15 22 29	6 13 20 27
W	6 13 20 27	3 10 17 24 31	7 14 21 28	5 12 19 26	2 9 16 23 30	7 14 21 28
T	7 14 21 28	4 11 18 25	1 8 15 22 29	6 13 20 27	3 10 17 24	1 8 15 22 29
F	1 8 15 22 29	5 12 19 26	2 9 16 23 30	7 14 21 28	4 11 18 25	2 9 16 23 30
S	2 9 16 23 30	6 13 20 27	3 10 17 24	1 8 15 22 29	5 12 19 26	3 10 17 24 31
S	3 10 17 24 31	7 14 21 28	4 11 18 25	2 9 16 23 30	6 13 20 27	4 11 18 25

1989

	January	February	March	April	May	June
M	2 9 16 23 30	6 13 20 27	6 13 20 27	3 10 17 24	1 8 15 22 29	5 12 19 26
T	3 10 17 24 31	7 14 21 28	7 14 21 28	4 11 18 25	2 9 16 23 30	6 13 20 27
W	4 11 18 25	1 8 15 22	1 8 15 22 29	5 12 19 26	3 10 17 24 31	7 14 21 28
T	5 12 19 26	2 9 16 23	2 9 16 23 30	6 13 20 27	4 11 18 25	1 8 15 22 29
F	6 13 20 27	3 10 17 24	3 10 17 24 31	7 14 21 28	5 12 19 26	2 9 16 23 30
S	7 14 21 28	4 11 18 25	4 11 18 25	1 8 15 22 29	6 13 20 27	3 10 17 24
S	1 8 15 22 29	5 12 19 26	5 12 19 26	2 9 16 23 30	7 14 21 28	4 11 18 25

	July	August	September	October	November	December
M	3 10 17 24 31	7 14 21 28	4 11 18 25	2 9 16 23 30	6 13 20 27	4 11 18 25
T	4 11 18 25	1 8 15 22 29	5 12 19 26	3 10 17 24 31	7 14 21 28	5 12 19 26
W	5 12 19 26	2 9 16 23 30	6 13 20 27	4 11 18 25	1 8 15 22 29	6 13 20 27
T	6 13 20 27	3 10 17 24 31	7 14 21 28	5 12 19 26	2 9 16 23 30	7 14 21 28
F	7 14 21 28	4 11 18 25	1 8 15 22 29	6 13 20 27	3 10 17 24	1 8 15 22 29
S	1 8 15 22 29	5 12 19 26	2 9 16 23 30	7 14 21 28	4 11 18 25	2 9 16 23 30
S	2 9 16 23 30	6 13 20 27	3 10 17 24	1 8 15 22 29	5 12 19 26	3 10 17 24 31

1990

	January	February	March	April	May	June
M	1 8 15 22 29	5 12 19 26	5 12 19 26	2 9 16 23 30	7 14 21 28	4 11 18 25
T	2 9 16 23 30	6 13 20 27	6 13 20 27	3 10 17 24	1 8 15 22 29	5 12 19 26
W	3 10 17 24 31	7 14 21 28	7 14 21 28	4 11 18 25	2 9 16 23 30	6 13 20 27
T	4 11 18 25	1 8 15 22	1 8 15 22 29	5 12 19 26	3 10 17 24 31	7 14 21 28
F	5 12 19 26	2 9 16 23	2 9 16 23 30	6 13 20 27	4 11 18 25	1 8 15 22 29
S	6 13 20 27	3 10 17 24	3 10 17 24 31	7 14 21 28	5 12 19 26	2 9 16 23 30
S	7 14 21 28	4 11 18 25	4 11 18 25	1 8 15 22 29	6 13 20 27	3 10 17 24

	July	August	September	October	November	December
M	2 9 16 23 30	6 13 20 27	3 10 17 24	1 8 15 22 29	5 12 19 26	3 10 17 24 31
T	3 10 17 24 31	7 14 21 28	4 11 18 25	2 9 16 23 30	6 13 20 27	4 11 18 25
W	4 11 18 25	1 8 15 22 29	5 12 19 26	3 10 17 24 31	7 14 21 28	5 12 19 26
T	5 12 19 26	2 9 16 23 30	6 13 20 27	4 11 18 25	1 8 15 22 29	6 13 20 27
F	6 13 20 27	3 10 17 24 31	7 14 21 28	5 12 19 26	2 9 16 23 30	7 14 21 28
S	7 14 21 28	4 11 18 25	1 8 15 22 29	6 13 20 27	3 10 17 24	1 8 15 22 29
S	1 8 15 22 29	5 12 19 26	2 9 16 23 30	7 14 21 28	4 11 18 25	2 9 16 23 30

1991

	January	February	March	April	May	June
M	7 14 21 28	4 11 18 25	4 11 18 25	1 8 15 22 29	6 13 20 27	3 10 17 24
T	1 8 15 22 29	5 12 19 26	5 12 19 26	2 9 16 23 30	7 14 21 28	4 11 18 25
W	2 9 16 23 30	6 13 20 27	6 13 20 27	3 10 17 24	1 8 15 22 29	5 12 19 26
T	3 10 17 24 31	7 14 21 28	7 14 21 28	4 11 18 25	2 9 16 23 30	6 13 20 27
F	4 11 18 25	1 8 15 22	1 8 15 22 29	5 12 19 26	3 10 17 24 31	7 14 21 28
S	5 12 19 26	2 9 16 23	2 9 16 23 30	6 13 20 27	4 11 18 25	1 8 15 22 29
S	6 13 20 27	3 10 17 24	3 10 17 24 31	7 14 21 28	5 12 19 26	2 9 16 23 30

	July	August	September	October	November	December
M	1 8 15 22 29	5 12 19 26	2 9 16 23 30	7 14 21 28	4 11 18 25	2 9 16 23 30
T	2 9 16 23 30	6 13 20 27	3 10 17 24	1 8 15 22 29	5 12 19 26	3 10 17 24 31
W	3 10 17 24 31	7 14 21 28	4 11 18 25	2 9 16 23 30	6 13 20 27	4 11 18 25
T	4 11 18 25	1 8 15 22 29	5 12 19 26	3 10 17 24 31	7 14 21 28	5 12 19 26
F	5 12 19 26	2 9 16 23 30	6 13 20 27	4 11 18 25	1 8 15 22 29	6 13 20 27
S	6 13 20 27	3 10 17 24 31	7 14 21 28	5 12 19 26	2 9 16 23 30	7 14 21 28
S	7 14 21 28	4 11 18 25	1 8 15 22 29	6 13 20 27	3 10 17 24	1 8 15 22 29

1992

	January	February	March	April	May	June
M	6 13 20 27	3 10 17 24	2 9 16 23 30	6 13 20 27	4 11 18 25	1 8 15 22 29
T	7 14 21 28	4 11 18 25	3 10 17 24 31	7 14 21 28	5 12 19 26	2 9 16 23 30
W	1 8 15 22 29	5 12 19 26	4 11 18 25	1 8 15 22 29	6 13 20 27	3 10 17 24
T	2 9 16 23 30	6 13 20 27	5 12 19 26	2 9 16 23 30	7 14 21 28	4 11 18 25
F	3 10 17 24 31	7 14 21 28	6 13 20 27	3 10 17 24	1 8 15 22 29	5 12 19 26
S	4 11 18 25	1 8 15 22 29	7 14 21 28	4 11 18 25	2 9 16 23 30	6 13 20 27
S	5 12 19 26	2 9 16 23	1 8 15 22 29	5 12 19 26	3 10 17 24 31	7 14 21 28

	July	August	September	October	November	December
M	6 13 20 27	3 10 17 24 31	7 14 21 28	5 12 19 26	2 9 16 23 30	7 14 21 28
T	7 14 21 28	4 11 18 25	1 8 15 22 29	6 13 20 27	3 10 17 24	1 8 15 22 29
W	1 8 15 22 29	5 12 19 26	2 9 16 23 30	7 14 21 28	4 11 18 25	2 9 16 23 30
T	2 9 16 23 30	6 13 20 27	3 10 17 24	1 8 15 22 29	5 12 19 26	3 10 17 24 31
F	3 10 17 24 31	7 14 21 28	4 11 18 25	2 9 16 23 30	6 13 20 27	4 11 18 25
S	4 11 18 25	1 8 15 22 29	5 12 19 26	3 10 17 24 31	7 14 21 28	5 12 19 26
S	5 12 19 26	2 9 16 23 30	6 13 20 27	4 11 18 25	1 8 15 22 29	6 13 20 27

1993

	January	February	March	April	May	June
M	4 11 18 25	1 8 15 22	1 8 15 22 29	5 12 19 26	3 10 17 24 31	7 14 21 28
T	5 12 19 26	2 9 16 23	2 9 16 23 30	6 13 20 27	4 11 18 25	1 8 15 22 29
W	6 13 20 27	3 10 17 24	3 10 17 24 31	7 14 21 28	5 12 19 26	2 9 16 23 30
T	7 14 21 28	4 11 18 25	4 11 18 25	1 8 15 22 29	6 13 20 27	3 10 17 24
F	1 8 15 22 29	5 12 19 26	5 12 19 26	2 9 16 23 30	7 14 21 28	4 11 18 25
S	2 9 16 23 30	6 13 20 27	6 13 20 27	3 10 17 24	1 8 15 22 29	5 12 19 26
S	3 10 17 24 31	7 14 21 28	7 14 21 28	4 11 18 25	2 9 16 23 30	6 13 20 27

	July	August	September	October	November	December
M	5 12 19 26	2 9 16 23 30	6 13 20 27	4 11 18 25	1 8 15 22 29	6 13 20 27
T	6 13 20 27	3 10 17 24 31	7 14 21 28	5 12 19 26	2 9 16 23 30	7 14 21 28
W	7 14 21 28	4 11 18 25	1 8 15 22 29	6 13 20 27	3 10 17 24	1 8 15 22 29
T	1 8 15 22 29	5 12 19 26	2 9 16 23 30	7 14 21 28	4 11 18 25	2 9 16 23 30
F	2 9 16 23 30	6 13 20 27	3 10 17 24	1 8 15 22 29	5 12 19 26	3 10 17 24 31
S	3 10 17 24 31	7 14 21 28	4 11 18 25	2 9 16 23 30	6 13 20 27	4 11 18 25
S	4 11 18 25	1 8 15 22 29	5 12 19 26	3 10 17 24 31	7 14 21 28	5 12 19 26

1994

	January	February	March	April	May	June
M	3 10 17 24 31	7 14 21 28	7 14 21 28	4 11 18 25	2 9 16 23 30	6 13 20 27
T	4 11 18 25	1 8 15 22	1 8 15 22 29	5 12 19 26	3 10 17 24 31	7 14 21 28
W	5 12 19 26	2 9 16 23	2 9 16 23 30	6 13 20 27	4 11 18 25	1 8 15 22 29
T	6 13 20 27	3 10 17 24	3 10 17 24 31	7 14 21 28	5 12 19 26	2 9 16 23 30
F	7 14 21 28	4 11 18 25	4 11 18 25	1 8 15 22 29	6 13 20 27	3 10 17 24
S	1 8 15 22 29	5 12 19 26	5 12 19 26	2 9 16 23 30	7 14 21 28	4 11 18 25
S	2 9 16 23 30	6 13 20 27	6 13 20 27	3 10 17 24	1 8 15 22 29	5 12 19 26

	July	August	September	October	November	December
M	4 11 18 25	1 8 15 22 29	5 12 19 26	3 10 17 24 31	7 14 21 28	5 12 19 26
T	5 12 19 26	2 9 16 23 30	6 13 20 27	4 11 18 25	1 8 15 22 29	6 13 20 27
W	6 13 20 27	3 10 17 24 31	7 14 21 28	5 12 19 26	2 9 16 23 30	7 14 21 28
T	7 14 21 28	4 11 18 25	1 8 15 22 29	6 13 20 27	3 10 17 24	1 8 15 22 29
F	1 8 15 22 29	5 12 19 26	2 9 16 23 30	7 14 21 28	4 11 18 25	2 9 16 23 30
S	2 9 16 23 30	6 13 20 27	3 10 17 24	1 8 15 22 29	5 12 19 26	3 10 17 24 31
S	3 10 17 24 31	7 14 21 28	4 11 18 25	2 9 16 23 30	6 13 20 27	4 11 18 25

1995

	January	February	March	April	May	June
M	2 9 16 23 30	6 13 20 27	6 13 20 27	3 10 17 24	1 8 15 22 29	5 12 19 26
T	3 10 17 24 31	7 14 21 28	7 14 21 28	4 11 18 25	2 9 16 23 30	6 13 20 27
W	4 11 18 25	1 8 15 22	1 8 15 22 29	5 12 19 26	3 10 17 24 31	7 14 21 28
T	5 12 19 26	2 9 16 23	2 9 16 23 30	6 13 20 27	4 11 18 25	1 8 15 22 29
F	6 13 20 27	3 10 17 24	3 10 17 24 31	7 14 21 28	5 12 19 26	2 9 16 23 30
S	7 14 21 28	4 11 18 25	4 11 18 25	1 8 15 22 29	6 13 20 27	3 10 17 24
S	1 8 15 22 29	5 12 19 26	5 12 19 26	2 9 16 23 30	7 14 21 28	4 11 18 25

	July	August	September	October	November	December
M	3 10 17 24 31	7 14 21 28	4 11 18 25	2 9 16 23 30	6 13 20 27	4 11 18 25
T	4 11 18 25	1 8 15 22 29	5 12 19 26	3 10 17 24 31	7 14 21 28	5 12 19 26
W	5 12 19 26	2 9 16 23 30	6 13 20 27	4 11 18 25	1 8 15 22 29	6 13 20 27
T	6 13 20 27	3 10 17 24 31	7 14 21 28	5 12 19 26	2 9 16 23 30	7 14 21 28
F	7 14 21 28	4 11 18 25	1 8 15 22 29	6 13 20 27	3 10 17 24	1 8 15 22 29
S	1 8 15 22 29	5 12 19 26	2 9 16 23 30	7 14 21 28	4 11 18 25	2 9 16 23 30
S	2 9 16 23 30	6 13 20 27	3 10 17 24	1 8 15 22 29	5 12 19 26	3 10 17 24 31

1996

	January	February	March	April	May	June
M	1 8 15 22 29	5 12 19 26	4 11 18 25	1 8 15 22 29	6 13 20 27	3 10 17 24
T	2 9 16 23 30	6 13 20 27	5 12 19 26	2 9 16 23 30	7 14 21 28	4 11 18 25
W	3 10 17 24 31	7 14 21 28	6 13 20 27	3 10 17 24	1 8 15 22 29	5 12 19 26
T	4 11 18 25	1 8 15 22 29	7 14 21 28	4 11 18 25	2 9 16 23 30	6 13 20 27
F	5 12 19 26	2 9 16 23	1 8 15 22 29	5 12 19 26	3 10 17 24 31	7 14 21 28
S	6 13 20 27	3 10 17 24	2 9 16 23 30	6 13 20 27	4 11 18 25	1 8 15 22 29
S	7 14 21 28	4 11 18 25	3 10 17 24 31	7 14 21 28	5 12 19 26	2 9 16 23 30

	July	August	September	October	November	December
M	1 8 15 22 29	5 12 19 26	2 9 16 23 30	7 14 21 28	4 11 18 25	2 9 16 23 30
T	2 9 16 23 30	6 13 20 27	3 10 17 24	1 8 15 22 29	5 12 19 26	3 10 17 24 31
W	3 10 17 24 31	7 14 21 28	4 11 18 25	2 9 16 23 30	6 13 20 27	4 11 18 25
T	4 11 18 25	1 8 15 22 29	5 12 19 26	3 10 17 24 31	7 14 21 28	5 12 19 26
F	5 12 19 26	2 9 16 23 30	6 13 20 27	4 11 18 25	1 8 15 22 29	6 13 20 27
S	6 13 20 27	3 10 17 24 31	7 14 21 28	5 12 19 26	2 9 16 23 30	7 14 21 28
S	7 14 21 28	4 11 18 25	1 8 15 22 29	6 13 20 27	3 10 17 24	1 8 15 22 29

1997

	January	February	March	April	May	June
M	6 13 20 27	3 10 17 24	3 10 17 24 31	7 14 21 28	5 12 19 26	2 9 16 23 30
T	7 14 21 28	4 11 18 25	4 11 18 25	1 8 15 22 29	6 13 20 27	3 10 17 24
W	1 8 15 22 29	5 12 19 26	5 12 19 26	2 9 16 23 30	7 14 21 28	4 11 18 25
T	2 9 16 23 30	6 13 20 27	6 13 20 27	3 10 17 24	1 8 15 22 29	5 12 19 26
F	3 10 17 24 31	7 14 21 28	7 14 21 28	4 11 18 25	2 9 16 23 30	6 13 20 27
S	4 11 18 25	1 8 15 22	1 8 15 22 29	5 12 19 26	3 10 17 24 31	7 14 21 28
S	5 12 19 26	2 9 16 23	2 9 16 23 30	6 13 20 27	4 11 18 25	1 8 15 22 29

	July	August	September	October	November	December
M	7 14 21 28	4 11 18 25	1 8 15 22 29	6 13 20 27	3 10 17 24	1 8 15 22 29
T	1 8 15 22 29	5 12 19 26	2 9 16 23 30	7 14 21 28	4 11 18 25	2 9 16 23 30
W	2 9 16 23 30	6 13 20 27	3 10 17 24	1 8 15 22 29	5 12 19 26	3 10 17 24 31
T	3 10 17 24 31	7 14 21 28	4 11 18 25	2 9 16 23 30	6 13 20 27	4 11 18 25
F	4 11 18 25	1 8 15 22 29	5 12 19 26	3 10 17 24 31	7 14 21 28	5 12 19 26
S	5 12 19 26	2 9 16 23 30	6 13 20 27	4 11 18 25	1 8 15 22 29	6 13 20 27
S	6 13 20 27	3 10 17 24 31	7 14 21 28	5 12 19 26	2 9 16 23 30	7 14 21 28

1998

	January	February	March	April	May	June
M	5 12 19 26	2 9 16 23	2 9 16 23 30	6 13 20 27	4 11 18 25	1 8 15 22 29
T	6 13 20 27	3 10 17 24	3 10 17 24 31	7 14 21 28	5 12 19 26	2 9 16 23 30
W	7 14 21 28	4 11 18 25	4 11 18 25	1 8 15 22 29	6 13 20 27	3 10 17 24
T	1 8 15 22 29	5 12 19 26	5 12 19 26	2 9 16 23 30	7 14 21 28	4 11 18 25
F	2 9 16 23 30	6 13 20 27	6 13 20 27	3 10 17 24	1 8 15 22 29	5 12 19 26
S	3 10 17 24 31	7 14 21 28	7 14 21 28	4 11 18 25	2 9 16 23 30	6 13 20 27
S	4 11 18 25	1 8 15 22	1 8 15 22 29	5 12 19 26	3 10 17 24 31	7 14 21 28

	July	August	September	October	November	December
M	6 13 20 27	3 10 17 24 31	7 14 21 28	5 12 19 26	2 9 16 23 30	7 14 21 28
T	7 14 21 28	4 11 18 25	1 8 15 22 29	6 13 20 27	3 10 17 24	1 8 15 22 29
W	1 8 15 22 29	5 12 19 26	2 9 16 23 30	7 14 21 28	4 11 18 25	2 9 16 23 30
T	2 9 16 23 30	6 13 20 27	3 10 17 24	1 8 15 22 29	5 12 19 26	3 10 17 24 31
F	3 10 17 24 31	7 14 21 28	4 11 18 25	2 9 16 23 30	6 13 20 27	4 11 18 25
S	4 11 18 25	1 8 15 22 29	5 12 19 26	3 10 17 24 31	7 14 21 28	5 12 19 26
S	5 12 19 26	2 9 16 23 30	6 13 20 27	4 11 18 25	1 8 15 22 29	6 13 20 27

1999

	January	February	March	April	May	June
M	4 11 18 25	1 8 15 22	1 8 15 22 29	5 12 19 26	3 10 17 24 31	7 14 21 28
T	5 12 19 26	2 9 16 23	2 9 16 23 30	6 13 20 27	4 11 18 25	1 8 15 22 29
W	6 13 20 27	3 10 17 24	3 10 17 24 31	7 14 21 28	5 12 19 26	2 9 16 23 30
T	7 14 21 28	4 11 18 25	4 11 18 25	1 8 15 22 29	6 13 20 27	3 10 17 24
F	1 8 15 22 29	5 12 19 26	5 12 19 26	2 9 16 23 30	7 14 21 28	4 11 18 25
S	2 9 16 23 30	6 13 20 27	6 13 20 27	3 10 17 24	1 8 15 22 29	5 12 19 26
S	3 10 17 24 31	7 14 21 28	7 14 21 28	4 11 18 25	2 9 16 23 30	6 13 20 27

	July	August	September	October	November	December
M	5 12 19 26	2 9 16 23 30	6 13 20 27	4 11 18 25	1 8 15 22 29	6 13 20 27
T	6 13 20 27	3 10 17 24 31	7 14 21 28	5 12 19 26	2 9 16 23 30	7 14 21 28
W	7 14 21 28	4 11 18 25	1 8 15 22 29	6 13 20 27	3 10 17 24	1 8 15 22 29
T	1 8 15 22 29	5 12 19 26	2 9 16 23 30	7 14 21 28	4 11 18 25	2 9 16 23 30
F	2 9 16 23 30	6 13 20 27	3 10 17 24	1 8 15 22 29	5 12 19 26	3 10 17 24 31
S	3 10 17 24 31	7 14 21 28	4 11 18 25	2 9 16 23 30	6 13 20 27	4 11 18 25
S	4 11 18 25	1 8 15 22 29	5 12 19 26	3 10 17 24 31	7 14 21 28	5 12 19 26

2000

	January	February	March	April	May	June
M	3 10 17 24 31	7 14 21 28	6 13 20 27	3 10 17 24	1 8 15 22 29	5 12 19 26
T	4 11 18 25	1 8 15 22 29	7 14 21 28	4 11 18 25	2 9 16 23 30	6 13 20 27
W	5 12 19 26	2 9 16 23	1 8 15 22 29	5 12 19 26	3 10 17 24 31	7 14 21 28
T	6 13 20 27	3 10 17 24	2 9 16 23 30	6 13 20 27	4 11 18 25	1 8 15 22 29
F	7 14 21 28	4 11 18 25	3 10 17 24 31	7 14 21 28	5 12 19 26	2 9 16 23 30
S	1 8 15 22 29	5 12 19 26	4 11 18 25	1 8 15 22 29	6 13 20 27	3 10 17 24
S	2 9 16 23 30	6 13 20 27	5 12 19 26	2 9 16 23 30	7 14 21 28	4 11 18 25

	July	August	September	October	November	December
M	3 10 17 24 31	7 14 21 28	4 11 18 25	2 9 16 23 30	6 13 20 27	4 11 18 25
T	4 11 18 25	1 8 15 22 29	5 12 19 26	3 10 17 24 31	7 14 21 28	5 12 19 26
W	5 12 19 26	2 9 16 23 30	6 13 20 27	4 11 18 25	1 8 15 22 29	6 13 20 27
T	6 13 20 27	3 10 17 24 31	7 14 21 28	5 12 19 26	2 9 16 23 30	7 14 21 28
F	7 14 21 28	4 11 18 25	1 8 15 22 29	6 13 20 27	3 10 17 24	1 8 15 22 29
S	1 8 15 22 29	5 12 19 26	2 9 16 23 30	7 14 21 28	4 11 18 25	2 9 16 23 30
S	2 9 16 23 30	6 13 20 27	3 10 17 24	1 8 15 22 29	5 12 19 26	3 10 17 24 31

23.2 World holidays

Since the dates of holidays vary each year according to the day of the week upon which they fall and other considerations, all dates should be regarded as **approximate**. When a date given refers specifically to the **1987** observance of a holiday it is marked *. The following list shows only **all-day** holidays and does not include regional and local holidays within countries.

Note: Certain countries do not observe Sunday as a general holiday; these include Afghanistan, Algeria, Bahrain, Bangladesh, Djibouti, Egypt, Iran, Iraq, Israel, Jordan, Kuwait, Libya, Maldives, Mauritania, Nepal, Oman, Pakistan, Qatar, Saudi Arabia, Somali, Sudan, Syria, United Arab Emirates, Yemen Arab Republic and Yemen People's Democratic Republic.

	JANUARY	
1	New Year's Day	all countries EXCEPT: Afghanistan, Bangladesh, Bhutan, Burma, Egypt, Ethiopia, Iran, Libya, Nepal, Oman, Pakistan, Qatar, Saudi Arabia, Sri Lanka, Tanzania, Yemen Arab Republic
	Day of Liberation	Cuba
	National Day	Haiti, Sudan
2	Ancestry Day	Haiti
	Bank Holiday	(1 day) New Zealand, Scotland; (2 days) Japan
	Public Holiday	(1 day) Botswana, Czechoslovakia, Grenada, Mauritius, Mongolia, Romania, St Lucia, Seychelles, Taiwan, Western Samoa, Yugoslavia; (2 days) South Korea
	Bank Holiday	Taiwan
3	Revolution Anniversary	Burkina Faso
4	Independence Day	Burma
	Martyrs of Independence	Zaire
5	*Epiphany	Venezuela
6	Epiphany	Andorra, Austria, Cyprus, Dominican Republic, Greece, Italy, Liechtenstein, Puerto Rico, San Marino, Spain, Sweden
	Army Day	Iraq
7	Christmas (Eastern Orthodox)	Egypt, Ethiopia

9	Day of National Mourning	Panama
10	*Twelfthtide	Finland
11	Hostos' Birthday	Puerto Rico
	King Prithvi Memorial Day	Nepal
	Republic Proclamation Day	Albania
13	Liberation Day	Togo
15	Adults' Day	Japan
16	Martyrs' Day	Benin
18	Revolution Day	Tunisia
19	Epiphany	Ethiopia
	*Martin Luther King's Birthday	Puerto Rico, USA (34 States and DC)
20	Army Day	Lesotho, Mali
	National Heroes' Day	Cape Verde Islands, Guinea-Bissau
21	Feast of Our Lady of Altagracia	Dominican Republic
22	Discovery Day	St Vincent
24	Economic Liberation Day	Togo
26	*Australia Day	Australia
	Duarte's Day	Dominican Republic
	Republic Day	India
27	St Devote's Day	Monaco
28	Democracy Day	Rwanda
29	*Chinese New Year	(1 day) Brunei, South Korea, Malaysia; (2 days) Singapore; (3 days) Hong Kong, Taiwan
	*Spring Festival	(3 days) Macao
30	*Spring Festival	(4 days) China
31	Independence Day	Nauru

FEBRUARY

1	Senegambia Day	Gambia, Senegal
2	Candlemas Day	Liechtenstein
3	Basanta Panchami	Nepal
	Heroes' Day	Mozambique, São Tome and Principe
	St Blás' Day	Paraguay

4	Commencement of the Armed Struggle	Angola
	Independence Day	Sri Lanka
5	Arusha Declaration Anniversary	Tanzania
	Constitution Day	Mexico
	St Agatha's Day	San Marino
6	Waitangi Day/ National Day	New Zealand
7	Independence Day	Grenada
8	8th February Revolution	Iraq
9	St Maron's Day	Lebanon
11	Armed Forces Day	Liberia
	National Foundation Day	Japan
	Youth Day	Cameroon
12	Lincoln's Birthday	USA (many States)
	*Macha Bucha Day	Thailand
	Union Day	Burma
16	*Washington's Birthday	Puerto Rico, USA
18	Independence Day	Gambia
19	Late King Tribhuvan Memorial and Democracy Day	Nepal
21	Shaheed Day	Bangladesh
22	Independence Day	St Lucia
23	National Day	Brunei
	Republic Day	Guyana
25	National Day	(3 days) Kuwait
	Revolution Day	Surinam
26	*Maha Shivarata	Nepal
	*Maha Sivarathri	Sri Lanka
27	Independence Day	Dominican Republic

MARCH

1	Heroes' Day	Paraguay
	Independence Movement Day	South Korea

2	*Carnival	(1 day) Andorra, St Lucia; (2 days) Bolivia, Brazil, Dominica, Ecuador, Panama, Uruguay, Venezuela
	Declaration of Establishment of Authority of People	Libya
	*Discovery Day	Guam
	Peasants' Day	Burma
	*Shrove Monday	Greece, Luxembourg
	Victory of Adwa Day	Ethiopia
3	*Carnival	Liechtenstein, Portugal
	*Mardi Gras	Haiti
	Martyrs' Day	Malawi
	*Shrove Tuesday	Monaco
	Throne Day	Morocco
	Unity Day	Sudan
4	*Ash Wednesday	Jamaica
5	Chiefs' Day	Vanuatu
6	Independence Day	Ghana
8	International Women's Day	Mongolia, USSR
	National Day	Libya
	Revolution Day	Syria
	Women's Day	Cape Verde Islands, Guinea-Bissau, Yemen PDR
9	Baron Bliss Day	Belize
	*Commonwealth Day	Swaziland
10	Labour Day	South Korea
11	*Decoration Day	Liberia
12	Anniversary of Renewal	Gabon
	Independence Day	Mauritius
	Moshoeshoe's Day	Lesotho
15	J J Roberts' Day	Liberia
17	St Patrick's Day	Irish Republic, Northern Ireland
18	Day of the Supreme Sacrifice	Congo
19	St Joseph's Day	Andorra, Costa Rica, Liechtenstein, San Marino, Venezuela

20	Independence Day	Tunisia
	Oil Day	Iran
21	Juárez' Birthday	Mexico
	New Year's Day	Afghanistan
	Now Rooz	(4 days) Iran
	Spring Day	Iraq
	Vernal Equinox	Japan
	*Youth Day	Zambia
23	Pakistan Day	Pakistan
	*Emancipation Day	Puerto Rico
	*St Joseph's Day Holiday	Colombia
25	Greek Independence Day	Cyprus, Greece
	Universal Vote	San Marino
26	Independence Day	Bangladesh
27	*Ascension of the Prophet Muhammad	Indonesia
	Resistance Day	Burma
28	Liberation Day (British Troops)	Libya
29	Anniversary of President Boganda's Death	Central African Republic
	Memorial Day	Madagascar
30	*Youth Day/Chinese Martyrs' Day	Taiwan
31	*Icaka New Year	Indonesia
	National Day	Malta

APRIL

1	Bank Holiday	Burma
	Captain Regent's Day	San Marino
	Islamic Republic Day	Iran
	*Liberation Day	Uganda
	Youth Day	Benin
2	13th of Farvardin	Iran
3	Proclamation of 2nd Republic	Guinea
4	National Day	Hungary, Senegal
5	Arbor Day	South Korea

6	Chakri Memorial Day	Thailand
	Ching Ming Festival	Hong Kong, Macao, Taiwan
	Founder's Day	South Africa
	Patriots' Day	Ethiopia
	Revolution Day	Sudan
7	Mozambican Women's Day	Mozambique
9	Martyrs' Day	Tunisia
10	*National Fast and Prayer Day	Liberia
11	National Heroes' Day	Costa Rica
12	*Palm Sunday (Eastern Orthodox)	Egypt
	*Redemption Day	Liberia
13	*Monday of Holy Week	Uruguay
	Songkran Festival Day	Thailand
14	Americas' Day	Haiti, Honduras
	Sinhala and Tamil New Year	Nepal, Sri Lanka
	*First Day of Passover	Israel
	*Thingyan Holiday	(3 days) Burma
	*Tuesday of Holy Week	Uruguay
15	Assumption of Power by Supreme Military Council	Niger
	*Bengali New Year	Bangladesh
	*Holy Wednesday	El Salvador, Uruguay
16	De Diego's Birthday	Puerto Rico
	*Holy Thursday	Argentina, Brazil, Colombia, Costa Rica, Denmark, Ecuador, El Salvador, Guatemala, Honduras, Iceland, Mexico, Nicaragua, Norway, Paraguay, Philippines, Spain, Uruguay, Venezuela
17	Burmese New Year	Burma
	Evacuation Day	Syria
	*Good Friday	most Western countries
18	*Easter/Holy Saturday	Australia, Belize, Botswana, Brazil, Chile, Costa Rica, Cyprus, Fiji, France, Ghana, Guatemala, Hong Kong, Macao, Malawi, Mexico, Papua New Guinea, Seychelles, Solomon Islands, Spain, Uganda, Western Samoa, Zambia
	Independence Day	Zimbabwe

19	Constitution Day	Venezuela
	*Easter Day	most Western countries
	Landing of the 33 Orientales	Uruguay
	Defence Forces Day	Zimbabwe
	Republic Day	Sierra Leone
20	*Easter Monday	most Western countries
	*Last Day of Passover	Israel
	*Sham Al-Naseem/El-Nassim	Egypt, Sudan
21	*Easter Tuesday	Nauru
	Independence Hero Tiradentes	Brazil
23	*First Day of Summer	Iceland
	National Sovereignty and Children's Day	Turkey
24	Victory Day	Togo
25	Anzac Day	Australia, New Zealand, Tonga, Western Samoa
	Liberation Day	Italy, Portugal, Macao
	National Flag Day	Swaziland
	Sinai Liberation Day	Egypt
26	*Day of Remembrance	Israel
	Union Day	Tanzania
27	Sawr Revolution Day	Afghanistan
	National Day	Togo
29	Emperor's Birthday	Japan
30	Queen's Birthday	Netherlands

MAY

1	International Labour Day/ May Day	(1 day) many countries; (2 days) Bulgaria, Yemen Arab Republic, USSR, Yugoslavia; (3 days) Romania
2	Birthday of HM Jigme Dorji Wangchuck	Bhutan
	King's Birthday	Lesotho
3	Constitution Day	Japan

4	*Bank Holiday	UK
	*Labour Day/May Day Holiday	Barbados, St Kitts-Nevis, St Vincent
5	Birthday of Crown Prince Tupouto'a	Tonga
	Children's Day	Japan, South Korea
	Coronation Day	Thailand
	Liberation Day	Netherlands
	Puebla Battle	Mexico
6	Martyrs' Day	Syria
8	*Armistice Day 1945	France, Monaco
9	National Day	Czechoslovakia
	Victory Day	USSR
11	*Visakha Bucha Day	Thailand
12	*Full Moon of Kason	Burma
	*Vesak Day	Malaysia, Singapore
13	*Waisak/Vesak Full Moon	Indonesia; (2 days) Sri Lanka
14	Independence Day	Israel
	Kamuzu Day	Malawi
	National Day	Paraguay
	National Unification Day	Liberia
15	*Revelation of the Koran	Brunei
	*General Prayer Day	Denmark
	Independence Day	Paraguay
17	Constitution Day	Nauru, Norway
18	Las Piedras Battle	Uruguay
	*Victoria Day	Canada
19	Youth and Sports Day	Turkey
20	Mouvement Populaire de la Revolution (MPR) Day	Zaire
	National Day	Cameroon
21	Battle of Iquique	Chile
22	National Heroes' Day	Sri Lanka
23	Fête Nationale	Morocco
	Labour Day	Jamaica

259

24	Day of Slav Literature, Bulgarian Education and Culture	Bulgaria
	Independence Battle	Ecuador
25	Africa Day	Chad, Mali, Mauritania, Zambia, Zimbabwe
	*Spring Bank Holiday	Gibraltar, UK
	Bermuda Day	Bermuda
	*Commonwealth Day Holiday	Belize
	Independence Day	Argentina, Jordan
	*Memorial Day	Puerto Rico, USA
27	*Ascension Eve	France, Ivory Coast, Madagascar
28	*Ascension	Andorra, Austria, Belgium, Botswana, Burkina Faso, Burundi, Cameroon, Central African Republic, Denmark, France, FRG, Haiti, Iceland, Indonesia, Ivory Coast, Lesotho, Liechtenstein, Luxembourg, Madagascar, Monaco, Namibia, Netherlands, Norway, Rwanda, Senegal, South Africa, Swaziland, Switzerland
	*Eid-al-Fitr	Jordan
29	*Bank Holiday	Belgium
	*Hari Raya Puasa	(1 day) Singapore; (2 days) Brunei
	*Feast of Fitr	(1 day) Ethiopia; (2 days) Algeria, Indonesia
	*Ramazan Bayram	Cyprus
30	*Feast of Fitr	Sri Lanka
31	Republic Day	Namibia, South Africa

JUNE

1	*Ascension Holiday	Colombia, Venezuela
	Children's Day	Cape Verde Islands
	Independence Holiday	(3 days) Western Samoa
	*June Holiday	Irish Republic
	Madaraka Day	Kenya
	Mother's Day	Central African Republic
	*Queen's Birthday Observance	New Zealand
	*Tuen Ng/Dragon Boat Festival	Hong Kong, Macao, Taiwan
	Victory Day	Tunisia

2	Coronation of the Fourth Hereditary King	Bhutan
	National Day	Italy
	Youth Day	Tunisia
3	*Pentecost	Israel
	The Supreme Head of State's Birthday	Malaysia
4	Emancipation Day	Tonga
	June 4th Revolution Day	Ghana
5	Constitution Day	Denmark
	15th Khordad Uprising	Iran
	*Labour Day Holiday	Bahamas
	Liberation Day	Seychelles
	President's Birthday	Equatorial Guinea
6	Flag Day	Sweden
	Memorial Day	South Korea
	*Whitsuntide	Finland, France
7	Liberation Day	Chad
8	*Whit Monday	Andorra, Austria, Bahamas, Barbados, Belgium, Burkina Faso, Central African Republic, Denmark, Dominica, France, FRG, Gabon, GDR, Greece, Grenada, Iceland, Ivory Coast, Liechtenstein, Luxembourg, Madagascar, Monaco, Netherlands, Norway, Rwanda, St Kitts-Nevis, St Lucia, St Vincent, Senegal, Solomon Islands, Sweden, Switzerland, Trinidad and Tobago
	*Queen's Birthday Observance	Australia (except Western Australia)
10	Camões and Portuguese Communities/Portugal Day	Macao, Portugal
	Great Arab Revolt and Army Day	Jordan
	Malvinas Islands Memorial	Argentina
11	Evacuation Day (US Troops)	Libya
12	Independence Day	Philippines
	Peace with Bolivia	Paraguay
	*Queen's Birthday Observance	Solomon Islands

261

13	*Queen's Birthday	Hong Kong, St Kitts-Nevis
15	*Bank Holiday	Macao
	*Queen's Birthday Observance	Bermuda, Fiji, Hong Kong
17	Independence Day	Iceland
	National Day	FRG
18	*Corpus Christi	Andorra, Austria, Bolivia, Brazil, Costa Rica, Dominican Republic, Equatorial Guinea, Grenada, Haiti, Liechtenstein, Macao, Paraguay, Poland, Portugal, St Lucia, Seychelles, Spain, Trinidad and Tobago
	Evacuation Day	Egypt
	Fête Dieu	Monaco
19	Artigas Day	Uruguay
	Labour Day	Trinidad and Tobago
	*Midsummer Eve	Finland, Sweden
	Righting Day	Algeria
20	Flag Day	Argentina
	*Midsummer Day	Finland, Sweden
22	Corrective Move	Yemen PDR
	*Corpus Christi Holiday	Colombia, Venezuela
23	National Day	Luxembourg
24	Anniversary of Currency, Promulgation, Constitution and Day of Fishers	Zaire
	Battle of Carabobo	Venezuela
	City of Macao Day	Macao
	St John's Day	Andorra
25	Independence Day	Mozambique
26	Independence Day	Madagascar, Somali
	*Independence Feast	(2 days) Djibouti
29	*Bank Holiday	El Salvador
	Independence Day	Seychelles
	Sts Peter and Paul	Chile, Colombia, Costa Rica, Peru, San Marino, Venezuela
30	Army Day	Guatemala
	Bank Holiday	Ecuador, El Salvador, India, Peru, Sri Lanka
	Independence Day	Zaire

JULY		
1	Bank Holiday	Bangladesh, Egypt, Guatemala, Pakistan, Taiwan
	Canada Day	Canada (except Newfoundland)
	*Caricom Day	St Vincent
	Day of Freedom	Surinam
	Independence Day	Burundi, Rwanda
	Mid-Year Holiday	Thailand
	Republic Day	Ghana
	Takeover Day	Nauru
	Union Day	Somali
2	*Carnival	St Vincent
3	*Independence Day Holiday	USA (many States)
4	Fighters' Day	Yugoslavia
	Independence Day	Puerto Rico, USA
	Philippine-American Friendship Day	Philippines
5	Independence Day	Algeria, Venezuela
	National Day	Rwanda
6	*Caribbean Day	Guyana
	*Family Day	Lesotho
	*Heroes' Day	Zambia
	*Republic Day	Malawi
7	Independence Day	Solomon Islands
	Saba Saba Peasants' Day	Tanzania
	*Unity Day	Zambia
9	Independence Day	Argentina
	Youth Day	Morocco
10	Armed Forces Day	Mauritania
	Full Moon of Waso	Burma
	Independence Day	Bahamas
11	National Day	(3 days) Mongolia
12	Independence Day	São Tome and Principe
13	*Buddhist Lent	Thailand
	*National Holiday	(2 days) Monaco
	*Law of 20 Dec. 1906	France
	*Orangeman's Day Holiday	Northern Ireland

14	Bastille Day	France
	14th July Revolution	Iraq
15	The Sultan of Brunei's Birthday	Brunei
17	Constitution Day	South Korea
	Munoz-Rivera's Birthday	Puerto Rico
	17th July Revolution	Iraq
18	Constitution Day	Uruguay
19	Anniversary of the Sandinista Revolution	Nicaragua
	Martyrs' Day	Burma
20	Independence Day	Colombia
	*President's Day	Botswana
21	First Sermon of Lord Buddha and Death of Jigme Dorji Wangchuck	Bhutan
	National Day	Belgium
	*Public Holiday	Botswana
22	King's Birthday	Swaziland
	National Day	Poland
23	Egyptian National Day	Egypt, Libya, Syria
24	Bolivar's Day	Ecuador, Venezuela
25	Annexation of Guanacaste	Costa Rica
	Constitution Day	Puerto Rico
	National Holiday	Cuba
	Republic Day	Tunisia
	St James' Day/Santiago Day	Spain
26	Independence Celebrations	Liberia; (2 days) Maldives
	National Rebellion Day	Cuba
27	Barbosa's Birthday	Puerto Rico
	*National Holiday	Cuba
28	Independence Celebrations	(2 days) Peru
	People's Holiday	San Marino
30	Independence Day	Vanuatu
	*Cup Match Holiday	Bermuda

| 31 | Revolution Day | Congo |
| | *Somers Day | Bermuda |

AUGUST

1	Discovery Day	Trinidad and Tobago
	Freedom Day	Guyana
	Harvest Day	Rwanda
	National Day	Switzerland
	Parents' Day	Zaire
	*Santa Domingo Day	Nicaragua
2	Our Lady of the Angels	Costa Rica
3	Armed Forces Day	Equatorial Guinea
	*August Holiday Monday	Dominica, Fiji, Iceland, Irish Republic, St Kitts-Nevis, Scotland
	Emancipation Day	Bahamas, Grenada, St Lucia, St Vincent
	Farmers' Day	Zambia
	*Independence Day	Jamaica, Niger
	*Kadooment Day	Barbados
	Martyrs of Colonialism	Guinea-Bissau
	President's Birthday	Tunisia
	*San Salvador Feast	(4 days) El Salvador
4	Arafa	Afghanistan
	*Fast of Av	Israel
	*Id-al-Adha	(3 days) Lebanon
	National Holiday	Burkina Faso
	Public Holiday	Grenada
	*Wakfet Arafet	Egypt
5	*Courban Bairam/ Kurban Bayram	(1 day) Cyprus; (2 days) Egypt; (4 days) Turkey
	*Eid Adha	(3 days) Afghanistan
	*Hari Raya Haji	Singapore
	*Id-al-Adha	Algeria, Ethiopia, Indonesia
6	*Id-ul-Azha	Sri Lanka
	Independence Day	Bolivia
7	National Holiday	Colombia

9	National Day	Singapore
10	Independence Day	Ecuador
	*Public Holiday	Singapore
11	Accession of King Hussein	Jordan
	Heroes' Day	(2 days) Zimbabwe
	Independence Day	Chad
12	Queen's Birthday	Thailand
13	Independence Day	Central African Republic
	The Three Glorious Days	(3 days) Congo
	Women's Day	Tunisia
14	Independence Day	Pakistan
	Mid-August Holiday	(2 days) Italy
	Oued-Ed-Dahab	Morocco
15	Assumption	most Roman Catholic countries
	Constitution Day	Equatorial Guinea
	Independence Day	India
	Liberation Day	South Korea
	Mothers' Day	Costa Rica
	National Constitution Day	Papua New Guinea
	St Mary's Day	Gambia
16	Restoration of the Republic	Dominican Republic
17	Anniversary of General San Martin's Death	Argentina
	*Assumption Holiday	Colombia, Luxembourg
	*Bank Holiday	Belgium
	Independence Day	Gabon, Indonesia
19	Independence Day	Afghanistan
20	Constitution Day	Hungary
23	National Day	Romania
24	*National Holiday	Liberia, Romania
25	Constitution Day	Paraguay
	Independence Day	Uruguay
26	*Muslim New Year	Algeria, Djibouti, Egypt, Indonesia, Malaysia
29	*Public Holiday	Hong Kong
30	St Rose of Lima Day	Peru

31	*Bank Holiday	Macao
	Independence Day	Trinidad and Tobago
	*Liberation Day	Hong Kong
	National Day	Malaysia
	*Summer Bank Holiday	UK (except Scotland)

SEPTEMBER

1	Anniversary of the Arrival of the Military Committee for National Recovery	Central African Republic
	Libya Unity Day	Libya, Syria
	President's Report	Mexico
2	Independence Day	Vietnam
3	*Ashora/Achoura	Afghanistan, Algeria
	Independence Day	Qatar
	Liberation Day	Monaco
	St Marinus Day	San Marino
	3 Sept. 1934 Commemoration	Tunisia
6	Armed Forces Day	São Tome and Principe
	Defence of Pakistan Day	Pakistan
	Independence Day	Swaziland
7	Independence Day	Brazil
	*Labour Day	Bermuda, Canada, Puerto Rico, USA
	*Settlers' Day	Namibia
	Victory Day	Mozambique
8	*Cultural Festival	Rwanda
	Our Lady of Meritxell	Andorra
9	National Day	(2 days) Bulgaria
10	National Day	Belize
11	Anniversary of the Death of Quaid-e-Azam	Pakistan
	Ethiopian New Year and Reunion of Eritrea with Ethiopia	Ethiopia
	National Liberation	Chile

12	Revolution Day	Ethiopia
	National Day	Cape Verde Islands, Guinea-Bissau
14	Battle of San Jacinto	Nicaragua
15	Independence Day	Costa Rica, El Salvador, Guatemala, Honduras, Nicaragua
	Respect for the Aged Day	Japan
16	Independence Day	Mexico, Papua New Guinea
17	Day of the National Hero	Angola
18	National Anniversary	Chile
	Victory of Uprona	Burundi
19	Armed Forces Day	Chile
	Independence Day	St Kitts-Nevis
21	Independence Day	Belize
22	National Day	Mali
23	Autumn Equinox	Japan
	National Day	Saudi Arabia
24	Establishment of the Republic	Guinea-Bissau
	Feast of Our Lady of Mercy	Dominican Republic
	*Jewish New Year 5748	(2 days) Israel
	Republic Day	Trinidad and Tobago
25	Armed Forces Day	Mozambique
	Referendum Day	Rwanda
26	YAR National Day	Yemen Arab Republic; Yemen People's Democratic Republic
27	Feast of the Finding of the True Cross	Ethiopia
28	Birthday of Confucius	Taiwan
	*Queen's Birthday Observance	Western Australia
29	Battle of Boqueron Day	Paraguay
30	Agricultural Reform Day	São Tome and Principe
	National Day	Botswana

OCTOBER

1	Armed Forces Day	South Korea
	Bank Holiday	Burma
	Captain Regent's Day	San Marino
	National Day	(1 day) Macao, Nigeria; (2 days) China
	Public Holiday	Botswana
2	Independence Day	Guinea
	Mahatma Gandhi's Birthday	India
3	*Day of Atonement	Israel
	Francisco Morazán's Birthday	Honduras
	National Foundation Day	South Korea
4	Independence Day	Lesotho
5	Constitution Day	Vanuatu
	*National Sports Day	Lesotho
	Portugal Republic Day	Macao, Portugal
	Thanksgiving Day	St Lucia
	*United Nations Day	Barbados
6	Armed Forces Day	Egypt
	Liberation Day	Syria
7	Constitution Day	USSR
	*End of Buddhist Lent	Burma
	Evacuation Day	Libya
	Foundation Day	GDR
	*Moon Festival	South Korea, Taiwan
8	*Chinese Mid-Autumn Festival	Hong Kong, Macao
	Combat of Angamos	Peru
	*Feast of Tabernacles (First Day)	Israel
9	Independence Day	Uganda
	Independence of Guayaquil	Ecuador
	Korean Alphabet Day	South Korea
10	Beginning of the Independence Wars	Cuba
	Health-Sports Day	Japan
	Kruger Day	Namibia, South Africa
	National Day	Fiji, Taiwan

12	*Columbus Day	Argentina, Belize, Colombia, Ecuador, El Salvador, Mexico, Puerto Rico, USA (most States), Uruguay, Venezuela
	Day of the Race	Chile, Costa Rica, Guatemala, Paraguay
	Discovery Day	Bahamas, Honduras
	Lotu-o-Tamai	Western Samoa
	National Day	Equatorial Guinea, Spain
	*Revolution Anniversary Observance	Panama
	*Thanksgiving	Canada
14	Founder's Day/Youth Day	Zaire
	Revolution Day	Yemen PDR
15	Evacuation Day	Tunisia
	*Feast of Tabernacles (Last Day)	Israel
17	Dessaline's Day	Haiti
	Mothers' Day	Malawi
19	*National Heroes' Day	Jamaica
20	Kenyatta Day	Kenya
	1944 Revolution Anniversary	Guatemala
21	Armed Forces Day	Honduras
	*Deepavali	Malaysia, Singapore, Sri Lanka
	Revolution Anniversary	(2 days) Somali
22	*Diwali	Fiji
23	Chulalongkorn Day	Thailand
24	Independence Day	Zambia
	United Nations Day	Haiti, Swaziland
25	Restoration Day	Taiwan
26	Armed Forces Day	Benin, Rwanda
	*Labour Day	New Zealand
	National Day	Austria
	*October Holiday	Irish Republic
	*Restoration Day Observance	Taiwan
27	Angam Day	Nauru
	Anniversary of the country's name change	Zaire
	Independence Day	St Vincent

28	Greek National Day	Cyprus, Greece
29	Turkish National Day	Cyprus, Turkey
31	*All Saints' Observance	Finland, Sweden
	Birthday of Chiang Kai-Shek	Taiwan
	Chung Yeung Festival	Hong Kong
	*Festival of Ancestors	Macao

NOVEMBER

1	All Saints' Day	most Roman Catholic countries
	Anniversary of the Revolution	Algeria
2	*All Saints' Observance	most Roman Catholic countries
	All Souls' Day	Ecuador, El Salvador, Haiti, Macao, Mexico, Uruguay
	*Arbor Day Observance	Western Samoa
	*Bank Holiday	Belgium
	Commemoration of the Dead	San Marino
	*Law of 23 Dec. 1904	France
	Memorial Day	Brazil
	*Prophet Mohammed's Birthday	Fiji
3	Culture Day	Japan
	Independence Day	Dominica
	Independence from Colombia	Panama
	Independence of Cuenca	Ecuador
	*Mouloud Al-Nabi	Djibouti
4	*Birthday of the Prophet	Cyprus, Indonesia, Malaysia
	Constitution Day	Tonga
	Flag Day	Panama
	St Charles' Day	Andorra
5	Anniversary of the First Cry of Independence	El Salvador
	*Full Moon of Tazaungdaing	Burma
	*Milad-Un-Nabi	Sri Lanka
	*Thanksgiving Day	Liberia
6	Al-Massira Day	Morocco

271

7	Anniversary of the October Socialist Revolution	Bulgaria, Hungary, Mongolia; (2 days) USSR
	National Revolution Day	Bangladesh
8	Queen's Birthday	Nepal
9	Iqbal Day	Pakistan
11	Armistice/Remembrance/ Veterans' Day	Belgium, Bermuda, Canada, France, Monaco Puerto Rico, USA
	Birthday of HM Jigme Singye Wangchuck	(3 days) Bhutan
	Independence Day	Angola
	Republic Day	(2 days) Maldives
12	Birthday of Dr Sun Yat Sen	Taiwan
14	King Hussein's Birthday	Jordan
	Maulid	Ethiopia
	Readjustment Day	Guinea-Bissau
	Proclamation of the Republic	Brazil
16	*Independence of Cartagena	Colombia
	*Prince Charles' Birthday	Fiji
17	Armed Forces Day	Zaire
18	*Day of Penance	FRG
	National Day	Morocco; (2 days) Oman
	Vertières Day	Haiti
19	Discovery Day	Puerto Rico
	Garifuna Day	Belize
	Liberation Day	Mali
	Prince of Monaco Holiday	Monaco
20	Mexican Revolution	Mexico
22	Independence Day	Lebanon
23	Labour Thanksgiving Day	Japan
24	National Day	Zaire
25	Independence Day	Surinam
26	*Thanksgiving	Puerto Rico, USA

28	Independence Day	Albania, Mauritania
	Independence from Spain	Panama
	Proclamation of the Republic	Chad
29	Liberation Day	Albania
	President Tubman's Birthday	Liberia
	Republic Day	(2 days) Yugoslavia
30	Independence Day	Barbados, Yemen PDR
	National Day	Benin
	National Heroes' Day	Philippines
	*Unity Day	Vanuatu

DECEMBER

1	Proclamation of the Republic	Central African Republic
	Restoration of Independence	Macao, Portugal
2	National Day	Laos; (2 days) United Arab Emirates
4	King Tupou I Day	Tonga
5	Discovery Day	Haitī
	King's Birthday	Thailand
6	Independence Day	Finland
7	Independence Day	Ivory Coast
	*King's Birthday Observance	Thailand
8	Immaculate Conception	most Roman Catholic countries
	Mothers' Day	Panama
9	Independence Day	Tanzania
10	Constitution Day	Thailand
	Human Rights Day	Equatorial Guinea
	Foundation of the Popular Movement for the Liberation of Angola (MPLA)	Angola
12	*National Holiday	Mauritania
	Independence Day	Kenya
	Our Lady of Guadalupe	Mexico

13	Republic Day	Malta
	St Lucia Day	St Lucia
16	Day of the Covenant	Namibia, South Africa
	King Mahendra Memorial Day and Constitution Day	Nepal
	National Day	Bahrain
	Victory Day	Bangladesh
17	National Day	Bhutan
18	National Day	Niger
21	Power of the People Day	São Tome and Principe
22	Tree Planting Day	Malawi
24	Christmas Eve	Austria, Cape Verde Islands, Denmark, Finland, Liechtenstein, Macao, Portugal, San Marino, Sweden, (and a half-holiday in most other countries)
25	Christmas Day	all countries EXCEPT: Afghanistan, Albania, Algeria, Bahrain, Bhutan, Bulgaria, China, Cuba, Egypt, Ethiopia, Iran, Iraq, Israel, Japan, Kuwait, Libya, Maldives, Mauritania, Mongolia, Morocco, Nepal, Oman, Qatar, Romania, Saudi Arabia, Somali, Thailand, Tunisia, Turkey, USSR, United Arab Emirates, Yemen Arab Republic, Yemen PDR, Yugoslavia
26	Boxing Day/Christmas Holiday/St Stephen's Day	most countries
28	*Boxing Day Observance/ Christmas Holiday/ St Stephen's Holiday	Irish Republic, Luxembourg, New Zealand, Nigeria, Papua New Guinea, UK, Vanuatu
29	Christmas Holiday	Irish Republic, Northern Ireland
	King's Birthday	Nepal
30	Bank Holiday	Colombia, El Salvador
	National Day	Madagascar
	Rizal Day	Philippines
31	Bank Holiday/New Year's Eve/St Sylvester's Day	many countries
	Feed Yourself Day	Benin
	Foundation of the Party and People's Republic of Congo	Congo
	Revolution Day	Ghana

24 MAPS

24.1 Europe and EEC

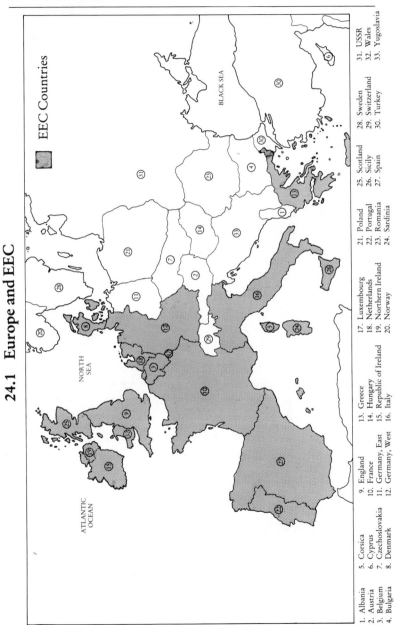

EEC Countries

1. Albania
2. Austria
3. Belgium
4. Bulgaria
5. Corsica
6. Cyprus
7. Czechoslovakia
8. Denmark
9. England
10. France
11. Germany, East
12. Germany, West
13. Greece
14. Hungary
15. Republic of Ireland
16. Italy
17. Luxembourg
18. Netherlands
19. Northern Ireland
20. Norway
21. Poland
22. Portugal
23. Romania
24. Sardinia
25. Scotland
26. Sicily
27. Spain
28. Sweden
29. Switzerland
30. Turkey
31. USSR
32. Wales
33. Yugoslavia

24.2 Counties and Regions of the UK and Ireland

SCOTLAND
48. Borders
49. Central
50. Dumfries and
    Galloway
51. Fife
52. Grampian
53. Highland
54. Lothian
55. Orkney
56. Shetland
57. Strathclyde
58. Tayside
59. Western Isles

NORTHERN
IRELAND
60. Antrim
61. Armagh
62. County Down
63. Fermanagh
64. Londonderry
65. Tyrone

REPUBLIC OF
IRELAND
74. Carlow
75. Cavan
76. Clare
77. Cork
78. Donegal
79. Dublin
80. Galway
81. Kerry
82. Kildare
83. Kilkenny
84. Laoighis
85. Leitrim
86. Limerick
87. Longford
88. Louth
89. Mayo
90. Meath
91. Monaghan
92. Offaly
93. Roscommon
94. Sligo
95. Tipperary
96. Waterford
97. Westmeath
98. Wexford
99. Wicklow

ENGLAND
1. Avon
2. Bedfordshire
3. Berkshire
4. Buckinghamshire
5. Cambridgeshire
6. Cheshire
7. Cleveland
8. Cornwall
9. Cumbria
10. Derbyshire
11. Devon
12. Dorset
13. Durham
14. East Sussex
15. Essex
16. Gloucestershire
17. Greater London
18. Greater Manchester
19. Hampshire
20. Hereford and
    Worcester
21. Hertfordshire
22. Humberside
23. Isle of Man (**NB**
    Crown Dependency
    not UK county)
24. Isle of Wight
25. Kent
26. Lancashire
27. Leicestershire
28. Lincolnshire
29. Merseyside
30. Norfolk
31. Northamptonshire
32. Northumberland
33. North Yorkshire
34. Nottinghamshire
35. Oxfordshire
36. Shropshire
37. Somerset
38. South Yorkshire
39. Staffordshire
40. Suffolk
41. Surrey
42. Tyne and Wear
43. Warwickshire
44. West Midlands
45. West Sussex
46. West Yorkshire
47. Wiltshire

WALES
66. Clwyd
67. Dyfed
68. Gwent
69. Gwynedd
70. Mid Glamorgan
71. Powys
72. South Glamorgan
73. West Glamorgan

24.3   UK Travel Networks

24.3A   Motorways of UK and Ireland

24.3B   British Rail InterCity Routes

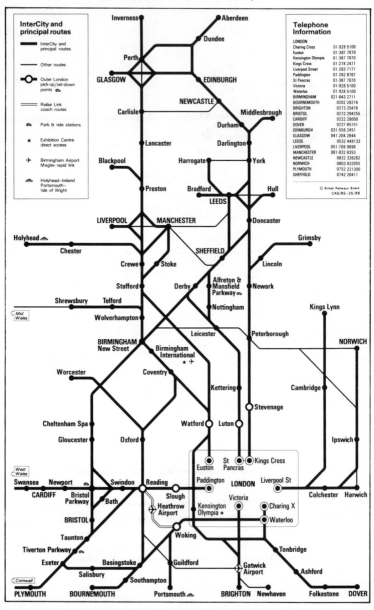

InterCity and principal routes

▬▬▬ InterCity and principal routes

──── Other routes

⊶ Outer London pick-up/set-down points ⇌

═══ Railair Link coach routes

⇌ Park & ride stations

✳ Exhibition Centre direct access

✈ Birmingham Airport Maglev rapid link

⇌ Holyhead–Ireland Portsmouth–Isle of Wight

Telephone Information

LONDON
Charing Cross	01-928 5100
Euston	01-387 7070
Kensington Olympia	01-387 7070
Kings Cross	01-278 2477
Liverpool Street	01-283 7171
Paddington	01-262 6767
St Pancras	01-387 7070
Victoria	01-928 5100
Waterloo	01-928 5100
BIRMINGHAM	021-643 2711
BOURNEMOUTH	0202 28216
BRIGHTON	0273 25476
BRISTOL	0272 294255
CARDIFF	0222 28000
DOVER	0227 65151
EDINBURGH	031-556 2451
GLASGOW	041-204 2844
LEEDS	0532 448133
LIVERPOOL	051-709 9696
MANCHESTER	061-832 8353
NEWCASTLE	0632 328262
NORWICH	0603 632055
PLYMOUTH	0752 221300
SHEFFIELD	0742 26411

© British Railways Board
CAS/BS-25/86

278

24.3C Airports of UK and Ireland

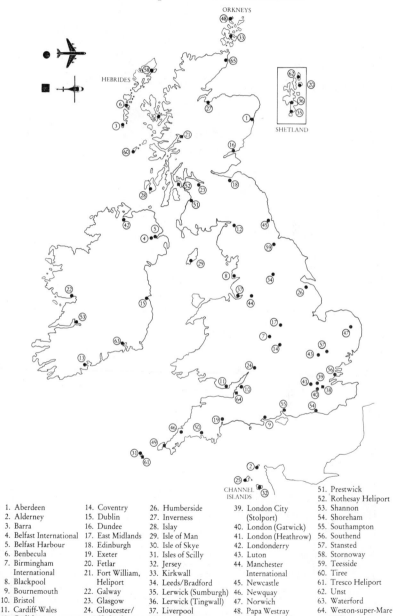

1. Aberdeen
2. Alderney
3. Barra
4. Belfast International
5. Belfast Harbour
6. Benbecula
7. Birmingham International
8. Blackpool
9. Bournemouth
10. Bristol
11. Cardiff-Wales
12. Carlisle
13. Cork
14. Coventry
15. Dublin
16. Dundee
17. East Midlands
18. Edinburgh
19. Exeter
20. Fetlar
21. Fort William, Heliport
22. Galway
23. Glasgow
24. Gloucester/Cheltenham
25. Guernsey
26. Humberside
27. Inverness
28. Islay
29. Isle of Man
30. Isle of Skye
31. Isles of Scilly
32. Jersey
33. Kirkwall
34. Leeds/Bradford
35. Lerwick (Sumburgh)
36. Lerwick (Tingwall)
37. Liverpool
38. London, Battersea Heliport
39. London City (Stolport)
40. London (Gatwick)
41. London (Heathrow)
42. Londonderry
43. Luton
44. Manchester International
45. Newcastle
46. Newquay
47. Norwich
48. Papa Westray
49. Penzance Heliport
50. Plymouth
51. Prestwick
52. Rothesay Heliport
53. Shannon
54. Shoreham
55. Southampton
56. Southend
57. Stansted
58. Stornoway
59. Teesside
60. Tiree
61. Tresco Heliport
62. Unst
63. Waterford
64. Weston-super-Mare Heliport
65. Wick

Note: this map shows CAA licensed airports which have at least one resident airline, and CAA licensed heliports. *(See also Chapter 22.4)*

24.4 Time Zones

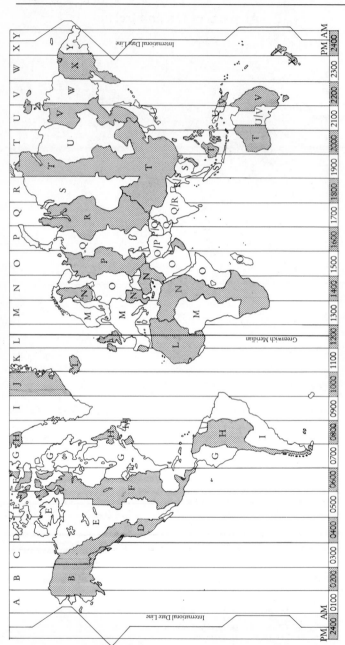

WORLD TIMES AT 12 NOON GMT

Note: some countries have adopted half-hour time zones which are indicated on the map as a combination of two coded zones. For example, it is 1730 hours in India at 1200 GMT. The standard times shown above are subject to variation in certain countries where Daylight Saving/Summer Time operates for part of the year. (*See also Chapter 22.2.*)

25 WEIGHTS AND MEASURES

25.1 Metric and imperial

Quick equivalents

Often it is only necessary to make approximate conversions between metric and imperial measurements and the following rough equivalents are useful. (For *precise* conversion figures consult the tables on p 282).

Length

1 in	2·5 cm	1 cm	0·4 in
1 ft	0·3 m	1 m	1·1 yd
1 yd	0·9 m	1 km	0·6 mile
1 fathom	1·8 m		
1 mile	1·6 km		
1 nautical mile	1·8 km		

Weight

1 oz	28 gm	1 g	0·03 oz
1 lb	0·4 kg	1 kg	2·2 lb
1 stone	6·3 kg	1 quintal	2 cwt
1 cwt	51 kg	1 tonne	0·9 ton
1 ton	1·02 tonnes		

Capacity

1 cu in	16 cm^3	1 cm^3	0·06 cu in
1 cu ft	0·03 m^3	1 m^3	1·3 cu yd
1 cu yd	0·75 m^3	1 litre	1·75 pints
1 pint	0·5 litres	1 hectolitre	2·75 bushels
1 quart	1·1 litres		
1 gallon	4·5 litres		
1 bushel	36·3 litres		

Area

1 sq in	6·5 cm^2	1 cm^2	0·15 sq in
1 sq ft	0·1 m^2	1 m^3	1·2 sq yd
1 sq yd	0·8 m^2	1 acre	120 sq yd
1 sq mile	259 hectares	1 hectare	2·5 acres
1 acre	4047 m^2	1 km^2	0·4 sq miles

Conversion tables

The following tables may be used to convert imperial units to metric units, and vice versa.

cm		in	m		ft	km		miles
2·54	1	0·3937	0·3048	1	3·28084	1·60934	1	0·62137
5·08	2	0·7874	0·6096	2	6·562	3·219	2	1·243
7·62	3	1·1811	0·9144	3	9·843	4·828	3	1·864
10·16	4	1·5748	1·2192	4	13·123	6·437	4	2·485
12·70	5	1·9685	1·5240	5	16·404	8·047	5	3·107
15·24	6	2·3622	1·8288	6	19·685	9·656	6	3·728
17·78	7	2·7559	2·1336	7	22·966	11·265	7	4·350
20·32	8	3·1496	2·4384	8	26·247	12·875	8	4·971
22·86	9	3·5433	2·7432	9	29·528	14·484	9	5·592

cm²		sq in	m²		sq ft	km²		sq miles
6·4516	1	0·155	0·0929	1	10·764	2·58999	1	0·3861
12·903	2	0·310	0·1858	2	21·528	5·18	2	0·772
19·355	3	0·465	0·2787	3	32·292	7·77	3	1·158
25·806	4	0·620	0·3716	4	43·056	10·36	4	1·544
32·258	5	0·775	0·4645	5	53·820	12·95	5	1·931
38·710	6	0·930	0·5574	6	64·583	15·54	6	2·317
45·161	7	1·085	0·6503	7	75·347	18·13	7	2·703
51·613	8	1·240	0·7432	8	86·111	20·72	8	3·089
58·064	9	1·395	0·8361	9	96·875	23·31	9	3·475

cm³		fl oz	litre		imp gal	g		oz
28·4131	1	0·0352	4·5456	1	0·21997	28·3495	1	0·03527
56·826	2	0·0704	9·092	2	0·4399	56·6990	2	0·07054
85·239	3	0·1056	13·638	3	0·6599	85·0485	3	0·10581
113·652	4	0·1408	18·184	4	0·8799	113·3980	4	0·14108
142·065	5	0·1760	22·730	5	1·0998	141·7475	5	0·17635
170·478	6	0·2112	27·277	6	1·3198	170·0970	6	0·21162
198·891	7	0·2464	31·823	7	1·5398	198·4465	7	0·24689
227·305	8	0·2816	36·369	8	1·7598	226·7960	8	0·28216
255·718	9	0·3168	40·915	9	1·9797	255·1455	9	0·31743

kg		lb	tonne		ton	newton		lbf
0·45359	1	2·20462	1·0160	1	0·984205	4·4482	1	0·2248
0·907	2	4·409	2·032	2	1·9684	8·896	2	0·4496
1·361	3	6·614	3·048	3	2·9526	13·345	3	0·6744
1·814	4	8·818	4·064	4	3·9368	17·793	4	0·8992
2·268	5	11·023	5·080	5	4·9210	22·241	5	1·1240
2·722	6	13·228	6·096	6	5·9052	26·689	6	1·3489
3·175	7	15·432	7·112	7	6·8894	31·138	7	1·5737
3·629	8	17·637	8·128	8	7·8736	35·586	8	1·7985
4·082	9	19·842	9·144	9	9·8578	40·034	9	2·0233

How to use the tables

The central figures can be read as either metric or imperial, e.g. on line 7 of the first table:

$$7 \text{ in} = 17.78 \text{ cm} \qquad 7 \text{ cm} = 2.7559 \text{ in.}$$

Values above 9 may be obtained by decimal point adjustment and addition, e.g. in the third table:

To convert 573 miles to km	500 miles = 804.7km
	70 miles = 112.65km
	3 miles = 4.828km
	573 miles = 922.178km

Such results should be treated as approximations. In the example given the conversion of 500 miles is correct only to the nearest 0.1 km, therefore the final sum can be correct only to the same degree; hence the conversion of 573 miles from the table is correctly stated as '922.2 km to the nearest 0.1 km'. The precise figure for 573 miles is 922.154 112 km.

25.2 International system of units

The Système International d'Unités has been internationally adopted as a coherent system of units (SI units of measurement) for the measurement of all physical quantities.

Base units

Seven independent quantities have been chosen which are measured in the *base units* of the system (Table 25.2   p 285).

Derived units

To measure any other quantity, a *derived unit* is formed by multiplying or dividing any two or more base units, or powers of them, together; e.g. speed is measured in metres per second, where the metre and the second are base units. The more frequently used derived units have been given names of their own for convenience, e.g. power is measured in watts, where one watt is derived from one kilogram multiplied by one metre squared divided by one second cubed.

Abbreviations

Each unit name has an agreed abbreviation (column 3 in Table 25.2). To abbreviate a unit compounded from more than one unit name, the abbreviations of the constituent units are written with a small space between them, e.g. a newton metre is abbreviated N m. Where a unit is raised to a power, the conventional algebraic indices are used, e.g. a metre squared, or square metre, is abbreviated m^2.

Division of units

The word *per* indicates division by all succeeding units. To abbreviate units which are to be divided, negative indices are preferred, but a solidus (/) may be used, e.g. metre per second is abbreviated $m\ s^{-1}$ or m/s, kilogram per metre cubed is $kg\ m^{-3}$ or kg/m^3.

Multiples and submultiples

To avoid the use of many zeros in either very large or very small numbers, prefixes indicating multiplication or division by some power of a thousand (Table 25.1) can be added to a unit, e.g. mega-: multiply by a million, so a megawatt (1 MW) is a million watts; milli-: divide by a thousand, so a milliwatt (1 mW) is a thousandth of a watt.

TABLE 25.1

prefix	abbrev.	factor	
exa-	E	10^{18}	= million million million
peta-	P	10^{15}	= thousand million million
tera-	T	10^{12}	= million million
giga-	G	10^{9}	= thousand million
mega-	M	10^{6}	= million
kilo-	k	10^{3}	= thousand
*hecto-	h	10^{2}	= hundred
*deca- *deka-	da	10	= ten
*deci-	d	10^{-1}	= tenth
*centi-	c	10^{-2}	= hundredth
milli-	m	10^{-3}	= thousandth
micro-	μ	10^{-6}	= millionth
nano-	n	10^{-9}	= thousand millionth
pico-	p	10^{-12}	= million millionth
femto-	f	10^{-15}	= thousand million millionth
atto-	a	10^{-18}	= million million millionth

*These prefixes are used only exceptionally where kilo- or milli- would be impractical; thus a centimetre ($\frac{1}{100}$ metre) is accepted as an everyday unit of convenient size, but it is not a preferred SI unit.

TABLE 25.2

Equivalents are given to four significant figures' accuracy, except where they are exact as indicated by bold figures.

Quantity	SI unit	abbreviation and derivation	equivalent in British units	SI equivalent of one British unit
Base units				
Length	**metre**	m	3·281 feet	**0·3048** m
Mass*	**kilogram**	kg	2·205 pounds	**0·453 592 37** kg
Time	**second**	s	—	—
Temperature interval	**kelvin**	K	$\frac{9}{5}$ °Fahrenheit	$\frac{5}{9}$ K
Current, electric	**ampere**	A	—	—
Amount of substance	**mole**	mol	—	—
Luminous intensity	**candela**	cd	0·9833 candle	1·017 cd
Some derived and additional units				
Length	kilometre	km	0·6214 mile	1·609 km
	centimetre	cm	0·3937 inch	**2·54** cm
*Mass	tonne, metric ton	t = Mg	0·9842 ton	1·016 t
Area	metre squared	m²	10·76 ft²	0·092 90 m²
	hectare	ha = 10 000 m²	2·471 acres	0·4047 ha
Volume	metre cubed	m³	1·308 yd³	0·7646 m³
	litre	l = dm³	0·2200 gal (UK)	4·546 litres
*Weight; Force	newton	N = kg m s⁻²	0·2248 lbf	4·448 N
Energy; Work; Heat	joule	J = m N = kg m² s⁻²	0·2388 calorie 0·7376 ft lbf 1 kJ = 0·9478 Btu	**4·1868** J 1·356 J 1·055 kJ
Power	watt	W = J s⁻² = kg m² s⁻³	0·001 341 hp	745·7 W
Velocity; Speed	metre per second	m s⁻¹	3·281 ft/s	**0·3048** m s⁻¹
	kilometre per hour	km h⁻¹	0·6214 mile/h	1·609 km h⁻¹
Pressure; Stress	pascal	Pa = N m⁻²	1 kPa = 0·1450 lbf/in²	6·895 k Pa
	bar	bar = 10⁵ Pa	14·50 lbf/in²	0·068 95 bar
Frequency	hertz	Hz = s⁻¹	1 c/s	1 Hz
Angle	radian	rad	57° 18′	$\frac{\pi}{180}$ rad
Solid angle	steradian	sr	—	—
Temperature, absolute	degree Celsius or Centigrade	°C	$(\frac{9}{5}$ t°C + 32) °F	$\frac{5}{9}$ (t °F − 32) °C
	kelvin	K	$\frac{9}{5}$ degree Rankine	$\frac{5}{9}$ K
Potential difference; Electromotive force	volt	V = kg m² s⁻³ A⁻¹ = W A⁻¹		
Resistance Reactance electrical Impedance	ohm	Ω = kg m² s⁻³ A⁻² = V A⁻¹		
Capacitance, electrical	farad	F = kg⁻¹ m⁻² s⁴ A² = A s V⁻¹		
Inductance, magnetic	henry	H = kg m² s⁻² A⁻² = V s A⁻¹		

*The mass of a body is the quantity of matter in it; its weight is the force with which the earth attracts it, and is directly proportional to its mass. The use of the term "weight", where "mass" is strictly intended, is acceptable in non-technical usage when referring to objects within the earth's atmosphere.

25.3 Mathematical symbols

+	plus	⊂	is a subset of
−	minus	∃	there exists
±	plus or minus	∀	for all values of
×	multiply by	*	denotes an operation
÷	divide by	⇔	is equivalent to; if and only if
=	is equal to	⇒	implies
≡	is identically equal to	{} ∅	empty set
≈ ≑	is approximately equal to	{x, y}	the set whose members are x and y
≠	is not equal to	E	universal set
>	is greater than	N	the set of natural numbers
≫	is much greater than	W	the set of whole numbers
≯	is not greater than	Z	the set of integers
<	is less than	Q	the set of rational numbers
≪	is much less than	R	the set of real numbers
≮	is not less than	C	the set of complex numbers
≥	is greater than or equal to	→	maps to
≤	is less than or equal to	∴	therefore
∩	intersection	∵	because
∪	union	∠	angle
∈	is member of set	∣	parallel
		L	perpendicular

25.4 Miscellaneous

Temperature conversion

°Celsius		°Fahrenheit
−17·78	0	32·0
−12·22	10	50·0
−6·67	20	68·0
−1·11	30	86·0
4·44	40	104·0
10·00	50	122·0
15·56	60	140·0
21·11	70	158·0
26·68	80	176·0
32·24	90	194·0
37·80	100	212·0

Boiling point of water 100°C/212°F   **Freezing point of water 0°C/32°F**

Clothing and shoe sizes

The following tables show equivalent sizes of clothes and shoes according to the British, American, and continental European measurement systems. The equivalents are only approximate.

Shoes

British	3	3½	4	4½	5	5½	6	6½	7
American	4½	5	5½	6	6½	7	7½	8	8½
Continental	36	36	37	38	38	39	39	40	41

British	7½	8	8½	9	9½	10	10½	11
American	8½	9½	9½	10½	10½	11½	11½	12
Continental	42	42	43	43	44	44	45	46

Men's shirts

British	14	14½	15	15½	16	16½	17	17½
American	14	14½	15	15½	16	16½	17	17½
Continental	35/36	37	38	39/40	41	42	43	44

Women's dresses

British	8	10	12	14	16	18	20	22
American	6	8	10	12	14	16	18	20
Continental	36	38	40	42	44	46	48	50

Women's sweaters

British	34	36	38	40	42	44
American	34	36	38	40	42	44

Men's sweaters

British	34	36	38	40	42	44
American	small	medium	large	extra large		

Inch/centimetre equivalents

inch	12	13	14	15	16	17	18	19	20	21
cm	30	33	35	38	41	43	45	48	51	53
inch	22	23	24	25	26	27	28	29	30	32
cm	55	58	61	63	66	69	71	74	76	81
inch	34	36	38	40	42	44	46	48	50	52
cm	85	91	97	102	107	112	117	122	127	132

Roman numerals

I	=	1		L	=	50
II	=	2		LI	=	51
III	=	3		LII, etc.	=	52, etc.
IV	=	4		LX	=	60
V	=	5		LXI	=	61
VI	=	6		LXII, etc.	=	62, etc.
VII	=	7		LXX	=	70
VIII	=	8		LXXI	=	71
IX	=	9		LXXII, etc.	=	72, etc.
X	=	10		LXXX	=	80
XI	=	11		LXXXI	=	81
XII	=	12		LXXXII, etc.	=	82, etc.
XIII	=	13		XC	=	90
XIV	=	14		XCI	=	91
XV	=	15		XCII, etc.	=	92, etc.
XVI	=	16				
XVII	=	17		C	=	100
XVIII	=	18		CC	=	200
XIX	=	19		CCC	=	300
XX	=	20		CD	=	400
XXI	=	21		D	=	500
XXII, etc.	=	22, etc.		DC	=	600
XXX	=	30		DCC	=	700
XXXI	=	31		DCCC	=	800
XXXII, etc.	=	32, etc.		CM	=	900
XL	=	40				
XLI	=	41		M	=	1000
XLII, etc.	=	42, etc.		MM	=	2000

The Greek alphabet

A	α	alpha	= a		N	ν	nū	= n
B	β	bēta	= b		Ξ	ξ	xī	= x *(ks)*
Γ	γ	gamma	= g		O	o	omicron	= o
Δ	δ	delta	= d		Π	π	pī	= p
E	ϵ	epsilon	= e		P	ϱ	rhō	= r
Z	ζ	zēta	= z		Σ	$s\,\sigma$	sigma	= s
H	η	ēta	= ē		T	τ	tau	= t
Θ	$\theta\ \vartheta$	thēta	= th *(th)*		Υ	υ	ūpsilon	= u *(yoo, oŏ, ü)*
					(often transcribed *y*)			
I	ι	iōta	= i		Φ	ϕ	phī	= ph *(f)*
K	$\varkappa$	kappa	= k		X	χ	chī	= kh *(hh)*
					(often transcribed *ch*, as in Latin)			
Λ	λ	lambda	= l		Ψ	ψ	psī	= ps
M	μ	mū	= m		Ω	ω	ōmega	= ō

The Greek alphabet, apart from its use as the official script in Greek-speaking areas, is of worldwide importance as a source of symbols used in all branches of science and mathematics. The equivalents in our alphabet given above are intended as a guide to transliteration and as an indication of the anglicised pronunciation of ancient Greek. We have not attempted to describe modern Greek pronunciation.

26 MEDIA

This chapter lists a selection of useful UK media addresses. The addresses and telephone numbers listed were correct at the time of going to press. For additional information on the media market consult:

Benn's Media Directory	PO Box 20, Sovereign Way, Tonbridge, Kent TN9 1RQ
Brad (British Rate & Data)	76 Oxford Street, London W1N 9FD

For local companies and contacts consult *Yellow Pages*. (See also Chapter 6: Advertising and Publicity.)

26.1 Magazines and journals

Business

The Banker	102-8 Clerkenwell Road, London EC1M 5SA
British Business	Millbank Tower, Millbank, London SW1P 4QU
Business	234 King's Road, London SW3 5UA
Business Bulletin	The Guildhall, Dartmouth, Devon TQ6 9RY
The Business Economist	11 Bay Tree Walk, Watford, Herts WD1 3RX
Business Graduate	John Wiley & Sons Ltd, Baffins Lane, Chichester, Sussex PO19 1UD
Business Traveller	49 Old Bond Street, London W1X 3AF
COMLON	LCCI Examinations Board, Marlowe House, Station Road, Sidcup, Kent DA15 7BJ
Economic Affairs	2 Lord North Street, London SW1P 3LB
Investors Chronicle	Greystoke Place, Fetter Lane, London EC4A 1ND
Link-Up	Mark Allen Publishing Ltd, Battersea Business Centre, 103-9 Lavender Hill, London SW11 5QL
Money Observer	The Observer Ltd, 8 St Andrew's Hill, London EC4V 5JA
Multinational Business	Economist Publications, 40 Duke Street, London W1A 1DW
Small Business	Small Business Bureau, 32 Smith Square, London SW1P 3HH
Stockmarket Confidential	57-61 Mortimer Street, London W1N 7TP
Venture UK	Cover Publications Ltd, PO Box 381, Mill Harbour, London E14 9TW

Business equipment

Buckley's Guide to Office Automation	IT Publishing Ltd, 6 Hanover Square, London W1R 9HH
Business Computing & Communications	Morgan-Grampian House, 30 Calderwood Street, London SE18 6QH
Business Equipment Digest	BED Business Journals Ltd, 44 Wallington Square, Wallington, Surrey SM6 8RG
Business Systems & Equipment	Maclean Hunter Ltd, 76 Oxford Street, London W1N 9FD
Communication Technology Impact	Elsevier International Bulletins, Mayfield House, 256 Banbury Road, Oxford OX2 7DH
Microinfo	Microinfo Ltd, PO Box 3, Alton, Hants GU34 2PG
Office Equipment Index	Maclaren Publishers Ltd, PO Box 109, Maclaren House, 19 Scarbrook Road, Croydon CR9 1QH
Office Equipment News	AGB Business Publications, Audit House, Field End Road, Eastcote, Ruislip, Middx HA4 9LT
Office Magazine	Patey Doyle (Publishing) Ltd, Wilmington House, Church Hill, Wilmington, Dartford, Kent DA2 7EF
Office Trade News	(address as above)
Office Weekly	Good Times Publishing, 4a Duke Street, Manchester Square, London W1M 6EA
Televisual	Centaur Ltd, 60 Kingly Street, London W1R 5LH
Wharton's Complete Office Automation Guide	Wharton Publishing Ltd, Regal House, London Road, Twickenham, Middx TW1 3QS
What to Buy for Business	What to Buy Ltd, 11 King's Road, Chelsea, London SW3 4RP

Current affairs

Contemporary Review	61 Carey Street, London WC2 2JG
The Economist	25 St James's Street, London SW1A 1HG
Encounter	44 Great Windmill Street, London W1V 7PA
New Internationalist	42 Hythe Bridge Street, Oxford OX1 2EP
New Socialist	150 Walworth Road, London SE17 1JT
New Society	5 Sherwood Street, London W1V 7RA
New Statesman	14-16 Farringdon Lane, London EC1R 3AU
Newsweek	25 Upper Brook Street, London W1Y 1PD
Parliamentary Affairs	Oxford University Press, Walton Street, Oxford OX2 6DP

The Spectator	56 Doughty Street, London WC1N 2LL
Time Magazine	Time & Life Building, New Bond Street, London W1Y 0AA
Tribune	308 Gray's Inn Road, London WC1X 8DY

Management and administration

Better Your Business	Causton Hall, Cross Road, Croydon, Surrey CR0 6TB
The British Journal of Administrative Management	40 Chatsworth Parade, Petts Wood, Orpington, Kent BR5 1RW
Business Express	22 Vineyard Road, Wellington, Telford, Shropshire TF1 1HB
Chief Executive	Morgan-Grampian House, 30 Calderwood Street, London SE18 6QH
Co-operative Marketing & Management	418 Chester Road, Manchester M16 9HP
The Director	10 Belgrave Square, London SW1X 8PH
First Voice	Yorkshire Communications Group, 17A Monckton Road, Wakefield, W Yorks WF2 7AL
Futures	PO Box 63, Bury Street, Guildford, Surrey GU2 5BH
Government Executive	342/362 Corn Exchange Buildings, Manchester M4 3BU
In Business Life	1 High Street, Christchurch, Dorset BH23 1AE
In Business Now	Millbank Tower, Millbank, London SW1P 4QU
Industrial Management & Data Systems	62 Toller Lane, Bradford, W Yorks BD8 9BY
International Management	McGraw Hill House, Shoppenhangers Road, Maidenhead, Berks SL6 2QL
Journal of General Management	Henley Management College, Greenlands, Henley-on-Thames, Oxon RG9 3AU
Long Range Planning	Headington Hill Hall, Oxford OX3 0BW
Management & Marketing Abstracts	(address as above)
Management News	British Institute of Management, Management House, Parker Street, London WC2B 5PT
Management Today	30 Lancaster Gate, London W2 3LP
Managerial & Decision Economics	Baffins Lane, Chichester, Sussex PO19 1UD
Mind Your Own Business	106 Church Road, London SE19 2UB

| Western Management | The Studio, Hinton Lane, Clifton, Bristol BS8 4NS |
| Works Management | Franks Hall, Horton Kirby, Kent DA4 9LL |

Personnel management

Employment Gazette	HMSO, PO Box 276, London SW8 5DT
IPM Digest	8 Lichfield Road, Kew, Surrey TW9 3JR
Journal of Management Development	62 Toller Lane, Bradford, W Yorks BD8 9BY
Manpower	Manpower House, 270-2 High Street, Slough SL1 1LJ
Personnel Management	1 Hills Place, London W1R 1AG
Personnel Resource Management	PO Box 45, Dorking, Surrey RH5 5YZ
Personnel Review	62 Toller Lane, Bradford, W Yorks BD8 9BY

26.2 Newspapers

Daily

Daily Express	121-8 Fleet Street, London EC4P 4JT
	01-353 8000
Daily Mail	Northcliffe House, Tudor Street, London EC4Y 0JA
	01-353 6000
Daily Mirror	33 Holborn, London EC1P 1DQ
	01-353 0246
Daily Record	40 Anderston Quay, Glasgow G3 8DA
	041-248 7000
Daily Telegraph	135 Fleet Street, London EC4P 4BL
	01-353 4242
Financial Times	10 Cannon Street, London EC4P 4BY
	01-248 8000
Glasgow Herald	195 Albion Street, Glasgow G1 1QP
	041-552 6255
The Guardian	119 Farringdon Road, London EC1R 3ER
	01-278 2332
The Independent	40 City Road, London EC1Y 2DB
	01-253 1222
Irish News & Belfast Morning News	113-7 Donegall Street, Belfast BT1 2GE
	(0232) 24164
Morning Star	75 Farringdon Road, London EC1M 3JX
	01-405 9542

The Scotsman	20 North Bridge, Edinburgh EH1 1YT 031-225 2468
The Star	Great Ancoats Street, Manchester M60 4HB 061-236 2112
The Sun	1 Pennington Street, London E1 9XP 01-481 4100
The Times	1 Pennington Street, London E1 9XN 01-481 4100
Today	70 Vauxhall Bridge Road, London SW1V 2RP 01-630 1333
Western Mail	Thomson House, Havelock Street, Cardiff CF1 1WR (0222) 33022

Sunday newspapers

The Mail on Sunday	Northcliffe House, London EC4Y 0JA 01-353 6000
News of the World	1 Pennington Street, London EC1 9BH 01-481 4100
News on Sunday	Caxton House, 13-16 Borough Road, London SE1 0AL 01-928 4902/4898
The Observer	8 St Andrew's Hill, London EC4V 5JA 01-236 0202
Press & Journal	PO Box 43, Lang Stracht, Mastrick, Aberdeen AB9 8AF (0224) 690222
Sunday Express	121-8 Fleet Street, London EC4P 4JT 01-353 8000
Sunday Mail	40 Anderston Quay, Glasgow G3 8DA 041-248 7000
Sunday Mirror	33 Holborn, London EC1P 1DQ 01-353 0246
Sunday News	51-9 Donegall Street, Belfast BT1 2GB (0232) 244441
Sunday People	9 New Fetter Lane, London EC4A 1AR 01-353 0246
Sunday Post	2 Albert Square, Dundee DD1 9QJ (0382) 23131
Sunday Telegraph	135 Fleet Street, London EC4P 4BL 01-353 4242
Sunday Times	1 Pennington Street, London E1 9XW 01-481 4100
Sunday Today	70 Vauxhall Bridge Road, London SW1V 2RP 01-630-1333

Evening newspapers

Belfast Telegraph	124 Royal Avenue, Belfast BT1 1EB
	(0232) 221242
The Evening Express	PO Box 43, Lang Stracht, Mastrick, Aberdeen AB9 8AF
	(0224) 690222
The Evening News	20 North Bridge, Edinburgh EH1 1YT
	031-225 2468
The Evening Times	195 Albion Street, Glasgow G1 1QP
	041-552 6255
The London Daily News	33 Holborn Circus, London EC4 1AR
	01-822 2323
The London Standard	121 Fleet Street, London WC1N 2QB
	01-353 8000
South Wales Echo	Thomson House, Havelock Street, Cardiff CF1 1WR
	(0222) 33022

National newspaper groups

Newspaper Publishing PLC	40 City Road, London EC1 2DB
	01-253 1222
Northcliffe Newspapers Group Ltd	Tudor Street, London EC4Y 0JA
	01-353 4000
Thomson Regional Newspapers Ltd	Pemberton House, East Harding Street, London EC4A 3AS
	01-353 9131

26.3 News agencies

Agence France Press (AFP)	Chronicle House, Fleet Street, London EC4Y 8BB
	01-353 7461
Anglo Danish Press (ADP)	Grosvenor Works, Mount Pleasant Hill, London E5 9NL
	01-806 3232
Associated Press (AP)	12 Norwich Street, London EC4A 1BP
	01-353 1515
Canadian Press (CP)	23 Norwich Street, London EC4A 1EJ
	01-353 6355
Deutsche Press-Agentur (DPA)	85 Fleet Street, London EC4P 1BE
	01-353 8594
Gemini News Service	40-43 Fleet Street, London EC4Y 1BT
	01-353 2567
Inter Press Service (IPS)	86-100 St Pancras Way, London NW1 9ES
	01-482 4951

Jewish Chronicle News & Feature Service	25 Furnival Street, London EC4A 1JT 01-405 9252
Jiji Press	IPC, 76 Shoe Lane, London EC4A 3JB 01-353 5417
Middle East News Agency (MENA)	Communications House, Gough Square, London EC4A 3DE 01-353 5455
Newslink Africa	IPC, Suite 441, 76 Shoe Lane, London EC4A 3JB 01-353 0186
New Zealand Associated Press (NZAP)	107 Fleet Street, London EC4A 2AN 01-353 2686
New Zealand Press Association (NZPA)	85 Fleet Street, London EC4Y 1DY 01-353 5430
Reuters	85 Fleet Street, London EC4P 4AJ 01-250 1122
Tass News Agency	Communications House, 12-16 Gough Square, London EC4A 3JH 01-353 9831
United Press International (UPI)	8 Bouverie Street, London EC4Y 8BB 01-353 2282

26.4 Radio

National radio

BBC Radio	Broadcasting House, London W1A 1AA 01-580 4468
BBC Radio North	Broadcasting Centre, 146/146a Woodhouse Lane, Leeds LS2 9PX (0532) 441188
BBC Radio North East	Broadcasting House, New Bridge Street, Newcastle upon Tyne NE1 8AA (0632) 320961
BBC Radio North West	Oxford Road, Manchester M60 1SJ 061-236 8444
BBC Radio Scotland	Queen Street, Edinburgh EH2 1JF 031-225 3131
BBC Radio Ulster	Ormeau Avenue, Belfast BT2 8HQ (0232) 244400
BBC Radio Wales	Llantrisant Road, Llandaff, Cardiff CF5 3YQ (0222) 564888

BBC local radio

BBC Radio Aberdeen	Broadcasting House, Beech Grove Terrace, Aberdeen AB9 2ZT
	(0224) 635233
BBC Radio Bedfordshire	PO Box 476, Luton LU1 5BA
	(0582) 459111
BBC Radio Bristol	PO Box 194, 3 Tyndalls Park Road, Bristol BS8 1PP
	(0272) 741111
BBC Radio Cambridgeshire	PO Box 96, Broadcasting House, Hills Road, Cambridge CB2 1LD
	(0223) 315970
BBC Radio Cleveland	PO Box 1548, Broadcasting House, Newport Road, Middlesbrough TS1 5DG
	(0642) 225211
BBC Radio Clwyd	The Old Schoolhouse, Glanrafon Road, Mold, Clwyd CH7 1PA
	(0352) 56821
BBC Radio Cornwall	Phoenix Wharf, Truro, Cornwall TR1 1UA
	(0872) 75421
BBC Radio Cumbria	Hilltop Heights, London Road, Carlisle CA1 2NA
	(0228) 31661
BBC Radio Derby	PO Box 269, Derby DE1 3HL
	(0332) 361111
BBC Radio Devon	PO Box 100, Exeter EX4 4DB
	(0392) 215651
	PO Box 5, Seymour Road, Plymouth PL3 5BD
	(0752) 260323
BBC Radio Essex	198 New London Road, Chelmsford CM2 9AB
	(0245) 262393
BBC Radio Foyle	PO Box 927, Rock Road, Londonderry BT48 7NE
	(0504) 69101
BBC Radio Furness	Hartington Street, Barrow-in-Furness, Cumbria LA14 5FH
BBC Radio Guernsey	Commerce House, Les Banques, St Peter Port, Guernsey
	(0481) 28977
BBC Radio Gwent	Powys House, Cwmbran, Gwent NP44 1YF
	(06333) 72727
BBC Radio Highland	7 Culduthel Road, Inverness IV2 4AD
	(0463) 221711

BBC Radio Humberside	63 Jameson Street, Hull HU1 3NU
	(0482) 23232
BBC Radio Jersey	Broadcasting House, Rouge Bouillon, St Helier, Jersey
	(0534) 70000
BBC Radio Kent	Sun Pier, Chatham, Kent ME4 4EZ
	(0634) 46284
BBC Radio Lancashire	King Street, Blackburn BB2 2EA
	(0254) 62411
BBC Radio Leeds	Broadcasting House, Woodhouse Lane, Leeds LS2 9PN
	(0532) 442131
BBC Radio Leicester	Epic House, Charles Street, Leicester LE1 3SH
	(0533) 27113
BBC Radio Lincolnshire	PO Box 219, Newport, Lincoln LN1 3DF
	(0522) 40011
BBC Radio London	35a Marylebone High Street, London W1A 4LG
	01-486 7611
BBC Radio Manchester	PO Box 90, New Broadcasting House, Oxford Road, Manchester M60 1SJ
	061-228 3434
BBC Radio Merseyside	55 Paradise Street, Liverpool L1 3BP
	051-708 5500
BBC Radio Nan Eilean	BBC Rosebank, Church Street, Stornoway, Isle of Lewis PA87 2LS
	(0851) 5000
BBC Radio Newcastle	Broadcasting Centre, Barrack Road, Newcastle upon Tyne NE99 1RN
	091-232 4141
BBC Radio Norfolk	Norfolk Tower, Surrey Street, Norwich NR1 3PA
	(0603) 617411
BBC Radio Northampton	PO Box 1107, Northampton NN1 2BE
	(0604) 20621
BBC Radio Nottingham	York House, Mansfield Road, Nottingham NG1 3JB
	(0602) 415161
BBC Radio Orkney	Castle Street, Kirkwall, Orkney KW15 1HD
	(0856) 3939
BBC Radio Oxford	242 Banbury Road, Oxford OX2 7DW
	(0865) 53411
BBC Radio Sheffield	Ashdell Grove, 60 Westbourne Road, Sheffield S10 2QU
	(0742) 686185

BBC Radio Shetland	Brentham House, Lerwick, Shetland ZE1 0LR (0595) 4747
BBC Radio Shropshire	2/4 Boscobel Drive, Shrewsbury SY1 3TT (0743) 248484
BBC Radio Solent	South Western House, Canute Road, Southampton SO9 4PJ (0703) 631311
BBC Radio Solway	Elmbank, Lover's Walk, Dumfries DG7 1NZ (0387) 68008
BBC Radio Stoke-on-Trent	Conway House, Cheapside, Hanley, Stoke-on-Trent ST1 1JJ (0782) 24827
BBC Radio Sussex	1 Marlborough Place, Brighton BN1 1TU (0273) 680231
BBC Radio Tweed	Municipal Buildings, High Street, Selkirk TD7 4BU (0750) 21884
BBC Radio WM (West Midlands)	PO Box 206, Birmingham B5 7SD 021-472 5141
BBC Radio York	20 Bootham Row, York YO3 7BR (0904) 641351

Independent local radio

Beacon Radio (**Wolverhampton**)	PO Box 303, 267 Tettenhall Road, Wolverhampton WV6 0DQ (0902) 757211
BRMB (**Birmingham**)	PO Box 555, Radio House, Aston Road North, Birmingham B6 4BX 021-359 4481/9
Capital Radio (**London**)	Euston Tower, Euston Road, London NW1 3DR 01-388 1288
Chiltern Radio (**Luton/Bedford**)	Chiltern Road, Dunstable LU6 1HQ (0582) 666001
County Sound (**Guildford**)	The Friary, Guildford, Surrey GU1 4YX (0483) 505566
Devonair Radio (**Exeter/Torbay**)	The Studio Centre, 35/37 St David's Hill, Exeter EX4 4DA (0392) 30703
Downtown Radio (**Belfast**)	Newtownards, Co. Down BT23 4ES (0247) 815555
Essex Radio (**Southend/Chelmsford**)	Radio House, Clifftown Road, Southend-on-Sea SS1 1SX (0702) 333711

GWR Radio (**Swindon/ Bristol/West Wilts**)	PO Box 2000, Swindon SN4 7EX (0793) 853222
Hereward Radio (**Peterborough/ Northampton**)	PO Box 225, 114 Bridge Street, Peterborough PE1 1XJ (0733) 46225
Invicta Radio (**Maidstone/ Medway/Kent**)	15 Station Road East, Canterbury CT1 2RB (0227) 67661
Leicester Sound (**Leicester**)	Granville House, Granville Road, Leicester LE1 7RW (0533) 551616
LBC (**London**)	PO Box 261, Communications House, Gough Square, London EC4P 4LP 01-353 1010
Manx Radio (**IOM**)	PO Box 219, Broadcasting House, Douglas Head, Douglas, IOM (0624) 73589
Marcher Sound (**Wrexham/Deeside**)	PO Box 238, Mold Road, Gwersyllt, Wrexham LL11 1BT (0978) 752202
Mercia Sound (**Coventry**)	Hertford Place, Coventry CV1 3TT (0203) 28451
Metro Radio (**Tyne & Wear**)	Radio House, Longrigg, Swalwell, Newcastle upon Tyne NE99 1BB 091-488 3131
Moray Firth Radio (**Inverness**)	PO Box 271, Inverness IV1 1UJ (0463) 224433
NorthSound Radio (**Aberdeen**)	45 King's Gate, Aberdeen AB2 6BL (0224) 632234
Pennine Radio (**Bradford/ Huddersfield/Halifax**)	PO Box 235, Pennine House, Forster Square, Bradford BD1 5NP (0274) 731521
Piccadilly Radio (**Manchester**)	127/131 The Piazza, Piccadilly Plaza, Manchester M1 4AW 061-236 9913
Plymouth Sound (**Plymouth**)	Earl's Acre, Alma Road, Plymouth PL3 4HX (0752) 27272
Radio Aire (**Leeds**)	PO Box 362, 51 Burley Road, Leeds LS3 1LR (0532) 452299
Radio Broadland (**Norwich/ Gt Yarmouth**)	St George's Plain, Colgate, Norwich NR3 1DD (0603) 630621
Radio City (**Liverpool**)	PO Box 194, 8–10 Stanley Street, Liverpool L69 1LD 051-227 5100
Radio Clyde (**Glasgow**)	Clydebank Business Park, Clydebank G81 2RX 041-941 1111

Radio Forth **(Edinburgh)**	Forth House, Forth Street, Edinburgh EH1 3LF 031-556 9255
Radio Hallam **(Sheffield/ Barnsley/Doncaster/ Rotherham)**	PO Box 194, Hartshead, Sheffield S1 1GP (0742) 71188
Radio Luxembourg	38 Hertford Street, London W1Y 8BA 01-493 5961
Radio Mercury **(Reigate/Crawley)**	Broadfield House, Brighton Road, Crawley RH11 9TJ (0293) 519161
Radio Orwell	Electric House, Lloyds Avenue, Ipswich IP1 3HZ (0473) 216971
Radio Tay **(Dundee/Perth)**	PO Box 123, Dundee DD1 9UF (0382) 29551
Radio Tees **(Teesside)**	74 Dovecot Street, Stockton-on-Trent TS18 1HB (0642) 615111
Radio Trent **(Nottingham)**	29/31 Castle Gate, Nottingham NG1 7AP (0602) 581731
Radio 210 **(Thames Valley/ Reading)**	PO Box 210, Reading RG3 5RZ (0734) 413131
Radio Victory **(Portsmouth)**	PO Box 257, Portsmouth PO1 5RT (0705) 827799
Radio West **(Bristol)**	PO Box 963, Watershed, Canons Road, Bristol (0272) 279900
Radio Wyvern **(Hereford/Worcester)**	5/6 Barbourne Terrace, Worcester WR1 3JM (0905) 612212
Red Dragon Radio **(Cardiff)**	Radio House, West Canal Wharf, Cardiff CF1 5XJ (0222) 384041
Red Rose Radio **(Preston/Blackpool)**	St Paul's Square, Preston PR1 1YE (0772) 556301
Saxon Radio **(Bury St Edmunds)**	Long Brackland, Bury St Edmunds (0284) 701511
Severn Sound **(Gloucester/Cheltenham)**	Old Talbot House, 67 Southgate Street, Gloucester GL1 1TX (0452) 423791
Signal Radio **(Stoke-on-Trent)**	Stoke Road, Stoke-on-Trent ST4 2SR (0782) 417111
Southern Sound **(Brighton)**	Radio House, Franklin Road, Portslade BN4 2SS (0273) 422288

Suffolk Group Radio **(Ipswich/Bury St Edmunds)**	Electric House, Lloyds Avenue, Ipswich IP1 3HZ (0473) 216971
Swansea Sound **(Swansea)**	Victoria Road, Gowerton, Swansea SA3 3AB (0792) 893751
Two Counties Radio **(Bournemouth)**	5/7 Southcote Road, Bournemouth BH1 3LR (0202) 294881
Viking Radio **(Humberside)**	Commercial Road, Hull HU1 2SG (0482) 25141
West Sound **(Ayr)**	54 Holmston Road, Ayr KA7 3BD (0292) 283662
Wiltshire Radio	Old Lime Kiln, High Street, Wootton Bassett, Swindon (0793) 853222

26.5 Television

BBC television

BBC Television	Television Centre, Wood Lane, London W12 7RJ 01-743 8000
BBC Breakfast Time	Television Centre, Lime Grove Studios, London W12 7RJ 01-743 8000
BBC TV East	St Catherine's Close, All Saints Green, Norwich NR1 3ND (0603) 619331
BBC TV Midlands	BBC Broadcasting Centre, Pebble Mill Road, Birmingham B5 7QQ 021-472 5353
BBC TV North	Broadcasting Centre, Woodhouse Lane, Leeds LS2 9PX (0532) 441188
BBC TV North East and Cumbria	Broadcasting House, 54 New Bridges Street, Newcastle upon Tyne NE1 8AA (0632) 321313
BBC North West	New Broadcasting House, Oxford Road, Manchester M60 1SJ 061-236 8444
BBC TV Northern Ireland	Ormeau Avenue, Belfast BT2 8HQ (0232) 244400

BBC TV Scotland	BBC Broadcasting House, Queen Margaret Drive, Glasgow G12 8DG 041-339 8844
BBC TV South	South Western House, Canute Road, Southampton SO9 1PF (0703) 26201
BBC TV South West	Broadcasting House, Seymour Road, Plymouth PL3 5BD (0752) 29201
BBC TV Wales	Llantrisant Road, Llandaff, Cardiff CF5 2YQ (0222) 654888
BBC TV West	Broadcasting House, Whiteladies Road, Bristol BS8 2LR (0272) 732211
BBC World Service	Bush House, Strand, London WC2B 4PH 01-257 2090

Independent television

Anglia TV	Anglia House, Norwich NR1 3JG (0603) 615151
Border TV	TV Centre, Carlisle CA1 3NT (0228) 25101
Central Independent TV	Central House, Broad Street, Birmingham B1 2JP 021-643 9898 East Midlands TV Centre, Lenton Lane, Nottingham NG7 2NA (0602) 863322
Channel TV	TV Centre, Rouge Bouillon, St Helier, Jersey, CI (0534) 73999
Channel 4	60 Charlotte Street, London W1P 2AX 01-631 4444
Grampian TV	Queen's Cross, Aberdeen AB9 2XJ (0224) 646464
Granada TV	TV Centre, Manchester M60 9EA 061-832 7211
HTV (Wales)	TV Centre, Cardiff CF5 6XJ (0222) 590590
HTV (West)	TV Centre, Bath Road, Bristol BS4 3HG (0272) 778366
Independent Television News (ITN)	48 Wells Street, London W1P 4DE 01-637 2424

London Weekend TV	South Bank TV Centre, Kent House, Upper Ground, London SE1 9LT
	01-261 3434
Scottish TV	Cowcaddens, Glasgow G2 3PR
	041-332 9999
Sianel Pedwar Cymru (S4C)	Sophia Close, Cardiff CF1 9XY
	(0222) 43421
Television South (TVS)	TV Centre, Northam Road, Southampton SO9 5HZ
	(0703) 34211
	TV Centre, Vinters Park, Maidstone ME14 5NZ
	(0622) 54945
Television South West (TSW)	Derry's Cross, Plymouth PL1 2SP
	(0752) 663322
Thames Television	Thames Television House, 303-316 Euston Road, London NW1 3BB
	01-387 9494
TV-AM	Breakfast TV Centre, Hawley Crescent, London NW1 8EF
	01-267 4300/4377
Tyne Tees Television	TV Centre, City Road, Newcastle upon Tyne NE1 2AL
	091-261 0181
Ulster Television	Havelock House, Ormeau Road, Belfast BT7 1EB
	(0232) 228122
Yorkshire Television	TV Centre, Leeds LS3 1JS
	(0532) 438283

26.6 Direct mail

(See also Chapters 6.4: Advertising and Publicity and 20.1: Royal Mail)

Advice and assistance on direct mail can be obtained from the following organisations:

Direct Mail Producers Association	34 Grand Avenue, London N10 3BP
	01-883 7229
Direct Mail Sales Bureau	12-13 Henrietta Street, London WC2E 8JJ
	01-836 4081
Direct Mail Services Standards Board	92 New Cavendish Street, London W1M 7FA
	01-636 7581

Some companies offering direct mail services
(See also *Yellow Pages* for local companies)

ADS (Marketing Resources)	72 Sackville Street, Manchester M1 3NJ 061-236 6564
Amherst Direct Mail Ltd	Amherst House, Ferring Street, Ferring, Worthing BN12 5JR (0903) 502251
Astro Mailing	3 Elmdon Road, Marston Green, Birmingham B37 7BS 021-779 6771
Avon Direct Mail Services Ltd	Unit 7, Harbour Road Estate, Portishead, Bristol BS20 9EG (0272) 842487
Bowker Mailing Services	Erasmus House, Epping CM16 4BU (0378) 77333
Britannica Mailing Service	Mappin House, 156-162 Oxford Street, London W1N 0HJ 01-637 3371
CCN Communications	70 Sackville Street, Manchester M1 3NJ 061-236 1862
Contract Mail Ltd	97 Kilburn Square, Kilburn High Road, London NW6 6PS 01-328 4447
Datamail Ltd	10 South Bank Business Centre, 140 Battersea Park Road, London SW1 4NB 01-720 1202
Distribution and Media Sales (UK) Ltd	30 Bridge Road, Haywards Heath RH16 1TU (0444) 414041
Halligan Advertising Services Ltd	66 Addison Road, Bromley BR2 9TT 01-646 6917
Hardings Mail Services Ltd	Unit 6, Elms Industrial Estate, St Martin's Way, London SW17 0JH 01-947 8477/8/9
Holborn Direct Mail Co.	Capacity House, 2-6 Rothsay Street, Tower Bridge Road, London SE1 4UD 01-407 6444
Ibis Information Services Ltd	Waterside, Lowbell Lane, London Colney, St Albans AL2 1DX (0727) 25209
Industrial Direct Mail Service	Windsor Court, East Grinstead House, East Grinstead RH19 1XA (0342) 26972
List Management Services Ltd	Nassau House, 122 Shaftesbury Avenue, London W1V 7DJ 01-439 3844

Marketforce Ltd	Advance House, Brent Crescent, London NW10 7XR
	01-961 1880
Pauline Marks Ltd	Postmark House, Cross Lane, London N8 7SD
	01-348 4294
Mastermail Direct Advertising Ltd	Mastermail House, 8 Morocco Street, London SE1 3HB
	01-403 2373
O E McIntyre Ltd	McIntyre House, Canning Place, Liverpool L1 8HY
	01-209 1566
Parade Direct Marketing Ltd	PO Box 145, 127 Hagley Road, Birmingham B16 8XT
	021-455 0223
Response Analysis & Mailing Ltd (RAM)	22 Stephenson Way, London NW1 2HD
	01-387 0832
Simmonds Direct Mail Group	82-84 Peckham Rye, London SE15 4HB
	01-639 0331
Streets Ahead Mailing Services	8 The Quadrant, Hoylake, Merseyside L47 2EE
	051-632 3162
Waterhouse Direct Mail Services	10 Peterborough Mews, New Kings Road, London SW6 3BL
	01-731 6900

27 GLOSSARIES

27.1 Business

acceptance (1) Agreement to enter into a contract. (2) Agreement to pay a bill of exchange, usually by signing it.

accepting house A financial institution which accepts bills of exchange as well as carrying out other financial activities.

annual accounts A company's financial statements, including the profit and loss account and the balance sheet. Public limited companies are required by law to publish annual accounts.

annual percentage rate (APR) A method of calculating the interest rates on hire-purchase agreements. The 1974 Consumer Credit Act prevented sellers from quoting misleading interest rates by requiring them to quote only the APR.

annual report The report which a company sends to its shareholders each year. It may include the annual accounts.

appreciation An increase in the value of an asset or commodity.

assessment (1) The valuation of property in order to calculate the amount to be paid in rates. (2) The examination of income and profit in order to calculate the amount to be paid in tax.

assurance A type of insurance which does not depend on a possible future occurrence. Regular premiums are paid, and a lump sum is paid out by the assurers, either on the death of the assured person or on a stated date.

audit A systematic examination of the financial records of a business, to check that transactions have been accurately recorded and to make sure that the company's statements and reports give a true and fair view of its financial position.

balance sheet A statement of a company's financial position at a specified time. It shows what the company *owns* (i.e. assets) and what it *owes* (i.e. liabilities).

bill of lading An official receipt for goods to be shipped stating the terms and conditions under which the goods will be transported.

black economy Ordinary economic activities carried on in such a way as to avoid the payment of taxes. No invoices or official documents are issued for work done, and payment is in cash or in kind.

black market A situation in which there is an illegal trade in certain goods or services. Shortages, rationing and strict price controls all tend to produce a black market, where prices are usually high.

bonded goods   Imported goods on which duty is payable. They must be stored in a bonded warehouse ('in bond') until the duty is paid or until they are re-exported.

break-even point   The stage in business activity where production and sales are such that total income equals total costs, and neither profit nor loss is made.

British Standards Institution (BSI)   An organisation which lays down minimum standards of quality for a wide range of manufactured goods. A product carrying the BSI 'Kite mark' is one that conforms to BSI quality specifications.

capital expenditure   The buying of machinery and other long-lasting assets which will be used in the production process over a long period of time.

capital gains   Profit obtained by selling an asset. It may be liable to tax.

capital-intensive   A production process or industry which requires a comparatively large amount of capital (money and equipment) in relation to the amount of labour required is called capital-intensive (e.g. oil-refining and car-manufacturing).

cartel   An association between two or more independent organisations producing the same product, arranged to pursue a common policy on controlling prices and production in order to reduce or eliminate competition between cartel members.

collateral security   Documents such as shares or the title deeds to property, given by a borrower to a lender as a safeguard for a loan and returned to the borrower when the loan is repaid.

compound interest   Interest which is calculated on the original amount *plus* any interest which has already accumulated.

cost-benefit analysis   A type of study which compares the cost of a particular course of action with the resulting benefits. It takes into account the 'social' costs and benefits as well as the strictly financial ones.

costing   The process of measuring and analysing the cost of a business activity, product, department, etc. Accurate costing is essential to business control and planning.

critical path analysis   A planning technique showing all the separate jobs within a project, and the time each job should take. The 'critical path' is the order of doing the jobs which will ensure the fewest delays and the minimum cost of the project.

current assets   Assets such as stock, cash in hand and debts owed, which change rapidly in the course of normal business.

current liabilities   Debts or amounts owing to others expected to be paid within twelve months from the date of the balance sheet (e.g. creditors and tax payable).

cybernetics A science which studies communication and control functions in humans and machines. The knowledge gained can be applied to the management of large groups of people or complex systems of machinery.

deed of covenant A legal agreement in which a person promises to pay a fixed sum for an agreed period of time. It enables the payer to deduct tax from the total payment.

deficit (1) The amount by which a company's liabilities are greater in value than its assets or its spending greater than its income. (2) A situation in which the balance of payments shows that imports exceed exports.

deflation A decrease in demand, production and prices, which can be achieved by restricting the amount of money available in the economy.

depreciation (1) A reduction in the value of an asset. (2) This reduction as reflected in a company's accounts. A set percentage of the asset's value is converted into an expense at the end of each accounting period.

devaluation A reduction in the value of a currency as compared with other currencies. It is achieved by lowering the exchange rate, and usually has the effect of reducing a country's imports.

diminishing returns The law of diminishing returns states that, beyond a certain point, *increased* use of a production facility will result in *decreased* output (because of break-downs, etc.).

dumping Selling goods in a foreign market at a price which is below the cost of production, or below the competitive price level in that market.

endowment assurance A combination of life assurance and long-term saving. In return for the payment of regular premiums, the assurance company agrees to pay a fixed sum on a specified future date or on the death of the assured person.

ergonomics The scientific study of man in relation to his working environment. The results obtained are used to make changes in equipment design, working routines and working environment in order to improve efficiency.

exchange control Government regulations concerning foreign currency transactions, designed to protect the stability of the national currency. Britain abolished exchange control in 1979.

exchange rate The ratio at which one currency can be exchanged for another (e.g. 1·50 US dollars to £1). Exchange rates affect the relative cheapness or expensiveness of imports and exports and therefore influence the economy in general.

ex gratia payment A payment which is a favour or goodwill gesture and not the result of any legal obligation or contract.

feasibility study A systematic investigation of a particular project to find out if it is technically possible and if it is desirable from a financial point of view.

fixed assets Assets which will be of use to a business over a long period of time (e.g. land, buildings, equipment and trademarks).

fixed capital Items such as premises and equipment, or the money used to buy them.

fixed costs Any costs which are not affected by the level of production (e.g. rent, rates and interest repayments).

float (1) To launch a company, by drawing up various documents and sending them to the Registrar of Companies for official clearance to proceed with selling shares in the company. (2) A reserve of cash for small expenses, giving change, etc.

flow chart A diagram showing all the stages in a process and the order in which they are performed. (See also under Computing p 320).

franchise An agreement allowing someone to sell someone else's product or service, subject to certain conditions. Franchise-buyers usually have to restrict their operations to a specific area.

freeze (1) A government order that prices and/or wages are to remain at a certain level. (2) A general restriction or ban placed on some activity (e.g. the giving of bank loans or the manufacturing of weapons).

frozen asset Any asset which cannot easily be sold or converted into cash.

gearing The ratio between a company's permanent capital and the total value of loans made to it. The higher the gearing, the greater the proportion of borrowed money to 'own' money.

goodwill (1) The part of the value of a business which results from its popularity and reputation, as opposed to its capital, stock, etc. (2) The difference between the actual price paid for a business and the total value of its assets.

green pound The agreed value of the pound used to express EEC agricultural prices in sterling and to measure the level of Britain's contribution under the Common Agricultural Policy. Its value differs from that of the pound sterling.

gross national product (GNP) The total value of the goods and services produced within a country (i.e. the gross domestic product) plus the income from property held in foreign countries.

group trading When a number of traders join together (e.g. in order to improve distribution) to make bulk buying possible or to cut administration costs, this is called group trading.

hidden price increase A reduction in the quality or quantity of a product or service without any change in price.

holding company A company whose main purpose is to exercise financial control over one or more other companies by acquiring a majority shareholding in it (or them).

hyperinflation A serious economic situation in which the rate of inflation rises very rapidly and the value of money falls steeply.

inflation An economic situation in which the general level of prices increases progressively. This causes the real value of money to fall since a certain amount of money can buy fewer goods and services.

inflationary spiral A situation in which inflation diminishes the real value of money, causing employees to demand higher wages: higher wages result in increased production costs, causing higher prices and raising inflation further.

information technology (IT) Electronic, telecommunications and computer technology as applied to the gathering, recording and communicating of information.

infrastructure Things such as transport systems, power, education, etc. which are essential to the functioning of an economy or the well-being of a nation.

intangible assets Assets such as trademarks and goodwill which have no physical existence but which are of financial benefit to a company.

interim accounts Financial information about a company relating to a period which is shorter than the financial year.

invisible exports and imports The export and import of services. Foreigners holidaying in Britain, or making use of British banking, insurance, shipping services, etc. are providing the country with invisible exports. British people holidaying abroad represent invisible imports.

J-curve A small initial deterioration or decrease followed by a larger improvement or increase. This appears as a J-shaped curve on a graph.

joint and several liability The responsibility of any one member of a group for the actions or debts of any or all of the others, and the responsibility of the group as a whole for the actions or debts of any one member.

Keynesian economics J. M. Keynes was an influential British economist of the 1930s. He argued that governments should spend money to counteract business recessions, and that greater investment in industry was necessary to achieve higher levels of national income.

labour-intensive Any business activity which requires a large amount of labour relative to capital is said to be labour-intensive (e.g. hand-tailoring and repair services).

limited company A company whose shareholders enjoy limited liability. This means that if the company has debts an individual shareholder is personally liable for those debts only up to the value of his or her shareholding.

limited liability See **limited company**.

liquid assets Cash and other assets that can quickly and easily be converted into cash (e.g. shares, bank deposits).

liquidation (1) The winding-up of a company which can no longer pay its debts. (2) The paying of a debt.

liquidator The official receiver appointed by the bankrupt company or by its creditors to make a list of the company's assets and liabilities, sell the assets, pay the debts and distribute any money left over to the shareholders.

liquidity (1) The amount of cash or liquid assets a company has, which can be used to pay debts. In general, a high liquidity is a good thing. (2) A measure of the ease with which an asset can be turned into cash.

loss leader A product in a shop sold at a very low price to attract customers, in the expectation that they will also buy other products and so provide an overall profit for the retailer.

M1 A term used in describing or measuring the UK money supply. M1 equals all notes and coins in current general circulation plus all instantly-withdrawable bank deposits.

M3 M3 equals M1 plus all privately-held bank deposits plus all privately-held foreign currency bank deposits.

macroeconomics The study of economics on a large scale, for example national income, international trade, etc.

microeconomics The study of economics on a small scale, for example, the prices of individual products or the performances of individual companies or industries.

minimum lending rate The minimum rate of interest at which the Bank of England agrees to lend money to discount houses. This in turn influences the rate at which banks and building societies lend money to individuals.

minority shareholding The holding of less than 50% of a company's shares (by an individual or group). Minority shareholders have little influence on the company's policy, but they are legally protected from 'unfair' actions of the majority.

mixed economy An economy in which the ownership of the means of production is partly public (nationalised industries) and partly private (individuals and companies).

monetarism An economic policy based chiefly on the control of a country's money supply, in the belief that this is the main factor influencing the rate of inflation and economic activity.

mutual insurance company A type of insurance company in which the policy-holders are also the shareholders, profits being distributed among them by means of either cash payments or reduced premiums.

net assets The total value of assets (both fixed and current) minus the current liabilities. This figure is usually shown on balance sheets and is an important indication of the value of the company.

net price The price to be paid after taking into account any discounts or deductions.

net profit The gross profit minus all operating and selling costs.

nominal partner A person who allows his or her name to be used in association with a business (e.g. to maintain goodwill) although he or she has no financial interest in it or other connection with it.

operational research Scientific techniques (such as critical path analysis) used to study and improve problem-solving and decision-making in an organisation.

overcapacity The state of having more workers, machinery, factory space, etc. than is needed to meet the existing demand for one's product.

public limited company A company having at least two members and shares which are available to the general public (but not necessarily quoted on the Stock Exchange). It must publish its accounts and must include the words 'public limited company' (or PLC) in its name.

per pro Short for *per procurationem*, a Latin phrase meaning 'by the agency of another'. It is written (in the form **pp**) next to a signature to show that the person is signing on behalf of (and with the full authority of) another.

personal allowance The sum of money a person is allowed to earn which is not subject to income tax. The actual amount is different for married and unmarried people.

price discrimination Pricing a product at different levels for different markets. This can be made possible by the markets being far apart geographically, or by the markets being divided into separate classes of consumer.

price-fixing (1) The setting of prices by the government. (2) An agreement between two or more producers, sellers, etc. to fix the price of a product at a level which is favourable to themselves. This is usually illegal.

prices and incomes policy Government measures to restrict (or ban) wage/salary increases and price increases, in an attempt to reduce inflation and unemployment.

profit and loss account A financial statement of a company's income and spending over an accounting period. A simple profit and loss account shows total sales value minus labour, raw materials, rent and rates costs, etc. to give the trading profit.

profit-sharing An agreement under which employees receive a share of the company's profits.

profit-taking The selling-off of shares in order to profit from the original rise in price.

quango The acronym for 'quasi-autonomous non-governmental (or national government) organisation'—a body set up and funded by the government to supervise or develop activity in areas of public interest.

quid pro quo A Latin phrase meaning 'something for something'. It is used to describe a favour or concession made by one party to a business transaction in return for a previous favour or concession made by the other party.

rationalisation The reorganising of a business activity or industry in order to achieve greater efficiency and savings.

real wages The value of wages expressed not in money but in terms of the goods and services that can be bought with them.

recession A period of decline in overall economic activity, usually accompanied by an increase in unemployment.

reflation An increase in overall economic activity, brought about by the government increasing the supply of currency, reducing interest rates, etc.

registered office The official address of a company, where legal documents, etc. should be sent and where certain records are kept for public inspection.

restrictive practice (1) Any activity which is designed to prevent or curtail competition, and which is therefore against the public interest e.g. price-fixing and agreements to sell only in certain areas. (2) Used to describe certain trade-union-related practices which are felt to be against the public interest.

revaluation (1) The setting of a new value on an asset, e.g. to reflect current market prices more accurately. (2) An increase in the value of a currency as compared with other currencies.

running costs The cost of materials and labour, and anything else required for the normal operation of a machine, a company department or the company as a whole.

secured creditor A creditor who has the right to take and dispose of the assets of a debtor if the debtor fails to pay.

sequestration The removal of an organisation's assets, e.g. to protect its creditors, or while a legal dispute is being settled.

simple interest Interest which is calculated on the original amount only (ignoring any interest which has already accumulated).

sinking-fund A fund formed by regularly setting aside sums of money (which accumulate interest) in order to pay off some future debt, e.g. the replacement of assets.

sole trader A person who owns and controls his or her own business. (See also Chapter 12.1).

standard costing A system in which actual costs are compared with a series of predetermined standard costs. Any major differences between the two sets of figures can then be investigated.

statutory income The estimate of income received during a financial year, which is used to calculate the amount of tax due.

statutory returns The annual return which must be sent to the Registrar of Companies after each annual general meeting. It includes copies of accounts, lists of shareholders, details of directors, etc.

takeover Gaining control of a company by buying the majority of its shares, usually achieved by offering shareholders a figure well above the existing market price for their shares.

tangible assets Assets which have a physical existence, such as equipment and buildings.

tax loss A loss that can be set against taxable profits in order to reduce the amount of tax which has to be paid.

tender An offer to do a job, supply goods, etc. for a certain price. Contracts involving the supply of large numbers of items or the carrying-out of major pieces of work are 'put out to tender' so that various firms compete for the contract.

throughput The amount of material handled by a process or the amount of production achieved, in a specified time.

tolerance The allowable range of variation in the size of a product. It is sometimes expressed as a percentage of the 'ideal' size.

trade cycle The pattern of alternating increase and decrease in general levels of business activity. Many factors affect trade cycles and both the 'slump' and the 'boom' parts of a cycle may vary in extent and in length of time.

trading account A document giving financial information about a company's operation during a specified accounting period.

trading certificate A document issued by the Registrar of Companies which allows a company to start its business activities.

undercapitalised If a company has not enough capital and reserves for it to continue trading at the desired level, it is said to be undercapitalised.

undersubscription The situation that exists when a company wishing to issue share capital seeks applications for shares and fewer shares are applied for than are available.

undistributed profits Profits that have not been paid to shareholders but have been retained in the company (all profits made are owed to shareholders, but directors do not have to pay all the profits to them).

unearned income Income gained from investments, etc. not from working. It is sometimes taxed at a different rate from earned income.

unpresented cheques Cheques written out by an account holder and sent to suppliers or paid for services received, but not yet passed to the account holder's bank for payment.

valuation Estimating the value (in money terms) of something, especially an official estimate made for insurance purposes, etc.

valuation of investment The realisable value of investments held.

value added The difference between the cost of the materials required for some manufacturing process and the money received from the sale of the finished goods.

value-added tax (VAT) A government indirect tax on goods and services, based on the 'value added' as a result of manufacturing and marketing, etc.

variable cost A cost which varies in direct proportion to the output or activity of a business.

vertical integration A situation in which a company merges with (or takes over) another company which is involved in a different stage of producing the same product.

wage differentials The differences in the wages paid to different classes or groups of workers, e.g. to skilled and unskilled workers or to workers doing similar jobs in different industries.

warranty (1) An undertaking in a contract of sale, the breach of which might give rise to a claim for damages. (2) An undertaking, generally written, guaranteeing that goods sold are fit for use, etc., and stating the manufacturer's responsibility to repair or replace the goods should they prove faulty. (3) A declaration by an insured person that statements made by him or her to the insurers are true and that stipulated conditions have been fulfilled.

wasting asset Any asset, especially a natural resource, whose value decreases as it is used up, and which cannot be replaced or renewed.

windfall profit A profit arising, usually suddenly or unexpectedly, as a result of matters not directly connected with the normal business of the company or organisation concerned.

winding-up The closing-down of a business, either voluntarily or by order of the court, with the selling-off of its assets and payments of its debts.

working capital The capital readily available to a company for the day-to-day running of its business. It is what remains when current liabilities are deducted from current assets.

work study The analysis of how jobs are done and the measurement of the time taken to do them, carried out in order to increase efficiency and productivity and to establish standard levels of performance. Also known as time and motion study.

yield gap The difference between what is received in dividends from ordinary shares and the yield from fixed-interest shares.

zero-rated A term denoting goods on which the purchaser pays no VAT and on which the seller can claim back any VAT he or she has already paid.

27.2 Computing

(See also 27.7: Word processing).

access To gain control of a computer system or to retrieve data from a storage device (e.g. main memory) or peripheral unit (e.g. magnetic disk drive).

access time The time taken to retrieve data or information from a storage device. Access times can vary according to the type of storage device used, e.g. access time from a magnetic disk is shorter than from magnetic tape.

acoustic coupler A device which converts electrical pulses from a key-operated machine to sound (acoustic waves) for transmission and reception along telephone lines to and from a computer, permitting computers to be connected with a terminal by a modem and telephone handset.

address As information is entered into a computer, each place in which the information is stored has an address. That address alters as information is moved around. An address is itself a number.

ALGOL Algorithmic Orientated Language. A high level computer programming language used especially for scientific and mathematical applications.

analogue computer A type of computer in which varying electrical currents or voltages, etc. are used to represent other quantities (e.g. forces, speeds) proportionally in working out problems.

applications software A computer program or set of programs designed to carry out specific tasks (e.g. a business application, a game, word processing).

archive (1) To archive is the process of storing data files on a computer in a retrievable form (e.g. hard or floppy disk). (2) Archives are files stored on hard or floppy disk, usually data files rather than software.

ASCII American Standard Code for Information Interchange. An international standard computer code in which eight binary bits are combined to represent letters, numbers and symbols on a computer keyboard. Most VDUs and printers use this code.

assembler A computer program which converts a symbolic language program automatically into a machine language program which can then be directly executed by the computer.

assembly language A programming language in which each statement corresponds to a machine language instruction. It is usually given some form of mnemonic (e.g. BASIC, COBOL).

audio response A spoken reply from a computer, using a pre-defined limited vocabulary.

backing storage Storage media, such as magnetic disks, apart from the computer's main memory. Data and programs held in backing storage have to be transferred into the core store before use.

back-up copy A copy made of the working disk so that, in the event of accident to the working disk, all data is not lost completely.

BASIC Beginner's All-purpose Symbolic Instruction Code. A high level programming language designed for use in a number of various forms for microcomputers.

batch processing The method of processing data by computer which groups together a collection of transactions and processes them as a single unit (a batch) rather than as individual items.

baud rate A measure of the number of bits per second travelling from one part of a computer system to another, or between computers.

binary A method of counting using only two alternative values: 1 or 0, on or off.

bit An acronym for *binary digit*. The smallest unit of information used in a computer, having one of two values, 1 or 0. The CPU of a computer is often described according to the number of bits that it can process or access at one time (e.g. a 32 bit CPU).

bootstrap A method of inputting data prior to the loading of a computer program in order that the program can be loaded.

buffer (1) Memory space in a printer which stores the characters for printing. A printer with a buffer memory can perform more complex printing functions than one that will only print characters as they are fed from the computer. (2) An area where data can be temporarily stored whilst being transferred from one unit to another.

bug An error or defect in a computer system or computer program.

byte An acronym for *by eight*. The most common unit of computer storage, a byte (a group of eight bits) is equivalent to one character, symbol or two numerical digits. One byte contains enough information to represent one ASCII character.

cathode ray tube/terminal (CRT) A screen similar to a television screen which displays text from a computer. As keys are struck by the operator, letters or symbols appear on the screen.

central processing unit (CPU) The part of the computer system which co-ordinates the whole system, where all parts of the computer system are linked together and where the calculations and manipulation of data take place.

chip A single integrated circuit formed on the surface of a piece of silicon etched with tiny electronic circuits. It is between 1 and 5 cm in length and can have between 6 and 40 external connections.

COBOL Common Business Orientated Language. A high level computer programming language designed for use in business applications and the manipulation of business data, using terms which are related to ordinary English words.

code A machine language representation of a character.

cold start A complete restart of a computer following major failure or breakdown.

computer output microfilm (COM) Sometimes called computer output microfiche. Instead of producing paper output, COM systems reduce the same information to microfilm (or microfiche).

compatibility The ability of two devices, whether hardware or software, to work in conjunction, e.g. if a magnetic disk used on one computer can be read by another computer, the two computers are said to be compatible.

corruption The unintended alteration or mutilation of computer data during processing, storage or transmission.

CP/M Control Program for Microprocessors. A widely used disk operating system for microcomputers.

crash When computer hardware or software malfunctions, or when a program which is running cannot be completed or re-started, a computer system is said to have crashed.

cursor A marker on a VDU indicating the point at which text should be entered. Appearances can vary, some cursors are boxes, triangles or underlines, and some flash on and off.

data Numbers or characters which provide the building blocks for information. Data is normally deemed to be input into a computer in order that information can be output.

database An organised collection of files of information that has been systematically recorded. The files can be interconnected and form the base of an organisation's data processing system, with specific reference to information retrieval.

data processing Clerical, arithmetical and logical operations on data. In the context of information technology, data processing implies the use of a computer in its operations.

debug To test a computer program or routine and to isolate and correct errors to get rid of bugs or faults.

default The value of a variable which is used by a computer system, unless it is specifically altered by the keyboard to use another value.

density The amount of storage space on a magnetic disk.

direct access The ability to access data in a storage and retrieval system directly without having to scan any part of the storage file first. Each record's storage location is completely unconnected with any other record storage.

disk A flat circular medium used for magnetic backing storage of information and programs. A disk is divided into recording tracks and sub-divided into sectors.

disk capacity The amount of storage space on a disk.

disk drive An electro-mechanical device which houses a magnetic disk effecting necessary movement and writing to or reading from the disk.

disk operating system (DOS) Software that manages the storage and retrieval of information on disk and controls the operation of all activities relating to the use of magnetic disks in a computer system.

dot matrix printer A printer capable of producing work at high speed which uses a series of electrically hammered moving pins to create characters made up of a pattern of dots. Printed output material is not considered to be of letter quality.

double density disk A magnetic disk with twice the storage capacity of a standard disk of the same dimension.

down In computing terms, a system is said to be down when it is not operating.

download The transference of data or programs from one computer to another, e.g. from a mainframe to a microcomputer.

downtime A period when computer equipment is not operating because of malfunction, maintenance, etc.

dump The transfer of data from one computer storage area to another or, more usually, to output.

dumping The copying of contents of a storage area onto another medium usually for the purpose of security or checking.

external storage Any storage medium which is portable (e.g. magnetic disks).

facsimile transmission (See p 223).

field A section of a computer record designated for the storage of specific information. A fixed field has a defined, unvarying length, whereas a variable field can be assigned different length values.

fifth generation computer The coming generation of computers with greatly increased processing power which facilitates the running of user-friendly artificial intelligence software.

file An organised and structured collection of information recorded as a unit with an identifying name.

fixed head Read/write heads in a CPU or disk drive which are kept stationary.

fixed head disk A disk memory with one read/write head for track on the disk.

floppy disk A thin disk made of a flexible material with one or both sides coated to accept magnetic recording, usually either 5¼ inches or 8 inches in diameter. Also known as a **magnetic disk**.

flowchart A graphical representation showing the sequence of events and choices which need to be made in the solution of a problem, using symbolic shapes and usually, although not exclusively, relating to a computer program.

flowcharting A method of representing a series of events with lines which represent inter-connection and symbols which represent events or processes. Systems flowcharts represent the relationship between events in a data processing system. Program flowcharts show the logical components of a computer program.

foreground A facility of some computers whereby high priority tasks can be carried out whilst those of low priority are also being carried out in the background.

format (1) To format is to arrange data or text according to specific instructions. (2) An arrangement of data, which may refer to the layout of a printed document, the order of instructions in a program or the arrangement of data in a computer file.

formula A term used in spreadsheet software. If several columns of figures have to be totalled, or a percentage of each calculated, a formula can be set up to do this and then run.

FORTRAN Formula Translator. A high level computer programming language used specifically for scientific, technical or mathematical applications.

fourth generation computers The majority of contemporary computers.

hard copy Permanent output from a computer and usually synonymous with print on paper.

hard disk A magnetic disk hermetically sealed to prevent contamination by dust and moisture offering large storage capacity and used for the bulk storage of computer data.

hard sectoring The marking of sector boundaries on a magnetic disk by the punching of holes in the disk. All available space can be used for data storage.

hardware The magnetic, electrical, mechanical and electronic components which make up a computer.

hash Data which is nonsense.

head A device which reads and records or erases information on a computer storage medium.

hexidecimal code A data code which uses the base 16 as compared with base 2 for binary code and base 10 for decimal code.

high level language A computer programming language which allows a user to employ instructions close to his/her own familiar language rather than machine code. The higher the level of the language, the nearer the language is to English language.

high resolution The fineness of detail distinguishable in an image and often referred to the screen of a VDU.

icon An image on the screen of an advanced microcomputer resembling a familiar office object (e.g. document, tray) and representing a work area in the computer. The work area is accessed by moving the cursor to the icon and then pressing a key to call up that work area.

image printer Using optical technology, a printer which will compose an image of a complete page from digital input, the final copy being produced as print on paper.

immediate access store A storage area in a computer into which information can be written and from which it can be instantly read no matter where it is in the store.

incompatibility If a program capable of running on one computer cannot be run on another computer, the software is said to be incompatible.

input The putting in of information to a computer by an operator from a keyboard and therefore being information received by a computer.

input device A piece of equipment which allows data and instructions to be entered into a computer's memory (e.g. keyboard, terminal, light pen, MICR, OCR).

integrated In reference to computer packages, sometimes called a suite, the linking together of a database, spreadsheet, word processing and graphics which can interact actively.

integrated circuit See **chip.**

intelligent terminal A terminal which has some processing or computing capabilities independent from the computer it is connected to.

interface The connecting link between two parts of a computer system, e.g. the cable that runs between a word processing terminal and its disk drive.

internal storage The internal **read only memory** of a computer where programs and data are stored.

joystick A device in the form of a unit with a small stick which moves the cursor on a VDU.

laser disk A form of video used to access information held on a disk rather than on a tape. The disk is read by decoding patterns produced by a laser light reflected off the disk's surface.

laser printer A printer using a laser light source to write on paper which is then passed through an ink powder. Ink is attracted to the area on the paper which has been written on and excess powder is removed. The ink is then fixed by chemical treatment or heat.

liquid crystal display (LCD) Liquid crystals can be switched from an opaque to a transparent state when interposed between a light source and an observer. LCD is often used on calculators.

load To enter information or a program into a computer from a storage device.

log on/off To initiate or terminate on-line interaction with a computer.

loop A series of instructions within a computer program which are performed continuously until a condition which has been pre-determined is met, when the computer will exit from the loop and carry on with the next instruction in the original program.

low level language   A computer language which is very close to the computer's own machine code. Each low level language instruction has its own direct machine code equivalent.

machine code   A binary code used in machine language for a machine's basic instructions which are directly acceptable to the CPU of a computer system.

machine language   A language used by a computer for internal communications with its related parts and the language in which a computer performs arithmetic and editing functions.

macro code   An instructional code capable of generating several machine instructions. Also known as macro.

magnetic card   A piece of cardboard or plastic with a magnetisable surface on which data can be recorded.

magnetic disk   See **floppy disk**.

mainframe   The CPU of a large computer installation with many terminals attached and distinguishing the computer from a minicomputer or microcomputer.

megabyte   1048576 bytes, frequently referred to as one million bytes and used to measure storage capacity of a computer or CPU.

memory   A device in the CPU of a computer which can store information for extraction by the computer when required. Memory is measured in **bytes**.

microcomputer   A category for the smallest computers which uses a microprocessor as its processing element, having sufficient peripherals and memory to link with the outside world and store information.

microprocessor   Sometimes a synonym for microcomputer but more correctly the central processor in which all elements of a control unit are contained on a single chip.

minicomputer   A medium-sized computer, smaller than mainframe but larger than micro, with either general or specialised usage including process control, often used by a medium sized company to keep records, payroll, stock, etc.

modem   An acronym for *modulator/demodulator*. A device for converting a digital signal from a computer into an analogue signal which can then be transmitted along a standard telephone line.

mouse   A device which can be rolled across the surface of a graphics table. When a button on the mouse is depressed, the computer will address the item in the mouse position. Commonly used with **icons**.

MS DOS   A commercial name for a **disk operating system.**

network   A computer system where a number of components at a physical distance from each other can be interconnected by telecommunications channels.

off-line   A terminal or other computer component not connected to or controlled by a CPU.

on-line   A terminal or other component directly connected to the CPU in a computer system and which will interact directly with the central processor.

operating system   A collection of programs contained in a computer used to control the sequencing of processing of other programs from the operation of various input and output devices.

optical character recognition (OCR)   A technique in which information in the form of characters, numbers or symbols is read by an optical scanning device, or optical character reader, which converts the information into computer readable form.

PASCAL   Program Appliqué à la Sélection et la Compilation Automatique de la Littérature. A large multi-disciplinary database compiled by the French Centre Nationale de la Recherche Scientifique. Sometimes referred to as a high level language used for general programming work.

peripheral   Any unit of a computer (e.g. disk drive, joystick, light pen, card reader, magnetic tape unit, printer) which connects in different ways to the central processor and memory and which forms input and output devices.

program   A set of instructions which a computer carries out in sequence enabling the computer to operate and carry out specific tasks.

programming language   The language in which coded instructions are written for a computer.

random access memory (RAM)   Memory into which information can be written and from which it may read in a random access fashion. The size of a computer's random access memory is a measure of the computer's power.

read   The copying of information from a storage medium, or the electronic retrieval of information.

read only   A term used in reference to memory and magnetic disks. If a disk has been write protected, its contents can be read but nothing can be written to it. This facility provides a safeguard against the accidental erasure of data, information and programs stored on a disk.

read only memory (ROM)   A store of memory from which

information can only be read or copied. Usually it is a permanent store holding software which is permanently or firmly in place. Sometimes referred to as firmware.

real time A computer system is said to be operating in real time if the system operates synchronously, responding to a request from a terminal and the processing of information which is fed in takes place straightaway.

retrieval The way in which a computer searches for particular files or parts of files in response to a request from a user and loads those files to the cursor or screen.

sequential access The storage and retrieval of records and information which has been recorded in sequence (e.g. on magnetic tape). Information to be accessed is searched for in an order of start to finish, until the required text is encountered. Also known as serial access.

sequential storage The storage of records in an order where the next available space after the storage of the previous record is used.

serial The travelling of electrical patterns of bits down a wire to a computer, one after the other. Often referred to as serial bit stream.

serial interface An interface in which access time involves a waiting time where serial bit transmission is used.

serial storage Storage on a magnetic device in which words appear in sequence often inferring that access time will include a waiting time.

shared facility A computer system in which several pieces of equipment use the same facility (e.g. a disk drive, a printer). Also known as shared resource.

shared logic A computer system consisting of work stations made up of keyboards and VDUs which are connected to a CPU, usually with a hard disk. The terminals operate under central control.

soft copy Computer output on a medium which cannot be read by an observer e.g. floppy disk or computer output as displayed on the screen of a VDU.

software A generic term for programs, operating systems, packages and compilers which are used to direct the operations of a computer or other hardware and which can be run on computer hardware, consisting of patterns of binary information.

speech generation The production of human speech by a computer using a limited vocabulary where often the computer can read back the information given to it.

split screen The displaying of more than one image on the screen of a VDU. Areas of the screen are referred to as 'windows'.

spreadsheet An application program which provides a matrix into which data can be entered and manipulated and intended for use in forecasting and financial planning.

storage Another word for memory in a computer system, or the medium on which information can be stored.

system An organised set of computer components which interact to allow the processing of data.

systems analyst A person trained in the investigation, analysis and design of computer systems (often for business applications) who can provide solutions to the most effective way of processing data.

systems analysis The task of analysing computer systems and determining how a computer system can be made more efficient (normally used for business applications).

systems software Software used to run the operating system of a computer. Also known as operating software.

tape An input or output storage device for a computer. There are two kinds of tape: paper and magnetic.

terminal A peripheral device consisting of a keyboard and screen, linked to a computer used to input data and receive output from the computer, or for sending and receiving data over a communications channel.

time sharing A computer system that allows many terminals or users to concurrently share a central computer, each user having the impression that he or she has the sole use of the computer.

touch screen A terminal with a screen which is sensitive to the touch of the user. Positions touched usually using a finger or a light pen are recorded by the computer as a signal allowing data to be input or a command to be followed.

variable (See under Word Processing p 366).

visual display unit (VDU) A cathode ray tube on which the output of a computer can be displayed.

Winchester disk A form of backing storage for a computer consisting of a magnetic disk in an hermetically sealed container which is very powerful. Sometimes referred to as a rigid or **hard disk**.

window A feature of some advanced microcomputer systems in which the VDU screen is split into sections, called 'windows', enabling the operation of different sections of the memory to be seen at the same time.

working disk A back-up copy of a disk is made and stored in a safe place and the original disk becomes the working disk, i.e. the disk which is being worked on at the present time. If for any reason the working disk is damaged, the back-up disk can be used to make another working copy.

27.3 Legal

abstract of title A summary of the title deeds and documents for unregistered land.

accessory One who aids or participates in a crime, but not as principal.

act of bankruptcy The action of a creditor which allows a debtor to present a bankruptcy petition to the court.

actus reus The guilty act as part of a criminal offence. Compare with **mens rea**.

ancient lights The right to light of windows which have enjoyed twenty years of unobstructed access to light, binding the owner of an adjacent property against building or planting so as to obstruct the light.

arbitration The settling of a dispute by a person or group agreed upon by the opposing parties in order to obtain a decision which is equitable.

artificial person An entity, such as a registered company or society, which is seen in the eyes of the law as a person, as opposed to a natural person i.e. an individual.

adjudication The act of a court in pronouncing judgment.

administrator One empowered by a court to take charge of the personal estate of a deceased person, in default of an executor.

affiliation order An order of a magistrates court requiring the alleged father of an illegitimate child to make payments to maintain the child.

age of consent The age at which a person is legally competent to give consent to certain acts, in particular marriage and sexual intercourse.

airspace The part of the atmosphere above a piece of land which in English and international law belongs to the owner of the land.

appellant A person who appeals to a higher tribunal or court for a previous decision to be changed.

arrestable offence (1) A criminal offence for which there is a mandatory fixed penalty. (2) A criminal offence carrying a prison sentence of at least five years for a first offender. A warrant is not necessary for arrest.

assignment The legal transfer for assigning of rights; the writing by which a transfer is made.

attest To testify or bear witness to; to affirm by signature or oath; to give proof of.

bankruptcy The state of one whom the court has adjudged insolvent and whose affairs are compulsorily administered in order to distribute any assets among the creditors.

beneficial owner One entitled to the use of land or income from the land.

battery An attack using force against a person, e.g. beating, wounding, or, irrespective of causing harm, threatening by touching clothes or body.

bona fide Evidence of good faith.

bond A written obligation to pay a sum or to perform a contract.

bylaw (1) The law of a local authority or private corporation. (2) A supplementary law or an inferred regulation.

care order A court order which entitles a local authority to care for a child in spite of claims made by a parent or guardian.

casus belli (1) An occurrence which gives rise to war. (2) Grounds for a quarrel.

caveat A warning; a notice given by an interested party in a case so as to halt proceedings until the party is given a hearing.

chattel Any kind of property which is not freehold.

circumstantial evidence Evidence of circumstances providing indirect or inferential evidence of a fact but not direct proof of it.

civil action A court case which is not a criminal prosecution; a case brought by a person or party against another party for an alleged wrong in order to obtain compensation.

cohabit To live together as if husband and wife.

collateral security An additional and separate security for repayment of money borrowed.

collusion A secret agreement to deceive, especially one made between parties apparently in conflict in a lawsuit.

committal The act of sending a person to court or to prison, usually temporarily.

common law The unwritten law of England which is embodied in reported cases and commentaries and administered by the royal courts.

common law marriage A marriage recognised as such by long association and repute, not by a marriage ceremony.

completion In conveyancing, the final stage in the sale of a property, when ownership is transferred from the seller to the purchaser.

commute To convert into a lighter penalty, as in the commutation of a sentence.

concurrent sentences Prison sentences for two or more offences which are served simultaneously, not consecutively.

consecutive sentences Prison sentences for two or more offences which are served one after another, not concurrently.

consideration A thing given or done or abstained from by one person in agreement with another, in exchange for that other person giving, doing or abstaining from something. It is an essential element in making an agreement legally binding, e.g. a contract.

contempt of court (1) In criminal law, conduct obstructing or tending to obstruct the administration of justice. (2) In civil law, disobedience of an order of court, or breach of an undertaking given to the court.

contract A legally binding agreement between two or more parties.

conveyancing The transference of property from the seller to the purchaser.

copyright The sole right to reproduce a literary, dramatic, musical, or artistic work—also to perform, translate, film or record such a work.

corroboration Oral or written evidence given in court which confirms other evidence given.

coverture The condition of a married woman as legally deemed under the protection of her husband.

debenture A written acknowledgment of a debt; the form in which loans are made to companies.

decree absolute In divorce, a decree which terminates a marriage and which takes effect immediately.

decree nisi In divorce, a conditional decree which becomes a **decree absolute** unless cause be shown to the contrary.

deed of covenant (See under Business p 308).

deed poll A deed executed by one party, especially one by which a person changes his or her name.

de facto Actual, if not rightful.

de jure By right, legally.

dies non A day on which judges do not sit, or one on which normal business is not transacted.

domicile A person's legally recognised place of residence.

easement The right to use something, particularly land, not one's own, or to prevent its owner from making an inconvenient use of it.

ejection (1) Expulsion of a possessor from his or her property, resulting in an action of ejection to recover it. (2) An action to remove persons illegally occupying property.

encumbrance (1) A debt secured over land. (2) A legal claim on an estate.

estoppel A conclusive admission which cannot be denied by the party whom it affects.

exchange of contracts In conveyancing, the point at which the purchaser and the vendor exchange signed identical copies of the sale of contract, making the sale legally binding.

execution (1) The carrying out by a law officer of e.g. a citation or contract. (2) The carrying out of a criminal sentence. (3) The authentication of a deed.

fee simple Unconditional inheritance or ownership of land.

fee tail An estate which may descend only to the direct heirs of the owner and cannot be disposed of by the immediate possessor.

femme sole An unmarried woman (spinster, widow or divorcée).

foreclosure The process by which a mortgagor, failing to repay the money lent on the security of an estate, is compelled to forfeit his right to redeem the estate.

freehold The right to hold property or land free of duty.

garnishee A person warned not to pay money owed to his or her direct creditor because the latter is indebted to the **garnisher** (who gives the warning).

'gazump' To raise the price of property after accepting an offer from a buyer but before the contract has been signed.

ground rent Rent paid to a landlord for the use of the ground for a specified term, usually ninety-nine years.

habeus corpus A writ requiring a jailer to produce a prisoner in person and to state the reasons for his or her detention.

hearsay evidence Evidence given by a witness based on the oral statements of someone else and not on his or her own knowledge.

hereditament Any property that may pass to an heir.

hire purchase agreement A credit agreement in which a hired article becomes the property of the hirer after a stipulated number of payments.

in camera Court proceedings conducted in the judge's private chambers, not in open court.

incorporation The formation of a company or other association which has a personality distinct from its members.

indictable offence An offence that could be tried on indictment in the Crown Court.

indictment The written accusation against one who is to be tried by jury.

injunction A writ by which a court stops or prevents some unfair or illegal act being done.

in loco parentis A term describing the role of a guardian or custodian who cares for children on behalf of their parents.

interlocutory Describing an intermediate stage before a final decision, e.g. interlocutory injunction, interlocutory proceedings, i.e. occurring at a hearing before the full court trial takes place.

intestate Without having made a valid will.

jointly and severally Describing two or more persons legally associated in obligation or ownership.

joint tenancy Property held by two or more persons as joint tenants.

laches Negligence or undue delay by a plaintiff in bringing an action to court to enforce his or her equitable right.

leading question A question so put as to suggest the desired answer, allowed only in cross-examination.

leasehold A tenure in land or property on a lease, for a fixed term.

letters of administration The authority granted to a person to administer or distribute the personal estate of a deceased person, in default of an executor.

libel A defamatory and untrue publication or statement in permanent form, such as print or film.

lien A right to retain possession of another's property until he or she pays a debt.

liquidation The process of dissolving a company. It can be initiated by members or creditors of the company, or by a court order.

litigant A person engaged in a lawsuit.

litigation The action of carrying on a lawsuit.

lump sum award Damages paid as a single sum of money and not in several smaller amounts.

maintenance In divorce, payment made either in a lump sum or in instalments to support children or the other spouse.

malfeasance An illegal deed, especially of an official.

mandamus A writ or command issued by a higher court to a lower.

mandate A right given to a person to act in the name of another.

manslaughter Unlawful homicide without intent or with mitigating circumstances.

mens rea The criminal intention that a defendant must be proved to have had when committing a crime if he or she is to be convicted.

misfeasance The negligent or improper performance of a lawful act.

mitigation Lessening the severity of a penalty or the seriousness of the offence.

mortgagee One to whom a mortgage is made or given.

mortgagor One who mortgages his or her property.

naturalise To grant the privileges of natural-born citizens to an alien.

negotiable instruments Documents which can be transferred from one person to another upon endorsement, e.g. cheques, promissory notes, bills of exchange.

next friend The person appointed to act in a legal action for a minor or a mental health patient.

notary public   An officer, usually a solicitor, authorised to certify deeds, contracts, copies of documents, affidavits, etc.

obiter dictum   A remark made by a judge in giving judgment which is not of central importance to the case but may be used in the future as persuasive authority.

patent (letters patent)   An official document conferring an exclusive right or privilege, such as the sole right for a term of years to the proceeds of an invention.

peppercorn rent   A trivial or nominal rent which by agreement the tenant does not pay to a landlord but which preserves the legal title of the landlord.

perjury   The breaking of an oath; the crime committed by one who, when giving evidence on oath or affirmation as a witness in a court of justice, gives evidence which he or she knows to be false.

petition   A written application to a court for some judicial action.

power of attorney   A power given to one person by another to act on his or her behalf.

precedent   A previous judicial instance or proceeding that is used as an authority for making the same decision in later cases.

prima facie   Describing evidence sufficient to support the bringing of a charge, or a case supported by such evidence.

pro indiviso   Describing rights which two or more persons hold in common.

pro rata   Proportionately.

promissory note   A written promise to pay a sum of money on some future day or on demand.

promoter   One who takes part in the setting up of a new company.

putative   Reputed, commonly supposed to be, e.g. as applied to a marriage supposed invalid by canon law but entered into in good faith by at least one of the parties, or to the alleged father of an illegitimate child.

quasi contract   An implied contract.

quid pro quo   Something done in exchange for something else.

receivership   The state of a bankrupt company or of property which is the subject of litigation when a court has appointed a receiver to administer the affairs of the company or property.

recognisance   A legal obligation entered into before a magistrate to do, or not to do, some particular act; money pledged for the performance of such an obligation.

respondent   A defendant, especially in a divorce suit.

salvage (money)   Compensation, usually assessed by the court, which is made to persons other than the ship's company for preserving a ship or cargo from danger of loss.

search The examination of records and registers to find encumbrances affecting title to property.

sequestration A writ allowing a court to seize control of a person's property.

sine die Without a day having been appointed,—pertaining to a meeting or other business indefinitely adjourned.

slander Injurious defamation by spoken words or by looks, signs or gestures.

statute law Law in the form of statutes, i.e. (in Britain) contained in the Acts of Parliament.

sue To take legal action, e.g. instituting a suit or making a claim.

summary offence An offence that must be tried before magistrates.

suspended sentence A sentence not served unless another crime is committed.

testator One who leaves a will.

title deeds Documents proving ownership of land and the terms of ownership.

tort Any wrong, not arising out of contract, for which there is a remedy by compensation or damages.

treasure trove Ownerless objects of intrinsic or historical value found hidden, which are the property of the Crown (in England, gold and silver only).

undischarged bankrupt A bankrupt who has not been given an order of discharge by the court and who is thus liable to certain restrictions and disqualifications.

venue (1) The county where a crime is alleged to have been committed. (2) The place where the cause is tried.

waiver A written statement formally indicating the abandonment or resignation of legal rights.

ward of court A minor in the care of a guardian who has been appointed by the court or the parents.

wardship The jurisdiction of the High Court to make a minor a ward of court.

warranty An undertaking in a contract which is additional to the main purpose of the contract, breach of which may lead to a claim for damages.

wasting assets Property in the estate of a deceased person which is declining in value and which cannot be replaced or renewed.

without prejudice A disclaimer used in correspondence and other documents indicating that if settlement of a case is not reached, the statements it relates to cannot be used as evidence without the agreement of both parties.

27.4 Medical

abrasion An injury in which the surface of the skin or lining of a part of the body has been lost or scraped off.

abscess A collection of pus in a cavity formed by the destruction of normal body tissue.

Achilles tendon A large tendon, which can be felt in the lower part of the back of the calf, and which runs down to the heel bone.

acne A common skin condition affecting in particular the face, back and chest, and consisting of small pus-filled boils and blackheads.

acupuncture The insertion of fine needles into particular parts of the body for the treatment of disease or the relief of pain.

adenoids Glandular tissue at the back of the nose, which is normally large in children and may cause breathing and hearing problems. Adenoids normally shrink as the child gets older.

adrenalin A hormone, the release of which is stimulated by factors such as emotion, pain and stress. The effect of adrenalin is to cause the heart's output to increase and blood to be redirected to tissues whose requirements are high in times of stress.

agoraphobia A fear of being in a large open space.

AIDS An illness caused by a virus which destroys the body's immune system. Thus infections and certain tumours can no longer be dealt with by the body and can overwhelm the patient, causing death. It is spread by sexual intercourse and by contact with infected blood, e.g. through the sharing of needles by drug addicts. Many carriers of the virus have not yet developed signs of the illness.

allergy A condition in which a substance causes symptoms in a susceptible individual not normally caused in the majority of people (e.g. skin rashes, diarrhoea, asthma).

amniocentesis A test performed to detect possible abnormalities in an unborn baby, in which a sample of the fluid surrounding the baby in the womb is removed through a needle inserted into the mother's abdomen.

anaemia A low level of haemoglobin in the blood due to deficiency of iron or vitamins.

analgesic A drug which relieves pain.

angina Pain felt usually in the chest on exertion or in response to emotion, caused by narrowing or blockage of one or more of the blood vessels which supply the heart.

anorexia nervosa A serious condition especially common in adolescent and young women in which loss of appetite and aversion to eating leads to marked weight loss. Emotional factors are thought to play a part in the development of this condition.

antibody A substance produced by the body as a defence against e.g. infection by a bacteria or virus, enabling the body to fight the infection.

antibiotic A drug which will destroy or inhibit the growth of bacteria and certain other micro-organisms which cause infectious disease.

arthritis Inflammation in one or many joints causing pain and restriction of movement.

asbestosis An incurable lung disease caused by inhaling asbestos particles.

asthma A breathing disorder in which the bronchial tubes are intermittently narrowed, causing breathlessness and a wheezing noise as air is expired through the narrowed tubes.

atherosclerosis Fatty deposits in the walls and the inside of blood vessels leading to hardening of arteries and their narrowing and blockage, thereby reducing blood supply to tissues.

athlete's foot A fungus infection of the skin of the feet, occurring especially between the toes and leading to redness, itching, soreness and cracking.

bacteria Micro-organisms which may be free-living or parasitic and which may or may not cause disease.

biopsy The removal of a piece of tissue for microscopic examination and subsequent diagnosis.

blood group This refers to hereditary differences in red blood cells and is important when blood transfusion is required; blood given to an individual must have red blood cells of that individual's group or a serious reaction will occur.

blood pressure The pressure of blood flow in the arteries consisting of two readings; one taken when the heart is contracting (systolic) and one taken when the heart is relaxed (diastolic).

bronchitis Inflammation in the bronchial tubes due to irritation from such agents as smoke or infection.

bulimia Compulsive eating of excessive quantities of food in response to emotional factors. Self-induced vomiting may occur.

cancer Excessive growth of abnormal cells which multiply more quickly than normal body cells, causing destruction of surrounding tissue and spreading to other parts of the body.

carcinogen A substance which causes cancer.

carcinoma A type of cancer arising in the surface layers of an organ or tissue.

cardiac Pertaining to the heart.

catheter A hollow tube, e.g. a urinary catheter which is a flexible tube passed from the outside into the bladder, allowing urine to be removed when a patient is unable to initiate or control urination.

cerebro-vascular accident A condition in which blood supply to an area of the brain is interrupted by a haemorrhage or arterial blockage, causing paralysis, loss of sensation or other symptoms, depending on the part of the brain affected. Also called a stroke.

chemotherapy Treatment of disease with drugs.

cerebral Pertaining to the brain.

cervical smear test A screening test for cancer of the cervix or neck of the womb, performed by examining under the microscope cells obtained from the cervix in a vaginal examination. The test picks up cell changes which may in time lead to cancer development at a treatable stage.

chiropractor A practitioner who believes that disease is caused by abnormalities of nerves and who is skilled in manipulation, in particular of the spine, in order to restore the normal function of nerves.

cholesterol A fat-like substance found in animal fats, oils and egg yolks. Raised levels in the blood are associated with atherosclerosis.

chromosomes Rod-shaped structures, 46 of which occur in the nuclei of all cells of the human body, 23 being passed on from each parent. Chromosomes carry on them the genes or hereditary factors which determine the characteristics of the person.

colic A strong involuntary contraction of the muscle of the bowel or of an abdominal organ which causes severe pain to be felt.

colostomy A surgical procedure in which the rectum and anus, which have been affected by disease, are bypassed and a new opening of the colon is created on the surface of the abdomen through which excrement is passed.

congenital Present at birth.

claustrophobia A fear of being shut up in a confined space.

coma A deeply unconscious state.

coronary thrombosis A 'heart attack' in which one or more arteries to the heart become blocked, causing loss of blood supply and therefore loss of oxygen to the heart muscles' supply by the artery. If the area involved is extensive, the heart will be unable to function and death will result. Lesser degrees of damage will heal.

cyst A bag-like structure containing fluid or semi-solid material.

delirium A state of diminished awareness in which a patient may be confused, restless, and may experience hallucinations or illusions.

dementia A condition in which intellectual functions such as memory, ability to learn new things, awareness of time, surroundings and people are gradually and irreversibly lost and deterioration of personality and behaviour occurs.

dermatitis Inflammation of the skin in response to irritation.

diabetes A disease, caused by lack of the hormone insulin, in which the level of glucose in the blood is abnormally high, causing symptoms ranging from increased thirst and passing more urine to coma and death.

dialysis A method by which waste products from protein breakdown can be removed from the blood when the kidneys, which normally perform this function, have failed.

dyslexia Impaired ability to read owing to malfunction in that part of the brain concerned with understanding the written word.

dysmenorrhoea Cramping pain in the lower abdomen felt at the time of mentrual periods.

ectopic pregnancy A pregnancy in which the fertilised egg becomes implanted somewhere other than the womb (often in the Fallopian tube).

embolism A condition in which a solid particle or air bubble becomes lodged in an artery, causing interruption of blood flow.

emphysema A condition in which there is increase in size of the smallest airways in the lungs, causing transfer of oxygen from the lungs to the bloodstream to be less efficient. The term also describes the presence of air in the tissues caused by, e.g. a penetrating chest wound.

epidural An injection of local anaesthetic into the lower spine causing loss of painful sensation in the lower part of the body, thus making it possible to perform surgery without a general anaesthetic.

epilepsy A disturbance in the brain caused by abnormal electrical activity and leading to 'fits' in which there may be symptoms such as loss of consciousness, jerking of limbs, and unusual sensations.

fibrositis Pain and stiffness of muscles and soft tissues usually of the neck, shoulders and trunk; of uncertain cause.

fracture A break, usually of a bone. A green-stick fracture is an incomplete break which occurs only in children.

gangrene The death of tissues of the body due to inadequate blood supply.

gastric Pertaining to the stomach.

gastro-enteritis An infection of the gastro-intestinal tract from the stomach downwards, causing vomiting, diarrhoea and abdominal pain.

glandular fever   A disease particularly affecting young adults due to a virus infection, leading to enlargement of the lymph glands and a large variety of symptoms including sore throat and extreme tiredness.

haemoglobin   The iron-containing part of the red blood cell which combines with oxygen.

haemophilia   A hereditary condition, almost always affecting males, in which a factor essential for blood clotting is present in a concentration lower than normal, and leading to excessive bleeding from minor injuries.

haemorrhoids   Dilated veins around the anus. Also known as piles.

hepatitis   Inflammation of the liver often caused by virus infection or excessive alcohol consumption. It may or may not be accompanied by jaundice.

hernia   The abnormal protrusion of an organ or part of it through an opening in surrounding structures. Hernias are often noticed as a lump in the groin, where the abdominal cavity lining, containing intestine, may protrude through the abdominal muscle.

herpes   A variety of virus which often infects the skin or nerves, causing a rash with characteristic blisters. It may affect the face (cold sores), the genitals (genital herpes), or cause shingles elsewhere on the body.

homeopathy   The treatment of disease with minute amounts of substances which themselves cause the symptoms which characterise the disease.

hormones   Chemical substances produced in the body which regulate the function of certain tissues and organs.

hypertension   Raised blood pressure.

hysterectomy   Surgical removal of the uterus or womb.

ileostomy   A surgical procedure in which the colon, rectum and anus are bypassed because of disease and an opening of the ileum or small bowel is created on the surface of the abdomen, through which excrement is passed.

immunity   A state of being not susceptible to an infection, usually because a past infection has stimulated production by the body of antibodies which remain and destroy the infecting organisms if they are encountered again.

inflammation   The response of tissues or organs to injury or infection, characterised by redness, swelling, pain and heat.

jaundice   A yellow appearance of the skin and whites of the eyes which occurs in liver-disease or where there is obstruction to the outflow of bile from the liver.

leukaemia　A variety of cancer affecting the blood, in which there is production of large numbers of abnormal white blood cells at the expense of red cells and platelets (which help blood-clotting). Characteristic symptoms are bleeding, anaemias and susceptibility to infections.

lumbago　Low back pain from any cause.

lymph　Fluid found in the lymphatic vessels (which run alongside blood vessels), the function of which is to fight infections and develop immunity to them.

malignant　A term used to describe cancer which, untreated, is likely to progress and result in death.

mastectomy　Surgical removal of the breast as part of treatment for breast cancer.

meningitis　An infection of the *meninges*, the tissue covering the brain and spinal cord.

menopause　The cessation of menstrual periods occurring around the age of 45-50. Also called the 'change of life'.

metabolism　The chemical changes which occur in the body in order to maintain life, involving the conversion of food to energy and the breakdown and repair of tissues.

metastatic　A term describing the spread, usually of cancer, from the source to other areas of the body.

micro-organism　A minute living organism, usually too small to be seen with the naked eye (e.g. bacterium, virus, fungus or yeast).

migraine　A throbbing headache, often on one side of the head, thought to be caused by dilation of cerebral arteries, sometimes associated with other symptoms, such as disturbance of vision or sensation and vomiting.

Mongol　A person with what is now usually known as Down's Syndrome, in which an extra chromosome is present in body cells. The syndrome is characterised by a typical appearance, mental retardation and other congenital abnormalities.

multiple sclerosis　A disease of the nervous system which may cause abnormalities of sensation, movement and co-ordination, and eyesight problems, all of which may be temporary in the initial stages but are subject to variable and progressive deterioration over the years.

muscular dystrophy　A disease which is usually inherited and which causes wasting of muscles and progressive weakness.

narcotic　A drug which induces very deep sleep to the point of unconsciousness.

neurosis A disorder of the mind usually caused by stress and anxiety in the patient's environment and characterised by severe and persistent anxiety.

osteopath A practitioner who attributes disease to disorder of the skeletal system and who applies suitable manipulation with the aim of correcting it.

pacemaker A battery-operated electrical device which is inserted into the body to stimulate the heart to beat in the presence of disease which has caused abnormal slowing of the heart.

paranoid Having an unreasonable belief that people wish or are doing harm to one.

paraplegia Paralysis of the legs and lower part of the body affecting movement and sensation and usually also leading to inability to urinate and defecate.

Parkinson's disease A disorder of the nervous system due to damage to the brain caused by, e.g. atheroscelerosis, infections or drugs. Characterised by muscular stiffness and rigidity and bodily shaking.

pertussis Whooping cough.

phlebitis The inflammation of a vein, usually just under the skin.

placebo A harmless and inactive substance given instead of a real drug; a dummy tablet which may work in the same way as an active tablet where a patient believes it will do so.

pleurisy Infection or inflammation of the surface coating of the lungs.

pneumonia Infection or inflammation of the lung tissues.

prognosis The likely outcome of an illness.

prolapse A falling down or out of place; a term often used of the womb, where pelvic muscles have become weak and no longer hold it up; it may therefore come down and be felt as a lump in the genital region. Also used of an inter-vertebral disc; a slipped disc is also called a prolapsed disc.

prophylaxis Preventative measure against disease.

psoriasis A skin disease characterised by redness and scaling of skin.

psychopath A person with an antisocial personality, unconcerned about the effect of his or her actions on others.

psychosis Serious mental illness, due to disturbance within the brain, in which the patient loses touch with reality and may have abnormal beliefs and hallucinations.

psychosomatic A term used to describe illnesses in which emotional factors produce physical symptoms.

quadriplegia Paralysis of all four limbs.

radiotherapy Treatment of disease, often cancer, by X-rays and other forms of radiation.

renal Pertaining to the kidney.

rubella German measles.

scarlet fever An infectious disease caused by a bacterium, the streptococcus, and consisting of a sore throat and a rash. It has become less common since the advent of penicillin treatment and nowadays is easily treatable.

schizophrenia A serious mental illness, of unknown cause, which leads to a variety of symptoms including disintegration of the personality, abnormal beliefs, hallucinations and paranoia.

sciatica Pain felt in the buttock and back of the leg caused by pressure on the sciatic nerve, often from a slipped disc in the lower spine.

senility A term describing changes occurring in old age, often referring to **dementia.**

shingles A common disease caused by the herpes virus, the symptoms of which are pain and a blistering skin rash in a confined area on one side of the body, the area being that supplied by a particular nerve in which the virus has lain dormant.

spina bifida A congenital abnormality in which the normal uniting into a tube of the spinal bones in the foetus does not occur throughout the length of the spine. The spinal cord may be exposed and damaged.

spastic A term used to describe involuntary muscular rigidity.

steroids Chemicals naturally occurring in the body, of which there are a wide variety including hormones and cholesterol. Artificially produced as drugs, they have a powerful action against inflammation, though used in excess they can lead to serious side-effects.

stroke See **cerebro-vascular accident.**

tennis elbow Inflammation in the tendons on the outer side of the elbow, possibly causing severe pain and difficulty in gripping and turning movements; not necessarily associated with tennis playing.

teratogen Anything which causes damage to a developing foetus in the womb.

thrombosis Clotting of blood within blood vessels.

thrush An infection caused by a yeast, affecting in particular the mouth, vagina, groin and skin folds.

tinnitus Ringing in the ears.

tracheostomy An artificial opening from the trachea (the windpipe) to the surface of the neck, created to allow a patient to breathe in circumstances where breathing is obstructed above the trachea.

tumour   A lump of new tissue growing independently of surrounding tissue. It may or may not be cancerous.

ulcer   An open sore, deeper than an abrasion.

urticaria   An itchy, bumpy rash caused by allergy, also called nettle rash or hives.

varicose veins   Abnormally dilated veins near the surface of the skin.

vasectomy   Male sterilisation achieved by dividing the *vas deferens* on both sides, thereby preventing sperm leaving the body in the ejaculate.

verucca   A wart; a small lump caused by a slow-growing virus.

virus   A minute micro-organism which lives in cells as a parasite, causing a wide range of infectious diseases and also certain tumours.

27.5 Printing

acknowledgments   The prelim in a book in which the author or editor thanks those who assisted in the preparation and publication of the book.

all edges gilt (aeg)   Describing a book having the top, side and bottom trimmed edges of the pages coloured gold.

art paper   Paper coated with a composition containing china clay, used for printing illustrations, especially fine-screen (i.e. 150 lines per inch) half-tones.

artwork   Illustrations and other decorative material suitable for reproduction.

ascender   The part of a letter which extends above the body of the letter. Contrast with **descender**.

bibliography   (1) The study, description or knowledge of books, in regard to their outward form, authors, subjects, editions and history. (2) A descriptive list of books. (3) A book containing such a list.

bleed   In bookbinding, the extent to which an illustration extends beyond the trimmed size of a page in order to ensure that the print will run off the page after trimming.

blind blocking   Blocking which produces a recessed surface which is not enhanced by the use of ink or metal foil.

blocking   In bookbinding, impressing letters or a design on a book cover using ink or metal foil. Contrast with **blind blocking**.

blurb   A brief description of a book, printed on the jacket or the back of the book.

bold (face)   Describing any style of typeface printed with very heavy strokes.

break off An instruction to a printer to begin text on the next line rather than run it on to the present line. Also called take over.

bulk The estimated thickness of a book, enabling the jacket to be designed with the correct width of spine.

camera-ready copy (CRC) Typescript copy which does not need to be typeset but which is ready for photographing. It is often produced on a word processor with a daisy wheel printer or a laser printer.

cancel A new reprinted leaf to be substituted for a suppressed leaf (containing a major error) after the book is printed.

caps An abbreviation for capitals (**upper-case** letters).

case The hard covers of a book i.e. the front, back and spine.

cased Machine-bound in hard covers.

cast-off An estimate of the length of copy, including number of words, illustrations, etc., expressed in the number of pages the copy will fill when printed.

catchword/phrase (1) A word or phrase in the text, e.g. an entry in a dictionary, which is repeated at the top of the column containing the entry. (2) A word or phrase repeated at the beginning of a textual note at the bottom of the page.

cedilla A mark placed under the letter 'c' to indicate an s-sound (in French and Portuguese), and in other languages, e.g. Turkish, to denote other sounds.

cold composition/type Typesetting by photographic methods i.e. filmsetting or photocomposition or by typewriter. Contrast with **hot-metal typesetting**.

collate (1) To place in order, as sheets of a book for binding, and to examine with respect to completeness and sequence of sheets. (2) To examine and compare books, and especially old manuscripts, in order to ascertain information about the history of composition and publication.

collotype A form of gelatine process in book illustration and advertising.

colophon An inscription at the end of a book or literary composition, often naming the author and scribe or printer, with place and date of execution, etc., as on a modern title-page.

compositor A person who sets up type.

copy Material to be printed (e.g. typescripts, photographs, line drawings).

copy preparer A person who marks up typescripts with the typographical specifications chosen by the designer.

cropping Cutting off or masking the areas of an illustration which are not to be reproduced.

dedication A prelim containing the author's inscription of the book to another person.

descender The part or 'tail' of a letter which comes below the line of type. Contrast with **ascender**.

diacritical marks Accents, cedillas and other marks attached to letters to indicate modified sound, value, etc.

diaeresis Two dots placed over the second of two adjacent vowels to show that each is to be pronounced separately (e.g. naïf).

displayed Describing typed matter, such as long quotations, set on separate lines, indented and preceded and followed by extra space to distinguish it from the rest of the text.

dummy A sample of a proposed job made up with the actual material and cut to correct size to show bulk, style of binding, etc.

duodecimo A book formed of sheets folded so as to make twelve leaves, usually written 12mo.

edition The number of copies of a book printed at a time, or at different times without significant alteration.

edition de luxe A splendid and expensive edition.

elite In typography, a measurement of length referring to twelve typewritten characters to the horizontal inch.

ellipsis Three dots indicating the omission of a word or words.

em The square of the body of any size of type. The 12 point em is the standard unit of typographic measurement.

em rule A rule which occupies the width of an em or the square of any size of type.

en Half of an em.

en point A point which is placed in the middle of a piece of type as wide as an en so that it is printed with space on either side.

en rule A rule which is half the width of an em rule.

endmatter The parts of a book which follow the text (e.g. appendices, bibliography, index).

endnotes Notes which come at the end of the relevant chapter or at the end of the book instead of being printed at the foot of the relevant page.

endpaper A folded sheet at the beginning or end of a book, one leaf of which is pasted to the binding, leaving the other as a flyleaf.

epigraph A quotation or motto at the beginning of a book or a chapter.

erratum/errata slip A list of corrections or errors in writing or printing tipped in to a book.

flyleaf A blank leaf at the beginning or end of a book.

folio (1) A sheet of paper folded in half. (2) A book made up of such sheets. (3) A manuscript leaf. (4) The particular number of such a leaf (e.g. folio 12).

format Strictly, the size of a trimmed page, but generally used to distinguish the form, shape and style in which a book is produced.

fount A complete assortment of types of one size and design, with all that is necessary for printing in that design. Also called (especially in the US) font.

full out Describing a passage which is not indented but adjoins the left or right margin.

furniture The pieces of wood, metal or plastic, of various lengths and widths, put round pages of type to make margins and fasten the matter in the chase.

galley proof A proof of text matter before it is made up into pages. Also called a slip proof.

gathering A folded section of pages comprised of one sheet or part of a sheet. Also called a signature.

half-title The first printed page of a book, containing only the title and preceding the title-page. Also called a bastard title.

half-tone A photographic process which represents light and shade by dots of different sizes, the image being photographed through a screen.

hanging indentation Describing the first line of a paragraph which is printed full out left, with the next lines indented. Also called reverse indent.

headline The line at the top of a page containing the title of the book or a chapter title.

histogram A statistical graph in which frequency distribution is shown by means of vertical columns (see p 77).

hot-metal typesetting Used to describe machines or methods using type made from molten metal (e.g. monotype, linotype).

imposition The assembling of pages prior to printing so that they will be in the right order when the sheet is folded.

impression A single printing of a book. A reprint having only minor corrections is a new impression.

imprint The name and address of the publisher and the printer, and the date and place of publication of a book. The publisher's imprint appears on the title-page, the printer's on the verso or on the last page of a book.

indentation/indention The blank space at the beginning of a line printed further in from the margin than subsequent lines.

insert Printed matter placed in a book and not secured in any way.

inset A printed section placed inside another before binding.

kern The part of a type that projects beyond the body and rests on an adjoining letter.

landscape A book or illustration having the longer sides at head and foot. Contrast with **portrait**.

layout A plan of a job showing position of type, illustrations and specifying type sizes and type faces.

leading Additional spacing between lines of type.

lemma A headword at the start of a textual note.

letterspacing Adding small spaces between characters, usually capitals or small capitals, to enhance the appearance of a line.

ligature A type of two or more letters joined together, e.g. æ, ff, fl.

line drawing A drawing comprised of black lines and solid and tint areas, without variable tones.

literal A wrong letter in printed or typed matter resulting from a mistake made by the typesetter.

lower-case The small letters of the alphabet.

make up The arrangement of composed types into columns or pages, including the insertion of illustrative matter, captions, headlines, notes, etc.

masking Covering the areas on the edge of a photograph which are not to be reproduced.

measure The width of a column or page of type, usually expressed in 12 point (or pica) ems.

Monotype A machine that casts and sets type letter by letter; a reproduction made by this process.

octavo (1) Having eight leaves to the sheet, usually written 8vo. (2) A book, or the size of a book, made up of such sheets.

offprint A reprint of a single article from a periodical.

offset lithography The most common form of photolithography, the process of lithographic printing from a photographically prepared plate using greasy ink; a rubber blanket receives the printed image and transfers it to paper.

opening The two pages exposed together when a book is opened.

overrunning Rearranging lines of type within a paragraph when a correction makes a line shorter or longer, achieved by moving words from one line to another and altering the spacing between them.

Ozalid A method of proofing film-set matter onto chemically treated paper; a reproduction made by this process.

page-on-galley proofs Proofs of pages which have not been imposed.

paste-up A layout in which galley proofs are pasted down to pages and outlines are drawn to show the size and position of illustrations.

perfect binding An unsewn book binding in which the backs of the gathered sections are sheared off and the leaves held in place by glue.

photogravure A method of photo-engraving in which the design etched on the metal surface is sunk into the surface, not relief.

pica In typography, a measurement of length, referring to ten typewritten characters to the horizontal inch.

pitch The number of characters that will fit into one inch of a line of text, typically 10, 12 or 15 when the typed text is monospaced.

plate (1) An engraved piece of metal used for printing. (2) An impression printed from it, an engraving. (3) An illustration separately printed, usually on different paper, and insetted in a book.

point A measurement of type sizes: 72 points to the inch.

portrait Describing the shape of a book or illustration with a height greater than its width. Contrast with **landscape**.

prelims The preliminary pages of a book, comprising the half-title, title, dedication, contents, etc.

print run The number of copies printed at a single printing.

proof One or more early impressions printed for the purpose of correcting errors. Also called a pull.

proportional spacing The spacing of typewritten characters in proportion to their size. Standard typewriters produce letters of uniform width, e.g. a capital L is given the same space as a lower case l, irrespective of their size.

pullout/foldout A folded sheet insetted into a book which, when unfolded, opens out beyond the pages of the book.

quarto (1) Having the sheet folded into four leaves or eight pages, usually written 4to. (2) A book, or the size of a book, made up of such sheets.

range To align, e.g. characters, lines of type.

recto The right-hand page of an open book. Contrast with **verso**.

reprint To print a new impression, especially with little or no change; an offprint.

repro pull A reproduction proof, of a quality good enough to be suitable for reproduction photographically.

retouching Work done by hand, especially on a photograph by pencil-work on the negative, to enhance the image or remove imperfections.

rough A rough sketch to give an impression of the original, or a drawing which needs to be redrawn.

rule A continuous printed line.

running head A headline which changes from page to page.

saddle stitched To stitch, normally with wire, through the back fold of insetted work.

sans serif   A style of typeface without serifs.

screen   A grid, of various gauges, through which images are photographed. The result, in which the image is broken up into dots, is called a **half-tone**.

serif   The finishing stroke at the top and bottom of a letter.

set   To arrange type by hand into words and lines.

sheet   A sheet which has not been folded.

signature   (1) A letter or figure at the foot of the first page (and usually on one or more successive pages) of each sheet in a book, indicating the order in which the sheets should be bound. (2) A folded section of pages comprising one sheet so marked.

solid   Describing type set without the insertion of spaces (leading) between the lines.

sort   One character of type.

special sort   An unusual character, or a character which is not part of the standard fount.

specification   The detailed description of typeface size, style, etc. which the designer determines for each book. Also called a type spec.

specimen   A specimen page giving examples of all the typographical styles, sizes, headings, etc. that a printer will encounter in setting a particular book.

spread/double-page spread   A table, illustration, etc. which extends across an opening.

stet   To restore text after marking for deletion, an instruction indicated to the printer by a row of dots below the text which is to be restored.

strip in   To join the ends of two pieces of film or paper.

tint   A mechanical tint: a pattern of dots, hatching, etc. or a solid panel in a second colour, which a draughtsman, blockmaker or printer can apply to an illustration.

tip in   Pasting a pullout, plate, errata slip, etc. to the adjoining page, rather than binding it in with the other pages.

transpose   To change the order of characters, words, paragraphs, etc.

turnovers   All the lines in a paragraph except the first.

type area   The area on a page occupied by the text and the notes (it may or may not include the headline and page number).

typeface   The printing surface of a type cut into one of a variety of styles.

umlaut   In German, the two dots placed over a letter representing a vowel change brought about by a vowel or semivowel, especially i, j, in the following syllable.

unit   The body width in which letters are cast in the Monotype method, calculated as one em = 18 units, or one en = 9 units.

upper-case   Capital letters.

variant/variant reading   One or more words and/or punctuation marks in an early version of a text which differ from the final version.

verso   The left-hand page of an open book. Contrast with **recto**.

web printing   Printing on a reel of paper as distinct from printing on individual sheets. Reeled paper is normally cut and folded on the printing press.

widow   The last line of a paragraph when it appears at the top of a page.

wordbreak   The division of a word at the end of a line.

wrap-round   A small group of pages, such as half-tones, folded around a signature so that half precede the signature and the rest follow it.

x height   The height of a lower-case x (i.e. a letter without an ascender or descender), used to gauge the height of a particular typeface.

27.6   Stock Exchange

above par   Describing a share or bond the market price of which is greater than its face value.

account   A division of the Stock Exchange calendar; an account usually runs for two weeks (ten working days).

accepting house   (See under Business p 306).

account day   The day on which the bargains done in the course of an individual account are settled, usually the second Monday after the end of the account.

accumulative dividend   A dividend which has not been paid out to shareholders and is therefore included in a company's liabilities.

after-hours dealings   Dealings conducted after the official close at 3.30 pm and which thus become the first deals done on the following day of business. Also known as early bargains.

aftermarket   The trading of bonds immediately after they have been issued.

agent   A trader who acts for an investor.

alpha securities   The largest industrial shares, called 'blue chip' stocks before the Big Bang.

application form   The document, issued by a company as part of its prospectus, for use by the public to apply for shares in the company.

arbitrage Buying stocks and shares in one country or market and selling them in another, in order to profit from price differences.

Articles of Association (See p 116).

assets A business's property or resources, such as buildings, machinery, stock, cash, debts, and goodwill.

asset-stripping The practice of taking over a company (usually one with a poor financial record) and selling off its assets in order to make a profit.

authorised capital The maximum amount of money that a company is allowed to raise by issuing shares to the general public. This amount is shown in the company's Memorandum of Association.

backwardation A situation which occurs when the bid price and offer price of a market maker deviate enough to allow an immediate profit to be made by simultaneously buying and selling.

banker's acceptance note A letter of credit or draft which is backed by a bank.

bargain Any deal or transaction taking place on the Stock Exchange.

bear A Stock Exchange dealer or other trader who sells shares, commodities, etc. in the hope that prices will fall before he or she is due to deliver. He or she can then buy them at a lower price and in this way make a profit. A market in which prices are falling is called a **bear market**. Compare with **bull**.

bearer bond A bond which has no registration of ownership and which is thus held by whoever possesses it.

bed and breakfast Sale and repurchase of the same stock at an agreed cost to establish a capital loan or loss for tax purposes, whilst retaining beneficial ownership.

beta securities Since the Big Bang, the name for secondary shares (more active than gamma securities).

bid An approach by one company to purchase another.

bid price The price at which a market maker will buy.

Big Bang The name given to the changes in the system and rules of the London Stock Exchange which came into effect on 27 October 1986, involving (among other things) the abolition of the distinction between stockbrokers and stock-jobbers, and of fixed commissions.

bond A security issued by a government or a commercial organisation on which the holder receives a rate of interest usually fixed until the repayment date.

bonus issue Extra shares issued free of charge by a company to its shareholders in proportion to the size of their current holdings. This is paid for from company reserves, and is done so that the company's share capital will more closely reflect the value of its assets.

boom market A period of rising prices, increased business activity, higher demand and increased profits.

broker A dealer or agent buying and selling (or arranging contracts for others to buy and sell) insurance, stocks and shares, shipping, etc.

brokerage The charge made by a broker for the work done in arranging a contract. It is usually calculated as a percentage of the value of the contract. More specifically, it is the charge made by a stockbroker for buying or selling shares on a client's behalf.

broker/dealer After the Big Bang, a member of the Stock Exchange able to carry out the functions previously performed by both stockbrokers and stock-jobbers (but only allowed to act in one or the other capacity in any particular deal).

bull A Stock Market dealer or other trader who buys shares, commodities, etc. in the hope that prices will rise before he or she is due to receive them. He or she can then resell them at the higher price and in this way make a profit. A market in which prices are rising is called a **bull market**. Compare with **bear**.

bulldog bond A bond denominated in sterling which is issued in the British market by a person not resident in Britain, usually guaranteed by a foreign government.

call An instalment of the total payment for newly-issued shares.

call option An option to buy shares or commodities at or within a specified time and at an agreed price.

capital (1) The total financial resources of an individual or organisation. (2) The total amount of money collected by the person(s) starting a company.

capitalisation issue An issue of shares which results from the conversion of a company's money reserves into share capital by means of a bonus issue. Also known as a free or scrip issue.

capital markets The money market which deals in securities which are generally medium or long-term, not short-term.

cash and new The amount paid by a seller for the privilege of postponing delivery of stocks and shares. Also known as **contango**.

CD Certificate of deposit. A certificate issued by a bank, usually for up to 90 days' maturity, which is negotiable and earns interest.

checking An automated facility offered by the Stock Exchange which matches up both parties to a bargain.

clearing system An institution which handles transactions and accepts securities for safe keeping.

close The time when a trading session ends.

closing prices The buying and selling prices of stocks and shares when the Stock Exchange finishes business for the day.

commercial paper Short-term bonds (i.e. up to 270 days) which are unsecured against the assets of the issuer.

commission Payment made to an agent or sales representative for business done, usually a percentage of the value of that business (e.g. of sales made).

common stock The American term for ordinary shares.

compensation fund The fund which the Stock Exchange maintains to reimburse investors when a member firm fails to meet its obligations.

consideration The monetary value of a Stock Exchange transaction.

contango See **cash and new**.

convertible bond A bond on which the holder exercises the option, usually for a limited time, to convert into the shares of the company which issued it, or the parent company.

coupon A dated slip (usually one of several) accompanying a bond. When it is presented to the company on the stated date it entitles the holder to a dividend or to interest due on the bond.

cum (1) Used in expressions (e.g. *cum cap.* capitalisation issue, *cum div.* dividend issue, *cum rights* rights issue) to indicate that the buyer is allowed to participate in the issue specified. (2) The abbreviation for 'cumulative' (e.g. cumulative preference share).

cumulative preference share A share with a fixed and guaranteed rate of dividend. If a company cannot afford to pay in a particular year, the dividend accumulates. Holders of cumulative preference shares must be paid in full before any payment is made to other shareholders.

current yield The return of a financial asset to a holder, expressed as the interest rate or coupon on the market price. Also known as interest yield or running yield.

debenture A particular type of loan to a company, or the document describing it. Debentures are not part of the company's share capital. They carry a fixed rate of interest (which must be paid whether the company makes a profit or not) and are usually redeemable on a set date.

deferred ordinary shares Shares whose holders are entitled to part of the company's profits only after all other shareholders have been paid.

direct placement Placing an issue of securities with a financial institution without the use of an underwriter.

discount The amount below the issue price at which a stock is trading.

discretionary account An account for which buying and selling can be undertaken without first obtaining the consent of the client.

dividend/dividend yield A proportion of a company's profits paid to shareholders. It is usually expressed as a percentage of the face value of the shares.

drop-lock A bond which automatically changes rates, changing to fixed-rate interest if the rates drop below a predetermined point.

dual capacity A situation, enabled by the Big Bang, which allows member firms of the Stock Exchange to act as agents and principals.

eligible liabilities In British banking, the liabilities that may be allowed in calculating the reserve-asset ratio.

equity The total assets of a company after liabilities are taken into account.

eurobonds Securities on which the named currency is not the currency of the country in which they have been issued.

eurodollar American currency held by an American not resident in the US, usually as a deposit with the foreign branch of an American bank or with a bank outside the US.

euronote Short-term notes (i.e. issued from three months to six months) structured as a medium-term loan in which the underwriter agrees to issue notes on request.

ex coupon Security without the right to the coupon, or the interest rate, on the bond.

face value The value printed on a share or similar document. It may be higher or lower than the market value.

Fed funds Deposits by member banks in the US Federal Reserve System, which consists of a board of governors, twelve Federal Reserve Banks and thousands of privately-owned banks who combine to control the supply of money and credit.

firm order An order to buy or sell a security that can be effected within the time allowed without further confirmation.

fixed interest security A security or bond which offers an annual guaranteed interest payment (e.g. UK gilts). There is usually a fixed date on which the bond is redeemed.

floating rate interest An interest rate which changes on a pre-determined regular basis to reflect changes in market rates, usually calculated at a certain number of points above the bank rate (e.g. floating-rate CDs, bonds or notes).

foreign bond A bond which a foreign borrower issues in the domestic market of a particular country and which is denominated in the currency of that country.

forward contract/delivery A contract for the settlement of a financial instrument or commodity on a mutually agreed date in the future. Unlike a **futures contract**, it is not standardised.

futures contract A standardised contract for the sale or purchase of a fixed quantity of commodity, financial instruments, cash, etc. at a future date.

gamma securities Stocks which are relatively inactive.

gilt-edged securities Securities such as government stocks which are regarded as very safe investments, issued to fund the deficit between a nation's taxes and revenues and government spending. Their fixed rate of interest is comparatively low, but repayment is guaranteed. Also known as gilts.

hedging Attempting to prevent losses caused by fluctuations in market prices, e.g. offsetting the cost of a purchase by selling a balancing amount before having to pay for the purchase.

insider dealing Buying and selling shares in a company on the basis of 'inside' knowledge, e.g. confidential information about the company's financial position. The Stock Exchange disapproves of insider dealing and has taken steps to outlaw it.

issue price The gross price placed on an issue of securities before commissions are deducted, expressed as a percentage of principal amount.

issuing house An institution which arranges the details of an issue of stock or shares as well as the compliance required by the Stock Exchange with its regulations governing the listing.

jobber See **market maker**.

liability Something which is owed to someone else. Typical liabilities include money owed to suppliers, money due to be paid to shareholders, money owed in tax to the Inland Revenue, and money—in the form of a loan or overdraft—owed to the bank.

LIBOR London Interbank Offered Rate: the interest rate offered by banks in the London eurodollar market, used as a point of reference for many international loans and floating-rate issues.

LIFFE London International Financial Futures Exchange. Market where financial futures and options on financial futures (e.g. bonds, interest rates and currencies) are traded.

listed security/stock A security (formerly called a quoted company) which has complied with certain requirements of the Stock Exchange and which is listed in the Stock Exchange Daily Official List.

longs/long-dated securities A security which is not due to be redeemed for at least fifteen years.

mandate The authorisation of the borrower to proceed with loan or bond issue under the terms agreed with the lead manager.

margin   Same as **spread**.

market maker   A Stock Exchange member who buys and sells stocks i.e. a broker/dealer. Before the Big Bang, this was the function of a stock-jobber, who was not allowed to deal with the public.

market order   An order to be executed immediately which is given to a broker or agent to buy or sell at the best price obtainable.

market valuation   The current value of a company or security, computed by multiplying the current price by the current number of shares issued.

maturity date   The time at which a loan or bond becomes due for payment.

member firm   A firm of broker/dealers which is a member of the Stock Exchange.

middle price   The price which is halfway between the two quoted in the Stock Exchange Daily Official List, or the average of the buying and selling prices offered by a market maker.

money market   Discount houses, banks, accepting houses and other financial institutions engaged in buying, selling, lending and borrowing money for profit.

net worth/assets   The total value of assets (both fixed and current) minus the current liabilities.

new time   Trading on the Stock Exchange for the next account period in the last two days of the present one.

nominal price   The estimated price for a security when no deals were done during a trading session.

nominal yield   The interest which can be earned on the face value of a bond. See also **current yield**.

nominee   A person named by and operating on behalf of another person, usually to preserve that person's anonymity.

note   A certificate of indebtedness usually used for short-term issues.

offer price   The price at which a market maker will sell, the best offer being the lowest obtainable from all the market makers who are quoting.

opening   The official start of a trading session, at which time an opening price is recorded.

option   The right to buy (**call option**) or sell (**put option**) at a specified price, at or within a specified time, whatever happens to the market price.

OTC   Over-the-counter: trading conducted outside stock exchanges.

par   The value stated on the front of a share, etc.

partly paid   Security on which a part of the issue price has been paid, with the remainder to be paid at a specified rate.

portfolio A collection of investments made by a person or institution.

preference shares Shares which give the owner the right to receive a fixed dividend each year before ordinary shareholders receive any profit. If the company goes into liquidation, preference shareholders receive their share capital before ordinary shareholders if sufficient funds are available.

preferred ordinary shares A type of share ranking between ordinary shares and preference shares in the 'queue' to receive payment of a dividend.

premium The amount paid for a share over and above its par value.

primary market The new market for a new issue of securities. Once dealing starts, the market is a secondary one.

principal A sum of money on which interest is paid.

prospectus A document giving details about a company and inviting the public to buy shares in the company. A copy must be sent to the Registrar of Companies beforehand.

proxy (1) A document authorising a person to act on another person's behalf (e.g. by voting on behalf of a shareholder at a company meeting). (2) A person who has been authorised to act in this way.

put option An option to sell shares or commodities at (or within) a specified time and at an agreed price. The option is usually acquired by paying a proportion of the value of the items.

quotation (1) A statement of the price and conditions relating to a (possible) business transaction. Often shortened to **quote**. (2) The listing of a company's shares in the official Stock Exchange publication (and the buying and selling of its shares in the Stock Exchange). To obtain such a quotation, usually regarded as a valuable privilege, a company must meet certain requirements (especially relating to giving information about itself).

redemption yield Annualised (or semi-annualised) yield which takes account of the flow of coupon payments on a stock as well as the amounts of profit or loss incurred on repayment of the principal on redemption.

repurchase agreement An agreement in which a security is sold and later bought back, the difference between the selling and repurchase prices being partly in lieu of interest. The seller is thus provided with cash during the interval.

reserves (1) Part of a company's profits which is retained within the company for various possible uses (i.e. not paid out to shareholders in the form of a dividend). (2) Amounts of gold and foreign currencies held by a country. They can be used to pay foreign debts, influence exchange rates, etc. (3) Amounts of cash held by banks and immediately available to customers.

roundtripping An action which enables a company to borrow and lend at a profit by taking advantage of a short-term rise in market rates to a higher level than its own rates of borrowing.

samurai bond The Japanese term for a bond issued in Japan by a foreign institution which is denominated in yen and purchasable by non-residents of Japan.

scrip issue Same as **capitalisation issue** and **bonus issue**.

SEAQ Stock Exchange Automated Quotations: an electronic system in operation since the Big Bang which displays the quotations of market makers.

securities Financial assets, such as shares or bonds, which can be bought and sold.

short The sale of a security which is not in the possession of the seller in the expectation that a profit can be made from falling prices between the selling and the delivery dates.

shorts/short-dated securities Securities which are due to be redeemed within five years.

split The process by which the number of shares in an issue is increased and the nominal value decreased so that the net effect to holders is nil. Utilised to make shares more marketable.

spread (1) In the bond markets, the difference between the selling and the buying price. (2) In the futures markets, the simultaneous sale and purchase of the same instrument for delivery in different months, and of different contracts in the same month.

stag A person who applies for new shares in the belief that they will be over-subscribed and that he or she will be able to sell his/her allotment immediately for a good profit.

stock-jobber See **market maker**.

stop-loss order An order to buy or sell at a certain price, either above or below the market price at the time the order was given.

straddle The practice of purchasing a futures contract in one market while simultaneously selling it in another.

straight bond A fixed-rate bond without conversion (i.e. not converted into gold or dollars at a fixed price).

subordinated debt In the event of liquidation, a debt that can be claimed by an unsecured creditor only after the claims of other debts have been met.

swap An agreement between two counter-parties to exchange debt obligations to enable each party to take advantage of differing interest rates or currency opportunities.

switching (1) Moving from one stock to another to take advantage of expected changes in interest rates and/or expectations, or of anomalies which may have developed. (2) Liquidating a position in the futures market while at the same time re-establishing the position in another future on the same commodity or financial instrument.

syndicate The body of managers, underwriters and selling agents of a bond.

talisman The acronym for Transfer Accounting, Lodgement for Investors, Stock Management for Jobbers: a service established in 1979 which automated much of the settlement of UK securities listed on the Stock Exchange.

tap stock A UK government bond, issued through the government broker, which can be adjusted to influence the gilts market.

traded options Options which can be traded throughout their life and exercised on the expiry date by the eventual holder.

transfers The form on which the seller of a security authorises the removal of his or her name from the register and the substitution of the name of the buyer.

turnover value The total monetary value of transactions, computed by multiplying the price by the number of shares traded.

underwriter/underwriting (1) A member of Lloyd's who accepts the risk of insuring by guaranteeing payment from his or her personal wealth in return for a share of the premium. (2) A person or institution who agrees to take up a proportion of a share issue should the investment public apply in an insufficient amount, in return for a fee.

unlisted companies Companies not listed in the Stock Exchange Daily Official List but which may be included in the USM.

USM Unlisted Securities Market. The market for the buying and selling of those shares, etc. which are not on the Stock Exchange's official list (i.e. which cannot be bought and sold on the Stock Exchange).

unsecured creditor A creditor who is entitled to payment only after secured creditors have been paid in full. If there is money left over for this, unsecured creditors are treated equally and paid in proportion to the amounts of their loans.

warrant A document issued by a company to a stockholder giving him or her the right to buy further stock at a stated price, either before a given date or at any future date.

Yankee bond A bond issued by a foreign entity in the US which is registered with the Securities and Exchange Commission.

yearling British stock which is issued by municipal authorities and which matures within a year.

yield/yield gap The difference between what is received in dividends from ordinary shares and the yield from fixed-interest shares.

zero coupon bond A bond issued without an interest coupon but at a discounted price: it will give a computed interest by the time it is redeemed at face value.

27.7 Word processing

(See also 27.2: Computing)

alphanumeric Describing any combination of letters of the alphabet and Arabic numerals which can be processed by a computer.

background A facility of some computers whereby low priority tasks can be performed whilst those of high priority are also being performed in the foreground.

bi-directional printing The printing of lines both right to left and left to right, eliminating the need for a return to the beginning of the line.

block In computing, a group of records or information units handled as a single unit and stored in adjacent locations on magnetic tape or disk. In many magnetic storage devices only complete blocks can be accessed or transferred.

boilerplate A passage of text used repeatedly in various contexts which can be inserted in different files.

centring Locating a heading or other words of text equidistant between the left and right margins.

central processing unit (CPU) The part of a computer system which co-ordinates the whole system, where all parts of the system are linked together and where the calculations and manipulation of data takes place.

character A generic expression for a letter of the alphabet, a number, a symbol or a punctuation mark printed or displayed on a screen.

character set The collection of numbers, letters, symbols and graphics that can be generated by a particular system.

command key A special key or set of keys on a keyboard which has been defined to carry out certain tasks (e.g. underscoring, saving data).

communicating word processors Word processors connected via a network to allow very rapid office-to-office and/or business-to-business communication of text.

communications A peripheral piece of hardware enabling a word processor to communicate with other equipment.

conditional page break A facility on most word processors that once the page length has been determined for a file, the word processor can be programmed to insert its own page break.

control key A key on a computer keyboard which when depressed with a variety of other keys gives additional facilities for the manipulation of files.

cpi Characters per inch. The number of characters to every horizontal inch of typing, usually 10, 12 or 15. Also known as **pitch**.

create The term given to the setting up of a new file in computing or word processing.

cursor A marker on a VDU indicating the point at which text should be entered.

cut and paste Marking the text to be repositioned (cut) and moving it to a new location (paste). A labour-saving feature when large blocks of text have to be moved.

daisy wheel The name given to a print where the type head is circular and the characters are attached round it on the ends of stalks.

daisy wheel printer A printer having a wheel which rotates at speed until the required character is brought before a hammer. The character is then struck by the hammer against the ribbon. Daisy wheels are interchangeable to facilitate different typefaces and produce letter-quality printout.

dictionary A library; a file of text with special applications (e.g. a spelling dictionary).

discretionary hyphen A hyphen inserted between syllables of a word which runs on from one line of text to the next and which is automatically deleted when the line length is changed.

display format The total number of characters visible on screen, expressed either as the total number or as the number of lines and characters in each line.

distributed logic Computer systems where logic or intelligence are distributed in the system rather than located centrally e.g. some word processing systems link intelligent terminals which may make shared use of other resources such as storage, printer.

document A medium and the data recorded on it. Most commonly refers to print on paper.

document based system A word processing program where each file is produced as a whole document and not divided on screen into pages.

document merge A facility of most word processors to join together two separate documents making one final document. If more than two documents are integrated, the process is referred to as document assembly.

dual pitch printer A printer which has the facility to switch from one type size to another by the movement of a switch.

edit The process of removing or inserting information by an operator when a record is passed through a computer.

erase To delete or obliterate a file or an item of data.

error detection A facility of communications which ensures that text has not been corrupted during transmission.

flag Information which can be added to computer data in order to characterise the data or to provide information about it. Sometimes called a marker, point or a tag.

footer A page number, catchword or other short piece of text printed at the bottom of each page, below the last line of text.

format The layout or arrangement of the text on screen or on paper.

free-form text database A facility of some word processing programmes whereby files can be organised in a specified manner and then any word or combination of words can be located, the items identified being scrolled in a window on screen.

function key One or more keys on a keyboard which allow a user to issue a series of commands with one key depression, provided that the keys have been allocated special functions.

global search A feature which activates the cursor to find every occurrence of a pre-determined character, word or phrase in a file.

global search and replace An editing function in word processing where the cursor will search for each occurrence of a particular character, word or phrase and replace it with another pre-determined character, word or phrase.

glossary Any set of frequently used passages of text (**boilerplates**).

header A page number, catchword or other short piece of text printed at the top of each page, above the first line of text.

help menu A facility which enables a WP operator to find information on available commands and their syntax without leaving the program in use and without having to refer to the manual.

impact printing A means of printing where the characters are formed on the paper by means of a hammer striking the ribbon (e.g. dot matrix printers, line printers).

insert The addition of a word, phrase or paragraph to any text that has already been produced.

insert mode Any text that is typed at a keyboard which is added to the version already appearing on the visual display unit.

justified text   Text which has an even right margin equal to the left margin and where the right hand margin appears vertically straight.

justify   To adjust the positions of words on a page, distributing additional space in lines so that the right margin forms a straight vertical and parallel edge to the left margin.

letter quality   The term usually refers to output from a printer where the printing is indistinguishable from that typed on a good electric typewriter.

letter quality printer   Any printer that can produce print of the same quality as a good electric typewriter.

line feed   A facility of most printers to automatically move the paper up through the printing mechanism one line at a time.

line graphics   A facility which enables some word processors to draw boxes or other horizontal or vertical lines round a passage of text.

list processing   A facility which enables word processors to automatically merge predetermined lists of data (e.g. names and addresses) in a standard passage of text, creating a new document.

logic-seeking   Describing a printer which automatically skips over blank spaces in the text and so prints faster.

mail merge   The process of combining a document file and a mailing list in word processing for the production of a standard letter.

mark (block)   A function which enables an operator to cut and paste passages of text by inserting special code markers at the beginning and end of a passage.

matrix printer   A printer in which each character is made up of a series of dots produced by a print head pushing a pattern of wires against a ribbon and onto the paper which also moves across the paper.

menu   A list of possible options or facilities presented to the user from data or word processing software on a computer.

merge   The combining of information from two or more sources (e.g. address lists or mailing lists with document files or form letters).

mnemonics   In word processing, a code of a few characters which initiates commands (e.g. erasing a file, moving a block, re-formatting a page).

mode   Any operating function on a word processor.

multi-access   Describing a system which enables several operators to use it simultaneously.

non-impact printing   Printers which do not require physical impact for printing characters on paper (e.g. ink jet printing and electrostatic printing).

numeric Describing a field or character only able to contain or indicate a numeral.

numeric keypad A keyboard containing only numerals.

output Information transmitted by a computer or its storage devices to a screen or printer. It may be in the form of print on paper, punched cards or paper tape.

output device A device capable of receiving information from a central processor or peripheral unit which translates computer information into another medium (e.g. a VDU, printer).

overwrite The writing of data into a computer's memory where data previously held in a location is replaced with the new data.

page The amount of text which can be displayed on screen, or a passage of text divided from another by a page break.

pagebased system A feature of some word processing programs where each file is produced in pages making up a whole document. The hard copy output is the same as it appears on the screen of a VDU.

page break An internal command which informs the printer to start a new page.

page control A feature which allows a WP operator to address the length of the typing page to suit the display of text, or omit pages of typed text which will still be numbered chronologically within the document, for the later insertion of diagrams or drawings.

page feed A facility of most printers to roll up the paper one page at a time through the printing mechanism.

pagination (1) The numbering of pages in a document. (2) A word processing function used to create and number pages.

pitch The number of characters per horizontal inch of typing (e.g. 10, 12 or 15). Also known as **cpi**.

printer An output device from a computer which produces hard copy (text on paper) concerned with speed, quality and price.

print out The reproduction of text (printed paper output) on paper which a computer produces via a printer.

print pause A command facility which stops the printer for paper change, ribbon change, paper jam, etc. automatically.

prompt A computer initiated message to the operator used to indicate that particular information is required before the program can proceed any further.

protocol A set of standards which govern a format of communications to be exchanged between two devices in a communications system.

queue The processing of jobs or items (e.g. data awaiting action, execution or transmission). If terminals in a multi-user system send a file for printing simultaneously, the files will be queued and printed in rotation.

recall   Transferring stored text to enable it to be edited or printed.

records management   A facility of some word processors which allows for the sorting, editing, storage, etc. of data which may not be related to text.

reformat   A feature whereby after the insertion, modification or deletion of text in a file, the format of the file can automatically be readjusted to give a good finished copy within the pre-set margins or line length.

repagination   Automatic alteration of page numbering and size—a feature which is normally used after the editing of text, particularly in document-based systems.

required hyphen   A hyphen in a compound word or expression which is not automatically deleted when the length of a line is altered.

reverse printer   A printer capable of printing right to left, and left to right. Also known as a bi-directional printer.

ruler line   A line across the top or bottom of a VDU screen which indicates the margin positions and the tabulation which has been set.

run   The execution of a computer program, suite of programs or routine.

save   A term used to refer to the storing of data on storage media (e.g. on magnetic disks).

scan   The examination of material e.g. a word processing document, a page of a document or the conversion of data into machine readable form.

scroll   The movement of text up and down or across a VDU so that the user can view the whole of a document or, on systems that display only half pages, the whole of a page.

search   An examination of information in computer file to find the occurrence of a character, word or phrase.

search and replace   A facility in which every occurrence of a specified character, word or phrase is replaced with a pre-defined character, word or phrase. Also known as global exchange or global search and replace.

shared logic   A computer system consisting of work stations made up of keyboards and VDUs which are connected to a CPU, usually with a hard disk. The terminals operate under central control.

sort   The arrangement of items of information into a meaningful order, often into alphabetical, numerical or chronological order.

spelling check In word processing, a program which uses a standard or specialised dictionary which can be added to by the user. When the program is run, the text is checked for spelling errors which the user can correct.

stand-alone A piece of equipment which can operate independently of any other equipment e.g. a work station which can operate on its own without being connected with a CPU is a stand-alone system. Often a category for word processors which are self contained and require no additional equipment.

standard paragraphs Text that is frequently used, stored and available for insertion into assembled documents.

standard text A facility which enables the operator to store and recall rapidly and easily words and phrases and often paragraphs that are used frequently.

stationery In word processing, single-sheet stationery describes the standard A4 format, fed into a printer sheet by sheet. Continuous stationery consists of a long strip of paper perforated at the end of each sheet and, at the sides with sprocket holes, allowing it to be fed into a printer by a tractor feed.

status line The line at the top or bottom of the screen which gives details of the work being performed (e.g. file name, page, line and column numbers, line spacing).

stop code (switch code) A special character identifying the location in the text at which data can be later inserted automatically.

strikeover A facility to type one character over another character, so that both characters (letters, numbers, symbols or a combination of these) appear in one type space.

string A group of items which are arranged in sequence according to a set of pre-defined rules (e.g. a set of consecutive characters in a computer memory).

string search A facility sometimes referred to as the find facility; when a string of characters is typed to the search, the file will be searched for where that string appears. Also known as search facility.

text editing The editing of text, which may be carried out on any form of computer from a mainframe with appropriate software to a dedicated word processor.

text editor Software which manipulates the text of computer programs themselves.

text processing Computer editing and subsequent production of text. Often used as a synonym for word processing, although text processing more commonly refers to the handling of very large quantities of text.

thermal printer A method of printing using paper coated with a dye that darkens at predetermined temperatures to produce a copy of an image.

tractor feed A piece of equipment which attaches to a printer using continuous stationery: two belts of circular studs catch the sprocket holes in the stationery to feed it through.

unconditional page break A feature of word processing programs where the operator works through a document checking page breaks and putting in unconditional page breaks where necessary.

underscore The underlining facility on word processing software.

variable block A piece of information that can be substituted for another piece of information if requested by the user. Often referred to as a variable.

visual display unit (VDU) A cathode ray tube, which looks similar to a television screen and which displays text from a computer.

word count facility Found on some document-based word processing systems, the number of words typed at any one time appears on the screen.

word processing The electronic storage, editing and manipulating of text using an electronic keyboard, computer and printer where text is stored on a magnetic medium except for final output which is in the form of print on paper.

word processor (WP) An electronic device used for the storage, editing and manipulation of text and consisting of a keyboard, an internal memory or storage, external storage, logic and printer. There are three main types: stand-alone, shared logic and distributed logic.

wordwrap A term referring to the way in which a partially typed word is automatically moved to a new line if the length of the word proves too long to fit into the existing line. Also known as wraparound.

write protect The covering of the exposed part of a floppy disk where information can be written to or read from, by a tag so that information can no longer be written on to the disk, but the reading of information from the disk is not interfered with.

write protect tag A tag used to prevent data being written onto a magnetic disk.

27.8 Foreign words and phrases

à bas Down, down with! *(Fr)*
ab initio From the beginning *(L)*

à compte   On account; in part payment *(Fr)*

ad finem   To the end *(L)*

ad gustem   According to taste *(L)*

ad hoc   For this special purpose *(L)*

ad infinitum   Without any apparent end *(L)*

ad interim   In the meanwhile *(L)*

ad libitum   At pleasure; as much as/in any way that one desires *(L)*

ad nauseam   To a sickening degree *(L)*

ad rem   To the point; to the purpose *(L)*

ad verbum   Word for word; literally *(L)*

affair d'amour/affaire de cœur   A love affair *(Fr)*

aficionado   An ardent follower, fan *(Sp)*

à fond   To the bottom; thoroughly *(Fr)*

agent provocateur   One paid to associate with a person, party or group, with the purpose of leading them to commit acts which will make them liable to punishment *(Fr)*

à la carte   According to the menu, each dish priced separately *(Fr)*

alter idem   Another precisely similar *(L)*

amor vincit omnia   Love conquers all things *(L)*

ante meridiem   Before noon *(L)*

à point   To the point; exactly right; opportunely *(Fr)*

apologia   A defence; justification *(L)*

au fait   Expert, knowledgeable about something *(Fr)*

au gratin   With breadcrumbs *(Fr)*

au pis aller   At the worst *(Fr)*

autre temps, autre mœurs   Other times, other manners *(Fr)*

avant-garde   Very modern; ahead of (artistic) fashion *(Fr)*

bête noir   What one hates most *(Fr)*

bona fide   In good faith; genuine *(L)*

bona vacantia   Unclaimed goods *(L)*

bonhomie   Easy good nature *(Fr)*

carpe diem   Enjoy the present day; seize the opportunity *(L)*

carte blanche   Freedom of action; (literally) a blank paper *(Fr)*

cause célèbre   A very famous trial *(Fr)*

caveat emptor   Let the buyer beware; at the buyer's risk *(L)*

ceteris paribus   Other things being equal *(L)*

chacun à son goût   Each to his own taste *(Fr)*

cherchez la femme   Look for the woman; there's a woman at the bottom of it *(Fr)*

cogito ergo sum   I think, therefore I am *(L)*

comme il faut   As it should be *(Fr)*

compos mentis   Of sound mind *(L)*

cordon bleu   Blue ribbon; a cook of the highest excellence *(Fr)*

corpus delicti   The body, substance or foundation of the offence *(L)*

cosi fan tutte   That is what all women do; women are all like that *(It)*

coup de main   A sudden enterprise or effort *(Fr)*

crème de la crème   The very best *(Fr)*

cri de cœur   A cry from the heart *(Fr)*

cui bono?   For whose benefit is it?; who gains by it? *(L)*

de bonne grâce   With good grace; willingly *(Fr)*

de haut en bas   From top to bottom; contemptuously *(Fr)*

déjà vu   A feeling of having previously experienced something as it happens *(Fr)*

Deo gratias   Thanks to God *(L)*

de rigueur   Absolutely necessary because of etiquette, fashion, etc. *(Fr)*

Dieu et mon droit   God and my right *(Fr)*

dolce far niente   Sweet doing-nothing; sweet idleness *(It)*

double entendre   A word or phrase with two meanings, one straightforward and one subtle or indecent *(Fr)*

dramatis personae   The characters of a drama or play *(L)*

dulce et decorum est (pro patria mori)   It is sweet and glorious (to die for one's country) *(L)*

dum spiro, spero   While I breathe, I hope *(L)*

ecce homo   Behold the man *(L)* (The words of Pontius Pilate)

embarras de richesses   Too much of a good thing *(Fr)*

enfant terrible   A child whose sayings embarrass his elders; a person who embarrasses his colleagues in a similar way *(Fr)*

en masse   In a body; all together *(Fr)*

en passant   In passing; by the way *(Fr)*

entente cordiale   A friendly agreement or relationship between states *(Fr)*

errare est humanum   To err is human *(L)*

esprit de corps   Regard for the honour of the body to which one belongs *(Fr)*

et ego in Arcadia   I too have lived in Arcadia; I too had that experience *(L)*

et tu, Brute!   You too, Brutus? *(L)* (Caesar's alleged exclamation when he saw Brutus amongst his assassins)

eureka!   I have found (it)! *(Gr)* (Archimedes' alleged exclamation when he thought of a way to determine the purity of the gold in the King of Syracuse's crown)

ex cathedra   From the episcopal or papal throne or professional chair; with high authority *(L)*

exempli gratia   By way of example *(L)*

ex libris   From the books of/library of *(L)*

fait accompli   An accomplished fact; a thing already done *(Fr)*

faux pas   A mistake; social blunder *(Fr)*

festina lente   Hasten gently; hurry slowly *(L)*

furor loquendi/scribendi   A rage for speaking/writing *(L)*

genius loci   The guardian spirit of the place *(L)*

gloria in excelsis   Glory to God in the highest *(L)*

grande dame   A lady of aristocratic manner and forceful personality *(Fr)*

hasta mañana   Until tomorrow *(Sp)*

hic sepultus   Here (is) buried *(L)*

hoi polloi   The masses; the rabble; the vulgar *(Gr)*

honi soit qui mal y pense   Shame to him who thinks evil; the shame be his who thinks ill of it *(L)*

ibidem (ibid.)   In the same place, thing or case *(L)*

idée fixe   A fixed idea; an obsession *(Fr)*

in extremis   At the point of death or in desperate circumstances *(L)*

in flagrante delicto   In the very act; (literally) while the crime is blazing *(L)*

infra dignitatem (infra dig)   Beneath one's dignity *(L)*

in re   In the matter of *(L)*

in statu quo   In the former state *(L)*

inter alia   Amongst other things *(L)*

inter nos   Between ourselves *(L)*

in toto   Entirely *(L)*

in vino veritas   In wine is truth; wine brings out the truth *(L)*

ipso facto   By that very fact; thereby *(L)*

joie de vivre   Joy of living *(Fr)*

Kirche, Küche, Kinder   Church, kitchen, children *(Ger)*

laissez faire   A general principle of non-interference *(Fr)*

le beau monde   The fashionable world *(Fr)*

magnum bonum   A great good *(L)*

magnum opus   A great work; someone's greatest achievement *(L)*

maître d'hôtel   A house-steward, major-domo, a manager or head-waiter of an hotel *(Fr)*

mala fide   With bad faith; treacherously *(L)*

mal à propos   Ill-timed *(Fr)*

mea culpa   By my own fault *(L)*

memento mori   Remember death; a reminder of death *(L)*

mens sana in corpore sano   A sound mind in a sound body *(L)*

mirabile dictu   Wonderful to tell *(L)*

modus operandi   Manner of operation; way of going about a job *(L)*

morituri te salutamus   We who are about to die salute you *(L)* (The greeting given by the gladiators to the emperor)

mot juste   The word which exactly fits the context *(L)*

nemine contradicente (nem con)   Without opposition, with no-one speaking to the contrary *(L)*

nemo me impune lacessit   No-one provokes me with impunity *(L)* (the motto of Scotland)

nihil ad rem   Nothing to the point *(L)*

nil desperandum   Never despair *(L)*

noli me tangere   Don't touch me *(L)* (the words of Jesus quoted from John's Gospel, but now often used as a general warning against interference)

nom de guerre   A pseudonym; (literally) a war name *(Fr)*

non sequitur   A remark or action unconnected with what has gone before; a conclusion that does not follow logically from the premises *(L)*

nota bene (NB)   Mark well; take good note *(L)*

nouveau riche   One who has only lately acquired wealth; an upstart *(Fr)*

obiter dictum   A thing said by the way; a cursory remark *(L)*

onus probandi   The burden of proving *(L)*

O tempora! O mores!   Oh the times! Oh the manners/customs!; What times! What conduct! *(L)*

pari passu   With equal pace; together *(L)*

per ardua ad astra   By steep and difficult ways to the stars; the way to the stars is not easy *(L)*

per diem   By the day *(L)*

persona non grata   An unacceptable person *(L)*

pièce de résistance   The best or most important item; the substantial course at dinner *(Fr)*

pied-à-terre   A dwelling kept for temporary, secondary or occasional use, usually in a city *(Fr)*

pis aller   Makeshift; the worst or last shift *(Fr)*

plus ça change, plus c'est la même chose   The more that it changes the more it is the same thing, i.e. no superficial or apparent change alters its essential nature *(Fr)*

post meridiem   After noon *(L)*

prima facie   At first sight *(L)* See also under Legal p 332.

pur sang   Of pure blood; total *(Fr)*

qui s'excuse s'accuse   He who excuses himself accuses himself; whoever makes too many or unnecessary excuses lays himself open to suspicion *(Fr)*

quid pro quo   (See under Business p 313).

quod erat demonstrandum   (the thing) which was to be proved or demonstrated *(L)*

raison d'être   The reason for the existence of something *(Fr)*

rara avis   A rare person or thing; (literally) a rare bird *(L)*

res judicata   A case or law suit already decided *(L)*

rien ne va plus   (Literally) nothing goes any more—used by croupiers to indicate that no more bets may be placed *(Fr)*

sang froid   Coolness of behaviour; calmness; (literally) cold blood *(Fr)*

sans souci   Without care or worry *(Fr)*

savoir faire   Knowledge of what to do and how to do it *(Fr)*

semper idem   Always the same *(L)*

se non è vero, è ben trovato   If it is not true, it is cleverly invented *(It)*

solvitur ambulando   It is solved in walking, i.e. the problem is solved by actually doing it, by practical experiment *(L)*

sub judice   Under (legal) consideration *(L)*

suum cuique   Let each have his own *(L)*

taedium vitae   Weariness of life *(L)*

tant mieux/pis   So much the better/worse *(Fr)*

tempus fugit   Time flies *(L)*

terra incognita   An unknown country *(L)*

tour de force   A feat of strength or skill *(Fr)*

tout court   Quite brief(ly), without preface; simply or brusquely *(Fr)*

ultima ratio regum   The last argument of kings—the cannon, war *(L)*

urbi et orbi   To the city (Rome) and the world; to everyone *(L)*

uti possidetis   The principle of letting e.g. belligerents keep what they have acquired; (literally) as you possess *(L)*

vade mecum   A handbook or pocket-companion; (literally) go with me *(L)*

veni, vidi, vici   I came, I saw, I conquered *(L)* (The words of Julius Caesar)

ventre à terre   Flat out; at full speed; (literally) belly to the ground *(Fr)*

verbatim (et literatim)   Word for word (and letter for letter) *(L)*

videlicet (viz)   To wit, namely *(L)*

vigilante   An unofficial peacekeeper or protector of a group; member of a vigilance committee *(SP)*

vivat rex/regina   Long live the king/queen *(L)*

vox populi, vox Dei   The voice of the people is the voice of God *(L)*

28 ABBREVIATIONS IN COMMON USE

(1) *It is now usual to spell abbreviations, especially of scientific terms and names of international organisations, without stops. In the list below, the stops are generally omitted, but it should be understood that in most cases neither method of writing (with or without stops) is wrong.*

(2) *Abbrevaitions for the names of societies and associations are given, but abbreviations for the designations of those belonging to any particular organisations—as Associate, Fellow, Associate Fellow, Member, or Associate Member—are not specifically included.*

A Associate ... see note (2) above; amateur; Academician; argon; ampere; angstrom; atomic (in **A-bomb**); denoting the first, or a high, class (as in **A-road**); advanced (in **A-level**); Austria (IVR)

Å Ångström

a are (metric measure); accepted; acre; active; afternoon; *annus* year; *ante* before

ā, āā in prescriptions, *ana* (Gr), i.e. of each a like quantity

AA Automobile Association; Alcoholics Anonymous; anti-aircraft

AAA Amateur Athletic Association; American Automobile Association

AAM air-to-air missile

AAQMG Assistant Adjutant and Quartermaster General

AAS *Academiae Americanae Socius* Fellow of the American Academy

AB able-bodied seaman; *Artium Baccalaureus* Bachelor of Arts

ABA Amateur Boxing Association

Abb. Abbess; Abbot; Abbey

abbr., abbrev. abbreviated; abbreviation

ABC Associated British Cinemas; American Broadcasting Corporation; Australian Broadcasting Corporation

abd abdicated; abridged

ABFM American Board of Foreign Missions

ab init *ab initio* from the beginning

abl ablative

ABM anti-ballistic missile

Abp Archbishop

abr abridged; abridgment

ABS Associate of the Building Societies Institute; Association of Broadcasting Staff

abs, absol. absolute(ly)

abs re *absente reo* the accused being absent

ABTA Association of British Travel Agents

AC aircraft(s)man; Aero Club; Alpine Club; *ante Christum* before Christ; (or **ac**) alternating current (*elect.*); Companion of the Order of Australia

Ac actinium

A/C, a/c account

ACA Associate of the Institute of Chartered Accountants

ACAS Advisory, Conciliation and Arbitration Service

acc (or **acct, a/c**) account; accountant; (or **accus**) accusative; according

ACGB Arts Council of Great Britain

ACP African, Caribbean and Pacific

ACT Australian Capital Territory

act. active; acting

ACTT Association of Cinematographic Television and Allied Technicians

ACU Association of Commonwealth Universities

ACW aircraft(s)woman

AD *anno Domini* in the year of the Lord; Dame of the Order of Australia

ad (or **advt**) advertisement; after date; *ante diem* before the day

ADC aide-de-camp; (or **AD and C**) advise duration and charge

ad fin *ad finem* at, towards, or to, the end

ad inf *ad infinitum* to infinity

ad init *ad initium* at or to the beginning

ad int *ad interim* in the meantime

adj adjective; adjourned; adjustment
Adjt Adjutant
Adjt-Gen Adjutant-General
ad lib *ad libitum* at pleasure
ad loc *ad locum* at the place
Adm Admiral
admin administration
ADP automatic data processing
adv advent; adverb; *adversus* against; advocate; advisory
ad val *ad valorem* according to value
advt advertisement
ae, aet *aetatis* of his age, aged (so many years)
AEA Atomic Energy Authority (UK)
AEB Associated Examining Board
AEC Atomic Energy Commission (US)
AEI Associated Electrical Industries
AERE Atomic Energy Research Establishment
AEU Amalgamated Engineering Union
AF Associate Fellow . . . see note (2) above; Admiral of the Fleet; audio frequency
AFA Amateur Football Association
AFC Air Force Cross
AFG Afghanistan (IVR)
AFL-CIO American Federation of Labor and Congress of Industrial Organizations
AFM Air Force Medal
AG Adjutant-General; (or **A-G**) Attorney-General; *Aktiengesellschaft* (Ger) joint stock company
Ag *argentum* silver
AGM, agm annual general meeting
AGR advanced gas-cooled reactor
agr, agric agriculture
Agt Agent
AH *anno Hegirae* in the year of Hegira—i.e. from the flight of Mohammed (AD 622, 13 Sept)
Ah ampere hour
AHA Area Health Authority
AHS *anno humanae salutis* in the year of human salvation
AI artificial insemination
AIBD Association of International Bond Dealers
AID artificial insemination by donor; Agency for International Development (US)
AIDS acquired immune deficiency syndrome

AIH artificial insemination by husband
AK Knight of the Order of Australia
AL Albania (IVR)
Al aluminium
Al(a) Alabama
Alas Alaska
Alba Alberta
Alcan Aluminium Company of Canada
Ald Alderman
alg algebra
alt alternate; altitude; alto
Alta Alberta
AM Associate Member . . . see note (2) above; *Artium Magister* Master of Arts; (or **am**) *ante meridiem* before noon; *Anno Mundi* in the year of the world; *Ave Maria* Hail Mary; amplitude modulation; Member of the Order of Australia
Am americium
Am, Amer America; American
AMC American Motors Corporation
AMDG *ad majorem Dei gloriam* to the greater glory of God
AMMA Assistant Masters' and Mistresses' Association
ammo ammunition
amp ampere
amt amount; air mail transfer
amu atomic mass unit
an. *anno* in the year; anonymous; *ante* before
anal analysis; analogy
anat anatomy
anc ancient(ly)
ANC African National Congress
Ang *Anglice* in English
anme *anonyme* (Fr) limited liability
anon anonymous
ans answer
antiq antiquities; antiquarian
Anzac (a soldier serving with the) Australian-New Zealand Army Corps
Anzus (the alliance between) Australia, New Zealand and the United States
AO Army Order; Officer of the Order of Australia
AOB any other business
AOCB any other competent business
AOC-in-C Air Officer Commanding-in-Chief
AOF Ancient Order of Foresters
aor aorist

AP Associated Press
APEX Association of Professional, Executive, Clerical and Computer Staff
apo apogee
Apoc Apocalypse; Apocrypha(l)
app appendix; apparent(ly); apprentice
appro approval; approbation
approx approximate(ly)
APR annual percentage rate
Apr April
APRC *anno post Romam conditam* in the year after the founding of Rome (753 BC)
AQ achievement quotient
aq *aqua* water
Ar argon
Ar, Arab Arabic
ar *anno regni* in the year of the reign
ar, arr arrive(s); arrival
ARA Associate of the Royal Academy
ARAMCO Arabian-American Oil Company
ARC Agricultural Research Council
arccos inverse cosine
arch archaic; architecture
archaeol archaeology; archaeological
Archd Archdeacon; Archduke
archit architecture
arcsin inverse sine
arctan inverse tangent
arg *argentum* silver
arith arithmetic(al)
Ariz Arizona
Ark Arkansas
ARP Air Raid Precautions
ARR *anno regni regis* or *reginae* in the year of the king's or the queen's reign
arr arranged; arrive(s); arrival
art article; artificial; (or **arty**) artillery
AS Anglo-Saxon; *anno salutis* in the year of salvation; Assistant Secretary
As arsenic
ASA Amateur Swimming Association; American Standards Association
asap as soon as possible
ASC American Society of Cinematographers
Asda Associated Dairies
Asdic an acronym from Allied (or Anti-) Submarine Detection and Investigation Committee, used for a particular device for locating submerged objects

ASE Amalgamated Society of Engineers; Association for Science Education
ASEAN Association of South-East Asian Nations
ASF Associate of the Institute of Shipping and Forwarding Agents
ASH Action on Smoking and Health
ASLEF Associated Society of Locomotive Engineers and Firemen
ASM air-to-surface missile
ASP accelerated surface post
Ass, Assoc Association
Asst Assistant
AST Atlantic Standard Time
ASTMS Association of Scientific, Technical and Managerial Staffs
astr, astron astronomy
astrol astrology
AT Alternative Technology
ATA Air Transport Auxiliary
ATC Air Training Corps; air traffic control; automatic train control
ATM automated teller machine
atm atmosphere
at no, at numb atomic number
Att Attic (Greek); Attorney
Att-Gen Attorney-General
attrib attribute(d); attributive(ly)
Atty Attorney
ATV Associated Television
at wt atomic weight
AU (or **ÅU**) Ångström unit (now usu. Ångström; abbrev. Å); astronomical unit
Au *aurum* gold
AUC *anno urbis conditae* or *ab urbe condita* in the year from the building of the city—Rome (753 BC)
AUEW Amalgamated Union of Engineering Workers
Aufl *Auflage* (Ger) edition
Aug August
AUS Australia, including Papua New Guinea (IVR)
AUT Association of University Teachers
aut, auto automatic
Auth Ver, AV Authorised Version
AV audio-visual
av *annos vixit* lived (so many) years
av (or **ave**) avenue; average
AVM Air Vice-Marshal
avoir, avdp avoirdupois
AWOL absent, or absence, without official leave

AWRE   Atomic Weapons Research Establishment

ax   axiom

az   azimuth

B   Baron; British; Bachelor; boron; bel; black (on lead pencils); Belgium (IVR)

2B, 3B   same as **BB, BBB** (on lead pencils)

b   born; book; bowled; breadth

BA   *Baccalaureus Artium* Bachelor of Arts; British America; British Association (for the Advancement of Science); British Academy; Buenos Aires; British Airways; Booksellers' Association (of Great Britain and Ireland)

Ba   barium

BAA   British Airports Authority

BABS   beam, or blind, approach beacon system

BAC   British Aircraft Corporation

Bach   Bachelor

BACIE   British Association for Commercial and Industrial Education

BACS   Bankers' Automated Clearing Service

BAFTA   British Academy of Film and Television Arts

BAgr(ic)   Bachelor of Agriculture

BAI   *Baccalaureus in Arte Ingeniaria* Bachelor of Engineering

bal   balance

BALPA   British Airline Pilots' Association

B and B   bed and breakfast

B and FBS   British and Foreign Bible Society

BAOR   British Army of the Rhine

Bap, Bapt   Baptist

bap, bapt   baptised

Bar   Barrister

bar   baritone

BArch   Bachelor of Architecture

Bart   Baronet

Bart's   St Bartholomew's Hospital, London

BASF   *Badische Anilin und Soda-Fabrik* (German chemical company)

BAT   British-American Tobacco Company

bat, batt   battalion; battery

BB   Boys' Brigade; double, or very, black (on lead pencils)

bb   books

BBB   triple black, blacker than **BB** (on lead pencils)

BBBC   British Boxing Board of Control

BBC   British Broadcasting Corporation (orig. Company)

BBFC   British Board of Film Censors

BC   before Christ; Board of Control; British Columbia; Battery Commander

BCAL   British Caledonian (Airways)

BCC   British Council of Churches

bcg   bacillus of Calmette and Guérin, an attenuated strain of the tubercle bacillus, used for inoculation

BCh   *Baccalaureus Chirurgiae* Bachelor of Surgery

BCL   Bachelor of Civil Law

BCom(m)   Bachelor of Commerce

BCS   British Computer Society

BD   Bachelor of Divinity

bd   bound

BDA   British Dental Association

Bde   Brigade

BDH   British Drug Houses

BDI   *Bundesverband der Deutschen Industrie* (Ger) Federation of German Industry

BDS   Bachelor of Dental Surgery

bds   boards

BE   Bachelor of Engineering; Board of Education

Be   beryllium

B/E, be   bill of exchange

BEAB   British Electrical Approvals Board

BEAMA   British Electrical and Allied Manufacturers' Association

BEd   Bachelor of Education

Beds   Bedfordshire

BEF   British Expeditionary Force

bef   before

Belg   Belgian; Belgium; Belgic

BEM   British Empire Medal

Benelux   a name for Belgium, the Netherlands and Luxembourg

BEng   Bachelor of Engineering

Berks   Berkshire

B ès L   *Bachelier ès Lettres* (Fr) Bachelor of Letters

B ès S   *Bachelier ès Sciences* (Fr) Bachelor of Sciences

bet.   between

BeV   billion electron-volt(s) (in USA, where billion means 1000 million, same as **GeV**)

bf   brought forward

BFPO British Forces Post Office
BG Bulgaria (IVR)
bhp brake horse-power
BHS British Home Stores
Bi bismuth
Bib Bible
Bibl Biblical
bibl bibliotheca (=a library, book-collection, or catalogue)
biblio, bibliog bibliography
BICC British Insulated Callender's Cables
BIFU Banking Insurance and Finance Union
BIM British Institute of Management
biog biography
biol biology
BIPM *Bureau International des Poids et Mesures* (Fr) International Bureau of Weights and Measures
BIR British Institute of Radiology
BIS Bank for International Settlements
bis bissextile (=having a day added, as a leap year)
bk book; bank; bark
bkg banking
bkt basket
BL Bachelor of Law; Bachelor of Letters; British Legion; British Leyland; British Library
bl barrel; bale; (or **B/L**) bill of lading
BLAISE British Library Automated Information Service
bldg building
BLESMA British Limbless Ex-Servicemen's Association
BLit(t) *Baccalaureus Lit(t)erarum* Bachelor of Literature or Letters
BLLD British Library Lending Division
BLMC British Leyland Motor Corporation
BLRD British Library Reference Division
Blvd Boulevard
BM Bachelor of Medicine; British Museum; Brigade Major
BMA British Medical Association
BMEWS ballistic missile early warning system
BMJ British Medical Journal
BML British Museum Library
BMus Bachelor of Music
BMW *Bayerische Motoren Werke* (Ger) Bavarian motor works

Bn Baron
bn battalion
BNEC British National Export Council
BNFL British Nuclear Fuels Limited
BNOC British National Oil Corporation
bo branch office; buyer's option; (or **BO**) body odour
BOA British Optical Association
BOC British Oxygen Company
BOCM British Oil and Cake Mills
Bol Bolivia
bor borough
BOSS Bureau of State Security (South Africa)
bot botany; bought; bottle
BOTB British Overseas Trade Board
Boul Boulevard
BP British Pharmacopoeia; British Petroleum; Baden-Powell; be prepared
Bp Bishop
bp boiling-point; bills of parcels; bills payable; (or **b pl**) birthplace; *bonum publicum* the public good
BPC British Printing Corporation; British Pharmaceutical Codex
BPharm Bachelor of Pharmacy
BPhil *Baccalaureus Philosophiae* Bachelor of Philosophy
BQ *bene quiescat* may he (or she) rest well
BR British Rail; Brazil (IVR)
Br bromine
Br Brother
br bank rate; branch; brig; brown; bridge
Braz Brazil; Brazilian
BRCS British Red Cross Society
BRD *Bundesrepublik Deutschland* (Ger) German Federal Republic
b rec bills receivable
Bret Breton
Brig Brigadier
Brig-Gen Brigadier-General
Brit Britain; Britannia; British; Briton
Bro Brother
Bros Brothers
BRS British Road Services
BS Bachelor of Science or of Surgery; Blessed Sacrament; balance sheet; (or **bs**) bill of sale; British Shipbuilders
BSA Building Societies Association; Birmingham Small Arms

BSAC British Sub Aqua Club
BSC British Steel Corporation; British Sugar Corporation
BSc Bachelor of Science
BSI British Standards Institution; Building Societies Institute
BSM British School of Motoring
BS(S) British Standards (Specification)
BST British Summer Time; British Standard Time
Bt Baronet
BT British Telecom
BTA British Tourist Authority
BTEC Business and Technical Education Council
Btu British thermal unit
bu. bushel(s)
Bucks Buckinghamshire
Bulg Bulgaria; Bulgarian
BUNAC British Universities North America Club
BUPA British United Provident Association
bus., bush. bushel(s)
BV *Beata Virgo* Blessed Virgin; *bene vale* farewell
BVM The Blessed Virgin Mary
BVM(&)S Bachelor of Veterinary Medicine and Surgery

C carbon; Conservative
°C degree(s) Celsius, centigrade
c centi-; *caput* chapter; cent; centime; *circa* about; caught
¢ cent(s)
© copyright
CA Chartered Accountant (Scotland); County Alderman
Ca calcium
ca *circa* about; cases
CAA Civil Aviation Authority
CAB Civil Aeronautics Board (USA); Citizens Advice Bureau
cad cash against documents
CAI computer-aided instruction
CAL computer-assisted learning
cal calorie
Cal, Calif California
Cam, Camb Cambridge
Cambs Cambridgeshire
CAMRA Campaign for Real Ale
CAN customs assigned number
Can Canada; Canadian; Canon; Canto

C and A Clemens and August (clothing stores)
C and G City and Guilds (of London Institute)
C & W country and western music
Cant Canterbury; Canticles
Cantab *Cantabrigiensis* of Cambridge
Cantuar *Cantuaria* Canterbury; *Cantuariensis* of Canterbury
CAP Common Agricultural Policy
cap capital; *caput* chapter; *capitulum* head, chapter; *capiat* let him (or her) take
caps capitals (in printing)
Capt Captain
CAR Central African Republic
Car. *Carolus* Charles
car. carat
CARD Campaign Against Racial Discrimination
Card. Cardinal
Cards Cardiganshire
CARE Co-operative for American Relief to Everywhere
Caricom Caribbean Community and Common Market
CASE Confederation for the Advancement of State Education
CAT College of Advanced Technology; computer-aided typesetting
cat. catechism; catalogue
Cath. Catholic
cath. cathedral
CB Companion of the Order of the Bath; confined (or confinement) to barracks; Citizens' Band (radio); cash book
CBC Canadian Broadcasting Corporation
CBE Commander of the Order of the British Empire
CBI Confederation of British Industry
CBM Californian Business Machines
CBS Confraternity of the Blessed Sacrament; Columbia Broadcasting System
CC County Council; Cricket Club; closed circuit (transmission); Companion of the Order of Canada; Chamber of Commerce
cc cubic-centimetre(s); *capita* chapters; carbon copy
CCA current cost accounting
CCCP see **USSR**

CCF   Combined Cadet Force
CCPR   Central Council of Physical Recreation
CCS   Corporation of Certified Secretaries
CD   *Corps Diplomatique* (Fr) Diplomatic Corps; Civil Defence; contagious disease(s)
Cd   cadmium
c/d   carried down
CDN   Canada (IVR)
Cdr   Commander
CDSO   Companion of the Distinguished Service Order
CDV   Civil Defence Volunteers
CE   Civil Engineer; Council of Europe
Ce   cerium
CEDO   Centre for Education Development Overseas (formerly **CREDO**)
CEGB   Central Electricity Generating Board
CEI   Council of Engineering Institutions
cel   celebrated
Celt.   Celtic
cen   central; century
CEng   Chartered Engineer
cent   *centum* a hundred; century; central
CENTO   Central Treaty Organisation
CERN   *Conseil Européen pour la Recherche Nucléaire* (Fr) European Organisation for Nuclear Research
cert   certainty; (or **certif**) certificate; certificated; certify
CET   Central European Time
cet par   *ceteris paribus* other things being equal
CF   Chaplain to the Forces
Cf   californium
cf   calf (book-binding)
cf   *confer* compare
cf (and) i   cost, freight, and insurance
CFAFr   Communauté Financière Africaine franc
CFPFr   Communauté Française du Pacific franc
cg   centigram(me)(s)
cg   centre of gravity
CG(L)I   City and Guilds (of London) Institute
CGPM   *Conférence Générale des Poids et Mesures* (Fr) General Conference of Weights and Measures
CGS   (or **cgs**) centimetre-gramme-second (unit or system); Chief of the General Staff

CGT   capital gains tax; *Confédération Générale du Travail* (Fr) General Confederation of Labour
CH   Companion of Honour; *Confederatio Helvetica* Switzerland (also IVR)
Ch   Chief; China; Church; Champion
ch   central heating; chaldron; chapter; child
Chamb.   Chamberlain
Chanc.   Chancellor; Chancery
Chap.   Chaplain; Chapter
CHAPS   Clearing House Automated Payments System
Chas   Charles
ChB   *Chirurgiae Baccalaureus* Bachelor of Surgery
chem   chemistry; chemical
Ch Hist   Church History
Chin.   China; Chinese
ChJ   Chief-Justice
ChM   *Chirurgiae Magister* Master of Surgery
choc   chocolate
Chr   Christ; Christian
chron   chronicle; chronology; chronological
CI   Channel Islands
CIA   Central Intelligence Agency (USA)
Cia   *Compagnia* (It) Company
CID   Criminal Investigation Department; Council of Industrial Design
CIE   *Córas Iompair Éireann* (Ir) Transport Organisation of Ireland
Cie   *Compagnie* (Fr) Company
cif   cost, insurance, freight
CIGS   Chief of Imperial General Staff (now **CGS**)
CII   Chartered Insurance Institute
CIM   Commission on Industry and Manpower
C-in-C   Commander-in-Chief
CIPFA   Chartered Institute of Public Finance and Accountancy
CIPM   *Comité International des Poids et Mesures* (Fr) International Committee of Weights and Measures
CIR   Commission on Industrial Relations
cir, circ   *circa, circiter, circum* about
circs   circumstances
CIS   Chartered Institute of Secretaries
CIT   Chartered Institute of Transport
cit   citation; citizen

civ civil; civilian
CJ Chief-Justice
Cl chlorine
cl centilitre(s); *cum laude* with praise; class; clause
class classical; classification
CLitt Companion of Literature
CLR computer language recorder
CLT computer language translator
CM Certificated Master: Corresponding Member; Common Metre; *Chirurgiae Magister* Master of Surgery; Member of the Order of Canada
Cm curium
cm centimetre(s)
CMG Companion of the Order of St Michael and St George
CMI computer-managed instruction
Cmnd Command Paper
CMRST Committee on Manpower Resources for Science and Technology
CMS Church Missionary Society
CNAA Council for National Academic Awards
CND Campaign for Nuclear Disarmament
CNR Canadian National Railway
CNS central nervous system
CO conscientious objector; Colonial Office (before Aug. 1966); Commonwealth Office (from Aug. 1966; see also **FCO**); Commanding Officer; Criminal Office; Crown Office
Co cobalt; Company; County
c/o care of
coad coadjutor
Cod. Codex
COD, cod cash (or collect) on delivery
co-ed co-educational
C of A Certificate of Airworthiness
C of E Church of England; Council of Europe
C of I Church of Ireland
C of S Church of Scotland; Chief of Staff
cog cognate
cog centre of gravity
COGB Certified Official Government Business
COHSE Confederation of Health Service Employees
COI Central Office of Information
COL computer-oriented language

Col Colonel; Colorado
col column
coll college; colleague; collector; colloquial
collat collateral(ly)
colloq colloquial(ly)
Colo Colorado
COM computer output microfilm
Com Commander; Commodore; Committee; Commissioner; Commonwealth; Communist
com common; comedy: commerce; committee; commune
Comdr Commander
Comdt Commandant
COMECON Council for Mutual Economic Aid, or Assistance (Communist Nations)
comm commentary; commander; communication
Commissr Commissioner
commn commission
Commy Commissary; Communist
comp comparative; compositor; compare; compound; compounded
compar comparative; comparison
COMSAT Communications Satellite (USA)
Com Ver Common Version
Con Consul
con *contra* against; *conju(n)x* consort; conclusion; conversation; convenience
conc concentrated; concentration
Cong Congress; Congregation(al)
conj conjunction; conjunctive
Conn Connecticut
conn connection; connected; connotation
cons consonant
Consols Consolidated Funds
cont, contd continued
contr contracted; contraction
contr bon mor *contra bonos mores* contrary to good manners or morals
conv conventional
co-op co-operative
Cop, Copt Coptic
Cor Corinthians; Coroner
Cor Mem Corresponding Member
corol, coroll corollary
Corp Corporation; Corporal
corr corrupted; corruption; correspond
Cor Sec Corresponding Secretary
CoS Chief of Staff

cos cosine
CP Clerk of the Peace; Common Pleas; carriage paid; College of Preceptors; Communist Party; Cape Province (S. Africa)
cp candle-power; compare
CPA Chartered Patent Agent
CPAC Consumer Protection Advisory Committee
CPAG Child Poverty Action Group
CPC Clerk of the Privy Council
CPI, cpi consumer price index; characters per inch
Cpl Corporal
cpp current purchasing power
CPR Canadian Pacific Railway
CPS *Custos Privati Sigilli* Keeper of the Privy Seal; (or **cps**) characters per second
CPSA Civil and Public Services Association
CPU central processing unit
CR *Carolus rex* King Charles; *civis romanus* a Roman citizen; *Custos Rotulorum* Keeper of the Rolls
Cr chromium
cr credit; creditor; crown
CRAC Careers Research and Advisory Centre
CRE Commission for Racial Equality
cres, cresc crescendo; crescent
CRMP Corps of Royal Military Police
CRO cathode-ray oscillograph; Commonwealth Relations Office (until 1966); Criminal Records Office
CRT cathode-ray tube
CS Court of Session; Clerk to the Signet; Civil Service; Christian Science; Chemical Society; orthobenzylidene malononitrile, an irritant 'gas' synthesised (1928) by *C*orson and *S*toughton; Czechoslovakia (IVR)
Cs caesium
c/s cycles per second (hertz)
CSE Certificate of Secondary Education
CSEU Confederation of Shipbuilding and Engineering Unions
CSIRO Commonwealth Scientific and Industrial Research Organisation
CSO community service order
CSP Council for Scientific Policy; Chartered Society of Physiotherapists
CST Central Standard Time
CSU Civil Service Union

CSV community service volunteer
CSYS Certificate of Sixth Year Studies
C/T credit transfer
Ct Connecticut
ct cent; carat
CTC Cyclists' Touring Club
CTOL conventional take-off and landing
CTT capital transfer tax
Cu *cuprum* copper
cu, cub cubic
CUP Cambridge University Press
cur, curt current (this month)
cusec cubic feet per second
CV, cv *curriculum vitae* (see Dict), or *cursus vitae* course, progress, of life
cva cerebrovascular accident
CVO Commander of the (Royal) Victorian Order
CWO, cwo cash with order
cwr continuous welded rail
CWS Co-operative Wholesale Society
cwt hundred-weight(s)—**c** (*centum* a hundred), **wt** (weight)

D deuterium; Federal Republic of Germany (IVR)
3-D three-dimensional
d day; diameter; *dele* delete; dead; died; deserted; degree; *denarius* or *denarii* a penny or pence (before 1971): duke
DA District Attorney; Diploma of Art
D(A)AG Deputy (Assistant) Adjutant-General
Dan Daniel; Danish
D and C dilatation and curettage (an operation which cleans out a body-cavity, esp. the womb)
DATEC data and telecommunications
dau daughter
dB decibel
DBE Dame Commander of the Order of the British Empire
DC *da capo* (It) return to the beginning (*mus*); District of Columbia; (or **dc**) direct current (*elect*): District Commissioner
DCL Doctor of Civil Law; Distillers Company Limited
DCM Distinguished Conduct Medal
DCMG Dame Commander of the Order of St Michael and St George
DCS Deputy Clerk of Session

DCVO Dame Commander of the (Royal) Victorian Order

DD *Divinitatis Doctor* Doctor of Divinity

dd, D/D days after date; day's date; direct debit

DDD *dat, dicat, dedicat* gives, devotes, and dedicates; *dono dedit dedicavit* gave and dedicated as a gift

DDR *Deutsche Demokratische Republik* (Ger) German Democratic Republic (also IVR)

DDS Doctor of Dental Surgery

DDT dichlorodiphenyltrichloroethane, an insecticide

DE Department of Employment

DEA Department of Economic Affairs

Dec December

dec deceased

dec, decl declaration; declension

DEd Doctor of Education

def definition; (or **deft**) defendant

deg degree(s)

Del Delaware

del delegate; (or **delt**) *delineavit* drew it

demon, demons demonstrative

DEng Doctor of Engineering

dent dental; dentist; dentistry

DEP Department of Employment and Productivity

Dep, Dept, dep, dept department; deputy

dep deposed; depart(s); departure

der, deriv derivation; derived

derv diesel engine fuel oil (from *d*iesel *e*ngined *r*oad *v*ehicle)

DES Department of Education and Science

DesRCA Designer of the Royal College of Art

DEW distant early warning

DF Defender of the Faith; Dean of the Faculty

DFC Distinguished Flying Cross

DFM Distinguished Flying Medal

dft defendant; draft

DG *Dei gratia* by the grace of God

dg decigram(me)(s)

dh *das heisst* (Ger) that is to say

DHSS Department of Health and Social Services (formerly Security)

dial dialect

diam diameter

DIC Diploma of the Imperial College

dict dictator; dictionary

diff different; difference

DIG Disabled Income Group

DIH Diploma in Industrial Health

dil dilute

DIN *Deutsche Industrie Normen* (Ger) German Industrial Standards

DIng *Doctor Ingeniariae* Doctor of Engineering

Dip Diploma, as eg **Dip Ed,** Diploma in Education, **Dip Tech,** Diploma in Technology

Dir Director

dis discontinued

disc discount; discoverer

diss dissertation

dist distance; distinguish; district; distilled

div divide; division; divine; divorced; dividend

DIY do-it-yourself

DJ disc-jockey

DK Denmark (IVR)

DL Deputy Lieutenant

dl decilitre(s)

DLit(t) *Doctor litterarum* or *litteraturae* Doctor of Letters or Literature

DM Deutsche Mark (Federal German currency)

dm decimetre(s)

DMus Doctor of Music

DMZ demilitarised zone

DNA deoxyribonucleic acids

DNB Dictionary of National Biography

do *ditto* (It) the same (aforesaid)

DOA dead on arrival

dob date of birth

DOC District Officer Commanding

DOE Department of the Environment

DOG Directory of Opportunities for Graduates

DOM *Deo optimo maximo* to God, best and greatest; *Dominus Omnium Magister* God the master of all; dirty old man

Dom *Dominus* Lord; Dominion

dom domestic

DOMS Diploma in Ophthalmic Medicine and Surgery

Dor Doric

doz dozen

DP Displaced Person; data processing; duly performed (the work of the class)

DPH Diploma in Public Health

DPh, DPhil *Doctor Philosophiae* Doctor of Philosophy

DPM Diploma in Psychological Medicine

dpm disintegrations per minute

DPP Director of Public Prosecutions

dpt department

Dr Doctor; debtor; drummer; driver; drachma (Greek currency)

dr dead reckoning; dram; drawer

DS *dal segno* (It) from the sign (*mus*); disseminated sclerosis

ds, D/S days after sight

DSC Distinguished Service Cross

DSc *Doctor Scientiae* Doctor of Science

DSM Distinguished Service Medal

DSO Distinguished Service Order

dsp *decessit sine prole* died without issue

DT data transmission; (or **dt, DT's, dt's**) delirium tremens

DTh *Doctor Theologiae* Doctor of Theology

DTI Department of Trade and Industry

DV *Deo volente* God willing

dvp *decessit vita patris* died in father's lifetime

dwt pennyweight—**d** (*denarius* a penny), **wt** (weight)

dyn dyne; dynamo; dynamometer

E East; English; Spain (IVR)

E energy

E and OE errors and omissions excepted

eaon except as otherwise noted

EAPS European Association of Professional Secretaries

Ebor *Eboracum* York; *Eboracensis* of York

EBU European Broadcasting Union

EC East Central; Established Church; European Community; Electricity Council

EC $ East Caribbean dollar

ECE Economic Commission for Europe

ECG electrocardiogram (-graph)

ECG(D) Export Credits Guarantee (Department)

ECO English Chamber Orchestra

ECSC European Coal and Steel Community

ECT electroconvulsive therapy

ECTU European Confederation of Trade Unions

ECU English Church Union; European currency unit

Ed Editor

ed, edit edited; edition

EdB Bachelor of Education

EDC European Defence Community

EDF European Development Fund

Edin Edinburgh

edit edited; edition

EDP electronic data processing

EDS English Dialect Society

EE errors excepted

EEC European Economic Community

EEG electroencephalogram (-graph)

EET Eastern European Time

EETS Early English Text Society

EFL English as a foreign language

EFT electronic funds transfer

EFTA European Free Trade Association

EFTPOS electronic funds transfer at point of sale

eg, eg, ex gr *exempli gratia* for example

EGU English Golf Union

EI East Indies

EIS Educational Institute of Scotland

El Al Israeli airline (lit. 'towards the sky')

elec, elect electric; electricity

ELT English language teaching

EMA European Monetary Agreement

EMF European Monetary Fund

emf electromotive force

EMI EMI Limited (formerly Electrical and Musical Industries Limited)

Emp Emperor, Empress

EMS European Monetary System

emu electromagnetic unit

enc(s) enclosure(s)

ENE east-north-east

ENEA European Nuclear Energy Agency

Eng England; English

eng engineer; engraver; engraving

Ens Ensign

ENSA Entertainments National Services Association

ENT Ear, Nose and Throat

Env Ext Envoy Extraordinary

EOC Equal Opportunities Commission

eod every other day

EP   extended play (record): electroplated
Ep   Epistle
EPA   European Productivity Agency
EPIC   Exchange Price Information Service
EPNS   electroplated nickel silver; English Place-Name Society
EPU   European Payments Union
ER   *Elisabeth Regina* Elizabeth, Queen
ER(I)   *Edwardus Rex (Imperator)* Edward, King (and Emperor)
ERNIE   *e*lectronic *r*andom *n*umber *i*ndicator *e*quipment (computer)
ESA   European Space Agency
Esc   escudo (Portuguese currency)
ESE   east-south-east
ESL   English as a second language
ESN   educationally subnormal
ESP   extra-sensory perception
esp, espec   especially
Esq, Esqr   Esquire
ESRC   Economic and Social Research Council
ESRO   European Space Research Organisation
ESSO   Standard Oil
EST   Eastern Standard Time; electric shock treatment
est   established; estimated
ESU   English-Speaking Union
ET   Arab Republic of Egypt (IVR)
ETA   estimated time of arrival
et al   *et alii, aliae,* or *alia* and others; *et alibi* and elsewhere
etc, &c   *et ceteri* or *cetera* and the others, and so forth
ETD   estimated time of departure
et seq or **sq** (sing), *et sequens* **et sqq** (pl) *et sequentes* or *sequentia* and the following
ETU   Electrical Trades Union
ety, etym   etymology; etymological
EU   Evangelical Union
Eu   europium
Euratom   *Eur*opean *Atom*ic Energy Community
eV   electron-volt
ex   examined; example: exception; executive; export
Exc   Excellency
exc   except; exception
ex div   *extra dividendum* without dividend
ex gr   *exempli gratia* for the sake of example
ex lib   *ex libris* from the books (of)—as on bookplates

ex officio   by virtue of his office (Lat)
exp   export; exponential
exr   executor
exrx   executrix
ext   extension; externally; extinct; extra; extract

F   Fellow . . . see note (2); Fahrenheit; fluorine; France (IVR)
F   force
f   following; farthing; feminine; fathom; foot; forte; folio
f   frequency
FA   Football Association; Faculty of Actuaries
Fa   Florida
fam   familiar; family
FAO   Food and Agriculture Organisation
FAS   Fellow of the Society of Arts; Fellow of the Antiquarian Society
fas   free alongside ship
FBA   Fellow of the British Academy
FBI   Federal Bureau of Investigation
FCA   Fellow of the Institute of Chartered Accountants
FCO   Foreign and Commonwealth Office (**FO** and **CO** combined in 1968)
fcp, fcap   foolscap
FD   *Fidei Defensor* Defender of the Faith
Fe   *ferrum* iron
Feb   February
fec   *fecit* did it, or made it (sing.)
fem   feminine
FET   field-effect transistor
feud   feudal
ff   *fecerunt* did it, or made it (pl); folios; following (pl)
ff   fortissimo
FH   fire hydrant
FIAT   *Fabbrica Italiana Automobile Torino* (It) Italian Motor Works in Turin
Fid Def   *Fidei Defensor* Defender of the Faith
FIDO   Fog Investigation and Dispersal Operation; Film Industry Defence Organisation
fi fa   *fieri facias* that you cause to be made (a writ of execution)
FIFA   *Fédération Internationale de Football Association* (Fr) International Association Football Federation

FIFO first in, first out
fig figure; figurative(ly)
FIS Family Income Supplement
fl *floruit* flourished; florin
Flor, Fla Florida
fl oz fluid ounce(s)
FM frequency modulation; Field-Marshal
Fm fermium
fm fathom
FO Foreign Office (see **FCO**); Field Officer; Flying Officer
fo, fol folio
fob free on board
FOC father of the chapel
foc free of charge
FOE Friends of Europe; Friends of the Earth
for free on rail
FP fireplug; former pupil; Free Presbyterian
fp forte-piano; freezing-point
FPA Family Planning Association
FPS foot-pound-second
Fr francium; franc; Father; France; French; Friar; Friday
fr fragment; franc; frequently
frat fraternise; fraternity
FRCP Fellow of the Royal College of Physicians (**Edin,** of Edinburgh; **Lond,** of London; **Irel,** of Ireland)
FRCPS Glas Fellow of the Royal College of Physicians and Surgeons of Glasgow
FRCS Fellow of the Royal College of Surgeons (**Ed,** of Edinburgh; **Eng,** of England; **Irel,** of Ireland)
F(R)FPSG (formerly) Fellow of the (Royal) Faculty of Physicans and Surgeons of Glasgow (now **FRCPS Glas**)
FRG Federal Republic of Germany
FRPS Fellow of the Royal Photographic Society
FRS Fellow of the Royal Society (**E,** of Edinburgh)
FSF Fellow of the Institute of Shipping and Forwarding Agents
FT Financial Times
ft foot, feet; fort
fth, fthm fathom
fur furlong(s)
fut future
fz sforzando (*mus*)

G Gauss; giga-
G constant of gravitation, the factor linking force with mass and distance
g gram(me)
g acceleration of gravity
GA General Assembly
Ga gallium; Georgia
Gael Gaelic
gal, gall gallon(s)
G and S Gilbert and Sullivan
GATT General Agreement on Tariffs and Trade
gaz gazette; gazetteer
GB Great Britain (also IVR)
GBE (Knight or Dame) Grand Cross of the British Empire
gbh grievous bodily harm
GBS George Bernard Shaw
GC George Cross
GCA ground control(led) approach system or control apparatus
GCB (Knight) Grand Cross of the Bath
GCE General Certificate of Education
GCH (Knight) Grand Cross of Hanover
GCHQ Government Communications Headquarters
GCM General Court-Martial; (or **gcm**) greatest common measure
GCMG (Knight) Grand Cross of the Order of St Michael and St George
GCVO (Knight or Dame) Grand Cross of the (Royal) Victorian Order
Gd gadolinium
GDI gross domestic income
gdns gardens
GDP gross domestic product
GDR German Democratic Republic
Ge germanium
GEC General Electric Company
Gen Genesis; (or **Genl**) General
gen gender; genitive; genus; general
gent gentleman
Geo Georgia; George
geog geography
geol geology
geom geometry
Ger German
GeV giga-electron-volt (the equivalent of a thousand million electron-volts, same value in Europe as **BeV** in USA)
GHQ General Headquarters
GI government (or general) issue (US Army); hence, common soldier
Gib Gibraltar

GIGO   garbage in, garbage out
Gk   Greek
GKN   Guest, Keen and Nettlefold
Gl   glucinum (now beryllium)
Glam   Glamorganshire
GLC   Greater London Council
Gld   guilder (Dutch currency)
GLORIA   Geological Long Range Asdic
Glos   Gloucestershire
GM   George Medal; (or **G-M**) Geiger-Müller counter; General Motors
gm   gram(me)
GMBATU   General, Municipal, Boilermakers and Allied Trades Union
GmbH   *Gesellschaft mit beschränkter Haftung* (Ger) limited liability company
GMC   General Medical Council
GMT   Greenwich Mean Time
GMWU   General and Municipal Workers Union (now **GMBATU**)
GNP   gross national product
GOC   General Officer Commanding
Gov   Governor; (or **Govt**) Government
GP   General Practitioner; Gallup poll; *Gloria Patri* glory to the Father
GPO   General Post Office
GR   Greece (IVR)
Gr   Greek
gr   grain; grammar; grouse; gunner
gram   grammar
GR(I)   *Georgius Rex (Imperator)* George, King (and Emperor)
GS   General Staff; General Service; Geological Society; Grammar School
GSM   gram(me)s per square metre
GSO   General Staff Officer
GSP   Good Service Pension
GT   *gran turismo* used of a fast motor-car built for touring in style
GUM   *Gosudarstvenni Universalni Magazin* (Russ) State Universal Store
GUS   Great Universal Stores

H   hydrogen; Henry; hydrant; hospital; hard (on lead pencils); Hungary (IVR)
2H   same as **HH** (on lead pencils)
h   hour
h   height
HA   Heavy Artillery
Ha   hahnium
ha   hectare; *hoc anno* this year

HAC   Honourable Artillery Company; high-alumina cement
h and c   hot and cold (water laid on)
Hants   Hampshire (*Hantshaving,* orig. name of county)
HB   hard black (on lead pencils)
hbar   hectobar
HBM   His (or Her) Britannic Majesty
HC   Heralds' College; House of Commons; Holy Communion
HCF   (or **Hon CF**) Honorary Chaplain to the Forces; (or **hcf**) highest common factor
HCM   His (or Her) Catholic Majesty
HE   His Excellency; His Eminence; high explosive; horizontal equivalent
He   helium
Heb, Hebr   Hebrew; Hebrews
HEH   His (or Her) Exalted Highness
her   heraldry; *heres* heir
Herts   Hertfordshire
HF   high frequency
Hf   hafnium
hf   half; **hf-bd** half-bound; **hf-cf** half-calf; **hf-mor** half-morocco
HG   His (or Her) Grace
Hg   *hydrargyrum* mercury
HGV   heavy goods vehicle
HH   His (or Her) Highness; very hard (on lead pencils)
HIDB   Highlands and Islands Development Board
Hi-Fi, hi-fi   high fidelity
HIH   His (or Her) Imperial Highness
HIM   His (or Her) Imperial Majesty
HIS   *hic iacet sepultus* here lies buried
hist   historian; history; historical
HJ(S)   *hic jacet (sepultus)* here lies (buried)
HK   House of Keys (Isle of Man); Hong Kong (also IVR)
hl   hectolitre(s)
HM   His (or Her) Majesty
HMA   Headmasters' Association
HMAS   His (or Her) Majesty's Australian Ship
HMC   His (or Her) Majesty's Customs; Headmasters' Conference
HMCS   His (or Her) Majesty's Canadian Ship
HMG   His (or Her) Majesty's Government
HMI   His (or Her) Majesty's Inspector, Inspectorate

HML His (or Her) Majesty's Lieutenant

HMP *hoc monumentum posuit* erected this monument

HMS His (or Her) Majesty's Ship or Service

HMSO His (or Her) Majesty's Stationery Office

HMV His Master's Voice (gramophone company)

HNC Higher National Certificate

HND Higher National Diploma

Ho holmium

ho house

Hon Honourable; Honorary

Hons Honours

Hon Sec Honorary Secretary

hor horizon; horology

hort, hortic horticulture; horticultural

HP hire-purchase; High Priest; half-pay; (or **hp**) horse-power

HQ headquarters

HR House of Representatives; Home Rule

Hr Herr

hr hour

HRE Holy Roman Emperor or Empire

HRH His (or Her) Royal Highness

HRIP *hic requiescit in pace* here rests in peace

HS *hic situs* here is laid

HSE Health and Safety Executive; *hic sepultus* (or *situs*) *est* here is buried (or laid)

HSH His (or Her) Serene Highness

HSS *Historiae Societatis Socius* Fellow of the Historical Society

HT high tension

HTV Harlech Television

Hunts Huntingdonshire

HWM high water mark

Hz Hertz (cycles per second)

I iodine; Island, Isle; Italy (IVR)

I electric current

IA Institute of Actuaries

Ia Iowa

IAAF International Amateur Athletic Federation

IAAS Incorporated Association of Architects and Surveyors

IAEA International Atomic Energy Agency

IAM Institute of Advanced Motorists

IAS Indian Administrative Service

IATA International Air Transport Association

IB Institute of Bankers

IBA Independent Broadcasting Authority

ib, ibid *ibidem* in the same place

IBM International Business Machines (computer manufacturers)

IBRD International Bank for Reconstruction and Development (World Bank)

IC integrated circuit

i/c in charge

ICA Institute of Contemporary Arts; Institute of Chartered Accountants

ICAO International Civil Aviation Organisation

ICBM intercontinental ballistic missile

ICE Institution of Civil Engineers; internal combustion engine

ICFC Industrial and Commercial Finance Corporation

IChemE Institution of Chemical Engineers

ICI Imperial Chemical Industries

ICJ International Court of Justice

ICL International Computers Limited

ICMA Institute of Cost and Management Accountants

ICRC International Committee of the Red Cross

ICS Indian Civil Service (in Republic of India, **IAS**)

ID Intelligence Department; identification; infectious diseases

Id Idaho

id *idem* the same

IDA International Development Association

IDD International direct dialling

IDN *in Dei nomine* in the name of God

IDV International Distillers and Vintners

i.e., ie *id est* that is

IEC International Electrotechnical Commission

IEE Institution of Electrical Engineers

IF intermediate frequency; insufficient funds

IFC International Finance Corporation

IHC, IHS for the Greek capitals **IHC** (**H**, capital eta (= **E**) and **C**, a form of sigma (= **S**)), first two and last letters of *Iesous* Jesus, often misread as *Jesus Hominum Salvator* Jesus Saviour of Men

ihp indicated horse-power
IL Institute of Linguists; Israel (IVR)
ILC irreversible letter of credit
ILEA Inner London Education Authority
Ill Illinois
ill illustration; illustrated
ILN Illustrated London News
ILO International Labour Organisation or (its secretariat) International Labour Office
ILP Independent Labour Party
IMechE Institution of Mechanical Engineers
IMF International Monetary Fund
imit imitative
IMM Institution of Mining and Metallurgy
Imp Imperial; *Imperator* Emperor
imp (or **imperf**) imperfect; (or **imper**) imperative; *imprimatur* let it be printed; (or **impers**) impersonal
IMunE Institution of Municipal Engineers
In indium
in inch(es)
inc including; incorporated
incl including; included
IND same as **IDN**; India (IVR)
Ind Indiana; Independent
ind, indic indicative
indecl indeclinable
indef indefinite
indiv individual
Ind Ter Indian Territory
inf *infra* below; infantry; infinitive
infra dig *infra dignitatem* beneath one's dignity
init *initio* in the beginning
in lim *in limine* on the threshold, at the outset
in loc *in loco* in its place
in loc cit *in loco citato* in the place cited
in pr *in principio* in the beginning
INRI *Jesus Nazarenus Rex Judaeorum* Jesus of Nazareth King of the Jews
Inst Institute
inst instant—the present month; institute
InstP Institute of Physics
instn institution
int interest; interior; interpreter; international; integral

Intelsat International Telecommunications Satellite Consortium
interj interjection
Interpol International Criminal Police Commission
interrog interrogation; interrogative(ly)
in trans *in transitu* in transit
intrans intransitive
intro, introd introduction
inv *invenit* designed it; invented; invoice
IOB Institute of Building
IOC International Olympic Committee
IoJ Institute of Journalists
IOM Isle of Man
IOU I owe you
IOW Isle of Wight
IPA Institute of Practitioners in Advertising; International Publishers' Association; International Phonetic Alphabet
IPC International Publishing Corporation
IPCS Institution of Professional Civil Servants
IQ Intelligence Quotient
iq *idem quod* the same as
IQPS Institute of Qualified Private Secretaries
IQS Institute of Quantity Surveyors
IR Iran (IVR)
Ir iridium; Irish
IRC International Red Cross
IRA Irish Republican Army
IRB Irish Republican Brotherhood
IRBM intermediate range ballistic missile
Irel. Ireland
IRL Ireland (IVR)
IRQ Iraq (IVR)
ISBN International Standard Book Number
ISCh Incorporated Society of Chiropodists
ISD international subscriber dialling
ISF Institute of Forwarding and Shipping Agents
Is(l) island
ISO Imperial Service Order; International Organisation for Standardisation
ISS International Social Service
ISSN International Standard Serial Number

ISTC Iron and Steel Trades Confederation
IT Information Technology
It Italian; Italian vermouth
ITA Independent Television Authority (now **IBA**)
ita initial teaching alphabet
ital italic; Italian
ITN Independent Television News
ITO International Trade Organisation
ITT International Telephone and Telegraph Corporation
ITU International Telecommunications Union
ITV Independent Television
IU international unit
IU(C)D intra-uterine (contraceptive) device
IUPAC International Union of Pure and Applied Chemistry
IUPAP International Union of Pure and Applied Physics
IVR International Vehicle Registration
IW Isle of Wight

J joule; Japan (IVR)
J Judge; Justice
JAL Japan Air Lines
Jan January
Jas James
JC *Juris Consultus* Jurisconsult; Jesus Christ; Justice Clerk
JCD *Juris Civilis Doctor* Doctor of Civil Law
JCR junior common room
JFK John Fitzgerald Kennedy
JHS same as **IHC**
JMB Joint Matriculation Board
Josh Joshua
JP Justice of the Peace
Jr, Jun, Junr Junior
JUD *Juris Utriusque Doctor* Doctor both of Canon and of Civil Law
Jul July
Jun June; Junior
junc junction
jurisp jurisprudence

K Kelvin (thermometer scale); kelvin; *kalium* potassium; kilobyte
k kilo-
Kan Kansas

KB Knight of the Bath; Knight Bachelor; King's Bench
KBE Knight Commander of the Order of the British Empire
KC King's Counsel; King's College; Kennel Club
KCB Knight Commander of the Bath
KCMG Knight Commander of the Order of St Michael and St George
KCVO Knight Commander of the (Royal) Victorian Order
Ken Kentucky
KG Knight of the Order of the Garter
kg kilogram(me)(s)
KGB *Komitet Gosudarstvennoi Bezopasnosti* (Russ) Committee of State Security
KGCB Knight of the Grand Cross of the Bath
kilo kilogram(me); kilometre
kk *kaiserlich-königlich* (Ger) Imperial-Royal
KKK Ku Klux Klan
KL Kuala Lumpur
KLH Knight of the Legion of Honour
KLM *Koninklijke Luchtvaart Maatschappij* (Du) Royal Dutch Airlines
KM Knight of Malta
km kilometre(s)
kn knot (nautical, etc, measure)
KO, ko knock out; kick off
K of L Knight of Labour
kpg, kph kilometres per gallon, hour
Kr krypton
kr kreutzer; krone
Ks Kansas
KT Knight of the Thistle
Kt Knight Bachelor
kV kilovolt
kW kilowatt
kWh kilowatt-hour
Ky Kentucky

L Lake; Latin; Liberal; lumen; learner (driver); *libra* pound; Luxembourg (IVR)
L symbol for inductance; luminance
l litre (the abbreviation, though the accepted one, is undesirable as liable to be misread); latitude; league; left; long; (or **lb**) *libra* pound
l length
LA Law Agent; Literate in Arts; Los Angeles; Library Association

La lanthanum; Louisiana
Lab Labour
lab laboratory
LAC Licentiate of the Apothecaries' Company
LAMDA London Academy of Music and Dramatic Art
Lancs Lancashire
lang language
LAR Libya (IVR)
LASER *l*ight *a*mplification by *s*timulated *e*mission of *r*adiation
Lat Latin
lat latitude
lb *libra* pound (in weight)
lb, lbw leg before wicket
LBC London Broadcasting Company
lc lower-case (in printing); *loco citato* in the place cited; left centre; letter of credit
LCCI London Chamber of Commerce and Industry
LCD liquid crystal display
LCh, LChir *Licentiatus Chirurgiae* Licentiate in Surgery
LCJ Lord Chief-Justice
LCM, lcm least common multiple
Ld Lord
Ldp, Lp Lordship
LDS Licentiate in Dental Surgery
LDV Local Defence Volunteers (later Home Guard)
LEA Local Education Authority
LEAP Life Education for the Autistic Person
lect lecture
LED light emitting diode
leg legal; legate; legislature
Leics Leicestershire
LEPRA Leprosy Relief Assocation
lex lexicon
LF low frequency
LGU Ladies Golf Union
lh left hand
LHD *Litterarum Humaniorum Doctor* Doctor of Humane Letters
LI Long Island; Light Infantry
Li lithium
Lib Liberal
lib *liber* book
lib cat library catalogue
Lieut Lieutenant
LIFO last in, first out
LILO last in, last out
Lincs Lincolnshire

liq liquid
lit literal(ly); literature
lith, litho, lithog lithograph; lithography
Lit Hum *litterae humaniores* humane letters, the humanities
Lit(t)D *Litterarum Doctor* Doctor of Letters
LJ Lord Justice
LLB *Legum Baccalaureus* Bachelor of Laws
LLCM Licentiate of the London College of Music
LLD *Legum Doctor* Doctor of Laws
LLM *Legum Magister* Master of Laws
LM long metre
lm lumen
ln natural logarithm
LNG liquefied natural gas
LOB Location of Offices Bureau
loc cit *loco citato* at the place quoted
L of C line of communication
log logarithm
lon, long longitude
Lond London
Lonrho *Lon*don *Rho*desian (industrial conglomerate)
loq *loquitur* speaks
LP long-playing (record); Lord Provost; low pressure; Labour Party
LPG liquefied petroleum gas
LPO London Philharmonic Orchestra
Lr lawrencium; lira (Italian currency)
LRAM Licentiate of the Royal Academy of Music
LRCP Licentiate of the Royal College of Physicians (**Edin,** of Edinburgh; **Lond,** of London; **Irel,** of Ireland)
LRCS Licentiate of the Royal College of Surgeons (**Ed,** of Edinburgh; **Eng,** of England; **Irel,** of Ireland)
LSA Licentiate of the Society of Apothecaries
LSD lysergic acid diethylamide (a hallucinatory drug)
L.S.D. *librae, solidi, denarii* pounds, shillings, pence
LSE London School of Economics
LSO London Symphony Orchestra
LT low tension
Lt Lieutenant
LTA Lawn Tennis Association
Lt-Col Lieutenant-Colonel
Ltd limited liability

Middx Middlesex

mil, milit. military

Min Ministry

min mineralogy; minimum; minute

Minn Minnesota

MIRV Multiple Independently Targeted Re-entry Vehicle (type of missile)

misc miscellaneous; miscellany

Miss Mississippi

MIT Massachusetts Institute of Technology

MJ megajoule(s)

MJI Member of the Institute of Journalists

MK (on cars) mark

Mkk markka (Finnish currency)

MKS metre-kilogram-second unit, or system

MKSA metre-kilogram-second-ampere unit, or system

ml millilitre(s)

MLA Member of Legislative Assembly; Modern Language Association

MLC Member of Legislative Council; Meat and Livestock Commission

MLitt *Magister Litterarum* Master of Letters or Literature

Mlle *Mademoiselle* (Fr) Miss;—pl **Mlles** *Mesdemoiselles.*

MLR minimum lending rate

MM (Their) Majesties; Martyrs; Military Medal

MM. *Messieurs* (Fr) Gentlemen, Sirs

mm millimetre(s)

Mme *Madame* (Fr) Mrs;—pl **Mmes** *Mesdames*

MN Merchant Navy

Mn manganese

MO Medical Officer

Mo molybdenum; Missouri

mo month

MOD Ministry of Defence

mod modern; moderate

mod con modern convenience

MOH Medical Officer of Health

mol mole (unit)

mol wt molecular weight

Mon Monmouthshire; Monday

Monsig Monsignor

Mont Montana; Montgomeryshire

mos months

MOS(T) metal oxide silicon (transistors)

MOT Ministry of Transport

MP Member of Parliament; Military Police; Metropolitan Police; Municipal Police (US); mounted police

mp mezzo-piano; melting-point

MPDS Market Price Display Service

mpg, mph miles per gallon, hour

MPharm Master of Pharmacy

MPS Member of the Pharmaceutical Society; Member of the Philological Society

MR Master of the Rolls

Mr Mister; Master

MRA Moral Rearmament

MRC Medical Research Council

MRCA multirole combat aircraft

MRG Minority Rights Group

Mrs Mistress (fem of **Mr,** Mister)

MS manuscript; Master of Surgery; *Memoriae Sacrum* Sacred to the Memory; milestone; multiple sclerosis

Ms see Dictionary

ms millisecond(s); (or **M/S**) months (after)

MSC Manpower Services Commission

MSc Master of Science

MSF medium standard frequency

msl mean sea-level

MSS manuscripts

MST mountain standard time

MSW Medical Social Worker

MT Mechanical Transport; mean time

Mt, mt mount

MTh Master of Theology

mth month

Mts, mts mountains

mus music; museum

MusB(ac) Bachelor of Music

MusD(oc) Doctor of Music

MusM Master of Music

mv merchant vessel; motor vessel; muzzle velocity

MVO Member of the Royal Victorian Order

MW medium wave

Mx Middlesex

myth mythology; mythological

N nitrogen; newton; North, Northern; Norway (IVR)

n name; noun; *natus* born; neuter; noon; nano-

Na *natrium* sodium

NAAFI Navy, Army, and Air-Force Institute(s) (providing canteens for the armed forces)

NABM National Association of British Manufacturers

NACRO National Association for the Care and Resettlement of Offenders

NALGO National and Local Government Officers' Association

N and Q Notes and Queries

NASA National Aeronautics and Space Administration (USA)

Nat National

nat *natus* born

nat hist natural history

NATO North Atlantic Treaty Organisation

nat ord natural order

Nat Phil natural philosophy

Nat Sci Natural Science(s)

NATSOPA National Society of Operative Printers, Graphical and Media Personnel

NATTKE National Association of Television, Theatrical, and Kinematographic Employees

Nat West NatWest, National Westminster Bank

naut nautical

nav naval; navigation

NAVAR combined navigation and radar system

Nazi *Nazionale Sozialisten* (Ger) German National Socialist Party

NB New Brunswick; North Britain; North British; North bag (in postal sorting); (or **nb**) *nota bene* note well, or take notice

Nb niobium

NBC National Broadcasting Company (USA)

NBL National Book League

NBS National Bureau of Standards (USA)

NC New Church; numerical control; North Carolina

NCB National Coal Board (now British Coal)

NCCL National Council for Civil Liberties

NCO non-commissioned officer

NCR National Cash Register Company; no carbon required

ncv no commercial value

Nd neodymium

ND, NDak North Dakota

nd no date, not dated

NDPS National Data Processing Service

NE north-east; New England

Ne neon

NEB New English Bible; National Enterprise Board

Neb, Nebr Nebraska

NEC National Executive Committee; National Exhibition Centre

NED New English Dictionary (now **OED**)

NEDC National Economic Development Council (Neddy)

NEDO National Economic Development Office

neg negative

NEI *non est inventus* has not been found

nem con *nemine contradicente* no one contradicting

nem diss *nemine dissentiente* no one dissenting

NERC Natural Environment Research Council

Neth Netherlands

neut neuter

Nev Nevada

New M New Mexico

N/F no funds

NF Norman French; Northern French; National Front; Newfoundland (also **Nfd**)

NFER National Foundation for Educational Research

NFS National Fire Service

NFT National Film Theatre

NFU National Farmers' Union

NFWI National Federation of Women's Institutes

NGA National Graphical Association

NH New Hampshire

NHBRC National House-Builders' Registration Council (or Certificate)

NHI National Health Insurance

NHS National Health Service

NI Northern Ireland; national insurance

Ni nickel

NIRC National Industrial Relations Court

NJ New Jersey

NKVD *Narodny Komitet Vnutrennikh Del* (Russ) People's Committee of Internal Affairs

NL Netherlands (IVR)
NLRB National Labor Relations Board (USA)
NM, N Mex New Mexico
n mile international nautical mile
NNE north-north-east
NNW north-north-west
NO New Orleans; natural order
no (or **No**) *numero* (in) number; not out
nom, nomin nominative
non-coll non-collegiate
non-com non-commissioned
Noncon Nonconformist
non obst *non obstante* notwithstanding
non pros *non prosequitur* does not prosecute
non seq *non sequitur* it does not follow
non-U not upper class
NOP National Opinion Poll
nop not otherwise provided
Northants Northamptonshire
Northd Northumberland
Nos, nos numbers
Notts Nottinghamshire
Nov November
NP Notary Public; New Providence; (or **np**) new paragraph
np no place (of publication)
NPFA National Playing Fields Association
NPG National Portrait Gallery
NPL National Physical Laboratory
npl noun plural
nr near
NRA National Rifle Association
NRDC National Research Development Corporation
NS New Style; Nova Scotia
ns nanosecond(s); not specified; nouns
NSB National Savings Bank
n sing noun singular
NSPCC National Society for Prevention of Cruelty to Children
NSRA National Small-Bore Rifle Association
NSW New South Wales
NT New Testament; Northern Territory; National Trust
NTDA National Trade Development Association
ntp normal temperature and pressure
NTS National Trust for Scotland
NU name unknown

NUGMW National Union of General and Municipal Workers
NUI National University of Ireland
NUJ National Union of Journalists
NUM National Union of Mineworkers
NUPE National Union of Public Employees
NUR National Union of Railwaymen
NUS National Union of Students; National Union of Seamen
NUT National Union of Teachers
NV New Version
NV(A)LA National Viewers' and Listeners' Association
nvd no value declared
NW north-west
NWT North-west Territory (Canada)
NY New York (city or state)
NYC New York City
NYO National Youth Orchestra
NZ New Zealand (also IVR)

O oxygen; Ohio
o/a on account of
O&C Oxford and Cambridge (Schools Examination Board)
O & M organisation and method
OAP Old Age Pension or Pensioner
OAPEC Organisation of Arab Petroleum-Exporting Countries
OAS on active service; Organisation of American States
OAU Organisation of African Unity
ob *obiit* died
obdt obedient
OBE Officer of the Order of the British Empire
obj object; objective
obl oblique; oblong
obs obsolete; observation
o/c overcharge
OC Officer Commanding; Officer of the Order of Canada
OCF Officiating Chaplain to the Forces
OCR optical character recognition or reader
Oct October
oct octavo
OCTU Officer Cadet Training Unit
OD Ordnance Datum or Data
O/D overdrawn

OE Old English
OECD Organisation for Economic Co-operation and Development
OED Oxford English Dictionary
OF Old French; Oddfellow
off. official; officinal
OFT Office of Fair Trading
OHMS On His (or Her) Majesty's Service
OK see Dictionary
Okla Oklahoma
OM Order of Merit; Old Measurement
OMR optical mark recognition
ono or near(est) offer
Ont Ontario
Op Opera; Opus
op out of print; opposite; operation
op cit *opere citato* in the work cited
OPEC Organisation of Petroleum-Exporting Countries
opp opposed; opposite
Ops Operations; Operations Officer; Operations room
OR other ranks; operations research
Or, Ore, Oreg Oregon
ord ordained; order; ordinary; ordnance
orig origin; original(ly)
OS Old Style; Ordinary Seaman; outsize; Ordnance Survey
O/S outstanding
osp *obiit sine prole* died without issue
OT Old Testament; occupational therapy
OTC Officers' Training Corps
OU Open University
OUP Oxford University Press
Oxbridge *Ox*ford and Cam*bridge*.
Oxf Oxford
OXFAM *Ox*ford Committee for *Fam*ine Relief
Oxon *Oxonia* Oxford; *Oxoniensis* of Oxford; Oxfordshire
oz ounce(s) (15th cent. It *ōz*, abbreviation of *onza*)

P phosphorus; parking; President; Prince; pedal; Portugal (IVR)
P power
p new penny; new pence; piano; pico-; page; participle
P&P postage and packing
PA Press Association; Publishers Association; personal assistant; Public Address (system)
Pa protactinium; pascal
Pa, Penn Pennsylvania
pa past
p.a. (or **pa**) per annum; participial adjective
PABX private automatic branch exchange
Pal Palestine
pam pamphlet
Pan Panama
Pan Am Pan-American (World Airways Incorporated)
P and O Peninsular and Oriental (Steamship Navigation Co)
pa p past participle
par paragraph; parallel; parish
pass passive
pa t past tense
Pat Off Patent Office
PAYE Pay As You Earn (Income Tax)
PB Pharmacopoeia Britannica; Plymouth Brethren
Pb *plumbum* lead
PBX private branch exchange
PC Police Constable; Privy Councillor; *Patres Conscripti* Conscript Fathers
pc postcard; per cent
pce piece
PCS Principal Clerk of Session
Pd palladium
pd paid
PDI pre-delivery inspection
PDR People's Democratic Republic
PDSA People's Dispensary for Sick Animals
PE Protestant Episcopal; physical education
p/e price-earnings ratio
PEC photoelectric cell
ped pedal
PEI Prince Edward Island
PEN Poets, Playwrights, Editors, Essayists, and Novelists
Pen Peninsula
Penn, Pa Pennsylvania
PEP Political and Economic Planning; personal equity plan
per period; person
per an per annum
per cent see Dictionary
perf perfect

per pro   *per procurationem* by the agency (of)

Pers   Persian

pers   person; personal

Pes   peseta (Spanish currency)

PF   Procurator Fiscal; Patriotic Front

Pf   pfennig (German currency)

pf   piano-forte

PG   paying guest

Pg   Portugal; Portuguese

PGA   Professional Golfers' Association

phar, pharm   pharmaceutical; pharmacopoeia; pharmacy

PhB   *Philosophiae Baccalaureus* Bachelor of Philosophy

PhD   *Philosophiae Doctor* Doctor of Philosophy

Phil   Philadelphia; philology; philological; philosophy; philosophical

phon, phonet   phonetics

phonog   phonography

phot   photography

phr   phrase

phys   physiology; physics; physician

PIA   Pakistan International Airlines

PIB   Prices and Incomes Board

pinx   *pinxit* painted it

PL   Poet Laureate; Public Library

pl   plural

PLA   Port of London Authority

PLC, plc   Public Limited Company

PLO   Palestine Liberation Organisation

PLP   Parliamentary Labour Party

PLR   public lending right

plu, plur   plural

plup   pluperfect

PM   Past Master; (or **pm**) *post meridiem* after noon; Postmaster; (or **pm**) *post mortem* after death; Prime Minister; Provost-Marshal

Pm   promethium

pm   premium

PMG   Postmaster-General; Paymaster-General

PMO   Principal Medical Officer

Pmr   Paymaster

PMRAFNS   Princess Mary's Royal Air Force Nursing Service

pn   promissory note

PNdB   perceived noise decibel

PO   Post Office; Petty Officer; Pilot Officer

Po   polonium

po   postal order; pole

pod   pay on delivery

Pol Econ   Political Economy

pop   population; popular

POP   Post Office preferred

pos, posit   positive

POUNC   Post Office Users' National Council

POW   prisoner of war

PP   parish priest; present pupil; past President

pp   pages; *per procurationem* by proxy (also *per pro* for and on behalf of); pianissimo; past participle

ppc   picture post-card

PPE   Philosophy, Politics and Economics

PPI   Plan Position Indicator; printed postage impression

PPS   *post postscriptum* a later additional postscript; Parliamentary Private Secretary

PQ   Province of Quebec

PR   prize ring; Puerto Rico; proportional representation; *Populus Romanus* the Roman people; public relations

Pr   Prince; priest; Provençal

pr   pair; per; present; price

PRA   pre-recorded address; President of the Royal Academy

Preb   Prebend; Prebendary

pref   preface

prep   preparation; preparatory; preposition

Pres   President

pres p   present participle

pret   preterite

Prin   Principal

PRN   *pro re nata* for special occasion arising

PRO   Public Relations Officer; Public Record Office

pro   professional; prostitute; probationary

prob   probably

Prof   Professor

pron   pronoun

PROP   Preservation of the Rights of Prisoners

prop   proper(ly); proposition; property

Prot   Protestant

pro tem   *pro tempore* for the time being

Prov   Proverbs; Provincial; Provost

RAC Royal Automobile Club; Royal Armoured Corps; Royal Agricultural College

Rad Radical

rad radian; *radix* root

RADA Royal Academy of Dramatic Art

RADC Royal Army Dental Corps

RAE Royal Aircraft Establishment

RAEC Royal Army Educational Corps

RAeS Royal Aeronautical Society

RAF Royal Air Force

RAM Royal Academy of Music; random access memory

ram relative atomic mass

RAMC Royal Army Medical Corps

RAN Royal Australian Navy

R and A Royal and Ancient (Golf Club) St Andrews

R and B rhythm and blues (type of popular music)

R and D research and development

RAOC Royal Army Ordnance Corps

RAPC Royal Army Pay Corps

RAS Royal Astronomical Society; Royal Asiatic Society

RAVC Royal Army Veterinary Corps

RBA Royal Society of British Artists

RBS Royal Society of British Sculptors

RC Roman Catholic; Red Cross; Royal College of Art

RCA Royal Canadian Academy; Radio Corporation of America

RCAF Royal Canadian Air Force

RCM Royal College of Music; Regimental Court-Martial

RCMP Royal Canadian Mounted Police

RCN Royal Canadian Navy

RCOG Royal College of Obstetricians and Gynaecologists

RCP Royal College of Physicians

RCS Royal College of Surgeons; Royal Corps of Signals; Royal College of Science

RCT Royal Corps of Transport

RCVS Royal College of Veterinary Surgeons

RD Rural Dean; Naval Reserve Decoration; (or **R/D**) refer to drawer

Rd Road; rand (S African currency)

RDC Rural District Council

RDI Designer for Industry of the Royal Society of Arts

RDS Royal Dublin Society

RE Royal Engineers; Royal Society of Etchers and Engravers; Royal Exchange

re with reference/regard to

Réau Réaumur's thermometric scale

rec *recipe* take; record; receipt

recd received

REconS Royal Economic Society

ref referee; reference

Ref Ch Reformed Church

reg, regd registered

Reg Prof Regius Professor

regt regiment

rel relating; relation; relative

rel d relative density

REME Royal Electrical and Mechanical Engineers

rep representative; republic; report; reporter

rept receipt; report

retd retired; returned

Rev revise(d); revision; (or **Revd**) Reverend

rev revolution

Rev Ver Revised Version

RF *République française* (Fr) French Republic; radio frequency

RFC Rugby Football Club

RFU Rugby Football Union

RGG Royal Grenadier Guards

RGN Registered General Nurse

RGS Royal Geographical Society

Rgt Regiment

RH Royal Highness

rh right hand

RHA Royal Horse Artillery; Royal Hibernian Academy; Road Haulage Association; Regional Health Authority

rhet rhetoric; rhetorical

RHF Royal Highland Fusiliers

RHG Royal Horse Guards

RHistS Royal Historical Society

RHM Rank Hovis McDougall

RHS Royal Humane Society; Royal Horticultural Society; Royal Historical Society; Royal Highland Show

RI Royal Institute of Painters in Water Colours; Rhode Island; religious instruction; Indonesia (IVR)

RIA Royal Irish Academy

RIAM Royal Irish Academy of Music

RIBA Royal Institute of British Architects

RIC Royal Irish Constabulary; Royal Institute of Chemistry

RICS Royal Institution of Chartered Surveyors

RIGB Royal Institution of Great Britain

RIP *requiescat in pace* may he (or she) rest in peace

RIPHH Royal Institute of Public Health and Hygiene

RJET remote job entry terminal

RL Lebanon (IVR); Rugby League

RLO returned letter office

RLS Robert Louis Stevenson

Rly, rly railway

RM Royal Mail; Royal Marines

RMA Royal Military Academy, Sandhurst; Royal Marine Artillery

RMetS Royal Meteorological Society

RMO Resident Medical Officer

RMP (Corps of) Royal Military Police

RMS Royal Mail Steamer; Royal Microscopical Society

RN Royal Navy

Rn radon

RNAS Royal Naval Air Service(s)

RNIB Royal National Institute for the Blind

RNLI Royal National Lifeboat Institution

RNR Royal Naval Reserve

RNVR Royal Naval Volunteer Reserve

RNZAF Royal New Zealand Air Force

RNZN Royal New Zealand Navy

ro *recto* on the right-hand page

ROC Royal Observer Corps

ROI Royal Institute of Oil Painters

ROM read only memory

Rom Romans

rom roman (in printing)

Ro-Ro roll-on-roll-off

RoSPA see **RSPA**

RP Reformed Presbyterian; Regius Professor; Received Pronunciation; Royal Society of Portrait Painters

RPA radiation protection adviser

RPI retail price index

RPM retail price maintenance

rpm, rps revolutions per minute, second

RPO Royal Philharmonic Orchestra

RPS Royal Photographic Society

RR Right Reverend

RRE Radar Research Establishment

RRP recommended retail price

RS Royal Society

RSA Royal Society of Antiquaries; Royal Society of Arts; Royal Scottish Academy or Academician; Republic of South Africa

RSC Royal Shakespeare Company

RSE Royal Society of Edinburgh

RSFSR Russian Soviet Federated Socialist Republic

RSG Regional Seats of Government

RSL Royal Society of Literature

RSM Regimental Sergeant-Major; Royal Society of Medicine; Royal School of Music

RSO railway sub-office; railway sorting office; rural sub-office; radiological safety officer; Resident Surgical Officer

RSPA, RoSPA Royal Society for the Prevention of Accidents

RSPB Royal Society for the Protection of Birds

RSPCA Royal Society for the Prevention of Cruelty to Animals

RSS (or **SRS**) *Regiae Societatis Socius* Fellow of the Royal Society; Royal Statistical Society

RSV Revised Standard Version

RSVP *répondez s'il vous plaît* (Fr) reply, if you please

RT radiotelephone, -phony

RTE *Radio Telefís Éireann* (Ir) Irish Television

Rt Hon Right Honourable

RTO Railway Transportation (or Traffic) Officer

RTPI Royal Town Planning Institute

Rt Rev Right Reverend

RTZ Rio Tinto Zinc Corporation Limited

RU Rugby Union

Ru ruthenium

RUC Royal Ulster Constabulary

R-unit Röntgen unit—unit of measurement of X-ray radiation

RV Revised Version

RWS Royal Society of Painters in Water Colours

Ry, ry railway

RYA Royal Yachting Association

RYS Royal Yacht Squadron

RZS Royal Zoological Society (**E**, of Edinburgh)

S sulphur; square; stokes; siemens; South; Sabbath; Saint; society; sun; Sweden (IVR)

s second(s)

$ dollar

SA South Africa; South America; South Australia; Salvation Army; sex-appeal; *Société anonyme* (Fr) limited liability company; Society of Arts; Society of Antiquaries (**Scot,** of Scotland)

sa *secundum artem* according to art; *sine anno* without date

sae stamped addressed envelope

Salop Shropshire

SALT Strategic Arms Limitation Talks

SAM surface-to-air missile

SARAH Search and Rescue and Homing

SAS *Societatis Antiquariorum Socius* Fellow of the Society of Antiquaries; Scandinavian Airlines System; Special Air Service

Sask Saskatchewan

Sat Saturday

S.A.T.B. soprano, alto, tenor, bass

SAYE save as you earn

Sb *stibium* antimony

SBN Standard Book Number

SC *senatus consultum* a decree of the Roman senate; Special Constable; Supreme Court; Staff College; Staff Corps; South Carolina

Sc scandium

sc *scilicet* namely; *sculpsit* (he) sculptured (this); (or **s. caps, sm. caps**) small capitals (in printing)

s/c self-contained

ScB *Scientiae Baccalaureus* Bachelor of Science

ScD *Scientiae Doctor* Doctor of Science

SCE Scottish Certificate of Education

SCF Save the Children Fund

Sch schilling (Austrian currency); school

sci fa *scire facias* that you cause to know

sci- fi science fiction

scil, sciz, *scilicet* namely (cf **viz**)

SCL Student of Civil Law

SCM Student Christian Movement; State Certified Midwife

Scot Scotland; Scottish

ScotBIC Scottish Business in the Community

SCR senior common room

Script Scripture

SCUBA self-contained underwater breathing apparatus

sculp, sculpt *sculpsit* (he) sculptured (this); sculpture; sculptor

SD, S Dak South Dakota

sd *sine die* without a day (fixed)

SDA Scottish Development Agency

SDC single data converter

SDLP Social and Democratic Labour Party

SDP social, domestic and pleasure; Social Democratic Party

SDR special drawing rights

SE south-east; Society of Engineers

Se selenium

SEAC South-East Asia Command

SEATO South-East Asia Treaty Organisation

Sec, Secy Secretary

sec secant; *secundum* in accordance with; second; section

sec leg *secundum legem* according to law

sec reg *secundum regulam* according to rule

sect section

SED Scottish Education Department

Sem seminary; Semitic

SEN State Enrolled Nurse

Sen Senator; senior

Sep, Sept September; Septuagint

seq *sequens* following (pl **seqq,** *sequentes* or *sequentia*)

SERC Science and Education Research Council

Serg, Sergt Sergeant

Sess Session

SF science fiction; Sinn Fein; signal frequency; Finland (IVR)

SFA Scottish Football Association; Sweet Fanny Adams (= nothing at all)

SFr Swiss franc

sfz sforzando

SG Solicitor-General

sg specific gravity

SGHWR steam-generating heavy water reactor

SGP Singapore (IVR)

SHAEF Supreme Headquarters of the Allied Expeditionary Force

SHAPE Supreme Headquarters Allied Powers Europe

shv *sub hoc verbo* or *sub hac voce* under this word

SI Système International (d'Unités)

Si silicon

sic so written

sig signature

sin sine

sing singular

SIPRI Stockholm International Peace Research Institute

SIS Secret Intelligence Service

SJ Society of Jesus

SL Solicitor at Law; Sergeant-at-Law; (or **S Lat**) South latitude

SLADE Society of Lithographic Artists, Designers, Engravers and Process Workers

sld sailed

slp *sine legitima prole* without lawful issue

SM Short Metre; Sergeant-Major

Sm samarium

Smith. Inst. Smithsonian Institution

SMLondSoc *Societatis Medicae Londiniensis Socius* Member of the London Medical Society

SMM *Sancta Mater Maria* Holy Mother Mary

SMMT Society of Motor Manufacturers and Traders

SMO Senior Medical Officer

SMP School Mathematics Project

smp *sine mascula prole* without male issue

Sn *stannum* tin

sn *secundum naturam* according to nature

SNCF *Société Nationale des Chemins de Fer français* (Fr) French national railways

SNO Scottish National Orchestra

SNP Scottish National Party

SO Staff Officer; Signal Officer; standing order; special order

so seller's option

Soc Society

SOGAT Society of Graphical and Allied Trades

Sol, Solr Solicitor

sol solution

Sol-Gen Solicitor-General

sop soprano

SOS see Dictionary

Sp Spanish

sp *sine prole* without issue; spelling; species (pl **spp.**)

SPCK Society for Promoting Christian Knowledge

SPG Special Patrol Group

sp gr specific gravity (now relative density)

SPQR *Senatus Populusque Romanus* the Senate and People of Rome

SPR Society for Psychical Research

sps *sine prole superstite* without surviving issue

spt seaport

SPUC Society for the Protection of the Unborn Child

sp vol specific volume

sq (or **Sq**) square; *sequens* following (in pl **sqq,** *sequentes* or *sequentia*)

sqn squadron

SR Southern Region

Sr senior; Sir; Señor; strontium

sr steradian

SRC Science Research Council; Student Representative Council

SRCh State Registered Chiropodist

SRI *Sacrum Romanum Imperium* Holy Roman Empire

SRN State Registered Nurse

SRS (or **RSS**) *Societatis Regiae Socius* Fellow of the Royal Society

SRU Scottish Rugby Union

SS Saints; *Schutzstaffel* (Ger) Hitler's bodyguard

ss steamship; screw steamer

SSAFA Soldiers', Sailors' and Airmen's Families Association

SSC Solicitor before the Supreme Court (Scotland); *Societas Sanctae Crucis* Society of the Holy Cross

SSD *Sanctissimus Dominus* Most Holy Lord (the Pope)

SSE south-south-east

SSM surface-to-surface missile

SSN Standard Serial Number

SSRC Social Science Research Council

SST supersonic transport

SSW south-south-west

St Saint; Strait; Street

st stone (weight)

Staffs Staffordshire

STD subscriber trunk dialling

std standard

Ste *Sainte* (Fr) fem of Saint

ster, stereo stereophonic; stereotype

ster, stg sterling

stet let it stand

STOL short take-off and landing

STP *Sanctae Theologiae Professor* Professor of Theology

stp standard temperature and pressure

str steamer

str strong

STS Scottish Text Society

STUC Scottish Trades Union Congress

STV Scottish Television; Single Transferable Vote

SU strontium unit—unit of measurement of strontium radiation; Scripture Union; Soviet Union (also IVR)

sub subject

subj subject; subjunctive

subst substitute; substantive

suf, suff suffix

sup superfine; superior; (or **superl**) superlative; supreme; *supra* above; supine; supplement

superl superlative

supp, suppl supplement

Supr Supreme

Supt Superintendent

Surg surgeon; surgery

sv *sub voce* under that heading; *sub verbo* under the word

SW south-west; small women('s); short wave

SWALK sealed with a loving kiss

SWAPO South West Africa People's Organisation

SWG standard wire gauge

syn synonym

T tritium

t tonne (cf **l**, litre)

t time

TA Territorial Army

tal qual *talis qualis* just as they come, average quality

tan tangent

TASS *Telegrafnoye Agentsvo Sovietskovo Soyuza* (Russ) telegraph agency of the Soviet Union; Technical, Administrative and Supervisory Section (of **AUEW**)

Tb terbium

TB tuberculosis

Tc technetium

TCCB Test and County Cricket Board

TCD Trinity College Dublin; Twentieth Century Dictionary

TCL Trinity College of Music, London

TCP trichlorophenylmethyliodosalicyl (a proprietary germicide)

TD Territorial Decoration; *Teachta Dála* (Ir) member of the Dail

Te tellurium

tech. technical; technology

TEFL teaching English as a foreign language

tel telephone

tel, teleg telegram; telegraph

temp temporal; *tempore* in the time of; temperature; temporary

Ten, Tenn Tennessee

ten tenor

Ter, Terr Territory; terrace

term termination

TES Times Educational Supplement

TESL teaching English as a second language

Test Testament

Teut Teutonic

Tex Texas

Text Rec *textus receptus* the revised text

TF Territorial Force

tf till forbidden

TFR Territorial Force Reserve

TGWU Transport and General Workers' Union

Th thorium; Thursday

ThD Doctor of Theology

theat theatrical

theol theology; theologian

THES Times Higher Educational Supplement

THF Trust Houses Forte

ThL Theological Licentiate

Tho, Thos Thomas

TI Tube Investments

Ti titanium

tid *ter in die* thrice a day

TIF *Transports Internationaux par Chemin de Fer* (Fr) International Rail Transport

TIR *Transports Internationaux Routiers* (Fr) International Road Transport

TIROS Television and Infrared Observation Satellite

Tl thallium

TLS Times Literary Supplement

TM transcendental meditation

Tm thulium

TN trade name

TNT trinitrotoluene (explosive)

TO turn over; Telegraph-office; Transport Officer

Toc H Talbot House

TPI Town Planning Institute

tpr teleprinter
TR Turkey (IVR)
tr transpose; transactions; translator; trustee; transfer
trans transitive; translated; translation; transpose
TRH Their Royal Highnesses
trig trigonometry
Trin Trinity
TSB Trustee Savings Bank
TSO town sub-office
TT teetotal; Tourist Trophy; tuberculin tested
Tu, Tues Tue Tuesday
TUC Trades Union Congress
TV television
TVA Tennessee Valley Authority
TVP texturised vegetable protein
TWA Trans-World Airlines
TWI Training within Industry
typ, typo typographer; typography

U uranium; Unionist; upper-class; Uruguay (IVR)
UAE United Arab Emirates
UAR United Arab Republic
UC, uc upper case (capital letters)
UCAR Union of Central African Republics
UCATT Union of Construction, Allied Trades and Technicians
UCCA Universities Central Council on Admissions
UCL University College London
UDA Ulster Defence Association
UDC Urban District Council; Universal Decimal Classification
UDI Unilateral Declaration of Independence
UDR Ulster Defence Regiment
UDT United Dominions Trust
UEFA Union of European Football Associations
UF United Free Church (of Scotland)
UFO unidentified flying object
UGC University Grants Committee
UHF ultra high frequency
UJD *Utriusque Juris Doctor* Doctor of both Laws (Canon and Civil)
UK United Kingdom
UKAEA United Kingdom Atomic Energy Authority
ULCC ultra large crude carriers

ult, ulto *ultimo* in the last (month); ultimate(ly)
UMIST University of Manchester Institute of Science and Technology
UN United Nations
UNA United Nations Association
UNCTAD, Unctad United Nations Commission for Trade and Development
UNEP United Nations Environment Programme
UNESCO United Nations Educational, Scientific and Cultural Organisation
UNICEF United Nations International Children's Emergency Fund—now United Nations Children's Fund
UNIDO United Nations Industrial Development Organisation
Unit Unitarian
Univ University; Universalist
UNO United Nations Organisation
UNRRA United Nations Relief and Rehabilitation Administration
UP United Presbyterian; United Press
UPU Universal Postal Union
UPW Union of Post Office Workers
Uru Uruguay
US United States; United Service(s); Under-secretary
us *ut supra* as above
US(A) United States (of America) (also IVR); United States Army
USAF United States Air Force
USCL United Society for Christian Literature
USDAW Union of Shop, Distributive and Allied Workers
USIS United States Information Service
USN United States Navy
USPG United Society for the Propagation of the Gospel
USS United States Ship or Steamer
USSR (also **CCCP** (Russ)) Union of Soviet Socialist Republics
usu usually
USW ultrasonic waves; ultrashort waves
usw *und so weiter* (Ger) and so forth
UT Universal Time
Ut Utah
ut dict *ut dictum* as said
ut sup *ut supra* as above
UU Ulster Unionist
uv ultraviolet

UVF   Ulster Volunteer Force
UWIST   University of Wales Institute of
Science and Technology

V   vanadium; volt
V   symbol for electric potential difference
v   velocity; *versus* against; *vide* see; verb;
verse; volume
VA   Royal Order of Victoria and Albert;
Vicar Apostolic; volt-ampere(s)
Va   Virginia
vac   vacuum; vacation
VAD   Voluntary Aid Detachment
val   value
V and A   Victoria and Albert Museum
var   variant; variety; variable
var lect   *varia lectio* variant reading
VAT   Value-added Tax
Vat   Vatican
vb   verb
VC   Victoria Cross; Vice-Chancellor;
Vice-Consul
VCR   video cassette recorder
VD   Venereal Disease(s); Volunteer
(Officers') Decoration
vd   various dates; vapour density
VDC   Volunteer Defence Corps
VDQS   *Vins délimités de qualité supérieure*
(Fr) wines of superior quality from
approved vineyards
VDU   visual display unit
VE   Victory in Europe (1945)
veg   vegetable(s)
Ven   Venerable
VERA   versatile reactor assembly; vision
electronic recording apparatus
verb sap   *verbum sapienti,* or **verb sat,**
verbum sat(is) a word to the wise is
enough
Vet, Veter   Veterinary
Vet Surg   Veterinary Surgeon
VF   voice frequency; video frequency
VG   Vicar-General; (or **vg**) very good
vg   *verbi gratia* for example
VHF   very high frequency
vi   verb intransitive
via   by way of
Vic   Vicar; Vicarage
Vict   Victoria; Victoria University
vid   *vide* see
vil(l)   village
VIP   Very Important Person
VIR   *Victoria Imperatrix Regina* (see **VRI**)

Vis, Visc   Viscount
viz   *videlicet* namely (z = mediaeval Latin
symbol of contraction)
VJ   Victory over Japan (1945)
vl   *varia lectio* variant reading (pl **vvll**)
VLCC   very large crude carrier
VLF   very low frequency
VN   voucher number
vo   *verso* on the left-hand page
voc   vocative
vocab   vocabulary
vol   volunteer; volume
VP   Vice-President
VR   *Victoria Regina* Queen Victoria
VRD   Volunteer Reserve Decoration
VRI   *Victoria Regina et Imperatrix*
Victoria, Queen and Empress
VRQ   verbal reasoning quotient
VS   Veterinary Surgeon; *volti subito* turn
quickly
VSO   Voluntary Service Overseas
VSOP   very special old pale
Vt   Vermont
v t   verb transitive
VTO(L)   vertical take-off (and landing)
VTR   video tape recorder
Vul, Vulg   Vulgate
vul, vulg   vulgar
vvll   see **vl**
VW   *Volkswagen* (Ger) people's car
vy   various years

W   *wolframium* tungsten; watt; West;
Welsh; women('s)
w   weak; with
WA   West Africa; Western Australia
WAAC   Women's Army Auxiliary Corps
(now **WRAC**)
WAAF   Women's Auxiliary Air Force
(earlier and later **WRAF**)
Wash   Washington
WASP   White Anglo-Saxon Protestant
Wb   weber
WBA   West Bromwich Albion Football
Club; World Boxing Association of
America
WBC   World Boxing Council
WC   water-closet; Western Central;
Wesleyan Chapel
WCC   World Council of Churches
W/Cdr   Wing-Commander
WCT   World Championship Tennis
W/E   week ending

WEA Workers' Educational Association
Wed Wednesday
wef with effect from
WEU Western European Union
wf wrong fount (in printing)
WFTU World Federation of Trade Unions
wg wire gauge
WHO World Health Organisation
WI West Indies; Women's Institute
Wilts Wiltshire
Wis Wisconsin
wk week
WLF Women's Liberal Federation
Wm William
WMO World Meteorological Organisation
WNP Welsh Nationalist Party
WNW west-north-west
WO War Office (1964 absorbed in Ministry of Defence); Warrant Officer; walk-over
Worcs Worcestershire
Wp, Wpfl Worshipful
WP Warsaw Pact; word processing
wp weather permitting; word processing
wpb wastepaper basket
wpm words per minute
WR Western Region
WRAC Women's Royal Army Corps
WRAF Women's Royal Air Force
WRI Women's Rural Institute
WRNS Women's Royal Naval Service
WRVS Women's Royal Voluntary Service (previously **WVS**)
WS Writer to the Signet
WSW west-south-west
wt weight
W Va West Virginia

WVS Women's Voluntary Service (now **WRVS**)
WWF World Wildlife Fund
Wy, Wyo Wyoming

X, Xt Christ. (X = Greek *Ch*)
x *ex* (Latin without), as in **x d,** ex dividend
Xe xenon
Xm, Xmas Christmas
Xn, Xtian Christian

Y yttrium; yen (Japanese currency)
y year; yard
Yb ytterbium
yd yard
ye the (the **y** not being a **y** but representing the old letter thorn, þ)
Yeo Yeomanry
YHA Youth Hostels Association
YMCA Young Men's Christian Association
Yn yen (Japanese currency)
Yorks Yorkshire
yr your; younger; year
yt that (*y* as in **ye** above)
YTV Yorkshire Television
YU Yugoslavia (IVR)
YWCA Young Women's Christian Association

ZA South Africa (IVR)
zB *zum Beispiel* (Ger) for example
Zn zinc
ZPG zero population growth
Zr zirconium
ZST Zone Standard Time

INDEX

Part VII
DICTIONARY

How to use this dictionary

Arrangement of words

Each entry begins with a headword in bold type. Under each of these you will find its part of speech and its meaning(s). After this come the meanings of other parts of speech which have the same form as the headword.

Then follows a list of words formed directly from the headword *eg* by adding **-ness, -ment, -ly** *etc.* Where these are easily understood from the word from which they are formed, no meanings are given but they are placed as close to that word as possible.

Following these is a list of compounds, also in alphabetical order. These are words consisting of two parts whose first part is the headword, *eg* **high-handed**, or a word directly formed from it, *eg* **highly-strung**. Sometimes these are written as one word, *eg* **hardware**, sometimes with a hyphen, *eg* **hard-hearted**, sometimes as two words, *eg* **hard labour**.

Next comes a list of phrases in alphabetical order. These are groups of words containing the headword, *eg* **hard of hearing**, or a word derived from the headword, *eg* **in keeping with**.

Meanings

Where a word has more than one meaning these are separated by a semi-colon (;). In some cases meanings are made clearer by a phrase or sentence in italics showing how the word is used. Sometimes to save space two meanings have been put together in one by the use of brackets, *eg* **move** to (cause to) change place or position.

The meanings of words which look alike and are pronounced in the same way appear under one headword, *eg* **jet, port**, except where this would result in a very complicated entry, *eg* **light, mean**.

Separate headwords have been given for words which look alike but are pronounced differently, *eg* **bow**[1], **bow**[2], **tear**[1], **tear**[2].

Spelling

Many verbs in English can be spelt with either **-ize** or **-ise** as their ending. Which you use is a matter of choice. This dictionary uses the **-ize** form.

Some words which can be spelt in different ways sometimes appear in the dictionary like this — **acknowledg(e)ment**. This means that this word is correctly spelt with or without the bracketed **e**. Sometimes both spellings have been written out in full, *eg* **omelette, omelet**.

Parts of verbs

The past tenses of verbs have been given where these are not formed by simply adding **-d** or **-ed**, *eg* **referred, flung**. The past participles have been given only where they are different from the past tense, *eg* **flown, drunk**.

Adverbs

In general adverbs have not been given unless they are very common.

Plurals

Common plurals have been given where these are not formed by simply adding **-s**, *eg* **bodies, glasses**.

Pronunciation

You will find that the pronunciation of some words has been given in square brackets. The special letters used for this are explained in the following table. In some cases the special letter has been used in the word itself, *eg* **mātron, lēver**.

The pronunciation of words in bold type in an entry follows the pattern of the headword unless a change is shown. This is done either by the use of the special letters or by a new pronunciation in square brackets. Any following words in bold type then follow the new pronunciation pattern.

Pronunciation key

A stress mark ' comes just before the part of the word which is sounded with greatest emphasis, as in **measure** ['mezhər]; **ex'plain**.

	sound	example	pronunciation
a	as in **hat**	passion	['pashən]
ä	as in **path**	calm	[käm]
ā	as in **play**	weigh	[wā]
		mātron	–
e	as in **leg**	head	[hed]
ē	as in **clean**	chief	[chēf]
		lēver	–
i	as in **stick**	women	['wimin]
ī	as in **side**	fight	[fīt]
		title	–
o	as in **hot**	cough	[kof]
ö	as in **fall**	caught	[köt]
ō	as in **toe**	dough	[dō]
		mōtor	–
oŏ	as in **book**	sugar	['shŏogər]
ōō	as in **moon**	group	[grōop]
oi	as in **boy**	quoits	[koits]
ow	as in **shout**	bough	[bow]
u	as in **run**	rough	[ruf]
ū	as in **tune**	queue	[kū]
		fūtile	–
ə	as in **infant**	again	[ə'gen]
ȫ	as in **bird**	heard	[hȫrd]
ch	as in **cheese**	nature	['nāchər]
j	as in **jam**	region	['rējən]
th	as in **thin**	through	[thrōo]
dh	as in **this**	blithe	[blīdh]
sh	as in **ship**	pressure	['preshər]
zh	as in **pleasure**	measure	['mezhər]
ŋ	as in **bring**	tongue	[tuŋ]
hh	as in **loch**	pibroch	['pēbrohh]

The letter **c** is usually pronounced [s], and **g** is usually pronounced [j], before **e**, **i** or **y**; elsewhere, **c** is usually pronounced [k] and **g** is usually pronounced [g].

Labels and abbreviations

Sometimes you will find a word or words in brackets before a meaning or word. The label (*old*) means that the word is no longer commonly used in modern English, *eg* **damsel, palfrey**; (*hist*) that the thing referred to is no longer in use, *eg* **halberd, musket**; (*myth*) that the thing, person or animal is found only in stories and never existed, *eg* **cockatrice, gorgon**; (*US*) that the word or meaning is American, *eg* **sidewalk, fender**; (*coll*) or (*slang*) that the word or meaning is common in spoken or informal English but not in formal written English, *eg* **chum, quid**.

A

a, an adjs one. A boy came into the garden;
any. An ant has six legs; in, to or for
each: four times a day. The form a is
used before words beginning with a
consonant, eg boy, or consonant
sound, eg eucalyptus; an is used before
words beginning with a vowel, eg ant,
or vowel sound, eg honour.

a'back: taken aback surprised.

'abacus n a frame with beads on wires for
counting: – pl **'abacuses**.

a'bandon v to leave, without meaning to
return to; to give up (an idea etc). – n
a'bandonment.

a'base v to humble. – n **a'basement**.

a'bashed adj embarrassed, confused.

a'bate v to make or grow less. – n
a'batement.

abattoir ['abətwär] n a (public)
slaughter-house.

'abbess n the female head of an abbey or a
convent: – pl **'abbesses**.

'abbey n a monastery or convent ruled by
an abbot or an abbess; the church now
or formerly attached to it: – pl
'abbeys.

'abbot n the male head of an abbey: – fem
'abbess.

ab'brēviate v to shorten (a word, phrase
etc). – n **abbrevi'ation** a shortened
form of a word etc used instead of the
whole word (eg maths for mathematics).

'abdicate v to give up (a duty, position,
esp that of king or queen). – n
abdi'cation.

'abdomen n the part of the human body
between the chest and the hips. – adj
ab'dominal.

ab'duct v to take away by force or fraud.
– n **ab'duction**.

a'bet v to help or encourage (usu to do
wrong): – pt **a'betted**.

abeyance [ə'bāəns]: **in abeyance** undecided, not to be dealt with for the time
being.

ab'hor v to look on with horror, to hate:
– pt **ab'horred**. – n **ab'horrence**. –
adj **ab'horrent** hateful.

a'bide v to put up with, tolerate. – adj
a'biding lasting. – **abide by** to keep,
act according to.

a'bility n power or means to do a thing;
talent: – pl **a'bilities**.

'abject adj miserable, degraded.

a'blaze adj burning fiercely; gleaming
like fire.

'āble adj having power, means etc (to do a
thing); clever. – adv **'ably**.

ablution [ə'blōoshən] n (usu pl) washing
of the body.

ab'normal adj not normal (in behaviour
etc); unusual. – n **abnor'mality**: – pl
abnor'malities.

a'board adv, prep on(to) or in(to) (a
means of transport).

a'bode n a dwelling place.

a'bolish v to do away with (eg a custom).
– ns **abo'lition**; **abo'litionist** one who
tries to do away with anything, esp
slavery.

a'bominate v to hate very much. – adj
a'bominable hateful. – n **abomi'nation** great hatred; anything hateful. –
the Abominable Snowman (also
'Yeti) a large animal which may exist in
the Himalayas.

aborigines [abə'rijinēz] npl the original
or native inhabitants of a country (esp
Australia). – adj **abo'riginal**.

a'bort v (of a plan etc) to come to
nothing; to stay undeveloped; to lose a
baby before birth. – n **a'bortion** the
(deliberate) loss of an unborn child. –
adj **a'bortive** coming to nothing, useless: an abortive attempt.

a'bound v to be very plentiful; (with **in**)
to have many or much.

a'bout prep around. Look about you; near
(in time, size etc): about ten o'clock:
about two metres; here and there in:
scattered about the room. – adv around.
They stood about waiting; in motion or
in action: running about; in the opposite
direction. He turned about and walked
away. – **about to** on the point of (doing
something).

above [ə'buv] prep over, in a higher
position than: above his head; greater
than: above average; too good for. He's
above jealousy. – adv overhead, on
high; earlier on (in a book etc). – adj,
adv **above board** open(ly).

a'brāsion n the act of rubbing off; a
graze on the body. – n **a'brasive**
something used for rubbing or polishing. – adj able to wear down; (of
persons) able to hurt people's feelings.

abreast [ə'brest] adv side by side. –
abreast of up to date with: abreast of
the times.

a'bridge v to shorten (a book, story etc).
– n **a'bridg(e)ment**.

abroad [ə'bröd] adv in another country;
outside. Witches go abroad after dark; in
all directions.

a'brupt adj sudden, without warning;

(of speech *etc*) bad-tempered, short, blunt.

abscess ['abses] *n* a boil or similar collection of pus in the body: – *pl* **'abscesses**.

ab'scond *v* to run away secretly.

'absent *adj* away, not present. – *v* **ab'sent** (with **oneself**) to keep away. – *ns* **'absence** the state of being away; **absen'tee** one who is absent. – *adj* **'absent-'minded** forgetful.

absolute ['absəlōōt] *adj* complete, not limited by anything: *absolute power*. – *adv* **abso'lutely** completely. – *n* **abso'lution** forgiveness, pardon.

absolve [əb'zolv] *v* to pardon.

absorb [əb'zörb] *v* to soak up; to take up the whole attention of. – *adjs* **ab'sorbed; ab'sorbent** able to soak up (liquid). – *n* **ab'sorption** the act of absorbing; complete mental concentration.

ab'stain *v* (with **from**) to hold oneself back. – *ns* **ab'stainer** one who abstains from something, *esp* from alcoholic drink; **ab'stention** a holding back from.

ab'stemious *adj* not greedy, sparing (in food, drink *etc*).

'abstinence *n* holding back (from alcoholic drink *etc*).

'abstract *adj* existing only as an idea, not as a real thing. – *n* a summary.

abstruse [əb'strōōs] *adj* difficult to understand.

ab'surd *adj* clearly wrong, ridiculous. – *n* **ab'surdity**: – *pl* **ab'surdities**.

a'bundance *n* a plentiful supply. – *adj* **a'bundant** plentiful.

abuse [ə'būz] *v* to use wrongly; to insult, speak unkindly to, treat badly. – *n* **abuse** [ə'būs] wrongful use; insulting language. – *adj* **a'busive**.

abyss [ə'bis] *n* a bottomless depth: – *pl* **a'bysses**. – *adj* **abysmal** [ə'bizməl] bottomless; (*coll*) very bad.

acacia [ə'kāshə] *n* a family of thorny shrubs and trees.

a'cademy *n* a college for special study or training; a society for encouraging science or art; in Scotland, a senior school: – *pl* **a'cademies**. – *adj* **aca'demic** learned; not practical: *purely of academic interest*; of universities *etc*. – *n* a university or college teacher.

accede [ək'sēd] *v* to agree (to).

accelerate [ək'selərāt] *v* to increase in speed. – *ns* **accele'ration; ac'celerator** a lever, pedal *etc* by which speed is increased.

accent ['aksənt] *n* (a mark used to show

the) stress on a syllable or word, or in French to show the quality of a vowel; emphasis. *The accent must be on hard work*; a special way of saying words in a particular region *etc*: *a Scottish accent*. – *v* **ac'centuate** to make more obvious, emphasize.

accept [ək'sept] *v* to take something offered; to agree; to submit to. – *adj* **ac'ceptable** satisfactory; pleasing. – *n* **ac'ceptance** the act of accepting.

access ['akses] *n* right or means of approach or entry. – *adj* **ac'cessible** easily approached or reached. – *ns* **accessi'bility; ac'cession** a coming to: *the accession of a king to his throne*; **ac'cessory** a (small) additional fitting (to a car *etc*) or article of dress (as a handbag *etc*); a helper (*esp* in crime): – *pl* **ac'cessories**.

accident ['aksidənt] *n* an unexpected event (often unwanted or causing injury *etc*). – *adj* **acci'dental** happening by chance.

ac'claim *v* to welcome enthusiastically. – *n* **accla'mation** noisy sign of approval.

ac'climatize *v* to accustom (*esp* to another climate). – *n* **acclimati'zation**.

ac'commodate *v* to find room for; to make suitable; to oblige; to supply (with). – *adj* **ac'commodating** obliging. – *n* **ac'commo'dation** space; lodgings.

accompany [ə'kumpəni] *v* to go or be with; to play an instrument (*eg* a piano) while a singer sings *etc*: – *pt* **ac'companied**. – *ns* **ac'companiment** that which goes along with (something); the music played while a singer sings *etc*; **ac'companist** one who plays an accompaniment.

ac'complice [ə'kumplis] *n* one who helps another (*esp* in crime).

ac'complish [ə'kumplish] *v* to complete; to bring about. – *adj* **ac'complished** completed; skilled (as in music *etc*). – *n* **ac'complishment** completion; something one is good at.

ac'cord *v* to agree (with); to give, grant. – *n* agreement. – *n* **ac'cordance** agreement. – *adv* **ac'cordingly** therefore. – **according to** as told by; in relation to: *paid according to your work*; **of one's own accord** of one's own free will.

ac'cordion *n* a type of small musical wind instrument with a keyboard.

ac'cost *v* to approach and speak to.

ac'count *v* to give a reason (for). – *n* a bill; a reckoning up of money; a description (of events *etc*); an explanation. – *adj* **ac'countable** answerable, responsible. – *n* **ac'countant** a keeper or inspector of accounts. – **on account of** because of.

accoutrements [ə'kōōtrəmənts] *npl* (*esp* military) dress and equipment.

ac'credited *adj* given the official power to act.

ac'crue *v* to be given or added to. *Interest accrues to savings deposited in a bank.* – *adj* **ac'crued**.

ac'cūmūlate *v* to collect; to increase. – *ns* **ac'cumu'lation** a collection; a mass or pile; **ac'cumulator** a type of battery (as in a car).

'accūrate *adj* correct, exact. – *n* **'accuracy**.

accursed [ə'kərsid] *adj* under a curse; hateful.

accuse [ə'kūz] *v* to bring a (criminal) charge against. – *ns* **accu'sation** a charge brought against anyone; **ac'cused** one charged with wrongdoing; **ac'cuser**.

ac'customed *adj* used to: *accustomed to travel*; usual.

ace *n* the one on playing cards; a person who is expert in anything.

a'cetylene *n* a kind of gas used for giving light and heat.

ache [āk] *n* a continuous pain. – *v* to be in continuous pain.

achieve [ə'chēv] *v* to get (something) done, accomplish; to win. – *n* **a'chievement**.

'acid *adj* (of taste) sharp; sarcastic. – *n* a substance containing hydrogen which will dissolve metals. – *v* **a'cidifȳ** to make or become acid: – *pt* **a'cidified**. – *n* **acidity** [ə'sidəti] the state of being acid.

acknowledge [ək'nolij] *v* to admit the truth of; to (write to) say one has received something. – *n* **ack'nowledg(e)ment**.

acme ['akmi] *n* the highest point, perfection.

acne ['akni] *n* a common skin disease with pimples.

'ācorn *n* the fruit of the oak tree.

acoustic [ə'kōōstik] *adj* of hearing or sound. – *npl* **a'coustics** the study of sound; the characteristics (of a hall *etc*) which affect the hearing of sound in it.

ac'quaint *v* to make (someone) familiar (with). – *n* **ac'quaintance** knowledge; a person whom one knows slightly.

acquiesce [akwi'es] *v* (*usu* with **in**) to agree (to). – *n* **acqui'escence**.

ac'quire *v* to get (as a possession), gain. – *adj* **ac'quired** gained, not born with.

– *n* **acqui'sition** the act of getting; something got. – *adj* **ac'quisitive** eager to get.

ac'quit *v* to declare (someone) innocent of a crime: – *pt* **ac'quitted**. – *n* **ac'quittal** a legal judgement of 'not guilty'. – **acquit oneself well, badly** to do well, badly; to be successful, unsuccessful.

acre ['ākər] *n* a land measure containing 4840 square yards or about 4000 square metres. – *n* **'acreage** the number of acres in a piece of land.

'acrid *adj* harsh, bitter.

'acrimony *n* bitterness of feeling or speech. – *adj* **acri'mōnious**.

'acrobat *n* one who performs feats of agility, rope-walking *etc*. – *adj* **acro'batic**.

'acronym *n* a word formed from the initial letters of other words (*eg radar* for radio detecting and ranging).

a'cross *adv, prep* to or at the other side (of). *They swam across the river. He saw her across the table.* – **across the board** involving all (things or persons).

a'crostic *n* a poem *etc* in which the first or last letters of each line, taken in order, spell a word or words.

act *v* to do something; to behave: *act foolishly*; to play a part (as in a play). – *n* something done; a government law; a part of a play. – *n* **'action** a deed, an act; a law-case; what happens (in a film, play *etc*). – *adj* **'actionable** likely to cause a law-case: *an actionable statement*. – *v* **'activate** to start (something) working. – *adj* **'active** busy; lively; able to work *etc*; of the form of a verb in which the subject performs the action of the verb as in 'The dog *bit* the man'. – *n* **ac'tivity**: – *pl* **ac'tivities**. – *n* **'actor** one who acts a part in a play or film: – *fem* **'actress**: – *pl* **'actresses**.

actual ['akchōōəl] *adj* real, existing in fact. – *n* **actu'ality**. – *adv* **'actually** really.

'actūary *n* one who works out the price of insurance: – *pl* **'actuaries**. – *adj* **actu'ārial**.

'actūate *v* to put into action; to drive or urge on.

'acūmen *n* quickness of understanding.

'acūpuncture *n* a method of treating illness by piercing the skin with needles.

a'cute *adj* quick at understanding; (of a disease) severe, but not lasting very long; (of an angle) less than a right angle. – *n* **a'cuteness**. – *n* **acute accent** a stroke leaning forwards placed over letters in some languages to show their pronunciation.

ad *n* short for **advertisement**.

'**adage** *n* an old saying, a proverb.

'**adamant** *adj* unwilling to give way.

'**Adam's 'apple** *n* the natural lump which sticks out from the throat.

a'**dapt** *v* to make suitable, to alter (so as to fit). – *adj* a'**daptable** easily altered to suit new conditions. – *ns* adap'**tation; a'daptor** device which enables an electrical plug to be used in a socket for which it was not designed, or several plugs to be used on the same socket.

add *v* to make one thing join another to give a sum total or whole; to mix in: *add eggs to the flour*; to say further. – *n* ad'**dition** the act of adding; something added. – *adj* ad'**ditional**.

ad'dendum *n* something added: – *pl* ad'**denda**.

'**adder** *n* the common name of the viper, a poisonous snake.

'**addict** *n* one who is dependent on something (often on a drug or alcohol), either physically or mentally. – **ad-dicted to** dependent on.

ad'**dress** *v* to speak to; to write the address on (a letter *etc*). – *n* the name of the house, street, and town where a person lives *etc*; a speech: – *pl* ad'**dresses**.

'**adenoids** *npl* swellings at the back of the nose which hinder breathing.

a'**dept** *adj* very skilful.

'**adequate** *adj* sufficient, enough. – *n* '**adequacy**.

ad'**here** *v* to stick (to); to give support (to) or be loyal (to). – *n* ad'**herence**. – *adj* ad'**herent** sticking (to). – *n* a follower, one who supports a cause *etc*.

ad'**hesion** *n* the act of sticking (to). – *adj* adhesive [əd'hēsiv] sticky, gummed. – *n* something which makes things stick to each other.

ad'**jacent** *adj* (with **to**) lying next to.

'**adjective** *n* a word which tells something about a noun (as 'The *black* dog bites. The work is *hard*'). – *adj* ad-jec'**tival**.

ad'**join** *v* to be joined to. – *adj* ad-'**joining**.

adjourn [ə'jörn] *v* to stop (a meeting *etc*) with the intention of continuing it at another time or place; to go to another place (*eg* another room). – *n* ad'**journ-ment**.

ad'**judicate** *v* to give a judgement on (a dispute *etc*); to act as a judge at a (musical *etc*) competition. – *ns* adjudi'**cation; ad'judicator** one who adjudicates.

'**adjunct** *n* something joined or added.

ad'**just** *v* to rearrange or alter to suit the circumstances. – *adj* ad'**justable**. – *n* ad'**justment**.

'**adjutant** *n* a military officer who assists a commanding officer.

'**ad-'lib** *v* to speak without plan or preparation. – *adj* without preparation.

ad'**minister** *v* to manage or govern; to carry out (the law *etc*); to give (help, medicine *etc*). – *v* ad'**ministrate** to manage or govern. – *n* adminis'**tration** management; (the body that carries on) the government of a country *etc*. – *adj* ad'**ministrative**. – *n* ad'**ministrator** one involved in the administration of a country *etc*.

'**admiral** *n* the commander of a navy. – *n* '**admiralty** the government office which manages naval affairs.

ad'**mire** *v* to think very highly of; to look at with pleasure. – *adj* **admirable** ['admərəbl] worthy of being admired. – *adv* '**admirably**. – *ns* admi'**ration**; ad'**mirer**.

ad'**mit** *v* to let in; to acknowledge the truth of, confess; (with **of**) to leave room for, allow. *This admits of no other explanation*: – *pt* ad'**mitted**. – *adj* ad'**missible** allowable. – *ns* ad'**mission** (the price of) being let in; anything admitted; ad'**mittance** the right or permission to enter.

ad'**monish** *v* to warn; to rebuke, scold. – *n* admo'**nition** a warning. – *adj* ad'**monitory**.

ado [ə'dōō] *n* trouble, fuss.

adolescent [adə'lesnt] *n*, *adj* (a person) between childhood and the adult state. – *n* ado'**lescence**.

a'**dopt** *v* to take as one's own (*esp* a child of other parents). – *n* a'**doption**.

a'**dore** *v* to love very much; to worship. – *adj* a'**dorable** worthy of being loved. – *adv* a'**dorably**. – *n* ado'**ration** worship; great love.

a'**dorn** *v* to decorate (with ornaments *etc*). – *n* a'**dornment** ornament.

a'**drift** *adv* drifting, floating.

a'**droit** *adj* skilful.

adū'**lation** *n* great flattery. – *adj* '**adulatory**.

'**adult** *adj* grown up. – *n* a grown-up person.

a'**dulterate** *v* to make impure by adding something else. – *n* a'**dulte'ration**.

a'**dultery** *n* breaking of the marriage promise, unfaithfulness to one's wife or husband. – *n* a'**dulterer**: – *fem* a'**dulteress**.

ad'**vance** *v* to go forward; to put forward (a plan *etc*); to help the progress of; to pay before the usual or agreed time. – *n* movement forward; improvement; a loan. – *adj* **ad'vanced** well forward in progress. – *n* **ad'vancement** progress. – **in advance** beforehand.

ad'vantage *n* a better position, superiority; gain or benefit. – *v* to help, benefit. – *adj* **advan'tāgeous** profitable; helpful. – **take advantage of** to make use of (a situation, person *etc*) in such a way as to benefit oneself.

'advent *n* coming, arrival: *the advent of television.*

adven'titious *adj* happening by chance.

ad'venture *n* a bold or exciting undertaking or experience. – *n* **ad'venturer** one who takes risks, *esp* in the hope of making a lot of money; a soldier who fights for any side who will pay him.

'adverb *n* a word which gives a more definite meaning to a verb, adjective, or other adverb (as 'He writes *neatly*. The sky is *beautifully* clear. He works *very* slowly'). – *adj* **ad'verbial** of or like an adverb.

'adversary *n* an enemy; an opponent: – *pl* **'adversaries.**

'adverse *adj* unfavourable. – *n* **ad'versity** misfortune: – *pl* **ad'versities.**

'advert *n* short for **advertisement**.

advertise ['advərtīz] *v* to make known to the public; to stress the good points of (a product for sale). – *n* **advertisement** [əd'vərtismənt] anything (as a film, picture) which is intended to persuade the public to buy a particular product.

ad'vice *n* something said as a help to someone trying to make a decision *etc*; a formal notice. – *v* **advise** [əd'vīz] to give advice to; to recommend (an action *etc*). – *adj* **ad'visable** wise, sensible. – *ns* **advisa'bility; ad'viser.** – *adj* **ad'visory** advice-giving.

'advocate *n* one who pleads for another; (in Scotland) a court lawyer. – *v* to plead or argue for; to recommend.

adze, (*US*) **adz** *n* a kind of axe used by a carpenter.

aeon, eon ['ēon] *n* a very long period of time, an age.

'aerate *v* to put air (or some other gas) into (a liquid).

'aerial *adj* of, in or from the air; placed high up or overhead (as an *aerial* railway). – *n* a wire or rod (or a set of these) by means of which radio or television signals are received or sent.

aerie see **eyrie**.

aero'batics *npl* stunts performed by an aircraft.

'aerodrome *n* an aeroplane station.

'aeroplane *n* a flying-machine heavier than air, with wings.

'aerosol *n* a container of liquid and gas under pressure, from which the liquid is squirted in the form of a mist.

aesthetic [is'thetik] *adj* of beauty or its appreciation; artistic, pleasing to the eye.

'affable *adj* pleasant, easy to speak to. – *n* **affa'bility.**

af'fair *n* events *etc* which are connected with one person or thing: *the Suez affair*; (often in *pl*) business, concern; a love affair.

af'fect *v* to act upon; to have an effect on; to move the feelings of; to pretend to feel *etc*. – *n* **affec'tation** pretence. – *adjs* **af'fected** moved in one's feelings; not natural, sham; **af'fecting** moving the feelings.

af'fection *n* a strong liking. – *adj* **af'fectionate** loving. – *adv* **af'fectionately.**

affi'dāvit *n* a written statement made on oath.

af'filiated *adj* (with **with** or **to**) connected, attached. – *n* **affili'ation.**

af'finity *n* a close likeness or agreement: – *pl* **af'finities.**

af'firm *v* to state firmly. – *n* **affir'mation** a firm statement. – *adj* **af'firmative** saying 'yes'.

af'fix *v* to attach to.

af'flict *v* to give continued pain or distress to. – *adj* **af'flicted** suffering. – *n* **af'fliction** great suffering, misery.

affluent ['aflōoənt] *adj* wealthy. – *n* a stream flowing into a river or lake. – *n* **'affluence** wealth.

af'ford *v* to be able to pay for; to give, yield.

af'forest *v* to cover land with forest. – *n* **affores'tation.**

af'fray *n* a fight, a brawl.

affront [ə'frunt] *v* to insult openly. – *n* an insult.

a'float *adv*, *adj* floating.

a'foot *adv* happening or about to happen.

aforesaid [ə'försed] *adj* said or named before.

a'fraid *adj* struck with fear; (*coll*) sorry to have to admit that.

aft *adv* near or towards the stern of a vessel.

'after *prep* later in time than: *after dinner*; following: *one after another: day after day*; in memory or honour of: *named after his father*; in pursuit of: *run after the bus*; about: *ask after someone's health*; despite. *After all his efforts, he still failed*; in the style of: *after (the manner of) Shakespeare*. – *adv* later in time or place. *They arrived soon after.* – *conj* later than the time when. *After she arrived, things improved greatly.* – *adj, prefix* **after(-)** later in time or place: *in after years*: *aftertaste.* – **after all** all things considered. *After all, he's not very well*; despite everything said or done before. *He's coming after all.*

'**aftermath** *n* the bad results of something, *eg* of war *etc*.

after'noon *n* the time between noon and evening.

afterthought ['äftərthöt] *n* a later thought.

'**afterwards** *adv* later.

again [ə'gen] *adv* once more. *Play the tune again*; in(to) the original state, place *etc: there and back again*; on the other hand. *Again, I might be wrong*; (*coll*) at another (later) time. *Goodbye, I'll see you again.*

against [ə'genst] *prep* in opposition to: *against the law. He fought against his brother*; in the opposite direction to: *against the wind*; on a background of: *against the sky*; close to, touching: *lean against the wall*; as protection from: *immunized against diphtheria.*

'**agate** *n* a kind of precious stone.

age *n* a long period of time; the time a person or thing has lived or existed. – *v* to grow or make (obviously) older. – *adj* **aged** ['ājid] old; **aged** [ājd] of the age of: *aged five.* – **of age** legally an adult.

a'**genda** *n* a list of things to be done, *esp* at a meeting.

'**agent** *n* a person or thing that acts; one who acts for another; a spy. – *n* '**agency** the office or business of an agent; action, means by which something is done: – *pl* '**agencies**.

ag'**grandize** *v* to make greater. – *n* **aggrandizement** [ə'grandizmənt].

'**aggravate** *v* to make worse; (*coll*) to annoy. – *adj* '**aggravating**. – *n* **aggra'vation**.

'**aggregate** *n* a total.

ag'**gressive** *adj* ready to attack first; quarrelsome. – *ns* ag'**gressiveness**; ag'**gression**; ag'**gressor**.

aggrieved [ə'grēvd] *adj* hurt, upset.

aghast [ə'gäst] *adj* struck with horror.

'**agile** *adj* active, nimble. – *n* **agility** [ə'jiləti].

'**agitate** *v* to stir up; to excite, disturb. – *ns* **agi'tation**; '**agitator** one who stirs up (*usu* political) feeling.

ag'**nostic** *n* one who believes that we cannot know whether God exists or not. – *n* ag'**nosticism**.

a'**go** *adv* in the past. *Two years ago I went*

to Rome.

a'**gog** *adj* eager, excited.

'**agony** *n* great pain: – *pl* '**agonies**. – *adjs* '**agonized** showing great pain; '**agonizing** causing great pain.

agora'**phobia** *n* great fear of open spaces.

a'**grarian** *adj* of farmland or farming.

a'**gree** *v* to be alike (*esp* in opinions, decisions *etc*); to say that one will do something, consent; (with **with**) to suit. – *adj* a'**greeable** pleasant; ready to agree. – *adv* a'**greeably**. – *n* a'**greement** likeness (*esp* of opinions); a written statement making a bargain.

'**agriculture** *n* the cultivation of the land, farming. – *adj* **agri'cultural**.

a'**ground** *adj, adv* (of boats) stuck on the bottom of the sea or a river. *The ship ran aground.*

ague ['āgū] *n* a fever.

ahead [ə'hed] *adv* in front; in advance: *ahead of time.*

aid *v* to help, assist. – *n* help.

aide-de-camp ['āddə'koŋ] *n* an officer who carries messages to and from a general on the field: – *pl* '**aides-de-'camp**.

ail *v* to be ill; to trouble. – *n* '**ailment** a trouble, disease.

'**aileron** *n* a hinged flap on the back edge of an aeroplane's wing, used to control balance.

aim *v* to point at (*esp* with a gun); to intend to do; to have as one's purpose. – *n* the act of, or skill in, aiming; the point aimed at, goal, intention. – *adj* '**aimless** without aim or purpose.

air *n* the mixture of gases (mainly oxygen and nitrogen) which we breathe, the atmosphere; a light breeze; fresh air; space overhead; a tune; the look or manner (of a person). – *v* to expose to the air; to make known (an opinion *etc*). – *n* '**airing** the act of exposing to the air. – *adjs* '**airless**; '**airy** of or like the air; well supplied with fresh air; light-hearted. – *adv* '**airily**. – *n* '**airbed** a mattress which can be blown up. – *adjs* '**airborne** in the air, flying; '**air-con'ditioned** of buildings *etc* in which the air is cleaned and kept to a certain temperature by a special system. – *n(pl)* '**aircraft** flying machine(s). – *ns* **air force** the branch of the armed forces using aircraft; '**air-gun** a gun worked by means of compressed air; **air hostess** a woman whose duty is to serve and look after the passengers on aircraft; '**airlock** a bubble in a pipe obstructing the flow of a liquid; a compartment with two doors for entering and leaving an airtight spaceship *etc*; **'airman** one who pilots an aircraft; **'airport** a place where aircraft land and take off, with buildings for customs, waiting-rooms *etc*; **'air-pump** a pump for forcing air in or out of something; **'air-raid** an attack by aeroplanes; **'airship** a large balloon which can be steered and driven. – *adj* **'airtight** made so that air cannot pass in or out. – **on the air** broadcasting.

aisle [īl] *n* the side part of a church; a passage between seats (*esp* in a church).

a'jar *adv* (of doors *etc*) partly open.

a'kimbo *adv* with hand on hip and elbow bent outward.

a'kin *adj* similar.

a'lacrity *n* briskness, cheerful readiness.

a'larm *n* sudden fear; something which rouses to action or gives warning of danger. – *v* to frighten. – *adj* **a'larming**. – *n* **a'larmist** one who frightens others needlessly.

a'las! a cry showing grief.

'albatross *n* a type of large sea-bird: – *pl* **'albatrosses**.

albino [al'bēnō] *n* a person or animal with no natural colour in their skin and hair (which are white) and eye pupils (which are pink): – *pl* **al'binos**.

'album *n* a book with blank pages for holding photographs, stamps *etc*; a long-playing record.

'albūmen *n* the white of eggs.

alchemy ['alkəmi] *n* (*hist*) the early form of chemistry which aimed to change other metals into gold. – *n* **'alchemist** one who practised alchemy.

'alcohol *n* the pure spirit in strong drinks. – *adj* **alco'holic** of or containing alcohol. – *n* a person suffering from alcoholism. – *n* **'alcoholism** dependence on alcoholic drinks.

'alcove *n* a recess in a room's wall.

alder ['öldər] *n* a type of tree which grows beside ponds and rivers.

alderman ['öldərmən] *n* a councillor next in rank to the mayor of a town *etc*; (*US*) a member of the governing body of a city.

ale *n* a drink made from malt, hops *etc*.

a'lert *n* signal to be ready for action. – *v* to make alert, warn. – *adj* watchful; quick-thinking. – **on the alert** on the watch (for).

al'falfa *n* a kind of grass.

al'fresco *adj, adv* in the open air.

algae ['aljē] *npl* a group of simple plants which includes seaweed.

'algebra *n* a method of counting, using

letters and signs.

'ālias *adv* otherwise known as: *Smith alias Jones*. – *n* a false name: – *pl* **'aliases**.

'alibi *n* the plea that a person charged with a crime was elsewhere when it was done; the state or fact of being elsewhere when a crime was committed.

alien ['āliən] *adj* foreign. – *n* a foreigner. – *v* **'alienate** to make (a person) strange or unfriendly. – **alien to** not in keeping with: *alien to his nature*.

alight [ə'līt] *v* to climb *etc* down; to settle, land. – *adj, adv* on fire, burning.

align [ə'līn] *v* to set in line; to take sides in an argument *etc*. – *n* **a'lignment** arrangement in a line.

a'like *adj* like one another, similar. – *adv* in the same way, similarly.

ali'mentary *adj* of food. – *n* **alimentary canal** the passage through the body which begins at the mouth.

a'live *adj* living; full of activity. – **alive to** aware of.

'alkali *n* a substance such as soda or potash (opposite of **acid**). – *adj* **'alkaline**.

all [öl] *adj, pron* every one (of). *All men are equal. All must go*; the whole (of). *He ate all the cake.* – *adv* wholly, completely. *She was dressed all in red.* – *n* **'all-'rounder** one who shows ability in many kinds of work, sport *etc*. – **all in** with everything included; (*coll*) exhausted; **all-in wrestling** wrestling in which no holds are against the rules; **all over** over the whole of; everywhere; finished, ended.

al'lay *v* to make less, relieve; to calm.

allege [ə'lej] *v* to say without proof. – *n* **alle'gation**.

al'lēgiance *n* loyalty.

'allegory *n* a story or fable which deals with a subject in a way which is meant to suggest a deeper, more serious subject. '*Pilgrim's Progress' is an allegory of the Christian's life*: – *pl* **'allegories**. – *adj* **alle'gorical**.

allergy ['alərji] *n* abnormal sensitiveness (of the body) to something: – *pl* **'allergies**. – *adj* **al'lergic**.

al'lēviate *v* to make lighter, to lessen. – *n* **allevi'ation**.

'alley *n* a narrow passage or lane; an enclosure for bowls or skittles: – *pl* **'alleys**.

alliance *see* **ally**.

'alligātor *n* a kind of large reptile like a crocodile.

alliteration [ə'litə'rāshən] *n* the repetition of the same sound at the beginning of two or more words close together (*eg* 'Sing a Song of Sixpence').

'**allocate** *v* to give to each his share. – *n* **allo'cation**.

al'lot *v* to give to each his share, distribute: – *pt* **al'lotted**. – *n* **al'lotment** the act of distributing; a small plot of ground for growing vegetables *etc*.

allow [ə'low] *v* to let (someone do something); (with **for**) to take into consideration (in sums, plans *etc*); to admit, confess; to give, *esp* at regular intervals. *She allows him £5 a week.* – *adj* **al'lowable**. – *n* **al'lowance** a fixed sum or amount given regularly. – **make allowance(s) for** to treat differently because of taking into consideration special circumstances *etc*.

'**alloy** *n* a mixture of two or more metals.

allude [ə'lood] *v* (with **to**) to mention in passing. – *n* **al'lusion**. – *adj* **al'lusive**.

al'lure *v* to tempt, draw on by promises *etc*. – *n* **al'lurement**. – *adj* **al'luring**.

alluvium [ə'looviəm] *n* earth, sand *etc* brought down and left by rivers in flood: – *pl* **al'luvia**. – *adj* **al'luvial**.

al'ly *v* to join oneself to (by treaty *etc*): – *pt* **al'lied**. – *adj* '**allied**. – *ns* '**ally** a friend, person *etc* in alliance with another: – *pl* '**allies; al'liance** a joining together of two people, nations *etc* (*esp* against an enemy of both).

almanac ['ölmənak] *n* a calendar of days, weeks, and months of any year, *usu* with information (about the phases of the moon *etc*).

almighty [öl'miti] *adj* having much power. – **the Almighty** God.

almond ['ämənd] *n* the kernel of the fruit of the almond-tree.

almost ['ölmōst] *adv* very nearly but not quite: *almost five years old*: *almost at our destination*.

alms [ämz] *npl* gifts to the poor.

a'loft *adv* on high; upward.

a'lone *adj* not accompanied by others, solitary. *He found he was alone again.* – *adv* only, without anything or anyone else. *That alone is bad enough*; not accompanied by others. *He lived alone.*

a'long *prep* over the length of. *He walked along the road.* – *adv* onward. *Hurry along!* – *prep* **a'long'side** beside. – *adv* near a ship's side. – **along with** together with.

a'loof *adj, adv* at a distance, apart; showing no interest in others. – *n* **a'loofness**.

a'loud *adv* so as to be heard.

'**alpha** *n* the first letter of the Greek alphabet.

'**alphabet** *n* letters of a language given in a fixed order. – *adjs* **alpha'betic(al)** in the order of the alphabet.

'**alpine** *adj* of the Alps or other high mountains.

already [öl'redi] *adv* before this or that time. *I've already done that*; now, before the expected time. *You haven't finished already, have you?*

al'sātian *n* a breed of large, wolf-like dog.

also ['ölsō] *adv* in addition, besides, too. *He also must go.* – *n* '**also-ran** a person or thing who competed (as in a race) but was not among the winners.

altar ['öltər] *n* a raised place for offerings to a god; in Christian churches, the communion table.

alter ['öltər] *v* to change. – *n* **alte'ration**.

altercation [öltər'kāshən] *n* an argument or quarrel.

alternate ['öltərnāt] *v* (of two things *etc*) to do or happen in turn. – *adj* **al'ternate** happening *etc* in turns. – *adv* **al'ternately**. – *n* **alter'nation**. – *adj* **al'ternative** offering a second possibility *etc*.

although [öl'dhō] *conj* though, in spite of the fact that.

'**altimēter** *n* an instrument for measuring height above sea level.

'**altitude** *n* height above sea level.

'**alto** *n* the male voice of the highest pitch; the female voice of lowest pitch (also **con'tralto**).

altogether [öltə'gedhər] *adv* considering everything, in all. *Altogether there were 20 of them*; completely. *I am not altogether satisfied.*

altruism ['altrooizəm] *n* unselfish concern for the good of others. – *adj* **altru'istic**.

alū'minium, (*US*) **aluminum** [ə'loominəm] *n* an element, a very light metal.

always ['ölwāz] *adv* for ever. *I'll always remember this day*; every time. *He always says the same thing.*

am *see* **be**.

a'malgam *n* a mixture (*esp* of metals). – *v* **a'malgamate** to join together, combine; to mix. – *n* **a'malga'mation**.

a'mass *v* to collect in large quantity.

amateur ['amətər] *n* one who takes part in a thing for the love of it, not for money (opposite of **professional**). – Also *adj*. – *adj* **ama'teurish** not done properly; not skilful.

a'maze *v* to surprise greatly. –

n a'mazement.

'**Amazon** *n* (*myth*) one of a nation of warrior women; a very strong or manlike woman.

am'**bassador** *n* a government minister sent to look after the interests of one country in another country; a representative.

'**amber** *n* a hard yellowish substance like resin used in making jewellery. – *adj* made of amber; of the colour of amber.

ambi'**dextrous** *adj* able to use both hands with equal skill. – *n* **ambidex'terity**.

am'**biguous** *adj* having two possible meanings; not clear. – *n* **ambi'guity**: – *pl* **ambi'guities**.

am'**bition** *n* the desire for success, power, fame *etc*. – *adj* **am'bitious**.

'**amble** *v* to walk without hurrying. – Also *n*.

ambrosia [am'brōziə] *n* (*myth*) the food of the gods, which gave eternal youth and beauty.

'**ambulance** *n* a vehicle for carrying the sick or injured.

ambush ['amboŏosh] *n* the act of lying hidden in order to make a surprise attack; the people hidden in this way; their place of hiding: – *pl* '**ambushes**. – *v* to attack suddenly from a position of hiding.

a'**menable** *adj* open to advice or suggestion.

a'**mend** *v* to correct, to improve; to alter slightly. – *n* a'**mendment** a change (*usu* in something written). – **make amends** to make up for having done wrong.

a'**menity** *n* a pleasant or convenient feature of a place *etc*: – *pl* a'**menities**.

amethyst ['aməthist] *n* a type of precious stone of a bluish-violet colour.

'**amiable** *adj* likeable; friendly. – *n* **amia'bility**.

'**amicable** *adj* friendly.

a'**mid**, a'**midst** *preps* in the middle of, among. *She seemed very calm amidst all the confusion.*

a'**miss** *adv* wrong(ly); badly.

'**amity** *n* friendship.

am'**monia** *n* a strong-smelling gas made of hydrogen and nitrogen.

ammū'**nition** *n* things with which guns *etc* are charged (such as gunpowder, bullets *etc*).

amnesia [am'nēziə] *n* loss of memory.

'**amnesty** *n* a general pardon of wrongdoers: – *pl* '**amnesties**.

amoeba [ə'mēbə] *n* a very simple form of animal life found in ponds *etc*: – *pls* a'**moebas**, **amoebae** [ə'mēbē].

a'**mok**, a'**muck**: **run amok** to become furious or mad and do a lot of damage.

among, **amongst** [ə'muŋ(st)] *preps* in the midst or in the middle of: *a house among trees: among friends*; in shares, in parts. *Divide the chocolate among all four*; in the group of. *Among all his novels, this is the best.*

a'**moral** *adj* non-moral, outside the domain of morality.

'**amorous** *adj* loving; ready or inclined to love.

a'**mount** *v* to add up (to). – *n* total, sum (*usu* of money).

amp, **ampère** ['amper] *n* the standard unit of electric current.

am'**phibian** *n* any animal that lives on land and in water; a vehicle for use on land and in water. – Also *adj*. – *adj* am'**phibious**.

amphitheatre ['amfithēətər] *n* (*hist*) a theatre with seats surrounding a central arena.

'**ample** *adj* plenty of; large enough.

'**amplify** *v* to increase; to make louder: – *pt* '**amplified**. – *ns* **amplifi'cation**; '**amplifier** an electrical device for increasing loudness.

'**amplitude** *n* largeness; size.

'**amputate** *v* to cut off (*esp* a human limb). – *n* **ampu'tation**.

amuck *see* **amok**.

amuse [ə'mūz] *v* to make to laugh; to give pleasure to. – *n* a'**musement**. – *adj* a'**musing** giving pleasure; funny.

an *see* **a**.

anachronism [ə'nakrənizəm] *n* the act of mentioning something which did not exist or was not yet invented at the time spoken about.

ana'**conda** *n* a type of large S. American water snake.

anaemia, (*US*) **anemia** [ə'nēmiə] *n* a shortage of red cells in the blood. – *adj* a'**naemic** suffering from anaemia; pale or ill-looking.

anaesthetic, (*US*) **anesthetic** [anəs'thetik] *n* a substance which produces lack of feeling for a time in a part of the body, or which makes a person unconscious. – *n* **anaesthetist** [ə'nēsthətist] a doctor who gives anaesthetics.

'**anagram** *n* a word or sentence formed by rewriting (in a different order) the letters of another word or sentence (*veil* is an anagram of *evil*).

a'**nalogy** *n* a likeness, resemblance in certain ways: – *pl* a'**nalogies**. – *adj* **analogous** [ə'naləgəs] similar, alike in some way.

a'**nalysis** *n* a breaking up of a thing into

its parts; a detailed examination (of something): – *pl* **a'nalysēs**. – *v* **'analyse**, (*US*) **'analyze**. – *n* **'analyst** a person who analyses.

anarchy ['anərki] *n* lack or absence of government; disorder or confusion. – *n* **'anarchist** one in favour of anarchy.

a'nathema *n* a curse; a hated person or thing.

a'natomy *n* the study of the parts of the body; the body. – *n* **a'natomist**.

ancestor ['ansistər] *n* one from whom a person is descended by birth, a forefather. – *adj* **an'cestral**. – *n* **'ancestry** line of ancestors.

anchor ['aŋkər] *n* a heavy piece of iron, with hooked ends, for holding a ship fast to the bed of the sea *etc*. – *v* to fix by anchor; to let down the anchor. – *n* **'anchorage** a place where a ship can anchor. – **cast anchor** to let down the anchor; **weigh anchor** to pull up the anchor.

'anchovy *n* a type of small fish of the herring family: – *pl* **'anchovies**.

ancient ['ānshənt] *adj* very old; of times long past.

ancillary [an'siləri] *adj* serving or supporting something more important.

and *conj* joining two statements, pieces of information *etc*. *I opened the door and went inside. The hat was blue and red*; in addition to. *2 and 2 make 4*.

'anecdote *n* a short, interesting or amusing story, *esp* a true one.

anemometer [ani'momitər] *n* an instrument for measuring the speed of the wind.

anemone [ə'neməni] *n* a type of woodland or garden flower.

aneroid barometer ['anəroid] *n* one in which the pressure of the air is measured without the use of mercury.

angel ['ānjəl] *n* a messenger or attendant of God; a very good or beautiful person. – *adj* **angelic** [an'jelik].

angelica [an'jelikə] *n* a plant whose candied leaf-stalks are used as cake decoration.

anger ['aŋgər] *n* a bitter feeling (against someone), annoyance, rage. – *v* to make angry. – *adj* **'angry**. – *adv* **'angrily**.

angina [an'jinə] *n* a type of painful heart disease.

'angle *n* a corner; the V-shape made by two lines meeting at a point; a point of view. – *v* to try to get by hints *etc*: *angling for a job*. – *n* **'angler** one who fishes with rod and line. – *adj* **'angular** having angles; thin, bony.

'Anglican *adj* of the Church of England.

'anglicize *v* to turn into the English language; to make English in character.

'Anglo-'Saxon *adj*, *n* (of) the people of England before the Norman Conquest; (of) their language.

an'gora *n* wool made from the hair of the Angora goat or rabbit. – *ns* **Angora cat, goat, rabbit** a type of cat, goat or rabbit with long silky hair.

angry *see* **anger**.

anguish ['aŋgwish] *n* very great pain or distress.

angular *see* **angle**.

'animal *n* a living being which can feel and move of its own accord; an animal other than man. – *adj* of or like an animal.

'animate *v* to give life to; to make lively. – *adj* living. – *adj* **'animated** lively; (of puppets, cartoon figures *etc*) made to move as if alive. – *n* **ani'mation**.

ani'mosity *n* bitter hatred, enmity.

'aniseed *n* a kind of seed with a flavour like that of liquorice.

'ankle *n* the joint connecting the foot and leg.

'annals *npl* (yearly) historical accounts of events.

an'neal *v* to soften (or toughen) glass or metal by heating strongly and cooling slowly.

an'nex *v* to take possession of; to add, attach. – *n* **'annex(e)** a building added to another. – *n* **annex'ation**.

an'nihilate *v* to destroy completely. – *n* **annihi'lation**.

anni'versary *n* the day of each year when some event is remembered: – *pl* **anni'versaries**.

'annotate *v* to make notes upon; to add notes or explanation to. – *n* **anno'tation**.

an'nounce *v* to make (publicly) known. – *ns* **an'nouncement; an'nouncer** in radio *etc* one who announces programmes or reads the news.

an'noy *v* to make rather angry, irritate. – *n* **an'noyance**.

'annūal *adj* yearly. – *n* a plant that lives only one year; a book published yearly. — *v* **annualize** to convert to a yearly rate, amount *etc*. — *adv* **'annually**.

an'nūity *n* a yearly payment made for a certain time or for life: – *pl* **an'nuities**.

an'nul *v* to put an end to, declare no longer valid: – *pt* **an'nulled**. – *n* **an'nulment**.

'anodȳne *n* something that soothes pain.

a'noint *v* to smear with ointment or oil (as part of a religious ceremony).

a'nomaly *n* something unusual, not according to rule: – *pl* **a'nomalies**. –

adj a'**nomalous**.

a'**non** short for **anonymous**, used when the author of a poem *etc* is not known.

a'**nonymous** *adj* without the name (of the author, giver *etc*) being known or given. – *n* ano'**nymity**.

'**anorak** *n* a hooded waterproof jacket.

another [ə'nudhər] *adj* a different (thing or person). *He moved to another job*; one more of the same kind. *Have another biscuit.* – Also *pron*.

answer ['änsər] *v* to speak, write *etc* in return or reply; to find the result or solution (of a sum, problem *etc*); (with **for**) to be responsible; (with **for**) to suffer, be punished. – *n* something said, written *etc* in return or reply; a solution. – *adj* '**answerable** able to be answered; responsible.

ant *n* a type of small insect, thought to be hard-working.

an'**tagonist** *n* an enemy; an opponent. – *n* an'**tagonism** hostility, opposition, enmity. – *adj* **antago'nistic** opposed (to) unfriendly, hostile. – *v* an'**tagonize** to make an enemy of, cause dislike.

Ant'**arctic** *adj* of the South Pole or regions round it.

ante- [anti] *prefix* before.

ante'cēdent *adj* going before in time. – *n* one who lived at an earlier time, an ancestor; (*pl*) previous conduct, history *etc*.

'**ante'date** *v* to date before the true time; to be earlier in date than.

antediluvian [antidi'lōōviən] *adj* very old or old-fashioned.

'**antelope** *n* a kind of graceful, swift-running, deer-like animal.

ante'nātal *adj* before birth.

an'**tenna** *n* a feeler of an insect; an aerial: – *pls* an'**tennas**, **antennae** [an'tenē].

'**anteroom** *n* a room leading into a large room.

'**anthem** *n* a piece of music for a church choir; any song of praise.

an'**thology** *n* a collection of specially chosen poems, stories *etc*: – *pl* an'**thologies**.

'**anthracite** *n* a kind of coal that burns with a hot, smokeless flame.

'**anthrax** *n* an infectious disease of cattle, sheep *etc*, sometimes caught by man.

'**anthropoid** *adj* (*esp* of apes) man-like.

anthro'pology *n* the study of mankind. – *n* **anthro'pologist**.

anti- *prefix* against; opposite.

'**antibi'otic** *n* a type of medicine taken to kill disease-causing bacteria.

an'**ticipate** *v* to look forward to, to expect; to see or know in advance; to act before (someone or something). – *n*

an'**tici'pation** expectation; excitement.

'**anti'climax** *n* a dull or disappointing ending.

'**anti'clockwise** *adj, adv* in the opposite direction to the hands of a clock.

'**antics** *npl* tricks, odd or amusing actions.

'**anti'cȳclone** *n* a circling movement of air or wind round an area of high air pressure *usu* causing calm weather.

'**antidote** *n* something given to act against the effect of poison.

antihistamine ['anti'histəmēn] *n* a medicine used to treat an allergy.

an'**tipathy** *n* dislike.

antipodes [an'tipədēz] *npl* places on the earth's surface exactly opposite each other, (*esp* Australia and New Zealand, which are opposite to Europe). – *adj* **antipodean** [an'tipə'dēən].

antique [an'tēk] *adj* old, from earlier times; old-fashioned. – *n* an old, *usu* interesting or valuable object from earlier times. – *adj* **antiquated** ['antikwātid] grown old, or out of fashion. – *n* an'**tiquity** ancient times, *esp* those of the Greeks and Romans; great age; (*pl*) an'**tiquities** objects from earlier times.

anti'septic *adj* germ-destroying. – *n* something which destroys germs.

antisocial ['anti'sōshəl] *adj* not fitting in with, harmful to other people; disliking the company of other people.

an'**tithesis** *n* the direct opposite: – *pl* an'**tithesēs**.

'**antler** *n* the horn of a deer.

'**anvil** *n* a metal block on which blacksmiths hammer metal into shape.

anxious ['aŋkshəs] *adj* worried about what may happen. – *n* **anxiety** [aŋ'ziəti]: – *pl* an'**xieties**.

any ['eni] *adj* one: *any book*; some: *any bread*; every, no matter which. *Any time you go, he's always there.* – *pron* some. *There aren't any left.* – *pron* '**anybody** any person. – *adv* '**anyhow** in any case. *Anyhow, I'll go and see him*; carelessly. *The papers were scattered anyhow over his desk.* – *prons* '**anyone** any person; '**anything** a thing of any kind. – *advs* '**anyway** in any case; '**anywhere** in any place. – **at any rate** in any case, whatever happens.

a'**part** *adv* aside; in or into pieces; in opposite directions. – **apart from** separate(ly) from; except for.

apartheid [ə'pärtāt] *n* (the policy of) keeping people of different races apart.

a'**partment** *n* a room in a house; a set of rooms, a flat.

'**apathy** *n* lack of feeling or interest. – *adj* **apa'thetic**.

ape *n* any of a group of animals related to monkeys, but larger, tail-less and walking upright. – *v* to imitate.

'**aperture** *n* an opening, a hole.

'**āpex** *n* the highest point of anything: – *pls* '**apexes**, '**apicēs**.

'**āphid** *n* a type of small insect which feeds on plants.

'**āpiary** *n* a place where bees are kept: – *pl* '**apiaries**. – *n* '**apiarist** one who keeps an apiary or who studies bees.

a'piece *adv* to or for each one.

aplomb [ə'plom] *n* self-confidence.

apocryphal [ə'pokrifəl] *adj* unlikely to be true.

a'pology *n* an expression of regret that one has done wrong: – *pl* **a'pologies**. – *adj* **a'polo'getic** showing regret about having done wrong. – *v* **a'pologize** to make an apology.

'**apoplexy** *n* sudden loss of ability to feel, move *etc*, a stroke. – *adj* **apo'plectic**.

apostle [ə'posl] *n* one sent to preach the gospel, *esp* one of the twelve disciples of Christ; a leader of a movement or cause (such as for free speech *etc*).

apostrophe [ə'postrəfi] *n* a mark (') to show possession: *John's hat*; or that a letter *etc* has been missed out: *isn't* (for *is not*).

a'pothecary *n* (*old*) one who makes and supplies medicines *etc*, a chemist: – *pl* **a'pothecaries**.

appal [ə'pöl] *v* to horrify, shock: – *pt* **ap'palled**. – *adj* **ap'palling** shocking.

appa'rātus *n* an instrument or machine; instruments, tools or material required for a piece of work.

ap'parel *n* clothing.

ap'parent *adj* easily seen, evident. – *adv* **ap'parently**.

appa'rition *n* something strange or remarkable which appears suddenly; a ghost.

ap'peal *v* to ask earnestly (for help *etc*); (in law) to take a case that one has lost to a higher court; to be pleasing (to). – Also *n*. – *adj* **ap'pealing** asking earnestly; arousing liking or sympathy.

ap'pear *v* to come into view; to arrive; to seem. – *n* **ap'pearance**.

appease [ə'pēz] *v* to soothe or satisfy, *esp* by giving what was asked for.

ap'pendix *n* a part added at the end of a book; a small worm-shaped part of the bowels: – *pls* **ap'pendicēs**, **ap'pendixes**. – *n* **ap'pendi'citis** a disease, an inflammation of this part of the body.

apper'tain *v* to belong (to).

'**appetite** *n* desire (for food). – *adj* '**appetizing** tempting to the appetite.

ap'plaud *v* to praise (by clapping the hands). – *n* **applause** [ə'plöz].

'**apple** *n* a type of round firm fruit, *usu* red or green.

ap'plȳ *v* to put on (an ointment *etc*); to use; to ask formally (for); to be suitable or relevant; (with **to**) to affect: – *pt* **ap'plied**. – *n* **ap'pliance** a tool, instrument *etc*. – *adj* '**applicable** able to be applied; suitable, relevant. – *ns* '**applicant** one who applies or asks; **appli'cation** the act of applying; the thing applied (*eg* an ointment); hard work, close attention; a formal request (*usu* on paper). – **apply oneself** to work hard.

ap'point *v* to fix (a date *etc*); to place in a job. *He was appointed manager.* – *n* **ap'pointment** the act of appointing; a job, a post; an arrangement to meet someone.

apportion [ə'pörshən] *v* to divide in fair shares.

apposite ['apəzit] *adj* suitable, appropriate.

appraise [ə'prāz] *v* to estimate the value or quality of. – *n* **ap'praisal**. – *adj* **ap'praising** (of a glance *etc*) quickly summing up.

appreciate [ə'prēshiāt] *v* to see or understand the good points, beauties *etc* of; to understand; to rise in value. – *n* **appreci'ation**. – *adj* **ap'preciable** noticeable, considerable.

appre'hend *v* to arrest; to understand. – *n* **appre'hension**. – *adj* **appre'hensive** afraid.

ap'prentice *n* one who is learning a trade. – *n* **ap'prenticeship** the time during which one is an apprentice.

ap'proach *v* to come near; to be nearly equal to; to speak to in order to ask for something. – *n* a coming near to; a way leading to a place: – *pl* **ap'proaches**. – *adj* **ap'proachable** able to be reached; (of persons) easy to speak to, friendly.

appro'bation *n* good opinion, approval.

ap'prōpriate *adj* suitable, fitting. – *v* to take possession of; to set (money *etc*) apart for a purpose. – *n* **appropri'ation**.

approve [ə'prōōv] *v* to agree to, permit; (with **of**) to think well of. – *n* **ap'proval**. – **on approval** (of goods) on trial, for return (to shop *etc*) if not bought.

ap'proximate *adj* more or less accurate. – *v* (with **to**) to be or come near (a number *etc*). – *n* **approxi'mation** a rough estimate.

'**āpricot** *n* a type of orange-coloured fruit

12

like a small peach.

April ['āprəl] *n* the fourth month of the year.

'**āpron** *n* a garment worn to protect the front of the clothes; a hard surface for aircraft to stand on. – *n* **apron stage** the part of the stage in front of the curtains in a theatre.

apropos [aprə'pō]: **apropos of** in connection with, concerning.

apse *n* a rounded domed section, *esp* at the east end of a church.

apt *adj* (with **to**) likely to; suitable, fitting. – *ns* '**aptitude** talent, ability; '**aptness** suitability.

'**aqualung** *n* a breathing apparatus worn by divers.

aquamarine [akwəmə'rēn] *n* a type of bluish-green precious stone.

a'**quārium** *n* a tank or tanks for keeping fish or water animals: – *pl* a'**quaria**.

a'**quatic** *adj* living, growing or taking place in water.

'**aqueduct** *n* a bridge for taking water, such as a canal, across a valley.

'**aquiline** *adj* like an eagle; (of a nose) curved or hooked.

'**arable** *adj* fit for ploughing; (of land *etc*) growing crops.

'**arbitrary** *adj* fixed not by rules but by someone's decision or opinion. – *v* '**arbitrate** to act as a judge between people or their claims *etc*. – *ns* **arbi'tration** the act of judging between claims *etc*; '**arbitrator** a judge.

arboreal [är'böriəl] *adj* of trees, living in trees.

arbour ['ärbər] *n* a seat in a garden shaded by tree-branches *etc*.

arc *n* part of the circumference of a circle, a curve. – *ns* '**arc-lamp**, '**arc-light** a bright lamp lit by a special kind of electric current.

ar'cade *n* a covered walk, *esp* one with shops on both sides.

arch *n* the curved part above one's head in a gateway or the curved support for a bridge, roof *etc*: – *pl* '**arches**. – *adj* mischievous, roguish. – *v* to raise or curve in the shape of an arch. – *n* '**archway** a passage or road beneath an arch.

arch- chief (as in '**arch-'enemy**).

archaeology [ärki'oləji] *n* the study of the people of earlier times from the remains of their buildings *etc*. – *adj* **archaeo'logical**. – *n* **archae'ologist**.

archaic [är'kāik] *adj* (*esp* of words) no longer used, old-fashioned.

archangel ['ärkānjəl] *n* a chief angel.

'**arch'bishop** *n* a chief bishop.

'**arch'deacon** *n* a clergyman next in rank below a bishop.

'**arch'duke** *n* (*hist*) the title of the ruling princes of Austria.

'**archer** *n* one who shoots arrows from a bow. – *n* '**archery** the art of shooting with a bow and arrows.

archipelago [ärki'peləgō] *n* a group of small islands: – *pls* **archi'pelago(e)s**.

architect ['ärkitekt] *n* one who plans and designs buildings. – *n* '**architecture** the style of a building; the study of building.

archives ['ärkīvz] *npl* (a place for keeping) historical papers, written records *etc*.

'**Arctic** *adj* of the district round the North Pole; '**arctic** very cold.

'**ardent** *adj* eager, passionate. – *n* '**ardour**.

'**ardūous** *adj* difficult. – *n* '**arduous-ness**.

are *see* **be**.

area ['āriə] *n* extent (of a surface) measured in square metres *etc*; a region, a piece of land or ground.

a'**rēna** *n* any place for a public contest, show *etc*; (*hist*) the centre of an amphitheatre *etc* where gladiators *etc* fought.

'**argosy** *n* a large trading-ship with a valuable cargo: – *pl* '**argosies**.

argue ['ärgū] *v* to quarrel in words; to (try to) prove by giving reasons (that); to suggest or urge. – *adj* '**arguable** that can be argued as being true. – *n* '**argument** a heated discussion, quarrel; reasoning (for or against something). – *adj* **argu'mentative** fond of arguing.

'**aria** *n* a song for solo voice in an opera *etc*.

'**arid** *adj* dry. – *ns* a'**ridity**, '**aridness**.

a'**rise** *v* to rise up; to come into being: – *pt* a'**rose**, *pp* **arisen** [ə'rizn].

aris'tocracy *n* those of the nobility and upper class. – *n* '**aristocrat** a member of the aristocracy. – *adj* **aristo'cratic** of the aristocracy; having a distinguished appearance.

a'**rithmetic** *n* a way of counting using numbers. – *adj* **arith'metical**.

ark *n* the covered boat in which Noah lived during the Flood.

arm *n* either of the two upper limbs of the human body; anything jutting out like this; (*pl*) weapons. – *v* to equip with weapons. – *adj* **armed** carrying a weapon, now *esp* a gun. – *ns* '**armchair** a chair with arms at each side; '**arm-pit** the hollow under the arm at the shoulder.

ar'mada *n* a fleet of armed ships.

arma'dillo *n* a type of small American animal whose body is protected by bony plates: – *pl* **arma'dillos**.

'armaments *npl* equipment for war, *esp* the guns of a ship, tank *etc*.

armistice ['ärmistis] *n* in war, a halt in the fighting, a truce.

armorial [är'möriəl] *adj* of a coat-of-arms.

armour ['ärmər] *n* (*hist*) a protective suit of metal worn by knights. – *adj* **'armoured** (of a vehicle) protected by metal plates. – *n* **'armoury** an arms store: – *pl* **'armouries**.

'army *n* a large number of men armed for war; a great number: – *pl* **'armies**.

a'roma *n* a sweet smell. – *adj* **aro'matic**.

arose *see* **arise**.

a'round *prep* in a circle about; on all sides of, surrounding. *Flowers grew around the tree*; all over, at several places in: *papers scattered around the room*; somewhere near in time, place, amount: *around here: around three o'clock*. – *adv* on every side. *Children stood around and sang.* – **get around** (of a fact, rumour *etc*) to become known to all; (of a person) to be active.

arouse [ə'rowz] *v* to awaken; to stir, move (a feeling or person).

arraign [ə'rān] *v* to accuse publicly.

arrange [ə'rānj] *v* to put in some order; to plan, to settle. – *n* **ar'rangement**.

'arras *n* a screen of tapestry.

ar'ray *n* order, arrangement; clothing. – *v* to put in order; to dress, to adorn.

ar'rears: in arrears not up to date, behindhand (with payments *etc*).

ar'rest *v* to seize, capture *esp* by power of the law; to stop; to catch (the attention *etc*). – *n* capture by the police; stopping. – *adj* **ar'resting** striking, capturing one's attention.

ar'rive *v* to reach a place. – *n* **ar'rival** the act of arriving; person or thing that arrives. – **arrive at** to reach, come to (a decision *etc*).

'arrogant *adj* proud, haughty, self-important. – *n* **'arrogance**.

arrow ['arō] *n* a straight, pointed weapon made to be shot from a bow; an arrow-shape (on road signs *etc*) showing direction.

'arsenal *n* a factory or store for weapons, ammunition *etc*.

'arsenic *n* an element that, combined with oxygen, makes a strong poison.

'arson *n* the crime of setting fire to a house *etc* on purpose.

art *n* drawing, painting, sculpture *etc*; cleverness, skill; cunning; (*pl*) non-scientific school or university subjects.

– *adjs* **'artful** wily, cunning; **'artless** simple, frank.

'artefact, 'artifact *n* an object made by man.

'artery *n* a tube which carries blood from the heart to pass through the body: – *pl* **'arteries**. – *adj* **ar'terial** of or like arteries. – *n* **arterial road** a main traffic road.

artesian well [är'tēziən] *n* one in which water rises to the surface by natural pressure.

'artichoke *n* a type of thistle-like plant, part of whose flower-head is eaten. – *n* **Jerusalem artichoke** a type of plant whose roots are used as food.

'article *n* a thing, object; a composition in a newspaper, journal *etc*; (in grammar) the name of the words *the, a, an*.

ar'ticulate *adj* expressing thoughts or words clearly. – *n* **articu'lation**. – *n* **articulated lorry** one with a cab which can turn at an angle to the main part of the lorry, making cornering easier.

artifact *see* **artefact**.

arti'ficial *adj* not natural; made by man. – *n* **artifici'ality**.

ar'tillery *n* big guns; the part of the army that uses these.

artisan [ärti'zan] *n* a skilled workman.

'artist *n* one who paints pictures; one skilled in anything; an artiste. – *adj* **ar'tistic** of artists; having or showing a talent for art. – *n* **'artistry** skill as an artist.

artiste [är'tēst] *n* one who performs in a theatre, circus *etc*.

as *adv, conj* in phrases expressing comparison or similarity: *as good as: the same as.* – *conj* while, when. *He fell as I watched*; because, since. *As it's wet we can't go*; in the same way that. *He thinks as I do.* – *adv* for instance. – **as for** concerning, regarding; **as if, as though** as it would be if; **as to** regarding; **as well (as)** too, in addition (to).

as'bestos [az'bestos] *n* a thread-like mineral which will not burn.

ascend [ə'send] *v* to climb, go up; to rise or slope upwards. – *n* **a'scendancy, a'scendency** control (over). – *adj* **a'scendant, a'scendent** rising. – *n* **a'scent** a going up; a slope upwards. – **ascend the throne** to be crowned king or queen.

ascertain [asər'tān] *v* to find out; to make certain.

ascetic [ə'setik] *n* one who keeps away from all kinds of pleasure. – Also *adj*.

as'cribe *v* to think of as belonging to (a person or thing) or due to (a cause).

ash *n* a type of hard-wood tree with silvery bark; (often in *pl*) what is left after anything is burnt: – *pl* '**ashes**. – *adj* '**ashen** very pale.

a'shamed *adj* feeling shame.

a'shore *adv* on (to the) shore.

a'side *adv* on or to one side; apart. – *n* words spoken (*esp* by an actor) which other persons nearby are supposed not to hear.

'**asinine** *adj* of an ass; stupid.

ask *v* to request information about: *Ask where to go*; to invite.

as'kance : **look askance at** to look at with suspicion.

askew [əs'kū] *adv* off the straight, to one side.

a'sleep *adj* sleeping; (of limbs) numbed.

asp *n* a small poisonous snake.

as'paragus *n* a type of plant whose young shoots are eaten as a vegetable.

'**aspect** *n* look, appearance; view, point of view; side of a building *etc* or the direction it faces in.

'**aspen** *n* a kind of poplar tree.

as'perity *n* harshness, sharpness of temper; bitter coldness.

'**asphalt** *n* a tarry mixture used to make pavements, paths *etc*.

as'phyxia *n* stoppage in breathing, suffocation (as by smoke or other fumes). – *v* **as'phyxiate** to suffocate. – *n* **asphyxi'ation**.

aspi'distra *n* a kind of pot-plant with large leaves.

as'pire *v* (with **to** or **after**) to try to achieve or reach (something difficult, ambitious *etc*). – *n* **aspiration**.

'**aspirin** *n* a pain-killing drug.

ass *n* a horse-like animal with long ears, a donkey; a stupid person: – *pl* '**asses**.

assagai, assegai ['asəgī] *n* a thin wooden spear, with an iron tip.

as'sail *v* to attack. – *n* **as'sailant** one who attacks.

as'sassin *n* one who assassinates, a murderer. – *v* **as'sassinate** to murder (*esp* a politically important person). – *n* **assassi'nation**.

as'sault *n* an attack, *esp* a sudden one. – Also *v*.

as'semble *v* to bring (people) together; to put together (a machine *etc*); to meet together. – *ns* **as'semblage** a collection (of persons or things); **as'sembly** a putting together; a gathering of people, *esp* for a special purpose: – *pl* **as'semblies**. – *n* **assembly line** series of machines and workers necessary for the manufacture of an article.

as'sent *v* to agree. – *n* agreement.

as'sert *v* to state firmly; to insist on (a right *etc*). – *n* **as'sertion**. – *adj* **as'sertive** not shy, inclined to assert oneself. – **assert oneself** to make oneself noticed, heard *etc*.

as'sess *v* to fix an amount (to be paid in tax *etc*); to estimate the value, power of *etc*. – *ns* **as'sessment; as'sessor** one who assesses.

'**asset** *n* an advantage, a help; (*pl*) the property of a person, company *etc*.

as'siduous *adj* persevering; hard-working.

assign [ə'sīn] *v* to give to someone as his share or task; to fix (a time or place). –*ns* **assignation** [asig'nāshən] an appointment to meet; **assignment** [ə'sīnmənt] an act of assigning; a task given.

as'similate *v* to take in. – *n* **assimi'lation**.

as'sist *v* to help. – *ns* **as'sistance; as'sistant** a helper, *esp* one who helps a senior worker; one who serves in a shop *etc*.

as'sizes *npl* the name of certain law courts in England.

as'sociate *v* to keep company with; to join (with) in partnership or friendship; to connect in thought. – *adj* joined or connected (with). – *n* a friend, partner, companion. – *n* **associ'ation** a club, society, union *etc*; a partnership, friendship; a connection made in the mind.

as'sorted *adj* various, mixed. – *n* **as'sortment** a variety, mixture.

assuage [ə'swāj] *v* to soothe, ease (pain, hunger *etc*).

as'sume *v* to take upon oneself; to take as true without further proof, take for granted; to put on (a disguise *etc*). – *adj* **as'sumed** taken upon oneself; pretended. – *n* **assumption** [ə'sumpshən] act of assuming; something taken for granted.

assure [ə'shōor] *v* to make (someone) sure; to state positively (that). – *n* **as'surance** a feeling of certainty; confidence; a promise; insurance. – *adj* **as'sured** certain; confident.

'**asterisk** *n* a star(*) used in printing for various purposes, *esp* to point out a note added.

as'tern *adv* (in ships) at or towards the back part.

asthma ['asmə] *n* an illness causing inability to breathe out properly. – *n*, *adj* **asth'matic** (one) suffering from asthma.

as'tonish *v* to surprise greatly. – *n* **as'tonishment** amazement, wonder.

as'tound *v* to surprise greatly, amaze. –

adj as'tounding.

astra'khan *n* lamb-skin with a curled wool.

'astral *adj* of the stars.

as'tray *adv* out of the right way, straying.

as'tride *adv* with legs apart. – *prep* with legs on each side of.

astringent [əs'trinjənt] *adj, n* (of) a type of lotion *etc* used for closing up the skin's pores. – *adj* (of a manner *etc*) sharp, sarcastic.

as'trology *n* the study of the stars and their supposed power over the lives of humans. – *n* as'trologer.

'astronaut *n* one who travels in space.

as'tronomy *n* the study of the stars and their movements. – *n* as'tronomer. – *adj* astro'nomical of astronomy; (of numbers) very large.

as'tute *adj* cunning, clever.

a'sunder *adv* apart, into pieces.

a'sylum *n* a place of refuge or safety; an old name for a home for the mentally ill.

at *prep* showing position, time *etc*: *at home*: *at 3 o'clock*; costing: *bread at 14 pence a loaf*. – at all in any way: *not worried at all*.

ate *see* eat.

atheism ['āthiizəm] *n* belief that there is no God. – *n* 'atheist one who does not believe in a God.

'athlete *n* one good at sport, *esp* running, gymnastics *etc*. – *adj* athletic [əth'letik] of athletics; good at sports, strong, powerful. – *npl* ath'letics running, jumping *etc* or competitions in these.

'atlas *n* a book of maps: – *pl* 'atlases.

'atmosphere *n* the air round the earth; any surrounding feeling: *a friendly atmosphere*. – *adj* atmospheric [atmə'ferik]. – *npl* atmos'pherics in radio *etc*, air disturbances causing crackling noises. – *n* atmospheric pressure the pressure exerted by the atmosphere at the surface of the earth, due to the weight of the air.

'atoll *n* a coral island or reef.

'atom *n* the smallest part of an element; anything very small. – *n* atomic energy very great force got by breaking up the atoms of some substances as in the atom(ic) bomb.

a'tone *v* to make up for wrong-doing. – *n* a'tonement.

a'trocious *adj* cruel or wicked; (*coll*) very bad. – *ns* a'trociousness; atrocity [ə'trosəti] a terrible crime; (*coll*) something very ugly: – *pl* a'trocities.

at'tach *v* to fasten or join (to); to think of (something) as having: *attach importance to the event*. – *adj* at'tached fastened; fond (of). – *n* at'tachment something attached; a joining by love or friendship.

attaché-case [ə'tashikās] *n* a small case for papers *etc*.

at'tack *v* to fall upon suddenly or violently; to speak or write against. – *n* an act of attacking; a fit (of an illness *etc*).

at'tain *v* to reach; to gain. – *adj* at'tainable able to be attained. – *n* at'tainment act of attaining; the thing attained, an achievement or accomplishment.

at'tempt *v* to try. – *n* a try or effort; an attack (on someone's life *etc*).

at'tend *v* to be present at; to pay attention to; to wait on, look after; to accompany. – *n* at'tendance act of waiting on or of being present; the number of persons present. – *adj* at'tendant going along with. – *n* one who attends; one employed to look after (something): *a cloakroom attendant*. – *n* at'tention careful notice; concentration; care; in (army) drill, a stiffly straight standing position. – *adj* at'tentive giving or showing attention; polite.

'attic *n* a room just under the roof of a house.

at'tire *v* to dress. –- *n* clothing.

'attitude *n* way of thinking or feeling; position of the body.

attorney [ə'tərni] *n* one who has legal power to act for another: – *pl* at'torneys.

at'tract *v* to draw to or towards; to arouse liking or interest. – *n* at'traction act or power of attracting; that which attracts. – *adj* at'tractive pleasing; good-looking, likeable.

at'tribute *v* to think of as belonging to, or due to (a person or cause). – *adj* at'tributable. – *n* 'attribute something that is part of the nature of a person or thing, a quality.

aubergine ['ōbərzhēn] *n* a type of plant whose dark purple fruit is used as a vegetable.

auburn ['ōbərn] *adj* (*esp* of hair) red-dish-brown in colour.

'auction *n* a public sale in which articles are sold to the person who offers the highest price. – *v* to sell by auction. – *n* auctio'neer one who sells by auction.

au'dacious *adj* daring, bold. – *n* audacity [ö'dasəti].

'audible *adj* able to be heard. – *n*

16

audi'bility. – *adv* **'audibly.**

'audience *n* a number of people gathered to watch or hear (a performance *etc*); a formal interview with someone important: *an audience with the Pope.*

'audio-'typist *n* a typist able to type from a recording on a tape-recorder *etc.*

audio-visual ['ödiō'vizhōōəl] *adj* needing to be heard and seen at the same time.

'audit *v* to examine accounts officially. – Also *n*. – *n* **'auditor** one who audits accounts.

'auditory *adj* of hearing. – *ns* **au'dition** a test given to an actor, singer *etc*; **auditorium** [ödi'töriəm] the part of a theatre *etc* where the audience sits: – *pls* **aud'itoria, audi'toriums.**

aug'ment *v* to increase in size, number or amount. – *n* **augmen'tation.**

'augur : augur well, augur ill to be a good, bad sign for the future.

'August *n* the eighth month of the year.

au'gust *adj* full of dignity, stately.

aunt [änt] *n* a father's or a mother's sister or an uncle's wife.

'aural *adj* pertaining to the ear. — *adv* **'aurally.** — *adj* **'auriform** ear-shaped.

auspices ['öspisiz]: **under the auspices of** under the control or supervision of.

auspicious [ös'pishəs] *adj* favourable; promising luck.

aus'tere *adj* severe; without luxury *etc*, simple. – *n* **austerity** [ös'terəti].

au'thentic *adj* true, real, genuine. – *v* **au'thenticate** to show to be true or real. – *n* **authen'ticity.**

'author *n* the writer of a book, poem, play *etc.*

au'thority *n* power or right; a person whose opinion is reliable, an expert; a person or body of people having control (over something); (*pl*) **au'thorities** persons in power. – *adj* **au'thoritative** said *etc* by an expert or someone in authority.

'authorize *v* to give (a person) the power or the right to do something; to give permission (for something to be done).

autobi'ography *n* the story of a person's life written by himself: – *pl* **autobi'ographies.** – *adj* **autobio'graphical.**

'autocrat *n* a ruler who has complete power. – *n* **au'tocracy** government by such a ruler. – *adj* **auto'cratic** of an autocrat; expecting complete obedience.

'autograph *n* one's own signature; one's own handwriting. – *v* to write one's own name (on).

auto'matic *adj* (of a machine *etc*) self-working; (of an action) unconscious, without thinking. – *n* something automatic (*eg* an automatic washing-machine); a kind of self-loading gun. – *adv* **auto'matically.** – *ns* **auto'mation** the use in factories *etc* of machines for controlling other machines. – **au'tomaton** a (human-shaped) machine that can be operated to move by itself; a person who acts like a machine: – *pls* **au'tomatons, au'tomata.**

automobile ['ötəməbēl] *n* (*US*) a motor car.

au'tonomy *n* the power or right of a country *etc* to govern itself. – *adj* **au'tonomous.**

'autopsy *n* an examination of the body after death: – *pl* **'autopsies.**

autumn ['ötəm] *n* the season of the year when leaves change colour and fruits *etc* are ripe. – *adj* **autumnal** [ö'tumnəl] of or like autumn.

auxiliary [ög'zilyəri] *adj* helping; additional. – *n* a helper: – *pl* **au'xiliaries.**

a'vail: avail oneself of to make use of; **to no avail** without any effect, of no use.

a'vailable *adj* able or ready to be made use of. – *n* **availa'bility.**

avalanche ['avəlänsh] *n* a mass of snow and ice sliding down from a mountain; a great amount: *an avalanche of work.*

avarice ['avəris] *n* greed, *esp* for riches. – *adj* **ava'ricious.**

avenge [ə'venj] *v* to take revenge for (a wrong). – *n* **a'venger.**

avenue ['avinū] *n* a (tree-bordered) street or approach to a house; means, way: *avenue of escape.*

average ['avərij] *n* the result got by adding several amounts and dividing the total by the number of amounts (The *average* of 3, 7, 9, 13 is 8 (32÷4)). – *adj* obtained by working out an average (of amounts *etc*): *average price*: *average temperature*; ordinary, usual; of medium size *etc*. – *v* to form an average; to find the average of.

a'verse *adj* not fond of, opposed (to). – *n* **a'version** dislike; something that is hated.

a'vert *v* to turn (one's eyes *etc*) away; to prevent.

'aviary *n* a place for keeping birds: – *pl* **'aviaries.**

āvi'ātion *n* (the science of) flying in aircraft. – *n* **'aviator** an airman.

'avid *adj* eager, greedy. – *n* **a'vidity.**

a'void *v* to escape, keep clear of. – *adj* **a'voidable.** – *n* **a'voidance.**

avoirdupois [avwärdōō'pwä] *adj, n* (of) the system of measuring weights in pounds and ounces.

avow [ə'vow] *v* to declare openly. – *n* **a'vowal**. – *adj* **a'vowed**.

a'wait *v* to wait for.

a'wake *v* to rouse (from sleep); to stop sleeping. – *adj* not asleep; watchful. – *v* **a'waken** to awake; to arouse (interest *etc*). – *ns* **a'wakening**, **a'waking**.

award [ə'wörd] *v* to give, grant (a prize *etc*); to grant legally. – *n* what is awarded (such as a payment, prize *etc*).

a'ware *adj* having knowledge (of), conscious (of); alert. – *n* **a'wareness**.

a'way *adv* to or at a distance from the person or thing spoken about. *Throw it away. He is away*; in the opposite direction. *He turned away*; into nothing. *The sound died away*; constantly: *working away*. – **do away with** to abolish, get rid of; **get away with** to do (something) without being punished; **make away with** to destroy; to steal and escape with; **right away** immediately.

awe [ö] *n* wonder mixed with fear; dread. – *adjs* **'awesome** causing fear; **'awestruck** full of fear and wonder.

'awful *adj* (*coll*) bad: *an awful headache*; bad; (*coll*) very great: *an awful lot*; terrible. – *adv* **'awfully** (*coll*) very (much): *awfully grateful*. – *n* **'awful-ness**.

'awkward *adj* clumsy, not graceful; difficult (to deal with). – *n* **'awkward-ness**.

awl *n* a pointed tool for boring small holes.

'awning *n* a covering (of canvas *etc*) to give shelter.

awry [ə'rï] *adj, adv* crooked; not according to plan, wrong.

axe *n* a tool for chopping: – *pl* **'axes**. – *v* to cancel (a plan *etc*); to reduce greatly (costs, services *etc*).

'axis *n* the line, real or imaginary, on which a thing turns (as the axis of the earth, from North to South Pole, around which the earth turns); a fixed line taken as a reference, as in a graph: – *pl* **'axēs**.

axle ['aksl] *n* the rod on which a wheel turns.

azure ['azhər] *adj* sky-coloured, clear blue.

B

'babble *v* to talk indistinctly or foolishly; (of a stream *etc*) to murmur. – Also *n*.

babe *n* a baby.

ba'boon *n* a kind of large monkey with a dog-like snout.

'bāby *n* a very young child, an infant: – *pl* **'babies**. – *ns* **'babyhood** the time when one is a baby; **'babysitter** someone who stays in the house with child(ren) while parents are out.

'bachelor *n* an unmarried man. – *ns* **Bachelor of Arts**, **Bachelor of Science** *etc* one who has passed examinations at a certain level in subjects at a university *etc*.

ba'cillus *n* a rod-shaped kind of germ: – *pl* **ba'cilli**.

back *n* the part of the body in man from the neck to the base of the spine; the upper part of the body in animals; the part of anything situated behind; one who plays behind the forwards in football, hockey *etc*. – *adj* of or at the back. – *adv* to or in the place from which a person or thing came; to or in a former time or condition *etc*. – *v* to move backwards; to bet on (a horse *etc*); (often with **up**) to help or support. – *ns* **'backer** a supporter;

'backing support; material used on the back of something (*esp* a picture); a musical accompaniment (*esp* on a record). – *n* **'backbone** the spine; the main support of anything; firmness. – *v* **back'fire** (of a motor car *etc*) to make an explosive noise in the exhaust pipe; (of a plan *etc*) to go wrong. – *ns* **'background** the space behind the principal figures *etc* (of a picture); details *etc* that explain something; one's family and upbringing; **'backhand** (in tennis *etc*) a stroke played with the back of the hand facing the ball. – *adj* **'back'handed** (of a compliment *etc*) having a double or unflattering meaning. – *ns* **'backlash** a (violent) reaction (against something); **'backstroke** stroke used in swimming on the back; **'back-wash** a backward current, such as that caused by a wave going out; **'backwater** a river pool not in the main stream; a place not affected by what is happening in the world outside. – **back down** to change one's opinion *etc*; **back out** to move out backwards; to excuse oneself from keeping to an agreement *etc*; **put one's back into** to work hard at; **put**

someone's **back up** to irritate someone; **with one's back to the wall** in desperate difficulties.

'**backgammon** *n* a game rather like draughts, played with dice.

'**backward** *adj* moving towards the back; slow in learning or development. – *adv* '**backward(s)** towards the back; towards the past.

'**bācon** *n* pig's flesh salted and dried, used as food.

bac'**tēria** *npl* kinds of germs found in the air, water, earth, in living and dead bodies, and *usu* in things going rotten. – *adj* bac'**terial**. – *ns* bacteri'**ology** the study of bacteria; bacteri'**ologist**.

bad *adj* not good; wicked; (*usu* with **for**) hurtful. *Smoking is bad for you*; (of food) rotten; severe, serious: *a bad cut in his foot*; faulty; unwell. – *adv* '**badly** not well; seriously. – *n* '**badness**. – *n* **bad language** swearing *etc*.

badge *n* a mark or sign or brooch-like ornament giving some information about the wearer.

'**badger** *n* a burrowing animal of the weasel family which comes out at night. – *v* to pester or annoy.

'**badminton** *n* a game rather like tennis, played with shuttlecocks.

baffle ['bafl] *v* to prevent (*eg* a plan) from being carried out, to hinder; to be too difficult or too clever for, to puzzle.

bag *n* a holder or container *usu* of a soft material; the quantity of fish or game caught. – *adj* '**baggy** (of clothes) large and loose.

baga'telle *n* a board game, in which balls are struck into numbered holes; something unimportant.

'**baggage** *n* luggage.

'**bagpipes** *npl* musical instrument made up of a bag and several pipes.

bail *v* (with **out**) to get an untried prisoner out of prison for the time being by giving money which will be returned only if he comes back for his trial; *see also* **bale**. – *n* money given to bail out a prisoner; in cricket, one of the crosspieces on the top of the wickets.

bailie ['bāli] *n* (in Scotland) formerly a burgh magistrate.

'**bailiff** *n* an officer who works for a sheriff; a landowner's agent.

bait *n* food put on a hook to make fish bite, or in a trap *etc* to attract animals; anything tempting. – *v* to put bait on a hook or trap; to worry, annoy.

baize *n* a coarse woollen cloth.

bake *v* to cook (in an oven); to dry or harden in the sun or in an oven. – *ns* '**baker** a person who bakes or sells

bread *etc*; '**bakery**, '**bakehouse** a place used for baking in. – *n* **baking powder** a powder added to flour to make cakes *etc* rise.

balalaika [balə'līkə] *n* a type of Russian musical instrument, like a guitar.

'**balance** *n* a weighing machine; the money needed to make the two sides of an account equal; steadiness. – *v* to be the same in weight; to make both sides of an account the same; to make or keep steady.

'**balcony** *n* a platform built out from the wall of a building; an upper floor or gallery in theatres, cinemas *etc*: – *pl* '**balconies**.

bald [böld] *adj* without hair; (of a statement *etc*) plain, bare.

balderdash ['böldərdash] *n* nonsense.

baldric ['böldrik] *n* a cross-belt from shoulder to waist, for carrying sword, bugle etc.

bale *n* a large tight bundle (of cotton, hay *etc*). – **bale out** to escape by parachute from an aircraft in an emergency; to scoop water out of a boat (also **bail out**).

'**baleful** *adj* harmful; full of hate.

balk [bö(l)k] *v* to hinder, to baffle; (with **at**) to refuse (to do something).

ball[1] *n* anything round; the round object used in playing many games. – *npl* '**ball**'**bearings** in machinery *etc*, small steel balls that sit loosely in grooves and ease the revolving of one part over another. – *n* '**ballpoint (pen)** a pen with a tiny ball as the writing point.

ball[2] *n* a formal party at which dancing takes place. – *n* '**ballroom**.

'**ballad** *n* a simple poem telling a story *usu* in verses of four lines; a simple song.

'**ballast** *n* heavy material (such as sand, gravel *etc*) put into a ship *etc* to steady it.

ballerina [balə'rēnə] *n* a female ballet dancer.

ballet ['balā] *n* a kind of graceful dancing which tells a story by mime.

bal'listic missile *n* one which moves under power and is guided on its way, but simply falls on to its target.

bal'loon *n* an airtight ball of thin rubber *etc*, which floats in the air when filled with light gas.

'**ballot** *n* a way of voting in secret by marking a paper and putting it into a special box.

balm [bäm] *n* anything that soothes; a sweet-smelling healing ointment. – *adj* '**balmy** mild, soothing; sweet-smelling. – *n* '**balminess**.

balsa ['bölsə] *n* a type of tropical American tree giving a very light wood ('**balsawood**).

balsam ['bölsəm] *n* a kind of flowering plant; an oily sweet-smelling substance obtained from certain trees.

balus'trade *n* a row of pillars (on a balcony *etc*) joined by a rail.

bam'boo *n* the hard, woody, jointed stem of a type of very tall Indian grass.

bam'boozle *v* to trick, puzzle.

ban *n* an order forbidding something. – *v* to forbid officially (the publication of a book *etc*): – *pt* **banned**.

ba'nal *adj* lacking originality or wit, commonplace. – *n* **ba'nality**.

ba'nana *n* the long yellow fruit of a type of tropical tree.

band *n* a group of people; a group of musicians playing together; a strip of some material to put round something; a stripe (of colour *etc*); (in radio) a group of wavelengths. – *v* to join together.

'**bandage** *n* a strip of cloth *etc* or special dressing for a wound *etc*.

bandeau ['bandō] *n* hairband: – *pl* '**bandeaux**.

'**bandit** *n* an outlaw, robber, *esp* a member of a gang of robbers.

bandolier, bandoleer [bandə'lēr] *n* a belt across the body for carrying cartridges.

'**bandy** *adj* (of legs) bent outward at the knee. – **bandy words** to argue.

bane *n* (a cause of) ruin or trouble.

bang *n* a sudden, loud noise; a heavy blow. – *v* to close with a bang, slam; to hit, strike. *He banged his head on the door.*

bangle ['bangl] *n* a large ring worn on arms (or legs).

'**banish** *v* to order to leave (a country); to drive away (doubts, fear *etc*). – *n* '**banishment**.

'**banister** *n* the posts and handrail of a staircase.

'**banjo** *n* a type of musical stringed instrument like a guitar, having a long neck and a round body: – *pls* '**banjo(e)s**.

bank *n* a mound or ridge of earth *etc*; the edge of a river *etc*; a place where money is put for safety; a place where blood *etc* is stored till needed. – *n* '**banker** one who manages a bank. – *ns* **bank holiday** a day on which all banks (and most other shops *etc*) are closed; '**banknote** a piece of paper money issued by a bank; '**bankrupt** one who has no money to pay his debts. – *adj* unable to pay one's debts; utterly

lacking (in ideas *etc*). – *n* '**bankruptcy**. – **bank on** to depend on, count on.

'**banner** *n* a kind of flag carried in processions *etc*, *usu* hung between two poles; any flag.

banns *npl* a public announcement that a marriage is to take place.

banquet ['bankwit] *n* a feast or ceremonial dinner.

'**bantam** *n* a small kind of hen.

'**banter** *v* to tease in fun. – Also *n*.

bap'tize *v* to sprinkle with water as a sign of being taken into the Christian church; to christen, give a name to. – *n* '**baptism**. – *adj* **bap'tismal**.

bar *n* a rod of anything solid; a broad line or band; a cake (of soap, chocolate *etc*); something standing in the way, a hindrance; a bank of sand *etc*, lying at the mouth of a river; the counter across which drinks are served in a public house; the rail at which prisoners stand for trial; the lawyers in a court; a division in music. – *prep* except: *the best runner bar none*. – *v* to fasten with a bar; to hinder or shut out: – *pt* **barred**. – *prep* '**barring** except for, but for. *They have all gone, barring you and me. Barring accidents he will be there.*

barb *n* the backward-pointing spike on an arrow, fish-hook *etc*. – *adj* **barbed** having a barb or barbs. – *n* **barbed wire** wire with clusters of sharp points placed regularly along it, used for fencing *etc*.

bar'bārian *adj, n* (of) an uncivilized person. – *adj* **barbaric** [bär'barik] uncivilized; cruel. – *n* **bar'barity**.

barbecue ['bärbikū] *n* a frame on which to grill meat *etc*, *esp* outdoors; a party at which a barbecue is used. – *v* to cook (meat *etc*) on a barbecue.

'**barber** *n* one who shaves beards and cuts hair, a men's hairdresser.

bard *n* a poet.

bare *adj* uncovered, naked; plain, simple; empty. – *v* to uncover or expose. – *adv* '**barely** hardly, scarcely. – *adj* '**barefaced** impudent.

bargain ['bärgin] *n* an agreement (about buying or selling something); something bought cheaply. – *v* to argue about a price *etc*. – **bargain for** to expect: *more than he bargained for*; **into the bargain** in addition, besides.

barge [bärj] *n* a flat-bottomed boat used on rivers and canals. – *v* to move or rush clumsily; to push or bump (into); to push one's way into rudely.

'**baritone** *n* (a male singer with) a voice between high (tenor) and low (bass).

bark *n* the sharp cry made by a dog *etc*; the rough outer covering of a tree's trunk and branches. – *v* to utter a bark; to speak sharply or angrily; to injure by scraping the skin.

barley *n* a type of grain used for food.

barn *n* a building in which grain, hay *etc* are stored.

barnacle *n* a type of shellfish which sticks to rocks, ships' hulls *etc*.

ba'rometer *n* an instrument which measures the weight or pressure of the air and shows changes in the weather.

baron *n* a nobleman, the lowest in the British peerage; (*hist*) a powerful nobleman. – *n* **'baroness** a baron's wife or a female baron: – *pl* **'baronesses**. – *adj* **ba'rōnial**.

baronet *n* the lowest title that can be passed on to an heir. – *n* **'baronetcy** the rank of baronet.

barracks *npl* a place for housing soldiers.

barrage ['baräzh] *n* something that hinders an enemy, *esp* heavy gunfire; an overwhelming number (of questions *etc*); a bar across a river to make the water deeper.

barrel *n* a wooden cask or vessel with curved sides; the metal tube of a gun through which the shot is fired.

barren *adj* not able to produce (fruit, crops, children *etc*), infertile. – *n* **'barrenness**.

barri'cāde *n* a barrier put up to block a street *etc*. – *v* to block (a street *etc*) in this way; to make (doors *etc*) strong against attack; to shut behind a barrier.

barrier *n* something (*eg* a strong fence *etc*) standing in the way; any obstacle.

barring see **bar**.

barrister *n* a lawyer who pleads cases in court.

barrow ['barō] *n* a small hand-cart; (*hist*) a mound raised over a grave.

barter *v* to give one thing in exchange for another. – *n* trading by exchanging goods without using money.

basalt ['basölt] *n* a hard, dark-coloured rock thrown up as lava from volcanoes.

base *n* that on which a thing stands or rests; the lowest part; a place from which a military or other action is carried on. – *v* to use as a foundation. *I base my opinion on what I have heard.* – *adj* worthless, cowardly. – *adj* **'base-less** without a foundation; untrue. – *n* **'basement** a storey below ground level in a building. – *n* **'baseball** an American ball game, rather like rounders.

bash *v* to hit hard. – Also *n*.

'bashful *adj* shy.

'bāsic *adj* of, forming a base; necessary, fundamental.

basil ['bazl] *n* a herb used as flavouring.

basilisk ['bazilisk] *n* (*myth*) a reptile whose look or breath killed; a type of American lizard.

'bāsin *n* a wide, open dish; any large hollow holding water (*eg* a dock); the land drained by a river and its tributaries.

'bāsis *n* that on which a thing rests, the foundation. *Mutual trust was the basis of their friendship*; the main ingredient: – *pl* **'basēs**.

bask *v* to lie in warmth; to enjoy, feel great pleasure (in).

'basket *n* a container made of strips of wood, rushes *etc* woven together; anything resembling a basket in shape. – *n* **'basket-ball** a team game like netball.

bass[1] [bās] *n* the low part in music; (a male singer with) a deep voice: – *pl* **'basses**. – *adj* low or deep in tone.

bass[2] [bas] *n* a kind of fish of the perch family: – *pls* **bass**, **'basses**.

bas'soon *n* a kind of musical wind instrument with low notes.

bāste *v* to spoon fat over (meat) while roasting to keep (it) from burning; to sew loosely together with big stitches, to tack.

'bastion *n* a defence (against something); a kind of tower on a castle *etc*.

bat *n* a shaped piece of wood *etc* for striking a ball in some games; a kind of mouse-like flying animal. – *v* to use the bat in cricket *etc*; to flutter (one's eyelids *etc*): – *pt* **'batted**. – *n* **'batsman** one who bats in cricket *etc*.

batch *n* a quantity of things made, sent off *etc* at one time: – *pl* **'batches**.

'bāted: with bated breath anxiously.

bath *n* a vessel which holds water in which to wash the body; a washing or soaking of the body in water *etc*. – *v* to wash (oneself or another) in a bath. – *n* **'bath'chair** an invalid's wheeled chair.

bathe [bādh] *v* to swim in water; to wash gently; to take a bath. – Also *n*. – **bathed in** covered with.

'bathyscāphe, 'bathysphere *ns* deep-sea observation chambers.

'batik *n* a method of dyeing patterns on cloth by waxing certain areas so that they remain uncoloured.

'batman *n* an army officer's servant.

'baton *n* a small wooden stick; a light stick used by a conductor of music.

bat'talion *n* a part of a regiment of foot soldiers.

'**batten** *n* a piece of sawn timber; in ships, a strip of wood used to fasten down the hatches.

'**batter** *v* to hit repeatedly. – *n* a beaten mixture *usu* of flour, milk and eggs, for cooking. – *adj* '**battered** beaten, ill-treated; worn out by use *etc*. – *n* '**battering-ram** (*hist*) in warfare, a machine with a heavy beam for breaking through walls *etc*.

'**battery** *n* in an army, a number of large guns; a device for storing and transmitting electricity; a series *etc* in which farm animals or birds are reared or fattened, or kept for egg-laying: – *pl* '**batteries**.

'**battle** *n* a fight, *esp* between armies. – Also *v*. – *ns* '**battleaxe** (*hist*) a kind of axe used in fighting; (*coll*) a fierce, domineering woman; '**battlefield**; '**battleship** a heavily armed and armoured warship.

'**battlement** *n* a wall on the top of a building, with openings or notches for firing guns *etc* from.

'**bauble** *n* a brightly-coloured ornament of little value.

bawl *v* to shout or cry out loudly. – Also *n*.

bay *n* a wide inlet of the sea in a coastline; a space in a room *etc* set back, a recess; a compartment in an aircraft; the laurel tree. – *v* (of dogs) to bark. – *n* **bay window** a window that forms a recess. – **hold at bay** to fight off; **stand at bay** to stand and face attackers *etc*.

'**bayonet** *n* a steel stabbing blade that can be fixed to the muzzle of a rifle. – *v* to stab with this.

ba'zaar, ba'zar *n* a sale of goods for charity *etc*; an Eastern market-place; a shop.

be *v* to live, exist. *There may be a few sweets left*; to have a position, quality *etc*. *He wants to be a dentist. He will be angry.* – Also used to form tenses of other verbs. – *pres tense* **am, are, is**, *pt* **was, were**, *pp* **been**. – *n* '**being** existence; any living person (or thing).

beach *n* the shore of the sea *etc*, *esp* when sandy or pebbly: – *pl* '**beaches**. – *v* to drive or haul a boat up on the beach. – *n* '**beachcomber** a person who searches beaches for useful or saleable articles.

'**beacon** *n* a (flashing) light or other warning signal; (*hist*) a fire on a hill used as a signal of danger.

bead *n* a small pierced ball of glass or other hard material (for threading along with others to form a necklace *etc*); a drop of liquid.

'**beadle** *n* an officer of a church or college.

'**beagle** *n* a small hound used in huntin hares.

beak *n* the hard, horny part of a bird' mouth with which it gathers food anything pointed or projecting.

'**beaker** *n* a tall cup or glass, *usu* without handle.

beam *n* a long, straight piece of wood o metal; a shaft of light; a radio signal the greatest breadth of a ship. – *v* t shine; to smile broadly; to divert b radio wave.

bean *n* a kind of pod-bearing plant; th seed of this used as food.

bear [bār] *n* a heavy animal with shagg fur and hooked claws. – *v* to carry; t endure, put up with; to produce (fruit children *etc*): – *pt* **bore**, *pp* **borne** (bu *usu* **born** of children, ideas *etc*. *Th baby was born last year*). – *ad* '**bearable** able to be borne or endured – *ns* '**bearer** a carrier or messenger '**bearing** behaviour; direction; con nection; part of a machine supporting moving part. – *n* '**bearskin** the hig fur cap worn by the Guards in th British Army. – **bear in mind** t remember, to take into account; **bea out** to confirm. *What has happene bears out what you said yesterday*; **bea with** to be patient with; **bring to bea** to bring into use.

beard *n* the hair that grows on a man' chin and cheeks. – *v* to face up to, defy.

beast *n* a four-footed animal; a bruta person. – *adj* '**beastly** like a beast i actions or behaviour; horrible; (*coll* unpleasant. – *n* '**beastliness**.

beat *v* to hit (repeatedly); to overcome o defeat; (of a heart or pulse) to move o throb in the normal way; to mar (time) in music *etc*; to stir (a mixture *etc*) with quick movements; to strike bushes *etc* to rouse birds: – *pp* '**beaten** *pt* **beat**. – *n* a stroke; a round or cours which one (*eg* a policeman) follow regularly. – *adj* '**beaten** (of metal shaped; (of earth) worn smooth b treading; defeated. – **beat up** to injur by repeated hitting, kicking *etc*.

beatific [bēə'tifik] *adj* of, or showing great happiness.

beauty ['būti] *n* (of a person or thing very pleasing appearance; (of music poetry, voices *etc*) pleasing sound; very attractive woman *etc*: – *p* '**beauties**. – *adjs* '**beautiful**, *esp* i poetry *etc* '**beauteous**. – *v* '**beautify** t make beautiful: – *pt* '**beautified**.

'**beaver** *n* a type of gnawing animal tha can dam streams; its fur.

becalmed [bi'kämd] *adj* (of a sailing

ship) unable to move for lack of wind.

ecause [bi'koz] for the reason that. *He didn't go because it was raining.* – *adv* (with **of**) on account of. *Because of his interference, I shall not succeed.*

eck: at one's beck and call obeying all one's orders or requests.

beckon *v* to make a sign (with the finger) to summon someone.

ecome [bi'kum] *v* to come to be. *He became angry;* to suit. *That dress becomes you.* – *adj* **be'coming** (of clothes *etc*) suiting well; (of behaviour) suitable.

ed *n* a place on which to rest or sleep; a plot (for flowers *etc*) in a garden; the bottom of a river *etc*. – *v* to plant in soil *etc*; to provide a bed for: – *pt* **'bedded**. – *n* **'bedding** mattress, bedcovers *etc*; straw *etc* for cattle to lie on. – *npl* **'bedclothes** bedcovers. – *adj* **'bedridden** kept in bed by weakness, illness *etc*. – *ns* **'bedrock** the solid rock under the soil; **'bedroom** a room for sleeping; **bedspread** ['bedspred] a top cover for a bed; **bedstead** ['bedsted] a frame for supporting a bed.

bedlam *n* a place of uproar, confusion.

be'draggled *adj* (wet and) untidy.

bee *n* a type of winged insect that makes honey in wax cells; a gathering for combined work *etc*. – *n* **'beehive** a (dome-shaped) case or box in which bees are kept. – **make a beeline for** to go directly towards.

beech *n* a type of forest tree with grey smooth bark: – *pl* **'beeches**.

beef *n* the flesh of an ox or cow, used as food. – *adj* **'beefy** stout, muscular. – *n* **'beefeater** a guardian of the Tower of London; a member (Yeoman) of the (Queen's or King's) Guard.

been *see* **be**.

beer *n* an alcoholic drink flavoured with hops.

beet *n* a kind of plant with a carrot-like root, one type (**sugar beet**) used as a source of sugar, the other with a root (**'beetroot**) used as a vegetable.

beetle *n* a kind of insect with four wings, the front pair forming hard covers for the back pair; a kind of hammer.

beetling *adj* (of cliffs *etc*) overhanging; (of eyebrows) heavy, frowning.

befall [bi'föl] *v* to happen (to). *A disaster befell him.*

be'fit *v* to be suitable or right for.

before [bi'för] *prep* in front of. *He stood before the entrance to the cave;* earlier than: *before three o'clock;* rather than, in preference to. *He would die before he would give in.* – *adv* in front; earlier. –

conj earlier than the time that. – *adv* **be'forehand** previously, before the time when something else is done.

befriend [bi'frend] *v* to act as a friend to, to help.

beg *v* to ask for money *etc*; to ask earnestly: – *pt* **begged**. – *n* **'beggar** one who begs; a very poor person. – *v* to make poor. – *adj* **'beggarly** poor; worthless. – **beggar description** to be greater than the speaker *etc* can find words to describe; **beg the question** to take as being proved the very point that needs to be proved.

began *see* **begin**.

be'get *v* to be the father of; to cause: – *pres p* **be'getting**, *pt* **be'gat**, *pp* **be'gotten**.

be'gin *v* to make a start on: – *pres p* **be'ginning**, *pt* **be'gan**, *pp* **be'gun**. – *n* **be'ginning**.

begone [bi'gon] *interj* be off, go away!

be'grudge *v* to grudge, envy. *He begrudged Jane her success.*

beguile [bi'gil] *v* to cheat; to pass (time) pleasantly; to amuse, entertain.

begun *see* **begin**.

behalf [bi'häf]: **on behalf of** as the representative of; in aid of: *collecting on behalf of the blind.*

be'have *v* to conduct oneself (well); to act (in a certain way). – *n* **be'haviour**. – *adj* **well- (badly-)behaved** having good (bad) manners.

behead [bi'hed] *v* to cut off the head of.

be'hest *n* command.

be'hind *prep* at or towards the back of: *behind the door;* after; in support of, encouraging. *His friends were behind him in his struggle.* – *adv* at the back; not up to date: *behind with his work.*

be'hōld *v* to look (at), see.

be'hōlden *adj* grateful because of a good turn done. *I felt beholden to them.*

be'hove: it behoves one to it is right for one to.

belabour [bi'lābər] *v* to beat, thrash. – **belabour the point** to discuss a subject at too great length.

be'lated *adj* arriving late.

be'lay *v* on ships, to fasten a rope round a peg.

belch *v* to bring up wind (noisily) from the stomach through the mouth; (of a fire *etc*) to send up (smoke *etc*) violently.

beleaguer [bi'lēgər] *v* to besiege.

belfry ['belfri] *n* the part of a steeple or tower in which the bells are hung: – *pl* **'belfries**.

be'lie *v* to prove false: – *pres p* **be'lying**, *pt* **be'lied**.

23

believe [bi'lēv] v to think of as true or as existing; to trust (in); to think or suppose. – n **be'lief** what we think to be true; faith. – **make believe** to pretend.

be'little v to make to seem small or unimportant.

bell n a hollow object usu of metal which gives a ringing sound when struck by the tongue or clapper inside.

bellicose ['belikōs] adj inclined to fight, quarrelsome.

belligerent [bi'lijərənt] adj carrying on war; quarrelsome, aggressive.

bellow ['belō] v to roar like a bull. – Also n.

bellows ['belōz] npl an instrument for making a blast of air.

'belly n the abdomen; the underpart of an animal's body; the bulging part of anything: – pl **'bellies**. – v to swell or bulge out: – pt **'bellied**.

be'long v to be one's property. That book belongs to me; to be a member of (a club etc); to be born in or live in. I belong to Glasgow; (of an object) to have its place in. Those knives belong in the kitchen drawer. – npl **be'longings** what one possesses.

beloved [bi'luvid] adj much loved, very dear. – Also n.

below [bə'lō] prep lower in position, rank etc than. Her skirt reached below her knees. A captain ranks below a major. – adv in a lower position. We looked down at the river below.

belt n a band or strip of leather, cloth etc worn around the waist; a continuous band of tough material used in machines or for conveying objects in a factory etc; a broad strip of anything (such as land). – v to put a belt round, to thrash with a belt; (coll) to beat, hit. – adj **'belted** wearing or having a belt.

be'moan v to weep about, mourn.

bench n a long seat; a work-table; the judges of a court: – pl **'benches**.

bend v to curve; (of persons) to stoop: – pt, adj **bent**. – n a turn (in a road etc).

be'neath prep under, in a lower position than. A toad sat beneath the dripping tap; covered by. Beneath her coat she wore a black dress; (felt to be) too low a task etc for. Sweeping floors was beneath him. – adv below.

benediction [benə'dikshən] n a blessing.

benefactor ['benəfaktər] n one who does good to another.

beneficial [benə'fishəl] adj bringing gain or advantage (to). – n **bene'ficiary** a person who receives a gift, a legacy, an advantage etc: – p **bene'ficiaries**.

benefit ['benəfit] n something good to receive or have done to one; money received under an insurance plan etc unemployment benefit. – v to do good to, to gain advantage.

be'nevolence n wish to do good; a kin act. – adj **be'nevolent** kindly.

benign [bi'nīn] adj gentle, kindly; (o disease) not causing death (opposite o **malignant**).

bent n a natural liking. – adj see **bend**.

bequeath [bi'kwēdh] v to leave by will. n **be'quest** money etc left by will.

be'rate v to scold.

be'reaved adj deprived by death of relative etc. – n **be'reavement**.

be'reft adj lacking, deprived (of).

beret ['berā] n a flat, round hat.

'berry n a (usu juicy) fruit enclosin seeds: – pl **'berries**.

ber'serk adv in a frenzy, mad.

berth n a room or sleeping place in a shi etc; the place where a ship is tied up in dock. – v to moor (a ship). – **give** **wide berth to** to keep well away from

'beryl n a type of precious stone such a an emerald or aquamarine.

be'seech v to ask earnestly.

be'set v to attack from all sides; t surround.

be'side prep by the side of, near: th house beside the river; compared with Beside her sister she seems plain; awa from, wide of: beside the point. – b **beside oneself** to lose self-control.

be'sides prep in addition to. Besides me there are plenty others; other than except: nothing at all besides water. – adv also, moreover. Besides, you can go; in addition: plenty more besides.

besiege [bi'sēj] v to surround (a tow etc) with an army; to crowd round.

be'smirch v to stain (a person's nam etc).

be'sotted: besotted with foolishly fon of.

be'spoke adj (of clothes) ordered to b made.

best adj good in the most excellent way. – adv in the most excellent way. – v t defeat. – ns **best man** one who attend a man who is being married; **best par** the largest or greatest part; **'best 'seller** a book etc which sells exceed ingly well. – **at best** under the mos favourable circumstances; **do one'** **best** to try as hard as one can; **mak** **the best of** do as well as possible with.

'bestial adj like a beast, beastly.

be'stir v to waken up, make lively.

bestow [bi'stō] *v* to give.

bet *n* money put down to be lost or kept depending on the outcome of a race *etc.* – *v* to place a bet: – *pt* **bet** or **'betted**.

be'take: betake oneself to go.

be'tray *v* to give up (secrets, one's friends *etc*) to an enemy; to show signs of. *His face betrayed no emotion.* – *n* **be'trayal**.

betroth [bi'trōdh] *v* to promise in marriage. – *n* **be'trothal**. – **betrothed to** engaged to be married to.

'better *adj* good to a greater degree, of a more excellent kind; (of persons) healthier; completely recovered (from an illness). – *adj* in a more excellent way. – *v* to improve. – **better off** in a better position, wealthier; **get the better of** to defeat, to overcome; **had better** would be wise to; ought to; **think better of** to change one's mind about.

be'tween *prep* in or through the space dividing (two persons, places, times *etc*): *between 3 o'clock and 6 o'clock*; in parts, in shares to (two people). *Divide the chocolate between you*; from one (thing) to another: *the road between the cities*; one or the other of. *Choose between the boys.*

'bevel *n* a slanting edge. – *v* to give a slanting edge to: – *pt, adj* **'bevelled**.

beverage ['bevərij] *n* a liquid for drinking.

'bevy *n* a group of women or girls; a flock of birds (*eg* quails): – *pl* **'bevies**.

be'wail *v* to mourn loudly over.

be'ware *v* to be watchful for (something dangerous).

be'wilder *v* to puzzle, confuse. – *n* **be'wilderment** confusion.

be'witch *v* to put under a spell; to charm. – *adj* **be'witching** charming; very beautiful.

be'yond *prep* on the far side of: *beyond the post office*; later than: *beyond three o'clock*; more than: *beyond what was required*; too far gone for: *beyond repair*; too difficult for. *The problem was beyond him.* – *adv* on or to the far side, further away.

bi- *prefix* twice; having two; occurring *etc* twice (in a period of time) or once in every two (periods of time).

'bias *n* a favouring of one person, one side of an argument *etc* rather than another; a tendency to move *etc* in a particular direction; a weight on or in an object making it move in a particular direction. – *v* to give a bias to: – *pt* **'bias(s)ed**. – *n* **bias binding** a piece of material cut on the slant and used for

finishing hems *etc.*

bib *n* a piece of cloth *etc* put under a child's chin to prevent his clothes being stained by food *etc*; the part (of an apron, overalls *etc*) covering the front, upper part of the body.

'Bible *n* the holy book of the Christian Church. – *adj* **Biblical** ['biblikəl].

bibli'ography *n* a list of books (about a subject): – *pl* **bibli'ographies**. – *n* **bibli'ographer** one who puts together a bibliography.

'bibliophile *n* a lover of books.

bicen'tenary *n* the two-hundredth year after an event *eg* someone's birth: – *pl* **bicen'tenaries**.

biceps ['biseps] *n* the muscle in front of the upper part of the arm.

'bicker *v* to quarrel (*usu* over small matters).

'bicycle *n* a cycle with two wheels and driven by foot-pedals.

bid *v* to offer a price (for); to tell, say: *I bid you farewell*; to command; to invite. – *n* an offer of a price; a bold attempt: *a bid for freedom.*

bi'ennial *adj* lasting two years; happening once every two years. – *n* a plant that flowers only in its second year.

bier [bēr] *n* a carriage or frame for carrying a dead body.

big *adj* large, great in size, amount, extent *etc*; important; boastful: – *comp* **'bigger**, *superl* **'biggest**.

'bigamy *n* the crime or state of having two wives or two husbands at once. – *n* **'bigamist**. – *adj* **'bigamous**.

bight [bit] *n* a small bay.

'bigot *n* one who too strongly believes or supports anything. – *n* **'bigotry**.

bike *n* short for **bicycle**.

bikini [bi'kēni] *n* a woman's brief two-piece bathing suit: – *pl* **bi'kinis**.

bi'lateral [bi'latərəl] *adj* having two sides; affecting two sides, parties *etc*: *a bilateral agreement.*

'bilberry *n* a type of plant with an edible dark-blue berry.

bile *n* a fluid coming from the liver. – *adj* **bilious** ['bilyəs] ill with too much bile; sick; greenish-yellow in colour. – *n* **'biliousness**.

bilge [bilj] *n* the broadest part of a ship's bottom; bilgewater; (*slang*) nonsense. – *n* **'bilgewater** water which lies in the ship's bottom.

bilingual [bi'lingwəl] *adj* speaking two languages (well).

bill *n* the beak of a bird; an account for money; an early version of a law before it has been passed by parliament; a printed sheet of information.

'billet *n* a lodging, *esp* for soldiers. – *v* to lodge (soldiers) in private houses.

'billiards *n* a game played with a **cue** and balls on a table.

'billion *n* a million millions (1,000,000,000,000); (*US*, now often in Britain) a thousand millions (1,000,000,000).

billow ['bilō] *n* a great wave. – *v* to rise in billows. – *adj* **'billowy**.

'billy, **'billycan** *n* a container for cooking, making tea *etc*, *esp* outdoors. – *n* **'billy-goat** a male goat.

bin *n* a container for storing corn, wine *etc* or for holding dust and ashes.

'binary *adj* made up of two. – *n* **binary system** a mathematical system in which numbers are expressed by two digits only, 1 and 0.

bind *v* to tie with a band; to fasten together; to make to promise: – *pt* **bound**. – *n* **'binding** anything that binds; the cover, stitching *etc* which holds a book together.

bingo ['biŋgō] *n* a popular gambling game using numbers.

bi'noculars *npl* a device with lenses and two eyepieces for seeing distant things more closely.

bi'ography *n* a written account of the life of a person: – *pl* **bi'ographies**. – *n* **bi'ographer** one who writes a biography. – *adj* **bio'graphical**.

bi'ology *n* the study of living things. – *adj* **bio'logical**.

biped ['biped] *n* an animal with two feet (*eg* a bird).

birch *n* a type of hardwood tree; a bundle of birch twigs, used for beating people: – *pl* **'birches**. – *v* to beat with a birch.

bird *n* a feathered, egg-laying creature. – *n* **'birdwatching** the study of birds in their natural surroundings. – **bird of prey** a bird (*eg* a hawk) which kills and eats animals (*esp* mammals) or birds; **bird's-eye view** a wide view, as would be seen from above.

'Biro® *n* a type of ballpoint pen.

birth *n* the very beginning of a person's (or animal's) life in the world. – *ns* **'birthday** the day on which one is born; the day of the same date each year; **'birthmark** a mark on the body from birth; **'birthright** the right which one may claim because of one's parentage.

biscuit ['biskit] *n* dough baked hard in small cakes.

bi'sect *v* to cut in two equal parts.

'bishop *n* a clergyman of high rank (next to an archbishop) in the Roman Catholic church and the Church of England. – *n* **'bishopric** the district ruled by a bishop.

'bison *n* a large wild ox of which there two types, the American one, commonly called **buffalo**, and the European one, which is almost extinct: – *pl* **'bison**.

bit *n* a small piece; a small tool for boring; the part of the bridle which the horse holds in its mouth.

bit *see* **bite**.

bitch *n* a female dog, wolf *etc*; (*coll*) an unpleasant, ill-tempered woman: – *pl* **'bitches**.

bite *v* to grip, cut or tear with the teeth: – *pt* **bit**, *pp* **'bitten**. – *n* a grip with the teeth; the part bitten off; (in fishing) a nibble at the bait; a wound on the body caused by an animal's or insect's bite.

'bitter *adj* unpleasant to the taste; harsh: *bitter cold*; resentful, angry through disappointment.

'bittern *n* a type of bird like a heron.

bivouac ['bivooak] *n* a rest for the night in the open air without tents. – *Also v*: – *pt* **'bivouacked**.

'bi-'weekly *adj* happening twice a week or once every two weeks.

bi'zarre *adj* odd, strange.

blab *v* to talk much; to let out a secret: – *pt* **blabbed**.

black *adj* dark and colourless. – *n* black colour. – *v* **'blacken** to make black or dark; to make to appear wicked. – *adj* **'black-and-'blue** badly bruised. – *ns* **black belt** an award for skill in judo; **'blackberry** a type of black-coloured soft fruit growing on a prickly stem; **'blackbird** a type of black, thrush-like bird; **'blackboard** a dark-coloured board for writing on in chalk; **'blackcock** a kind of grouse; **black eye** a bruised area round the eye *usu* as result of a blow; **blackguard** ['blagärd] a wicked person; **'blackleg** one who works when other workers are on strike; **'blackmail** the crime of threatening to reveal a person's secrets unless he pays money; **'blackmailer**; **black market** illegal or dishonest buying and selling. – *Also adj*. – *n* **'blackout** (a period of) total darkness caused by putting out or obscuring all lights; a faint, loss of consciousness. – *v* **black out** to become unconscious. – *ns* **black sheep** a person who is less successful, or less righteous than others in his group (*usu* a family); **'blacksmith** a man who makes or repairs articles of iron; **black widow** a type of very poisonous American spider.

'bladder *n* a thin bag of skin *etc*, *esp* that in which urine collects in the body.

blade *n* the cutting part of a knife, sword *etc*; a leaf of grass or corn.

blame *v* to find fault with; to consider responsible for. – *n* fault; responsibility (for something bad). – *adjs* **'blameless; 'blameworthy** deserving blame.

blancmange [blə'monzh] *n* a type of jelly-like pudding made with milk.

bland *adj* polite, gentle; mild, not irritating; dull, not exciting.

'blandishments *npl* acts or words meant to flatter.

blank *adj* (of paper *etc*) without writing or marks; expressionless: *a blank look.* – *n* an empty space; a cartridge without a bullet. – *n* **blank verse** poetry without rhyme.

'blanket *n* a bed-covering of wool *etc*; a covering. – *adj* covering a group of things: *a blanket agreement.* – *v* to cover (with something thick).

blare *v* to sound loudly. – Also *n*.

'blarney *n* flattery or coaxing talk.

blas'pheme *v* to speak lightly or wickedly of God; to curse and swear. – *ns* **blas'phemer; blasphemy** ['blasfəmi]: – *pl* **'blasphemies.** – *adj* **'blasphemous**.

blast *n* a blowing or gust of wind; a loud note (as on a trumpet); an explosion. – *v* to break (stones, a bridge *etc*) by explosion; to wither, destroy; to produce a loud noise. *Music blasted from the radio.* – *ns* **blast furnace** a furnace (such as is used in iron-smelting) into which hot air is blown; **'blast-off** the moment of the launching of a rocket. – Also *v*. – **at full blast** as quickly, strongly *etc* as possible.

'blatant *adj* very obvious; shameless. – *adv* **'blatantly**.

blaze *n* a rush of light or flame. – *v* to burn with a strong flame; to throw out a strong light. – *n* **'blazer** a kind of jacket worn by schoolchildren, sportsmen *etc*.

'blazon *v* to make known publicly; to display very obviously.

bleach *v* to whiten, remove the colour from. – *n* a substance which bleaches, used for cleaning, whitening clothes *etc*: – *pl* **'bleaches**.

bleak *adj* dull and cheerless; cold, unsheltered. – *n* **'bleakness**.

'bleary *adj* (of eyes) tired and inflamed.

bleat *v* to cry like a sheep; to complain in an irritating or whining way. – Also *n*.

bleed *v* to lose blood; to draw blood from: – *pt* **bled**. – *n* **'bleeding** a flow of blood.

bleep *v* to give out a high-pitched intermittent sound. – Also *n*.

'blemish *n* a stain; a fault or flaw: – *pl* **'blemishes**. – *v* to stain or spoil.

blend *v* to mix together. – Also *n*. – *n* **'blender** an electric machine which mixes thoroughly and liquidizes.

bless *v* to wish happiness to; to make happy; to make holy. – *adjs* **blessed** [blest, 'blesid], (in poetry *etc*) **blest** happy; fortunate; made holy, consecrated. – *n* **'blessing** a wish or prayer for happiness or success; any means or cause of happiness. *The children were a blessing to them.*

blight [blīt] *n* a disease in plants which withers them; anything that destroys. – *v* to destroy.

blind *adj* unable to see. – *n* a window screen; something which deceives. – *v* to make blind; to dazzle. – *n* **'blindness**. – *n* **blind alley** a street open only at one end; anything which leads nowhere. – *adj* **'blindfold** having the eyes bandaged, so as not to see. – *n* **blindman's buff** a game in which a blindfold person tries to catch others.

blink *v* to close the eyes for a moment; to shine unsteadily. – *npl* **'blinkers** pieces of leather over a horse's eyes to prevent it seeing in any direction except in front.

bliss *n* very great happiness. – *adj* **'blissful**.

'blister *n* a thin bubble on the skin full of watery matter. – *v* to rise up in a blister.

blithe [blīdh] *adj* happy, gay.

blitz *n* a sudden violent attack (*esp* from the air).

'blizzard *n* a fierce storm of wind and snow.

'bloated *adj* swollen, puffed out. – *n* **'bloater** a type of smoked herring.

blob *n* a drop of liquid; a round spot.

block *n* a lump (of wood, stone *etc*); a connected group (of buildings *etc*); something which hinders or obstructs: *a road block*; an engraved piece of wood or metal for printing; (*hist*) the wood on which people were beheaded. – *v* to hinder, prevent from going on. – *n* **'blockhead** a stupid person. – *npl* **block letters** capital letters written in imitation of printing type (*eg* NAME).

bloc'kade *v* to surround a fort or country so that food *etc* cannot reach it. – Also *n*.

blonde *adj*, *n* (of) a woman of fair skin and light-coloured hair. – *adj* **blond** light-coloured; fair-haired.

blood [blud] *n* the red liquid which flows in the bodies of men and animals; one's descent or parentage: *royal blood.* – *adjs* **'bloodless; 'bloody.** – *ns* **blood donor** one who gives blood which is stored and given to ill people; **blood group** any one of the types into which human blood is divided; **'bloodhound** a breed of large dog with a good sense of smell; **'bloodshed** the shedding of blood, slaughter. – *adjs* **'bloodshot** (of eyes) inflamed with blood; **'blood-thirsty** cruel, eager to kill. – *n* **'blood-vessel** a vein or artery (of the body) in which the blood circulates.

bloom *v* (of plants) to flower; to be in good health. – *n* a blossom or flower; rosy colour; freshness, perfection; a powder on the skin of fresh fruits.

'blossom *n* a flower; the flowers on a fruit tree. – *v* to put forth flowers; to open out, develop, flourish.

blot *n* a spot or stain (of ink *etc*). – *v* to spot or stain; to dry writing with **blotting paper:** – *pt* **'blotted.** – **blot out** to remove or conceal from sight or memory.

blotch *n* a spot or patch of colour *etc*: – *pl* **'blotches.** – *v* to mark with blotches. – *adjs* **blotched; 'blotchy.**

blouse [blowz] *n* a loose piece of clothing for the upper body.

blow [blō] *n* a hard stroke or knock (*eg* with the fist); (*coll*) a sudden piece of bad luck. – *v* (of air or wind) to move; to drive air upon or into; to sound (a wind instrument); to breathe hard or with difficulty: – *pt* **blew** [blōō], *pp* **blown.** – *adj* **'blowy** windy. – *ns* **'blowfly** a fly which lays its eggs in dead flesh *etc*, a bluebottle; **'blow-lamp, 'blowtorch** a lamp for aiming a very hot flame at a particular spot. – **blow over** to pass and be forgotten; **blow up** to destroy by explosion.

'blubber *n* the fat of whales and other sea animals.

'bludgeon *n* a short stick with a heavy end.

blue [blōō] *adj, n* (of) the colour of a clear sky; (*coll*) unhappy, depressed. – *ns* **'bluebell** the wild hyacinth; (in Scotland) the harebell; **'bluebottle** a large fly with a blue abdomen; **Blue Peter** a blue flag with white centre, raised when a ship is about to sail; **'blueprint** a sketch-plan of work to be done; **'bluestocking** a learned lady. – **out of the blue** unexpectedly.

bluff *adj* rough and jolly in manners, outspoken. – *v* to (try to) deceive (by a display of self-confidence). – *n* a high steep bank overlooking the sea or a river; deception, trickery.

'blunder *v* to make a bad mistake. – Also *n.*

'blunderbuss *n* a short hand gun with a wide mouth: – *pl* **'blunderbusses.**

blunt *adj* having an edge or point that is not sharp; rough in manner. – *v* to make less sharp or less painful. – *adv* **'bluntly.**

blur *n* a spot, thing *etc* that cannot be seen clearly; a smudge, a smear. – Also *v.* – *adj* **blurred.**

blurt *v* (*usu* with **out**) to speak suddenly and without thinking.

blush *n* a red glow on the face caused by shame *etc*; a reddish glow: – *pl* **'blushes.** – *v* to go red in the face.

'bluster *v* to blow strongly; to boast noisily (but without good reason). – *n* a blast or roaring as of the wind; words of noisy, empty boasting.

boa ['bōə] *n* a long scarf of fur or feathers. – *n* **boa (con'strictor)** a type of large snake which kills its prey by winding itself round it and crushing it.

boar *n* the male pig; a wild pig.

board *n* a sheet of wood; a group of people who run a business *etc*: *board of directors*; stiff card used in the binding of books; food. – *v* to cover with boards; to supply with food at fixed terms; to enter (a ship *etc*). – *n* **'boarder** one who receives food and lodging. – *ns* **'boarding-house** a house where paying guests receive meals at a fixed price; **'boarding-school** a school in which food and lodging is given.

boast *v* to brag, to speak proudly and exaggeratedly, *esp* about oneself and one's actions. – *n* something said in a bragging or boasting manner. – *adj* **'boastful** fond of boasting.

boat *n* a vessel for sailing or rowing; a ship; a boat-shaped dish: *a sauceboat.* – *v* to sail about in a boat. – *n* **'boater** a straw hat with a brim.

boatswain, bosun ['bōsn] *n* an officer who looks after a ship's boats, rigging *etc*.

bob *v* to move up and down; to cut (hair) to about neck level: – *pt* **bobbed.**

'bobbin *n* a small cylindrical piece of wood *etc* on which thread is wound.

bobsleigh ['bobslā] *n* a long sledge or two short sledges joined together with one long seat.

bode : **bode well, ill** to be a good, bad sign.

bodice ['bodis] *n* the (close-fitting) part of a woman's or a child's dress above the waist.

'bodkin *n* a large blunt needle.

'body *n* the whole or main part of a man

or animal; a corpse; the main part of anything; a mass (*esp* of persons): – *pl* **'bodies**. – *adj* **'bodily** of the body. – *adv* all in one piece, as one whole. – *n* **'bodyguard** a person or group of people whose job is to protect another person from harm or attack.

'boffin *n* (*coll*) a (research) scientist.

bog *n* a marsh. – *adj* **'boggy**. – **bog down** to hinder, prevent from making progress.

bogey ['bōgi] *n* something greatly feared.

'boggle *v* to be astonished at, refuse to believe.

'bōgus *adj* false.

boil *v* (of a liquid) to reach the temperature at which it turns to vapour; to bubble up owing to heat; (*coll*) to be hot; (*coll*) to be angry. – *n* a kind of inflamed swelling. – *n* **'boiler** a container in which water is heated or steam is produced.

'boisterous *adj* wild, noisy; (of weather) stormy.

bōld *adj* daring, full of courage; cheeky; striking, well-marked: *a picture in bold colours*; (of printing type) thick and clear.

'bollard *n* on ships or quays, a post for fastening ropes to; in a street, a short post used in controlling traffic.

'bōlster *n* a long pillow or cushion. – *v* (with **up**) to support.

bōlt *n* a (small) metal sliding bar used to fasten a door *etc*; a large screw or pin; a roll of cloth. – *v* to fasten with a bolt; to swallow (food) hurriedly; to rush away, escape. – **bolt upright** (sitting) with a very straight back.

bomb [bom] *n* a case containing explosive or other harmful material, thrown, dropped, timed to go off automatically *etc*. – *v* to drop bombs on. – *ns* **'bomber** an aeroplane built for bombing; a person who throws, plants *etc* bombs; **'bombshell** formerly, a bomb; a startling piece of news.

bom'bard [bɔm'bärd] *v* to attack with artillery; to batter or pelt. – *n* **bom'bardment**.

'bombast *n* high-sounding language. – *adj* **bom'bastic**.

bond *n* (often *pl*) that which binds (*eg* chains, ropes *etc*); that which brings people together. *Their interest in ballet was a bond between them*; a (written) promise to pay or do something. – *n* **'bondage** slavery. – **bonded store, bonded warehouse** one where goods are kept until taxes have been paid on them; **in bond** in a bonded warehouse.

bone *n* a hard material forming the skeleton of animals; one of the connected pieces of a skeleton: *the hip bone*. – *v* to take the bones out of (meat *etc*). – *adj* **'bony** (of food) full of bones; not fleshy, thin; made of bone or bone-like substance.

'bonfire *n* a large fire in the open air.

'bonnet *n* a type of hat for women, *usu* fastened by ribbons *etc*; the covering over a motor-car engine.

'bonny *adj* good-looking; healthy-looking.

'bōnus *n* an extra payment in addition to wages *etc*; something extra: – *pl* **'bonuses**.

boo *v* make a sound of disapproval. – Also *n*.

'booby *n* a silly or stupid person. – *ns* **booby prize** a prize for the person who is last in a competition; **booby trap** an explosive or other harmful device hidden or disguised as something harmless, intended to injure the first person to come near it.

book *n* (printed) pages bound together; a written work which has appeared, or is intended to appear, in the form of a book. *I read your book and enjoyed it.* – *v* to order (places *etc*) beforehand. – *ns* **'book-keeping** the keeping of accounts; **'booklet** a small (paper-covered) book; **'book-maker** (also (*coll*) **'bookie**) one who takes bets and pays winnings; **'bookworm** a person who is very fond of reading; a grub that eats holes in books.

boom *v* to make a hollow sound or roar; to increase in prosperity, success *etc*. – *n* a loud, hollow sound; a rush or increase of trade, prosperity *etc*: *the oil boom*; a pole by which a sail is stretched.

'boomerang *n* a curved piece of wood which when thrown returns to the thrower, used as a hunting weapon by Australian aborigines.

boon *n* a blessing or favour to be grateful for. – *n* **boon companion** a close friend with whom one makes merry.

boor *n* a rough or rude person. – *adj* **'boorish**.

boost *v* to push up, raise, increase: *boost the sales of shampoo*: *boost resistance to polio*. – Also *n*. – *n* **'booster** that which boosts; a device for increasing the power of a machine *etc*; the first of several stages of a rocket.

boot *n* a covering (of leather *etc*) for the foot and lower part of the leg; a place for stowing luggage in a car. – *v* to kick. – *n* **'boo'tee** a (knitted) boot for a baby.

– **to boot** in addition, as well.

booth [boōodh] *n* a covered stall (at a fair or market); a small (enclosed) compartment (for telephoning, voting etc).

'**bootlegger** *n* one who deals illegally in alcoholic drink.

'**booty** *n* plunder or gains *usu* taken in war *etc*.

'**border** *n* the edge or side of anything; the boundary of a country; a flowerbed in a garden. – *v* (*usu* with **on, upon**) to be near to. *His behaviour borders on madness.* – *adj* '**bordered** edged.

bore[1] [bōr] *v* to make a hole by piercing; to weary, seem tiresome or dull to. – *n* a hole made by boring; the size across the tube of a gun; a tiresome person or thing; a flood or wave that rushes up some river mouths at high tide. – *n* '**boredom** lack of interest, weariness.

bore[2] *see* **bear**.

born *adj* by birth, natural: *a born athlete.* Also *see* **bear**. – **be born** (of a baby) to come out of the mother's womb; to come into existence.

borne *see* **bear**.

borough ['burə] *n* (*hist*) a town with special privileges granted by royal charter; a town that elects Members of Parliament.

borrow ['borō] *v* to get (from another) on loan.

'**borzoi** *n* a breed of long-haired dog.

bosh *n* nonsense.

bosom ['boōzəm] *n* the breast; midst, centre: *the bosom of his family.* – *adj* (of friends *etc*) close.

boss *n* a leader or master: – *pl* '**bosses**. – *v* to manage, order about in a high-handed way. – *adj* '**bossy** tending to boss others too much, domineering.

bosun *see* **boatswain**.

'**botany** *n* the study of plants. – *adjs* bo'**tanic(al)**. – *n* '**botanist** one who studies or is an expert in botany. – *n* **botanic garden** a large public garden where plants and trees of different countries are grown.

botch *v* to mend clumsily; to do badly. – *n* a badly done piece of work.

both *adj, pron* the two, the one and the other. *We both went. Both of us went. Both (the) men are dead. The men are both dead. Both are dead.* – *adv* equally, together. *He is both dishonest and cunning.*

bother ['bodhər] *v* to be a nuisance to; to trouble (oneself or others). – *n* trouble, inconvenience.

'**bothy** *n* (in Scotland) a hut to give shelter to climbers *etc*; a simply furnished hut for farm labourers: –

pl '**bothies**.

'**bottle** *n* a hollow narrow-necked vessel for holding liquids. – *v* to put in a bottle. – *n* '**bottleneck** a narrow part of a road likely to become crowded with traffic; any stage in a process where progress is held up. – **bottle up** to keep in, hold in (one's feelings).

'**bottom** *n* the lowest part or underside of anything; the sitting part of the body, the buttocks. – *adj* '**bottomless** extremely deep.

boudoir ['boōdwär] *n* a lady's private room.

bough [bow] *n* a branch of a tree.

bought *see* **buy**.

boulder ['bōldər] *n* a large stone.

bounce *v* to (cause to) jump or spring up after striking the ground *etc*; to move about noisily. – Also *n*. – *n* '**bouncer** a person whose job it is to force troublemakers (at a club *etc*) to leave. – *adj* '**bouncing** (large and) lively.

bound *n* a leap, a jump; (*usu pl*) borders, limits. – *v* to jump, leap; to limit; to surround; *see* also **bind**. – *n* '**boundary** (line *etc* marking) the edge or limit: – *pl* '**boundaries**. – *adj* '**boundless** having no limit, vast. – **bound for** ready to go to, on the way to; **bound to** certain to. *He is bound to notice it*; **out of bounds** beyond the permitted limits.

'**bounty** *n* a gift; generosity; money given as a help: – *pl* '**bounties**. – *adjs* **bounteous** ['bowntiəs], '**bountiful** generous; plentiful.

bouquet [boō'kā] *n* a bunch of flowers; a scent (of wine).

bourgeois ['boōrzhwä] *n, adj* (a person) of the middle class.

bout *n* a (round in a) fight or contest; a period, spell, fit (of illness *etc*).

boutique [boō'tēk] *n* a small shop *usu* selling goods (*esp* clothes) of the latest fashion.

'**bovine** *adj* of or like cattle; stupid.

bow[1] [bow] *v* to bend; to nod the head or bend the body in greeting; to give in; to weigh down, crush. – *n* a bending of the head or body; (*usu pl*) the front part of a ship.

bow[2] [bō] *n* anything in the shape of a curve or arch; a weapon for shooting arrows, made of a stick of springy wood bent by a string; a looped knot; a wooden rod with horsehair stretched along it, by which the strings of a violin *etc* are played. – *adj* '**bow-'legged** having legs curving outwards. – *ns* '**bowman** a soldier *etc* who uses a bow; **bow window** a window built in a curve.

bowels ['bowəlz] *npl* in the body, the large and small intestines; the innermost parts of anything: *in the bowels of the earth.*

bower ['bowər] *n* a shady spot in a garden.

bowl [bōl] *n* a basin for holding liquids *etc*; a basin-shaped hollow in anything; a heavy wooden ball for rolling along the ground, as in the game skittles; (*pl*) a game played on a green with specially weighted bowls. – *v* to play at bowls; to move speedily like a bowl; (in cricket) to send the ball at the wicket; to put out a batsman by knocking his wicket with the ball. – *n* '**bowler** one who bowls in cricket; a (black) hat with a rounded top. – **bowl over** to knock down; to surprise greatly.

box *n* a case for holding anything; a hardwood tree; an evergreen shrub; (in a theatre) private closed-in seats: – *pl* '**boxes**. – *v* to enclose, confine in a box or any small space; to strike with the hand or fist; to fight with the fists, wearing padded gloves, as a sport. – *ns* '**boxing** the name of this sport; '**boxer** one who boxes as a sport; a breed of large smooth-haired dog with a head like a bulldog's. – *ns* **Boxing Day** December 26, the day after Christmas Day; **box office** an office where theatre tickets *etc* may be bought.

boy *n* a male child; a male servant. – *adj* '**boyish**. – *ns* '**boyhood** the time of being a boy; **Boy Scout** *see* **Scout**.

'**boycott** *v* to refuse to do business or trade with. – Also *n*.

bra short for **brassière**.

brace *n* anything that draws together and holds tightly; a pair or couple (*esp* of pheasant, grouse *etc* when shot); a carpenter's tool used in boring; (*pl*) shoulder-straps for holding up trousers. – *v* to tighten or strengthen, give firmness to. – *adj* '**bracing** giving strength.

'**bracelet** *n* an ornament for the wrist.

'**bracken** *n* a coarse kind of fern.

'**bracket** *n* a support for something fastened to a wall; in printing *etc* a mark (*eg* ( ), [ ]) used to group together several words *etc*. – *v* to enclose in brackets; to group together.

'**brackish** *adj* (of water) rather salty.

'**bradawl** *n* a tool to pierce holes.

brag *v* to boast. – Also *n*.

braid *v* to plait (the hair). – *n* decorative ribbon used as trimming; a plait of hair.

braille [brāl] *n* a system of raised marks

on paper which blind people can read by feeling.

brain *n* the part of the body inside the skull, the centre of feeling and thinking. – *v* to knock out the brains of; to hit on the head. – *adj* '**brainy** (*coll*) clever. – *ns* '**brainwashing** forcing (a person) to change his views; '**brain-wave** a good idea.

braise [brāz] *v* to stew (meat) in little liquid.

brake *n* a part of a vehicle, used for stopping or slowing down. – *v* to slow down by using the brake(s).

'**bramble** *n* the blackberry bush; (in Scotland) its fruit.

bran *n* the inner husks of wheat *etc, usu* separated from flour after grinding.

branch *n* a shoot or arm-like limb of a tree; a small shop, bank, library *etc* belonging to a bigger one: – *pl* '**branches**. – *v* to divide or spread out like branches.

brand *n* a make of goods (having a special trademark); a burning piece of wood; a permanent mark *esp* one made by a red-hot iron. – *v* to mark with a brand; to put a permanent mark on, impress deeply; to mark with disgrace: *branded as a thief.* – *adj* '**brand-**'**new** absolutely new.

'**brandish** *v* to wave (a weapon *etc*) about.

'**brandy** *n* a strong drink, a spirit made from wine: – *pl* '**brandies**.

brass *n* metal made by mixing copper and zinc; (in music) brass wind instruments: – *pl* '**brasses**. – *adj* of, made of brass; playing brass musical instruments. – *adj* '**brassy** like brass; showily dressed or harsh-voiced. – *n* **brass plate** a nameplate on a door *etc*.

brassière ['brasiər] *n* an article of women's underwear for supporting the breasts.

brat *n* a disapproving name for a child.

bra'**vado** *n* a show of bravery, bold pretence.

brave *adj* ready to meet danger, pain *etc* without showing fear, courageous; noble. – *v* to face or meet boldly and without fear. – *n* a Red Indian warrior. – *n* **bravery** ['brāvəri].

'**bra**'**vo** *interj* well done!

brawl *n* a noisy quarrel; a fight. – Also *v*.

brawn *n* muscle power. – *adj* '**brawny** big and strong.

bray *n* a cry (like that) of an ass. – Also *v*.

'**brazen** *adj* of or like brass; impudent, shameless. – **brazen (it) out** to face (a difficult situation) with bold impudence.

'**brāzier** *n* a kind of iron basket for holding burning coals.

bra'zil-nut *n* the three-sided nut from a type of tree found in Brazil.

breach *n* a break or gap; a breaking of a law, of a promise *etc*; a quarrel: – *pl* '**breaches**. – *v* to make a breach or opening in. – **breach of the peace** a breaking of the law by noisy, offensive behaviour.

bread [bred] *n* food made of flour or meal and baked; necessary food, means of living. – *n* '**breadwinner** one who earns a living for a family.

breadth [bredth] *n* distance from side to side, width; extent.

break [brāk] *v* to (cause to) fall to pieces or apart; to act against (a law, promise *etc*); to interrupt (a silence *etc*); to tell (news); to check, soften the effect of (a fall); to cure (of a habit); (of a teenage boy's voice) to drop to a deep male tone; (often with **in**) to tame or train (a horse): – *pt* **broke**, *pp* '**broken**. – *n* an opening; a pause; (*coll*) a lucky chance. – *adj* '**breakable**. – *ns* '**breakage** the act of breaking; the thing broken; '**breaker** a large wave. – *ns* '**break-in** illegal entry (by force) of a house *etc* with intent to steal; '**break-through** a sudden success after effort; '**breakwater** a barrier to break the force of the waves. – **break down** (*n* '**breakdown**) to divide into parts; (of engines *etc*) to fail; to be overcome with weeping or (nervous) exhaustion; **break into** to get into by force; **break out** to appear suddenly; to escape; (with **in**) to become covered (with a rash *etc*); **break up** to (cause to) fall to pieces or apart; to separate, depart. *The meeting broke up.*

breakfast ['brekfəst] *n* the first meal of the day. – Also *v*.

bream *n* a type of small fish.

breast [brest] *n* the front part of a human or animal body between neck and belly; either of the milk-producing parts of the body of a woman. – *n* '**breastplate** a piece of armour for the breast.

breath [breth] *n* the air drawn into and then sent out from the lungs; one act of breathing; a very slight breeze. – *adj* '**breathless** breathing very fast, panting; excited. – *n* '**breathalӯser** a device into which one breathes to indicate the amount of alcohol in the blood.

breathe [brēdh] *v* to draw in and send out air from the lungs; to whisper: – *pres p* '**breathing**. – *n* '**breather** a rest or pause.

bred *see* **breed**.

breech *n* the back part, *esp* of a gun; (*pl*) **breeches** ['brichiz] trousers (*esp* those coming just below the knee).

breed *v* to produce (children, a family); to mate and rear (animals); to cause. *Dirt breeds disease*: – *pt* **bred** [bred]. – *n* a group (of animals or people) alike in looks *etc*, being descended from the same ancestor, race, type; kind, sort: *a new breed of salesmen.* – *n* '**breeding** act of producing or rearing; good manners; education and training.

breeze *n* a gentle wind. – *adj* '**breezy** windy; bright, lively.

brethren ['bredhrən] *n* old *pl* of **brother**.

'**brevity** *n* shortness.

brew [broō] *v* to make beer; to make (tea *etc*); (of a storm, trouble *etc*) to be gathering or forming; to plot, plan: *brewing mischief.* – *n* '**brewery** a place where beer is made: – *pl* '**breweries**.

'**briar**, '**brier** *n* the wild rose; a type of heather plant whose wood is used for making tobacco pipes.

bribe *n* a gift (*usu* money) given to persuade a person to do something *usu* dishonest. – *v* to win over with a bribe. – *n* **bribery** ['brībəri].

'**bric-à-brac** *n* small odds and ends.

brick *n* an (oblong) block of baked clay for building; a toy building-block of wood *etc*.

bride *n* a woman about to be married, or newly married. – *adj* '**bridal** of a bride or a wedding. – *ns* '**bridegroom** a man about to be married, or newly married; '**bridesmaid** an unmarried woman who attends the bride at a wedding.

bridge *n* something built to carry a track or road across a river *etc*; the captain's platform on a ship; a card game; the bony part of the nose; a thin piece of wood holding up the strings of a violin *etc*. – *v* to be or build a bridge over; to get over (a difficulty).

'**bridle** *n* the harness on a horse's head to which the reins are attached. – *v* to put on a bridle; to toss the head indignantly. – *n* '**bridle-path** a path for horseriders.

brief [brēf] *adj* short; taking a short time. – *n* (a set of notes giving) information or instructions, *esp* to a lawyer about a law case; (*pl*) women's short-legged knickers; short underpants. – *v* to instruct or inform. – **in brief** in a few words.

brier *see* **briar**.

brig *n* a sailing vessel with two masts and square-cut sails.

bri'gade *n* a body (*usu* two battalions) of soldiers. – *n* **brigadier** [brigə'dēr] a senior army officer.

'brigand *n* a robber, bandit.

bright [brit] *adj* shining; full of light; clever; cheerful. – *v* **'brighten** to make or grow bright.

'brilliant *adj* very clever; sparkling; splendid. – *n* **'brilliance**.

brim *n* the edge (of a cup *etc*); the outer edge of a hat which sticks out. – *v* to be full: – *pt* **brimmed**. – *adj* **'brim'ful** full to the brim.

'brimstone *n* sulphur.

brine *n* salt water. – *adj* **'briny**.

bring *v* to fetch, lead or carry (to a place); to cause to come. *The medicine brings him relief*: – *pt* **brought** [bröt]. – **bring about** to cause; **bring home to** to make (someone) realize (something); **bring off** to do (something) successfully; **bring to** to revive; **bring up** to rear, to feed and educate; to mention. *He brought up that point in his speech.*

brink *n* the edge (of a cliff, *etc*). – **on the brink of** almost at the point of, on the verge of: *on the brink of war*.

brisk *adj* moving quickly; lively and efficient: *a brisk manner*. – *n* **'briskness**.

bristle ['brisl] *n* a short, stiff hair (as of a pig). – *v* (of hair *etc*) to stand on end; to show anger and indignation. – *adj* **'bristly** having bristles; rough.

'brittle *adj* hard but easily broken.

broach *v* to begin to talk about (a subject *etc*); to open, begin using (*eg* a cask of wine).

broad [bröd] *adj* wide, extensive; (of an accent *etc*) strong, obvious. – *v* **'broaden** to make or grow broader. – *n* **'broadness**. – *v* **'broadcast** to send out by radio *etc*. – Also *n*. – *n* **'broadside** a shot by all the guns on one side of a ship; a strong attack (in an argument *etc*).

bro'cade *n* a silk cloth on which fine patterns are sewn.

'broccoli *n* a type of green vegetable.

brochure ['brōshoŏr] *n* a booklet: *a holiday brochure*.

brogue [brōg] *n* a strong shoe; a broad accent (*esp* Irish) in speaking.

broil *v* to grill; to make or be very hot.

broke *adj* (*coll*) without money. – *v* see **break**.

broken see **break**.

'broker *n* one who buys and sells (stocks and shares *etc*) for others.

bronchitis [broŋ'kitis] *n* an illness (affecting the windpipe) in which breathing is difficult. – *adj* **bronchial** ['broŋkiəl] having to do with the windpipe.

'bronco *n* (*US*) a half-tamed horse.

bronto'saurus *n* a type of large extinct dinosaur.

bronze *n* a golden-brown mixture of copper and tin. – Also *adj*. – *adj* **bronzed** sunburnt (to a colour like that of bronze).

brooch [brōch] *n* an ornament pinned to the clothing: – *pl* **'brooches**.

brood *v* (of a hen *etc*) to sit on eggs; to think (anxiously) for some time. – *n* a number of young birds hatched at one time; young animals or children of the same family.

brook *n* a small stream. – *v* to put up with, endure.

broom *n* a type of shrub with yellow flowers; a brush for sweeping. – *n* **'broomstick** the handle of a broom.

broth *n* soup, *esp* one made with vegetables.

brother ['brudhər] *n* a male born of the same parents as oneself; a companion, a fellow-worker *etc*. – *adj* **'brotherly** of or like a brother; affectionate. – *ns* **'brotherhood** an association of men; **'brother-in-law** the brother of one's husband or of one's wife; the husband of one's sister or of one's sister-in-law.

brought see **bring**.

brow [brow] *n* the forehead; an eyebrow; the edge of a hill. – *v* **'browbeat** to bully.

brown [brown] *adj* of a dark colour made by mixing red, yellow, black *etc*; suntanned. – Also *n*.

brownie ['browni] *n* (*myth*) a helpful fairy or goblin; a Brownie Guide. – *n* **Brownie Guide** a junior Girl Guide.

browse [browz] *v* to feed (on the shoots or leaves of plants); to glance through (books), reading here and there.

bruise [broŏz] *n* a mark, a discoloured area (*eg* on the body) where it has been struck *etc*. – *v* to cause bruises (to).

brunette [broŏ'net] *n* a woman with dark hair.

brunt: bear, take the brunt to take the chief strain.

brush *n* an instrument with tufts of bristles, hair, wire *etc* for smoothing the hair, cleaning, painting *etc*; a disagreement, a brief quarrel or fight; the tail of a fox; undergrowth: – *pl* **'brushes**. – *v* to pass a brush over; to remove by sweeping; to touch lightly in passing. – *n* **'brushwood** broken branches, twigs *etc*; undergrowth.

brusque ['broŏsk] *adj* sharp and short in

manner, rude. – *n* '**brusqueness**.

Brussels sprouts *npl* a type of vegetable with sprouts like small cabbages on the stem.

brute [broot] *n* an animal; a cruel person. – *adj* '**brutal** like a brute, cruel. – *n* **bru'tality**. – *adj* '**brutish** like a brute, savage, coarse. – *n* **brute strength** pure physical strength.

'**bubble** *n* a thin ball of liquid blown out with air. – *v* to rise in bubbles. – *adj* '**bubbly**.

bucca'neer *n* (*hist*) pirate. – *adj* **bucca'neering** like a pirate.

buck *n* the male of the deer, goat, hare and rabbit; (*US coll*) a dollar. – *v* (of a horse *etc*) to attempt to throw a rider by rapid jumps into the air.

'**bucket** *n* a container for water *etc*.

'**buckle** *n* a clip (of metal *etc*) for fastening straps or belts. – *v* to fasten with a buckle. – *n* '**buckler** a small shield.

'**buckshot** *n* large lead shot fired from a shotgun.

bud *n* the first shoot of a tree or plant. – *v* to produce buds. – *adj* '**budding** showing signs of becoming: *a budding author.*

Buddhism ['boodizəm] *n* a religion whose followers worship Buddha. – *n*, *adj* '**Buddhist**.

budge *v* to move slightly, stir.

'**budgerigar** *n* a kind of small parrot often kept as a pet.

'**budget** *n* the plan for a government's spending made each year by parliament; anyone's plan of their future spending. – *v* to allow for in a budget.

'**budgie** *n* short for **budgerigar**.

buff *n* a light yellowish brown colour. – *v* to polish.

'**buffalo** *n* a large kind of ox, *esp* one used in Asia to draw loads; (*US*) the American bison. – *pl* '**buffaloes**.

'**buffer** *n* something which lessens the force of a blow or collision.

'**buffet** *n* a slap or a blow. – *v* to strike, knock about.

buffet² ['boofā] *n* a counter or café where food and drink may be bought; a (cold) meal set out on tables for people to serve themselves.

buf'foon *n* a clown, fool. – *n* **buf'- foonery**.

bug *n* a name for any small insect, *esp* one which is disliked; a tiny device which may be concealed in a room to record conversations. – *v* to put such a device in (a room *etc*): – *pt* **bugged**. – *n* '**bugbear** a thing that frightens or annoys.

'**bugle** *n* a type of small trumpet. – *n* '**bugler** one who plays the bugle.

build [bild] *v* to put together the parts of anything: – *pt* **built**. – *n* (of persons) physical type: *a heavy build.* – *ns* '**builder**; '**building** the act or trade of building (houses *etc*); a house or other built dwelling *etc*. – *n* **building society** a kind of bank which lends people money to buy a house. – *adj* '**built-'up** (of an area *etc*) containing houses and other buildings.

bulb *n* the rounded part of the stem of certain plants (*eg* hyacinth, onion) which store their food; a pear-shaped glass globe surrounding the element of an electric light. – *adj* '**bulbous** bulb-shaped.

bulge [bulj] *n* a swelling; a (temporary) noticeable increase. – *v* to swell out.

bulk *n* (large) size; the greater part. – *adj* '**bulky** taking up much room. – *n* '**bulkhead** a wall in the inside of a ship, meant to keep out water in a collision.

bull [bool] *n* the male of animals of the ox family, also of the whale, elephant *etc*. – *n* '**bulldog** a breed of strong, fierce-looking dog. – *v* '**bulldoze** to use a bulldozer on; to force. – *ns* '**bull-dozer** a machine for levelling land and clearing away obstacles; '**bullfight** (in Spain *etc*) a public entertainment in which a bull is angered and *usu* finally killed; '**bullfinch** a small pink-breasted bird; '**bullfrog** a type of large frog; '**bullring** the arena in which bullfights take place; '**bull's-eye** the mark in the middle of a target; a striped sweet.

bullet ['boolit] *n* the piece of metal fired from a gun. – *adj* '**bullet-proof** not able to be pierced by bullets.

bulletin ['boolətin] *n* a report (as of a person's health, of news *etc*).

bullion ['boolian] *n* gold and silver in the form of bars *etc*.

bullock ['boolək] *n* a young bull.

bully ['booli] *n* one who unfairly uses his size and strength to hurt or frighten weaker persons: – *pl* '**bullies**. – *v* to act like a bully. – *v* '**bully-'off** (in hockey *etc*) to put the ball in play.

bulrush ['boolrush] *n* a type of large strong reed which grows on wet land or in water: – *pl* '**bulrushes**.

bulwark ['boolwərk] *n* anything strong for defence (such as a wall).

'**bumble-bee** *n* a type of large bee.

bump *v* to strike heavily; to knock by accident. – *n* the sound of a heavy blow; the act of striking (by accident); a raised lump. – *n* '**bumper** a bar round the front and back of a car's body to protect it from damage. – *adj* large: *a bumper crop.*

'**bumpkin** *n* a clumsy, awkward, country person, often used insultingly.

bumptious ['bumpshəs] *adj* self-important.

bun *n* a kind of cake; hair wound into a rounded mass.

bunch *n* a number of things tied together or growing together: – *pl* '**bunches**. – *v* to crowd together.

'**bundle** *n* a number of things loosely bound together. – *v* to tie in a bundle; to push roughly. *He bundled the children into the car.*

bung *n* the stopper of the hole in a barrel, bottle *etc.* – *v* to stop up with a bung. – *n* '**bung-hole**.

bungalow ['buŋgəlō] *n* a house of one storey, *usu* standing by itself.

bungle ['buŋgl] *v* to do a thing badly or clumsily. – Also *n.*

'**bunion** *n* a lump or swelling on the joint of the big toe.

bunk *n* a narrow bed *esp* in a ship's cabin. – *n* '**bunker** a large box for keeping coal; a sandpit on a golf course; an underground shelter. – *n* '**bunk-'bed** one of a pair of narrow beds one above the other.

'**bunkum** *n* nonsense.

'**bunny** *n* a child's name for a rabbit: – *pl* '**bunnies**.

'**bunting** *n* a thin cloth used for making flags; flags; a type of bird of the finch family.

buoy [boi] *n* a floating mark which acts as a guide or as a warning for ships; something which acts as a float (*eg* a lifebuoy). – *n* '**buoyancy** ability to float, lightness; ability to recover quickly. – *adj* '**buoyant** light; cheerful.

bur(r) *n* the prickly seedcase or head of certain plants.

'**burden** *n* a load; something difficult to bear (*eg* poverty, sorrow); (*old*) the chorus of a song. – *adj* '**burdensome**.

bureau ['būrō] *n* a writing table; an office: – *pls* **bureaux**, **bureaus** ['būrōz].

bureaucracy [bū'rokrəsi] *n* government by officials: – *pl* **bu'reaucracies**. – *n* '**bureaucrat** an administrative official. – *adj* **bureau'cratic**.

burgh ['burə] *n* (in Scotland) a borough.

'**burglar** *n* one who breaks into a house to steal. – *n* '**burglary**: – *pl* '**burglaries**.

burial *see* **bury**.

burlesque [bər'lesk] *n* a piece of writing, acting *etc*, making fun of somebody.

'**burly** *adj* broad and strong.

burn *v* to set fire to; to be on fire, or scorching; to injure by burning: – *pt* **burnt, burned**. – *n* a hurt or mark caused by fire; (in Scotland) a small stream. – *n* '**burner** the part of a lamp or gas-jet from which the flame rises.

'**burnish** *v* to polish. – Also *n.*

burnt *see* **burn**.

burrow ['burō] *n* a hole or passage in the ground dug by certain animals for shelter. – *v* to make a passage beneath the ground.

burst *v* to break suddenly (after increased pressure); to move, speak *etc* suddenly or violently. – Also *n.*

bury ['beri] *v* to put beneath the earth (*esp* a dead body); to cover, hide: – *pt* '**buried**. – *n* '**burial**.

bus *n* a (public) road vehicle for carrying passengers: – *pl* '**buses**. – *n* **bus stop** an official stopping place for buses.

busby ['buzbi] *n* a tall, fur hat worn by certain soldiers: – *pl* '**busbies**.

bush [boosh] *n* a growing thing between a plant and a tree in size; wild, un-farmed country (*esp* in Africa *etc*): – *pl* '**bushes**. – *adj* '**bushy** full of bushes; like a bush. – *ns* '**bush-baby** a type of small lemur; '**bush-ranger** in Australia, an outlaw living in the wilds; **bush telegraph** the quick passing-on of news from person to person.

business ['biznis] *n* one's work or job; trade. *Business is good just now*; something that concerns a person. *This is my business*: – *pl* '**businesses**.

busk *v* to play or sing in the street *etc* for money. – *n* '**busker**.

bust *n* a work of art (*usu* a sculpture) showing only the head and shoulders of the person; a woman's breasts.

'**bustard** *n* a kind of large, swift-running bird similar to a turkey.

bustle ['busl] *v* to busy oneself noisily. – *n* noisy activity, fuss; a stuffed pad once worn by ladies under the skirt of their dress.

busy ['bizi] *adj* having a lot to do: – *comp* '**busier**, *superl* '**busiest**. – *adv* '**busily**. – *n* '**busybody** one too concerned with others' affairs. – **busy oneself with** to occupy oneself with.

but *conj* showing a contrast between two ideas *etc*. *John was there but Peter was not*: *not brown but blue*; except that, without that. *It never rains but it pours.* – *prep* except, with the exception of. *No one but John had any money*: *the next road but one* (*ie* the second road). – *adv* only. *She's but a girl. We can but hope.* –

but for were it not for. *But for your help we would have been late.*

butcher ['boŏchər] *n* one whose work is to (kill animals for food and) sell meat. – *v* to kill cruelly. – *n* '**butchery** great or cruel slaughter.

'**butler** *n* the chief manservant in a household who looks after the wines *etc*, and who serves them.

butt *n* a large cask, a barrel; one of whom others make fun; the thick heavy end of a rifle *etc*; the end of a finished cigarette or cigar; a push with the head. – *v* to strike with the head. – **butt in** to interrupt or interfere.

'**butter** *n* a fatty food made by churning cream. – *v* to spread over with butter. – *ns* '**buttercup** a plant with a cup-like yellow flower; '**buttermilk** the milk that is left after butter has been made; '**butterscotch** a kind of hard toffee made with butter.

'**butterfly** *n* a kind of insect with large (*usu* coloured) wings: – *pl* '**butterflies**.

'**buttocks** *see* **bottom**.

'**button** *n* a knob of metal, plastic *etc* used to fasten clothing; a knob pressed to work an electrical device (*eg* a door-bell). – *v* to fasten by means of buttons. – *n* '**buttonhole** a hole through which a button is passed. – *v* to catch the attention of (someone) and force (him) to listen.

'**buttress** *n* a support (as on the outside of a wall): – *pl* '**buttresses**. – *v* to support, as by a buttress.

'**buxom** *adj* plump and pretty.

buy [bī] *v* to get by giving money for: – *pt* **bought** [böt]. – *n* '**buyer**.

buzz *v* to make a humming noise like bees; (of aircraft) to fly close to. – Also *n*. – *n* '**buzzer** a device which makes a buzzing noise as a signal.

'**buzzard** *n* a type of large bird of prey.

by [bī] *adv* near. *A crowd stood by, watching*; past. *A dog trotted by*; aside: *money put by for an emergency*. – *prep* next to, near: *standing by the door*; past: *passing by the house*; through, along, across. *We came by the main road*; showing person *etc* who does something: *written by him*; (of time) not after. *Do it by four o'clock*; during the (time of): *by day*: *by moonlight*; by means of: *by train*; to the extent of: *taller by a head*; used to express measurements, compass directions *etc*: *a room 6 metres by 4 metres*: *North by East*; in the quantity of. *We sell potatoes by the pound. They're paid by the week.* – *n* '**by-election** an election for parliament during a parliamentary session. – *adj* '**by-gone** past. – *npl* '**by-gones** old grievances or events that are or should be forgotten. – *ns* '**by-law**, '**bye-law** a local (not a national) law; '**by-pass** a road built round a town *etc* so that traffic need not pass through it; '**bypath**, '**byroad**, '**byway** a side road; '**by-product** something useful obtained during the manufacture of something else; '**bystander** one who stands watching something; '**byword** a common saying; someone or something well-known for some special quality.

bye [bī] *n* in cricket, a ball bowled past the wicket; a run made from this.

C

cab *n* a taxi; (*hist*) a hired carriage.

cabaret ['kabərā] *n* an entertainment with dancing, singing *etc*.

'**cabbage** *n* a type of vegetable, the leaves of which are eaten.

'**cabin** *n* a hut; a small room, *esp* in a ship.

'**cabinet** *n* a cupboard with shelves and doors; a similar container for storage *etc*; a wooden case with drawers; a number of government ministers who decide on policy. – *n* '**cabinet-maker** a maker of fine furniture.

'**cable** *n* a strong rope or thick metal line; a line of covered telegraph wires laid under the sea or underground; a telegram sent by such a line; an under-ground wire. – *v* to telegraph by cable. – *n* **cable television** the transmission of television programmes to people's houses by cable.

cacao [kə'kāō] *n* a tree from whose seeds cocoa and chocolate are made.

cache [kash] *n* a store or hiding place of treasure, arms *etc*; things hidden.

'**cackle** *n* the sound made by a hen or goose; a laugh which sounds like this.

ca'cophony *n* an unpleasant noise. – *adj* **ca'cophonous**.

'**cactus** *n* a type of prickly plant: – *pls* '**cactuses**, '**cacti**.

cad *n* a low, despicable person.

cadaverous [kə'davərəs] *adj* corpse-like; very pale and thin.

'**caddie** *n* a golfer's assistant (and adviser) who carries his clubs.

'**caddy** *n* a box in which tea is kept.

'**cādence** *n* the fall of the voice (as at the end of a sentence); a group of chords which ends a piece of music.

ca'**det** *n* a youth training to be an officer in the armed forces or to be a police officer; a schoolboy who takes military training.

cadge *v* to get by begging; to beg. – *n* '**cadger**.

café ['kafā] *n* a small restaurant where coffee, tea, snacks *etc* are served.

cafeteria [kafə'tēriə] *n* a self-service restaurant.

caffeine ['kafēn] *n* a drug found in coffee and tea *etc*.

'**caftan** *n* a kind of long-sleeved garment reaching to the ankles.

cage [kāj] *n* a box made of metal *etc* rods in which birds or animals are enclosed; in a mine, a lift used by the miners. – *v* to close up in a cage.

cagey, cagy ['kāji] *adj* unwilling to speak freely, wary. – *n* '**caginess**.

cairn *n* a heap of stones, *esp* one set up over a grave, or as a mark on a mountain-top; a breed of small terrier. – *n* '**cairn'gorm** a brown or yellow variety of quartz, used for brooches *etc*.

ca'**jole** *v* to coax by flattery. – *n* ca'**jolery** [kə'jōləri].

cake *n* a baked piece of dough *etc*, *usu* sweetened; anything pressed into a lump: *a cake of soap*. – *v* to form into a mass, harden. – **have one's cake and eat it** to enjoy both of two alternative things.

'**calamine** *n* a pink powder containing a zinc salt, used in lotion or ointment to soothe skin.

ca'**lamity** *n* a great disaster, a misfortune: – *pl* ca'**lamities**. – *adj* ca-'**lamitous**.

calcium ['kalsiəm] *n* an element, a metal which forms the chief part of lime.

'**calcūlate** *v* to count, work out by mathematics; to think out in an exact way. – *adjs* '**calculable** able to be counted or measured; '**calculating** thinking selfishly. – *ns* calcu'**lation** a mathematical reckoning, a sum; '**calculator** a machine which makes mathematical calculations; '**calculus** a mathematical system of calculation.

'**calendar** *n* a table or list showing the year divided into months, weeks and days.

calf [käf] *n* the young of cattle *etc*; its skin cured as leather; the back of the lower part of a person's leg:

– *pl* **calves**.

'**calibrate** *v* to mark the scale on (a measuring instrument); to check or adjust the scale of (a measuring instrument).

'**calibre**, (*US*) '**caliber** *n* measurement across the opening of a tube or gun; (of a person) quality of character, ability.

'**calico** *n* a kind of cotton cloth. – Also *adj*.

'**cal(l)ipers** *npl* an instrument like compasses, used for measuring thicknesses of tubes *etc*; (*sing*) a splint to support the leg, made of two metal rods.

call [köl] *v* to cry aloud; to name; to summon; to make a short visit; (*US*) to telephone. – Also *n*. – *n* '**calling** one's trade or job.

cal'**ligraphy** *n* (beautiful) handwriting. – *n* cal'**ligrapher**. – *adj* calli'**graphic**.

cal'**losity** *n* a hard thickening of the skin.

'**callous** *adj* cruel, hardhearted. – *n* a callosity. – *n* '**callousness**.

callow ['kalō] *adj* not mature, inexperienced.

'**callus** *n* a callosity: – *pl* '**calluses**.

calm [käm] *adj* still or quiet; not anxious or flustered. – *n* absence of wind; quietness, peacefulness. – *v* to make peaceful. – *n* '**calmness**.

calorie ['kaləri] *n* a measure of heat; a measure of the energy-giving value of food. – *n* calo'**rimeter** an instrument for measuring heat.

'**calumny** *n* a false accusation or lie about a person: – *pl* '**calumnies**.

calve [käv] *v* to give birth to a calf.

ca'**lypso** *n* a West Indian folksong made up as the singer goes along: – *pl* ca'**lypsos**.

'**cālyx** *n* the outer covering or cup of a flower: – *pls* **calyces** ['kālisēz], '**calyxes**.

'**camber** *n* a slight curve or bulge on a road *etc*, making the middle higher than the sides.

came *see* **come**.

'**camel** *n* a type of animal of Asia and Africa with a humped back, used for both carrying and riding.

camelopard ['kamiləpärd] *n* the giraffe.

cameo ['kamiō] *n* a gem or other stone on which a carved figure or design stands out: – *pl* '**cameos**.

'**camera** *n* an instrument for taking photographs. – **in camera** in private.

'**camomile** *n* a type of plant, or its dried flowers, used in medicine.

camouflage ['kaməfläzh] *n* the disguising of the appearance of (something) so that it is not easily seen against its background; such an appearance occurring naturally (in animals *etc*), protective colouring. – Also *v*.

camp *n* a group of tents, huts *etc* in which people (holidaymakers, explorers *etc*) live for a short time; fixed military quarters or settlement. – *v* to pitch tents; to set up a temporary home. – *ns* **camp bed** a small portable folding bed; **'campsite** (official) place for pitching tents.

campaign [kam'pān] *n* organized action in support of a cause or movement; a war or part of a war. – *v* to organize support; to serve in a military campaign.

campa'nology *n* the study or art of bell-ringing.

'campus *n* the grounds of a university, college *etc*: – *pl* **'campuses**.

can[1] *v usu* used with another verb to express the ability to do something. *He can play the guitar*; used to express permission given. *You can go swimming tomorrow*: – *pt* **could** [kŏŏd].

can[2] *n* a tin container for liquids, preserved food *etc*. – *v* to put (food) into a closed tin to keep it from going bad. – *n* **'cannery** a place where food is canned.

ca'nal *n* a waterway for boats, made by man.

ca'nāry *n* a type of yellow-feathered songbird kept as a pet: – *pl* **ca'naries**.

ca'nasta *n* a kind of card-game.

'cancan *n* a high-kicking dance.

'cancel *v* to put off permanently, call off: *cancel one's holiday plans*; to cross out by crossing with lines. – **cancel out** to make ineffective by balancing each other. *His sins and good deeds cancel one another out.*

'cancer *n* a disease which eats away part of the body. – *adj* **'cancerous**.

'candid *adj* saying just what one thinks, frank. – *n* **candour** ['kandər].

'candidate *n* one who enters for an examination or competition for a job, prize *etc*. – *n* **'candidature**.

candied *see* **candy**.

'candle *n* a stick of wax, containing a wick, used for giving light. – *ns* **'candle-power** the amount of light given by one candle; **'candlestick** a holder for a candle; **'candlewick** a cotton tufted material, used for bedspreads *etc*.

candour *see* **candid**.

'candy *n* sugar crystallized by boiling; (*US*) a sweet. – *v* to preserve in sugar, to coat with sugar. – *adj* **'candied**.

cane *n* the stem of certain kinds of plant (such as bamboo and sugar cane); a walking stick. – *v* to beat with a cane. – *n* **'caning** a thrashing with a cane. – **cane sugar** sugar got from the sugar cane.

'cānine *adj* of dogs. – *n* **canine (tooth)** any of the four sharp-pointed teeth, one on each side of the upper and lower jaw.

'canister *n* a box or case, *usu* of tin, for holding tea *etc*.

'canker *n* a spreading sore; a disease in trees, plants *etc*.

'cannabis *n* a preparation made from hemp, used as a drug.

'cannibal *n* a person who eats human flesh; an animal that eats its own kind. – *n* **'cannibalism**.

'cannon *n* a large, *usu* mounted gun. – *v* to run into, collide with. – *n* **'cannonball** a solid metal ball to be shot from a cannon.

'cannot *v usu* used with another verb to express the inability to do something. *I cannot understand this*; used to refuse permission. *I've told him he cannot go today*. – **cannot but** can only, cannot avoid (doing something). *We cannot but wait.*

'canny *adj* wise, shrewd, cautious. – *n* **'canniness**.

canoe [kə'nōō] *n* a light narrow boat driven by paddles.

'canon *n* a law or rule; a standard to judge by; a clergyman connected with a cathedral; a list of saints. – *v* **'canonize** to put someone on the list of saints.

cañon *see* **canyon**.

'canopy *n* a covering over a throne, bed, pulpit *etc*: – *pl* **'canopies**.

cant *n* words understood by people in a particular occupation *etc* only; talk which is not sincere; a slope; a tilted position. – *v* to tilt something from a level position.

can't short for **cannot**.

can'tankerous *adj* bad-tempered, quarrelsome.

can'tata *n* a short piece of music for a choir of singers.

can'teen *n* a place where drink and food may be bought and eaten (*usu* in some place of work); a water-flask; a case containing cutlery.

'canter *v* to move at an easy gallop. – Also *n*.

'cantilēver *n* a large projecting bracket used in building for holding up heavy parts like balconies and stairs. – *n* **cantilever bridge** a bridge made of a row of upright piers with cantilevers extending to meet one another.

'**canton** *n* one of the Swiss federal states.

'**canvas** *n* a coarse, strong cloth used for sails, tents *etc* and for painting on: – *pl* '**canvases**.

'**canvass** *v* to go round asking for votes, money *etc*.

canyon, cañon ['kanyɔn] *n* a deep, steep-sided valley containing a river or stream.

cap *n* a soft hat *usu* with a peak; a cover or top (as of a bottle, pen *etc*). – *v* to put a cap on; to give a university degree to; to choose (a player) for a national sports team (*esp* football or cricket); to do better than, improve on. *He capped my story with a better one*: – *pt* **capped**.

'**cāpable** *adj* able to cope with difficulties without help; (often with **of**) able or likely (to): *capable of doing great things*. – *n* **capa'bility**: – *pl* **capa'bilities**.

ca'pācious *adj* roomy, wide.

ca'pacitor *n* an apparatus for collecting and storing electricity.

ca'pacity *n* power of understanding; ability to do a thing; the amount that something can hold; position: *in his capacity as leader*: – *pl* **ca'pacities**. – **to capacity** to the greatest extent possible: *filled to capacity*: *working to capacity*.

cape *n* a covering for the shoulders; a point of land running into the sea.

'**cāper** *v* to leap, dance about. – *n* a leap; (*coll*) a prank or adventure; the flower-bud of a shrub which, when pickled, is used in sauces.

capercaillie,   **capercailzie** [kapər'kāl(y)i] *n* a kind of large grouse.

ca'pillary *adj* very fine, like a hair. – *n* a very fine tube; a tiny blood vessel: – *pl* **ca'pillaries**.

'**capital** *adj* chief, most important; involving death; excellent. – *n* the chief city (of a country); a large letter (as that which begins a sentence); money for carrying on a business; money invested, accumulated wealth. – *ns* '**capitalism** a system in which the country's wealth is owned by individuals, not by the State; '**capitalist** one who supports or practises capitalism. – *v* '**capitalize** to write in capitals; to turn to one's advantage. – *n* **capital punishment** punishment by death. – **make capital out of** to turn to one's advantage.

ca'pitūlate *v* to give in (*eg* to an enemy). – *n* **ca'pitu'lation**.

'**cāpon** *n* a young fattened cock.

caprice [kə'prēs] *n* a sudden, impulsive change of mind or mood. – *adj* **capricious** [kə'prishəs] full of caprice,

apt to change one's mind often.

cap'size *v* to upset, to overturn.

'**capstan** *n* on a ship or quay, a machine turned by spokes or by a steam engine, used for winding or hauling.

'**capsule** *n* the case containing the seeds of a plant; a small gelatine case for powdered medicine; the part of a space rocket which contains the crew.

'**captain** *n* the commander of a company of soldiers, a ship or an aircraft; the leader of a team, club *etc*. – *v* to lead. – *n* '**captaincy** the rank of a captain.

'**caption** *n* a heading (for a newspaper article, photograph *etc*).

'**captious** *adj* ready to find fault.

'**captivate** *v* to charm, fascinate.

'**captive** *n* a prisoner. – *adj* taken or kept as a prisoner; not able to get away: *a captive audience*. – *ns* **cap'tivity** the state of being a prisoner; '**captor** one who takes a prisoner. – *v* '**capture** to take by force; to get hold of, seize: *capture the imagination*. – *n* the act of capturing; the thing captured.

car *n* a motor-car; (*esp US*) a carriage of a train. – *n* **car park** a place where motor-cars *etc* may be left for a time.

carafe [kə'raf] *n* a bottle for serving wine, water *etc*.

'**caramel** *n* sugar melted and browned; a kind of sweet, made of sugar and butter.

'**carat** *n* a measure of the purity of gold; a measure of the weight of gems.

'**caravan** *n* a house on wheels drawn originally by horse, now *usu* by car; a number of travellers *etc* crossing the desert together. – *n* **caravanserai** [karə'vansəri] an inn where desert caravans stop.

'**caraway** *n* a type of plant whose spicy seeds are used to flavour cakes *etc*.

'**carbine** *n* a short light musket.

'**carbo'hȳdrate** *n* one of a group of substances containing carbon, hydrogen and oxygen, such as sugar, starch *etc*.

car'bolic acid *n* an acid used to kill germs.

'**carbon** *n* an element of which charcoal is one form. – *adjs* **car'bonic** (made) of carbon;   **carboniferous** [kärbə'nifərəs] producing or containing coal or carbon. – *ns* **carbon copy** a copy of a piece of typing *etc* made by using carbon paper; an exact copy; **carbon dioxide** a gas present in the air and breathed out by men and animals; **carbon monoxide** a poisonous gas with no smell; **carbon paper** a paper coated with black ink for making copies in typing *etc*.

'**carbuncle** *n* a type of fiery-red precious stone; an inflamed swelling under the skin.

'**carbūrettor**, '**carbūretter**, (*US*) '**car-būretor** *n* the part of a motor-car engine which changes the petrol into vapour.

carcass, carcase ['kärkɔs] *n* the dead body (of an animal).

card *n* (a piece of) pasteboard or very thick paper; a tool for combing wool *etc*; (*pl*) any of the many types of games played with a pack of special cards. – *v* to comb wool *etc*. – *n* '**cardboard** stiff pasteboard.

'**cardiac** *adj* of the heart: *cardiac failure*.

'**cardigan** *n* a knitted woollen jacket.

'**cardinal** *adj* principal, important. – *n* a person of high rank in the Roman Catholic Church. – *npl* **cardinal numbers** numbers telling how many (1, 2, 3 *etc*).

care *n* close attention; worry, anxiety; protection, keeping: *in my care*. – *v* to be concerned or worried; (with **for**) to look after; to feel affection or liking (for). – *adjs* '**carefree** having no worries; '**careful** attentive, taking care; '**careless** paying little attention, not taking care. – *n* '**carelessness**. – *n* '**caretaker** one who looks after a building. – *adj* in temporary charge: *a caretaker government*. – *adj* '**careworn** looking very worried, worn out by anxiety. – **care of, c/o** at the house of.

ca'reer *n* one's life's work, trade, profession; course, progress through life, headlong rush. – *v* to move or run rapidly and wildly.

ca'ress *v* to touch gently and lovingly. – Also *n*: – *pl* **ca'resses**.

'**cargo** *n* a ship's load: – *pl* '**cargoes**.

caribou ['karibōo] *n* the N. American reindeer.

'**caricature** *n* a picture of someone which exaggerates certain of their features. – *v* to draw a caricature of. – *n* '**caricaturist**.

caries ['kāriĕz] *n* rottenness, *esp* of the teeth. – *adj* '**carious**.

'**carillon** *n* a set of bells on which tunes can be played; the tune played on these.

'**carmine** *adj, n* (of) a bright red colour.

'**carnage** *n* slaughter, killing.

car'nātion *n* a type of garden flower, often pink, red or white.

'**carnival** *n* a celebration with merriment, feasting *etc*.

'**carnivore** *n* a flesh-eating animal: – *pl* **car'nivora**. – *adj* **car'nivorous**.

'**carol** *n* a song of joy or praise (*esp* one sung at Christmas).

carouse [kɔ'rowz] *v* to take part in a drinking bout.

carp *n* a freshwater fish found in ponds. – *v* to find fault with small errors, complain about nothing.

'**carpenter** *n* a worker in wood, *esp* as used in buildings *etc*. – *n* '**carpentry** the trade of a carpenter.

'**carpet** *n* the woven covering of floors, stairs *etc*. – *v* to cover with a carpet.

carriage ['karij] *n* the act or cost of carrying; a vehicle for carrying people; way of walking. *She has a dignified carriage*.

'**carrion** *n* rotting animal flesh.

'**carrot** *n* a type of vegetable whose long orange-coloured root is eaten.

'**carry** *v* to pick up and take to another place; to contain and take to a destination: *cables carrying electricity*; to bear, have as a mark: *carry a scar*; (of a voice *etc*) to be able to be heard at a distance; to win, succeed: *carry the day*; to keep for sale: *carry cigarettes*: – *pt* '**carried**. – *n* '**carrier** one who carries goods; a machine or container for carrying; one who passes on a disease. – *n* **carrier pigeon** a pigeon which carries letters. – **carried away** overcome by one's feelings; **carry on** to continue (doing); **carry out** to bring to a successful finish.

cart *n* a vehicle (drawn by a horse) used on farms; a small wheeled vehicle pushed by hand. – *v* to carry (in a cart); to drag (off). – *n* '**carter** one who drives a cart. – *ns* '**cart-horse** a large, heavy horse, used for working; '**cartwheel** the wheel of a cart; a sideways somersault with hands touching the ground; '**cartwright** a maker of carts.

'**cartilage** *n* gristle, a strong elastic material in the bodies of men and animals.

car'tography *n* the science of map-making.

'**carton** *n* a container made of cardboard, plastic *etc*.

car'toon *n* a comic drawing with a comic caption; a (*usu* amusing) film made of a series of drawings of animals *etc* which gives an impression of their movement; a large drawing on paper, later to be copied in its final form. – *n* **car'toonist**.

'**cartridge** *n* a case holding the powder and bullet fired by a gun; a spool of film or tape enclosed in a case; a tube of ink for loading a pen; the part of a record-player which holds the stylus.

carve *v* to make or shape by cutting; to cut up (meat) into slices.

cas'cade *n* a waterfall. – *v* to fall like or in a waterfall.

case *n* a container or outer covering; that which happens, an occurrence; statement of facts, argument; state of affairs, what is true; a trial in a law-court: *a murder case.*

'casement *n* a window-frame; a window that swings on hinges.

cash *n* money in the form of coins and notes. – *v* to turn into, or change for, money. – *n* **cashier** [ka'shēr] one who looks after the receiving and paying of money. – *v* to dismiss (*esp* from the army or navy) in disgrace. – *n* **cash register** a machine for holding money that records the amount put in. – **cash in on** to profit from (in terms of money or advantage).

cashew ['kashoo] *n* a type of kidney-shaped nut, or the large tropical tree that bears it.

'cashmere *n* fine soft goats' wool.

casino [kə'sēnō] *n* a building in which gambling takes place: – *pl* **ca'sinos.**

cask *n* a barrel (*usu* containing wine *etc*).

'casket *n* a small box (for holding jewels *etc*); (*US*) a coffin.

cas'sava *n* a kind of tropical plant from whose roots tapioca is obtained.

'casserole *n* a covered dish in which food can be cooked and served; the food cooked in it.

cas'sette *n* a holder for film, magnetic tape for recording sound *etc*; the magnetic tape itself.

'cassock *n* a long robe worn by priests.

cassowary ['kasəwəri] *n* a type of large, flightless bird of Australia and New Guinea.

cast *v* to throw or fling (objects, light *etc*); to throw off, drop, shed; to shape (*esp* metal) in a mould; to choose (actors *etc*) for a play or film; to give a part to (an actor *etc*): – *pt* **cast.** – *n* something shaped in a mould; the actors in a play; a small heap of earth thrown up by a worm; a type: *cast of mind*; a squint (in the eye). – *ns* **'castaway** a deserted or shipwrecked person; **cast iron** unpurified iron melted and moulded into shape. – *adjs* **cast down** depressed; **'cast-off** used by someone else, second-hand.

casta'nets *npl* hollow shells of ivory or hard wood, which are clicked together to accompany a dance.

caste [käst] *n* a class or rank of people (*esp* in India).

castellated *see* **castle.**

caster *see* **castor.**

'castigate *v* to scold; to punish. – *n* **casti'gation.**

castle ['käsl] *n* a fortified house or fortress. – *adj* **castellated** ['kastəlātid] having walls, towers *etc* like those of a castle.

'castor *n* a small wheel (as on the legs of furniture). – Also **'caster.** – *ns* **'castor-'oil** an oil made from a kind of palm, used as a medicine; **castor sugar, caster sugar** very fine granulated sugar.

cas'trate *v* to remove the testicles (of a male animal) and deprive of the ability to reproduce.

casual ['kazhōōəl] *adj* happening by chance; not regular, temporary: *casual labour*; (of clothes) informal. *She wears casual clothes at the weekend*; not careful, unconcerned: *a casual attitude to work*. – *n* **'casualty** a person who is killed or wounded. – *n* **casualty department** a hospital department for treating accidental injuries *etc*.

cat *n* a sharp-clawed furry animal kept as a pet; one of the cat family which includes, lions, tigers *etc*. – *ns* **'cat-burglar** a burglar who breaks into houses by climbing walls *etc*; **'catgut** cord made from the stomachs of sheep, used as strings for violins *etc*; **'cat-o'-'nine-tails** a whip with nine tails or lashes; **cat's cradle** a children's game with string; **'cat's-eye®** a small mirror fixed in the surface of a road to reflect light and so guide drivers at night.

cataclysm ['katəklizəm] *n* a great flood of water; a violent change.

catacomb ['katəkoōm] *n* an underground burial place.

catalogue ['katəlog] *n* a list of names, books, objects for sale *etc* set out in some order. – *v* to list in order.

'catalyst *n* any substance which helps or prevents a chemical reaction without itself changing; anything that brings about a change.

catama'ran *n* a boat with two parallel hulls.

'catapult *n* a small forked stick with a length of elastic fixed to the two prongs, used for firing small stones *etc*; (*hist*) a weapon for throwing heavy stones in warfare.

'cataract *n* a waterfall; a disease of the outer eye.

catarrh [kə'tär] *n* inflammation of the lining of the nose and throat causing a discharge; the discharge caused.

catastrophe [kə'tastrəfi] *n* a sudden

disaster. – *adj* **catas'trophic**.

catch *v* to take hold of, capture; to take (a disease): *catch a cold*; to be in time for: *catch the train*; to surprise (in an act): *catch him stealing*: – *pt* **caught** [köt]. – *n* a haul (of fish); something one is lucky to have got or won; a hidden flaw or disadvantage; something which fastens: *a window-catch*. – *adjs* **'catching** infectious, liable to be caught; **'catchy** (of a tune) not easily forgotten. – *ns* **catchment area** an area from which a river or a reservoir draws its water supply; an area from which the pupils in a school are drawn; **'catch-phrase, 'catchword** phrase or word which is popular for a while. – **catch on** to become popular; **catch up on** to draw level with, overtake; to get up-to-date with (work *etc*).

catechize ['katikīz] *v* to ask many questions. – *n* **catechism** ['katikizəm] a book (*esp* a religious one) which teaches by asking questions and giving the answers; a series of searching questions.

category ['katəgəri] *n* a class or division of things (or people) of the same kind: – *pl* **'categories**. – *adj* **cate'gorical** allowing of no doubt or argument. – *adv* **cate'gorically**.

'cāter *v* to provide food; to supply what is required: *cater for all tastes*. – *ns* **'caterer; 'catering**.

'caterpillar *n* the larva of an insect that feeds upon the leaves of plants. – *adj* moving on endless metal belts: *a caterpillar tractor*.

'caterwaul *v* to howl or yell like a cat. – *n* **'caterwauling**.

catgut *see* cat.

ca'thēdral *n* the church of a bishop; the chief church in the district ruled by a bishop.

catherine-wheel ['kathərinwēl] *n* a firework which turns like a wheel when burning.

'cathode ray tube *n* a device in which a narrow beam of electrons strikes against a screen, as in a television set.

'catholic *adj* wide, comprehensive: *catholic taste in books*; **'Catholic** (short for **Roman Catholic**) of the Roman Catholic Church.

'catkin *n* a tuft or spike of small flowers on certain trees, *esp* the willow and hazel.

'cattle *npl* animals that eat grass, *esp* oxen, bulls and cows.

caught *see* catch.

'cauldron *n* a large pan.

cauliflower ['koliflowər] *n* a kind of cabbage, of which one eats the white flower-head.

cause [köz] *n* that which makes something happen; a reason (for action): *cause for complaint*; an aim for which a group or person works: *the cause of peace*. – *v* to make happen.

causeway ['közwā] *n* a raised road over wet ground or shallow water.

'caustic *adj* burning, corroding; bitter, severe: *caustic wit*.

'cauterize *v* to burn away flesh with a caustic substance or a hot iron in order to make a sore heal cleanly.

'caution *n* a warning; carefulness (owing to presence of some danger). – *v* to warn. – *adjs* **'cautionary** giving a warning; **'cautious** careful, showing caution.

caval'cade *n* a procession on horseback, in cars *etc*.

cavalier [kavə'lēr] *n* (*hist*) a supporter of the king in the Civil War of the 17th century. – *adj* offhand: *in a cavalier fashion*.

'cavalry *n* horse soldiers.

cave *n* a hollow place in the earth or in rock. – *n* **'caveman** prehistoric man who lived in caves. – **cave in** (to cause) to fall or collapse inwards.

'cavern *n* a deep hollow place in the earth. – *adj* **'cavernous** huge and hollow; full of caverns.

caviare, caviar ['kaviär] *n* the pickled eggs of the sturgeon.

'cavil *v* to make objections over small, unimportant details: – *pt* **'cavilled**.

'cavity *n* hollow place, a hole: – *pl* **'cavities**.

ca'vort *v* to dance or leap around.

caw *v* to call like a crow. – Also *n*.

cayenne [kā'en] *n* a type of very hot red pepper.

'cayman *n* any of various kinds of alligator, *esp* those of S. America.

cease *v* to come or bring to an end. – *adj* **'ceaseless** without stopping.

'cēdar *n* a type of large evergreen tree with a hard sweet-smelling wood.

cede *v* to yield or give up (to another).

ceiling ['sēliŋ] *n* the inner roof of a room; the upper limit.

'celandine *n* a type of small yellow wild flower.

celebrate ['seləbrāt] *v* to feast and make merry in honour of a marriage, birthday or other happy event. – *adj* **'celebrated** famous. – *ns* **cele'bration; ce'lebrity** a famous person; fame: – *pl* **ce'lebrities**.

celery ['seləri] *n* a type of vegetable the stalks of which are eaten.

ce'lestial *adj* of the sky. *Stars are celestial bodies*; heavenly.

'celibacy *n* the state of not being married. – *adj* **'celibate**.

cell *n* a small room in a prison, monastery *etc*; the smallest, fundamental part of living things; the part of an electric battery containing electrodes. – *adj* **'cellular** made of or having cells or small hollow spaces.

'cellar *n* an underground room, *esp* one for storing coal, wine *etc*.

cello ['chelō] *n* (short for **violoncello**) a type of large musical, stringed instrument similar in shape to a violin. – *n* **'cellist** one who plays the cello.

'cellophaneⓇ *n* a kind of transparent wrapping material.

cellular *see* **cell**.

'celluloid *n* a very hard elastic substance used for making film *etc*.

'cellulose *n* a substance found in plants and wood used to make paper, textiles *etc*.

ce'ment *n* the mixture of clay and lime used to stick bricks together in buildings; anything that makes two things stick together. – *v* to put together with cement; to join firmly.

cemetery ['semətri] *n* a place where the dead are buried: – *pl* **'cemeteries**.

'cenotaph *n* a monument to a person or persons buried elsewhere.

'censor *n* one whose job is to remove from books, films *etc* anything which might be found offensive. – *adj* **censorious** [sen'söriəs] fault-finding.

censure ['senshər] *n* blame, expression of disapproval. – *v* to blame, criticize.

'census *n* a counting of the people in a country: – *pl* **'censuses**.

cent *n* a coin which is the hundredth part of a larger coin (*eg* of a dollar).

'centaur *n* (*myth*) a monster, half man and half horse.

cen'tenary *n* a hundredth birthday; the hundredth year since an event took place: – *pl* **cen'tenaries**. – *n* **cente'nārian** a person a hundred or more years old. – *adj* **centennial** [sən'teniəl] having lasted a hundred years; happening every hundred years.

'centigrade *adj* having a hundred degrees; as measured on a centigrade thermometer: *5 degrees centigrade*. – **centigrade thermometer** a thermometer which shows the temperature at which water freezes as 0 degrees, and that at which it boils as 100 degrees.

'centigramme *n* a hundredth part of a gramme.

centilitre ['sentilētər] *n* a hundredth part of a litre.

'centimētre *n* a hundredth part of a metre.

'centipede *n* a small crawling creature with many legs.

'centre, (US) **'center** *n* the middle point or part; a place built or used for some special activity or service: *sports centre*. – *adj* **'central** belonging to the centre; chief. – *v* **'centralize** to group in a single place: to bring (government authority) under one central control. – *n* **central heating** heating of a building by water, steam or air from a central point.

cen'trifugal *adj* moving away from the centre.

centripetal [sen'tripitl] *adj* moving towards the centre.

cen'tūrion *n* (*hist*) a commander of 100 Roman soldiers.

century ['senchŏŏri] *n* a hundred years; a hundred in number (such as runs in cricket): – *pl* **'centuries**.

ce'ramic *adj* of (the making of) pottery. – *n* something made of pottery; (*pl*) the art of pottery.

cereal ['sēriəl] *n* grain used as food; a (breakfast) food prepared from grain.

cerebral ['serəbrəl] *adj* of the brain.

ceremony ['serəməni] *n* the formal acts and solemn show or display that goes with an important event: *the marriage ceremony*: – *pl* **'ceremonies**. – *n* **cere'mōnial** *adj* with or of ceremony. – *adj* **cere'monious** full of ceremony.

cerise [sə'rēs] *adj, n* (of) the colour of cherries, red.

'certain *adj* sure; not to be doubted; fixed, settled; some or one, not definitely named: *certain places*: *a certain shop*. – *adv* **'certainly**. – *n* **'certainty**.

cer'tificate *n* a written or printed statement that something has happened or been done: *birth certificate*. – *v* **'certify** to put down in writing as an official promise, statement *etc*: – *pt* **'certified**.

ces'sation *n* a ceasing or stopping.

'cesspool *n* a pool or tank in which liquid waste or sewage is collected.

chafe *v* to make hot or sore by rubbing; to wear away by rubbing; to become annoyed.

chaff *n* the husks of corn after threshing; anything of no great value; good-natured teasing. – *v* to tease jokingly.

'chaffinch *n* a type of small bird: – *pl* **'chaffinches**.

chagrin ['shagrin] *n* annoyance.

chain *n* a number of links or rings (*esp* of

metal) passing through one another; (*pl*) these used to tie prisoners' limbs, fetters; a number of connected things: *a mountain chain*; a group of things owned by one person or firm: *a chain of shops*; a number of atoms of an element joined together; a measure of distance (22 yards, 20·1 metres). – *v* to fasten or imprison with a chain. – *ns* **chain reaction** a (chemical) process in which each reaction in turn causes a similar reaction; **'chain-store** one of several shops under the same ownership.

chair *n* a seat for one person with a back to it; an official position (as of the person in charge of a meeting or of a university professor). – *ns* **'chairlift** a row of chairs on an endless cable for carrying people up mountains *etc*; **'chairman** one who presides at or is in charge of a meeting.

chalcedony [kal'sedəni] *n* a type of precious or semi-precious stone.

chalet ['shalā] *n* a small wooden house often used by holidaymakers; a summer hut used by Swiss herdsmen in the Alps.

chalice ['chalis] *n* a cup for wine, *esp* that used in church services.

chalk [chök] *n* a type of limestone; a similar substance used for writing, drawing. – *v* to mark with chalk. – *adj* **'chalky** of chalk; white, pale.

'challenge *v* to question another's right to do a thing *etc*; to ask (someone) to take part in a contest of some kind *eg* to settle a quarrel. – *n* a call to a contest of any kind, *esp* to a duel. – *n* **'challenger**. – *adj* **'challenging** (of a problem *etc*) interesting but difficult.

'chamber *n* a room; the place where an assembly (such as parliament) meets, or where legal cases are heard by a judge; an enclosed space or cavity; the part of a gun that holds the cartridges. – *n* **chamber music** music for a small group of players, suitable for performance in a room rather than in a large hall.

'chamberlain *n* one appointed by a king or local authority to carry out certain duties.

chameleon [kə'mēliən] *n* a type of small lizard able to change its colour to match its surroundings.

chamois ['shamwä] *n* a type of goat-like deer living in mountainous country; (also **shammy** ['shami]) a soft kind of leather made from its skin.

champ *v* to chew noisily. – **champing at the bit** impatient to act.

champagne [sham'pān] *n* a type of white sparkling wine.

'champion *n* a person, animal *etc* who has beaten all others in a competition; one who strongly supports a cause (such as freedom of speech *etc*). – *v* to support the cause of (a person, freedom *etc*). – *n* **'championship** the act of championing; a contest to find a champion; the title of champion.

chance *n* a risk, possibility; something unexpected, not planned; an opportunity. – *v* to risk; to happen by accident. – *adj* happening by accident. – *adj* **'chancy** risky. – **by chance** not arranged, unexpectedly; **chance upon** to meet or find unexpectedly.

'chancel *n* the part of a church near the altar.

'chancellor *n* a high government minister (*eg Chancellor of the Exchequer* who is in charge of government spending, *Lord Chancellor* the head of the English legal system); the head of a university.

chancery ['chansəri] *n* (in England) the Lord Chancellor's court.

chandelier [shandə'lēr] *n* a fixture hanging from the ceiling with branches for holding lights.

change [chānj] *v* to make or become different; to give up or leave one thing for another (*eg* one's job, house); to put on different clothes; to give or get (money of one kind) in exchange for (money of another kind). – *n* the act of making or becoming something different; another set of clothing; money in the form of coins; money given back by a shopkeeper when a buyer gives more than the price of an article. – *adj* **'changeable** likely to change; often changing. – *n* **'changeling** a child secretly taken or left in place of another.

'channel *n* the bed of a stream; a passage for ships; a narrow sea; a groove; a gutter; a band of frequencies for radio or television signals. – *v* to direct into a particular course.

chant *v* to sing; to recite in a singing manner. – Also *n*.

chanty *see* **shanty**.

chaos ['kāos] *n* disorder, confusion. – *adj* **cha'otic**.

chap *n* (*coll*) a man. – *adj* **chapped** (of skin) cracked by cold or wet weather.

'chapel *n* a small part of a larger church; a small church for (private) worship.

chaperone ['shapərōn] *n* an older lady who attends a younger one when she goes out in public. – *v* to act as a chaperone to.

chaplain ['chaplin] *n* a clergyman with the army, navy, or air force or on a ship *etc*.

chapter *n* a division of a book; (a meeting of) the clergy of a cathedral. – **chapter of accidents** a series of accidents.

char *v* to burn until black; to do odd jobs of housework, cleaning *etc*: – *pt* **charred**. – *n* **charwoman** a woman hired to do housework for other people.

charabanc ['sharəbaŋ] *n* a long motor-coach with rows of seats.

character ['karəktər] *n* the nature and qualities of a person *etc*; the good points and bad points which make up a person's nature; self-control, firmness; a person noted for odd or strange ways; reputation; a person in a play, story, film *etc*. – *n* **characte'ristic** a point or feature which is typical of a person *etc* and easily noticed. – *adj* typical. – *v* **characterize** to be typical of; to describe (as).

charade [shə'räd] *n* a word-guessing game, in which the syllables of a word and then the whole word are acted.

charcoal *n* wood burnt black.

charge [chärj] *v* to accuse. *He was charged with murder*; to ask (a price); to attack; to load (a gun *etc*); to fill (with); to lay a task upon a person. – *n* blame, accusation (for a crime); price, fee; an attack; the gunpowder in a shell or bullet; care. *The money was given into my charge*; someone looked after by another person. – *n* **charger** a horse used in battle. – **in charge** in command or control; **take charge of** to take command of.

chariot *n* (*hist*) (two-wheeled) carriage used in battle. – *n* **chario'teer** chariot-driver.

charity *n* giving of money to the poor *etc*; an organization which collects money and gives it to those in need; love for all people; kindness: – *pl* **charities**. – *adj* **charitable** giving to the poor; kindly; of a charity.

charlatan ['shärlətən] *n* one who claims greater powers, abilities *etc* than he really has.

charm *n* something thought to have magical powers; a spell; power to attract (by appearance, manner *etc*). – *v* to please greatly, delight; to put under a spell.

charnel-house *n* a place where the bones of the dead are put.

chart *n* a table or diagram giving some form of information (*eg* a temperature chart); a map, *esp* one of seas or lakes, showing rocks, islands, currents, depth *etc*; a rough map. – *v* to make a chart of; to plan.

charter *n* a written paper showing the granting of rights, favours, lands *etc*, *esp* by a king or a government. – *v* to hire (a boat, aeroplane *etc*). – *adj* **chartered** having a charter; (of an aeroplane *etc*) hired for a special purpose.

charwoman *see* **char**.

chary *adj* cautious, careful (of).

chase *v* to run after, pursue; to hunt. – *n* a pursuit; a hunt.

chasm ['kazəm] *n* a deep hole or drop between high rocks *etc*; a wide difference.

chassis ['shasi] *n* the frame, wheels, and machinery of a motor-car; an aeroplane's landing carriage: – *pl* **chassis** ['shasiz].

chaste *adj* pure, virtuous. – *n* **chastity** ['chastəti].

chasten ['chāsn] *v* to make humble; to punish, *usu* by scolding. – *adj* **chastened**.

chastise *v* to punish, *usu* by whipping or beating. – *n* **chastisement** ['chastizmənt].

chat *v* to talk in an easy, friendly way (about unimportant things): – *pt* **chatted**. – Also *n*. – *adj* **chatty** willing to talk, talkative.

chateau ['shatō] *n* a French castle or country house: – *pl* **chateaux** ['shatōz].

chattels *npl* movable possessions. – **goods and chattels** personal possessions.

chatter *v* to talk idly, rapidly or indiscreetly; (of teeth) to rattle together through cold *etc*. – Also *n*. – *n* **chatterbox** one who chatters a great deal.

chauffeur ['shōfər] *n* a person employed to drive a motor-car.

cheap *adj* low in price, inexpensive; of little value, worthless. – *v* **cheapen** to make cheap.

cheat *v* to deceive; to act dishonestly to gain an advantage. – *n* one who cheats; a dishonest trick.

check *v* to bring to a stop; to hinder or hold back; to see if something (*eg* a sum) is correct or accurate; to see if something (*eg* a machine) is in good condition or working properly. – *n* a sudden stop; something that hinders; a test of the correctness or accuracy of; a square (*eg* on a draughtboard); (a fabric with) a pattern of squares. – *adj* **checked**. – *ns* **checkmate** in chess, a position from which the king cannot escape; '**checkout** a place where payment is made in a supermarket. – **check in, check out** to record one's arrival at or departure from (*eg* work, an airport *etc*).

checkers *see* **chequers**.

cheek *n* the side of the face below the eye; insolence, disrespectful speech or behaviour. – *adj* '**cheeky** impudent, insolent. – *n* '**cheekiness**.

cheep *v* to make a faint sound like a small bird. – Also *n*.

cheer *n* a shout of approval or welcome. – *v* to shout approval; to encourage, urge on; to comfort, gladden. – *adjs* '**cheerful** happy, in good spirits; '**cheerless** sad, gloomy; '**cheery** lively and merry. – **cheer up** to make or become less gloomy.

'**cheeri'o** *interj* goodbye!

cheese [chēz] *n* a solid food made from milk. – *adj* '**cheeseparing** mean.

'**cheetah** *n* a type of swift-running animal like the leopard.

chef [shef] *n* a male head cook.

chemistry ['kemistri] *n* the study of the elements and the ways they combine or react with each other. – *adj* '**chemical** of chemistry or reactions between elements *etc*. – *n* a substance which is formed by or used in a chemical process. – *n* '**chemist** one who studies chemistry; one who makes up and sells medicines.

cheque, (*US*) **check** [chek] *n* a written order to a banker telling him to pay money from one's bank account to another person. – *n* **cheque book** a book containing cheques.

chequers, checkers ['chekərz] *n* a pattern of squares, as on a chessboard; the game of draughts. – *adj* '**chequered**, '**checkered** marked like a chessboard; partly good, partly bad: *a chequered life*.

'**cherish** *v* to protect and treat with fondness or kindness; to keep in one's mind or heart: *cherish a hope*.

cheroot [shə'rōōt] *n* a small cigar.

'**cherry** *n* a type of small bright-red fruit with a stone, or the tree that bears it: – *pl* '**cherries**.

'**cherub** *n* an angel having wings and the plump face and body of a child; a beautiful child: – *pls* '**cherubs**, '**cherubim**.

chess *n* a game for two persons, played with pieces ('**chessmen**) which are moved on a board marked off into alternate black and white squares ('**chessboard**).

chest *n* a large strong box; the part of the body between the neck and the stomach. – **chest of drawers** a piece of furniture fitted with a set of drawers.

chesterfield ['chestərfēld] *n* a kind of sofa.

chestnut ['chesnut] *n* a type of reddish-brown nut, or the tree that bears it; a reddish-brown horse; an old joke.

'**cheviot** *n* a kind of sheep.

chevron ['shevrən] *n* a V-shape (*esp* on a badge, road-sign *etc*).

chew *v* to break up (food) with the teeth before swallowing.

chic [shēk] *adj* smart and fashionable. – *n* style, fashionable elegance.

chicanery [shi'kānəri] *n* dishonest cleverness.

chick, 'chicken *ns* the young of (domestic) fowls, *esp* of the hen. – *adj* '**chicken-'hearted** cowardly. – *n* '**chickenpox** an infectious disease which causes red, itchy spots.

'**chicory** *n* a type of plant whose root is ground to mix with coffee and whose leaves are used as a vegetable.

chide *v* to scold by words.

chief [chēf] *adj* head; main, most important; largest. – *n* a leader or ruler; the head (of a department, organization *etc*). – *adv* '**chiefly** mainly, for the most part. – *n* '**chieftain** the head of a clan or tribe.

chiffon ['shifon] *n* a thin flimsy material.

'**chilblain** *n* a painful swelling which occurs in cold weather on hands and feet.

child *n* a young human being; a son or daughter (of any age): – *pl* **children** ['childrən]. – *n* '**childhood** the time of being a child. – *adjs* '**childish** of or like a child; silly; '**childlike** innocent.

chill *n* coldness; an illness that causes shivering, a feverish cold; (of manner *etc*) lack of warmth or enthusiasm. – *adj* cold. – *v* to make cold (without freezing). – *adj* '**chilly** cold.

'**chilli**, '**chili** *n* the dried, hot-tasting pod of a kind of pepper; a sauce made with this.

chime *n* the sound of bells ringing; (*pl*) a set of bells (as in a clock). – *v* to ring; (of clocks) to strike.

'**chimney** *n* a passage for the escape of smoke or heated air from a fire: – *pl* '**chimneys**. – *ns* '**chimneypot** a pipe of earthenware, iron *etc* placed at the top of a chimney; '**chimneystack** a number of chimneys built up together; '**chimneysweep(er)** one who sweeps or cleans chimneys.

chimpan'zee *n* a type of African ape.

chin *n* the part of the face below the mouth.

'china *n* fine kind of earthenware, porcelain; articles make of this.

chin'chilla *n* a type of small S. American animal, valued for its soft grey fur.

chink *n* a narrow opening; a sound like that of coins striking together.

chintz *n* a cotton cloth with brightly coloured patterns.

chip *v* to break or cut small pieces (from or off): – *pt* **chipped**. – *n* a small piece chipped off; a part damaged by chipping; a long thin piece of potato fried; (*US*) a (potato) crisp.

'chipmunk *n* a kind of N. American squirrel.

chipo'lata *n* a type of small sausage.

chiropodist [ki'ropɔdist] *n* one who treats minor disorders and diseases of the feet (*eg* corns). – *n* **chi'ropody** the treatment of these.

chirp, 'chirrup *n* the sharp, shrill sound (of birds *etc*). – Also *v*. – *adj* **'chirpy** merry, cheerful.

chisel ['chizl] *n* an iron or steel tool to cut or hollow out wood, stone *etc*. – *v* to cut with a chisel: – *pt* **'chiselled**.

chit *n* a short note; a child, a young woman: *chit of a girl*. – *n* **'chit-chat** gossip, talk.

chivalry ['shivɔlri] *n* kindness, *esp* towards women or the weak; (*hist*) the standard of behaviour expected of knights in medieval times. – *adj* **'chivalrous**.

chive *n* a herb like the leek and onion, used as flavouring.

chlorine ['klörēn] *n* an element, a yellowish-green gas with a sharp, distinctive smell, used as a bleach and disinfectant. – *v* **chlorinate** ['klorināt] to add chlorine, or a substance containing it, to (*eg* water).

chloroform ['klorɔförm] *n* a liquid, the vapour of which when breathed in, causes unconsciousness.

'chock-a-'block, 'chock'full *adjs* completely full.

'chocolate *n* a paste got from the seeds of the cacao-tree, used in sweet-making; a sweet made from this paste when hardened; a drink made from it. – *adj* dark brown in colour, like chocolate.

choice *n* the act or power of choosing; something chosen. – *adj* of a high quality: *choice vegetables*.

choir ['kwir] *n* a group or society of singers; the part of a church where the choir sits. – *adj* **choral** ['körɔl] of or for a choir.

choke *v* to stop or partly stop the breathing of; to block or clog (a pipe *etc*); to have one's breathing stopped or interrupted (*eg* by smoke or chemicals). – *n* a valve in a petrol engine which controls the flowing-in of air.

cholera ['kolɔrɔ] *n* a deadly disease commonest in hot countries.

choose [chōōz] *v* to pick out and take (one) from two or several things, to select; to decide, prefer to. *We chose to go*: – *pt* **chose** [chōz], *pp* **'chosen**.

chop *v* to cut into small pieces; to cut with a sudden blow: – *pt* **chopped**. – *n* a chopping blow; a slice of mutton, pork *etc*, containing a bone. – *n* **'chopper** a knife or axe for chopping; (*coll*) a helicopter. – *adj* **'choppy** (of the sea) not calm, having small waves. – **chop and change** to keep changing.

'chopsticks *npl* two small sticks of wood, ivory *etc* used by the Chinese *etc* instead of a knife and fork.

choral *see* **choir**.

chord [körd] *n* a musical sound made by the playing of several notes together; a straight line joining any two points on a curve.

chore [chör] *n* dull, boring job; (*pl*) housework.

choreography [kori'ogrɔfi] *n* the arrangement of dancing and dance steps (in a ballet *etc*). – *n* **chore'ographer**.

chorister ['koristɔr] *n* a member of a choir.

'chortle *v* to laugh, chuckle.

chorus ['körɔs] *n* a band of singers and dancers; a choir or choral group; the repeated part of a song: – *pl* **'choruses**.

chose, chosen *see* **choose**.

chow [chow] *n* a breed of dog from China with a bushy coat and a blue-black tongue.

christen ['krisn] *v* to baptize and give a name to. – *n* **'christening**.

Christian ['krischɔn] *n* a follower of Christ. – Also *adj*. – *n* **Christianity** [kristi'anɔti] the religion having Christ as its centre. – *n* **Christian name(s)** one's first name (or names): *John William* Smith.

Christmas ['krismɔs] *n* a yearly holiday or festival, in memory of the birth of Christ, held on December 25. – *ns* **Christmas Eve** December 24; **Christmas tree** an evergreen tree hung with lights, decorations and gifts at Christmas.

chromatic [krɔ'matik] *adj* of colours; coloured. – *n* **chromatic scale** a series of musical notes, each separated from the next by a semitone.

chromium ['krōmiəm] *n* an element, a metal which does not rust.

chronic ['kronik] *adj* (*esp* of a disease) lasting a long time.

chronicle ['kronikl] *n* a record of events in order of time. – *v* to write down events in order. – *n* '**chronicler**.

chronological [kronə'lojikəl] *adj* arranged in the order of the time of happening.

chronometer [krə'nomitər] *n* an instrument for measuring time.

chrysalis ['krisəlis] *n* an insect (*esp* a butterfly or moth) at an early part of its life when it is without wings and shut up in a soft covering (**cocoon**).

chrysanthemum [kri'santhəməm] *n* a type of garden flower with a large, bushy head.

'**chubby** *adj* plump: – *comp* '**chubbier**, *superl* '**chubbiest**. – *n* '**chubbiness**.

chuck *v* to throw, toss; to pat gently (under the chin).

'**chuckle** *n* a quiet laugh. – *v* to laugh quietly.

chum *n* (*coll*) a close friend.

chunk *n* a thick piece.

church *n* a building used for public, *esp* Christian, worship; any group of people of the same beliefs who meet together for worship: – *pl* '**churches**. – *n* '**churchyard** the burial ground round a church.

'**churlish** *adj* rude, bad-mannered.

churn *n* a machine used for making butter. – *v* to make (butter) in a churn; to shake or stir about violently.

chute [shōot] *n* a sloping trough for sending things down to a lower level (*eg* water, logs, parcels); a similar structure with steps in a playground, for children to slide down.

'**chutney** *n* any of various sauces made from vegetables, fruits, vinegar: – *pl* '**chutneys**.

'**cider** *n* an alcoholic drink made from the juice of apples.

ci'gar *n* a roll of tobacco leaves for smoking. – *n* **ciga'rette** a tube of fine tobacco enclosed in thin paper.

'**cinder** *n* a burnt-out piece of coal.

cinema ['sinəmə] *n* a place where films are shown; (with **the**) films generally, or films regarded as a form of art.

'**cinnamon** *n* a yellowish-brown spice got from the bark of a tree.

'**cipher** *n* a secret writing, code; nought, 0; a person of no importance.

'**circa** *prep* about: *circa 5,000 men*.

'**circle** *n* a figure formed from an endless curved line, ○ ; something in the form

of a circle, a ring; any society or group of people; a balcony or tier of seats in a theatre *etc*. – *v* to enclose in a circle; to move round (something). – *n* '**circlet** a little circle, *esp* one used as an ornamental headband.

circuit ['sɔrkit] *n* a movement in a circle; a connected group of places, sporting events *etc*: *the American tennis circuit*; the path of an electric current. – *adj* **circuitous** [sɔr'kūitəs] (of a route *etc*) not direct, roundabout.

'**circular** *adj* round, like a circle. – *n* a letter sent round to a number of persons. – *v* '**circularize** to send a circular to.

'**circulate** *v* to move round (as the blood moves in the body); to send round. – *n* **circu'lation** the act of circulating; the movement of the blood; the total sales of a newspaper, magazine *etc*.

cir'cumference *n* (the length of) the outside line of a circle.

circumlo'cution *n* a roundabout way of saying something.

circum'navigate *v* to sail round (*eg* the world). – *n* **circum'navigator**.

'**circumscribe** *v* to draw a line round; to lay down limits (*eg* for a person's actions), restrict. – *n* **circum'scription**.

'**circumspect** *adj* wary, looking carefully at circumstances, cautious. – *n* **circum'spection** caution.

'**circumstance** *n* a condition (of time, place, manner *etc*) which affects a person, an action or an event; (*pl*) the state of a person's (financial) affairs. – *v* **circum'stantiate** to prove by giving details. – *n* **circumstantial evidence** evidence which points to a conclusion but does not give proof of it.

circum'vent *v* to get round (a difficulty); to outwit. – *n* **circum'vention**.

'**circus** *n* a travelling company of performing animals, acrobats, clowns *etc*; a large arena for sports events.

'**cirrus** *n* a fleecy kind of cloud.

'**cistern** *n* a tank for holding or storing water.

'**citadel** *n* fortress, *esp* one in a city.

cite *v* to quote as an example or as proof; to summon a person to appear in court. – *n* **ci'tation** something quoted; a summons to appear in court; official recognition of an achievement, a brave act *etc*.

'**citizen** *n* one who lives in a city, town or state. – *n* '**citizenship** the rights of or state of being a citizen.

'**citric acid** *n* a type of sharp-tasting acid

found in citrus fruits.

'**citron** *n* a type of fruit similar to a lemon.

'**citrus fruit** *n* any one of certain fruits including the orange, lemon and lime.

'**city** *n* a large town; a town with a cathedral: – *pl* '**cities**. – **the City** that part of London regarded as the centre of business.

'**civic** *adj* having to do with a city or a citizen. – *npl* '**civics** the study of one's duties as a citizen.

'**civil** *adj* of the ordinary people of a country, not its armed forces; polite. – *ns* ci'**vilian** one who is not in the armed forces; ci'**vility** politeness, good manners. – *ns* **civil engineer** an engineer who plans bridges, roads *etc*; **civil law** law concerned with the rights of a citizen, not concerned with criminal acts; **civil list** the expenses of the king's or queen's household; **civil marriage** a marriage which does not take place in church; **civil rights** the rights of a citizen; **civil service** the paid administrative officials of the country who are not in the armed forces; **civil war** war between citizens of a country.

'**civilize** *v* to bring (a people) under a regular system of laws, education *etc* from a primitive state. – *adj* '**civilized** living under such a system; not savage. – *n* civili'**zation** making or becoming civilized; life under a civilized system; the civilized nations as a whole.

clad *adj* clothed (in).

claim *v* to demand as a right; to state as a truth, assert (that). – Also *n*. – *n* '**claimant** one who makes a claim.

clairvoyance [klār'voians] *n* the supposed power to see into the future or into the world of spirits. – *n, adj* clair'**voyant**.

clam *n* a type of large shellfish with two shells hinged together.

'**clamber** *v* to climb awkwardly or with difficulty.

'**clammy** *adj* moist and sticky.

clamour ['klamər] *n* a loud, continuous noise or outcry. – *v* to cry aloud; to make a loud demand (for). – *adj* '**clamorous** noisy.

clamp *n* a piece of timber, iron *etc* used to fasten things together. – *v* to bind with a clamp. – **clamp down on** to stop (something, *eg* vandalism) by forceful action.

clan *n* (in Scotland) a tribe, or a number of families, under a chieftain *usu* having the same surname. – *adj* '**clannish** loyal to one another, like the members of a clan. – *n* '**clansman** a

member of a clan.

clandestine [klan'destin] *adj* hidden, secret, underhand.

clang *v* to make a loud, deep, ringing sound. – Also *n.*

clank *n* a sound like that made by metal hitting metal. – Also *v.*

clap *n* the noise made by the sudden striking together of two things (*esp* the hands); a burst of sound, *esp* thunder. – *v* to strike noisily together (*esp* the hands to show pleasure); to put or place suddenly. *Clap him in jail*: – *pt* **clapped**. – *n* '**clapper** the tongue of a bell. – *n* '**claptrap** meaningless words, nonsense.

'**claret** *n* a type of red wine.

'**clarify** *v* to make clear and understandable; to make (*eg* a liquid) clear and pure: – *pt* '**clarified**.

clari'net *n* a type of musical wind instrument, *usu* of wood. – *n* clari'**nettist** one who plays the clarinet.

'**clarion** *n* (*old*) a kind of trumpet; a shrill, rousing noise. – *n* **clarion call** a loud, clear call to action.

'**clarity** *n* clearness.

clash *n* a loud noise, as of the striking together of weapons; a disagreement or fight: – *pl* '**clashes**. – *v* to bang noisily together; to disagree; (of events) to take place at the same time; (*usu* with **with**) not to look well together. *The two shades of red clashed with each other.*

clasp *n* a hook *etc* for fastening; a fastening for the hair; a handshake; an embrace. – *v* to hold closely; to grasp; to fasten.

class *n* a rank or order of persons or things; a number of schoolchildren or students who are taught together; (of animals, plants *etc*) a group of different kinds, all of which have something in common: – *pl* '**classes**. – *v* to place in a class; to arrange in some order. – *v* '**classify** to arrange in classes; to put into a class or category: – *pt* '**classified**. – *n* classifi'**cation**.

'**classic** *n* any great writer, book or other work of art; (*pl*) (the study of) ancient Greek and Latin writers' works. – *adjs* '**classic** excellent; standard: *the classic example*; simple and elegant in style; '**classical** of a classic or the classics; (of music) serious, not light.

'**clatter** *n* noise as of plates *etc* banged together.

clause [klöz] *n* a part of a sentence containing a finite verb; a part of a will, act of parliament *etc*.

claustrophobia [klöstrə'fōbiə] *n* an abnormal fear of enclosed spaces. –

adj **claustro'phobic**.

claw *n* one of the hooked nails of an animal or bird; the foot of an animal or bird with hooked nails. – *v* to scratch or tear.

clay *n* soft, sticky earth, different kinds of which are used in making pottery, bricks *etc*. – *adj* **'clayey**.

'claymore *n* (*hist*) a a kind of large sword once used by the Scottish Highlanders.

clean *adj* free from dirt; pure; neat; complete: *a clean break*. – *adv* completely. *He got clean away*. – *v* to make clean, or free from dirt. – *n* **'cleaner** one whose job is to clean; something which cleans. – *adv* **'cleanly**. – *ns* **cleanliness** ['klenlinəs]; **cleanness** ['klɛnnis].

cleanse [klenz] *v* to make clean.

clear *adj* bright, undimmed; free from mist or cloud; transparent; free from difficulty or hindrance; easy to see or hear or understand; after deductions and charges have been made: *clear profit*; without a stain; without touching, without being caught by: *clear of the rocks: clear of the enemy*. – *v* to make clear; to empty: *clear the streets of snow*; to free from blame; to leap over (without touching); (of the sky, weather) to become bright. – *ns* **'clearance** act of clearing; **'clearing** land free of trees; **'clearness**. – *adj* **'clear-'cut** distinct, obvious. – **clear out, clear off** to go away.

cleave *v* to divide, split; to crack; to stick (to): – *pt* **clove, cleft**, *pp* **'cloven, cleft**. – *ns* **'cleavage** the act of splitting; the way in which two things are split or divided; **'cleaver** that which cleaves, a chopper.

clef *n* a musical sign fixing the pitch of the notes.

cleft *n* an opening made by splitting; a crack. – *v see* **cleave**.

cleg *n* a type of horsefly.

'clematis *n* a flowering, climbing shrub.

'clement *adj* mild; merciful. – *n* **'clemency** readiness to forgive; mercy.

clench *v* to press firmly together. *He clenched his teeth*.

'clergy *n* the ministers of the Christian religion. – *ns* **'clergyman, 'cleric** one of the clergy, a minister.

clerk [klärk, (*US*) klȯrk] *n* one who works in an office, writing letters, keeping accounts *etc*. – *v* to act as clerk. – *adj* **clerical** ['klerikəl] of office work; of the clergy.

'clever *adj* quick in learning and understanding; skilful. –

n **'cleverness**.

cliché ['klēshā] *n* something (*esp* an idea, phrase *etc*) that has been used too much and has little meaning.

click *n* a short, sharp sound. – Also *v*.

client ['klīənt] *n* a customer of a shopkeeper *etc*; one who goes to a lawyer *etc* for advice. – *n* **clientele** [klēon'tel] the customers of a lawyer, shopkeeper *etc*.

cliff *n* a very steep, rocky slope, *esp* one by the sea.

'climate *n* the weather conditions (heat, cold, rain, wind *etc*) of a place or country; the conditions (*eg* economic) in a country *etc*. – *adj* **cli'matic**.

'climax *n* (of events *etc*) the point of greatest interest, feeling or importance: – *pl* **'climaxes**.

climb [klim] *v* to go to the top of; to go up using the hands or feet or both; to slope upward. – *n* an act of climbing; a place for climbing. – *n* **'climber** one who climbs; a plant which climbs up other plants, walls *etc*.

clinch *v* to grasp tightly; to settle (an argument, bargain *etc*). – *n* (in boxing) a position in which the boxers hold each other with their arms; a passionate embrace: – *pl* **'clinches**.

cling *v* to stick or hang on (to): – *pt* **clung**.

'clinic *n* a place or part of a hospital where a particular kind of medical advice or treatment is given. – *adj* **'clinical** of a clinic; based on observation: *clinical medicine*; objective, cool and unemotional: *a clinical view of the situation*.

clink *n* a ringing sound. – Also *v*.

'clinker *n* the waste stuff when iron is smelted or coal burnt.

clip *v* to cut (off); to fasten with a clip. – *n* the thing clipped off; a small fastener (*eg* for paper); (*coll*) a smart blow. – *n* **'clipper** a fast-sailing vessel; (*pl*) tool for clipping.

clique [klēk] *n* a small group of people who help each other but keep others at a distance.

cloak *n* a loose outer garment; something which hides: *cloak of darkness*. – *v* to cover as with a cloak; to hide. – *n* **'cloakroom** a place where coats, hats *etc* may be left for a time.

cloche [klosh] *n* a transparent frame for protecting plants: – *pl* **'cloches**.

clock *n* a machine for measuring time. – *adj* **'clockwise** turning or moving in the same direction as the hands of a clock. – *adj, n* **'clockwork** (worked by) machinery such as that of a clock. –

clock in, clock out (or **on, off**) to record one's time of arrival or departure (*usu* at one's place of work). – **like clockwork** smoothly, without difficulties.

clod *n* a thick lump, *esp* of turf; a stupid man. – *n* **'clodhopper** a stupid clumsy person. – *adj* **'clodhopping**.

clog *n* a shoe with a wooden sole. – *v* to block (pipes *etc*): – *pt* **clogged**.

cloister *n* a covered-in walk in a monastery or convent; a monastery or convent. – *adj* **'cloistered** shut up in a monastery *etc*; sheltered.

close¹ *adj* near in time, place *etc*; shut up, with no opening; without fresh air, stuffy; narrow, confined; mean; secretive; beloved, very dear: *a close friend*; decided, won by a small amount: *a close contest*. – *n* a narrow passage off a street; the gardens, walks *etc* near a cathedral. – *n* **'closeness**. – *n* **'close-up** a film or photograph taken very near the subject.

close² [klōz] *v* to shut; to finish; to come closer to and fight (with). – *n* the end. – *n* **closure** ['klōzhər] the act of closing. – *ns* **closed-circuit television** a system of television cameras and receivers for private use (as in shops *etc*); **closed shop** a place of work where only members of a (particular) trade union are employed.

closet ['klozit] *n* (*US*) a cupboard. – *v* to take into a room *etc* for a private conference. – **closeted with** in private conference with.

closure see **close**².

clot *n* a lump or thickening that forms in some liquids (*eg* blood, cream). – *v* to form into clots: – *pt* **'clotted**.

cloth *n* woven material of cotton, wool, linen, silk *etc*; a piece of this; a table-cover.

clothes [klōdhz] *npl* things worn to cover the body and limbs (as shirt, trousers, skirt *etc*); bedclothes. – *v* **clothe** to put clothes on; to provide with clothes. *He has barely enough money to clothe the children*; to cover. – *n* **'clothing** clothes.

cloud *n* a mass of tiny drops of water or ice floating in the sky; a great number or quantity of anything small in the air (*eg* locusts, dust). – *v* to blot out, hide or become dark, as with a cloud. – *adjs* **'clouded; 'cloudless; 'cloudy** darkened with clouds; not clear or transparent. – *n* **'cloudburst** a sudden heavy fall of rain.

clout *n* (*coll*) a blow. – *v* (*coll*) to hit.

clove *n* a flower bud of the clove tree,

used as a spice; a small section of a bulb of garlic *etc*. – *v* see **cleave**.

'cloven-'hoofed *adj* having the hoof divided, as the ox, sheep *etc*.

'clover *n* a type of field plant with leaves *usu* in three parts, common in pastures. – **in clover** in luxury.

clown [klown] *n* a comedian with a painted face and comical clothes in a circus; a fool. – *n* **'clowning** silly or comical behaviour. – *adj* **'clownish** like a clown; awkward.

cloy *v* (of *eg* something sweet) to become unpleasant when too much is taken. – *adj* **'cloying**.

club *n* a heavy stick; a bat or stick used in certain games, *esp* golf; a group of people who meet for study, games, entertainment *etc*; the place where these people meet sometimes provided with refreshments, entertainment *etc*; (*pl*) one of the four suits in playing-cards. – *v* to beat with a club: – *pt* **clubbed**. – **club together** (of a group of people) to put money into a joint fund for some purpose.

cluck *n* a sound like that made by a hen. – Also *v*.

clue [klōō] *n* any sign or piece of evidence that helps to solve a mystery, problem *etc*.

clump *n* a cluster of trees or shrubs. – *v* to walk heavily.

clumsy ['klumzi] *adj* awkward in movement or actions; tactless, not skilfully carried out: *a clumsy apology*: – *comp* **'clumsier**, *superl* **'clumsiest**. – *n* **'clumsiness**.

clung see **cling**.

'cluster *n* a bunch; a crowd. – *v* to group together in clusters.

clutch *v* to hold firmly; to seize or grasp. – *n* a grasp; part of a motor-car engine used in changing the gears: – *pl* **'clutches**.

'clutter *n* a collection (of objects) in a crowded or confused state; disorder, confusion, untidiness. – *v* to crowd together untidily; (with **up**) to fill or cover in an untidy, disordered way.

cō- *prefix* joint, working *etc* with as in **'co-'author, 'co-'driver**.

coach *n* a bus for long-distance travel; a large, closed, four-wheeled horse carriage; a railway carriage; a private teacher, *esp* one who trains sportsmen: – *pl* **'coaches**. – *v* to prepare (someone) for an examination, sports contest *etc*.

coagulate [kō'agūlāt] *v* to (cause to) become a thickened mass (as when milk goes sour or blood clots).

coal *n* a black substance (the wood of prehistoric trees *etc*) dug out of the earth and used for burning, making gas *etc*. – *ns* '**coalfield** a district where there is coal to be mined; **coal gas** the mixture of gases, obtained from coal, used for lighting and heating; '**coalmine** a mine from which coal is dug.

coalesce [kōə'les] *v* to come together and unite.

coalition [kōə'lishən] *n* a joining together of different parts or parties.

coarse *adj* not fine in texture *etc*, rough; harsh; vulgar. – *v* '**coarsen** to make coarse. – *n* '**coarseness**.

coast *n* the side or border of land next to the sea. – *v* to sail along or near a coast; to move without the use of any power (as downhill on a bike, car *etc*). – *adj* '**coastal**. – *n* '**coastguard** one who acts as a guard along the coast to prevent smuggling and help those in danger in boats.

coat *n* an outer garment with sleeves; hair or wool (of an animal); a covering (*eg* paint). – *v* to cover with a coat or layer. – *n* '**coating** a covering. – **coat of arms** the badge or crest of a family.

coax *v* to get (someone) to do what is wanted without using force.

cob *n* a head of corn, wheat *etc*; a male swan.

cobalt ['kōbölt] *n* an element, a silvery metal; a blue colouring got from it.

cobble *n* a rounded stone once used in paving roads. – Also '**cobblestone**. – *v* to mend (shoes); to repair, patch roughly or hurriedly. – *n* '**cobbler** one who mends shoes.

cobra *n* a type of poisonous snake, found in India and Africa.

cobweb *n* a spider's web.

cocaine *n* a type of drug used to deaden pain.

cochineal *n* a scarlet dye, used to colour food, made from the dried bodies of certain insects.

cock *n* the male of most kinds of bird, *esp* the male of the farmyard hen; a tap or valve for controlling the flow of a liquid *etc*; a hammer-like part of a gun which, when the trigger is pulled, fires the shot; a small heap (of hay). – *v* to draw back the cock of a gun; to set upright (ears *etc*); to tilt to one side (*eg* one's head). – *adj* '**cocky** conceited, self-confident. – *ns* '**cockerel** a young cock; **cocker spaniel** a breed of small spaniel; '**cockpit** the space for the pilot or driver in an aeroplane, small boat or racing car; a pit or enclosed space where game cocks fight; '**cockroach** a

type of crawling insect: – *pl* '**cockroaches**; '**cockscomb** the comb or crest on a cock's head; a fop, a conceited person. – *adj* '**cock'sure** quite sure, often without cause. – *n* '**cocktail** a mixed alcoholic drink.

coc'kade *n* a knot of ribbons or something similar worn on the hat.

cocka'too *n* a kind of parrot.

'**cockatrice** *n* (*myth*) a monster like a cock with a dragon's tail.

cockerel *see* **cock**.

'**cockle** *n* a type of shellfish. – *n* '**cockleshell** the shell of a cockle.

'**cockney** *n* one born in the East End of London, *esp* one born within the sound of Bow Bells; the way of speaking in this area: – *pl* '**cockneys**. – Also *adj*.

'**cocoa** *n* a drink made from the ground seeds of the cacao tree.

'**coconut** *n* the large, hard-shelled nut of a type of palm tree.

co'coon *n* a covering or case of silk spun by the larva (grub) of certain insects to protect it while it turns into a butterfly, moth *etc*.

cod *n* a fish much used as food, found in the northern seas.

'**coddle** *v* to treat as an invalid, pamper, over-protect.

code *n* a way of signalling or sending secret messages, using words, letters *etc* agreed on beforehand; a book or collection of laws, rules *etc*. – *v* '**codify** to arrange in an orderly way, classify: – *pt* '**codified**.

'**codicil** *n* a note added to a will or treaty.

coeducation ['kōedū'kāshən] *n* the education of boys and girls together. – *adj* '**coedu'cational**.

coelacanth ['sēləkanth] *n* a type of primitive fish.

co'erce *v* to make (to do), to compel. – *n* **coercion** [kō'ərshən]. – *adj* **co'ercive** using force.

co'eval *adj* of the same age or time.

coexist ['kōig'zist] *v* to exist at the same time. – *n* '**coex'istence**. – *adj* '**coex'istent**.

'**coffee** *n* a drink made from the ground beans or seeds of the coffee shrub; a pale brown colour.

'**coffer** *n* a chest for holding money, gold *etc*. – *n* '**coffer-dam** a watertight dam placed in a river inside which the foundations of a bridge are built.

'**coffin** *n* the box in which a dead body is buried or cremated.

cog *n* a tooth on a wheel. – *n* '**cogwheel** a toothed wheel.

'**cogent** *adj* (of speaking or writing) convincing, having the power to make people believe what is said. – *n* '**cogency**.

'**cogitate** *v* to think carefully. – *n* **cogi'tation**.

cognac ['konyak] *n* a kind of French brandy.

'**cognizance** *n* awareness, notice. – **take cognizance of** to take notice of, take into consideration.

co'here *v* to stick together. – *n* **co'herence** connection (between thoughts, ideas *etc*). – *adj* **co'herent** sticking together; clear and logical in thought or speech. – *n* **co'hesion** the act of sticking together. – *adj* **co'hesive**.

'**cohort** *n* (*hist*) a tenth part of a Roman legion.

coiffure [kwa'für] *n* a style of hairdressing.

coil *v* to wind in rings, to twist. – *n* a coiled arrangement (of rope *etc*).

coin *n* a piece of stamped metal used as money. – *v* to make metal into money; to make up (a new word *etc*). – *n* '**coinage** the act of coining; coins; the system of coins used in a country; a newly-made word.

coincide [kōin'sid] *v* (sometimes with **with**) to be like or the same as. *Their interests coincide. His story coincides with hers*; (sometimes with **with**) to happen at the same time as. *Her arrival coincided with his departure.* – *n* **coincidence** [kō'insidəns] the happening of one thing at the same time as another, by chance or without planning. – *adj* **coinci'dental**.

coir *n* outside fibre of the coconut.

coke *n* a type of fuel made by heating coal till the gas is driven out.

colander ['kuləndər] *n* a kind of bowl with small holes in it for straining vegetables *etc*.

cōld *adj* low in temperature; lower in temperature than is comfortable; causing shivering; unfriendly. – *n* the state of being cold or of feeling the coldness of one's surroundings; a disease, due to germs, causing shivering, running nose *etc*. – *n* '**coldness**. – *adj* '**cold-'blooded** (of fishes *etc*) having cold blood; cruel; lacking in feelings. – *ns* **cold feet** lack of courage; **cold war** a struggle between nations for power without the use of open warfare.

'**cole-slaw** *n* a salad made from raw cabbage.

'**colic** *n* a severe stomach pain.

col'laborate *v* to work together (with); to work with (an enemy) to betray one's country *etc*. – *ns* **col'labo'ration**; **col'laborator**.

collage [ko'läzh] *n* a design made of scraps of paper and other odds and ends pasted on paper *etc*.

col'lapse *v* to fall or break down; to cave or fall in; to become unable to continue. – Also *n*. – *adj* **col'lapsible** (of a chair *etc*) able to be folded up.

'**collar** *n* a band, strip *etc* worn round the neck by man or animals; the part of an article of clothing at the neck. – *v* (*coll*) to seize. – *n* '**collarbone** either of two bones joining the breast bone and shoulderblade.

col'late *v* to examine and compare. – *n* **col'lation** a light (often cold) meal; a comparison.

collateral [kə'latərəl] *adj* side by side; parallel.

colleague ['kolēg] *n* a person who does the same kind of work as another or who works in the same firm *etc* as another.

col'lect *v* to bring together; to gather together. – *adj* **col'lected** gathered together; (of persons) calm. – *n* **col'lection** the act of collecting; a number of objects or people; money gathered at a meeting, *esp* a church service. – *adj* **col'lective** acting together; of several persons or persons, not of one. – *n* **col'lector** one who collects (tickets, money, stamps *etc*).

college ['kolij] *n* (a building used by) a group of people gathered together to learn and study; a building which is part of a university *etc*. – *adj* **col'lēgiate**.

col'lide *v* (of moving things *etc*) to come together with great force. – *n* **col'lision** a violent meeting of two moving things, *esp* vehicles; a disagreement, clash (of interests *etc*).

'**collie** *n* a breed of long-haired dog with a pointed nose, a sheepdog.

collier ['koliər] *n* one who works in a coalmine; a coal ship. – *n* '**colliery** a coalmine: – *pl* '**collieries**.

col'lōquial *adj* used in everyday talk but not in very correct writing or speaking. – *n* **col'loquialism** an example of colloquial speech.

collusion [kə'lōōzhən] *n* a secret agreement (*usu* for some dishonest purpose).

'**cōlon** *n* in punctuation, the mark (:), used to show a break in a sentence; a part of the bowel.

colonel ['kйrnl] *n* an officer next below brigadier who has command of a regiment.

colon'nade *n* a row of columns or pillars.

'colony *n* a group of settlers or the settlement they make in another country; any group of people, animals *etc* of the same type living together: – *pl* **'colonies**. – *adj* **co'lōnial** of colonies abroad. – *n* **'colonist** a settler. – *v* **'colonize** to set up a colony in.

co'lossal *adj* huge, enormous. – *n* **co'lossus** anything enormous (*eg* a huge statue).

colour, (*US*) **color** ['kulər] *n* a quality that an object shows in the light, as redness, blueness *etc*; any shade or tint; vividness, brightness; (*pl*) a flag or standard. – *v* to put colour on; to blush; to influence. *Unemployment coloured his attitude to life*. – *adjs* **'coloured** having colour; not white-skinned; **'colourful** brightly coloured; vivid, interesting. – *n* **'colouring** the putting on of colours; the effect of combining colours; complexion. – *adj* **'colourless** without colour; dull. – *adj* **'colour-blind** unable to distinguish certain colours (*eg* red and green). – **off colour** unwell.

cōlt *n* a young horse.

column ['koləm] *n* a stone (or wooden) pillar standing upright; anything of a long or tall, narrow shape; a line of print, figures *etc* stretching from top to bottom of a page; an arrangement (of troops, ships *etc*) one behind the other.

'cōma *n* unconsciousness lasting a long time. – *adj* **'comatose** in or of a coma; drowsy, sluggish.

comb [kōm] *n* a toothed instrument for separating, smoothing or cleaning hair, wool, flax *etc*; the crest of certain birds; a collection of cells for honey. – *v* to arrange, smoothe or clean with a comb; to search (a place) thoroughly.

'combat *v* to fight or struggle against. – *n* a fight or struggle. – *n, adj* **'combatant** (one who is) fighting. – *adj* **'combative** quarrelsome.

com'bine *v* to join together. – *n* **'combine** a number of traders *etc* who join together. – *n* **combi'nation** a joining together of things or people; a set of things or people combined; the series of letters or figures dialled to open a safe; (*pl*) an article of underwear for the body and legs. – *n* **'combine 'harvester** a machine that both cuts and threshes crops.

com'bustible *adj* liable to catch fire and burn. – *n* anything that will catch fire. – *n* **com'bustion** burning.

come [kum] *v* to move towards this place (opposite of **go**). *Come here!*; to draw near. *Christmas is coming*; to arrive. *We'll have tea when you come*; to happen, occur. *The index comes at the end of the book*: – *pt* **came**, *pp* **come**. – **come about** to happen; **come across, come upon** to meet, find accidentally; **come by** to obtain; **come into** to get (by inheriting); **come of age** to reach the age at which one becomes an adult for legal purposes; **come round, come to** to recover (from a faint *etc*); **come upon** *see* **come across**; **to come** in the future.

comedy ['komədi] *n* a play of light-hearted or amusing kind (opposite of **tragedy**): – *pl* **'comedies**. – *n* **co'mēdian** a performer who tells jokes, acts in comedy *etc*.

comely ['kumli] *adj* pleasing, good-looking. – *n* **'comeliness**.

'comet *n* a kind of star which has a tail of light.

comfort ['kumfərt] *v* to help, soothe (someone in pain or distress). – *n* ease, quiet enjoyment; state of being comfortable; anything that makes one happier or more at ease. – *adj* **'comfortable** at ease, free from trouble, pain, hardship *etc*; giving comfort.

'comic *adj* of comedy; funny. – *n* someone amusing, *esp* a professional comedian; a (comic) picture paper. – *adj* **'comical** funny, amusing. – *n* **comic strip** a strip of small pictures showing stages in an adventure.

'comma *n* in punctuation, the mark (,).

com'mand *v* to give an order; to be in charge of; to look over or down upon (a view *etc*). – *n* an order; control. – *ns* **comman'dant** an officer who has command of a place or of troops; **com'mander** one who commands; in the navy, an officer next in rank below captain. – *adj* **com'manding** powerful; having a wide view. – *n* **com'mandment** an order or command.

comman'deer *v* to seize (something) *esp* for the use of an army.

com'mando *n* (a soldier serving in) a unit of the army trained for hard or dangerous tasks: – *pl* **com'mandoes**.

com'memorate *v* to bring to memory by some solemn act; to serve as a memorial of. – *n* **commemo'ration**.

com'mence *v* to begin. – *n* **com'mencement**.

com'mend *v* to praise; to give into the care of. – *adj* **com'mendable** praiseworthy. – *n* **commen'dation** praise. – *adj* **com'mendatory**

praising.

commensurate [kə'menshərət] *adj* (with **with**) equal in size, importance *etc*, in proportion to.

'**comment** *n* a remark or series of remarks; a criticism. – Also *v*. – *ns* '**commentary** a description of an event *etc* (by one who is watching it) (also **running commentary**); a set of explanatory notes for a book *etc*: – *pl* '**commentaries**; '**commentator** one who gives or writes a commentary.

'**commerce** *n* the buying and selling of goods between people or nations; trade, dealings. – *adj* **com'mercial** of commerce; (of radio, TV *etc*) paid for by advertisements.

commiserate [kə'mizərāt] *v* to sympathize (with). – *n* **commise'ration** pity.

commis'sar *n* (in USSR) the head of a government department.

commis'sāriat *n* that part of an army or other organization that looks after the food supply.

com'mission *n* the act of committing; a warrant or document giving authority to an officer in the armed forces; an order *esp* for a work of art; a fee for doing business *etc* on another's behalf; a body of persons appointed to investigate something. – *v* to give a commission or power to. – *ns* **commissio'naire** a uniformed doorkeeper; **com'missioner** one who represents high authority in a district *etc*; a member of a commission. – **in** (**out of**) **commission** in (not in) use.

com'mit *v* to give or hand over; to entrust; (with **oneself** *etc*) to promise; to do (something *usu* wrong): *commit a crime*: – *pt* **com'mitted**. – *ns* **com'mitment** a promise; a task that must be done; **com'mittal** the act of committing. – *adj* **com'mitted** pledged to support (something): *a committed Communist*. – *n* **com'mittee** a number of people chosen from a larger body to attend to some special business.

com'mōdious *adj* roomy, spacious.

com'modity *n* an article to be bought or sold; (*pl*) **com'modities** goods, produce.

'**commodore** *n* an officer next above a captain in the navy.

'**common** *adj* shared by all or by many; seen or happening often; ordinary; without special rank. – *n* land belonging to the people of a town, parish *etc*. – *n* '**commoner** one who is not a noble. – *n* '**Commons** (**House of**

Commons) the lower House of Parliament. – *ns* **common law** unwritten law based on custom; **Common Market** an association of certain European countries to establish free trade (without duty, tariffs *etc*) among them; **common noun** a name for any one of a class of things (opposite of **proper noun**). – *adj* '**commonplace** ordinary. – *ns* '**common-room** in a school *etc*, a sittingroom for the use of a group; **common sense** practical good sense; '**commonwealth** an association of self-governing states.

com'mōtion *n* a disturbance *esp* among people.

'**commune** *n* a group of people living together, sharing work *etc*. – *v* **com'mune** to talk together. – *adj* '**communal** common, shared.

com'mūnicate *v* to make known, tell; to give, pass on. *He communicated his fear to the rest*; to get in touch (with); to have a connecting door. – *adj* **com'municable** able to be passed on to others: *a communicable disease*. – *n* **communi'cation** an act or means of conveying information; a message; a way of passing from place to place. – *adj* **com'municative** willing to give information, talkative.

communiqué [kə'mūnikā] *n* an official announcement.

Com'mūnion *n* in the Christian Church, the celebration of the Lord's supper; **com'munion** the act of sharing (thoughts, feelings *etc*), fellowship.

'**commūnism** *n* the kind of socialism developed in Russia or China where industry is controlled by the state. – *n* '**communist** of communism; one who believes in communism.

com'mūnity *n* a group of people living in one place; the public in general: – *pl* **com'munities**.

com'mute *v* to travel regularly between two places *esp* to work (in a city *etc*) from one's home; to change (a punishment) for one less severe. – *n* **com'muter** one who travels regularly to work from his home in a different place.

com'pact *adj* fitted or packed closely, neatly together. – *n* '**compact** a bargain or agreement.

com'panion *n* someone or something that accompanies; a friend. – *adj* **com'panionable** friendly. – *n* **com'panionship** friendship; the act of accompanying. – *n* **com'panionway**

on a ship, a staircase from deck to cabin.

company ['kumpəni] *n* a gathering of persons; a number of persons who have joined together for trade *etc*, a business firm; part of a regiment; a ship's crew; companionship: – *pl* '**companies**.

com'pare *v* to set things together to see how far they are or are not alike; to liken. – *adjs* '**comparable; comparative** [kəm'parətiv] judged by comparing with something else: *a comparative improvement*; (*gram*) the degree of adjective or adverb between positive and superlative (*eg* blacker, better, more courageous). – *n* **com'parison** the act of comparing. – **beyond compare** much better than all rivals.

com'partment *n* a separate part or division (*eg* of a railway carriage).

compass ['kumpəs] *n* an instrument with a magnetized needle for showing direction; (*usu pl*) '**compasses** an instrument (made up of a fixed leg and a movable leg) for drawing circles.

compassion [kəm'pashən] *n* pity for another's suffering; mercy. – *adj* **com'passionate** pitying, merciful.

com'patible *adj* able to live with, agree with *etc*. – *n* **com'pati'bility**.

com'patriot *n* a fellow-countryman.

com'pel *v* to force (someone to do something): – *pt* **com'pelled**.

'**compensate** *v* to make up for wrong or damage done, *esp* by giving money. – *n* **compen'sation** something (*usu* money) given to make up for wrong or damage.

compère ['kompɛr] *n* one who introduces different acts of an entertainment. – Also *v*.

com'pete *v* to try to beat others (in a race *etc*). – *ns* **compe'tition; competitor** [kəm'petitər] one who competes; a rival. – *adj* **com'petitive** (of sport *etc*) based on competitions; (of a person) fond of competing.

'**competent** *adj* capable, efficient; skilled; properly trained or qualified. – *n* '**competence**.

com'pile *v* to make (a book *etc*) from information that one has collected. – *ns* **compi'lation; com'piler**.

com'placent *adj* satisfied (with oneself). – *ns* **com'placence; com'placency**.

com'plain *v* to express dissatisfaction (about something); to grumble. – *n* **com'plaint** a statement of one's dissatisfaction, sorrow *etc*; an illness. *The common cold is not a serious complaint*.

'**complement** *n* that which completes or

fills up; the full number or quantity needed to fill (something); the angle that must be added to a given angle to make up a right angle. – *adj* **comple'mentary** completing; together making up a whole; (of an angle) making up a right angle.

com'plete *adj* having nothing missing; finished; whole. – *v* to finish; to make perfect. – *ns* **com'pleteness; com'pletion** the act of completing.

'**complex** *adj* made up of many parts; complicated, difficult. – *n* a set of repressed emotions and ideas which affect a person's behaviour; an exaggerated reaction (to something), an obsession: *a complex about her weight*; a group of related buildings *etc*: *a shopping complex*: – *pl* '**complexes**. – *n* **com'plexity**: – *pl* **com'plexities**.

com'plexion *n* the colour or look of the skin of the face; appearance.

compliance *see* **comply**.

'**complicate** *v* to make difficult. – *adj* '**complicated** difficult to understand; detailed. – *n* **compli'cation** a (new) difficulty; a development (in an illness *etc*) which makes things worse.

com'plicity *n* a share in a crime or other misdeed.

'**compliment** *n* an expression of praise or flattery; (*pl*) good wishes. – *v* **compli'ment** to praise, to congratulate (on). – *adj* **compli'mentary** flattering, praising; given free: *a complimentary ticket*.

com'plȳ *v* (to agree) to do something that someone else orders or wishes: – *pt* **com'plied**. – *n* **com'pliance**. – *adj* **com'pliant** yielding, giving agreement.

com'pōnent *adj* forming one of the parts of a whole. – *n* a part (of a machine *etc*).

compose [kəm'pōz] *v* to put together or in order, to arrange, form; to create (a piece of music, a poem *etc*). – *adjs* **com'posed** quiet, calm; **composite** ['kompəzit] made up of parts. – *ns* **compo'sition** the act of composing; the thing composed, *esp* a piece of writing or music; a mixture of substances; **com'positor** a person who puts together the types for printing; **com'pōsure** calmness.

'**compost** *n* a gardener's mixture of natural manures.

'**compound** *adj* made up of a number of different parts; not simple. – *n* (in chemistry) a substance formed from two or more elements; an enclosure (round a building).

compre'hend *v* to understand; to

include. – *adj* **compre'hensible** able to be understood. – *n* **compre'hension** the act or power of understanding. – *adj* **compre'hensive** taking in or including much or all. – *n* **comprehensive school** a school providing all types of secondary education.

com'press *v* to press together; to force into a narrower or smaller space. – *n* **'compress** a folded cloth or pad used to create pressure on a part of the body or to reduce inflammation. – *n* **com'pression**.

comprise [kəm'priz] *v* to include, contain; to consist of.

'compromise ['komprəmiz] *n* a settlement, an agreement reached by both sides giving up something. – *v* to make a compromise; to put in a difficult or embarrassing position.

com'pulsion *n* a force driving a person to do a thing. – *adj* **com'pulsory** requiring to be done; forced upon one.

com'punction *n* regret.

com'pute *v* to count, calculate. – *n* **compu'tation**. – *n* **com'puter** an electronic machine that carries out many stages of calculations and stores and sorts information of various kinds.

comrade ['komrid] *n* a companion, a friend.

con *v* to trick, play a confidence trick on. – *ns* **'con-man** one who (regularly) cons people; **'con-trick** a confidence trick.

'concave *adj* hollow or curved inwards (opposite of **convex**). – *n* **concavity** [kon'kavəti] a hollow.

con'ceal *v* to hide, keep secret. – *n* **con'cealment** the act of hiding; a hiding-place.

con'cede *v* to give (up), yield; to admit (the truth of something). *I concede that you may be right.*

conceit [kən'sēt] *n* a too high opinion of oneself or of one's abilities. – *adj* **con'ceited** having a very good opinion of oneself, vain. – *n* **con'ceitedness**.

conceive [kən'sēv] *v* to form in the mind, to imagine; to become pregnant. – *adj* **con'ceivable** able to be imagined.

'concentrate *v* to direct all one's attention or effort towards (something); to bring together to one place. – *adj* **'concentrated** (of an acid *etc*) made stronger or less dilute. – *n* **concen'tration**.

con'centric *adj* (*esp* of circles placed one inside the other) having the same point for centre.

'concept *n* a general idea about something. – *n* **con'ception** the act of conceiving; an idea.

con'cern *v* to have to do with; to make uneasy; to interest, to affect; (with **oneself** *etc*) to be interested or anxious. – *n* that which concerns; anxiety; a business. – *prep* **con'cerning** about: *concerning your inquiry*.

'concert *n* a musical entertainment, performance or show. – *adj* **con'certed** planned or practised together. – **in concert** together.

concertina [konsər'tēnə] *n* a type of musical wind instrument, with bellows and keys.

concerto [kən'chɜrtō] *n* a long piece of music for solo instrument with an accompaniment from an orchestra: – *pl* **con'certos**.

con'cession *n* a granting or allowing of something; that which is granted, allowed.

conch *n* a kind of sea-shell: – *pl* **'conches**.

con'ciliate *v* to win over (someone previously unfriendly or angry). – *n* **con'cili'ation**. – *adj* **con'ciliatory**.

concise [kən'sīs] *adj* brief, in a few words. – *n* **con'ciseness**.

conclude [kən'klōōd] *v* to end; to reach a decision or a judgement; to settle. – *adj* **con'cluding** last, final. – *n* **con'clusion** end; decision, judgement. – *adj* **con'clusive** settling, deciding: *conclusive proof*.

con'coct *v* to mix (a food or drink); to make up, invent: *concoct a story*. – *n* **con'coction**.

'concord *n* agreement.

concourse ['koŋkörs] *n* a crowd; a crowding together; a large open space in a building *etc*.

'concrete *adj* solid, real; made of concrete. – *n* a mixture of gravel, cement *etc* used in building.

con'cur *v* to agree: – *pt* **con'curred**. – *n* **con'currence**. – *adj* **con'current** happening *etc* together; agreeing.

con'cussion *n* temporary harm done to the brain when one receives a knock on the head.

condemn [kən'dem] *v* to blame; to give judgement against or to sentence to a certain punishment; to declare (houses *etc*) unfit for use. – *n* **condem'nation**. – *n* **condemned cell** a cell for a prisoner condemned to death.

con'dense *v* to make to go into a smaller space; (of steam, vapour) to turn to liquid. – *n* **conden'sation** the act of condensing; drops of liquid formed from vapour.

condescend [kondi'send] *v* to act towards someone as if one is better than he is; to make oneself humble. – *adj* **conde'scending**. – *n* **conde'scension**.

'condiment *n* something that seasons or flavours food, *esp* salt or pepper.

con'dition *n* the state in which anything is; something that must happen or be done before some other thing happens or is done; a term of or a point in a bargain, treaty *etc*. – *adj* **con'ditional** depending on certain things happening.

con'dole *v* to share another's sorrow, to sympathize. – *n* **con'dolence**.

con'done *v* to forgive, allow (an offence) to pass unchecked.

con'dūcive *adj* helping, favourable (to): *conducive to peace*.

con'duct *v* to lead, guide; to control, be in charge of, organize; to direct (an orchestra *etc*); to pass on, transmit (electricity *etc*); (with **oneself**) to behave. – *ns* **'conduct** act or method of controlling or organizing; behaviour; **con'duction** a passing on, transmission of heat, electricity *etc*; **con'ductor** one who directs an orchestra *etc*; one in charge of a bus *etc*: – *fem* **con'ductress**; something that transmits (heat, electricity *etc*).

conduit ['kondit] *n* a channel or pipe to carry water, electric wires *etc*.

cone *n* a shape or figure, round at the bottom and coming to a point; anything cone-shaped (*eg* a fir-cone). – *adj* **conical** ['konikəl] cone-shaped.

coney *see* **cony**.

con'fectioner *n* one who makes or sells sweets, cakes *etc*. – *n* **con'fectionery** sweets, cakes *etc*; the shop or business of a confectioner.

confederate [kən'fedərət] *adj* joined together by treaty. – *n* a person who has agreed to act with others (often for an evil purpose). – *ns* **con'federacy** a league, alliance: – *pl* **con'federacies**; **con'fede'ration** a union, a league (of states *etc*).

con'fer *v* to talk together; to give, grant: – *pt* **con'ferred**. – *n* **'conference** a meeting for discussion.

con'fess *v* to own up, to admit (*eg* that one has done wrong). – *adj* **con'fessed** admitted, not secret. – *n* **con'fession** owning up to (a crime or fault).

con'fetti *n* small pieces of coloured paper thrown at weddings or other celebrations.

con'fide *v* (with **in**) to tell (secrets *etc*) to; to hand over to someone's care. – *ns* **confidant** [konfi'dant] one trusted with a secret: – *fem* **confi'dante**; **'confidence** trust or belief; self-reliance; boldness; something told privately. – *adjs* **'confident** very sure; bold; **confi'dential** to be kept as a secret: *confidential information*; having to keep secrets: *confidential secretary*; **con'fiding** trusting. – *n* **confidence trick** a trick to get money *etc* from someone by first gaining his trust.

con'fine *v* to shut up, imprison; to keep within limits. – *npl* **'confines** limits. – *n* **con'finement** the state of being confined; imprisonment; (the time of) giving birth to a child.

con'firm *v* to make firm, strengthen; to make sure; to show to be true; to take into the Church. – *n* **confir'mation** a making sure; proof; the ceremony in which a person is made a full member of the Church. – *adj* **con'firmed** settled in a habit *etc*: *a confirmed bachelor*.

'confiscate *v* to take away, as a punishment. – *n* **confis'cation**.

confla'gration *n* a big fire.

'conflict *n* a struggle or contest; a battle. – *v* **con'flict** (of statements *etc*) to contradict each other. – *adj* **con'flicting**.

confluence ['konflōōəns] *n* a place where rivers join.

con'form *v* to follow the example of most other people (in behaviour, dress, religion *etc*). – *ns* **confor'mation** form, shape or structure; **con'formity** likeness; the act of conforming.

con'found *v* to puzzle, confuse.

confront [kən'frunt] *v* to face, meet (*eg* an enemy, a difficulty); to bring face to face (with). *He was confronted with the evidence*. – *n* **confron'tation**.

confuse [kən'fūz] *v* to mix up, to put in disorder; to mix up in the mind; to puzzle; to embarrass. – *n* **con'fusion**.

con'geal *v* to become solid *esp* by cooling; to freeze.

con'gēnial *adj* agreeable, pleasant.

con'genital *adj* (of a disease *etc*) present in a person from birth.

conger ['koŋgər] *n* a kind of large sea-eel.

con'gested *adj* overcrowded; clogged; (of a part of the body) too full of blood. – *n* **con'gestion** (of traffic *etc*) overcrowded condition; a gathering of too much blood in one part of the body.

conglomeration [kənglomə'rāshən] *n* a heap or collection.

con'gratulate *v* to express one's joy (to a

person) at his success. – n **congratu-'lation** (often in pl). – adj **con-'gratulatory**.

congregate ['koŋgrigāt] v to come together in a crowd. – n **congre'gation** a gathering esp of people in a church.

congress ['koŋgres] n a large meeting of persons from different places for discussion: – pl **'congresses**; **'Congress** the name given to the parliament of the United States.

congruent ['koŋgrŏŏənt] adj (of triangles etc) exactly matching.

congruous ['koŋgrŏŏəs] adj suitable, appropriate. – n **con'gruity**.

conical see **cone**.

'conifer n a cone-bearing tree. – adj **co'niferous**.

con'jecture n a guess. – v to guess. – adj **con'jectural**.

conjugal ['konjŏŏgəl] adj of marriage.

conjugate ['konjŏŏgāt] v to give the different parts of a verb. – n **conju'gation**.

con'junction n a word that joins sentences, phrases etc (eg and, but); a union, combination with. – **in conjunction with** together with, acting with.

conjuncti'vitis n a kind of inflammation of the inside of the eyelid and surface of the eye.

conjure ['kunjər] v to do tricks that seem magical. – n **'conjuror** one who does conjuring tricks.

'conker n a horse-chestnut, esp one used in a game (**'conkers**) in which one tries to hit one's opponent's chestnut.

con'nect v to join or fasten together. – n **con'nection** something that connects; a state of being connected; a train, aeroplane etc which takes one on the next part of one's journey; a friend, relation etc. – **in connection with** concerning.

'conning-tower n the place on a warship or submarine from which orders for steering are given.

con'nive v (with **at**) to take no notice of, disregard (a misdeed etc). – n **con'nivance**.

connoisseur [konə'sör] n one who has an expert knowledge (of pictures, music, wines etc).

conno'tation n a meaning; what is suggested by a word in addition to its simple meaning.

con'nūbial adj of marriage.

conquer ['koŋkər] v to gain by force; to overcome. – ns **'conqueror** one who conquers; **conquest** ['koŋkwest] something won by force or effort; an act of

conquering.

conscience ['konshəns] n one's inward sense of what is right and wrong. – adj **consci'entious** careful and earnest in one's work etc. – n **consci'entiousness**.

conscious ['konshəs] adj aware of oneself and one's surroundings, awake (after being unconscious); aware, knowing; deliberate, intentional. – n **'consciousness**.

'conscript n a person who is obliged by law to serve in the armed forces. – v **con'script** to compel to serve (in the armed forces). – n **con'scription**.

'consecrate v to set apart for a holy use. – n **conse'cration**.

con'secutive adj coming in order, one after the other.

con'sensus n an agreement (of opinion).

con'sent v to agree (to). – n agreement; permission.

'consequence n that which comes after, result; importance. – adjs **'consequent** following as a result; **conse'quential** following as a result; important.

con'serve v to keep from being wasted, spoilt or lost. – ns **conser'vation** the act of conserving (old buildings, countryside, wild animals and flowers etc); **conser'vationist** one who encourages and practises conservation. – adj **con'servative** not liking changes; (of a guess or estimate) moderate, not exaggerated. – n, adj **Con'servative** (a supporter) of the Conservative Party. – n **con'servatory** a glass-house for plants: – pl **con'servatories**. – n **Conservative Party** one of the main political parties of the UK.

con'sider v to think; to think about (carefully); to think of as, regard as; to pay attention to the wishes etc of (someone). – adjs **con'siderable** (fairly) large; important; **con'siderate** thoughtful about others' wishes etc, kind. – n **conside'ration** serious thinking; thoughtfulness for others; a small payment. – prep **con'sidering** taking into account: considering his age.

consign [kən'sin] v to give into the care of. – n **con'signment** a load (eg of goods).

con'sist v to be made up of. – n **con'sistency** thickness or firmness; the quality of (always) being the same: – pl **con'sistencies**. – adj **con'sistent** not changing, regular; (of statements etc) not contradicting each other.

con'sole v to comfort, cheer up. – n **conso'lation** something that makes trouble etc more easy to bear.

con'solidate v to make or become solid or strong; to unite. – n **consoli'dation**.

'consonant n a letter of the alphabet that is not a vowel (eg b, c).

'consort n a husband or wife; a companion. – v **con'sort** to keep company (with).

con'spicuous adj clearly seen, noticeable.

con'spire v to plan or plot together. – ns **conspiracy** [kən'spirəsi] a plot by a group of people: – pl **con'spiracies**; **con'spirator** one who takes part in a conspiracy.

constable ['kunstəbl] n a policeman; (hist) a high officer of state or the keeper of a castle. – n **con'stabulary** the police force.

'constant adj never stopping; never changing; faithful. – n **'constancy**. – adv **'constantly** always; often.

constel'lation n a group of stars.

conster'nation n dismay, astonishment.

consti'pation n too slow working of the bowels. – v **'constipate** to cause constipation.

'constitute v to set up, establish; to form or make up. – n **con'stituency** (the voters in) a district which has a member of parliament: – pl **con'stituencies**. – adj **con'stituent** making or forming. – n a necessary part; a voter in a constituency. – n **consti'tution** the way in which a thing is made up; the natural condition of a body with regard to strength, health etc; a set of rules, laws etc by which a country or body of people is governed. – adj **consti'tutional** of a constitution. – n a short walk for the sake of one's health.

con'strain v to force (a person) to act in a certain way. – n **con'straint** compulsion, force; embarrassment.

con'strict v to press together tightly, to cramp; to surround and squeeze.

con'struct v to build, make. – n **con'struction** the act of constructing; anything built; the arrangement of words in a sentence; meaning. – adj **con'structive** of construction; helping to improve: constructive criticism.

'consul n a person who looks after his country's affairs in a foreign country; in ancient Rome, a chief ruler. – adj **'consular**. – n **'consulate** the official residence of a consul; the duties and authority of a consul.

con'sult v to seek advice or information from. – n **con'sultant** one (esp a doctor) who gives professional or expert advice. – Also adj. – n **consul'tation** the act of consulting (for

expert advice). – n **consulting room** a room where a doctor etc sees his patients.

con'sume v to eat up; to use (up); to destroy. – n **con'sumer** one who buys, eats or uses (goods etc).

'consummate v to complete. – adj complete, perfect.

con'sumption n the act of consuming; the amount consumed; (old) tuberculosis.

'contact n touch; meeting; communication; an acquaintance, esp one who can be of help; a person who has been with someone suffering from an infectious disease. – v to get into contact with.

con'tagious adj (of disease etc) spreading from person to person (esp by touch).

con'tain v to hold or have inside; to hold back: contain her anger. – n **con'tainer** a box, tin, jar etc for holding anything.

con'taminate v to make impure or dirty. – n **contami'nation**.

'contemplate v to look at or think about attentively; to intend. – n **contem'plation**.

con'temporary adj, n (of) a person living at or belonging to the same time.

con'tempt n complete lack of respect, scorn. – adjs **con'temptible** deserving scorn, worthless; **con'temptuous** scornful. – **contempt of court** deliberate disobedience to and disrespect for the law and those who carry it out.

con'tend v to struggle against; to hold firmly to a belief, maintain (that). – n **con'tention** an opinion strongly held; a quarrel, dispute. – adj **con'tentious** quarrelsome.

con'tent adj happy, satisfied. – n happiness, satisfaction. – v to make happy or to satisfy. – n **'content** (often pl) that which is contained in anything. – adj **con'tented** happy, content. – n **con'tentment** happiness, content.

contention, contentious see contend.

con'test v to fight for, argue against. – n **'contest** a fight, a competition. – n **con'testant** one who contests.

'context n the place in a book, speech etc to which a certain part belongs; the setting, background of an event etc.

con'tiguous adj touching, close. – n **conti'guity**.

'continent n one of the five great divisions of the earth's land surface (Europe, Asia, Africa, Australia, America). – adj **conti'nental** of or like a continent; European. – **the Continent** the mainland of Europe.

con'tingent adj depending (on something else). – *n* a batch, a group (*esp* of soldiers). – *n* **con'tingency** a chance happening: – *pl* **con'tingencies**.

continue [kən'tinū] *v* to keep on, go on (doing something). – *adj* **con'tinual** going on without stop. – *ns* **con'tinuance** the state of going on without interruption; **continu'ation** the act of carrying something farther or continuing; a part that continues, an extension; **conti'nuity** the state of having no gaps or breaks. – *adj* **con-'tinuous** coming one after the other (without a gap or break).

con'tort *v* to twist or turn violently. – *ns* **con'tortion** a violent twisting; **con-'tortionist** one who can twist his body violently.

contour ['kontōōr] *n* (often *pl*) outline, shape. – *n* **contour line** a line drawn on a map through points all at the same height above sea-level.

'contraband *n* goods, legally forbidden to be brought into a country; smuggled goods. – Also *adj*.

contra'ception *n* the prevention of conceiving children. – *adj*, *n* **contra'ceptive** (of) a drug or device which prevents the conceiving of children.

con'tract *v* to become or make smaller; to bargain for; to promise in writing. – *ns* **'contract** a (written) agreement; **con'traction** a shortening; a shortened form (*esp* of a word); **con'tractor** one who promises to do work, or supply goods, at an arranged price.

contra'dict *v* to say the opposite of; to deny. – *n* **contra'diction**. – *adj* **con-tra'dictory**.

con'tralto *n* the deepest or lowest singing voice in women: – *pl* **con'traltos**.

con'traption *n* a machine, a device.

contrapuntal *see* **counterpoint**.

'contrary[1] *adj* opposite. – *n* the opposite. – **on the contrary** just the opposite.

con'trāry[2] *adj* always doing or saying the opposite, perverse. – *n* **con'trariness**.

con'trast *v* to compare so as to show differences; to show a marked difference from. – *n* **'contrast** a difference between (two) things.

contra'vene *v* to break (a law *etc*). – *n* **contravention** [kontrə'venshən].

contretemps ['kontrətöŋ] *n* a mishap at an awkward moment.

con'tribute *v* to give (money, help *etc*) along with others; to supply, give (written articles to a magazine *etc*); to help to cause (something). – *ns* **contri-'bution; con'tributor**.

'contrite *adj* very sorry for having done

wrong. – *n* **contrition** [kən'trishən].

con'trive *v* to plan; to bring about (with difficulty), manage. – *n* **con'trivance** an act of contriving; an invention.

con'trōl *n* power or authority to guide, rule, manage, restrain *etc*; (often *pl*) means by which a driver keeps a machine under his power or guidance. – *v* to exercise control over; to have power over. – *adj* **con'trolled**. – *n* **con'troller**. – *n* **control tower** an airport building from which landing and take-off instructions are given.

con'troversy *n* an argument, a disagreement: – *pl* **con'troversies**. – *adj* **contro'versial** likely to cause argument.

co'nundrum *n* a riddle, a question.

conur'bation *n* a group of towns forming a single built-up area.

convalesce [konvə'les] *v* to recover health gradually after being ill. – *n* **conva'lescence** a gradual return to health and strength. – *adj*, *n* **conva-'lescent** (of) a person convalescing.

con'vection *n* the spreading of heat by movement of heated air or water. – *n* **con'vector** a heater which works by convection.

con'vene *v* to call or come together. – *n* **con'vener** one who calls a meeting.

con'vēnient *adj* suitable; easy to reach or use, handy. – *n* **con'venience** suitableness, handiness; any means of giving ease or comfort; (*coll*) a (public) lavatory. – **at your convenience** when it suits you best.

'convent *n* a dwelling for nuns (or monks).

con'venticle *n* (*hist*) a secret meeting (for worship).

con'vention *n* a way of behaving that has become usual, a custom; a large meeting or assembly; a treaty or agreement. – *adj* **con'ventional** done by habit or custom.

converge [kən'vörj] *v* to come together, meet at a point. – *n* **con'vergence**. – *adj* **con'vergent**.

con'verse *v* to talk. – *n* **'converse** talk; the opposite. – *adj* opposite. – *n* **conver'sation** talk, exchange of ideas, news *etc*. – *adj* **conver'sational** of or used in conversation; talkative.

con'vert *v* to change (from one thing into another); to turn from one religion to another, or from an evil to a religious life. – *ns* **con'version** the act of converting; something converted to another use; **'convert** one who has been converted. – *adj* **con'vertible** able to be changed (from one thing to another). – *n* a car with a folding roof.

'**convex** *adj* curved on the outside (opposite of **concave**). – *n* **con'vexity**.

convey [kən'vā] *v* to carry, transport; to send; (in law) to hand over: *convey property*. – *n* **con'veyance** the act of conveying; a vehicle of any kind. – *n* **conveyor belt** an endless moving band for conveying articles, *esp* in a factory.

con'vict *v* to declare or to prove that a person is guilty. – *ns* **'convict** one found guilty of a crime (and sent to prison); **con'viction** (in a law court) the passing of a sentence upon a guilty person; a strong belief.

con'vince *v* to make (someone) believe that something is true; to persuade (someone) by showing.

con'vivial *adj* jolly, festive. – *n* **convivi-'ality**.

convo'cation *n* a meeting *esp* of bishops, or of heads of a university.

con'volvūlus *n* a kind of twining plant with trumpet-shaped flowers.

'**convoy** *v* to go along with and protect. – *n* merchant ships protected by warships; a line of army lorries with armed guard.

con'vulse *v* to cause to shake violently: *convulsed with laughter.* – *n* **con'vulsion** a sudden stiffening or jerking of the muscles; a violent disturbance. – *adj* **con'vulsive**.

'**cōny, 'coney** *n* a rabbit or its fur.

coo *v* to make a sound like that of a dove. – Also *n*.

cook *v* to prepare (food) by heating; (*coll*) to alter (accounts *etc*) dishonestly. – *n* one who cooks and prepares food ready for table. – *ns* **'cooker** a stove for cooking; an apple *etc* used in cooking, not for eating raw; **'cookery** the art of cooking.

cool *adj* slightly cold; calm, not excited; rather cheeky. – *v* to make or grow cool; to calm. – *adv* **'coolly**. – *n* **'coolness**.

coop *n* a box or cage for hens *etc*. – *v* to shut (up) as in a coop. – *n* **'cooper** one who makes barrels.

cō-'operate *v* to work or act together. – *n* **co-ope'ration** a working together; willingness to act together. – *n* **co-operative society** a trading organization in which the profits are shared among members.

cō-'opt *v* to choose (someone) to join a committee or other body.

cō-'ordinate *v* to make things fit in or work smoothly together. – *n* **co-ordi'nation**.

coot *n* a type of water-bird with a white spot on the forehead.

cope *v* to struggle or deal successfully (with), manage.

'**cōping** *n* the top layer of stone in a wall. – *n* **'coping-stone** the top stone of a wall.

'**cōpious** *adj* plentiful.

'**copper** *n* an element, a hard reddish-brown metal; a coin made from (metal containing) copper; a large vessel made of copper, *usu* to boil water in. – *n* **'copperplate** very fine and regular handwriting.

'**copra** *n* the dried kernel of the coconut, yielding coconut oil.

copse, coppice [kops], ['kopis] *n* a wood of low-growing trees.

'**copy** *n* an imitation; a print or reproduction (of a picture *etc*); an individual example of a certain book *etc*: – *pl* **'copies**. – *v* to make a copy of; to imitate. – *n* **'copyright** the right of one person or body to publish a book, perform a play, print music *etc*. – *adj* or protected by the law of copyright.

coquette [kə'ket] *n* a woman who flirts.

'**coral** *n* a hard substance made up of the skeletons of a kind of tiny animal, gradually building up from the sea-bottom to form a rock-like mass (**coral reef**).

cord *n* thin rope or strong string; anything of cord-like appearance:

'**cordial** *adj* cheery, friendly. – *n* a refreshing drink. – *n* **cordi'ality** friendliness.

'**cordite** *n* a kind of explosive.

'**cordon** *n* a line of guards, police *etc* to keep people back. – *adj, n* **cordon bleu** ['kördoŋ'blə] (of) a first class cook.

cordu'roy *n* a ribbed cloth (*usu* cotton) looking like velvet.

core [kör] *n* the inner part of anything, *esp* of fruit. – *v* to take out the core of fruit.

co-respondent [ko·rə'spond·ənt] *n* a man or woman charged with adultery, and proceeded against along with the wife or husband who is the **respondent**.

'**corgi** *n* a breed of short-legged dog.

cork *n* the outer bark of the cork-tree (an oak found in southern Europe *etc*); a stopper for a bottle *etc* made of cork. – *adj* made of cork. – *v* to plug, to stop up (with a cork). – *n* **'corkscrew** a tool with a screw-like spike for taking out corks. – *adj* shaped like a cork-screw.

corm *n* the bulb-like underground stem of certain plants.

'**cormorant** *n* a type of big sea-bird.

corn *n* (a grain or seed of) wheat, oats or

maize; a little lump of hard skin *usu* on a toe. – *ns* '**corncrake** a kind of bird with a harsh croaking cry; **corned beef** salted (tinned) beef; '**cornflour** finely ground (maize) flour; '**cornflower** a type of plant, with a blue flower.

cornea ['körniə] *n* the transparent covering of the eyeball.

'**corner** *n* the point where two lines, walls, roads *etc* meet; a small (quiet) place; (*coll*) a difficult situation. – *v* to drive into a place from which there is no escape. – *n* '**corner-stone** the stone at the corner of (the foundation of) a building; something upon which much depends.

'**cornet** *n* a type of musical instrument like a trumpet; an ice-cream in a cone-shaped wafer.

cornice ['körnis] *n* an ornamental border round a ceiling.

co'rolla *n* the petals of a flower.

co'rollary *n* something which may be taken for granted when something else has been proved; a natural result: – *pl* **co'rollaries**.

'**coronary** *n* (short for **coronary thrombosis**) a heart disease caused by blockage of one of the arteries supplying the heart: – *pl* '**coronaries**.

coro'nation *n* the crowning of a king or queen.

'**coroner** *n* a government officer who holds inquiries into the causes of sudden or accidental deaths.

'**coronet** *n* a small crown; a crown-like head-dress.

'**corporal** *n* in the British Army, the rank next below sergeant. – *adj* of the body. – *n* **corporal punishment** beating, caning *etc*.

'**corporate** *adj* of or forming a whole, united. – *n* **corpo'ration** a body of people acting as one, *eg* for administrative or business purposes.

corps [kör] *n* a division of an army; an organized group: – *pl* **corps** [körz].

corpse *n* a dead body.

'**corpulence** *n* fatness of body. – *adj* '**corpulent**.

corpuscle ['körpusl] *n* a very small particle or cell in a fluid (*esp* blood).

cor'ral *n* (*US*) a fenced space for (captured) animals; (*US*) a circle of wagons formed for defence.

cor'rect *v* to remove faults and errors from; to set right; to punish. – *adj* having no errors; true. – *n* **cor'rection** the putting right of a mistake; punishment. – *adj* **cor'rective**.

corres'pond *v* to write letters to; to be similar (to), to match. – *ns*

corres'pondence letters; likeness to; **corres'pondent** one who writes letters; one who contributes reports to a newspaper *etc*.

'**corridor** *n* a passage-way.

corrigendum [kori'jendəm] *n* a correction to a book *etc*: – *pl* **corri'genda**.

cor'roborate *v* to give evidence which strengthens evidence already given. – *n* **corrobo'ration**.   – *adj* **cor'roborative**.

cor'rode *v* to rust; to eat away, as acid eats into metal. – *n* **cor'rosion**. – *adj* **cor'rosive**.

'**corrugated** *adj* folded or shaped into ridges: *corrugated iron*.

cor'rupt *v* to make evil or rotten; to bribe. – *adj* dishonest, taking bribes; bad, rotten. – *adj* **cor'ruptible** able to be corrupted or bribed. – *n* **cor'ruption** evil, sin; bribery.

'**corsair** *n* a pirate; a pirate-ship.

'**corset** *n* a tight-fitting under-garment to support the body.

cortege [kör'tezh] *n* a (funeral) procession.

cor'vette *n* a type of small swift warship, used against submarines.

cosh *n* a short heavy stick: – *pl* '**coshes**. – *v* to hit with a cosh.

cosmetic [koz'metik] *n* something designed to improve the appearance, *esp* of the face. – *adj* improving the appearance of.

cosmic ['kozmik] *adj* of the universe or outer space. – *n* '**cosmonaut** an astronaut.

cosmopolitan [kozmə'politən] *adj* belonging to all parts of the world; made up of people of many races; used to, feeling at home in, many different parts of the world.

'**cosset** *v* to treat with too much kindness, pamper.

cost *v* to be priced at; to cause loss (of something) as though in payment. *War costs lives*: – *pt, pp* **cost**. – *n* what must be spent or suffered in order to get something. – *adj* '**costly** high-priced, valuable. – *n* '**costliness**.

'**coster(monger)** *n* a street-seller of fruit *etc*.

'**costume** *n* (a set of) clothes. – *n* **costume jewellery** inexpensive, imitation jewellery.

cosy ['közi] *adj* warm and comfortable. – *n* a covering used for a teapot *etc* to keep it warm.

cot *n* a small bed with high sides for children; (*US*) a small bed which can be folded away, a camp bed; (in poetry *etc*) a cottage.

coterie ['kōtəri] *n* a number of persons interested in the same things who tend to exclude other people.

'**cottage** *n* a small house, *usu* in the countryside or a village. – *n* '**cottager** one who lives in a cottage.

'**cotton** *n* a soft fluffy substance got from the seeds of the cotton plant; cloth made of cotton. – Also *adj*. – *n* '**cotton'wool** cotton in a fluffy state, used for wiping, absorbing.

couch *n* a sofa: – *pl* '**couches**. – *v* to express (in words). *The letter was couched in old-fashioned English.* – *n* **couch grass** a kind of grass, a troublesome weed.

'**couchant** *adj* (in heraldry) lying down: *lion couchant*.

cougar ['kōōgər] *n* (*esp US*) the puma.

cough [kof] *n* a noisy effort of the lungs to throw out air and harmful matter from the throat. – *v* to make this effort.

could [kōod] *v* the form of the verb **can** used to express a condition. *He could do it if he tried. I could understand a small mistake, but this is ridiculous*; *see* also **can**[1].

coulomb ['kōōlom] *n* a unit of electric charge.

'**council** *n* a group of (elected) persons who meet to discuss or give advice about policy, government *etc*. – *n* '**councillor** a member of a council.

'**counsel** *n* advice; one who advises in matters of law, a lawyer. – *v* to give advice to. – *n* '**counsellor** one who gives advice.

count *v* to find the total number of, add up; to say numbers in order (1, 2, 3, *etc*); to think, consider. *Count yourself lucky!* – *n* the act of counting; the number counted; a charge, accusation; a point being considered; a nobleman in certain countries: – *fem* '**countess**. – *n* '**counter** a person who or a thing which counts; a token used in counting; a small plastic disc used in ludo *etc*; a table on which money is counted or goods are laid for show. – *adj* '**countless** too many to be counted, very many. – **count on** to rely on, depend on.

'**countenance** *n* the face; the look on a person's face. – *v* to allow, encourage.

'**counter** *v* to answer or oppose (a move, act *etc*) by another. – *adv* in the opposite direction. – *adj* opposed; opposite. – *n see* **count**.

counter- *prefix* against, opposing; opposite.

counte'ract *v* to block or defeat (an action) by doing the opposite.

'**counterattack** *n* an attack made by the defenders upon an attacking enemy. – Also *v*.

'**counterattraction** *n* something which draws away the attention from something else.

'**countercharge** *v* to bring a charge against someone who has accused one. – Also *n*.

counterfeit ['kowntərfit] *adj* not genuine, not real; made in imitation *esp* with a dishonest purpose: *counterfeit money*. – Also *n*. – *v* to make a copy of for dishonest purposes.

'**counterfoil** *n* a part of a cheque, postal order *etc* kept by the payer or sender.

counter'mand *v* to give an order which goes against one already given.

'**counterpane** *n* a top cover for a bed.

'**counterpart** *n* something which is just like or which corresponds to something or someone.

'**counterpoint** *n* the combining of two or more melodies to make a piece of music. – *adj* **contra'puntal**.

'**counterpoise** *n* a weight which balances another weight.

countersign ['kowntərsīn] *v* to sign one's name after another has done so to show that a document is genuine.

countess *see* **count** and **earl**.

country ['kuntri] *n* a nation; a land under one government; the land in which one lives; a district which is not in a town or city; an area or stretch of land: – *pl* '**countries**. – *adj* belonging to the country. – *n* '**countryside** the parts of the country other than towns and cities.

'**county** *n* a division of a country: – *pl* '**counties**.

coup [kōō] *n* any sudden outstandingly successful move or act; a sudden and violent change in government. *The president was killed during the coup.*

couple ['kupl] *n* a pair, two of a kind together; husband and wife. – *v* to join together. – *ns* **couplet** ['kuplit] two lines of rhyming verse; '**coupling** a kind of link for joining parts of machinery, railway carriages *etc*.

coupon ['kōōpon] *n* a part of a ticket *etc* that can be torn off *esp* a piece cut from an advertisement *etc* which may be exchanged for goods or money; (**football coupon**) a form in which one tries to forecast the result of football matches in the hope of winning money.

courage ['kurij] *n* bravery, lack of fear. – *adj* **cou'rageous**.

courgette [kōōr'zhet] *n* a type of vegetable, a small marrow.

courier ['kooriər] *n* one who acts as guide for tourists; a messenger.

course [körs] *n* a path in which anything moves; the act of moving from point to point; the road or ground on which one runs, travels, plays games *etc*; the direction to be followed. *The ship held its course*; line of action (what one should do); a part of a meal; a number of things following each other: *a course of twelve lectures*; one of the rows of bricks in a wall. – *v* to move quickly; to hunt. – *ns* 'courser a swift horse; 'coursing the hunting of hares with greyhounds. – **in due course** after a while, when it's the proper time; **in the course of** during.

court [kört] *n* a shut-in space (*eg* one surrounded by houses, or one used for certain sports such as tennis); the persons who attend a king, queen *etc*; any place where a king, queen *etc* lives; the place where legal cases are heard or tried. – *v* to try to persuade (a woman) to marry one, to woo; to try to gain (*eg* admiration) or seem to be trying to gain (danger *etc*). – *adj* **courteous** ['körtiəs] polite; obliging. – *n* **courtier** ['körtiər] a member of a royal court. – *adj* 'courtly having fine manners. – *ns* 'court-'martial a court held by navy or army officers to try those who break navy or army laws: – *pl* 'courts-'martial; 'courtship the act or time of courting or wooing; 'courtyard a court or enclosed space beside a house.

courtesy ['körtəsi] *n* politeness.

courtier *see* **court**.

cousin ['kuzn] *n* the son or daughter of an uncle or aunt.

cove *n* a small inlet on the sea coast; a bay.

coven ['kuvən] *n* a gathering of witches.

covenant ['kuvənənt] *n* an important agreement or promise between people to do or not to do something.

cover ['kuvər] *v* to put or spread something on, over or about; to hide; to stretch over (an area or a length of time). *Trees covered the land. His diary covered three years*; to include; to be enough for. *Five pounds should cover the cost*; to travel over. *He covers 3 kilometres a day*; to point a weapon at. *He had the gangster covered.* – *n* something that covers, hides or protects. – *ns* 'coverage the area covered; the amount or extent of news covered by a newspaper *etc*; the amount of protection given by an insurance policy; 'covering something which covers; 'coverlet a bed cover. – **cover up** to

cover completely; to conceal deliberately (a wrong, an illegal or dishonest deed *etc*) (*n* 'cover-up).

covert ['kuvərt] *adj* secret, not done openly. – *n* a hiding place (trees, bushes *etc*) for animals or birds when hunted.

covet ['kuvit] *v* to desire eagerly, *esp* something belonging to another person. – *adj* 'covetous. – *n* 'covetousness.

covey ['kuvi] *n* a flock of birds, *esp* partridges.

cow [kow] *n* the female animal of the ox kind used for giving milk; the female of certain other animals (*eg* elephant, whale). – *v* to frighten. – *adj* cowed. – *ns* 'cowboy a man who has the charge of cattle on a ranch in America; 'cowherd one who looks after cows.

coward ['kowərd] *n* person who has no courage and shows fear easily. – *adj* 'cowardly. – *n* cowardice ['kowərdis] lack of courage.

cowed *see* **cow**.

cower ['kowər] *v* to crouch down or shrink back, through fear.

cowl [kowl] *n* a cap or hood, *esp* that of a monk; a cover for a chimney.

cowslip ['kowslip] *n* a type of yellow wild flower.

cox short for **coxswain**.

coxcomb ['kokskōm] *n* (*hist*) a strip of red cloth notched like a cock's comb, which court jesters used to wear; a person who is conceited *esp* about his dress.

coxswain ['koksn] *n* one who steers a boat; an officer in charge of a boat and crew.

coy *adj* too modest or shy.

coyote [koi'ōti] *n* a type of small wolf of N. America: – *pls* coy'ote, coy'otes.

coypu ['koipoo] *n* a type of large, beaver-like animal living in rivers and marshes.

crab *n* a kind of sea animal with a shell and five pairs of legs, the first pair of which have large claws. – *adj* **crabbed** ['krabid] bad-tempered. – *n* **crab apple** a type of small, bitter apple. – *adj, adv* 'crabwise (moving) sideways like a crab.

crack *v* to (cause to) make a sharp sudden sound; to break partly without falling to pieces; to break into (a safe); to solve, decipher (a code); to break open (a nut); to make (a joke). – *n* a sharp sound; a split or break; a narrow opening; (*coll*) a sharp, witty remark. – *adj* excellent: *a crack tennis player.* – *adj* **cracked** split, damaged, crazy. – *n* 'cracker a hollow tube of paper, often containing a small gift, which breaks with a bang when the ends are pulled; a thin, crisp biscuit. – **crack up** to fail suddenly, go to pieces, collapse.

'crackle to make a continuous cracking noise. – n **'crackling** a cracking sound; the rind or outer skin of roast pork.

'cradle n a baby's bed *esp* one in which it can be rocked; anything shaped like a cradle in which something is laid (*eg* a frame under a ship that is being built).

craft n a trade or skill; a boat or small ship; slyness. – n **'craftsman** one who works at a trade. – adj **'crafty** cunning, sly.

crag n a rough steep rock. – adj **'craggy** rocky; (*usu* of faces) with strong or rough features.

cram v to fill full, stuff; to learn up in a short time facts for an examination: – pt **crammed**.

cramp n a painful stiffening of the muscles. – v to put into too narrow or small a space; to hinder, restrict. – adj **cramped** without enough room; (of handwriting) small and closely-written.

'crampon n a metal plate with spikes, fixed to the boots when climbing on ice *etc.*

'cranberry n a type of red, sour berry.

crane n a kind of large wading bird with long legs, neck and bill; a machine for lifting heavy weights. – v to stretch out the neck (to see round or over something).

'cranium n the skull: – pls **'crania, 'craniums**.

crank n a handle with which something (*eg* an axle) can be made to turn; a lever or arm which turns movement to and fro into movement round and round; a person with unusual or odd ideas. – v to start (an engine) with a crank. – adj **'cranky** odd, with unusual ideas *etc*; cross, irritable.

'cranny n a small opening or crack: – pl **'crannies**.

crape see **crêpe**.

crash n a noise of heavy things breaking or banging together; a collision, a violent meeting together of a vehicle (*eg* car, train, aeroplane) with another vehicle or another object (*eg* a tree, the ground) *usu* resulting in damage; the failure of a business: – pl **'crashes**. – v (of a car *etc*) to be involved in a crash; (of a business) to fail; to force one's way noisily through; (*coll*) to attend (a party) uninvited (also **'gatecrash**). – n **'crash-helmet** a covering for the head worn for protection by motor-cyclists

etc. – v **'crash-'land** to land (an aircraft), *usu* in an emergency, in a way which damages it. – n **'crash-'landing**.

crass adj stupid.

crate n an openwork container, *usu* made of wooden slats, for carrying goods, sometimes with compartments for bottles.

'crater n the bowl-shaped mouth of a volcano; a hole in the earth made by an explosion.

cra'vat n a scarf worn in place of a tie.

crave v to long for. – n **'craving**.

'craven adj cowardly.

crawfish see **crayfish**.

crawl v to move on hands and knees; to move slowly; to be covered (with): *crawling with wasps*; to behave in too humble a manner. – n the act of crawling; a kind of swimming stroke.

'crayfish, 'crawfish n a kind of shellfish, something like a small lobster.

'crayon n a coloured pencil or stick used for drawing.

craze n a temporary fashion or enthusiasm. – adj **'crazy** mad, unreasonable. – n **crazy paving** paving made with stones of irregular shape.

creak v to make a sharp, grating sound like the sound of a hinge in need of oiling.

cream n the fatty substance which forms on milk and gives butter when churned; anything like cream: *cold cream*: *ice cream*; the best part of anything: *cream of society*. – v to take off the cream; to take away the best part of anything. *The school creamed off the best pupils and put them in one class.* – adj **'creamy** full of or like cream.

crease n a mark made by folding or doubling anything; (in cricket) a line showing the position of a batsman and bowler. – v to make creases in; to become creased.

create [kri'āt] v to bring into being; to make; (*coll*) to make a fuss. – n **cre'ation** the act of creating; that which is created. – adj **cre'ative** having the ability to create, artistic. – n **cre'ator** one who creates. – **the Creator** God.

creature ['krēchər] n an animal or person.

creche [kresh] n a (public) nursery for children.

cre'dentials npl evidence, *esp* letters which a person carries to show people that they may trust him.

'credible adj able to be believed. – n **credi'bility**.

credit *n* recognition of good qualities, achievements *etc*. *Give him credit for some common sense*; good qualities, honour; source of honour: *a credit to the school*; trustworthiness regarding ability to pay for goods *etc*; time allowed for payment of goods *etc*; the sale of goods to be paid for at a later time; the side of an account on which payments received are entered; a sum of money which one has in an account at a bank; belief, trust; (*pl*) (the giving of) the names of people who have helped in a film *etc*. – *v* to believe; to enter on the credit side of an account; (with **with**) to give credit for; to think (someone) has. *I credited him with more sense*. – *adj* '**creditable** bringing honour or good reputation to. – *n* '**creditor** one to whom money is due.

'**credulous** *adj* believing too easily. – *n* **cre'dulity**.

creed *n* what is believed, *esp* in one's religion.

creek *n* a small inlet or bay on the sea coast; a short river.

creep *v* to move slowly or secretly and silently; to move on hands and knees or with the body close to the ground; to shiver with fear or disgust. *It makes your flesh creep*; (of a plant *etc*) to grow along the ground or a wall *etc*: – *pt* **crept** [krept]. – *n* a moving in a creeping way; (*coll*) a person one dislikes; (*pl*) great fear or disgust. *Spiders give me the creeps*. – *n* '**creeper** a plant growing along the ground, or up a wall. – **creep up on** to approach (*usu* from behind) unseen.

cre'mate *v* to burn (a dead body). – *ns* **cre'mation**; **crematorium** [kreməˈtöriəm] a place where dead bodies are burnt.

crenellated [ˈkrenəlātid] *adj* having battlements.

'**creosote** *n* an oily liquid made from wood tar, used to keep wood from rotting.

crêpe, crape [krāp] *n* a type of fine, crinkly material. – *n* **crêpe paper** paper with a crinkled appearance.

crept *see* **creep**.

crescent [ˈkresnt] *adj* curve-shaped, like the new or old moon, not the full moon. – *n* anything shaped in a curve; a name for a curved road or street.

cress *n* a type of plant with leaves of a slightly bitter taste, used in salads.

crest *n* the tuft on the head of a cock or other bird; the top of a hill, wave *etc*; feathers on the top of a helmet; a badge. – *adj* '**crestfallen** down-hearted, dis-

couraged.

cre'vasse *n* a deep crack or split in snow or ice.

crevice [ˈkrevis] *n* a crack or narrow opening.

crew [krōō] *n* the people who man a ship, aircraft, bus *etc*; a gang or mob. – *v* to act as a member of a crew; *see* **crow**. – *n* '**crewcut** a hairstyle in which the hair is very, very short.

crib *n* a manger; a child's bed; a ready-made translation *etc* used by school-children to avoid preparing their own. – *v* to copy the work of another: – *pt* **cribbed**.

'**cribbage** *n* a type of card game.

crick *n* a sharp pain (in the neck). – *v* to produce a crick in.

'**cricket** *n* an outdoor game played with bats, a ball and wickets, between two sides of 11 each; a kind of insect similar to a grasshopper. – *n* '**cricketer** one who plays cricket. – *n* **cricket match** a game of cricket.

cried *see* **cry**.

crier [ˈkrīər] *n* short for **town-crier**.

crime *n* an act or deed which is against the law. – *adj* **criminal** [ˈkriminl] forbidden by law; very wrong. – *n* one guilty of a crime.

crimson [ˈkrimzn] *adj, n* (of) a deep red colour.

cringe [krinj] *v* to crouch or shrink back in fear *etc*; to behave in too humble a way.

'**crinkle** *v* to wrinkle, crease; to make a crackling sound. – *adj* '**crinkly** having a wrinkled appearance.

crinoline [ˈkrinəlēn] *n* a petticoat or skirt made to stick out all round by means of hoops.

'**cripple** *n* a lame or disabled person. – *v* to make lame; to make less strong, less efficient *etc*, throw out of action. *The strike crippled the country*. – *adj* '**crippled**.

'**crisis** *n* a deciding moment or turning point; a time of great danger or suspense: – *pl* '**crises**.

crisp *adj* stiff and so dry as to be crumbled easily, brittle; cool and fresh: *crisp air*; curly, wavy; firm and fresh: *a crisp lettuce*; sharp, clearly defined. – *v* to make crisp. – *n* a thin crisp piece of fried potato eaten cold. – *n* '**crispness**. – *adj* '**crispy**.

'**criss-cross** *adj, n* (having) a pattern of crossing lines. – Also *adv*.

cri'terion *n* a means or rule by which something can be judged, a test, a standard: – *pl* **cri'teria**.

'**critic** *n* one who judges the good points

or faults in a thing (such as a picture, play, book *etc*); one who finds faults in a thing or person. – *adj* '**critical** fault-finding; of criticism; of or at a crisis; very ill; serious; very important. – *n* '**criticism** a judgement or opinion on (something) *esp* one showing up faults; the act of criticizing. – *v* '**criticize** to find fault with; to give an opinion or judgement on.

croak *v* to make a low, hoarse sound. – Also *n*. – *adj* '**croaky**.

crochet ['krōshā] *n* a kind of knitting done with one hooked needle.

crock *n* an earthenware pot or jar; a worthless, old and decrepit person or thing. – *n* '**crockery** china or earthenware dishes.

'**crocodile** *n* a type of large reptile found in rivers in Asia, Africa *etc*; a procession (*usu* of children) walking two by two. – *npl* **crocodile tears** pretended tears.

'**crōcus** *n* a type of yellow, purple or white flower which grows from a bulb: – *pl* '**crocuses**.

croft *n* a small farm with a cottage *esp* in the Scottish Highlands. – *n* '**crofter**.

crone *n* an ugly old woman.

'**crōny** *n* (*coll*) a close friend: – *pl* '**cronies**.

crook *n* anything bent (such as a shepherd's or bishop's stick bent at the end); a criminal; a cheat. – *v* to bend or form into a hook. – *adj* **crooked** ['krōōkid] bent like a crook; not straight; not honest. – *n* '**crookedness**.

croon *v* to sing or hum in a low voice. – *ns* '**crooner;** '**crooning**.

crop *n* that which is gathered for food from fields, trees or bushes; a part of a bird's stomach; a kind of riding whip; the hair on the head; a short haircut. – *v* to cut short; to gather a crop (of wheat *etc*): – *pt* **cropped**. – **come a cropper** to fail badly; to have a fall; **crop up** to happen unexpectedly.

croquet ['krōkā] *n* a game in which the players, using long-handled wooden hammers, try to drive wooden balls through hoops in the ground.

cross *n* anything shaped like this: + or ×; a frame consisting of two bars of wood *etc* placed across each other, of the type on which Christ and criminals were nailed; a monument in a street, often but not always cross-shaped, where proclamations used to be made and markets held; the result of breeding an animal or plant with one of another kind: *a cross between a horse and*

a donkey; a trouble or grief that one must bear. – *v* to mark with a cross; to go to the other side of (a room, road *etc*); to lie or pass across; to meet and pass; to go against the wishes of, annoy; to draw two lines across (cheques); to breed (one kind) with (another). – *adj* ill-tempered, angry. – *ns* '**crossing** a place where a street, river *etc* may be crossed; a journey over the sea; '**crossness** bad temper, sulkiness. – *n* '**crossbow** (*hist*) a bow fixed to a wooden stand with a device for pulling back the bowstring. – *n, adj* '**cross-'country** (a race) across fields *etc*, not on roads. – *vs* '**cross-ex'amine,** '**cross-'question** to test the truth of someone's words (in a court) by close questioning. – *adj* '**cross-'eyed** having a squint. – *ns* '**cross-'reference** in a book such as a dictionary, a statement that what is looked for will be found in another place; '**crossroads** a place where roads cross each other; '**cross-'section** a section made by cutting across (something); a sample, a part or quantity taken as being representative of the whole: *a cross-section of voters*; '**crossword** a form of word puzzle.

'**crotchet** *n* a note of a certain length in music. – *adj* '**crotchety** bad-tempered.

crouch *v* to stand with the knees well bent; (of an animal) to lie close to the ground.

croup [krōōp] *n* a disease of children causing difficulty in breathing and a harsh cough; the hindquarters of a horse.

croupier ['krōōpiā] *n* a person who collects the money and pays the winners at gambling.

crow [krō] *n* a type of large bird, generally black; the cry of a cock; the happy sounds made by a baby. – *v* to cry like a cock: – *pt* **crew** [krōō], **crowed**; to boast: – *pt* **crowed**; (of a baby *etc*) to make happy noises: – *pt* **crowed**. – *ns* '**crowbar** a large iron bar used as a lever; **crow's foot** one of the wrinkles near the eye, produced by ageing; '**crow's-'nest** a sheltered and enclosed platform near the mast-head of a ship for a man to keep a lookout. – **as the crow flies** in a straight line.

crowd [krowd] *n* a number of persons or things together (without order or arrangement). – *v* to gather into a crowd; to fill (a room *etc*) too full; to give too little space to, to hinder by being too close.

crown [krown] *n* the jewelled head-dress

worn by kings or queens on great occasions; the best or most magnificent part of anything; the highest part or top of anything (*eg* of the road, the head); an old coin which was worth five shillings. – *v* to set a crown on; to make king; (*coll*) to hit on the head; to reward, finish happily. *Her efforts were crowned with success.*

crucial ['krōōshəl] *adj* testing, involving making a decision: *the crucial moment*; of great and far-reaching importance. *The crucial question is whether he will succeed.*

crucible ['krōōsibl] *n* a small container for melting metals *etc*.

crucify ['krōōsifi] *v* to put to death by fixing the hands and feet to a cross: – *pt* '**crucified**. – *ns* '**crucifix** a figure or picture of Christ fixed to the cross: – *pl* '**crucifixes**; **cruci'fixion** the act of crucifying; death on the cross, *esp* that of Christ.

crude [krōōd] *adj* raw, not purified or refined: *crude oil*; roughly made or done; rude, blunt, tactless. – *ns* '**crudeness**, '**crudity**.

cruel ['krōōəl] *adj* causing pain or distress; having no pity for others' sufferings. – *n* '**cruelty**: – *pl* '**cruelties**.

cruet ['krōōit] *n* a small jar for salt, pepper, sauces *etc*; two or more such jars on a stand.

cruise [krōōz] *v* to travel (by car, ship *etc*) at a steady speed. – *n* a journey by ship made for pleasure and relaxation. – *n* '**cruiser** a middle-sized warship.

crumb [krum] *n* a small bit of anything, *esp* bread. – *v* '**crumble** ['krumbl] to break into crumbs or small pieces; to fall to pieces. – *adj* '**crumbly**.

'**crumpet** *n* a kind of soft cake, baked on a griddle and eaten with butter.

'**crumple** *v* to crush into creases or wrinkles; to become creased; to collapse.

crunch *v* to chew anything hard, and so make a noise; to crush. – *n* a noise as of crunching; (*coll*) a testing moment or turning-point.

crusade [krōō'sād] *n* any movement undertaken for some good cause; (*hist*) an expedition of Christians to win back the Holy Land from the Turks. – *n* **cru'sader** one who goes on a crusade.

crush *v* to squeeze together; to beat down or overcome; to crease or crumple (a dress *etc*). – *n* a violent squeezing; a vast crowd of persons or things; a drink made by squeezing fruit. – *adj* **crushed** squeezed, squashed; completely defeated or miserable.

crust *n* the hard outside coating of anything (such as bread, a pie, the earth *etc*). – *adj* '**crusty** having a crust; (of people) cross.

crustacean [krus'tāshən] *n* any of a large group of animals, often having a hard shell, including crabs, lobsters, shrimps *etc*.

crutch *n* a stick with a bar across the top for lame people; any support: – *pl* '**crutches**.

crux *n* the difficult or most important part of a problem.

cry *v* to make a loud sound, as in pain or sorrow; to weep; to call loudly: – *pt* **cried**. – Also *n*: – *pl* **cries**. – *adj* '**crying** weeping; calling loudly; calling for, requiring notice or attention: *a crying need*. – **cry off** cancel: *cry off a match*; **cry over spilt milk** to be worried about a misfortune that is past and cannot be helped.

crypt *n* an underground cell or chapel, *esp* one used for burial. – *adj* '**cryptic** full of mystery, secret; difficult to understand: *a cryptic remark*.

'**crystal** *n* a special kind of very clear glass often used for cut-glass ornaments *etc*; the regular shape taken by each small part of certain substances (*eg* salt, sugar). – *adj* '**crystalline** made up of (or like) crystals. – *v* '**crystallize** to form into the shape of a crystal; to take a form or shape, become clear. – *n* **crystalli'zation**.

cub *n* the young of certain animals (such as foxes); a Cub Scout. – *n* **Cub Scout** a junior Scout.

cube *n* a solid body having six equal square sides; the answer to a sum in which a number is multiplied by itself twice (8 is the cube of 2). – *adj* '**cubic** of cubes; having the shape of a cube.

'**cubicle** *n* a small room closed off in some way from a larger one.

'**cubit** *n* (*hist*) the distance from elbow to middle-finger tip, once used as a means of measurement.

cuckoo ['kōōkōō] *n* a type of bird, named after its call, which visits Britain in summer and lays its eggs in the nests of other birds.

'**cucumber** *n* a creeping plant with a long green fruit used in salads.

cud *n* food brought back from the stomach and chewed a second time by certain animals (*eg* the sheep, cow).

'**cuddle** *v* to put one's arms round, hug. – Also *n*.

'**cudgel** *n* a heavy stick, a club. – *v* to beat with a cudgel.

cue [kū] *n* a hint or sign (telling a person

when to speak, or what to say next); the stick used in billiards and snooker.

cuff *n* the end of a sleeve (of a shirt, coat *etc*) near the wrist; the turned back hem of a trouser leg; a blow with the open hand. – *v* to hit with the hand. – *n* **'cufflinks** two ornamental buttons *etc* joined by a small bar, chain *etc* used to fasten a shirt cuff. – **off the cuff** without planning or rehearsal.

cuisine [kwi'zēn] *n* (the art of) cookery.

'cul-de-sac *n* a street closed at one end.

'culinary *adj* of kitchen or cookery.

cull *v* to gather; to choose from a group; to pick out (seals, deer *etc*) from a herd and kill for the good of the herd. – *n* such a killing.

'culminate *v* to reach the highest point; to reach the most important or greatest point, to end (in). – *n* **culmi'nation**.

'culpable *adj* guilty, blameworthy.

'culprit *n* a person who is to blame for something; (in English and US law) a prisoner accused but not yet tried.

cult *n* worship or religious belief; a strong devotion to or enthusiasm for a person, thing or idea: *the cult of physical fitness*.

'cultivate *v* to grow (vegetables *etc*); to plough, sow *etc* (land); to try to develop and improve. *He cultivated their friendship.* – *adj* **'cultivated** having been cultivated; educated, informed. – *n* **culti'vation** ploughing *etc*; education and refinement.

'culture *n* a form or type of civilization of a certain race or nation and the customs associated with it: *Jewish culture*; improvement or development of the mind *etc* by education, training *etc*; educated tastes in art, music, literature; cultivation (of plants *etc*). – *adj* **'cultured** well-educated *esp* in literature, art *etc*.

'culvert *n* an arched drain for carrying water under a road, railway *etc*.

cumbersome ['kumbərsəm] *adj* heavy, difficult to manage, handle *etc*.

'cummerbund *n* a sash worn around the waist.

'cūmūlative *adj* increasing as parts *etc* are added on.

'cūmūlus *n* a kind of cloud common in summer, made up of rounded heaps.

'cunning *adj* sly, clever in a deceitful way; skilful, clever. – *n* slyness; skill, knowledge.

cup *n* a hollow container to hold liquid for drinking; an ornamental vessel *usu* of metal, given as a prize in sports events *etc*. – *v* to make or put in the shape of a cup. *She cupped her hands*: – *pt* **cupped**. – *n* **'cupful** as much as fills

a cup: – *pl* **'cupfuls**. – *n* **'cup-tie** (in football *etc*) one of a series of games *eg* in a competition for which the prize is a cup.

cupboard ['kubərd] *n* a recess in a room with a door and shelves or a box with doors, often hung on walls, used for storing things.

cū'pidity *n* greed.

'cūpola *n* a curved ceiling or dome on the top of a building.

cur *n* a dog of mixed breed; a cowardly person.

curare [kū'räri] *n* a kind of poison used by some S. American Indians on the tips of their arrows.

'cūrate *n* a Church of England clergyman assisting a rector or a vicar.

cū'rātor *n* one who has charge of a museum, art gallery *etc*.

curb *v* to hold back, try to prevent from going on. – Also *n*.

curd *n* milk thickened by acid; the cheese part of milk, as opposed to the **whey**. – *v* **'curdle** to turn into curd. – **curdle someone's blood** to shock or terrify someone.

cure *n* the act of freeing from disease, healing; that which heals. – *v* to heal; to get rid of (a bad habit *etc*); to preserve, *eg* by drying, salting *etc*. – *adjs* **'curable**; **'curative** likely to cure.

curfew ['kɔrfū] *n* an order forbidding people to be in the streets after a certain hour; (*hist*) the ringing of an evening bell, as a signal to put out all fires and lights.

'cūrio *n* an article valued for its oddness or rareness: – *pl* **'curios**.

'cūrious *adj* anxious to find out; unusual, odd. – *n* **curi'osity** strong desire to find out; anything unusual: – *pl* **curi'osities**.

curl *v* to twist (hair) into small coils or rolls; (of hair) to grow naturally in small coils; (of smoke *etc*) to move in a spiral; to twist out of shape, form a curved shape; to play at the game of curling. – *n* a small coil or roll as of hair. – *n* **'curling** a game played by throwing round, flat stones along a sheet of ice. – *adj* **'curly** having curls.

curlew ['kɔrlū] *n* a type of wading bird with very long slender bill and legs.

'currant *n* a kind of small black raisin; any of various kinds of small, soft, round fruit: *redcurrant*.

'current *adj* belonging to the present time: *the current year*; passing from person to person, generally accepted. *That story is current.* – *n* a stream of water, air or electrical power moving in a certain direction. – n '**currency** the money (notes and coins) of a country; state or time of being current or well-known. *The story gained currency*: – pl '**currencies**. – n **current account** a bank account from which money may be withdrawn by cheque.

cur'**riculum** n the course of study at a university, school etc. – n **curriculum vitae** ['vēti] a brief account of the main events of a person's life.

'**curry** n a kind of food (meat, vegetables etc) containing a mixture of spices which gives a strong, peppery flavour: – pl '**curries**. – v to cook (meat etc) using the spices necessary for a curry; to rub down (a horse): – pt '**curried**. – n **curry powder** a selection of spices ground together used in making a curry. – **curry favour** to try hard to be someone's favourite.

curse v to use swear words; to wish evil on (someone). – n a wish for evil or a magic spell. *The witch put a curse on him*; an evil or a great misfortune or the cause of this. – adjs **cursed** under a curse; **cursed** ['kɔrsid] hateful.

'**cursory** adj hurried.

curt adj impolitely short, abrupt. – n '**curtness**.

cur'**tail** v to make less, reduce. – n cur'**tailment**.

'**curtain** n a piece of material hung to cover a window, stage etc.

'**curtsy**, '**curtsey** n a bow made by women by bending the knees: – pl '**curtsies**.

curve n a rounded line, like part of the edge of a circle: anything shaped like this: *curve in the road*. – v to bend; to form into a curve. – n '**curvature** a curving or bending; a curved piece (of something); an abnormal curving, as of the spine.

cushion ['kŏoshən] n a casing of some soft material filled with stuffing (rags, foam rubber etc) for resting on; any soft pad.

cushy ['kŏoshi] adj (*coll*) easy and comfortable: *a cushy job*.

'**custard** n a dish consisting of milk, eggs etc flavoured, and cooked together.

'**custody** n care, guardianship; imprisonment. – n **cus'tōdian** a keeper; a caretaker (*eg* of a museum).

'**custom** n something done by habit or because it is usual; the regular or frequent doing of something; habit; the regular buying of goods at the same shop etc; (*pl*) taxes on goods coming into a country; (*pl*) the department of the government that collects these or

the place where they are collected. – adj '**customary** usual. – n '**customer** one who buys (regularly) from a shop; (*coll*) a person: *an awkward customer*. – adj '**custom-'built** built to suit a particular demand or purpose.

cut v to make a slit or opening in, or divide, with something sharp (*eg* scissors, a knife): *cut a hole in*: *cut a slice of bread*; to wound; to remove with something sharp (*eg* scissors, lawnmower): *cut hair*: *cut the grass*; to reduce in amount; to shorten (a play, book etc) by removing parts (of it); to ignore (a person one knows); to divide in two (a pack of cards); to stop filming; (*coll*) to stay away from: *cut school for the day*: – pres p '**cutting**, pt **cut**. – n a slit or opening made by cutting; a wound made with something sharp; a stroke or blow; a thrust with a sword; the way a thing is cut; the shape and style (of clothes); a piece (of meat). – n '**cutting** a piece cut from a newspaper; a trench or passage, cut in the earth or rock for a railway or road; a twig or shoot of a tree or plant. – adj '**cut-and-'dried** (of plans etc) arranged carefully and exactly. – n **cut glass** glass with ornamental patterns cut on the surface, used for vases, drinking-glasses etc. – adj '**cut-'price** sold at a price lower than usual. – n '**cut-throat** a wicked dangerous person. – adj '**cut-'up** distressed. – **cut down** to take down by cutting; to reduce (supply, amount taken etc); **cut in** to interrupt; **cut off** to separate. *They were cut off from the mainland by the tide*; to stop: *cut off supplies*; **cut out** to shape (a dress etc) by cutting; (*coll*) to stop; of an engine, to fail.

cute adj smart, clever; pretty and pleasing.

'**cuticle** n the skin at the bottom and edges of finger and toe nails.

'**cutlass** n a short broad sword: – pl '**cutlasses**.

'**cutlery** n knives, forks, spoons etc.

'**cutlet** n a slice of meat usu with the bone attached.

'**cuttlefish** n a type of sea creature like a squid.

'**cyanide** n a kind of poison.

'**cycle** n short for **bicycle**; a number or round of events coming one after the other, over and over again: *the cycle of the seasons*; a period of time in which events happen in this way; a number of poems, songs, stories, written about one main person or event. – v to ride a bicycle. – n '**cyclist** one who rides a bicycle.

'**cyclone** *n* a whirling windstorm; a system of winds blowing in a spiral. – *adj* **cyclonic** [si'klonik].

'**cygnet** *n* a young swan.

'**cylinder** *n* a solid or hollow tube-shaped object; in machines, motor-car engines *etc*, the hollow tube in which a piston works. – *adj* **cy'lindrical** shaped like a cylinder.

'**cymbals** *npl* brass, plate-like musical instruments, beaten together in pairs.

'**cynic** *n* one who believes the worst about people. – *n* '**cynicism**. – *adj* '**cynical** sneering; believing the worst of people.

cynosure ['sinəzūr] *n* centre of attraction.

'**cypress** *n* a type of evergreen tree.

cyst *n* a kind of liquid-filled blister on an internal part of the body or just under the skin.

cys'titis *n* inflammation of the bladder.

czar *see* **tsar**.

D

dab *v* to touch gently with a pad, cloth *etc*, *eg* to soak up moisture: – *pt* **dabbed**. – *n* the act of dabbing; a small lump of anything soft or moist; a gentle blow, pat; a small kind of flounder. – *n*, *adj* '**dab-'hand** (*coll*) expert.

'**dabble** *v* to play in water with hands or feet; to do (something) in a half-serious way or as a hobby. *He dabbles in witchcraft.* – *n* '**dabbler**.

dace *n* a type of small river fish.

dachshund ['daks-hoōnd] *n* a breed of dog with short legs and a long body.

dad, '**daddy** *ns coll* or child's names for **father**.

'**dādo** *n* the lower part of an inside wall when decorated in a different way from the rest: – *pl* '**dado(e)s**.

'**daffodil** *n* a type of yellow flower which grows from a bulb.

daft *adj* silly.

'**dagger** *n* a short sword for stabbing.

dahlia ['dālyə] *n* a type of garden plant with large flowers.

'**daily** *adj*, *adv* every day. – *n* a paper published every day; a person who is paid to clean a house regularly (also **daily help**): – *pl* '**dailies**.

'**dainty** *adj* small and neat; pleasant-tasting. – *n* anything pleasant (*esp* tasty food): – *pl* '**dainties**. – *n* '**daintiness**.

'**dairy** *n* the place where milk is kept, and butter and cheese are made; a shop which sells milk *etc*: – *pl* '**dairies**. – *ns* **dairy cattle** cows kept for their milk, not their meat; **dairy farm** a farm mainly concerned with the production of milk, butter *etc*; '**dairymaid**, '**dairyman** woman, man working in a dairy.

dais ['dāis] *n* a raised floor at the upper end of a hall *etc*: – *pl* **daises** ['dāisiz].

daisy ['dāzi] *n* a type of small common flower with white petals: – *pl* '**daisies**.

dale *n* low ground between hills.

'**dally** *v* to waste time by idleness or play; to play (with): – *pt* '**dallied**. – *n* '**dalliance**.

Dal'matian *n* a breed of large spotted dog.

dam *n* a bank or wall of earth, concrete *etc* to keep back water; the water kept in like this; a mother, *esp* of animals. – *v* to keep back by a dam; to hold back, control (tears *etc*): – *pt* **dammed**.

'**damage** *n* hurt or injury *esp* to a thing; (*pl*) money paid, by order of a law court, by one person to another to make up for injury, insults *etc*. – *v* to spoil, make less effective or unusable.

'**damask** *n* silk, linen or cotton cloth, with figures and designs.

dame *n* a comic woman in a pantomime, *usu* played by a man dressed up as a woman; **Dame** the title of a woman of the same rank as a knight.

damn [dam] *v* to sentence to unending punishment (in hell); to condemn as wrong, bad *etc*. – *adj* **damnable** ['damnəbl] deserving to be condemned; hateful. – *n* **dam'nation** unending punishment; condemnation.

damp *n* moist air; wetness. – *v* to wet slightly; to make less fierce or intense (*eg* a fire). – *adj* moist, slightly wet. – *n* '**dampness**. – *v* '**dampen** to make or become damp or moist; to lessen (enthusiasm *etc*). – *n* '**damper** that which damps or dampens.

damsel ['damzəl] *n* (*old*) an unmarried girl.

damson ['damzən] *n* a type of small dark-red plum.

dance *v* to move in time to music. – Also *n*. – *n* '**dancer**.

'**dandelion** *n* a type of common plant with a yellow flower.

'**dandruff** *n* dead skin which collects under the hair and falls off in small pieces.

'**dandy** *n* a man who pays great attention to his dress and looks: – *pl* '**dandies**.

danger ['dānjər] *n* something which may harm. *The canal is a danger to children*; a state in which one may be harmed. *He is in danger.* – *adj* '**dangerous** unsafe, likely to cause harm; full of risks.

dangle ['daŋgl] *v* to hang loosely.

dank *adj* moist, wet.

'**dapper** *adj* small and neat.

'**dappled** *adj* marked with spots or splashes of colour.

dare *v* to be brave or bold enough (to); to lay oneself open to, to risk: *dare his anger*; to challenge. *He dared him to cross the railway line.* – *adj* '**daring** bold, fearless. – *n* boldness. – *n* '**dare-devil** a rash person fond of taking risks. – Also *adj.* – **I dare say** I suppose. *I dare say you're right.*

dark *adj* without light; black or of a colour near to black; gloomy; evil: *dark deeds.* – *ns* **dark**, '**darkness**. – *v* '**darken** to make or grow dark or darker. – *adj* '**dark-'haired** having dark-brown or black hair. – **a dark horse** a person about whom little is known; **in the dark** knowing nothing (about something); **keep dark** to keep (something) secret.

'**darling** *n* a word showing affection; one dearly loved; a favourite.

darn *v* to mend (clothes) with crossing rows of stitches. – *n* the place so mended.

dart *n* a pointed, arrow-like weapon for throwing or shooting; something which pierces; (*pl*) a game in which small darts are aimed at a board ('**dartboard**) marked off in circles and numbered sections. – *v* to move quickly and suddenly.

dash *v* to throw, knock *etc* violently, *esp* so as to break; to ruin (*esp* hopes); to depress, sadden (spirits *etc*); to rush with speed or violence. – *n* a rush; a short race; a small amount (as of soda water *etc*); liveliness; in writing, a short line (–) to show a break in a sentence *etc*: – *pl* '**dashes**. – *adj* '**dashing** hasty; spirited, smart.

'**dastardly** *adj* cowardly.

'**data** *npl* available facts (from which conclusions may be drawn): – *sing* '**datum**.

date¹ *n* a statement of time expressed in terms of the day, month and year (*eg* 23 December 1946); the time at which an event occurs or occurred; the period of time to which something belongs; an appointment. *I have a date with her next Wednesday.* – *v* to give a date to; to belong to a certain time. *This castle dates from the 12th century*; to become old-fashioned. *That dress will date quickly.* – **out of date** old-fashioned; no longer used; no longer valid; **up to date** in fashion, modern; including, or knowledgeable about, the latest information; at the point (in work *etc*) that one should be.

date² *n* a type of palm-tree, or its fruit.

datum *see* **data**.

daub *v* to smear; to paint roughly or without skill.

daughter ['dötər] *n* a female child (when spoken of in relation to her parents). – *n* '**daughter-in-law** a son's wife.

daunt *v* to frighten; to be discouraging. – *adj* '**dauntless** unable to be frightened.

'**Davy-lamp** *n* a kind of safety lamp for coalminers.

daw short for **jackdaw**.

'**dawdle** *v* to move slowly. – *n* '**dawdler**.

dawn *n* beginning (*esp* of a day). – *v* to become day; to begin to appear. – *n* '**dawning** dawn. – **dawn on** to become suddenly clear to (someone).

day *n* the time of light, from sunrise to sunset; twenty-four hours, from one midnight to the next; the time or hours *usu* spent at work; (sometimes *pl*) a particular time or period: *in the days of steam.* – *n* '**daydream** a dreaming or imagining of pleasant events while awake. – Also *v.* – *ns* '**daylight** the light of day, of the sun; '**day-re'lease** time off from work for education. – **day in, day out** on and on, continuously; **the other day** recently.

daze *v* to make to feel confused *eg* by a blow, to stun; to bewilder.

'**dazzle** *v* (of a strong light) to prevent one from seeing clearly; to shine brilliantly; to fascinate, impress deeply.

'**deacon** *n* the lowest rank of clergyman in the Church of England; a church official in other churches: – *fem* '**deaconess**.

dead [ded] *adj* without life; cold and cheerless; numb; (of an engine *etc*) not working; no longer in use; complete: *dead silence*; exact: *dead centre*; certain: *a dead shot.* – *adv* completely: *dead certain*; suddenly and completely: *stop dead.* – *n* those who have died. *Speak well of the dead*; the time of greatest stillness, coldness, darkness *etc*: *the dead of night.* – *n* '**deadness**. – *v* '**deaden** to lessen pain *etc*. – *adj* '**deadly** likely to cause death, fatal; intense, very great. – *adv* intensely, extremely. – *n* '**deadliness**. – *adjs* '**dead-and-a'live** dull, having little life; '**dead-'beat** having no strength left; '**dead-'end** of a road *etc* closed at one end; of a job *etc* not leading to promotion. – *ns* **dead heat** a race in which two or more runners are equal; '**deadline** a date by which something must be done; '**deadlock** a standstill resulting from a complete failure to agree. – *adj* '**deadpan** without expression on the face.

deaf [def] *adj* unable to hear; refusing to listen. – *v* '**deafen** to make deaf; to have an unpleasant effect on the hearing; to make (walls *etc*) soundproof. – *n* '**deafness**. – *n* '**deaf-'mute** one who is both deaf and dumb.

deal *n* a (business) agreement or arrangement; an amount or quantity: *a good deal of paper*; the dividing out of playing cards in a game; a kind of softwood. – *v* to divide, give out; to trade (in); to do business (with); (with **with**) to take action concerning, cope with. *He deals with all the problems.* – *n* '**dealer** one who deals; a trader.

dean *n* the chief clergyman in a cathedral church; an important official of a university.

dear *adj* high in price; highly valued; much loved. – *n* one who is loved; one who is lovable or charming. – *adv* at a high price. – *adv* '**dearly**. – *n* '**dearness**.

dearth [dörth] *n* a scarcity, shortage.

death [deth] *n* the state of being dead, the end of life; the end (of something): *the death of music halls*. – *adj, adv* '**deathly** like death; very pale or ill-looking. – *ns* '**death-blow** a blow that causes death; an event *etc* that causes the end of something; '**death-mask** a plastercast taken of a dead person's face; **death rattle** a rattling in the throat which is sometimes heard before a person's death; **death roll** a list of the dead; **deathwatch beetle** a kind of insect that makes a ticking noise and whose larva destroys wood.

de'bar *v* to keep from, prevent: – *pt* **de'barred**.

de'base *v* to lessen in value; to make bad, wicked *etc*. – *adj* **de'based**. – *n* **de'basement**.

de'bate *n* a discussion, *esp* a formal one before an audience; an argument. – Also *v*. – *adj* **de'batable** able to be argued about, doubtful: *a debatable point*.

debauchery [di'böchəri] *n* excessive indulgence in drunkenness and other (immoral) pleasures. – *adj*

de'bauched given to, inclined to debauchery.

de'bilitate *v* to make weak. – *n* **de'bility** weakness of the body.

'**debit** *n* a debt. – *v* to mark something down as a debt.

debo'nair *adj* of pleasant and cheerful appearance and manners.

de'bouch *v* to come out from a narrow or confined place.

debrief ['dē'brēf] *v* to gather information (from an astronaut, spy *etc*) after a mission.

débris ['dābrē] *n* the remains of something broken, destroyed *etc*; rubbish.

debt [det] *n* what one owes to another. – *n* '**debtor** one who owes a debt. – **in debt** owing money; **in someone's debt** under an obligation to someone, owing someone a favour *etc*.

début ['dābū] *n* the first public appearance (*eg* of an actor). – *n* **debutante** ['debūtänt] a young woman making her first appearance in upper-class society.

'**decade** *n* a period of ten years; a set or series of ten.

'**decadence** *n* a falling (from high) to low standards in morals, the arts *etc*. – *adj* '**decadent**.

de'camp *v* to run away.

de'cant *v* to pour (wine) from a bottle into a decanter. – *n* **de'canter** a bottle (*usu* ornamental) with a glass stopper for wine, whisky *etc*.

de'capitate *v* to cut the head from. – *n* **decapi'tation**.

de'cathlon *n* a contest consisting of ten events in the Olympic Games *etc*.

de'cay *v* to become bad, worse or rotten. – Also *n*. – *adj* **de'cayed**.

de'cease *n* death. – *adj* **de'ceased** dead. – *n* (with **the**) a dead person.

deceit [di'sēt] *n* the act of deceiving. – *adj* **de'ceitful**.

deceive [di'sēv] *v* to tell untruths so as to mislead; to cheat. – *n* **de'ceiver**.

decelerate [dē'selərāt] *v* to slow down.

De'cember *n* the twelfth month of the year.

'**decent** *adj* respectable; good enough, adequate: *a decent salary*; kind. *It's decent of you to help*. – *n* '**decency**.

de'ception *n* the act of deceiving, cheating; something that deceives or is intended to deceive. – *adj* **de'ceptive** different from what it seems or looks, misleading. *Appearances may be deceptive*. – *adv* **de'ceptively**.

'**decibel** *n* a unit of loudness of sound.

de'cide *v* to make up one's mind (to do something); to settle (an argument *etc*). – *adj* **de'cided** clear: *a decided difference*; with one's mind made up. – *adv* **de'cidedly** definitely.

de'cidūous *adj* (of trees) having leaves that fall in autumn.

'decimal *adj* numbered by tens; of ten parts or the number 10. – *n* a decimal fraction. – *v* **'decimalize** to convert (figures or a country's currency) to decimal form. – *n* **decimali'zation**. – *ns* **decimal currency** a system of money in which each coin or note is either a tenth of another or ten times another in value; **decimal fraction** a fraction expressed as so many tenths, hundredths, thousandths *etc* and written using a **decimal point** like this $0 \cdot 1 = \frac{1}{10}$, $2 \cdot 33 = 2^{33}/_{100}$.

'decimate *v* to make much smaller in numbers, *esp* by destruction.

de'cipher *v* to translate (writing in code) into ordinary, understandable language; to make out the meaning of (something difficult to read).

decision [dĭ'sizhən] *n* the act of deciding; the ability to decide; judgement; firmness. *He acted with decision*. – *adj* **de'cisive** final, putting an end to a contest *etc*: *a decisive defeat*; showing decision and firmness: *a decisive manner*.

deck *v* to put ornaments *etc* on, adorn. – *n* a platform extending from one side of a ship *etc* to the other and forming the floor; a floor on a bus *etc*; a pack (of playing cards). – *n* **'deck-chair** a collapsible chair of wood and canvas *etc*.

de'claim *v* to make a speech in impressive dramatic language; to speak violently (against someone). – *n* **decla'mation**. – *adj* **declamatory** [di'klamətəri].

de'clare *v* to make known (*eg* goods on which duty is payable, income on which tax is payable); to announce *esp* formally or publicly: *declare war*; to say firmly; (in cricket) to end an innings before ten wickets have fallen. – *n* **decla'ration**.

declension [di'klen·shən] *n* a system of cases and case-endings (*gram*); a class of words similarly declined; decay, descent.

de'cline *v* to say 'no' (to an invitation, offer *etc*), refuse; to become less strong, less good *etc*; to slope down. – *n* a downward slope; a gradual worsening (of health *etc*).

de'clivity *n* a downward slope: – *pl* **de'clivities**.

dē'code *v* to translate (a coded message)

into ordinary, understandable language.

decompose [dēkəm'pōz] *v* to rot, decay; to separate in parts or elements. – *n* **decompo'sition**.

décor ['dākör] *n* the decoration of a room *etc* and the arrangement of objects in it.

'decorate *v* to add some form of ornament to (someone or something); to make more beautiful, impressive *etc*; to paint, paper the walls of (a room *etc*); to pin a badge or medal on (someone) as a mark of honour. – *n* **deco'ration**. – *adj* **'decorative** ornamental; pretty. – *n* **'decorator** one who decorates houses, rooms *etc*.

'decorous *adj* behaving in an acceptable or dignified way. – *n* **de'corum** good behaviour.

de'coy *v* to lead into a trap or into evil. – *n* ['dēkoi] anything intended to lead another into a trap.

de'crease *v* to make or become less in number. – *n* **'dēcrease** a growing less.

de'cree *n* an order or law; a judge's decision. – *v* to give an order: – *pt* **de'creed**.

de'crepit *adj* weak and infirm because of old age; in ruins or disrepair. – *n* **de'crepitude**.

de'crȳ *v* to make (something) seem worthless, belittle; to express disapproval of: – *pt* **de'cried**.

'dedicate *v* to give up wholly to, devote to: *dedicated to teaching*: *dedicated to football*; to set apart *esp* for a holy or sacred purpose; to name a person in the front page of a book. *I dedicate this book to my father*. – *n* **dedi'cation**.

de'duce *v* to find out something by putting together all that is known. – *n* **deduction** [di'dukshən].

de'duct *v* to subtract, take away (from). – *n* **de'duction** a subtraction; an amount subtracted.

deed *n* something done, an act; (in law) a signed statement or bargain.

deep *adj* being or going far down; hard to understand; cunning; occupied or involved to a great extent: *deep in debt*; intense, strong: *of a deep red colour*; heartfelt: *deep love*; low in pitch. — *n* (with **the**) the sea. — *v* **'deepen** to make deep. — *adj* **'deep-seated** firmly fixed, not easily removed. — **in deep water** in difficulties or trouble.

deer *n* a kind of animal with antlers (*usu* in the male only), such as the reindeer: – *pl* **deer**.

de'face *v* to spoil the appearance of, disfigure. – *n* **de'facement**.

de'fame *v* to (try to) harm the reputation

of. – *n* **defamation** [defə'māshən]. – *adj* **defamatory** [di'famətəri].

de'fault *v* to fail to do something one ought to do, *eg* to pay a debt. – Also *n*. – *n* **de'faulter**.

de'feat *v* to beat, win a victory over (in a fight, competition *etc*). – Also *n*.

'defect *n* a lack of something necessary for completeness or perfection, a flaw. – *v* **de'fect** to desert a country, political party *etc* to join or go to another: *defect to the West.* – *n* **de'fection** failure in duty; desertion. – *adj* **de'fective** faulty; incomplete; (of a person) not having normal mental or physical ability.

de'fence, (*US*) **de'fense** *n* the act or action of defending against attack; a means or method of protection; a person's answer to a charge made against him, *esp* in a law-court. – *adj* **de'fenceless** without defence.

de'fend *v* to guard or protect against attack; to conduct the defence of in a law-court. – *n* **de'fendant** one who resists attack; the accused person in a law case. – *adjs* **de'fensible** able to be defended; **de'fensive** defending or protecting. – **on the defensive** prepared to defend oneself against attack or criticism.

de'fer *v* to put off to another time; to give way (to the wishes *etc* of another): – *pt* **de'ferred**. – *n* **'deference** respect, willingness to consider the wishes *etc* of others; the act of giving way to another. – *adj* **defe'rential** showing deference or respect.

de'fiance *n* open disobedience or opposition. – *adj* **de'fiant**.

de'ficient *adj* lacking in what is needed. – *n* **de'ficiency** lack, want; the amount lacking: – *pl* **de'ficiencies**.

'deficit *n* amount by which something (*eg* a sum of money) is too little.

de'file *v* to make dirty, to soil; to corrupt, make bad or evil. – *n* **de'filement**.

de'fine *v* to fix the bounds or limits of; to outline or show clearly; to state the exact meaning of. – *adj* **definite** ['definit] having clear limits, fixed; exact; certain; clear. – *ns* **'definiteness; defi'nition** an explanation of the exact meaning of a word or phrase; sharpness or clearness of outline. – *adj* **de'finitive** quite fixed, final, settling once and for all. – *n* **definite article** the name given to the adjective *the*.

de'flate *v* to let the air or gas out of (a tyre *etc*); to reduce (a person's) self-importance or self-confidence.

– *n* **de'flation**.

de'flect *v* to turn aside (from a fixe course or direction). – *n* **de'flection**

de'form *v* to spoil the shape of; to mak ugly. – *adj* **de'formed** badly or abnor mally formed. – *n* **de'formity** a par abnormal in shape; state of being badl shaped: – *pl* **de'formities**.

de'fraud *v* to cheat; (with **of**) to take b cheating or fraud.

de'fray *v* to pay for (the expenses o anything).

'de'frost *v* to remove frost or ice (from refrigerator), thaw.

deft *adj* clever (*esp* with the fingers). – **'deftness**.

de'funct *adj* no longer active or in use

de'fy *v* to dare someone (to d something), to challenge; to resis boldly or openly; to make impossible *Her beauty defies description*: – p **de'fied**.

degenerate [di'jenərət] *adj* having be come immoral or very bad. – *v* t become or grow bad or worse. – *n* **degene'ration**.

de'grade *v* to lower in grade, rank *etc*; t disgrace. – *adj* **de'grading**. – *n* **degra dation** [degrə'dāshən].

de'gree *n* a step or stage in a process *etc* rank or grade; amount, extent: *a degre of certainty*; a unit of temperature; a unit by which angles are measured, one 360th part of the circumference of a circle; a title or certificate given by a university (gained by examination or as an honour).

'dehy'drate *v* to remove water from (*esp* food), dry out. – *n* **'dehy'dration**.

deify ['dāifi] *v* to worship as a god: – *pt* **'deified**.

deign [dān] *v* to do as a favour, or act as if one is doing a favour. *She deigned to answer us.*

deity ['dāəti] *n* a god or goddess: – *pl* **'deities**.

de'jected *adj* gloomy, dispirited. – *n* **de'jection**.

de'lay *v* to put off to a later time; to keep back, hinder. – Also *n*.

de'lectable *adj* delightful, pleasing.

delegate ['deligāt] *v* to give (a task) to someone else to do. – *n* ['deligət] someone acting on behalf of another or others, a representative. – *n* **dele'gation** a group of delegates.

de'lete *v* to rub or strike out (*eg* a piece of writing). – *n* **de'letion**.

deleterious [deli'tēriəs] *adj* harmful.

deliberate [di'libərāt] *v* to think carefully or seriously (about). – *adj* [di'libərət] intentional, not by acci-

dent; slow in deciding; not hurried. –
adv **de'liberately**. – *n* **delibe'ration**
careful thought; calmness, coolness;
(*pl*) formal discussions.

delicate *adj* not strong, frail; easily
damaged; of fine texture; dainty, done
by fine work; pleasing to the senses, *esp*
the taste; tactful; requiring careful
handling. – *n* **'delicacy** the state of
being delicate; tact; something delicious to eat: – *pl* **'delicacies**.

delica'tessen *n* a shop selling food
cooked or prepared ready for serving.

delicious [di'lishəs] *adj* pleasant to the
taste; giving pleasure. – *n*
de'liciousness.

delight [di'lit] *v* to please highly; to take
great pleasure (in). – Also *n*. – *adjs*
de'lighted; de'lightful.

delinquent [di'liŋkwənt] *adj* guilty of an
offence or misdeed; not carrying out
one's duties. – *n* a person who is guilty
of an offence; a person who fails in his
duty. – *n* **de'linquency** wrongdoing,
misdeeds; failure in duty.

de'lirious *adj* raving, wandering in the
mind (*usu* as a result of fever); wildly
excited. – *n* **de'lirium** state of being
delirious; wild excitement. — *n*
delirium tremens a delirious disorder of the brain produced by over-
absorption of alcohol.

de'liver *v* to hand over; to give out (*eg* a
speech, blow); to set free; to rescue; to
assist at the birth of (a child). – *ns*
de'liverance a freeing; **de'livery** a
handing over (as of letters, parcels *etc*);
the birth of a child; way of speaking: –
pl **de'liveries**.

del'phinium *n* a kind of branching
garden plant, *usu* with blue flowers.

'delta *n* the triangular stretch of land at
the mouth of a river which reaches the
sea in two or more branches.

delude [di'lōōd] *v* to deceive. – *n*
de'lusion the act of deluding; a false
belief, *esp* as a symptom of mental
illness.

deluge ['delūj] *n* a great flow of anything, *esp* water (also work to be done,
letters to be answered *etc*). – *v* to flood
(with water, work *etc*).

delve *v* to dig; to search deeply and
carefully.

de'mand *v* to ask, or ask for, firmly or
sharply; to insist; to require, call for.
This demands instant attention. – *n* a
request which seems like a command;
urgent claim: *demands on my time*; a
wish or willingness to buy or a need for
(certain goods *etc*).

de'mean *v* to lower, degrade (*esp*

oneself).

de'meanour *n* behaviour, conduct.

de'mented *adj* out of one's mind, insane.

de'mise *n* death.

'dē'mob short for **demobilize** or **de-
mobilization**.

dē'mōbilize *v* to break up an army after
a war is over; to free (a soldier) from
army service. – *n* **demobili'zation**.

de'mocracy *n* government of the people
by the people through their elected
parliament. – *n* **'democrat** one who
believes in this kind of government;
(*US*) **'Democrat** a member of the
American Democratic Party. – *adj*
demo'cratic. – *adj*, *n* (*US*)
Demo'cratic (of, belonging to) one of
the two chief political parties in the
USA.

de'molish *v* to lay in ruins, pull or tear
down (a building *etc*). – *n* **demo-
'lition**.

'dēmon *n* an evil spirit, a devil.

'demonstrate *v* to show clearly; to
prove; to show (a machine *etc*) in
action; to express a (*usu* political)
opinion by marching, showing placards
etc in public. – *adj* **'demonstrable** able
to be shown clearly. – *n*
demon'stration a show; a display;
proof; a public expression of opinion
by processions, mass-meetings *etc*. –
adj **de'monstrative** pointing out;
proving; (in the habit of) showing
one's feelings openly. – *n* **'demon-
strator** one who shows (*eg* the working of a machine); a person who takes
part in a public demonstration.

de'moralize *v* to take away the confidence of.

de'mote *v* to reduce to a lower rank or
grade. – *n* **de'motion**.

de'mur *v* to object, say 'no': – *pt*
de'murred.

de'mure *adj* shy and modest. – *n*
de'mureness.

den *n* the lair or cave of a wild animal; a
small private room for working *etc*.

denier ['deniər] *n* a unit of weight of
nylon, silk, rayon yarn.

'denigrate *v* to attack the reputation of,
defame.

'denim *n* a type of cotton cloth used for
jeans, overalls *etc*.

'denizen *n* a dweller, an inhabitant.

denomi'nation *n* name or title; a value
(as of a coin, stamp *etc*); a group of
people of the same religious beliefs. –
adj **denomi'national**. – *n*
de'nominator the lower number in a
vulgar fraction by which the upper
number is divided (as the 3 in $^2/_3$).

de'note *v* to mean, be a sign of.

dénouement [dā'nōōmōŋ] *n* the most important part of a story (*eg* where a mystery is solved).

de'nounce *v* to accuse (of a crime *etc*) publicly; to inform against. *He denounced him to the enemy.* – *n* denunciation [dinunsi'āshən].

dense *adj* closely packed together; thick; very stupid. – *ns* 'denseness; 'density the state of being dense; the weight of a standard volume of something (*eg* water): – *pl* 'densities.

dent *n* a hollow made by a blow or pressure. – *v* to make a dent in.

'dental *adj* of a tooth or teeth.

'dentist *n* one who cures tooth troubles (by filling, taking teeth out *etc*). – *ns* 'dentistry the work of a dentist; 'denture (often *pl*) a set of false teeth.

de'nūde *v* to make bare, strip (something) of a covering of any kind. *The wind denuded the trees of leaves.* – *n* dēnu'dation.

denunciation *see* denounce.

de'nȳ *v* to declare to be untrue. *I deny that I did it*; to refuse, forbid. *I deny you the right to leave*: – *pt* de'nied. – *n* de'nial. – deny oneself to do without (things that one desires or needs).

dē'ōdorant *n* something that removes or hides unpleasant smells.

de'part *v* to go away; to turn aside from: *depart from one's plans.* – *n* de'parture. – a new departure a new course of action of some kind.

de'partment *n* a separate part or branch (of a shop, university, government *etc*).

de'pend *v* (with on or upon) to rely on; (with on) to receive necessary support (*esp* financial) from; (with on or upon) to be controlled or decided by. *It all depends on the weather.* – *adj* de'pendable to be trusted. – *ns* de'pendant one who is kept or supported by another; de'pendence the state of being dependent. – *adj* de'pendent depending; relying on another for (*esp* financial) support.

de'pict *v* to draw, paint *etc*; to describe.

de'plete *v* to make smaller in amount, number *etc*. – *n* de'pletion.

de'plore *v* to feel or express disapproval or regret about (something). – *adj* de'plorable regrettable; very bad.

de'ploy *v* to place in position ready for action.

dē'popūlate *v* to reduce greatly the number of people in (an area *etc*). – *adj* de'populated empty of people; reduced in population.

deport *v* to send (a person) out of a country. – *n* depor'tation. – *n* de'portment way of carrying or holding oneself; behaviour.

de'pose *v* to remove from a high position (*esp* a king from his throne). – *n* depo'sition the act of deposing; *see* also deposit.

deposit [di'pozit] *v* to place; to put or set down; to put in for safe keeping (*eg* money in a bank). – *n* money paid in part payment of something which one means to buy; money put in a bank; a solid that has settled at the bottom of a liquid; a layer (of coal, iron *etc*) occurring naturally in rock *etc*. – *ns* depo'sition a written piece of evidence; de'pository a place where anything is deposited: – *pl* de'positories. – *n* deposit account a bank account from which money must be withdrawn in person, not by cheque.

depot ['depō] *n* a storehouse; a military station where stores are kept; the place where railway engines, buses *etc* are kept and repaired.

de'prave *v* to make wicked. – *adj* de'praved wicked. – *n* depravity [di'pravəti].

'deprecate *v* to show disapproval of, condemn as bad. – *n* depre'cation.

depreciate [di'prēshiət] *v* to lessen the value of; to fall in value. – *n* depreci'ation.

depre'dation *n* (often *pl*) plundering.

de'press *v* to make gloomy, unhappy or of low spirits; to press down; to lower in value, amount *etc*. – *n* de'pression low spirits, gloominess; a hollow; a lowering in value *etc*; a period in which the economic situation of a country is bad with unemployment, lack of trade *etc*; a region of low atmospheric pressure.

de'prive *v* to take away. *They deprived the king of his power.* – *n* deprivation [depri'vāshən] the act of depriving; the state of being deprived. – *adj* de'prived suffering from hardship *etc*, disadvantaged.

depth *n* deepness; a deep place; the deepest part; the middle: *depth of winter*; intensity, strength. – in depth thorough(ly), careful(ly); out of one's depth in water deeper than one can stand up in; concerned in problems too difficult to understand.

depū'tation *n* persons chosen (and sent) to speak or act for others. – *n* 'deputy one acting in place of another; a delegate, representative: – *pl* 'deputies. – *v* 'deputize to take another's place for a time, act as substitute.

de'rail v to cause to leave the rails. – n **de'railment**.

de'range v to put out of place or out of working order. – adj **de'ranged** out of one's mind, insane; out of order. – n **de'rangement**.

derelict ['derilikt] adj broken-down, abandoned (esp buildings, ships etc). – n **dere'liction** the neglecting of what should be attended to: dereliction of duty.

de'ride v to laugh at, mock. – n **derision** [di'rizhən] act of deriding; mockery. – adj **de'risive**.

de'rive v to be descended or formed (from); to trace (a word) back to the beginning of its existence; to receive, obtain: derive satisfaction. – n **derivation** [deri'vāshən]. – n, adj **de'rivative** (something) derived from something else, not original; a word made from another word (eg fabulous from fable).

derma'titis n inflammation of the skin.

derma'tology n the study and treatment of skin diseases. – n **derma'tologist**.

de'rogatory adj harmful to one's reputation, dignity etc; scornful, belittling, disparaging.

derrick n a kind of crane for lifting weights; a framework over an oil well that holds the drilling machinery.

descant n (in music) a tune played or sung above the main tune.

descend [di'send] v to go or climb down; to slope downwards; to be passed down from parent to child; to have as one's ancestor. I'm descended from Napoleon; to go from a greater to a lesser or worse state. – ns **de'scendant** a person descended from another; **de'scent** the act or state of descending; a downward slope; the way down.

des'cribe v to give an account of in words; to draw the outline of, trace. – n **description** [dis'kripshən] the act of describing; an account in words; sort, kind: people of all descriptions. – adj **des'criptive**.

des'crȳ v to notice, see: – pt **des'cried**.

desecrate ['desikrāt] v to spoil (something sacred); to treat without respect. – n **dese'cration**.

desert[1] [di'zərt] v to run away (from) (eg the army); to leave, abandon. He deserted his family. His courage deserted him. – ns **de'serter** one who deserts esp from the army etc; **de'sertion** the act of deserting (esp from the army etc).

desert[2] ['dezərt] n a stretch of barren country, usu hot, dry and sandy with very little water. – n **desert island** an

uninhabited island in a tropical area.

deserve [di'zərv] v to have earned as a right by one's actions etc, be worthy of. – adj **de'serving**. – adv **deservedly** [di'zərvidli] justly.

'desiccate v to dry up; to preserve by drying: desiccated coconut.

design [di'zīn] v to make a plan or a sketch of something (eg a building) before it is made; to intend. – n a plan or sketch; a painted picture, pattern etc; an intention or plan. – adj **de'signing** crafty, cunning. – **have designs on** to plan to get (someone or something) for oneself.

designate ['dezignāt] v to point out, indicate; to name; to appoint, select (for a duty etc). – adj appointed to a post but not yet occupying it: director designate. – n **desig'nation** a name, title.

desire [di'zīr] v to wish for (greatly). – n a longing for; a wish. – adj **de'sirable** pleasing; worth having. – n **desira'bility**. – **desirous of** wishing for, wanting something.

desist [di'zist] v to stop (doing something).

desk n a table for writing, reading etc.

'desolate adj lonely; sorrowful, unhappy; empty of people, deserted; barren. – adj **'desolated** overcome by grief; made desolate. – n **deso'lation** the state of being desolated; loneliness; deep sorrow; barren land; ruin.

des'pair v to give up hope. – n lack of hope; that which causes despair. He was the despair of his parents. – adj **des'pairing** having no hope.

despatch see **dispatch**.

despe'rado n a bold or violent criminal, a gangster: – pls **despe'rado(e)s**.

'desperate adj having lost all hope, despairing; very bad; reckless; violent. – n **despe'ration**.

des'picable adj contemptible, worthless and hateful.

des'pise v to look upon with contempt, regard as worthless or hateful.

des'pite prep in spite of. Despite the rain they went to the seaside.

des'poil v to rob, plunder. – n **despōli'ation**.

des'pondent adj downhearted, dejected. – n **des'pondency**.

'despot n one (usu king or ruler of a country) with unlimited power, a tyrant. – adj **des'potic**. – n **'despotism**.

dessert [di'zərt] n fruits, sweets etc served at the end of a meal; the sweet course in a meal.

destine ['destin] v to set apart for a

certain use *etc.* – *adj* 'destined bound (for a place); intended (as if by fate): *destined to succeed.* – *ns* desti'nation the place to which someone or something is going; 'destiny what is destined to happen; fate: – *pl* 'destinies.

'destitute *adj* in need of food, shelter *etc*; (with of) completely lacking in: *destitute of kindness.* – *n* desti'tution.

des'troy *v* to pull down, knock to pieces; to ruin; to kill. – *n* des'troyer one who destroys; a type of fast warship.

des'truction *n* the act of destroying or being destroyed; ruin; death. – *adjs* des'tructible able to be destroyed; des'tructive causing destruction; doing great damage; (of criticism *etc*) pointing out faults without suggesting improvements.

'desultory *adj* moving from one thing to another without a fixed plan; (of conversation *etc*) changing from subject to subject, rambling.

de'tach *v* to unfasten, remove (from). – *adjs* de'tachable able to be taken off: *a detachable lining*; de'tached standing apart, by itself: *a detached house*; separated; not personally involved, showing no emotion or prejudice. – *n* de'tachment state of being detached; the act of detaching; a body or group (*eg* of troops on special service).

'detail *n* a small part, fact, item *etc.* – *v* to describe fully, give particulars of; to set (a person) to do a special job or task. *The airman was detailed for night-flying.* – *adj* 'detailed with nothing left out. – in detail giving attention to details, item by item.

de'tain *v* to hold back; to keep late; to keep under guard. – *n* de'tention imprisonment; a forced stay (as a punishment at school at the end of the day).

de'tect *v* to discover; to notice. – *ns* de'tection; de'tective one who tries to find criminals or watches suspected persons.

détente [dā'tönt] *n* a lessening of hostility between nations.

detention *see* detain.

de'ter *v* to discourage or prevent from (by frightening): – *pt* de'terred. – *adj*, *n* de'terrent (of) something (*esp* a weapon) which deters.

de'tergent *n* a (soapless) substance used with water for washing dishes *etc*.

de'teriorate *v* to grow worse. *His health is deteriorating rapidly.* – *n* deterio'ration.

determine [di'tẽrmin] *v* to decide; to fix or settle. *He determined his course of action.* – *n* determi'nation the state of being determined; the act of determining; stubbornness, firmness of character and purpose. – *adj* de'termined having one's mind made up, decided: *determined to succeed*; stubborn; fixed, settled.

deterrent *see* deter.

de'test *v* to hate greatly. – *adj* de'testable very hateful. – *n* dētes'tation great hatred.

dē'throne *v* to remove from a throne. – *n* de'thronement.

'detonate *v* to (cause to) explode. – *n* deto'nation an explosion; 'detonator something which sets off an explosive.

detour ['dētoor] *n* a wandering from the main route.

de'tract *v* to take away (from), lessen (an achievement, value *etc*). – *n* de'traction.

'detriment *n* harm, damage, disadvantage. – *adj* detri'mental disadvantageous, causing harm or damage.

deuce [dus] *n* a playing card with two pips; (in tennis scoring) having forty points each.

'devastate *v* to lay waste, leave in ruins; to overcome (a person) with grief *etc.* – *n* devas'tation.

de'velop *v* to (make to) grow bigger or to a more advanced state; to acquire gradually (an interest *etc*); to become active, visible *etc. Spots developed on her face*; to unfold gradually; to use chemicals (called de'veloper) to make a photograph appear. – *n* de'velopment.

'dēviate *v* to turn aside, *esp* from the right, normal or standard course. – *n* devi'ation.

de'vice *n* something made for a purpose *eg* a tool or an instrument; a plan; a picture or design on a coat of arms.

'devil *n* the spirit of evil, Satan; any evil spirit or person. – *adj* 'devilish of or like a devil; very wicked. – *ns* 'devilment, 'devilry mischief. – *adj* 'devil-may-'care not caring what happens.

'dēvious *adj* not direct, roundabout; not straightforward.

de'vise *v* to make up, put (quickly) together; to plan or plot.

de'void *adj* (with of) empty of, free from: *devoid of generosity*.

de'volve *v* to fall as a duty (upon someone).

de'vote *v* to give up wholly (to). – *adj* de'voted loving and loyal; given up (to): *devoted to his work.* – *ns* de'votee keen follower; de'votion great love.

de'vour *v* to eat up greedily; to destroy.

de'vout *adj* earnest, sincere; religious. – *n* **de'voutness**.

dew [dū] *n* tiny drops of water coming from the air as it cools at night. – *adj* **'dewy**.

dex'terity *n* skill, quickness. – *adj* **'dext(e)rous**.

diabetes [diə'bētēz] *n* a disease in which there is too much sugar in the blood. – *adj*, *n* **diabetic** [diə'betik].

dia'bolic(al) *adj* devilish, very wicked.

diadem *n* a kind of crown.

diagnose [diəg'nōz] *v* to say what is wrong (with a sick person) after making an examination. – *n* **diag'nosis**: – *pl* **diag'nosēs**. – *adj* **diagnostic** [diəg'nostik].

di'agonal *n*, *adj* (a line) going from one corner to the opposite corner.

diagram *n* a drawing to explain something.

dial *n* the face of a clock or watch; the turning disc over the numbers on a telephone; any disc *etc* containing numbers and a pointer. – *v* to turn a telephone dial to get a number: – *pt* **'dialled**.

dialect *n* a way of speaking found only in a certain district or among a certain class or group of people.

dialogue ['diəlog] *n* a talk between two (or more) people.

diameter [di'amitər] *n* the line (drawn) across a circle, passing through its centre.

diamond *n* a very hard, precious stone; a kind of four-cornered shape: ◇; a playing card bearing red marks of this shape.

diaper *n* (*US*) a baby's nappy.

diaphragm ['diəfram] *n* a layer of muscle separating the lower part of the body from the chest; any thin dividing layer.

diarrhoea [diə'rēə] *n* looseness of bowel movements.

diary *n* a (small book containing a) record of daily happenings: – *pl* **'diaries**.

diatribe *n* an angry attack in words or writing.

dice *n* a small cube *usu* with numbered sides or faces, used in certain games (also **die**): – *pl* **dice**.

Dictaphone® ['diktəfōn] *n* a type of machine which records what is spoken into it.

dic'tate *v* to read out (something) so that another may write (it) down; to give firm commands. – *n* **'dictate** an order, command. – *ns* **dic'tation**; **dic'tator**

an all-powerful ruler. – *adj* **dictatorial** [diktə'töriəl] of or like a dictator; domineering, in the habit of giving orders.

'diction *n* manner of speaking; choice of words.

'dictionary *n* a book having the words of a language in (alphabetical) order, along with their meanings; a book containing other information alphabetically arranged: – *pl* **'dictionaries**.

did *see* **do**.

die *v* to lose life; to wither: – *pres p* **'dying**, *pt* **died**. – *n* a stamp or punch for making raised designs on money *etc*; *see* also **dice**.

diesel engine ['dēzəl] *n* an internal combustion engine in which heavy oil is ignited by heat generated by compression.

diet ['diət] *n* food; a course of recommended foods *eg* for the purpose of losing weight; a meeting of a court *etc*. – *v* to eat certain kinds of food only, *esp* to lose weight. – *adj* **die'tetic** of a diet or diets.

'differ *v* (with **from**) to be unlike; to disagree: – *pt* **'differed**. – *n* **'difference** a point in which things are unlike; the amount by which one number is greater than another; a disagreement. – *adj* **'different** unlike. – *v* **differentiate** [difə'renshiāt] to make a difference or distinction between.

'difficult *adj* not easy, hard to do, understand or deal with; hard to please. – *n* **'difficulty** lack of easiness, hardness; anything difficult; anything which makes something difficult, an obstacle, hindrance *etc*; (*pl*) **'difficulties** troubles.

'diffident *adj* shy, not confident. – *n* **'diffidence**.

diffuse [di'fūz] *v* to spread in all directions. – *adj* **diffuse** [di'fūs] widely spread.

dig *v* to turn up (earth) with a spade *etc*; to make (a hole) by this means; to poke or push (something) into: – *pres p* **'digging**, *pt* **dug**. – *n* a poke or thrust; a digging up (or the place dug) to find archaeological remains. – *n* **'digger** a machine for digging.

di'gest *v* to break up food (in the stomach) and turn it into a form in which the body can make use of it; to think over. – *n* **'digest** a summing-up; a collection of written material. – *adjs* **di'gestible** able to be digested; **di'gestive** making digestion easy. – *n* **di'gestion** the act or power of digesting.

'**digit** *n* a finger or toe; any of the numbers 0–9. – *adj* '**digital** (of an electronic calculator, clock *etc*) using the numbers 0–9.

digi'tālis *n* a family of plants, including the foxglove, from which a medicine used in heart disease is obtained.

'**dignified** *adj* stately, serious. – *ns* '**dignity** a stately or serious manner; manner showing a sense of one's own worth or of the seriousness of the occasion; high rank; '**dignitary** a person of high rank or office: – *pl* '**dignitaries**.

di'gress *v* to wander from the point in speaking or writing. – *n* **di'gression**.

dike, dyke *n* a wall; an embankment; a ditch.

di'lapidāted *adj* falling to pieces, needing repair.

di'late *v* to make or grow larger, swell out. – *ns* **dila'tation, di'lation**.

dilatory ['dilətəri] *adj* slow (in doing things), inclined to delay.

di'lemma *n* a position or situation giving a choice of two things, neither of which is pleasant.

dilettante [dili'tanti] *n* one who has a slight but not serious interest in several subjects.

'**diligent** *adj* hard-working, industrious. – *n* '**diligence**.

'**dilly-'dally** *v* to loiter, waste time.

di'lūte *v* to lessen the strength of a liquid *etc, esp* by adding water. – Also *adj*. – *adj* **di'luted**. – *n* **di'lution**.

dim *adj* not bright or clear; not seeing or understanding clearly. – *v* to make or become dim: – *pt* **dimmed**. – *n* '**dimness**.

dime *n* the tenth part of an American dollar, ten cents.

di'mension *n* a measurement (of length, width or thickness); (*pl*) size, measurements.

di'minish *v* to make or grow less. – *n* **dimi'nūtion** a lessening. – *adj* **di'minutive** very small.

'**dimple** *n* a small hollow, *esp* on the cheek or chin.

din *n* a loud, lasting noise. – *v* (with **into**) to put (information *etc*) into someone's mind by constant repetition: – *pt* **dinned**.

dine *v* to take dinner.

dinghy ['diŋgi] *n* a small rowing boat, *esp* one carried on board a bigger boat: – *pl* '**dinghies**.

dingy ['dinji] *adj* dull, faded, dirty-looking. – *n* '**dinginess**.

'**dinner** *n* the main meal of the day.

'**dinosaur** *n* any of various types of extinct (giant) reptile.

dint *n* a hollow made by a blow, a dent. – **by dint of** by means of.

diocese ['diəsis] *n* a bishop's district.

dip *v* to plunge into any liquid for a moment; to lower (*eg* a flag) and raise again; to slope down; to look briefly into (a book *etc*): – *pt* **dipped**. – *n* a liquid substance in which anything is dipped; a downward slope; a hollow; a short bathe.

diphtheria [dif'thēriə] *n* an infectious throat disease.

diphthong ['difthoŋ] *n* two vowel-sounds pronounced as one syllable (as in *out*).

di'plōma *n* a written statement giving an honour, or saying that one has passed a certain examination.

di'plōmacy *n* the business of making agreements, treaties *etc* between countries; cleverness in making people agree, tact. – *n* '**diplomat** one engaged in diplomacy. – *adj* **diplo'matic** of diplomacy; tactful.

'**dire** *adj* dreadful: *in dire need*.

di'rect *adj* straight, not roundabout; (of a person's manner) straightforward, outspoken. – *v* to point or aim at; to show the way; to order, instruct; to control, organize; to put a name and address on (a letter). – *ns* **di'rection** the act of directing; the place or point to which one moves, looks *etc*; an order; guidance; (*pl*) instructions; **di'rectness**; **di'rector** one who directs, *esp* one who guides or manages (a business *etc*); **di'rectory** a book of names and addresses *etc*: – *pl* **di'rectories**. – *ns* **direct speech** speech reported in the speaker's exact words; **direct tax** a tax on income or property.

dirge [dörj] *n* a lament; a funeral hymn.

dirk *n* a kind of dagger.

dirt *n* any unclean substance, such as mud, dust, dung *etc*. – *adj* '**dirty** not clean, soiled; bad, evil. – *v* to soil with dirt: – *pt* '**dirtied**. – *adv* '**dirtily**. – *n* '**dirtiness**. – *n* **dirt track** an earth track for motor-cycle racing.

dis'āble *v* to take away (wholly or partly) the power or strength from, cripple. – *ns* **disability** [disə'biləti] something which disables: – *pl* **dis'abilities**; **dis'ablement** the act of disabling; state of being disabled.

disabuse [disə'būz] *v* to set right (someone) about a wrong belief or opinion. *You must disabuse him of that idea.*

disad'vantage *n* an unfavourable circumstance, a drawback. – Also *v*. – *adjs* **disad'vantaged** having a disadvantage

of some kind *esp* poverty, homelessness;
disadvantageous ['dɪsədvən'tājəs].

disaf'fected *adj* discontented, rebellious. – *n* **disaf'fection**.

disa'gree *v* (sometimes with **with**) to hold different opinions *etc* (from another); to quarrel; (of food) to be unsuitable (to someone) and cause pain. – *adj* **disa'greeable** unpleasant. – *n* **disa'greement**.

disallow [dɪsə'low] *v* not to allow.

disap'pear *v* to go out of sight, vanish. – *n* **disap'pearance**.

disap'point *v* to fail to come up to the hopes or expectations (of); to fail to fulfil. – *adj* **disap'pointed**. – *n* **disap'pointment**.

disapprove [dɪsə'prōōv] *v* to have an unfavourable opinion (of). – *n* **disap'proval**.

dis'arm *v* to take weapons away from; to get rid of war weapons; to make less angry *etc*, to charm. – *n* **dis'armament** the act of doing away with war weapons. – *adj* **dis'arming** gaining friendliness, charming: *a disarming smile*.

disarrange [dɪsə'rānj] *v* to throw out of order, make untidy. – *n* **disar'rangement**.

disar'ray *n* disorder.

disaster [di'zästər] *n* an extremely unfortunate happening, *esp* one that causes great damage, loss *etc*. – *adj* **di'sastrous**.

dis'band *v* to (cause to) break up. *The gang disbanded.* – *n* **dis'bandment**.

disbelieve [disbi'lēv] *v* not to believe. – *ns* **disbe'lief**; **disbe'liever**.

dis'burse *v* to pay out. – *n* **dis'bursement**.

disc, disk *n* a flat, round shape; a gramophone record. – *n* **disc jockey** one who introduces and plays recorded music (for radio programmes *etc*).

dis'card *v* to throw away as useless.

discern [di'sörn] *v* to see, realize. – *adjs* **di'scernible** able to be seen (or understood); **di'scerning** quick or clever at noticing or understanding. – *n* **di'scernment** the state of quality of being discerning.

discharge [dis'chärj] *v* to unload (cargo); to set free; to dismiss; to fire (a gun); to perform (duties); to pay (a debt); to give off (*eg* smoke), let out (*eg* pus). – *n* **'discharge** unloading; setting free; firing (of a gun); dismissal; something discharged (*eg* pus); the performance (of duties); payment.

disciple [di'sipl] *n* one who believes in another's teaching, *esp* one of the followers of Christ.

discipline ['disiplin] *n* training in an orderly way of life; order kept by means of control. – *v* to bring to order; to punish. – *n* **discipli'narian** one who insists on strict discipline. – *adj* **disci'plinary** of or enforcing discipline (by punishment).

dis'claim *v* to refuse to have anything to do with, deny. – *n* **dis'claimer** a denial.

disclose [dis'klōz] *v* to uncover, reveal, make known. – *n* **disclosure** [dis'klōzhər] the act of disclosing; something disclosed.

'disco short for **discothèque**.

discolour, (*US*) **discolor** [dis'kulər] *v* to change or spoil the colour of; to stain. – *n* **disco'loration**.

discomfiture [dis'kumfichər] *n* embarrassment; defeat.

discomfort [dis'kumfərt] *n* want of comfort, uneasiness.

discon'cert *v* to upset, embarrass.

discon'nect *v* to separate, break the connection between. – *adj* **discon'nected** separated, no longer connected; (of speech *etc*) not well joined together, rambling.

dis'consolate *adj* sad, disappointed.

discon'tent *n* dissatisfaction. – *adj* **discon'tented** dissatisfied, cross. – *n* **discon'tentment**.

discon'tinue *v* to stop, cease to continue.

'discord *n* disagreement, quarrelling; (in music) a jarring of notes. – *adj* **dis'cordant**.

discothèque ['diskətek] *n* a club, hall *etc* at which recorded music is played for dancing.

'discount *n* a small sum taken off the price of something. *He received a 10% discount on his order.* – *v* **dis'count** to leave out, not to consider; to allow for exaggeration in (*eg* a story).

discourage [dis'kurij] *v* to take away the confidence, hope *etc* of. *His low marks discouraged him*; to try to prevent (by showing disapproval of). *She discouraged his attempts.* – *n* **dis'couragement**. – *adj* **dis'couraging** giving little hope or encouragement.

discourse ['diskörs] *n* a speech, sermon, lecture; an essay; a conversation. – *v* **dis'course** to talk.

discourteous [dis'körtiəs] *adj* not polite, rude. – *n* **discourtesy** [dis'körtəsi].

discover [dis'kuvər] *v* to find out; to find by chance, *esp* for the first time. – *ns* **dis'coverer**; **dis'covery** the act of finding or finding out; the thing discovered: – pl dis'coveries.

dis'credit n loss of good reputation, disgrace; disbelief. – v to refuse to believe; to cause disbelief in; to disgrace. – adj dis'creditable disgraceful.

dis'creet adj wise, cautious, tactful. – n discretion [dis'kreshən].

dis'crepancy n a difference, disagreement (between two stories, amounts of money etc): – pl dis'crepancies.

discretion see discreet.

dis'criminate v to make differences (between), to distinguish; to treat (people) differently. – adj dis'criminating showing good sense in judging things etc. – n discrimi'nation the act of or ability in discriminating.

'discus n a heavy disc thrown in a kind of athletic competition.

dis'cuss v to talk about. – n dis'cussion.

dis'dain v to look down on, scorn (something); to be too proud (to do something). – n scorn. – adj dis'dainful.

disease [di'zēz] n illness. – adj di'seased.

disem'bark v to put or go ashore. – n 'disembar'kation.

disembodied [disim'bodid] adj (of a spirit, soul etc) separated from the body.

disen'gage v to separate, free. – adj disen'gaged separated, freed; not busy; vacant, not engaged.

disentangle [disin'taŋgl] v to free from entanglement, to unravel.

disfavour [dis'fāvər] n the state of being out of favour; dislike.

disfigure [dis'figər] v to spoil the beauty or appearance of. – n dis'figurement.

dis'franchise v to take away the right to vote.

dis'gorge v to vomit; to throw out; to give up (what has been taken).

dis'grace n the state of being out of favour; shame. – v to bring shame upon. – adj dis'graceful shameful; very bad.

disgruntled [dis'gruntld] adj sulky, discontented.

disguise [dis'gīz] v to change the appearance of, by a change of dress etc; to hide (feelings etc). – n a disguised state; that which disguises.

dis'gust n strong dislike, loathing; indignation. – v to arouse dislike, loathing or indignation. – adj dis'gusting sickening; causing disgust.

dish n a plate, bowl etc for food; food prepared for table: – pl 'dishes. – v to

put into a dish, serve out.

dishearten [dis'härtn] v to take away courage or hope from. – adjs dis'heartened; dis'heartening.

dishevelled [di'shevəld] adj untidy, with hair etc disordered.

dishonest [dis'onist] adj not honest, deceitful. – n dis'honesty.

dishonour [dis'onər] n disgrace, shame. – v to cause shame to. – adj dis'honourable having no sense of honour; disgraceful.

disillusion [disi'lōōzhən] v to take away a false belief from. – Also n. – adj disil'lusioned. – n disil'lusionment.

disin'clined adj unwilling.

disin'fect v to destroy disease-causing germs in. – n disin'fectant a substance that kills germs.

disin'herit v to take away the rights of an heir.

dis'integrate v to fall into pieces; to break up into parts. – n disinte'gration.

disinterested [dis'intristid] adj unselfish, not influenced by private feelings or interests.

dis'jointed adj (esp of speech etc) not well connected together.

disk see disc.

dis'like v not to like, to disapprove of. – Also n.

'dislocate v to put (a bone) out of joint; to upset, to put out of order. – n dislo'cation.

dis'lodge v to drive from a place of rest, hiding or defence; to knock out of place accidentally.

dis'loyal adj not loyal, unfaithful. – n dis'loyalty.

dismal ['dizməl] adj gloomy; sorrowful, sad.

dis'mantle v to strip off or take down fittings, furniture etc; to take to pieces.

dis'may v to surprise and upset. – Also n.

dis'member v to tear to pieces; to cut the limbs from. – n dis'memberment.

dis'miss v to send or to put away; to send (a person) from a job, sack; to stop, close (a law-case etc). – n dis'missal.

dis'mount v to come down off a horse, bicycle etc.

disobey [disə'bā] v to fail or refuse to do what is commanded. – adj disobedient [disə'bēdyənt] refusing or failing to obey. – n diso'bedience.

diso'bliging adj not willing to carry out the wishes of others.

dis'order n lack of order, confusion; disturbance; disease. – v to throw out of order. – adj dis'orderly out of order; behaving in a lawless (noisy) manner. – *n* **dis'orderliness**.

disown [dis'ōn] *v* to refuse or cease to recognize as one's own.

dis'parage *v* to speak of as being of little worth or importance, belittle. – *n* **dis'paragement**. – *adj* **dis'paraging**.

dis'parity *n* great difference, inequality: – *pl* **dis'parities**.

dispassionate [dis'pashənət] *adj* favouring no one, unbiassed; judging calmly, cool.

dis'patch, des'patch *v* to send off (a letter *etc*); to kill, finish off; to do or deal with quickly. – *n* the act of sending off; a report (*eg* to a newspaper); speed in doing something; killing; (*pl*) **dis-'patches** official papers (*esp* military or diplomatic). – *n* **dispatch rider** a carrier of military dispatches by motor cycle.

dis'pel *v* to drive away, make to disappear: – *pt* **dis'pelled**.

dis'pense *v* to give or deal out; to prepare (medicines, prescriptions) for giving out. – *adj* **dis'pensable** able to be done without. – *ns* **dis'pensary** a place where medicines are given out; **dispen'sation** special leave to break a rule *etc*; **dis'penser** one who dispenses; a machine which dispenses. – **dispense with** to do without.

dis'perse *v* to scatter; to spread; to (cause to) vanish. – *ns* **dis'persal**, **dis'persion** a scattering.

dis'pirited *adj* sad, discouraged.

dis'place *v* to put out of place; to disarrange; to put (a person) out of office. – *n* **dis'placement** a movement out of place; the quantity of water moved out of place by a ship *etc* when floating. – *n* **displaced person** a person forced to leave his own country because of war, political opinions *etc*.

dis'play *v* to set out for show. – *n* a show, exhibition.

displease [dis'plēz] *v* not to please; to offend, annoy. – *n* **displeasure** [dis'plezhər] annoyance, disapproval.

dispose [dis'pōz] *v* to arrange, settle; to get rid (of); to make inclined. – *adj* **dis'posable** intended to be thrown away. – *n* **dis'posal** the act of disposing. – *adj* **dis'posed** inclined, willing. – **at one's disposal** available for one's use.

disposition [dispə'zishən] *n* arrangement; nature, personality; (in law) a giving over of (property *etc*) to another.

dispossess [dispə'zes] *v* to take away from, deprive (someone) of ownership (of).

disproportionate [disprə'pörshənət] *adj* too big or too little, not in proportion.

disprove [dis'prŏov] *v* to prove to be false.

dis'pūte *v* to argue (about). – *n* an argument, quarrel. – *adj* **dis'putable** not certain, able to be argued about. – *n* **dispu'tation** an argument.

disqualify [dis'kwolifi] *v* to put out of a competition *etc* for breaking rules; to take away a qualification or right: – *pt* **dis'qualified**. – *n* **disqualifi'cation**.

dis'quiet [dis'kwiət] *n* uneasiness, anxiety. – Also *v*.

disre'gard *v* to pay no attention to, ignore. – *n* want of attention, neglect.

disre'pair *n* the state of being out of repair.

disre'pūte *n* bad reputation. – *adj* **dis-'reputable** having a bad reputation, not respectable.

disres'pect *n* rudeness, lack of politeness. – *adj* **disres'pectful**.

dis'rupt *v* to break up; to throw (a meeting *etc*) into disorder. – *n* **dis'ruption**. – *adj* **dis'ruptive** breaking up or causing disorder.

dis'satisfȳ *v* not to satisfy, to displease. – *adj* **dis'satisfied**. – *n* **dissatis'faction**.

dis'sect *v* to cut into parts in order to examine; to study and criticize. – *n* **dis'section**.

dis'semble *v* to hide, disguise (one's true intentions *etc*).

dis'seminate *v* to scatter, spread. – *n* **dissemi'nation**.

dis'sent *v* to have a different opinion; to refuse to agree. – *n* disagreement. – *ns* **dis'sension** disagreement, quarrelling; **dis'senter** a member of a church that has broken away from the officially established church.

disser'tation *n* a long piece of writing or talk on a particular (often scholarly) subject.

disservice [dis'sɜrvis] *n* harm, an ill turn.

dis'similar *adj* not the same. – *n* **dissimi'larity**: – *pl* **dissimi'larities**.

dis'simūlate *v* to pretend; to disguise, hide (one's true intentions *etc*).

'dissipate *v* to (cause to) disappear; to waste. – *adj* **'dissipated** having wasted one's energies *etc* on too many pleasures. – *n* **dissi'pation**.

dissociate [di'sōshiāt] *v* to separate. – **dissociate oneself from** to refuse to be associated with or to give one's support to.

dissolve [di'zolv] *v* to melt; to break up;

to put an end to. – *n* **dissolution** [disə'lōoshən].

dissolute ['disəlōot] *adj* having bad habits, wicked.

'**dissonance** *n* discord, *esp* when deliberately used in music; disagreement. – *adj* '**dissonant**.

dissuade [di'swād] *v* to stop (from doing something) by advice or persuasion. – *n* **dis'suasion**.

'**distaff** *n* the stick which holds the bunch of flax or wool in spinning. – *adj* of women, female: *on the distaff side.*

'**distance** *n* the space between things *etc*; a far-off place or point: *in the distance*; coldness of manner. – *adj* '**distant** far off or far apart in place or time; not close: *a distant cousin*; cold in manner.

dis'taste *n* dislike. – *adj* **dis'tasteful** disagreeable, unpleasant.

dis'temper *n* a kind of paint used chiefly for walls; a disease of dogs. – *v* to paint with distemper.

dis'tend *v* to swell; to stretch outwards. – *n* **dis'tension**.

dis'til *v* to get (a liquid) in a pure state by heating to a steam or vapour and cooling; to extract the spirit or essence from something by this method; to (cause to) fall in drops: – *pt* **dis'tilled**. – *ns* **distil'lation** the act of distilling; **dis'tillery** a place where distilling (of whisky, brandy *etc*) is done: – *pl* **dis'tilleries**.

dis'tinct *adj* clear; easily seen or made out; different. – *adj* **dis'tinctive** different, special. – *ns* **dis'tinctiveness**; **dis'tinction** a difference; outstanding worth or merit; a mark of honour.

distinguish [dis'tiŋgwish] *v* to recognize a difference (between); to mark off as different; to make out, recognize; to give distinction to. – *adj* **dis'tinguished** outstanding, famous.

dis'tort *v* to twist out of shape; to turn or twist (a statement *etc*) from the true meaning; to cause (a sound) to be unclear and harsh. – *n* **dis'tortion**.

dis'tract *v* to draw aside (the attention); to trouble, confuse; to make mad. – *adj* **dis'tracted** mad (with pain, grief *etc*). – *n* **dis'traction** something which draws away attention; anxiety, confusion; amusement; madness.

distraught [dis'trôt] *adj* extremely agitated or anxious.

dis'tress *n* pain, trouble, sorrow; a cause of suffering. – *v* to cause pain or sorrow to. – *adjs* **dis'tressed**; **dis'tressing**.

dis'tribute *v* to divide among several, deal out; to spread out widely. – *n* **distri'bution**.

'**district** *n* a region of a country or town.

dis'trust *n* lack of trust or faith; suspicion. – *v* to have no trust in – *adj* **dis'trustful**.

dis'turb *v* to throw into confusion; to worry, make anxious; to interrupt. – *n* **dis'turbance** an act of disturbing; a noisy or disorderly happening; an interruption.

disuse [dis'ūs] *n* the state of being no longer used. – *adj* **disused** [dis'ūzd] no longer used.

ditch *n* a long narrow hollow trench dug in the ground, *esp* one for water: – *pl* '**ditches**.

dither ['didhər] *v* to hesitate, be undecided; to act in a nervous, uncertain manner. – *n* a state of indecision or nervousness.

'**ditto** often written **do.**, the same as already written or said.

'**ditty** *n* a simple, little song: – *pl* '**ditties**.

di'van *n* a long, low couch without a back; a kind of bed without a headboard.

dive *v* to plunge headfirst into water; to swoop through the air; to go down steeply and quickly. – Also *n*. – *n* '**diver** one who dives; one who works under water using special breathing equipment *etc*; any of several types of diving bird.

di'verge *v* to separate and go in different directions; to differ. – *n* **di'vergence**. – *adj* **di'vergent**.

di'verse *adj* different, various. – *v* **di'versify** to make or become different or varied: – *pt* **di'versified**.

di'version *n* a turning aside; an alteration to a traffic route; (an) amusement.

di'versity *n* difference; variety.

di'vert *v* to turn aside, change the direction of; to amuse. – *adj* **di'verting** amusing.

di'vest *v* to strip or deprive of. *They divested him of his authority.*

di'vide *v* to separate into parts; to share (among); to (cause to) go into separate groups; in arithmetic, to find out how many times one number contains another. – *npl* **di'viders** measuring compasses used in geometry.

'**dividend** *n* that which is to be divided (see **divisor**); a share of profit (of a business *etc*).

di'vine *adj* of God; holy. – *v* to guess; to foretell, predict. – *ns* **divination** [divi'nāshən] (the art of) foretelling; **di'viner** one who claims a special ability in finding hidden water or metals; **divinity** [di'vinəti] a god; the nature of a god; religious studies: – *pl* di'**vinities**; **Di'vinity** God. – *n* di'**vining rod** a (hazel) stick, used by water diviners.

di'**vision** *n* the act of dividing; a barrier, something which divides or separates; a part or section (of an army *etc*); separation; disagreement. – *adjs* di'**visional** of a division; **divisible** [di'vizəbl] able to be divided. – *ns* divisi'**bility**; **divisor** [di'vizər] the number by which another number (the '**dividend**) is divided.

di'**vorce** *n* the legal ending of a marriage; a complete separation. – *v* to end one's marriage with; to separate (from).

di'**vulge** *v* to let out, make known (a secret *etc*).

'**dizzy** *adj* giddy, confused; causing giddiness: *dizzy heights.* – *n* '**dizziness**.

do [dōō] *v* to carry out, perform (a job *etc*); to carry out some action on, *eg* to wash or clean (dishes *etc*), to cook or make (a meal *etc*), to comb (hair), (*slang*) to swindle; to act. *Do as you please*; to get on. *He is doing well*; to be enough. *A penny will do*; used to avoid repeating a verb. *I sometimes see her, but when I do, she runs away*; used with a more important verb (1) in questions. *Do you see?* (2) in sentences with **not**. *I do not know*; (3) to emphasize. *I do hope*: – *pres t* **do, does** [duz], *pt* **did**, *pp* **done** [dun]. – *n* (*coll*) an affair; a festivity, party. – *n* **doer** ['dōōər]. – *npl* **doings** ['dōōiŋz] actions. – *adj* **done** [dun] finished. – **do away with** to put an end to, destroy.

do. *see* **ditto**.

'**docile** *adj* (of a person or animal) easy to manage. – *n* **docility** [də'siləti].

dock *n* (often *pl*) a deepened part of a harbour *etc* where ships go for loading, unloading, repair *etc*; the box in a law court where the accused person stands; a kind of weed with large leaves. – *v* to put in or enter a dock; to clip or cut short. – *n* '**docker** one who works in the docks. – *n* '**dockyard** a naval harbour with docks, stores *etc*.

'**docket** *n* a label or note giving the contents of something.

'**doctor** *n* one who is trained to treat ill people; one who has the highest university degree in any subject. – *v* to treat, as a doctor does a patient; to tamper with, add something harmful to.

doctrine ['doktrin] *n* a belief that is taught.

'**document** *n* a written statement, giving proof, evidence, information *etc*. – *adj* docu'**mentary** of or found in documents; of a documentary. – *n* a film,

programme *etc* giving information about a certain subject: – *pl* docu'**mentaries**.

'**dodder** *v* to shake, tremble, *esp* as a result of old age.

dodge *v* to avoid (by a sudden or clever movement). – *n* a trick.

'**dōdō** *n* a type of large extinct bird: – *pls* '**dodo(e)s**.

doe *n* the female of certain animals (as deer, rabbit, hare).

doer, does *see* **do**.

doff *n* to take off (one's hat *etc*).

dog *n* a type of animal often kept as a pet; one of the dog family which includes wolves, foxes *etc*; the male of this animal. – *adj* (of animal) male. – *v* to follow and watch constantly. – *n* '**dogcollar** a collar for dogs; a clergyman's collar. – *adj* '**dog-eared** (of the pages of a book) turned down at the corner. – *ns* '**dogfish** a kind of small shark; '**dog-rose** the wild rose; '**dogsbody** (*coll*) a person who is given odd jobs, *esp* unpleasant ones; **dog's life** a life of misery. – *adj* '**dog-'tired** completely worn out. – *n* '**dog-watch** on a ship, the period of lookout from 4 to 6 a.m. or 6 to 8 p.m.

dogged ['dogid] *adj* refusing to give in, determined. – *n* '**doggedness**.

'**doggerel** *n* bad poetry.

'**dogma** *n* an opinion accepted or fixed by an authority (such as the Church); opinion that is not to be contradicted. – *adj* dog'**matic** of dogma; forcing one's opinions on others.

'**doily**, '**doyley** *n* a fancy napkin (as on plates in a cakestand).

'**doldrums** *npl* those parts of the ocean about the equator where calms and variable winds are common; low spirits.

dole *v* to deal (out) in small pieces. – *n* money given by a country to unemployed people. – *adj* '**doleful** sad, unhappy. – *n* '**dolefulness**.

doll *n* a toy in the shape of a small human being.

'**dollar** *n* the main unit of money in some countries, *esp* that of N. America.

'**dolmen** *n* an ancient tomb in the shape of a stone table.

'**dolphin** *n* a type of sea animal like a porpoise.

dōlt *n* a stupid person. – *adj* '**doltish**.

do'main *n* kingdom; land in the country, an estate; area of interest or knowledge.

dome *n* anything shaped like a half-ball (*esp* a roof). – *adj* **domed**.

do'mestic *adj* of the home or household;

(of animals) tame, sharing man's life or used by man; not foreign, of one's own country: *domestic products*. – *n* a servant in a house. – *adj* **do'mesticated** (of an animal) accustomed to live near man; (of a person) fond of doing jobs associated with running a house. – *n* **domes'ticity** fondness for home. – *ns* **domestic help** (a person paid to give) assistance with housework; **domestic science** the study of subjects associated with running a house (*eg* cookery, sewing).

'**domicile** *n* the country, place *etc* in which a person lives permanently.

'**dominant** *adj* ruling; most powerful, most important. – *n* '**dominance**.

'**dominate** *v* to have command or influence over; to be most strong, or most noticeable *etc*; to tower above, overlook. – *n* **domi'nation**.

domi'neering *adj* overbearing, like a tyrant.

do'minion *n* lordship, rule; an area with one ruler, owner, or government.

'**domino** *n* a hooded cloak with a mask for the face; one of the pieces used in dominoes; (*pl*) '**dominoes** a game played with wooden or ivory pieces marked with dots.

don *n* a college or university lecturer *etc*. – *v* to put on (a coat *etc*): – *pt* **donned**.

do'nation *n* a gift of money or goods. – *v* **do'nate** to present a gift.

done *see* **do**.

'**donkey** *n* an ass, a type of animal with long ears, related to the horse: – *pl* '**donkeys**.

donor ['dōnər] *n* a giver of a gift or of a part of the body to replace a diseased part of someone else's body.

don't [dōnt] short for **do not**.

doom *n* judgement; fate; ruin. – *adj* **doomed** condemned; destined, certain (to fail, be destroyed *etc*).

door [dōr] *n* the hinged barrier, *usu* of wood, which closes the entrance to a room, house *etc*; the entrance itself. – *ns* '**doorstep** the step in front of the door of a house; '**doorway** the space *usu* filled by a door, entrance.

dope *v* to drug. – *n* (*coll*) any drug or drugs; a kind of quick-drying paint or varnish used *eg* in making models of aeroplanes.

'**dormant** *adj* sleeping; not active: *a dormant volcano*.

'**dormer** *n* (also **dormer window**) a small window jutting out from a sloping roof.

'**dormitory** *n* a room with beds for several people: – *pl* '**dormitories**.

'**dormouse** *n* a type of small animal which hibernates: – *pl* '**dormice**.

'**dorsal** *adj* of the back: *dorsal fin*.

dose *n* the quantity of medicine to be taken at one time; any unpleasant thing (*eg* an illness, punishment) that must be endured. – *v* to give medicine to.

doss *v* (*coll*) to lie down to sleep in a makeshift or temporary place. – *n* '**doss-house** (*coll*) a cheap lodging-house.

dossier ['dosiā] *n* a set of papers containing information about a person or subject.

dot *n* a small, round mark. – *v* to mark with a dot; to scatter: – *pt* '**dotted**.

'**dōtage** *n* the foolishness and childishness of old age.

dote: dote on to be foolishly fond of.

double ['dubl] *v* to multiply by two; to fold. – *n* twice as much. *He ate double the amount*; a person so like another as to be mistaken for him. – *adj* containing *etc* twice as much: *a double dose*; made up of two of the same sort together; folded over; deceitful: *a double game*. – *adv* '**doubly**. – *ns* **double agent** a spy paid by each of two countries hostile to each other, but who is loyal to only one of them; **double bass** a type of large stringed musical instrument. – *adj* '**double-'breasted** (of a suit or coat) having one half of the front overlapping the other and a double row of buttons but a single row of bottonholes. – *v* '**double'cross** to cheat. – Also *n*. – *ns* '**double-'dealer** a deceitful, cheating person; '**double-'dealing**; '**double-'decker** a vehicle (*usu* a bus) with two floors; **double glazing** two sheets of glass in a window to keep in the heat or keep out noise. – **at the double** very quickly; **double back** to turn sharply and go back the way one has come.

doublet ['dublit] *n* (*hist*) a close-fitting jacket, once worn by men.

doubloon [dub'lōon] *n* (*hist*) an old Spanish gold coin.

doubt [dowt] *v* to be unsure or undecided about; not to trust. – *n* a feeling of not being sure; suspicion, a thing doubted. – *adj* '**doubtful**. – *adv* '**doubtless**.

dough [dō] *n* a mass of flour, moistened and kneaded. – *n* '**doughnut** a ring-shaped cake with a hole in the middle fried in fat.

doughty ['dowti] *adj* strong; brave.

dove [duv] *n* a pigeon. – *n* **dovecote** ['duvkot] a pigeon house. – *v* '**dovetail** to fit one thing exactly into another.

dowdy ['dowdi] *adj* not smart, badly dressed.

down [down] *adv* towards or in a lower place or position; to a smaller size *etc*: *to grind down*; from an earlier to a later time: *handed down from father to son*; on the spot, in cash: *£2 down. – prep* towards or in the lower part of; along: *down the road. – adj* descending, going, *etc* downwards: *the down escalator. – n* light, soft feathers; (*pl*) low, grassy hills. – *adj* '**downy** soft like feathers. – *adjs* '**down-at-'heel** (of shoes) worn down at the heel; shabby; '**downcast** sad. – *n* '**downfall** (of a person) ruin, defeat. – *adj* **down'hearted** discouraged. – *n* '**downpour** a heavy fall of rain. – *adj, adv* '**down'stairs** on or to a lower floor (of a house *etc*). – *adv* '**down'stream** further down a river or stream (in the direction of its flow). – *adj* '**downtrodden** kept in a humble, inferior position. – *adv* '**downwards** moving, leading *etc* down. – **go, be down with** to become or be ill with. *He has gone down with flu.*

dowry ['dowri] *n* money and property brought by a woman to her husband on their marriage: – *pl* '**dowries**.

doyley *see* **doily**.

doze *v* to sleep lightly. – Also *n*.

dozen ['duzn] *adj, n* twelve.

drab *adj* of dull colour.

draft *n* a rough sketch or outline of something; a group (*eg* of soldiers) picked out for a special purpose; (*US*) conscription into the army *etc*; an order for payment of money. – *v* to make a rough plan; to pick out (*esp* soldiers) for some special purpose; (*US*) to conscript into the army *etc*. – *n* '**draftsman** (also '**draughtsman**) one who draws plans.

drag *v* to pull *esp* roughly or by force; to move slowly and heavily; (to cause) to trail along the ground *etc*; to search (the bed of a lake *etc*) by means of a net or hook.

'**dragon** *n* (*myth*) a winged, fire-breathing serpent; a fierce or rather frightening person. – *n* '**dragonfly** a kind of winged insect with a long body and double wings.

dra'goon *n* a heavily-armed horse soldier. – *v* to force or bully (a person into doing something).

drain *v* to clear (land) of water by trenches or pipes; to drink everything in (a cup *etc*); to use up completely (money, strength *etc*). – *n* anything (such as a ditch, waterpipe, trench) in which liquids may flow away. – *n*

'**drainage** the drawing-off of water by rivers, pipes etc. – *adj* **drained** emptied of liquid; with no strength left.

drake *n* the male of the duck.

'**drama** *n* a play for acting on the stage; an exciting or tense happening. – *adj* **dra'matic** having to do with plays; exciting, thrilling; unexpected; sudden. – *n* '**dramatist** a writer of plays. – *v* '**dramatize** to turn (a story) into a play for acting; to make real events seem like scenes from a play; to make vivid, striking or sensational. – *n* **dramati'zation**.

drank *see* **drink**.

'**draper** *n* a dealer in cloth and cloth goods. – *v* **drape** to arrange (cloth coverings) to hang gracefully. – *n* '**drapery** cloth goods; a draper's shop. – *npl* **drapes** (*US*) curtains.

'**drastic** *adj* severe; thorough.

draught [dräft] *n* the act of drawing or pulling; something drawn out; an amount of liquid drunk at once, without stopping; a current or rush of air; *see* also **draft**; (*pl*) a game for two, played by moving pieces on a squared board. – *adj* '**draughty** full of air currents, cold. – *n* '**draughtsman** same as **draftsman**.

draw *v* to make a picture (*esp* with pencil, crayons *etc*); to pull after or along; to attract (a crowd, attention *etc*); to obtain money from a fund *etc*: *to draw a pension*; to require depth for floating. *This ship draws 20 feet*; to move or come (near *etc*). *Night draws near*; to score equal points in a game. *Their team might draw with ours*: – *pt* **drew** [drōō], *pp* **drawn**. – *ns* '**drawer** one who draws; a sliding box for clothes *etc* which fits into a chest, cabinet, table *etc*; '**drawing** a picture made by pencil, crayon *etc*. – *ns* '**drawback** a disadvantage; '**drawbridge** a bridge (at the entrance to a castle) which can be drawn up or let down; '**drawing-pin** a pin with a large flat head for fastening paper on a board *etc*; '**drawing-room** a sitting-room. – **draw a conclusion** to form an opinion from evidence heard; **drawn and quartered** (*hist*) having the body cut in pieces after being hanged; **draw up** (of a car *etc*) to stop; to move closer; to plan, write out (a contract *etc*).

drawl *v* to speak in a slow, lazy manner. – Also *n*.

drawn *see* **draw**.

dread [dred] *n* great fear. – *adj* terrifying. – *v* to be greatly afraid of. – *adj* '**dreadful** terrible; (*coll*) very bad. – *n*

dreadnought ['drednöt] (*hist*) a kind of battleship.

dream *n* thoughts, pictures in the mind that come mostly during sleep; something imagined, not real; something very beautiful; a hope or ambition. – *v* to see visions and pictures in the mind while asleep: – *pt*, *pp* **dreamed** or **dreamt** [dremt]. – *adj* **'dreamy** looking as if not quite awake; vague, dim; beautiful. – **dream up** to invent.

'dreary *adj* gloomy, cheerless.

dredge *v* to drag a net, bucket *etc* along the bed of a river or sea in order to bring up fish, mud *etc*; to sprinkle with (*eg* sugar). – *n* an instrument for dredging a river *etc*. – *n* **'dredger** a ship which deepens a channel *etc* by lifting mud from the bottom; a box or jar with a sprinkler top (*eg* a sugar dredger).

dregs *npl* sediment, the solid part that falls to the bottom of a liquid: *dregs of wine*; the least useful part of anything; the last remaining part.

drench *v* to soak.

dress *v* to put on clothes or a covering; to prepare (food *etc*) for use *etc*; to arrange (hair); to treat and bandage (wounds). – *n* covering for the body; a lady's gown, frock *etc*; style of clothing: – *pl* **'dresses**. – *adj* (of clothes *etc*) for wearing on formal occasions. – *ns* **'dresser** a kitchen sideboard for dishes *etc*; **'dressing** something put on as a covering; a seasoned sauce added to salads *etc*; a bandage *etc* to cover a wound. – *adj* **'dressy** fond of stylish clothes; stylish, smart. – *ns* **'dress-'coat** a black tailcoat; **'dressing-gown** a loose, light coat worn indoors over pyjamas *etc*; **dress rehearsal** the final rehearsal of a play, in which the actors wear their costumes.

drew *see* **draw**.

drey [drā] *n* a squirrel's nest: – *pl* **dreys**.

'dribble *v* to (cause to) fall in small drops; to let saliva run down the chin; (in football) to kick the ball on, little by little. – Also *n*.

dried *see* **dry**.

drift *n* something driven by wind (such as ice, snow, sand); the direction in which a thing is driven; (of words spoken or written) the general meaning. – *v* to go with the tide or current; (of snow *etc*) to be driven into heaps by the wind; to wander or live aimlessly. – *n* **'drifter** one who drifts; a fishing boat which uses nets (**'drift-nets**) which remain near the surface of the water. – *n* **'driftwood** wood driven on to the seashore by winds or tides.

drill *v* to make a hole in; to make with a drill; to exercise soldiers *etc*; to sow (seeds) in rows. – *n* a tool for making holes in wood *etc*; exercise, practice *esp* of soldiers; a row of seeds or plants.

drink *v* to swallow (a liquid); to take alcoholic drink, *esp* to too great an extent: – *pt* **drank**, *pp* **drunk**. – *n* something to be drunk; alcoholic liquids. – **drink in** to take eagerly into the mind, listen eagerly; **drink to** to wish (someone) well while drinking, to toast; **drink up** drink (a liquid) to the last drop.

drip *v* to fall in drops; to let (water *etc*) fall in drops: – *pt* **dripped**. – *n* a drop; a continual dropping (*eg* of water); liquid that drips; a device for adding liquid slowly to a vein *etc*. – *n* **'dripping** fat from meat in roasting *etc*. – *v* **drip-'dry** to dry (a garment) by hanging it up to dry without squeezing moisture out of it in any way; (of a garment) to dry in this way. – *adj* able to be dried in this way.

drive *v* to control or guide (*eg* a car *etc*); to go in a vehicle; to force or urge along; to hurry on; to hit hard (a ball, nail *etc*); to bring about: *drive a bargain*: – *pt* **drove**, *pp* **driven** ['drivn]. – *n* a journey in a car; a private road to a house; an avenue or road; energy, enthusiasm; a campaign: *a drive to put an end to racialism*; a hard stroke with a club or bat (in golf, cricket, tennis *etc*). – *n* **'driver** one who drives; a wooden-headed golf club. – *n* **'drive-in** (*US*) a cinema, restaurant where people are catered for while remaining in their cars. – **what are you driving at?** what are you suggesting or implying?

drivel ['drivl] *n* (*coll*) nonsense. – *v* (*coll*) to talk nonsense: – *pt* **'drivelled**.

driven *see* **drive**.

'drizzle *n* rain in small drops. – Also *v*. – *adj* **'drizzly**.

drōll *adj* funny, amusing; odd.

dromedary ['droməɗəri] *n* a type of Arabian camel with one hump: – *pl* **'dromedaries**.

drone *v* to make a low humming sound; to speak in a dull boring voice. – *n* a low humming sound; a dull boring voice; the low-sounding pipe of a bagpipe; the male of the honey-bee; a lazy, idle person.

drool *v* to let saliva flow in anticipation of food; to anticipate (something) in a very obvious way.

droop *v* to hang down. *The hem of her dress is drooping*; to grow weak, faint or discouraged.

drop *n* a small round or pear-shaped particle of liquid, *usu* falling: *raindrop*: *teardrop*; a small quantity (of liquid); a fall or descent from a height: *a drop of six feet*; a small sweet: *acid drop*. – *v* to fall suddenly; to let fall; to fall in drops; to set down from a car *etc*; to give up, abandon (a friend, habit *etc*): – *pt* **dropped**. – *n* **'droplet** a tiny drop. – *npl* **'droppings** dung (of animals or birds). – **drop off** to fall asleep; **drop out** to withdraw (*eg* from a university course).

dross *n* the scum which metals throw off when melting; waste matter, impurities; anything worthless.

drought [drowt] *n* a period of time when no rain falls, *esp* when this causes hardship.

drove *n* a number of moving cattle or other animals; a crowd (of people). – *v see* **drive**. – *n* **'drover** one who drives cattle.

drown [drown] *v* to sink in water and so die; to kill (a person or animal) in this way; to flood or soak completely; to cause (a sound) not to be heard by making a louder sound.

drowsy ['drowzi] *adj* sleepy.

drub *v* to beat or thrash: – *pt* **drubbed**. – *n* **'drubbing** a thrashing.

drudge *v* to do very humble or boring work. – *n* one who does such work. – *n* **'drudgery** hard, uninteresting work.

drug *n* a substance used in medicine (*eg* to kill pain); a substance taken habitually by people to achieve a certain effect *eg* great happiness or excitement. – *v* to give a drug or drugs to; to make to lose consciousness by a drug: – *pt* **drugged**. – *n* **'druggist** one who deals in drugs; a chemist. – *n* **'drugstore** (*US*) a shop which sells various articles (*eg* cosmetics, newspapers, soft drinks) as well as medicines.

drum *n* a musical instrument of skin *etc* stretched on a round frame of wood or metal, and beaten with sticks; anything shaped like a drum (*eg* a container for oil). – *v* to beat a drum; to tap continuously (with the fingers): – *pt* **drummed**. – *n* **'drummer**; **'drumstick** a stick for beating a drum; the lower part of the leg of a cooked chicken *etc*.

drunk *adj* suffering from or showing the effects (giddiness, unsteadiness *etc*) of taking too much alcoholic drink. – *n* one who is drunk; one who is often drunk. – *v see* **drink**. – *n* **'drunkard** one who is in the habit of drinking too

much alcohol. – *adj* **'drunken** drunk; in the habit of being drunk. – *n* **'drunkenness**.

dry *adj* not moist or wet; thirsty; uninteresting; (of manner) reserved, matter-of-fact; (of wine) not sweet. – *v* to make or become dry: – *pt* **dried**. – *adv* **'dryly, 'drily**. – *v* **'dry-'clean** to clean (clothes *etc*) with chemicals, not with water. – *n* **'dry-'rot** a disease of wood, in which it becomes dry and crumbly. – *adj* **'dry-'stone** (of walls) built of stone without cement or mortar.

'dryad *n* (*myth*) a nymph of the woods.

'dual *adj* double; made up of two. – *n* **dual carriageway** a road divided by a central barrier or boundary, with each side used by traffic moving in one direction. – *adj* **'dual-'purpose** able to be used for more than one purpose.

dub *v* to declare (someone) a knight by touching each shoulder with a sword; to name or nickname; to add sound-effects to a film *etc*; to provide (a film) with a new sound-track (*eg* in a different language): – *pt* **dubbed**.

'dubbin, 'dubbing *n* a grease for softening leather or making it waterproof.

'dubious *adj* doubtful, uncertain; probably not honest: *dubious dealings*. – *n* **du'biety**.

'ducal *adj* of a duke.

'ducat *n* (*hist*) an old European gold coin.

'duchess *n* the wife, or widow, of a duke; a woman of the same rank as a duke in her own right: – *pl* **'duchesses**.

'duchy *n* the land owned, or ruled over, by a duke: – *pl* **'duchies**.

duck *n* a kind of web-footed bird, with a broad flat beak; (in cricket) a score of no runs. – *v* to push (someone's head) under water; to lower the head quickly as if to avoid a blow. – *n* **'duckling** a baby duck.

duck-billed platypus *see* **platypus**.

duct *n* a tube or pipe for carrying liquids (*eg* in the human body), electric cables *etc*.

dudgeon ['dujən]: **in high dudgeon** very angry, indignant.

due *adj* owed, that ought to be paid *etc*; expected to be ready, to arrive *etc*; proper: *due care*. – *adv* directly: *due south*. – *n* that which is owed; what one has a right to; (*pl*) the amount of money charged for some service or for belonging to a club *etc*. – **due to** brought about by, caused by. *His success was due to hard work*; because of. *The game was cancelled due to rain*.

duel ['dūəl] *n* (*hist*) a fight (with pistols or swords) between two people. – Also *v. - n* '**duellist** one who fights in a duel.

du'et *n* musical piece for two singers *etc*.

'**duffel-coat,** '**duffle-coat** *n* a coat of coarse woollen cloth, *usu* with toggles instead of buttons.

dug *see* **dig**.

'**dugout** *n* a boat made by hollowing out the trunk of a tree; a rough shelter dug out of a slope or bank or in a trench.

duke *n* a nobleman next in rank below a prince. - *n* '**dukedom** the title, rank, or lands of a duke.

'**dulcet** *adj* sweet to the ear; melodious.

'**dulcimer** *n* a type of musical instrument with stretched wires which are struck with small hammers.

dull *adj* not lively; (of persons) slow to understand or learn; not exciting or interesting; (of weather) cloudy, not bright or clear; not bright in colour; (of sounds) not clear or ringing; blunt, not sharp. - Also *v*. - *adv* '**dully**. - *n* '**dullness** the state of being dull.

dulse *n* a type of eatable seaweed.

'**duly** *adv* at the proper or expected time; as expected. *He duly handed it over.*

dumb [dum] *adj* without the power of speech; silent; (*coll*) stupid. - *adv* '**dumbly** in silence. - *n* '**dumbness**. - *v* **dumb'found** to astonish. - *n* **dumb show** acting without words.

'**dummy** *n* one who is dumb; something which seems real but is not (*eg* an empty package for shop-window display), a model of a human used for displaying clothes *etc*; an artificial teat put in a baby's mouth to comfort it.

dump *v* to throw down heavily; to unload and leave (rubbish *etc*); to sell at a low price. - *n* a place for leaving rubbish; (*pl*) depression, low spirits. *He's in the dumps today.*

'**dumpling** *n* a ball of cooked dough.

'**dumpy** *adj* short and thick or fat.

dun *adj* greyish-brown, mouse-coloured. - *v* to demand payment: - *pt* **dunned**.

dunce *n* one slow at learning; a stupid person.

dune *n* a low hill of sand.

dung *n* the waste matter passed out of an animal's body, manure. - *n* '**dunghill** a heap of dung in a farmyard.

dungarees [dungə'rēz] *npl* trousers made of coarse, hard-wearing material with a bib.

dungeon ['dunjən] *n* a dark underground prison.

dupe *n* one easily cheated. - *v* to deceive; to trick.

'**duplicate** *adj* exactly the same. - *n* another of exactly the same kind; an exact copy. - *v* to make a copy or copies of. - *n* **dupli'cation**.

du'plicity *n* deceit, double-dealing.

'**durable** *adj* lasting, able to last; wearing well.

du'ration *n* the time a thing lasts.

du'ress *n* illegal force used to make someone do something. - **under duress** under the influence of force, threats *etc*.

'**during** *prep* throughout all or part of. *We lived here during the war*; at a particular point within (a period of time). *He died during the war.*

dusk *n* twilight, partial dark. - *adj* '**dusky** dark-coloured. - *n* '**duskin₃ss**.

dust *n* fine grains or specks of earth, sand *etc*; anything in the form of fine powder. - *v* to free from dust. *She dusted the table*; to sprinkle lightly with powder. - *n* '**duster** a cloth for removing dust. - *adj* '**dusty** covered with dust. - *ns* '**dustbin** a container for household rubbish; '**dust-bowl** an area with little rain in which the wind raises storms of dust; **dust jacket** a paper cover on a book; '**dustman** one whose job it is to collect household rubbish.

'**duty** *n* something one ought to do; an action or task required to be done; a tax; (*pl*) '**duties** the various tasks involved in a job. - *adjs* '**dutiable** (of goods) on which tax is to be paid; '**dutiful** obedient; careful to do what one should. - *adj* '**duty-'free** not taxed.

duvet ['dōōvā] *n* a kind of quilt stuffed with feathers, down *etc*, used instead of blankets.

dux *n* (in Scotland) the top boy or girl in a school or class.

dwarf [dwörf] *n* an under-sized person, animal or plant. - *v* to make to appear small. *A seven-foot man dwarfs one of ordinary height.* - *adj* not growing to full or usual height.

dwell *v* to live or stay (somewhere); (with **on**) to think or speak for a long time (about something). *Don't dwell on the past.*

'**dwindle** *v* to grow less, waste away.

dye [dī] *v* to give a colour to clothes, cloth *etc*. - *n* a powder or liquid for colouring. - *n* '**dyeing** the putting of colour into cloth.

dying *see* **die**.

dyke *see* **dike**.

dy'namic *adj* of force; (of a person) forceful, energetic. - *n* **dy'namics** the scientific study of movement and force.

'**dynamite** *n* a type of powerful explosive.

'**dynamo** *n* a machine for turning the

energy produced by movement into electricity: – *pl* '**dynamos**.

'**dynasty** *n* a succession of kings *etc* of the same family: – *pl* '**dynasties**. – *adj* **dy'nastic**.

'**dysentery** *n* an infectious disease caus-ing fever, pain and diarrhoea.

dyslexia [dis'leksiə] *n* great difficulty in learning to read and in spelling.

dys'pepsia *n* indigestion. – *n, adj* **dys-'peptic** (a person) suffering from indigestion.

E

each *adj* (of two or more things *etc*) every one taken individually: *on each side of the fence*: *on each occasion*. – *pron* every one individually. *Each of them received a prize*. – **each other** used when an action takes place between two (loosely, between more than two) people. *He and I don't see each other often.*

'**eager** *adj* keen, anxious to do or get (something). – *n* '**eagerness**.

'**eagle** *n* a kind of large bird of prey. – *n* '**eaglet** a young eagle.

'**eagre** *n* the rise of the tide in a river.

ear *n* the part of the body through which one hears sounds; the ability to tell one sound from another: *a good ear (for music)*; a spike or head (of corn *etc*). – *n* '**eardrum** the middle part of the ear. – *v* '**earmark** to mark or set aside for a special purpose. – *adj* '**ear-piercing** very loud or shrill. – *ns* '**earshot** the distance at which a sound can be heard; '**earwig** a type of insect with pincers at its tail. – **lend an ear** to listen.

earl [ɔrl] *n* a British nobleman ranking between a marquis and a viscount: – *fem* '**countess**. – *n* '**earldom** the lands or title of an earl.

early ['ɔrli] *adj* in good time; at or near the beginning (of a period of time, an event, a book *etc*); sooner than ex-pected; soon: – *comp* '**earlier**, *superl* '**earliest**. – Also *adv*. – *n* '**earliness**. – *n* **early bird** an early riser; one who gains an advantage by acting more quickly than his rivals.

earn [ɔrn] *v* to get (money) by work; to deserve. – *npl* '**earnings** pay for work done.

earnest ['ɔrnist] *adj* serious, serious-minded. – *n* seriousness; something (*usu* money) given to make sure that a bargain will be kept. – *n* '**earnestness**. – **in earnest** meaning what one says or does.

earth [ɔrth] *n* the planet on which we live; its surface; soil; the hole of a fox, badger *etc*; an electrical connection (*usu* a wire) with the ground. – *v* to connect electrically with the ground. –

adjs '**earthen** made of earth or clay; '**earthly** of the earth as opposed to heaven; '**earthy** like soil; covered in soil; (of persons *etc*) coarse, not re-fined. – *ns* '**earthenware** pottery, dis-hes made of clay; '**earthquake** a shak-ing of the earth's crust; '**earth-tremor** a slight earthquake; '**earthwork** a man-made fortification (*usu* a bank) of earth; '**earthworm** the common worm.

ease [ēz] *n* freedom from difficulty; freedom from pain, worry or embar-rassment; rest from work. – *v* to make or become less painful, strong, difficult *etc*; to put carefully and gradually (into or out of a position). – *adj* '**easy** not hard to do; free from pain, worry or discomfort: – *comp* '**easier**, *superl* '**easiest**. – *adv* '**easily**. – *n* '**easiness**. – **stand at ease** to stand with the legs apart and arms behind one's back.

easel ['ēzl] *n* a stand for an artist's picture, a blackboard *etc*.

east *n* one of the four chief directions, that in which the sun rises. – Also *adj*. – *adjs* '**easterly** coming from or facing the east; '**eastern** of the east; '**eastward(s)** towards the east. – Also *adv*.

'**Easter** *n* the time when Christ's rising from the dead is celebrated.

eat *v* to chew and swallow (food); to destroy gradually, waste away: – *pt* **ate**, *pp* '**eaten**. – *adj* '**eatable** fit to eat, edible.

eaves *npl* the edge of a roof overhanging the walls. – *v* '**eavesdrop** to listen secretly to a private conversation. – *n* '**eavesdropper**.

ebb *n* the flowing away of the tide after high tide; a lessening, a worsening. – *v* to flow away; to grow less or worse.

'**ebony** *n* a type of black, hard wood. – *adj* made of ebony; black as ebony.

ebullient [i'bulyənt] *adj* lively and en-thusiastic. – *n* **e'bullience**.

eccentric [ik'sentrik] *adj* odd, acting strangely; (of circles) not having the same centre. – *n* **eccentricity** [eksen'trisəti] oddness of manner or conduct: – *pl* **eccen'tricities**.

ecclesiastic(al) [iklēzi'astik(ǝl)] *adj* of the church or clergy.

echo ['ekō] *n* the repeating of a sound caused by its striking a surface and coming back: – *pl* '**echoes**. – *v* to send back sound; to repeat (a thing said); to imitate.

e'clipse *n* the disappearance of the whole or part of a heavenly body, as of the sun when the moon comes between it and the earth; loss of glory or brilliance. – *v* to throw into the shade; to blot out (a person's success *etc*) by doing better.

e'cology *n* the study of plants, animals *etc* in relation to their natural surroundings. – *adj* **eco'logical**. – *n* **e'cologist**.

e'conomy *n* the management of the money affairs of a country *etc*; the careful use of something *esp* money: – *pl* **e'conomies**. – *adjs* **eco'nomic** concerning economy or economies; making a profit; **eco'nomical** careful in spending or using *esp* money, not wasteful. – *ns* **eco'nomics** the study of the manner in which men and nations make and spend money; **e'conomist** one who studies or is an expert on economics. – *v* **e'conomize** to be careful in spending or using.

'ecstasy *n* very great joy or pleasure: – *pl* **'ecstasies**. – *adj* **ec'static**.

eczema ['eksimǝ] *n* a type of skin disease.

'eddy *n* a current of water, air *etc* running against the main stream, causing a circular movement: – *pl* **'eddies**. – Also *v*.

edelweiss ['ādlvīs] *n* a kind of Alpine plant with white flowers.

edge *n* the border of anything, the part farthest from the middle; the cutting side of a knife, weapon *etc*; sharpness, as of appetite, mind *etc*; advantage. – *v* to put an edge or border on; to move little by little: *edge forward*. – *n* **'edging** a border or fringe. – *adj* **'edgy** on edge, unable to relax, irritable. – *adv* **'edgeways** sideways.

'edible *adj* fit to be eaten.

'ēdict *n* an order, command.

edifice ['edifis] *n* a large building.

'edifȳ *v* to improve the mind: – *pt* **'edified**. – *adj* **'edifying**. – *n* **edifi'cation** progress in knowledge.

'edit *v* to prepare matter for printing, broadcasting *etc*. – *ns* **e'dition** the form in which a book *etc* is published after being edited; the number of copies of a book, newspaper *etc* printed at one time; an issue of a newspaper altered in some way for a particular area (*eg* with

local news added); **'editor** one who edits a book *etc*. – *adj* **edi'torial** of an editor. – *n* the part of a newspaper *etc* written by its editor.

'edūcate *v* to teach (persons), *esp* in a school, college *etc*. – *n* **edu'cation**. – *adj* **edu'cational** of education.

eel *n* a kind of long ribbon-shaped fish.

'eerie *adj* causing fear of the unknown.

ef'face *v* to rub out; (with **oneself**) to keep from being noticed.

ef'fect *n* the result of an action; strength, power (of a drug *etc*); an impression produced: *the effect of the lighting*; general meaning; use, operation. *That law is not yet in effect*; (*pl*) goods, property. – *v* to bring about. – *adjs* **ef'fective** producing the desired effect; actual; **ef'fectūal** able to do what is required.

ef'feminate *adj* unmanly, womanish.

effervesce [efǝr'ves] *v* to froth up; to be very lively, excited *etc*. – *n* **effer'vescence**. – *adj* **effer'vescent**.

effi'cācious *adj* effective. – *n* **'efficacy**.

ef'ficient *adj* able to do things well, fit, capable. – *n* **ef'ficiency**.

'effigy *n* a likeness of a person, *esp* made of stone, wood *etc*: – *pl* **'effigies**.

effluent ['eflōōǝnt] *n* a stream flowing from another stream or lake; sewage.

'effort *n* a try, *esp* one using all one's strength, ability *etc*; hard work.

effrontery [i'fruntǝri] *n* impudence.

ef'fūsive *adj* pouring forth words.

egg *n* an almost round object, laid by birds, insects *etc* from which their young are produced. – **egg on** to urge.

'egoism *n* the habit of considering only one's own interests, selfishness; egotism. – *n* **'egoist**. – *adj* **ego'istic**. – *ns* **'egotism** the habit of speaking much of oneself, boastfulness; **'egotist**.

eider(-duck) ['īdǝr(duk)] *n* a northern sea duck. – *n* **'eiderdown** soft feathers from the eider; a quilt.

eight [āt] *n* the number 8. – *adj* 8 in number. – *adj* **eighth** [ātth] the last of eight. – *n* one of eight equal parts.

eighteen ['ā'tēn] *n* the number 18. – *adj* 18 in number. – *adj* **'eigh'teenth** the last of eighteen (things *etc*). – *n* one of eighteen equal parts.

eighty ['āti] *n* the number 80. – *adj* 80 in number. – *adj* **'eightieth** the last of eighty. – *n* one of eighty equal parts.

either ['īdhǝr] *adj*, *pron* one or other of two. *Either bus will take you there. Either of the boys can play*; each of two, both. *Trees grow on either side of the river*. – *conj* used with **or** to show alternatives. *Either you go or he does*. – *adv* any more than another. *I cannot go either. That doesn't work either.*

e'jacūlate *v* to shout out, exclaim. – *n* **ejacu'lation**.

e'ject *v* to throw out; to make (someone) leave a house, job *etc.* – *n* **e'jection**.

eke: eke out to make enough (by adding to in some way). *She eked out the stew by adding vegetables.*

e'laborate *v* to work out in detail. *You must elaborate your escape plan*; (often with **on**) to explain (too) fully. – *adj* done with fullness and exactness, often too much so; having much ornament or decoration. – *n* **elabo'ration**.

élan [ā'lan] *n* enthusiasm, dash.

'eland *n* a type of African deer.

e'lapse *v* (of time) to pass.

e'lastic *adj* able to stretch and spring back again, springy. – *n* a piece of cotton *etc* made springy by having rubber, woven into it. – *n* **ēlas'ticity**.

e'lated *adj* in high spirits, very pleased. – *n* **e'lation**.

elbow ['elbō] *n* the joint where the arm bends. – *v* to push with the elbow, jostle. – *ns* **elbow grease** hard rubbing; **'elbow-room** plenty of room to move.

'elder *adj* older; having lived a longer time. – *n* one who is older; an office-bearer in certain churches; a type of tree with purple-black berries ('**elderberries**). – *adjs* **'elderly** nearing old age; **'eldest** oldest.

e'lect *v* to choose (someone) by voting; to choose (to). – *adj* chosen; chosen for a post but not yet in it: *president elect.* – *n* **e'lection** the choosing, *usu* by voting (of people to sit in parliament *etc*). – *v* **e'lectio'neer** to try to get votes in an election. – *n* **e'lectorate** all those who have the right to vote.

elec'tricity *n* a form of energy used to give light, heat and power. – *adjs* **e'lectric, e'lectrical** [ə'lektrik(əl)] of, produced by, worked by *etc* electricity. – *n* **electrician** [elek'trishən] one skilled in working with electricity. – *vs* **e'lectrifȳ** to supply with electricity; to excite or surprise greatly: – *pt* **e'lectrified**; **e'lectrocute** to kill by an electric current. – *n* **electric charge** a quantity of electricity *eg* that stored in a battery.

e'lectrode *n* a conductor through which an electric current enters or leaves a battery *etc.*

e'lectron *n* a very light particle within an atom, having the smallest possible charge of electricity. – *adj* **elec'tronic** of or using electrons or electronics. – *n*

elec'tronics a branch of physics dealing with the movement and effects of electrons, and with their application to machines *etc.*

'elegant *adj* graceful, well-dressed, fashionable; (of clothes *etc*) well-made and tasteful. – *n* **'elegance**.

elegy ['eliji] *n* a poem about sad things, such as the death of a friend: – *pl* **'elegies**.

'element *n* a part of anything; a substance that cannot be split into simpler substances by chemical means, as oxygen, iron *etc*; surroundings necessary for life or those which suit one best; the heating wire carrying the current in an electric heater *etc*; (*pl*) first steps in learning; (*pl*) the powers of nature, the weather. – *adjs* **ele'mental** of the elements; **ele'mentary** at the first stage; simple.

'elephant *n* a type of very large animal, with a thick skin, a trunk and two ivory tusks. – *adj* **ele'phantine** big and clumsy.

'elevate *v* to raise to a higher position; to make cheerful; to improve (the mind). – *ns* **ele'vation** the act of raising up; rising ground; height; a drawing of a building as seen from the side; an angle measuring height: *the sun's elevation*; **'elevator** (*US*) a lift in a building.

eleven [i'levn] *n* the number 11. – *adj* 11 in number. – *adj* **e'leventh** the last of eleven (things *etc*). – *n* one of eleven equal parts; a team (for cricket *etc*) of eleven people. – *n* **e'levenses** coffee, biscuits *etc* taken around eleven o'clock in the morning.

elf *n* (*myth*) a mischief-working fairy: – *pl* **elves**. – *adjs* **'elfin**, **'elfish**, **'elvish**.

e'licit *v* to draw out (information *etc*).

'eligible *adj* fit or worthy to be chosen. – *n* **eligi'bility**.

e'liminate *v* to get rid of; to exclude, omit. *He was eliminated at the first interview.* – *n* **e'limi'nation**.

élite [ā'lēt] *n* those thought to be the best people, as the richest, best educated *etc.*

e'lixir *n* a liquid which people once thought would make them live for ever or would turn iron *etc* into gold.

elk *n* a very large kind of deer.

ell *n* an old measure of length.

el'lipse *n* an oval shape: – *pl* **el'lipsēs**. – *adjs* **el'liptic, el'liptical** oval; having part of the words or meaning left out.

elm *n* a type of tree with a rough bark and leaves with saw-like edges.

elo'cūtion *n* the art of what is thought to be correct speech; style of speaking.

'**ēlongate** v to stretch out lengthwise, make longer. – n **elon'gation**.

e'**lope** v to run away from home to get married. – n e'**lopement**.

'**eloquent** adj good at putting one's thoughts etc into spoken words (to influence others). – n '**eloquence**.

else adv otherwise. Eat or else you will starve; apart from the person or thing mentioned. Someone else has taken her place. – adv '**else'where** in or to another place.

elucidate [i'lōōsidāt] v to make (something) easy to understand.

elude [i'lōōd] v to escape (by a trick); to be too difficult to remember or understand. – adj **elusive** [i'lōōsiv] hard to catch.

'**elver** n a young eel.

elves, elvish see elf.

e'**māciated** adj very thin, like a skeleton.

'**emanate** v to flow, come out from. – n **ema'nation** something given out by a substance, as gas, rays etc.

e'**mancipate** v to set free, as from slavery or strict or unfair social conditions. – n **emanci'pation**.

embalm [im'bäm] v to preserve (a dead body) from decay by treating it with spices or drugs.

em'bankment n a bank of earth or stone to keep water back, to carry a railway etc over low-lying places etc.

em'bargo n an official order forbidding something, esp trade with another country: – pl **em'bargoes**.

em'bark v to put or go on board ship; (with on) to start (a new career etc). – n **embar'kation**.

em'barrass v to make to feel uncomfortable and self-conscious; to put difficulties (sometimes lack of money) in the way of. – n **em'barrassment**.

'**embassy** n the offices etc of an ambassador in a foreign country: – pl '**embassies**.

em'bellish v to make beautiful, to decorate; to add details to (a story etc). – n **em'bellishment**.

'**ember** n a piece of wood or coal glowing in a fire.

em'bezzle v to use for oneself money given to one to look after. – n **em'bezzlement**.

em'blāzon v to set out in bright colours or in some very noticeable way.

'**emblem** n an object, picture etc which represents something. The dove is the emblem of peace. The leek is the emblem of Wales; a badge.

em'body v to include; to give form or expression (to an idea etc). His first

novel embodies the hopes of youth: – pt **em'bodied**. – n **em'bodiment**.

em'boss v to make a pattern which stands out from a flat surface (of leather, metal etc). – adj **em'bossed**.

em'brace v to throw the arms round in affection; to include; to accept, adopt eagerly (a political party etc). – Also n.

embro'cation n an ointment for rubbing on the body (for stiffness etc).

em'broider v to ornament with designs in needlework; to add (untrue) details to (a story etc). – n **em'broidery**.

em'broil v to get (a person) into a quarrel, or into a difficult situation etc; to throw into confusion.

embryo ['embriō] n the young of an animal or plant in its earliest stages in the womb, egg or seed; the beginning of anything: – pl '**embryos**. – adj **embryonic** [embri'onik] in an early stage of development.

ē'**mend** v to remove faults or errors from. – n **emen'dation**.

emerald ['emərəld] n a type of gem of a bright green colour.

e'**merge** v to come out; to become known or clear. – ns e'**mergence**; e'**mergency** an unexpected happening, usu dangerous or worrying, requiring very quick action: – pl e'**mergencies**. – adj e'**mergent** arising; newly formed or newly independent: emergent nation. – n **emergency exit** a way out of a building if anything goes wrong.

emery ['eməri] n a very hard mineral, for smoothing and polishing, used in **emery paper, emery board** etc.

e'**metic** adj causing vomiting. – Also n.

'**emigrate** v to leave one's country to settle in another. – ns **emi'gration**; '**emigrant** one who emigrates.

'**eminent** adj famous, notable. – n '**eminence** distinction, fame; a title of honour; a rising ground, hill. – adv '**eminently** very, obviously: eminently suitable.

'**emissary** n one sent on private (often secret) business: – pl '**emissaries**.

e'**mit** v to send, give out (light, sound etc): – pt e'**mitted**. – n e'**mission** the act of emitting.

e'**mollient** adj, n softening and smoothing (substance).

e'**molument** n wages, salary.

e'**mōtion** n any feeling that disturbs or excites the mind (fear, love, hatred etc). – adj e'**motional** moving the feelings; (of persons) having feelings easily excited. – adj e'**motive** causing emotion (rather than thought).

'**empathy** n the ability to share another

person's feelings *etc.* – *v* '**empathize**.

'**emperor** *n* the ruler of an empire: – *fem* '**empress**.

'**emphasis** *n* greater force of voice used on some words or parts of words to make them more noticeable; greater attention or importance. *The emphasis is on freedom.* – *v* '**emphasize** to put emphasis on; to call attention to. – *adj* em'**phatic** spoken strongly.

'**empire** *n* a large and powerful nation or group of nations (*usu* ruled by an emperor); area of power or control.

em'**pirical** *adj* based on experiment and experience, not on theory alone. – *n* em'**piricism**.

em'**ploy** *v* to give work to; to use; to occupy the time of. – *ns* em'**ploy** employment; **employ'ee** one who works for an em'**ployer**; em'**ploy-ment** work, trade, occupation.

em'**porium** *n* a market; a shop, *esp* a big shop: – *pls* em'**poria**, em'**poriums**.

empress *see* **emperor**.

'**empty** *adj* having nothing (or no one) in it; unlikely to result in anything: *empty threats*. – *v* to make or become empty: – *pt* '**emptied**. – *n* an empty bottle *etc*: – *pl* '**empties**. – *n* '**emptiness**.

'**ēmū** *n* a type of Australian bird which cannot fly.

'**emūlate** *v* to try to do as well as, or better than. – *n* emu'**lation**.

e'**mulsion** *n* a milky liquid, *esp* that made by mixing oil and water.

e'**nāble** *v* to make it possible for, allow. *The money enabled him to retire.*

e'**nact** *v* to act, perform; to make a law.

e'**namel** *n* any thin, hard, glossy coating, as paint on metal; the smooth white coating of the teeth *etc*. – *v* to coat or paint with enamel: – *pt* e'**namelled**. – *n* e'**namelling**.

enamoured [i'namərd]: **enamoured of** fond of.

en'**campment** *n* a camp for troops *etc*.

en'**chant** *v* to delight, please greatly; to put a spell or charm on. – *ns* en'**chanter**: – *fem* en'**chantress**; en'**chantment** state of being enchanted; act of enchanting.

en'**close** [in'klōz] *v* to put inside an envelope *etc* with a letter *etc*; to put (*eg* a wall) around. – *n* **enclosure** [in'klōzhər] the act of enclosing; something enclosed.

en'**compass** [in'kumpəs] *v* to surround; to include.

en'**core** ['oŋkör] *n* an extra performance of a song *etc* given in reply to a call from an audience; this call.

en'**counter** *v* to meet, *esp* unexpectedly;

to come up against (a difficulty, enemy *etc*). – *n* a meeting, a fight.

en'**courage** [in'kurij] *v* to give hope or confidence to; to urge (to do). – *n* en'**couragement**.

en'**croach** *v* to go beyond one's rights or land and interfere with another's. – *n* en'**croachment**.

en'**cumbrance** *n* something which hinders or weighs heavily on (someone).

encyclop(a)edia [insiklə'pēdiə] *n* a book or books containing much information, either on all subjects or on one particular subject. – *adj* **encyclo'p(a)edic** giving complete information.

end *n* the last point or part; death; the farthest point of the length of something, as of a table *etc*; purpose or object aimed at, the result; a small piece left over. – *v* to bring or come to an end. – *n* '**ending** the last part. – **on end** standing *etc* on one end; in a row or series, without a stop. *He fasted for days on end.*

en'**danger** [in'dānjər] *v* to put in danger or at risk.

en'**dear** *v* to make dear or more dear. – *n* en'**dearment** a word of love.

en'**deavour** [in'devər] *v* to try hard (to). – *n* a determined attempt.

en'**demic** *adj* of a disease *etc* found regularly in a certain area.

en'**dive** ['endiv] *n* a type of plant whose curly leaves are eaten as a salad.

en'**dorse** *v* to give one's support to something said or written; to write on the back of a cheque to show that money has been received for it; to indicate on a motor licence that the owner has broken a driving law. – *n* en'**dorsement**.

en'**dow** [in'dow] *v* to give money for the buying and upkeep of. *He endowed a bed in the hospital*; to give a talent, quality *etc* to. *Nature endowed her with a good brain.* – *n* en'**dowment**.

en'**dūre** *v* to bear without giving way; to last. – *adj* en'**durable** bearable. – *n* en'**durance** the power of enduring.

enemy ['enəmi] *n* a person who wishes to harm one; a person, army *etc* armed to fight against one; one who is against (something): *an enemy of Communism*: – *pl* '**enemies**. – *n* '**enmity**.

'**energy** *n* strength to work; vigour; ability to work, play *etc* very actively; power (such as electricity, heat *etc*): – *pl* '**energies**. – *adj* ener'**getic** active, lively.

'**enervate** *v* to take strength out of.

en'**force** *v* to cause (a law *etc*) to be

carried out.

en'gage v to begin to employ (workmen etc); to book in advance; to take or keep hold of (one's attention etc); to be busy with, occupied in; (of machine parts) to fit together; to begin fighting. – adj **en'gaged** bound by a promise esp of marriage; busy (on something); in use. – n **en'gagement** a promise of marriage; an appointment (to meet someone); a fight: naval engagement. – adj **en'gaging** pleasant, charming.

engine ['enjin] n a machine in which heat or other energy is used to produce motion; the part of a train which pulls the coaches etc. – n **engi'neer** one who makes or works with any kind of engine or machine; one who designs machines, engines etc; one who designs or makes bridges, roads, canals etc. – v to bring about by clever or cunning planning. – n **engi'neering** the science of machines, roadmaking etc.

en'grave v to write or draw with a special tool on wood, steel etc; to make a deep impression on. The event was engraved on his memory. – n **en'graving** (a print made from) a cut-out drawing etc in metal or wood.

en'gross v to take up the whole interest or attention.

en'gulf v to swallow up wholly.

en'hance v to make to appear greater or better. Candlelight enhances her beauty.

e'nigma n anything or anyone difficult to understand, a mystery. – adj **enig'matic**.

en'joy v to find or take pleasure in; to be in the habit of having, esp something of advantage. He enjoys good health. – adj **en'joyable**. – n **en'joyment**. – **enjoy oneself** to have a pleasant time.

en'large v to make larger; (with **on**) to say much or more about something. – n **en'largement** an increase in the size of anything; a larger photograph made from a smaller one.

enlighten [in'litn] v to give more knowledge or information to. – n **en'lightenment**.

en'list v to join an army etc; to obtain the support and help of.

en'liven v to make more active or cheerful.

enmity see **enemy**.

enormous [i'nörməs] adj very large. – n **e'normity** hugeness; great wickedness; ability to shock. The enormity of his remarks silenced all.

enough [i'nuf] adj, pron (in) the number or amount wanted or needed: enough pages: enough money. He has quite enough now. – adv as much as is wanted or necessary. She's been there often enough to know her way.

enquire see **inquire**.

en'rage v to make angry.

en'rōl, en'rōll v to enter (a name) in a register or list: – pt **en'rolled**. – n **en'rolment**.

en'sconce: ensconce oneself to settle comfortably.

ensemble [ön'sömbl] n all the parts of a thing taken together; an outfit of clothes; (a performance given by) a group of musicians etc.

ensign ['ensīn] n the flag of a nation, regiment etc: the White Ensign of the Royal Navy; (hist) a young officer who carried the flag.

ensue [in'sū] v to follow, come after; to result (from).

ensure [in'shōōr] v to make sure

en'tail v to leave land so that the heir cannot sell any part of it; to bring as a result, involve. The exam entailed extra work.

entangle [in'taŋgl] v to make tangled or complicated; to involve (in difficulties).

'enter v to go or come in or into; to put (a name etc) into a list; to take part (in); to begin (on, upon).

'enterprise n anything new (esp if risky or difficult) undertaken; a spirit of boldness in trying new things; a business concern. – adj **'enterprising** showing boldness esp in attempting new things.

enter'tain v to amuse; to receive as a guest; to give a party; to consider (eg a suggestion); to hold in the mind. He entertained the belief that he was Napoleon. – n **enter'tainer** one who entertains, esp one paid to amuse people. – adj **enter'taining** amusing. – n. **enter'tainment** something that entertains, as a theatrical show, a party etc.

enthral [in'thröl] v to give great delight to: – pt **en'thralled**.

en'thusiasm n great interest and keenness. – n **en'thusiast**. – adj **en'thusi'astic** acting with all one's powers; greatly interested, keen. – adv **enthusi'astically**. – v **en'thuse** to be enthusiastic (over).

en'tice v to draw on by promises, rewards etc. – n **en'ticement** a bribe, promise or reward. – adj **en'ticing**.

en'tire adj whole, complete. – n **entirety** [in'tirəti].

en'title v to give a name to a book etc; to give (a person) a right to.

'**entity** *n* something which exists: – *pl* '**entities**.

ento'**mology** *n* the study of insects. – *n* ento'**mologist**.

'**entrails** *npl* the inner parts of an animal's body, the bowels.

'**entrance**¹ *n* a place for entering (*eg* a door); the act of coming in; the right to enter. – *n* '**entrant** one who comes in; one who goes in for a race, competition *etc*.

en'**trance**² *v* to fill with great delight; to bewitch. – *adj* en'**trancing** charming.

en'**treat** *v* to ask earnestly. – *n* en'**treaty**: – *pl* en'**treaties**.

en'**trenched** *adj* firmly established, difficult to move or change.

en'**trust, in'trust** *v* to trust (something) to the care of (someone else).

'**entry** *n* the act of entering; a place for entering; something written in a book, as a name *etc*: – *pl* '**entries**.

e'**numerate** *v* to count; to mention individually. – *n* enume'**ration**.

e'**nunciate** *v* to pronounce distinctly; to state formally. – *n* enunci'**ation**.

en'**velop** *v* to cover by wrapping; to surround entirely: *enveloped in mist*. – *n* '**envelope** a wrapping or cover, *esp* for a letter.

en'**vironment** *n* surroundings, circumstances in which a person or animal lives.

envisage [in'vizij] *v* to picture in one's mind and consider.

'**envoy** *n* a messenger, *esp* one sent to deal with a foreign government.

'**envy** *v* to look greedily at someone and wish that one had what he has: – *pt* '**envied**. – Also *n*. – *adjs* '**enviable** worth envying, worth having; '**envious** feeling envy.

'**enzyme** *n* a substance produced in a living body which affects the speed of chemical changes without itself changing.

eon *see* **aeon**.

'**epaulet**, '**epaulette** *n* a shoulder ornament on a uniform.

ephemeral [i'femərəl] *adj* lasting a very short time.

'**epic** *n* a long poem, story, film *etc* about great deeds. – *adj* of or like an epic; heroic; greater than usual.

'**epicure** *n* one who is fond of eating and drinking good things. – *adj* epicu'**rean**.

epi'**demic** *n* an outbreak (*eg* of disease or crime) which affects many people.

epi'**dermis** *n* the top covering of the skin.

epi'**glottis** *n* a piece of skin at the back of the tongue which closes the windpipe during swallowing.

epigram *n* any short, neat, witty saying in prose or verse. – *adj* epigram-'**matic**.

'**epilepsy** *n* an illness causing attacks of unconsciousness and (*usu*) fits. – *adj* epi'**leptic** suffering from epilepsy; of epilepsy: *an epileptic fit*. – *n* one suffering from epilepsy.

epilogue, (*US*) **epilog** ['epilog] *n* the very end part of a book, programme *etc*; a speech at the end of a play *etc*.

e'**piscopal** *adj* of or ruled by bishops. – *adj* e'**pisco'palian** believing in e'**piscopacy**, the ruling of the Church by bishops.

'**episode** *n* one of several parts of a story *etc*; an interesting event or happening. – *adj* **episodic** [epi'sodik] of episodes; happening at irregular intervals.

epistle [i'pisl] *n* a (formal) letter *esp* one from an apostle of Christ in the Bible.

'**epitaph** *n* words about a dead person put on a gravestone.

'**epithet** *n* a describing word, an adjective.

epitome [i'pitəmi] *n* something or someone that represents something on a small scale. *He is the epitome of politeness*; a summary (of a book, story). – *v* e'**pitomize** to make or be the epitome (of something).

epoch ['ēpok] *n* an event or time marking the beginning of a new period in history, development *etc*; an extended period of time, *usu* marked by an important series of events. – *adj* '**epochmaking** marking an important point in history.

'**equable** *adj* of calm temper; (of climate) neither very hot nor very cold.

'**equal** *adj* of the same size, value, quantity *etc*; evenly balanced; (with **to**) able, fit for: *equal to the job*. – *n* a person of the same rank, cleverness *etc* (as another). – *v* to be or make equal to; to be the same as: – *pt* '**equalled**. – *n* **equality** [i'kwoləti] the state of being equal. – *v* '**equalize** to make equal.

equa'**nimity** *n* evenness of temper, calmness.

e'**quate** *v* to regard or treat as being in some way the same; to state the equality of. – *n* **equation** [i'kwāzhən] a statement, *esp* in mathematics, that two things are equal.

e'**quator** *n* an imaginary line around the earth, halfway between the North Pole and South Pole. – *adj* **equa'torial** of, situated on or near, the equator.

'**equerry** *n* an official who attends a king

or prince *etc*: – *pl* **'equerries**.

e'**questrian** *adj* of horse-riding; on horseback. – *n* a horseman.

ēqui- *prefix* equal. – *adjs* **'equi'distant** equally distant; **'equi'lateral** having all sides equal.

ēqui'**librium** *n* a state of equal balance between weights, forces *etc*; a balanced state of mind or feelings.

'**equine** *adj* of or like a horse or horses.

'**equinox** *n* either of the times (about 21st March and 23rd September) when the sun crosses the equator, making night and day equal in length. – *adj* **equi'noctial**.

e'**quip** *v* to supply with everything needed (for a task): – *pt* e'**quipped**. – *ns* '**equipage** carriages, attendants *etc* for a rich or important person; e'**quipment** a set of articles needed to equip (a person or thing).

'**equity** *n* fairness, just dealing. – *adj* '**equitable** fair, just.

e'**quivalent** *adj* equal in value, power, meaning *etc*. – Also *n*.

e'**quivocal** *adj* having more than one meaning; uncertain, doubtful. – *v* e'**quivocate** to use words with more than one meaning in order to mislead, to tell lies cleverly.

'**ēra** *n* a number of years counting from an important point in history: *the Elizabethan era*; a period of time marked by an important event or events: *the era of steam*.

e'**radicate** *v* to get rid of completely. – *n* **eradi'cation**.

erase [i'rāz] *v* to rub out; to remove. – *ns* e'**raser** something which erases, a rubber; **erasure** [i'rāzhǝr] the act of erasing; something erased.

ere [ār] *prep, conj* before: *ere long*.

e'**rect** *v* to build; to set upright. – *adj* standing straight up. – *n* e'**rection** the act of erecting; anything erected.

ermine ['ȫrmin] *n* a stoat; its white fur.

e'**rode** *v* to wear away, destroy gradually. – *n* e'**rosion**.

e'**rotic** *adj* of or arousing sexual desire.

err *v* to make a mistake; to sin. – *adj* **er'ratic** irregular, wandering, not following a fixed course; not steady or reliable in behaviour. – *n* **er'ratum** an error in a book: – *pl* **er'rata**.

'**errand** *n* a (*usu* short) journey on which a person is sent to say or do something for someone else; the purpose of this journey.

'**errant** *adj* doing wrong; straying; wandering in search of adventure: *a knight errant*.

erratic, erratum *see* **err**.

'**error** *n* a mistake; wrongdoing. – *adj* **er'rōneous** wrong.

erudite ['eroŏdit] *adj* clever, having learned much from books. – *n* **eru'dition**.

e'**rupt** *v* to break out or through. – *n* e'**ruption** a breaking or bursting forth, as a volcano, a rash on the body *etc*.

'**escalate** *v* to increase in amount, intensity *etc*. – *ns* **esca'lation**; '**escalator** a moving stairway.

es'**cape** to get away safe or free; (of gas *etc*) to leak; to slip from (the memory *etc*). – *n* the act of escaping. – *ns* **esca'pade** a mischievous adventure; es'**capement** something which controls the movement of a watch *etc*; es'**capism** the (habit of) trying to escape from reality into daydreaming *etc*.

es'**carpment** *n* the steep, cliff-like side of a hill *etc*.

'**escort** *n* person(s), ship(s) *etc* accompanying others for protection, courtesy *etc*. – *v* es'**cort** to act as escort to.

es'**cutcheon** *n* a shield on which a coat of arms is shown.

'**Eskimo** *n* one of a people inhabiting the Arctic regions: – *pl* '**Eskimos**.

eso'**teric** *adj* of or understood by a small number of people.

es'**parto** *n* a type of strong grass grown in Spain and N. Africa, used for making paper, ropes *etc*.

especial [is'peshǝl] *adj* more than ordinary; particular. – *adv* es'**pecially**.

espionage ['espiǝnäzh] *n* spying; the use of spies, *esp* by one country to find out the secrets of another.

espla'nade *n* a level roadway, *esp* one along a seafront.

Esq *see* **Esquire**.

Es'**quire** *n* (*usu* written **Esq**) a title of politeness after a man's name: *John Brown, Esq*.

'**essay** *n* a written composition; an attempt. – *v* es'**say** to try. – *n* '**essayist** a writer of essays.

'**essence** *n* the most important part or quality; substance got from a plant *etc* in concentrated form: *vanilla essence*.

es'**sential** *adj* absolutely necessary. – Also *n*. – *adv* es'**sentially** basically; necessarily.

es'**tablish** *v* to settle in position; to found, set up; to show to be true, prove (that). – *adj* es'**tablished** firmly set up; accepted, recognized; (of a church) officially recognized as national. – *n* es'**tablishment** anything established, *esp* a place of business, residence *etc*. – **The Establishment** the people holding important, influential positions in a community.

es'tate *n* a large piece of land owned by a person or group of people; a person's total possessions; land developed for houses, factories *etc.* – *ns* **estate agent** one whose job it is to sell houses; **estate car** a car with a large inside luggage compartment and an additional door at the back.

es'teem *v* to think highly of, to value. – Also *n.* – *adj* **es'teemed**.

'estimate *v* to judge the size, amount, value of something *esp* roughly, without measuring. – Also *n.* – *n* **esti'mation** opinion, judgement.

estranged [is'trānjd] *adj* no longer friendly.

'estūary *n* the wide lower part of a river, up which the tide travels: – *pl* **'estuaries**.

etc *see* **et cetera**.

et cetera [it'setrə] (written **etc**) and other things of the same sort.

etch *v* to make drawings on metal, glass *etc* by eating out the lines with acid. – *n* **'etching** the picture from the etched plate.

e'ternal *adj* lasting for ever; seemingly endless. – *n* **e'ternity** time without end; the time or state after death.

'ēther *n* a colourless liquid used to dissolve fats, to deaden feeling *etc.* – *adj* **ethereal** [i'thēriəl] delicate, fairy-like.

'ethical *adj* having to do with right behaviour, justice, duty; right, just, honourable. – *n* **'ethics** the study of right and wrong; (belief in) standards leading to right, ethical behaviour.

'ethnic *adj* of race; of the customs, dress, food of a particular race or group.

eth'nology *n* the study of the different races of mankind.

etiquette ['etiket] *n* (rules setting out) polite or correct behaviour.

ety'mology *n* the study of the history of words; a (short) description of the history of a word: – *pl* **ety'mologies**. – *adj* **etymo'logical**. – *n* **ety'mologist**.

euca'lyptus *n* a type of large Australian evergreen tree giving timber, oils, gum: – *pls* **euca'lyptuses, euca'lypti**.

'eulogize *v* to praise greatly. – *n* **'eulogy** great praise, written or spoken: – *pl* **'eulogies**.

'euphemism *n* a pleasant name for something unpleasant (*eg* 'passed on' for 'died'). – *adj* **euphe'mistic**.

eu'phōnious *adj* pleasant in sound. – *n* **'euphony**. – *n* **eu'phonium** a brass musical instrument with a low tone.

eu'phoria *n* a feeling of great happiness, joy. – *adj* **euphoric** [ū'forik].

eurhythmics [ū'ridhmiks] *n* the art of graceful movement of the body, *esp* to music.

eutha'nāsia *n* the killing of someone painlessly, *esp* to end suffering.

e'vacūate *v* to (cause to) leave *esp* because of danger; to make empty. – *ns* **evacu'ation; evacu'ee** a person who has been evacuated (from danger).

e'vade *v* to avoid or escape *esp* by cleverness or trickery. – *n* **e'vasion**. – *adj* **e'vasive** with the purpose of evading; not straightforward: *an evasive answer*.

e'valūate *v* to find or state the value of.

evanescent [evə'nesnt] *adj* passing away quickly.

ēvan'gelical *adj* spreading Christ's teaching. – *n* **e'vangelist**.

e'vaporate *v* to (cause to) change into vapour. *Heat evaporates water*; to vanish. – *n* **evapo'ration**.

evasion *see* **evade**.

eve *n* the evening or day before a festival: *Christmas Eve*; the time just before an event: *on the eve of the battle*.

'ēven *adj* level, smooth; (of numbers) able to be divided by 2 without a remainder; calm. – *adv* used to emphasize a word or words. *The job was even harder than before. Even young children could understand that*; exactly, just. – *v* to make even or smooth. – *n* **'evenness**. – **get even with** to harm (someone) who has harmed one.

'ēvening *n* the last part of the day and early part of the night.

e'vent *n* something (*esp* something important) that happens; an item in a sports programme *etc.* – *adjs* **e'ventful** exciting; **e'ventūal** final; happening as a result. – *n* **e'ventu'ality** a possible happening: – *pl* **e'ventu'alities**. – *adv* **e'ventually** at last, finally.

'ever *adv* always; at any time. – *n* **'evergreen** a kind of tree *etc* with green leaves all the year round. – *adv* **'ever'more** for ever.

'every *adj* each (of several things *etc*) without exception. – *prons* **'everybody, 'everyone** every person. – *adj* **'everyday** daily; common, usual. – *pron* **'everything** all things. – *adv* **'everywhere** in every place. – **every other** one out of every two, alternate.

e'vict *v* to put (someone) out of house and home *esp* by force of law. – *n* **e'viction**.

'evident *adj* easily seen or understood. – *adv* **'evidently**. – *n* **'evidence** a clear sign; proof; information given in a law case.

'ēvil *adj* wicked; harmful; unpleasant. – *n* wickedness.

e'vince *v* to show. *The men evinced surprise at these words.*

e'voke to draw out, produce. *The house evoked memories of their childhood.* – *adj* **evocative** [i'vokətiv] evoking, *eg* memories, a certain atmosphere.

e'volve *v* (to cause) to develop; to work out (a plan *etc*). – *n* **evolution** [ēvə'lōōshən] gradual development; the teaching or belief that the higher forms of life have gradually developed out of the lower. – *adj* **evo'lutionary**.

ewe [ū] *n* a female sheep.

ewer ['ūər] *n* a large jug with a wide spout.

ex- *prefix* no longer, former: *the ex-president*; outside, not in: *an ex-directory (telephone) number.*

ex'act *adj* accurate; punctual; careful. – *v* to compel to pay, give *etc*. – *adj* **ex'acting** asking too much; tiring. – *n* **ex'actness** accuracy, correctness.

exaggerate [ig'zajərāt] *v* to make (something) seem larger, greater *etc* than it is. – *n* **exagge'ration**.

exalt [ig'zölt] *v* to raise in rank; to praise; to make joyful. – *n* **exal'tation**.

examine [ig'zamin] *v* to put questions to (pupils *etc*) to test knowledge; to question (a witness); to look at closely, inquire into; (of a doctor) to look at (one's body) to check for illness or disease. – *ns* **exami'nation** a test of knowledge (also **ex'am**); a close inspection or inquiry; formal questioning; **ex'aminer**.

ex'ample *n* one case given to show what other things of the same kind are like; a warning. *Let this be an example to you.*

ex'asperate *v* to make very angry. – *n* **exaspe'ration**.

'excavate *v* to dig, scoop out; to uncover by digging. – *ns* **exca'vation** the act of digging out; a hollow made by digging; **'excavator** a machine used for excavating.

exceed [ik'sēd] *v* to go beyond, be greater than. – *adv* **ex'ceedingly** very.

excel [ik'sel] *v* to do very well; to be better than: – *pt* **ex'celled**. – *ns* **'excellence** the state of being excellent, very high quality; **'Excellency** a title of ambassadors *etc*: – *pl* **'Excellencies**. – *adj* **'excellent** unusually or extremely good.

except [ik'sept] *prep* leaving out, not counting. – *conj* with the exception (that). – *v* to leave out, not to count. – *prep* **ex'cepting** except. – *n*

ex'ception something left out; something that is unlike the rest: *an exception to the rule.* – *adj* **ex'ceptional** standing out from the rest. – *adv* **ex'ceptionally** very. – **except for** with the exception of; **take exception to** to object to, be offended by.

excerpt ['eksörpt] *n* a part chosen from a whole work: *an excerpt from a play.*

excess [ik'ses] *n* a going beyond what is usual or proper; the amount by which one thing is greater than another; (*pl*) **ex'cesses** very bad behaviour. – *adj* beyond the amount allowed. – *adj* **ex'cessive** too much, too great *etc*. – *adv* **ex'cessively**.

exchange [iks'chānj] *v* to give one thing and get another in return. – *n* the act of exchanging; exchanging money of one country for that of another; the difference between the value of money in different places; a central office or building (*eg* where telephone lines are connected); a place where business shares are bought and sold.

exchequer [iks'chekər] *n* the part of government that has to do with the money affairs of a country. – **Chancellor of Exchequer** *see* **chancellor**.

excise[1] [ik'sīz] *v* to cut off or out. – *n* **excision** [ik'sizhən].

excise[2] ['eksīz] *n* tax on goods *etc* made and sold within a country and on certain licences *etc*.

excite [ik'sīt] *v* to rouse the feelings of; to move to action. – *adjs* **ex'citable** easily excited; **ex'citing**. – *n* **ex'citement**.

ex'claim *v* to cry or shout out. – *n* **excla'mation** a sudden shout. – *adj* **ex'clamatory**. – *n* **exclamation mark** in punctuation, a mark (!) to show that an exclamation has been made.

ex'clude *v* to shut out; to prevent from sharing; to leave out (of consideration). – *n* **ex'clusion**. – *adj* **ex'clusive** shutting out unwanted persons, select: *an exclusive club*; not obtainable elsewhere: *an exclusive offer.* – **exclusive of** not including.

excom'mūnicate *v* to expel from membership of a church, to forbid to take part in church sacraments. – *n* **excommuni'cation**.

excrescence [iks'kresns] *n* something unwanted which grows outwards (such as a wart).

ex'crete *v* to cast out, discharge waste matter from the body. – *n* **'excrement** the waste matter cast out by humans or animals.

excruciating [iks'krōōshiátiŋ] *adj* (of pain *etc*) very severe.

ex'cursion *n* an outing, *usu* for pleasure (such as a picnic).

excuse [iks'kūz] *v* to forgive, pardon; to set free from a duty or task. – *n* **excuse** [iks'kūs] one's reason or explanation for having done something wrong. – *adj* **excusable** [iks'kūzəbl] pardonable.

'**execrable** *adj* very bad.

'**execūte** *v* to perform: *execute a dance step*; to carry out: *execute commands*; to put to death legally. – *ns* **exe'cution** a doing or performing; killing by order of the law; **exe'cutioner** one whose duty it is to put to death condemned persons. – *adj* **ex'ecutive** having power to act, carry out laws. – *n* the part of a government (or society) having such power; a person in a business organization who has the power to act on important decisions. – *n* **ex'ecutor** a person who sees to the carrying out of what is stated in a will.

ex'emplary *adj* worth following as an example: *exemplary conduct*; acting as a warning: *exemplary punishment*.

ex'emplifȳ *v* to be an example of; to show by giving example: – *pt* **ex'emplified**.

ex'empt *v* to grant freedom from some duty, task, payment, *etc*. – *adj* free (from), not liable (to do something that others have to do). – *n* **ex'emption**.

'**exercise** *n* a task for practice; training for body, mind *etc*. – *v* to give exercise to; to use. *Exercise great care!*

ex'ert *v* bring into action, use. *He exerts great influence on her*. – *n* **ex'ertion** effort; hard work. – **exert oneself** to make a great effort.

ex'hale *v* to breathe out. – *n* **exha'lation**.

exhaust [ig'zöst] *v* to tire out; to use up completely: *exhaust our supplies*; to say all that can be said about (a subject *etc*). – *n* the way out for the waste products of fuel-using engines (steam, fumes *etc*). – *adj* **ex'hausted** tired out; emptied; used up. – *n* **ex'haustion** great tiredness, weariness; the act of exhausting. – *adj* **ex'haustive** saying all that can be said.

exhibit [ig'zibit] *v* to show (in public). – *n* anything shown (*eg* a picture in a picture gallery). – *ns* **exhibition** [eksi'bishən] a public show, an open display; **exhi'bitionism** a tendency to try to attract people's attention; **exhi'bitionist; exhibitor** [ig'zibitər].

exhilarate [ig'zilərāt] *v* to make joyful or lively, refresh. – *adj* **ex'hilarating**.

exhort [ig'zört] *v* to urge (to do). – *n* **exhor'tation**.

ex'hūme *v* to dig out (*esp* a body from a grave). – *n* **exhu'mation**.

'**exigent** *adj* demanding immediate attention, urgent. – *n* **ex'igency** an urgent need or demand. *He was forced by the exigencies of the situation to sell his house*: – *pl* **ex'igencies**.

'**exile** *n* a person who lives outside his own country, either by choice or unwillingly; a (*usu* long) stay in a foreign land. – *v* to drive (a person) away from his own country, to banish.

exist [ig'zist] *v* to be, have life; to live; to live in poor circumstances. – *n* **ex'istence**. – *adj* **ex'istent**.

'**exit** *n* a way out; the act of going out.

'**exodus** *n* a going away of many people (*esp* those leaving a country for ever).

exonerate [ig'zonərāt] *v* to free from blame. – *n* **exone'ration**.

exorbitant [ig'zörbitənt] *adj* going beyond what is usual or reasonable: *an exorbitant price*. – *n* **ex'orbitance**.

'**exorcize** *v* to drive out (an evil spirit or spell); to free (someone or something) from an evil spirit dwelling in them. – *ns* '**exorcism** the act of driving away evil spirits or spells; '**exorcist**.

exotic [ig'zotik] *adj* coming from a foreign country; unusual, colourful.

ex'pand *v* to grow wider or bigger; to open out. – *ns* **ex'panse** a wide stretch (as of land *etc*); **ex'pansion** a growing, stretching or spreading. – *adj* **ex'pansive** spreading out; (of persons) talkative, telling much.

expatiate [iks'pāshiāt] *v* to talk a great deal (about something).

ex'pātriate *adj* living outside one's native country. – Also *n*.

ex'pect *v* to think of as likely to happen, come *etc* soon; to think, assume. *I expect he's too busy*. – *adj* **ex'pectant** hopeful, expecting; expecting to become (*esp* a mother). – *ns* **ex'pectancy** state of expecting; hope; **expec'tation** state of expecting; what is expected. – *adj* **ex'pecting** (*coll*) pregnant.

ex'pēdient *adj* suited to the time and to the occasion but sometimes not just or fair. – *n* something done to get round a difficulty. – *ns* **ex'pedience, ex'pediency**.

'**expedite** *v* to hasten, hurry on. – *adj* **expe'ditious** swift, speedy.

expe'dition *n* a journey with a purpose (often exploration); people making such a journey.

ex'pel *v* to drive or force out; to send away in disgrace (*esp* from a school): –

pt ex'**pelled**. – *n* ex'**pulsion**.

ex'**pend** *v* to spend, use up. – *n* ex'**penditure** amount spent or used up, *esp* money.

ex'**pense** *n* cost; cause of spending. *The house was a continual expense;* (*pl*) money spent in carrying out a job *etc*. – *adj* ex'**pensive** costing much money.

experience [iks'pēriəns] *n* any event in which one is involved: *a horrible experience;* wisdom, knowledge gained from events, practice *etc*. – *v* to go through, undergo. – *adj* ex'**perienced** skilled, knowledgeable.

ex'**periment** *n* a trial, test (of an idea, machine *etc*). – *v* to carry out experiments. – *adj* experi'**mental**.

'**expert** *adj* highly skilful or knowledgeable (in a particular subject). – *n* one who is highly skilled or knowledgeable. – *n* **expertise** [eksər'tēz] skill.

'**expiate** *v* to make up for (a crime *etc*). – *n* **expi'ation**.

ex'**pire** *v* to die; to come to an end. – *n* ex'**piry** the end or finish.

ex'**plain** *v* to make clear; to give reasons for. – *n* expla'**nation** a statement which makes clear something difficult or puzzling; a reason (*eg* for one's behaviour). – *adj* ex'**planatory** meant to make clear.

ex'**plētive** *n* an exclamation, *esp* a swear word.

ex'**plicable** *adj* able to be explained.

ex'**plicit** *adj* plainly stated; outspoken.

ex'**plode** *v* to blow up like a bomb with loud noise; to prove (a theory *etc*) to be wrong. – *n* ex'**plosion** a sudden burst or blow-up, with a loud noise. – *adj* ex'**plosive** liable to explode; hot-tempered. – *n* anything (such as gunpowder) that will explode.

'**exploit** *n* a daring deed; a feat. – *v* ex'**ploit** to make use of selfishly; to make good use of (resources *etc*). – *n* exploi'**tation**.

ex'**plore** *v* to make a journey of discovery. – *ns* explo'**ration**; ex'**plorer**.

explosion *see* **explode**.

ex'**pōnent** *n* one who shows skill in a particular art or craft: *an exponent of karate*. — *adj* expon'**ential**.

ex'**port** *v* to sell goods *etc* in a foreign country. – *ns* '**export** act of exporting; something exported; expor'**tation**.

ex'**pose** *v* to place (something) where all can see it; to show up (a hidden evil, crime *etc*); to lay open to sun, wind, cold *etc*; to allow light to reach and act on (a film). – *ns* ex'**posure**; expo'**sition** a public show; a statement which makes clear a writer's meaning.

ex'**postūlate** *v* to protest. – *n* expostu'**lation**.

ex'**pound** *v* to explain fully.

ex'**press** *v* to show by action; to put into words; to press or squeeze out. – *adj* clearly stated: *express instructions;* sent in haste: *express messenger*. – *n* a fast train. – *n* ex'**pression** the look on one's face; showing meaning, feeling by means of language, art *etc*; a show of feeling in a performance of music *etc*; a word or phrase: *a slang expression;* pressing or squeezing out. – *adj* ex'**pressive** expressing; expressing meaning or feeling clearly.

ex'**prōpriate** *v* to take (property *etc*) away from its owner.

expulsion *see* **expel**.

ex'**punge** *v* to rub out, remove.

exquisite ['ekskwizit] *adj* of great beauty; excellent; (of pleasure *etc*) very great; keen, sharp.

ex'**tant** *adj* still existing.

extempore [iks'tempəri] *adv, adj* at a moment's notice, without preparation. – *v* ex'**temporize** to make up (music, a speech *etc*) as one plays, speaks *etc*.

ex'**tend** *v* to stretch, make longer; to hold out: *he extended his hand;* to last. *This holiday extends into next week*. – *n* ex'**tension** a part added (to a building, a holiday *etc*); a telephone connected with a main one. – *adj* ex'**tensive** wide; covering a large space; happening or being in many places. – *n* ex'**tent** the space something covers; degree: *to a great extent*.

ex'**tenūate** *v* to lessen; to make to seem less bad. – *n* extenu'**ation**.

ex'**tērior** *adj* lying *etc* on the outside, outer: *an exterior wall*. – *n* the outside (of something).

ex'**terminate** *v* to destroy completely, kill off (a race, a type of animal *etc*). – *n* extermi'**nation**.

ex'**ternal** *adj* outside; on the outside.

ex'**tinct** *adj* no longer active: *an extinct volcano;* of a kind no longer found alive. *The dodo is extinct*. – *n* ex'**tinction** making or becoming extinct.

extinguish [iks'tiŋgwish] *v* to put out (fire *etc*); to put an end to. – *n* ex'**tinguisher** a spray containing chemicals for putting out fires.

ex'**tōl** *v* to praise greatly: – *pt* ex'**tolled**.

ex'**tort** *v* to take by force or threats. – *n* ex'**tortion**. – *adj* ex'**tortionate** (of a price) much too high.

'**extra** *adj* more than is usual or necessary; additional. – *adv* unusually. – *n* anything extra; a person employed to be one of a crowd in a film.

extra- *prefix* outside, beyond, as in 'extra-ter'restrial outside, or from outside the earth.

ex'tract *v* to draw or pull out *esp* by force; to choose and take out parts of a book *etc*; to take out (a substance forming part of something else) by pressure *etc* or by chemical means. – *ns* 'extract a part chosen (from a book *etc*); a substance obtained by extraction; ex'traction act of extracting; one's descent. *He was of English extraction.*

'extradite *v* to hand over to the police of another country (someone wanted by them). – *n* extra'dition.

ex'trāneous *adj* having nothing to do with the subject: *extraneous information.*

extraordinary [iks'trördənəri] *adj* not usual, exceptional; very surprising; specially employed: *ambassador extraordinary.*

extra'sensory *adj* beyond the range of the ordinary senses.

ex'travagant *adj* spending too freely; wasteful; too great: *extravagant praise.* – *n* ex'travagance.

'extravert, 'extrovert *n* one who is chiefly interested in matters outside of himself.

ex'treme *adj* far from the centre; far from the ordinary or usual; very great. – *n* an extreme point. – *ns* ex'trēmist one who carries ideas foolishly far;

extremity [iks'treməti] the farthest-off part or place; great distress or pain; (*pl*) ex'tremities farthest-off parts of the body, as hands, feet.

'extricate *v* to set free (from difficulties *etc*).

extrovert *see* extravert.

exuberant [ig'zūbərənt] *adj* in very high spirits. – *n* ex'uberance.

exude [ig'zūd] *v* to give off (in great amounts): *exude sweat: exude happiness.*

exult [ig'zult] *v* to be very glad, rejoice greatly. *They exulted in their victory.* – *adj* ex'ultant. – *n* exul'tation.

eye [i] *n* the part of the body with which one sees; the ability to notice: *an eye for detail*; sight; anything like an eye (*eg* the hole in a needle *etc*). – *v* to look at. – *ns* 'eyeball the round part of the eye; the eye itself (the part between the eyelids); 'eyebrow the hairy ridge above the eye; 'eyeglass a lens to correct faulty eyesight; 'eyelash one of the hairs on the edge of the eyelid; 'eyelet a small hole for a lace *etc*; 'eyelid the skin cover of the eye; 'eye-opener that which shows up something unexpected; 'eyesore anything that is ugly (*esp* a building); 'eyewitness one who sees a thing done (*eg* a crime committed).

eyrie, eyry, aerie ['iri] *n* the nesting place of eagles or other birds of prey.

F

'fāble *n* a story (about animals *etc*) that has a lesson or moral. – *adj* fabulous ['fabūləs] existing (only) in fable. *The griffin is a fabulous creature*; (*coll*) very good.

'fabric *n* cloth; the outside parts (walls *etc*) of a building.

'fabricate *v* to make up (lies). – *n* fabri'cation.

façade [fə'säd] *n* the front of a building; a deceptive appearance.

face *n* the front part of the head; the front of anything; appearance. – *v* to turn, stand *etc* in the direction of; to stand opposite to; to put an additional surface ('facing) on. – *n* 'facepowder powder put on the face to improve the appearance. – face up to to meet or accept boldly. *He faced up to his responsibilities.*

'facet *n* a side of a many-sided object, *esp* a cut gem.

fa'cētious *adj* funny, joking. – *n* fa'cetiousness.

facial ['fāshəl] *adj* of the face.

'facile *adj* not deep or thorough, superficial; easily persuaded; (too) fluent. – *n* facility [fə'siləti] ease; skill in doing a thing; (*pl*) fa'cilities the means for doing a thing (easily). – *v* fa'cilitate to make easy.

facsimile [fak'siməli] *n* an exact copy.

fact *n* something known or held to be true; reality; (in law) a deed. – in fact actually, really.

'faction *n* a group of people (part of a larger group) acting together. *The rival factions hated each other.* – *adj* 'factious trouble-making, riotous.

'factor *n* something which affects the

course of events; one who does business for another; a number which exactly divides into another (*eg* 3 is a factor of 6). – *v* '**factorize** to find factors of.

'**factory** *n* a workshop where goods are made in large quantities: – *pl* '**factories**.

fac'**tōtum** *n* a person employed to do all kinds of work.

'**faculty** *n* power of the mind, *eg* reason *etc*; a natural power of the body, as hearing *etc*; ability, aptitude; a department of study in a university *etc*: *Faculty of Science*: – *pl* '**faculties**.

fad *n* an odd like or dislike. – *adj* '**faddy**.

fade *v* to (make to) lose colour, strength *etc*; to go from sight, hearing *etc*.

faeces ['fēsēz] *n* solid waste material excreted from the body.

fag *v* to work hard; to weary; (*coll*) to work as a school fag: – *pt* **fagged**. – *n* any tiresome bit of work; (*coll*) a young schoolboy forced to do jobs for an older one; (*slang*) a cigarette.

'**faggot**, '**fagot** *n* a bundle of sticks.

Fahrenheit ['farənhit] *adj* as measured on a Fahrenheit thermometer: *50 degrees Fahrenheit*. – **Fahrenheit thermometer** a thermometer which shows the temperature at which water freezes as 32 degrees, and that at which it boils as 212 degrees.

fail *v* to (declare to) be unsuccessful; to break down, stop; to lose strength; to be lacking, not to be enough; to disappoint. – *ns* '**failing** a fault; a weakness; '**failure** the act of failing; someone or something which fails. – **without fail** certainly. *Do it without fail by tomorrow.*

fain *adv* (in poetry *etc*) willingly.

faint *adj* lacking in strength, brightness, courage *etc*; about to lose consciousness. – *v* to become faint; to fall down unconscious. – *n* a loss of consciousness. – *adv* '**faintly** dimly, not clearly. – *n* '**faintness**.

fair¹ *adj* of a light colour *esp* of hair; free from rain; not favouring one side, just; good enough but not excellent; beautiful. – *n* '**fairness**. – *adj* '**fair-'haired** having light-coloured hair, blond. – *n* '**fairway** the deep-water part of a channel, river *etc*; the mown part on a golf course, between the tee and the green.

fair² *n* a large market held at fixed times; an exhibition of goods from different countries, firms *etc*; a sale of goods for charities; a collection of entertainments (merry-go-rounds *etc*) which moves

from place to place.

'**fairy** *n* (*myth*) a (small) being like a man or woman with magical powers: – *pl* '**fairies**. – *ns* **fairy light** a small coloured light for decoration (of Christmas trees *etc*); **fairy story**, **fairy tale** an old story of fairies, giants *etc*; (*coll*) a lie.

faith *n* trust, belief (*eg* in God); loyalty to a promise. *He kept faith with them.* – *adjs* '**faithful** loyal; keeping one's promises; true, accurate: *a faithful account of events*; believing (in God); '**faithless**.

fake *v* to make an imitation of (*esp* in order to deceive). – *adj* not genuine, forged. – *n* one who pretends to be something he is not; a forgery.

falcon ['fölkən] *n* a kind of bird of prey. – *n* '**falconry** the training of falcons for hunting.

fall [föl] *v* to drop down; to become less; (of a fortress *etc*) to be captured; to die in battle; to happen, occur. *Christmas falls on Tuesday this year:* – *pt* **fell**, *pp* '**fallen**. – *n* a dropping down; something that falls: *a fall of snow*; lowering (in value *etc*); (*US*) autumn; an accident in which one falls (as from a horse, when running *etc*); ruin, downfall, surrender; (*pl*) a waterfall. – *n* '**fallout** radioactive dust resulting from the explosion of an atomic bomb *etc*. – **fall flat** to fail to have the intended effect; **fall in love** to begin to be in love; **fall out with** to quarrel with; **fall through** (of plans *etc*) to fail, come to nothing.

'**fallacy** *n* a wrong idea or belief; something which is thought to be true but is really false; unsound argument or reasoning: – *pl* '**fallacies**. – *adj* fal'**lācious** misleading, false; not showing sound reasoning.

'**fallible** *adj* liable to make a mistake or to be wrong. – *n* **falli'bility**.

fallow ['falō] *adj* (of land) left unsown for a time after being ploughed; of a yellowish-brown colour. – *n* **fallow deer** a type of yellowish-brown deer.

false [föls] *adj* untrue; not real, fake; not natural: *false teeth*. – *ns* '**falsehood** a lie, an untruth; '**falseness**, '**falsity** quality of being false. – *v* '**falsifȳ** to make false, alter for a dishonest purpose. *He falsified the firm's accounts:* – *pt* '**falsified**.

falter ['föltər] *v* to stumble or hesitate.

fame *n* the quality of being well-known or much talked about, renown. – *adjs* **famed**, '**famous** well-known, having fame. – *adv* '**famously** (*coll*) very well.

fa'**miliar** *adj* well-known; seen, known

etc before; well-acquainted (with); too friendly, cheeky. – *n* **famili'arity**. – *v* **fa'miliarize** to make quite accustomed or acquainted (with).

family *n* a man, his wife and their children; the children alone; a group of people related to one another; a group (such as plants, animals, languages) having some likeness: – *pl* **'families**.

famine ['famin] *n* great shortage *esp* of food or water.

famished *adj* very hungry.

famous *see* **fame**.

fan *n* an instrument or device for making a rush of air; a small hand-held device, *usu* shaped like part of a circle, for cooling the face; an admirer (of an actor, singer *etc*). – *v* to cause a rush of air with a fan; to increase the strength of: *fan his anger*: – *pt* **fanned**. – *n* **'fanlight** a window above a door, *esp* one shaped like a half circle. – **fan out** to spread out in the shape of a fan.

fa'natic *n* a person who is over-enthusiastic or eager about something (*esp* religion). – *adj* **fa'natic(al)** wildly or excessively enthusiastic.

fancy *n* a sudden liking or desire; the power of the mind to imagine things *esp* things unlike reality; something imagined: – *pl* **'fancies**. – *adj* not plain; ornamented. – *v* to picture, imagine; to have a sudden wish for; to think without being sure: – *pt* **'fancied**. – *n* **'fancier** one whose hobby is to keep prize animals, birds *etc*. – *adj* **'fanciful** inclined to have fancies; imaginary, not real.

fanfare *n* a great blowing of trumpets or bugles.

fang *n* a tooth of a wild animal (*esp* a fierce one); the poison-tooth of a snake.

fantasy *n* an imaginary (*esp* unreal) scene, story *etc*; an idea not based on reality: – *pl* **'fantasies**. – *adj* **fan'tastic** very unusual, strange; (*coll*) very great; (*coll*) excellent.

far *adv* at or to a long way: *far off*; very much: *far better*. – *adj* a long way off, distant: *a far country*; more distant: *the far side*. – *adjs, advs* **'farther**, **'farthest**. – *adjs* **far-'fetched** very unlikely: *a far-fetched story*; **far-'flung** extending over a great distance; **far-'sighted** foreseeing what is likely to happen and preparing for it.

farce *n* a play with unlikely and ridiculous characters and plot; anything silly and useless. – *adj* **'farcical** absurd, ridiculous.

fare *v* to get on (well, badly). *He fared well in the competition*. – *n* the price of a journey; a person who pays to be carried on a journey; food. – *interj, n* **fare'well** goodbye.

farm *n* an area of land used for growing crops, breeding and feeding cows, sheep *etc*; a place where certain animals, fish *etc* are reared: *an oyster farm*. – *v* to work the lands *etc* of a farm. – *n* **'farmer** the owner or tenant of a farm who works the land *etc*. – *ns* **'farmhouse** the house where a farmer lives; **farmstead** ['färmsted] a farm and farmhouse; **'farmyard** the yard surrounded by farm buildings. – **farm out** to give (work) to others to do for payment.

farrow ['farō] *n* a family of baby pigs. – *v* to give birth to a family of pigs.

farthing ['färdhiŋ] *n* an old coin, ¼ of an old penny.

fascinate ['fasināt] *v* to charm, attract or interest irresistibly; to make (a victim) still and powerless. *The snake fascinated the rabbit*. – *adj* **'fascinating**. – *n* **fasci'nation**.

fashion ['fashən] *n* the make or cut of a thing (*esp* clothes); a way of behaving, dressing *etc* which is popular for a time; a way of doing a thing: *acting in a strange fashion*. – *v* to shape (according to a pattern). – *adj* **'fashionable** agreeing with the latest style of dress, way of living *etc*. – **in fashion** fashionable.

fast *adj* quick-moving; (of a clock *etc*) showing a time in advance of the correct time; of colour (in clothes *etc*) fixed, not likely to be removed by washing. – *adv* quickly; firmly: *stand fast*. – *v* to go without food (of one's own free will). – Also *n*. – *n* **'fastness** quickness, speed; a stronghold, fortress, castle.

fasten ['fäsn] *v* to fix: *fasten it to the wall*; to make firm (by tying, nailing *etc*).

fas'tidious *adj* difficult to please.

fat *n* an oily substance made by the bodies of animals and by plants. – *adj* having much fat; plump; thick, wide. – *v* **'fatten** to make or become fat.

'fātal *adj* causing death or disaster. – *n* **fatality** [fə'taləti] (an accident causing) death: – *pl* **fa'talities**.

fate *n* what the future holds for one, fortune, luck; end or death. *He met his fate bravely*. – *adjs* **'fated** controlled by fate; doomed; **'fateful** having important results.

father ['fädhər] *n* a male parent; a priest; a person who first makes, invents *etc* something. *Jules Verne is the father of science fiction*. – *ns* **'father-in-law** the

father of one's husband or wife;
'**fatherland** one's native land.
fathom ['fadhəm] *n* a measure of depth
(6 feet, 1·83 metres). – *v* to understand, get to the bottom of (a mystery
etc).
fatigue [fə'tēg] *n* great tiredness; weakness or strain (of metals *etc*) caused by
use. – *v* to tire out.
'**fatuous** *adj* very foolish.
'**faucet** *n* (*US*) a tap.
fault *n* a mistake; a flaw, something bad
or wrong (*eg* with a machine). – *adjs*
'**faultless**; '**faulty** having a fault or
faults.
faun *n* (*myth*) an imaginary creature,
half man, half animal.
'**fauna** *n* the animals of a district or
country as a whole.
favour ['fāvər] *n* a kind action; goodwill,
kindness, approval; gift, token, badge
etc. *The knight wore his lady's favour.* –
v to show preference for; to be an
advantage to. *The darkness favoured his
escape.* – *adj* '**favourable** friendly;
showing approval; advantageous, helpful (to). – *n* **favourite** ['fāvərit] a liked
or best-loved person or thing; one, *esp*
a horse, likely to win. – Also *adj.* – *n*
'**favouritism** showing favour toward
one person *etc* more than another. – **in
favour of** in support of; for the benefit
of.
fawn *n* a young deer; its colour, a light
yellowish-brown. – *adj* of this colour. –
v to show affection as a dog does; (with
upon) to flatter in too humble a way.
fear *n* a feeling caused by danger, evil *etc*.
– *adj* '**fearful** timid; afraid; terrible;
(*coll*) very bad: *a fearful headache*;
'**fearless** brave, daring.
feasible ['fēzəbl] *adj* able to be done,
likely. – *n* **feasi'bility**.
feast *n* a rich and plentiful meal; a
festival day on which some event is
remembered. – *v* to hold or eat a feast.
feat *n* a deed difficult to do.
feather ['fedhər] *n* one of the growths
which form the outer covering of a
bird. – *adj* '**feathery** having or covered
in feathers; soft; light.
feature ['fēchər] *n* a mark by which
anything is known, a characteristic; an
important or special article in a newspaper *etc*; the main film *etc* in a
programme; a special attraction; (*pl*)
the various parts of a person's face
(eyes, nose *etc*). – *v* to show or exhibit
as a feature; to take part (in).
February ['febrŏŏəri] *n* the second
month of the year.
'**fecund** *adj* fertile. – *n* **fe'cundity**.

fed *see* **feed**.
federal ['fedərəl] *adj* joined by treaty or
bargain. – *adj* '**federated** joined after
an agreement is made. – *n* **fede'ration**
those joined together for a common
purpose, a league.
fee *n* a price paid for work done, or for
some special service or right.
'**feeble** *adj* weak. – *n* '**feebleness**. – *adv*
'**feebly**.
feed *v* to give food to; to eat food; to
supply with necessary materials: – *pt*
fed [fed]. – *n* food for animals: *cattle
feed*. – **fed up** tired, bored and dis-
gusted.
feel *v* to explore by touch; to experience,
be aware of (pain, pleasure *etc*); to
believe, consider; to think (oneself) to
be. *I feel ill*; to be sorry (for). *I feel for
you in your sorrow*: – *pt* **felt** [felt]. – *ns*
'**feeler** one of two thread-like parts of
an insect's body (on the head) by which
it senses danger *etc*; '**feeling** sense of
touch; emotion. *He spoke with great
feeling*; affection; an impression, belief; (*pl*) what one feels inside one such
as love, anger. – **feel like** to want, have
an inclination to or for. *He feels like
going out. He feels like an apple.*
feet *see* **foot**.
feign [fān] *v* pretend to feel or be. *He
feigned illness.*
feint [fānt] *n* a pretence; a move to put
an enemy off his guard. – Also *v*.
fe'licity *n* happiness. – *npl* **felici'tations**
good wishes, congratulations. – *adj*
fe'licitous lucky; well-chosen, suiting
well.
'**feline** *adj* cat-like; of the cat family.
fell *n* a barren hill. – *v* to bring to the
ground; to cut down; *see* also **fall**. –
adj cruel, fierce.
fellow ['felō] *n* an equal; one of a pair; a
member of a learned society, college
etc; a man, boy. – *n* '**fellowship** state
of being on equal terms; friendship; an
award to a university graduate.
'**felon** *n* one who has committed a serious
crime. – *n* '**felony** serious crime: – *pl*
'**felonies**.
felt *n* a type of rough cloth made of rolled
and pressed wool. – *v see* **feel**.
'**female** *n*, *adj* (one) of the sex which
produces young.
feminine ['feminin] *adj* womanly; having to do with women. – *ns*
femi'ninity; '**feminism** the movement which aims to win rights for
women equal to those of men; '**femin-
ist** a supporter of this movement.
'**femur** *n* the thigh bone.
fen *n* low marshy land, often covered

with water.

'ence *n* a railing, hedge *etc* for closing in animals or land; (*slang*) a receiver of stolen goods. – *v* to close in with a fence; to fight with swords; to give answers that tell nothing. – *n* 'fencing fences; material for fences; the sport of fighting with swords, using blunted weapons.

end: fend for oneself to look after, provide for oneself.

'ender *n* a low guard round a fireplace to keep in coals *etc*; something (a piece of matting *etc*) lowered over a ship's side to act as a buffer against the quay; (*US*) the bumper of a car *etc*.

'ermen'tation *n* the change which takes place when certain substances are brought together (as when yeast is added to the dough in the making of bread); a state of great excitement. – *v* fer'ment (of a mixture) to change by fermentation; to stir up trouble *etc*. – *n* 'ferment.

'ern *n* a kind of plant with no flowers and feather-like leaves.

'e'rōcious *adj* fierce, savage. – *n* ferocity [fə'rɒsəti].

'erret *n* a type of small weasel-like animal used to chase rabbits out of their warrens. – *v* to search busily and persistently.

'errule ['ferool] *n* a metal ring or cap on the tip of a walking stick or umbrella.

'erry *v* to carry (people, cars *etc*) over water by boat or overland by aeroplane *etc*. – *n* a crossing place for boats; the boat which crosses: – *pl* 'ferries.

'ertile *adj* fruitful, producing much; full of ideas. – *v* fertilize ['fɜrtilīz] to make (soil *etc*) fertile or more fertile. – *ns* fer'tility fruitfulness, ability of land to produce crops *etc*, ability of a woman or female animal to produce children; fertili'zation; 'fertilizer a substance (*eg* manure, chemicals) for making fields (more) fertile.

'ervent *adjs* very eager; intense. – *n* fervour ['fɜrvər].

'ester *v* (of a cut, sore) to have pus in it because of infection.

'estive ['festiv] *adj* of a feast; in a happy, celebrating mood, joyful. – *n* 'festival a celebration; a feast; a season of musical, theatrical or other performances; fes'tivity joyfulness, merrymaking: – *pl* fes'tivities.

'es'toon *v* to decorate with chains of ribbons, flowers *etc*.

'etch *v* to go and get; to bring in (a price). *The vase fetched £100 at the auction.*

fête [fāt] *n* an occasion with stalls, competitions, displays *etc* to raise money (often for charity). – *v* to entertain lavishly, make much of (a person).

fetid, foetid ['fētid] *adj* having a rotten smell, stinking.

'fetish *n* something of which a person is excessively (and unnaturally) fond: – *pl* 'fetishes.

'fetlock *n* the part of a horse's leg just above the foot.

'fetters *npl* chains, bonds (for imprisonment).

'fettle: in fine fettle in good health or condition.

feud [fūd] *n* a private, drawn-out war *esp* between families, clans, tribes *etc*.

feudal ['fūdl] *adj* (*hist*) of the system by which, in earlier times, certain services were given to the overlord by the tenants, as a return for their lands. – *n* 'feudalism.

'fēver *n* (any illness causing) high body temperature and quickened pulse. – *adjs* 'feverish; 'fevered having a fever; very excited.

few *adj, n* not many: *a few (pounds) left; the few (pounds) which were left.* – *n* 'fewness the state of being few. – a good few, quite a few several, a considerable number.

fez *n* a close-fitting red hat (shaped like a flowerpot) with a tassel and formerly the national head-dress of the Turks: – *pl* 'fezzes.

fiancé [fi'önsā] *n* a person to whom one is engaged to be married: *her fiancé*: – *fem* fi'ancée: *his fiancée*.

fi'asco *n* a complete failure: – *pl* fi'ascos.

fib *v* to lie about something unimportant: – *pt* fibbed. – Also *n*.

'fibre *n* any fine thread or threadlike stuff. – *adj* 'fibrous. – *n* 'fibreglass a material made of very fine threadlike pieces of glass used for many purposes *eg* building boats.

'fickle *adj* changeable, not constant or loyal.

'fiction *n* stories *etc* which tell of imagined characters and events; an untruth, a lie. – *adjs* 'fictional (of novels, stories *etc*) about imagined characters and events; fic'titious not real, imaginary; untrue.

'fiddle *n* a violin. – *v* to play the violin; to make restless, aimless movements (with); to interfere, tamper (with); (*coll*) to falsify (accounts *etc*) with the intention of cheating.

fi'delity *n* faithfulness; truth; accuracy.

'**fidget** *v* to move (the hands, feet *etc*) restlessly.

field [fēld] *n* a piece of ground enclosed for pasture, crops, sports *etc*; an area of land which contains a natural resource (*eg* coal, gold); an area or branch of interest, knowledge *etc*; those taking part in a race, competition *etc*. – *v* (in cricket *etc*) to catch the ball and return it. – *n* '**field-day** a day of unusual activity or success. – *npl* '**fieldglasses** a small double telescope. – *ns* '**field-gun** a light, mobile cannon; '**field-'marshal** an officer of the highest rank in the army.

fiend [fēnd] *n* an evil spirit; a wicked person. – *adj* '**fiendish**.

fierce [fērs] *adj* very angry-looking, hostile, likely to attack; intense, strong: *fierce competition*. – *n* '**fierce-ness**.

fiery ['fīri] *adj* like fire; easily made angry; high-spirited.

fife *n* a type of small flute.

'**fif'teen** *n* the number 15. – *adj* 15 in number. – *adj* '**fif'teenth** the last of fifteen (things *etc*). – *n* one of fifteen equal parts.

fifth *see* **five**.

'**fifty** *n* the number 50. – *adj* 50 in number. – *adj* '**fiftieth** the last of fifty (things *etc*). – *n* one of fifty equal parts.

fig *n* a soft, pear-shaped fruit containing many seeds and often eaten dried; the tree which bears it.

fight [fīt] *v* to struggle (with) with fists, weapons *etc*; to quarrel; to go to war with: – *pt* **fought** [föt]. – *n* a struggle; a battle. – *n* '**fighter** one who fights; a fast military aircraft armed with guns.

'**figment** *n* a made-up story or an idea which has no real existence.

figure ['figər] *n* outward form or shape; a number; a geometrical shape; a person. *A mysterious figure approached*; (in a book *etc*) a diagram or drawing; a set of movements (as in skating *etc*). – *v* to appear. *He figures in the story*; (*usu* with **out**) to work out, understand. – *adjs* '**figurative** (of words) used not in the ordinary meaning but to show likenesses (*eg* in 'He was a lion in battle' for 'He was as brave as or like a lion in battle.'); '**figured** marked with a design: *figured silk*. – *n* '**figurehead** a person who does little but who serves as a leader.

'**filament** *n* a slender threadlike object (*eg* the thin wire in an electric-light bulb).

filch *v* to steal.

file *n* a folder, loose-leaf book *etc* to hold papers; a line of soldiers *etc* walking one behind another; a steel tool with a roughened surface for smoothing or wearing away wood, metal *etc*. – *v* to put (papers *etc*) in a file; to rub with a file; to walk in a file.

'**filial** *adj* of or natural to a son or daughter.

'**filibuster** *n* a very long speech made to delay the passing of a law. – Also *v*.

'**filigree** *n* very fine gold or silver thread lace-work.

fill *v* to put (something) into (until there is no room for more). *He fills the bucket with water*; to become full. *Her eyes filled with tears*; to satisfy, fulfil (a requirement *etc*); to occupy: *fill a post*: *fill time*; to appoint a person to (a job *etc*). *Have you filled the vacancy?*; to put something in a hole (in a tooth *etc*) to stop it up. – *n* as much as is needed to fill. *He ate his fill*. – *ns* '**filler**; '**filling** anything used to fill a hole or gap. – *n* '**filling-station** a garage where petrol is sold. – **fill in** to fill (*esp* a hole); to complete (a form *etc*); to do another person's job while they are absent. *I'm filling in for George*; **fill up** to fill completely.

'**fillet** *n* a piece of meat or fish without bones. – *v* to remove the bones from.

'**fillip** *n* an encouragement.

'**filly** *n* a young female horse: – *pl* '**fillies**.

film *n* a thin skin or coating; a thin celluloid strip with a chemical coating on which photographs are taken; a story, play *etc* photographed on film and shown in a cinema, on television *etc*. – *v* to photograph on a film. – *n* '**filmstar** a famous actor or actress in films.

'**filter** *n* a strainer or other device for removing solid material from liquids; a green arrow on a traffic light which allows one lane of traffic to move while the main stream is held up. – *v* to purify by a filter; to come in drops or gradually; (of cars *etc*) to join gradually a stream of traffic; (of a lane of traffic) to move in the direction shown by the filter.

filth *n* dirt. – *adj* '**filthy** foul, very dirty.

fin *n* a part of a fish's body with which it balances itself and swims.

'**final** *adj* last; allowing of no argument. *The judge's decision is final*. – *n* the last contest in a competition. – *n* fi'**nality** the quality of being final and decisive. – *v* '**finalize** to get or put (*eg* plans) in a final or finished form.

finale [fi'näli] *n* the last part of anything (*eg* a concert).

fi'nance *n* money affairs; the study or management of these; (*pl*) the money one has to spend. – *v* to supply with sums of money. – *adj* **fi'nancial**. – *n* **fi'nancier** one who manages (public) money.

finch *n* a kind of small bird: – *pl* **'finches**.

find *v* to come upon or meet with either accidentally (*I found this ring in the street*) or after searching (*After looking everywhere I found my book under the bed*); to discover; to judge to be. *I find it difficult*: – *pt* **found**. – *n* something found *esp* something of interest or value. – **find out** to discover; detect.

fine *n* money to be paid as a punishment. – Also *v*. – *adj* made up of very small pieces, drops *etc*; not coarse: *fine linen*; thin, delicate; slight: *a fine distinction*; beautiful, handsome; of good quality; pure; bright, not rainy; well, healthy. – *n* **'finery** splendid clothes *etc*. – *n* **fine arts** painting, sculpture, music.

fi'nesse *n* cleverness and subtlety (in handling situations *etc*).

finger ['fiŋgər] *n* one of the five branching parts of the hand. – *v* to touch with the fingers. – *n* **'fingering** (in music) the positioning of the fingers in playing an instrument; the showing of this by numbers. – *n* **'fingerprint** the mark made by the tip of a finger, used by the police as a means of identification.

finish *v* to end or complete the making *etc* of; to stop: *finish work for the day*. – *n* the end (*eg* of a race); the last touch (of paint, polish *etc*) that makes a perfect job. – *adj* **'finished** ended; complete; perfect; (of a person) ruined, not likely to achieve further success *etc*.

finite *adj* having an end or limit.

fiord, fjord [fyörd] *n* a long narrow inlet between steep hills (*esp* in Norway).

fir *n* a kind of cone-bearing tree. – *n* **'fir-cone**.

fire *n* the heat and light given off by something burning; a mass of burning material, objects *etc*; a heating device: *electric fire*; eagerness, keenness. – *v* to set on fire; to make eager: *fired by his enthusiasm*; to make (a gun) explode, to shoot. – *ns* **fire alarm** a device (*eg* a system of bells) to give warning of a fire; **fire brigade** a company of firemen; **'fire-damp** a dangerous gas found in coal mines; **fire engine** a vehicle carrying firemen and their equipment; **fire escape** a means of escape (*esp* an outside metal staircase) from a building in case of fire; **'firefly** a

type of insect which glows in the dark; **'fire-guard** a framework of iron placed in front of a fireplace for safety; **'fireman** one whose job it is to put out fires; **'fireplace** a recess in a room below a chimney for a fire; **'firewood** wood for burning on a fire. – *npl* **'fireworks** squibs, rockets *etc* sent up at night for show; (*coll*) angry behaviour.

'firkin *n* a small barrel.

firm *adj* not easily moved or shaken; with mind made up. – *n* a business company. – *n* **'firmness**.

'firmament *n* the heavens, sky.

first *adj, adv* before all others in place, time or rank. – *adv* before doing anything else. – *ns* **'first-'aid** treatment of a wounded or sick person before the doctor's arrival; **'first-born** the eldest child. – *adjs* **'first-'class** of the highest standard, best kind *etc*; **'first-'hand** direct; **'first-'rate** first class.

firth *n* a narrow arm of the sea, *esp* at a river mouth.

'fiscal *adj* of the public revenue; of financial matters.

fish *n* a kind of animal that lives in water, and breathes through gills: – *pl* **fish** or **'fishes**. – *v* to (try to) catch fish with rod, nets *etc*; to search (for). *She fished for a handkerchief in her bag*; to try cunningly to obtain: *fish for compliments*. – *adj* **'fishy** like a fish; doubtful, arousing suspicion. – *ns* **'fisherman** one who fishes (*esp* for a living); **'fishmonger** one who sells fish.

fission ['fishən] *n* splitting.

fissure ['fishər] *n* a crack.

fist *n* a tightly-shut hand. – *npl* **'fisticuffs** a fight with the fists.

fit *adj* suited to a purpose; proper; in good training or health. – *n* a sudden attack or spasm of laughter, illness *etc*. – *v* to be of the right size or shape; to be suitable: – *pt* **'fitted**. – *adj* **'fitful** coming or doing in bursts or spasms. – *n* **'fitness**. – *adj* **'fitting** suitable. – *n* something fixed or fitted *esp* in a room, house *etc*.

five *n* the number 5. – *adj* 5 in number. – *adj* **fifth** the last of five (things *etc*). – *n* one of five equal parts.

fives *npl* a handball game played in a walled court.

fix *v* to make firm; to fasten; to mend, repair. – *adj* **fixed** settled; set in position. – *adv* **fixedly** ['fiksidli] steadily, intently. *He stared fixedly at me*. – *n* **'fixture** anything fixed (such as a shelf); a match or race that has been arranged.

fizz *v* to make a hissing sound. – *n* a hissing sound. – *adj* **'fizzy** of a drink in which tiny bubbles form on the surface.

'fizzle: fizzle out to fail, coming to nothing.

fjord *see* **fiord**.

'flabbergasted *adj* very surprised.

'flabby *adj* not firm, soft, limp; weak, feeble. – *n* **'flabbiness**.

flaccid ['flaksid] *adj* hanging in loose folds, not firm, limp.

flag *n* a banner, standard, or ensign; a flat paving-stone; a type of water-plant, *esp* an iris. – *v* to become tired or weak: – *pt* **flagged**.

flagellation [flajə'lāshən] *n* whipping.

'flagon *n* a large container for liquid.

'flagrant *adj* conspicuous; openly wicked. – *n* **'flagrancy**.

flail *v* to wave or swing in the air. – *n* a tool for threshing corn made of a wooden bar (the **swingle**) tied to a handle.

flair *n* talent, skill: *a flair for organizing*.

flak *n* anti-aircraft fire; strong criticism.

flake *n* a thin slice or chip of anything; a very small piece (as of snow *etc*). – *v* to form into flakes. – **flake off** to break off in flakes.

flam'boyant *adj* splendidly coloured; too showy, intended to attract notice.

flame *n* the bright leaping light of a fire. – *v* to burn brightly. – *adj* **'flaming** burning; red; violent: *a flaming temper*.

flamingo [flə'miŋgō] *n* a type of long-legged bird of pink or bright-red colour: – *pl* **fla'mingo(e)s**.

'flammable *adj* easily set on fire.

flan *n* a flat, open tart.

flange *n* a raised edge on the rim of a wheel.

flank *n* the side of anything (as of a person's or animal's body, of an army *etc*). – *v* to go by the side of; to be situated at the side of.

flannel *n* loosely woven woollen cloth; a small piece of material used *esp* for washing the face; (*pl*) trousers of this or similar material. – *n* **flanne'lette** cotton cloth made in imitation of flannel.

flap *n* anything broad and loose-hanging: *the flap of a tent*; the sound made when such a thing moves; a time of feverish activity; a panic. – *v* to hang down loosely; to (cause to) move with a flapping noise; to get into a panic: – *pt* **flapped**.

flare *v* to blaze up. – *n* a bright light, *esp* one used at night as a signal, to light up an enemy country *etc*.

flash *n* a quick burst of light; a moment, instant; a distinctive mark on a uniform: – *pl* **'flashes**. – *v* to shine out suddenly; to pass quickly. – *adj* **'flashy** dazzling for a moment; showy, gaudy cheaply smart. – *n* **'flashlight** a burst of light in which a photograph is taken an electric torch. – **in a flash** suddenly.

flask *n* a narrow-necked bottle.

flat *adj* level: *a flat surface*; (of drinks) not fizzy; leaving no doubt, downright: *a flat denial*; below the right musical pitch; (of a tyre) punctured; dull, uninteresting. – *adv* stretched out: *lying flat on her back*. – *n* an apartment which lies on one storey of a building; a sign (*b*) in music which lowers a note; a punctured tyre. – *n* **'flatness**. – *v* **'flatten** to make or become flat. – *ns* **'flatfish** a sea fish with a flat body (*eg* a sole); **flat race** a race over level ground without hurdles; **flat rate** a rate which is the same in all cases. – **flat out** as fast as possible, with as much effort as possible.

'flatter *v* to praise insincerely; to make out (a person or thing) to be better than he (or it) really is. – *n* **'flattery**.

'flatulence *n* wind in the stomach. – *adj* **'flatulent**.

flaunt *v* to display in an obvious way.

'flautist *n* a flute-player.

flavour ['flāvər] *n* taste: *the flavour o, lemons*; quality or atmosphere. *The celebrations had an Eastern flavour.* – *v* to give a taste to. – *n* **'flavouring** anything used to give a special taste.

flaw *n* a fault, an imperfection, a defect. – *adj* **'flawless** without fault or blemish.

flax *n* a type of plant whose fibres are woven into linen cloth. – *adj* **'flaxen** made of or looking like flax; (of hair) fair.

flay *v* to strip the skin off.

flea *n* a type of small, wingless, blood-sucking insect having great jumping power.

fleck *n* a spot, a speck. – *adj* **flecked** marked with spots or patches.

fled *see* **flee**.

fledgling ['flejliŋ] *n* a young bird with fully-grown feathers.

flee *v* to run away (from danger *etc*): – *p* **fled** [fled].

fleece *n* a sheep's coat of wool. – *v* to clip wool from; (*coll*) to rob by cheating. – *adj* **'fleecy** soft and fluffy like wool.

fleet *n* a number of ships; a number of vehicles (taxis *etc*). – *adj* swift; nimble, quick in movement. – *adj* **'fleeting** passing quickly. – *n* **'fleetness**

swiftness.

flesh *n* the soft substance (muscle *etc*) which covers the bones of animals; meat; the body; the soft eatable part of fruit. – *adj* '**fleshy** fat, plump. – **flesh and blood** relations, family; human nature.

flew *see* **fly**.

flex *v* to bend. – *n* a length of covered wire attached to electrical devices. – *adj* '**flexible** easily bent; (of persons) willing or able to adapt to new or different conditions. – *n* **flexi'bility** ease in bending; willingness *etc* to adapt. – *n* '**flexitime** a system in which a worker does an agreed number of hours' work at times partly chosen by himself.

flick *v* to strike lightly with a quick, sharp movement; to remove (dust *etc*) with a movement of this kind. –*n* a quick, sharp movement: *a flick of the wrist.*

flicker *v* to burn unsteadily. – Also *n*.

flight [flīt] *n* the act of flying; a journey by plane; the act of fleeing or escaping; a flock (of birds); a number (of steps). – *adj* '**flighty** changeable, impulsive.

flimsy ['flimzi] *adj* thin; easily torn or broken *etc*; weak: *a flimsy excuse.*

flinch *v* to move or shrink back in fear, pain *etc*.

fling *v* to throw: – *pt* **flung**. – *n* a throw; a casual attempt; a period of time devoted to pleasure.

flint *n* a kind of hard stone. – *adj* made of flint. – *n* '**flintlock** a gun fired by sparks from a flint.

flip *v* to toss lightly: – *pt* **flipped**. – *n* a light toss or stroke. – *n* '**flipper** a limb of a seal, walrus *etc*.

flippant *adj* joking, not serious. – *n* '**flippancy**.

flirt *v* to play at courtship without any serious intentions. – *n* one who flirts. – *n* **flir'tation**. – *adj* **flir'tatious** fond of flirting.

flit *v* to move quickly and lightly from place to place: – *pt* '**flitted**.

float *v* to keep on the surface of a liquid; to set going: *float a fund.* – *n* a cork *etc* on a fishing line; a raft; a van (for milk *etc*); a large lorry for transporting cattle *etc*; a platform on wheels, used in processions *etc*; a sum of money set aside for giving change *etc*.

flock *n* a number of animals or birds together; a large number of people; the congregation of a church; a shred or tuft of wool; wool or cotton waste. – *v* (*usu* with **together**) to gather in a crowd; to go in a crowd.

floe *n* a sheet of floating ice.

flog *v* to beat, lash: – *pt* **flogged**. – *n* '**flogging**.

flood [flud] *n* a great flow (*esp* of water); the rise or flow of the tide; a great quantity: *a flood of letters.* – *v* to (cause to) overflow; to cover or fill with water. – *n* '**floodlighting** strong lighting from many sources.

floor [flör] *n* the part of a room on which one walks; a storey of a building. – *v* to make a floor; (*coll*) to knock flat; (*coll*) to puzzle.

flop *v* to sway or swing about loosely; to fall or sit down suddenly and heavily; to move about in a heavy, clumsy way; to fail badly: – *pt* **flopped**. – Also *n*. – *adj* '**floppy** flopping, soft and flexible.

'**flora** *n* the plants of a district or country as a whole. – *adj* **floral** ['flörəl] (made) of flowers. – *n* **florist** ['florist] a seller or grower of flowers.

'**florid** *adj* (of persons) high-coloured, flushed; too ornate.

floss *n* fine silk thread.

flo'tilla *n* a fleet of small ships.

'**flotsam** *n* floating objects washed from a ship or wreck.

flounce *v* to walk (away) suddenly and impatiently (*eg* in anger). – *n* a plaited decorative strip on the hem of a dress.

'**flounder** *v* to struggle to move one's legs and arms (in water, mud *etc*); to have difficulty in speaking or thinking clearly or in acting efficiently. – *n* a small flatfish.

'**flour** *n* finely-ground wheat; anything crushed to powder. – *adj* '**floury**.

flourish ['flurish] *v* to be successful, *esp* financially; (of flowers *etc*) to grow well, thrive; to be healthy; to wave (something) as a show or threat. – *n* fancy strokes in writing; a sweeping movement (with the hand, sword *etc*); showy splendour; an ornamental passage in music: – *pl* '**flourishes**.

flout *v* to treat with contempt, defy openly.

flow [flō] *v* to run, as water; to move smoothly; (of the tide) to rise. – Also *n*.

flower ['flowər] *n* the part of a plant or tree from which fruit or seed grow; the best of anything. – *v* (of plants *etc*) to produce a flower; to be at one's best, flourish. – *adj* '**flowery** full of, decorated with flowers; of a piece of writing, using fine-sounding, fancy language.

flown *see* **fly**.

flu [flōō] short for **influenza**.

'**fluctuate** *v* to vary (in number, price *etc*); to be always changing. – *n* **fluctu'ation**.

flue [flōō] *n* a passage for air and smoke

in a stove or chimney.

fluent ['flŏŏənt] *adj* finding words easily in speaking or writing without any awkward pauses. – *n* '**fluency**.

fluff *n* any soft, downy stuff. – *adj* '**fluffy**.

fluid ['flŏŏid] *n* a substance whose particles can move about freely – a liquid or gas; a liquid. – *adj* flowing; not settled.

fluke [flŏŏk] *n* a type of small worm which harms sheep; the part of an anchor which holds fast in sand; a success due to chance.

flung *see* **fling**.

fluoride ['flŏŏorid] *n* a substance containing the element **fluorine** ['flŏŏorēn] which prevents tooth decay. – *vs* '**fluoridize**, '**fluoridate** to add fluoride to drinking water. – *n* **fluori-**'**dation**.

'**flurry** *n* a sudden rush (of wind *etc*): – *pl* '**flurries**. – *v* to excite: – *pt* '**flurried**.

flush *n* a reddening of the face; freshness, glow: – *pl* '**flushes**. – *v* to become red in the face; to clean by a rush of water. – *adj* (with **with**) having the surface level (with the surface around); (*coll*) well supplied with money.

'**fluster** *n* excitement caused by hurry. – Also *v.*

flute [flŏŏt] *n* a type of high-pitched musical wind instrument. – *adj* '**fluted** decorated with grooves.

'**flutter** *v* to move (*esp* wings) quickly. – *n* a quick beating (of pulse *etc*); nervous excitement.

flux *n* an ever-changing flow. *Events are in a state of flux.*

fly *n* a type of small winged insect; a fish-hook made to look like a fly; a flap of material with buttons or a zip *esp* at the front of trousers: – *pl* **flies**. – *v* to move through the air on wings or in an aeroplane; to run away: – *pt* **flew** [flŏŏ], *pp* **flown** [flōn]. – *ns* **flying squad** a branch of the police using fast cars; '**flyover** a road *etc* built on pillars to cross over another; '**flysheet** the outer covering of a tent; '**flywheel** a heavy wheel which enables a machine to run at a steady speed.

foal *n* a young horse. – *v* to give birth to a foal.

foam *n* a mass of small bubbles on liquids. – *v* to produce foam. – *n* **foam rubber** sponge-like form of rubber for stuffing chairs, mattresses *etc*.

fob *n* a small watch pocket; a fancy chain hanging from the watch pocket. – *v* to make (someone) accept (something worthless *etc*). *I was fobbed off with a silly excuse*: – *pt* **fobbed**.

fo'c'sle *see* **forecastle**.

'**fōcus** *n* meeting point for rays of light; point to which light, a look, attention is directed: – *pls* '**focuses, foci** ['fōsi] – *v* to get the right length of ray of light for a clear picture; to direct (one's attention *etc*) to one point. – *adj* '**foca** of or at a focus.

'**fodder** *n* dried food (hay, oats *etc*) fo farm animals.

foe *n* an enemy.

foetid *see* **fetid**.

fog *n* thick mist. – *v* to cover in fog; to bewilder, confuse. – *adj* '**foggy**. – *r* '**foghorn** a horn used as a warning to or by ships in fog.

foil *v* to defeat, disappoint. – *n* metal in the form of paper-thin sheets; a dul person or thing against which someone or something else seems brighter; blunt sword with a button at the end used in fencing practice.

foist *v* to pass off as genuine.

fōld *n* a part laid on top of another; an enclosure for sheep *etc*. – *v* to lay one part on top of another. – *n* '**folder** a cover to hold papers.

'**fōliage** *n* leaves.

folk [fōk] *n* people; a nation, race; (*pl*) one's family or relations. – *ns* '**folklore** the study of the customs, beliefs, fairy tales *etc* of a people; '**folksong** a song passed on from person to person over a period of time.

follow ['folō] *v* to go or come after; to happen as a result; to act according to; to understand; to work at (a trade). – *ns* '**follower**; '**following** supporters. – *prep* '**following** after, as a result of *Following the fire, the house collapsed.*

'**folly** *n* foolishness: – *pl* '**follies**.

fo'ment *v* to stir up, encourage growth of (a rebellion *etc*).

fond *adj* loving; tender. – *n* '**fondness**. – **fond of** having a liking for.

'**fondle** *v* to caress.

font *n* the basin holding water for baptism.

food *n* that which living beings eat. – *n* '**foodstuff** something used for food. – *n* **food processor** electrical appliance for chopping, blending *etc* food.

fool *n* a silly person; (*hist*) a court jester; a pudding made of fruit, sugar and cream. – *v* to deceive; to play the fool. – *adj* '**foolish**. – *ns* '**foolishness**, '**foolery** foolish behaviour. – *adjs* '**foolhardy** rash, taking foolish risks; '**foolproof** (of engines, plans *etc*) unable to go wrong. – **fool about** to behave in a playful or silly manner.

'**foolscap** *n* a large size of paper for

writing or printing.

foot *n* the part of the leg below the ankle; the lower part of anything; twelve inches, 30 centimetres: – *pl* **feet**. – *v* to pay (a bill *etc*). – *n* '**footing** balance; degree of friendship, seniority *etc*. – *ns* '**football** (a game played by kicking) a large ball; '**foothill** a smaller hill at the foot of a mountain; '**foothold** a place to put the foot in climbing; a firm position from which one can begin to do something; '**footlight** a light at the front of a stage, which shines on the actors; '**footnote** a note at the bottom of a page; '**footpad** (*hist*) a highway robber; '**footplate** a driver's platform on a railway engine; '**footprint** a mark of a foot; '**footstep** the sound of a person's foot when walking; '**footwear** shoes *etc*.

fop *n* a person who is vain about dress. – *adj* '**foppish**.

for *prep* sent to or to be given to: *a letter for you*; towards. *They headed for home*; during (a period). *They waited for three hours*; on behalf of. *Do it for me*; because of: *for good reason*; as the price of: *£1 for a saucepan*; (in order) to have. *He did it for the money*.

'**forage** *n* food for horses and cattle. – *v* to search for food, fuel *etc*.

'**foray** *n* a sudden raid for plunder.

forbade *see* **forbid**.

forbearance [för'bārəns] *n* control of temper. – *adj* **for'bearing** patient.

for'bid *v* to order not to: – *pt* **forbade** [fər'bad]. – *adjs* **for'bidden**; **for'bidding** rather frightening.

force *n* strength; violence; the police; a group of workers, soldiers *etc*; (*pl*) soldiers, sailors, airmen. – *v* to make, compel. *They forced him to go*; to get by violence: *force an entry*; to break open; to hurry on; to make vegetables *etc* grow more quickly. – *adjs* **forced** done unwillingly, with effort: *a forced laugh*; '**forceful** acting with power; '**forcible** done by force.

'**forceps** *n* a tool with two arms for gripping.

ford *n* a shallow crossing place in a river. – *v* to cross (water) on foot.

fore- *prefix* before; beforehand; in front.

forearm[1] ['förärm] *n* the lower part of the arm.

fore'arm[2] *v* to prepare beforehand.

fore'boding *n* a feeling of coming evil.

'**forecast** *v* to tell (about) beforehand, to predict. – Also *n*.

forecastle, fo'c'sle ['fōksl] *n* a raised deck at the front of a ship; the part of ship under the deck where the crew live.

'**forefather** ['förfädhər] *n* an ancestor.

'**forefinger** ['förfiŋgər] *n* the finger next to the thumb.

forefront ['förfrunt] *n* the very front.

foregone ['förgon]: **a foregone conclusion** a result that can be guessed rightly in advance.

'**foreground** *n* the part of a view (or picture of one) nearest the front or nearest the person looking at it.

forehead ['forid] *n* the part of the face above the eyebrows.

foreign ['forən] *adj* belonging to another country; not belonging naturally in a place *etc*: *a foreign body in an eye*; not familiar. – *n* '**foreigner** a person from another country; somebody unfamiliar.

'**foreleg** *n* a front leg (of an animal).

'**forelock** *n* the lock of hair next to the forehead.

'**foreman** *n* an overseer or leader of a group (such as workmen, jury): – *pl* '**foremen**.

'**foremast** *n* ship's mast nearest the bow.

'**foremost** *adj* the most famous or important.

fo'rensic *adj* having to do with courts of law: *forensic medicine*.

'**forerunner** *n* a person or thing which is a sign of what is to follow.

fore'see *v* to see or know beforehand: – *pt* **fore'saw**, *pp* **fore'seen**. – *n* '**foresight** ability to see what will happen later; a fitting on the front of the barrel of a rifle to make correct aiming possible.

'**foreshore** *n* the part of the shore between high and low tidemarks.

foresight *see* **foresee**.

forest ['forist] *n* a large piece of land covered with trees; a stretch of country kept for game (such as deer). – *ns* '**forester** a worker in a forest; '**forestry** (the science of) forest-growing.

forestall [för'stöl] *v* to upset someone's plan by acting earlier than he expects. *He forestalled him*.

'**foretaste** *n* a sample of what is to come.

fore'tell *v* to tell before, to prophesy: – *pt* **fore'told**.

forethought ['förthöt] *n* thought or care for the future.

foretold *see* **foretell**.

forewarn [för'wörn] *v* to warn beforehand. – *n* **fore'warning**.

forewoman ['förwoomən] *n* a woman overseer; a head woman in a shop or factory.

foreword ['förwörd] *n* a piece of writing at the beginning of a book.

forfeit ['förfit] *v* to lose (a right) as a result of doing something. – *n* that which must be given up for some (criminal) action; a fine. – *n* 'forfeiture the loss of something as a punishment.

forge *n* a blacksmith's workshop; a furnace in which metal is heated. – *v* to hammer (metal) into shape; to imitate for criminal purposes; to move steadily on. *He forged ahead with his plans.* – *n* 'forgery something imitated for criminal purposes; the act of criminal forging: – *pl* 'forgeries.

for'get *v* to lose or put away from the memory: – *pt* **forgot**, *pp* for'gotten. – *adj* for'getful likely to forget. – *n* for'getfulness.

forgive [fər'giv] *v* to be no longer angry with (someone); to overlook (a fault, debt *etc*). – *n* for'giveness pardon; readiness to pardon. – *adj* for'giving.

for'go *v* to give up, do without.

forgot, forgotten *see* **forget**.

fork *n* a pronged tool for piercing and lifting things; anything divided like a fork (*eg* a road, tree branch). – *v* to divide into two branches *etc*.

for'lorn *adj* pitiful, unhappy. – *n* **forlorn hope** a wish which seems to have no chance of being granted.

form *n* shape or appearance; kind, type; a paper with printed questions and space for the answers; a long seat; a school class; the nest of a hare. – *v* to give shape to; to make. – *adj* 'formal (of a person's manner) cold, business-like; done according to established rule, custom or convention. – *ns* for'mality something which must be done but has little meaning. *The chairman's speech was only a formality*; cold correctness of manner: – *pl* for-'malities; for'mation the act of forming; arrangement (as ot aeroplanes when flying). – *n* **formal dress** the kind of clothes required to be worn on certain social (ceremonial) occasions *eg* balls, banquets *etc*.

'format *n* (of books) the size, shape, kind of print *etc*; the design or arrangement of an event *etc* (such as a television programme).

'former *adj* of an earlier time; of the first-mentioned of two (opposite of **latter**). – Also *n*. – *adv* 'formerly in earlier times.

'formidable *adj* causing fear; difficult to overcome.

'formula *n* a set of rules to be followed; an arrangement of signs or letters used in chemistry, arithmetic *etc* to express an idea briefly (such as H_2O = water): – *pls* **formulae** ['förmülē], 'formulas. – *v* 'formulate to set down clearly; to make into a formula.

for'sake *v* to desert: – *pt* for'sook. – *adj* for'saken left alone; miserable.

forswear [för'swār] *v* to give up (something).

fort *n* a place of defence against an enemy.

forte ['förtā] *n* that at which one is very good.

forth *adv* forward; onward. – *adjs* forth-'coming happening or appearing soon; (of person) willing to tell what he knows; friendly and open; 'forthright outspoken, straightforward. – *adv* forth'with immediately.

'fortify *v* to strengthen (against attack): – *pt* 'fortified. – *npl* fortifi'cations walls *etc* built to strengthen a position.

'fortitude *n* courage in meeting danger or bearing pain.

fortnight ['förtnit] *n* two weeks. – *adj, adv* 'fortnightly once a fortnight.

'fortress *n* a fortified place: – *pl* 'fortresses.

for'tuitous *adj* happening by chance.

'fortune *n* luck (good or bad); large sum of money. – *adj* 'fortunate lucky.

'forty *n* the number 40. – *adj* 40 in number. – *adj* 'fortieth the last of forty (things *etc*). – *n* one of forty equal parts.

'forum *n* (*hist*) market-place in ancient Rome; any public place where speeches are made; a meeting to talk about a particular subject.

'forward *adj* advancing: *a forward movement*; near or at the front; (of fruit *etc*) ripe earlier than usual; too ready in word or action. – *v* to help (toward success): *forward one's plans*; to send on (*eg* letters). – *advs* 'forward, 'forwards onward; towards the front.

foss, fosse *n* a ditch round an ancient fort or castle.

'fossil *n* the hardened remains of the shape of a plant or animal found in rock. – *v* 'fossilize to change into a fossil.

'foster *v* to bring up or nurse (*esp* a child not one's own); to help on, encourage (something). – *ns* 'foster-child (·brother, -sister) a boy or girl fostered by a family; 'foster-mother (-father) mother (father) who brings up a fostered child.

fought *see* **fight**.

foul *adj* very dirty; smelling or tasting bad; (of weather, temper) stormy. – *v* to become entangled with; to dirty; to play unfairly. – *n* a breaking of the rules of a game. – *n* **foul play** a criminal act.

found *v* to establish, set up; to shape by pouring melted metal into a mould; *see also* **find**. – *ns* **foun'dation** that on which anything rests; a sum of money left or set aside for a special purpose *eg* to support an organization *etc*; an organization *etc* supported in this way; **'founder** one who founds; **'foundry** workshop where metal founding is done: – *pl* **'foundries**.

'founder *v* (of a ship) to sink; (of a horse) to stumble or go lame. – *n see* **found**.

'foundling *n* a child abandoned by its parents.

'fountain *n* a jet of water rising up; the pipe or structure from which it comes; the beginning of anything.

four [för] *n* the number 4. – *adj* 4 in number. – *adj* **fourth** the last of four (things *etc*). – *n* one of four equal parts.

'four'teen *n* the number 14. – *adj* 14 in number. – *adj* **'four'teenth** the last of fourteen (things *etc*). – *n* one of four-teen equal parts.

fowl [fowl] *n* a bird, *esp* of the farmyard or poultry kind.

fox *n* a type of dog-like reddish-brown animal of great cunning: – *pl* **'foxes**. – *v* to trick by cleverness or cunning; to puzzle, baffle. – *adj* **'foxy** cunning. – *ns* **'foxglove** a tall wild flower; **'foxhound** a breed of dog trained to chase foxes; **fox terrier** a breed of dog trained to drive foxes from their earths; **'foxtrot** a dance made up of walking steps and turns.

foyer ['foiā] *n* an entrance hall to a theatre, hotel *etc*.

fracas ['frakā] *n* uproar; a noisy quarrel.

'fraction *n* a part, not a whole number (such as $\frac{1}{2}$, $\frac{2}{5}$, $\frac{7}{8}$ *etc*); a small part.

'fractious *adj* cross, quarrelsome.

'fracture *n* a break in something hard, *esp* in a bone of the body.

'fragile *adj* easily broken.

'fragment *n* a part broken off; something not complete. – *v* **frag'ment** to break into pieces. – *adj* **'fragmentary** broken.

'fragrant *adj* sweet-smelling. – *n* **'frag-rance** sweet scent.

'frail *adj* weak; easily tempted to do wrong. – *n* **'frailty** weakness: – *pl* **'frailties**.

frame *v* to put a frame round; to put together, to construct; (*slang*) to make (someone) appear to be guilty of a crime. – *n* a case or border round anything; build of human body; state (of mind). – *n* **'framework** the out-

line, shape, or skeleton of anything.

franc *n* the standard unit of French, Belgian and Swiss money.

'franchise *n* the right to vote (*esp* in a general election).

frank *adj* open, speaking one's mind. – *v* to mark a letter by machine to show that postage has been paid.

'frankfurter *n* kind of smoked sausage.

'frankincense *n* a sweet-smelling resin used as incense.

'frantic *adj* wildly excited or anxious.

fra'ternal *adj* brotherly; of a brother. – *n* **fra'ternity** a company of persons who regard each other as equals: – *pl* **fra'ternities**. – *v* **'fraternize** to make friends with.

'fratricide *n* the murder or murderer of a brother.

fraud *n* deceit, dishonest dealing; one who pretends to be other than he is; a fake. – *adj* **'fraudulent**.

fraught [fröt] *adj* anxious, tense; (with **with**) filled.

fray *n* a fight, a brawl. – *v* to wear away.

freak *n* an unusual event; an odd or unconventional person or thing.

'freckle *n* a brown spot on the skin.

free *adj* not bound or shut in; generous; frank (in manner); costing nothing. – *v* to make or set free; (with **from** or **of**) to get rid of. – *n* **'freedom** liberty. – *adj* **'freehand** (of drawing) done without the help of rulers, tracing *etc*. – *ns* **'freelance** a person working on his own (such as a writer who is not employed by any one newspaper); **'Freemason** a member of a certain men's society, sworn to secrecy. – *adj* **'free-'range** (of poultry) allowed to move about freely and feed out of doors; (of eggs) laid by poultry of this kind. – *n* **free speech** the right to express opinions of any kind. – *adj* **'freestyle** (of swimming race *etc*) in which any style may be used.

freeze *v* to turn into ice; to make (food) very cold in order to preserve; to go stiff (as with cold, fear); to fix (prices, wages *etc*) at a certain level: – *pt* **froze**, *pp* **frozen**. – *n* **'freezer** a type of cabinet in which food is made, or kept, frozen.

freight [frāt] *n* load, cargo; charge for carrying a load. – *v* to load with goods. – *n* **'freighter** a ship or aircraft that carries cargo. – *n* **freight train** a goods train.

French: *ns* **French polish** a kind of varnish for furniture; **French win-dow** a long window also used as a door. – **take French leave** to go or remain absent without permission.

fre'netic *adj* frantic.

'frenzy *n* a fit of madness; wild excitement. – *adj* **'frenzied** mad.

'frēquent *adj* happening often. – *v* fre-'quent to visit often. – *n* **'frequency** the rate at which something happens; the number per second of vibrations, waves *etc* : – *pl* **'frequencies**.

'fresco *n* a picture painted on a wall while the plaster is still damp: – *pl* **'fresco(e)s**.

fresh *adj* new, unused; (of food) newly made, gathered *etc*, not preserved; (of weather) cool, refreshing; (of persons) not tired; cheeky. – *adv* newly: *fresh-laid eggs*. – *v* **'freshen** to make fresh; to grow strong. – *ns* **'freshman, 'fresher** a first-year university student. – *adj* **'freshwater** of inland rivers, lakes *etc*, not of the sea.

fret *v* to worry or show discontent: – *pt* **'fretted**. – *n* one of the ridges on the fingerboard of a guitar. – *adj* **'fretful**.

'fretwork *n* decorated cut-out work in wood. – *n* **'fretsaw** a narrow-bladed, fine-toothed saw for fretwork.

'friar *n* a member of one of the brotherhoods of the Church, *esp* one who has vowed to live in poverty. – *n* **'friary** the friars' house: – *pl* **'friaries**.

'friction *n* rubbing of two things together; the wear caused by rubbing; bad feeling, quarrelling.

'Friday *n* sixth day of the week.

fridge *n* (*coll*) refrigerator.

fried *see* **fry**.

friend [frend] *n* one who likes and knows well another person. *He is my friend. We are good friends*; sympathizer, helper. – *adj* **'friendly** kind; (with **with**) on good terms. – *ns* **'friendliness; 'friendship**.

frieze [frēz] *n* a part of a wall below the ceiling, often ornamented with designs; a picture on a long strip of paper *etc*, often displayed on a wall.

'frigate *n* a small warship.

fright [frīt] *n* sudden fear. *It gave me a fright. He took fright and ran away*. – *v* **'frighten** to make afraid. – *adj* **'frightful** causing terror; (*coll*) very bad.

'frigid *adj* frozen, cold; cold in manner. – *n* **fri'gidity** coldness.

frill *n* an ornamental edging (of linen, lace *etc*); something unnecessary added on (to thing, action *etc*).

fringe *n* a border of loose threads; hair cut to hang over the forehead; a border (*esp* of soft material, paper etc). – *v* to edge round.

Frisbee® ['frizbi] *n* a plastic plate-like

object skimmed through the air as a game.

frisk *v* to skip about playfully; (*coll*) to search (person) for weapons *etc*. – *adj* **'frisky**.

'fritter *n* a piece of fried batter containing fruit *etc*. – *v* (with **away**) to waste time *etc*.

'frivolous *adj* playful, not serious. – *n* **fri'volity**: – *pl* **fri'volities**.

'frizzy *adj* (of hair) massed in small curls.

fro: to and fro forwards and backwards.

frock *n* a woman's or girl's dress; a monk's wide-sleeved garment. – *n* **'frock-coat** a man's long coat.

frog *n* a small greenish jumping animal living on land and in water. – *n* **'frogman** an underwater swimmer wearing flippers and breathing apparatus.

'frolic *n* merrymaking or an outburst of gaiety. – *v* to play gaily: – *pt* **'frolicked**. – *adj* **'frolicsome**.

from *prep* used before the place, thing, person *etc* that is the starting point of an action, period of time *etc*: *from England to France: from Friday to Monday: from the first of March* (*onwards*): *made from fruit and sugar*; used to show separation: *to keep away from there*: *take it from him*.

frond *n* a leaf-like growth *esp* a branch of a fern or palm.

front [frunt] *n* the part of anything nearest the person who sees it; the part which faces the direction in which the thing moves; (in war) the fighting line. – Also *adj*. – *n* **'frontage** front part of a building. – **in front of** at the head of, before.

frontier ['fruntēr] *n* a boundary between countries. – Also *adj*.

frontispiece ['fruntispēs] *n* a picture at the very beginning of a book.

frost *n* frozen dew; the coldness of weather needed to form ice. – *v* to cover with frost or anything sparkling like it. – *adjs* **'frosted; 'frosty**.

froth *n* foam on liquids. – *v* to throw up foam. – *adj* **'frothy**.

frown [frown] *v* to wrinkle the brows (in deep thought, disapproval *etc*). – Also *n*. – **frown on** to look upon with disapproval.

frowzy ['frowzi] *adj* rough and tangled.

froze, frozen *see* **freeze**.

frugal ['frōōgəl] *adj* careful in spending, thrifty; costing little, small: *a frugal meal*. – *n* **fru'gality**.

fruit [frōōt] *n* the part of a plant containing the seed; result. *Their hard work* *bore fruit.* – *n* **'fruiterer** one who sells fruit. – *adj* **'fruitful** producing (much) fruit; producing good results. – *n* **fruition** [froo'ishən] ripeness; a good result. – *adj* **'fruitless** useless, done in vain. – *n* **fruit machine** a gambling machine into which coins are put.

frump *n* a plain badly or unfashionably dressed woman. – *adj* **'frumpish**.

frus'trate *v* to make (someone feel) powerless; to bring to nothing. *They frustrated his wishes.* – *n* **frus'tration**.

frỹ *v* to cook in hot fat: – *pt* **fried**. – *n* anything fried; young fishes. – **small fry** people or things of little importance.

fuchsia ['fūshə] *n* a type of shrub with long hanging flowers.

fuddle *v* to make stupid (with drink).

fudge *n* a soft, sugary sweet.

fuel ['fūəl] *n* any substance (*eg* coal, oil, petrol, gas) by which a fire, engine *etc* is kept going.

'fūgitive *adj* running away (from police *etc*). – *n* one who is running away (from someone or something): *a fugitive from justice.*

fugue [fūg] *n* a piece of music with several interwoven tunes.

fulcrum ['foolkrəm] *n* the point on which a lever turns, or a balanced object rests.

fulfil [fool'fil] *v* to carry out (a task, promise *etc*): – *pt* **ful'filled**. – *n* **ful'filment**.

full [fool] *adj* holding as much as can be held; (with **of**) having plenty; plump: *full face.* – *adv* (used with *adjs*) fully: *full-grown.* – *n* **'fullness**. – *adv* **'fully**. – *ns* **full moon** the moon when it appears at its largest; **full stop** point placed at the end of a sentence *etc*.

fulmar ['foolmər] *n* a type of white seabird.

'fulminate *v* to flash like lightning; (with **against**) to speak fiercely. – *n* **fulmi-'nation**.

fulsome ['foolsəm] *adj* overdone: *fulsome praise.*

'fumble *v* to use the hands awkwardly; to drop (something thrown, as a ball).

fūme *n* (*usu pl*) smoke or vapour. – *v* to give off smoke or vapour; to be (quietly) in a rage.

'fūmigate *v* to kill germs by means of strong fumes. – *n* **fumi'gation**.

fun *n* enjoyment, a good time: *to have fun.* – *adj* **'funny** amusing; odd. – *adv* **'funnily**. – *ns* **'funfair** amusement park; **funny bone** part of the elbow. – **make fun of** to tease, make others laugh at.

'function *n* a special job, use or duty (of a machine, person, part of the body *etc*); (large) arranged gathering of people. – *v* (of a machine *etc*) to work, operate; to carry out usual duties. – *n* **'functionary** one holding an office, an official: – *pl* **'functionaries**.

fund *n* a sum of money for a special purpose; a store or supply.

funda'mental *adj* of great or far-reaching importance; going to the very bottom of the matter. – *n* a necessary part; (*pl*) the groundwork or first stages.

'fūneral *n* the ceremony of burial or cremation. – *adj* **funereal** [fū'nēriəl] mournful.

fungus ['fuŋgəs] *n* a soft, spongy plant growth (*eg* toadstool, mushroom); disease-growth on animals and plants: – *pl* **'fungi**.

fū'nicular railway *n* a kind of railway in which carriages are pulled uphill by a cable.

'funnel *n* a wide-mouthed filler by which liquids are poured into bottles; a tube or passage for escape of smoke, air *etc*.

fur *n* the short fine hair of certain animals; their skins covered with fur (used for clothing); a coating on the tongue, on the inside of kettles, boilers *etc*. – *v* to line or cover with fur: – *pt* **furred**. – *adj* **'furry**. – *n* **'furrier** one who buys, sells, or works with furs.

'furbish *v* to rub up until bright.

furious *see* **fury**.

'furlong *n* one-eighth of a mile (220 yards, 201·17 metres).

'furnace *n* a very hot oven or closed-in fireplace for melting iron ore, making steam for heating *etc*.

'furnish *v* to fit up (a room or house) completely; to supply. *He was furnished with enough food for a week.* – *ns* **'furnishings** (*pl*) fittings of any kind; **'furniture** movable articles in a house *etc* (as tables, chairs).

furore [fū'ror] *n* uproar; excitement.

furrow ['furō] *n* the groove made by a plough; any groove; a deep wrinkle. – *v* to cut deep grooves in; to wrinkle.

further ['fərdhər] *adv, adj* to a greater distance or degree; in addition. – *v* to help on or forward. – *adv* **'further'more** in addition to what has been said. – *adj* **'furthest** to the greatest distance or degree.

'furtive *adj* stealthy, sly; done slyly.

'fūry *n* violent anger. – *adj* **'furious**.

furze another name for **gorse**.

fuse [fūz] *v* to melt; to join together; to put a fuse in (a plug *etc*); (of a circuit *etc*) to stop working because of the melting of a fuse. – *n* easily-melted wire put in an electric circuit for safety; any device for causing an explosion to take place automatically. – *n* **'fusion** a melting; close union of things, as if melting into one another.

fuselage ['fūzəläzh] *n* the body of an aeroplane.

fuss *n* unnecessary activity, excitement or attention, often about something unimportant; strong complaint. – *v* to

be unnecessarily concerned about details; to worry overmuch. – *adj* **'fussy**.
'fusty *adj* mouldy; stale-smelling.
'fūtile *adj* useless; having no effect. – *n* **futility** [fū'tiləti] uselessness.
future ['fūchər] *adj* happening *etc* later in time. – *n* (with **the**) the time to come; (in grammar) the future tense.
fuzz *n* fine, light hair, feathers *etc*; (*slang*) the police. – *adj* **'fuzzy** covered with fuzz, fluffy; curly.

G

'gabble *v* to talk fast, chatter. – Also *n*.
gaberdine [gabər'dēn] *n* a kind of cloth; a kind of coat.
'gāble *n* the triangular area of wall at the end of a building with a ridged roof.
'gadabout *n* a person who loves travelling about.
'gadfly *n* a fly which bites cattle.
'gadget *n* a (small) simple machine or tool.
Gaelic ['gālik] *n* the language of the Scottish Highlanders and the Irish.
gaff *n* a large hook used for landing fish, such as salmon; a spar made from a mast, for raising the top of a sail. – **blow the gaff** (*coll*) to let out a secret.
gag *v* to silence by stopping the mouth: – *pt* **gagged**. – *n* something put in a person's mouth to silence him; (*coll*) a joke or funny story.
'gaggle *n* a flock (of geese).
gaiety, gaily *see* **gay**.
gain *v* to win; to reach; to get closer, *esp* in a race; (of clocks, watches) to go ahead (of correct time); to take on (*eg* weight). – *n* something gained; profit.
gait *n* way or manner of walking.
'gaiter *n* a cloth ankle-covering, fitting over the shoe, sometimes reaching to the knee.
gala *n* a time of rejoicing and merrymaking; a sports meeting: *swimming gala*.
'galaxy *n* a system of stars; a splendid gathering (*eg* of women, famous people): – *pl* **'galaxies**. – *n* **'Galaxy** the Milky Way.
gale *n* a strong wind.
gall [göl] *n* bile (a bitter fluid coming from the liver and stored in the **'gallbladder**); bitterness of feeling; a growth (caused by insects) on oaks and other trees and plants. – *v* to annoy. – *adj* **'galling**.

'gallant *adj* brave; noble; paying great attention to ladies. – *n* a man who is a favourite with ladies because of his fine manners. – *n* **'gallantry** bravery; politeness to ladies.
galleon ['galiən] *n* (*hist*) a large Spanish sailing ship.
'gallery *n* a long passage; the top floor of seats in a theatre; a room for showing paintings *etc* (also **art gallery**): – *pl* **'galleries**.
'galley *n* (*hist*) a long, low-built ship driven by oars; a place where cooking is done on board ship: – *pl* **'galleys**. – **'galley-slave** (*hist*) a prisoner condemned to work at the oars of a galley.
'gallon *n* a measure for liquids (8 pints, 3·636 litres).
'gallop *v* to move by leaps; to (cause to) move very fast. – *n* a fast pace.
gallows ['galōz] *n* wooden framework on which criminals were hanged.
ga'lore *adv* in great plenty: *whisky galore*.
ga'losh, go'losh *n* a rubber shoe worn over ordinary shoes in wet weather: – *pl* **ga'loshes**.
'galvanism *n* electricity got by action of chemicals (*usu* acids) on metal. – *adj* **gal'vanic**. – *v* **'galvanize** to stir into activity; to stimulate by electricity; to coat (iron *etc*) with zinc. – *n* **galva'nometer** an instrument for measuring electric currents.
'gambit *n* a first move (as in chess) in which something is lost in order to make one's position stronger; an opening move in a transaction or an opening remark in a conversation.
'gamble *v* to play games for money; to risk money on the result of a game, race *etc*; to take a wild chance. – Also *n*.
'gambol *v* to leap playfully. – Also *n*.
game *n* a contest played according to

rules; (*pl*) athletic competition: *Olympic Games*; wild animals and birds hunted for sport. – *adj* plucky; (of limbs *etc*) lame. – *n, adj* '**gaming** gambling. – *n* '**gamekeeper** one who looks after game birds, animals, fish *etc*. – **big game** large hunted animals (*eg* lions).

gammon *n* leg of a pig, salted and smoked.

gamut *n* the whole range of notes which a voice or instrument can produce; the whole extent of anything.

'**gander** *n* a male goose.

gang *n* any group of people who meet regularly; a team of criminals; a number of labourers. – *ns* '**ganger** foreman of a company of workmen (*eg* labourers); '**gangster** one of a gang of criminals.

gangrene ['gaŋgrēn] *n* the rotting of some part of the body. – *adj* **gangrenous** ['gaŋgrənəs].

gangster *see* gang.

gangway *n* a passage between rows of seats; a movable bridge leading from a quay to a ship.

'**gannet** *n* a type of large white sea bird.

'**gantry** *n* a platform or structure for supporting (a travelling crane *etc*).

gaol, gaoler *see* jail, jailer.

gap *n* an opening or space between things.

gape *v* to open the mouth wide (as in surprise); to be wide open.

garage ['garäj] *n* a building for storing a car (or cars); a shop where car repairs are done, and petrol, oil *etc* sold.

garb (*old*) *n* dress. – *v* to clothe.

'**garbage** *n* rubbish.

'**garble** *v* to mix up, muddle: *a garbled account of what happened*.

'**garden** *n* a piece of ground on which flowers or vegetables are grown. – *v* to work in a garden; to take care of a garden. – *n* '**gardener**. – *n* **garden party** a large tea party, held out of doors.

gar'gantūan *adj* very large, huge.

'**gargle** *v* to wash the throat with (but without swallowing) a soothing or germ-killing liquid.

'**gargoyle** *n* a jutting-out roof-spout, carved in the shape of a human or animal head.

'**gārish** *adj* over-bright.

'**garland** *n* flowers or leaves tied or woven into a circle.

'**garlic** *n* an onion-like plant with a strong smell and taste, used in cooking.

'**garment** *n* any article of clothing.

'**garnet** *n* a semi-precious stone *usu* red in colour.

'**garnish** *v* to decorate (a dish of food). – Also *n*: – *pl* '**garnishes**. – *n* '**garnishing**.

'**garret** *n* a room next to the roof of a house.

'**garrison** *n* a body of troops for guarding a fortress.

gar'rotte *v* to strangle (by tightening a noose of rope *etc* round someone's neck, *orig* by tightening an iron collar).

'**garrulous** *adj* fond of talking. – *ns* **garrulity** [gə'rōōləti], '**garrulousness**.

'**garter** *n* a broad elastic band to keep a stocking up.

gas *n* a substance like air (though some gases may be smelled); natural or manufactured form of this which will burn and is used as a fuel; (*US*) petrol: – *pl* '**gases**. – *v* to poison with gas: – *pt* **gassed**. – *adj* **gaseous** ['gasiəs]. – *ns* **gas mask** a covering for the face to prevent breathing in of poisonous gas; **gasoline, gasolene** ['gasəlēn] (*US*) petrol; **ga'someter** a tank for storing gas; '**gasworks** place where gas is made.

gash *n* a deep, open wound: – *pl* '**gashes**. – Also *v*.

gasp *n* sound made by a sudden intake of the breath. – *v* to breathe with difficulty; to say breathlessly; (*coll*) to want badly: *gasping for a drink*.

'**gastric** *adj* of the stomach.

gate *n* (that which closes) the opening in a wall, fence *etc*; the number of people at a (football) match; the total sum they pay to get in. – *n* '**gatecrasher** one who comes to a party uninvited. – *v* '**gatecrash**. – *n* '**gateway** an opening containing a gate; an entrance.

gâteau ['gatō] *n* a fancy cake.

gather ['gadhər] *v* to bring together, or to meet, in one place; to pick (flowers *etc*); to increase in. *The car gathered speed*; to learn, come to the conclusion (that). *I gather that you have finished*. – *n* '**gathering** a crowd.

gauche [gōsh] *adj* awkward and clumsy in people's company.

gaucho ['gowchō] *n* a cowboy of the S. American plains, noted for horse-riding.

'**gaudy** *adj* showy; vulgarly bright in colour. – *n* '**gaudiness**.

gauge [gāj] *v* to measure; to make a guess. – *n* a measuring device. – *ns* '**broad-**, '**narrow-gauge** railways having the distance between rails greater or less than the *standard gauge* (4 ft 8½ in, 1·435 metre).

gaunt *adj* thin, haggard.

'gauntlet *n* a long glove (often of leather) with a guard for the wrist used by motor cyclists *etc*; (*hist*) the iron glove of armour.

gauze *n* thin cloth that can be seen through.

ga'votte *n* (music for) a type of lively dance.

'gawky *adj* awkward.

gay *adj* lively; merry, full of fun; brightly coloured. – *n* **gaiety** ['gāəti]. – *adv* **'gaily**.

gaze *v* to look steadily. – *n* a fixed look.

ga'zelle *n* a type of small deer.

ga'zette *n* a newspaper, *esp* one having lists of government notices. – *n* **gazetteer** [gazə'tēr] a geographical dictionary.

gear [gēr] *n* anything needed for a particular job, sport (*eg* harness, tools, clothes); (in cars *etc*) a connection by means of a set of toothed wheels between the engine or source of power and the wheels. – *v* (with **to**) to adapt to, design for what is needed.

geese *see* **goose**.

geisha ['gāshə] *n* a Japanese girl trained to entertain.

gelatine ['jelətēn] *n* a jelly-like substance made from hooves, animal bones *etc*, and used in food. – *adj* **gelatinous** [jə'latənəs] jelly-like.

gelding ['geldiŋ] *n* a castrated horse.

gem *n* any precious stone, *esp* when cut to shape; anything greatly valued.

'gender *n* (in grammar, *esp* in languages other than English) any of three types of noun – masculine, feminine or neuter.

gene *n* the basic unit of heredity responsible for passing on specific characteristics from parents to offspring. – *adj* **genetic** [jə'netik].

genealogy [jēni'alɔji] *n* history of families from generation to generation; the ancestors of a person or family shown as a plan: – *pl* **gene'alogies**. – *adj* **genea'logical**. – *n* **gene'alogist** one who studies or makes genealogies.

general ['jenərəl] *adj* not detailed, broad: *a general idea of the person's interests*; involving everyone: *a general election*; to do with several different things: *general knowledge*; of most people: *the general opinion*. – *n* a high-ranking army officer. – *n* **generali'zation** a (too) general view, statement *etc*. – *v* **'generalize** to make a broad general statement (meant to cover all individual cases). – *adv* **'generally, in general** usually; in most cases; by most people. – *n* **general practitioner** a doctor who treats most ordinary illnesses.

generate ['jenərāt] *v* to produce, bring into being: *generate electricity*: *generate hatred*. – *ns* **gene'ration** act of creating or making; a step in family descent; people born at about the same time; **'generator** a machine for making electricity *etc*.

generic *see* **genus**.

generous ['jenərəs] *adj* giving plentifully; kind. – *n* **gene'rosity**.

genesis ['jenəsis] *n* beginning.

genetic *see* **gene**.

'genial *adj* good-natured.

genie ['jēni] *n* a guardian spirit: – *pl* **genii** ['jēnii].

'genius *n* unusual cleverness; a person who is unusually clever: – *pl* **'geniuses**.

gen'teel *adj* (too) good-mannered.

'gentile *n* (in the Bible) anyone not a Jew.

gen'tility *n* noble birth, aristocracy; good manners, refinement often to too great an extent.

'gentle *adj* (of persons) soft in manner, not brutal; (of things) mild, not extreme: *gentle breeze*. – *n* **'gentleness**.

'gentleman *n* a man (opposite of **lady**), *esp* one of noble birth; a well-mannered man. – *adj* **'gentlemanly** behaving in a polite manner.

'gentry *n* a wealthy, land-owning class of people.

genuine ['jenūin] *adj* real, not fake; (of persons) honest and straightforward. – *n* **'genuineness**.

'genus *n* a group (*usu* of living things) made up of a number of kinds: – *pl* **genera** ['jenərə]. — *adj* **generic** general, applicable to any member of a group or class.

ge'ography *n* the study of the surface of the earth and its inhabitants. – *n* **ge'ographer** one who studies geography. – *adjs* **geo'graphic(al)**.

ge'ology *n* the study of the earth's history as shown in its rocks and soils. – *adj* **geo'logical**. – *n* **ge'ologist**.

ge'ometry *n* the branch of mathematics which deals with the study of lines, angles, and figures. – *adjs* **geo'metric(al)** having regular shape; (of patterns *etc*) made up of angles and straight lines.

ge'rānium *n* a kind of plant, often with bright red flowers.

gerbil ['jərbl] *n* a type of small, rat-like desert animal, often kept as a pet.

germ *n* a very small living thing which may cause a disease; the smallest form of what will become a living thing (as a fertilized egg, a flower bud); that from which anything grows: *germ of an idea.* – *n* '**germicide** a germ-killer. – *v* '**germinate** to begin to grow, to sprout. – *n* germi'**nation**.

ger'**mane** *adj* closely related.

ges'**ticulate** *v* to wave hands and arms about in excitement *etc*. – *n* gesticu'**lation**.

'**gesture** *n* a movement of the hands, head *etc*; an action made to show one's feelings: *a gesture of friendship.*

get [get] *v* to obtain; to go or move; to cause to be done: *get your hair cut*; to receive: *get a letter*; to cause to be in some condition: *get the car going*; to arrive: *get home*; to catch, or have (a disease); to become: *get old*: – *pt, pp* **got**, (*US*) *pp* '**gotten**. – **get at** to reach; to hint at; to criticize continually; (*slang*) to try to influence by bribes or threats; **get away with** to do and escape punishment for; **get on with** to be on friendly terms with; **get over** to recover from; **get up** to stand up; to get out of bed.

geyser ['gēzər] *n* a hot spring which spouts water into the air; a gas or electric water heater.

ghastly ['gästli] *adj* very pale, death-like; ill: *feeling ghastly*; horrible, ugly; (*coll*) very bad. – *n* '**ghastliness**.

gherkin ['gərkin] *n* a small pickled cucumber.

ghetto ['getō] *n* a (poor) part of a city *etc* in which a certain group (*esp* of immigrants) lives: – *pl* '**ghettos**.

ghost [gōst] *n* a spirit, *usu* of a dead person. – *adj* '**ghostly** like a ghost. – *n* '**ghostliness**.

ghoul [gool] *n* an evil spirit which plunders dead bodies; a person unnaturally interested in death and disaster. – *adj* '**ghoulish**.

'**giant** *n* (in old stories) a huge, man-like being; a person of great height or size: – *fem* '**giantess**. – *adj* huge.

'**gibber** *v* to speak nonsense; to make meaningless noises. – *n* '**gibberish** words without meaning.

'**gibbet** *n* (*hist*) a gallows on which criminals used to be executed or hung up after execution.

gibbon ['gibən] *n* a large, tail-less ape.

gibe *see* **jibe**.

'**giblets** *npl* eatable parts from the inside of a fowl *etc*.

giddy ['gidi] *adj* unsteady, dizzy; causing dizziness: *from a giddy height*. – *n* '**giddiness**.

gift [gift] *n* something freely given (*eg* a present); a natural talent: *a gift for music*; (*coll*) something easily done *etc*. *The examination paper was a gift*. – *adj* '**gifted** having special natural power or ability. – **look a gift horse in the mouth** to find fault with a gift.

gi'**gantic** *adj* huge, of giant size.

giggle ['gigl] *v* to laugh in a nervous or silly manner. – Also *n*.

gila ['hēlə] *n* (also **gila monster**) a type of poisonous lizard.

gild [gild] *v* to cover with gold; to make bright. – *n* **gilt** the gold covering used in gilding. – *adj* covered with thin gold; coloured like gold. – *adj* '**gilt-'edged** not risky, safe to invest in: *gilt-edged stocks*. – **gild the lily** to try to improve something already beautiful enough.

gill[1] [jil] *n* a measure (¼ pint, 11·36 cubic centimetres) for liquids.

gill[2] [gil] *n* one of the openings on the side of a fish's head through which it breathes.

gillie ['gili] *n* a man who helps and guides a sportsman while fishing or shooting (*esp* in Scotland).

gilt *see* **gild**.

'**gimcrack** *adj* cheap and badly-made.

gimlet ['gimlit] *n* a small tool for boring holes by hand.

gimmick ['gimik] *n* something meant to attract attention.

gin *n* an alcoholic drink made from grain, and flavoured with juniper berries; a trap or snare.

ginger ['jinjər] *n* a hot-tasting root, used as a seasoning in food. – *adj* flavoured with ginger; reddish-brown in colour (*esp* hair). – *adv* '**gingerly** very carefully. – *n* '**gingerbread** cake flavoured with ginger.

gingham ['giŋəm] *n* a striped or checked cotton cloth.

gipsy *see* **gypsy**.

gi'**raffe** *n* a type of African animal with very long legs and neck.

gird [gərd] *v* to bind round. – *ns* '**girder** a beam of iron, steel, or wood used in building; '**girdle** belt, cord *etc* which goes round something (*usu* the waist).

girl [gərl] *n* a female child or young woman. – *n* '**girlhood** the state or time of being a girl. – *adj* '**girlish** like a girl. – *n* **Girl Guide** *see* **Guide**.

giro ['jīrō] *n* a system by which payment may be made through banks, post offices *etc*; (also '**girocheque**) a form like a cheque by which such payment is made.

girth [gərth] *n* measurement round the middle; a strap that keeps a saddle on a horse *etc*.

gist *n* the main points or ideas (of a story, argument *etc*).

give [giv] *v* to hand over freely or in exchange; to utter (a shout, cry); to break or crack. *The bridge gave under the weight of the train*; to produce. *This lamp gives a good light*: – *pt* **gave**, *pp* **'given**. – *n* **'giver**. – **give away** to hand over (something) to someone without payment; to betray; **give in** to yield; **give over** (*coll*) to stop (doing something); **give rise to** to cause; **give up** to hand over; to yield; to stop, abandon (a habit *etc*); **give way** to yield; to collapse; to let traffic crossing one's path go before one.

glacé ['glasā] *adj* iced or sugared.

glacier ['glasiər] *n* a slowly-moving river of ice in valleys between high mountains. – *adj* **'glacial** of ice or glaciers.

glad *adj* pleased; giving pleasure: *the glad news*. – *v* **'gladden** to make glad. – *n* **'gladness**.

glade *n* an open space in a wood.

'gladiator *n* (*hist*) in ancient Rome, a man trained to fight with other men or with animals for the amusement of spectators.

glamour ['glamər] *n* fascination, charm, beauty, *esp* artificial. – *adj* **'glamorous**.

glance *n* a quick look. – *v* to take a quick look at; (with **off**) to hit and fly off sideways.

gland *n* a part of the body which takes substances from the blood and stores them either for use or so that the body may get rid of them. – *adj* **'glandular**.

glare *n* an unpleasantly bright light; an angry or fierce look. – *v* to shine with an unpleasantly bright light; to look angrily. – *adj* **'glaring** dazzling; very clear, obvious: *a glaring mistake*.

glass *n* a hard transparent substance made from certain metal oxides and other oxides; anything made of glass *esp* a glass drinking vessel or a mirror; (*pl*) **'glasses** a pair of lenses set in a frame used to correct bad eyesight, spectacles. – *adjs* **glass** made of glass; **'glassy** (of eyes) without expression. – *n* **'glasshouse** a greenhouse.

glaze *v* to cover with a thin coating of glass or other shiny stuff; to make shiny; to put panes of glass in a window; of eyes, to become glassy. – *n* a shiny surface; a sugar-coating. – *n* **glazier** ['glāziər] one who sets glass in window-frames.

gleam *v* to glow; to flash. – *n* a beam of light; brightness.

glean *v* to collect (*esp* things overlooked before); (*old*) to gather corn in handfuls after the reapers.

glee *n* joy; a song in parts. – *adj* **'gleeful** merry.

glen *n* in Scotland, a long narrow valley.

glib *adj* speaking smoothly and fluently (often insincerely and superficially); (of a reply *etc*) quick and ready, but showing little thought. – *n* **'glibness**.

glide *v* to move smoothly and easily; to travel by glider. – *n* the act of gliding. – *n* **'glider** an aeroplane without an engine.

'glimmer *v* to burn or shine faintly. – *n* a faint light; a faint appearance (of): *a glimmer of hope*.

glimpse *n* a brief view. – *v* to get a brief look at.

glint *v* to sparkle, gleam. – Also *n*.

glisten ['glisn] *v* to sparkle.

'glitter *v* to sparkle. – Also *n*.

'gloaming *n* twilight, dusk.

gloat *v* to look at or think about with wicked joy. *She gloated over his defeat.*

globe *n* a ball; the earth; a ball with a map of the world drawn on it; a glass covering for a lamp. – *adjs* **'global** of, or affecting, the whole world; applying generally: *global increase in earnings*; **globular** ['globūlər] ball-shaped. – *n* **'globule** a drop; a small ball-shaped piece.

gloom *n* dullness, darkness; sadness. – *adj* **'gloomy** dimly lighted; sad, depressed.

'glory *n* fame, honour; great show, splendour: – *pl* **'glories**. – *v* to rejoice, take great pleasure (in). – *v* **'glorify** to make glorious; to praise highly: – *pt* **'glorified**. – *adj* **'glorious** splendid; deserving great praise; delightful.

gloss *n* brightness on the surface. – *v* to make bright; to explain; (with **over**) to try to hide (a fault *etc*) by treating (it) rapidly or superficially or by giving (it) a false appearance. – *n* **'glossary** a list of words with their meanings: – *pl* **'glossaries**. – *adj* **'glossy** shiny, highly polished.

glove [gluv] *n* a covering for the hand with a separate covering for each finger; a boxing glove.

glow [glō] *v* to burn without flame; to give out a steady light; to be flushed (from heat, cold *etc*); to tingle (with an emotion): *glowed with pride*. – *n* a glowing state; great heat; bright light. – *adj* **'glowing** giving out a steady light; tingling; flushed; full of praise. *I hear glowing accounts of his bravery.* – *n* **'glow-worm** a kind of beetle which glows in the dark.

glower ['glowǝr] *v* to stare (at) with a frown. – *adj* **'glowering** scowling; threatening.

glucose ['glookōs] *n* a kind of sugar found in the juice of fruits.

glue [gloo] *n* a substance for sticking things together. – *v* to join with glue. – *adj* **'gluey** sticky.

glum *adj* sad, gloomy.

glut *v* to take one's fill greedily; to supply too much to (a market): – *pt* **'glutted.** – *n* an over-supply (of something): *a glut of fish on the market.*

'glutton *n* one who eats too much; one eager (for anything): *a glutton for punishment.* – *adj* **'gluttonous** fond of overeating; eating greedily. – *n* **'gluttony** greediness in eating.

glycerine ['glisǝrēn] *n* a colourless, sticky, sweet-tasting liquid.

gnarled [närld] *adj* knotty, twisted.

gnash [nash] *v* to grind (the teeth).

gnat [nat] *n* a small (blood-sucking) fly, a midge.

gnaw [nö] *v* to bite at with a scraping action.

gnome [nōm] *n* (*myth*) a goblin who lives underground, often guarding treasure.

gnu [noo] *n* a type of African antelope.

go *v* to move: *go home: go to London*; to leave: *time to go*; to lead. *The road goes north*; to become: *go mad*; to work. *The machine is going at last*; to intend (to do). *I'm going to eat an apple*; to be removed, taken away *etc. The food's all gone*; to be given, awarded *etc. The prize has gone to John*: – *pt* **went**, *pp* **gone** [gon]. – *n* the act or process of going; energy, spirit; (*coll*) attempt, try; (*coll*) fashion, style. – *adj* **'go-ahead** eager to succeed. – *n* permission to act. – *n* **'go-between** one who helps two people to communicate with each other. – *adj* **'go-go** energetic. – *n* **'go-kart** a small low-powered racing car. – **from the word go** from the start; **go about** to try, set about; **go ahead** to proceed, to begin on an action *etc*; **go along with** to agree with; **go back on** to fail to keep (a promise *etc*); **go for** to aim to get; to attack; **go off** to explode; to become rotten; to come to dislike (a person *etc*); **go on** to continue; to talk too much; **go round** to be enough for everyone. *Will the food go round?*; **go steady (with)** to court (a person); **go the whole hog** to do (something) thoroughly; **go under** to be ruined; **on the go** very active.

goad *n* a sharp-pointed stick for driving oxen *etc*; anything that urges on. – *v* to urge on by annoying.

goal *n* the upright posts between which the ball is to be driven in football and other games; a score in football; anything aimed at or wished for.

goat *n* a type of animal of the sheep family with horns and a long-haired coat.

'gobble *v* to swallow quickly; to make a noise like a turkey.

'goblet *n* (*hist*) a large cup without handles; a drinking glass with a stem.

'goblin *n* (*myth*) a mischievous and ugly spirit.

god *n* a being who is worshipped, an idol: – *fem* **'goddess; God** the creator and ruler of the world in the Christian, Jewish *etc* religions. – *adj* **'godly** holy, good living. – *ns* **'godfather** a man who says that he will see that a child is brought up according to the beliefs of the Christian Church: – *fem* **'godmother; 'godsend** a very welcome piece of unexpected good fortune; **'godspeed** a wish for success or for a safe journey.

'goggle-eyed *adj* with staring eyes.

'goggles *npl* spectacles for protecting the eyes from dust, glare, water *etc*.

go-go *see* **go.**

goitre ['goitǝr] *n* a swelling in the neck.

gōld *n* an element, a precious yellow metal; riches. – *adj* of, or like, gold. – *adj* **'golden** of, or like, gold; very fine. – *ns* **'gold-digger** a woman who views men merely as a source of wealth; **golden wedding** *see* **wedding; 'goldfield** a place where gold is found; **'goldfinch** a type of small many-coloured bird; **'goldfish** a kind of golden-yellow Chinese carp, often kept as a pet; **'gold-'leaf** gold beaten to a thin sheet; **'goldsmith** a maker of gold articles.

golf *n* a game in which a ball is struck with various clubs. – *n* **'golfer** one who plays golf. – *n* **golf club** a club used in golf; a society of players of golf; the place where they meet.

'gollywog *n* a doll with a black face and bristling hair.

golosh *see* **galosh.**

'gondola *n* a boat used on Venice canals; the car suspended from an airship, cable railway *etc*. – *n* **gondolier** [gondǝ'lēr] a boatman who rows a gondola.

gone *see* **go.**

gong *n* a metal plate which, when struck, gives a booming sound, used *eg* to call people to meals.

good *adj* having the qualities which the

speaker wants in the thing or person spoken of: *a good fire, hammer, engineer, butcher etc*; virtuous: *a good person*; kind. *She was good to me*; pleasant, enjoyable: *a good time*; large: *a good income*. – *npl* **goods** one's belongings; things to be bought and sold. – *n* **'goodness** the quality of being good. – *adj* **'good-for-'nothing** useless, lazy. – *n* **good name** (good) reputation. – *adj* **good-'natured** kind, cheerful. – *ns* **good morning, good-'day, good afternoon, good evening, good night, good'bye** words used as greeting when meeting or leaving someone; **good'will** kind wishes; a good reputation in business.

goose *n* a web-footed bird larger than a duck: – *pl* **geese**. – *npl* **'goosepimples** small bumps on the skin caused by cold or fear.

gooseberry ['goozbəri] *n* an eatable *usu* green berry.

gore *n* (a thick mass of) blood; a triangular-shaped piece of cloth in a garment *etc*. – *v* to pierce with horns, tusks *etc*. – *adj* **'gory** covered with blood; of blood or bloodshed.

gorge *n* the throat; a narrow valley between hills. – *v* to swallow greedily till one is full.

gorgeous ['görjəs] *adj* showy, splendid; beautiful, very attractive; (*coll*) excellent, enjoyable, very fine *etc*.

'gorgon *n* (*myth*) a monster whose glance turned people to stone; any very stern-looking person.

gorgon'zola *n* a kind of strong cheese.

go'rilla *n* the largest kind of ape.

gorse *n* a kind of prickly bush with yellow flowers.

goshawk ['gos-hök] *n* a short-winged hawk.

gosling ['gozliŋ] *n* a young goose.

'gospel *n* the teaching of Christ; the absolute truth.

'gossamer *n* fine spider-threads floating in the air or lying on bushes; any very thin material.

'gossip *n* (one who listens to and passes on) talk, not necessarily true, about someone's personal affairs *etc*. – *v* to pass on gossip; to chatter.

got *see* **get**.

gouache [goo'äsh] *n* a kind of paint containing water, gum and honey; a painting done with this paint.

gouge [gowj] *n* a chisel with a hollow blade for cutting grooves. – *v* to scoop (out).

goulash ['goolash] *n* a stew of meat and vegetables, highly seasoned: – *pl* **'goulashes**.

gourd [goord] *n* a large fleshy fruit; the skin of a gourd used as a bottle, cup *etc*.

gourmand ['goormön] *n* a glutton.

gourmet ['goormä] *n* one with a taste for good wines or food.

gout *n* a painful swelling of the smaller joints, *esp* of the big toe. – *adj* **'gouty**.

govern ['guvərn] *v* to rule, control; to put into action the laws *etc* of a country. – *ns* **'governess** a woman who teaches young children at their home; **'government** rule; control; the persons who rule and administer the laws of a country; **'governor** one who rules.

gown [gown] *n* a woman's dress; a loose robe worn by clergymen, lawyers, teachers *etc*.

grab *v* to seize or grasp suddenly; to lay hands on, *esp* by rough or unjust means: – *pt* **grabbed**. – *n* a sudden grasp or catch.

grace *n* beauty of form or movement; a short prayer at a meal; the title of a duke or archbishop; favour or mercy: *God's grace*. – *adjs* **'graceful** beautiful in appearance; done in a neat way; **gracious** ['grāshəs] kind, polite. – **with good** (or **bad**) **grace** willingly (or unwillingly).

grade *n* a step or placing according to quality or rank; class. – *v* to arrange in order (*eg* from easy to difficult). – *ns* **gra'dation** arrangement in order (of rank, difficulty *etc*); **gradient** ['grādiənt] a slope (on a road, railway *etc*). – *adj* **gradual** ['gradüəl] step by step; going slowly but steadily. – *adv* **'gradually**. – **make the grade** to do as well as is necessary (in a job, examination *etc*).

'graduate *v* to divide into regular spaces; to pass university examinations and receive a degree. – *n* one who has done so. – *n* **gradu'ation** the act of getting a degree from a university.

graffiti [grə'fētē] *npl* words or drawings scratched or painted on a wall *etc*.

graft *v* to fix a shoot or twig of one plant upon another, so that it may grow there; to fix (skin) from one part of the body upon another part; to transfer (a part of the body) from one person to another; to get illegal profit by graft. – *n* living tissue (*eg* skin) which is grafted; a shoot *etc* grafted; hard work; profit gained by illegal or unfair means.

Grail *n* the plate said to be used by Christ at the Last Supper.

grain *n* a seed (*eg* of wheat, oats); corn in general; a very small quantity; a very small measure of weight; the run of the

lines of fibre in wood, leather *etc*. –
against the grain against (a person's)
natural feelings.

gram *see* **gramme**.

'**grammar** *n* (the study of) the correct
use of words in speaking or writing. *His
grammar is bad.* – *n* gram'**mārian** an
expert on grammar. – *adj* **grammati-**
cal [grə'matikəl] correct according to
rules of grammar. – *n* **grammar**
school a kind of secondary school.

gramme, gram *n* the basic unit of
weight in the metric system.

'**gramophone** *n* an older name for a
record-player.

'**granary** *n* a storehouse for grain: – *pl*
'**granaries**.

grand *adj* great; noble; fine. – *ns*
'**grandchild**,   '**grand-daughter**,
'**grandson** one's son's or daughter's
child; **grand duke** in some countries a
duke of specially high rank;
'**grandfather** one's father's or mother's
father; **grand master** a chess-player of
the greatest ability; '**grandmother**
one's father's or mother's mother;
grand opera opera without spoken
dialogue; **grand piano** a piano with a
large flat top; '**grandstand** rows of
raised seats at a sports ground giving a
good view.

gran'dee *n* a man of high rank.

grandeur ['granjər] *n* greatness.

gran'diloquent *adj* speaking in a high-
sounding language.

'**grandiose** *adj* planned on a large scale.

granite ['granit] *n* a hard rock of greyish
or reddish colour.

'**granny** *n* (*coll*) a grandmother: – *pl*
'**grannies**.

grant *v* to give; to allow (something
asked for); to admit as true. – *n*
something given (normally money) for
a special purpose. – *conjs* '**granted**,
'**granting** (often with **that**) (even) if,
assuming: *granted that you are right.* –
take for granted, to assume (that
something will happen) without checking; to treat (a person) casually, without respect or kindness.

'**granule** *n* a tiny grain or part. – *adjs*
'**granular** made up of grains; '**granu-**
lated broken into grains.

grape *n* the green or black smooth-
skinned berry from which wine is
made. – *ns* '**grapefruit** a fruit like a
large yellow orange; '**grapeshot** shot
which scatters when fired.

graph *n* line (or lines) drawn on squared
paper to show changes in quantity (*eg*
in temperature, money spent). – *adj*
'**graphic** vivid, well told.

'**graphite** *n* a form of carbon used in
making pencils.

'**grapple** *v* to struggle (with); to try to
deal (with a problem *etc*).

grasp *v* to clasp and grip with the fingers
or arms; to understand. – *n* a grip with
one's hand *etc*; one's power of understanding. – *adj* '**grasping** greedy,
mean.

grass *n* the plant covering fields of pasture; a kind of plant with long narrow
leaves (*eg* wheat, reeds, bamboo):
– *pl* '**grasses**. – *adj* '**grassy** covered
with grass. – *ns* '**grasshopper** a type of
jumping insect; '**grass-snake** a type of
green harmless snake; '**grass-'widow**
a woman whose husband is away.

grate *n* a framework of iron bars for
holding a fire. – *v* to rub down into
small pieces; to make a harsh, grinding
sound; to irritate. – *ns* '**grater** an
instrument with a rough surface for
rubbing cheese *etc* into small pieces;
'**grating** a frame of iron bars.

'**grateful** *adj* feeling thankful; showing
or giving thanks. – *n* **gratification**
[gratifi'kāshən] pleasure; satisfaction.
– *v* '**gratify** to please; to satisfy: – *pt*
'**gratified**. – *n* '**gratitude** thankfulness; desire to repay kindness shown.

gratis ['gratis] *adv* for nothing, without
payment.

gra'tūity *n* a money gift in return for
something done, a tip: – *pl* **gra'tuities**.
– *adj* **gra'tuitous** uncalled-for, done
without good reason or excuse: *a
gratuitous insult.*

grave *n* a pit in which a dead person is
buried. – *adj* serious, important: *grave
problems*; not gay, dignified, solemn. –
adv '**gravely**. – *ns* '**graveness, gravi-**
ty ['gravəti]. – *ns* '**gravestone** a stone
placed to mark a grave; '**graveyard** a
place where the dead are buried, a
cemetery.

'**gravel** *n* small stones or pebbles.

'**grāven** *adj* (*old*) carved: *graven images.*

'**gravity** *n* seriousness, importance: *the
gravity of the situation*; seriousness, lack
of gaiety, solemnity; weight; the force
which attracts things towards earth and
causes them to fall to the ground. – *v*
'**gravitate** to move towards as if strongly attracted (to). – *n* **gravi'tation**.

'**grāvy** *n* the juices from meat that is
cooking; a sauce made from these.

gray *see* **grey**.

graze *v* to feed on (growing grass); to
scrape the skin of; to touch lightly in
passing. – *n* a scraping of the skin; a
light touch. – *n* '**grazing** grass land for
animals to graze in.

grease n thick animal fat; oily substance of any kind. – v to smear with grease, apply grease to. – adj **'greasy**. – n **'greasepaint** a kind of make-up used by actors etc.

great [grāt] adj very large; powerful; very important, distinguished; very talented: a great singer; of high rank, noble. – n **'greatness**. – ns **'great-'grandchild** the son or daughter of a grandson or granddaughter; **'great-'grandparents** the father and mother of a grandfather or grandmother.

grebe n a fresh-water diving bird.

greed n great and selfish desire (for food, money etc). – adj **'greedy**. – n **'greediness**.

green adj of the colour of growing grass etc; without experience; easily fooled. – n the colour of growing grass; a piece of ground covered with grass; (pl) green vegetables for food. – ns **'greenery** green plants; **'greenness**. – ns **green belt** open land surrounding a city etc; **'greenfly** the aphid; **'greengage** a kind of plum, green but sweet; **'greengrocer** one who sells fresh vegetables; **'greenhouse** a building, usu of glass, in which plants are grown. – **the green light** permission to begin (anything).

greet v to meet a person with kind words; to say 'Hullo,' 'Good-day,' etc; to react to, respond to. They greeted his speech with approval; to meet (the eyes etc). – n **'greeting** words of welcome or kindness; reaction, response.

gre'gārious adj living in flocks and herds; liking the company of others.

gre'nade n a small bomb thrown by hand.

grew see **grow**.

grey, gray adj, n (of) a colour between black and white; grey-haired, old. – n grey colour; a grey horse. – ns **'greybeard** an old man; **'greyhound** a breed of fast-running dog; **grey matter** (coll) brains.

grid n a grating of bars; a network of lines, eg for helping to find a place on a map; a network of wires carrying electricity through the country. – n **'gridiron** a frame of iron bars for cooking food over a fire.

grief [grēf] n deep sorrow. – **come to grief** to meet with misfortune or ruin.

grieve [grēv] v to feel sorrow; to make sorrowful. – n **'grievance** a cause for complaining. – adj **'grievous** painful; serious; causing grief.

'griffin, **'griffon** n (myth) an animal with the body and legs of a lion and the beak and wings of an eagle.

grill v to cook directly under heat (provided by an electric or gas cooker); to cook on a gridiron over a fire; to question (someone) closely. – n a frame of bars for grilling food on; grilled food; the part of a cooker used for grilling; a restaurant serving grilled food.

grille [gril] n a metal grating over a door, window etc.

grim adj stern, fierce-looking; terrible; very unpleasant: a grim sight; unyielding, stubborn: grim determination. – n **'grimness**.

gri'mace n a twisting of the face in fun or pain. – Also v.

grime n dirt. – adj **'grimy**.

grin v to smile broadly: – pt grinned. – Also n. – **grin and bear it** to suffer something without complaining.

grind v to crush to powder; to sharpen by rubbing; to rub together (eg the teeth): – pt **ground**. – n hard or unpleasant work. – n **'grinder** a person or thing that grinds. – n **'grindstone** a revolving stone for grinding or sharpening tools. – **back to the grindstone** back to work; **keep one's nose to the grindstone** to work, or make someone work, without stopping.

grip n a firm hold, grasp; a way of holding or grasping; control; the handle or part by which anything is held; a travelling bag, a holdall. – v to take a firm hold of: – pt **gripped**.

gripe n a sharp pain in the stomach; a complaint. – v to complain.

grisly ['grizli] adj frightful, hideous.

grist n corn for grinding. – **grist to the mill** something which brings profit or advantage.

gristle ['grisl] n a tough elastic substance in meat. – adj **'gristly**.

grit n tiny pieces of stone; courage. – v to apply grit to (eg icy roads); to clench (one's teeth): – pt **gritted**. – adj **'gritty**.

grizzled ['grizld] adj grey, or mixed with grey. – adj **'grizzly** of a grey colour. – n **'grizzly (bear)** a type of large bear of N. America: – pl **'grizzlies**.

groan v to utter a moaning sound (in pain, disapproval etc); to be loaded: a table groaning with food.

groats npl oat grains without the husks.

'grocer n a dealer in certain kinds of food and household supplies. – npl **'groceries** food (sold by grocers).

'groggy adj weak and staggering (from blows or illness).

groin *n* the part of the body where the inner part of the thigh joins the rest of the body.

groom *n* one who has charge of horses; a man who is being married (*usu* **'bridegroom**). – *v* to look after (*esp* a horse); to make smart and tidy.

groove *n* a furrow, a long hollow. – *v* to cut a groove.

grope *v* to search (for) by feeling as if blind.

gross *adj* coarse; very fat; great, obvious: *gross error*; (of sums of money) total, before any deductions (*eg* income tax) are made: *gross profit*. – *n* the whole taken together; twelve dozen. – *n* **'grossness** coarseness.

grotesque [grə'tesk] *adj* very odd or strange looking.

'grotto *n* a cave: – *pl* **'grotto(e)s**.

ground *n* the surface of the earth; a good reason: *ground(s) for complaint*; (*pl*) lands surrounding a castle, large house *etc*; (*pl*) dregs: *coffee grounds*. – *v* (of ships) to strike the sea-bed *etc* and remain stuck; to prevent (aeroplanes) from flying; *see* also **grind**. – *adj* **'grounded** (of aeroplanes) unable to fly. – *n* **'grounding** the first steps in learning something. – *adj* **'groundless** without reason. – *ns* **ground floor** the storey of a building at street level; **'groundhog** same as **marmot**; **'ground-swell** broad ocean waves; **'groundwork** the first stages of a task.

groundsel ['grownsl] *n* a type of common wild plant with small yellow flowers.

group [grōōp] *n* a number of persons or things together. – *v* to form or gather into a group; to classify.

grouse *n* a kind of game bird hunted on moors and hills (*pl* **grouse**); a grumble, complaint (*pl* **'grouses**). – *v* to grumble, complain.

grove *n* a small group of trees.

'grovel *v* to crawl or lie on the ground; to make oneself too humble: – *pt* **'grovelled**.

grow [grō] *v* to become bigger or stronger; to become: *grow old*; to rear, cause to grow (plants, trees *etc*): – *pt* **grew** [grōō], *pp* **grown**. – *n* **growth** growing; increase; something that grows; something abnormal that grows on the body.

growl [growl] *v* to utter a deep sound like a dog. – Also *n*.

grown *see* **grow**.

grub *n* the form of an insect after being hatched from the egg (*eg* a caterpillar); (*coll*) food. – *v* to dig. – *adj* **'grubby** dirty. – *n* **'grubbiness**.

grudge *v* to be unwilling to give, grant, allow *etc*. *I grudge him his success*; to give *etc* unwillingly, with reluctance. – *n* feeling of resentment. *I bear a grudge against him*.

gruel ['grōōəl] *n* a thin mixture of oatmeal boiled in water. – *adj* **'gruelling** very tiring.

gruesome ['grōōsəm] *adj* horrible.

gruff *adj* rough in manner; (of voice *etc*) deep and harsh.

'grumble *v* to complain in a badtempered, discontented way. – Also *n*.

'grumpy *adj* cross, badtempered.

grunt *v* to make a sound like that of a pig. – Also *n*.

guarantee [garən'tē] *n* a (written) promise (to do something); a statement by the maker that something will work well; money put down which will be given up if a promise is broken. – *v* to give a guarantee. – *n* **guaran'tor** one who promises to pay if another person fails to keep an agreement to pay.

guard [gärd] *v* to keep safe from danger or attack. – *n* a man or group of men whose duty it is to protect; something (*eg* a fireguard) which protects from danger; one in charge of railway train or coach; a position of defence (in boxing, cricket, fencing *etc*). – *adj* **'guarded** careful. – *n* **'guardian** one who has the legal right to take care of an orphan; one who protects or guards.

guava ['gwävə] *n* a type of yellow pear-shaped fruit, or the tree that bears it.

gudgeon ['gujən] *n* a type of small freshwater fish.

guerrilla [gə'rilə] *n* a member of a small band which makes sudden attacks on a larger army but does not fight openly. – *adj* of a method of fighting in which many small bands acting independently make sudden raids on an enemy.

guess [ges] *v* to say without sure knowledge; to say what is likely to be the case. – Also *n*: – *pl* **'guesses**. – *n* **'guesswork** guessing.

guest [gest] *n* a visitor received and entertained in another's house or in a hotel *etc*.

guf'faw *v* to laugh loudly. – Also *n*.

guide [gīd] *v* to show the way to, lead, direct; to influence. – *n* one who shows the way (to travellers *etc*); one who points out interesting things about a place; a book (**'guidebook**) telling about a place; **Guide** a girl belonging to the Girl Guides organization. – *n* **'guidance** help or advice towards doing something *etc.* – *n* **guided mis-sile** an explosive rocket which after being fired can be guided to its target by radio waves.

guild [gild] *n* a company or association of persons working in the same trade or profession or sharing the same inter-ests; a name used by some societies or clubs.

guile [gīl] *n* cunning, deceit.

guillemot ['gilimot] *n* a type of diving sea-bird.

guillotine ['gilətēn] *n* (*hist*) an instru-ment for beheading (formerly used in France); a machine for cutting paper. – *v* to behead with the guillotine; to cut (paper) with a guillotine.

guilt [gilt] *n* a sense of shame; blame for wrongdoing (*eg* breaking the law). – *adj* **'guilty**.

guinea ['gini] *n* (*hist*) a British gold coin; now a word for £1·05, sometimes used in expressing prices, fees *etc.* – *ns* **'guinea-fowl** a bird, something like a pheasant, having white-spotted feath-ers; **'guinea-pig** a gnawing animal about the size of a rabbit; a person used as the subject of an experiment.

guise [gīz] *n* appearance, dress *esp* a disguised or false appearance: *in the guise of a priest.*

guitar [gi'tär] *n* a type of stringed musical instrument.

gulch *n* a narrow rocky valley.

gulf *n* a large inlet of the sea.

gull *see* **seagull**.

'gullet *n* a passage by which food goes down into the stomach.

'gullible *adj* easily tricked.

'gully *n* a channel worn by water: – *pl* **'gullies**.

gulp *v* to swallow eagerly or in large mouthfuls. – Also *n*.

gum *n* the firm flesh in which the teeth grow; sticky juice got from some trees and plants; a kind of sweet. – *v* to stick with gum. – *adj* **'gummy** sticky.

'gumption *n* good sense.

gun *n* any weapon firing bullets or shells. – *ns* **'gunboat** a small warship with heavy guns; **'gun-carriage** a wheeled support for a field-gun; **gun dog** a dog trained to fetch birds *etc* after they have been shot; **'gunfire** the firing of guns; **'gun-metal** a mixture of copper and tin; **'gunpowder** an explosive in pow-

der form; **'gun-running** bringing guns into a country illegally. – **stick to one's guns** to keep determinedly to one's opinion.

gunwale, gunnel ['gunl] *n* the upper edge of a boat's side.

'gurgle *v* to flow making a bubbling sound; to make such a sound. – Also *n*.

gush *v* to flow out in a strong stream; to talk at great length, exaggerating one's emotions, enthusiasms *etc. She would gush about her daughter's wedding for hours.* – *n* a strong or sudden flow: – *pl* **'gushes**.

'gusset *n* a cornered piece of cloth put into a garment to strengthen part of it.

gust *n* a sudden blast (such as wind). – *adj* **'gusty** windy.

'gusto *n* enthusiasm.

gut *n* a narrow passage in the lower part of the body; animal intestines made for use as violin-strings *etc.* – *v* to take out the inner parts of: *gut a fish*; to destroy completely (often by fire): *a gutted building*: – *pt* **'gutted**.

'gutter *n* a water channel (on the roof, at the edge of a roadside *etc*). – *n* **'guttersnipe** a poor child who spends most of his time in the streets.

'guttural *adj* harsh in sound, as if formed in the throat.

guy [gī] *n* a steadying rope for a tent *etc*; an image of Guy Fawkes made of old clothes *etc*, burned in Britain on 5th November; (*coll*) a man.

'guzzle *v* to eat or drink greedily.

gym [jim] *n* short for **gymnasium** or **gymnastics**.

gymkhana [jim'känə] *n* a meeting for competitions (often between horse-riders).

gymnasium [jim'nāziəm] *n* a building or room fitted out for physical exer-cises: – *pls* **gym'nasiums, gym'nasia**. – *n* **'gymnast** one who does gymnastics. – *adj* **gym'nastic**. – *npl* **gymnastics** [jim'nastiks] exercises to strengthen the body.

gypsum ['jipsəm] *n* a softish chalk-like mineral.

gypsy, gipsy ['jipsi] *n* a member of a wandering people; a Romany: – *pl* **'gypsies**.

gyrate [ji'rāt] *v* to whirl round. – *n* **gy'ration**. – *adj* **gyratory** ['jirətəri].

H

'haberdashery *n* materials for sewing, mending *etc.* – *n* **'haberdasher** a person who sells haberdashery.

'habit *n* something one is used to doing; one's ordinary behaviour; dress: *a monk's habit.* – *adj* **ha'bitūal** usual, formed by habit. – *v* **ha'bituate** to make accustomed.

'habitable *adj* that may be lived in. – *ns* **'habitat** the natural home of an animal or plant; **habi'tation** a dwelling place.

hack *v* to cut or chop up roughly; to ride on horseback *esp* along ordinary roads. – *n* a rough cut, gash; person who does hard work for low pay, *esp* a writer; an ordinary riding horse (kept for hire). – *n* **'hacksaw** a saw for cutting metal.

'hackles *npl* the feathers on the neck of a farmyard cock; the hair on a dog's neck. – **make someone's hackles rise** to make someone angry.

hackneyed ['haknid] *adj* (*esp* of sayings *etc*) too much used, not fresh or original. – *n* **hackney carriage, hackney cab** a carriage or taxi let out for hire.

'haddock *n* a kind of small eatable sea-fish: – *pls* **'haddock, 'haddocks**.

Hades ['hādēz] *n* (*myth*) the dwelling place of the dead, hell.

haemoglobin, (*US*) **hemoglobin** [hēmə'glōbin] *n* the oxygen-carrying substance in the red blood cells.

haemorrhage, (*US*) **hemorrhage** ['hemərij] *n* bleeding, *esp* in great quantity.

haft *n* a handle (of a knife *etc*).

hag *n* an ugly old woman; a witch.

'haggard *adj* thin-faced, hollow-eyed *etc*, with tiredness.

'haggis *n* a Scottish food made from the chopped-up heart, lungs and liver of a sheep and cooked in a sheep's stomach: – *pl* **'haggises**.

'haggle *v* to argue in a determined way (*esp* over a price).

'ha-ha *n* a sunken fence round a garden or park.

hail *v* to greet, welcome; to call to. – *n* a call from a distance; greeting; welcome; frozen raindrops; a shower (*eg* of bullets, things thrown *etc*). – *v* to shower with hail. *It's hailing*; to pour down. *Arrows hailed down.* – *n* **'hailstone** a piece of hail. – **hail from** to come from, belong to (a place).

hair *n* a thread-like growth on the skin of an animal; the whole mass of these (as on the head). – *adj* **'hairy** covered with

hair. – *ns* **'hair-breadth, 'hair's-breadth** a very small distance; **'hairdresser** one who cuts, washes and sets hair. – *adj* **'hair-raising** causing great fear. – *n* **'hairspring** a very fine spring in a watch *etc*. – **split hairs** to be very particular over unimportant details.

hake *n* a kind of eatable sea-fish something like a cod.

'halberd *n* (*hist*) a battle-axe fixed on a long pole. – *n* **halberdier** [halbər'dēr] a soldier armed with a halberd.

halcyon ['halsiən] : **halcyon days** a time of peace and happiness.

hale: hale and hearty healthy.

half [häf] *n* one of two equal parts: – *pl* **halves** ['hävz]. – *adj* being one of two equal parts; not full or complete: *half measures: a half smile.* – *adv* partly, to some extent. – *v* **halve** to cut, divide in two. – *ns* **'half-breed, 'half-caste** a person having father and mother of different races, *esp* white and black; **'half-brothers, 'half-sisters** brothers or sisters sharing only one parent; **'half-'crown** a coin in old British money of the value of two shillings and sixpence ($12\frac{1}{2}$ pence). – *adj* **'half-'hearted** not eager. – *adv* **'half-'mast** (of flags) hoisted half-way up the mast to show that some well-known person has died. – *ns* **'halfpenny** the lowest value British coin; **'half-'time** ['häf'tim] in sport, a short rest half-way through a game. – *adv, adj* **'half-'way** at or of a point equally far from the beginning and the end (of a distance, journey, period of time, task *etc*). – *adj* **'half-'witted** weak in the mind.

'halibut *n* a kind of large eatable flatfish.

hali'tōsis *n* bad breath.

hall [höl] *n* a passage or large room at the entrance to a house; a large public room; a large country house, the home of a squire or landowner. – *n* **'hall-mark** a mark put on gold and silver articles to show the quality of the gold or silver; any mark which shows that a thing is good.

hallo *see* **hello**.

hallow ['halō] *v* to make holy; to set apart for holy use. – *n* **Hallowe'en** ['halō'ēn] the evening of October 31st, when witches and spirits are supposed to be around.

hallucination [həlōōsi'nāshən] *n* the seeing of something that is not really there. *He had hallucinations after he took* *the drugs.* – *adj* **hal'lucinatory** causing hallucinations.

'**hālo** *n* a circle of light round the sun or moon or around a person's head (as in the pictures of a saint) : – *pl* '**halo(e)s**.

halt [hölt] *v* to come or bring to a stop; to be lame, limp; to hesitate, be uncertain. – *adj* lame. – *n* a stop, standstill; stopping place. – *adv* '**haltingly** hesitantly.

halter ['höltər] *n* a head-rope for holding and leading a horse.

halve *see* **half**.

'**halyard** *n* a rope for raising or lowering a sail or flag.

ham *n* the thigh of a pig salted and dried; the back of the thigh; (*coll*) an amateur radio operator. – *n* '**hamburger** a round cake of minced beef, usually fried. – *adj* '**ham-'fisted** clumsy.

'**hamlet** *n* a small village.

'**hammer** *n* a tool for beating or breaking hard substances or driving nails; a striking piece in a clock, piano, pistol *etc.* – *v* to drive or shape with a hammer; to defeat overwhelmingly. – **hammer and tongs** violently.

'**hammock** *n* a length of netting, canvas *etc* hung up by the corners, and used as a bed.

'**hamper** *v* to hinder. – *n* a large basket with a lid.

'**hamster** *n* a kind of animal, similar to a rat, with large cheek pouches.

'**hamstring** *n* a tendon at the back of the knee. – *v* to lame by cutting this; to make ineffective or powerless.

hand *n* the part of the human body at the end of the arm; a pointer (*eg* of a clock); help: *lend a hand*; a measure (four inches, 10·16 centimetres) used for measuring the height of horses; a workman; one's style of handwriting; side or direction: *left-hand side*; a set of playing cards dealt to a person; clapping, applause: *a big hand*. – *v* to pass (something) with the hand; (with **over**) to give. – *ns* '**handbag** a small bag carried by women for personal belongings; '**handbill** a small printed notice; '**handbook** a small book giving information or directions (a guidebook); '**handcuffs** steel bands, joined by a short chain, put round the wrists of prisoners; '**handful** as much as can be held in one hand; a small amount; '**handhold** something which the hand can grip (*eg* in climbing). – *adj* '**hand-'picked** chosen carefully. – *n* '**handwriting** writing with pen or pencil. – **at hand** near by; **hand-to-hand fighting** fighting in which those

involved are in close contact with each other; '**hand-to-'mouth** (of an existence *etc*) with barely enough to live on and nothing to spare; **in hand** in one's possession: *cash in hand*; in preparation; under control; **out of hand** out of control; at once.

'**handicap** *n* something that makes doing something more difficult; (in a race, competition *etc*) a disadvantage (*eg* having to run a greater distance in a race) given to the best competitors so that others have a better chance of winning; the race, competition *etc*; a physical or mental disability. – Also *v*. – *adj* '**handicapped** having or given a handicap; physically or mentally disabled.

'**handicraft** *n* skilled work done by hand, not machine.

handiwork ['handiwȯrk] *n* thing(s) made by hand; work done by, or a result of the action of a particular person *etc*. *This is the handiwork of a vandal.*

handkerchief ['haŋkərchif] *n* a cloth for wiping the nose *etc*.

'**handle** *v* to touch, hold or use with the hand; to manage, cope with. – *n* that part of anything meant to be held in the hand. – *npl* '**handlebars** (on a bicycle) a bar at the front with a handle at each end, used for steering.

handsome ['hansəm] *adj* good-looking; generous: *a handsome gift*.

'**handy** *adj* useful or convenient to use; easily reached, near; clever with the hands. – *ns* '**handiness**; '**handyman** a man who does odd jobs.

hang *v* to fix or be fixed to some point off the ground *esp* with string *etc*; to remain more or less still in the air (*eg* of a hawk, a cloud); (with **down**) to droop, fall or incline downwards; to depend (on); to attach wall-paper to a wall: – *pt* **hung**; to put a criminal to death by putting a rope round his neck and letting him fall: – *pt* **hanged**. – *ns* '**hanger** that on which a coat *etc* is hung; '**hanging** the killing of a criminal by hanging. – *adj* '**hangdog** guilty-looking. – *ns* '**hanger-'on** one who stays near someone in the hope of gaining some advantage: – *pl* '**hangers-'on**; '**hangman** the man who hangs criminals; '**hangover** uncomfortable after-effects of being drunk; something remaining (from). – **get the hang of** to understand, learn how to use; **hang about, around** to remain near, loiter; **hang back** to hesitate; **hang fire** to delay.

'**hangar** *n* a shed for aeroplanes.

hank *n* a coil or loop of string, rope, wool *etc*.

'**hanker** *v* to long for.

'**hankie**, '**hanky** short for **handker-chief**.

'**hansom-cab** *n* a light two-wheeled cab with the driver's seat raised behind.

'**hap'hazard** *adj* depending on chance, without planning or system. – Also *adv*.

'**hapless** *adj* unlucky.

'**happen** *v* to take place; to occur by chance; to chance to do. *I happened to find him.* – *n* '**happening** an event.

'**happy** *adj* joyful; contented; lucky: *a happy chance*; willing: *happy to help*: – *comp* '**happier**, *superl* '**happiest**. – *adv* '**happily**. – *n* '**happiness**. – *adj* '**happy-go-'lucky** easy-going, taking things as they come.

hara-kiri ['harə'kērē] *n* suicide as practised in Japan in earlier times.

harangue [hə'raŋ] *n* an intense, rousing speech (to a crowd). – Also *v*.

'**harass** *v* to annoy (often); to make sudden attacks on. – *n* '**harassment**.

harbinger ['härbinjər] *n* a sign of something to come: *harbinger of spring*.

harbour ['härbər] *n* a place of shelter for ships; any place of shelter or safety. – *v* to give shelter or refuge; to store (*eg* unkind thoughts) in the mind.

hard *adj* solid, firm; not easily broken or put out of shape; not easy to do, understand *etc*; not easy to please; not easy to bear; having no kind or gentle feelings; (of water) containing many minerals and so not lathering well when soap is added; (of drugs) habit-forming. – *adv* strongly, violently. – *v* '**harden** to make hard. – *adv* '**hardly** scarcely; only just; with difficulty. – *n* '**hardness** the state of being hard. – *adjs* '**hard-'headed** clever, shrewd; '**hard-'hearted** having no kind feelings. – *ns* **hard labour** tiring work given to prisoners as part of their punishment; '**hardship** something not easy to bear (*eg* cold, lack of money); '**hardware** goods such as pots and pans; equipment (machinery, weapons *etc*); part or parts of a computer (*see* **software**); '**hardwood** the wood of certain trees (as oak, ash, elm *etc*). – **hard and fast** (*esp* of rules) strict; **hard hit** hurt, badly affected (as by a loss of money); **hard of hearing** rather deaf; **hard up** short of money.

'**hardy** *adj* daring, brave; strong, tough. – *n* '**hardiness**.

hare *n* a type of fast-running animal, like a large rabbit. – *n* '**harebell** a plant with blue, bell-shaped flowers. – *adj* '**hare-brained** careless about what one does; mad, foolish. – *n* '**hare-'lip** a split in the upper lip at birth, like that of a hare.

harem ['härəm] *n* the women's rooms in a Muslim house; the women who occupy these.

haricot ['harikō] *n* a type of bean.

hark *interj* listen! – **hark back** to refer back to what was being spoken of earlier.

harlequin ['härlikwin] *n* a comic character in a dress of several colours, in a pantomime or comedy.

harm *n* hurt; damage. – *v* to cause damage; to do a wrong to. – *adjs* '**harmful**; '**harmless**.

'**harmony** *n* agreement of one part, colour or sound with another; agreement between people: *living in harmony*: – *pl* '**harmonies**. – *adj* **har'monic** having to do with harmony. – *n* **har'monica** a mouth organ. – *adj* **har'mōnious** pleasant-sounding; peaceful; without disagreement. – *n* **har'mōnium** a type of musical wind instrument like a small organ. – *v* **harmonize** ['härmənīz] to be in, or bring into, harmony; to agree, go well (with); (in music) to add the different parts to a melody.

'**harness** *n* the leather and other fittings for a horse at work. – *v* to put harness on a horse; to use (a source of power *etc*) for a special purpose. – **in harness** working, not on holiday or retired.

harp *n* a musical instrument played by plucking the strings with the fingers. – *n* '**harpist**. – **harp on** to talk too much about.

har'poon *n* a spear tied to rope, used for killing whales. – *v* to strike with a harpoon.

harpsichord ['härpsikörd] *n* a kind of musical instrument something like a piano.

'**harpy** *n* (*myth*) a monster with the body of a woman, and the wings, feet and claws of a bird of prey; a cruel woman: – *pl* '**harpies**.

'**harrier** *n* a breed of small dog for hunting hares; a kind of bird of prey; a cross-country runner.

harrow ['harō] *n* a frame with iron spikes for breaking up lumps of earth in ploughed land. – *v* to drag a harrow over; to distress greatly. – *adj* '**harrowing** very distressing.

'**harry** *v* to plunder, lay waste (an area, country *etc*); to harass, worry (a person): – *pt* '**harried**.

harsh *adj* rough, bitter; cruel. – *n* '**harshness**.

hart *n* the stag or male deer, *esp* from the age of six years.

'**hart(e)beest** *n* a type of S. African antelope.

'**harvest** *n* the time of the year when the ripened crops are gathered in; the crops gathered at this time. – *v* to gather in (a crop). – *n* '**harvester** a person or machine that harvests; a kind of creature like a spider. – *n* **harvest home** the feast held when the harvest is gathered in.

hash *n* a dish of chopped meat *etc*. – **make a hash of** to spoil completely.

hasp *n* a clasp (of a padlock *etc*).

'**hassock** *n* a thick cushion used as a footstool or for kneeling on.

hāste *n* speed, hurry. – *v* **hasten** ['hāsn] to hurry (on); to drive forward. – *adj* **hasty** ['hāsti] hurried; done without thinking. – *adv* '**hastily**. – **make haste** to hurry.

hat *n* a kind of covering for the head. – *n* '**hatter** one who makes or sells hats. – *n* '**hat-trick** (in cricket) the putting out of three batsmen by three balls in a row; (in football *etc*) three goals scored by the same player; any action performed three times in a row. – **keep (something) under one's hat** to keep secret.

hatch *n* (the door or cover of) an opening in a floor, wall *etc*: – *pl* '**hatches**. – *v* to produce young from eggs; to form and set working a plan (*usu* evil); to shade (part of a picture *etc*) with fine lines. – *ns* '**hatchery** a place for hatching eggs (*esp* of fish): – *pl* '**hatcheries**; '**hatchway** an opening in a floor or ship's deck.

'**hatchet** *n* a small axe. – *adj* '**hatchet-'faced** thin-faced, with sharp features. – **bury the hatchet** to put an end to a quarrel.

hate *v* to dislike very much. – *n* great dislike. – *adj* '**hateful** causing hatred. – *n* **hatred** ['hātrid] extreme dislike.

haughty ['hŏti] *adj* proud, looking on others with scorn. – *n* '**haughtiness**.

haul *v* to drag, pull with force. – *n* a strong pull; (*coll*) a difficult or tiring job: *a long haul*; that which is caught at one pull: *a haul of fish*; a rich find, booty. – *n* '**haulage** (money charged for) the carrying of goods.

haunch *n* the fleshy part of the hip; a leg and loin of meat (*esp* venison): – *pl* '**haunches**.

haunt *v* to visit often; (of a ghost) to stay

about a place. *A ghost haunts this house.* – *n* a place often visited. – *adj* '**haunted** inhabited by ghosts.

have [hav] *v* used with another verb to show that an action is in the past and completed. *I have bought a shirt*; to own or possess. *I have a fur coat*; to hold, contain. *This house has three bedrooms*; to give birth to: *to have a baby*; to suffer from: *to have a cold*; to cause (to be done): *have your hair cut*; to put up with. *I won't have her being so rude*: – *pt* **had**. – **have done with** to finish; **have it out** to settle (as an argument).

'**hāven** *n* a safe harbour; a place of safety.

'**haversack** *n* a bag made of canvas *etc* with shoulder-strap, for carrying food *etc*.

'**havoc** *n* great destruction.

haw *see* **hawthorn**.

hawk *n* a bird of prey of the falcon kind. – *v* to hunt birds with trained hawks; to carry goods about for sale. – *n* '**hawker** a door-to-door salesman.

'**hawthorn** *n* a type of prickly tree, with white flowers and small red berries (**haws**).

hay *n* grass, cut and dried, used as cattle food. – *ns* '**hay-cock** a pile of hay in a field; '**hay-'fever** an illness like a bad cold caused by pollen *etc*; '**hay-fork** a long-handled fork used in turning and lifting hay; '**hayrick, -stack** hay built up into a house-like block. – *adj* '**haywire** tangled, in a state of disorder.

'**hazard** *n* chance; risk of harm or danger. – *v* to risk; to put forward (a guess *etc*) at the risk of being wrong. – *adj* '**hazardous** dangerous, risky.

haze *n* a thin mist. – *adj* '**hazy** misty; not clear, vague. – *n* '**haziness**.

'**hāzel** *n* a type of light-brown nut, or the tree that bears it.

he [hē] *pron* some male person or animal already spoken about (used only as the subject of a verb). *He ate a banana.*

head [hed] *n* the uppermost part of the body, containing the brain, jaw *etc*; the chief part, place or person. – *v* to lead; to go in front of; to go in the direction of. *They headed for home*; to hit (a ball) with the head; (with **off**) to turn aside: *head off an attack*. – *ns* '**header** a dive, head first; '**heading** that which stands at the head (such as the title of a book or chapter). – *adj* '**heady** exciting. – *ns* '**headache** a pain in the head; a worrying problem; '**headband** a band worn round the head; '**headboard** a board across the top end of a bed; '**head-dress** a covering for the head. – *adv* '**head'first** with the head first; rashly, without thinking. – *ns* '**headland** a point of land running out into the sea, a cape; '**headlight** a strong light on the front of a motor car *etc*; '**headline** a line in large letters at the top of a page in a newspaper *etc*. – *adj, adv* '**headlong** with the head first; without stopping; without thought. – *n* '**head'master** the principal master of a school: – *fem* '**head'mistress**. – *adj, adv* '**head-'on** with the head or front first. – *ns* '**head'quarters** place from which the chief officers of an army *etc* control their operations; the chief office (of a business *etc*); '**headstone** a gravestone. – *adj* '**headstrong** determined to do as one likes. – *ns* '**headway** forward movement; '**headwind** a wind blowing straight in one's face. – **head over heels** in a somersault; completely, thoroughly.

heal *v* to make or become healthy or sound, cure. – *n* **health** [helth] the state of one's body *etc*; soundness of body *etc*; a wish (said while drinking) that someone may have good health. – *adj* '**healthy** in good health or condition; encouraging good health.

heap *n* a pile of things thrown one on top of another; a great many (of). – *v* to throw in a pile.

hear *v* to receive (sounds, news, music) by the ear; to listen to: – *pt* **heard** [hŏrd]. – *n* **hearing** ['hēriŋ] the act or power of listening; a court case. – *n* '**hearsay** what one hears people say, rumour. – **Hear! Hear!** a cry to show agreement with a speaker; **will not hear of** will not allow. *He would not hear of her going home alone.*

hearse [hŏrs] *n* a car for carrying a dead body to the grave.

heart [härt] *n* the part of the body which acts as a blood pump; the inner or chief part of anything; courage; eagerness; one of the signs on playing cards. – *v* '**hearten** to cheer on, encourage. – *adjs* '**heartless** cruel; '**hearty** strong, healthy; (of a meal) large; done eagerly; over-cheerful. – *adv* '**heartily**. – *n* '**heartache** sorrow. – *adj* '**heartbroken** very upset, very sad. – *ns* '**heartburn** a burning feeling in the chest after eating, indigestion; '**heart-failure** (death caused by) the sudden stopping of the heart's beating. – *adj* '**heartfelt** felt deeply, sincere.

hearth [härth] *n* (the floor of) the fireplace.

heat *n* (high) temperature; anger; a division or round in a competition, race

etc. – *v* to make or become hot. – *n* **heat wave** a period of hot weather. – **in heat** (of female animals) sexually excited in the breeding season.

heath *n* barren, open country; heather.

heathen ['hēdhən] *n* one who does not believe in God, *esp* one who worships idols. – Also *adj*.

heather ['hedhər] *n* a plant with small purple or white flowers growing on moorland. – *adj* of the colour of purple heather.

heave *v* to lift by force; to throw; to rise and fall; to produce, let out (*esp* a sigh). – Also *n*.

heaven ['hevn] *n* the sky (often in *pl*); the dwelling place of (the Christian) God; the place of reward of the good after death; any place of great happiness. – *adj* '**heavenly** dwelling in heaven; (*coll*) delightful. – **heavenly bodies** the sun, moon and stars.

heavy ['hevi] *adj* of great weight; great in amount, force *etc*: *heavy rainfall*; not easy to bear; slow; sleepy: – *comp* '**heavier**, *superl* '**heaviest**. – *adv* '**heavily**. – *n* '**heaviness**.

'**heckle** *v* (in an election) to ask awkward questions of a public speaker. – *n* '**heckler** one who heckles.

hectare ['hektär] *n* 10,000 square metres.

'**hectic** *adj* rushed; feverish.

'**hector** *v* to bully.

hedge *n* a fence of bushes, shrubs *etc*. – *v* to make a hedge; to shut in with a hedge; to avoid giving a straight answer. – *ns* '**hedgehog** a small prickly-backed animal; '**hedgerow** a row of bushes forming a hedge.

heed *v* to give attention to, listen to. – *adj* '**heedless** careless. – **pay heed to** to take notice of.

heel *n* the back part of the foot. – *v* to hit (*esp* a ball) with the heel; to put a heel on (a shoe); (of ships) to lean over. – **take to one's heels, show a clean pair of heels** to run away.

'**hefty** *adj* (of persons) powerful, muscular; heavy.

heifer ['hefər] *n* a young cow.

height [hit] *n* the state of being high; distance from bottom to top; the highest point; (often *pl*) a high place. – *v* '**heighten** to make higher.

heinous ['hānəs] *adj* very wicked.

heir [ār] *n* one who by law receives a title or property on the death of the owner: – *fem* '**heiress**. – *ns* '**heir-ap'parent** one who is expected to receive a title or property when the present holder dies; '**heirloom** something valuable that has been handed down in the family from generation to generation.

held *see* **hold**.

'**helicopter** *n* a flying machine kept in the air by propellers rotating on a vertical axis.

'**hēliograph** *n* a means of signalling, using the sun's rays.

'**hēliotrope** *n* a plant with small, sweet-smelling, lilac-blue flowers; a light purple colour.

'**hēlium** *n* an element, a very light gas.

hell *n* in some religions, the place of punishment of the wicked after death; the dwelling place of the Devil; any place of great misery or pain. – *adj* '**hellish**. – **hellbent on** determined to.

hel'lo, hal'lo, hul'lo *n* a greeting used between people. *I said hello to him. Hello! How are you?*

helm *n* the wheel or handle by which a ship is steered. – *n* '**helmsman** the one who steers.

'**helmet** *n* an armoured covering for the head.

help *v* to aid, do something necessary or useful for; to give the means for doing something to; to stop oneself from (doing). *I cannot help liking him.* – *n* aid, assistance; one who assists. – *adj* '**helpful** useful, able to help. – *n* '**helping** a share (of food). – *adj* '**helpless** useless; powerless. – *n* '**helpmate** a partner. – **help oneself** serve oneself (with food).

'**helter-'skelter** *adv* in a great hurry, in confusion. – *n* a spiral slide in a fairground *etc*.

hem *n* the border of a garment doubled down and stitched. – *v* to put or form a hem on; (with **in**) to surround: – *pt* **hemmed**.

'**hemisphere** *n* a half of the earth or a map of it: *western, eastern, northern* or *southern hemisphere.* – *adj* **hemi'spherical** like half a ball in shape.

'**hemlock** *n* a type of poisonous plant.

hemoglobin *see* **haemoglobin**.

hemorrhage *see* **haemorrhage**.

hemp *n* a type of plant used for making ropes, bags, sails *etc* and which supplies a drug. – *adj* '**hempen**.

hen *n* a female bird; a female domestic fowl. – *v* '**henpeck** (of a wife) to worry (a husband) into always giving way.

hence *adv* from this place or time: *ten years hence*; for this reason. *Hence, I shall have to stay.* – *advs* '**hence'forth**, '**hence'forward** from now on.

'**henchman** *n* a follower; a servant.

'**henna** *n* a reddish dye taken from a plant for colouring the hair *etc*.

'**heptagon** *n* a seven-sided figure. – *adj* **hep'tagonal**.

her *pron* a female person already spoken about (used only as the object in a sentence). *He helps her.* – *adj* belonging to such a person: *her house.* – *pron* **hers**. *This house is hers.* – *pron* **her'self** used reflexively. *She washed herself;* used for emphasis. *She herself won't be there but her brother will.*

'**herald** *n* something that is a sign of future things; (*hist*) a person who carries and reads important notices. – *v* to announce loudly; to be a sign of. – *adj* **he'raldic** of heraldry. – *n* '**heraldry** the study of coats of arms, badges, crests *etc*.

herb *n* a plant the stem of which dies every year; a plant used in the making of medicines or in cooking. – *adjs* **herbaceous** [hɜr'bāshəs] of herbs: *herbaceous border*; '**herbal** of or using herbs: *herbal remedy*. – *n* '**herbalist** one who sells herbs used in cooking or medicine. – *adj* **her'bivorous** eating or living on grass *etc*.

Herculean [hɜrkū'lēən] *adj* needing or showing great strength *etc*; very strong.

herd *n* a group of animals of one kind; (with **the**) most people. – *v* to treat or group together like a herd of animals.

here *adv* at, in or to this place. *He's here already. Come here!* – *advs* **here-a'bouts** approximately in this place; **here'after** after this. – *n* (with **the**) life after death. – *adv* **here'by** by this means.

he'redity *n* the passing on of qualities (appearance, intelligence *etc*) from parents to children. – *adj* **he'reditary** passed on in this way.

heresy ['herəsi] *n* an opinion which goes against the official (*esp* religious) view: – *pl* '**heresies**. – *n* '**heretic** one who holds or teaches such an opinion. – *adj* **he'retical**.

'**heritage** *n* something passed on by or inherited from an earlier generation, a parent *etc*.

her'maphrodite *n* an animal which has the qualities of both male and female sexes.

her'metically: hermetically sealed closed completely and airtight.

'**hermit** *n* one who lives alone (*esp* for religious reasons). – *n* '**hermitage** the dwelling of a hermit. – *n* **hermit crab** a kind of crab which lives in the abandoned shell of a shellfish.

'**hēro** *n* one admired (by many) for his brave deeds; the chief male person in a story *etc*: – *pl* **'heroes**, *fem* **heroine** ['herōin]. – *adj* **he'roic** brave as a hero; of heroes. – *n* **'heroism** bravery.

'heron *n* a type of large water bird, with long legs and neck.

'herring *n* an eatable sea fish: – *pls* **'herring**, **'herrings**.

hers, herself *see* **her**.

hertz *n* a unit of frequency, used of radio waves *etc*.

hesitate ['hezitāt] *v* to pause because of uncertainty; to be unwilling (to do something). – *ns* **'hesitancy, hesi'tation**. – *adj* **'hesitant**.

'hessian *n* a type of coarse cloth.

het: het up (*coll*) excited.

hew *v* to cut with blows; to shape with blows: – *pt* **hewed**, *pp* **hewed, hewn**.

'hexagon *n* a six-sided figure. – *adj* **hex'agonal**.

heyday ['hādā] *n* the time of greatest strength, the prime.

'hibernate *v* to pass the winter in rest, as some animals do. – *ns* **hiber'nation**, **'hibernator**.

hiccup, hiccough ['hikup] *n* a sharp gasp, caused by laughing, eating, drinking; (*pl*) a fit of such gasping. – Also *v*.

'hickory *n* a N. American tree.

hide *v* to put or keep out of sight: – *pt* **hid** [hid], *pp* **'hidden**. – *n* a place of hiding from which birds *etc* are watched; the skin of an animal. – *adj* **'hidden** out of sight; unknown. – *n* **'hiding** a thrashing. – *adj* **'hidebound** (of persons *etc*) not open to new ideas.

hideous ['hidiəs] *adj* frightful; very ugly.

hierarchy ['hirärki] *n* a number of things or persons arranged in order of rank.

hieroglyphics [hirə'glifiks] *npl* ancient Egyptian writing, in which pictures are used as letters; writing difficult to read.

'hi-fi short for **high fidelity**.

higgledy-piggledy ['higldi'pigldi] *adv, adj* in great disorder.

high [hī] *adj* raised far above; of (great) extent upward, tall; well up on any scale of measurement, judgement, rank *etc*; great, large: *high hopes: high prices*; (of sound) shrill, acute in pitch; (of food, *esp* meat) beginning to go bad. – *adv* far above in the air; well up on any scale; to a high degree. – *adv* **'highly** very: *highly delighted*; in a high position or degree. – *n* **'highness** height; **'Highness** a title of a king *etc*. – *adj* **'high-born** of noble birth. – *ns* **'highbrow** a person of intellectual tastes; **High Court** a supreme court. –

adjs **'high-ex'plosive** (of shells, bombs) causing great damage; **high fidelity** reproducing sound very clearly; **'high-'flown** (of language, style) using words that sound too grand or pompous; **'high-'handed** (of actions) done without thought for others. – *ns* **'Highlands** a mountainous region, *esp* the north of Scotland; **'Highlander** one who comes from the Highlands; **'highlight** a bright spot or area in a picture; a colour (in hair *etc*) made obvious by bright light; (most) memorable event or experience. – *adj* **'highly-'strung** nervous, easily excited. – *n* **'highroad** a main road. – *adj* **'high-'spirited** bold, lively. – *ns* **high tea** a cooked meal in the late afternoon; **high tide, high water** the time when the tide is farthest up the shore; **high treason** the crime of acting against the safety of one's own country; **'highway** the public road; **'highwayman** (*hist*) a robber who attacks people on the public road. – **Highway Code** a set of official rules for road users in Britain; **the high seas** the open seas.

'hijack *v* to steal (a car, aeroplane *etc*) while it is moving; to force the driver or pilot (of a vehicle) to head for a place chosen by the **'hijacker**. – Also *n*.

hike *v* to travel on foot. – Also *n*. – *n* **'hiker**.

hi'lārious *adj* very funny; very merry. – *n* **hi'larity** [hi'larəti].

hill *n* a mound of high land, less high than a mountain. – *adj* **'hilly**. – *n* **'hillock** a small hill.

hilt *n* the handle, *esp* of a sword. – **up to the hilt** thoroughly, completely.

him *pron* a male person already spoken about (used only as the object in a sentence): *help him: say to him.* – *pron* **him'self** used reflexively. *He has cut himself*; used for emphasis. *He himself could not do the job but his friend could.*

hind *n* a female deer. – *adj* placed behind. – *adj* **'hindmost** farthest behind. – *n* **'hindsight** wisdom or knowledge got only after something has happened.

'hinder *v* to keep back, delay, prevent. – *n* **'hindrance** something that hinders.

hinge *n* a joint on which a door, lid *etc* turns. – *v* to move on a hinge; to depend (on). *Everything hinges on the weather.*

hint *n* a mention which suggests one meaning without stating it clearly; a slight impression, or one not clearly stated: *a hint of fear in his words.* – Also *v*. *He hinted that he might go.*

'**hinterland** *n* the district lying inland from the coast.

hip *n* the part of the side of the body just below the waist; the fruit of the (wild) rose.

hippo'potamus *n* a large African animal living in and near rivers: – *pls* **hippo-'potamuses, hippo'potami**.

'**hire** *n* money paid for work done, or for the use of something belonging to another person. – *v* to give or get the use of something by paying money. – *n* '**hire-'purchase** a way of buying an article by paying for it in weekly or monthly parts or instalments.

'**hirsute** *adj* hairy, shaggy.

his [hiz] *adj* belonging to him: *his book*. – *pron. This book is his*.

hiss *v* to make a sound like a snake. – *n* such a sound, made to show anger or displeasure: – *pl* '**hisses**.

'**history** *n* the study of the past; a description in speech or (*esp*) writing of past events, ways of living *etc*: – *pl* '**histories**. – *n* **historian** [his'tōrian] one who writes history. – *adjs* **his'toric** [his'torik] important, likely to be remembered; **his'torical** of history; true of something in the past.

histri'onic *adj* having to do with stage-acting or actors. – *npl* **histri'onics** a dramatically exaggerated display of strong feeling.

hit *v* to strike with a blow *etc*; (with **upon**) to come upon, discover: – *pres p* '**hitting**, *pt* **hit**. – *n* a blow; a stroke; a shot which hits a target; a success (*esp* a successful song, recording, play *etc*). – *n* **hit parade** (weekly) list of best-selling records.

hitch *v* to fasten (by a hook *etc*); to lift with a jerk; to hitch-hike. – *n* a jerk; an unexpected stop or delay; one of several kinds of knot: – *pl* '**hitches**. – *v* '**hitch-hike** to travel by relying on lifts in other people's vehicles. – *n* '**hitch-hiker**.

hither ['hidhər] *adv* to this place. – *adv* '**hither'to** up till now. – **hither and thither** back and forward.

hive *n* a place where bees live; a busy place: *hive of industry*.

hoard *n* a (hidden) store (of treasure, food *etc*). – *v* to store up (in secret).

'**hoarding** *n* a fence of boards.

hoarse *adj* having a harsh voice, as from a cold or cough.

'**hoary** *adj* white with age; of great age. – *n* '**hoar-frost** white frost.

hoax *n* a trick played to deceive people: – *pl* '**hoaxes**. – *v* to play a hoax on.

hob *n* a small shelf next to a fireplace on which pans *etc* may be kept hot; the top of an electric *etc* stove.

'**hobble** *v* to walk with difficulty with short steps. – Also *n*.

'**hobby** *n* a favourite way of passing one's spare time: – *pl* '**hobbies**. – *n* '**hobby-horse** a wooden horse on rockers or in a merry-go-round; a favourite subject, which one continually talks about.

'**hobgoblin** *n* (*myth*) a mischievous fairy.

'**hobnail** *n* a big-headed nail used for horseshoes and in the soles of heavy boots.

'**hobnob** *v* to be on very friendly terms (with): – *pt* '**hobnobbed**.

hock *n* a kind of white wine; a joint on the hind leg of an animal, below the knee.

'**hockey** *n* an eleven-a-side ball game played with clubs curved at one end.

'**hōcus-'pōcus** *n* a juggler's trick; deception, trickery.

hod *n* a wooden trough on a pole, for carrying bricks and mortar; a container for coal.

hoe *n* a tool used for weeding, loosening earth *etc*. – *v* to use a hoe.

hog *n* a pig. – *v* (*coll*) to take or use selfishly: – *pt* **hogged**.

'**Hogmanay** *n* (in Scotland) the last day of the year (December 31) when many parties are held and people visit each other.

hoist *v* to lift, to raise. – *n* a lift, an elevator for goods.

hōld *v* to keep in one's hand or power; to have; to contain; to think, believe; to cause to take place: *hold a meeting*; to apply (still). *That rule doesn't hold any longer*; celebrate: *not to hold Christmas*: – *pt* **held**. – *n* grip, grasp; influence. *He has a hold over the others*; (in ships) a large space where cargo is carried. – *ns* '**holder** something made to hold something else; one who holds; '**holding** the amount held (*eg* land, shares in a company). – *ns* '**holdall** a (large) bag with a zip; '**holdup** an attack with intent to rob. – **hold forth** to speak at length; **hold good** to be true; **hold out** to continue to fight; **hold over** to keep till later; **hold up** to support; to hinder; to attack and demand money from.

hole *n* an opening in something solid; a pit or burrow; a miserable place; (*coll*) a difficulty.

'**holiday** *n* a day (or longer time) of rest and amusement.

hollow ['holō] *adj* having empty space inside, not solid; fake, unreal: *a hollow victory*. – *n* a sunken place; a dip in the land. – *v* to scoop (out).

'**holly** *n* a type of evergreen shrub with scarlet berries and prickly leaves.

'**hollyhock** *n* a type of tall garden plant.

'**holocaust** *n* a great destruction (by fire).

'**hōlster** *n* the (leather) case for a pistol.

hōlt *n* an otter's den.

'**hōly** *adj* of or like God; religious; set apart for use in worshipping God. – *n* '**holiness** the state of being holy. – *n* **Holy Writ** the Bible.

'**homage** *n* a sign of respect: *to pay homage to the king.*

home *n* the place where one *usu* lives or where one's family lives; the place from which anything comes originally. *America is the home of jazz*; a place where children or elderly or sick people live and are looked after. – *adj* of one's dwelling place or one's country. – *adv* to one's home; to the full length. *He drove the nail home.* – *adjs* '**homely** plain but pleasant; (*US*) plain, not attractive; '**homing** (*esp* of pigeons) having the habit of making for home. – *npl* **home economics** the study of how to run a home. – *adj* '**home-'made** made at home. – *n* **Home Secretary** (in Britain) the government minister who looks after matters relating to law and order, immigration *etc.* – *adj* '**homesick** longing for home. – *ns* **homestead** ['hōmsted] farmhouse; **home truth** a plain statement of something true but unpleasant made to a person's face. – *adv* '**homewards** towards home. – *n* '**homework** work (*usu* for school) done at home. – **bring home** to make (someone) realize (something).

'**homicide** *n* the killing of a human being; one who kills a human being. – *adj* **homi'cidal**.

ho'mogenize *v* to treat (milk) so that the cream does not separate itself and rise to the surface. – *n* **ho'mogeni'zation**.

'**homonyms** *npl* words having the same sound but a different meaning (*eg there, their*).

hone *v* to sharpen (a knife *etc*).

honest ['onist] *adj* truthful; not inclined to steal, cheat *etc.* – *n* '**honesty**.

honey ['huni] *n* a sweet, thick fluid made by bees from the nectar of flowers. – *n* '**honeycomb** a network of wax cells in which bees store honey. – *adj* '**honeycombed** having holes like the cells in an empty honeycomb. – *ns* '**honeymoon** a holiday spent immediately after marriage; '**honeysuckle** a climbing shrub with sweet-smelling flowers.

honk *n* a noise like the cry of the wild goose or the sound of a motor horn. – Also *v*.

honorary ['onərəri] *adj* done to give honour; acting without payment. – *n* **hono'rārium** a gift or fee for services not paid for by wages.

honour, (*US*) **honor** ['onər] *n* respect for truth, honesty *etc*; fame, glory; reputation, good name; a title which shows respect: *Your Honour*; a privilege; (often *pl*) recognition given for exceptional achievements *etc.* – *v* to give respect to (what is good); to give high rank to; to pay money when due: *honour a debt.* – *adj* '**honourable** worthy of honour.

hood *n* a covering for the head; anything which covers or protects like a hood; a folding cover over seats in a carriage, car *etc*; (*US*) the bonnet of a car.

'**hoodwink** *v* to deceive.

hoof *n* the horny part on the feet of certain animals (*eg* horses): – *pls* **hooves, hoofs**.

hook *n* a bent piece of metal *etc* for hanging things on (*eg* coats) or for catching things (*eg* fish). – *v* to catch, hold or drag with (anything like) a hook. – *adj* **hooked** curved like a hook; caught (by a hook); (*slang*) addicted to, fascinated by. – **by hook or by crook** by one means or another, whatever the cost.

'**hookah**, '**hooka** *n* a tobacco pipe through which smoke is drawn through water, used by Turks and Arabs.

'**hooligan** *n* a wild, unruly person. – *n* '**hooliganism** unruly behaviour.

hoop *n* a thin ring of wood or metal.

hoopoe ['hōōpōō] *n* a kind of bird with a large crest.

hooray *see* **hurrah**.

hoot *v* to sound a motor horn *etc*; (of an owl) to call, cry; (of persons) to make a similar sound, *esp* in laughter. – *n* the sound made by a motor horn, siren or owl; a shout of scorn *etc.* – *n* '**hooter** a device which makes a hooting sound (*eg* a motor horn).

'**Hoover**® *n* a kind of vacuum cleaner. – *v* '**hoover** to use a vacuum cleaner on (a floor *etc*).

hop *v* to leap on one leg: – *pt* **hopped**. – *n* a short jump on one leg; a climbing plant, the bitter fruits of which are used in brewing beer. – *n* '**hopper** a box or funnel for shaking down corn *etc* to the grinding (or other) machinery. – *n* '**hopscotch** a hopping game over lines drawn on the ground (scotches).

hope *n* a state of mind in which one

expects or wishes good to come; something desired. – v to expect or wish good to happen. – adjs '**hopeful**; '**hopeless** without hope; very bad.

horde [hörd] n a large crowd or group.

ho'rizon n the line which seems to be formed by the meeting of the earth and sky; the limit of what a person can see or understand. – adj **hori'zontal** lying level or flat.

horn n a hard growth on the heads of certain animals (eg oxen, sheep, deer); something made of horn or curved or sticking out like an animal's horn; part of a motor car which gives a warning sound; a kind of wind instrument, once made of horn, now of brass. – adjs **horned** having horns or something like horns; '**horny** hard like horn.

'**hornet** n a kind of large wasp.

'**hornpipe** n a lively sailor's dance.

'**horoscope** n the telling of a person's fortune by studying the position of the stars at his birth.

'**horror** n great fear, terror; something which causes fear; someone who causes great dislike (esp a child). – adjs '**horrible** causing horror; very unpleasant or bad; '**horrid** hateful; very unpleasant. – v '**horrify** to frighten greatly; to shock. I was horrified by the child's behaviour: – pt '**horrified**.

horse n a type of four-footed animal with hooves and a mane; a wooden frame for hanging clothes to dry; an apparatus for vaulting etc in a gymnasium. – ns '**horse-'chestnut** a type of tree or its brown, shiny nut; '**horsefly** a large fly which bites; **horse laugh** a loud, harsh laugh; '**horseplay** rough play, fooling around; '**horsepower** a unit of mechanical power used in giving power of cars etc (usu shortened to **h.p.**); '**horse-radish** a type of plant, the root of which has a sharp taste, used in sauces; '**horseshoe** a shoe for horses, made of a curved piece of iron; a horseshoe-shaped thing.

'**horticulture** n the study and art of gardening. – adj **horti'cultural** having to do with gardening. – n **horti-'culturist** one skilled in gardening.

hosanna [hə'zanə] n an exclamation of praise to God.

hose [hōz] n a covering for the legs or feet: – pl **hose**; a tubing of rubber etc for carrying water: – pl '**hoses**. – n **hosiery** ['hōziəri] knitted goods (such as tights).

hospice ['hospis] n a home which provides special nursing care for incurable invalids.

hos'pitable adj showing kindness to guests or strangers. – n **hospi'tality** a friendly welcome often including food, drink etc for guests or strangers.

'**hospital** n a building for the treatment of the ill and injured.

hōst n one who welcomes and entertains guests; an innkeeper or hotelkeeper: – fem '**hostess**; a very large number.

'**hostage** n a person held prisoner by an enemy or opponent to make sure that an agreement will be kept to or a condition fulfilled.

'**hostel** n a building providing rooms for students etc. – ns '**hostelry** an inn: – pl '**hostelries**; **hostler, ostler** ['oslər] (hist) the servant who looks after the horses at an inn.

'**hostile** adj of an enemy; not friendly; showing dislike or opposition (to). – n **hostility** [hos'tiləti] unfriendliness; opposition; the state of being an enemy; (pl) **hos'tilities** acts of warfare.

hot adj very warm; (of food) having much spice; passionate; radioactive; (slang) stolen; (slang) not safe: – comp '**hotter**, superl '**hottest**. – n '**hotbed** a place where there is much disease, wickedness etc: a hotbed of rebellion. – adj '**hot-'blooded** passionate, easily roused to anger etc. – n '**hot-'dog** a hot sausage in a roll. – adv '**hot-foot** in great haste. – adj '**hot-'headed** inclined to act rashly without thinking. – ns '**hothouse** a heated glasshouse for plants; **hot line** a direct telephone line between heads of government. – **in(to) hot water** in(to) trouble.

'**hotchpotch** n a confused mixture.

ho'tel n a building where travellers etc may stay for payment.

hound n a dog used in hunting. – v to hunt, pursue.

hour [owr] n sixty minutes, the 24th part of a day; a time or occasion: the hour of reckoning. – adj '**hourly** happening or done every hour. – Also adv. – n '**hour-glass** an instrument for measuring the hours by the running of sand from one glass into another.

house n a building in which people (often a single family) live; a family household; a business firm; a building where school boarders stay. – v **house** [howz] to provide a house for; to shelter. – n '**housing** accommodation eg houses, flats etc; a casing or covering for machines etc. – ns **houseboat** ['howsbōt] a river barge with a cabin for living in; '**housebreaker** a person who breaks into a house to steal;

'**household** the people who live together in a house; a family; '**householder** one who owns or pays the rent of a house; the chief person in a family; '**housekeeper** one paid to look after the running of a house; '**housewarming** a party held when someone moves into a new house; '**housewife** a woman who looks after a house and her husband and family. – **a household word** something which everyone is talking about.

'**hovel** *n* a small dirty dwelling.

'**hover** *v* (of birds *etc*) to remain in the air in the same spot; to stay near, linger (about); to be undecided or uncertain. – *n* '**hovercraft** a craft able to travel over land or sea supported on a cushion of air.

how [how] *adv* in what manner. *How is she dressed?*; to what extent. *How old are you?*; to a great extent. *How beautifully she sings*; by what means. *How do you do it?*; in what state of health, condition *etc. How are you?* – *adv* **how'ever** no matter how; in spite of that.

howdah ['howdə] *n* a seat fixed on an elephant's back.

howitzer ['howitsər] *n* a short cannon used to attack a besieged town or trench.

howl [howl] *v* to make a long, loud sound like that of a dog or wolf; to yell (as in pain, anger, joy). – Also *n*. – *n* '**howler** (*coll*) a very silly mistake.

hub *n* the centre part of a wheel through which the axle passes; the centre of much traffic, business *etc*.

'**hubbub** *n* a confused sound of many voices.

'**huddle** *v* to crowd together. – *n* a close group.

hue *n* colour. – **hue and cry** an alarm and general chase.

huff *n* a fit of bad temper and sulking. – *adj* '**huffy**.

hug *v* to hold tightly with the arms; to keep close to. *The ships hug the shore*: – *pt* **hugged**.

huge [hūj] *adj* of great size. – *n* '**hugeness**.

hula-hoop ['hōōləhōōp] *n* a light hoop for spinning round the waist.

hulk *n* an old ship unfit for use; anything big and clumsy. – *adj* '**hulking** big and clumsy.

hull *n* the body or framework of a ship.

hullaba'loo *n* noisy disturbance.

hullo *see* **hello.**

hum *v* to make a buzzing sound like that of bees; to sing with the lips shut; (of a place *etc*) to be noisily busy: – *pt* **hummed**. – *ns* **hum**, '**humming** the noise of bees; any buzzing, droning sound. – *n* '**humming-bird** a type of small brightly-coloured bird whose rapidly moving wings make a humming noise.

'**human** *adj* having to do with mankind as opposed to God or animals; (of persons) having the qualities, feelings *etc* natural to mankind. – *n* a man, woman or child. – *adj* **humane** [hū'mān] kind, showing mercy, gentle. – *ns* **humanism** ['hūmənizəm] a set of ideas about or interest in ethics and mankind, not including religious belief; '**humanist**. – *adj* **hu'mani'tārian** kind to one's fellowmen. – *n* **hu'manity** men and women in general; kindness, gentleness.

'**humble** *adj* modest, meek; not of high rank, unimportant. – *v* to make to feel low and unimportant. – **eat humble pie** to acknowledge openly that one has made a mistake.

'**humbug** *n* a fraud; nonsense; a kind of hard sweet.

'**humdrum** *adj* dull, not exciting.

'**humid** *adj* (of air, climate) moist, damp. – *n* **hu'midity** moisture; amount of wetness.

hū'mility *n* humble state of mind, meekness. – *v* **hu'miliate** to make to feel humble or ashamed, hurt someone's pride. – *adj* **hu'miliating**. – *n* **humili'ation** something which humiliates; shame.

humour, (*US*) **humor** ['hūmər] *n* the ability to see things as amusing or ridiculous (also **sense of humour**); funniness; the amusing side of anything; one's state of mind, temper, mood. – *v* to do as another wishes. – *n* '**humorist** one who can bring out the amusing side of things. – *adj* '**humorous** funny, causing laughter.

hump *n* a lump (*eg* on the back). – *n* '**humpback** a back with a hump; a person with a hump on his back. – *adj* '**humpbacked** having a hump on the back; (of a bridge *etc*) rising and falling so as to form a hump shape.

'**hūmus** *n* soil made of rotted leaves *etc*.

hunch *n* a hump; a suspicion that something is untrue or is going to happen *etc*: – *pl* '**hunches**. – *n* '**hunchback** humpback. – *adj* '**hunchbacked** humpbacked.

hundred ['hundrəd] *n* the number 100. – *adj* 100 in number. – *adj* '**hundredth** the last of a hundred (things *etc*). – *n* one of a hundred equal parts.

hundredweight ['hundrədwāt] *n* 112 lb, 50·8 kilogrammes (*usu* written **cwt**).

hunger ['huŋgər] *n* desire for food; a strong desire for anything. – *v* to go without food; to long (for). – *adj* '**hungry** wanting or needing food. – *n* '**hunger-strike** a refusal to eat (*eg* by prisoners) as a protest.

hunt *v* to chase animals or birds for food or for sport; to search (for). – *n* chasing wild animals; a search. – *n* '**hunter** one who hunts: – *fem* '**huntress**; a horse trained for hunting. – *n* '**huntsman** one who hunts.

'**hurdle** *n* a frame to be jumped over in a race; any difficulty which must be overcome.

'**hurdy'gurdy** *n* a musical instrument played by turning a handle, a hand-organ, a barrel organ.

hurl *v* to throw with force.

'**hurly'burly** *n* a great stir, uproar.

hur'rah, hur'ray, hoo'ray *interj* a shout of joy, approval *etc*.

'**hurricane** *n* a violent storm of wind blowing at a speed of over 75 miles (120 kilometres) per hour. – *n* **hurricane lamp** a lamp specially made to keep alight in strong wind.

'**hurry** *v* to act or move quickly; to make (someone) act *etc* quickly: – *pt* '**hurried**. – *n* eagerness to act or move quickly, haste. – *adj* '**hurried** done in a hurry.

hurt *v* to cause pain or distress; to wound; to damage. – *n* a wound; damage. – *adj* '**hurtful** causing pain, distress or damage.

'**hurtle** *v* to (cause to) move at great speed.

husband ['huzbənd] *n* a married man (the partner of a **wife**). – *v* to spend or use (*eg* one's money, strength) carefully. – *n* '**husbandry** farming; care with one's money, thrift.

hush *inter* be quiet! – *n* (*coll*) silence. – *v* to make quiet. – *adj* '**hush-'hush** (*coll*) top secret. – **hush up** to stop (a scandal *etc*) becoming public.

husk *n* the dry thin covering of certain fruits and seeds.

'**husky** *adj* (of the voice) hoarse, rough in sound; big and strong. – *n* a Canadian sledge dog: – *pl* '**huskies**.

hussar [hə'zär] *n* a light-armed horse soldier.

'**hussy** *n* a forward, cheeky girl: – *pl* '**hussies**.

'**hustings** *npl* speeches, campaigning *etc* which take place just before an election.

hustle ['husl] *v* to push rudely; to hurry. – Also *n*.

hut *n* a small wooden building; a simple dwelling place.

hutch *n* a box in which pet rabbits are housed: – *pl* '**hutches**.

'**hȳacinth** *n* a type of sweet-smelling flower which grows from a bulb.

hyaena *see* **hyena**.

'**hȳbrid** *n* something (*usu* an animal or plant) made or bred from two different kinds (*eg* a mule, which is a hybrid from a horse and an ass); a word formed of parts from different languages. – Also *adj*.

'**hȳdra** *n* (*myth*) a many-headed water serpent that grew two heads for each one cut off; a water creature that can divide and redivide itself.

'**hȳdrant** *n* a connection to which a hose can be attached to draw water off the main water supply.

hȳ'draulic *adj* carrying water; worked by water or other fluid.

hȳdrō- *prefix* water. – *n* '**hydro** (short for **hydro'pathic**) a type of hotel (originally with special swimming baths *etc* for health improvements); **hydroelec'tricity** electricity got from water-power. – *adj* **hydroe'lectric**.

'**hȳdrogen** *n* an element, the lightest gas, which with oxygen makes up water. – *n* **hydrogen bomb** an exceedingly powerful bomb using hydrogen.

hȳdro'phōbia *n* fear of water, a symptom of rabies; rabies.

hyena, hyaena [hī'ēnə] *n* a dog-like wild animal with a howl sounding like laughter.

hygiene ['hījēn] *n* (the study of) cleanliness as a means to health. – *adj* **hy'gienic**.

hymn [him] *n* a song of praise, *esp* one sung to God. – *ns* **hymnal** ['himnəl], '**hymnary** a book of hymns: – *pl* '**hymnaries**.

hȳper- *prefix* to a greater extent than usual, excessive as in **hyper'active**.

hyperbole [hī'pörbəli] *n* exaggeration. – *adj* **hyper'bolical**.

'**hȳpermarket** *n* a very large super-market.

'**hȳphen** *n* a short stroke (-) used to link or separate parts of a word or phrase: *sweet-and-sour*: *re-create*.

'**hypnotize** *v* to put a person into a sleep-like state in which he obeys suggestions. – *n* **hyp'nōsis** a hypnotized state; hypnotism. – *adj* **hypnotic** [hip'notik] of hypnosis or hypnotism; causing hypnosis or a sleep-like state. – *ns* '**hypnotism** the production of a hypnotized state; hypnosis; **'hypnotist**.

hȳpō- *prefix* below, under.

hypochondria [hipɔ'kondriə] *n* overanxiety about one's own health. – *n, adj* **hypo'chondriac**.

hypocrite ['hipɔkrit] *n* a person who pretends to be good but is not. – *n* **hy'pocrisy** false pretence of goodness. – *adj* **hypo'critical**.

hȳpo'dermic *n* a hypodermic syringe. – *n* **hypodermic syringe** an instrument with a fine, hollow needle (**hypodermic needle**) for giving an injection of a drug just below the skin.

hȳ'potenūse *n* the longest side of a right-angled triangle.

hȳ'pothesis *n* something taken as true (for the sake of argument): – *pl* **hy'pothesēs**. – *adj* **hypo'thetical** supposed.

hys'tēria *n* nervous excitement causing uncontrollable laughter, crying *etc*; a nervous illness. – *npl* **hysterics** [his'teriks] a fit of hysteria. – *adj* **hys'terical**.

I

I [i] *pron* the word used by a speaker or writer in mentioning himself (as the subject of a verb). *He and I went together.*

'ibex *n* a wild mountain goat: – *pl* **'ibexes**.

ice *n* frozen water; ice cream. – *v* to cover with icing; to freeze. – *n* **'icing** melted sugar, flavoured and allowed to set. – *adj* **'icy** covered with ice; very cold. – *adv* **'icily**. – *ns* **ice age** an age when the earth was mostly covered with ice; **'iceberg** a huge mass of floating ice; **'icebox** (*US*) refrigerator; **ice cream** a sweet creamy mixture, flavoured and frozen; **ice floe** a piece of floating ice; **ice hockey** hockey played with a rubber disc (**puck**) on an ice rink. – **dry ice** solid carbon dioxide.

ichthyology [ikthi'olɔji] *n* the study of fishes.

'icicle *n* a hanging, pointed piece of ice formed by the freezing of dropping water.

'icon, 'ikon *n* a painted or mosaic image (*eg* of Christ or of a saint).

i'conoclasm *n* the act of breaking images; the attacking of long established beliefs.

I'd [id] short for **I would, I should, I had**. *I'd sooner go than stay.*

idea [i'dēə] *n* a thought, notion; mental picture; plan.

ideal [i'dēəl] *adj* perfect; existing in imagination only (opposite of **real**). – *n* that which is highest and best; a standard of perfection. – *ns* **i'dealism; i'dealist** one who thinks that perfection can be reached. – *v* **i'dealize** to think of as perfect. – *n* **ideali'zation**. – *adv* **i'deally** in ideal circumstances. *Ideally all under-fives should attend a play group.*

i'dentifȳ *v* to (claim to) recognize, prove to be the same. *He identified the man as his attacker*; to think of as the same. *He identifies money with happiness*: – *pt* **i'dentified**. – *n* **identifi'cation**. – *adj* **i'dentical** the same in all details. – **identify (oneself) with** to feel close to or involved with.

i'dentikit picture *n* a rough picture of a wanted person which police put together from descriptions.

i'dentity *n* who or what a person or thing is; the state of being the same: – *pl* **i'dentities**.

idē'ology *n* a set of (usually political) ideas: – *pl* **ide'ologies**. – *adj* **ideo'logical**.

idiocy *see* **'idiot**.

'idiom *n* a common form of expression whose meaning cannot be guessed from the actual words. '*The boy turned up unexpectedly one day*'. – *adj* **idio'matic**.

idio'syncrasy *n* a personal oddness of behaviour: – *pl* **idio'syncrasies**. – *adj* **idiosyn'cratic**.

'idiot *n* a feeble-minded person; a fool. – *n* **'idiocy** feeble-mindedness, foolishness. – *adj* **idi'otic**.

'idle *adj* without work to do; lazy; meaningless: *idle chatter*. – *v* to spend (time) in doing nothing; (of an engine) to run without doing any work. – *ns* **'idler; 'idleness**. – *adv* **'idly**.

'idol *n* an image worshipped as a god; a person or thing loved or honoured too much. – *v* **'idolize** to love (too) greatly.

idyllic [i'dilik] *adj* very happy in a simple way.

if *conj* on condition that, supposing that. *If you go, he will go*; whether. *I don't know if he's going.*

'igloo *n* an Eskimo's snow hut.

igneous ['igniəs] *adj* having to do with fire; (of rock) formed by the action of great heat within the earth.

ig'nite *v* to set on fire; to catch fire. – *n* **ig'nition** the act of setting on fire or catching fire; the sparking part of a motor engine.

ig'nōble *adj* dishonourable; of low birth.

'ignominy *n* (public) disgrace. – *adj* **igno'minious** dishonourable, disgraceful.

igno'rāmus *n* an ignorant person.

ig'nore *v* to take no notice of. – *adj* **'ignorant** knowing very little; (with **of**) not knowing, not aware. – *n* **'ignorance**.

iguana [i'gwänə] *n* a type of tree lizard.

ikon *see* **icon**.

I'll [il] short for **I shall**, **I will**. *I'll be there soon.*

ill *adj* unwell; evil, bad; unlucky. – *adv* badly. •– *n* evil; (*pl*) misfortunes. – *n* **'illness** disease, sickness. – *adjs* **'ill-at-'ease** uncomfortable; **'ill-'gotten** (of profits *etc*) obtained in a wrongful way; **'ill-'humoured**, **'ill-'natured** bad-tempered; **'ill-'starred** unlucky. – *ns* **'ill-'will**, **'ill-'feeling** dislike, resentment. – *vs* **'ill-'treat**, **'ill-'use** to treat badly.

il'lēgal *adj* against the law. – *n* **ille'gality**: – *pl* **ille'galities**.

il'legible *adj* (almost) impossible to read, indistinct.

ille'gitimate *adj* born of parents not married to each other.

il'licit *adj* unlawful, forbidden.

il'literate *adj* not able to read or write. – *n* **il'literacy**.

il'logical *adj* not logical, not showing sound reasoning.

il'lūminate *v* to light up; to make (more) clear. – *adj* **il'luminated** (of a document *etc*) decorated with (coloured) lettering *etc*. – *n* **illumi'nation**; (*pl*) a decorative display of lights.

illusion [i'lōōzhən] *n* something which deceives the mind or eye; a mistaken belief. – *adjs* **il'lusive**; **il'lusory**.

'illustrate *v* to draw pictures for (a book *etc*); to explain, show (through examples, diagrams, slides *etc*). – *n* **illus-'tration** a picture in a book *etc*; an example which illustrates. – *adj* **'illustrative**. – *n* **'illustrator** one who illustrates.

il'lustrious *adj* famous, distinguished.

I'm [im] short for **I am**. *I'm older now.*

'image *n* a likeness made of someone or something; a striking likeness; a picture in the mind; public reputation. – *n* **'imagery** pictures suggested by words that help to make a piece of writing more vivid.

i'magine *v* to form a picture in the mind often of something that is not present or does not exist; to think, suppose. – *adj* **i'maginary** existing only in the imagination, not real. – *n* **i'magi'nation** the power of forming pictures in the mind (of things not present); the creative ability of an artist *etc*. – *adj* **i'maginative** having a lively imagination; done with imagination: *an imaginative piece of writing.*

imago *see* **pupa**.

imbecile ['imbəsēl] *n* a feeble-minded person; a fool. – *n* **imbecility** [imbə'siləti] feeble-mindedness, stupidity.

im'bibe *v* to drink (in).

im'būe *v* to fill the mind (with). *The general's actions imbued his troops with feelings of patriotism.*

'imitate *v* to try to be the same as, to copy. – *n* **imi'tation** a copy. – *adj* made to look like: *imitation leather.* – *n* **'imitator**.

im'maculate *adj* spotless; very clean and neat.

imma'tērial *adj* of little importance.

imma'tūre *adj* not mature.

im'mēdiate *adj* happening straight away: *immediate reaction*; close: *immediate family*; direct: *his immediate successor.* – *adv* **im'mediately** without delay. – *n* **im'mediacy**.

imme'morial *adj* going further back in time than can be remembered.

im'mense *adj* very large. – *n* **im'mensity**.

im'merse *v* to plunge into liquid. – *n* **im'mersion**. – *n* **immersion heater** an electric water-heating instrument (inside the hot water tank). – **immerse oneself in** to give one's whole attention to.

'immigrate *v* to come into a country and settle there. – *n* **immi'gration**. – *adj*, *n* **'immigrant** (of) one who immigrates.

'imminent *adj* about to happen: *imminent danger.*

im'mōbile *adj* without moving; not easily moved. – *n* **immo'bility**. – *v* **im'mobilize** put out of action.

immoderate [i'modərət] *adj* going beyond reasonable limits.

im'moral *adj* wrong, evil; indecent: *immoral suggestions.* – *n* **immo'rality**.

im'mortal *adj* living for ever; famous for ever. – *n* **immor'tality** unending life or fame. – *v* **im'mortalize** to make immortal or famous for ever.

immovable [i'mōōvəbl] *adj* not able to be moved or changed.

im'mūne *adj* not likely to catch (a disease) or be affected by: *immune to measles: immune to his charm.* – *n* **im'munity.** – *v* **'immunize** to make a person immune from (a disease) (*esp* by an injection of something to fight the disease).

imp *n* a mischievous child or fairy. – *adj* **'impish.**

'impact *n* the blow of one thing striking another; a collision; strong effect. *Her appearance made an impact on the audience.* – *v* **im'pact** to press firmly together.

im'pair *v* to damage, weaken. – *n* **im'pairment.**

im'pala *n* a large African antelope.

im'pale *v* to pierce through (with a spear *etc*).

im'part *v* to tell to others (what one knows).

im'partial *adj* not favouring one side more than another; just. – *n* **imparti-'ality.**

im'passable *adj* (of roads *etc*) not able to be passed.

impasse [am'päs] *n* a situation from which there seems to be no way out.

im'passioned *adj* moved by strong ·feeling.

im'passive *adj* not easily moved either by pleasure or pain.

inpatient [im'pāshənt] *adj* restlessly eager; short-tempered. – *n* **im'patience.**

im'peach *v* to accuse publicly (*esp* a high official) of misconduct. – *n* **im'peachment.**

im'peccable *adj* faultless. – *adv* **im-'peccably**: *impeccably dressed.*

impe'cūnious *adj* having no money.

im'pede *v* to hinder, keep back. – *n* **impediment** [im'pedimənt] a hindrance; a defect in a person's speech *eg* a stutter or stammer.

im'pel *v* to urge; to drive on: – *pt* **im'pelled.**

im'pending *adj* about to happen: *an impending storm.*

im'perative *adj* necessary, urgent; (*gram*) expressing command.

imper'ceptible *adj* so small as not to be noticed.

im'perfect *adj* having a fault or flaw, not perfect. – *n* **imper'fection** a fault or a flaw.

im'pērial *adj* of an emperor or empire. – *ns* **im'perialism** the policy of gaining the territory of, and ruling other people; **im'perialist.**

im'peril *v* to put in danger: – *pt* **im'perilled.**

im'pērious *adj* having an air of authority, haughty.

impermeable [im'pərmiəbl] *adj* not able to be passed through. *Clay is impermeable by water.*

im'personal *adj* not showing or influenced by personal feelings; not connected with any person.

im'personate *v* to dress up as, or act the part of, someone. – *ns* **imperso'nation; im'personator.**

im'pertinent *adj* cheeky, bad-mannered; not pertinent. – *n* **im'pertinence.**

imper'turbable *adj* not easily worried, calm.

im'pervious *adj* (with **to**) able to remain unaffected by. *He is impervious to hints.*

impe'tigo *n* a kind of skin disease.

im'petūous *adj* rushing into action, rash. – *n* **impetu'osity.**

'impetus *n* moving force. *The impetus of the blow sent him flying*; impulse.

im'piety *n* lack of respect for holy things. – *adj* **impious** ['impiəs] wicked.

im'pinge *v* (with **on, upon**) come in contact with; trespass (on) (*eg* another person's rights or privacy).

im'placable *adj* not able to be soothed or calmed.

im'plant *v* to fix in, plant firmly. – Also *n.*

'implement *n* a tool (*eg* a spade, a painter's brush). – *v* to carry out, to fulfil (*eg* a promise).

'implicate *v* to bring in, involve (a person). *The statements of other gang members implicate you in the crime.* – *n* **impli'cation** the act of implicating; something meant though not actually said.

im'plicit *adj* understood, meant though not actually said; unquestioning: *implicit obedience.*

im'plȳ *v* to suggest. *His silence implied disapproval*: – *pt* **im'plied.**

impo'lite *adj* not polite, rude.

im'port *v* to bring in (goods) from abroad (for sale). – *ns* **'import** act of importing; something imported; meaning; importance; **impor'tation** act of importing.

im'portant *adj* worth taking notice of; special. – *n* **im'portance.**

impor'tūne *v* to keep asking for something. – *adj* **im'portunate** repeatedly asking. – *n* **impor'tunity.**

im'pose *v* to place something (as a tax burden *etc*) on (someone or something); (with **on**) to take advantage (of a person), to deceive. – *adj* **im'posing** impressive, making much show. – *n* **impo'sition** a burden; an exercise given as a punishment.

im'possible *adj* not able to be done or to happen; (of a person *etc*) not able to be dealt with, intolerable. – *n* **impossi-'bility**.

im'postor *n* one who pretends to be someone else in order to deceive. – *n* **im'posture** (the act of) deceiving in this way.

'impotent *adj* without power, strength or effectiveness; (of males) without sexual power. – *n* **'impotence**.

im'pound *v* to take possession of (something) by law (*eg* furniture in payment of the rent).

impoverish [im'povərish] *v* to make (a person *etc*) poor; to make poor in quality. – *n* **im'poverishment**.

im'practicable *adj* not able to be done. – *n* **im'practica'bility**.

im'practical *adj* lacking common sense. – *n* **im'practi'cality**.

im'pregnable *adj* too strong to be taken by, or overthrown by, attack.

impre'sario *n* the organizer of a (musical) entertainment: – *pl* **impre-'sarios**.

im'press *v* to arouse (someone's) interest or admiration; to mark by pressing upon; to fix deeply in the mind. – *n* **im'pression** what a person thinks or feels about something. *The play left a lasting impression on me. My impression is that it's likely to rain*; a mark made by impressing; a quantity of copies of a book printed at one time. – *adj* **im'pressionable** easily influenced or affected. – *n* **im'pressionism** the attempt, in painting, writing, *etc* to reproduce the actual effect of something. – *adj* **im'pressive** having a great effect on the mind.

im'print *v* to print; to mark; to set a permanent mark on (the mind *etc*). – *n* **'imprint** that which is imprinted; the printer's name on a book.

imprison [im'prizn] *v* to shut up as in a prison. – *n* **im'prisonment**.

im'probable *adj* not likely to happen. – *n* **improba'bility**.

im'promptu *adj, adv* without preparation or rehearsal.

im'proper *adj* not suitable; wrong; indecent. – *n* **impro'priety** something improper: – *pl* **impro'prieties**. – *n* **improper fraction** a fraction greater than 1 (as $^5/_4$, $^{21}/_8$).

improve [im'proov] *v* to make or become better. – *n* **im'provement**.

im'provident *adj* taking no thought for future needs. – *n* **im'providence**.

'improvise *v* to put together, produce from available materials or on the spur of the moment: *improvised stretcher: an improvised tune*. – *n* **improvi'sation**.

'impudent *adj* cheeky, insolent. – *n* **'impudence**.

'impulse *n* sudden force such as a push; a sudden urge resulting in sudden action. – *adj* **im'pulsive** acting on impulse, without time to consider. – *n* **im'pulsiveness**.

im'punity *n* freedom from punishment, injury or loss.

im'pure *adj* mixed with other substances; not clean. – *n* **im'purity**: – *pl* **im'purities**.

im'pute *v* to think of (something blameworthy) as being caused, done *etc* (by someone). – *n* **impu'tation** suggestion of fault, blame.

in *prep* showing position in space or time: *in the garden: in the year 1921*; showing state, condition, manner *etc*: *in part: in a high voice*. – **be in for** to be trying to get; to be about to receive (something unpleasant).

in- *prefix* into, on, towards as in **in-shore**; not, as in **inaccurate**.

ina'bility *n* lack of power, means *etc* (to do something): – *pl* **ina'bilities**.

inaccessible [inak'sesəbl] *adj* not able to be (easily) reached, approached or obtained.

in'accurate *adj* not correct; not exact. – *n* **in'accuracy**: – *pl* **in'accuracies**.

in'active *adj* not active; not working, doing nothing. – *ns* **in'action** lack of action; **inac'tivity** idleness; rest.

in'adequate *adj* not enough; unable to cope (in an emergency *etc*).

inad'missible *adj* not allowable.

inad'vertent *adj* unintentional. – *adv* **inad'vertently**.

i'nane *adj* silly, foolish. – *n* **inanity** [i'nanəti].

in'animate *adj* without life.

in'applicable *adj* not applicable.

inap'propriate *adj* not suitable.

in'apt *adj* not apt; unfit or unqualified. – *ns* **in'aptitude**, **in'aptness** unfitness, awkwardness. – *adv* **in'aptly**.

inar'ticulate *adj* unable to express oneself (clearly); uttered indistinctly.

inasmuch [inəz'much]: **inasmuch as** *conj* because, since.

inat'tentive *adj* not paying attention. – *n* **inat'tention**.

in'audible *adj* not loud enough to be heard.

i'naug**ū**rate v to make a start on, usu with show or ceremony. – adj i'naugural. – n inaugu'ration.

inaus'picious adj unlucky, unlikely to end in success.

'in'bred adj natural; resulting from 'in-'breeding repeated mating within the family.

in'calc**ū**lable adj not able to be counted or estimated.

incandescent [inkan'desnt] adj white-hot.

incan'tation n (words sung or said as) a spell.

in'c**ā**pable adj unable (to do what is expected); helpless (through drink etc).

inca'pacitate v to take away power, strength or rights; to disable. – n inca'pacity inability; disability.

incarcerate [in'kärs**ə**rāt] v to imprison.

in'carnate adj having human form. – n incar'nation appearance in the form of a human body.

in'cendiary adj meant for setting (buildings etc) on fire: an incendiary bomb.

in'cense v to make angry. – n 'incense spices etc burned (esp in religious ceremonies) to give off a pleasant smell.

in'centive n that which encourages one to do something.

in'ception n beginning.

in'cessant adj going on without pause.

inch n one twelfth of a foot (about 2·5 centimetres): – pl 'inches. – v to move very gradually.

'incident n a happening. – n 'incidence how often or in what quantity a thing occurs; a falling (of a ray of light etc). – adj inci'dental happening in connection with something: an incidental expense; casual. – adv inci'dentally by the way.

incinerate [in'sin**ə**rāt] v to burn to ashes. – ns incine'ration; in'cinerator an apparatus for burning rubbish etc.

in'cipient adj beginning to exist: an incipient dislike.

in'cision n the act of cutting into something; a cut, a gash. – adj in'cisive (of words, manner etc) sharp, clear, firm. – ns in'cisiveness; in'cisor a front tooth.

in'cite v to move to action; to urge on. – n in'citement.

inci'vility n impoliteness: – pl inci'vilities.

in'clement adj (of weather) stormy. – n in'clemency.

in'cline v to lean or slope (towards); to

bend, bow; to (cause to) have a liking, tendency, (slight) desire for. – n 'in-cline a slope. – adj in'clined. – n inclination [inkl**ə**'nāsh**ə**n] liking, tendency; slope; bending.

include [in'kl**ōō**d] v to count in, along with others. – n in'clusion. – adj in'clusive including everything mentioned etc. From Tuesday to Thursday inclusive is 3 days.

incognito [inkog'nētō] adj, adv with one's identity concealed (by use of a disguise, false name etc). – n a disguise: – pl incog'nitos.

inco'herent adj (of a speech etc) not coherent, unconnected, rambling; (of a person) speaking in this way. – n inco'herence.

incom'bustible adj not able to be burned by fire.

income ['i**ŋ**k**ə**m] n a person's earnings; gain or profit.

incoming ['inkumi**ŋ**] adj approaching; new, next.

incom'mode v to cause bother or trouble to.

incommūni'cado adj, adv without means of communicating with others.

in'comparable adj without equal. – adv in'comparably.

incom'patible adj (of statements etc) contradicting each other; (of persons) bound to disagree. – n incompati-'bility.

in'competent adj not good enough at doing a job. – n in'competence.

incom'plete adj not finished.

incompre'hensible adj not able to be understood, puzzling. – n incom-prehension.

incon'ceivable adj not able to be imagined or believed.

inconclusive [i**ŋ**k**ə**n'kl**ōō**siv] adj not leading to a definite decision or conclusion.

incongruous [i**ŋ**'kongr**ōō**əs] adj not matching well; out of place, unsuitable. – n incon'gruity: – pl incon-'gruities.

inconse'quential adj unimportant.

inconsiderable [inkən'sid**ə**rəbl] adj slight, unimportant.

inconsiderate [inkən'sid**ə**rət] adj not thinking of others.

incon'sistent adj not consistent, contradicting.

incon'sōlable adj not able to be comforted.

incon'spicuous adj not noticeable.

in'constant adj often changing. – n in'constancy.

in'continent adj unable to control one's

bladder and bowels; uncontrolled.

incon'venient *adj* causing awkwardness or difficulty. – *n* **incon'venience**. – *v* to cause inconvenience, trouble to.

incontro'vertible *adj* not to be doubted.

in'corporate *v* to contain as part of a whole. *The new sports complex will incorporate a gymnasium, swimming pool etc*; to include within a group *etc*. – *adj* **in'corporated** (shortened to **inc**) formed into a company or society.

incor'rect *adj* wrong.

in'corrigible *adj* too bad to be put right or reformed.

incor'ruptible *adj* not able to be bribed; that can never decay.

in'crease *v* to grow, to make greater or more numerous. – *n* **'increase** growth; the amount added by growth. – *adv* **in'creasingly** more and more.

in'credible *adj* impossible to believe. – *adv* **in'credibly**. – *n* **incredi'bility**.

in'credulous *adj* not believing (what is said). – *n* **incre'dulity**.

'increment *n* an increase, *esp* one added annually to a salary.

in'criminate *v* to show that a person has taken part in a crime or misdeed.

'incubātor *n* a large heated box for hatching eggs or one for rearing premature babies. – *v* **'incubate**. – *n* **incubation period** the time (between being infected and the appearance of the symptoms) that it takes for a disease to develop.

'inculcate *v* to impress something on (a person's mind) by much repeating.

in'cumbent *adj* resting on (someone) as a duty. *It is incumbent upon me to warn you*. – *n* one who holds an office, *esp* in the church.

in'cur *v* to bring something (as blame, debt *etc*) upon oneself: – *pt* **in'curred**.

in'curable *adj* unable to be cured.

in'cursion *n* an invasion, raid.

indebted [in'detid] *adj* having cause to be grateful (to someone for something received). – *n* **in'debtedness**.

in'dēcent *adj* offending (often in a sexual sense) against normal or usual standards of behaviour. – *n* **in'decency**.

inde'cision *n* slowness in making up one's mind, hesitation. – *adj* **inde'cisive** not coming to a definite result; unable to make up one's mind.

in'deed *adv* in fact; (used for emphasis) really. – *interj* expressing surprise *etc*.

inde'fatigable *adj* untiring.

inde'fensible *adj* unable to be defended; (of behaviour *etc*) inexcusable.

inde'finable *adj* not able to be stated or described clearly.

in'definite *adj* not fixed, uncertain; without definite limits. – *adv* **in'definitely** for an indefinite period of time. – *n* **indefinite article** the name given to the adjectives *a, an*.

in'delible *adj* unable to be rubbed out or removed.

in'delicate *adj* impolite, rude. – *n* **in'delicacy**.

in'demnity *n* money paid to make up for (possible) damage or loss.

in'dent *v* to begin a new paragraph by going in from the margin; (with **for**) to apply for (stores, equipment *etc*). – *ns* **inden'tation** a hollow, dent; a notch or inward curve in an outline, coastline *etc*; **in'denture** a written agreement or contract.

inde'pendent *adj* free to think or act for oneself; not relying on someone (or something) else for support, guidance *etc*. – *n* **inde'pendence**.

indes'cribable *adj* not able to be described.

indes'tructible *adj* not able to be destroyed.

inde'terminate *adj* not fixed, indefinite.

'index *n* an alphabetical list giving the page number of subjects dealt with in a book; an indication: – *pl* **'indexes**; (in mathematics) an upper number which shows how many times a number is multiplied by itself (*eg* 4^3 means $4 \times 4 \times 4$): – *pl* **'indicēs**.

'Indian: *ns* **Indian corn** maize; **Indian ink** a very black ink used by artists; **Indian summer** a period of summer warmth in autumn.

'india'rubber *n* rubber, *esp* a piece for rubbing out pencil *etc*.

'indicate *v* to point out, show. – *n* **indi'cation** a sign. – *adj* **in'dicative** pointing out, being a sign of: *indicative of his attitude*. – *n* **'indicator** that which indicates; a pointer; a name given to many instruments *etc* that give information (*esp* by means of a pointer or the like, as the left and right flashing lights on a vehicle).

indict [in'dīt] *v* to accuse of a crime *esp* formally or in writing. – *n* **in'dictment**.

in'different *adj* neither very good nor very bad; (with **to**) showing no interest in. – *n* **in'difference**.

indigenous [in'dijinəs] *adj* native to a country or area.

'indigent *adj* living in want, poor. – *n* **'indigence**.

indi'gestion *n* discomfort or pain experienced in digesting food. – *adj* **indi'gestible** difficult to digest.

in'dignant *adj* angry (*usu* because of wrong done to oneself or others). – *ns* **indig'nation; in'dignity** loss of dignity; insult: – *pl* **in'dignities**.

'indigo *adj, n* (of) a purplish-blue colour.

indi'rect *adj* not straight or direct; not affecting or affected directly. – *ns* **indirect speech** speech reported not in the speaker's actual words; **indirect tax** a tax on particular goods, paid by the customer in the form of a higher price.

indis'creet *adj* rash, not cautious; giving away too much information. – *n* **indis-cretion** [indis'kreshən] a rash or unwise saying or act.

indis'criminate *adj* making no (careful) distinction between one thing (or person) and another: *indiscriminate killing*: *indiscriminate buying*.

indis'pensable *adj* not able to be done without, necessary.

indis'posed *adj* unwell. – *n* **indispo'sition**.

indis'pūtable *adj* not able to be denied.

indis'tinct *adj* not clear.

indis'tinguishable *adj* difficult to make out; too alike to tell apart.

indi'vidūal *adj* of a person or thing (out of a group) taken singly; distinctive; unusual. – *n* a single person, animal or thing. – *ns* **indi'vidualist** one who believes in independent actions *etc*; **individu'ality** separate existence; quality of standing out from others.

indivisible [indi'vizəbl] *adj* not able to be divided.

in'doctrinate *v* to fill with a certain teaching or set of ideas.

'indolent *adj* lazy. – *n* **'indolence**.

in'domitable *adj* unconquerable, unyielding.

indoor ['indör] *adj* done *etc* inside a building. – *edv* **'in'doors** in or into a building *etc*.

in'dūbitable *adj* not to be doubted. – *adv* **in'dubitably**.

in'dūce *v* to persuade; to bring on, cause. – *n* **in'ducement** something which encourages or persuades. *Money is an inducement to work*.

in'duction *n* the formal installing (of someone, *esp* a clergyman) in a new post; the production of electricity in something by placing it near something else containing electricity; the process of drawing a conclusion from particular cases. – *adj* **in'ductive**.

in'dulge *v* to be in the habit of giving in to the wishes of (someone). *She indulges that child too much*; to give way to, not to restrain. *He indulged in grief in*

private. – *n* **in'dulgence** the act of indulging; a pardon for a sin. – *adj* **in'dulgent** not strict, kind.

'industry *n* (any branch of) trade or manufacture: *steel industry*: *clothing industry*; steady attention to work: – *pl* **'industries**. – *adj* **in'dustrial**. – *n* **in'dustrialist** someone involved in organizing an industry. – *adj* **in'dustrious** hard-working.

i'nēbriated *adj* drunk.

in'edible *adj* not eatable.

in'effable *adj* not able to be described.

inef'fective *adj* useless, having no effect. – *n* **inef'fectiveness**.

ineffectual [ini'fekchōoəl] *adj* achieving nothing.

inefficient [ini'fishənt] *adj* not efficient, not capable; wasting time, energy *etc*. – *n* **inef'ficiency**: – *pl* **inef'ficiencies**.

inelegant [in'eligənt] *adj* not graceful. – *n* **in'elegance**.

in'eligible *adj* not qualified, not suitable (to be chosen).

i'nept *adj* clumsy; foolish. – *n* **i'neptitūde**.

inequality [ini'kwoləti] *n* lack of equality, unfairness; unevenness: – *pl* **ine'qualities**.

i'nert *adj* without the power of moving; disinclined to move or act; not lively; chemically inactive. – *ns* **i'nertness; inertia** [i'nərshiə].

ines'cāpable *adj* unable to be avoided.

in'estimable *adj* too good *etc* to be estimated.

in'evitable *adj* not able to be avoided. – *n* **inevita'bility**. – *adv* **in'evitably**.

inex'cūsable *adj* not to be excused.

inexhaustible [inig'zöstəbl] *adj* very plentiful; not likely to become used up.

in'exorable *adj* not able to be persuaded or moved by pleading, relentless.

inex'pensive *adj* cheap in price.

inex'pērience *n* lack of (skilled) knowledge or experience. – *adj* **inex'perienced**.

inex'plicable *adj* not able to be explained.

inex'pressible *adj* not able to be told or described in words.

inex'tricable *adj* not able to be disentangled. – *adv* **inex'tricably**.

in'fallible *adj* never making an error; certain to produce the desired result expected: *an infallible remedy*. – *n* **infalli'bility**.

'infamous *adj* having a very bad reputation; disgraceful. – *n* **'infamy** (public) disgrace.

'infant *n* a baby. – *n* **'infancy** the state or time of being an infant; the beginning of anything. *Civilization was still in its infancy.* – *n* in'**fanticide** the murder of a child; one who murders a child. – *adj* '**infantile** of babies; childish.

'**infantry** *n* foot-soldiers.

in'**fatuated** *adj* filled with foolish love. – *n* infatu'**ation**.

in'**fect** *v* to fill with disease-causing germs; to pass on disease to; to pass on, spread (*eg* enthusiasm). – *n* in'**fection** the means (*usu* germs) by which disease is spread; a disease; anything that spreads widely and affects many people. – *adj* in'**fectious** likely to spread from person to person.

in'**fer** *v* to reach a conclusion (from facts or reasoning); to hint: – *pt* in'**ferred**. – *n* '**inference**.

in'**ferior** *adj* lower in any way; not of best quality. – *n* one lower in rank *etc*. – *n* inferi'**ority**. – *n* inferiority complex a constant feeling that one is less good in some way than others.

in'**fernal** *adj* of hell; (*coll*) annoying. – *n* in'**ferno** hell; any place of horror or fire.

in'**fertile** *adj* (of soil *etc*) not producing much; (of persons or animals) not able to bear young. – *n* infer'**tility**.

in'**fest** *v* to swarm over. *The dog is infested with lice.*

'**infidel** *adj* one who does not believe in religion (*esp* Christianity). – *n* infi'**delity** unfaithfulness, disloyalty.

'**in-fighting** *n* rivalry or quarrelling between members of the same group.

'**infiltrate** *v* to pass into in small amounts. *Enemy soldiers infiltrated our lines.* – *n* infil'**tration**.

infinite ['infinit] *adj* without end or limit. – *adj* infini'**tesimal** very small. – *ns* in'**finitive** part of the verb that expresses the action but has no subject (*eg* I hate *to lose*); in'**finity** space or time stretching so far as to be beyond our power of thinking.

in'**firm** *adj* feeble, weak. – *ns* in'**firmary** a name given to some hospitals: – *pl* in'**firmaries**; in'**firmity** a weakness of the body or of the character: – *pl* in'**firmities**.

in'**flame** *v* to make hot or red; to cause violent feelings *esp* anger. – *adjs* in'**flamed**; **inflammable** [in'flaməbl] easily set on fire; easily excited. – *n* **inflammation** [inflə'māshən] heat in a part of the body, with pain, redness and swelling. – *adj* in'**flammatory** rousing to anger or excitement.

in'**flate** *v* to blow up (a balloon, tyre *etc*); to puff up (with pride), exaggerate. *She has an inflated sense of her own impor-*

tance; to increase to a great extent. – *n* in'**flation** the act of inflating; the state of a country's economy in which prices and wages keep forcing each other to increase.

in'**flexible** *adj* not yielding, unbending.

in'**flexion**, in'**flection** *n* a change of tone in the voice.

in'**flict** *v* to bring down (something unpleasant *eg* blows, punishment) on. – *n* in'**fliction**.

influence ['inflooəns] *n* the power to affect other persons or things. – *v* to have power over. – *adj* influ'**ential**.

influenza [infloo'enzə] *n* an infectious illness with fever, headache, a cold *etc*.

'**influx** *n* a flowing in; (of people *etc*) a coming in in large numbers.

in'**form** *v* to give knowledge to; (with **on**) to tell (something) against (someone), betray. – *ns* in'**formant** one who informs; infor'**mation** knowledge, news. – *adj* in'**formative** giving information. – *n* in'**former** one who gives information (to the police, authorities *etc*).

in'**formal** *adj* not formal; relaxed, friendly. – *n* infor'**mality**.

infra- *prefix* below, beneath.

'**infra-red** *adj* of rays of heat with wavelengths longer than visible light.

in'**fringe** *v* to break (a rule or law). – *n* in'**fringement**.

in'**furiate** *v* to drive into a rage.

in'**fuse** *v* to pour upon or over; to fill the mind (with a desire *etc*). – *n* in'**fusion** the act of infusing; liquid (such as tea) formed by pouring water on something.

ingenious [in'jēniəs] *adj* skilful in inventing; cleverly thought out. – *n* **ingenuity** [injə'nūəti] cleverness; quickness of ideas.

ingenuous [in'jenūəs] *adj* open, frank; without cunning. – *n* in'**genuousness**.

'**inglenook** *n* a fireside corner.

ingot ['iŋgət] *n* a lump (*usu* cast in oblong shape) of unworked metal, *esp* of gold or silver.

'**in grained** *adj* deeply fixed: *ingrained laziness*.

ingratiate [in'grāshiāt] *v* to get oneself into the favour of someone. – *adj* in'**gratiating**.

in'**gratitude** *n* lack of gratitude or thankfulness.

in'**gredient** *n* one of the things of which a mixture is made.

in'**habit** *v* to live in. – *n* in'**habitant** someone who lives permanently in a place.

in'**hale** *v* to breathe in. – *ns* in'**halant** a

medicine which is inhaled; **inhalation** [in(h)ə'lāshən] the act of inhaling; a medicine which is inhaled.

in'**hērent** adj inborn, belonging naturally.

in'**herit** v to receive property etc as an heir; to possess the qualities of one's parents etc. She inherits her quick temper from her mother. – ns in'**heritance** that which one gets (by will) when a relative dies; in'**heritor** an heir.

in'**hibit** v to hold back, prevent. – adj in'**hibited** unable to let oneself go. – n inhi'**bition** a holding back (of natural impulses etc), restraint.

inhos'**pitable** adj unwelcoming, unfriendly.

in'**hūman** adj not human; brutal. – n inhu'**manity**.

inhū'**mane** adj cruel.

i'**nimical** adj unfriendly, hostile.

i'**nimitable** adj impossible to imitate.

i'**niquity** n wickedness; a sin: – pl i'**niquities**. – adj i'**niquitous** unjust; wicked.

initial [i'nishəl] adj of or at a beginning. There were initial problems in running the new school. – n the letter beginning a word esp a name. – v to put the initials of one's name to: – pt i'**nitialled**.

initiate [i'nishiāt] v to begin, start. It was he who initiated the reforms; to give first lessons to; to admit (esp with secret ceremonies) to a society etc. – ns initi'**ation**; i'**nitiative** (the right to take) the first step; readiness to take a lead.

in'**ject** v to force (a fluid etc) into the veins or muscles by means of a needle and syringe; to put (eg enthusiasm) into. – n in'**jection**.

injudicious [injōo'dishəs] adj unwise.

in'**junction** n an order or command.

injure ['injər] v to harm, damage; to wrong. – adj '**injured** hurt; offended. – n '**injury** hurt, damage, harm; a wrong: – pl '**injuries**.

in'**justice** n unfairness; a wrong.

ink n a coloured (often dark blue or black) liquid used in writing, printing etc. – v to mark with ink. – adj '**inky** of or covered in ink; very dark.

'**inkling** n a hint or slight sign.

inlaid see inlay.

'**inland** adj not beside the sea; carried on etc inside a country (as **inland revenue** taxes etc collected within the country). – adv in'**land** toward the inner part of a country.

'**inlay** n a kind of decoration done by fitting pieces of different shapes and colours into a background. – v to do

this kind of work. – adj '**inlaid**.

'**inlet** n a small bay.

'**inmate** n a resident or occupant (esp of an institution): the inmates of the mental hospital.

'**inmost** adj the most inward, the farthest in.

inn n a house for the lodging of travellers, a small country hotel. – n '**innkeeper** one who keeps an inn.

in'**nate** adj inborn, natural.

'**inner** adj farther in; (of feelings etc) hidden. – adj '**innermost** farthest in; most secret.

'**innings** n a team's turn for batting in cricket; a turn or a go (at something).

'**innocent** adj not guilty, blameless; harmless; (with of) lacking, without: innocent of make-up. – n '**innocence**.

in'**nocuous** adj not harmful.

inno'**vation** n something new.

innū'**endo** n (a remark containing) a disagreeable hint: – pl innu'**endoes**.

in'**nūmerable** adj too many to be counted.

in'**nūmerate** adj having no understanding of arithmetic or mathematics. – n in'**numeracy**.

i'**noculate** v to give (a person etc) a mild form of a disease (by injecting germs in his blood) so that he may not easily catch it. – n i'**nocu'lation**.

inof'**fensive** adj harmless, giving no offence.

in'**opportūne** adj at a bad or inconvenient time.

i'**nordinate** adj going beyond the limit, unreasonably great.

inor'**ganic** adj not having the characteristics of living bodies.

in-patient ['inpāshənt] n a patient who lives in, as well as being treated in a hospital.

input ['inpŏot] n an amount (of energy, labour etc) that is put into something; information fed into a computer.

inquest n a legal inquiry into a case of sudden death.

in'**quire**, en'**quire** v to ask. – adj in'**quiring**, en'**quiring** questioning; eager to find out. – ns in'**quirer**, en'**quirer**; in'**quiry**, en'**quiry** a question; a search for information; an investigation: – pl in'**quiries**, en'**quiries**.

inqui'**sition** n a careful questioning or investigation. – n in'**quisitor** an official investigator.

in'**quisitive** adj eager to find out; fond of prying into the affairs of others.

'**inroad** n a raid, an advance (into). – **make inroads into** to use up large amounts of. *While unemployed he made inroads into his savings.*

in'sane *adj* mad, not sane. – *n* **insanity** [in'sanəti].

in'sanitary *adj* not sanitary, likely to help the spread of disease.

insatiable [in'sāshiəbl] *adj* not able to be satisfied.

in'scribe *v* to write or engrave on (*eg* a name on the first page of a book, or on a monument). – *n* **in'scription** the writing on a book, monument *etc*.

inscrutable [in'skrōōtəbl] *adj* not able to be searched into and understood, mysterious.

'insect *n* any small six-legged creature with wings and a body divided into sections. – *n* **in'secticide** powder or liquid for killing insects. – *adj* **insec-'tivorous** (of plants and animals) feeding on insects.

inse'cūre *adj* not safe; not firm; not feeling secure or settled. – *n* **inse-'curity**.

in'sensible *adj* unconscious, unaware (of); not having feeling.

in'sensitive *adj* (with **to**) not feeling: *insensitive to cold*; unsympathetic (to): *insensitive to her grief*; unappreciative of (*eg* beauty).

in'separable *adj* not able to be separated or kept apart.

in'sert *v* to put in or among. – *ns* **'insert; in'sertion** the act of putting in; something put in.

'inset *n* something set in (*eg* a small picture, map *etc* in a corner of a larger one).

'in'shore *adj* (of fishing *etc*) carried on near the shore. – *adv* to or near the shore.

'in'side *n* the side, space or part within; indoors. – *adj* being on or in the inside; indoor; coming from or done by someone within an organization *etc*: *inside information*. – *adv* to, in or on the inside. – *prep* to the inside of; within.

in'sidious *adj* likely to trap those who are not careful, treacherous; (of a disease *etc*) coming on gradually and unnoticed.

insight ['insīt] *n* power of looking into a matter and understanding clearly.

in'signia *npl* signs or badges showing that one holds an office, award *etc*.

insig'nificant *adj* of little importance. – *n* **insig'nificance**.

insin'cere *adj* not sincere. – *n* **insincerity** [insin'serəti].

in'sinūate *v* to hint (at a fault); to put in (something) gradually (and secretly); to work oneself into (favour). – *n*

insinu'ation a sly hint.

in'sipid *adj* dull, without liveliness; tasteless.

in'sist *v* to urge something strongly: *insist on punctuality*; to refuse to give way, to hold firmly to one's intentions *etc*. *He insists on walking there*; to go on saying (that). *He insists that he saw a ghost.* – *adj* **in'sistent** holding fast to what one claims; compelling attention. – *n* **in'sistence**.

'insolent *adj* rude, impertinent, insulting. – *n* **'insolence**.

in'solūble *adj* not able to be dissolved; (of a problem *etc*) not able to be solved.

in'solvent *adj* not able to pay one's debts. – *n* **in'solvency**.

in'somnia *n* sleeplessness. – *adj*, *n* **in'somniac** (of) one who suffers from insomnia.

in'spect *v* to look carefully into, to examine; to look over (troops *etc*) ceremonially. – *ns* **in'spection** careful examination; **in'spector** an official who inspects; a police officer below a superintendent and above a sergeant in rank.

in'spire *v* to encourage, rouse; to be the source of (poetic) ideas; to breathe in. – *n* **inspiration** [inspə'rāshən] something or someone that influences or encourages; a very good idea; breathing in. – *adj* **in'spired** [in'spird] seeming to be aided by higher powers; brilliantly good.

insta'bility *n* lack of steadiness or stability (*esp* in the personality).

install, instal [in'stöl] *v* to place in position, or put in ready for use (as electricity into a house); to introduce formally to a new job *etc* : – *pt* **in'stalled**. – *n* **instal'lation** the act of installing; something installed.

instalment [in'stölmənt] *n* a part of a sum of money paid at fixed times until the whole amount is paid; one part of a serial story.

'instance *n* an example, a particular case. – *v* to mention as an example. – **at the instance of** at the request of.

'instant *adj* immediate, urgent; able to be prepared *etc* almost immediately: *instant coffee*. – *n* a very short time, a moment; a point or moment of time. – *adj* **instan'tāneous** done, happening very quickly. – *adv* **'instantly** immediately.

instead [in'sted] *adv* in place of someone or something. *He will go instead.* – **instead of** in place of. *Walk instead of running.*

'instep *n* the arching, upper part of the

foot.

'instigate v to stir up, encourage. – n **insti'gation**.

in'stil v to put in little by little (esp ideas into the mind): – pt **in'stilled**.

'instinct n a natural feeling or knowledge, which living things seem to have without thinking and without being taught. – adj **in'stinctive** due to instinct.

'institute v to set up, establish, start. – n a society, organization etc or the building it uses. – n **insti'tution** a society, organization, building etc established for a particular purpose (esp care or education); an established custom. – adj **insti'tutional**.

in'struct v to teach; to direct or command. – n **in'struction** teaching; a command; (pl) rules showing how something is to be used. – adj **in'structive** containing or giving information or knowledge. – n **in'structor**.

'instrument n a thing used in doing something, a tool; something for producing musical sounds (such as a piano, trumpet). – adj **instru'mental** helpful in bringing (something) about; belonging to or produced by musical instruments. – n **instru'mentalist** one who plays on a musical instrument.

insu'bordinate adj rebellious, disobedient. – n **insubordi'nation**.

in'sufferable adj not able to be endured.

insuf'ficient adj not enough. – n **insuf'ficiency**.

'insular adj of an island or islands; (of opinions) narrow, prejudiced.

'insulate v to cover (something) with a material that will not let through electrical currents, or heat, or sound; to cut off, isolate. – n **insu'lation**.

'insulin n a substance used in the treatment of diabetes.

in'sult v to treat with scorn or rudeness. – n **'insult**. – adj **in'sulting** scornful, rude.

in'superable adj that cannot be overcome.

insure [in'shoor] v to arrange for payment of a sum of money on (something) if it should be lost, damaged, stolen etc. – n **in'surance**.

in'surgent adj rising up in rebellion. – n a rebel.

insur'mountable adj not able to be got over.

insur'rection n a rising up in rebellion.

in'tact adj whole, unbroken.

'intake n a thing or quantity taken in.

in'tangible adj not able to be felt by touch; difficult to define or describe, not clear.

integer ['intijər] n a whole number, not a fraction. – adj **integral** ['intigrəl] of or essential to a whole: an integral part of the machine; made up of parts forming a whole. – v **'integrate** to fit parts together to form a whole; to enable (racial) groups to mix freely with each other and live on equal terms. – ns **inte'gration; in'tegrity** honesty; state of being whole.

'intellect n the thinking power of the mind. – adj **intel'lectual** showing or requiring intellect. – n a person of natural ability or with academic interests.

in'telligent adj clever, quick at understanding. – n **in'telligence** mental ability; information sent, news. – adj **in'telligible** able to be understood.

in'temperate adj going beyond reasonable limits, uncontrolled; having the habit of drinking too much. – n **in'temperance**.

in'tend v to mean or plan to (do something). – n **in'tent** purpose. – adj with all one's mind (on), attentive; determined (on). – n **in'tention** what one means to do; meaning. – adj **in'tentional** done on purpose. – adv **in'tentionally**.

in'tense adj very great; (of a person) over-serious, inclined to feel strongly. – n **in'tensity**. – v **in'tensify** to increase: – pt **in'tensified**. – adj **in'tensive** very thorough, concentrated.

inter- prefix between, among, together as in **intertwine**.

in'ter v to bury: – pt **in'terred**. – n **in'terment**.

inter'act v to act on one another.

inter'cede v to act as peacemaker between two persons, nations etc. – ns **inter'cession; inter'cessor**.

inter'cept v to stop or seize on the way; to cut off, interrupt (a view, the light etc).

inter'change v to put each in the place of the other; to (cause to) alternate. – n **'interchange** the act of interchanging; a junction of two or more major roads on separate levels to allow cars etc to transfer from one to another without lines of traffic crossing each other. – adj **inter'changeable** able to be used one for the other.

'intercom n a telephone system within a building, aeroplane etc.

intercourse ['intərkörs] n communication; dealings between people etc; sexual intercourse.

'interdict n an order forbidding something.

'interest *n* special attention, curiosity; a thing with which one concerns oneself; advantage, benefit; a sum paid for the loan of money. – *v* to catch or hold the attention of. – *adjs* **'interested** having or taking an interest; **'interesting** holding the attention.

inter'fere *v* (with **in**) to take part in what is not one's business, meddle; (with **with**) to get in the way of, hinder: *interfere with the progress of the plan.* – *n* **inter'ference** the act of interfering; the spoiling of radio or television reception by another station or local disturbance (lightning, traffic *etc*).

'interim *n* time between; the meantime. – *adj* temporary.

in'tērior *adj* inner; inside a building; inland. – *n* the inside of anything; the inland part of a country.

inter'ject *v* to throw a remark in (to a conversation); to exclaim. – *n* **inter'jection** word or words of exclamation (*eg* Ah! Oh dear!).

inter'lock *v* to lock or clasp together; to fit into each other.

'interlōper *n* one who goes in where he has no right, an intruder. – *v* **inter'lope**.

interlude [′intərlōōd] *n* an interval, or what happens in it; a short piece of music played between the parts of a play, film *etc*.

'inter'marry *v* (of a race or group) to marry with members of another race *etc*; to marry with members of the same group, race *etc*.

inter'mēdiary *n* one who acts between two persons (*eg* in trying to settle a quarrel): – *pl* **inter'mediaries**.

inter'mēdiate *adj* in the middle; coming between.

interment *see* **inter**.

in'terminable *adj* never ending, boringly long.

inter'mission *n* an interval, a pause.

inter'mittent *adj* ceasing every now and then and starting again.

in'tern *v* to keep someone from the enemy side prisoner in a country while a war is going on. – *ns* **inter'nee** someone who is confined in this way; **in'ternment**.

in'ternal *adj* of the inner part *esp* of the body; inside, within (a country, organization *etc*).

inter'national *adj* happening between nations; world-wide. – *n* a match between teams of two countries.

inter'nēcine *adj* (of feuds *etc*) within a group) causing deaths on both sides.

interplanetary [intər′planətəri] *adj* between the planets.

'interplay *n* the action of one thing on another.

inter'pose *v* to place or come between, to put in (a remark *etc*) by way of interruption.

in'terpret *v* to explain the meaning of something; to translate; to bring out the meaning of something (as music, a part in a play *etc*) in one's performance; to take the meaning of something to be. – *ns* **in'terpre'tation; in'terpreter** one who translates (on the spot) the words of a speaker into the language of his hearers.

inter'regnum *n* the time between the end of one reign and the beginning of the next.

in'terrogate *v* to examine by asking questions, to question. – *ns* **in'terro'gation; inter'rogative** a word used in asking a question (*eg* Why? Who?). – *adj* questioning. – *n* **in'terrogator**.

inter'rupt *v* to stop (a person) while he is saying or doing something; to stop (something that one is doing); to get in the way of, cut off (a view *etc*). – *n* **inter'ruption**.

inter'sect *v* (of lines *etc*) to meet and cross. – *n* **inter'section** the point where two lines cross; a crossroads.

inter'sperse *v* to scatter here and there in. – *n* **inter'spersion**.

interstice [in′tərstis] *n* a small space between things placed close together, a chink.

inter'twine *v* to twine or twist together.

'interval *n* a time or space between; a short pause in a programme *etc*.

inter'vene *v* to come or be between, or in the way; to join in (in order to stop) a fight or quarrel between other persons or nations. – *n* **intervention** [intər′venshən].

interview [′intərvū] *n* a formal meeting of one person with one or more others for purposes of business (*eg* an appointment to a job) or of broadcasting information. – Also *v*.

in'testate *adj* without having made a will. *He died intestate.*

intestines [in′testinz] *npl* the inside parts of the body, *usu* the bowels and passages leading to them. – *adj* **in'testinal**.

'intimate *adj* knowing much about, familiar (with); (of friends) close; private, personal. – *n* a close friend. – *v* to hint; to announce. – *ns* **'intimacy** close friendship; familiarity; **inti'mation** a hint; an announcement.

in'timidate *v* to frighten (*esp* by threatening violence). – *adj* **in'timidating**. – *n* **intimi'dation**.

into ['intoo] *prep* to the inside: *into the room*; to a different state. *A tadpole changes into a frog;* (*maths*) expressing the idea of division. *2 into 4 goes twice.*

intolerable [in'tolərəbl] *adj* not able to be endured. – *adj* **in'tolerant** not willing to put up with (people of different ideas, race, religion *etc*). – *n* **in'tolerance**.

in'tone *v* to speak in a singing manner, to chant. – *n* **into'nation** the rise and fall of the voice.

in'toxicate *v* to make drunk; to excite. – *ns* **in'toxicant** a strong drink; **intoxi-'cation** drunkenness.

intra- *prefix* within.

in'tractable *adj* difficult, stubborn.

in'transigent *adj* refusing to come to an agreement. – *n* **in'transigence**.

in'transitive *adj* (of verbs) not of the kind that can take an object (as *to go, to fall*).

in'trepid *adj* without fear, brave. – *n* **intre'pidity**.

'intricate *adj* complicated, having many twists and turns. – *n* **'intricacy** the state of being intricate; something intricate: – *pl* **'intricacies**.

intrigue [in'trēg] *n* a secret plot or scheming; a secret love affair. – *v* to plot; to rouse the curiosity of, fascinate. – *adj* **in'triguing**.

in'trinsic *adj* belonging to a thing as part of its nature.

intro'duce *v* to bring in or put in; to make (a person) known (to another). – *n* **introduction** [intrə'dukshən] the introducing of a person or thing; something written (or said) at the beginning of a book (or speech *etc*) briefly explaining its contents *etc*. – *adj* **intro'ductory** coming at the beginning.

intro'spective *adj* inward-looking, fond of examining one's thoughts, feelings *etc*. – *n* **intro'spection**.

intrude [in'trood] *v* to thrust (oneself) in uninvited or unwanted. – *ns* **in'truder** someone who breaks in or intrudes; **in'trusion**. – *adj* **in'trusive**.

intu'ition *n* the power of grasping a fact or idea without thinking it out; an idea so grasped.

'inundate *v* to flood; to overwhelm. *I'm inundated with work.* – *n* **inun'dation**.

i'nure *v* to make accustomed (to pain *etc*).

in'vade *v* to enter (a country *etc*) as an enemy intending to take possession; to interfere with (someone's rights, priv-acy *etc*). – *ns* **in'vader; invasion**.

in'valid¹ *adj* (of a passport *etc*) not valid, not legally effective. – *v* **in'validate** to make invalid. – *n* **inva'lidity**.

'invalid² *n* a person who is ill or disabled. – Also *adj.* – *v* to cause to be an invalid; (with **out**) to discharge as an invalid (*esp* out of the army).

in'valuable *adj* too precious to have its value estimated, priceless.

in'variable *adj* unchanging. – *adv* **in'variably** always.

invasion *see* **invade**.

in'vective *n* words of scorn or hate, violent abuse.

inveigle [in'vēgl] *v* to coax, entice. – *n* **in'veiglement**.

in'vent *v* to make or think up (a machine, scheme *etc*) for the first time; to make up (a story, an excuse). – *ns* **in'vention** something invented; **in'ventor**. – *adj* **in'ventive** good at inventing, resourceful.

'inventory *n* a detailed list of articles (as the contents of a house *etc*): – *pl* **'inventories**.

in'vert *v* to turn upside down; to reverse the order of. – *adj* **'inverse** opposite, reverse. – *n* the opposite. – *adv* **in'versely**. – *n* **in'version** a turning upside-down; a reversal. – *npl* **inverted commas** commas upside down ("—", '—') or similar marks used in writing to show where direct speech begins and ends.

in'vertebrate *adj* (of animals) having no backbone (*eg* worms, insects). – Also *n.*

in'vest *v* to put money in a firm *etc* (*usu* in the form of shares) to make a profit; to clothe, surround something with a quality; to surround, lay siege to (a stronghold *etc*). – *ns* **in'vestiture** a ceremony of giving (the robes *etc* of) high office to someone; **in'vestment** something (*esp* money) invested; something in which money is invested; a siege; **in'vestor** one who invests.

in'vestigate *v* to search into with care. – *ns* **investi'gation** a careful search; **in'vestigator**.

inveterate [in'vetərət] *adj* firmly fixed in a habit by long practice: *an inveterate gambler;* (of a quality, habit *etc*) deep-rooted. – *n* **in'veteracy**.

in'vidious *adj* likely to cause ill-will or envy.

in'vigilate *v* to supervise (an examination *etc*). – *n* **in'vigilator**.

in'vigorate *v* to strengthen, refresh. – *adj* **in'vigorating**.

in'vincible *adj* not able to be defeated or surmounted. – *n* **invinci'bility**.

in'violable *adj* (of an oath, a right, a person) to be treated as sacred, not to be broken or disregarded or harmed. – *n* **inviola'bility**. – *adj* **in'violate** not violated, free from harm *etc*.

invisible [in'vizəbl] *adj* not able to be seen. – *n* **invisi'bility**.

in'vite *v* to ask a person politely to do something, *esp* to come (to one's house, to a meal *etc*); to ask for or to seem by one's behaviour to be asking for. *His behaviour invites punishment.* – *n* **invit-ation** [invi'tāshən] a (written) request (to come). – *adj* **in'viting** tempting, attractive.

invocation *see* **invoke**.

'invoice *n* a letter sent with goods with details of price and quantity. – *v* to make such a list.

in'voke to call upon (in prayer); to ask for (*eg* help); to call forth (a spirit). – *n* **invo'cation**.

in'voluntary *adj* not done willingly or intentionally. – *adv* **in'voluntarily**.

in'volve *v* to have as a consequence, to require; to (cause a person to) take part (in) or be concerned (in): *involved in social work*: *involved in the disgrace.* – *adj* **in'volved** complicated. – *n* **in-'volvement**.

'inward *adj* placed within; situated in the mind or soul. – *advs* **'inward**, **'inwards** towards the inside; **'inward-ly** within; in the heart, privately.

iodine ['iədēn] *n* an element, used in liquid form to kill germs.

'ion *n* an electrically-charged atom or group of atoms.

i'ota *n* a little bit.

IOU ['iō'ū] *n* short for *I owe you*, a note given as a receipt for money borrowed.

irascible [i'rasibl] *adj* easily made angry. – *n* **irasci'bility**.

'ire *n* anger. – *adj* **i'rate** angry.

iridescent [iri'desnt] *adj* coloured like a rainbow; shimmering with changing colours. – *n* **iri'descence**.

'iris *n* the coloured part of the eye round the pupil; a type of lily-like flower which grows from a bulb: – *pl* **'irises**.

irk *v* to weary, annoy. – *adj* **'irksome** tiresome.

iron ['iərn] *n* an element, the most common metal, widely used to make tools *etc*; an instrument of iron (such as one for smoothing clothes, a golf club *etc*); (*pl*) a prisoner's chains. – *adj* made of iron; like iron; stern; (of a rule *etc*) not to be broken. – *v* to smooth with an iron; (with **out**) to smooth out (difficulties). – *n* **ironmonger** ['iərnmuŋgər] a dealer in articles made

of iron ('**ironmongery**).

'irony *n* a form of deliberate mockery in which one says the opposite of what is obviously true; apparent mockery in a situation, words *etc*. *The irony of it was that she would have given him the money if he hadn't stolen it*: – *pl* **'ironies**. – *adjs* **i'ronic**; **i'ronical**.

irrational [i'rashənl] *adj* against (the rules of) common-sense.

ir'regular *adj* not regular; uneven, variable; against the rules. – *n* **irregu'lari-ty**: – *pl* **irregu'larities**.

irrelevant [i'relivənt] *adj* not having to do with what is being spoken about. – *n* **ir'relevancy**.

ir'reparable *adj* not able to be repaired.

irre'placeable *adj* too good, precious rare *etc* to be replaced.

irre'pressible *adj* (of high spirits *etc*) not able to be kept in check.

irre'proachable *adj* not able to be found fault with.

irresistible [iri'zistəbl] *adj* too strong or too charming to be resisted.

irresolute [i'rezəlōōt] *adj* not able to make up one's mind or keep to one's decision.

irres'pective *adj* taking no account of. *He went every day irrespective of the weather.*

irres'ponsible *adj* having no sense of responsibility, thoughtless.

irreverent [i'revərənt] *adj* having no respect (*eg* for holy things). – *n* **ir'reverence**.

ir'revocable *adj* not to be changed.

'irrigate *v* to supply (land) with water (by canals *etc*). – *n* **irri'gation**.

'irritate *v* to annoy; to cause discomfort, inflammation (to the skin, eyes *etc*). – *adj* **'irritable** cross, easily annoyed. – *n* **irri'tation** annoyance; discomfort *etc* of the skin *etc*.

island ['ilənd] *n* land surrounded with water; anything resembling this, as a **traffic island**, built in the middle of a street for pedestrians to stand on. – *n* **'islander** an inhabitant of an island.

isle [il] *n* an island.

'isobar *n* a line on the map connecting places where atmospheric pressure is the same.

'isolate *v* to place a person by himself; to consider a thing by itself. – *n* **iso'lation**.

isosceles [i'sosəlēz] *adj* (of a triangle) having two sides equal.

'isotherm *n* a line on the map connecting places which have the same tempera-ture.

issue ['ishōō] *v* to go, flow, or come out

to give out (orders *etc*); to publish. – *n* a flow; children: *he died without issue*; publication; the copies of a book published at one time; one number in the series (of a magazine *etc*); result, consequence; the actual question which is being argued about or discussed. – **to take issue** to disagree (with).

isthmus ['isməs] *n* a narrow neck of land connecting two larger portions: – *pl* **'isthmuses**.

it *pron* the thing spoken of. *My hat disappeared but I found it again*; used in sentences that have no real subject. *It snowed today. It is too late*; used in phrases as a kind of object. *Go it alone. Brave it out.* – *adj* **its** belonging to it. – *pron* **it'self** used reflexively. *The cat licked itself*; used for emphasis. *When we've seen the garden we'll see the house itself.*

i'talics *npl* a kind of type which *slopes to the right.* – *v* **i'talicize** to print in italics.

itch *n* an irritating feeling in the skin which is made better by scratching; a strong desire. – *v* to have an itch; to long (to). – *adj* **'itchy**.

'item *n* a separate article or detail (in a list).

itinerant [i'tinərənt] *adj* making journeys from place to place (on business *etc*), travelling. – *n* one who travels around, *esp* a tramp, gypsy, pedlar *etc*.

itinerary [i'tinərəri] *n* a route or plan of a journey: – *pl* **i'tineraries**.

its, itself *see* **it**.

it's [its] short for **it is**.

'ivory *n* the hard white substance which forms the tusks of the elephant, walrus *etc*.

'ivy *n* a creeping evergreen plant.

J

jab *v* to poke, stab: – *pt* **jabbed**. – Also *n*.

'jabber *v* to talk rapidly (and indistinctly). – Also *n*.

jack *n* an instrument for raising heavy weights such as motor cars; the playing card between ten and queen, the knave. – *v* (*usu* with **up**) to raise with a jack. – *ns* **'jackboots** large boots reaching above the knee; **'jack-in-the-box** a figure that is fixed to a spring inside a box and leaps out when the lid is opened; **'jack-knife** a large folding knife; a dive resembling a jack-knife's action. – *v* (of a vehicle and its trailer) to swing together to form a sharp angle.

jackal ['jaköl] *n* a dog-like wild animal.

'jackass *n* a male ass; a stupid person. – *n* **laughing jackass** the Australian giant kingfisher or kookaburra.

'jackdaw *n* a type of small crow.

'jacket *n* a short coat; a covering, *esp* a loose paper cover for a book.

'jackpot *n* a fund of prize money which has mounted up because of being so far unwon.

jade *n* hard green mineral substance, used for ornaments. – *adj* **'jaded** tired.

jagged ['jagid] *adj* rough-edged, uneven.

'jaguar *n* a type of South American animal like a leopard.

jail, gaol [jāl] *n* a prison. – *n* **'jailer,**

'gaoler one who has charge of a jail or of prisoners. – *n* **'jailbird, gaolbird** a person who has been in jail.

jam *n* fruit boiled with sugar till it is set; a crush; a stopping or blockage caused by crowding together; (*coll*) a difficult situation. – *v* to press or squeeze tight; to crowd full; to stick and so be unable to move. *This wheel has jammed*; to cause interference with another radio station's broadcast: – *pt* **jammed**.

jamb [jam] *n* the side post of a door.

jambo'ree *n* a large, lively gathering; a rally of Boy Scouts.

jangle ['jaŋgl] *v* to sound harshly with a ringing noise; to irritate.

'janitor *n* a caretaker; a doorkeeper.

'Januāry *n* the first month of the year.

jar *n* a glass or earthenware bottle with a wide mouth. – *v* to have a harsh, startling effect; to hurt by a sudden (violent) movement: – *pt* **jarred**. – *adj* **'jarring** harsh, startling.

'jargon *n* special words used within a particular trade, profession *etc*; grand-sounding but meaningless talk.

jasmine ['jazmin] *n* a shrub with white or yellow sweet-smelling flowers.

'jaundice *n* a disease which causes yellowness of the skin *etc*. – *adj* **'jaundiced** having jaundice; discontented, bitter.

jaunt *n* a journey, *esp* one for pleasure. –

adj **'jaunty** cheerful, gay.

javelin ['javəlin] *n* a long spear for throwing.

jaw *n* the mouth, chin *etc*, the lower part of the face; (*pl*) mouth (*esp* of an animal).

jay *n* a brightly-coloured bird of the crow kind. – *n* **'jaywalker** one who walks carelessly among traffic.

jazz *n* popular music of American Negro origin.

jealous ['jeləs] *adj* wanting to have what someone else has, envious; carefully looking after what one thinks much of. – *n* **'jealousy**.

jeans *npl* denim trousers.

jeep *n* a small army motor vehicle.

jeer *v* to make fun of, scoff. – Also *n*.

'jelly *n* the juice of fruit boiled with sugar till it becomes firm; a transparent wobbly food *usu* fruit-flavoured; anything in a jelly-like state: – *pl* **'jellies**. – *n* **'jellyfish** a sea animal with a jelly-like body.

'jemmy *n* a burglar's iron tool: – *pl* **'jemmies**.

'jenny wren *n* a female wren.

jeopardy ['jepərdi] *n* danger. – *v* **'jeopardize** to put in danger or at risk.

jer'bōa *n* a small rat-like desert animal with very long hindlegs.

jerk *v* to give a sudden sharp movement. – Also *n*. – *adj* **'jerky** moving or coming in jerks.

'jerkin *n* a type of short coat.

jersey ['jörzi] *n* a sweater, pullover: – *pl* **'jerseys**.

jest *n* a joke. – *v* to joke. – *n* **'jester** (*hist*) a court fool, once employed by kings, nobles *etc* to amuse them. – **in jest** jokingly, for a joke.

jet *n* a hard black mineral substance, used for ornaments *etc*; a spout of flame, air or liquid; a jet plane. – *adj* **'jet-'black** very black. – *ns* **jet plane** one driven by jet propulsion; **jet propulsion** high speed forward motion produced by sucking in air, liquid *etc* and forcing it out from behind.

'jetsam *n* goods thrown overboard and washed ashore.

'jettison *v* to throw overboard; to abandon.

'jetty *n* a small pier: – *pl* **'jetties**.

Jew *n* one who is of the race or religion of the Israelites. – *adj* **'Jewish** of the Jews. – *n* **Jew's harp** a small harp-shaped musical instrument played between the teeth.

'jewel *n* a precious stone; anything or anyone highly valued. – *adj* **'jewelled**,

(*usu US*) **'jeweled** set with jewels. – *ns* **'jeweller**, (*usu US*) **'jeweler** one who makes or deals in articles made of precious jewels and metals; **'jewellery**, (*usu US*) **'jewelry** articles made or sold by a jeweller.

jib *n* a three-cornered sail in front of a ship's foremast; the jutting-out arm of a crane. – *v* (with **at**) to refuse to (do something), object to: – *pt* **jibbed**.

jibe, gibe *v* to jeer, scoff. – Also *n*.

jig *n* a lively dance. – *v* to jump about: – *pt* **jigged**.

'jigsaw (puzzle) *n* a puzzle consisting of many differently shaped pieces that fit together to form a picture.

jilt *v* to cast aside (someone with whom one has been in love).

jingle ['jiŋgl] *n* a clinking sound (as of coins); a simple rhyme. – Also *v*.

job *n* a person's daily work; any piece of work. – *adj* **'jobbing** doing odd jobs of work for payment: *jobbing gardener*. – *n* **'job-'lot** a collection of odds and ends. – **it is a good job (that)** it is fortunate that.

'jockey *n* one who rides horses in a race: – *pl* **'jockeys**. – *v* to push one's way (into a good position).

'jocūlar *adj* joking, merry. – *n* **jocu'larity**.

jodhpurs ['jodpərz] *npl* riding breeches, fitting tightly from knee to ankle.

jog *v* to nudge, push slightly; to travel slowly; to run at a gentle pace: – *pt* **jogged**. – *n* **'jogging**.

'joggle *v* to shake slightly. – Also *n*.

join *v* to put or come together; to connect, fasten; to become a member of; to come and meet. – *n* the place where two or more things join. – *ns* **'joiner** one who joins; a worker in wood; **joint** the place where two or more things join; the place where two bones are joined (*eg* elbow, knee); meat containing a (joint) bone. – *adj* united; shared among more than one. – *adv* **'jointly** together. – **join battle** to begin fighting in battle.

joist *n* the beam to which the boards of a floor or the laths of a ceiling are nailed.

joke *n* anything said or done to cause laughter. – Also *v*. – *n* **'joker** one who jokes; an extra card in a pack.

'jolly *adj* merry. – *ns* **jollifi'cation** noisy (feasting and) merriment; **'jolliness**, **'jollity** merriment.

'jollyboat *n* a small boat belonging to a ship.

jōlt *v* to shake suddenly; to go forward with sudden jerks. – *n* a sudden jerk.

'joss-stick *n* a stick of gum which gives

158

off a sweet smell when burned.

jostle ['josl] *v* to push or knock against.

jot *n* a very small part. – *v* to write down hurriedly or briefly: – *pt* '**jotted**. – *n* '**jotter** a book for note-taking.

joule [jool] *n* a unit of energy.

journal ['jərnl] *n* an account kept of each day's doings, a diary; a newspaper, a magazine. – *ns* '**journalism** the business of running, or writing for, papers and magazines; '**journalist** one who writes for newspapers *etc*.

journey ['jərni] *n* a distance travelled: – *pl* '**journeys**. – *v* to travel. – *n* '**journeyman** one whose apprenticeship is finished.

joust *n* (*hist*) the armed contest between two knights on horseback at a tournament. – *v* to fight on horseback at a tournament.

'**jovial** *adj* cheerful, good-humoured. – *n* jovi'**ality**.

jowl [jowl] *n* the lower part of the jaw or cheek.

joy *n* gladness. – *adjs* '**joyful**, '**joyous** full of joy; '**joyless** dismal.

jubilant ['joobilənt] *adj* full of rejoicing, triumphant. – *n* jubi'**lation**.

jubilee ['joobilē] *n* celebrations arranged in memory of some event (such as a wedding, coronation *etc*).

judge *v* to hear the evidence *etc* in a question of law and make a decision on it; to form an opinion; to decide which is best in a competition *etc*. – *n* (in the courts of law) one who hears cases and decides on them according to the country's laws; one skilled in finding out good and bad points (*esp* of those in a competition). – *n* '**judg(e)ment** a decision (in a court of law *etc*); an opinion; good sense in forming opinions.

judicial [joo'dishəl] *adj* of a judge or court of justice.

judiciary [joo'dishiəri] *n* the judges of a country taken as a whole.

judicious [joo'dishəs] *adj* wise.

judo ['joodō] *n* a Japanese form of wrestling.

jug *n* a dish for liquids *usu* with a handle and a shaped lip for pouring.

'**juggernaut** *n* a vast and dangerous force; a large (articulated) lorry.

'**juggle** *v* to toss a number of things (balls, clubs *etc*) into the air and catch them; to handle or present in a deceitful way. – *n* '**juggler**.

'**jugular vein** *n* the large vein at the side of the neck.

juice [joos] *n* the liquid in vegetables, fruits *etc*. – *adj* '**juicy**.

ju-jitsu [joo'jitsoo] *n* an earlier form

of **judo**.

jukebox ['jookboks] *n* a coin-operated machine which plays selected records automatically.

July [joo'lī] the seventh month of the year.

'**jumble** *v* to throw together without order, muddle. – *n* a confused mixture. – *n* '**jumble-sale** a sale of odds and ends, cast-off clothing *etc*.

'**jumbo** *n* a child's name for an elephant: – *pl* '**jumbos**. – *adj* very large: *jumbo-jet*.

jump *v* to leap; to make a sudden (startled) movement (upwards). – Also *n*. – *adj* '**jumpy** easily startled.

'**jumper** *n* a sweater or jersey.

'**junction** *n* a place or point of joining (*eg* of roads or railway lines).

'**juncture** *n* point. *At this juncture he collapsed.*

June [joon] *n* the sixth month of the year.

jungle ['juŋgl] *n* a dense growth of trees and plants in tropical areas.

junior ['joonyər] *adj* younger; in a lower class or rank. – Also *n*.

juniper ['joonipər] *n* a type of evergreen shrub with berries and prickly leaves.

junk *n* a Chinese flat-bottomed sailing ship, high in the bow and stern; worthless articles, rubbish.

'**junket** *n* a dish made of curdled milk sweetened and flavoured. – *n* '**junketing** feasting, merriment.

jurisdiction [jooris'dikshən] *n* legal authority or power; the district over which a judge, court *etc* has power.

jurisprudence ['joorisproodəns] *n* the study or knowledge of law.

jury ['joori] *n* a group of men or women selected to reach a decision on whether an accused prisoner is guilty or not; a group of judges for a competition *etc*: – *pl* '**juries**. – *ns* '**juror**, '**juryman** one who serves on a jury.

just *adj* not favouring one more than another, fair; in keeping with one's rights; correct. – *adv* exactly; not long since; merely, only; really: *just longing to see you*.

'**justice** *n* fairness in making judgements; what is right or rightly deserved; a judge. – **Justice of the Peace** (shortened to **JP**) a citizen who acts as a judge for certain matters.

'**justify** *v* to prove or show to be just, right or desirable: – *pt* '**justified**. – *adj* '**justifiable** able to be justified or defended. – *n* justifi'**cation** good reason.

jut *v* to stand or stick out: – *pt* '**jutted**.

159

jute [jōōt] *n* the fibre from certain plants for making sacking, canvas *etc.*

juvenile ['jōōvənil] *adj* young, of young people; childish. – *n* a young person.

juxta'pose *v* to place side by side. – *n* **juxtapo'sition**.

K

kale *n* a cabbage with open curled leaves.

kaleidoscope [kə'lidəskōp] *n* a tube-shaped toy in which loose, coloured shapes reflected in two mirrors can be seen changing patterns. – *adj* **kaleidoscopic** [kəlidə'skopik] with changing colours; changing quickly.

kangaroo [kaŋgə'rōō] *n* a large Australian animal with long hindlegs and great power of leaping. The female carries its young in a pouch on the front of its body.

'kāpok *n* light waterproof fibre fluff got from the seeds of a tropical tree, used for stuffing pillows *etc.*

karate [kə'räti] *n* a Japanese form of unarmed fighting using blows and kicks.

kart *see* **go-kart**.

kayak ['kiak] *n* a canoe *esp* an Eskimo canoe made of sealskins stretched on a frame.

ke'bab *n* small pieces of meat *etc usu* cooked on a skewer.

kedgeree [kejə'rē] *n* a dish made with rice, fish and other ingredients.

keel *n* the long supporting piece of a ship's frame that lies lengthways along the bottom. – *v* (with **over**) to overturn; to fall (over). – *v* **'keelhaul** (*hist*) to punish by hauling under the keel of a ship by ropes.

keen *adj* eager, enthusiastic; very sharp; biting cold. – *n* **'keenness**.

keep *v* to hold on to, not to give or throw away; to look after; to feed and clothe; to have or use; to fulfil (one's promise); to stay, (cause to) remain in any position or state; (sometimes with **on**) to continue (doing something); (of food) to remain in good condition; to celebrate: *keep Christmas:* – *pt* **kept** [kept]. – *n* food and other necessities; a castle stronghold. – *ns* **'keeper** one who looks after something; **'keeping** care; charge. – *n* **'keepsake** a gift in memory of the giver or an occasion *etc.* – **in keeping with** suited to; **keep out** to exclude; to stay outside; **keep up** to go on with, to continue (something); **keep up with** to go as fast *etc* as.

keg *n* a small cask or barrel.

kelp *n* a type of large brown seaweed.

'kelvin *n* a measure of temperature.

ken *n* the amount or extent of one's knowledge or understanding: *beyond the ken of the average person.*

'kennel *n* a hut for a dog; (*pl*) a place where dogs can be looked after.

kept *see* **keep**.

kerb *n* the edge of something, *esp* a pavement.

kerchief ['kɜrchif] *n* a square of cloth used in dress to cover the head *etc.*

'kernel *n* the softer substance in the shell of a nut or inside the stone of a pulpy fruit; the important part of anything.

'kerosene *n* paraffin oil.

'kestrel *n* a type of small falcon which hovers.

ketch *n* a two-masted sailing vessel: – *pl* **'ketches**.

'ketchup *n* a flavouring sauce made from tomatoes *etc.*

'kettle *n* a metal pot *usu* with a spout for heating liquids. – *n* **'kettledrum** a drum made of a metal bowl covered with stretched skin *etc.*

key [kē] *n* that by which something (*eg* a door lock, a nut) is turned or screwed; in musical instruments, one of the small parts for sounding the notes; in a typewriter, one of the parts which one presses to type a word; the chief note of a piece of music; that which explains a mystery, code *etc*; a book containing answers to exercises *etc.* – *adj* important, essential. – *ns* **'keyboard** the keys in a piano or organ arranged along a flat board; **'keyhole** the hole in which a key of a door *etc* is placed; **'keynote** the chief note of a piece of music; the chief point about anything; **'keystone** the stone at the highest point of an arch holding the rest in position. – *adj* **'keyed-'up** excited.

khaki ['käki] *adj, n* (of) greenish-brown. – *n* cloth of this colour used for soldiers' uniforms.

kibbutz [ki'bōōts] *n* a (farming) settlement in modern Israel in which all share the work: – *pl* **kibbutzim** [ki'bōōtsēm].

kick *v* to hit or strike out with the foot;

(of a gun) to spring back violently when fired. – *n* a blow with the foot; the springing-back of a gun when fired. – *n* 'kick-off the start (of a football game). – for kicks for fun.

kid *n* a young goat; goatskin; (*coll*) a child. – *adj* made of kid leather.

kidnap *v* to carry off (a person or child) by force, often demanding money in exchange for them: – *pt* 'kidnapped. – *n* 'kidnapper.

kidney *n* one of a pair of urine-controlling organs placed in the lower part of the back, one on each side. Some animals' kidneys are used as meat: – *pl* 'kidneys.

kill *v* to put to death; to put an end to. – *n* the act of killing; the animals killed by a hunter. – *n* 'killer. – be at the kill to be there at the most exciting moment.

kiln *n* a large oven or furnace for baking pottery, bricks *etc* or for drying grain, hops *etc*.

kilogramme *n* a measure of weight – 1000 grammes (about 2¹⁄₅ lb).

kilomĕtre *n* a measure of length – 1000 metres (about ⁵⁄₈ of a mile).

kilowatt ['kiləwot] *n* a measure of electrical power.

kilt *n* (in Scotland) a pleated tartan skirt reaching to the knee, traditionally worn by men.

ki'mōno *n* a loose Japanese robe, fastened with a sash: – *pl* ki'monos.

kin *n* persons of the same family, relations. – kith and kin *see* kith; next of kin one's nearest relative.

kind *n* a sort, type; goods, not money: *paid in kind*. – *adj* having good feelings towards others; generous; gentle. – *adv* 'kindly like a king; royal. – *ns* 'kindness; 'kindliness. – *adj* 'kind'hearted kind.

kindergarten *n* a school for very young children.

kindle *v* to light a fire; to catch fire; to stir up (feelings). – *n* 'kindling material for starting a fire.

kindred ['kindrid] *n* one's relatives. – *adj* of the same sort; related.

ki'netic *adj* of motion.

king *n* the male ruler of a nation, inheriting his position by right of birth; the playing card with a picture of a king; the most important chess piece. – *adj* 'kingly like a king; royal. – *ns* 'kingcup marsh marigold; 'kingdom the area ruled by a king; any of the three great divisions of natural objects – animal, vegetable or mineral; 'kingfisher a type of fish-eating bird

with brightly-coloured feathers; 'kingpin the most important person in an organization.

kink *n* a bend or curl in a rope, hair *etc*; a peculiarity of the mind.

kinsman ['kinzmən] *n* a man of the same family as oneself: – *fem* 'kinswoman. – *npl* 'kinsfolk one's own people, relations.

kiosk ['kēosk] *n* a small stall for the sale of papers, sweets *etc*; a telephone box.

'kipper *n* a smoked and dried herring.

kirk *n* (in Scotland) a church.

kiss *v* to touch lovingly with one's lips; to touch gently. – Also *n*: – *pl* 'kisses. – kiss of life a mouth-to-mouth method of restoring breathing.

kit *n* an outfit of clothes, tools *etc* (necessary for a particular job *etc*).

'kitchen *n* a room where food is cooked. – *n* kitche'nette a small kitchen. – *n* 'kitchen-'garden a vegetable garden.

kite *n* a light frame, covered with paper or other material, for flying in the air; a kind of hawk.

kith: kith and kin friends and relatives.

'kitten *n* a young cat.

'kittiwake *n* a type of gull.

'kitty *n* a sum of money set aside for a purpose.

kiwi ['kēwē] *n* a swift-running almost wingless bird of New Zealand.

klepto'mānia *n* an uncontrollable desire to steal. – *n*, *adj* klepto'maniac.

knack [nak] *n* a special clever ability.

knacker ['nakər] *n* a buyer of old horses for slaughter.

knapsack ['napsak] *n* a bag for food, clothes *etc* slung on the back.

knave [nāv] *n* a cheating rogue; (in cards) the jack. – *n* 'knavery dishonesty. – *adj* 'knavish cheating, wicked.

knead [nēd] *v* to work (dough *etc*) by pressing with the fingers; to massage.

knee [nē] *n* the joint at the bend of the leg. – *n* 'kneecap the flat round bone on the front of the knee joint.

kneel [nēl] *v* to go down on one or both knees: – *pt* knelt [nelt].

knell [nel] *n* the tolling of a bell for a death or funeral; a warning of a sad end or failure.

knickerbockers ['nikərbokərz] *npl* loose breeches tucked in at the knee.

knickers ['nikərz] *npl* women's and girls' underwear for the lower part of the body; knickerbockers.

knick-knack ['niknak] *n* a small, ornamental article.

knife [nif] *n* a tool for cutting: – *pl* knives [nivz]. – *v* to stab.

knight [nit] *n* (*hist*) one of noble birth,

trained to use arms; a rank, with the title *Sir*, which does not go down from father to son; a piece used in chess. – *v* to raise to the rank of knight. – *adj* **'knightly** of knights; gallant, courageous. – *ns* **'knight-'errant** (*hist*) a knight who travelled in search of adventures; **'knighthood** the rank of a knight.

knit [nit] *v* to form a garment or fabric from yarn or thread (by means of knitting needles); to join closely: – *pt* **'knitted**. – *n* **'knitting** work done by knitting. – *npl* **knitting needles** (a pair of) thin pointed rods used in knitting.

knob [nob] *n* a hard rounded part standing out from the main part; a (door-)handle.

knock [nok] *v* to strike, hit; to drive or be driven against; to tap on a door to have it opened. – *n* a sudden stroke; a tap (on a door). – *n* **'knocker** a hinged weight on a door for knocking with. – *adj* **'knock-'kneed** having knees that touch in walking. – **knock out** to hit (someone) hard enough to make him unconscious.

knoll [nōl] *n* a small rounded hill.

knot [not] *n* a hard lump, *esp* one made by tying string *etc*, or one in wood at the join between trunk and branch; a tangle; a small gathering, cluster (*eg of people*); a measure of speed for ships (about 1·85 kilometre per hour). – *v* to tie in a knot: – *pt* **'knotted**. – *adj* **'knotted** full of knots; **'knotty** having knots; difficult.

know [nō] *v* to be aware or sure of; to recognize: – *pt* **knew**. – *adj* **'knowing** clever; cunning. – *adv* **'knowingly** intentionally. – *n* **knowledge** ['nolij] that which is known; information; ability, skill. – *adj* **'knowledgeable** showing or having knowledge.

knuckle ['nukl] *n* a joint of the fingers. – *v* (with **under**) to give in, yield.

kō'ala bear *n* an Australian tree-climbing animal that looks like a small bear.

kookaburra *see* **jackass**.

Ko'ran *n* the holy book of the Mohammedans.

'kösher *adj* pure and clean according to Jewish law.

kowtow ['kow'tow] *v* (with **to**) to treat with too much respect.

kung-fu ['kuŋ'fōō] *n* a form of self-defence, developed in China.

kraal [kräl] *n* a South African village.

'kūdos *n* fame, glory.

L

lab short for **laboratory**.

'läbel *n* a small written note fixed on to something (to tell its contents, owner *etc*). – *v* to fix a label to; to call something by a certain name: – *pt* **'labelled**.

'läbial *adj* of the lips.

la'boratory *n* a scientist's workroom: – *pl* **la'boratories**.

labour, (*US*) **labor** ['läbər] *n* (hard) work; workmen on a job; (in a pregnant female) the process of childbirth. – *v* to work hard; to move slowly or with difficulty; emphasize (a point) too greatly. – *adjs* **laborious** [lə'böriəs] requiring hard work; wearisome; **'läboured** showing signs of effort. – *n* **'labourer** one who does heavy unskilled work. – *n* **Labour Party** one of the chief political parties of Great Britain.

la'burnum *n* a kind of tree with large hanging clusters of yellow flowers and poisonous seeds.

labyrinth ['labərinth] *n* a place full of puzzling windings, a maze.

lace *n* a string or cord, for fastening shoes *etc*; decorative openwork fabric made with fine thread. – *v* to fasten with a lace.

lacerate ['lasərāt] *v* to tear, wound. – *n* **lace'ration**.

lack *v* to be in want; to be without. – *n* want, need.

lacka'daisical *adj* bored, half-hearted.

'lackey *n* a manservant; one who acts like a slave: – *pl* **'lackeys**.

la'conic *adj* using few words to express one's meaning. – *adv* **la'conically**.

lacquer ['lakər] *n* a varnish. – Also *v*.

la'crosse *n* a twelve-a-side ball game played with sticks having a shallow net at the end.

'lactic *adj* of milk.

lad *n* a boy, a youth.

'ladder *n* a set of rungs or steps between two supports, for climbing up or down; a run from a broken stitch, in a stocking *etc*.

lade *n* a channel for leading water to a millwheel.

'läden *adj* loaded, burdened. – *n* **'lading** that which is loaded; cargo.

'**lādle** *n* a large spoon for lifting out liquid. – *v* to lift with a ladle.

'**lādy** *n* a woman (of good manners); a title of the wives of knights, lords and baronets, and of the daughters of noblemen: – *pl* '**ladies**. – *n* '**ladybird** a small beetle, usually red with black spots. – **Her Ladyship** the title of a lady.

lag *v* to move slowly and fall behind; to cover (a boiler or pipes) with a warm covering: – *pt* **lagged**. – *n* a delay. – *n* '**lagging** material for covering pipes *etc*.

lager ['lägɔr] *n* a light beer.

la'goon *n* a shallow stretch of water separated from the sea by low sand-banks, rocks *etc*.

laid *see* **lay**¹.

lain *see* **lie**.

lair *n* the den of a wild beast.

laird *n* (in Scotland) a land-owner, squire.

laity *see* **lay**².

lake *n* a large stretch of water surrounded by land.

'**lama** *n* a Buddhist priest of Tibet.

lamb [lam] *n* a young sheep; the meat of this animal; one gentle as a lamb.

lame *adj* unable to walk, crippled; not good enough: *a lame excuse*. – *v* to make lame. – *n* '**lameness**.

la'ment *v* to mourn, feel or express grief for; to regret. – *n* a show of grief (also **lamen'tation**); a mournful poem or piece of music. – *adj* '**lamentable** pitiful; very bad.

lamp *n* a (glass-covered) light.

lam'poon *n* a violent criticism (in writing) of a person.

'**lamprey** *n* a type of fish like an eel: – *pl* '**lampreys**.

lance *n* a long shaft of wood, with a spearhead. – *v* to cut open (a boil *etc*) with a knife. – *n* '**lancer** a light cavalry soldier. – *n* '**lance-'corporal** a soldier with rank just below a corporal.

land *n* the solid portion of the earth's surface; ground, soil; a (part of a) country. – *v* to set or come on land or on shore. – *adj* '**landed** consisting of or owning lands and estates: *landed property*: *landed gentry*. – *n* '**landing** a coming ashore or to ground; a place for getting on board; the level part of a staircase between the flights of steps. – *n* '**landfall** an approach to land after a voyage; the land approached. – *adj* '**landlocked** almost shut in by land. – *ns* '**landlord** the owner of land or houses; the master of an inn: – *fem* '**landlady**; '**landlubber** one who

lives, works *etc* on land and knows little about the sea; '**landmark** any object on land that serves as a guide; an important event; '**landscape** a (picture of a) view of inland scenery; '**landslide** a mass of land that slips down from the side of a hill; **landslide victory** (in elections *etc*) one in which a great mass of votes goes to one side.

landau ['landö] *n* a kind of carriage with a removable top.

lane *n* a narrow road, street or passage; a course or part of the road, sea *etc* to which cars, ships, aircraft *etc* must keep.

language ['laŋgwij] *n* human speech; the speech of a particular people or nation.

languid ['laŋgwid] *adj* lacking liveliness and spirit. – *v* **languish** ['laŋgwish] to grow weak, to droop; to long (for). – *adj* '**langu̇shing**. – *n* **languor** ['laŋgɔr] state of being languid.

lank *adj* tall and thin; (of hair) straight and limp. – *adj* '**lanky** tall and thin.

'**lantern** *n* a case for holding or carrying a light. – *adj* '**lantern-'jawed** hollow-cheeked, long-jawed.

'**lanyard**, '**laniard** *n* (on a ship) a short rope used for fastening; a cord for hanging a whistle *etc* round the neck.

lap *v* to lick up with the tongue; to wash or flow against; (with **up**) to accept (praise *etc*) greedily; to wrap round, surround; to make (something) lie partly (over); in a race, to get a lap ahead of other competitors: – *pt* **lapped**. – *n* the front part (from waist to knees) of a person seated; the clothes covering that part; a fold; one round of a racetrack or other competition course. – *n* '**lapdog** a small pet dog.

la'pel *n* the part of a coat joined to the collar and folded back on the chest.

'**lapidary** *n* one who cuts, polishes and shapes (precious) stones: – *pl* '**lapidaries**. – *adj* engraved on stone.

lapse *v* to fall (into evil ways or careless habits); to cease. – *n* a mistake, a failure; a passing away (of time).

'**lapwing** *n* a type of bird of the plover family (also '**peewit**).

'**larboard** *n* the left side of a ship looking from the stern, now called **port**.

'**larceny** *n* stealing, theft.

larch *n* a kind of cone-bearing deciduous tree: – *pl* '**larches**.

lard *n* the melted fat of the pig. – *v* to put strips of bacon *etc* in meat before cooking; to smear, lay on thickly.

'**larder** *n* a room or place where food is kept; stock of food.

large *adj* great in size, amount *etc*. – *adv* **'largely** mainly, to a great extent. – *n* **'largeness**. – **at large** at liberty, free; in general: *the public at large*.

largesse [lär'jes] *n* a generous giving away of money *etc*.

'lariat *n* a rope for fastening horses while they are grazing; a lasso.

lark *n* a general name for several kinds of singing bird; a piece of fun or mischief. – *v* to fool about, behave mischievously.

'larkspur *n* a tall plant with blue, white or pink spurred flowers, a kind of delphinium.

'larva *n* an insect in its first stage after coming out of the egg, a grub: – *pl* **larvae** ['lärvē].

larynx ['lariŋks] *n* the upper part of the windpipe containing the cords that produce the voice. – *n* **laryngitis** [larin'jitis] a disease of the larynx.

lascivious [lə'siviəs] *adj* full of indecent desires, lustful.

laser ['lāzər] *n* (an instrument that concentrates light into) a very narrow powerful beam.

lash *n* a thong or cord of a whip; a stroke with a whip: – *pl* **'lashes**. – *v* to strike with a whip; to fasten with a rope *etc*; to attack with bitter words.

lass *n* a girl: – *pl* **'lasses**.

'lassitude *n* lack of energy, weariness.

lasso [la'sōō] *n* a long rope with a loop that tightens when the rope is pulled, used for catching wild horses *etc*: – *pl* **las'so(e)s**. – *v* to catch with a lasso.

last *adj* coming after all the others. *He was the last person to arrive. The audience left before the last act*; most recent, next before the present. *His last job was boring.* – Also *adv*. – *v* to continue, go on; to remain in good condition. – *n* a foot-like shape on which shoes are made or repaired. – *adv* **'lastly** finally. – **at last** in the end; **on one's last legs** completely worn out, about to collapse; **to the last** to the end.

latch *n* a catch of wood or metal used to fasten a door: – *pl* **'latches**. – *v* to fasten with a latch. – *n* **'latchkey** a door-key (to raise the latch of a door).

late *adj* coming after the expected time. *The train was late*; far on (in time). *It's getting late*; recent: *our late disagreement*; recently dead: *the late king*; recently, but no longer, holding an office or position: *the late chairman*. – Also *adv*. – *adv* **'lately** recently. – *n* **'lateness**. – **of late** recently.

'latent *adj* hidden, undeveloped but capable of becoming developed or active:

latent ability: *latent hostility*.

'lateral *adj* of, at, to, or from the side.

'latex *n* the milky juice of plants *esp* of the rubber tree.

lath *n* a thin narrow strip of wood.

lathe [lādh] *n* a machine for turning and shaping articles of wood, metal *etc*.

lather ['lädhər] *n* a foam or froth (*eg* from soap and water). – *v* to cover with lather.

'Latin *n* the language of ancient Rome.

'latitude *n* the distance, measured in degrees on the map, of a place north or south from the equator; freedom of action or choice. *His new job allows him far more latitude than his previous one.*

'latter *adj* the last of two mentioned; recent. – *adv* **'latterly** recently. – *adj* **'latter-day** of recent times.

lattice ['latis] *n* a network of crossed wooden *etc* strips (also **'lattice-work**); a window having this.

'laudable *adj* worthy of being praised. – *adj* **'laudatory** expressing praise.

laugh [läf] *v* to make sounds with the voice in showing amusement, happiness, scorn *etc*. – *n* the sound of laughing. – *adj* **'laughable** comical, ridiculous. – *n* **'laughter** the act or noise of laughing. – *n* **laughing stock** an object of scornful laughter.

launch *v* to cause a boat, ship, to slide into the water; to start (someone or something) off on a course; to throw or hurl. – *n* the act of launching; a large motor boat: – *pl* **'launches**.

'launder *v* to wash and iron clothes. – *ns* **launderette** [lön'dret] a shop where customers may wash clothes in washing machines; **'laundry** a place where clothes are washed (*pl* **'laundries**); clothes to be washed.

'laurel *n* the bay tree, from which wreaths were made for crowning victors *etc*; (*pl*) honours or victories gained.

'lava *n* molten rock *etc* thrown out by a volcano, becoming solid as it cools.

'lavatory *n* a toilet: – *pl* **'lavatories**.

'lavender *n* a plant with small pale-purple, sweet-smelling flowers; a pale-purple colour.

'lavish *v* to spend or give very freely. – *adj* too free in giving or spending, very generous.

law *n* the collection of rules according to which a country is governed; any one of such rules; (in science) a rule that says that in certain conditions certain things always happen. – *adjs* **'lawful** allowed by law; **'lawless** paying no attention to, and not observing the laws. – *n*

'lawyer one whose work it is to give advice in matters of law. – *adj* **'law-abiding** obeying the law. – *ns* **law court** a place where people accused of crimes are tried; **'lawsuit** a quarrel or dispute to be settled by a court of law.

lawn *n* an area of smooth grass *eg* as part of a garden; a kind of fine linen. – *ns* **'lawnmower** a machine for cutting grass; **lawn tennis** tennis played on a grass court.

lax *adj* not strict; careless, negligent. – *ns* **'laxity; 'laxness; 'laxative** a medicine which loosens the bowels.

lay¹ *v* to place or set down; to put (*eg* a burden, duty) on (someone); to beat down; to cause to disappear or subside: *lay a ghost*; to set in order, arrange; (of hens) to produce eggs; to bet, wager: – *pt* **laid**. – *adj* **'laid-'up** ill in bed. – *ns* **'layabout** a lazy idle person; **'layby** a parking area at the side of a road. – **lay about someone** to deal blows on all sides; **lay off** to dismiss (workers) temporarily; (*coll*) to stop: *lay off arguing*; to talk at great length; **lay up** to store for future use; **lay waste** to ruin, destroy.

lay² *adj* not of the clergy; without special training in or special knowledge of a particular subject. – *ns* **laity** ['lāəti] ordinary people, not clergymen; **'layman** one of the laity; someone without special training in a subject.

lay³ *n* (*hist*) a short poem; a song.

'layer *n* a thickness or covering.

lay'ette *n* a baby's complete outfit.

'lazy *adj* not caring for work; idle: – *comp* **'lazier**, *superl* **'laziest**. – *v* **laze** to be lazy. – *n* **'laziness**.

lea *n* (*old*) a meadow.

lead¹ *v* to show the way by going first; to direct; to guide; to persuade; to live (a busy *etc* life); (of a road) to form a way (to), go (to): – *pt* **led**. – *n* the first or front place; guidance, direction; a leash for a dog *etc*. – *ns* **'leader** one who leads or goes first; a chief; a column in a newspaper expressing the editor's opinions; **'leadership** the state of being a leader; the ability to lead. – *n* **leading question** a question asked in such a way as to suggest the desired answer.

lead² [led] *n* an element, a soft bluish-grey metal; the part of a pencil that writes, really made of graphite; a weight used for sounding depths at sea *etc*. – *adj* **'leaden** made of lead; lead-coloured; dull, heavy.

leaf *n* a part of a plant growing from the side of a stem, *usu* green, flat and thin but of various shapes according to the plant; anything thin like a leaf; a page of a book; a hinged flap or movable extra part of a table *etc*: – *pl* **leaves** [lēvz]. – *adj* **'leafy**. – *n* **'leaflet** a small printed sheet. – **turn over a new leaf** to begin again and do better.

league [lēg] *n* a union of persons, nations *etc* for the benefit of each other; an association of clubs for games; an old measure of distance, *usu* 3 miles (about 4·8 kilometres). – **in league with** allied with.

leak *n* a hole through which liquid passes; an escape of gas *etc* or of secret information. – Also *v*. – *n* **'leakage** that which enters or escapes by leaking.

lean *v* to slope over to one side, not to be upright; to rest (against); to rely (on): – *pt* **leant** [lent]. – *adj* thin; poor, scanty; (of meat) not fat. – *ns* **'leaning** a liking (for something); **'leanness** thinness; poorness. – *n* **'lean-to** a shed *etc* built against another building or wall.

leap *v* to move with jumps; to jump (over): – *pt* **leapt** [lept]. – *n* a jump. – *ns* **'leapfrog** a game in which one player leaps over another's bent back; **leap year** a year which has 366 days (February having 29), occurring every fourth year.

learn [lėrn] *v* to get to know (something); to gain skill: – *pp* and *pt* **learned**, **learnt**. – *adj* **learned** ['lėrnid] having or showing great knowledge. – *ns* **'learner; 'learning** knowledge.

lease *n* (the period of) an agreement giving the use of a house *etc* on payment of rent. – *v* to let or rent. – *n* **'leasehold** property, or land, held by lease.

leash *n* a lead by which a dog *etc* is held: – *pl* **'leashes**. – *v* to put (a dog *etc*) on a leash.

least *adj*, *n* the smallest (of), amount (of): *least money. He has least*. – *adv* (often with **the**) the smallest or lowest degree. *I like her least*. – **at least** at any rate, anyway; **not in the least** not at all.

leather ['ledhər] *n* the skin of an animal, prepared (by tanning) for use. – *v* to beat. – *n* **'leathering** a thrashing. – *adj* **'leathery** like leather; tough.

leave *n* permission to do something (*eg* to be absent); (*esp* of soldiers, sailors) a holiday. – *v* to allow to remain; to abandon, forsake; to depart (from); to make a gift to a person by one's will; to give to a person's charge, care *etc*. *Leave the decision to him*: – *pt* **left**. – *npl* **'leavings** things left over. – **take one's**

leave (of) to part from; to say goodbye to.

'**lecherous** *adj* lustful in a sexual way. – *n* '**lechery**.

'**lectern** *n* a stand for a book to be read from.

lecture ['lekchər] *n* something written or read to an audience, on a certain subject; a scolding. – *v* to deliver a lecture; to scold. – *n* '**lecturer** one who lectures, *esp* to students.

led *see* **lead**¹.

ledge *n* a shelf or an object that sticks out like a shelf: *a window-ledge*; an underwater ridge.

'**ledger** *n* the book of accounts of an office or shop.

lee *n* the side away from the wind, the sheltered side. – *adj, adv* '**leeward** in the direction towards which the wind blows. – *n* '**leeway** a drift (of a ship) off course; lost time, lost ground *etc. He has a lot of leeway to make up since he has been off ill.*

leech *n* a kind of blood-sucking worm: – *pl* '**leeches**.

leek *n* a long green and white vegetable of the onion family.

leer *n* a sly, sidelong or lustful look. – Also *v*.

lees *npl* dregs that settle at the bottom of liquid.

left¹ *adj* on, for, or belonging to the side of the body that in most people has the less skilful hand (opposite to **right**). – Also *adv*. – *n* the left side; a group with left-wing ideas *etc*. – *adjs* '**left-'handed** using the left hand rather than the right; awkward; '**left-'wing** extremely socialist or radical in political views, ideas *etc*.

left² *see* **leave**.

leg *n* one of the limbs by which animals (including man) walk; a long slender support of anything (as of a table); one stage in a journey, contest *etc*. – *npl* '**leggings** outer coverings for the lower legs. – *adj* '**leggy** having long legs.

'**legacy** *n* something which is left by will; something left behind by someone who had one's job, house *etc* previously: – *pl* '**legacies**. – *n* lega'**tee** one to whom a legacy is left.

'**legal** *adj* allowed by law, lawful; of law. – *n* le'**gality** the state of being legal: – *pl* le'**galities**. – *v* '**legalize** to make lawful.

le'**gation** *n* (the headquarters of) an official body of people acting on behalf of the government of their own country *etc* in another country, an embassy.

'**legend** *n* a story handed down from long

ago, a myth; the words accompanying picture, a caption. – *adj* '**legendary** legend; famous; not to be believed.

legerdemain ['lejərdəmān] *n* conjurir by quickness of the hand.

'**legible** *adj* (of writing) that can be rea (easily). – *n* legi'**bility**.

'**legion** *n* (*hist*) a body of Roman soldie of from three to six thousand; a grea many, a very large number. – '**legionary** a soldier of a legion.

'**legislate** *v* to make laws. – *n* legis'**la tion**. – *adj* '**legislative** law-making. *ns* '**legislator** one who makes laws '**legislature** the part of the governmer which has the powers of making laws

le'**gitimate** *adj* lawful; (of a child) bor of parents married to each other; cor rect, reasonable. – *n* le'**gitimacy**.

leisure ['lezhər] *n* time free fror work, spare time. – *adj* '**leisured** n occupied with business. – *adj, ad* '**leisurely** taking plenty of time.

'**lemming** *n* a kind of small rat-lik animal of the arctic regions.

'**lemon** *n* an oval fruit with pale yellov rind and very sour juice, or the tree tha bears it. – *n* lemo'**nade** a (fizzy) drin flavoured with lemons.

'**lemur** *n* a kind of animal related to th monkey but with a pointed nose.

lend *v* to give use of (something) for time; to give, add (a quality) to some one or something. *His presence lent a air of respectability to the occasion: – p* **lent**. – **lend itself to** to be suitable for adapt easily to.

length *n* the extent from end to end i space or time; the quality of being long a great extent; a piece (of cloth *etc*). – '**lengthen** to make or grow longer. *advs* '**lengthways**, '**lengthwise** in th direction of the length. – *adj* '**lengthy** long; tiresomely long. – **at length** i detail; at last.

'**lenient** *adj* merciful, punishing onl lightly. – *ns* '**lenience**; '**leniency**.

lens [lenz] *n* a piece of glass *etc* curved o one or both sides, used in spectacles contact lenses, cameras *etc*; a part of th eye: – *pl* '**lenses**.

Lent *n* (in the Christian church) a perio of fasting before Easter lasting fort days.

lent *see* **lend**.

'**lentil** *n* the seed of a pod-bearing plant used in soups *etc*.

'**leonine** *adj* like a lion.

leopard ['lepərd] *n* a type of animal o the cat family with a spotted skin.

'**leotard** *n* a kind of tight-fitting garmen worn for dancing, gymnastics *etc*.

leper *n* a person with leprosy; an outcast. – *n* **'leprosy** a contagious skin disease.

leprechaun ['leprəkön] *n* (*myth*) a kind of Irish fairy.

ess *adj* not as much: *less time*; smaller. *Think of a number less than 40.* – *adv* not as much, to a smaller extent. *He goes less (often) than he should.* – *n* a smaller portion, amount. *He has less than I have.* – *prep* minus: *5 less 2 equals 3.* – *v* **'lessen** to make smaller. – *adj* **'lesser** smaller.

lesson *n* that which is learned or taught; a part of the Bible read in church; a period of teaching.

lest *conj* for fear that, in case.

let *v* to allow; to grant use of (*eg* a house, shop, farm) in return for payment: – *pres p* **'letting**, *pt, pp* **let**. – **let down** to fail to help *etc*, disappoint; **let off** to excuse, not to punish *etc*; **let up** to become less.

lethal *adj* causing death.

lethargy *n* lack of energy or interest; sleepiness. – *adj* **le'thargic**.

letter *n* a mark expressing a sound; a written message; (*pl*) learning: *a man of letters.* – *n* **'lettering** the way in which letters are formed; the letters formed. – **(to) the letter** (according to) the exact meaning of the words. *He followed his father's instructions to the letter.*

lettuce ['letis] *n* a kind of green plant whose leaves are used in a salad.

leukaemia [loo'kēmiə] *n* a disease of the white blood cells in the body.

levee ['levi] *n* a reception, meeting *etc* held by a king or queen.

level *n* a flat, smooth surface; a height, position, strength *etc* in comparison with some standard: *water level*; a kind of instrument for showing whether a surface is level: *spirit level*; suitable or appropriate position or rank. – *adj* flat, even, smooth or horizontal. – *v* to make flat, smooth or horizontal; to make equal; to aim (a gun *etc*); to pull down (a building *etc*): – *pt* **'levelled**. – *adj* **'level-'headed** having good sense. – *n* **level crossing** a place where a road crosses a railway track.

lever *n* a bar of metal, wood *etc* used to raise up or shift something heavy; a bar or handle for operating a machine *etc*; any method of gaining advantage. *He used the information as a lever to get a better job.*

leveret ['levərit] *n* a young hare.

le'viathan *n* a kind of huge (sea) monster; anything huge or powerful.

levi'tation *n* (the illusion of) raising a heavy body in the air without support. – *v* **'levitate** to (cause to) float in the air.

'levity *n* lack of seriousness, frivolity.

'levy *v* to collect by order (*eg* a tax, men for an army): – *pt* **'levied**. – *n* money, troops *etc* collected by order: – *pl* **'levies**.

lewd *adj* taking delight in indecent thoughts or acts. – *n* **'lewdness**.

lexi'cographer *n* a maker of a dictionary.

'liable *adj* legally responsible (for) or bound to do something; likely or apt (to do something or happen); (with **to**) likely to have, get, suffer from: *liable to colds.* – *n* **lia'bility** (legal) responsibility; a debt; a disadvantage: – *pl* **lia'bilities**.

liaison [lē'āzon] *n* contact, communication.

liar *see* **lie**.

'libel *n* anything written with the purpose of hurting a person's reputation. – Also *v*: – *pt* **'libelled**. – *adj* **'libellous**.

liberal ['libərəl] *adj* generous; broadminded, tolerant. – *ns* **'Liberal** a member of the Liberal Party; **libe'rality**. – *n* **Liberal Party** one of the chief political parties of Great Britain.

liberate ['libərāt] *v* to set free. – *n* **libe'ration**.

libertine ['libərtēn] *n* one who lives a wicked, immoral life.

'liberty *n* freedom; too great freedom of speech or action; (*pl*) **'liberties** rights, privileges. – **take liberties** to behave rudely or impertinently.

'library *n* (a building or room containing) a collection of books or some other collection (*eg* gramophone records): – *pl* **'libraries**. – *n* **li'brarian** the keeper of a library.

li'bretto *n* (a book of) the words of an opera, musical show *etc*: – *pl* **libretti** [li'bretē] or **li'brettos**.

lice *see* **louse**.

'licence *n* a (printed) form giving permission to do something (*eg* to keep a dog, television set *etc*, to drive a car *etc*); too great freedom of action *etc*. – *v* **'license** to permit. – *n* **licen'see** one to whom a licence (*esp* one to keep a hotel or public house) is given. – *adj* **li'centious** given to behaving immorally or improperly. – *n* **li'centiousness**.

lichen ['likən] *n* a large group of moss-like plants that grow on rocks *etc*.

lick *v* to pass the tongue over; (of flames) to reach up, to touch. – *n* the act of licking; a tiny amount. – **lick into**

shape to make vigorous improvements on.

lid *n* a cover for a box, pot *etc*; the cover of the eye.

lie *n* a false statement meant to deceive. – *v* to tell a lie: – *pres p* 'lying, *pt* lied; to rest in a flat position: – *pt* lay, *pp* lain; to be or to remain in a state or position: – *pt* lay, *pp* lain. – *n* the position or situation in which something lies. – *n* 'liar one who tells lies. – *adj, n* 'lying. – **lie in wait (for)** to keep hidden in order to surprise someone (with an attack); **lie low** to keep quiet or hidden; **the lie of the land** the state of affairs.

liege [lēj] *n* a loyal subject; a lord or superior. – *n* 'liege-lord (*hist*) an overlord.

lieu [lōō]: **in lieu (of)** instead of.

lieutenant [ləf'tenənt] *n* in the army, an officer next below captain, in the navy, an officer below a lieutenant-commander; a rank below a higher officer, as **lieu'tenant-'colonel.**

life *n* the period between birth and death; the state of being alive; liveliness; manner of living; the story of a person's life; living things: *animal life*: – *pl* **lives.** – *adj* 'lifeless dead; not lively. – *ns* 'lifebelt a ring or belt made of cork or filled with air for keeping a person afloat; 'lifeboat a boat for saving shipwrecked persons; **life cycle** the various stages through which a living thing passes. – *adjs* 'life-like like a living person; 'lifelong lasting the length of a life; 'life-size (of a portrait *etc*) full size.

lift *v* to bring to a higher position, raise; to take up; (*coll*) to steal; (of fog *etc*) to disappear. – *n* a platform *etc* that moves up and down (between floors) carrying goods or people; a ride in someone's car *etc*; a raising (of spirits *etc*), a boost. – *n* 'lift-off the take-off of a rocket *etc*.

'**ligament** *n* a tough substance that connects the bones of the body.

'**ligature** *n* something which binds.

light[1] [līt] *n* the brightness given by the sun, moon, lamps *etc* that makes things able to be seen; a source of light (*eg* a lamp); a flame (of a match *etc*); knowledge. – *adj* bright; (of a colour) pale; having light, not dark. – *v* to give light to; to set fire to: – *pt* lit or 'lighted. – *v* 'lighten to make or become brighter; (of lightening) to flash. – *ns* 'lightening a making or becoming lighter or brighter; 'lighter something used for lighting (a cigarette *etc*); 'lighting a means of providing

light. — *ns* 'lighthouse a tower-like building with a flashing light to warn or guide ships; 'lightship a ship anchored in a fixed position to serve as a lighthouse; 'light-year the distance light travels in a year (6 billion miles). — **bring to light** to reveal, cause to be noticed; **come to light** to be revealed or discovered; **in the light of** taking into consideration (information acquired *etc*).

light[2] [līt] *adj* not heavy; easy to bear or to do; easy to digest; nimble, lively; not grave, gay; not serious: *light music*; (of rain *etc*) little in quantity. – *v* 'lighten to make less heavy. – *n* 'lighter a large open boat used in unloading and loading ships. – *adv* 'lightly. – *adjs* 'light-'fingered apt to steal; 'light-'headed dizzy; 'light-'hearted cheerful.

light[3] [līt] *v* (with **on, upon**) to land, settle on; to come upon by chance: – *pt* 'lighted or **lit.**

lightning ['lītnin] *n* an electric flash in the clouds. – *n* **lightning conductor** a metal rod that protects buildings *etc* from the electricity of lightning by conducting it down to earth.

'**lignite** *n* brown, woody coal.

like[1] *adj* the same as or similar to. – *adv* in the same way as. *He runs like a hare.* – *n* something or someone that is the equal of another. *You won't see his like again*; the same thing: *do the like.* – *v* 'liken to think of as similar, to compare. – *adj* 'likely probable; promising; liable (to do something). – *adv* probably. – *ns* 'likelihood probability; 'likeness a similarity, a resemblance; a portrait, photograph *etc* of someone. – *adv* 'likewise in the same way; also.

like[2] *v* to be pleased with; to be fond of. – *adj* 'lik(e)able attractive, lovable. – *n* 'liking a fondness; satisfaction: *to my liking.*

'**lilac** *n* a small tree with hanging clusters of pale purple or white flowers. – *adj* of pale purple colour.

lilt *n* (a tune *etc* with) a striking rhythm or swing. – Also *v*.

'**lily** *n* a tall plant grown from a bulb with large white or coloured flowers: – *pl* 'lilies. – *n* 'lily-of-the-'valley a plant with small white bell-shaped flowers.

limb [lim] *n* a leg or arm; a branch.

'**limber** *adj* easily bent, supple. – **limber up** to exercise so as to become supple.

'**limbo: in limbo** forgotten, neglected.

lime *n* the white substance, quicklime, left after heating limestone, used in making cement; a type of tree related to the lemon or its greenish-yellow fruit;

another name for the **linden** tree. – **in the limelight** attracting publicity or attention.

'**limit** *n* the farthest point or place; a boundary; largest (or smallest) extent, degree *etc*; restriction. – *v* to set or keep to a limit. – *n* **limi'tation** that which limits; the act of limiting; a weak point about a person or thing.

limousine ['limǝzēn] *n* a kind of large motor car, *esp* one with a separate compartment for the driver.

limp *adj* lacking stiffness; weak. – *v* to walk lamely; of a damaged ship *etc* to move with difficulty. – *n* the act of limping; a limping walk.

'**limpet** *n* a small cone-shaped shellfish that clings to rocks; a person who is difficult to get rid of.

'**limpid** *adj* clear, transparent.

'**linchpin** *n* a pin-shaped rod used to keep a wheel on an axle.

'**linden** *n* (also called **lime**) a tree with small flowers and heart-shaped leaves.

line *n* a cord, rope *etc*; a long thin stroke or mark; a wrinkle; a row (of printed words, ships, soldiers *etc*); a service of ships or aircraft; a railway; a telephone wire *etc*, or any connected system; a short letter; a family from generation to generation; course, direction; a kind or sort (of thing, activity *etc*); (*pl*) army trenches; (*pl*) a written school punishment exercise. – *v* to mark out with lines; (*esp* with **up**) to place in a row or alongside of; to form lines along (a street); to cover on the inside: *line a dress*. – *n* **lineage** ['liniij] one's descent, traced back to one's ancestors. – *adj* **lineal** ['liniǝl] directly descended through the father, grandfather *etc*. – *n* '**lineament** a feature, *esp* of the face. – *adj* '**linear** made of lines; (of measurement) in one dimension (length, breadth or height) only. – *ns* '**liner** a ship or aeroplane working on a regular service; '**lining** a covering on the inside. – *n* '**linesman** (in sport) an umpire at a boundary line. – **(ship, regiment) of the line** (a ship or regiment) belonging to the regular fighting forces.

'**linen** *n* cloth made of flax; articles made of linen (*eg* tablelinen, bedlinen).

ling *n* a type of long slender fish like the cod; heather.

linger ['lingǝr] *v* to remain for a long time or for longer than the expected time; to loiter, delay.

lingerie ['lönzhǝri] *n* women's underwear.

lingua franca ['lingwǝ'frankǝ] *n* any

(often simplified) language used amongst people from different nations *etc* so that they can talk together.

linguist ['lingwist] *n* one skilled in languages; one who studies language. – *adj* **lin'guistic**. – *n* **lin'guistics** the scientific study of languages and of language in general.

'**liniment** *n* an oil or ointment rubbed into the skin to cure stiffness in the muscles, joints *etc*.

'**lining** *n* the cover of the inside of anything.

link *n* a ring of a chain; a single part of a series; anything connecting two things. – *v* to connect as by a link; to join closely; to be connected.

links *npl* a stretch of flat or slightly hilly ground near the seashore; a golfcourse.

'**linnet** *n* a type of small songbird of the finch family.

'**lino** *n* short for **linoleum**. – *n* '**linocut** a design for printing cut into a block of linoleum.

linoleum [li'nōliǝm] *n* a type of smooth, hard-wearing covering for floors.

'**linseed** *n* flax seed. – *n* **linseed oil** oil from flax seed.

lint *n* linen scraped into a soft woolly material for putting over wounds; fine pieces of fluff.

'**lintel** *n* a timber or stone over a doorway or window.

'**lion** *n* a type of powerful animal of the cat family, the male of which has a shaggy mane: – *fem* '**lioness**. – *v* '**lionize** to treat (someone) as a celebrity. – **the lion's share** the largest share.

lip *n* the fleshy rim of the mouth; the edge of an opening, container *etc*. – *ns* '**lip-reading** reading what a person says from the movement of the lips; '**lip-service** saying one thing but believing another. *He pays lip-service to the rules*; '**lipstick** a stick of red, pink *etc* colouring for the lips.

'**liquefȳ** *v* to make or become liquid: – *pt* '**liquefied**. – *n* **lique'faction**.

liqueur [li'kūr] *n* a strong alcoholic drink, strongly flavoured and *usu* sweet.

'**liquid** *n* a flowing, water-like substance. – *adj* flowing; looking like water; soft and clear. – *v* '**liquidate** to close down, wind up the affairs of (a bankrupt business company); to get rid of by violence. – *ns* **liqui'dation**; '**liquidator**.

liquor ['likǝr] *n* any alcoholic drink, *esp* a strong kind (*eg* whisky).

liquorice, licorice ['likǝris] *n* a plant with a sweet root; a black, sticky sweet made from this root.

lira ['lērə] *n* the standard unit of Italian money.

lisp *v* to say *th* for *s* or *z* because of being unable to pronounce these letters correctly; to speak imperfectly, like a child. – Also *n*.

'lissom(e) *adj* nimble, bending easily.

list[1] *n* a series *eg* of names, numbers, prices *etc* written down one after the other. – *v* to write (something) down in this way. – *n* **listed building** one protected from being knocked down because it is of architectural or historical interest.

list[2] *v* (of a ship) to lean over to one side. – *n* a slope to one side.

listen ['lisn] *v* to give attention to so as to hear or to pay attention to the advice of. – *n* **'listener**.

'listless *adj* weary, without energy or interest. – *n* **'listlessness**.

lists *npl* (*hist*) the ground enclosed for a battle between knights on horseback.

lit *see* **light**[1] and **light**[3].

'litany *n* a set form of prayer: – *pl* **'litanies**.

literal ['litərəl] *adj* following the exact or most obvious meaning word for word with no exaggeration and nothing added by the imagination. – *adv* **'literally** exactly as stated. *He was literally blinded by the flash* means he actually lost the power of sight.

literary ['litərəri] *adj* of writing, books, authors *etc*; knowledgeable about books. – *n* **'literacy** ability to read and write. – *adj* **'literate** able to read and write.

literature ['litərəchər] *n* the books *etc* that are written in any language, *esp* novels, poetry *etc*; anything in written form on a subject.

lithe [lidh] *adj* (of a person or body) bending easily, supple, flexible.

'lithograph *n* a picture made from a drawing done on stone or metal. – *ns* **li'thographer**; **li'thography** printing done by this method.

liti'gation *n* a law case. – *adj* **li'tigious** fond of taking one's troubles to court.

litre ['lētər] *n* a metric measure of liquids (1·76 pint).

'litter *n* an untidy mess of paper, rubbish *etc*; a heap of straw as bedding for animals *etc*; a number of animals born at one birth; (*hist*) a kind of bed for carrying the sick and injured. – *v* to scatter carelessly about, *esp* rubbish *etc*; to produce a litter of young.

'little *adj* small in quantity or size. – *adv* in a small quantity or degree; not

much; not at all. *Little does he know.* – *pron* a small quantity, amount, distance *etc*. *Have a little more. Move a little to the right.*

'liturgy *n* the form of service of a church: – *pl* **'liturgies**. – *adj* **li'turgical**.

live[1] [liv] *v* to have life; to dwell; to pass one's life; to continue to be alive; to survive; (with **on**) to keep oneself alive; (with **on**) to be supported by; to be lifelike or vivid. – *n* **livelihood** ['livlihŏŏd] one's means of living (as one's daily work). – **live and let live** to allow others to live as they please; **live down** (*eg* one's past) to live until one's past acts are forgotten; **live up to** to be as good as expected.

live[2] [liv] *adj* having life, not dead; full of energy; (of a television broadcast *etc*) seen as the event takes place, not recorded; apt to burn, explode, or give an electric shock. – *adj* **'lively** full of life, high spirits, movement. – *n* **'liveliness**. – *v* **'liven** to make lively. – *ns* **'livestock** farm animals; **'livewire** a very lively, energetic person.

livelong ['livlong] *adj* whole: *the livelong day*.

liver ['livər] *n* a large gland in the body that carries out several important functions including purifying the blood. The liver of some animals is used as meat.

livery ['livəri] *n* the uniform of a manservant *etc*: – *pl* **'liveries**.

'livid *adj* of a bluish lead-like colour; (of a person) very angry.

'living *adj* having life; active, lively; (of a likeness) exact. – *n* means of living. – *ns* **'living-room** a sitting-room; **living wage** a wage on which it is possible to live comfortably.

'lizard *n* a kind of four-footed reptile.

llama ['lämə] *n* a type of S. American animal of the camel family without a hump.

lo! *interj* look!

loach *n* a type of small river fish: – *pl* **'loaches**.

load *v* to put on what is to be carried; to put the ammunition in (a gun); to put a film in (a camera); to weight for some purpose: *loaded dice.* – *n* as much as can be carried at once; cargo; a heavy weight or task; the power carried by an electric circuit. – *ns* **loaded question** one meant to trap a person into making an admission which is harmful to him; **'loadline** a line along a ship's side to mark the waterline when fully loaded.

loaf *n* a shaped mass of bread: – *pl* **loaves** [lōvz]. – *v* to pass time idly or lazily. – n 'loafer.

loam n a rich soil. – adj 'loamy.

loan n anything lent esp money. – v to lend.

loath, lōth adj unwilling (to).

loathe [lōdh] v to dislike greatly. – n 'loathing great hate or disgust. – adj 'loathsome causing loathing or disgust, horrible.

loaves see loaf.

lob n (in cricket) a slow, high ball bowled underhand; (in tennis) a ball high overhead dropping near the back of the court. – v to send such a ball; (coll) to throw: – pt **lobbed**.

'lobby n a small entrance hall; a passage off which rooms open; group of people who try to influence the government or other authority in a particular way: – pl 'lobbies.

lobe n the hanging-down part of an ear; a division of the brain, lungs etc.

'lobster n a kind of shellfish with large claws, used for food. – n **lobster pot** a basket in which lobsters are caught.

lobworm ['lobwōrm] n a kind of sea worm.

'lōcal adj of or confined to a certain place. – n (coll) one's nearest public house; (usu pl) the people living in a particular place or area. – n **locale** [lə'käl] the scene (of an) event. – n **locality** [lə'kaləti] a particular place and the area round about. – vs **localize** ['lōkəliz] to keep (something) to one area, keep from spreading; **lo'cate** to find; to set in a particular place: house located in north London. – n **lo'cation** the act of locating; situation. – ns **local colour** details in a story which make it more interesting and realistic; **local government** administration of the local affairs of a district etc by elected inhabitants. – **on location** (of filming) in natural surroundings, not in a studio.

loch [lohh] n (in Scotland) a lake; an arm of the sea.

lock n a fastening for doors etc (needing a key to open it); a part of a canal for raising or lowering boats; the part of a gun by which it is fired; a tight hold; a section of hair; (pl) hair. – v to fasten with a lock; to become fastened; (with **up**) to shut in (with a lock). – ns 'locker a small cupboard; 'locket a little ornamental case hung round the neck. – ns 'lockjaw a form of the disease tetanus which stiffens the jaw muscles; 'lockout the act of locking out (esp of factory workers etc by their employer during wages disputes);

'locksmith a smith who makes locks. – **lock, stock and barrel** completely.

locomotive [lōkə'mōtiv] n a railway engine. – adj of or capable of locomotion. – n loco'motion movement from place to place.

locum ['lōkəm] n one taking another's place (esp a doctor, dentist etc) for a time: – pl 'locums.

'lōcust n a type of large insect of the grasshopper family which destroys growing plants.

lodge n a small house (esp one at the entrance to a larger building); a beaver's dwelling; a house occupied during the shooting or hunting season; (the meeting place of) a branch of some societies. – v to live in rented rooms; to become fixed (in); to put in a safe place; to make (a complaint, appeal etc) officially. – ns 'lodger one who stays in rented rooms; 'lodging a place to stay, sleep etc; (pl) a room or rooms rented in another's house.

loft n a room or space just under a roof; a gallery in a hall, church etc. – adj 'lofty high up; noble, proud. – n 'loftiness

log n a thick, rough piece of wood, part of a felled tree; a device for measuring a ship's speed; a logbook. – v to write down (events) in a logbook: – pt **logged**. – n 'logbook a daily record of (a ship's or aeroplane's) progress.

'lōganberry n a kind of fruit like a large raspberry: – pl 'loganberries.

loggerhead ['logərhed]: **at loggerheads** quarrelling.

'logic n the study of reasoning correctly; correctness of reasoning. – adj 'logical according to the rules of logic or sound reasoning. – adv 'logically.

loin n the back of an animal cut for food; (pl) the lower part of the back. – n 'loincloth a piece of cloth worn round the hips, esp in India and south-east Asia.

'loiter v to proceed, move slowly; to linger; to stand around.

loll v to lie lazily about; (of the tongue) to hang down or out.

lone adj alone; standing by itself. – adj 'lonely lone; lacking or wanting companionship; (of a place) having few people. – n 'loneliness. – adj 'lonesome lone; feeling lonely.

long adj not short, measuring much from end to end; measuring a certain amount in distance or time: 2 cm long: 2 minutes long; far-reaching; slow to do something. – adv for a great time; through the whole time: all day long. – v to wish (for) very much. – n 'longing an eager desire. – *ns* '**longboat** the largest and strongest boat of a ship; '**longbow** a large bow bent by the hand in shooting; '**longhand** ordinary writing, not shorthand. – *adjs* '**long-'playing** (of a record) playing for a long time because of very fine grooves; '**long-'range** able to reach a great distance; (of a forecast) looking a long way into the future; '**long-'sighted** able to see things at a distance but not those close at hand; '**long-'suffering** putting up with troubles without complaining; '**long-'term** taking the future, not just the present, into account; '**long-'winded** using too many words. – **before long** soon; **in the long run** in the end.

lon'gevity [lon'jevəti] *n* great length of life.

longitude ['loŋgitūd] *n* the distance, measured in degrees on the map, of a place east or west of the Greenwich meridian.

loo *n* (*coll*) toilet.

look *v* to turn the eye towards so as to see; to seem; to face. *This room looks south.* – *n* the act of looking; the expression on one's face; appearance; (*pl*) personal appearance. – *ns* '**looking-glass** a mirror; '**lookout** (one who keeps) a careful watch; a high place for watching from; concern, responsibility. – **look down on** to despise, think of as being inferior; **look for** to search for; **look into** to investigate; **look on** to stand by and watch; to think of (as). *He looks on you as his mother*; **look out!** be careful! **look over** to examine briefly.

loom *n* machine for weaving cloth. – *v* to appear indistinctly, often threateningly.

loop *n* a doubled-over part in a piece of rope, string *etc*; a U-shaped bend (as in a river). – *n* '**loophole** a narrow slit in a wall; means of escaping or avoiding. – **loop the loop** to fly (an aircraft) upwards, backwards and down.

loose *adj* not tight, slack; not tied; free; not closely packed; vague, not exact; careless. – *adv* '**loosely**. – *vs* **loose**, '**loosen** to make loose, to slacken; to untie. – **break loose** to escape; **on the loose** free.

loot *n* goods stolen or plundered. – *v* to plunder, ransack.

lop *v* to cut off the top or ends of (*esp* a tree). – *pt* **lopped**. – *adjs* '**lop-'eared** having ears hanging down; '**lop-'sided** leaning to one side, not having the sides the same.

lope *v* to run with a long stride.

loquacious [lə'kwāshəs] *adj* talkative. – *ns* **lo'quaciousness**, **loquacity** [lə'kwasəti].

lord *n* the owner of an estate; a title given to noblemen, bishops and judges and used in other titles (as **Lord Mayor**); (*mainly hist*) a master, a ruler; **Lord** (with **the**) God. – *adj* '**lordly** like or belonging to a lord; noble, proud. – *ns* **Lord's day** Sunday; '**lordship** power, rule; used to or of a lord: *his lordship*. – **(House of) Lords** the upper (non-elected) house of the British parliament; **lord it over (someone)** to act like a lord, domineer.

lore *n* knowledge, beliefs *etc* handed down.

lorgnette [lör'nyet] *n* eyeglasses with a handle.

'**lorry** *n* a motor vehicle for carrying heavy loads: – *pl* '**lorries**.

lose [lōōz] *v* to cease to have, have no longer; to have (something) taken away from; to put (something) where it cannot be found; to waste (time); to miss (the train, a chance *etc*); not to win (a game *etc*): – *pt* **lost** [lost]. – *ns* **loser** ['lōōzər] one who loses; **loss** [los] the act of losing; that which is lost; waste, harm, destruction: – *pl* '**losses**. – *adj* **lost** not able to be found; no longer possessed; not won; thrown away; ruined; (with **in**) with attention totally taken up (by): *lost in thought*. – **at a loss** uncertain what to do.

loss, lost *see* **lose**.

lot *n* a large number or quantity; one's fortune or fate; a separate portion. – **cast** (or **draw**) **lots** to decide who is to do something by drawing names out of a box *etc*.

loth *see* **loath**.

'**lotion** *n* a liquid for soothing or cleaning the skin.

'**lottery** *n* the sharing-out of money or of prizes won by chance, through drawing lots: – *pl* '**lotteries**.

'**lotus** *n* kind of water-lily; (*myth*) a tree whose fruit was said to cause forgetfulness: – *pl* '**lotuses**.

loud *adj* making a great sound; noisy; showy, over-bright. – *advs* **loud**, '**loudly**. – *n* '**loud'speaker** an instrument for increasing the loudness of the voice *etc* to make it more widely heard.

lounge [lownj] *v* to lie back at one's ease; to move about lazily. – *n* a sitting room. – *n* '**lounger** a lazy person. – *n* **lounge suit** a man's suit for ordinary everyday (but not casual) wear.

lour *see* **lower**.

louse *n* a small blood-sucking insect sometimes found on the bodies of animals and people: – *pt* **lice**.

lout *n* a clumsy, awkward fellow.

love [luv] *n* great fondness, liking, affection; a loved person; (in tennis *etc*) no score, nothing. – *v* to be very fond of, to like very much. – *adjs* **'lovable** worthy of love; **'lovely** beautiful; delightful. – *n* **'lover** one who loves (someone); an admirer (of something); a person who is having a love affair with someone. – *adj* **'loving** full of love. – *n* **love affair** a (temporary) relationship between people in love but not married. – **in love (with)** feeling love and desire (for); having a great liking (for).

low [lō] *adj* not high, not lying or reaching far up; (of a voice) not loud; cheap; feeling sad; humble; mean, unworthy. – *v* to make the noise of cattle, to bellow or moo. – *adv* in or to a low position; not loudly; cheaply. – *n* **'lowness**. – *adj* **'lower** less high. – *v* to make less high; to let or come down. – *n* **'lowing** bellowing, mooing. – *adj* **'lowly** low in rank, humble. – *ns* **'lowliness; 'lowland** low or level country, without hills.

lower¹ *see* **low**.

lower², **lour** ['lowər] *v* (of the sky) to become dark and cloudy; to frown. – *adj* **'lowering**.

'loyal *adj* faithful, true. – *ns* **'loyalty**: – *pl* **'loyalties; 'loyalist** one who is true to his king and country.

'lozenge *n* a diamond-shaped figure; a small sweet for sucking.

lubricate ['lōobrikāt] *v* to oil (a machine *etc*) to make it move more easily and smoothly. – *ns* **lubri'cation; 'lubricant** something which lubricates, oil.

lucerne [lōo'sərn] *n* a type of plant used for feeding cattle, alfalfa.

lucid ['lōosid] *adj* easily understood; (of a mind) clear, not confused. – *n* **lu'cidity**.

luck *n* fortune, whether good or bad; chance; good fortune. – *adjs* **'luckless** unfortunate, unhappy; **'lucky** fortunate, having good luck; bringing good luck: – *comp* **'luckier**, *superl* **'luckiest**.

lucrative ['lōokrətiv] *adj* giving gain or profit.

lucre ['lōokər] *n* gain; money.

ludicrous ['lōodikrəs] *adj* ridiculous.

ludo ['lōodō] *n* a game played with counters on a board.

lug *v* to pull or drag with effort: – *pt* **lugged**. – *n* **'lugger** a type of small sailing vessel.

'luggage *n* suitcases and other baggage of a traveller.

lugubrious [lə'gōobriəs] *adj* mournful, dismal.

lugworm ['lugwərm] *n* a kind of large worm found on the seashore, used for bait by fishermen.

lukewarm ['lōokwörm] *adj* neither hot nor cold; not very eager, not enthusiastic.

lull *v* to soothe or calm. – *n* a period of calm. – *n* **'lullaby** a song to lull children to sleep: – *pl* **'lullabies**.

lum'bāgo *n* a pain in the lower part of the back.

'lumbar *adj* of or in the lower part of the back.

'lumber *n* useless old furniture *etc*; timber sawn up. – *v* to move about clumsily, heavily. – *n* **'lumberjack** one who fells, saws and shifts trees.

luminous ['lōominəs] *adj* giving light; shining; clear. – *n* **lumi'nosity**.

lump *n* a small, solid mass of no particular shape; a swelling; the whole taken together: *considered in a lump*; a heavy, dull person. – *v* to form into lumps; to treat as being alike, class (together). – *adjs* **'lumpish** heavy; dull; **'lumpy** full of lumps. – *n* **lump sum** an amount of money given all at once, not in instalments.

lunacy *see* **lunatic**.

lunar ['lōonər] *adj* of the moon.

lunatic ['lōonətik] *n, adj* (one who is) insane or crazy. – *n* **'lunacy**.

lunch *n* a midday meal: – *pl* **'lunches**. – *v* to eat lunch. – *n* **luncheon** ['lunchən] lunch.

lung *n* one of two bag-like parts of the body which fill and empty with air in the course of breathing.

lunge [lunj] *n* a sudden thrust or push. – Also *v*.

lupin ['lōopin] *n* a type of plant with flowers on long spikes.

lurch *v* to roll or pitch suddenly to one side, stagger. – *Also n.* – **leave in the lurch** to leave in a difficult position without help.

lure [lōor] *n* that which attracts or leads on, bait. – *v* to attract, entice away.

lurid ['lōorid] *adj* (of colour *etc*) glaring; horrifying, sensational; pale, like a ghost.

lurk *v* to keep out of sight; to be hidden; to move or act secretly and slyly. – *adj* **'lurking** (of a feeling) vague, hidden.

luscious ['lushəs] *adj* sweet, delicious, juicy.

lush *adj* (of grass *etc*) green, thick and plentiful.

lust *n* greedy desire (for power, riches *etc*); a strong sexual desire. – Also *v*. – *adj* '**lustful**.

lustre ['lustər] *n* brightness, splendour; gloss. – *adj* '**lustrous** bright, shining.

'**lusty** *adj* lively, strong.

lute [lŏot] *n* an old type of stringed musical instrument.

luxury ['lukshəri] *n* something pleasant (and expensive) but not necessary; the use or enjoyment of things of this sort: – *pl* '**luxuries**. – *adj* **luxuriant** [lug'zūriənt] having very great growth of leaves, branches *etc*; richly ornamented. – *v* **lu'xuriate** to be luxuriant; to enjoy, take delight (in). – *adj* **lu'xurious** supplied with luxuries; very comfortable.

'**lychgate** *n* a churchyard gate with a porch.

lying *see* **lie**.

lymph *n* a colourless fluid in the body. – *n* **lymph gland** one of the glands carrying lymph.

lynch *v* to condemn and put to death without legal trial.

lynx *n* a kind of wild animal of the cat family, noted for its keen sight: – *pl* '**lynxes**.

'**lȳre** *n* an old kind of musical instrument like the harp. – *n* '**lyrebird** a type of Australian bird with a lyre-shaped tail.

'**lyric** *n* a short poem (expressing the poet's feelings); (*pl*) the words of a song. – *adjs* '**lyric** of a lyric; full of (joyful) feeling; '**lyrical** lyric; song-like; full of enthusiastic praise.

M

macabre [mə'käbr] *adj* gruesome, horrible.

ma'cadamize *v* to surface (a road) with small broken stones.

maca'rōni *n* dried wheat paste made into long tubes and cooked.

maca'roon *n* a sweet cake or biscuit made mainly of almonds and sugar.

ma'caw *n* a kind of long-tailed brightly-coloured parrot.

mace *n* a heavy staff with an ornamental head (carried as a sign of office); (*hist*) a heavy stick; a spice made from the covering of a nutmeg.

Mach number [mähh] *n* the ratio of the speed of an aircraft to the velocity of sound (*eg* Mach 5 means 5 times the speed of sound).

machete [mə'cheti] *n* a kind of heavy knife used as a weapon *etc*.

machination [maki'nāshən] *n* (often *pl*) a crafty scheme, plot.

machine [mə'shēn] *n* a working arrangement of wheels, levers, or other parts; a (motor) bicycle. – *v* to sew (or do other jobs) with a machine. – *ns* **machinery** [mə'shēnəri] machines; the working parts of a machine; organization: *machinery of local government*; **ma'chinist** one who makes or works machinery. – *n* **ma'chine-gun** a gun which fires bullets very quickly one after the other.

'**mackerel** *n* a type of eatable seafish with wavy markings.

'**mackintosh** *n* a kind of waterproof overcoat: – *pl* '**mackintoshes**.

mad *adj* out of one's mind, insane; wildly foolish; furious with anger. – *n* '**madness**. – *v* '**madden** to make angry or mad. – *ns* '**madcap** a rash, hot-headed person; '**madhouse** any place of confusion and noise; (*hist*) a house for mad people; '**madman** one who is mad. – **like mad** very quickly, very energetically *etc*.

'**madam** *n* a polite form of address used to a woman.

made *see* **make**.

madeira [mə'dērə] *n* a kind of wine; a kind of sponge cake.

Ma'donna *n* the mother of Jesus, *esp* as shown in statues, pictures *etc*.

'**madrigal** *n* a part-song for several voices.

maelstrom ['mālstrəm] *n* a whirlpool; any place of great confusion.

maestro ['mīstrō] *n* one highly skilled in some art, *esp* a conductor or composer of music: – *pl* '**maestros**.

magazine [magə'zēn] *n* a paper published weekly, monthly *etc*, containing articles, stories, pictures *etc*; a storage place for military equipment, gunpowder *etc*; in a rifle, a place for extra cartridges.

ma'genta *adj, n* (of) a reddish-purple colour.

'**maggot** *n* a small worm-like creature, the grub of a blue-bottle *etc*. – *adj* '**maggoty** full of maggots.

'**magic** *n* any influence which produces results which cannot be explained or which are remarkable; conjuring tricks. – *adj* using magic; used in magic; magical. – *adj* 'magical of, produced by magic; very mysterious and beautiful; very wonderful or mysterious. – *n* **magician** [məˈjishən] one skilled in magic. – *n* **magic lantern** a device which throws pictures on a screen. – **black magic** magic which is done for an evil purpose, witchcraft.

'magistrate *n* one who has the power of putting the law into force in a police court, or as a Justice of the Peace. – *adj* **magis'tērial** of magistrates; having an air of authority.

magna'nimity *n* generosity. – *adj* **mag'nanimous** very generous.

'magnate *n* a person of great power or wealth.

magnesium [magˈnēziəm] *n* an element, a white metal which burns with a dazzling white light. – *n* **mag'nesia** a white powder formed from magnesium.

'magnet *n* a piece of iron, steel *etc* which has the power to attract other pieces of iron *etc*; a person or thing that attracts strongly. – *adj* **mag'netic** having the powers of a magnet; (of a person) strongly attractive. – *n* 'magnetism the power of a magnet; the science which deals with magnets; attraction, great charm. – *v* 'magnetize to make magnetic; to attract, influence. – *ns* **magnetic north** the direction in which the magnetized needle of a compass points; **magnetic tape** tape on which sound, pictures, computer material *etc* can be recorded.

mag'nēto *n* a device producing electric sparks, *esp* one for lighting the fuel in a motor-car engine: – *pl* **mag'netos.**

magnification *see* **magnify.**

mag'nificent *adj* splendid in appearance; great or noble in deeds; excellent, very fine. – *n* **mag'nificence.**

'magnifȳ *v* to make something appear larger (by using a magnifying glass); to exaggerate: – *pt* 'magnified. – *n* 'magnitude *n* greatness; size.

mag'nōlia *n* a type of tree with large white or purplish sweet-scented flowers.

'magpie *n* a black-and-white chattering bird of the crow family, known for its habit of collecting objects.

Maha'rajah *n* the title given to a great Indian prince: – *fem* **Maha'rani, Maha'ranee.**

ma'hogany *n* a type of tropical American tree or its hard reddish-brown wood, much used for furniture.

maid *n* a female servant; an unmarried

woman, a young girl. – *n* 'maiden an unmarried girl. – *adj* of a maiden, unmarried; first: *maiden speech*: *maiden voyage.* – *ns* **maiden name** the surname of a married woman before her marriage; **maiden over** (in cricket) an over in which no runs are made.

mail *n* letters, parcels *etc* carried by post; body armour of steel rings or plates; armour. – *v* to post.

maim *v* to cripple, disable.

main *adj* chief, most important. – *n* the ocean; (often *pl*) a chief pipe, wire *etc* supplying gas, water or electricity. – *adv* 'mainly chiefly, mostly. — *n* 'mainframe the central processing unit and storage unit of a computer. — *adj* (of a computer) of the large, powerful type rather than the small-scale kind. — *ns* 'mainland a large piece of land off whose coast smaller islands lie; 'mainsail the principal sail of a ship or boat; 'mainspring the chief spring, *esp* one which causes the wheels to move in a watch or clock; the chief cause of action; 'mainstay the chief support. — **in the main** for the most part.

main'tain *v* to keep (something) as it is; to continue to keep in good working order; to support (a family *etc*); to state (an opinion) firmly. – *n* 'maintenance the act of maintaining; upkeep, repair; means of support, *esp* money for food, clothing *etc.*

maize *n* a type of cereal crop grown widely in America.

'majesty *n* greatness of rank or manner; a title used to or of a king or queen (*eg* **Your Majesty**): – *pl* 'majesties. – *adj* **ma'jestic** stately.

'mājor *adj* greater or great in size, importance *etc*; opposite of **minor.** – *n* a senior army officer. – *n* **majority** [maˈjorəti] the greater number or quantity; the difference in amount between the greater and the lesser number; the age when one becomes legally an adult, in UK 18: – *pl* **ma'jorities.**

make *v* to form, construct; to cause to be. *You make me angry*; to bring about: *make trouble*; to amount to. *2 and 2 make 4*; to earn. *He makes £5 a day*; to force. *I made him do it*; to perform (a journey, an attempt *etc*); to prepare (*eg* a meal): – *pt* **made.** – *n* kind; shape, form; brand. – *n* 'maker. – *n, adj* 'makeshift (a thing) used for a time for want of something better. – *n* 'make-up cosmetics for a woman, or for an actor or actress. – **make believe** to pretend (n 'make-believe); make good to do well; to carry out (a promise); to make up for (a loss); make light of to treat as unimportant; make much of to fuss over, treat as important; make nothing of not to be able to understand, do etc; make light of; make off to run away; make up to see (in the distance or indistinctly); to declare, prove; to write out (a bill etc) formally; make up to form a whole. Eleven players make up the side; to put together, invent (a false story); to put make-up on the face; to be friendly again after a quarrel; make up for to give or do something in return for damage etc that one has done.

maladjusted [malə'justid] adj unable to fit in happily in one's work, way of life etc.

'maladminis'tration n bad management, esp of public affairs.

'malady n illness, disease: – pl 'maladies.

malaise [ma'lāz] n a feeling of discomfort.

'malapropism n the use of a wrong word which sounds something like the one intended eg contemptuous for contemporary.

ma'lāria n a fever caused by the bite of a certain type of mosquito.

male adj of the sex that is able to father children or young, masculine. – Also n.

malefactor ['malifaktər] n an evildoer.

malevolent [mə'levələnt] adj wishing ill to others, spiteful. – n ma'levolence.

malfor'mation n faulty or wrong shape.

malice ['malis] n ill will, spite. – adj malicious [mə'lishəs].

malign [mə'lin] v to speak evil of, esp falsely.

ma'lignant adj wishing to do great harm, spiteful; (of a disease etc) likely to cause death.

malinger [mə'lingər] v to pretend to be ill (to avoid work etc). – n ma'lingerer.

'mallard n the (male of the) common wild duck.

malleable ['maliəbl] adj (of metal etc) able to be beaten out by hammering; (of people) easy to influence.

'mallet n a kind of wooden hammer.

malnū'trition n underfeeding or poor feeding.

ma'lōdorous adj having a bad smell.

malpractice ['mal'praktis] n wrongdoing; failure to practise one's profession in a correct or proper way.

malt [mōlt] n barley or other grain prepared for making beer or whisky.

mal'treat v to treat roughly or unkindly. – n mal'treatment.

ma'm(n)a n a name sometimes used for mother.

'mammal n any of the kinds of animals of which the female feeds her young with her own milk.

'mammoth n a type of very large elephant, now extinct. – adj huge.

man n a human being; the human race; a grown-up human male; a husband; a piece in chess or draughts: – pl men. – v to supply with men: man the boats: – pt manned. – adj 'manful courageous. – adv 'manfully. – adjs 'manly brave, strong; 'mannish (of a woman) behaving, looking like a man. – n 'man-at-'arms a soldier. – v 'manhandle to handle roughly. – ns 'manhole a hole (into a drain, sewer etc) large enough to let a man through; 'manhood the state of being a man; manly quality; 'mankind the human race; 'man-of-'war a warship; 'manpower the number of people available for work; 'manslaughter the unintentional but blameworthy killing of a man. – Also v. – the man in the street the ordinary person; to a man every single one.

'manacle n a handcuff. – Also v.

'manage v to have control or have charge of; to deal with; to cope; to succeed. – adj 'manageable easily managed or controlled. – ns 'management the people in charge of organizing a business etc; the art of managing a business etc; 'manager a person who looks after a business etc: – fem 'manage'ress.

'mandarin n a type of fruit like a small orange; (hist) a senior Chinese official.

'mandate n a command; power given to person or nation to act in the name of another. – adj 'mandatory compulsory.

'mandible n the jaw or lower jawbone.

'mandolin(e) n a kind of round-backed stringed musical instrument like a guitar.

mane n long hair on the head and neck eg on the horse and the male of the lion.

maneuver see manoeuvre.

manganese [mangə'nēz] n an element, a hard easily-broken metal of a greyish-white colour.

mange [mānj] n a skin disease of dogs, cats etc. – adj 'mangy.

'mangel-wurzel n a kind of beetroot, grown as food for cattle.

manger ['mānjər] n a box or trough holding dry food for horses and cattle.

mangle ['mangl] n a machine for squeezing water out of clothes or for smoothing them. – *v* to squeeze (clothes) through a mangle; to smooth (clothes) by means of a mangle; to crush, tear, damage badly.

mango ['maŋgō] *n* a type of tree found in India or its reddish, juicy fruit: – *pl* '**mangoes**.

mangrove ['maŋgrōv] *n* a type of tree which grows on swamps in hot countries.

'**mānia** *n* a form of mental illness in which the sufferer is over-active, over-excited and unreasonably happy; (too) great fondness or enthusiasm (for something): *a mania for collecting records.* – *n* '**maniac** a madman; a very rash or over-enthusiastic person. – *adj* **manic** ['manik] suffering from mania; very energetic, very active, very excited.

'**manicure** *n* the care of hands and nails. – Also *v.* – *n* '**manicurist** one who cares for and treats hands and nails.

'**manifest** *adj* easily seen or understood. – *v* to show plainly. – *ns* **manifes'tation**; **mani'festo** a public announcement of intentions (*esp* by a political party): – *pl* **mani'festo(e)s**.

'**manifōld** *adj* many and various.

ma'nipūlate *v* to handle or manage skilfully, cunningly or dishonestly.

mankind, manly *see* **man**.

'**manna** *n* in the Bible, the food provided miraculously for the Israelites in the wilderness; any unexpected or delicious treat.

mannequin ['manikin] *n* a person, *usu* a woman, who wears clothes to show intending buyers how they look, a model.

'**manner** *n* the way (in which anything is done); the way in which a person behaves; (*pl*) (polite) behaviour *usu* towards others. – *n* '**mannerism** an odd and obvious habit in someone's behaviour *etc.* – *adj* '**mannerly** polite. – **all manner of** all kinds of.

manoeuvre, (*US*) **maneuver** [mə'nōōvər] *n* a planned movement of troops, ships or aircraft; a trick, a cunning plan. – *v* to perform a manoeuvre; to move or manage cunningly.

'**manor** *n* (*hist*) the land belonging to a lord or squire; a large house *usu* attached to a country estate. – *adj* **ma'norial**.

manse *n* (in Scotland) the house of a clergyman.

mansion ['manshən] *n* a large house.

mantelpiece ['mantlpēs] *n* a shelf over a fireplace.

mantilla [man'tilə] *n* a kind of veil covering the head and shoulders sometimes worn by Spanish women.

'**mantle** *n* a cloak or loose outer garment; a covering: *a mantle of snow*; a piece of thin, transparent, material round the light in gas or some paraffin lamps.

'**manūal** *adj* of the hand or hands; worked by hand; working with the hands: *manual worker.* – *n* a handbook used *eg* to give instructions as to how to use something: *a car manual*; the keyboard of an organ *etc.*

manū'factūre *v* to make (articles, materials *etc*), formerly by hand, now *usu* by machinery, and in large quantities. – *n* the process of manufacturing; anything manufactured. – *n* **manu'facturer**.

ma'nure *n* a substance, *esp* animal dung, used to make soil more fertile. – *v* to treat (soil, plants) with manure.

'**manūscript** *n* the prepared material for a book *etc* before it is printed; a book or paper written by hand.

Manx cat [maŋks] *n* a type of cat that has no tail.

many ['meni] *adj* a large number of: *many people were present.* – *pron* a large number. *Many survived.* – **many a** (followed by a *sing* noun) a large number of. *Many a man had to die before the war ended.*

map *n* a flat drawing of (part of) the earth's surface, showing various details *eg* rivers, mountains *etc.* – *v* to make a map of; (with **out**) to plan: – *pt* **mapped**.

'**māple** *n* any of several kinds of tree of the same type as the sycamore, one of which produces sugar; its hard light-coloured wood used for furniture *etc.*

mar *v* to spoil *eg* the appearance of someone. *The scar marred her beauty*: – *pt* **marred**.

ma'raud *v* to plunder, raid. – *n* **ma'rauder** a plundering robber. – *adj* **ma'rauding**.

'**marble** *n* any kind of limestone that takes a high polish, used for sculpture, decorating buildings *etc*; a little ball, now *usu* of glass, used in a children's game.

'**marcasite** *n* crystals formed from iron and used in jewellery.

March *n* the third month of the year.

march *v* (to cause) to walk in time with regular step; to go on steadily. – *n* a marching movement; a piece of music for marching to; the distance covered by marching; a steady going forward (of events *etc*): *the march of time*; a boundary: – *pl* '**marches**.

marchioness *see* **marquess**.

mare *n* the female of the horse.

margarine ['märjərēn] *n* a substance like butter, made mainly of vegetable fats.

'**margin** *n* an edge, border; the blank edge on the page of a book; something extra (*eg* time, money *etc*) beyond what seems to be needed. – *adj* '**marginal** placed in the margin; of or in a margin; borderline, close to a limit; (of a political constituency *etc*) without a clear majority for any one candidate or party; of little effect or importance: *a marginal improvement*.

marguerite [märgə'rēt] *n* a kind of large daisy.

'**marigōld** *n* a kind of plant with a yellow flower.

marijuana [mari'wänə] *n* a drug made from the plant hemp.

marina [mə'rēnə] *n* a place with moorings for yachts, sailing dinghies *etc*.

marine [mə'rēn] *adj* of the sea. – *n* a soldier serving on board a ship; shipping in general. – *n* **mariner** ['marinər] a sailor.

mario'nette *n* a puppet moved by strings.

'**marital** *adj* of marriage.

'**maritime** *adj* of the sea or ships; lying near the sea.

'**marjoram** *n* a type of sweet-smelling herb used as a flavouring.

mark *n* a sign that can be seen; a stain, spot *etc*; a target, a thing aimed at; trace; a point or unit used in establishing how good a piece of work is (*esp* in schools); the starting-line in a race: *on your marks*; the standard unit of German money. – *v* to make a mark on; to observe, watch; to stay close to (an opponent in football *etc*); to award marks to (a piece of schoolwork *etc*); (with **off**) to separate, distinguish. – *adj* **marked** easily noticed: *a marked improvement*. – *adv* **markedly** ['märkidli] noticeably. – *n* '**marker** one who marks the score at games; any object (as a counter *etc*) used to mark the score. – *n* '**marksman** one who shoots well. – **mark time** to move the feet up and down, as if marching, but without going forward; **up to the mark** coming up to the required standard.

'**market** *n* a public place for buying and selling; (a country, place *etc* where there is) a need or demand (for certain types of goods); sale. *His house is on the market.* – *v* to put on sale. – *n*

'**market-'garden** a garden in which fruit and vegetables are grown to be sold.

marlinspike ['märlinspik] *n* a spike for separating the strands of a rope *etc*.

'**marmalade** *n* a jam made from oranges, grapefruit or lemons.

marmoset ['märmɔzet] *n* a type of small monkey found in America.

'**marmot** *n* a kind of burrowing animal of the squirrel family (also **woodchuck** or **groundhog**).

ma'roon *adj*, *n* (of) a brownish-red colour. – *n* a firework used as a distress signal *etc*. – *v* to leave on an island without means of escape; to leave in a helpless or uncomfortable position.

marquee [mär'kē] *n* a large tent used for large gatherings (*eg* a wedding reception) or public entertainment (*eg* a circus).

'**marquess**, '**marquis** *n* a nobleman below a duke in rank: – *pl* '**marquesses**, '**marquises**: – *fem* **marchioness** ['märshənis]: – *pl* **marchio'nesses**.

marriage *see* **marry**.

marrow ['marō] *n* the soft substance in the hollow parts of bones; a type of long thick-skinned vegetable.

'**marry** *v* to join (or be joined) together as husband and wife: – *pt* '**married**. – *n* **marriage** ['marij] the ceremony by which a man and woman become husband and wife; a joining together. – *adj* '**marriageable** suitable or old enough for marriage.

marsh *n* a piece of low-lying wet ground: – *pl* '**marshes**. – *adj* '**marshy**. – *ns* **marsh'mallow** a type of marsh plant with pink flowers; a foam-like sweet sticky substance; **marsh marigold** a type of marsh plant with yellow flowers (also **kingcup**).

'**marshal** *n* a high-ranking officer in the army or air force; one who directs processions *etc*; (*US*) a kind of lawcourt official; (*US*) a head of a police force. – *v* to arrange (troops, facts, arguments *etc*) in order; to show the way, conduct, lead: – *pt* '**marshalled**. – *n* **marshalling yard** a place where railway wagons are shunted about to make up trains.

mar'sūpial *n* any animal which carries its young in a pouch (*eg* the kangaroo, opossum).

mar'tello tower *n* a round coastal fort.

'**marten** *n* a kind of animal related to the weasel, with valuable fur.

martial ['märshəl] *adj* warlike; of, or suitable for war. – *n* **martial law** the government of a country by army rules and rulers.

'**martin** *n* a kind of bird of the swallow family.

marti'**net** *n* one who keeps strict order.

'**martyr** *n* one who suffers death or hardship for what he believes. – *v* to put a person to death or make him suffer for his beliefs. – *n* '**martyrdom** the death or suffering of a martyr.

'**marvel** *n* anything astonishing or wonderful. – *v* to feel amazement (at): – *pt* '**marvelled**. – *adj* '**marvellous** astonishing, extraordinary; (*coll*) excellent, very good.

marzi'**pan** *n* a mixture of ground almonds, sugar *etc*, used in the making of sweets and cakes.

'**mascot** *n* a person, animal or thing that is supposed to bring good luck. *The football team's mascot was a teddy bear.*

masculine ['maskūlin] *adj* of the male sex; manly. – *n* mascu'**linity**.

mash *v* to beat or crush into a pulp-like mixture. – *n* mashed potato; a mixture, *esp* one of bran, meal *etc*, used as food for animals.

mask *n* a cover for the face (for disguise or protection); something pretended, disguise. – *v* to cover the face with a mask; to hide.

masochism ['masɔkizm] *n* unnatural pleasure taken in being dominated or cruelly treated. – *n* '**masochist** one who takes such pleasure.

'**mäson** *n* a worker in stone; a Freemason. – *adj* ma'**sonic**. – *n* '**masonry** stonework.

masque [mäsk] *n* an old type of theatre show in which the actors wore masks.

masquerade [maskə'räd] *n* a dance at which masks are worn; pretence. – *v* to pretend to be someone else. *He masqueraded as a butler.*

mass *n* a lump or quantity gathered together; a large quantity; the main part or body: – *pl* '**masses**; **Mass** (in some Christian Churches) the celebration of Christ's last supper with his disciples; music for this celebration. – *adj* of a mass; of or consisting of large numbers or quantities. – *v* to form into a mass. – *adj* '**massive** bulky, heavy, huge. – *ns* **mass media** means of communicating information to a large number of people *eg* television; **mass production** production in large quantities of articles all exactly the same.

massacre ['masɔkɔr] *n* the cruel killing of great numbers of people. – *v* to kill (large numbers) in a cruel way.

massage ['masäzh] *n* the rubbing of parts of the body (muscles, knees *etc*)

esp to remove pain or stiffness. – Also *v*. – *n* **masseur** [ma'sör] one who massages: – *fem* **masseuse** [ma'söz].

mast *n* a long upright pole, *esp* one holding up the sails *etc* in a ship or one holding an aerial, flag *etc*.

'**master** *n* one who controls or commands; an owner (of a dog *etc*); an employer; a male teacher; the commander of a merchant ship: one very skilled in something, an expert; a degree awarded by universities, as **Master of Arts, Science** *etc*. – *adj* chief; controlling: *master switch*. – *v* to overcome, defeat; to become able to do (a thing) thoroughly. – *adjs* '**masterful** strong-willed; '**masterly** showing the skill of an expert or master, clever. – *n* '**mastery** victory (over); control (of); great skill (in). – *n* '**master-key** a key which is so made that it opens a number of different locks. – *v* '**mastermind** to plan, work out the details of (a scheme *etc*). – Also *n*. – *ns* '**masterpiece** the best example of someone's work, *esp* a very fine picture, book, piece of music *etc*; '**masterstroke** a clever act or move.

'**masticate** *v* to chew. – *n* masti'**cation**.

'**mastiff** *n* a breed of large, powerful dog.

mat *n* a piece of material (coarse plaited plant fibre, carpet *etc*) for wiping shoes on, covering the floor *etc*; a piece of material, wood *etc* put below dishes at table. – *adj see* **matt**. – *adj* '**matted** thickly tangled. – *n* '**matting** material from which mats are made.

'**matador** *n* the man who kills the bull in bullfights.

match *n* a small stick of wood or other material ('**matchstick**) tipped with a substance which easily catches fire when rubbed against something hard; a person or thing similar to or the same as another; a person or thing agreeing with or suiting another; an equal; a (person suitable for) marriage; a contest or game: – *pl* '**matches**. – *v* to be of the same make, size, colour *etc*; to set (two things, teams *etc*) against each other; to hold one's own with, be equal to. – *adj* '**matchless** having no equal. – *ns* '**matchbox** a box for holding matches; '**matchwood** wood broken into small pieces.

mate *n* a companion or fellow-worker; a husband or wife; either the male or female of a pair of animals, birds *etc*; a merchant ship's officer, next in rank to the captain. – *v* to marry; (of animals or birds) to bring or come together for breeding purposes.

ma'tērial *adj* made of matter, able to be seen and felt; not spiritual, concerned with physical comfort, money *etc*: *a material outlook on life*; important, essential: *a material difference.* – *n* something out of which anything is, or may be, made; cloth. – *adv* **ma'terially** to a large extent, greatly. – *ns* **ma'terialism** a tendency to attach too much importance to material things (*eg* physical comfort, money); the belief that only things we can see or feel really exist or are important. – *n* **ma'terialist.** – *adj* **materia'listic.** – *v* **ma'terialize** to appear in bodily form; to happen, come about.

ma'ternal *adj* of a mother; like a mother, motherly; related through one's mother: *maternal grandmother.* – *n* **ma'ternity** the state of being a mother, motherhood. – *adj* of or for a woman having or about to have a baby: *maternity clothes.*

mathematics [mathə'matiks] *n* the study of measurements, numbers and quantities. – *adj* **mathe'matical** of or done by mathematics; very exact. – *n* **mathema'tician** one good at mathematics; one whose job is concerned with mathematics.

matinée ['matinā] *n* an afternoon performance in a theatre *etc.* – *n* **matinée coat** a baby's short jacket.

'matins *npl* the morning service in certain churches.

'matricide *n* the killing of one's own mother; one who kills his own mother.

ma'triculate *v* to admit, or be admitted to a university.

'matrimony *n* marriage. – *adj* **matri'mōnial.**

'mātrix *n* a mould in which metals, *etc* are shaped; a mass of rock in which gems *etc* are found: – *pl* **matrices** ['mātrisēz].

'mātron *n* a married woman; a senior nurse in charge of a hospital; a woman in charge of housekeeping or nursing in a school, hostel *etc.* – *adj* **'matronly** (of a woman) dignified, staid; plump.

matt, mat *adj* having a dull surface, not shiny or glossy.

'matter *n* anything that takes up space, can be seen, felt *etc*; material, substance; a subject written or spoken about; (sometimes *pl*) affair, business; trouble, difficulty. *What is the matter?*; importance. *It is of no great matter*; pus. – *v* to be of importance. *It does not matter*; to give out pus. *His wound is mattering.* – *adj* **'matter-of-'fact** keeping to the actual facts, not imaginative;

uninteresting. – **a matter of course** something that is to be expected. *His promotion came as a matter of course*; **a matter of opinion** a subject on which different opinions are held; **as a matter of fact** in fact.

'mattock *n* a kind of tool like a pickaxe.

'mattress *n* a thick firm layer of padding covered in cloth *etc*, for lying on, *usu* as part of a bed: – *pl* **'mattresses**.

ma'ture *adj* fully grown or developed; ripe, ready for use. – *v* to (cause to) become mature; of an insurance policy *etc* to be due to be paid out. – *n* **ma'turity** ripeness.

'maudlin *adj* silly, sentimental.

maul *v* to hurt badly by rough or savage treatment.

mauso'lēum *n* a very fine tomb.

mauve [mōv] *adj, n* (of) a purple colour.

'mawkish *adj* weak and sentimental.

'maxim *n* a general truth or rule showing how one should behave *etc.*

'maximum *adj* greatest, most. – *n* the greatest number or quantity; the highest point or degree: – *pl* **'maxima**.

May *n* the fifth month of the year. – *ns* **'Mayday** the first day of May; **'may-day** an international distress signal; **'maypole** a decorated pole for dancing round on Mayday.

may *v usu* used with another verb to express permission, possibility *etc*. *Yes, you may watch the film. I may find him there*; used to express a wish. *May you always be happy!*: – *pt* **might** [mit].

'maybē *adv* perhaps.

mayonnaise [māə'nāz] *n* a sauce made of eggs, oil, vinegar or lemon juice *etc.*

mayor [mār] *n* the chief public official of a city or town. – *n* **'mayoress** a mayor's wife; a mayor who is a woman.

maze *n* a series of winding paths in a park *etc* deliberately laid out in such a way that it is difficult to find the way out; something complicated and confusing: *a maze of regulations.*

ma'zurka *n* (the music for) a kind of lively Polish dance.

mē *pron* the word used by a speaker or writer in mentioning himself (as the object in a sentence). *He hit me. Give it to me.*

mead *n* an alcoholic drink made with honey.

meadow ['medō] *n* a field of grass. – *n* **'meadowsweet** a type of wild flower with sweet-smelling cream-coloured flowers.

'meagre, (*US*) **'meager** *adj* thin; poor in quality; scanty, not enough. – *n* **'meagreness**.

meal *n* the food taken at one time (*eg* breakfast, dinner, supper); grain ground to a coarse powder. – *adj* **'mealy-'mouthed** not frank and straightforward in speech.

mean[1] *adj* not generous with money *etc*; unkind, selfish; lowly, humble. – *n* **'meanness**.

mean[2] *adj* middle, coming midway between two other things, points, quantities *etc*; average. – *n* something lying midway between two other things *etc*; (*pl*) a method, instrument, action *etc* by which anything is brought about; money, property *etc*: *a man of means*. – **by all means** certainly, of course; in any or every way possibly; **by no means** certainly not; not at all; (**in the**) **'meantime, 'meanwhile** in the time between two happenings.

mean[3] *v* (to intend) to express, indicate. *'Halt' means 'stop'. By 'several' I mean three or more*; to intend: – *pt, pp* **meant** [ment]. – *n* **'meaning** what is (intended to be) expressed or conveyed; purpose, intention. – *adj* (of a look, glance *etc*) full of a certain meaning indicating a certain feeling. – *adjs* **'meaningful; 'meaningless**. – **mean well (ill)** to have good (bad) intentions.

me'ander *v* (of a river) to flow in a winding course; to wander about slowly and aimlessly.

measles ['mēzlz] *n sing* a kind of infectious disease, with red spots. – *adj* **'measly** (*coll*) ungenerous, mean.

measure ['mezhǝr] *n* size or amount (found by measuring); an instrument, container *etc* for measuring; musical time; (often *pl*) a plan of action. *They took measures to prevent their house from being burgled*; a law brought before parliament to be considered. – *v* to find out the size, quantity *etc* by using some form of measure; to be of a certain length, amount *etc*. *This wall measures 2 metres across*; to indicate the measurement of (something). *A thermometer measures temperature*; to mark (off), weigh (out) *etc* in portions. – *adj* **'measured** steady, unhurried. – *n* **'measurement** the act of measuring; the size, amount *etc* found by measuring.

meat *n* flesh of animals used as food. – *adj* **'meaty** full of meat; tasting of meat; (of a book *etc*) full of information.

mechanic [mi'kanik] *n* a skilled worker with tools or machines. – *adj* **me'chanical** of machinery: *mechanical engineer-*

ing; worked by machinery; done without thinking. – *adv* **me'chanically**. – *n* **me'chanics** the study of forces and motion; the study and art of constructing machinery; the actual details of how something works. *The mechanics of his plan are beyond me*. – *n* **'mechanism** a piece of machinery; the way a piece of machinery works; an action by which a result is produced – *v* **'mechanize** to equip (a factory *etc*) with machinery; to supply (troops) with armoured vehicles. – *n* **mechani'zation**.

'medal *n* a piece of metal *etc* in the form of a coin or a coin-like object, with a design, inscription *etc* stamped on it, made in memory of an event or given as a reward for merit. – *ns* **me'dallion** a large medal; **'medallist** one who has gained a medal.

'meddle *v* to concern oneself with things that are not one's business, to interfere or tamper (with). – *n* **'meddler**. – *adj* **'meddlesome** fond of meddling.

media *see* **medium**.

mediaeval *see* **medieval**.

'mediate *v* to act as a peacemaker (between). – *ns* **medi'ation; 'mediator** one who tries to make peace between people who are quarrelling.

medicine ['medsin] *n* something given to a sick person in order to make him better; the science of the treatment of illnesses. – *adj* **medical** ['medikǝl] of doctors or their work. – *n* **me'dicament** a medicine. – *adj* **medicated** ['medikātid] mixed with a healing or disinfecting substance. – *n* **medi'cation** medical treatment; a medicine. – *adj* **medicinal** [mǝ'disinl] used in medicine; used as a medicine; having the power to cure. – *n* **medicine man** a witch doctor.

medieval mediaeval [medi'ēvǝl] *adj* of the Middle Ages.

medi'ocre *adj* not very good, ordinary. – *n* **mediocrity** [mēdi'okrǝti].

'meditate *v* to think deeply and in quietness; to consider, think about. – *n* **medi'tation** deep, quiet thought. – *adj* **'meditative** thoughtful.

'medium *n* something (a means, a substance, a material *etc*) through which an effect is produced: – *pl* **'media** or **'mediums**; a means (*esp* television, radio or newspapers) by which news *etc* is made public: – *pl* **'media**; a person through whom spirits (of dead people) are said to speak: – *pl* **'mediums**. – *adj* middle or average in size, quality *etc*.

'medley *n* a mixture; a piece of music put

together from a number of other pieces: – *pl* '**medleys**.

meek *adj* gentle, uncomplaining. – *n* '**meekness**.

meerschaum ['mĕrshəm] *n* a fine white clay used to make tobacco pipes; a pipe made of this.

meet *v* to come face to face (with); to come together, join; to make the acquaintance of; to pay (bills *etc*) fully; to be suitable for, satisfy (requirements, a demand *etc*): – *pt* **met**. – *n* a meeting of huntsmen or other sportsmen. – *adj* proper, suitable. – *n* '**meeting** a coming together, *esp* of people; an assembly, gathering.

mega- *prefix* great, huge.

'**megalith** *n* a huge stone set up in prehistoric times.

megalo'mānia *n* an exaggerated idea of one's own importance or abilities.

'**megaphone** *n* a large trumpet-like device for making louder the sound of the voice.

megaton ['megətun] *adj* of a bomb with an explosive force equalling a million tons of TNT.

melancholy ['melənkəli] *n* lowness of spirits, sadness. – *adj* sad, depressed.

mélée ['melā] *n* a confused fight between two groups of people.

mellifluous [mə'liflooəs] *adj* sweet-sounding.

mellow ['melō] *adj* (of fruit) ripe, juicy, sweet; having become pleasant or agreeable with age; (of light, colour *etc*) soft, not harsh. – *v* to make or become mellow. – *n* '**mellowness**.

'**melodrama** *n* a type of play, intended to arouse great sympathy, horror *etc*. – *adj* **melodra'matic** of or like a melodrama, sensational, over-dramatic.

'**melody** *n* a tune; sweet music: – *pl* '**melodies**. – *adjs* **me'lodic** of melody; **me'lōdious** pleasing to the ear; tuneful.

'**melon** *n* a type of large juicy fruit or the plant that bears it.

melt *v* to make or become liquid, *esp* by heat; to soften; to disappear. *The crowd melted away*; to become tender in feeling. *His heart melted at the sight of the orphan*.

'**member** *n* one who belongs to any group, society *etc*; a limb of the body. – *n* '**membership** the members of a club *etc*; the state of being a member. – *n* **Member of Parliament** (shortened to **MP**) a person elected to the House of Commons.

'**membrane** *n* a thin skin which covers or lines parts of a human or animal body,

plants *etc*.

me'mento *n* something by which an event is remembered: – *pl* **me'mentos**

'**memo** short for **memorandum**: – *pl* '**memos**.

memoir ['memwär] *n* a written statement of what has happened; (*pl*) person's account of his own life, an autobiography.

memo'randum *n* a note which helps one to remember; a written statement of matter being discussed; a brief note sent round colleagues in an office *etc*: – *pl* **memo'randa**.

'**memory** *n* the power to remember; the mind's store of remembered things; something remembered; what is remembered about a person, his reputation: – *pl* '**memories**. – *adj* '**memorable** worthy of being remembered, famous. – *n* **me'morial** something (*eg* a monument) which helps us to remember persons or events of the past. – *adj* commemorating, honouring the memory of a person *etc*. – *v* **memorize** ['meməriz] to learn by heart. – **in memory of** in remembrance of or as a memorial of.

menace ['menəs] *n* harm or danger that may happen; a threat. – *v* to be danger to; to threaten. – *adj* '**menacing** evil-looking; threatening.

ménage [mā'näzh] *n* household.

menagerie [mi'najəri] *n* (a place for keeping) a collection of wild animals.

mend *v* to put right something broken torn *etc*, to repair; to make or grow better. – *n* a part which has been mended. – **on the mend** getting better

mendacious [men'dāshəs] *adj* untruthful. – *n* **mendacity** [men'dasəti].

'**mendicant** *n* a beggar. – Also *adj*.

menhir ['menhĕr] *n* a tall upright prehistoric stone.

'**mēnial** *adj* (of work) humble, uninteresting, not requiring skill.

menin'gitis *n* an illness caused by inflammation of the covering of the brain

menstruation [menstroo'āshən] *v* (in women) the monthly discharge of blood from the womb. – *adj* '**menstrual** of menstruation. – *v* '**menstruate**.

mensū'ration *n* the act or art of measuring length, height *etc*.

'**mental** *adj* of the mind; done, made happening *etc* in the mind; (of illness) affecting the mind. – *n* **men'tality** mental power; personality: – *pl* **men'talities**. – *n* **mental hospital** hospital for people suffering from mental illness.

menthol *n* a sharp-smelling substance got from peppermint oil.

mention *v* to speak of briefly; to remark (that). – *n* (act of) mentioning or remarking.

mentor *n* a (wise) giver of advice.

menū *n* (a card with) a list of dishes to be served at a meal: – *pl* **'menus**.

mercantile *adj* of buying and selling, trading.

mercenary ['mɜrsɪnərɪ] *adj* working for money; influenced by the desire for money. – *n* a soldier who is paid by a foreign country to fight in its army: – *pl* **'mercenaries**.

merchant *n* one who carries on a business in the buying and selling of goods, a trader. – *adj* of trade. – *n* **'merchandise** goods to be bought and sold. – *ns* **'merchantman** a trading ship; **merchant navy** ships and crews employed in trading.

mercūry *n* an element, a heavy, silvery liquid metal (also **quicksilver**). – *adj* **mer'curial** lively, often changing.

mercy *n* kindness, forgiveness towards an enemy, wrongdoer *etc*; pity; (*coll*) a bit of good luck. – *adjs* **'merciful** willing to forgive or to punish only lightly; **'merciless** cruel. – **at one's mercy** in one's power.

mere *n* a pool or a lake. – *adj* nothing more than, no more than: *mere nonsense*. – *adv* **'merely** only, simply.

merge *v* to (cause to) combine or join together; to blend, come together gradually. – *n* **'merger** a joining together *esp* of business firms *etc*.

me'ridian *n* a (semi-)circle drawn round the globe passing through the north and south poles; the highest point of the sun's course; the highest point of success *etc*.

meringue [mə'raŋ] *n* a cake made of sugar and white of egg.

merino [mə'rēnō] *n* a kind of sheep which has very fine wool; soft cloth made from its wool: – *pl* **me'rinos**.

merit *n* that which deserves praise or reward; worth, value; (*pl*) the rights and wrongs (of a case, affair *etc*). – *v* to deserve. – *adj* **meri'torious** deserving honour or reward.

mermaid *n* an imaginary sea creature with a woman's body down to the waist, and a fish's tail: – *masc* **'merman**.

merry *adj* full of fun, cheerful and lively; slightly drunk. – *n* **'merriment** fun; laughter. – *ns* **'merry-go-round** a kind of roundabout with wooden horses, seats *etc* for riding on; **'merrymaking** cheerful celebrating, festivity.

mesh *n* the opening between the threads of a net; network: – *pl* **'meshes**.

mesmerize ['mezmərɪz] *v* to hypnotize; to hold the attention of completely, fascinate. – *n* **'mesmerism**.

mess *n* an untidy or disgusting sight; disorder, confusion; (in the army, navy *etc*) a number of persons who take their meals together; the place where they eat: – *pl* **'messes**. – *v* (*usu* with **up**) to make untidy, dirty, muddled. – *npl* **'messmates** those who eat together.

'message *n* a piece of news or information sent from one person to another; a lesson, moral. – *n* **'messenger** a person who carries a message.

'metal *n* any of a group of substances (*eg* gold, silver, iron *etc*) *usu* shiny and able to conduct heat and electricity. – *adj* **me'tallic** made of metal; like metal. – *n* **me'tallurgy** the study of metals. – *adj* **metal'lurgic(al)**.

metamorphosis [metə'mörfəsɪs] *n* a change in appearance, form, character *etc*, a transformation; a change that takes place in some creature during growth (*eg* a tadpole into a frog): – *pl* **metamorphoses** [metə'mörfəsēz].

'metaphor *n* a way of describing something by suggesting that it is, or has the qualities of, something else. *The camel is the ship of the desert.* – *adj* **meta'phorical**.

mete *v* (with **out**) to deal out (punishment *etc*).

meteor ['mētiə] *n* a small mass, body *etc*, moving rapidly through space, becoming bright as it enters the earth's atmosphere, a shooting star. – *adj* **mete'oric** of, like a meteor; rapid; rapidly and brilliantly successful. – *ns* **'meteorite** a meteor which falls to the earth in the form of a piece of rock; **meteo'rologist** one who studies or makes forecasts about the weather. – *adj* **meteoro'logical**. **meteo'rology** the study of weather and climate.

'mēter *n* an instrument for measuring the amount of gas, electricity, water *etc* used; *see also* **metre**.

'method *n* a (planned or orderly) way of doing something; orderly arrangement. – *adj* **me'thodical** orderly, done or acting according to some plan.

'methylāted 'spirit(s) *n* a type of alcohol used as fuel in lamps, stoves *etc*.

me'ticulous *adj* (too) careful and accurate about small details.

'mètre, (*US*) **'mēter** *n* the chief unit of length in the metric system (about 1·1 yard); (in poetry, music) the arrangement of syllables or notes in a regular rhythm. – *adjs* **metric** ['metrik] of the metric system; metrical; **metrical** (in poetry) of, in metre; arranged in the form of verse. – *n* **metri'cation** the change-over of a country's units of measurements to the metric system. – *v* **'metricate**. – *n* **metric system** the system of weights and measures based on tens (1 metre = 10 decimetres = 100 centimetres *etc*).

'metronome *n* an instrument that keeps a regular beat, used for music practice.

me'tropolis *n* the capital city of a country; a chief centre: – *pl* **me'tropolises**. – *adj* **metro'politan**.

'mettle *n* courage, pluck. – **on one's mettle** out to do one's best.

mew *n* the cry of a cat; *see* **sea-mew**; (*pl*) stables (now often used as flats) built round a yard or in a lane. – *v* to make the cry of a cat.

mezzo-soprano ['metsōsə'pränō] *n* (a person with) a singing voice between alto and soprano: – *pl* **'mezzo-so'pranos**.

miaow [mi'ow] *n* the sound made by a cat. – Also *v*.

'mica *n* a type of mineral which glitters and divides easily into thin transparent layers.

mice *see* **mouse**.

Michaelmas daisy ['miklməs] *n* a kind of large daisy, a kind of aster.

micro- *prefix* very small.

'microbe *n* a kind of very tiny living thing; a germ.

'microchip *n* a tiny piece of silicon *etc* designed to act as a complex electronic circuit.

microcom'puter *n* a very small computer containing a microprocessor.

microcosm ['mikrəkozəm] *n* a version on a small scale. *The misery in the household was a microcosm of the misery to be found throughout the whole country.*

'microfilm *n* a very narrow photographic film on which whole books, documents *etc* can be reproduced on a tiny scale.

mi'crometer *n* an instrument used for measuring tiny distances or angles.

'microphone *n* an instrument for picking up sound waves to be broadcast, recorded or amplified.

micro'processor *n* a microcomputer (or part of one) consisting of one or more microchips.

'microscope *n* an instrument (containing magnifying glass) which makes small objects easily seen. – *adj* **microscopic** [mikrə'skopik] very tiny.

microwave oven *n* an oven in which

food is cooked by the heat produced by the passage of **'microwaves** (very short waves).

mid- *adj, prefix* placed or coming in the middle. – *n* **'mid'day** noon. – *adj* **'midland** in the middle of a country, away from the coast. – *ns* **'midnight** twelve o'clock at night; **'midshipman** formerly a junior naval officer, below sub-lieutenant; **'mid'summer** the time about June 21 which is the longest day of the year. – *adj, adv* **'mid'way** half-way. – *n* **'mid'winter** the time about December 21 which is the shortest day of the year.

'midden *n* a rubbish or dung heap.

'middle *adj* equally distant from the ends or edges; coming between. – *n* the middle point or part, centre; the course (of an action, job *etc*). – *adj* **'middling** of middle size, quality *etc*; not very good or bad. – *adj* **'middle-'aged** between youth and old age. – *ns* **Middle Ages** the time roughly between the years AD 500 and AD 1500; **'middle-class** the class of people between the working and upper classes.

midge *n* any of several kinds of small fly.

'midget *n* a person who has not grown up to the normal size. – *adj* very small.

'midriff *n* the middle of the body, just below the ribs.

midst *n* the middle (*eg* of a job). – **in our midst** among us.

'midwife *n* a woman who helps at the birth of babies: – *pl* **'midwives**. – *n* **midwifery** [mid'wifəri] the art of assisting at the birth of babies.

mien [mēn] *n* look or appearance.

might [mīt] *n* power, strength. – *v see* **may**. – *adj* **'mighty** having great power; very great: – *comp* **'mightier**, *superl* **'mightiest**. – *adv* (*coll*) very. – *n* **'mightiness** greatness. – **with might and main** with all possible effort.

migraine ['mēgrān] *n* a very severe type of headache.

mi'grate *v* to change one's home to another region or country; to pass regularly from one region to another, as certain birds *etc* do. – *n* **mi'gration**. – *adj, n* **'migrant** (of) a person, bird *etc* that migrates. – *adj* **'migratory** migrating; wandering.

mike short for **microphone**.

mild *adj* gentle; (of a taste) not sharp or bitter; not harsh or severe; (of weather) not cold. – *n* **'mildness**.

'mildew *n* a mark on plants, cloth, leather *etc* caused by tiny fungi.

mile *n* a measure of length (1·61 kilometre or 1760 yards). – *ns* **'mileage**

distance in miles; travel expenses (counted by the mile); **'milestone** a stone beside the road showing the number of miles to a certain place; something which marks an important event.

milieu ['mēlyȳ] *n* surroundings.

'military *adj* of, for soldiers or warfare. – *n* the army. – *adj* **'militant** fighting, warlike; aggressive, favouring or taking part in forceful action. – *n* a person who is militant. – *v* **'militate** to fight, work (against); to work (against), act to one's disadvantage. – *n* **militia** [mi'lishə] a body of men (not regular soldiers) trained to fight in emergencies.

milk *n* a white liquid produced by female animals as food for their young. – *v* to draw milk from; to force, take (money *etc*) from. – *adj* **'milky** of, like milk. – *ns* **'milkmaid** (*old*) woman who milks cows; **'milkman** a man who sells or delivers milk; **'milksop** a weak, unmanly man; **Milky Way** bright band of stars stretching across the sky.

mill *n* a machine for grinding or crushing grain, coffee *etc*; a building where grain is ground; a factory where things are made. – *v* to grind; to put grooves round the edge of (a coin); to move round and round in a crowd. – *n* **'miller** a person who grinds grain. – *ns* **'millrace** the stream of water which turns a millwheel and so drives the machinery of a mill; **'millstone** one of two heavy stones between which grain was ground; a great trouble or difficulty which keeps one from making progress; **'millwheel** a wheel, *esp* a waterwheel, used for driving a mill.

mil'lennium *n* a period of a thousand years; a period of great happiness hoped for on earth: – *pl* **mil'lennia**.

'millet *n* a type of grain used for food.

milli- *prefix* thousand; a thousandth part of.

'milligramme *n* a thousandth of a gramme.

millilitre ['mililētər] *n* a thousandth of a litre.

'millimētre *n* a thousandth of a metre.

milliner ['milinər] *n* one who makes and sells women's hats. – *n* **'millinery** the goods sold by a milliner.

'million *n* a thousand thousands (1,000,000). – *n* **millio'naire** a person who has a million pounds (or dollars) or more.

'millipede *n* a type of small crawling creature with a long body and very many legs.

mime *n* the use of, or the art of using actions, movements of the arms *etc* in place of speech; a play performed through mime; an action in such a play. – *v* to act using actions and movements but no words. – *v* **mimic** ['mimik] to imitate *esp* in a mocking way: – *pt* **'mimicked**. – *n* one who mimics. – *n* **'mimicry** the act of mimicking; (in an animal) a likeness to its surroundings or to another animal.

mimosa [mi'mōzə] *n* a type of tree with bunches of yellow, scented flowers.

mina'ret *n* a slender tower on a Mohammedan mosque.

mince *v* to cut or chop into small pieces; to walk in a prim way with short steps. – *n* meat chopped finely. – *n* **'mincer** a machine for mincing. – *ns* **'mincemeat** a chopped-up mixture of dried fruit, suet *etc*; **'mince-'pie** a pie filled with mincemeat. – **not to mince matters** not to try to soften an unpleasant statement by using tactful words.

mind *n* the power by which we think *etc*; intelligence, understanding; intention. *I have a (good) mind to tell him so.* – *v* to see to, look after. *Mind the baby*; to watch out for, be careful of. *Mind the step*; to object to. *I don't mind your saying so.* – *adjs* **'mindful** paying attention (to); **'mindless** foolish; without reason or thought. – **change one's mind** to change one's opinion or intention; **in two minds** undecided; **make up one's mind** to decide; **out of one's mind** mad; **presence of mind** ability to act calmly and sensibly; **speak one's mind** to speak frankly.

mine *pron* a thing or things belonging to me. *That book is mine.* – *n* a place (*usu* a pit or system of underground tunnels) from which metals, coal *etc* are dug; a heavy charge of explosive material for blowing up (a vehicle, ship *etc*). – *v* to dig or work a mine; to lay explosive mines in. – *n* **'miner** one who works in a (coal) mine. – *ns* **'minefield** an area covered with explosive mines; **'minelayer**, **'minesweeper** a ship which places mines in, or removes them from, the sea.

mineral ['minərəl] *adj*, *n* (of) any of the substances (coal, metals, gems *etc*) that are found in the earth and mined. – *ns* **mine'ralogy** the study of minerals; **mine'ralogist**. – *n* **mineral water** water containing small amounts of minerals; a fizzy type of soft drink.

mingle ['mingl] *v* to mix.

mini- *prefix* small (as in **minibus** *etc*). – *n* **'Mini** ® a type of small car.

miniature ['minichər] *n* a painting (or

something else) made on a small scale. – *adj* on a small scale.

'**minibus** *n* a type of small bus: – *pl* '**minibuses**.

'**minim** *n* (in music) a note equal to two crotchets in length.

'**minimize** *v* to make to seem small or unimportant. *He minimized the help he received*; to make as little as possible. – *n* '**minimum** the smallest possible quantity: – *pl* '**minima**. – *adj* the least possible.

'**minion** *n* a slave-like follower.

'**minister** *n* the head of one of the divisions or departments of the government; a clergyman; a representative of a government in a foreign country. – *v* (with **to**) to help, supply the needs of. – *adj* **minis'terial** of a minister. – *n* '**ministry** a department of government or its headquarters; the work of a clergyman: – *pl* '**ministries**.

mink *n* a small weasel-like kind of animal or its fur.

'**minnow** ['minō] *n* a type of very small river or pond fish.

'**minor** *adj* of less importance, size *etc*; small, unimportant; opposite of **major**. – *n* a person who has not come of age legally, in UK a person under 18 years old. – *n* **mi'nority** the smaller number or part; the state of being a minor: – *pl* **mi'norities**.

'**minster** *n* a large church or cathedral.

'**minstrel** *n* (*hist*) a (travelling) musician; a singer, entertainer. – *n* '**minstrelsy** a collection of songs.

mint *n* a type of plant with strong-smelling leaves, used as flavouring; a place where coins are made; (*coll*) a large sum (of money). – *v* to make coins. – **in mint condition** in perfect condition, as good as new.

minu'et *n* (the music for) an earlier kind of slow, graceful dance.

'**minus** *prep* used to show subtraction and represented by the sign (−). *Five minus two equals three, or* 5−2=3; (*coll*) without. *I'm minus my car today.* – *adj*, *n* (of) a quantity less than zero.

minute[1] ['minit] *n* the sixtieth part of an hour; in measuring an angle, the sixtieth part of a degree; a very short time; (*pl*) the notes taken of what is said at a meeting.

mi'nute[2] *adj* very small; very exact.

minx *n* a cheeky young girl: – *pl* '**minxes**.

'**miracle** *n* a wonderful act beyond the power of men; a fortunate happening that has no natural cause or explanation. – *adj* **mi'raculous**.

mirage ['miräzh] *n* something not really there that one imagines one sees, *esp* an expanse of water imagined by travellers in the desert.

'**mire** *n* deep mud. – *adj* '**miry**.

'**mirror** *n* a surface that reflects light, *esp* a piece of glass which shows the image of the person looking into it. – *v* to reflect as a mirror does.

'**mirth** *n* merriment, laughter. – *adjs* '**mirthful**; '**mirthless**.

mis- *prefix* wrong(ly), bad(ly).

misad'venture *n* an unlucky happening.

misanthropist [mi'zanthrəpist] *n* one who hates mankind. – *adj* **misan'thropic**. – *n* **mi'santhropy**.

misap'propriate *v* to put to a wrong use *esp* to use (someone else's money) for oneself.

misbe'have *v* to behave badly. – *n* **misbe'haviour**.

mis'carry *v* to go wrong or astray; to be unsuccessful; in pregnancy, to have a miscarriage: – *pt* **mis'carried**. – *n* **mis'carriage** a going wrong, failure; in pregnancy, the loss of the baby from the womb before it is able to survive.

miscellaneous [misə'lāniəs] *adj* assorted, made up of several kinds. – *n* **mis'cellany** a mixture or collection of things (*esp* writings) of different kinds: – *pl* **mis'cellanies**.

mis'chance *n* an unlucky accident.

mischief ['mischif] *n* naughtiness; evil, harm, damage. – *adj* '**mischievous** naughty; teasing; causing trouble.

miscon'ception *n* a wrong idea, a misunderstanding.

mis'conduct *n* bad or immoral behaviour.

misconstrue [miskən'strōō] *v* to take a wrong meaning from, misunderstand.

miscreant ['miskriənt] *n* a wicked person.

mis'deed *n* a bad deed; a crime.

misde'meanour *n* a misdeed or offence (*esp* against the law).

miser ['mīzər] *n* one who hoards his money and spends very little on himself or others; a mean person. – *adj* '**miserly** very mean.

misery ['mizəri] *n* great unhappiness, pain, poverty *etc*: – *pl* '**miseries**. – *adj* '**miserable** very unhappy; very poor, worthless or wretched.

mis'fire *v* (of guns *etc*) to fail to go off; (of a plan *etc*) to go wrong.

'**misfit** *n* a person who cannot fit in happily at home, work *etc*; a thing that fits badly.

misfortune [mis'förchən] *n* bad luck; an unlucky accident.

misgiving [mis'giviŋ] *n* a feeling of fear or doubt (*eg* about the result of an action).

misguided [mis'gīdid] *adj* led astray, mistaken.

mis'handle *v* to treat badly or roughly.

mishap ['mis-hap] *n* an unlucky accident.

mis'lay *v* to put (a thing) aside and forget where it is, to lose: – *pt* **mis'laid**.

mis'lead *v* to give a false idea (to), to deceive: – *pt* **mis'led**. – *adj* **mis-'leading**.

mis'nōmer *n* a wrong or unsuitable name.

misogynist [mi'soj∂nist] *n* one who hates women.

'**misprint** *n* a mistake in printing.

mis'quote *v* to make a mistake in repeating what someone has written or said.

misrepresent [misrepri'zent] *v* to give a wrong idea (of someone's words, actions *etc*).

miss *n* a form of address used before the name of an unmarried woman; a young woman or girl: – *pl* '**misses**. – *v* to fail to hit, reach, catch, find, see, hear, take (an opportunity), understand; to discover the loss or absence of; to feel the lack of. *He misses his old friends*; (with **out**) to leave out. – *n* the act of missing; a failure to hit the target; a loss. – *adj* '**missing** lost.

'**missal** *n* the Mass book of the Roman Catholic Church.

'**mis'shāpen** *adj* badly, abnormally shaped.

'**missile** *n* a weapon or other object that is thrown or fired.

'**mission** *n* a task, duty *etc* that a person or group is sent to do; a group of representatives sent (to another country) for negotiations *etc*, or one sent to spread a religion; the headquarters of such groups; one's chosen task or purpose. *His mission in life is to make people happy*. – *n* '**missionary** one who is sent to spread a religion: – *pl* '**missionaries**.

missive ['misiv] *n* something sent, *esp* a letter.

'**mis'spell** *n* to spell wrongly. – *n* '**mis'spelling**.

'**mis'spent** *adj* spent in the wrong way, wasted: *misspent youth*.

mist *n* a cloud of moisture seen in the air, thin fog or drizzle; anything that blurs one's sight, judgement *etc*. – *v* (with **up** or **over**) to cover or become covered with mist. – *adj* '**misty**.

mis'take *v* to misunderstand, be wrong or make an error about; to take (one thing or person) for another: – *pt* **mis'took**, *pp* **mis'taken**. – *n* a wrong action, statement *etc*, an error. – *adj* **mis'taken** making an error, unwise: *mistaken belief*.

mister *see* **Mr.**

mistletoe ['misltō] *n* a type of plant with white berries, used as a Christmas decoration.

'**mistress** *n* a female employer; a female teacher; a female owner (of a dog); a woman skilled in an art *etc*: *a mistress of sculpture*; a woman who is the lover though not the legal wife of a man; *see* **Mrs**: – *pl* '**mistresses**.

mis'trust *n* lack of trust or confidence in. – *v* not to trust, not to have confidence in.

misunder'stand *v* to take a wrong meaning from what is said or done. – *n* **misunder'standing** a mistake about a meaning; a slight disagreement.

'**mis'ūse** *n* bad or wrong use. – *v* **misuse** ['mis'ūz] to use wrongly; to treat badly.

mite *n* anything very small (*eg* a little child); a kind of very tiny spider; (*hist*) a very small coin.

'**mitigate** *v* to make (trouble, punishment, anger *etc*) less great or severe. – *n* **miti'gation**.

'**mitre** *n* the pointed head-dress worn by archbishops and bishops; a slanting joint between two pieces of wood.

'**mitt(en)** *n* a kind of glove without separate divisions for the four fingers.

mix *v* to unite or blend two or more things together to form one mass; (often with **up**) to confuse, muddle; to go into the company of others, associate (with). *He does not mix with his neighbours*. – Also *n*. – *adj* **mixed** jumbled together; confused, muddled; made up of, including different kinds (or sexes). – *ns* '**mixer** a machine (or person) that mixes; **mixture** ['mikschɔr] the act of mixing; the state of being mixed; a number of things mixed together; a medicine. – **mixed up** confused; bewildered.

'**mizzen-mast** *n* the mast nearest the stern of the ship.

mnemonic [ni'monik] *n* something (*eg* a rhyme *etc*) which helps one to remember (something).

moan *v* to make a low sound of grief or pain. – Also *n*.

moat *n* a deep trench round a castle *etc*, *usu* filled with water.

mob *n* a noisy crowd. – *v* to crowd round, or attack, in a disorderly way: – *pt* **mobbed**.

'**mōbile** *adj* able to move; moving or moved easily; changing quickly. – *n* a decorative object hung so that it moves slightly in the air. – *n* **mobility** [mə'bɪləti].

'**mōbilize** *v* to gather (troops *etc*) together ready for active service. – *n* **mobili'zation**.

'**moc(c)asin** *n* a soft leather shoe of the type worn by the N. American Indians.

mock *v* to laugh at, make fun of. – *adj* false, pretended, imitation: *a mock battle*. – *n* '**mockery** the act of mocking; a ridiculous imitation.

mode *n* manner (of doing or acting); kind, sort; fashion. – *adj* '**modish** fashionable, smart.

'**model** *n* a design, pattern *etc* to be copied; a copy of something made in a small size: *model railway*; a living person who poses for an artist; someone who is employed to wear and show off new clothes. – *adj* acting as a model; fit to be copied, perfect: *model behaviour*. – *v* to make a model of; to shape; to form according to a particular pattern; to wear and show off (clothes): – *pt* '**modelled**.

moderate ['modəreit] *v* to make or become less great or severe. – *adj* ['modərət] keeping within reasonable limits, not going to extremes; of medium or average quality, ability *etc*. – *adv* '**moderately**. – *ns* **mode'ration** a lessening or calming down; the practice of not going to extremes; '**moderator** the chairman at a meeting (*esp* of clergymen).

'**modern** *adj* belonging to the present or to a time not long past, not old. – *n* **mo'dernity**. – *v* '**modernize** to bring up to date.

'**modest** *adj* not exaggerating one's achievements *etc*, not boastful; not very large: *a modest salary*; behaving in a decent way, not shocking. – *n* '**modesty**.

'**modicum** *n* a small quantity or amount: *a modicum of kindness*: – *pl* '**modicums**.

'**modifȳ** *v* to make a change in. *He modified the design*; to make less extreme. *He modified his demands*: – *pt* '**modified**. – *n* **modifi'cation**.

'**modūlate** *v* to vary or soften the tone or pitch of (the voice *etc*). – *n* **modu'lation**.

'**module** *n* (in architecture) a standard unit of size; a separate, self-contained section of a spacecraft.

'**mōhair** *n* (fabric made from) the long silky hair of an Angora goat.

Mo'hammedan *n* one who follows the religion founded by Mohammed. – Also *adj*. – *n* **Mo'hammedanism**.

moist *adj* damp, very slightly wet. – *v* **moisten** ['mɔɪsn] to make slightly wet or damp. – *n* **moisture** ['mɔɪschər] slight wetness; water or other liquid in tiny drops in the atmosphere or on a surface. – *v* '**moisturize** to add moisture to. – *n* '**moisturizer**.

'**mōlar** *n* a back tooth which grinds one's food.

mo'lasses *n sing* a type of thick syrup left when sugar is made, treacle.

mole *n* a kind of small burrowing animal, with very small eyes and soft fur; a small (often dark brown) spot on the skin; a stone jetty or pier. – *n* '**molehill** a little heap of earth cast up by a burrowing mole.

molecule ['molikūl] *n* the smallest part of a substance that has the same qualities as the substance itself.

mo'lest *v* to annoy or torment.

'**mollifȳ** *v* to calm down, soothe, or lessen the anger of: – *pt* '**mollified**.

'**mollusc** *n* the name of a group of boneless animals *usu* with hard shells (*eg* shellfish, snails).

'**mollycoddle** *v* to pamper, over-protect.

'**mōlten** *adj* (of metal, lava *etc*) melted.

'**mōment** *n* a very short space of time, an instant; importance. – *adjs* '**momentary** lasting for a moment; **mo'mentous** of great importance. – *n* **mo'mentum** the force of a moving body: – *pl* **mo'menta**.

monarch ['monərk] *n* a king, queen, emperor or empress. – *n* '**monarchy** government by a monarch; an area governed by a monarch: – *pl* '**monarchies**.

'**monastery** *n* a house where a group of monks live: – *pl* '**monasteries**. – *adj* **mo'nastic** of or like monasteries or monks. – *n* **mo'nasticism** the way of life in a monastery.

Monday ['mundi] *n* the second day of the week.

monetary ['munitəri] *adj* of money or coinage.

money ['muni] *n* the coins and banknotes which are used for payment; wealth: – *pls* '**moneys**, '**monies**. – *adj* '**moneyed**, '**monied** wealthy.

mongoose ['mongōōs] *n* a type of small weasel-like animal which kills snakes: – *pl* '**mongooses**.

mongrel ['mungrəl] *adj*, *n* (of) an animal, *esp* a dog, of mixed breed.

'**monitor** *n* any of several kinds of instruments used for checking if some system, apparatus *etc* is working correctly; a pupil who helps in the running of a school; a screen in a television studio showing the picture being transmitted; a kind of large lizard. – *v* to use, or to be, a monitor; to check, keep a check on something; to listen to and report on foreign broadcasts *etc*.

monk [muŋk] *n* one of a male religious group that lives apart from the world in a monastery.

monkey ['muŋki] *n* the type of animal most like man, *usu* the small long-tailed kind walking on four legs (unlike the apes); a mischievous child: – *pl* '**monkeys**. – *v* to meddle, tamper with something. – *ns* '**monkey-nut** a peanut, groundnut; '**monkey-'puzzle** a kind of pine tree with prickly spines along its branches.

mono- *prefix* one, single.

'**monocle** *n* a single eyeglass.

mo'nogamy *n* marriage to one wife or husband only at a time. – *adj* **mo'nogamous**.

'**monogram** *n* two or more letters (often a person's initials) made into a single design. *He wore his monogram on his shirt.*

monologue ['monəlog] *n* a long speech by one person.

'**monoplane** *n* an aeroplane having one pair of wings.

mo'nopoly *n* the right, not shared by others, of doing, making or selling something; complete unshared possession, control *etc*: – *pl* **mo'nopolies**. – *v* **mo'nopolize** to have the full, unshared rights in anything; to take up the whole of (*eg* someone's attention, a conversation *etc*).

'**monorail** *n* a railway on which the trains run along a single rail.

'**monosyllable** *n* a word of one syllable. – *adj* **monosyl'labic**.

'**monotone** *n* a single, unchanging tone; dull. – *n* **mo'notony** lack of variety.

mon'soon *n* a wind that blows in the Indian Ocean; the rainy season caused by the south-west monsoon in summer.

'**monster** *n* anything of unusual size or appearance; a huge creature, causing fear; a very wicked person. – *adj* huge. – *n* **mons'trosity** something not natural; something very ugly: – *pl* **mons'trosities**. – *adj* '**monstrous** huge; horrible.

month [munth] *n* a twelfth part of a year, about four weeks. – *adj, adv* '**monthly** happening once a month. – *n* a paper published once a month: – *pl* '**monthlies**.

'**monūment** *n* a building, pillar, tomb *etc* built in memory of a person or an event. – *adj* **monu'mental** of or acting as a monument; very great in size, quantity *etc*. – *n* **ancient monument** any structure (such as a dwelling-place, grave *etc*) remaining from ancient times.

moo *n* the sound made by a cow. – Also *v*.

mood *n* the state of a person's feelings or temper. – *adj* '**moody** often changing one's mood; ill-tempered, cross.

moon *n* the heavenly body which travels round the earth once each month and reflects light from the sun. – *v* to wander (about); to gaze dreamily (at). – *ns* '**moonbeam** a beam of light from the moon; '**moonlight** the light of the moon; '**moonshine** the shining of the moon; rubbish, foolish ideas or talk; '**moonstone** a precious stone with a pearly shine.

moor *n* a large stretch of open ground, often covered with heather. – *v* to tie up or anchor (a ship *etc*). – *npl* '**moorings** the place where a ship is moored; the anchor, rope *etc* holding it. – *ns* '**moorhen** a kind of water bird, a female coot; '**moorland** a stretch of moor.

moose *n* a large kind of deer-like animal, found in N. America: – *pl* **moose**.

moot point a debatable point, a question with no obvious solution.

mop *n* a pad of sponge or a bunch of short pieces of coarse yarn *etc* on a handle for washing or cleaning; a thick head of hair. – *v* to clean with a mop; to clean or wipe. *He mopped his brow*: – *pt* **mopped**. – **mop up** clean or wipe up.

mope *v* to be unhappy and gloomy.

'**mōped** *n* a pedal bicycle with a motor.

mo'raine *n* a line of rocks and gravel left by a glacier.

'**moral** *adj* having to do with right and wrong behaviour and character; having to do with right behaviour or character. – *n* the lesson of a fable or story; (*pl*) one's character and behaviour. – *n* **mo'rality** (the right) moral standards. – *v* '**moralize** to draw a lesson from a story or happening. – *ns* **moral support** encouragement without active help; **moral victory** a failure that can really be seen as a success.

morale [mə'räl] *n* spirit and confidence.

mo'rass *n* a marsh or bog; something that bewilders (someone) or is difficult to cope with: *involved in a morass of government regulations*: – *pl* **mo'rasses**.

'**morbid** *adj* (of a person, thoughts *etc*)

too concerned with gloomy, unpleasant things; diseased, unhealthy.

more *adj* a greater number, amount of: *more cakes: more money.* – *adv* to a greater extent: *more beautiful. I love you more than I can say.* – *n* a great proportion, amount; a further or additional number, amount. *There's more where this came from.* – *adv* **more'over** besides.

morgue [mörg] *n* a place where dead bodies are laid, awaiting identification *etc.*

'**moribund** *adj* in a dying state.

morn *n* (in poetry *etc*) morning.

'**morning** *n* the first part of the day. – *adj* taking place in the morning. – *n* **morning star** Venus or another planet, when it rises before the sun.

mo'rocco *n* a fine goat-skin leather first brought from Morocco.

'**moron** *n* a person of low mental ability, an idiot. – *adj* **mo'ronic**.

mo'rose *adj* gloomy, bad-tempered.

'**morphia** *n* a kind of drug which causes sleep or deadens pain (also **morphine** ['mörfēn]).

'**morris-dance** *n* a kind of country dance in which dancers wear traditional clothes, decorated with bells.

morrow ['morō] *n* (in poetry *etc*) the next day, the day after.

morse *n* a code of signals (made up of dots and dashes) used in signalling and telegraphy.

'**morsel** *n* a small piece, *esp* of food.

'**mortal** *adj* liable to die; causing death, deadly. – *n* a human being. – *n* **mor'tality** the state of being mortal; the number of deaths; deaths in proportion to the population, death-rate: – *pl* **mor'talities**. – *adv* '**mortally** fatally: *mortally wounded.*

'**mortar** *n* a kind of bowl in which substances are crushed and ground *usu* by a **pestle**; a short gun for throwing shells; a mixture of lime, sand and water, used for fixing stones in a building *etc.* – *n* '**mortarboard** a university or college cap with a square flat top.

mortgage ['mörgij] *n* a sum of money lent through a legal agreement for buying buildings, land *etc* (which the borrower must give up if he fails to repay the loan). – *v* to offer buildings *etc* as security for money borrowed.

mortice *see* **mortise**.

'**mortify** *v* to make to feel ashamed or humble; (of a part of the flesh) to die: – *pt* '**mortified**. – *n* **mortifi'cation**.

mortise ['mörtis] *n* a hole made in a piece of wood to receive the shaped end (**tenon**) of another piece.

mortuary ['mörchōōəri] *n* a place where dead bodies are kept before burial or cremation: – *pl* '**mortuaries**.

mosaic [mə'zāik] *n* a picture or design made up of many small pieces of coloured glass, stone *etc.*

Moslem, Muslim ['mozləm] *adj, n* Mohammedan.

mosque [mosk] *n* a Mohammedan place of worship.

mosquito [məs'kētō] *n* any of several types of biting or blood-sucking insects, some carrying disease: – *pl* **mos'quito(e)s**.

moss *n* any of several kinds of very small flowerless plant, found in moist places; a bog: – *pl* '**mosses**. – *adjs* '**mossy**; '**moss-grown**.

mōst *adj* the greatest number of, amount of: *most boys: most food.* – *adv* very, extremely. *I'm most grateful*; (often with **the**) to the greatest extent. *He was the most ill of the family.* – *n* the greatest number, amount. *He got most.* – *adv* '**mostly** mainly, chiefly. – **at most** not more than; **for the most part** mostly.

moth *n* the name of a family of insects like butterflies, seen mostly at night; the cloth-eating grub of the **clothes moth**. – *n* '**mothball** a small ball of a chemical used to protect clothes from moths. – *adj* '**moth-eaten** (of cloth) full of holes made by moths; old, shabby.

mother ['mudhər] *n* a female parent; the female head of a convent. – *v* to give birth to, be the mother of; to care for as a mother does. – *adj* '**motherly** of, like a mother. – *ns* '**mother-country, -land** the country of one's birth; '**motherhood** the state of being a mother; '**mother-in-law** the mother of one's husband or wife; '**mother-of-'pearl** the shining, hard, smooth substance which forms inside certain shells; '**mother-'tongue** a person's native language.

motif [mō'tēf] *n* a distinctive, important feature or idea in a piece of music, a play, a design *etc.*

'**motion** *n* the act, state or power of moving; a single movement; a suggestion put before a meeting for discussion. – *v* to make a signal or sign by a movement or gesture; to direct (a person) in this way. *The policeman motioned him forward.* – *adj* '**motionless** without movement.

'**mōtive** *n* that which causes a person to

act or to do something, a reason. – *v*
'motivate to cause (someone) to act in
a certain way.

motley *adj* made up of different colours
or kinds.

mōtor *n* a machine (*usu* an engine
worked by petrol) which brings about
motion or does work; a motor-car. –
Also *adj*. – *v* to go by motor vehicle. – *n*
'motorist one who drives a motor-car.
– *v* **'motorize** to supply with an
engine. *He motorized his bicycle*. – *ns*
**'motor-bicycle (-bike, -cycle, -boat,
-bus, -car)** a bicycle (boat *etc*) driven
by an engine worked by petrol; **'motor-
way** a special kind of dual carriageway
on which traffic is allowed to drive
faster than on other roads.

mottled *adj* marked with spots of many
colours or shades.

motto *n* a short sentence or phrase,
which acts as a guiding principle or rule
of behaviour. *'Death before defeat' was
the family motto:* – *pl* **'mottoes**.

mould [mōld] *n* a shape into which a
substance in liquid form is poured so
that it may take on that shape when it
cools or sets: *a jelly mould*; soil
(containing rotted leaves *etc*); a fluffy
growth found on stale food *etc*. – *v* to
form in a mould; to shape. – *v*
'moulder to crumble away to dust. – *n*
'moulding a decorated border (*usu* of
moulded plaster) round a ceiling, picture frame *etc*. – *adj* **'mouldy** affected
by mould.

moult [mōlt] *v* (of birds) to shed the
feathers.

mound *n* a bank of earth or stones; a hill;
a heap.

mount *v* to go up; to get up, or place, on
a horse, bicycle *etc*; to fix (a jewel *etc*) in
a holder, or (a picture *etc*) on to a
backing, for display; to fix anything on
to a support; to prepare, organize (an
exhibition). – *n* a mountain; a support
or backing on which something is
displayed; a horse, bicycle *etc* to ride
on. – **The Mounties** ['mowntiz] the
Canadian mounted police.

mountain *n* a large hill; a large heap or
quantity. – *n* **mountai'neer** a climber
of mountains. – *adj* **'mountainous**
having many mountains; huge. – *n*
'mountain-'ash the rowan tree.

mountebank ['mowntibaŋk] *n* one who
makes untrue claims about himself, his
abilities *etc*.

mourn [mōrn] *v* to grieve for (a person,
loss *etc*); to be sorrowful. – *n*
'mourner. – *adj* **'mournful** sad. – *n*
'mourning the showing of grief; the
dark-coloured clothes traditionally
worn by mourners; a period of time
during which signs of grief (*eg* dark-
coloured clothes) are shown.

mouse *n* a type of little gnawing animal
(often greyish-brown) found in houses
and in the fields; a shy, timid, uninteresting person: – *pl* **mice**. – *adj* **'mousy**
of a light-brown colour; (of a person)
shy, timid, uninteresting.

mousse [mōōs] *n* a mixture, often containing cream, that has been whipped
up and set.

moustache [mɔs'täsh] *n* the hair upon
the upper lip of men.

mouth *n* the opening in the head by
which an animal or person eats and
utters sounds; that part of a river where
it flows into the sea; an opening or
entrance (of a bottle, a cave *etc*). – *v*
mouth [mowdh] to speak; to shape
words in an exaggerated way. – *ns*
mouthful ['mowthfōōl] as much as
fills the mouth: – *pl* **'mouthfuls;
'mouth-organ** a kind of small musical
instrument played by the mouth;
'mouthpiece the part of a musical
instrument, tobacco-pipe *etc* held in
the mouth; one who speaks for others.

move [mōōv] *v* to (cause to) change
place or position; to change one's
house; to rouse or affect the feelings of.
He was moved by the beautiful music; to
rouse into action; to propose, suggest.
– *n* an act of moving; a step or action; a
shifting of pieces in a game (of chess
etc). – *adj* **'movable** able to be moved,
lifted, changed *etc*. – *n* **'movement** the
act or manner of moving; a change of
position; a division of a piece of music;
a group of people united to achieve
some aim: *the Communist movement*; an
organized attempt to achieve an aim.
*He took part in the movement to reform
the divorce laws*. – *n* **'movie** a cinema
film. – *adj* **'moving** in motion; causing
emotion (*eg* pity).

mow [mō] *v* to cut grass, hay *etc* with a
scythe or machine; to destroy in great
numbers. – *n* **'mower** machine for
mowing.

Mr ['mistər] (short for **mister**) the form
of address used before the surname of
men.

Mrs ['misiz] (short for **mistress**) the
form of address used before the surname of married women.

Ms [miz] a form of address sometimes
used before the surnames of married or
unmarried women.

much *adj* a great amount of. – *adv* to, by
a great extent: *much loved*: *much faster*.

– *pron* a great amount; something important. *He made much of it.* – **much the same** nearly the same.

muck *n* dung, dirt, filth.

'**mūcus** *n* the slimy fluid from the nose *etc.* – *adj* '**mucous** like or covered by mucus.

mud *n* wet, soft earth. – *adj* '**muddy** covered with or containing mud. – *n* '**mudguard** a shield or guard over wheels to catch mudsplashes.

'**muddle** *v* to confuse, bewilder; to mix up; to make a mess of. – *n* a mess; a (state of) confusion.

muezzin [moo'ezin] *n* a Mohammedan priest who calls out the hour of prayer from a mosque.

muff *n* a tube-shaped (often furry) cover to keep the hands warm. – *v* to fail in trying to do something (*eg* catch a ball *etc*).

'**muffin** *n* a round, flat spongy cake to be toasted and eaten hot with butter; (*US*) a small, round cake made of flour, bran *etc* eaten with butter.

'**muffle** *v* to wrap up for warmth *etc*; to deaden (a sound). – *n* '**muffler** a scarf; (*US*) a silencer for a car *etc*.

'**mufti** *n* clothes worn when he is off duty by someone normally in uniform.

mug *n* a straight-sided cup. – *v* to attack and rob (someone) in the street: – *pt* **mugged**. – *n* '**mugger**.

'**muggy** *adj* (of the weather) close and damp.

mū'latto *n* a person one of whose parents was coloured, the other white: – *pl* **mu'lattoes**.

'**mulberry** *n* a kind of tree on whose leaves silkworms are fed; its purple berry: – *pl* '**mulberries**.

mulch *n* loose straw *etc* laid down to protect the roots of plants. – *v* to cover with mulch.

mule *n* an animal whose parents are a horse and an ass; a backless kind of slipper. – *adj* '**mulish** stubborn.

mull *v* to think or ponder (över). – *adj* **mulled** (of wine *etc*) sweetened, spiced and warmed.

'**mullet** *n* a type of eatable small sea fish.

'**mullion** *n* an upright (often stone) division in a window.

multi- *prefix* many.

multi-coloured ['multikulərd] *adj* many-coloured.

multi'fārious *adj* of many kinds.

multimillionaire ['multimiljə'nār] *n* one who has property worth several million pounds.

multi'national *adj*, *n* (of) a company which has branches in several different countries.

'**multiple** *adj* having or affecting many parts: *multiple injuries*; involving many things of the same sort, as vehicles in a *multiple crash*. – *n* a number or quantity which contains another an exact number of times.

'**multiplȳ** *v* to increase; to increase a number by adding it to itself a certain number of times, as 2 multiplied by 3 (or 2 × 3) = 2 + 2 + 2 = 6: – *pt* '**multiplied**. – *ns* **multipli'cation** the act of multiplying; **multi'plicity** a great number; the state of being many or varied; '**multiplier** the number by which another is to be multiplied.

'**multitude** *n* a great number; a crowd. – *adj* **multi'tudinous** very many.

mum *n coll* for **mother**. – *adj* silent.

'**mumble** *v* to speak indistinctly.

'**mummy** *n coll* or child's name for **mother**; a dead body kept whole for a very long time by wrapping in bandages and treating with wax, spices *etc*: – *pl* '**mummies**. – *v* '**mummifȳ** to make into a mummy: – *pt* '**mummified**.

mumps *n sing* an infectious disease affecting certain glands at the side of the neck, causing swelling.

munch *v* to chew (with the mouth shut).

mun'dane *adj* dull, ordinary.

mū'nicipal *adj* of, belonging to, owned by a city or town.

mū'nificent *adj* very generous. – *n* **mu'nificence**.

mū'nitions *npl* weapons, ammunition *etc* used in war.

'**mūral** *adj* of or on a wall. – *n* a painting, design *etc* made on a wall.

'**murder** *v* to kill a person unlawfully and on purpose. – *n* the act of murdering. – *n* '**murderer**: – *fem* '**murderess**. – *adj* '**murderous** capable of, guilty of murder; wicked.

'**murky** *adj* dark, gloomy.

'**murmur** *n* a low, indistinct, continuous sound; a low muttering or grumbling; hushed speech or tone. – *v* to make a murmur; to complain, grumble.

muscle ['musl] *n* fleshy, bundle-like parts of the body which, by drawing together or stretching out, cause the movements of the body. – *adj* **muscular** ['muskūlər] of muscles; strong.

muse [mūz] *v* to think (over) in a quiet, leisurely way. – *n* (*myth*) one of the nine goddesses of poetry, music, dancing *etc*.

museum [mū'zēəm] *n* a building in which objects of artistic, scientific or historic interest are kept and displayed:

– *pl* **mu'seums**.

mush *n* anything soft and pulpy; anything (*eg* a film, song) over-sentimental. – *adj* **'mushy**.

mushroom *n* a kind of (eatable) fungus, *usu* umbrella-shaped. – *adj* growing or springing up very quickly. – *v* to grow very quickly. *New buildings mushroomed all over the town.*

music ['mūzik] *n* the art of arranging, combining *etc* certain sounds able to be produced by the voice, or by instruments; an arrangement of such sounds or its written form; any sweet or pleasant sound. – *adj* **'musical** of music; sounding sweet, pleasant; having a talent for music. – *n* **musician** [mū'zishən] someone skilled in music; someone who plays a musical instrument. – *n* **music centre** apparatus consisting of a record-player, tape-recorder, and radio, with loudspeakers.

musk *n* a strong perfume, obtained from the male **'musk-deer** (a small hornless deer found in Central Asia). – *n* **'musk-rat** same as **musquash**.

musket *n* (*hist*) a kind of gun once used by soldiers. – *n* (*hist*) **muske'teer** a soldier armed with a musket.

Muslim ['moŏzlim] same as **Moslem**.

muslin ['muzlin] *n* a kind of fine, soft, cotton cloth.

musquash ['muskwosh] *n* a type of large N. American water-rat or its fur (also **musk-rat**): – *pl* **'musquashes**.

mussel *n* a kind of shellfish, used as food and having two separate halves to its shell.

must *v usu* used with another verb to express necessity. *You must learn to cross the road safely*; to express compulsion. *You must do as you're told*; to express certainty or probability. *This sum must be right.* – *n* something that must be done, a necessity.

mustang *n* a kind of wild horse found in America.

mustard *n* a type of plant with a sharp taste; a hot, dark yellow-coloured seasoning (for meat, *etc*) made from its seeds.

muster *v* to gather up or together (*eg* troops, courage). – **pass muster** to be accepted as satisfactory.

musty *adj* smelling old and stale.

mute *adj* dumb; silent; (of a letter in a word) not sounded. – *n* a dumb person. – *adj* **'muted** (of sounds) made quieter, hushed; (of colours) not bright.

mūtilate *v* to cut off (a limb *etc*) from; to damage greatly. – *n* **muti'lation**.

nūtiny *v* to rise against those in power;

to refuse to obey the commands of officers in the army, navy or air force: – *pt* **'mutinied**. – *n* refusal to obey commands, *esp* in the armed forces: – *pl* **'mutinies**. – *n* **muti'neer** one who takes part in a mutiny. – *adj* **'mutinous** rebellious; refusing to obey orders.

'mutter *v* to speak words in a low voice; to grumble.

'mutton *n* the flesh of the sheep used as food.

mutual ['mūchoŏol] *adj* given by each to the other(s): *mutual trust*: *mutual help*; common to two or more, shared by two or more: *mutual friend*.

'muzzle *n* the nose and mouth of an animal; a fastening placed over the mouth of an animal to prevent biting; the open end of a gun. – *v* to put a muzzle on (a dog *etc*); to prevent from speaking (freely). *The president muzzled the press.*

'muzzy *adj* cloudy, confused.

mȳ *adj* belonging to me. *This is my book.* – *pron* **my'self** used reflexively. *I hurt myself*; used for emphasis. *I myself can't go, but my brother can.*

mȳ'ōpia *n* short-sightedness. – *n, adj* **myopic** [mī'opik].

'myriad *n* a very great number. – *adj* very many, countless.

myrrh [mɔ̄r] *n* a kind of resin with a bitter taste, used in medicines, perfumes *etc*.

'myrtle *n* a type of evergreen shrub.

myself *see* **my**.

'mystery *n* something that cannot be or has not been explained, something puzzling; a deep secret: – *pl* **'mysteries**. – *adjs* **mys'tērious** puzzling, difficult to understand; secret, hidden; **'mystic(al)** having a secret or sacred meaning beyond ordinary human understanding. – *n* **'mystic** a person who tries to commune with God or obtain knowledge of sacred or mystical things *esp* by going into a state of spiritual ecstasy. – *v* **'mystifȳ** to puzzle greatly; to confuse, bewilder: – *pt* **'mystified**. – *n* **mystique** [mis'tēk] an atmosphere of mystery about someone or something.

myth *n* a story about gods, heroes *etc* of ancient times; a fable; something imagined or untrue. – *adjs* **'mythical** of a myth; invented, imagined, never having existed; **mytho'logical** of myth or mythology; mythical. – *ns* **my'thology** a collection of myths; the study of myths; **my'thologist**.

myxoma'tōsis *n* a contagious disease of rabbits.

N

'nābob *n* a title given to certain Indian princes.

nadir ['nādēr] *n* the point of the heavens opposite the **zenith**; the lowest point of anything.

nag *v* to find fault with constantly: – *pt* **nagged**. – *n* a (small) horse.

naiad ['nīad] *n* (*myth*) a goddess of rivers.

nail *n* a horny covering, protecting the tips of the fingers and toes; a thin pointed piece of metal for fastening wood *etc*. – *v* to fasten with nails; to fasten (something up) in this way (*eg* in a box); (*coll*) to catch, trap.

naive [nī'ēv] *adj* simple in thought, manner or speech; inexperienced and lacking knowledge of the world. – *n* **naiveté** [nī'ēvtā].

'nāked *adj* without clothes; having no covering. – *n* **'nakedness**.

'namby'pamby *adj* childish, insipid, lacking liveliness.

name *n* a word by which a person, place or thing is known or called; fame, reputation. *He has made a name for himself*; authority. *I arrest you in the name of the king.* – *v* to give a name to; to speak of by name, mention; to appoint. – *adj* **'nameless** without a name, not named. – *adv* **'namely** that is to say. – *ns* **'nameplate** a piece of metal or other material, having on it the name of a person, house *etc*; **'namesake** one having the same name as another.

'nanny *n* a children's nurse: – *pl* **'nannies**.

'nanny-goat *n* a female goat.

nap *n* a short sleep; a woolly or fluffy surface on cloth; a kind of card game. – *v* to take a short sleep: – *pt* **napped**. – **caught napping** taken unawares.

napalm ['nāpam] *n* petrol in a jelly-like form, used in bombs.

nape *n* the back of the neck.

naphtha ['naftha] *n* a kind of clear liquid which readily catches fire, obtained from coal and other substances.

'napkin *n* a small piece of cloth or paper for wiping the lips at meals; *see* also **nappy**.

'nappy *n* a piece of cloth folded and put between a baby's legs to absorb urine *etc*; a thick piece of absorbent paper for the same purpose.

nar'cissus *n* a type of plant like a daffodil with a white, star-shaped flower: – *pls*

nar'cissi, nar'cissuses.

nar'cotic *n* a type of drug that brings on sleep or stops pain.

nar'rate *v* to tell a story. – *ns* **nar'ration** the telling of a story; **narrative** ['narativ] a story. – *adj* telling a story. – *n* **nar'rātor** one who tells a story.

narrow ['narō] *adj* of small extent from side to side, not wide: *a narrow road*; with little to spare: *a narrow escape*; lacking wide interests or experience: *narrow views.* – *v* to make or become narrow. – *adv* **'narrowly** closely; barely. – *npl* **'narrows** a narrow sea passage, a strait. – *adj* **'narrow-'minded** unwilling to accept ideas different from one's own.

narw(h)al ['närwal] *n* a kind of whale with a large tusk.

nasal ['nāzal] *adj* of the nose; sounded through the nose.

nasturtium [nas'tûrsham] *n* a climbing plant with brightly-coloured flowers.

'nasty *adj* dirty; very disagreeable or unpleasant; (of a problem *etc*) difficult to deal with. – *n* **'nastiness**.

'nātal *adj* of birth.

'nātion *n* the people living in the same country, or under the same government; a race of people: *the Jewish nation.* – *adj* **national** ['nashanal] of or belonging to a nation or race. – *n* a person belonging to a nation: *a British national.* – *ns* **'nationalism** the desire to bring the people of a nation together under their own government; **'nationalist; natio'nality** state of being a member of a particular nation. – *v* **'nationalize** to make (something *esp* industries) the property of the nation. – *n* **nationali'zation**. – *n* **national anthem** any nation's official song or hymn.

native ['nātiv] *adj* born in a person: *native intelligence*; of one's birth: *my native land.* – *n* a person born in a certain place: *a native of Scotland*; one of those inhabiting a country from earliest times before the discovery by explorers, settlers *etc*. – **The Nativity** the birth of Christ.

'natty *adj* trim, tidy, smart.

nature ['nāchar] *n* the world around us (animals, trees, grass, streams, mountains *etc*); the qualities which make a thing, person, animal what it or he is. *She has a kindly nature.* – **-natured** (used with another word) having a certain temper or personality: *good-natured*: *ill-natured* etc. – *adj* **natural** ['nachərəl] of nature; produced by nature, not artificial; (of a quality, ability *etc*) in one at birth, not learned afterwards; (of manner, personality) unaffected, simple; (of a result *etc*) expected, normal. – *n* an idiot; one having a natural ability; (in music) a note which is neither a sharp nor a flat (shown by the sign ♮). – *adv* **'naturally** by nature; simply; of course. – *n* **'naturalist** one who studies animal and plant life. – *v* **'naturalize** to give the rights of a citizen to (one born in another country). – *ns* **natural gas** gas suitable for burning found in the earth or under the sea; **natural history** the study of animals and plants; **natural resources** the natural wealth of a country (as forests, minerals, water for power *etc*).

naught [nöt] *n* nothing; *see* also **nought**.

naughty ['nöti] *adj* bad, misbehaving. – *n* **'naughtiness**.

nausea ['nöziə] *n* a feeling of sickness. – *v* **'nauseate** to make sick, to fill with disgust. – *adj* **'nauseous** sickening; disgusting.

'nautical *adj* of ships or sailors. – *n* **nautical mile** 1·85 kilometre (6080 ft).

'nautilus *n* a small type of sea creature related to the octopus.

naval *see* **navy**.

nave *n* the middle or main part of a church.-

'navel *n* the small hollow in the centre of the front of the stomach.

'navigate *v* to direct, steer or pilot a ship, aircraft *etc* on its course; to sail on, over or through. – *adj* **'navigable** able to be used by ships. – *ns* **navi'gation** the art of navigating; **'navigator** one who steers or sails a ship *etc*.

'navvy *n* a labourer working on roads *etc*: – *pl* **'navvies**.

'nāvy *n* a nation's fighting ships; the men serving on these: – *pl* **'navies**. – *adj* **'naval** of the navy. – *adj* **'navy-'blue** dark blue.

nay (*old*) no.

neap *adj* (of the tide) having the smallest extent between its low and high level.

near *adj* not far away in place or time; close in relationship, friendship, *etc*; nearside; barely avoiding or almost reaching (something): *a near disaster*. – *adv* to, at a little distance (also **near'bȳ**) *He lives quite near*(*by*). – *prep* close to. – *v* to approach. – *adv* **'nearly** almost:

nearly four o'clock; closely: *nearly related*. – *n* **'nearness**. – *adjs* **'near'side** (of the side of a vehicle *etc*) furthest from the centre of the road; **'near-'sighted** short-sighted.

neat *adj* trim, tidy; skilfully done; (of liquor *esp* alcoholic) not diluted with water *etc*.

'nebūla *n* shining cloud-like appearance in the night sky, produced by very distant stars or by a mass of gas and dust: – *pl* **nebulae** ['nebūlē]. – *adj* **'nebulous** hazy, vague.

necessary ['nesisəri] *adj* not able to be done without. – *n* something that cannot be done without, as food, clothing *etc*: – *pl* **'necessaries**. – *v* **ne'cessitate** to make necessary; to force. – *n* **ne'cessity** that which cannot be done without; great need; want, poverty: – *pl* **ne'cessities**.

neck *n* the part between the head and body; anything like the neck: *the neck of a bottle*: *a neck of land*. – *ns* **'necklace** a string of beads or precious stones *etc* worn round the neck; **'necktie** (*US*) a man's tie. – **neck and neck** (in a race *etc*) running side by side, staying exactly equal.

'necromancer *n* one who deals in magic. – *n* **'necromancy**.

ne'cropolis *n* a cemetery. – *pl* **ne'cropolises**.

'nectar *n* the sweet liquid collected from flowers by bees to make honey; (*myth*) the drink of the ancient Greek gods; a delicious drink.

nectarine ['nektərēn] *n* a kind of peach.

née [nā] *adj* born, used in stating a woman's surname before her marriage: *Mrs Jane Brown, née Black*.

need *v* to be without, to be in want of; to require. – *n* state of needing; necessity; difficulty, want, poverty. – *adjs* **'needful** necessary; **'needless** unnecessary; **'needy** poor.

'needle *n* a small, sharp piece of steel, with a small hole (**eye**) at the top for thread, used in sewing; a similar, longer object with no hole, used for various purposes, *eg* in knitting, hypodermic syringes *etc*; (in a compass) the moving pointer; the long, sharp-pointed leaf of a pine, fir *etc*.

ne'er [när] *adj* (in poetry *etc*) never. – *adj*, *n* **'ne'er-do-well** (of) a lazy, worthless person who makes no effort.

ne'fārious *adj* very wicked.

negative ['negətiv] meaning or saying 'no', as an answer; (of a person, attitude *etc*) timid, lacking spirit or ideas. – *n* a word or statement by which something is denied; the photographic film, from which prints are made, in which light objects appear dark and dark objects appear light. – *v* to prove the opposite; to refuse to accept, to reject (a proposal made at a meeting *etc*).

ne'glect *v* to treat carelessly; to fail to give proper attention to; to fail to do. – *n* lack of care and attention. – *adj* **ne'glectful**.

negligée ['neglizhā] *n* a type of loose dressing gown *usu* made of thin material, worn by women.

'negligence *n* lack of proper care. – *adjs* **'negligent** careless; **'negligible** not worth thinking about, very small: *negligible amount*.

ne'gōtiate *v* to bargain (with), discuss a subject (with), in order to reach agreement; to arrange (a treaty, a payment *etc*); to get past (an obstacle or difficulty). – *ns* **negoti'ation**; **ne'gotiator**. – *adj* **ne'gotiable** able to be negotiated.

'Nēgro *n* a member of an African race with black skin and tightly curling hair: – *pl* **'Negroes**. – *adj* **'negroid** of, like a Negro.

neigh [nā] *v* to cry like a horse. – Also *n*.

neighbour, (*US*) **neighbor** ['nābər] *n* one who lives near another. – *n* **'neighbourhood** (surrounding) district or area: *in the neighbourhood of Paris: a poor neighbourhood*. – *adjs* **'neighbouring** near or next in position; **'neighbourly** friendly. – **in the neighbourhood of** approximately, nearly.

neither ['nīdhər] *adj, pron* not either. *Neither bus goes that way. Neither of us feels well.* – *conj* used (often with **nor**) to show alternatives in the negative. *Neither John nor David is tall. He neither talks nor laughs.*

nemesis ['nemisis] *n* fate, punishment that is bound to follow wrongdoing.

neo- [nēō] *prefix* new as in **neo'natal** of newborn babies.

nē'ologism *n* a new word or expression.

'nēon lighting *n* a form of lighting in which an electric current is passed through a small quantity of gas, used in advertising signs *etc*.

'nephew *n* the son of a brother or sister, or of a brother-in-law or sister-in-law.

nerve *n* one of the fibres which carry feeling from all parts of the body to the brain; courage, coolness; (*coll*) impudence. – *v* to strengthen the nerve or will of. – *adjs* **'nervous** of the nerves; easily excited or frightened; timid; **'nervy** excitable, jumpy. – *n* **nervous system** the brain, spinal cord and

nerves of an animal or human being.

nest *n* structure or place in which birds (and some animals and insects) live and rear their young; a shelter or den. – *v* to build a nest and live in it. – *v* **nestle** ['nesl] to lie close together as in a nest; to settle comfortably. – *n* **nestling** ['nestliŋ] a young newly hatched bird.

net *n* cord, string or finer material knotted so as to form a loose arrangement of crossing lines and spaces, used for catching birds, fish *etc* or for wearing over the hair *etc*; fine material made like a net, with meshes. – *adj* (also **nett**) (of a profit *etc*) remaining after expenses *etc* have been paid; (of the weight of something) not including packaging. – *v* to catch or cover with a net; to put (a ball) into a net; to make by way of profit: – *pt* **'netted**. – *n* **'netting** fabric of netted string, wire *etc*. – *ns* **'netball** a type of game in which a ball is thrown into a high net; **'network** an arrangement of lines crossing one another; a widespread organization; a system of linked radio stations *etc*.

nether ['nedhər] *adj* lower. – *adj* **'nethermost** lowest.

nett *see* **net**.

'nettle *n* a type of plant covered with hairs which sting sharply. – *v* to make angry, provoke. – *n* **'nettlerash** a skin rash, like that caused by a sting from a nettle.

neur(o)- [nūr(ō)] *prefix* of the nerves.

neuralgia [nū'raljə] *n* a pain in the nerves, *esp* in those of the head and face.

neurosis [nū'rōsis] *n* a type of mental illness in which the patient suffers from extreme anxiety.

neurotic [nū'rotik] *adj* suffering from neurosis; in a bad nervous state. – Also *n*.

neuter ['nūtər] *adj* (in grammar) neither masculine nor feminine; (of animals) neither male nor female; unable to bear or father young. – *v* to make (a horse *etc*) unable to bear or father young.

neutral ['nūtrəl] *adj* taking no side (in a quarrel or war); (of a colour) not strong or definite. – *n* a person or nation that takes no side in a war *etc*; the gear position *usu* used when a vehicle is remaining still. – *n* **neu'trality**. – *v* **'neutralize** to make neutral; to make useless or harmless.

neutron ['nūtron] *n* one of the particles (without electrical charge) which with protons make up the nucleus of an atom.

'never *adv* not ever; at no time; under no

circumstances. – *adv* **neverthe'less** in spite of that. *I feel ill. Nevertheless I shall come with you.*

new *adj* recent; not before seen or known; different; not used or worn; fresh. – *adv* **'newly**. – *n* **'newness**. – *n* **'newcomer** one who has lately arrived. – *adj* **newfangled** ['nūfaŋgld] (of things, ideas *etc*) new and not thought very good.

news *n sing* report of a recent event; new information. – *ns* **'newsagent** a shopkeeper who sells newspapers; **'newspaper** a paper printed daily or weekly containing news.

newt *n* a small lizard-like kind of animal, living on land and in water.

next *adj* nearest, closest in place, time *etc*: *the next page*. – *adv* in the nearest place or at the nearest time. *She led and I came next. Do that sum next.*

nib *n* a pen point.

'nibble *v* to take little bites (of). – *n* a little bite.

nice *adj* agreeable, pleasant; careful, precise, exact. – *adv* **'nicely** pleasantly; very well. – *n* **nicety** ['nisəti] a small fine detail: – *pl* **'niceties**. – **to a nicety** with great exactness.

niche [nich] also [nēsh] *n* a hollow in a wall for a statue, vase *etc*; a suitable place in life.

nick *n* a little cut, notch; (*slang*) prison, jail. – *v* to cut notches in; (*slang*) to steal.

'nickel *n* an element, a greyish-white metal used *esp* for mixing with other metals and for plating: *nickel-plating*; (in *US*) a 5-cent coin.

'nickname *n* a name used instead of a person or thing's real name, *usu* in fun or scorn.

nicotine ['nikətēn] *n* a substance contained in tobacco.

niece [nēs] *n* the daughter of a brother or sister, or of a brother-in-law or sister-in-law.

'niggardly *adj* mean, ungenerous.

'niggling *adj* unimportant, trivial, fussy; (of a worry, fear, *etc*) small but always present.

nigh [nī] *adj* (*old*) near.

night [nīt] *n* the period of darkness between sunset and sunrise; darkness. – *adj* of, for night; happening, active *etc* at night: *nightshift: a night worker*. – *adj, adv* **'nightly** by night; every night. – *ns* **'nightdress, -gown** a kind of garment worn in bed; **'nightfall** the beginning of night; **'nightjar** a kind of bird like a swallow which is active at night; **'nightmare** a frightening

dream; **'nightshade** a family of plants some of which have poisonous berries, *eg* deadly nightshade; **'night-'watchman** one who looks after a building during the night.

nightingale ['nītiŋgāl] *n* a type of small bird, the male of which sings beautifully by night and day.

nil *n* nothing.

'nimble *adj* quick and neat (in action or thought). – *n* **'nimbleness**.

'nimbus *n* a rain cloud.

'nincompoop *n* a weak, foolish person.

nine *n* the number 9. – *adj* 9 in number. – *adj* **ninth** the last of nine (things *etc*). – *n* one of nine equal parts.

'ninepins *n* a game in which nine bottle-shaped objects, *usu* wooden, are set up and knocked down by a ball.

'nine'teen *n* the number 19. – *adj* 19 in number. – *adj* **'nine'teenth** the last of nineteen (things *etc*). – *n* one of nineteen equal parts.

'ninety *n* the number 90. – *adj* 90 in number. – *adj* **'ninetieth** the last of ninety (things *etc*). – *n* one of ninety equal parts.

'ninny *n* a fool.

nip *v* to pinch, squeeze tightly (*eg* to the skin); to be stingingly painful; to bite, cut (off); to check the growth of, to damage (plants *etc*); (*coll*) to go nimbly or quickly: – *pt* **nipped**. – *n* a pinch; a sharp coldness in the weather; a small quantity: *a nip of whisky.*

'nipple *n* the pointed part of the breast from which a baby sucks milk.

nit *n* the egg of a louse or other small insect; (*coll*) a nitwit.

'nitwit *n* a very stupid person.

'nitric acid *n* a kind of strong acid containing nitrogen. – *n* **'nitrate** any of several substances formed from nitric acid, often used as soil fertilizers.

'nitrogen *n* an element, a type of gas forming nearly four-fifths of the air we breathe. – *n* **'nitro-'glycerine** a powerful kind of explosive.

no *adj* not any. *We have no food*; not a. *She is no beauty.* – *adv* not at all. *The patient is no better.* – *interj* expressing a negative. *Are you feeling better today? No.* – *n* a refusal; a vote against: – *pl* **noes**. – *prons* **'nobody** not any person; a person of no importance. *He is a nobody in politics*; **'no-one** not any person, nobody.

'noble *adj* great and good, fine; brave; of high birth or rank. – *n* a person of high rank or birth (also **'nobleman**). – *adv* **'nobly**. – *n* **no'bility** the nobles of a country; goodness, greatness of mind or character.

nobody see **no**.

noc'turnal adj happening or active (as certain kinds of animals) at night. – n **'nocturne** a piece of music intended to give a feeling of night-time.

nod v to bend the head forward quickly (often as a sign of agreement); to let the head drop in weariness: – pt **'nodded**. – n an action of nodding. – **nod off** to fall asleep.

node n the swollen part of a branch or twig where leaf-stalks join it; a swelling. – n **nodule** ['nodūl] a small rounded lump.

Noël, Nowell [nō'el] n Christmas.

noise [noiz] n a sound, often one which is loud or harsh. – v to spread (a rumour etc). – adjs **'noiseless; 'noisy** making a loud sound.

'nōmad n one of a group of people without a fixed home who wander about with flocks of sheep etc in search of pasture; someone who wanders from place to place. – adj **no'madic**.

'no-man's-land n land owned by no-one, esp that lying between two opposing armies.

nom de plume ['nomdə'ploom] n a name used by an author instead of his own name, a pen-name: – pl **'noms de 'plume**.

nomenclature [nə'menklōchər] n (system of) naming; names.

'nominal adj in name only; very small: a nominal fee.

'nominate v to propose (someone) for a post or for election; to appoint. – ns **nomi'nation; nomi'nee** one whose name is put forward for a post.

non- prefix not – used with a great many words to change their meaning to the opposite.

nonagenarian [nonəji'nāriən] n a person between ninety and ninety-nine years old.

nonchalant ['nonshələnt] adj not easily roused or upset, cool. – n **'nonchalance**.

non-commissioned ['nonkə'mishənd] adj belonging to the lower ranks of army officers, below second-lieutenant.

'non-com'mittal adj unwilling to express, or not expressing, an opinion.

noncon'formist n one who does not agree with those in authority, esp in church matters. – Also adj.

'nondescript adj not easily described, lacking anything noticeable or interesting.

none [nun] adv not at all: none the worse. – pron not one, not any.

no'nentity n a person of no importance: – pl **no'nentities**.

'non-ex'istent adj not existing, not real.

'non'plussed adj taken aback, confused.

'nonsense n words that have no sense or meaning; foolishness. – adj **non'sensical**.

'non-'stop adj going on without a stop.

'noodle n (usu pl) a strip of dough, eaten in soup etc or served with a sauce.

nook n a corner; a small recess.

noon n twelve o'clock midday.

no-one see **no**.

noose n a kind of loop in a rope etc that tightens when pulled.

nor conj used (often with **neither**) to show alternatives in the negative. Neither Mary nor Susan has been here.

norm n a pattern or standard to judge other things from. – adj **'normal** ordinary, usual according to a standard.

north n one of the four chief directions, that to the left of someone facing the rising sun (opposite to **south**). – Also adj, adv. – adjs **northerly** ['nördhərli] of, from or towards the north; **'northern** of the north; **northward(s)** ['nörthwərd(z)] towards the north. – Also adv. – ns **'north-'east (-'west)** the point of the compass midway between north and east (or west); **north pole** see **pole**.

nose n the part of the face by which people and animals smell and breathe; a jutting-out part of anything (eg the front of an aeroplane). – v to track by smelling; (coll) to interfere in others' affairs, to pry (into); to push a way through. The ship nosed through the ice. – adj **'nos(e)y** inquisitive, fond of prying. – n **'nosedive** a headfirst dive (by an aeroplane). – Also v. – n **'nosegay** a bunch of flowers.

nos'talgia n a longing for past times; a longing for home. – adj **nos'talgic**.

'nostril n one of the openings of the nose.

not adv expressing negative, refusal or denial. I am not going. Give it to me, not to him. I did not break the window.

'notable adj worth taking notice of; important, remarkable. – n an important person. – n **nota'bility** a well-known person: – pl **nota'bilities**. – adv **'notably** in a notable or noticeable way; particularly.

'nōtary (public) n an official whose job is to see that written documents or statements are drawn up in a way required by law: – pl **'notaries (public)**.

no'tation n the showing of numbers, musical sounds etc by signs: sol-fa *notation*; a set of such signs.

notch *n* a small V-shaped cut: – *pl* **'notches**. – *v* to make a notch. – *adj* **notched**.

note *n* a sign or piece of writing to draw someone's attention; (*pl*) ideas, details (for a speech, from a talk *etc*) set down in a short form; a short explanation; a short letter; a piece of paper used as money (*eg* a £1 note); a single sound or the sign standing for it in music; a key on the piano *etc*. – *v* to make a note of; to notice. – *adjs* **'noted** well-known; **'noteworthy** notable, remarkable. – *ns* **'notebook** a small book in which to make notes; **'notepaper** writing paper. – **of note** well-known, distinguished; **take note (of)** to notice particularly.

nothing ['nuthiŋ] *n* no thing, not anything; (in arithmetic) nought; something of no importance. – *adv* not at all. *He's nothing like his father.* – *n* **'nothingness** state of being nothing or of not existing; space, emptiness.

notice ['nōtis] *n* an announcement, made or shown publicly; attention. *The bright colour attracted my notice*; a warning given *eg* before leaving or before dismissing someone from a job, house *etc*. – *v* to see, observe, take note of. – *adj* **'noticeable** (likely to be) easily noticed.

'notify *v* to inform; to give notice of: – *pt* **'notified**. – *adj* **'notifiable** that must be reported: *a notifiable disease.* – *n* **notification** [nōtifi'kāshən].

'notion *n* an idea; a vague belief or opinion.

no'torious *adj* well known because of badness. *He is a notorious thief.* – *n* **notoriety** [nōtə'riəti].

notwith'standing *prep* in spite of. *Notwithstanding his poverty, he refused all help.*

nougat ['nōōgä] *n* a sticky kind of sweet (containing nuts *etc*).

nought [nöt] *n* nothing; naught; the figure 0.

noun *n* (in grammar) the word used as the name of any person or thing (as *John* and *box* in the sentence *John opened the box*).

nourish ['nurish] *v* to feed; to encourage the growth of. – *adj* **'nourishing** giving the body what is necessary for health and growth. – *n* **'nourishment** food; an act of nourishing.

'novel *adj* new and strange. – *n* a book telling a long story. – *ns* **'novelist** a writer of novels; **'novelty** something new and strange; newness; a small, *usu* cheap, manufactured article, *orig* of

unusual design, sold as a souvenir or toy. *These crackers have novelties inside them*: – *pl* **'novelties**.

No'vember *n* the eleventh month of the year.

novice ['novis] *n* a beginner.

now [now] *adv* at the present time. *I can see him now*; immediately before the present time. *I thought of her just now*; in the present circumstances. *I can't go now because my mother is ill.* – *conj* (*usu* **now that**) because, since. *I can go out now that it's fine.* – *adv* **'nowadays** in present times. – **now and then, now and again** sometimes, from time to time. *I see him now and again.*

nowhere ['nōwär] *adv* not in, or to, any place.

noxious ['nokshəs] *adj* harmful: *noxious fumes.*

'nozzle *n* a spout fitted to the end of a pipe, tube *etc*.

nuance ['nūöns] *n* a slight difference in meaning or colour *etc*.

nucleus ['nūkliəs] *n* the central part of an atom; the central part round which something collects or from which something grows: *the nucleus of his collection of books*; the part of a plant or animal cell that controls its development: – *pl* **'nuclei**. – *adj* **nuclear** ['nūklér] of a nucleus, *esp* that of an atom; produced by the splitting of the nuclei of atoms. – *ns* **nuclear energy** atomic energy; **nuclear missile** a missile whose warhead is an atomic bomb; **nuclear reactor** apparatus for producing nuclear energy.

nude *adj* without clothes, naked. – *n* an unclothed human figure; a painting or statue of such a figure. – *ns* **'nudism**; **'nudist** one who approves of going without clothes; **'nudity** the state of being nude. – **in the nude** naked.

nudge *n* a gentle push, *usu* with the elbow. – Also *v*.

'nugget *n* a lump, *esp* of gold.

nuisance ['nūsns] *n* a person or thing that is annoying or troublesome.

null: null and void having no legal force.

'nullify *v* to make useless or of no effect; to declare to be null and void: – *pt* **'nullified**.

numb [num] *adj* having lost the power to feel or move. – *v* to make numb.

'number *n* a word or figure showing how many, or showing a position in a series (as house numbers in a street); a collection of things or persons; one issue of a newspaper or a magazine; a popular song or piece of music. – *v* to count; to give numbers to; to amount to in number. – *adj* **'numberless** more than can be counted.

numeral ['nūmərəl] *n* a figure (*eg* 1, 2 *etc*) used to express a number. – *n* **'numerator** (in vulgar fractions) the number above the line (as 2 in ²/₃). – *adjs* **nu'merical** of, in, using or consisting of numbers; **'numerous** many.

numerate ['nūmərət] *adj* having some understanding of mathematics and science.

numismatist [nū'mizmətist] *n* one who collects and studies coins. – *n* **numis-'matics** the study of coins.

'numskull *n* a stupid person.

nun *n* a member of a female religious group living in a convent. – *n* **'nunnery** a house where a group of nuns live: – *pl* **'nunneries**.

nuptial ['nupshəl] *adj* of marriage. – *npl* **'nuptials** a wedding ceremony.

nurse *n* a person who looks after sick or injured people, or small children. – *v* to look after sick people *etc*, *esp* in hospital; to give (a baby) milk from the breast; to hold or look after with care. *He nurses his tomato plants*; to encourage (feelings, as anger, hope *etc*) in oneself. *He nurses a grudge against her.* – *n* **nursery** ['nərsəri] a room for young children; a place where young plants

are reared: – *pl* **'nurseries**. – *n* **nursery school** a school for very young children; **nursing home** a small private hospital.

nurture ['nərchər] *v* to bring up, rear; to nourish: *nurture resentment.* – *n* care, upbringing; food, nourishment.

nut *n* a fruit having a hard shell and, in it, a kernel; a small block *usu* of metal with a hole in it for screwing on the end of a bolt. – *adj* **'nutty** containing, or having the flavour of nuts; (*coll*) mad. – *n(pl)* **'nutcracker(s)** any of several types of instruments for cracking nuts open. – *n* **'nuthatch** a small kind of bird living on nuts and insects: – *pl* **'nuthatches**. – **in a nutshell** expressed very briefly.

'nutmeg *n* a hard kind of seed used as a spice in cooking.

'nutrient *adj*, *n* (of) a substance giving nourishment. – *n* **'nutriment** nourishment, food. – *adjs* **nu'tritious**, **'nutritive** valuable as food, nourishing.

'nuzzle *v* to press, rub or caress with the nose; to lie close to, snuggle, nestle.

'nylon *n* a type of material made from chemicals; (*pl*) stockings made of nylon.

nymph *n* (*myth*) a goddess of the rivers, trees *etc*; a beautiful girl; an insect not yet fully developed.

O

O!, Oh! [ō] *interj* expressing surprise, admiration, pain *etc*.

oaf *n* a stupid or clumsy person: – *pl* **oafs**.

oak *n* a type of tree having acorns as fruit; its hard wood. – *adjs* **oak**, **'oaken** made of oak. – *n* **oak apple** a kind of growth on the leaves and twigs of oaks, caused by insects.

oar *n* a pole for rowing, with a flat, blade-like end. – *v* to row. – *n* **'oarsman** one who rows. – **put one's oar in** to interfere in.

oasis [ō'āsis] *n* in a desert, a place where water is found and trees *etc* grow: – *pl* **oases** [ō'āsēz].

oast *n* a large oven to dry hops. – *n* **'oast-house**.

oath *n* a solemn promise to speak the truth, to keep one's word, to be loyal *etc*; a swear word: – *pl* **oaths** [ōdhz].

oats *npl* a type of grassy plant or its grain, used as food. – *ns* **'oatcake** a thin flat cake made of oatmeal; **'oatmeal** meal made by grinding down oat grains.

'obdurate *adj* stubborn, firm, unyielding.

obedience, obedient *see* **obey**.

obeisance [ə'bāsəns] *n* a bow or curtsy showing respect.

obelisk ['obəlisk] *n* a tall four-sided pillar with a pointed top.

o'bese [ə'bēs] *adj* very fat. – *n* **o'besity**.

obey [ə'bā] *v* to do what one is told to do: *obey one's father*: *obey an order.* – *n* **o'bēdience** the act of obeying; willingness to obey. – *adj* **o'bedient**.

o'bituary *n* a notice (*usu* in a newspaper) of a person's death, sometimes with an account of his career: – *pl* **o'bituaries**.

'object *n* anything that can be seen or felt; an aim or purpose. *His main object was to make money*; (in grammar) the word in a sentence which stands for the person or thing on which the action of the verb is done (as *me* in the sentences *He hit me. He likes me.*). – *v* **ob'ject** (often with **to**) to feel or show disapproval of. – *n* **ob'jection** the act of objecting; a reason for objecting. – *adjs*

ob'jectionable nasty, disagreeable; **ob'jective** not influenced by personal interests, fair. – *n* aim, purpose, goal.

o'blige *v* to force or compel. *I was obliged to go home*; to do a favour or service to. *Oblige me by shutting the door.* – *n* **obligation** [obli'gāshən] a promise or duty by which one is bound. *I am under an obligation to help him*; a debt of gratitude for a favour received. – *adjs* **o'bligatory** compulsory; required as a duty; **obliged** [ə'blījd] owing or feeling gratitude; **'obliging** ready to help others.

oblique [ə'blēk] *adj* slanting; not straight or direct; not straightforward: *an oblique reference.*

obliterate [ə'blitərāt] *v* to blot out; to destroy completely. – *n* **oblite'ration**.

o'blivion *n* forgetfulness; state of being forgotten. – *adj* **o'blivious** (with **of** or **to**) unaware, not paying attention; forgetful.

'oblong *n* a figure of this shape: ▭ . – Also *adj*.

obnoxious [əb'nokshəs] *adj* offensive, causing dislike.

'ōboe *n* a type of high-pitched woodwind instrument: – *pl* **'oboes**. – *n* **oboist** ['ōbōist] one who plays the oboe.

obscene [əb'sēn] *adj* (sexually) indecent; disgusting. – *n* **obscenity** [əb'senəti]: – *pl* **ob'scenities**.

ob'scure *adj* dark; not clear or easily understood; unknown, humble: *an obscure painter.* – *v* to darken; to make less clear. – *n* **ob'scurity**.

ob'sēquious *adj* trying to win favour by being too humble or too ready to agree, flatter *etc*.

observe [əb'zörv] *v* to notice; to watch with attention; to remark; to obey (a law *etc*); to keep, preserve: *observe a tradition.* – *n* **ob'servance** the act of keeping (a law, a tradition *etc*). – *adj* **ob'servant** good at noticing. – *ns* **obser'vation** the act or habit of seeing and noting; attention; a remark; **ob'servatory** a place for making observations of the stars, weather *etc*: – *pl* **ob'servatories**; **ob'server** one who sees or observes; one who is sent to listen to, but not take part in, a discussion *etc*.

ob'sess *v* to fill the mind completely. – *n* **ob'session** a feeling or idea from which the mind cannot get away; the state of being obsessed. – *adj* **ob'sessive** of obsession; having or liable to have an obsession.

'obsolete *adj* gone out of use. – *adj* **obsolescent** [obsə'lesnt] going out-of-date. – *n* **obso'lescence**.

'obstacle *n* something which stands in the way and hinders. – *n* **obstacle race** a race in which obstacles are laid across the course.

ob'stetrics *npl* the study and act of helping women before, during and after the birth of babies. – *adjs* **ob'stetric, ob'stetrical** of obstetrics. – *n* **obste'trician** a doctor trained in this.

'obstinate *adj* stubborn; not yielding. – *n* **'obstinacy** stubbornness.

obstreperous [əb'strepərəs] *adj* noisy, unruly.

ob'struct *v* to block up, keep from passing; to hold back. – *n* **ob'struction** something which hinders; something which blocks up.

ob'tain *v* to get, gain; to be in use. *This rule still obtains.* – *adj* **ob'tainable** able to be got.

obtrude [əb'trōōd] *v* to thrust (something unwanted on someone); to thrust (oneself) forward when not wanted. – *n* **ob'trusion**. – *adj* **ob'trusive** too noticeable; pushing, impudent.

ob'tuse *adj* (of an angle) greater than a right angle; blunt, not pointed; stupid, not quick to understand.

'obverse *n* the side of a coin on which is the head or main design.

'obviate *v* to remove, prevent or get round (a difficulty *etc*).

'obvious *adj* easily seen or understood, plain, evident.

occasion [ə'kāzhən] *n* a particular time: *on that occasion*; a special event: *a great occasion*; a cause or reason; opportunity. – *v* to cause. – *adj* **oc'casional** happening (or used) now and then. – *adv* **oc'casionally**.

Occident ['oksidənt] *n* the West. – *adj* **occi'dental**.

oc'cult *adj* secret, mysterious; supernatural. – Also *n*.

'occūpy *v* to dwell in; to keep busy; to take up, fill (space, time, a place *etc*); to seize, capture (a town, fort *etc*): – *pt* **'occupied**. – *ns* **'occupancy** the act, fact, or period of occupying; **'occupant; occu'pation** state of being occupied; that which occupies one; one's trade or job; possession (of a house *etc*); **'occupier** one who has possession (of a house *etc*).

oc'cur *v* to happen; to appear or to be found; (with **to**) to come into the mind of. *That never occurred to me*: – *pt* **oc'curred**. – *n* **oc'currence** a happening or event; the act or fact of occurring.

201

ocean ['ōshən] *n* the stretch of salt water surrounding the land of the earth; one of its five great divisions (Atlantic, Pacific, Indian, Arctic, Antarctic).

ochre ['ōkər] *n* a type of fine pale-yellow or red clay, used for colouring.

octa- octo- oct- *prefix* eight.

'**octagon** *n* an eight-sided figure. – *adj* **oc'tagonal**.

'**octave** *n* (in music) a series or stretch of eight notes (as from one C to the C next above it).

oc'tet *n* a group of eight (lines of poetry, singers *etc*).

Oc'tōber *n* the tenth month of the year.

octogenarian [oktəji'nāriən] *n* a person between eighty and eighty-nine years old.

'**octopus** *n* a type of sea creature with eight arms: – *pl* '**octopuses**.

'**ocūlar** *adj* of the eye.

'**ocūlist** *n* one who specializes in diseases and defects of the eye.

odd *adj* (of a number) not even, leaving a remainder of one when divided by two (*eg* the numbers 1, 17, 315); unusual, strange; not one of a matching pair, set or group *etc*, something left out or left over: *an odd glove: odd screw: odd minute*; (*pl*) chances or probability. *The odds are that he will win*; (*pl*) difference. *It makes no odds.* – *n* '**oddity** queerness, strangeness; a queer person or thing: – *pl* '**oddities**. – *npl* '**oddments** scraps. – **at odds** quarrelling; **odd jobs** jobs of different kinds, not part of regular employment; **odds and ends** objects, scraps *etc* of different kinds.

ode *n* a type of poem, *usu* written to a person or thing.

'**ōdious** *adj* hateful. – *n* '**odium** dislike, hatred.

odour ['ōdər] *n* smell (pleasant or unpleasant). – *adj* '**odourless** without smell.

of [ov] *prep* belonging to: *the house of my parents*; from (a place, person *etc*): *within two miles of his home*; from among: *one of my pupils*; made from, made up of: *a house of bricks*; indicating an amount, measurement *etc*: *a gallon of petrol*; about, concerning: *talk of old friends*; with, containing: *a class of twenty children*: *a cup of water*; as a result of: *die of hunger*; indicating removal or taking away. *He robbed her of her jewels*; indicating a connection between an action and its object: *the joining of the pieces*; indicating character, qualities *etc*. *He is a man of judgement. It was good of you to come*;

(*US*) (in telling the time) before, to: *ten* (*minutes*) *of eight.*

off *adv* away (from a place, from a particular state, standard, position *etc*). *He walked off rudely. Your work has gone off. The light was switched off*; entirely, completely. *Finish off your work.* – *adj* cancelled. *The expedition is off*; not up to the required or normal standard or condition. *The meat is off*; not working, not on. *The control is in the off position*; not quite pure in colour: *off-white.* – *prep* not on, away from. *I fell off the table*; taken away: *10% off the usual price*; below the normal standard: *off his game.* – **badly off, well off** poor, rich; **off and on** occasionally.

'**offal** *n* the parts of an animal unfit for use as food; certain internal organs of an animal (heart, liver *etc*) that are eaten.

'**off-'chance** *n* a slight chance.

'**off-colour** ['of'kulər] *adj, adv* not feeling well.

of'fend *v* to make angry or hurt the feelings of; to displease; to do wrong. – *ns* **of'fence** (any cause of) anger, displeasure, hurt feelings; a crime, a sin; **of'fender**; **of'fensive** the position of one who attacks; an attack. – *adj* annoying; insulting, disgusting; used in attacking or assaulting: *an offensive weapon.* – **take offence at** to be angry or feel hurt at.

'**offer** *v* to put forward (a gift, payment *etc*) for acceptance or refusal; to lay (a choice, chance *etc*) before; to say that one is willing to do something. – *n* an act of offering; a bid of money; something proposed. – *n* '**offering** a gift; collection of money in church.

'**off'hand** *adj* said or done without thinking or preparation; lacking politeness. – *adv* without previous preparation.

office ['ofis] *n* a place where business is carried on; the people working in such a place; a duty, a job; a position of authority, *esp* in the government; (*pl*) services, helpful acts. – *n* '**officer** a person who carries out a public duty; a person holding a commission in the army, navy or air force. – *adj* **official** [ə'fishəl] done, given out by those in power: *official announcement*: *official action*; forming part of one's task when holding a job or office: *official duties*; having full and proper authority. – *n* one who holds an office in the service of the government *etc*. – *adv* **of'ficially** as an official, formally; as announced or said in public (though not necessarily truthfully). – *v* **officiate** [ə'fishiāt] to perform a duty or service, *esp* as a clergyman at a wedding *etc.* – *adj* **of'ficious** fond of interfering *esp* in a pompous way.

offing: in the offing at a place or time not far off.

off-licence *n* a shop selling alcohol which must not be drunk on the premises.

off'set *v* to weigh against, to make up for. *The high cost of the project was partly offset by a government grant.*

offshoot *n* a shoot growing out of the main stem; anything (of lesser importance) growing out of or starting from something else. *That firm is an offshoot of an international firm.*

off'side *adj, adv* (in football) in a position between the ball and the opponent's goal; (of the side of a vehicle *etc*) nearest to the centre of the road.

offspring *n* one's child or children; the young (of animals *etc*).

oft *adv* (in poetry *etc*) often.

often ['ofn] *adv* many times.

ōgle *v* to eye (someone) impudently in order to show admiration.

ogre ['ōgər] *n* (*myth*) a (man-eating) giant; someone or something that frightens or threatens.

oil *n* a greasy liquid, got from plants (*eg* olive oil), from animals (*eg* whale oil), and from minerals (*eg* petroleum); (*pl*) oil colours for painting. – *v* to smear with oil, put oil on or in. – *adj* **'oily** of or like oil; (of person, manner *etc*) trying to be too friendly or flattering. – *ns* **oil colour** paint made by mixing a colouring substance with oil; **'oilfield** an area where mineral oil is found; **oil painting** a picture painted in oil colours; **'oilrig** a structure set up for drilling an oil-well; **'oilskin** cloth made waterproof by means of oil; a garment of this; **'oil-well** a hole drilled into the earth's surface or into the sea bed to obtain petroleum.

'ointment *n* any of many greasy substances rubbed on the skin to soothe, heal *etc*.

OK, okay ['ō'kā] *interj, adv* all right. – *v* **'o'kay** to mark or pass as being all right: – *pt* **'o'kayed**.

ōld *adj* advanced in age, aged; having a certain age: *ten years old*; not new, having existed a long time; belonging to far-off times; worn, worn-out; out-of-date, old-fashioned. – *n* **old age** the later part of life. – *adj* **'old-'fashioned** in a style common in the past, out-of-date. – **of old** long ago.

olive ['oliv] *n* a type of fruit which gives an oil used for cooking; the tree that bears it. – *adj* of a yellowish-green colour. – *n* **olive branch** a sign of a wish for peace.

Ombudsman ['ombŏŏdzmən] *n* an official appointed to look into complaints against the government.

omega ['ōmigə] *n* the last letter of the Greek alphabet.

omelette, omelet ['omlit] *n* beaten eggs fried (and *usu* folded over) in a pan.

omen ['ōmən] *n* a sign of future events. – *adj* **ominous** ['ominəs] suggesting future trouble.

o'mit *v* to leave out; to fail to do: – *pt* **o'mitted**. – *n* **o'mission** something omitted; the act of omitting.

'omnibus *n* a large public motor vehicle for passengers (*usu* shortened to **bus**): – *pl* **'omnibuses**.

om'nipotent *adj* having absolute, unlimited, power: *the omnipotent ruler.* – *n* **om'nipotence**.

omniscient [om'nisiənt] *adj* knowing everything. – *n* **om'niscience**.

omnivorous [om'nivərəs] *adj* feeding on all kinds of food.

on *prep* touching, fixed *etc* to the outer or upper side *etc* of a thing or person: *on the table*; supported by: *standing on one foot*; receiving, taking *etc*: *on half-pay*: *on drugs*; occurring in the course of a specified time *etc*: *on the following day*; about: *a book on churches*; with. *He had his wallet on him*; next to, near: *a city on the Thames*; indicating membership of. *He is on the committee*; in the condition, process or state of: *on sale*: *on show*; by means of. *He played the tune on the piano*; followed by: *disaster on disaster.* – *adv* so as to be touching, or fixed to the outer or upper side *etc* of a thing. *Put your coat on*; onwards, further. *They carried on towards London: from now on*; at a further point: *later on.* – *adj* working, performing. *The television is on*; arranged, planned. *Do you have anything on this afternoon?*

once [wuns] *adv* at an earlier time in the past. *Men once lived in caves*; for one time only. *I've read this book only once.* – *n* one time only. *Do it just this once.* – *conj* when. *Once you've finished, go!* – **all at once** suddenly. *All at once he appeared from nowhere; see* also **at once; at once** without delay. *Come here at once!*; (sometimes with **all**) at the same time, together. *She did several things (all) at once*; **once (and) for all** for the last time; **once upon a time** at some time in the past, often used at the beginning of stories.

oncoming ['onkumiŋ] *adj* approaching

from the front: *oncoming traffic.*

one [wun] *n* the number 1; a particular member of a group. *She's the one I hate most.* – *pron* a single particular person or thing: *one of my cats*; in formal or pompous English used instead of **you**, meaning anyone. *One must beware of thieves.* – *adj* 1 in number; a single. *Only one man survived*; identical, the same. *We're all of one mind*; some (unnamed time): *one day soon.* – *pron* **one'self** used reflexively: *wash oneself*; used for emphasis. *One always has to go oneself, because nobody else will.* – *adjs* **'one-'sided** (of a contest *etc*) with one person, side *etc* having a great advantage over the other; **'one-'way** (of a road, street) meant for traffic moving in one direction only. – **one another** used when an action takes place between more than two (loosely, between two) people. *They hit one another.*

onerous ['ōnərəs] *adj* heavy, hard to bear or do: *an onerous task.*

'ongōing *adj* continuing: *an ongoing task.*

onion ['unyən] *n* a type of vegetable with a strong taste and smell.

'onlooker *n* one who watches (an event).

'ōnly *adv* not more than: *only two matches left*; alone, solely. *Only you went*; not longer ago than. *I saw him only yesterday*; indicating the unavoidable result (of an action). *He'll only be offended if you mention it*; (with **too**) extremely. *I'll be only too pleased to come.* – *adj* single, solitary: *an only child.* – *conj* (*coll*) but, except that. *I'd like to go, only I have to work.*

'onrush *n* a rush forward.

'onset *n* beginning; a fierce attack.

onslaught ['onslöt] *n* a fierce attack.

'ōnus *n* burden; responsibility.

'onward *adj* going forward in place or time. – *advs* **'onward, 'onwards**.

onyx ['oniks] *n* a type of precious stone with layers of different colours.

ooze *v* to flow gently or slowly. – *n* soft mud; a gentle flow.

opacity *see* **opaque**.

'ōpal *n* a type of bluish-white precious stone, with flecks of various colours.

opaque [ə'pāk] *adj* not able to be seen through. – *n* **opacity** [ə'pasəti].

'ōpen *adj* not shut, allowing entry or exit; not enclosed or fenced; showing the inside or inner part; uncovered; not blocked; free for all to enter; honest, frank; (of land) without many trees. – *v* to make open; to unlock; to begin. – *ns* **'opener** something that opens (something): *a tin opener*; **'opening** a hole or gap; an opportunity; a vacant

job. – *adv* **'openly** without trying to hide or conceal anything. – *n* **open ai**[r] any place not indoors or undergroun[d] *etc*. – *adjs* **'open-'air**; **'open-'minde**[d] ready to take up new ideas. – **in th**[e] **open** out-of-doors, in the open air; **open to** likely or willing to receive *etc*; *open to attack*: *open to criticism.*

opera ['opərə] *n* a play in which music b[y] voices and orchestra is of the greates[t] importance. – *adj* **ope'ratic**.

operate ['opərāt] *v* to act, work; to brin[g] about an effect; to perform an opera[-] tion. – *adj* **'operating** of or for a[n] operation on a person's body. – *n* **ope'ration** action; method or way o[f] working; the cutting of a part of th[e] human body in order to cure disease[;] (*pl*) movements of armies, troops. – *adj* **'operative** working, in action; (of [a] rule *etc*) in force, having effect. – *n* [a] workman in a factory *etc*. – *n* **'operator** one who works a machine; one wh[o] connects telephone calls.

operetta [opə'retə] *n* a play with musi[c] and singing.

ophthalmic [of'thalmik] *adj* of the eye[:] *an ophthalmic surgeon.* – *n* **ophthal'mologist** a doctor wh[o] specializes in diseases of and injuries t[o] the eye.

opiate ['ōpiət] *n* a drug containin[g] opium used to make a person sleep [;] anything that calms or dulls the min[d] or feelings.

o'pinion *n* what one thinks or believes[;] (professional) judgement, point o[f] view. *He wanted another opinion on hi*[s] *son's case*; what one thinks of the wort[h] or value of someone or something. *[I] have a very low opinion of his work.* – *ad*[j] **o'pinionated** having strong opinions which one is confident are right.

'ōpium *n* a drug made from the drie[d] juice of a type of poppy.

o'possum *n* a type of small America[n] animal that carries its young in a pouc[h]

opponent *see* **oppose**.

'opportune *adj* coming at the right or convenient time. – *ns* **oppor'tunism** the state of being an opportunist; **oppor'tunist** a person who takes ad[-] vantage of any opportunity or cir[-] cumstance which will be to his advan[-] tage; **oppor'tunity** a chance (to do[)] something).

oppose [ə'pōz] *v* to struggle against, resist; to stand against, compete against. – *n* **opponent** [ə'pōnənt] one who opposes; an enemy; a rival. – *adj* **opposite** ['opəzit] facing, across from; lying on the other side (of); as different as possible. – *prep* facing, across from. *He lives opposite the post office*; acting a role (in a play, opera *etc*) corresponding in importance to. *She played Ophelia opposite his Hamlet.* – *n* something as different as possible (from something else). *Black is the opposite of white.* – *n* **opposition** [opə'zishən] resistance; those who resist; (in parliament) the party which is against the governing party.

op'press *v* to govern harshly like a tyrant; to treat cruelly; to distress or worry greatly. – *adj* op'pressive oppressing; cruel, harsh; (of weather) close, tiring. – *n* op'pression.

op'probrium *n* great or public disgrace; something that brings great disgrace. – *adj* op'probrious disgraceful; scornful.

opt *v* (with **for**) to choose; to decide (to do). – **opt out** to decide not to (do something).

optic, 'optical *adjs* having to do with the eye or sight. – *ns* optician [op'tishən] one who makes and sells spectacles; 'optics the science of light. – *n* optical illusion an impression that something seen is different from what it is.

optimism *n* the habit of taking a bright, hopeful view of things (opposite of pessimism). – *n* 'optimist one who is in the habit of taking such a view. – *adj* opti'mistic.

optimum *adj* best, most favourable: *optimum conditions*.

option *n* choice; the right or power to choose; the thing chosen. – *adj* 'optional left to one's choice.

opulent *adj* wealthy; luxurious. – *n* 'opulence riches.

opus *n* a work, *esp* a musical composition: – *pl* opera ['opərə].

or *conj* used (often with **either**) to show alternatives. *You can either go out or stay in: tea or coffee*; because if not. *You'd better go or you'll miss your bus.*

'oracle *n* a person thought to be very wise or knowledgeable; (*hist*) a holy place where a god was thought to give answers to difficult questions; an answer of this kind; a person through whom such answers were made known.

oral ['örəl] *adj* spoken, not written; having to do with the mouth. – *adv* 'orally. – *n* an oral examination or test.

orange ['orinj] *n* a type of juicy citrus fruit, with a thick reddish-yellow skin.

orang-utan ['oraŋ'ootan] *n* a type of large, man-like ape.

o'ration *n* a public speech *esp* one in fine, formal language. – *ns* orator ['orətər] a

public speaker, *esp* a very eloquent one; 'oratory the art of speaking well in public.

oratorio [orə'töriō] *n* a sacred story set to music, performed by soloists, choir and *usu* orchestra: – *pl* ora'torios.

orb *n* anything in the shape of a ball, a sphere.

'orbit *n* the path of a planet *etc* round another heavenly body, of a space capsule round the earth *etc*; range or area of influence: *within his orbit.* – *v* to go round the earth *etc* in space. *The spacecraft orbited the earth.*

'orchard *n* a large garden of fruit trees.

orchestra ['örkəstrə] *n* a group of musicians playing together under a conductor. – *v* 'orchestrate to arrange (a piece of music) for an orchestra.

orchid ['örkid] *n* a kind of plant *usu* with brightly coloured or unusually shaped flowers.

or'dain *v* to declare something to be law; to receive (a clergyman) into the Church. – *ns* ordinance ['ördinəns] a command; a law; ordi'nation the receiving of a clergyman into the church.

or'deal *n* a hard trial or test; suffering, painful experience.

'order *n* an instruction to act (made from a position of authority). *The captain gave his orders to his lieutenants*; a request, list of requests. *He left his order with the grocer*; an arrangement according to a system; an accepted way of doing things; a tidy or efficient state; peaceful conditions: *law and order*; rank, position, class; a society or brotherhood (*eg* of monks). – *v* to tell (to do something) from a position of authority; to give an order for; to arrange. – *adj* 'orderly in proper order; well-behaved, quiet. – *n* a soldier who carries the orders and messages of an officer; a hospital attendant who does routine jobs: – *pl* 'orderlies. – **in order** correct according to what is regularly done; in a tidy arrangement; **in order to** for the purpose of. *In order to live you must eat*; **out of order** not working; not the correct way of doing things; not in a tidy arrangement.

'ordinal numbers *npl* those showing order (as first, second, third *etc*).

'ordinary *adj* common, usual; normal; not unusually good *etc*. – **out of the ordinary** unusual.

'Ordnance 'Survey *n* a government office which produces official detailed maps.

ore [ör] *n* a mineral from which a metal is obtained (*eg* iron ore).

'organ *n* a part of the body (*eg* the liver); a large musical wind instrument with a keyboard; a means of spreading information, *eg* a newspaper: *an organ of Communism*. – *adj* **or'ganic** of or produced by the bodily organs; of living things; made up of parts all having their own work to do; (of food) grown without the use of artificial fertilizers *etc*. – *ns* **'organism** any living thing; **'organist** one who plays the organ.

organdie ['örgəndi] *n* a fine thin stiff muslin.

'organize *v* to arrange, set up (an event *etc*); to form into a whole. – *n* **organi'zation** the act of organizing; a body of people working together for a purpose.

orgy ['örji] *n* a drunken or other unrestrained celebration: – *pl* **'orgies**.

Orient ['öriənt] *n* the East. – *adj* **ori'ental**.

orientate ['öriəntāt] *v* to find one's position and sense of direction; to set or put facing a particular direction. – *ns* **orien'tation**; **orien'teering** the sport of finding one's way across country with the help of map and compass.

orifice ['orifis] *n* an opening.

'origin *n* the starting point; the place from which a person or thing comes; cause. – *adj* **o'riginal** first in time; not copied; able to think or do something new. – *n* the earliest version; a model from which other things are made. – *v* **o'riginate** to bring or come into being; to produce.

'ornament *n* anything that adds, or is supposed to add, beauty. – *v* to adorn, decorate. – *adj* **orna'mental** used for ornament; beautiful. – *n* **ornamen'tation**.

or'nate *adj* richly decorated.

orni'thologist *n* one who studies or is an expert on birds. – *n* **orni'thology**.

'orphan *n* a child who has lost one or both parents (*usu* both). – *n* **'orphanage** a home for orphans.

'orthodox *adj* holding (*esp* religious) views that are held generally in one's country, religion *etc*. – *n* **'orthodoxy**.

or'thography *n* correct or usual spelling.

orthopaedics, (*US*) **orthopedics** [örthə'pēdiks] *n* the branch of medicine which deals with bone diseases and injuries. – *adj* **ortho'paedic**.

oscillate ['osilāt] *v* to swing to and fro like the pendulum of a clock; to keep changing one's mind. – *n* **oscil'lation**.

osier ['ōziər] *n* a type of willow tree, the twigs of which are used in making baskets *etc*; one of the twigs.

osprey ['ospri] *n* a type of hawk which eats fish: – *pl* **'ospreys**.

os'tensible *adj* (of reasons *etc*) outwardly shown, apparent, but not always real or true.

osten'tātious *adj* showy, meant to catch the eye. – *n* **osten'tation**.

osteopath ['ostiəpath] *n* a person who treats injuries to bones, muscles *etc* by manipulating the patient's body, not by drugs or surgery.

ostler *see* **hostler**.

'ostracize *v* to banish (someone) from the company of a group of people. – *n* **'ostracism**.

'ostrich *n* a type of large bird which cannot fly: – *pl* **'ostriches**.

other ['udhər] *adj* second of two: *the other shoe*; remaining, not previously mentioned: *the other men*; different, additional: *some other reason*; (with *every*) second: *every other day*; recently past: *the other day*. – *pron* the second of two; those remaining, those not previously mentioned. *The others went home later*; the previous one: *one after the other*. – **other than** except: *no hope other than to retreat*; **someone, something or other** a person, thing not named or specified. *There's always someone or other here*.

'otter *n* a type of river animal living on fish.

'ottoman *n* a kind of low, cushioned seat without a back.

ought [öt] *v* used with other verbs to indicate duty or need. *He ought to set an example. You ought to keep yourself tidy*; or to indicate what can be reasonably expected. *The weather ought to be fine.*

ounce *n* a unit of weight, one-sixteenth of a pound, 28·35 grammes.

our *adj* belonging to us: *our house*. – *pron* **ours**. *The green car is ours*. – *pron* **our'selves** used reflexively. *We exhausted ourselves playing football*; used for emphasis. *We ourselves don't like it, but other people may.*

oust *v* to drive out (from position or possessions); to take the place of. *He ousted him as leader of the party.*

out *adv* into, towards the open air. *Go out for a walk*; from within. *Take out a pencil*; not inside. *He's out of prison now*; far from here: *out at sea*; not at home, not in the office *etc*. *He's out at the moment*; aloud: *shouted out*; to or at an end. *Hear me out*; inaccurate. *The calculation was two miles out*; (*coll*) on strike; published. *The book isn't out yet*; no longer hidden or secret; dismissed from a game (of cricket, baseball *etc*); finished, having won (at cards *etc*); no longer in power or office; determined: *out to win.* – *adjs* '**outer** nearer the edge, surface *etc*; further away; '**outermost** nearest the edge *etc*; furthest. – *n* '**outing** a trip, excursion. – *adj* '**out-and-**'**out** complete, thorough: *an out-and-out villain.*

outback *n* (in Australia) wild inland areas.

out'**bid** *v* to offer a higher price than (somebody else): – *pres p* **out**'**bidding**, *pt* **out**'**bid**.

outboard *adj* outside of a ship or boat: *an outboard motor.*

outbreak ['owtbrāk] *n* beginning (of a war, of disease *etc*).

outbuilding ['owtbildiŋ] *n* a shed or building separate from the main buildings.

outburst *n* a bursting out, *esp* of angry feelings.

outcast *adj, n* (of) a person driven away from friends and home.

outcome ['owtkum] *n* result.

outcrop *n* the part of a rock formation that can be seen at the surface of the ground.

outcry *n* a show of anger, disapproval *etc* (*esp* by the general public): – *pl* '**outcries**.

outdo [owt'dōō] *v* to do better than: – *pt* **out**'**did**, *pp* **out**'**done**.

outdoor ['owtdör] *adj* of or in the open air. – *adv* '**out**'**doors**.

outfit *n* a set of clothes worn together (sometimes for a special occasion *etc*): *her wedding outfit.* – *n* '**outfitter** a seller of outfits, *esp* men's clothes.

outgoings *npl* money spent or being spent.

outgrow [owt'grō] *v* to get too big or old for (clothes, toys *etc*).

out-house *n* a shed.

out'**landish** *adj* looking or sounding very strange.

outlaw *n* someone put outside the protection of the law; a robber or bandit. – *v* to place someone beyond the protection of the law; to ban, forbid.

outlay *n* money paid out.

outlet *n* a passage outwards *eg* for a water-pipe; a means of letting something out (*esp* a feeling, energy *etc*). *Football was an outlet for his high spirits*; a market for goods.

outline *n* the outer line (as of a figure in a drawing); a sketch showing only the main lines; a rough sketch; a brief description. – *v* to draw or describe an outline of.

outlive [owt'liv] *v* to live longer than.

outlook *n* a view (from a window *etc*); what is thought likely to happen: *the weather outlook.*

outlying *adj* far from the centre, distant.

out'**number** *v* to be greater in number than. *Their team outnumbered ours.*

out-patient ['owtpāshənt] *n* a patient who does not live in a hospital while receiving treatment.

outpost *n* a military station in front of or far from the main army; an outlying settlement.

output ['owtpōōt] *n* the goods produced by a machine, factory *etc*; the amount of work done by a person.

outrage *n* a wicked act of great violence; an act which hurts the feelings or that causes offence. – *v* to injure, hurt by violence; to insult, shock. – *adj* **out**'**rageous** violent, very wrong; not moderate.

outright [owt'rīt] *adv* completely. – *adj* '**outright** complete, thorough.

outset *n* start, beginning.

out'**side** *n* the outer surface or place: *the outside of the box.* – *adj* in, on, or of the outer surface or place: *the outside seat*; connected with leisure *etc* rather than one's full-time job: *outside interests*; slight: *an outside chance of winning.* – *adv* beyond the limits (of): *outside the walls*: *outside working hours*; out-of-doors, in(to) the open air. – *prep* beyond the borders *etc* of, not within. – *n* '**out**'**sider** a stranger; a person who is not included in a particular social group *etc*; a runner *etc* whom no-one expects to win. – **at the outside** at the most: *ten miles at the outside.*

outsize *adj* of a very large size. – Also *n.*

outskirts *npl* the outer borders of a city *etc.*

out'**spoken** *adj* bold and frank in speech.

out'**standing** *adj* well-known; very good; (of accounts, debts) unpaid.

outstretched *adj* (*esp* of one's hand) reaching out.

out'**vote** *v* to defeat (*eg* in an election *etc*) by a greater number of votes.

outward *adj* toward or on the outside; (of a journey) away from home, not towards it. – *advs* '**outwardly**, '**outwards**.

outweigh [owt'wā] *v* to be more important than. *The advantages outweigh the disadvantages.*

out'**wit** *v* to defeat by cunning: – *pt* **out**'**witted**.

oval ['ōval] *adj* having the shape of an egg. – Also *n.*

ovary ['ōvari] *n* the part of the female body in

which eggs are formed: – *pl* **'ovaries**.

o'**vation** *n* an outburst of cheering, hand-clapping *etc*.

oven ['uvn] *n* a covered place for baking; a small furnace.

'**over** *prep* higher than, above in position, number, rank *etc*: *over the door*: *over £10*: *ruling over the people*; across: *going over the bridge*; on the other side of: *the house over the road*; on top of. *He threw his coat over the body*; here and there on: *paper scattered over the carpet*; about. *They quarrelled over their money*; by means of: *over the telephone*; during, throughout: *over the years*; while doing, having *etc*. *He fell asleep over his dinner*. – *adv* above, higher in position or movement. *Two birds flew over*; across (a distance). *He walked over and spoke*; downwards. *I fell over*; above in number *etc*: *anyone aged four and over*; as a remainder: *three left over*; through: *read the passage over*. – *adj* finished. *The war is over*. – *n* (in cricket) a fixed number of balls bowled from one end of the wicket. – **over again** once more.

over- *prefix* often meaning too much, to too great an extent: *overcook*: *over-excited*: *over-payment*.

overall ['ōvərōl] *n* a garment worn over ordinary clothes to protect them against dirt; trousers with a bib made of hard-wearing material worn by workmen *etc*. – *adj* from one end to the other: *overall length*; including everything: *overall cost*.

ōver'awe *v* to make silent by fear or astonishment.

ōver'balance *v* to (make to) lose one's balance and fall.

overbearing [ōvər'bāriŋ] *adj* too sure that one is right, domineering.

'**overboard** *adv* out of a ship into the water. *Man overboard!*

'**over'cast** *adj* (of the sky) cloudy.

'**over'charge** *v* to charge too great a price; to fill or load too heavily.

'**overcoat** *n* an outdoor coat worn over all other clothes.

overcome [ōvər'kum] *v* to get the better of, conquer: – *pt* **over'came**. – *adj* helpless (from exhaustion, emotion *etc*).

overdo [ōvər'dōō] *v* to do too much; to exaggerate. *They rather overdid the sympathy*; to cook (food) too long: – *pt* **overdone** [ōvər'dun].

'**overdose** *n* too great an amount (of medicine *etc*).

'**ōver'draw** *v* to draw more money from the bank than one has in it. – *n* '**overdraft** the amount of money over-

drawn from a bank, sometimes by official arrangement.

'**over'due** *adj* later than the stated time. *The train is overdue*; (of a bill *etc*) still unpaid although the time for payment has passed.

overflow [ōvər'flō] *v* to flow over the edge or limits of. *The river overflowed its banks. The crowd overflowed into the next room*; to be so full as to flow over. – *n* '**overflow** a running-over of liquid; a pipe or channel for getting rid of extra or waste water *etc*.

overgrown ['ōvər'grōn] *adj* covered (with wild growth of plants); grown too large.

'**ōver'hang** *v* to jut out over.

ōver'haul *v* to examine carefully and carry out repairs. – *n* '**overhaul**.

overhead [ōvər'hed] *adv* above, over one's head. – *adj* '**overhead**. – *npl* the general expenses of a business *etc*.

ōver'hear *v* to hear what one was not meant to hear.

ōver'joyed *adj* filled with great joy.

ōver'land *adv* on or by land, not sea. – *adj* '**overland**.

ōver'lap *v* to extend over and cover a part of. *The two pieces of cloth overlapped*; (of work *etc*) to cover a part of the same area or subject (as another), partly to coincide. – *n* '**overlap** the amount by which something overlaps.

'**ōver'load** *v* to load or fill too much.

ōver'look *v* to look down upon from a higher point, to have or give a view of. *The hill overlooked the town*; to fail to see, to miss; to pardon, not to punish.

'**overlord** *n* (*hist*) a lord, *esp* one who may command other lords.

'**ōver'much** *adv* too much.

overnight ['ōvər'nīt] *adv* during the night. *He stayed overnight with a friend*; in a very short time. *He changed completely overnight*. – *adj* for the night: *an overnight bag*; got or made in a very short time: *an overnight success*.

'**overpass** *n* a road going over above another road, railway, canal *etc*.

overpower [ōvər'powər] *v* to defeat by a greater strength; to overwhelm, make helpless. – *adj* **over'powering** unable to be resisted; overwhelming, very strong *etc*: *an overpowering smell*.

'**over'rate** *v* to value more highly than one ought.

ōver'reach: overreach oneself to try to do or get more than one can and so fail.

ōver'ride *v* to ignore, set aside. *He overrode the teacher's authority*.

overrule [ōvə'rōōl] *v* to go against or cancel an earlier judgement or request.

over'run *v* to grow or spread over. *The garden is overrun with weeds and the house with mice*; to take possession of (a country).

over'seas *adj, adv* abroad; beyond the sea.

over'see *v* to watch over, supervise. – *n* **'overseer**.

overshadow [ōvər'shadō] *v* to lessen the importance of by doing better than.

oversight ['ōvərsit] *n* a mistake (*eg* when something has been left out); failure to notice.

over'step *v* to go further than (a set limit, rules *etc*).

o'vert *adj* not hidden or secret; openly done.

over'take *v* to catch up with and pass.

overthrow [ōvər'thrō] *v* to defeat.

overtime *n* time spent in working beyond one's set hours; payment, *usu* at a special rate, for this.

overture *n* a proposal or offer often intended to open discussions: *overtures of peace*; a piece of music played as an introduction to an opera *etc*.

over'whelm *v* to defeat completely; to load, cover *etc* with too great an amount: *overwhelmed with work*; (of emotion *etc*) to overcome, make helpless: *overwhelmed with grief*.

– *adj* **over'whelming**.

overwork ['ōvər'wərk] *v* to work more than is good for one. – *adj* **'over'worked**.

overwrought [ōvə'rōt] *adj* excessively nervous or excited, agitated.

'ōvum *n* the egg from which the young of animals and people develop: – *pl* **'ova**.

owe [ō] *v* to be in debt to. *He owes John ten pence*; to have (a person or thing) to thank for. *I owe my success to my family*. – **owing to** because of.

owl [owl] *n* a kind of bird of prey which comes out at night. – *n* **'owlet** a young owl.

own [ōn] *v* to have as a possession; to admit, confess to be true. – *adj* belonging to the person mentioned. *Is that your own penknife?* – *ns* **'owner** one who possesses; **'ownership** possession. – **on one's own** by one's own efforts; alone.

ox *n* the male of the cow (*usu* castrated) used for drawing loads *etc*: – *pl* **'oxen** used for both male and female cattle.

'oxygen *n* an element, a gas without taste, colour or smell, forming part of the air and of water.

'oyster *n* a type of eatable shellfish.

'ōzone *n* a form of oxygen.

P

pace *n* a step; rate (of walking *etc*). – *v* to measure by steps; to walk backwards and forwards.

pachyderm ['pakidərm] *n* a thick-skinned animal such as an elephant.

pacifȳ *v* to make peaceful; to calm, soothe. – *pres p* **'pacifying**, *pt* **'pacified**. – *n* **'pacifist** one who is against war and works for peace.

pack *n* a bundle, *esp* one carried on one's back; a set of playing cards; a number of animals (*esp* dogs, wolves *etc*). – *v* to place (clothes *etc*) in a case or trunk for a journey; to press or crowd together closely. – *n* **'package** a bundle or parcel. – *v* to put into a container; to wrap. – *ns* **'packet** a small parcel; a container made of paper, cardboard *etc*; **'packing** the act of putting things in cases, parcels *etc*; material for wrapping goods to pack; something used to fill an empty space. – *ns* **package holiday, package tour** a holiday or tour arranged by an organizer before it is advertised; **'pack-ice** a mass of large

pieces of floating ice driven together by wind, currents *etc*; **packing case** a wooden box in which goods are transported. – **send packing** to send (a person) away roughly.

pact *n* an agreement; a bargain or contract.

pad *n* a soft cushion-like object to prevent jarring or rubbing *etc*; sheets of paper fixed together; the paw of certain animals; a rocket-launching platform. – *v* to stuff or protect with anything soft; (often with **out**) to fill up (*eg* a book) with unnecessary material; to walk making a dull, soft, noise: – *pt* **'padded**. – *n* **'padding** stuffing material; (in writing or speech) words, sentences put in just to fill space or time.

'paddle *v* to move forward by the use of paddles; to row; to wade in shallow water. – *n* a short, broad spoon-shaped oar. – *n* **'paddle-steamer** a steamer driven by two large wheels made up of paddles.

'paddock *n* a small closed-in field *usu*

near a house or stable, used for pasture.

paddy-field ['padifēld] *n* a muddy field in which rice is grown.

'padlock *n* a removable lock with hinged hook.

'pāgan *n* a person who does not believe in any religion; a heathen. – Also *adj.* – *n* **'paganism**.

page [pāj] *n* one side of a blank, written or printed sheet of paper; a boy servant; a boy who carries the train of the bride's dress in a marriage service.

pageant ['pajənt] *n* a show or procession made up of scenes from history; any fine show. – *n* **'pageantry** splendid show or display.

pa'gōda *n* an Eastern temple, *esp* in China and India.

paid *see* **pay**.

pail *n* an open vessel of tin, zinc, plastic *etc* for carrying liquids, a bucket.

pain *n* feeling caused by hurt to mind or body; threat of punishment: *under pain of death*; (*pl*) care. *He takes great pains with his work.* – *v* to cause suffering to, distress. – *adjs* **pained** showing pain or distress; **'painful**; **'painless**. – *adj* **'painstaking** very careful.

paint *v* to put colour on in the form of liquid or paste; to describe in words. – *n* something in liquid form used for colouring and put on with a brush, a spray *etc.* – *ns* **'painter** one whose trade is painting; an artist; a rope used to fasten a boat; **'painting** the act or art of covering with colour or making a picture; a painted picture.

pair *n* two of the same kind; a set of two. – *v* to join to form a pair; to go two and two; to mate.

pal *n* (*coll*) a friend.

palace ['paləs] *n* the house of a king, queen, archbishop or nobleman.

pal(a)eolithic [paliə'lithik] *adj* of the early Stone Age when man used stone tools.

'palate *n* the roof of the mouth; taste. – *adj* **'palatable** pleasant to the taste; acceptable, pleasing. *He does not find the truth palatable.*

palatial [pə'lāshəl] *adj* like a palace, magnificent.

pa'laver *n* light, idle talk; (*hist*) a conference, *esp* with African chiefs.

pale[1] *n* a piece of wood, a stake, used in making a fence to enclose ground. – *n* **'paling** a row of stakes of wood *etc* in the form of a fence; a pale.

pale[2] *adj* light or whitish in colour; not bright. – *v* to make or turn pale.

'palette *n* a little oval board on which an artist mixes his paints.

palfrey ['pōlfri] *n* (*old*) a horse for riding (not a warhorse).

'palindrome *n* a word *etc* that reads the same backwards as forwards (*eg* level).

paling *see* **pale**.

pali'sade *n* a fence of pointed (wooden) stakes.

pall [pōl] *n* the cloth over a coffin at a funeral; a dark covering or cloud: *a pall of smoke.* – *v* to become dull or uninteresting.

'pallet *n* a straw bed or mattress.

palliative ['paliətiv] *adj* making less severe or harsh. – *n* something which lessens pain, *eg* a drug.

'pallid *adj* pale. – *n* **'pallor** paleness.

palm [päm] *n* a kind of tall tree, with broad, spreading fan-shaped leaves, which grows in hot countries; the inner surface of the hand between the wrist and the start of the fingers. – *ns* **'palmist** someone who claims to tell fortunes by the lines and markings of the hand; **'palmistry** the telling of fortunes in this way. – **palm off** to give with the intention of cheating. *That shopkeeper palmed off a foreign coin on me.*

'palpable *adj* able to be touched or felt; easily noticed, obvious.

'palpitate *v* (of the heart) to beat rapidly, to throb. – *n* **palpi'tation** uncomfortable rapid beating of the heart.

palsy ['pōlzi] *n* a loss of power and feeling in the muscles. – *adj* **'palsied**.

paltry ['pōltri] *adj* of little value.

'pampas *npl* the vast treeless plains of S. America.

'pamper *v* to spoil (a child *etc*) by giving too much attention to.

'pamphlet *n* a small book not bound in a cover.

pan *n* a broad shallow pot used in cooking; a saucepan; a shallow dent in the ground. – *v* to move a television or film camera so as to follow an object or give a wide view: – *pt* **panned**. – *n* **'pancake** a thin cake of eggs, sugar and milk, fried in a pan. – **pan out** to turn out (well or badly).

pan- *prefix* all, whole, as in **'Pan-A'merican** including all America or Americans, North and South.

panacea [panə'sēə] *n* a cure for all things.

panache [pə'nash] *n* a sense of style, swagger. *He always does things with great panache.*

pancake *see* **pan**.

'panda *n* a large black-and-white bear-like animal found in Tibet *etc*; a raccoon-like animal found in the

Himalayas.

pan'demic *adj* (of a disease *etc*) occurring over a wide area and affecting a large number of people.

pande'mōnium *n* a state of confusion and uproar.

'pander *v* (with **to**) to be over-anxious to give way (to other people or their wishes).

pane *n* a sheet of glass.

panegyric [panə'jirik] *n* a speech praising highly (a person, achievement *etc*).

'panel *n* a flat rectangular piece of wood such as is set into a door or wall; a group of people chosen for a particular purpose *eg* to judge a contest, take part in a television quiz *etc*. – *adj* **'panelled**.

pang *n* a sudden sharp pain.

'panic *n* a sudden and great fright; fear that spreads from person to person. – *v* to throw into panic; to act wildly through fear: – *pt* **'panicked**.

'pannier *n* a basket, *esp* one slung on a horse's back.

'panoply *n* all the splendid and magnificent dress, equipment *etc* associated with a particular event *etc*: *the panoply of a military funeral*; (*hist*) a full suit of armour: – *pl* **'panoplies**.

pano'rama *n* a wide view of a landscape, scene *etc*.

pansy ['panzi] *n* a kind of flower like the violet but larger: – *pl* **'pansies**.

pant *v* to gasp for breath; to say breathlessly; to wish eagerly (for). – *npl* **pants** underpants; women's short-legged knickers; trousers.

pantechnicon [pan'teknikən] *n* a large van for transporting furniture.

'panther *n* a large leopard; (*US*) a puma.

'pantomime *n* a Christmas play, with songs, jokes and dancing, based on a popular fairy tale *eg* Cinderella.

'pantry *n* a room for storing food: – *pl* **'pantries**.

pa'pa *n* a name sometimes used for father.

'pāpacy *n* the position or the power of the Pope. – *adj* **'papal**.

'pāper *n* a material made from rags, grass, wood *etc* used for writing, wrapping *etc*; a single sheet of this; a newspaper; an essay on a learned subject; a set of examination questions; (*pl*) documents proving one's identity, nationality *etc*. – *v* to cover (*esp* walls) with paper. – *ns* **'paperback** a book bound in a paper cover; **'paper-chase** a game in which one runner leaves a trail of paper so that others may track him; **'paperweight** a heavy glass, metal *etc* object used to keep a pile of papers in place.

papier-mâché ['papiā'mashā] *n* a substance consisting of paper pulp and some sticky liquid or glue, shaped (by moulding) into models, bowls, boxes *etc*.

pa'poose *n* a N. American Indian baby.

'paprika *n* a type of red pepper powder.

pa'pȳrus *n* a type of reed from which people used to make paper.

par *n* an accepted standard, value, level *etc*; (in golf) the number of strokes allowed for each hole if the play is perfect. – **below par** not up to standard; not feeling very well; **on a par with** equal to or comparable with.

'parable *n* a story (*esp* in the Bible) which teaches a moral lesson.

parachute ['parəshōōt] *n* an umbrella-shaped arrangement made of a light material and rope with which a person may drop slowly and safely to the ground from an aeroplane. – *v* to drop by parachute. – *n* **'parachutist** a person dropped by parachute from an aeroplane.

pa'rade *n* an orderly arrangement of troops for inspection or exercise; a procession of people, vehicles *etc* often in celebration of some event. – *v* to arrange (troops) in order; to march in a procession; to display in an obvious way.

paradigm ['parədim] *n* an example showing a certain pattern.

'paradise *n* any place or state of great happiness; **'Paradise** heaven.

'paradox *n* a saying which seems to contradict itself but which may be true: – *pl* **'paradoxes**. – *adj* **para'doxical**. – *adv* **para'doxically**.

'paraffin *n* an oil which burns and is used as a fuel (for heaters, lamps, *etc*).

'paragon *n* a model of perfection or excellence. *This boy is a paragon of good manners*.

'paragraph *n* a division of a piece of writing shown by beginning the first sentence on a new line, *usu* leaving a short space at the beginning of the line; a short item in a newspaper.

'parakeet *n* a type of small parrot.

'parallel *adj* (of lines) going in the same direction and never meeting, always remaining the same distance apart; similar or alike in some way. *The judge treats all parallel cases in the same way.* – *n* a parallel line; something comparable in some way with something else; a line drawn east and west across a map or round a globe at a set distance from the equator to mark latitude. – *n*

paral'lelogram a four-sided figure, the opposite sides of which are parallel and equal in length.

'paralyse v to affect with paralysis; to make helpless or ineffective; to bring to a halt. *The strike paralysed production at the factory.* – n **paralysis** [pə'raləsis] loss of the power to move and feel in one or more parts of the body. – adj **para'lytic** suffering from paralysis. – n a paralysed person.

'paramount adj above all others in rank or power; the very greatest: *of paramount importance.*

paramour ['parəmōōr] n (old) a lover esp of a married person.

parapet ['parəpit] n a low wall on a bridge or balcony to prevent persons from falling off.

parapher'nālia npl one's belongings, equipment etc.

paraphrase ['parəfrāz] v to express (a piece of writing) in other words. – Also n.

paraplegia [parə'plējə] n paralysis of the lower part of the body and legs. – adj, n **para'plegic** (of) one who suffers from this.

'parasite n an animal, plant or person which lives on another without being any use in return. – adj **parasitic** [parə'sitik].

'parasol n a light umbrella used as a sunshade.

'paratroops npl soldiers carried by air to be dropped by parachute into enemy country. – n **'paratrooper**.

'parboil v to boil (food) slightly.

'parcel n thing(s) wrapped and tied, usu to be sent by post. – v (usu with **out**) to divide into portions: – pt **'parcelled**. – **part and parcel** an absolutely necessary part.

parch v to make hot and very dry; to make thirsty. – adj **parched**.

'parchment n the dried skin of a goat or sheep used for writing on; paper resembling this.

'pardon v to forgive; to free from punishment; to allow to go unpunished. – n forgiveness; the act of pardoning. – adj **'pardonable** able to be forgiven.

pare v to peel or cut off the edge, outer surface or skin of; to make smaller little by little. – npl **'parings** small pieces cut away or peeled off.

'parent n a father or mother. – n **'parentage** descent from parents or ancestors: *of noble parentage.* – adj **parental** [pə'rentl] of parents; with the manner or attitude of a parent.

pa'renthesis n a word or group of words inserted in a sentence as an explanation, comment etc, usu separated from the rest of the sentence by brackets, dashes etc. *His father (so he said) was dead;* (pl) **parentheses** [pə'renthəsēz] brackets. – adj **paren'thetical**.

pa'riah n one driven out from a community or group, an outcast.

'parish n a district having its own church and minister: – pl **'parishes**. – n **pa'rishioner** a member of a parish.

'parity n the state of being equal.

park n a public place for walking with grass and trees; an enclosed piece of land surrounding a country house. – v to stop and leave (a car etc) in a place for a time.

'parka n a type of thick jacket with a hood.

'parley v to hold a conference, esp with an enemy: – pt **'parleyed**. – n a meeting between enemies to settle terms of peace etc: – pl **'parleys**.

parliament ['pärləmənt] n the chief law-making council of a nation – in Britain, the House of Commons and the House of Lords. – adj **parlia'mentary**.

parlour ['pärlər] n a sitting room in a house. – n **'parlourmaid** a woman or girl whose job is to wait at table.

parochial [pə'rōkiəl] adj having to do with a parish; interested only in local affairs; narrow-minded.

'parody n an amusing imitation of a serious author's subject and style: – pl **'parodies**. – v to make a parody of: – pt **'parodied**.

pa'role n the release of a prisoner before the end of his sentence on condition that he will have to return if he breaks the law.

paroxysm ['parəksizəm] n a fit of pain, rage, laughter etc.

parquet ['pärkā] n a type of flooring of wooden blocks arranged in a pattern.

parr n a young salmon before it leaves a river for the sea.

'parricide n the murder of a parent or a close relative; a person who commits such a crime.

'parrot n a kind of bird found in warm countries with a hooked bill and usu brightly coloured feathers, a good imitator of human speech.

'parry v to keep off, turn aside (a blow, question etc): – pt **'parried**.

parse [pärz] v to name the parts of speech of (words in a sentence) and say how the words are connected with each other.

'parsimony n great care in spending

one's money, meanness.

'parsley *n* a type of bright green leafy herb, used in cookery.

'parsnip *n* a type of plant with an eatable, yellowish root shaped like a carrot.

'parson *n* a clergyman, *esp* one in charge of a parish. – *n* **'parsonage** a parson's house.

part *n* a portion or share; a piece, something which, together with other things, makes up a whole: *the various parts of a car engine*; character taken by an actor in a play; a role in an action, campaign *etc*: *the part he played in the war*; (in music) the notes to be played or sung by a particular instrument or voice; (*pl*) talents: *a man of many parts.* – *v* to divide; to separate, to send or go in different ways; to put or keep apart. – *n* **'parting** the act of separating or dividing; a place of separation; a going away (from each other), a leave-taking; a line dividing hair on the head brushed in opposite directions. – *adv* **'partly** not wholly or completely. – *n* **'part-song** a song in which singers sing different parts in harmony. – **in good part** without being hurt or taking offence; **part of speech** one of the grammatical groups into which words are divided, *eg* noun, verb, adjective, preposition; **part with** to let go, be separated from. *He refused to part with his stick*; **take someone's part** to support someone in an argument *etc*.

par'take *v* (*usu* with **of**) to eat or drink some of something; to take a part (in): – *pt* **par'took**, *pp* **par'taken**.

partial ['pärshəl] *adj* in part only, not total or complete: *partial payment*; having a liking for (a person or thing): *partial to cheese.* – *n* **partiality** [pärshi'aləti] the favouring of one side *etc* more than another, bias; a particular liking for.

par'ticipate *v* to take part (in); to have a share in. – *ns* **par'ticipant**, **par'ticipator** one who takes part in; **par'ticipation** the act of taking part.

'participle *n* a form of a verb which can be used with other verbs to form tenses. 'He was *eating*. He had *turned*'; used as an adjective: '*stolen* jewels'; used as a noun. '*Running* makes me tired'.

particle *n* a very small piece: *a particle of sand.*

par'ticular *adj* of, relating to *etc* a single definite person, thing *etc* considered separately from others: *this particular waiter*: *this particular question*; special: *particular friend*: *particular care*; very exact, difficult to please: *particular*

about his food. – *npl* the facts or details about any thing or person.

partisan [pärti'zan] *adj* giving strong and enthusiastic support or loyalty to a particular cause, theory *etc*, *esp* without considering other points of view. – Also *n*.

partition [pər'tishən] *n* a division; something which divides, as a wall between rooms. – *v* to divide into parts; to divide by making a wall *etc*.

'partner *n* one who shares the ownership of a business *etc* with another or others; one of a pair *esp* in games, dancing *etc*; a husband or wife. – *v* to act as someone's partner. – *n* **'partnership** state of being partners: *business partnership*: *dancing partnership*; a joining of people as partners.

partridge ['pärtrij] *n* a type of bird which is shot as game.

'party *n* a gathering of guests: *a birthday party*; a group of people travelling *etc* together: *a party of tourists*; a number of people having the same plans or ideas: *a political party*; a person taking part in, knowing of, or approving an action: – *pl* **'parties**. – *n* **party line** a shared telephone line; policy laid down by the leaders of a political party.

pass *v* to go, move, travel *etc*. *He passed out of sight over the hill*; to cause to go or move (to another person or place): *pass the salt*; to go by. *I saw the bus pass our house*; to overtake. *He passed me because I slowed down*; (of parliament *etc*) to put (a law) into force; to be (declared) successful in an examination *etc*; to be declared healthy or in good condition (in an inspection); to come to an end. *The feeling of sickness soon passed*; to hand on, give. *He passed the story on to his son*; to spend (time). *He passed a pleasant hour by the river*; to make, utter (*eg* a remark): – *pt* **passed**. – *n* a narrow passage, *esp* over or through a range of mountains; a ticket or card allowing one to go somewhere; success in an examination. – *adjs* **'passable** fairly good; (of a river, ford *etc*) able to be crossed; **'passing** going by: *a passing car*; not lasting long: *a passing interest*; casual: *a passing remark.* – *n* the act of someone or something which passes; a going away, coming to an end; death. – *ns* **'passer-'by** one who happens to pass by when something happens: – *pl* **'passers-'by**; **'passport** a card or booklet which gives the name and description of a person, and which is needed to travel in another country; **'password** a secret word which allows those who know it to pass.

'**passage** n the act of passing: *passage of time*; a journey (*esp* in a ship); a long narrow way, a corridor; a way through; a part of what is written in a book.

passenger ['pasinjər] n a traveller, not a member of the crew, in a train, ship, aeroplane *etc*.

passion ['pashən] n strong feeling, *esp* anger or love; '**Passion** the sufferings (*esp* the death) of Christ. – *adj* '**passionate** easily moved to passion; full of passion.

passive ['pasiv] *adj* making no resistance; acted upon, not acting. – *ns* '**passiveness, pas'sivity**.

past n (with **the**) the time gone by; a person's previous life or career; (in grammar) the past tense. – *adj* of an earlier time. *He thanked me for past kindnesses*; just over, recently ended: *the past year*; gone, finished. *The time for argument is past.* – *prep* after. *It's past midday*; up to and beyond, further than. *Go past the church.* – *adv* by. *He marches past, looking at no-one.*

'**pasta** n a dough used in making spaghetti, macaroni *etc*.

pāste n a mixture of flour, water *etc* used for pies, pastry *etc*; a sticky liquid for sticking paper *etc* together; any soft mixture: *almond paste*; a kind of fine glass used in making imitation gems. – n '**pasteboard** cardboard.

'**pastel** *adj* (of colours) soft, pale. – n a chalk-like crayon used in drawing; a drawing made with this.

pasteurize ['paschəriz] v to heat food (*esp* milk) in order to kill harmful germs in it.

pastille ['pastəl] n a small sweet sucked as a medicine *etc*.

'**pastime** n a hobby, a spare-time interest.

'**pastor** n a clergyman. – *adj* '**pastoral** having to do with country life; of a clergyman or his work.

'**pastry** n flour paste used in the making of pies, tarts *etc*: – *pl* '**pastries**.

'**pasture** n ground covered with grass on which cattle graze. – n '**pasturage** grazing land.

pasty[1] ['pāsti] *adj* like paste; pale.

pasty[2] ['pasti] n a pie containing meat and vegetables in a covering of pastry.

pat n a light, quick blow or tap, *usu* with the hand; a small lump (*esp* of butter). – v to strike gently: – *pt* '**patted**. – **off pat** memorized thoroughly, ready to be said when necessary.

patch v to mend (clothes) by putting in a new piece of material to cover a hole;

(with **up**) to mend, *esp* hastily or clumsily: *patch up the roof*; (with **up**) to settle (a quarrel). – n a piece of material sewn on to mend a hole; a small piece of ground: – *pl* '**patches**. – *adj* '**patchy** uneven, mixed in quality. *Her work is very patchy.* – n '**patchwork** a piece of material formed of small patches or pieces of material sewn together.

pate n the head: *a bald pate*.

pâté ['patā] n a paste made of finely minced meat or fish, flavoured with herbs, spices *etc*.

'**pātent** n an official written statement which gives to one person or business for a stated number of years the sole right to make or sell something that they have invented. – *adj* protected from copying by a patent; open, easily seen. – v to obtain a patent for. – *adv* '**patently** openly, clearly: *patently obvious*. – n **patent (leather)** leather with a very glossy surface.

pa'ternal *adj* of a father; like a father, fatherly; on one's father's side of the family: *my paternal grandfather.* – n **pa'ternity** the state or fact of being a father.

path n a way made by people or animals walking on it, a track: *a hill-path*; the route to be taken (by a person or vehicle): *in the lorry's path*; a course of action, way of life. – n '**pathway** a path.

pa'thology n the study of diseases. – n **pa'thologist** a doctor who studies the causes and effects of disease; a doctor who makes post-mortem examinations.

'**pāthos** n the quality (of something) that causes one to feel pity. *The pathos of the situation made me weep.* – *adj* **pathetic** [pə'thetik] causing pity; causing contempt, totally useless or inadequate: *a pathetic attempt.*

patient ['pāshənt] *adj* suffering delay, pain, discomfort *etc* without complaint or anger. – n a person under the care of a doctor *etc*. – n '**patience** the ability or willingness to be patient; a card game played *usu* by one person.

patio ['patiō] n a paved open yard attached to a house: – *pl* '**patios**.

patois ['patwä] n a dialect of language spoken by the ordinary people of a certain area.

patriarch ['pātriärk] n the male head of a family or tribe; the head of the Greek Orthodox Church *etc*. – *adj* **patri'archal**.

patrician [pə'trishən] *adj* aristocratic.

'**patricide** n the murder of one's own father; one who commits such a murder.

patrimony *n* property handed down from one's father or ancestors.

patriot *n* one who loves (and serves) his country. – *n* '**patriotism** love of and loyalty to one's country. – *adj* **patri'otic**.

pa'trōl *v* to keep guard or watch by moving (on foot or in a vehicle) to and fro: – *pt* **pa'trolled**. – *n* the act of keeping guard in this way; the people *etc* keeping watch; a small group of Scouts or Girl Guides. – Also *adj*: *the patrol van*.

patron *n* one who protects or supports (a person, an artist, a form of art *etc*); a customer of a shop *etc*. – *n* **patronage** ['patrənij] the support given by a patron. – *v* '**patronize** to act as a patron toward. *He patronizes his local shop*; to treat a person as if one is superior to him. *He patronizes his brother-in-law.* – *n* **patron saint** a saint chosen as a protector. *St Patrick is the patron saint of Ireland.*

patter *v* (of falling rain, footsteps *etc*) to make a quick tapping sound. – *n* the sound of falling rain, of footsteps *etc*; chatter, rapid talk, *esp* that used by salesmen to encourage people to buy their goods.

pattern *n* an example suitable to be copied; a model or guide for making something; a decorative design; a sample: *a book of tweed patterns*. – *adj* '**patterned** having a design, not self-coloured.

patty *n* a small flat cake of chopped meat *etc*: – *pl* '**patties**.

paucity *n* smallness of number or quantity. *There's a paucity of good builders.*

paunch *n* a fat stomach: – *pl* '**paunches**.

pauper *n* a very poor person.

pause [pöz] *n* a short stop, an interval; a break or hesitation in speaking or writing; (in music) (a mark showing) the holding of a note or rest. – *v* to stop for a short time.

pave *v* to lay (a street or pathway) with stone or concrete pieces to form a level surface for walking on. – *n* '**pavement** a paved surface *esp* a paved footway at the side of a road for pedestrians. – **pave the way for** to prepare or make the way easy for.

pa'vilion *n* a building in a sports ground in which sportsmen change their clothes; a large ornamental building; a large tent.

paw *n* the foot of an animal. – *v* to scrape with the forefoot; to handle or touch roughly, clumsily or rudely; to strike

out wildly with the hand: *paw the air.*

pawn *v* to put (an article of some value) in someone's keeping in exchange for a sum of money which, when repaid, buys back the article. – *n* (in chess) a small piece of the lowest rank; a person who lets himself be used by another for some purpose: the state of having been pawned. *My watch is in pawn.* – *ns* '**pawnbroker** one who lends money in exchange for pawned articles; '**pawnshop** a pawnbroker's place of business.

pay *v* to give (money) in exchange for (goods *etc*). *He paid £10 for it*; to suffer the punishment (for); to be advantageous or profitable. *It pays to be careful*; to give (*eg* attention): – *pt* **paid**. – *n* money given or received for work *etc*, wages. – *adj* '**payable** requiring to be paid. – *ns* **pay'ee** one to whom money is paid; '**payment** the act of paying; money paid (or its value in goods *etc*). – *adj* '**pay-as-you-'earn** of a system of collecting income tax by deducting it from the pay or salary before this is given to the worker. – **pay off** to pay in full and discharge (workers) owing to lack of work *etc*; to have good results. *His hard work paid off*; **pay out** to spend; to give out (a length of rope *etc*).

pea *n* a kind of climbing plant, having round green seeds in pods; the seed itself, eaten as a vegetable.

peace *n* quietness; freedom from war or disturbance; a treaty bringing this about. – *adjs* '**peaceable** of a quiet nature, fond of peace; '**peaceful** quiet; calm. – *n* '**peace-offering** something offered to bring about peace.

peach *n* a type of juicy, velvet-skinned fruit, orangey-pink in colour; the tree that bears it: – *pl* '**peaches**.

'**peacock** *n* a type of large bird, noted for its splendid feathers, *esp* in its tail: – *fem* '**peahen**.

peak *n* the pointed top of a mountain or hill; the highest point; the jutting-out part of the brim of a cap. – *v* to rise to a peak; to reach the highest point. *Prices peaked in July and then fell steadily.* – *adjs* **peaked** pointed; (of a hat, cap) having a peak; '**peaky** looking pale and unhealthy.

peal *n* a set of bells tuned to each other; the changes rung on such bells; a loud sound or succession of loud sounds: *peals of laughter.* – *v* to sound loudly.

'**peanut** *n* a type of nut similar to a pea in shape (also '**groundnut,** '**monkeynut**). – *n* **peanut butter** a paste of ground roasted peanuts, spread on bread *etc.*

pear [pār] *n* a type of fruit narrowing towards the stem and bulging at the end; the tree that bears it. – *adj* **'pear-shaped**: *a pear-shaped woman*.

pearl [pėrl] *n* a gem formed in the shell of the oyster and several other shellfish; something resembling a pearl in shape, size, colour or value: *pearls of wisdom*.

peasant ['peznt] *n* one who works and lives on the land, *esp* in a primitive or underdeveloped area.

peat *n* a kind of turf, cut out of boggy places, dried and used as fuel.

'pebble *n* a small, roundish stone. – *adj* **'pebbly** full of pebbles. – *n* **pebble dash** a kind of coating for outside walls.

pe'can *n* a kind of oblong, thin-shelled nut, common in N. America; the tree bearing it.

pecca'dillo *n* a wrong or sin felt to be unimportant: – *pl* **pecca'dillo(e)s**.

peck *v* to strike with the beak; to pick up with the beak; to eat little, nibble (at); to kiss quickly and briefly. – *n* a sharp blow with the beak; a brief kiss. – *adj* **'peckish** slightly hungry.

'pectoral *adj* of or on the breast or chest.

pe'cūliar *adj* belonging to one person or thing in particular and to no other: *a custom peculiar to France*; strange, odd. *He is a very peculiar person.* – *n* **peculi'arity** that which marks a person or thing off from others in some way; something odd: – *pl* **peculi'arities**. – *adv* **pe'culiarly**.

pe'cūniary *adj* of money.

pedagogue ['pedəgog] *n* a teacher. – *adj* **pedagogic** [pedə'gojik] of a teacher or of education.

'pedal *n* a lever worked by the foot, as on a bicycle, piano *etc*; (on an organ) a key worked by the foot. – *v* to work the pedals of; to ride on a bicycle: – *pt* **'pedalled**.

'pedant *n* one who makes a great show of his knowledge; one who considers minor details to be of great importance. – *adj* **pe'dantic**. – *n* **'pedantry** too great a concern with unimportant details; a display of knowledge.

'peddle *v* to travel from door to door selling small objects. – *n* **'pedlar** one who peddles, a hawker.

pedestal ['pedistl] *n* the foot or support of a pillar, statue *etc*.

pe'destrian *adj* going on foot; for those on foot; unexciting, dull: *a pedestrian account of his adventures*. – *n* one who goes or travels on foot. – *n* **pedestrian crossing** a place where pedestrians

may cross the road when the traffi stops.

'pedigree *n* a list of the ancestors fro whom a person or animal is descended (distinguished) descent or ancestry. *adj* of an animal, pure-bred, from long line of ancestors of the same breed

pedlar *see* **peddle**.

pe'dometer *n* an instrument for measu ing the distance covered by a walker

peek *v* to peep, glance *esp* secretively. Also *n*.

peel *v* to strip off the outer covering c skin of: *peel an apple*; (of skin, pain bark *etc*) to come off in small pieces; t lose skin in small flakes (as a result c sunburn *etc*). – *n* skin, rind.

peep *v* to look through a narrow oper ing, round a corner *etc*; to look slyly c quickly (at); to begin to appear. *Th sun peeped out*; to make a high, sma sound. – *n* a quick look, a glimpse (*us* from a hidden position); a high, sma sound.

peer *v* to look at with half-closed eyes (as if) with difficulty. – *n* one's equal i rank, merit or age; a nobleman of th rank of baron upwards; a member c the House of Lords. – *n* **'peerage** peer's title; the peers as a group. – *ad* **'peerless** without any equal, bette than all others.

'peevish *adj* ill-natured, cross, fretful.

'peewit *n* the lapwing.

peg *n* a pin or stake of wood, metal *etc*; hook fixed to a wall for hanging clothe *etc*. – *v* to fasten with a peg; to fi (prices *etc*) at a certain level: – *p* **pegged**.

pejorative [pə'jorətiv] *adj* showing dis approval, dislike, scorn *etc*: *a pejorativ remark*.

Pekin(g)ese [pēki'nēz] *n* a breed c small dog with long coat and flat face

'pelican *n* a type of large waterbird with pouched bill for storing fish.

'pellet *n* a little ball (of shot *etc*); a smal pill.

'pell-'mell *adv* in great confusion; head long.

'pelmet *n* a strip or band (of wood *etc* hiding a curtain rail.

pelt *n* the (untreated) skin of an animal. *v* to throw (things) at; to run fast; (o rain, sometimes with **down**) to fal heavily. – **at full pelt** at top speed.

'pelvis *n* the frame of bone which circle the body below the waist.

'pemmican *n* dried meat, pressed har into cakes.

pen *n* an instrument for writing in ink: small enclosure, for sheep, cattle *etc*;

female swan. – *v* to shut up, enclose in a pen; to write (*eg* a letter): – *pt* **penned**. – *adj* **pent** (also **'pent-'up**) shut up, not allowed to go free; (of emotions *etc*) not freely expressed. – *ns* **'pen-friend** a person one has never seen (*usu* living abroad) with whom one exchanges letters; **'penknife** a pocket knife with folding blades; **'pen-name** a name adopted by a writer instead of his own name.

'**pēnal** *adj* of, or as, punishment. – *v* '**penalize** to punish; to put under a disadvantage. – *n* **penalty** ['penlti] punishment; a disadvantage put on a player or team which breaks a rule of a game. – *n* **penal servitude** imprisonment with hard labour as an added punishment.

'**penance** *n* punishment willingly suffered by a person to make up for a wrong.

pence *see* **penny**.

'**pencil** *n* an instrument containing a length of graphite or other substance for writing, drawing *etc*. – *v* to draw, mark *etc* with a pencil: – *pt* '**pencilled**.

'**pendant** *n* an ornament hung from a necklace *etc*.

'**pendent** *adj* hanging.

'**pending** *adj* awaiting a decision or attention. *This matter is pending*. – *prep* awaiting, until the coming of: *in jail pending further evidence*.

'**pendūlum** *n* a swinging weight which drives the mechanism of a clock.

penetrate ['penitrāt] *v* to pierce or pass into or through; to enter (*usu* by force). – *adj* '**penetrating** (of a sound) piercing; keen, probing: *a penetrating look*. – *n* **pene'tration** the act of breaking through or into; cleverness in understanding.

penguin ['peŋgwin] *n* a kind of large sea bird of Antarctic regions, which cannot fly.

penicillin [peni'silin] *n* a medicine got from mould, which kills many germs.

pe'ninsūla *n* a piece of land almost surrounded by water. – *adj* **pe'ninsular**.

'**pēnis** *n* the part of the body of a male human or animal used in sexual intercourse and for urinating.

'**penitent** *adj* sorry for one's sins. – *n* a penitent person. – *n* **penitentiary** [peni'tenshəri] (*US*) a prison.

'**pennant** *n* a long flag coming to a point at the end.

penny *n* a coin worth $^1/_{100}$ of £1: – *pls* '**pennies** used for a number of coins. *I need three pennies for the coffee machine;*

pence used to show an amount in pennies. *A ticket costs ten pence.* – *adj* '**penniless** having no money.

pension ['penshən] *n* a sum of money paid regularly to a retired person, a widow, one wounded in a war *etc*. – *adj* '**pensionable** having or giving the right to a pension: *pensionable age*: *pensionable post*. – *n* '**pensioner** one who receives a pension. – **pension off** to dismiss or allow to retire with a pension.

pensive ['pensiv] *adj* thoughtful.

pent, pent-up *see* **pen**.

'**pentagon** *n* a five-sided figure. – *adj* **pen'tagonal**.

pen'tathlon *n* a five-event contest in the Olympic Games *etc*.

penthouse ['pent-hows] *n* a (luxurious) flat at the top of a building.

pe'nultimate *adj* last but one.

'**penūry** *n* poverty, want.

'**pēony** *n* a type of garden plant with large red, white or pink flowers: – *pl* '**peonies**.

people ['pēpl] *n* the men, women and children of a country or nation; persons generally. – *v* to fill with living beings, *esp* people; to inhabit, make up the population of.

'**pepper** *n* a type of plant whose berries are dried, powdered and used as seasoning; the powder so used; any of several hollow fruits containing many seeds, used as a food either raw, cooked or pickled. – *v* to sprinkle with pepper; (with **with**) to throw at or hit. *He peppered him with bullets.* – *adj* '**peppery** containing much pepper; inclined to be hot-tempered. – *adj* '**pepper-and-'salt** mixed black and white: *pepper-and-salt hair*. – *ns* '**peppercorn** the dried berry of the pepper plant; **pepper mill** a small device for grinding peppercorns for flavouring food; '**peppermint** a type of plant with a powerful taste and smell; a flavouring taken from this and used in sweets *etc*.

pep-talk ['peptök] *n* a talk meant to encourage or arouse enthusiasm.

per *prep* in, out of: *five per cent* (often written as *5%*) *ie* five out of every hundred; for each: *£1 per dozen*; in each: *six times per week*. – **per annum** in each year; **per head** for each person.

peradventure [perəd'venchər] *adv* (*old*) by chance.

perambulator *see* **pram**.

perceive [pər'sēv] *v* to become aware of through the senses; to see; to understand. – *adj* **perceptible** [pər'septəbl] able to be seen *etc* or understood. – *n*

per'ception the act of perceiving; the ability to perceive; understanding. – *adj* **per'ceptive** able or quick to perceive or understand.

per'centage *n* the rate per hundred.

perch *n* a type of freshwater fish; a rod on which birds roost; any high seat or position: – *pl* **'perches**. – *v* to roost.

per'chance *adv* (*old*) by chance; perhaps.

'percolate *v* (of a liquid) to drip or drain through small holes; to cause (a liquid) to do this; (of news *etc*) to pass slowly down or through. – *n* **'percolator** a device for percolating: *a coffee percolator*.

percussion [pər'kushən] *n* a striking of one object against another; musical instruments played by striking, *eg* drums, cymbals *etc*.

per'dition *n* utter loss or ruin; everlasting punishment.

peregrine ['perigrin] *n* a type of falcon used in hawking.

pe'remptory *adj* urgent; (of a command *etc*) to be obeyed at once; (of a manner) commanding in an arrogant way, dictatorial.

pe'rennial *adj* lasting through the year; everlasting, perpetual; (of plants) growing from year to year without replanting or sowing. – *n* a perennial plant.

'perfect *adj* complete; finished; faultless; exact. – *v* **per'fect** to make perfect; to finish. – *ns* **per'fection** the state of being perfect; complete freedom from flaws; the highest state or degree; **per'fectionist** one who is satisfied only by perfection.

per'fidious *adj* treacherous, unfaithful. – *ns* **per'fidiousness**; **'perfidy**.

'perforate *v* to make a hole or holes through. – *adj* **'perforated** pierced with holes.

perforce [pər'förs] *adv* (*old*) of necessity, unavoidably.

per'form *v* to do or act; to act (a part), as on the stage; to provide any kind of entertainment for an audience; to play (a piece of music). – *ns* **per'formance** an entertainment (in a theatre *etc*); the act of doing something; the level of success of a machine, a car *etc*; **per'former** one who acts or performs.

'perfume *n* sweet smell, fragrance; a liquid which gives off a sweet smell when put on the skin, scent. – *v* **per'fume** to put scent on or in; to give a sweet smell to. – *n* **per'fumery** the shop or factory where perfume is sold or made.

per'functory *adj* done carelessly or half-heartedly. – *adv* **per'functorily**.

per'haps *adv* it may be (that), possibly. *Perhaps I'll forget to do it.*

peri- *prefix* around.

'peril *n* great danger. – *adj* **'perilous** very dangerous. – **at one's peril** at one's own risk.

perimeter [pə'rimitər] *n* the outside line enclosing a figure or shape: *perimeter of a circle*; the outer edge of any area. *He went outside the perimeters of the city.*

'period *n* any stretch of time; the time during which something (*eg* a revolution of the earth round the sun) takes place; a stage in the earth's development or in history; a full stop, as after a sentence; a sentence; an occurrence of menstruation. – *adjs* **peri'odic** of a period; happening at regular intervals (*eg* every month, year); happening every now and then: *a periodic clearing out of rubbish*; **peri'odical** issued, done *etc*, at regular intervals; periodic. – *n* a magazine which appears at regular intervals.

peripa'tetic *adj* moving from place to place: *a peripatetic salesman.*

pe'riphery *n* the line surrounding something; the outer boundary or edge (of something): – *pl* **pe'ripheries**. – *adj* **pe'ripheral** of or on a periphery; away from the centre; not essential, of little importance.

'periscope *n* a tube with mirrors by which an observer in a trench or submarine is able to see objects on the surface.

'perish *v* to be destroyed or pass away completely; to die; to decay, rot. – *adj* **'perishable** liable to go bad quickly.

'periwig *n* (*hist*) a wig.

'periwinkle *n* a type of small shellfish, shaped like a small snail, eaten as food when boiled; a type of creeping evergreen plant, with a small blue flower.

perjure ['përjər] *v* (with **oneself** *etc*) to tell a lie when one has sworn to tell the truth, *esp* in a court of law. – *ns* **'perjurer**; **'perjury**.

perk *n* short for **perquisite**. – *adj* **'perky** jaunty, in good spirits. – **perk up** to recover one's energy or spirits.

perm *n* short for **permanent wave**. – *v* to give a permanent wave to (hair).

'permanent *adj* lasting, not temporary. – *ns* **'permanence**; **'permanency** the state of being permanent; person or thing that is permanent. – *n* **permanent wave** a wave or curl put into the hair by a special process and *usu* lasting for some months.

permeate ['pərmiət] *v* to pass into through small holes, to soak into; to fill every part of. – *adj* 'permeable.

per'mit *v* to agree to another's action, to allow; to make possible: – *pt* per'mit-ted. – *n* 'permit a written order, allowing a person to do something. – *adj* permissible [pər'misəbl] allowable. – *n* permission [pər'mishən] freedom given to do something. – *adj* per'missive allowing something to be done; (too) tolerant.

permū'tation *n* the arrangement of things, numbers, letters *etc* in a certain order; the act of changing the order of things.

pernicious [pər'nishəs] *adj* destructive.

per'nickety *adj* fussy about small details.

pero'ration *n* the closing part of a speech; a speech.

pe'roxide *n* a chemical (hydrogen peroxide) used for bleaching hair *etc*.

perpen'dicular *adj* standing upright, vertical; at right angles (to). – *n* a line at right angles to another.

'perpetrate *v* to do or commit (a sin, error *etc*). – *ns* perpe'tration; 'perpet-rator.

perpetual [pər'pechoōəl] *adj* everlasting, unending. – *adv* per'petually. – *v* per'petuate to cause to last for ever or for a long time. – *n* perpetuity [pərpə'choōəti]. – in perpetuity for ever; for the length of one's life.

per'plex *v* to puzzle, bewilder; to make more complicated. – *n* per'plexity a puzzled state of mind; something which puzzles.

perquisite ['pərkwizit] *n* something of value one is allowed in addition to one's pay.

persecute ['pərsikūt] *v* to harass, worry, *usu* over a period of time; to kill, make to suffer, *esp* because of religious beliefs. – *ns* perse'cution; 'persecutor.

persevere [pərsi'vēr] *v* to keep trying to do a thing (in spite of difficulties). – *n* perse'verance the act of persevering.

per'sist *v* to hold fast to something (*eg* an idea); to continue to do something in spite of difficulties; to survive, last. *The idea that snakes are slimy still persists.* – *adj* per'sistent (of persons) obstinate, refusing to be discouraged; lasting, not dying out. – *n* per'sistence.

person *n* a human being; one's body. *He had jewels hidden on his person*; form, shape. *Trouble arrived in the person of Jeremy.* – *adj* 'personable goodlooking. – *n* 'personage a (wellknown) person. – *adj* 'personal one's own; private; (of remarks) insulting, offensive to the person they are aimed at. – *n* perso'nality all of a person's characteristics (of feeling, mind, body *etc*) as seen by others; a well-known person. – *adv* 'personally speaking from one's own point of view; by one's own act, not using an agent or representative. *He thanked me personally.* – *v* per'sonify to talk about things, ideas *etc* as if they were living persons (as in 'Time marches on.'); to be typical or a perfect example of: – *pt* per'sonified. – *n* per'sonifi'cation. – in person personally, not represented by someone else.

person'nel *n* the people employed in a firm *etc*.

perspective [pər'spektiv] *n* a point of view; in painting *etc*, (the art of giving) a sense of depth, distance *etc* like that in real life. – in perspective (of an object *etc* in a photograph *etc*) having the size *etc* in relation to other things that it would have in real life; (of an event *etc*) in its true degree of importance *etc* when considered in relation with other events *etc*. *You must learn to see things in perspective.*

'Perspex® *n* a transparent plastic which looks like glass.

perspicacious [pərspi'kāshəs] *adj* of clear or sharp understanding. – *n* perspicacity [pərspi'kasəti] keenness of understanding.

perspi'cūity *n* clearness in expressing one's thoughts.

per'spire *v* to sweat. – *n* perspi'ration sweat.

persuade [pər'swād] *v* to bring a person to do or think something, by arguing with him or advising him. – *n* persuasion [pər'swāzhən] act of persuading; a firm belief *esp* a religious belief. – *adj* persuasive [pər'swāsiv] having the power to convince. – *n* per'suasive-ness.

pert *adj* saucy, cheeky.

per'tain *v* (with to) to belong, have to do with: *duties pertaining to the job.*

pertinacious [pərti'nāshəs] *adj* holding strongly to an idea, obstinate. – *n* pertinacity [pərti'nasəti].

'pertinent *adj* connected with the subject spoken about, to the point.

per'turb *v* to disturb greatly; to make anxious or uneasy. – *n* pertur'bation great worry, anxiety.

peruse [pə'roōz] *v* to read (with care). – *n* pe'rusal.

per'vade *v* to spread through. *Silence pervaded the room.*

per'verse *adj* obstinate in holding to the wrong point of view; unreasonable. – *ns* **per'verseness, per'versity** stubbornness; wickedness.

per'vert *v* to turn away from what is normal or right: *pervert the course of justice*; to turn (a person) to crime or evil. – *n* **'pervert** one who commits unnatural or perverted acts. – *n* **per'version** the act of perverting; an unnatural or perverted act.

peseta [pə'sātə] *n* the standard unit of Spanish currency.

'pessimism *n* the habit of thinking that things will always turn out badly (opposite of **optimism**). – *n* **'pessimist** a person who tends to think in this way. – *adj* **pessi'mistic**.

pest *n* a troublesome person or thing; a creature that is harmful or destructive, *eg* a mosquito. – *ns* **'pesticide** any substance which' kills animal pests; **'pestilence** a deadly, spreading disease. – *adj* **'pestilent** very unhealthy; troublesome.

'pester *v* to annoy continually.

pestle ['pesl] *n* a tool for pounding things to powder.

pet *n* a tame animal *usu* kept in the home (such as a cat *etc*); a favourite (child); a fit of sulks. – *adj* kept as a pet; favourite; chief: *my pet hate.* – *v* to fondle: – *pt* **'petted**. – *adj* **'pettish** sulky. – *n* **pet name** one used to express affection or love.

'petal *n* one of the leaf-like parts of a flower.

'pēter: peter out to fade or dwindle away to nothing.

petite [pə'tēt] *adj* small and neat in appearance.

pe'tition *n* a request, *esp* one signed by many people and sent to a government or authority. – Also *v*. – *n* **pe'titioner**.

'petrel *n* a kind of small, long-winged sea-bird.

'petrifȳ *v* to turn into stone; to turn (someone) stiff, *esp* with fear: – *pt* **'petrified**. – *n* **petri'faction**.

pe'trōleum *n* oil in its raw, unrefined form, extracted from natural wells below the earth's surface. – *n* **'petrol** petroleum when refined as fuel for use in motor-cars *etc*.

petticoat *n* an underskirt worn by women.

'petty *adj* of little importance, trivial. – *n* **'pettiness**. – *ns* **petty cash** money paid or received in small sums; **petty officer** a rank of officer in the navy (equal to a non-commissioned officer in the army).

'petūlant *adj* cross, irritable; unreasonably impatient. – *n* **'petulance**.

pew [pū] *n* a seat or bench in a church.

pewter ['pūtər] *n* a mixture of tin and lead.

'phalanx *n* a company of foot soldiers, drawn up for battle in an oblong-shaped body; a group of supporters: – *pl* **'phalanxes**.

phantasy *see* **fantasy**.

'phantom *n* a ghost.

Pharaoh ['fārō] *n* (*hist*) a ruler of Egypt in ancient times.

pharmaceutical [färmə'sūtikəl] *adj* having to do with the making up of medicines and drugs. – *ns* **'pharmacist** one who prepares and sells medicines; **'pharmacy** the art of preparing medicines; a chemist's shop.

pharmacology [färmə'koləjı] *n* the scientific study of drugs and their effects – *n* **pharma'cologist**.

'pharynx *n* the back part of the throat behind the tonsils. – *n* **pharyn'gitis** an illness in which the pharynx becomes inflamed.

phase [fāz] *n* one in a series of changes in the shape, appearance *etc* of something (*eg* the moon); a period, stage in the development of something (*eg* a war, a scheme *etc*).

pheasant ['feznt] *n* a type of bird with brightly-coloured feathers which is shot as game.

phenomenon [fə'nomənən] *n* any happening or fact (*esp* in nature) that is observed by the senses: *the phenomenon of lightning*; anything remarkable or very unusual, a wonder: – *p* **phe'nomena**. – *adj* **phe'nomenal** very unusual, remarkable.

'phial *n* a small glass bottle.

phi'lander *v* to make love, to flirt. – *n* **phi'landerer**.

phi'lanthropy *n* the love of mankind *usu* as shown by money given or work done for the benefit of others. – *adj* **philan'thropic** doing good to one's fellow men. – *n* **phi'lanthropist** one who does good to others.

philately [fi'latəli] *n* the study and collecting of stamps. – *n* **phi'latelist**.

philharmonic [filər'monik] *adj* (*usu* in names of orchestras *etc*) music-loving.

phi'lology *n* the study of words and their history. – *n* **phi'lologist**.

phi'losopher *n* one who studies philosophy. – *adjs* **philo'sophic, philo'sophical** of philosophy; calm, not easily upset. – *n* **phi'losophy** the study of the nature of the universe, or of man and his behaviour; a person's view of life.

phlegm [flem] *n* the thick slimy matter brought up from the throat by coughing; coolness of temper, calmness. – *adj* **phlegmatic** [fleg'matik] not easily aroused.

phlox *n* a type of garden plant with flat white or purplish flowers.

'**phōbia** *n* an intense (*usu* irrational) fear, dislike or hatred.

phoenix ['fēniks] *n* (*myth*) a bird which was said to burn itself and to rise again from its ashes.

phone short for **telephone**.

phonetic [fə'netik] *adj* of the sounds of language; spelt according to sound (as *feeniks* for **phoenix**). – *n* **pho'netics** the study of the sounds of language; a system of writing according to sound.

'**phōn(e)y** *adj* (*coll*) fake, not genuine.

'**phosphorus** *n* an element, a wax-like, poisonous substance that gives out light in the dark. – *ns* '**phosphate** a kind of soil fertilizer containing phosphorus; **phosphorescence** [fosfə'resns] faint glow of light in the dark. – *adj* **phospho'rescent**.

'**phōtocopy** *n* a copy of a document *etc* made by a device which photographs and develops images of the document. – Also *v*.

phōto'genic *adj* being a good or striking subject for a photograph.

pho'tography *n* the art of taking pictures by means of a camera, making use of the action of light on special films or plates. – *n* '**phōtograph** (*coll* '**phōtō**) a picture so made. – *v* to take a picture with a camera. – *ns* **photographer** [fə'togrəfər]; '**Phōtostat** ⓡ a type of special camera for making photographic copies of documents, pages of books *etc*; a photographic copy so made.

phrase [frāz] *n* a small group of words expressing a single idea: *after dinner*: *on the water*; a short saying or expression; (in music) a short group of bars forming a distinct unit. – *v* to express in words. *You could have phrased your excuse more tactfully.* – *n* **phraseology** [frāzi'oləji] one's choice of words and phrases used in expressing oneself.

physical ['fizikəl] *adj* of the body: *physical strength*: *physical exercises*; of things that can be seen or felt. – *adv* '**physically**. – *ns* **physician** [fi'zishən] a doctor (specializing in medical rather than surgical treatment); **physicist** ['fizisist] one who specializes in physics; **physics** ['fiziks] the science which includes the

study of heat, light, sound, electricity, magnetism *etc*.

physiognomy [fizi'onəmi] *n* (the features or expression of) the face.

physiology [fizi'oləji] *n* the study of the way in which living bodies work (including blood circulation, food digestion, breathing *etc*). – *n* **physi'ologist**.

physiotherapy [fizio'therəpi] *n* the treatment of disease by bodily exercise, massage *etc* rather than by drugs. – *n* **physio'therapist**.

physique [fi'zēk] *n* the build of one's body; bodily strength.

pi'ano *n* a type of large musical instrument played by striking keys: – *pl* **pi'anos**. – *n* **pianist** ['pēənist] one who plays the piano.

piazza [pi'atsə] *n* a market-place, square in a town *etc* surrounded by buildings.

pibroch ['pēbrohh] *n* a kind of bagpipe music.

'**picador** *n* a bullfighter armed with a lance and mounted on a horse.

'**piccolo** *n* a kind of small, high-pitched flute: – *pl* '**piccolos**.

pick *v* to choose; to pluck, gather (flowers, fruit *etc*); to peck, bite, nibble (at); to poke, probe (teeth *etc*); to open (a lock) with a tool other than a key. – *n* choice; the best or best part; a kind of heavy tool for breaking ground *etc* pointed at one end or both ends; any instrument for picking (*eg* a toothpick). – *ns* '**pickaxe** a pick; '**pickpocket** one who robs people's pockets. – **pick a quarrel** to start a quarrel deliberately; **pick on** to single out *usu* for something unpleasant; to nag at; **pick up** to lift up; to learn (a language, habit *etc*); to take into a vehicle, give someone a lift; to find or get by chance; to improve, gain strength.

'**picket** *n* a pointed stake; a small sentry-post or guard; a number of men on strike who prevent others from working or from going into work. – *v* to fasten (a horse *etc*) to a stake; to place a guard of soldiers or a group of strikers at (a place).

'**pickle** *n* a liquid in which food is preserved; vegetables preserved in vinegar; (*coll*) an awkward, unpleasant situation. – *v* to preserve with salt, vinegar *etc*.

'**picnic** *n* a meal eaten out-of-doors, *usu* during an outing *etc*. – Also *v*: – *pt* '**picnicked**.

pictorial *see* **picture**.

picture ['pikchər] *n* a painting or

drawing; a portrait; a photograph; a film; (*pl*) the cinema; a vivid description; representation. – *v* to make a picture of; to form a likeness of in the mind, to imagine. – *adjs* **pictorial** [pik'töriəl] having pictures; consisting of pictures; calling up pictures in the mind; **picturesque** [pikchə'resk] such as would make a good or striking picture, pretty, colourful.

pie *n* meat, fruit or other food baked in a casing or covering of pastry.

piebald ['pīböld] *adj* (*esp* of horses) white and black in patches; spotted.

piece [pēs] *n* a part or portion of anything; a single article or example: *a piece of paper*; a composition in music, writing, painting or other form of art: *a piece of popular music*; a coin; a man in chess, draughts *etc*. – *v* to put (together). – *adv* **'piece'meal** by pieces, little by little. – *n* **'piecework** work paid for according to how much work is done, not according to the time spent on it.

pied *adj* with two or more colours in patches.

pier [pēr] *n* a platform of stone, wood *etc* stretching from the shore into the sea *etc* as a landing place for ships; a pillar (supporting an arch, bridge *etc*).

pierce [pērs] *v* to make a hole through; to force a way into; to move (the feelings) deeply. – *adj* **'piercing** shrill, loud; sharp.

pierrot ['perō] *n* a comic entertainer with a white face and loose white clothes.

piety *see* **pious**.

'piffle *n* nonsense.

pig *n* a type of farm animal, from whose flesh ham and bacon are made; an oblong moulded piece of metal (*eg* pig-iron). – *ns* **'piggery**, **'pigstȳ** a place where pigs are kept. – *adj* **'pig'headed** stubborn. – *ns* **'pigskin** a kind of leather made from a pig's skin; **'pigtail** the hair of the head formed into a plait.

pigeon ['pijən] *n* a kind of bird of the dove family. – *n* **'pigeon-hole** a small division in a case or desk for papers *etc*. – *v* lay aside; to classify, put into a category.

'pigment *n* paint or other substance used for colouring; a substance in animals and plants that gives colour to the skin *etc*. – *n* **pigmen'tation** colouring (of skin *etc*).

pigmy *see* **pygmy**.

pike *n* a type of freshwater fish; a weapon like a spear, with a long shaft and a sharp head.

'pilchard *n* a small type of herring-like sea fish used as food.

pile *n* a number of things lying one on top of another, a heap; a great quantity; a large building; a large stake or pillar driven into the earth as a foundation for a building, bridge *etc*; the thick, soft surface on carpets *etc* and on certain kinds of cloth, *eg* velvet. – *v* (often with **up**) to make or form a pile or heap.

'pilfer *v* to steal small things. – *n* **'pilfering**.

'pilgrim *n* a traveller to a holy place. – *n* **'pilgrimage** a journey to a holy place.

pill *n* a little tablet, ball *etc* of medicine; (sometimes with **the**) a contraceptive in the form of a small tablet.

'pillage *v* to seize goods, money *etc esp* as loot in war. – *n* the act of plundering in this way.

'pillar *n* an upright support for roofs, arches *etc*; an upright post or column as a monument *etc*; anything or anyone that supports. *He is a pillar of the church*. – *n* **'pillarbox** a pillar-shaped box with a slot through which letters *etc* are posted.

'pillion *n* a seat for a passenger on a motor-cycle; (*old*) a light saddle for a passenger on horseback, behind the main saddle.

'pillory *n* (*hist*) a wooden frame (with holes for the head and hands) in which wrongdoers were placed in a standing position: – *pl* **'pillories**. – *v* to mock in public: – *pres p* **'pillorying**, *p* **'pilloried**.

pillow ['pilō] *n* a kind of cushion for the head. – *v* to rest or support on, or as if on, a pillow. – *ns* **'pillowcase**, **'pillowslip** a cover for a pillow.

'pilot *n* one who steers a ship in or out of a harbour; the person flying an aeroplane; a guide, leader. – *v* to steer or guide. – *ns* **'pilot-light** a small gas-light from which larger jets are lit; an electric light showing that a current is switched on; **pilot scheme** a scheme introduced on a small scale to act as a guide to a full-scale one.

'pimpernel *n* a kind of plant of the primrose family, with small pink or scarlet flowers.

'pimple *n* a small round swelling on the skin. – *adjs* **'pimpled**, **'pimply** having pimples.

pin *n* a short pointed piece of metal with a small round head, used for fastening *esp* in dressmaking; a wooden or metal peg or nail; a skittle. – *v* to fasten with a pin; to hold fast, pressed against some